Fodor's Road Guide USA

Idaho

Montana

Nevada

Utah

Wyoming

First Edition

Fodor's Travel Publications
New York Toronto London Sydney Auckland
www.fodors.com

Fodor's Road Guide USA: Idaho, Montana, Nevada, Utah, Wyoming

Fodor's Travel Publications
President: Bonnie Ammer
Publisher: Kris Kliemann
Executive Managing Editor: Denise DeGennaro
Editorial Director: Karen Cure
Director of Marketing Development: Jeanne Kramer
Associate Managing Editor: Linda Schmidt
Senior Editor: Constance Jones
Director of Production and Manufacturing: Chuck Bloodgood
Creative Director: Fabrizio LaRocca

Contributors
Editor: Susan Walton
Additional Editing: Stephanie Adams, Jane Glennon
Writing: Peggy Ammerman Sailors (Idaho), Deke Castleman (Nevada), Stacey Clark (Utah), John Curtas (Nevada restaurants), Linda Fischvogt (Nevada restaurants), Tom Griffith (Montana), and Candy Moulton (Wyoming), with Karen Bosnick, Satu Hummasti, Tareek Jones, Kristin Rodine, and Brian Rohan
Research: Alexei Manheimer-Taylor
Black-and-White Maps: Rebecca Baer, Robert Blake, David Lindroth, Todd Pasini
Production/Manufacturing: Bob Shields
Cover: Rich Franco/Foto Factory Inc. (background photo), Bart Nagel (photo, illustration)
Interior photos: Photodisc (Idaho), Siobhan O'Hare (Montana), Nevada Commission on Tourism (Nevada), Artville (Utah), Photodisc (Wyoming)

Copyright
Copyright © 2001 by Fodors LLC

Color-map atlas copyright © 2001 by Maps.com and Fodors LLC. All other maps copyright © 2001 by Fodors LLC.

Fodor's is a registered trademark of Random House, Inc.

All rights reserved under International and Pan-American Copyright Conventions. Published in the United States by Fodor's Travel Publications, a unit of Fodors LLC, a subsidiary of Random House, Inc., and simultaneously in Canada by Random House of Canada Limited, Toronto. Distributed by Random House, Inc., New York.

No maps, illustrations, or other portions of this book may be reproduced in any form without written permission from the publisher.

First Edition
ISBN 0-679-00506-4
ISSN 1528-1485

Special Sales
Fodor's Travel Publications are available at special discounts for bulk purchases for sales promotions or premiums. Special editions, including personalized covers, excerpts of existing guides, and corporate imprints, can be created in large quantities for special needs. For more information, contact your local bookseller or write to Special Markets, Fodor's Travel Publications, 280 Park Avenue, New York, NY 10017. Inquiries from Canada should be directed to your local Canadian bookseller or sent to Random House of Canada, Ltd., Marketing Department, 2775 Matheson Boulevard East, Mississauga, Ontario L4W 4P7. Inquiries from the United Kingdom should be sent to Fodor's Travel Publications, 20 Vauxhall Bridge Road, London SW1V 2SA, England.

PRINTED IN THE UNITED STATES OF AMERICA
10 9 8 7 6 5 4 3 2 1

CONTENTS

v **GREAT ROAD TRIPS**

vi **HOW TO USE THIS BOOK**

3 **IDAHO**

    Boxes Basques in Idaho...27
             Silver City...32
             Useful Extras You May Want to Pack...43
             Famous Potatoes...44
             Kodak's Tips for Photographing Weather...57
             Whitewater Running...82
             Eating Well Is the Best Revenge...103
             Beyond T-Shirts and Key Chains...103
    Maps Lewis and Clark Country and the North Woods Driving Tour...16
             Sun, Salmon, and Silver Loop Driving Tour...19

105 **MONTANA**

    Boxes Packing Ideas for Cold Weather...135
             Kodak's Tips for Photographing Landscapes and Scenery...151
             The Corps of Discovery: America's Great Adventure...165
             As Clear as a Glacier...180
             Self-Reliance: A Montanan Hallmark...182
             Five Days in the Saddle...188
             Big Sky, Big Screen...194
    Maps Beartooth Highway Drive...117
             Bozeman Trail Driving Tour...119
             Glacier National Park...156–157

211 **NEVADA**

    Boxes Basque Food...232
             Southern Nevada...246
             Kodak's Tips for Photographing the City...264
             Kodak's Tips for Photographing People...266
             Divorce, Reno-Style...277
    Maps Into the Desert Driving Tour...221
             A Lakeside Drive...223

291 **UTAH**

    Boxes Liquor Laws...294
             Sweet Things—Utahns, Jell-O, and Ice Cream...307
             Hoodoos, and Bridges, and Arches. Oh My!...318
             Packing Ideas for Hot Weather...332
             The Sanpete Valley...341
             Kodak's Tips for Night Photography...397
    Maps From Salt Lake into the Mountains Drive...301
             A Color-Country Drive...303
             Arches National Park...305
             Bryce Canyon National Park...316
             Canyonlands National Park...319
             Zion National Park...398

401 **WYOMING**

Boxes Wyoming's Cowboy Symbol...431
Upper North Platte River Valley Scenic Drives...474
Let's Rendezvous...483

Maps From the Powder River to the Parks Driving Tour...416–417
Historic Trails Trek Driving Tour...418–419
Grand Teton National Park...454
Yellowstone National Park...508–509

512 **INDEX**

COLOR ATLAS

Great Road Trips

Of all the things that went wrong with Clark Griswold's vacation, one stands out: The theme park he had driven across the country to visit was closed when he got there. Clark, the suburban bumbler played by Chevy Chase in 1983's hilarious *National Lampoon's Vacation,* is fictional, of course. But his story is poignantly true. Although most Americans get only two precious weeks of vacation a year, many set off on their journeys with surprisingly little guidance. Many travelers find out about their destination from friends and family or wait to get travel information until they arrive in their hotel, where racks of brochures dispense the "facts," along with free city magazines. But it's hard to distinguish the truth from hype in these sources. And it makes no sense to spend priceless vacation time in a hotel room reading about a place when you could be out seeing it up close and personal.

Congratulate yourself on picking up this guide. Studying it—before you leave home—is the best possible first step toward making sure your vacation fulfills your every dream.

Inside you'll find all the tools you need to plan a perfect road trip. In the hundreds of towns we describe, you'll find thousands of places to explore. So you'll always know what's around the next bend. And with the practical information we provide, you can easily call to confirm the details that matter and study up on what you'll want to see and do, before you leave home.

By all means, when you plan your trip, allow yourself time to make a few detours. Because as wonderful as it is to visit sights you've read about, it's the serendipitous experiences that often prove the most memorable: the hole-in-the-wall diner that serves a transcendent tomato soup, the historical society gallery stuffed with dusty local curiosities of days gone by. As you whiz down the highway, use the book to find out more about the towns announced by roadside signs. Consider turning off at the next exit. And always remember: In this great country of ours, there's an adventure around every corner.

HOW TO USE THIS BOOK

Alphabetical organization should make it a snap to navigate through this book. Still, in putting it together, we've made certain decisions and used certain terms you need to know about.

LOCATIONS AND CATEGORIZATIONS

Color map coordinates are given for every town in the guide.

Attractions, restaurants, and lodging places are listed under the nearest town covered in the guide.

Parks and forests are sometimes listed under the main access point.

Exact street addresses are provided whenever possible; when they were not available or applicable, directions and/or cross-streets are indicated.

CITIES

For state capitals and larger cities, attractions are alphabetized by category. Shopping sections focus on good shopping areas where you'll find a concentration of interesting shops. We include malls only if they're unusual in some way and individual stores only when they're community institutions. Restaurants and hotels are grouped by price category then arranged alphabetically.

RESTAURANTS

All are air-conditioned unless otherwise noted, and all permit smoking unless they're identified as "no-smoking."

Dress: Assume that no jackets or ties are required for men unless otherwise noted.

Family-style service: Restaurants characterized this way serve food communally, out of serving dishes as you might at home.

Meals and hours: Assume that restaurants are open for lunch and dinner unless otherwise noted. We always specify days closed and meals not available.

Prices: The price ranges listed are for dinner entrées (or lunch entrées if no dinner is served).

Reservations: They are always a good idea. We don't mention them unless they're essential or are not accepted.

Fodor's Choice: Stars denote restaurants that are Fodor's Choices—our editors' picks of the state's very best in a given price category.

LODGINGS

All are air-conditioned unless otherwise noted, and all permit smoking unless they're identified as "no-smoking."

AP: This designation means that a hostelry operates on the American Plan (AP)—-that is, rates include all meals. AP may be an option or it may be the only meal plan available; be sure to find out.

Baths: You'll find private bathrooms with bathtubs unless noted otherwise.

Business services: If we tell you they're there, you can expect a variety on the premises.

Exercising: We note if there's "exercise equipment" even when there's no designated area; if you want a dedicated facility, look for "gym."

Facilities: We list what's available but don't note charges to use them. When pricing accommodations, always ask what's included.

Hot tub: This term denotes hot tubs, Jacuzzis, and whirlpools.

MAP: Rates at these properties include two meals.

No smoking: Properties with this designation prohibit smoking.

Opening and closing: Assume that hostelries are open year-round unless otherwise noted.

Pets: We note whether or not they're welcome and whether there's a charge.

Pools: Assume they're outdoors with fresh water; indoor pools are noted.

Prices: The price ranges listed are for a high-season double room for two, excluding tax and service charge.

Telephone and TV: Assume that you'll find them unless otherwise noted.

Fodor's Choice: Stars denote hostelries that are Fodor's Choices—our editors' picks of the state's very best in a given price category.

NATIONAL PARKS

National parks protect and preserve the treasures of America's heritage, and they're always worth visiting whenever you're in the area. Many are worth a long detour. If you will travel to many national parks, consider purchasing the National Parks Pass ($50), which gets you and your companions free admission to all parks for one year. (Camping and parking are extra.) A percentage of the proceeds from sales of the pass helps to fund important projects in the parks. Both the Golden Age Passport ($10), for those 62 and older, and the Golden Access Passport (free), for travelers with disabilities, entitle holders to free entry to all national parks, plus 50% off fees for the use of many park facilities and services. You must show proof of age and of U.S. citizenship or permanent residency (such as a U.S. passport, driver's license, or birth certificate) and, if requesting Golden Access, proof of your disability. You must get your Golden Access or Golden Age passport in person; the former is available at all federal recreation areas, the latter at federal recreation areas that charge fees. You may purchase the National Parks Pass by mail or through the Internet. For information, contact the National Park Service (Department of the Interior, 1849 C St. NW, Washington, DC 20240-0001, 202/208—4747, *www.nps.gov*). To buy the National Parks Pass, write to 27540 Ave. Mentry, Valencia, CA 91355, call 888/GO—PARKS, or visit www.national-parks.org.

IMPORTANT TIP

Although all prices, opening times, and other details in this book are based on information supplied to us at press time, changes occur all the time in the travel world, and Fodor's cannot accept responsibility for facts that become outdated or for inadvertent errors or omissions. So always confirm information when it matters, especially if you're making a detour to visit a specific place.

Let Us Hear from You

Keeping a travel guide fresh and up-to-date is a big job, and we welcome any and all comments. We'd love to have your thoughts on places we've listed, and we're interested in hearing about your own special finds, even the ones in your own back yard. Our guides are thoroughly updated for each new edition, and we're always adding new information, so your feedback is vital. Contact us via e-mail in care of roadnotes@fodors.com (specifying the name of the book on the subject line) or via snail mail in care of Road Guides at Fodor's, 280 Park Avenue, New York, NY 10017. We look forward to hearing from you. And in the meantime, have a wonderful road trip.

THE EDITORS

Important Numbers and On-Line Info

LODGINGS

Adam's Mark	800/444—2326	www.adamsmark.com
Baymont Inns	800/428—3438	www.baymontinns.com
Best Western	800/528—1234	www.bestwestern.com
	TDD 800/528—2222	
Budget Host	800/283—4678	www.budgethost.com
Clarion	800/252—7466	www.clarioninn.com
Comfort	800/228—5150	www.comfortinn.com
Courtyard by Marriott	800/321—2211	www.courtyard.com
Days Inn	800/325—2525	www.daysinn.com
Doubletree	800/222—8733	www.doubletreehotels.com
Drury Inns	800/325—8300	www.druryinn.com
Econo Lodge	800/555—2666	www.hotelchoice.com
Embassy Suites	800/362—2779	www.embassysuites.com
Exel Inns of America	800/356—8013	www.exelinns.com
Fairfield Inn by Marriott	800/228—2800	www.fairfieldinn.com
Fairmont Hotels	800/527—4727	www.fairmont.com
Forte	800/225—5843	www.forte-hotels.com
Four Seasons	800/332—3442	www.fourseasons.com
Friendship Inns	800/453—4511	www.hotelchoice.com
Hampton Inn	800/426—7866	www.hampton-inn.com
Hilton	800/445—8667	www.hilton.com
	TDD 800/368—1133	
Holiday Inn	800/465—4329	www.holiday-inn.com
	TDD 800/238—5544	
Howard Johnson	800/446—4656	www.hojo.com
	TDD 800/654—8442	
Hyatt & Resorts	800/233—1234	www.hyatt.com
Inns of America	800/826—0778	www.innsofamerica.com
Inter-Continental	800/327—0200	www.interconti.com
La Quinta	800/531—5900	www.laquinta.com
	TDD 800/426—3101	
Loews	800/235—6397	www.loewshotels.com
Marriott	800/228—9290	www.marriott.com
Master Hosts Inns	800/251—1962	www.reservahost.com
Le Meridien	800/225—5843	www.lemeridien.com
Motel 6	800/466—8356	www.motel6.com
Omni	800/843—6664	www.omnihotels.com
Quality Inn	800/228—5151	www.qualityinn.com
Radisson	800/333—3333	www.radisson.com
Ramada	800/228—2828	www.ramada.com
	TDD 800/533—6634	
Red Carpet/Scottish Inns	800/251—1962	www.reservahost.com
Red Lion	800/547—8010	www.redlion.com
Red Roof Inn	800/843—7663	www.redroof.com
Renaissance	800/468—3571	www.renaissancehotels.com
Residence Inn by Marriott	800/331—3131	www.residenceinn.com
Ritz-Carlton	800/241—3333	www.ritzcarlton.com
Rodeway	800/228—2000	www.rodeway.com

Sheraton	800/325—3535	www.sheraton.com
Shilo Inn	800/222—2244	www.shiloinns.com
Signature Inns	800/822—5252	www.signature-inns.com
Sleep Inn	800/221—2222	www.sleepinn.com
Super 8	800/848—8888	www.super8.com
Susse Chalet	800/258—1980	www.sussechalet.com
Travelodge/Viscount	800/255—3050	www.travelodge.com
Vagabond	800/522—1555	www.vagabondinns.com
Westin Hotels & Resorts	800/937—8461	www.westin.com
Wyndham Hotels & Resorts	800/996—3426	www.wyndham.com

AIRLINES

Air Canada	888/247—2262	www.aircanada.ca
Alaska	800/426—0333	www.alaska-air.com
American	800/433—7300	www.aa.com
America West	800/235—9292	www.americawest.com
British Airways	800/247—9297	www.british-airways.com
Canadian	800/426—7000	www.cdnair.ca
Continental Airlines	800/525—0280	www.continental.com
Delta	800/221—1212	www.delta.com
Midway Airlines	800/446—4392	www.midwayair.com
Northwest	800/225—2525	www.nwa.com
SkyWest	800/453—9417	www.delta.com
Southwest	800/435—9792	www.southwest.com
TWA	800/221—2000	www.twa.com
United	800/241—6522	www.ual.com
USAir	800/428—4322	www.usair.com

BUSES AND TRAINS

Amtrak	800/872—7245	www.amtrak.com
Greyhound	800/231—2222	www.greyhound.com
Trailways	800/343—9999	www.trailways.com

CAR RENTALS

Advantage	800/777—5500	www.arac.com
Alamo	800/327—9633	www.goalamo.com
Allstate	800/634—6186	www.bnm.com/as.htm
Avis	800/331—1212	www.avis.com
Budget	800/527—0700	www.budget.com
Dollar	800/800—4000	www.dollar.com
Enterprise	800/325—8007	www.pickenterprise.com
Hertz	800/654—3131	www.hertz.com
National	800/328—4567	www.nationalcar.com
Payless	800/237—2804	www.paylesscarrental.com
Rent-A-Wreck	800/535—1391	www.rent-a-wreck.com
Thrifty	800/367—2277	www.thrifty.com

Note: Area codes are changing all over the United States as this book goes to press. For the latest updates, check www.areacode-info.com.

Fodor's Road Guide USA

Idaho
Montana
Nevada
Utah
Wyoming

Idaho

Utter the word Idaho, and the humble potato, staple of the American dinner table, immediately comes to mind. Idaho spuds may be famous, but most everything else about the state is a mystery to many people. You might expect otherwise from a place wedged between the Pacific Northwest states of Washington and Oregon, famed for coffee, computer software, and grunge fashion, and the Rocky Mountain–cowboy states of Wyoming and Montana. Yet despite standing shoulder to shoulder with these heavyweights, Idaho weighs in as somewhat independent in nature and an unknown.

Novelist Ernest Hemingway, who first visited the Gem State in 1939 and penned part of his seminal *For Whom the Bell Tolls* in a room at the Sun Valley Lodge, said "A lot of state this Idaho, I didn't know about . . ." Despite, or perhaps because of, this imperfect understanding, Hemingway found the place so much to his liking that he sought out its grassy high prairies and mountain streams to indulge a few of his passions— bird hunting and fishing—and spent time at his home in Ketchum, also his final resting place.

If much of Idaho remains terra incognita, it's largely due to its sheer size and relative political youth. The thirteenth-largest state, Idaho spreads across the Northern Rockies, touching the base of Canada's British Columbia province with its narrow Panhandle. The heart of the state remains wild, a huge expanse of mountains and raging rivers; the 2.3-million-acre Frank Church–River of No Return Wilderness Area (the largest such area in the lower 48 states) claims much of the state's midsection. Farther north, in Idaho's Panhandle, are deep woods, mountains rich with precious ores, and huge lakes. Idaho became a state only a little over a century ago, and today just 1.1 million

CAPITOL: BOISE	POPULATION: 1,100,000	AREA: 83,557 SQUARE MI
BORDERS: CANADA, WA, OR, NV, UT, WY, MO	TIME ZONE: MOUNTAIN	POSTAL ABBREVIATION: ID
WEB SITE: WWW.VISITID.ORG		

people fill its boundaries; roughly 12 people share each square mile and only 4% of the land is considered urban and developed.

A 16,000-mi network of rivers and streams (3,100 mi of white water, the most of any state) winds through the mountain, valley, and plains terrain. Explorers Meriwether Lewis and William Clark supposedly coined the nickname for the Main Salmon River: "River of No Return." After the duo's boatmen witnessed the waters churn in 1805, "with great violence from one rock to another on each side foaming and roaring, so as to render the passage of any thing impossible," the expedition party backtracked to Montana and pursued an alternate route via the Lolo Pass over the Continental Divide. Today, the Main Salmon and its Middle Fork are ranked among the world's toughest by river runners. Idaho also claims the most mountain ranges of any state, with 80 of them wrinkling the landscape.

This Rocky Mountain state is also characterized by the vast Snake River Plain, a stark desert crescent that swings across the southern third of the state. Here are both the state's most desolate stretches as well as its lushest, with more than 4,600 irrigation projects crisscrossing farm fields that grow the famous potatoes along with alfalfa hay, sugar beets, legumes, and grain. Ranches in the south-central region also raise cattle and trout. Idaho is the biggest commercial producer of trout in the world. The 800-mi Snake River is king of the Idaho rivers. Of Idaho's fifteen largest towns, all but one are within 25 mi of the Snake. The stream carves a wide, steady course through valleys and deep canyons as the river and its aquifer, deep under the plains, pump the lifeblood to Idaho's potato fields in the southeastern and south-central regions of the state. Along the Snake's course there are waterfalls higher than Niagara Falls, springs gushing from canyon walls, and, in Hells Canyon, a gorge deeper than the Grand Canyon. Roughly in the middle of the state, desert and alpine climes converge. On the upper reaches of the Snake River Plain, a highly unusual mix of geologic phenomena can be found. A great volcanic rift zone ripples across the area, leaving in its wake spatter cones, calderas, and a blackened landscape as far as the eye can see.

Idaho has indeed staked much of its identity on its famed potatoes, the state's biggest cash crop, weighing in as a $526-million industry every year. J. R. Simplot, patriarch of the potato industry, began to devise ways to add value to the simple potato—by freezing, frying, and drying them, among other treatments—in the 1940s; he is now a billionaire. These measures transformed the common spud into Idaho's "Famous Potatoes."

In southwestern Idaho around Boise, chips of a different kind are now driving the economy. With microchip and computer giant Micron firmly rooted here, along with others growing the technology industry, it's clear that the climate and conditions are right for yet another type of cash crop in Idaho.

Although Idaho is short on famous sons and daughters, the few that it claims are particularly noteworthy. America's fresh-faced alpine skier Picabo (pronounced *peek-a-boo*) Street captured the world's hearts during the 1998 Olympic Games when she demonstrated her trademark gung-ho style and took the gold medal in the women's super giant slalom race. Picabo grew up skiing at Sun Valley and was born in the community known as Triumph, a former mining village just outside Ketchum. Idaho also claims another alpine skier in 1948 Olympics medalist Gretchen Fraser, who lived her later and final years in Sun Valley, although she was born in Washington. On the literary scene, in addition to claiming Hemingway, Idaho was the birthplace of the influential and controversial poet Ezra Pound.

It's Idaho simple, rugged character that seems to feed the heart and soul of Idahoans and nurtures the popular notion that Idaho is the last true vestige of the Western frontier. Today, there is a meeting of the minds and spirits in Idaho. It is busy

INTRODUCTION
HISTORY
REGIONS
WHEN TO VISIT
STATE'S GREATS
RULES OF THE ROAD
DRIVING TOURS

tempering a staunch, decades-old agricultural demeanor focused on dominating and cultivating the land. Its sights are set on the virtues of technology with an untamed spirit that is deeply rooted in its own private wild patch of the Rocky Mountain landscape. The Idaho of tomorrow is no doubt carving its unique niche in the psyche of the new American West. Idaho seems to have settled comfortably into its sterling setting, part polished gem and part diamond in the rough.

History

Although Native Americans, most notably the Shoshone and Bannock in the south and Nez Percé and Coeur d'Alene in the north, claimed the lands of Idaho for centuries, the state's recorded history begins with the 1805 Lewis and Clark Expedition. In 1805, Meriwether Lewis and William Clark approached Idaho's vast, uncharted wilderness along the Bitterroot Mountains at the Montana border, in what is now the state's north-central region. That was the first time that the Native Americans had seen the white man. In 1803, President Thomas Jefferson had dispatched Lewis and Clark up the Missouri River to explore the United States' Northwest region, west of the Rocky Mountains. In 1805, they stepped across the Lolo Pass and followed Indian trails and the Clearwater and Lochsa River valleys to the Snake River at Idaho's western border.

Like much of the Northwest, Idaho was opened to further exploration and exploitation by fur trappers. In 1810 Fort Henry was established near Saint Anthony and became the first American fur-trading post west of the Rocky Mountains. A year earlier the Kullyspell House near Lake Pend Oreille was built, the first non-native establishment in the Northwest. The Lake Pend Oreille area, with its lush woodlands and lakes, became a popular trapping area; British, American, and Canadian groups all cut trails through the region. The British were a dominant force in the area. Under David Thomson, the North West Company established a trading post on Lake Pend Oreille.

By 1810, exploration began on the Oregon Trail route and in 1818 the United States and Great Britain signed a Joint Occupation Treaty for Oregon Territory that included what is today Idaho. It would be another 71 years before Idaho would become a state. Idaho's southern boundary was determined in 1819 under the Adams-Onis treaty between Spain and the United States. The treaty put the southern boundary at the 42nd Parallel. That same year Goodale's Cutoff of the Oregon Trail was explored.

Over the next two decades Forts Boise and Hall were established in Idaho. As the demand for furs waned in the late 1830s, fur-trading interests left the area, and missionaries like Jesuit priest Henry H. Spalding established missions in the Panhandle region. Spalding's mission near Lapwai was the site of Idaho's first school and its first irrigation system, which supported the state's first crop of potatoes. In the same

ID Timeline

Pre-history	1805	1806	
From 13,000 BC, evidence suggests that Native American cultures inhabit Idaho, as shown in in rock shelters, petroglyphs, and stone tools.	Captain Meriwether Lewis and William Clark (who would retire as a brigadier general) enter the area of present-day Idaho at Lemhi Pass, cross into north Idaho over the Lolo Trail, then meet with Nez Percé Indians at Weippe Prairie.	Lewis and Clark spend more than six weeks with the Nez Percé Indians in the Kamiah area before returning eastward across the Lolo Trail. Canadian David Thompson establishes a fur-trading post near Bonners Ferry. Missouri Fur	Company establishes Fort Henry near St. Anthony, the first American trading post.

year, 1836, Narcissa Whitman and Eliza Spalding became the first white women to cross the Continental Divide.

The year 1843 marked the start of the great western migration across Idaho via emigrant trails. Oregon Trail wagons first crossed the state in that year, and six years later 20,000 gold seekers joined the rush to California, traveling through southeastern Idaho on the California Trail. For many years following, the Oregon and California trails saw heavy traffic, with way stations and supply centers along the routes becoming pioneer towns.

The discovery of gold along the Pend Oreille River by French Canadians in 1852 marked the beginning of the state's mining boom. A year later, the Washington Territory was created, and in 1859 Oregon was admitted as a state. By 1863 Idaho had become a territory. Within a few years of the establishment of Idaho's first town, Franklin, in 1860, major gold strikes were made in both Idaho's north-central region and in Idaho City, near Boise. The next 20 years saw several major battles with Native American tribes, including the 1877 Nez Percé War, the Bannock War in 1878, and the 1879 Sheepeater campaign. By this time the territory's population was 32,610, and both Boise and Lewiston had established school districts. The mining industry hit the mother lode in 1884 when silver ore was discovered in the Coeur d'Alene mining district, one of the nation's richest. A century later, the Silver Valley, as the district was known, would out-produce the rest of the nation in silver. Idaho rode this wave into statehood in 1890, becoming the 43rd state, with a population 88,548.

The railroads also laid track to Idaho beginning in the 1880s, supporting the booming mining industry and spurring development of communities across the state. Another region also struck it rich around the turn of the century, this time with water. The Carey Act of the early 1900s opened the way for completion of Milner Dam, near Twin Falls, in 1904, and spawned major irrigation projects that would turn the Snake River Plain into fertile farmland. By 1900 though, Idaho's population had only reached 161,722.

In the 1930s and '40s, the travel and agriculture industries began to make a mark on Idaho's economy. In 1936, as the Union Pacific Railroad was putting the finishing touches on a sparkling Austrian village–style destination ski resort, the first of its kind in the United States, it also constructed the world's first ski chairlift there. Ten years later Idaho's potato king, J. R. Simplot, began potato-dehydration operations in Caldwell. By this time, the state's population had reached a little over a half-million. By the 1980s, Idaho had added a few high-tech industries to the economic pot. Most of these are in the Boise Basin and southeastern Idaho. It wasn't until 1990, as the state was approaching its centennial, that population hit the 1 million mark.

1810–11	1818		1820	1824
The Pacific Fur Company expedition explores the Snake River valley en route to the Columbia River and discovers the Boise Valley.	Trappers explore southern Idaho on a Snake River expedition, and a treaty of joint occupancy between Great Britain and the United States maintains that the Oregon region, including Idaho, is	open to settlement by citizens of both nations.	A treaty between Spain and the United States establishes the southern boundary of Idaho at the 42nd Parallel.	Alexander Ross and Jedediah Smith lead expeditions throughout the Salmon River region; Russia cedes the Northwest Territory to the United States.

Regions

INTRODUCTION
HISTORY
REGIONS
WHEN TO VISIT
STATE'S GREATS
RULES OF THE ROAD
DRIVING TOURS

1. THE PANHANDLE: NORTH WOODS AND LAKES

Glaciers carved this area's pristine north-woods setting, where deep pine forests with pockets of ancient cedars drape across softly sculpted mountains that reach upward from 7,000 to 10,000 ft. Sapphire-blue lakes, the most of any region in the Western United States and some of the state's largest, dot the bumpy emerald-green terrain. This is timber country and an angler's big-fish paradise, with hardworking logging towns and rustic cabin resorts tucked in the woods. Though some areas like Sandpoint and Coeur d'Alene are modern vacation destinations with ski resorts, golf courses, the state's only theme park, and other travelers' pursuits, much of the region is still remote and rugged. Priest Lake is particularly secluded, mostly accessible via minor roadways. A state highway rims only a quarter of the lake's shoreline.

Towns listed: Bonners Ferry, Coeur d'Alene, Kellogg, Priest River, St. Maries, Sandpoint, Wallace

2. NORTH-CENTRAL: LEWIS AND CLARK TRAIL AND HELL'S CANYON

Of all the regions, the north-central area defies categorization. The world's deepest gorge, Hell's Canyon of the Snake River, dives down more than a mile along the Oregon border; over on the eastern border is the lofty Lemhi Pass, where Lewis and Clark stepped across the Continental Divide at more than 7,000 ft. In between are the lower 48 states' largest wilderness area and a network of wild rivers like the Selway, Salmon, with its Middle Fork, and the Clearwater, which lure white-water enthusiasts. The rolling hills of the Palouse spread in all directions from Moscow, and nearby Lewiston is home to a seaport that is 470 mi inland. The highlands east of Lewiston are home to the Nez Percé tribe.

Towns listed: Grangeville, Lewiston, Moscow

3. SOUTHWEST: SAGEBRUSH FLATS AND CANYONS

In striking contrast to the adjacent north-central region, the southwestern corner of the state is swept by an arid sagebrush flat, interrupted only occasionally by the deep canyons of the Snake and Bruneau Rivers. Huge Owyhee County, in the extreme southwest corner, is a desert wilderness. Alpine mountain ranges with towering ponderosa pines rim the east and west edges of the region and look down on the Boise Basin, where irrigation has turned patches of the dry plain into a checkerboard of farm fields

1832	1834–42	1843	1848	1849
Captain B.L.E. Bonneville leads covered wagons across the Rocky Mountains.	Fort Hall becomes a hub for trails and roads to the western United States, while several Jesuit missions are established in north-central Idaho and the Panhandle.	The Oregon Trail is established, entering the state to the east near Montpelier, passing by Fort Hall, and continuing westward along the Snake River before crossing into Oregon.	The Oregon Territory, which includes Idaho, is established.	Over 20,000 gold-rush immigrants pass through southeastern Idaho on the California Trail.

with fruit and vegetable crops and vineyards that drape across the foothills around Weiser, Caldwell, and Nampa.

Towns listed: Bruneau, Caldwell, Glenns Ferry, Idaho City, Mountain Home

4. CENTRAL: LAVA ROCK AND THE ROCKIES

In the central region, a majestic alpine setting collides with a seemingly endless amount of volcanic debris that colors the landscape black and barren as far as the eye can see. Among the state's eighty recognized mountain ranges, the jagged Sawtooth Mountains are also among the most beloved and give the central Idaho Rockies the look and feel of the Swiss Alps. One hundred miles away, the craggy lava beds that blanket the northern reaches of the Snake River plain are just as impressive, with eerie formations dotting the volcanic landscape. In the middle of the region is the resort of Sun Valley, which straddles high desert and alpine climes. River runners flock to the Salmon, the "White-Water Capital of the World," for white-water excursions on its Middle Fork, which crashes through the huge Frank Church–River of No Return Wilderness area, the largest in the lower 48 states. Here too are Idaho's tallest peak, Mount Borah, rising more than 12,000 ft, and remnants of mining towns in the Yankee Fork area.

Towns listed: Arco, Challis, Ketchum, McCall, Salmon, Stanley, Sun Valley, Weiser

5. EASTERN: GATEWAY TO YELLOWSTONE AND THE TETONS

Eastern Idaho is known as the backside of the Tetons and is a gateway to Yellowstone Country. To the west are sand dunes; running diagonally through the region is the Snake River. Scenic byways along the west side of the Tetons let you glimpse waterfalls and the peaks. Unlike busy Yellowstone, Montana, and Jackson, Wyoming, on the other side of the eastern Idaho peaks, tiny towns like Driggs cling to their easygoing, rural character. The waterways are favorite wintering areas for migrating trumpeter swans; big-game wildlife like moose and elk roams the woodlands of Targhee National Forest. Henry's Fork, a Snake River tributary, draws fly-fishers from around the globe for record-breaking cutthroat trout. The town of Island Park sits in the forested center of an ancient caldera 18 mi long and 23 mi wide, a hint at the volcanic activity in nearby Yellowstone. Two of the last undisturbed waterfalls of consequence in the West, 65-ft Lower Mesa Falls and 114-ft Upper Mesa Falls, are just south of Targhee Pass, where Montana, Idaho, and Wyoming come together. This region is also home to Idaho Falls, the second-largest city in the state, which surrounds its namesake falls along the Snake River.

Towns listed: Ashton, Driggs, Rexburg, St. Anthony

1852	1857–59	1863–65	1877–78	1880–84
French Canadians discover gold on the Pend Oreille River.	Oregon's eastern boundary is established and Oregon becomes a state, leaving all of Idaho in the Washington Territory. Gold is discovered on Orofino Creek and Lewiston becomes a mining supply town.	The Idaho Territory is organized, with Lewiston as its capital. The town of Boise is laid out and replaces Lewiston as the capital. Idaho's population climbs to 17,804.	Indian War with battles at White Bird.	Idaho's population almost doubles in 10 years to 32,619. Lead and silver lodes are discovered in the Wood River valley. The Northern Pacific railroad is completed across the northern part of the Territory and the Oregon Short

INTRODUCTION
HISTORY
REGIONS
WHEN TO VISIT
STATE'S GREATS
RULES OF THE ROAD
DRIVING TOURS

6. SOUTH-CENTRAL: SNAKE RIVER PLAIN AND CANYON

The Snake River and its deep canyon and wide plain are the focus of south-central Idaho. The Snake's deepest canyons and a waterfall higher than famed Niagara are just outside Twin Falls. Below the plain is the Snake River Plains aquifer, one of the world's largest; it puts on a display at the Thousand Springs area where water gushes from the verdant canyon walls. Irrigation enterprises set in motion in the early 1900s have turned much of the plain into one of the richest farming regions in the nation. Fish hatcheries and commercial farms that produce the most trout in the nation are also spread across the plain. Ancient zebralike horses once roamed the area, and their fossilized remains, in one of the four most significant fossil beds in the United States, rest along the canyon. In the remote southern part of the region, rounded rock monoliths rise like skyscrapers at the City of Rocks, a favorite destination of rock climbers.

Towns listed: Almo, American Falls, Buhl, Burley, Gannett, Gooding, Hagerman, Jerome, Malta, Rupert, Shoshone, Thousand Springs, Twin Falls

7. SOUTHEASTERN: PIONEER BYWAYS

The southeast corner of the state was settled early on, with the Oregon and California trails, among others, carving deep ruts into the landscape as they brought pioneers to the western frontier. Wagons carrying immigrants stopped at way stations like Montpelier, the trading post at Fort Hall, American Falls, and Lava Hot Springs, where geothermal water today fills a huge complex of pools. The region was also settled by Mormon farmers who moved here from Salt Lake City in the late 1800s. Along with pioneer towns that have a genuine Old West feel, the region is filled with natural wonders like turquoise-blue Bear Lake and Minnetonka Cave. Long before the pioneers settled here, the Shoshone and Bannock Indian tribes hunted and established villages here. After the crude trails were laid, the railroad chugged into the area and made Pocatello the "Gate City," the largest rail center west of the Mississippi. Today stately depots recall railroading's heyday.

Towns listed: Blackfoot, Fort Hall, Idaho Falls, Lava Hot Springs, Montpelier, Pocatello

When to Visit

Even within a given region, the varied landscape usually brings a wide range of weather conditions and microclimates. Generally though, Idaho enjoys a dry, moderate climate with very low relative humidity. The southwest corner of the state is true desert wilderness and is inhospitable in the summertime as temperatures soar, often above 90°F. The Boise Basin enjoys a moderate climate with surprisingly scant rainfall and snowfall while the mountain slopes that fringe the region have an alpine, four-season climate that brings snowy winters. The other stretch of desert with hot dry

1887	1890	1893	1900
Line is completed through the southern region. The Coeur d'Alene rush creates boomtowns in the Silver Valley.	A bill to annex north Idaho to Washington Territory passes Congress, but is not signed by President Cleveland and therefore does not become law.	Idaho reaches a population of 88,548 and is admitted to the Union as the 43rd state.	The Panic of '93 causes lead and silver prices to collapse and Coeur d'Alene's mines shut down.	Idaho's population reaches 161,772.

summers is in the central region among the lava flows of the Snake River Plain. In contrast, within the same region, the coldest temperatures in the state, sometimes dipping to −50°F, are registered at Stanley on the northern end of the Sawtooth Range.

Although Sun Valley is now as popular as a summer vacation destination as it is a winter skiing resort, most tourists avoid the Rockies in the spring, called "slack" by locals, when rain and thawing snows hamper any sort of outdoor recreation. The south-central region shares much of the same climate as the Boise Basin, with a moderate climate along the Snake River Plain. As it is the most mountainous of the Western states, most of Idaho's remaining regions feature terrain that brings short but warm summers with cool nights, and a dry climate and snowy winters. For outdoor recreation, the summer is optimum with temperatures from mid-May to mid-September generally averaging in the daytime 70–80°F and mountain climates about 10°F cooler. Most nighttime temperatures reach the low 50s°F in midsummer, and the mountains can be chilly at the upper 40s°F. The autumn follows the summer and winter as the most popular vacation season, particularly for anglers and hunters.

CLIMATE CHART

Average High/Low Temperatures (°F) and Monthly Precipitation (in inches)

	JAN.	FEB.	MAR.	APR.	MAY	JUNE
BOISE	37/21	44/27	52/31	61/37	71/44	80/51
	1.4	1.1	1.2	1.2	1.2	.9
	JULY	AUG.	SEPT.	OCT.	NOV.	DEC.
	90/58	88/66	78/48	65/39	48/30	39/23
	.28	3.2	.59	.79	1.3	1.3

	JAN.	FEB.	MAR.	APR.	MAY	JUNE
COEUR D'ALENE	34/21	40/24	48/28	59/34	68/42	75/48
	3.3	2.5	2.3	1.7	1.7	1.9
	JULY	AUG.	SEPT.	OCT.	NOV.	DEC.
	85/53	85/52	74/44	60/37	44/30	37/25
	.75	.92	1.3	2	3.1	3.6

	JAN.	FEB.	MAR.	APR.	MAY	JUNE
POCATELLO	32/15	39/20	47/26	58/33	68/41	77/47
	1.1	.9	1.2	1.1	1.3	1.1
	JULY	AUG.	SEPT.	OCT.	NOV.	DEC.
	88/53	87/52	76/43	63/34	45/25	35/18
	.54	.63	.78	.88	1.1	1.1

1903–06
The Carey Act supports irrigation projects around Twin Falls. The largest sawmill in the nation opens at Potlatch.

1910
Idaho's population reaches 325,594. Fires consume almost 20 percent of northern Idaho's forests and destroy many communities.

1915
Arrowrock Dam, the tallest in the world, is completed on the Boise River. Irrigation contributes to the development of three important crops—potatoes, peas, and sugar beets.

1920
The northern and southern portions of the state are connected for the first time by an improved roadway, Whitebird Hill grade. The state capitol is completed.

1924
Craters of the Moon National Monument is established.

INTRODUCTION
HISTORY
REGIONS
WHEN TO VISIT
STATE'S GREATS
RULES OF THE ROAD
DRIVING TOURS

	JAN.	FEB.	MAR.	APR.	MAY	JUNE
SUN VALLEY	30/30	36/04	40/10	52/22	64/29	71/35
	2.6	1.6	1.2	1.	1.6	1.7
	JULY	AUG.	SEPT.	OCT.	NOV.	DEC.
	83/38	82/37	72/30	61/23	44/14	32/4
	.73	.84	.9	.93	1.6	2.6

FESTIVALS AND SEASONAL EVENTS

WINTER

Dec. Climb aboard a climate-controlled boat for a view of the lighting displays that bedeck the lakefront during the Coeur d'Alene Fantasy in **Lights & Laser Extravaganza.** Along with a lighting ceremony that includes fireworks and a lighted parade, the cruises end with a laser show. 208/773–9797.

Jan. The **Sandpoint Winter Carnival** features five days of winter fun and festivities with a parade, snow sculptures, snowshoe softball, and cross-country and telemark races. 208/263–2161.

Feb. For years, residents in the town of McCall have displayed ice carvings in their front yards. The annual event now features world-class ice sculptures, the highlight of the weeklong **Winter Carnival,** which also schedules snowmobile races, parades, pyrotechnics, a Snowflake Ball, a wine tasting, sled-dog races, and a variety show. 208/634–7631.

The **Lionel Hampton/Chevron Jazz Festival** draws an international roster of jazz musicians for workshops and performances at the University of Idaho in Moscow. 208/885–6765.

SPRING

Apr. The **Lewiston Dogwood Festival** celebrates blossom time with an art show and crafts fair, wine and beer tasting, garden tours, crafts, concerts, and plays. 208/799–2243.

May The community of Twin Falls hosts **Western Days** with old-fashioned family fun featuring a carnival, music, an arts and crafts show, and a parade. 208/733–3974 or 800/255–8946.

Near McCall, the **Payette Apple Blossom Festival** includes an apple-bobbing competition, the Apple Core Open Golf Tournament, a talent show, an ice-cream social, a pie-eating contest, and an arts and crafts show.208/642–2362.

1925	1930s	1936	1939–45	
The Union Pacific Railroad begins service to Boise.	Idaho's population reaches 445,032. Gold- and silver-mining industries redevelop and Idaho becomes the top producer of silver in the nation.	The Union Pacific Railroad establishes Sun Valley, the nation's first destination ski resort, near the mining town of Ketchum. Former Gov. William E. Borah becomes the state's first presidential candidate.	During World War II Idaho contributes timber, silver, lead, and agricultural products to the war effort. Idaho becomes a relocation center for 10,000 Japanese nationals and Japanese-Americans from Washington and Oregon.	The state is also the site of 18 German and Italian prisoner-of-war camps.

SUMMER

June	The lifestyles of pioneer days are reenacted with a tepee village, trader's row, black-powder shoots, and a knife-throwing contest at Massacre Rocks State Park, American Falls, during the **Massacre Rocks Rendezvous.** 208/548–2672.
	Known as "America's Finest Family Festival," the **Boise River Festival** features more than 400 events, including six stages of continuous entertainment and the largest giant inflatable parade west of the Mississippi. 208/338–8887.
	The most prestigious fiddling event in the nation, the **National Oldtime Fiddlers Contest and Festival** in Weiser is the "Superbowl of Fiddling." 208/549–0452.
July	The two-day **Teton Valley Hot Air Balloon Festival** features more than 30 hot-air balloons racing across the picturesque Teton valley, with balloon rides, and a craft and antiques fair. 208/354–2500.
	The huge **Snake River Stampede** is two decades old and one of the top 20 rodeos in the country. 208/466–8497.
	The **International Folkdance Festival** attracts hundreds of dancers from around the world for a weeklong festival with showy opening and closing ceremonies.208/356–5700.

AUTUMN

Sept.	The highlight of **Ketchum Wagon Days** is a Big Hitch parade, the longest non-motorized parade in the Northwest. You'll also find pancake breakfasts, evening Western dances, antiques shows, an arts and craft fair, live entertainment, food, a rodeo, and a collectors' car auction. Sun Valley and Ketchum. 208/726–3423.
	In Blackfoot, the **Eastern Idaho State Fair** presents a rodeo, top names in country music, amusement rides, and a demolition derby. 208/785–2483.
	The **Lewiston Round Up** is the area's largest and oldest community event with three days of professional rodeo action. 208/743–3531.
Nov.	The **Coeur d'Alene Fall Craft Show** showcases handicrafts and art at Coeur d'Alene's Silver Lake Mall. 208/772–6296.

1970s		**1980s**	**1981**	**1990s**
Environmental concerns become a top political issue. Governor Cecil Andrus spearheads the passage of legislation emphasizing the conservation of natural resources, rivers, and streams. Many parts of Idaho	are designated national forests or wilderness areas, including the Hells Canyon National Recreation Area, the River of No Return, and Sawtooth National Wilderness Areas.	The mining industry continues a steady decline that started in the mid-1960s. Tourism becomes increasingly important in the state, helping to offset the decline in mining and timber revenues.	One of Idaho's largest employers, Bunker Hill Mine and Smelter, near Kellogg, shuts down leaving 2,000 workers unemployed.	Idaho ranks 42nd in the United States with a population of a little over 1 million. The state is the 6th most sparsely populated state. Food processing is the state's chief industry. Second is the manufacture of industrial machinery, and

State's Greats

INTRODUCTION
HISTORY
REGIONS
WHEN TO VISIT
STATE'S GREATS
RULES OF THE ROAD
DRIVING TOURS

Rugged and remote describes much of the Gem State. Yet Idaho's nature is surprisingly varied, from the continent's deepest gorge, **Hell's Canyon,** to the lower 48 states' largest wilderness area and its namesake stream, the River of No Return (also known as the **Salmon River**). The 2.3-million-acre mountain wilderness that surrounds the Salmon is largely untouched, remaining as untamed as when Lewis and Clark encountered the raging Salmon and were forced to reroute their trek across north-central Idaho in 1805. A network of rivers, many of them designated "wild and scenic," overlays the mountainous landscape, making the state tops in river excursions, with more than 3,100 mi of white-water rivers. They attract river runners from around the world for challenging rapid runs as well as leisurely scenic floats. The king of all Idaho rivers is the **Snake River,** which carves an 800-mi course through southern Idaho before making a dramatic departure by gouging out 1-mi-deep Hells Canyon along the Oregon border.

Although much of the state is laced with pioneer trails such as the Oregon and California, Idaho remains sparsely settled, with a total population of just over 1.1 million; its largest city, **Boise,** has only 145,000 residents. Here you'll still find genuine frontier towns with an Old West feel. About two-thirds of Idaho's land is in the hands of the federal government, which manages millions of acres of forest, lakes, and even desert, making the entire state one big playground for all sorts of outdoor recreation.

A broad-reaching wave of lava crashed across southern Idaho as recently as 2,000 years ago and created an eerie blackened landscape with peculiar volcanic formations that form a sharp contrast to the alpine climes less than 100 mi away in the central Rockies region. Along with one of the nation's largest sections of wilderness, a huge stretch of the Snake River Plain in southeastern Idaho has been irrigated and cultivated, transforming the once-barren flats into one of the richest farming regions in the world. The light volcanic soil here produces bushels of Idaho's famous potatoes. In the north woods of Idaho's Panhandle, dozens of lakes, some large, draw scores of anglers, boating enthusiasts, and others for water recreation.

Beaches, Forests, and Parks

It may come as a surprise, but many of Idaho's 2,000 lakes, particularly in the north-woods Panhandle region (the prime examples being **Lake Coeur d'Alene** and **Lake Pend Oreille**), are ringed by white, sandy beaches. This is a water state, with more than 16,000 mi of rivers and 239,000 acres of reservoirs. More than half of the state's 83,557 square mi is forested. The National Forest Service manages eleven forests and more than 16 million acres. The properties are evenly distributed, making the wooded preserves readily accessible. The state oversees almost 50,000 acres among twenty-three parks that range from pristine wooded lake settings to mining districts and ghost towns.

The state has purposely kept the national park designation out of its vocabulary, resisting efforts to make wilderness areas such as Sawtooth in the central Rockies a

lumber and wood production rank third. The manufacture of electronic and electrical equipment is the fourth-largest industry.

1992 Randy Weaver, a white separatist living in the northern Panhandle region draws national attention during an 11-day siege and shoot-out with federal officials. During the siege, several persons are killed including a federal

officer. Weaver and Kevin Harris are tried and acquitted, and the Weaver family wins a multi-million-dollar lawsuit against the federal government for using lethal force during the siege.

National Park. The **Frank Church–River of No Return Wilderness** holds national status as the largest in the lower 48 states, and Idaho has a national historical park (**Nez Perce National Historic Park**), two national monuments (**Hagerman Fossil Beds National Monument** and **Craters of the Moon National Monument**) and one national reserve (**City of Rocks National Reserve**). Amid all of this wild and rugged terrain is the state's only theme park (Silverwood), with an Old West mining town theme and a huge wooden roller coaster in the north-woods Panhandle.

Culture, History, and the Arts

Idaho's early history was shaped by great tribes like the Bannock, Shoshone, and Nez Percé; by Lewis and Clark, who explored portions of the white-water state; and later by pioneers brought west by the great trails like the Oregon and California. Like most Western states, boom times linked to mining and the railroad were colorful periods in Idaho's history. The state's Native American and settlement history is commemorated at the **Nez Perce National Historical Park,** at the re-created trading post **Fort Hall Replica** near Blackfoot, and at historic sites along the Oregon Trail such as **Massacre Rocks** and **Three Island Crossing,** both state parks along the Snake River.

Throughout the 30-mi Silver Valley—near Coeur d'Alene and one of the richest silver-ore regions in the world—some half-dozen museums recall the heydays of mining, among them the bawdy but tasteful **Oasis Bordello Museum** in Wallace, a mining town lined with Victorian buildings. Living towns like **Idaho City,** nestled in the foothills east of Boise, were born of the mining boom. The block-long town looks much as it did at the turn of the 20th century. The **Land of Yankee Fork Historical Area,** on the scenic Custer Motorway between Challis and Sunbeam along the Salmon River corridor, preserves remnants of the mining town of Custer, a mining camp, and a gold-mining dredge.

The railroad played an important role in the state's development, and several historic depots have been preserved, including the grand depot at **Pocatello,** once the West's rail center. The depot still operates as a passenger and freight station. Nampa's 1903 turreted depot is now the **Canyon County Historical Society Museum,** and Wallace's **Northern Pacific Depot Railroad Museum** recalls the role of the railroad in north-central Idaho's settlement and mining around the turn of the century. Admittedly, few artists hail from Idaho, and the state claims only one art museum, in Boise. The state prefers to rank its natural wonders among works of art. Among the more notable artists associated with the state is author Ernest Hemingway, who lived in Idaho and is buried in Ketchum. The **Ernest Hemingway Memorial** in Ketchum is a tribute to the novelist.

Sports

Idaho is one big outdoor playground, with a range of outdoor sports and recreation. Practically every region of the state has great **fishing** holes, from rushing rivers to tranquil alpine lakes. The catch is usually some species of trout. **Lake Pend Oreille** in the Panhandle is known for giant Kamloops; mackinaw topping 50 pounds have been hooked in **Priest Lake,** one of the most secluded of the northern lakes. Fishing is one of the top pastimes here. Even in cities like Boise and Idaho Falls one can find good fishing within a couple of miles. Some of the more notable fishing spots are **Silver Creek,** a cold-spring-fed high-desert stream south of Bellevue and the Sun Valley Area. This catch-and-release area is known for elusive huge rainbows. **Henry's Fork** of the Snake River is one of the world's premier streams for cutthroat trout.

Another popular water sport is **river running,** which usually means rafting or kayaking. With more than 3,100 mi of white water, kayakers, rafters, and boaters flock to the remote **Selway,** legendary **Middle Fork Salmon,** and **Main Salmon Rivers,** and in the extreme southwestern desert wilderness, the **Bruneau** and **Jarbridge Rivers.** These

INTRODUCTION
HISTORY
REGIONS
WHEN TO VISIT
STATE'S GREATS
RULES OF THE ROAD
DRIVING TOURS

streams reach peak flow in the spring, with the Bruneau passing through a narrow and dark rock-walled canyon 800 ft deep. City types who are looking for a river experience can try more leisurely floats, such as day trips on the **Boise River. Hot springs** dot Idaho too, ideal for end-of-the-day soaks. **Lava Hot Springs** has made a seemingly endless flow of geothermal spring water the focus of a mammoth pool complex in the state's southeast corner.

The national forests and state parks maintain networks of **foot trails,** and you can use the more than 13,000 mi of trails maintained specifically for **mountain biking.** The well-organized **Idaho Outfitters and Guides Association** (800/49–IDAHO; www.ioga.org) is a nonprofit association that represents 70 percent of the state's 390 licensed outfitters and guides. The organization can point vacationers to all sorts of outdoor adventures, from guest ranches, hunting, fishing, rock climbing, and river running to winter snowmobile outings.

Idaho claims the nation's first destination **ski resort, Sun Valley,** now popular year-round, along with more than a dozen other downhill skiing areas. **Targhee,** on the back side of the Tetons, is known for deep powder snowfall, and **Brundage,** outside McCall, features wooded glade runs. The world's largest **snowmobile trail system** is in **Silver Valley,** with a 1,000-mi network spanning the tri-state area of Idaho, Montana, and Washington. **Cross-country skiing** and **snowshoeing** are enjoying increasing popularity. Most winter resort areas groom trails.

Rules of the Road

License Requirements: To drive in Idaho you must be at least 16 years old and have a valid driver's license (15-year-olds may drive during daylight hours only). Residents of Canada and most other countries may drive with valid licenses from their home countries.

Right Turn on Red: Throughout the state, a right turn on red is permitted after a full stop, unless otherwise indicated by a no-turn-on-red sign.

Seat Belt and Helmet Laws: Drivers and front-seat passengers must wear seat belts. Children under the age of 5 must use a federally approved child safety seat. Only motorcyclists under the age of 18 are required to wear helmets.

Speed Limits: The speed limit on most interstate highways is 70 mph, except for portions of road that travel through urban or congested areas.

For More Information: Contact the Idaho Transportation Department | Office of Public Affairs, Box 7129, Boise, ID | 208/334–8005.

Lewis and Clark Country and the North Woods
FROM LOLO PASS TO SANDPOINT

Distance: 367 miles   Time: 4 days
Breaks: Stop overnight in Coeur d'Alene or Lewiston, both roughly midway along the tour and areas with a range of lodgings from lakeside hotels to cabin resorts and guest ranches.

Deep, cool woods sprinkled with lakes—some of the state's largest and the color of a deep blue winter sky—drape across the folded mountains of north-central Idaho and the slender Panhandle region. Along with the mostly north-woods features though, this region is anchored on the eastern and western edges by surprisingly varied

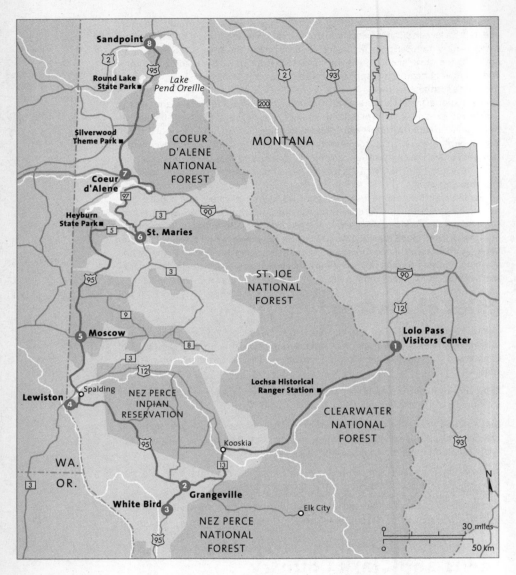

terrain, from the continent's deepest gorge to the high pass charted by Lewis and Clark on their 1805 trek through the Northwest. This tour travels the path that early explorers took across the Continental Divide and wilderness mountain ranges, then explores the native lands of the Nez Percé before stopping at Hell's Canyon, the state's lowest point and the site of an inland seaport. The route then heads north through the north woods of Idaho, where the Coeur d'Alene tribe hunted and fished. Avoid this tour in the winter, when snow and wintry conditions can make the roads impassable.

❶ Begin your tour at Lolo Pass (on the Montana-Idaho border on U.S. 12). The **Lolo Pass Visitors Center,** a refurbished log cabin, has exhibits and information on the Lolo Trail, which roughly parallels U.S. 12 and is the trail that Lewis and Clark followed on their epic journey. Originally it was a trail of the Lolo tribe, who used it to travel between the

INTRODUCTION
HISTORY
REGIONS
WHEN TO VISIT
STATE'S GREATS
RULES OF THE ROAD
DRIVING TOURS

buffalo hunting grounds in Wyoming and the Weippe Prairie of Idaho. Trappers, gold miners, and settlers also followed the path over a century ago. Remnants of the trail are still visible today. Roughly halfway to Grangeville, the **Lochsa Historical Ranger Station** (208/926–4275) recalls how rangers lived and operated one of the state's earliest U.S. Forest Service stations, which you could reach only on foot until the mid-1900s.

❷ Your drive from Lolo Pass to **Grangeville** (Box 212, Grangeville | 208/983–0460) will run 80 mi on U.S. 12 to Kooksia, then another 16 mi on Route 13. **White Bird Road,** as U.S. 95 is known between Grangeville and White Bird, was an engineering marvel when it was built in the late 1930s, climbing 4,429 ft in elevation within 14 mi. The **White Bird Hill Battlefield Auto Tour** (at Nez Perce National Historical Park, | 208/843–2261) recalls the fascinating story of the first battle of the Nez Percé War in the hills near White Bird. At the White Bird Interpretive Shelter, you can see exhibits that explain the sequence of the battle.

❸ At **White Bird** (12 mi south of Grangeville on U.S. 95), a gravel road, Route 493, will take you 12 mi to the northern rim of the continent's deepest gorge, Hells Canyon. At 1 mi deep, it surpasses the Grand Canyon. **Pittsburg Landing** (Hells Canyon National Recreation Area, Box 699, 2535 Riverside Dr., Clarkston, WA | 509/758–0616) is the only year-round access point to the 71-mi steep-walled basalt canyon. Picnic at the shady area near the river's edge. You can explore the canyon by jet boat and raft on trips from one to six days. Call the Idaho Outfitters and Guides Association for a list of licensed guides and outfitters serving Hells Canyon (208/342–1919).

❹ When you're finished at White Bird and Pittsburg Landing, backtrack 24 mi north to Grangeville, then 47 mi north on U.S. 95 to Spalding and the **Lewiston** area. Exhibits and a huge collection of artifacts tell the poignant story of the Nee-Me-Poo people or Nez Percé Indians and their legacy at the **Nez Perce National Historical Park and Museum** (Box 93, Spalding; 11 mi east of Lewiston | 208/843–2261). Nez Percé Chief Joseph is known for his words, "My heart is sick and sad. From where the sun now stands, I will fight no more forever." The park includes 38 sites in Idaho, Montana, Oregon, and Washington. The **Luna House Historical Museum** displays exhibits on the history of Nez Perce County and the surrounding area, including a pioneer kitchen and room setting in a building that was originally a hotel catering to miners en route to the northern goldfields. Lewiston, at an elevation of 738 ft, is the lowest point in the state. It is also the state's only seaport and most inland port in the nation, welcoming boats that have traveled 460 mi up the Snake River.

❺ From Lewiston, proceed 26 mi north on U.S. 95 to **Moscow** and the **Appaloosa Museum and Heritage Center.** The museum highlights the history of Appaloosa horses, which the Nez Percé bred centuries ago. Regalia, saddles, and artifacts used with the Appaloosa are on display, including Native American items. The **McConnell Mansion** was built in 1886 and reflects Eastlake, Queen Anne, and Victorian Gothic styles. Period furnished rooms display artifacts and Victorian-style furniture from the early 1900s to 1930s. Changing exhibits also tell the county history. The town is cradled by mountains to the east and the Palouse Hills to the west. The Palouse, as the area is known, is a picturesque rolling landscape with extremely fertile soil that at the height of growing season looks like a sea of green velvet. Moscow is known as the dry pea and lentil capital of the world—the crops carpet the hills. From Moscow Mountain, a few miles northeast of town via Mountain View Road, you get a panoramic view of the area.

❻ Leaving Moscow, head 51 mi north on U.S. 95, then 6 mi east on Route 3 to **St. Maries** and **Heyburn State Park.** The park occupies 5,505 acres at the foot of sprawling Lake

Coeur d'Alene on a lakelet known as Chatcolet Lake. Herons and ospreys are often seen nesting here. Six hiking trails cover 20 mi, some of which pierce thick stands of 400-year-old ponderosa pines.

❼ From Heyburn State Park, continue 7 mi north on Route 3, 21 mi north on Route 92, and 7 mi west on I–95 to **Coeur d'Alene.** A busy vacation resort area surrounds much of the northern tip of the lake, which includes the world's only floating golf green. The picturesque lake is 2½ mi wide and 25 mi long, and is nestled in a glacially sculpted setting of soft mountains and pine forests. **Lake Coeur d'Alene Cruises, Inc.** takes visitors on two-hour sightseeing tours and sunset dinner cruises, departing from the city dock. In town near the waterfront, the **Museum of North Idaho** has major exhibits on the region's rich history of Native American culture, steamboating, the logging industry, and nearby communities. The Fort Sherman Museum behind the museum is the reconstructed Fort Sherman Powder House, with artifacts and exhibits that tell the story of the fort, which operated until 1901. Fifteen miles north of town on U.S. 95 is **Silverwood Theme Park.** Silverwood is a charming Victorian-style park patterned after an 1880s mining town and the state's only amusement theme park. It offers a narrow-gauge steam train, a wooden roller coaster, a log flume, and 24 other rides, as well as an antique airplane museum and midway games.

❽ From Coeur d'Alene, proceed 43 mi north on U.S. 95 into **Sandpoint.** The state's largest lake, **Pend Oreille,** is nearby, and dips to an amazing depth of 1,200 ft, making it an angler's paradise for big fish and "fish stories" about the lake's own "Nessie." When asked, locals can spin a tale or two about the fabled lake monster. The authentic fish that inhabit the lake's depths are the giant Kamloops species of trout. The 65-mi-long lake has more than 300 mi of shoreline and at the northern end, the resort town of Sandpoint. The city beach features a sweeping stretch of sparkling white sand and a view to the east of Montana's Cabinet Mountains. Also along the lake is a shopper's paradise, the **Cedar St. Bridge,** with dozens of shops lining an enclosed rustic timbered bridge across Sand Creek. On the west side of the lake are tiny **Round Lake** and **Round Lake State Park,** one of the state's smallest. A little more than 140 acres of land surrounds the 58-acre lake. Since the lake is only 37 ft deep, it warms enough for comfortable swimming.

To return to Lolo Pass, leave Sandpoint on U.S. 95 and proceed for about 30 mi to Coeur d'Alene. From there either backtrack the way you came, or head east on I–90 for about 130 mi to Missoula, Montana, and then proceed south on U.S. 93 into Lolo and west on U.S. 12 to the pass.

Sun, Salmon, and Silver Loop Driving Tour

ROCKY MOUNTAIN RESORTS AND HIGH SAGEBRUSH DESERT

Distance: 202 miles   Time: 3 days
Breaks: Stop overnight in Sun Valley or the Sawtooth Valley area; both have a range of lodgings from hotels to cabin resorts and guest ranches.

The loop tour of the Rockies and sagebrush-dotted high desert and plains of central Idaho highlights where the fortunes of the heart of Idaho lie, in ample sunshine, a world-famous ski resort, the Salmon River's white water, and the craggy lava beds of Craters of the Moon National Monument.

❶ Begin the tour in **Ketchum** and the Sun Valley Area. The quaint 1880s-vintage mining town of Ketchum is 1 mi from world-renowned Sun Valley, the nation's first destination ski resort, which has a block-long Austrian-style village edging a grassy mall with a shady pond. Although Sun Valley is perhaps best known as a wintertime resort, summer has become equally popular. You can mountain-bike and go in-line skating on the Wood River Trails system, hike Bald Mountain, or take the chairlift to the top in the summer. In addition to fishing and golf, you can browse the shops and galleries in the polished frontier-era town of Ketchum and Sun Valley village. Author Ernest Hemingway fell in love with the Sun Valley area and is buried at the Ketchum Cemetery. North of Sun Valley village is the **Ernest Hemingway Memorial,** a bust of Hemingway and a passage taken from an epitaph Hemingway wrote for a friend who had died in a hunting accident during Hemingway's first visit to Idaho.

INTRODUCTION
HISTORY
REGIONS
WHEN TO VISIT
STATE'S GREATS
RULES OF THE ROAD
DRIVING TOURS

❷ From Ketchum, proceed 15 mi northwest on Route 75 to the **Sawtooth National Recreation Area (SNRA),** but stop first at SNRA headquarters (7 mi north of Ketchum) and borrow the cassette audio-tape tour describing U.S. Forest Service management of the SNRA, geology, and natural history along the route to Stanley. The 8,700-ft Galena summit marks the southern end of the Sawtooth Valley. Here, the spiny Sawtooth Range gathers more than 40 gray granite spires that reach more than 10,000 ft and face the White Cloud peaks across a 10-mi-wide valley that forms a 30-mi-long corridor that stretches north to Stanley. At the Galena overlook, the headwaters of the Salmon River look like a squiggly dribble of a stream. By the time the Salmon reaches the town of Stanley, the lapping dark blue river is 25 ft wide. The SNRA includes 756,000 acres, 217,000 of which are part of the Sawtooth Wilderness Area. Two other mountain ranges, the Boulders and Smokies, and central Idaho's major rivers, the Salmon, the South Fork of the

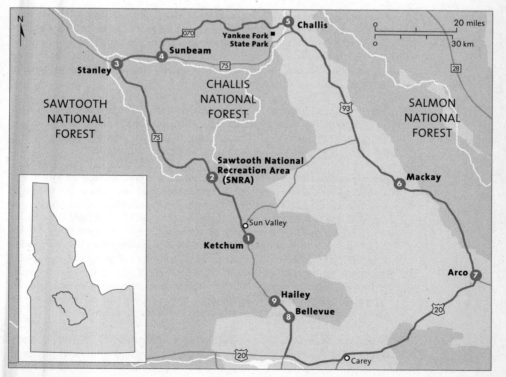

Payette, the Boise, and the Big Wood are also located within the SNRA. The area has more than 300 lakes and 250 mi of trails.

❸ Leaving the Sawtooth National Recreation Area, head north on Route 75 for approximately 30 mi into **Stanley.** The dirt-street, four-by-four-block community feels like an Old West frontier town. In the summer, the town of fewer than 100 permanent residents heats up as river runners and outfitters swarm the place on weekends. Stanley is a chief launching point for white-water excursions on the Salmon River. For information on kayaking and rafting trips or guided outdoor fishing and hunting trips contact the **Idaho Outfitters and Guides Association** (Box 95, Boise | 208/342–1919), which represents more than 400 licensed outfitters, guides, and related services.

❹ When you've finished exploring Stanley, proceed east on Route 75 for about 13 mi to **Sunbeam** and the Sunbeam and Custer Motorway. At Sunbeam, interpretive signs describe the Salmon River and the remnants of the Sunbeam Dam, the only dam ever constructed on the Salmon. From the dam, the **Custer Motorway** started a little more than a century ago as miners rushed to the Yankee Fork gold mines in the 1870s. By 1879, Alex Toponce, an enterprising freighter, had built a toll road from Challis to Bonanza. Town sites, mines, and several way stations sprang up along the road. Today, the historic mining road includes remnants of Custer, Bonanza, and the rusted metal skeletal remains of the 112-ft-long, 988-ton Yankee Fork dredge, which was used for digging into the mountainsides. The area is part of **Yankee Fork State Park,** a 6,000-acre region that was the scene of an important chapter in the state's mining history.

❺ From Sunbeam, take Forest Service Road 75 northeast for approximately 35 mi to **Challis.** Challis is lined with old brick buildings from the late 1800s, and local history buffs have compiled a walking tour of about fifty historic structures, including those in the former Chinatown district, residences, shops, and even the central hitching post. Be sure to visit the **Land of the Yankee Fork State Park Interpretive Center,** a building styled after the old mining mills, where displays tell the Yankee Fork mining story. Today Challis is an important base camp for Salmon River trips and pack trips into the high mountains of the 2.3-million-acre **Frank Church–River of No Return Wilderness,** the largest such area in the lower 48 states.

❻ From Challis, head south on U.S. 93 for approximately 46 mi into **Mackay.** This two-block community is dwarfed by the state's highest peaks in the Lost River Range, among them Mount Borah, which rises 12,662 ft just north of town. You can fish and take day hikes among the 10,000- to 12,000-ft peaks.

❼ Continue south on U.S. 93 for about 22 mi into **Arco.** Arco grew at the junction of routes followed by the Blackfoot–Wood River Stage Lines and the Blackfoot-Salmon Stage Lines. Twenty miles southeast of the quiet agricultural town, the eerie black lava fields that spread across the northern reaches of the wide Snake River Plain are an astonishing contrast to the high-peaked, alpine landscape just north of Arco. Much of the lava flow is within **Craters of the Moon National Monument,** a 60-mi crack in the earth's crust that spawned volcanic cones, spewing rivers of lava as recently as 2,000 years ago. Exploring the 83 square mi of the Great Rift Zone in Craters Monument is like a voyage to another planet. The 7-mi loop drive in the preserve lets you glimpse cinder cones, lava tubes, and caves. The visitor center explains the difference between aa and pahoehoe lava and other oddities and quirks of the volcanic world.

❽ The next stop, **Bellevue,** is 58 mi west of Craters of the Moon on U.S. 20, then 7 mi north on Route 75. It's a sleepy community astride the highway that was a bustling mining center and the gate city to the Wood River valley mining district in the 1880s. The mountainsides lining the valley still bear the zigzag etchings of roads inching up steep slopes to the mines. Although only 20 mi from cosmopolitan Sun Valley, the town maintains its easygoing, pioneer character. Today Bellevue is a hub community of the southern Wood River valley, serving big ranches that surround it.

○ From Bellevue, proceed 5 mi north on Route 75 into **Hailey.** This is where the locals who work in Ketchum and Sun Valley live and shop. Only 11 mi from Ketchum and the Sun Valley Area, the county-seat town appeals to families and vacationers looking for more homey, low-key surroundings. Several restaurants and shops dot the streets in this friendly town of 2,800. Hailey started as a major mining hub in the 1880s, and street names like Bullion reflect this heritage. The **Blaine County Museum** is in a narrow redbrick building downtown dating from the late 1880s. Here you can see old-time photographs and memorabilia from the mining and early settlement years.

To return to Ketchum, head north on Route 75 for 25 mi.

AMERICAN FALLS

MAP 3, E8

(Nearby towns also listed: Burley, Pocatello)

Waterfalls where the Snake River cascaded 50 ft over basalt boulders gave this town its name, long before dams and a huge reservoir were built here. Immigrants following the Oregon Trail across the Snake River Plain often wrote of the music of the falls in their diaries. One traveler recalled, "The sound of the falls was heard some time before reaching them. The scene was truly magnificent. Here was an entire change in the face of the country as well as the river." The look of the town and the river changed again beginning in 1901, as power plants and later a dam were built on the Snake, eventually slowing the falls to a trickle. By 1925 the town of 4,000 packed up and moved south to make way for flooding and what would become a 36-mi long reservoir. At the time, this was one of the largest towns ever relocated for such a project.

Today the town sits at the southern tip of the lake. When the water level is low you can still see the original town's skeletal remains—streets, sidewalks, and the foundations of buildings—in the northwestern section of the lake. Some buildings, such as the brick church at Fort Hall Avenue and Polk Street, were taken apart, moved, and reconstructed in the new town. American Falls is now a major agricultural processing and shipping center surrounded by huge farming operations that produce potatoes, grain, and sugar beets.

Information: American Falls Chamber of Commerce | 239 Idaho St. | 208/226–7214 | fax 208/226–7214 | www.governet.net/id/ci/amf/area.cfm.

Attractions
American Falls Dam. Two dams once spanned the the American Falls. The new dam was built over one of the old ones in 1989 by the Idaho Power Company, at a cost of $23 million. The current dam is 86 ft high and 2,900 ft long. Route 39 travels across it. | I–86 Exit 40, then follow signs on Rte. 39 Bypass | 208/226–7214 | Free | Daily dawn to dusk.

Great Rift Natural Landmark. A series of newer-looking lava flows and deep rifts reaches down 800 ft below the earth's surface. The Great Rift is the longest such geologic system in United States and the world's deepest. The flows are thought to be 2,000 years old. | Rte. 39, on Idaho Power Company grounds | 208/529–1020 | Free | Daily dawn to dusk.

Massacre Rocks State Park. Rugged lava rocks with almost 300 species of desert plants and 200 species of birds fill this 900-acre preserve. A ¼-mi walk along the Oregon Trail leads to the huge Register Rock, which is 2½ mi from the park, is inscribed with the names of pioneers who traveled through here. The visitor center has exhibits on the Oregon Trail, Shoshone Indians, the geology of the area, and fur trapping. From Memorial Day through Labor Day, costumed performers depict pioneer days during Living History Campfire Programs. | 3592 N. Park La.; I–86 Exit 28 | 208/548–2672 or 208/548–2472 | www.idahoparks.org | $2 per car | Daily.

Trenner Memorial Park. Also called Three Layer Park and situated along the Snake River just below the dam, Trenner is maintained by the Idaho Power Company and has picnic tables, access to fishing docks, and views of American Falls Dam and the Snake River. During high water, the falls that gave the town its name flow just below the dam. | At the end of Falls Ave. | 208/226–7214 | Free | Daily.

ON THE CALENDAR
JUNE: *Portneuf Muzzleloader Blackpowder Rendezvous.* The pioneer way of life is reenacted by mountain men with a tepee village, a traders' row, black-powder shoots, and a knife-throwing contest. | Massacre Rocks State Park | 208/548–2672.

ARCO

MAP 3, D7

(Nearby towns also listed: Idaho Falls, Rexburg)

In 1953, the town of Arco, which sits at about 5,900 ft in elevation, was the first in the world to be lighted by atomic power. Roughly 2,000 kilowatts of electricity were generated by the Boiling Water Reactor No. 3 (BORAX III) and sent 20 mi away to the tiny town wedged between the northern desert stretches of the vast Snake River Plain and the foot of the Lost River Mountain Range and Idaho's tallest peak, Mount Borah (elevation 12,662 ft). Two years earlier, the Experimental Breeder Reactor No. 1 (EBR-1) had been the first to generate usable electricity from nuclear power. BORAX III and EBR-1 started at the National Reactor Testing Station (NRTS), which opened in 1949. For nearly 25 years the NRTS functioned as an isolated laboratory for building and testing various kinds of nuclear reactors. Among the stated missions was showing how atomic power could safely generate electricity. The facility is now known as the Idaho National Engineering and Environmental Laboratory (INEEL) and sits on a tract of desert that is almost the size of the state of Rhode Island. More nuclear reactors have been produced here than anywhere else in the world. Today, in addition to nuclear reactor and fuel-cycle technology research, INEEL's work focuses on geothermal, low-head hydroelectric applications and other non-nuclear energy development. Arco is also known for the low-tech work of Mother Nature, a mysterious installation that spreads across the sagebrush flat 20 mi from town, the desolate volcanic landscape of Craters of the Moon National Monument. When confronted with the monolithic black buttes and ancient volcano cones that dot the blackened, jagged terrain, one early visitor to Craters noted that these are "the strangest 83 square miles on earth."

Information: Lost River Tourism | 132 W. Grand Ave. (Box 46), Arco 83213 | 208/527–8977 | fax 208/527–8546 | www.atcnet.net/'arco.

Attractions
★ **Craters of the Moon National Monument.** Once used for early moon-mission training by U.S. astronauts, the stark, black lava-flow area does indeed resemble a lunar landscape. The national monument covers 53,120 acres and is part of a 60-mi-long crack system that occurred as recently as 2,000 years ago. A 7-mi drive passes cinder cones, lava flows, spatter cones, and lava tubes. The visitor center's displays cover volcanic geology and include a video presentation and Native American history of the area. The preserve is particularly

showy during the spring wildflower season. You can hike trails that range from less than a mile to 7 mi. | Box 29 | 208/527–3257 | ww.nps.gov-crmo.com | $4 | Visitor center: June–Aug., daily 8–6; Sept.–May, daily 8–4:30.

Experimental Breeder Reactor Number 1 (EBR-1). In 1951, EBR-1 was the first power plant to generate usable electricity from atomic energy. When you visit, you can find out how the non-operating reactor plant once functioned. Exhibits also explain the Three Mile Island incident and newer nuclear technologies. | 208/526–0050 | www.inel.gov/resources/tours/ebr1.htm | Free | Memorial Day–Labor Day, daily 9–5.

ON THE CALENDAR
JAN.: *Winterfest.* Cross-country skiing, snow sculptures, snowshoeing, snow golf, food, and entertainment are all part of this celebration at Craters of the Moon National Monument. | Last weekend in Jan. | 208/527–3257.

Lodging
Arco Inn. Basic road motel with modest accommodations. Standard-size chain rooms and small but well maintained grounds. In-room phones. Cable TV. | 540 W. Grand | 208/527–3100 | 12 rooms | $32–45 | AE, DC, MC, V.

DK Motel. Very reasonable rates and a convenient location two blocks from the town center make this older motel a good stopping point. Rooms are well maintained and clean. Picnic area. No-smoking rooms. Cable TV. Laundry facilities. Business services. Pets allowed. | 316 S. Front St. | 208/527–8282 or 800/231–0134 | www.atcnet.net/~dkm | 24 rooms, 6 suites | $28–$49, $35–$65 suites | AE, D, MC, V.

ASHTON

MAP 3, F7

(Nearby town also listed: St. Anthony)

Ashton owes its name and its very existence to the Oregon Short Line railroad. Back in the early 1900s, to avoid the high prices being put on right-of-way land at Marysville, the railroad moved its tracks 2 mi west. In 1906, roughly a month after the first train arrived, the village of Ashton was established. The town was named for the railroad's chief engineer, Bill Ashton, who homesteaded here. Today, it is the northern gateway to the back side of the Grand Tetons range, anchoring the Mesa Falls and the Teton Scenic Byway routes near the famed trout stream Henry's Fork of the Snake River.

Information: Ashton Chamber of Commerce | Box 151, Ashton 83420 | 208/652–3987.

Attractions
★ **Harriman State Park.** The 4,330-acre park was once the Railroad Ranch, a working cattle ranch owned by Roland and Averell Harriman, who were associated with the Union Pacific railroad. Many of the ranch's log cabins and other original structures from the 1920s are preserved. You can see elk, moose, beavers, muskrats, bald eagles, ospreys, trumpeter swans, and other waterfowl. About 12 mi of the world-famous Henry's Fork, the tributary of the Snake River known for its fly fishing, winds through the preserve. The park includes 21 mi of trails and overnight facilities. | 19 mi north on U.S. 20 | 208/558–7368 | www.idahoparks.org | $3 per car | Daily dawn to dusk.

Henry's Lake State Park. Henry's Fork of the Snake River begins at Henry's Lake, a mountain lake 6,427 ft high and just a few miles south of Targhee Pass. You go to Henry's Fork to fish. The 6,200-acre lake is one of the larger high-country lakes, and it is known for large brook, rainbow, and cutthroat trout. Trumpeter swans from Canada winter here. | HC66, Box 20, Island Park; 37 mi north on U.S. 20, then 1 mi west | 208/558–7532 or 208/558–7532 | www.idahoparks.org | $3 per car | Late May–late Oct., daily.

Island Park caldera. Henry's Fork of the Snake River empties into a prehistoric collapsed volcano now known as the Island Park caldera. The former cone is 18 mi long and 23 mi wide. It is marked by a 1,200-ft scarp on the south and west rims. U.S. 20 climbs the scarp at Big Bend Ridge. | 25 mi south of Ashton off U.S. 20 | 208/374–5476 | Free | Daily dawn to dusk.

Covering almost 2 million acres, the **Targhee National Forest** includes both semi-desert arid land and alpine-timbered highlands with 10,000-ft peaks and mountain streams, lakes, and meadows. A portion of the forest is in Wyoming, bordering Yellowstone and Grand Teton national parks. It is known for its campgrounds and attracts backcountry hikers with its network of trails. | 420 North Bridge St., St. Anthony | 208/624–3151 | Free | Daily dawn to dusk.

The **Big Springs and Big Springs National Recreation Water Trail** runs through a unique area at the headwaters of Henry's Fork of the Snake River, where you'll find rainbow trout year-round. The Big Springs National Recreation Water Trail is a popular float trip of two to four hours. The water flows are gentle, taking you past tree-lined shores and marshy islands, and you can watch birds and other wildlife along the way. The dock is ¾ mi below Big Springs. | 33 mi north on U.S. 20/191 to Mack's Inn, then 5 mi east on paved road | 208/558–7301.

Upper Mesa Falls are a dramatic set of waterfalls and the last major free-flowing falls in the Columbia River watershed. You can see them just off the Mesa Falls Scenic Byway, Route 47. A narrow gorge squeezes the Snake River to produce the **Lower Mesa Falls,** which drop some 65 ft. You get the best view from the Grandview Campground and Overlook. Fishing is optimum at this secluded spot. You can reach both the Upper and Lower falls from the Mesa Falls Scenic Byway. | 208/558–7301.

Aspen Acres, This 18-hole golf course is laid out around a expansive old farm, with lush greens and and aspen trees. Executive-length course plays par-60. | 4179 E. 1100 N | 208/652–3524 or 800/845–2374 | Greens fee $10 | Closed in winter.

Lodging

Three Rivers Ranch. A fishing lodge popular with fly-fishing fanatics. Sprawled on the banks of three rivers, whose crisp, serene waters are the main attraction. Free airport shuttle. Fishing docks. Boating. | PO 856, Ashton 83420 | 208/652–3750 | www.threeriversranch.com | 7 cabins, 1 lodge for groups of 8 | $2,480/wk per person (based on double occupancy); all-inclusive | AE, DC, MC, V | Closed Nov.–Apr. | AP.

BELLEVUE

MAP 3, C7

(Nearby towns also listed: Hailey, Ketchum, Sun Valley Area)

The Queen of the Hills and Minnie Moore mines gave rise to the town of Bellevue in May 1880. Called the gate city to the Wood River valley mining belt, a few months after its founding, the town had a population of 600. For just eight years in the 1880s, the Wood River valley enjoyed fame as the state's leading mining area, producing about $60 million in lead, silver, and gold. The town's charter was granted by the territorial legislature. Today it is the only one of three towns so chartered to retain that status, which means that it operates somewhat independently of the rest of the state. The town's population now tops 1,500, and even though it is less than 20 mi from cosmopolitan Sun Valley it still clings to its pioneer character.

Information: Sun Valley/Ketchum Chamber of Commerce | Box 2420, Sun Valley 83353 | 800/634–3347 | www.visitsunvalley.com.

Attractions

Shoshone Indian Ice Caves. As you might expect, it's cold in these caves, which are 90 ft below the surface. The temperature averages a chilly 22°F. The caves are actually lava tubes that are encrusted with flowstone. | 26 mi south on Rte. 75 | 208/886–2058 or 208/886–2030 | $5 | May–Sept., daily 8–8.

Lodging

Come on Inn. This cluster of individual log cabins with homey country furnishings is near the center of town and close to Sun Valley and Ketchum. You can walk to downtown Bellevue. Kitchenettes, no in-room phones. Cable TV. Laundry facilities. Pets allowed. | 414 N. Main St. | 208/788–0825 | 5 cabins | $50–$65 | AE, D, MC, V.

BLACKFOOT

MAP 3, E8

(Nearby towns also listed: Idaho Falls, Pocatello)

Blackfoot is known as the potato capital of the world. The title is fair; more than 30% of the nation's potatoes are grown in the irrigated fertile fields that surround the town. At the confluence of the Blackfoot and Snake Rivers, surrounded by an oasis of trees, the town was first called Grove City. In 1878 the name was changed to Blackfoot for the Native American tribe that lived in the area. Two years later, the town missed becoming the state capital by only a single vote. In the 1870s a military post, Fort Hall, was established about 7 mi from town, but was abandoned 13 years later. The town preserves several buildings from the early 1900s, when the town was settled by homesteaders. On the "day of the run" in 1907, thousands of sagebrush "sooners" rushed to Blackfoot to file their land claims.

Information: Blackfoot Chamber of Commerce | Box 801, Blackfoot 83221–0801 | 208/785–0510 or 208/785–7974.

Attractions

Bingham County Historical Museum. The 15-room house occupied by the museum would look right at home on a Southern plantation. The lava stone structure with gingerbread detailing and a columned portico was built in 1905 by John G. and Mary Brown, originally from Tennessee. Exhibits include a collection of antique dolls and other artifacts pertaining to local history. The mansion has Victorian-era woodwork and and fancy ironwork. | 190 N. Shilling Ave. | 208/785–8065 | Donations accepted | Mar.–Nov., Wed.–Fri. 10–4.

Idaho Potato Expo. Housed in a 1913 train depot, this downtown, must-see museum is dedicated to Idaho's famous potatoes. You can see curiosities of the spud world such as the world's largest potato chip, as well as exhibits on potato farming, potato trivia and history, and video presentations. The Spud Seller Gift Shop stocks potatoes, potato fudge, and potato-related novelties. | 130 N.W. Main St. | 208/785–2517 | $3 | May–Sept., Mon.–Sat. 10–5, Sun. 12–5.

ON THE CALENDAR

JUNE: *Tater Tour de Cure.* A bicycle tour benefits local charities and the Idaho Potato Expo with rides of 10, 25, 60, or 100 mi. 208/785–2517.

AUG.: *Shoshone-Bannock Indian Festival.* At Fort Hall Replica on the Fort Hall Reservation, this is a celebration of Native American culture with traditional dress, an art show, high-stakes bingo, a fun run, Indian crafts, and traditional handgames. 208/238–3700.

SEPT.: *Eastern Idaho State Fair.* Top-name stars, a rodeo, pig racing, and a demolition derby are just a few of the events that attract more than 210,000 visitors to the fairgrounds each year. 208/785–2483.

Dining

Homestead Family Restaurant. American. A farm-like setting with a big farmhouse and barn-inspired buildings serves home-style food. Locals come here for the popular breakfasts. | 1335 Parkway Dr. | 208/785–0700 | Reservations not accepted | $4–$8 | MC, V | Closed Sun.

Lodging

Best Western Blackfoot Inn. Modern accommodations in a newer motel. Complimentary Continental breakfast. In-room data ports. Cable TV. Pool. Hot tub. Gym. Business services, Pets allowed. | 750 Jensen Grove Dr. | 208/785–4144 or 800/528–1234 | fax 208/785–4304 | 60 rooms | $40–$85 | AE, D, MC, V.

BOISE

MAP 3, B7

(Nearby towns also listed: Caldwell, Nampa)

From a distance, Boise looks like a dreamy desert oasis rising above the seemingly endless sagebrush flats of the Boise Basin. The welcoming patch of green attracted Captain B.L.E. Bonneville and his party of French trappers as they trudged across the barren Snake River Plain in 1833, causing them to exclaim, "Les bois! Les bois!" ("Trees!"). The French name stuck, though it is now pronounced *boy*-see.

Today the city still looks more like a tuft of dense forest than a bustling metropolitan center. The largest of Idaho's cities, Boise still numbers only a modest 125,000 souls. Although it's the state capital, Boise is an easygoing city where few high-rises manage to tower above the dense canopy. The shimmering blue Boise River rushes through the heart of downtown and gives the city an unspoiled and almost wild feel. Boise nestles at the eastern edge of a broad valley beneath 8,000-ft peaks. Across the valley, roughly 30 mi from downtown, rise still more mountains at the Oregon state line.

A year after Bonneville's group discovered the riverside oasis, the Hudson Bay Company, a British fur-trading enterprise, constructed a fort near the mouth of the Boise River. By the 1840s, pioneers were steering Conestogas along the Oregon Trail across southern Idaho and through what is now downtown Boise. The longest of the pioneer roads, the 2,020-mi Oregon Trail, joined the state of Missouri with Oregon. The trail's deep ruts can still be seen in spots along its route through Idaho.

Gold-rush trails leading to the Boise Basin and Owyhee mines also brought settlement to the Boise area. But it was not until 1863 that Boise actually became a town. With an endless stream of pioneers passing through the Oregon Trail and swarms of miners, the U.S. military decided to build a fort to protect the new settlers in the region. Construction on Fort Boise was begun, and within a year, when the regional legislature held its second session in Lewiston, Montana, Boise was incorporated and named the capital of the Idaho Territory. Although gold fever gripped Boise and the town had grown to 1,658 by 1864, five years later it had shrunk back to just under 1,000. It resumed its growth in the 1870s, and by 1887, three years before Idaho became a state, it had a functioning streetcar system.

Like that of most Western frontier towns, Boise's growth was spurred by a succession of transportation links, including the railroad. A branch of the Oregon Short Line reached Boise in 1887. While the Boise Basin was becoming a booming rail center, irrigation was turning stretches of the once barren valley into lush farmland. By 1910, after construction of a dam and a canal, Ada County had 1,500 irrigated farms. When the Arrowrock Dam on the Middle Fork of the Boise River was completed in 1930, it was the tallest dam in the world. Today, it is included in a major recreation area south of Boise surrounding Lucky Peak and Arrowrock reservoirs.

Beginning in the late 1800s, another wave of immigrants hit Boise, this time Basques from the western Pyrenees. Basques are primarily sheepherders, and in southwestern Idaho they found a terrain and climate similar to those of their homeland. Their immigration peaked in the 1930s, but still today the Snake River Plain has the largest concentration of Basques in the United States, many of them carrying on the sheepherding traditions of their forefathers. Colorful Basque traditions are displayed at a cultural center in Boise and in annual Basque festivals held in several towns in south-central and southwestern Idaho.

Boise's governmental center is anchored by the stunning State Capitol, which was modeled after the U.S. Capitol and built of native sandstone between 1905 and 1912. A soaring 208-ft dome and polished marble columns inside grace the structure. For all the presence of state government and the high-tech giants Micron Electronics, Micron Technology, and Hewlett-Packard, Boise is still a major agricultural center, and as such is the home of the supermarket giant Albertson's and J. R. Simplot Co., one of the world's foremost processors of food, most notably potatoes. With a robust economy based on such diverse industries, Boise has the polish of a modern city but still manages to be a modest and unassuming town with an easygoing manner.

With the Boise River surging through the center of town and thousands of acres of national forest, lakes, and rugged mountain wilderness within an hour's drive, Boise is known for its outdoor sports and recreation opportunities. Just outside the city limits there are dozens of state and federal recreation properties and nature preserves, ranging from Bruneau Dunes State Park to the vast Boise National Forest. Roughly 40 mi southwest, the Snake River and its tributaries offer all manner of water sports.

BASQUES IN IDAHO

Euskadi, the country that the Basques hail from, is a 100-mi-long patch of land in the Pyrenees, the mountain range that makes up the border between Spain and France. The ancient Romans named the mountain people Vascones, which led to the name Basque or Vascos. The Basques themselves prefer to call themselves Euskaldunak, their country Euskal-Herria, and their language Euskara. Many Basques immigrated to Idaho to herd sheep, leading their flocks to the high pastures of sparsely populated mountain valleys in the summer months. Idaho is now home to roughly 20,000 Euskaldunak (the largest concentration of them anywhere). Towns like Ketchum, with its Trailing of the Sheep event celebrating the herding of sheep through the valley, offer a taste of Basque life with food and wool demonstrations. The finale is the actual passage of flocks of sheep through town on their way from the highlands toward ranches in south-central Idaho. The Basques are also known for their dancing and music, and Boise is home to the world-renowned Oinkari dancers. The Basque Museum in Boise's Basque Block, which dates back to the time when Basques first lived there in boarding houses, is in one of the former tenements, and has exhibits on Basque life and culture. On the same block is Bar Gernika, a Basque restaurant and tavern.

© Corbis

With all of this going for it, it is no wonder that Boise is one of the Northwest's upstart cities. The media have not failed to recognize its virtues. *Money* magazine touted the City of Trees as "the fourth-best place to live in America." *USA Today* ranked Boise among the six "cities of the '90s." Yet there are those who think enough is enough. Reporter Marianne Flagg of the Idaho *Statesman* appealed to her media colleagues in 1992 to "please stop writing about us," complaining that "it's tough to be the object of so much swooning, so much rosy wooing."

Information: Boise Convention and Visitors Bureau | Box 2106, 83701 | 208/344–6236 | boisecvb@boise.org | www.boise.org.

NEIGHBORHOODS

Downtown. Boise's historic downtown and state government center are concentrated along the east bank of the Boise River, much of it a 10 by 15 block area around the State Capitol. Within three blocks of the Capitol is Old Boise, a 3-block-long section of the original downtown around Broadway Boulevard and Main Street. Beside the sleek city hall, the city's tallest high-rise, a 19-story banking center, and other modern buildings sit grand old stone and brick landmarks, many with turrets and fancy archways dating from the city's pioneer years, the 1870s to 1890s. The 1920s Egyptian Theater was saved from the wrecking ball as was the Victorian-era Idanha Hotel, whose six stories made it the tallest building in Boise until 1978. Many of the historic landmarks are now filled with restaurants, bars, galleries, and shops. The century-old Book Shop, the state's oldest bookstore, is at the corner of Ninth and Main Streets. Old-fashioned cast-iron street lamps with big glass globes add nostalgic charm to the modest district.

South of Main Street. The area south of Main Street is filled with newer buildings. Near Eighth and Main, the Grove is a new fountain plaza that serves as a gathering place for the downtown brown-bag lunch crowd and also the scene of evening concerts and special events during the summer. A block away, between Capitol Boulevard and 6th Street, is Boise's original Basque Block, where boardinghouses and merchants serving the city's huge Basque population were concentrated up until the 1930s. The Basque Museum and Cultural Center and the bar Gernika, a narrow and noisy tavern and grill serving Basque specialties, anchor the area today.

Warm Springs District. Boise's true historic downtown neighborhood is the Warm Springs District, which runs east from Broadway Avenue along Warm Springs Avenue for roughly six blocks. The charming neighborhood claims to be the first residential district to be heated by geothermal water since Pompeii. Beginning in 1890, the Boise Hot and Cold Artesian Water Company started siphoning off 172-degree water from an underground aquifer. Today the State Capitol, government buildings, and about 400 homes enjoy a practically endless supply of hot water, as more than 750,000 gallons of geothermal water continues to be pumped each day. Among the homes that line the neighborhood's quiet, shady streets are French chateaus, English country manors, and stately Gothic mansions.

The I–84 Corridor. Most of Boise's development since the early 1970s has been along the interstate corridor extending about 20 mi west and south. As housing developments have stretched across the landscape, towns like Nampa that were once distinctly separate communities have been absorbed into the metropolitan Boise area.

Attractions

Basque Museum. Boise is home to the largest community of Basques outside Europe. This museum is in a former rooming house that served young Basque sheepherders and other immigrants from 1910 to the 1970s. The exhibits cover Basque culture and traditions and the story of the Basques in Idaho. | 611 Grove St. | 208/343–2671 | $3 | Tues.–Fri., 10–4, Sat. 11–3.

Bogus Basin Ski Resort. The mountains here reach 7,600 ft and are typically blanketed with 250 inches of snowfall each year. The resort has 2,600 acres of skiable and snowboardable terrain and a vertical drop of 1,800 ft. You can ski on wide, machine-groomed runs or areas that are kept natural. Bogus has more lighted terrain for night skiing than any other area in the northwestern United States. Beyond the learning area and 2 high-speed quad lifts, 4 doubles, 1 triple, and 1 rope tow take you to intermediate, bump, and tree-skiing areas. Or try the snowboard park and 32 km of cross-country skiing trails. | 2405 Bogus Basin Rd. | 800/367–4397 or 208/332–5100 | www.bogusbasin.com | Mid-Nov.–Apr., weekdays 10–10, weekends 9 AM–10 PM.

Boise National Forest. North and east of Boise, most of the forest land is within the Idaho Batholith, a large, eroded geologic formation. Through uplifting, faulting, and subsequent dissection by streams, a mountainous subalpine landscape developed. Elevations range from 2,600 to 9,800 ft. Evergreens dominate, and the nontimbered areas are covered with grass. You can see big-game species such as mule deer and Rocky Mountain elk, while streams and lakes are home to trout. The Boise and Payette rivers run through the forest, as do the South and Middle Fork drainages of the Salmon River. | 18 mi southeast of Boise on Rte. 21 | 208/364–4100 | Free | Daily dawn to dusk.

Eagle Island State Park. Close to Boise, this park is popular for day use. There's a swimming beach, a waterslide, and a grassy picnic area, plus walking paths and horseshoe pits. | 2691 Mace Rd., Eagle | 208/939–0696 | www.idoc.state.id.us/irti/stateparks | $3 | Memorial Day–Labor Day, daily.

Greenbelt (Wheels R Fun). The Greenbelt, a 25-mi paved path along the Boise River, attracts lots of in-line skaters, cyclists, and walkers. You can also simply float down the river in an inner tube. Bicycles, in-line skates, and rafts are available for rent. | 831 S. 13th St. | 208/343–8228 | Free | Memorial Day–Labor Day, daily; May and Sept., weekends; closed in winter.

Idaho Botanical Garden. Wander through the twelve specialty gardens, rest on benches and watch the fountains, or walk the trail through the foothills. | 2355 Old Penitentiary Rd. | 208/343–8649 | $3.50 | Apr.–Oct., weekdays 9–5, weekends 10–6; Nov.–Mar., weekdays 9–5, weekends 12–4.

Museum of Mining and Geology. Artifacts and old photographs tell the story of the state's colorful history of gold, silver, and gemstone mining. You can also take field trips to nearby geological sites. | 2445 Old Penitentiary Rd. | 208/368–9876 | $2 | Apr.–Oct., weekdays 9–5, weekends 12–5.

Idaho Museum of Military History. At Gowen Field, next to the airport, this museum is dedicated to Idahoans who served in military conflicts. Displays include firearms, Idaho naval history exhibits, and displays on the development of Gowen Field and the Idaho Army and National Air Guard. | 4040 W. Guard St., Building 924 | 208/422–6128 | www.inghro.state.id.us¢museum | Free; donations accepted | Fri.–Wed., 12–4.

Julia Davis Park. This large city park is spread along the Boise River downtown and has a playground, band shell, picnicking, formal rose garden, and several cultural facilities. | 700 S. Capital Blvd. | 208/384–4240 | www.boisecity.org | Free | Daily dawn to dusk.

Zoo Boise. Zebras and other more exotic animals join native species from Idaho and the rest of North America at this facility that appeals to children. The Jack and Esther Simplot Education Center features wildlife exhibits. | 355 N. Julia Davis Dr. | 208/384–4260 | www.sunvalleyski.com/zooboise/info.html | $4 | Daily 10–5.

At the edge of the Julia Davis Park, the **Discovery Center of Idaho** is a science museum with more than 130 hands-on exhibits. | 131 Myrtle St. | 208/343–9895 | $4; special rates for seniors and children | Tues.–Fri. 10–5, Sat. 10–5, Sun. 12–5.

The **Idaho State Historical Museum** contains exhibits and artifacts that tell of the influence of Native American, Basque, and Chinese cultures, fur trading, the gold rush, and mining. The small cluster of wood-frame and log buildings next door evokes the pioneer settlement of the area. | 610 N. Julia Davis Dr. | 208/334–2120 | Free | Mon.–Sat., 9–5, Sun. 1–5.

The **Boise Art Museum,** the only such facility in the state, mounts more than 15 temporary exhibitions exploring historical and contemporary themes each year. | 670 S. Julia Davis Dr. | 208/345–8330 | $4 | Tues.–Sat. 10–5, weekends 12–5.

The **Boise Tour Train.** Narrated one-hour tours leave from Julia Roberts Park, where you board an 1890s-style train that rides on tires and takes you through downtown. En route, you see Boise's first log cabin, the original sandstone gates of Fort Boise, the Old Penitentiary, the botanical gardens, and, across the river, part of the Oregon Trail. | 208/342–4796 | www.boisetourtrain.com | $6.50 | Daily.

Lucky Peak State Park. Ten mi south of Boise on Route 21, near Lucky Peak Reservoir, this park lies at an elevation of 3,000 ft. Its Discovery Unit features for picnicking and fishing for bull trout, Kokanee salmon, and rainbow trout. Sandy Point, at the foot of Lucky Peak Dam, has the park's most popular beach, picnicking, and concessions. The Spring Shores Unit has boat docks, a ramp, boat trailer parking, a marina, and concession services. There are guided nature walks and interpretive programs. The nearby Oregon Trail is popular for mountain biking, and the Discovery and Sandy Point units are connected to the Boise Greenbelt. | 208/344–0240 | www.idahoparks.org | $3 | May–Oct., daily.

M-K Nature Center. This facility at the Idaho Department of Fish and Game (the M-K stands for Morrison-Knudsen) features a short interpretive nature trail and a visitor center with windows onto the underwater world of a living river, hands-on displays, and changing exhibits. | 600 S. Walnut St. | 208/368–6060 or 334–2225 | Free | Call for hours.

Old Idaho Territorial Penitentiary. Built in 1870 and used until 1973, the penitentiary now welcomes visitors for shorter stays. Lady Bluebeard and Diamondfield Jack are among the more notorious of the 13,000 felons who did time at the prison, which is listed on the National Register of Historic Places and is one of only three territorial prisons of this vintage left in the United States. On your walk through the prison buildings you'll see exhibits on the history of transportation and electricity in Idaho. The prison grew from its original single cell house into a complex of Old West buildings surrounded by a high, hand-cut stone wall with turrets and guard towers. | 2445 Penitentiary Rd. | 208/368–6080 | $4 | Sept.–May, daily 12–5; June–Aug., daily 10–6.

Owyhee River. The state's most remote river brings together canyons and sagebrush desert of Idaho, Nevada, and Oregon. The name Owyhee (pronounced *oh*-why-he) is a phonetic version of "Hawaii." Five portions of the river are known for white water. The upper reaches include a deep canyon with majestic scenery; the middle portion is a challenging course for serious boaters that includes the perilous Widowmaker, the river's most famous rapids. The East Fork is challenging Class II to Class III white water with a couple of Class IV rapids, and worth the effort for sweeping high-country views of the deep gorge, bighorn sheep, falcons, and mountain lions. Owyhee river trips are best from spring through early summer, generally April to June, and usually take two to three days. | 208/384–3300 | Free | Daily dawn to dusk.

State Capitol. In the center of the downtown business district, the neo-Classical building was started in 1905 and and completed in 1920. It features marble from Alaska, Georgia, Italy, and Vermont and is topped by a 5-ft-7-inch copper eagle. Exhibits on the first floor display the state's agricultural, timber, gemstone, and mining products. The second floor has a statue of George Washington carved from yellow pine and covered in gold leaf. You can take guided tours. | 8th and Jefferson Sts. | 208/334–2470 or 208/334–2000 | www.state.id.us | Free | Weekdays 8–5, weekends 9–5.

Veterans Memorial State Park. The memorial is a 78-acre day-use park with picnic tables and a small lake. The park connects with the Greenbelt. | 960 Veterans Way | 208/334–2812 | www.idoc.state.id.us/irti/stateparks | Free | Daily dawn to dusk.

World Center for Birds of Prey. The 7,200-square-ft center studies habits and propagation of raptors and also has exhibits, some of live birds. There is also a Tropical Birds of Prey building. | 5666 W. Flying Hawk La.; I–84 Exit 50 to S. Cole Rd., then 6 mi south | 208/362–8687 | www.pregrinefund.org | $4 | Mar.–Oct., daily 9–5; Nov.–Feb., daily 10–4.

TOUR COMPANIES

Birds of Prey Float. An easy scenic float covering 15 mi of Class I to Class II water that takes four hours. The main attraction is the chance to see birds of prey in their natural river-canyon habitat. The best times to take the float are spring and fall. You can rent equipment there. | Meridian exit off I–84, then south on Rte. 69 to Kuna, Swan Falls Rd. to dam | 208/384–3300 | www.id.blm.gov | Free water access | Daily dawn to dusk.

Boise River Tours. These are gentler raft trips aboard self-bailing craft, designed to be both informative and fun. Along the way, guides explain the plant and animal life of the dense forest. Unlike white-water raft trips, these three- to four-hour tours are relaxed and smooth cruises; you don't even get wet. Daytime temperatures average around 60°F in spring and fall and around 90°F in summer. A shuttle service and refreshments are provided. | 111 Broadway | 208/333–0003 | www.boiserivertours.com | $40 | Mid-Apr.–Nov.

River Trips–Idaho Outfitters and Guides Association. This group can give you information on river trips; their list includes more than 400 outfitters, guides, and services. | Box 95 | 208/342–1919 | www.ioga.org.

ON THE CALENDAR

JUNE: *Boise River Festival.* Known as "America's Finest Family Festival," the celebration throughout Boise features more than 400 events, including six stages of continuous entertainment, hot-air balloon rally, the largest giant inflatable parade west of the Mississippi, and another glittering parade at night with spectacularly lit floats. 208/338–8887.

JUNE: *Gene Harris Jazz Festival.* Jazz pianist Gene Harris has been Idaho's musical ambassador to the world for more than 40 years. Concerts and dances are held over four days. 208/385–1203.

JUNE–SEPT.: *Idaho Shakespeare Festival.* The summer festival presents a full season of the Bard, plus one contemporary work, in a riverside setting ideal for picnicking under the stars. | 5657 Warm Springs | 208/336–9221.

AUG.: *Western Idaho Fair.* Idaho's largest fair has 4-H exhibits, a carnival, food, games, and top entertainers nightly, all at the Boise Fairgrounds. 208/376–3247.

Dining

INEXPENSIVE

Bar Gernika Basque Pub and Eatery. Basque, American. A popular downtown bar and café in an old, columned storefront is a window on Idaho's long history of Basque culture. The menu features exotic Basque cuisine with spicy meat and tomato sauces, also burgers, salads, and Basque wines. | 202 S. Capitol Blvd. | 208/344–2175 | $6–$8 | MC, V | Closed Sun.

Brick Oven Beanery. American. Crusty fresh-baked bread, homemade soup, and slow-roasted meats top the menu at this well-known casual downtown eatery with dine-in and carry-out service. Try the Louisiana Cajun gumbo with sausage, turkey, and ham. | 801 Main St. | 208/342–3456 | $6–$10 | AE, D, DC, MC, V.

Chapala. Mexican. Traditional dishes and great service make this small Mexican restaurant a standout. | 105 S. 6th St. | 208/331–7886 | $5–11 | No credit cards.

Moon's Kitchen Cafe. American. This casual downtown family café was voted among the best for burgers and milk shakes by Boiseans. Breakfast draws an especially large crowd. | 815 W. Bannock St. | 208/385–0472 | $4–$7 | AE, D, MC, V | Closed Sun. No supper.

Murphy's Oyster Bar and Grill. American. Upscale sports bar and restaurant with several big-screen televisions with satellite hookups. Full bar with large selection of microbrews. | 15555 Broadway Ave. | 208/344–3691 | $12–18 | AE, DC, MC, V.

Rick's Cafe Americain at the Flicks. Contemporary. Place an order for grilled Italian bread with toppings from a menu with a long list of appetizers, sandwiches, and salads, then take a seat by the fire or on the patio and watch a flick while dining. The interior is inspired by the café of the same name in the movie *Casablanca*. Beer and wine only. | 646 Fulton St. | 208/342–4288 | $5–$10 | AE, D, MC, V | No lunch weekdays.

MODERATE

Angell's Bar and Grill. Eclectic. Dark wood and hunter green create a relaxed setting downtown for inventive steak and seafood fare, ethnically inspired dishes and Northwest cuisine such as applewood-grilled salmon steaks. Try the Cantonese chicken salad—with sautéed chunks of chicken breast, water chestnuts, almonds, Chinese noodles, lettuce, scallions, and celery snow peas with a Cantonese dressing. Weather permitting, you can eat on the two covered patios. | 1 Capitol Center | 208/342–4900 | $16–$24 | AE, MC, V | No lunch Sat.–Mon.

B.B. Strands. Continental. A Former grocery store provides a tranquil atmosphere with lush greenery, large booths, and hardwood floors. Favorites are roasted poblano chile, filet mignon, and vegetable Wellington. | 310 N. 4th St. | 208/342–3777 | $14–20 | AE, DC, MC, V.

Chart House. American. The riverbank provides a perfect backdrop for the nautically inspired interior. Favorites are the steak, prime rib, swordfish, and mud pie. | 2288 N. Garden St. | 208/336–9370 | $14–24 | AE, D, DC, MC, V.

SILVER CITY

A 500-pound sample of ruby silver crystals from Silver City's Poorman's Mine won a gold medal at the Paris Exposition of 1866, and investment money from as far away as England pour in to the town from those who sought to strike it rich.
But like the remains of many once decadent, now decaying mining towns in this part of the country, this one's most lasting message is the fleeting nature of fortune. Silver City is probably now best known for "Long John's," which resembles a two-story outhouse but actually is only a very tall one-story privy.

Silver City, in the rugged high-desert mountains southwest of Boise, was once Idaho's equivalent of the Big Apple. It had more than 2,000 citizens crowding every flat space in the valley, and some even occupying niches in the vertical spaces in the gulch where the town lies. One of Idaho's major banks started here, and Col. William Dewey built the first hydroelectric dam on the Snake River to power the mines here. The electrical system eventually evolved into the Idaho Power Company.

Like many mining towns, Silver City also had its share of shoot-outs. An underground war ensued in 1869 when miners from two competing companies discovered that they were mining the same vein. About 141 bullets were found at the timbers at the intersection, according to Idaho historian Arthur Hart.

World War II nearly did in the town, as buildings were torn down and mill equipment collected for scrap drives. Today only about 75 structures remain. But to walk among them is a definite step back in time. A jumble of rickety buildings with rusty metal and peeling paint evokes a sense, if not the reality, of what used to be here. Besides the outhouse, check out the Masonic Lodge, which spans Jordan Creek (miners used to go in one door and out the other, joking that they'd crossed over the Jordan. The 137-year-old Idaho hotel was moved to Silver City from the nearby mining town of Ruby City on sleds and skids across the snow in 1866. The Catholic Church is probably the most photographed site in Silver City.

The graveyard is now home to some of the city's famous and infamous residents, like the schoolmarm who was killed in the 1878 Indian War. An open house is held in September. To get there from Boise, drive to Nampa and take Hwy. 45 across the Snake River to Hwy. 78. Turn right, or south, five mi east of Murphy. The 23-mi, single-lane gravel road from here to Silver City takes about an hour to drive.
—Karen Bosick

The Gamekeeper. Continental. With its wide selection of meats, this restaurant is geared toward the carnivores. A piano player greets you nightly in the lounge. | 1109 Main St. | 208/343–4611 | $15–20 | AE, MC, V | Closed Sun.

Lock, Stock and Barrel. Steak/Seafood. This long-standing restaurant is known for hand-carved steaks, prime rib, and fresh seafood served in a casual atmosphere, with live music on weekends and local microbrews on tap. | 4705 Emerald St. | 208/336–4266 | $10–$20 | AE, D, DC, MC, V | No lunch.

Oñati—The Basque Restaurant. Basque. A no-smoking, family restaurant set in the back of a casual bar, this roomy eatery serves authentic Basque dishes and is known for its savory lamb stew, chorizo sausage and rice, ink fish (squid) in savory tomato sauce, and Basque wines. Also try the red-bean soup. | 3544 Chinden Blvd., Garden City | 208/343–6464 | $10–$20 | AE, D, DC, MC, V | Closed Sun.

★ **Peter Schott's.** American. Many regard this small, elegant restaurant, run by a local cooking-show celebrity, as Idaho's best. Inventive American cuisine with a Northern Italian flair is Schott's specialty; fresh fish dominates the menu, and the wine list is complete. | 928 W. Main | 208/336–9100 | $16–$22 | AE, DC, MC, V | Closed Sun.

Sandpiper. Contemporary. One of three in a chain of Idaho restaurants (other locations: Idaho Falls and Twin Falls), this restaurant is great for special occasions, with candlelight, high ceilings, and oak tables. The menu favorites are steaks, prime rib, and seafood, such as the Hawaiian crunch halibut topped with chive-lime butter sauce. There's live music on weekends. | 1100 W. Jefferson St. | 208/342–7701 | $12–$25 | AE, D, DC, MC, V.

Tablerock Brewpub and Grill. American. A combination brewpub and casual restaurant with an upbeat atmosphere, decorated with light wood and Southwestern-inspired furnishings and colors. Plates are heaped with tasty basic fare of onion rings, chili, salads, burgers, pastas, and chicken. Try the shepherd's pie or the lemon-peppered chicken salad. Dine on the patio in the summer. Kids' menu. | 705 Fulton St. | 208/342–0944 | $10–$15 | AE, D, MC, V.

EXPENSIVE

Desert Sage. Contemporary. Striking contemporary decor and architectural details create a swanky atmosphere for the inventive and Northwest regional-inspired cuisine served in this downtown restaurant. | 750 W. Idaho St. | 208/333–8400 | $25–$40 | AE, D, MC, V | No lunch Sat.

Milford's Fish House. Seafood. In the historic warehouse district, this is a casual place has a long list of daily fresh-fish specials. You can eat on the patio in summer. | 405 S. 8th St. | 208/342–8382 | $25–$35 | AE, MC, V | Closed Sun. No lunch.

Lodging

INEXPENSIVE

Best Western Airport Motor Inn. Next to the airport, this low-slung building is stucco with dark wood trim and has newly redecorated rooms. There's a restaurant nearby. Complimentary Continental breakfast. In-room data ports, some refrigerators. Cable TV. Outdoor Pool. Laundry facilities. Airport shuttle. No pets allowed. | 2660 Airport Way | 208/384–5000 or 800/727–5004 | fax 208/384–5566 | www.bestwestern/airportmotorinn.com | 50 rooms | $68 | AE, D, DC, MC, V.

Best Western Safari. An older hotel in downtown's Old Boise area, this is within walking distance of the Convention Center and government offices. Complimentary Continental breakfast. Refrigerators. Cable TV. Pool. Hot tub, sauna. Business services. Laundry services. Airport shuttle. Pets allowed. | 1070 Grove St. | 208/344–6556 | fax 208/344–7240 | www.safari1@bigplanet.com | 103 rooms | $59–$85 | AE, D, DC, MC, V.

Best Western Vista. A newly remodeled hotel near the airport, this place has contemporary gray, blue, and brown print upholstered sofas, gray carpet, and light-wood furniture. Complimentary chocolate-chip cookies are served from 8–10 PM. Complimentary Continental breakfast. In-room data ports. Cable TV. Indoor pool. Hot tub. Exercise equipment. Business services. Laundry facilities. Airport shuttle. No pets allowed. | 2645 Airport Way | 208/336–8100 | fax 208/342–3060 | www.bestwestern/vista.com | 87 rooms | $70–$90 | AE, D, DC, MC, V.

Boise River Inn. Both quiet and close to downtown, this older motel has a dark wood-shingled exterior. Some rooms overlook the courtyard pool. On the bank of Logger Creek, it's less than ½ block from the Boise River and the Greenbelt. Guest rooms are furnished in dark wood and shades of blue, rose, and gray. Complimentary Continental breakfast, picnic area. Kitchenettes. Pool. Laundry facilities. No pets allowed. | 1140 Colorado Ave. | 208/344–9988 | fax 208/336–9471 | 88 suites | $55–$65 suites | AE, D, DC, MC, V.

Comfort Inn. Proximity to the airport makes this a good choice if you're just passing through town. This brick and stucco modern hotel has rooms done in rose and tan, with light oak furnishings. Complimentary Continental breakfast. Refrigerators (in suites). Cable TV. Indoor pool. Hot tub. Airport shuttle. No pets. | 2526 Airport Way | 208/336–0077 | fax 208/342–6592 | 62 rooms | $57–$69 | AE, D, DC, MC, V.

Inn America. Near the airport and overlooking the interstate highway, this motel has simple contemporary furnishings. Guest rooms are decorated with dark blue and rose floral fabrics against light-wood furniture, framed prints, and brass lamps. Complimentary Continental breakfast. In-room data ports. Cable TV. Pool. Laundry facilities. Business services. Airport shuttle. No pets. Free parking. | 2275 Airport Way | 208/389–9800 or 800/469–4667 | fax 208/338–13083 | www.innamerica.com | 73 rooms | $39–$56 | AE, D, DC, MC, V.

Seven K. The extremely modest rates are a lure at this contemporary hotel. Rooms are standard size. Cable TV. Pool. | 3633 Chinden Blvd. | 208/343–7723 | 23 rooms | $30 | AE, DC, MC, V.

Sunrise Inn B&B. This small, family-owned and -operated bed-and-breakfast overlooks the city. The combination of scenic mountain views and a tranquil, rustic setting is restful. In-room refrigerators. | 2730 W. Sunrise Rim Rd. | 208/344–0805 | 2 rooms | $40 | Closed winter.

MODERATE

Amerisuites Hotel. At this new all-suites hotel near Boise Towne Square Mall, all rooms have sleeper sofas, making it an especially good choice for families. A free shuttle serves a 5-mi radius that will get you to both shopping and restaurants. You're also close to museums and the Roaring Springs Water Park. Complimentary Continental breakfast. In-room data ports, microwaves, refrigerators. In-room VCRs. Indoor pool. Fitness center. Laundry service. Business services. Airport shuttle, bus shuttles. | 925 N. Milwaukee Ave. | 208/375–1200 or 800/833–1516 | fax 208/375–2900 | www.amerisuites.com | 128 suites | $59–$109 suites | AE, D, DC, MC, V.

Boise Park Suite Hotel. Business travelers will appreciate the spacious rooms with ample work space and in-room data ports. Kitchenettes. In-room data ports. Cable TV. Pool. Fitness center. Business services. Airport shuttle. | 424 E. Parkcenter Blvd. | 208/342–1044 | 243 rooms | $115 | MC, V.

Courtyard by Marriott. Reliably bright accommodations and service in a well-run, friendly atmosphere characterize this new hotel that's downtown next to shopping and restaurants. Café. Cable TV. Indoor pool. Hot tub. Gym. Laundry facilities. Airport shuttle. No pets. Free parking. | 222 S. Broadway Ave. | 208/331–2700 | fax 208/331–3296 | www.courtyard.com | 162 rooms | $99–$109 | AE, D, DC, MC, V.

Doubletree. This downtown high-rise hotel has contemporary furnishings and an upbeat feel. Restaurant, bar, room service. Cable TV. Pool. Exercise equipment. Downhill skiing. Business services. Airport shuttle, pets allowed (fee). Free parking. | 1800 Fairview Ave. | 208/344–7691 | fax 208/336–3652 | www.hiltonhonors.com | 182 rooms | $69–$104 | AE, D, DC, MC, V.

Doubletree Club Hotel. On the edge of downtown, the contemporary high-rise hotel stands in a parklike setting near Boise State University and less than one block from the bank of the Boise River and Greenbelt. Bar, Au bon Pain. Refrigerators (in suites). Cable TV. Pool. Exercise equipment. Business services. Airport shuttle. Free parking. | 475 W. Park Center Blvd. | 208/345–2002 or 888/444–CLUB | fax 208/345–8354 | www.doubletree.com | 158 rooms | $59–$104 | AE, D, DC, MC, V.

Fairfield Inn by Marriott. This hotel, built in 1995, is close to the mall and the airport and set back from the highway. Designed with business travelers in mind, the rooms have ample work space. Complimentary Continental breakfast. Some microwaves, some refrigerators. Cable TV. Indoor pool. Spa. Meeting room. No pets allowed. | 3300 S. Shoshone St. | 208/331–5656 | fax 208/424–3169 | www.faifieldinn.com | 63 rooms | $54–$79 | AE, D, DC, MC, V.

★ **Idaho Heritage Inn.** This is an imposing turn-of-the-century governor's mansion close to downtown. The dignified Governor's Suite features dark walls and shiny white woodwork, an heirloom quilt on the oak sleigh bed, and an enclosed sun porch. A skylight brightens a roomy executive suite furnished with antique iron beds, striped wallpaper, and wicker. The Carriage House is a private hideaway complete with a microwave, refrigerator, and deck. In the Warm Springs district of Boise, the inn enjoys a seemingly endless supply of natural geothermal spring water and features deep tiled tubs in the baths. The nicely landscaped grounds enhance the setting, and you're within walking distance of downtown. Complimentary breakfast, picnic area. No TV in some rooms, in-room phones. No pets. No smoking. | 109 W. Idaho St. | 208/342–8066 | fax 208/343–2325 | info@idahoheritageinn.com | www.idheritageinn.com | 6 rooms (2 with shower only), 2 suites, 1 carriage house | $65–$105, $95 suites and carriage house | AE, D, MC, V.

Owyhee Plaza Hotel. One of the original big hotels downtown was built in 1910 and has since been renovated. Guest rooms have stylish, brightly painted walls, dark floral spreads, and warm copper-color carpeting. 2 restaurants, bar (with entertainment), room service. In-room data ports. Cable TV. Pool. Beauty salon. Business services. Laundry services. Airport shuttle. Pets allowed (fee). Free parking. | 1109 Main St. | 208/343–4611, 800/233–4611 (outside Idaho), or 800/821–7500 | fax 208/336–3860 | www.owyheeplaza.com | 100 rooms | $59–$132 | AE, MC, V.

Quality Inn Airport Suites. An older motel next to the airport, this has dark green plush carpeting and floral spreads accented with dark wood, brass lamps in guest rooms, and a pool surrounded by trees for a seclusion. Complimentary Continental breakfast. Many kitchenettes, refrigerators. Cable TV. Pool. Laundry facilities. Airport shuttle. Some pets allowed (fee). | 2717 Vista Ave. | 208/343–7505 | fax 208/342–4319 | 79 suites | $58–$70 suites | AE, D, DC, MC, V.

Ramada Inn. In-room whirlpool tubs are a nice plus since you also have use of the Valley Athletic Club. The furnishings are contemporary. Restaurant, country-western bar. Pool. Sauna. Free use of the Valley Athletic Club. | 1025 S. Capitol Blvd. | 208/344–7971 | 127 rooms | $60–75 | AE, DC, MC, V.

Shilo Inn Airport. This is a relatively new hotel near the airport. The rooms are comfortable and the amenities standard. Complimentary Continental breakfast. Some refrigerators. Cable TV. Pool. Hot tub. Exercise equipment. Laundry facilities. Business services. Airport shuttle. Pets allowed. | 4111 Broadway | 208/343–7662 | fax 208/344–0318 | 126 rooms | $60–$71 | AE, D, DC, MC, V.

Sleep Inn. Close to the airport, this is a good choice for those planning only a short stay. The rooms are standard size and comfortable. Complimentary Continental breakfast. Some refrigerators. Cable TV, in-room VCRs and movies. Laundry facilities. Business services. Airport shuttle. No pets. | 2799 Airport Way | 208/336–7377 or 800/321–4661 | fax 208/336–2035 | www.innamerica.com | 69 rooms (with shower only) | $55–$70 | AE, D, DC, MC, V.

Super 8 Lodge–Boise Airport. Standard chain accommodations at the airport. Snack shop. Cable TV. Pool. Laundry facilities. Business services. Airport shuttle. Some pets allowed (fee). | 2773 Elder St. | 208/344–8871 | fax 208/344–8871, ext. 444 | www.super8.com | 108 rooms | $55–$65 | AE, D, DC, MC, V.

BOISE

INTRO
ATTRACTIONS
DINING
LODGING

University Inn. Next to Boise State University on the edge of downtown and ½ block from the Boise River and Greenbelt. Bar, complimentary Continental breakfast. Cable TV. Pool. Hot tub. Business services. Airport shuttle. Free parking. | 2360 University Dr. | 208/345–7170 or 800/345–7170 | fax 208/345–5118 | 82 rooms | $45–$90 | AE, D, DC, MC, V.

VERY EXPENSIVE

Ameritel Inn. A newer contemporary hotel with dark green trim on stucco. The rooms have comfortable, upholstered easy chairs, light floral-print spreads, and dark-wood furniture. You're one block from the Boise Towne Square Mall. In-room data ports, some kitchenettes. Cable TV. Indoor pool. Hot tub. Gym. Laundry facilities. Business services. | 7965 W. Emerald St. | 208/378–7000 or 800/808–4667 | fax 208/378–7040 | 124 rooms | $75–$129 | AE, D, MC, V.

Doubletree-Riverside. A mile from downtown and overlooking the Boise River. Guest rooms are decorated in dark rose with floral fabrics and blue-gray carpeting. Restaurant, bar. In-room data ports, some refrigerators, room service. Cable TV. Pool, wading pool. Hot tub. Exercise equipment. Business services. Airport shuttle. Some pets allowed (fee). | 2900 Chinden Blvd. | 208/343–1871 | fax 208/344–1079 | 264 rooms, 40 suites | $79–$159 rooms, $145–$395 suites | AE, D, DC, MC, V.

Holiday Inn. Near the airport, with a Holidome recreation center featuring a 25-ft video wall. Rooms are newly redecorated in light rose and blue floral upholstery and light-wood contemporary furniture. Restaurant, bar, room service. Cable TV. Indoor pool. Hot tub. Exercise equipment. Laundry facilities. Business services. Airport shuttle. Pets allowed. | 3300 Vista Ave. | 208/344–8365 | fax 208/343–9635 | www.bhr.com | 266 rooms | $79–$99 | AE, D, DC, MC, V.

★ **J. J. Shaw House Bed and Breakfast Inn.** Downtown in a historic district, this stately restored 1907 Queen Anne–Victorian home is brick and sandstone, with columns, decorative moldings, French doors, and original leaded glass. The gracious three-story structure has spacious guest rooms elegantly furnished with poster beds, floral-bordered wallpaper, and antiques. Shaw's Retreat on the third floor features an elegantly draped king-size bed, sitting and dining areas, skylights, bay windows, and a bath with a double shower. Complimentary breakfast. In-room data ports, no-smoking rooms. Business services. | 1411 W. Franklin St. | 208/344–8899 or 877/344–8899 | fax 208/344–6677 | jjshaw@earthlink.net | www.jjsahw.com | 6 rooms | $79–$109 | AE, D, MC, V.

Residence Inn by Marriott. An all-suites hotel with fully equipped kitchens and living rooms, most with brick fireplaces. Studio, one- and two-bedroom, and two-bath units; contemporary upholstered wood furniture, framed Western prints, and warm earth-tone carpeting make the loft suites with fireplaces especially warm and comfortable. Picnic area. Refrigerators. Cable TV. Pool. Hot tub. Laundry facilities, dry cleaning. Business services. Airport shuttle. Some pets allowed ($10 fee). | 1401 Lusk Ave. | 208/344–1200 | fax 208/384–5354 | www.residenceinn.com/boiio | 104 suites | $105–$135 suites | AE, D, DC, MC, V.

Shilo Inn Riverside. In a parklike setting on the bank of the Boise River and close to downtown. There is a free shuttle, and the driver will take people anywhere in the area. Complimentary Continental breakfast. Microwaves and refrigerators in every room. Cable TV. Indoor pool. Exercise equipment. Laundry facilities. Business services. Airport shuttle. Pets allowed (fee). | 3031 Main St. | 208/344–3521 or 800/222–2244 | fax 208/384–1217 | www.shiloinn.com | 112 rooms | $55–$95 | AE, D, DC, MC, V.

Statehouse Inn. Downtown across from the convention center. New country-inspired decor features contemporary furnishings with bold striped wallpaper and floral fabrics in rose, cream, and shades of brown. Guest rooms are spacious and airy with comfortable upholstered side chairs and ottomans. Restaurant, bar, complimentary full breakfast (with suites). Minibars, some refrigerators, Cable TV, in-room VCRs. Exercise equipment. Laundry services. Business services. Airport shuttle. No pets. | 981 Grove St. | 208/342–4622 or 800/243–4622 | fax 208/344–5751 | 112 rooms | $70–$100 | AE, D, DC, MC, V.

Wapiti Meadow Ranch. People come here for the solitude, beauty, and outdoor activities. Lush meadows edged with forests and streams surround this wilderness retreat. Trail rides, gold panning, and ghost-town tours are just some of the diversions. Don't be surprised if you see an elk or moose or coyote strolling the grounds. All meals are included in the rate. Restaurant. No in-room phones. Spa, hot tub. Horseback riding. Fishing. Laundry facilities. No pets. | HC 72, Cascade; 50 mi north on Rte. 55 | 208/633–3217 | fax 208/633–3219 | www.guestranches.com/wapiti.htm | 7 cabins | $850–$1,600/wk (7–day minimum stay) | No credit cards | AP.

West Coast Park Center Suites. An all-suite hotel near the Boise River and Greenbelt in a quiet setting on the edge of downtown. Bar, complimentary Continental breakfast. In-room data ports, kitchenettes, minibars. Cable TV. Pool. Hot tub. Exercise equipment. Laundry facilities. Business services. Airport shuttle. | 424 E. Park Center Blvd. | 208/342–1044 or 800/342–1044 | fax 208/342–2763 | www.cavanaughs.com | 238 rooms | $84–$125 | AE, D, DC, MC, V.

BONNERS FERRY

MAP 3, B1

(Nearby town also listed: Sandpoint)

An 1863 gold rush to Canada's Wildhorse district gave rise to the town of Bonners Ferry, a convenient stopover on the banks of the Kootenai River. The town, roughly 35 mi from the Canadian border, is named after Edwin L. Bonner, who built a ferry on the river in 1864. When the Fry brothers bought the ferry operation a few years later, they tried to change the name to Fry but were unsuccessful. Long before gold miners and settlers founded the town, the area was inhabited by the lower band of the Kootenai (pronounced *koot*-n-nee) Nation. In 1855, the Kootenai were not represented at the Hellgate Treaty and were left without a claim to lands. In retaliation, they declared war, which forced the U.S. government to give them some 18 acres of land where a casino resort stands today. The town is also surrounded by the densely wooded mountains of the Panhandle National Forests. Less than 20 mi from the Montana border, it is also a starting point for excursions to Glacier National Park.

Information: **Greater Bonners Ferry Chamber of Commerce** | Bonners Ferry, 83805 | 208/267–5922 | www.bonnersferrychamber.com.

Attractions

Kootenai National Wildlife Refuge. Less than 20 mi from the Canadian border, just outside of Bonner's ferry, this 3,000-acre refuge includes ponds, grasslands, cultivated croplands, shrubs, and a timbered region to the west. The large variety of wetland birds includes many species of ducks—mallards, the main nesting species, and wigeon and pintails, which are migratory. Canada geese typically number 2,500 in the fall. In spring you can see migrating tundra swans. Both white-tailed and mule deer and coyotes are common; rarely seen are black bears, elk, and moose. | HCR 60, Box 283, Bonners Ferry | 208/267–3888 | fax 208/267–5570 | www.fws.gov | Free | Daily dawn to dusk.

Moyie Falls. The frothy white waterfall is tightly wedged between canyon walls. The Moyie Bridge spans the canyon 450 ft up, providing a dramatic view of the spectacular waterfall. | 10 mi east via U.S. 2 | 208/267–5922 | www.idoc.state.id.us | Free | Daily dawn to dusk.

ON THE CALENDAR

JUNE: *Kootenai Days.* A summer festival that takes over the town includes a rodeo, raft races, street dances, live music, and food. 209/267 5922.

Dining

Alberto's Restaurant. Mexican. A friendly atmosphere and Mexican folk art set the scene for the authentically prepared Mexican gourmet specialties at this restaurant on the edge of town. Try the mole poblano with nuts, peppers, chocolate and spices. The house special is shrimp mojo served in garlic sauce. | 6536 S. Main St. | 208/267–7493 | $5–$10 | D, MC, V.

Feist Creek Falls Resort. Contemporary. In a secluded woodsy setting along the Moyie River near Feist Creek Falls, this place is known for steaks, seafood, and barbecue ribs. | Rte. 34 and Meadow Creek Rd.; 45 mi north on U.S. 95 to Good Grief, then 3 mi south on Rte. 34 (near Canadian border) | 208/267–8649 | $10–$15 | AE, MC, V.

Panhandle. American. This homey downtown cafe serves country-style food at modest prices. | 7168 Main St. | 208/267–2623 | $10–$15 | D, MC, V.

Lodging

Bear Creek Lodge. You can choose between the newer motel and a bed-and-breakfast here. The motel offers roomy, modern log cabin–style rooms while the B&B has more luxurious accommodations. Complimentary Continental breakfast. In-room phones. Cable TV. | 5952 U.S. 95 S | 208/267–7268 | 5 motel rooms, 7 B&B rooms | $59–$69 motel rooms, $79 B&B suite | AE, D, DC, MC, V.

Best Western Kootenai River Inn. Off I–95 in the center of town, on Kootenai River Plaza. All rooms have a river view. Restaurant, bar, room service. Cable TV. Indoor pool. Hot tub. Exercise equipment. | Kootenai River Plaza | 208/267–8511 | fax 208/267–3744 | 69 rooms | $83–$100 | AE, D, DC, MC, V.

Bonners Ferry Log Inn. Guests are greeted by lush greenery and landscaped grounds at this modern inn with log cabin–style accommodations. Spacious, comfortable rooms. Hot tub. | U.S. 95 W | 208/267–3986 | 27 rooms | $69 | AE, DC, MC, V.

Kootenai Valley Motel. A smaller, older motel 1 mi from downtown that appeals to families, with fireplace units, all overlooking a grassy picnic area. A laundromat and restaurant are nearby. Some kitchenettes. Cable TV. Hot tub. Playground. Business services. No pets. | U.S. 95 S | 208/267–7567 | fax 208/267–2600 | 22 rooms | $65 | MC, V.

Paradise Valley Inn Bed and Breakfast. A log lodge with a cathedral ceiling set on 55 wooded acres, this secluded retreat only 10 minutes from Bonners Ferry features light and airy guest rooms, most with log walls and views. Contemporary furnishings have Native American and Western motifs. Cheop's Chamber features meadow and mountain views and a sunroom. Athena's Room overlooks the valley and has a private deck. Cleopatra's Bedroom is the premier accommodation, with views, a fireplace, a vintage clawfoot bathtub for two, and a private deck. The Inn's restaurant (reservations required) serves regionally inspired cuisine such as fresh salmon with lemon pepper, and pan-seared fillet of beef served either with a green peppercorn mustard sauce or a brandy-cream sauce. Complimentary full breakfast. In-room phones. TV, VCRs with movie selection. Hot tub. Laundry facilities. No pets. | 300 Eagle Way; 10 mi south off U.S. 95 | 208/267–4180 or 888/447–4180 | fax 208/267–3673 | info@ParadiseValleyInn.com | www.paradisevalleyinn.com | 5 rooms | $110–$175 (2–night minimum) | AE, MC, V.

BRUNEAU

MAP 3, B8

(Nearby town also listed: Hagerman, Mountain Home)

This tiny hamlet, founded in 1881, is believed to have gotten its name from the French word "brun," or brown, or perhaps an early French trapper named Baptiste or Pierre Bruneau. The placid farming community gives no clue about the spectacular vistas a few miles away. Bruneau is also a good gateway for exploring Owyhee county, Idaho's southernmost county. The county covers acres of ranchland, mining ghost towns, and rugged canyon lands full of hoodoos, which are strange rock formations.

ATTRACTIONS

Bruneau Sand Dunes Park. This is a giant sandbox with the largest single-structure sand dunes in North America. Taller than the Great Pyramid in Egypt, they reach a height of 470 ft. Scientists believe that the sand began collecting in the basin about 12,000 years ago, following the Lake Bonneville Flood, probably the second-largest flood in the world after northern Idaho's Lake Missoula flood. The water slammed against a lava wall on the park's outskirts and swirled around in what is now called Eagle Cove. The huge eddy deposited the sand, which formed the dunes. The sands don't shift and change with changes in air current because they're trapped by the basin and the prevailing winds. If you are a photographer, they are a wonderful subject.

Within the park's 2,800 acres, you can camp, monitor the wildflowers (prince's plum, storkbill, and pale evening primrose, among others). It is also a stopover for migrating water fowl. You can fish for blue gill, sunfish, and largemouth bass in the nearby lakes, hike, and ski down the dunes on your rock skis. | 3 mi southeast of Bruneau on Hwy. 51 | 208/366–7919 | $2 per car (day use); fees for camping.

Bruneau Overlook. The Bruneau River cuts a deep gash across the desert plateau carving a canyon with vertical walls 800 ft deep and 1,300 ft wide. Bighorn sheep hang on the cliffs, antelope bounce across the sagebrush plateau, and miners dig for a unique rock known as Bruneau jasper. If you're a history buff, you can search for petroglyphs left by the Paiute Indians. The Indian Bathtub hot springs, which you'll pass en route to the overlook, dried up several years ago after a drought and damage to the rock around it. You'll also pass through Saylor Creek Aerial Gunnery Range and see some nerve-wracking signs warning you to look out for objects falling from the sky. | Take the paved road off Hwy. 51 just south of Bruneau. At the eight-mi point, there's a fork; stay to the left, and continue for three mi, where the road dead-ends at the overlook.

C. J. Strike Dam. This 132-ft-high earth-filled dam was completed in 1952 at the confluence of the Bruneau and Snake Rivers, just west of Bruneau. You can camp and fish for bluegill, bass, crappie, and trout in the 8,000-acre horseshoe-shaped lake that was formed by the dam. Free tours are offered daily. | 2 mi west of Bruneau on Hwy. 78 | 208/834–2295 | Free; fees for camping.

Hughes River Expeditions. Between April and June, snowpack permitting, this outfitter in Cambridge offers multiday river trips along the Class IV rapids on the Bruneau River. | 800/262–1882 | fax 208/257–3476.

BUHL

MAP 3, C8

(Nearby town also listed: Twin Falls)

Buhl is the trout capital of the state, home of the nation's largest trout farm. The town is named after Frank H. Buhl, an investor and land developer from the East who helped start the Twin Falls Land Tract, which brought irrigation projects to the arid land along the south shore of the Snake River. Today the flat fields high above the river near the Thousand Springs section of the Snake are teaming with trout and crops and the area has earned the nickname Melon Valley. Trout farming started in 1928, 23 years after the town was platted, and today there are more than 60 hatcheries and fish farms in the area. At this point, the Oregon Trail travels along the south rim of the Snake River canyon, while along the north rim a few miles west of Buhl are the 2 mi of the so-called Thousand Springs, which spill some 200 ft down the verdant canyon wall.

Information: Buhl Chamber of Commerce | 716 U.S. 30 E, 83316 | 208/543–6682.

Attractions

Balanced Rock. A mushroom-shape rock with a top portion at 48 ft across on a base that is just 3 ft 17 inches in diameter. The formation stands at 200 ft and the base has been reinforced with concrete. Neighboring Balanced Rock Park stretches ½ mi along Salmon Falls Creek and has picnic tables and fire rings. | 6 mi west of Castleford on Rte. 74, 1 mi north on 900 East Rd., then 4 mi west on 3700 North Rd. | 208/543–6682 | Free | Daily dawn to dusk.

Clear Springs Food. The world's largest commercial trout farm produces nearly 18 million pounds of rainbow trout each year. There is a picnic area near a fish pond with underwater window viewing. You can take tours. | Clear Springs Rd.; off U.S. 30 | 800/635–8211 | Free | Daily.

ON THE CALENDAR
JULY: *Buhl Sagebrush Days.* An event in celebration of the desert shrub with food, fairs, and a fireworks display. 208/543–6682.

Dining

Harvest Cafe. American. This modest local diner is the favorite of residents. Steak and hamburgers are good choices. | 114 S. Broadway | 208/543–8892 | $6–12 | AE, DC, MC, V.

Lodging

Amsterdam Inn Bed & Breakfast. This turn-of-the-century home has a European-influenced interior and a homey feel. Each bedroom is tasteful decorated with antiques. Complimentary breakfast. | Clear Lakes Rd. | 208/543–6754 | 3 rooms | $35–50 | No credit cards.

BURLEY

MAP 3, D9

(Nearby towns also listed: American Falls, Twin Falls)

A river-straddling town, Burley sits on 20 mi of the most approachable shoreline of the Snake River. Its easy river access draws scores of boaters, anglers, and others for water recreation. It is also the site of one of the few powerboat races on the Snake. A farming community, Burley is also a sizable (population 8,918) base camp for those venturing to the City of Rocks for rock climbing or to Pomerelle during the winter for skiing in the 10,000-ft mountains that tower above the valley along the Utah state line.

Information: **Mini-Cassia Chamber of Commerce** | Box 640, Heyburn, 83336 | 208/ 679–4793 | fax 208/679–4794 | www.minicassiachamber.org.

Attractions

Caldron Linn. This geologic feature forces the Snake River through a passage less than 40 ft wide near the Oregon Trail. The Wilson Price Hunt exploration party of 1811 capsized on the river several times at this point and made the rest of their journey on foot. | North of Murtagh | 208/679–4793 | Free | Daily dawn to dusk.

Cassia County Historical Museum. The museum displays Native American artifacts, fossils, a stagecoach, and early farming tools. The main attraction is a mural-size map of Cassia County presented with an audio tape that traces the five pioneer trails that crossed it. On the grounds is a miniature pioneer village with a furnished log cabin, general store, and schoolhouse, all dating from the 1880s. | Main St. and Highland Ave. | 208/678–7172 | Free, donations accepted | Apr.–mid-Nov., Tues.–Sat. 10–5.

City of Rocks National Reserve. The reserve is also called the Silent City of Rocks and sits at an elevation of 5,800 ft. Recently named a National Historic Reserve and now part of the National Park system, the 14,000-acre park includes a 500-acre "city" of rock pinnacles that rise up some 60 to 70 stories. (This is among the top rock climbing areas in the U.S.) The tall, smooth columns with rounded edges are weathered granitic formations more than 2.5 billion years old, some of the oldest rocks in North America. The reserve is near the junction of the Oregon and California trails and was often mentioned in pioneers' diaries. Many left their names written in axle grease on rocks near the trail. The Kelton-Boise stage route also traveled through the reserve, and remains of the station are still visible. | 22 mi south on Rte. 27 to Oakley, then 16 mi southeast; follow signs | 208/678–7230 | www.nps.gov/ciro | Free | Visitor Center: daily 8–4:30.

The **Pomerelle Ski Area** is a no-frills vintage alpine skiing operation that is affordable and appeals to families. It is nestled in the Sawtooth National Forest in the Albion Mountain division. The peaks reach 9,000 ft; most of the 24 groomed runs are at 8,000 ft and the mountains usually have 500 inches of snowfall each year. The vertical drop is about 1,000 ft. You can rent equipment. There's a restaurant, ski school, downhill and cross-country skiing, weekend night skiing, and snowboarding. | Box 158, Albion; 50 mi east of Twin Falls, or take Heyman exit off I-84 and go south on Rte. 77 | 208/673–5599 | $22 | Mid-Dec.–mid-Apr., Tues., Sun. 11–4, Fri., Sat. 11–10.

Sawtooth National Forest—Burley Ranger District. The Burley District includes five units, each named for the mountain ranges it encompasses: Albion Mountain, Black Pine, Sublett, Raft River, and Cassia. The five units include more than 70,000 acres south of Burley in Idaho and below Utah state line. Peaks here reach 9,600 ft, and the terrain is both sagebrush-dotted grassland and forested mountains. There are six alpine lakes, three reservoirs, and many streams within the district, which is one of the less visited ones. You can see mule deer, moose, elk, wild turkeys, bobcats, cougars, many small mammals, and a wide variety of birds. You can camp, hike, and go mountain biking. In the Albion Mountain division, Lake Cleveland is one of two high alpine lakes south of the Snake River. | 3650 S. Overland Ave. | 208/678–0430 | www.northrim.net/sawtoothnf/index1.htm | Free | Daily dawn to dusk.

ON THE CALENDAR

JUNE: *Idaho Powerboat Regatta.* Six classes of 140-mph powerboats and four top drag boats race at the Burley Marina, reaching speeds of more than 200 mph. 208/679–4793.
AUG.: *Cassia County Fair and Rodeo.* A six-day hoedown at the fairgrounds with rides, games, food, exhibits, and a rodeo. 208/436–4793.

Dining
Charlie's Cafe. Mexican/American. Charlie's is the town's most frequented restaurant. Traditional Mexican dishes dominate the menu—huevos rancheros are popular—but locals also come for the prime rib. | 615 E. Main | 208/678–0112 | $6–$12 | AE, DC, MC, V.

Lodging
Best Western Burley Inn. A playground and volleyball court make this very well maintained hotel a good choice for families. Rooms overlook the pool and a shady courtyard. There is a small shopping mall nearby. Restaurant, bar, room service. Cable TV, some VCRs. Pool. Volleyball. Playground. Laundry facilities. Business services. Pets allowed. | 800 N. Overland Ave.; I-84 Exit 208 | 208/678–3501 | fax 208/678–9532 | 126 rooms | $60–$80 | AE, D, DC, MC, V.

CALDWELL

MAP 3, A7

(Nearby town also listed: Boise)

The snow-capped Owyhee Mountains along the Oregon border look down on fields lush with bright-green alfalfa hay, sugar beets, and big squares of land that are striped by vineyards and orchards, a sight that bears little resemblance to what one would have seen here in the 1880s, when the area surrounding the new town was little more than a dry alkaline basin dotted with sagebrush. The town grew and continued to develop irrigation projects that transformed the area into fertile farmland. Key to the development were efforts led by Idaho and Oregon Land Improvement Co. president Alexander Caldwell, from whom the town took its name, and his publicity agent Robert "Pard" Strahorn. They bought acreage along the railroad tracks and sold lots, helping the town grow. The company also owned water rights to an irrigation ditch that carried water from the Boise River. The completion of the Deer Flat dams and Lake Lowell in 1908 further boosted agricultural development in Caldwell, making Canyon County one of the most productive in the nation. Potato baron J. R. Simplot Co. started dehydrating onions and later potatoes at a Caldwell plant in the 1940s. This was the start of Simplot's food-processing operations, among the biggest in the world today. Simplot plants here now produce frozen, dehydrofrozen, and dehydrated products.

Information: **Caldwell Chamber of Commerce** | 914 Blaine St., 83605 | 208/459–7493 | fax 208/454–1284 | www.caldwellid.org.

Attractions

Albertson College of Idaho. Albertson College of Idaho is a private, liberal arts institution. Founded as The College of Idaho in 1891, Albertson is home to about 700 undergraduates and is the state's oldest four-year institution of higher learning. | 2112 Cleveland Blvd. | 208/459–5500 | www.acofi.edu | Free | Sept.–May.

Ste. Chapelle Winery and Vineyards. Idaho's largest winery is surrounded by the Winery Hill Vineyard and overlooks the Snake River valley. The winery began small in 1976, and now produces 130,000 cases of premium varietal wines each year. You can take a tour that explains the fermentation, aging, and bottling processes and includes a complimentary wine tasting. In summer, there's a Sunday afternoon jazz concert series at a 2-acre park below the winery. | 19348 Lowell Rd. | 208/459–7222 | fax 208/459–9738 | www.idahowines.com | Free | Mon.–Sat. 10–5, Sun. 12–5.

Warhawk Air Museum. The museum at the airport features a rare collection of WW II memorabilia and aircraft. | 4917 Aviation Way | 208/454–2854 | www.caldwellid.org | $2 | Daily 10–4.

ON THE CALENDAR

JUNE–SEPT.: *Jazz at the Winery.* World-class jazz is presented in an outdoor setting at the Ste. Chappelle Winery in the Sunnyslope Valley. 208/459–7222.
AUG.: *Night Rodeo.* One of the top 20 professional rodeos in the nation, featuring leading cowboys. This long-standing Idaho rodeo is held outdoors at the Rodeo Grounds. 208/459–7493.

Dining

Caldos y Mariscos el 7 Mares. Mexican. A mounted marlin dominates the decor of this gourmet seafood restaurant with a Mexican twist. House favorites are the *camarones al mojo de ajo* (garlic prawns) and the *pulpo* (octopus). | 420 N. 5th Ave. | 208/459–2190 | $4–11 | AE, DC, MC, V.

Tacos Michoacan. Mexican. A small restaurant popular with with locals because of its prompt service and inexpensive dishes, traditional Mexican fare. | 605 N. 5th Ave. | 208/454–1583 | $4–13 | AE, DC, MC, V.

Lodging

Best Inn and Suites. Just off I-84, with coffee and cookies in the evening and a 24-hour recreation facility including an indoor pool. Natural stone accents against yellowish tan siding, planters with flowers, and old wagon wheels resting against a split rail fence give the hotel a rustic flavor. Picnic area, complimentary Continental breakfast. Minibars, some refrigerators. Cable TV. Indoor pool. Hot tub. Exercise equipment, health club privileges. Laundry facilities. Pets allowed ($10 deposit). | 901 Specht Ave. | 208/454–2222 | fax 208/454–9334 | bestinn@cyberhighway.net | 65 rooms | $58–$100 | AE, D, DC, MC, V.

Best Western Caldwell Inn and Suites. A new hotel with mini, executive, and spa suites, along with standard guest rooms. For Albertson College fans, the Albertson College Room mini-suite features college memorabilia and decor. Located just off I–84 near other motels. Complimentary Continental breakfast. Indoor pool. Spa. Exercise equipment. Business services. | 908 Specht Ave.; I–84 Exit 29 | 208/454–7225 or 800/528–1234 (reservations) | fax 208/454–3522 | 69 rooms, 14 suites | $59–$140, $89–$129 suites | AE, D, DC, MC, V.

Harvey House Bed and Breakfast. Five miles from town, this converted farmhouse offers scenic views of the rural countryside. The well-kept gardens are pleasant, and and rooms are furnished with antiques. The owners will prepare prix-fixe dinners on request. Deck, Jacuzzi. | 13466 Hwy. 44; I–84 Exit 25, then 2 mi east | 208/454–9874 | 4 rooms | $85–110 | No credit cards.

Holiday Motel. This budget motel has contemporary design and standard chain-sized rooms. Picnic grounds. | 512 Frontage Rd. | 208/454–3888 | 36 rooms | $37 | AE, DC, MC, V.

Sundowner Motel. This older, independent motel downtown is close to everything and has spacious rooms. Complimentary Continental breakfast. Some refrigerators. Cable TV. Pool. Pets allowed (fee). | 1002 Arthur St.; I–84 Exit 28 | 208/459–1585 or 800/454–9487 | fax 208/454–9487 | 67 rooms | $40–$100 | AE, D, DC, MC, V.

USEFUL EXTRAS YOU MAY WANT TO PACK

- ❏ Adapters, converter
- ❏ Alarm clock
- ❏ Batteries
- ❏ Binoculars
- ❏ Blankets, pillows, sleeping bags
- ❏ Books and magazines
- ❏ Bottled water, soda
- ❏ Calculator
- ❏ Camera, lenses, film
- ❏ Can/bottle opener
- ❏ Cassette tapes, CDs, and players
- ❏ Cell phone
- ❏ Change purse with $10 in quarters, dimes, and nickels for tollbooths and parking meters
- ❏ Citronella candle
- ❏ Compass
- ❏ Earplugs
- ❏ Flashlight
- ❏ Folding chairs

- ❏ Guidebooks
- ❏ Luggage tags and locks
- ❏ Maps
- ❏ Matches
- ❏ Money belt
- ❏ Pens, pencils
- ❏ Plastic trash bags
- ❏ Portable TV
- ❏ Radio
- ❏ Self-seal plastic bags
- ❏ Snack foods
- ❏ Spare set of keys, not carried by driver
- ❏ Travel iron
- ❏ Travel journal
- ❏ Video recorder, blank tapes
- ❏ Water bottle
- ❏ Water-purification tablets

*Excerpted from *Fodor's: How to Pack: Experts Share Their Secrets*
© 1997, by Fodor's Travel Publications

CHALLIS

MAP 3, C6

(Nearby towns also listed: Salmon, Stanley)

As central Idaho's gateway to the rugged river and mountain wilderness, the tiny town of 1,200 is surrounded by the 2.3-million-acre Frank Church–River of No Return Wilderness, the largest such area in the lower 48 states, and sits near the Salmon River, one of the top white-water rivers in the country. Trappers first settled the Challis area in 1822, and some 50 years later gold brought a mining boom to the town that lasted almost three decades. The town was laid out by Alvah P. Challis in 1876 and became an important trading and shipping center, serving mining camps and ranches. The Challis mineral belt is still mined today for gold, silver, molybdenum, and 40 other minerals. You can take a self-guided driving tour along the Salmon River valley that traces

FAMOUS POTATOES

The humble potato was first grown in the north woods of Idaho by a Presbyterian missionary, Henry Harmon Spalding, at a Lapwai mission in the 1830s. The next notable milestone in the potato's history in Idaho was in 1860, when Mormon pioneers from Salt Lake City settled in the southeastern corner of the state near Franklin. The settlers lived in their wagons, built irrigation ditches, and harvested bushels of potatoes and onions the first year. Just 16 years later, farmers from the same area shipped more than 2.5 million pounds of potatoes to mining camps as far away as California. By the early 1870s, botanist Luther Burbank had developed the Burbank tuber, which was then succeeded by the Russet Burbank, developed by a scientist in Denver. Idaho would make the Russet Burbank famous. The University of Idaho established an agricultural experimentation station for potato research at Aberdeen in 1911. Seed-piece size, spacing, storage, bruising, and fertilizer levels and other factors were all tested and refined. Thanks to widespread irrigation initiatives in the early 1900s and ongoing research, the Snake River Plain, once an arid, sagebrush-dotted region, began producing enormous harvests of high-quality potatoes. Today Idaho's receipts from agriculture top $3.1 billion each year. It was J. R. Simplot who became the true spud king. After reaping a handsome profit on a small hog operation at age 17, he rented 160 acres near Declo (in the heart of today's potato country) and planted potatoes. Simplot applied his business savvy to adding value to the simple tuber, thereby becoming a billionaire who heads up the second-largest producer of frozen potatoes in the world. He produced freeze-dried potatoes for the troops in World War II and backed the development of frozen french fries in the 1940s. It's estimated that processors multiply the value of the raw spud six times over (from 5 cents to 30 cents a pound). Today's farmers in southern Idaho raise the nation's largest crop of potatoes, about 30 percent of the total yield in the United States. In addition to starting with good potatoes and abundant water, they can rely on the porous, fertile volcanic soil and arid growing conditions to produce uniform growth with few imperfections.

Yankee Fork mining history, also walking tour in Challis that recalls the town's early days.

Information: **Challis Area Chamber of Commerce** | 700 N. Main St., Challis, 83220 | 208/879–2771 | fax 208/879–5836.

Attractions

Challis National Forest. At more than 2.5 million acres, Challis is one of the larger national forests in Idaho. The property stretches nearly 125 mi east and west by 92 mi north and south, and includes a range of terrain from the rugged peaks of Mount Borah and the surrounding Lost River Range at 10,500 to 12,000 ft to the lower canyon of the Middle Fork of the Salmon River at 3,790 ft. Over 1,600 mi of trails run through the forest, including the Knapp Creek–Loon Creek Trail and the Mill Creek Lake Trail, both designated National Recreation Trails. The forest also includes one-third of the 2.3-million-acre Frank Church–River of No Return Wilderness, the largest wilderness in the continental United States. You can camp at the 26 developed campgrounds with more than 260 individual campsites. Each campground has its own special attractions, such as launching sites for river trips, fishing and boating on Mosquito Flat Reservoir, or nearby ghost towns like Custer and Bonanza. | Challis Ranger District, HC 63, Box 1669, | 208/879–4321 | fax 208/879–4199 | www.fs.fed.us/r4/sc | Free | Daily dawn to dusk.

The **Middle Fork of the Salmon Wild and Scenic River** is considered the standard by which other stretches of white water in the nation are measured. The Salmon River system is the longest undammed river system in any single state. The Middle Fork is 100 mi long and put-in points are at 6,000 ft, take-out points at 3,000 ft. The river is considered Class III+, depending on water levels, and has many technical rapids, although it still offers a well-rounded family experience. The course passes through alpine forest and grassland habitats with bighorn sheep, mule deer, and river otters. The optimum time for river trips is April through September, and they typically take from four to eight days. You can also visit hot springs, do some catch-and-release fishing, and hike—trailheads are along the side of the stream. The more popular hikes are Waterfall Creek, Veil Falls, and Loon Creek. The river corridor is also rich in archaeological and historical sites such as petroglyphs, pioneer homesteads, and gold dredging ruins. | 208/879–5204 | www.idoc.state.id.us/irti/Rivers | Free | Daily dawn to dusk.

The 79-mi **Main Salmon Wild and Scenic River** rushes through the Frank Church–River of No Return Wilderness Area. The river was called Tom-Agit-Pah, or "Big Fish Water," by the Shoshoni tribes who lived here during the annual salmon run. These native cultures considered the river too dangerous for canoe travel and developed an extensive trail system to reach the narrow canyon. The Nez Percé tribe used the lower river, and the Sheepeater Shoshoni lived upstream. The Main Salmon features big waves and many streamside campsites on sandy beaches. You can hike in the Salmon Canyon and, because the river corridor is not part of the wilderness, jet boats are permitted. River trips are scheduled from spring through fall, running Class III to Class IV rapids and usually taking five to seven days. | 208/756–3724 | www.idoc.state.id.us/irti/Rivers | Free | Daily dawn to dusk.

Just north of Mackay off U.S. 93 is Idaho's tallest peak, Mount Borah, which rises to 12,662 ft. A marker at the base of the peak notes the still-visible **1983 Challis Earthquake Fault Line** from the earthquake measuring 7.3 on the Richter Scale that shook the area on October 28, 1983, damaging Challis and Mackay. The earthquake was the largest to hit the continental United States since 1959. | 208/588–3400 | www.fs.fed.us/r4/sc | Free | Daily dawn to dusk.

Land of the Yankee Fork State Park. This 6,000-acre state park showcases Idaho's frontier mining history. Beginning in 1870, the Land of the Yankee Fork area attracted gold seekers, and within six years the mining communities of Custer and Bonanza were established. The 1880s brought rapid growth, as the Lucky Boy, General Custer, and Montana mines gave up their ore. Custer reached a population of 600. But by 1911 Custer and Bonanza were ghost towns. At the town sites are the Bonanza Cemetery and the Custer Museum, where artifacts and photographs are displayed. Nearby is the Yankee Fork Gold Dredge, a 988-

ton barge that searched the gravel of the Yankee Fork for gold until 1953. Guided tours are available during the summer. An interpretive center near Challis has displays telling the Yankee Fork mining story in a building styled after the old mining mills. The Custer Motorway, an old toll road that once saw freighters and stages on their way to Custer and Bonanza, parallels Route 75 in the backcountry en route to Yankee Fork, 35 mi away. Along the route, historic sites, overlooks, and interpretive signs point out the history of the region. At Sunbeam, interpretive signs describe the Salmon River and the remnants of the Sunbeam Dam, the only dam ever constructed on the Salmon. The park contains no designated campgrounds but you'll find camping areas along the Salmon River between the interpretive center and Custer and Bonanza. | 25 mi west of Challis; gold dredge and town sites 10 mi north of Rte. 75 | 208/879–5244 | Free | Daily.

Lodging

Northgate Inn. A large, older, well maintained motel on the north end of town, this place is close to both the Salmon River and to restaurants and shopping. Both rates and the amenities are basic. Satellite TV. Pets allowed (fee). | HC 63, Box 1665 | 208/879–2490 | fax 208/879–5767 | 56 rooms | $34–$51 | AE, D, MC, V.

Village Inn. A modern hotel with a restaurant, air-conditioned rooms, and a large hot tub. Restaurant. Some kitchenettes, some refrigerators. Cable TV. Hot tub. Pets allowed. | U.S. 93 | 208/879–2239 | fax 208/879–2813 | 54 rooms | $34–$68 | AE, D, DC, MC, V.

COEUR D'ALENE

MAP 3, A2

(Nearby town also listed: Kellogg)

Ancient glaciers sculpted Idaho's Panhandle, leaving behind a lake-studded terrain of low-lying rounded mountains draped in a forested mantle. The crown jewel of the Panhandle's southern reaches, pristine Lake Coeur d'Alene sparkles like a sapphire against the emerald-green landscape. The resort town of 28,158 that goes by the name of the lake it surrounds first attracted vacationers as a destination resort in the early 1900s. The cool north woods of Idaho and its sparkling centerpiece lake lured vacationers from Spokane and other Washington cities that had hot, dry summers. Luxuriously appointed steamers like the 197-ft *Idaho,* the largest in its day, sailed on overnight cruises. Today Coeur d'Alene's economy is still centered on vacationers. One of the most recognizable landmarks is a high-rise hotel that towers over the lakefront above a ³/₄-mi-long floating boardwalk, the world's longest. Coeur d'Alene claims another world record with the only floating golf green on the planet. There are several other golf courses nearby. Despite its commercialization though, the lake retains much of its wild nature. The largest population of ospreys in the western United States lives on the lake, and in December and January migrating bald eagles swoop across the water's surface to catch kokanee salmon.

The origin of the name Coeur d'Alene is subject to debate; in French it means "heart of awl." About 4 million acres around Coeur d'Alene and in the southern portion of the Panhandle were once held by the Coeur d'Alene Indian tribe, which gave Jesuit missionary Father Pierre De Smet a warm reception in the 1840s. About 20 years later, John Mullan and his crew started hacking the Mullan Road out of the wooded wilderness. It was rerouted in 1861 and is today part of Sherman Avenue.

In 1877, the Mullan Road carried General William Tecumseh Sherman to the area, where he surveyed the lakefront for potential sites for a military fort. A tent city was followed in 1878 by a military stockade, Fort Coeur d'Alene, on the north shore near the Spokane River inlet. Pioneers soon began settling in the area, which was incorporated as a town in 1887 with a population of 1,000. The discovery of gold, silver, and lead brought a rush of miners from 1883 to 1885. Today sightseeing cruisers troll the waters, offering a modern-day look at a thriving resort community spread along the lakeshore.

Another view of the town and lake is from atop Tubbs Hill, a 135-acre park that was once the 1882 homestead of German immigrant Tony Tubbs. Fortunately, Tubbs Hill and other lakefront and surrounding mountain wilderness pockets have been saved from development by a grassroots effort. Since the 1980s there has been a ground swell of support against development along the lakeshore, and for now the "Save the Shores" supporters have managed to keep overdevelopment at bay.

Information: Coeur d'Alene and Post Falls Convention and Visitors Bureau | Box 908, Post Falls, 83854 | 208/773–4080 or 800/292–2553 | www.info£cda-pfcvb.com.

Attractions

Canefield Mountain Trail System. Thirty miles of trails open to hikers, motorcycles, mountain bikes, and equestrians. | Fernan Ranger District, 2502 E. Sherman Ave.; East off I–90 | 208/664–2318 | Free.

Farragut State Park. The 4,000-acre park is 2,054 ft high, beneath the Coeur d'Alene Mountains in the Bitterroot Range. One of Idaho's largest state parks, it edges Lake Pend Oreille and has several beaches. You can often see whitetail deer, badgers, black bears, coyotes, bobcats, and an occasional elk. You can hike, fish, boat, and swim, and also take nature walks and go horseback riding. | E. 13400 Ranger Rd., Athol | 208/683–2425 | www.idoc.state.id.us/irti/stateparks | $2 per car | Daily dawn to dusk.

Idaho Panhandle National Forests. The combined forests total 2.5 million acres in the state's northern Panhandle, eastern Washington, and western Montana. The Panhandle Forest administers approximately half the total forested acres in the Panhandle region of Idaho. The forests' most notable features are the old stands of cedars at Hanna Flats and Roosevelt Grove near Priest Lake. Other highlights include the Settlers Grove of ancient cedars near Prichard and Hobo Cedar Grove near Clarkia. At the East Fork of Emerald Creek, 8 mi southeast of Route 3 near Clarkia, you can collect gem-quality garnets for a fee. The Idaho Panhandle National Forests include the Coeur d'Alene and portions of the Kaniksu and St. Joe national forests. | 3815 Schreiber Way | Forest Supervisor's Office: 208/765–7223 | fax 208/765–7307 | Free | Daily dawn to dusk.

Lake Coeur d'Alene. Glaciers carved out the basin for this lake, elevation 2,152 ft, that extends south of town for about 25 mi. The shimmering blue lake is just 2½ mi wide, tucked in among softly sculpted and forested mountains. Most of its water comes from the Coeur d'Alene, St. Joe, and St. Maries rivers, which rise along the Pend Oreille Divide and the Bitterroot Range. The lake's outlet is the Spokane River, a tributary to the Columbia. The south end of the lake is a bay-like area named Lake Chatcolet. The highly developed shoreline offers lakeside restaurants, marinas, and hotels. The lake is home to one of the world's largest populations of ospreys, which nest here. | www.idoc.state.id.us | Free | Daily dawn to dusk.

Museum of North Idaho. The museum's major exhibits highlight Native American culture, steamboats, the logging industry, and nearby communities. | 115 Northwest Blvd. | 208/664–3448 | www.coeurdalene.org | $1.50 | Apr.–Oct., Tues.–Sat. 11–5.

Fort Sherman Museum. Within the Museum of North Idaho, the Fort Sherman Powder House contains artifacts and information on Fort Sherman, which was founded in 1878. It also contains an original Forest Service smoke-chaser's cabin. | 208/664–3448 | Included in museum admission | May–Sept., Tues.–Sat. 1–4:45.

Silverwood Theme Park. The theme of this amusement park is an 1880s mining town. Within it are a narrow-gauge steam train, a wooden roller coaster, a log flume, and 24 other rides, including the newest roller-coaster ride Tremors, which spends much of the time in underground caves. Also an antique airplane museum and midway games. | 26225 U.S. 95 N, Athol | 208/683–3400 | fax 208/683–2268 | www.silverwood4fun.com | $24 | Call for hours.

Tubbs Hill. Come to this 120-acre wooded preserve to find century-old pine and fir trees, as well as hidden coves and beaches. Open to foot traffic only. | P.O. Box 7200 | 208/769–2252 | Free | Daily dawn till dusk.

ON THE CALENDAR

MAY: *Fred Murphy Days.* Locals honor the legendary steamboat captain with food, drink, a parade, tests of strength and skill, and street dances. 208/773–4080.

JULY: *July-amsh Powwow.* Hundreds of Native American drummers, horsemen, and dancers come together during one of the nation's largest outdoor powwows. More than 200 booths feature traditional goods, clothing, jewelry, drums, and furs for sale. Also, storytelling demonstrations, rodeo events, and traditional bareback riding. 208/773–5016.

NOV.: *Coeur d'Alene Fall Craft Show.* Handcrafted arts and crafts are presented at a show and sale. | Silver Lake Mall | 208/772–6296.

NOV.–DEC.: *Coeur d'Alene Fantasy in Lights and Laser Extravaganza.* A spectacular lighting ceremony with fireworks, a lighted parade downtown, and cruises aboard a climate-controlled boat are some of the offerings during this holiday festival. Each cruise ends with a laser show. 208/765–4000.

DEC. *Coeur d'Alene Festival of Trees.* A juried show of 40 trees and 100 holiday wreaths, also dinner and dance, auction, and style show at the Coeur d'Alene Resort. 208/666–8733.

Dining

Beverly's. Contemporary. The inspired Northwest cuisine is made even more enjoyable by the lake views through window walls. The 7th-floor restaurant, part of the Coeur d'Alene Resort, has a contemporary design with copper and dark wood accents. Try the grilled salmon drizzled with huckleberry salsa or the char-broiled tenderloin of beef served with a peppered panchetta chip, Beverly scalloped potatoes, and a truffle merlot sauce. Kids' menu. | 208/765–4000 | $19–$31 | AE, D, MC, V.

Capone's. American. Sports bar and grill where the interior tells the history of American sport. With hanging baseball mitts, nostalgic photos, and live music, the atmosphere is decidedly casual. Try the gourmet pizza. | 751 N. 4th St. | 208/667–4843 | $7–$11 | AE, DC, MC, V.

The Cedars. Contemporary. The rustic wood building sits on the lake at the end of a pier and is the town's only floating restaurant. Steaks and seafood predominate on the menu. | ¼ mi south of I-90 on U.S. 95 | 208/664–2922 | $30–$40 | AE, DC, MC, V | No lunch.

Chef in the Forest. Continental. A chalet building in a secluded pine-forest setting houses this fine dining restaurant that's out of town and next to a lake. Try the roast duckling with brandied raspberry sauce. | 7900 E. Hauser Lake Rd., Post Falls | 208/773–3654 | $18–$22 | MC, V | Closed Sun.–Tues. No lunch.

Hudson's Hamburgers. American. A lunch counter and local downtown landmark dating to 1907 with a six-item menu, counter, and some table seating for handmade double cheeseburgers, hot ham and cheese, and fried egg sandwiches. | 207 Sherman Ave. | 208/664–5444 | $3–$6 | No credit cards | Closed Sun., Mon. No supper.

Iron Horse Bar and Grill. Contemporary. Fun, family dining with old-time photographs, local history memorabilia. The menu is basic with steaks, prime rib, seafood, and burgers. You can eat on the patio in nice weather. | 407 Sherman Ave. | 208/667–7314 | $10–$16 | AE, D, DC, MC, V.

Jimmy D's. Contemporary. This establishment is across from the lakefront. Inside, the red-brick walls are hung with the work of local artists. At dinner, Northwest specialties are served by candlelight. Menu highlights are the creative pastas, seafood fettuccine, grilled steaks, and fresh fish. You can eat on the patio in season. | 320 Sherman Ave. | 208/664–9774 | $15–$20 | AE, D, DC, MC, V.

Mad Mary's. Thai. The brightly colored flames on the exterior wall reflect the causal atmosphere of this inexpensive restaurant that is a favorite with locals. The menu features standard Thai dishes. | 1801 Sherman Ave. | 208/667–3267 | $7–$11 | AE, DC, MC, V.

Moon Time. American. Casual is the word at this restaurant. There's a wide selection of microbrews and appetizers, such as fresh clams steamed in beer, along with a typical menu. | 1602 Sherman Ave. | 208/667–2331 | $6–$10 | AE, DC, MC, V.

Monarch Fisheries. Seafood. With direct shipments from Alaska and Seattle, this casual establishment may be the best place for well-prepared seafood in town. | 445 Cherry La. | 208/765–6744 | $8–$14 | AE, DC, MC, V.

Wolf Lodge Inn. Contemporary. Cherry and tamarack wood are used for open-pit grilled steaks, seafood, and food with a Western flair in the rustic, comfortable dining room in a quiet wooded setting. | 12025 E. Frontage Rd.; I–90 and Rte. 97 | 208/664–6665 | $21–$54 | AE, D, MC, V.

Lodging

Ameritel Inn. This is a good place to stay if your principal reason for stopping is Wild Water Water Park—it's right next door. Just off I–90, the new hotel is among a cluster of other lodging options. Complimentary Continental breakfast. Cable TV. Pool. Hot tub. Gym. Laundry facilities. No pets. | 333 Ironwood Ave. | 208/665–997 or 800/600–6001 | fax 208/665–9900 | www.ameritelinns.com | 118 rooms | $79–$149 | AE, D, DC, MC, V.

Baragar House. In the pristine area of Sherman, this family-owned and -operated bed-and-breakfast offers a luxurious yet homey atmosphere. Guest rooms are decorated in various motifs; the favorite seems to be the room that has the Milky Way painted on the ceiling in fluorescent paint. Complimentary breakfast. Sauna. | 316 Military Dr. | 800/615–8422 or 208/664–9125 | www.baragarhouse.com | 3 rooms | $100–$130 | AE, DC, MC, V.

Berry Patch Inn. Five minutes from town, this bed-and-breakfast is furnished in an elegant country style, with a stone fireplace and open beam ceiling. Complimentary breakfast. | 1150 Four Winds Rd. | 208/765–4994 | fax 208/765–4994 | www.bbhost/berrypatchinn | 3 rooms | $115–$135 | MC, V.

Best Western Templin's Resort. Older and well maintained, this hotel is good if you plan to do a lot of hiking. It's a five-minute walk from the Centennial Trail, which runs from Couer d'Alene to Spokane. On the bank of the Spokane River, many rooms overlook the marina and private beach. Restaurant, bar (with entertainment), picnic area, room service. In-room data ports, some refrigerators. Cable TV. Indoor pool. Hot tub. Tennis. Exercise equipment, beach, dock, marina, boating. Business services. Laundry facilities. Some pets allowed [fee]. | 414 E. 1st Ave., Post Falls; I–90 Exit 5 | 208/773–1611 | fax 208/773–4192 | www.bestwestern.com | 167 rooms | $84–$139 | AE, D, DC, MC, V.

★ **Blackwell House.** This B&B is in an elegant, charming Victorian estate built in 1904 by W. A. Blackwell, a wealthy timber merchant, as a wedding gift for his son. The three-story whitewashed wedding-cake home has rich wood paneling and patterned wallpaper in rose and burgundy. Guest rooms are furnished with antique beds and upholstered wingback chairs. The sunny Rosenberry Suite has huge double windows with lace curtains, a fireplace, and a sitting area. The roomy Blackwell Suite has an antique oak spool bed, soft-pink floral wallpaper, and a sitting area. Restaurant nearby, complimentary breakfast and afternoon snacks. No air-conditioning (in some rooms), no room phones, no TV in rooms. TV in lobby. Kids over 12 only. | 820 Sherman Ave. | 208/664–0656 | 11 rooms (2 with shared bath) | $75–$140 | AE, D, MC, V.

★ **Clark House on Hayden Lake.** This huge Colonial-style white house with green shutters stands in a cluster of cedars beside Hayden Lake. When it was built in 1910 as the summer home of F. Lewis Clark and his wife Winifred, the 15,000-square-ft home was on 1,400 acres and was the most expensive home in Idaho. Now restored, the interior has golden yellow walls and white woodwork, polished wood floors, framed art prints, and antiques.

The guest rooms are furnished with antiques and heavy traditional furniture in ivory, black, and gold. Four have fireplaces, and three overlook the garden or a small cedar forest. A formal, two-course breakfast is served, and six-course candlelight dinners are available by reservation only. Dining room, complimentary full breakfast. Hot tub. No pets. | E. 4550 S. Hayden Lake Rd. | 208/772–3470 or 800/765–4593 | fax 208/772–6899 | info@clarkhouse.com | www.clarkhouse.com | 10 rooms | $100–$225 | AE, D, DC, MC, V.

Coeur d'Alene Budget Saver Motel. Families traveling on a limited budget get a good deal with the two-room accommodations here. In-room TV. | 1519 Sherman Ave. | 208/667–9505 | 27 rooms | $30–44 | DC, MC, V.

Coeur D'Alene Inn and Conference Center. The room furnishings are striking at this new hotel—dark fabrics against light-wood contemporary furniture and short looped-pile carpet. The reasonably priced inn is five minutes from downtown and close to the interstate. Restaurant, bar (with entertainment), room service. In-room data ports, some refrigerators and microwaves. Cable TV with pay-per-view. Pool. Business services. Laundry services. Pets allowed (fee). | 414 W. Appleway St. | 208/765–3200 or 800/251–7829 | fax 208/664–1962 | www.cdainn.com | 122 rooms | $59–$119 | AE, D, DC, MC, V.

★ **Coeur D'Alene, a Resort on the Lake.** Everything is here; you never have to leave the resort. Restaurants and lounges, a European spa, a championship golf course, tennis, a recreation center, and lake cruises are all on the property. You can stay in the oversized rooms in the 18-story Lake Tower, the deluxe Park Wing, the west rooms that overlook the pool and floating boardwalk, or the east rooms that look toward Tubbs Hill. Economy rooms have limited views but are tastefully appointed. The resort's condominiums are two blocks away, and executive and penthouse suites are also available. The Beverly restaurant and a second restaurant sit on the water's edge. 2 restaurants (see Beverly's), 3 bars (with entertainment), room service. In-room data ports, refrigerators. Cable TV, in-room VCRs (movies available). 2 pools (1 indoor), wading pool. Hot tub, spa, massage. Gym. 18-hole golf course, tennis. Bowling, marina, boating. Shops. Children's programs (ages 5–12). Business services. | 115 S. 2nd St. | 208/765–4000 or 800/688–5253 | fax 208/664–7276 | resortinfo@cdaresort.com | www.cdaresort.com | 329 rooms | $79–$2,500 | AE, D, DC, MC, V.

Days Inn. A well-maintained older inn off I–90 and near the center of downtown. Complimentary Continental breakfast. Cable TV, VCRs available. Hot tub, sauna. Exercise equipment. Pets allowed ($25 deposit). | 2200 Northwest Blvd. | 208/667–8668 | fax 208/765–0933 | www.the.daysinn.com/coeurdalene06805 | 61 rooms | $50–$107 | AE, D, DC, MC, V.

Fairfield Inn by Marriott. This hotel just ½ mile from Lake Coeur d'Alene has easy access to I–90. Designed for business travelers, the spacious rooms have well-lighted work desks and in-room data ports. Complimentary Continental breakfast. In-room data ports, some microwaves and refrigerators. Cable TV. Indoor pool. Hot tub. Laundry facilities. No pets. | 2303 N. 4th St. | 208/664–1649 | fax 208/664–1649 | www.fairfieldinn.com | 69 rooms | $35–$100 | AE, D, DC, MC, V.

Flamingo Motel. One block from downtown, this older strip motel has both standard rooms and bungalow units. You can walk to the lake, restaurants, and shopping. Some kitchenettes, some refrigerators. Cable TV. Pool. No pets. | 718 Sherman Ave. | 208/664–2159 or 800/955–2159 | fax 208/667–8576 | 14 rooms, 4 bungalows | $72–$95, $130 bungalows | AE, D, DC, MC, V.

Hawthorne Inn and Suites. A very child-friendly place that's just off the interstate, this inn has some spa rooms, some kitchenettes, and an indoor pool. The freshly baked cookies served in the evening make it even nicer. Wednesday night socials have free hors d'oeuvres. Complimentary full breakfast. Some microwaves, some refrigerators. Cable TV. Indoor pool. Sauna, spa. Laundry facilities. Pets allowed. | 2209 E. Sherman Ave.; I–90 Exit 15 | 208/667–6777 | fax 208/769–7332 | www.nwhotels.com | 62 rooms | $50–$100 | AE, D, DC, MC, V.

Holiday Inn Express, Post Falls. You can get microwaves and refrigerators on request here, a nice amenity if you're traveling with a family. The newly remodeled hotel is close to the lake with a convenient location off the interstate but near downtown. Complimentary Continental breakfast. Microwaves and refrigerators available upon request. Health club privileges. Pool privileges. laundry services. Pets allowed (deposit). | 3105 E. Seltice Way, Post Falls | 208/773–8900 or 800/779–7789 | fax 208/773–0890 | 47 rooms | $60–$110 | AE, D, DC, MC, V.

Riverbend Inn, Post Falls. Attention shoppers! You're next door to the factory outlet mall here, as well as being close to the interstate and near the Spokane Airport and restaurants. Complimentary Continental breakfast. Some kitchenettes. Cable TV. Pool (seasonal). Hot tub. Laundry facilities. No pets. | W. 4105 Riverbend Ave., Post Falls | 208/773–3583 or 800/243–7666 | fax 208/773–1306 | 71 rooms | $52–$75 | AE, D, DC, MC, V.

Rockford Bay Marina. Stay in cabins or in the main building at this medium-size lakeside resort complex. You can boat, fish, swim, and hike. Restaurant. Marina. | 8700 Rockford Bay Rd. | 208/664–6931 | fax 208/666–6018 | rockford4@juno.com | www.presys.com/highway or www.ohwy.com/id/r/rockford.htm | 4 cabins | $70–$125 | D, MC, V.

Rodeway Inn Pines Resort. You're next to Winton Park and picnic facilities here at this newly remodeled motel ½ mile from I-90 south. Walk to downtown shops and restaurants. Complimentary Continental breakfast. Refrigerators on request. Indoor and outdoor pools. Hot tub. Laundry facilities. Boat dock. Cable TV. | 1422 Northwest Blvd. | 208/664–8244 or 800/651–2510 | fax 208/664–5547 | rodeway@ior.com | www.roadwayinncda.com | 65 | $49–$69 | AE, D, DC, MC, V.

Shilo Inn. This all-suites hotel has very reasonable rates. Off I-90, in a cluster of other newer hotels. Complimentary Continental breakfast. Kitchenettes. Cable TV. Indoor pool. Hot tub. Exercise equipment. Laundry facilities. Business services. | 702 W. Apple Way | 208/664–2300 | fax 208/667–2863 | www.shiloinns.com | 139 suites | $69 suites | AE, D, DC, MC, V.

Sleep Inn of Post Falls. Rates and rooms are basic at this new 84-room inn with an indoor pool. Complimentary Continental breakfast. Indoor pool. Hot tub. | 100 N. Pleasant View Rd., Post Falls | 208/777–9694 or 800/851–3178 | fax 208/777–8994 | 84 rooms | $50–$70 | AE, D, MC, V.

Someday House. High above the city, with panoramic views of the skyline and Lake Coeur d'Alene, this bed-and-breakfast has extra-large rooms with modern furnishings. Complimentary breakfast. Hot tub. | 790 Kidd Island Rd. | 208/664–6666 | 3 rooms | $95 | MC, V.

Stoneridge Resort. This condominium complex has a secluded setting with studio, 1-, and 2-bedroom condos and cabins. All the rooms have nice views, and you're near Silverwood Theme Park. You can shoot a few hoops on the basketball court. Gym. Basketball. | 250 Chatwold, Blanchard | 208/437–2451 | fax 208/437–5822 | www.ohwy.com/id/s/stonerid.htm | 25 apartments | $70 apartments | AE, D, MC, V.

Super 8. A multistory motel, conveniently located off I-90 and set in a cluster of other hotels. Cable TV. | 505 W. Apple Way; I-90 Exit 12 | 208/765–8880 | 95 rooms | $59–$65 | AE, D, DC, MC, V.

DRIGGS

MAP 3, F7

(Nearby towns also listed: Rexburg, Idaho Falls)

Two Mormons from Salt Lake City were so impressed with the potential for farming the land around what today is Driggs that they convinced their attorney friend B. W. Driggs to invest in property here as well. In 1889 a wagon train of Mormon emigrants from Salt Lake arrived. Undeterred by the harsh winters, the settlers harvested wild hay and dug irrigation ditches, and soon the farming community of Driggs was established. In 1915 tiny Driggs became the seat of Teton County. Along with Victor and Tetonia, Driggs sits in a quiet valley on the back side of the Grand Tetons, making it as picturesque though more subdued than towns like Jackson, Wyoming, and Yellowstone National Park on the east side of the range. Years before the Mormons settled Driggs, fur traders had regularly met about 1 mi south of town, in the valley known as Pierre's Hole, for about 20 years until 1840. The most famous gathering was the 1832 Rendezvous, by all accounts a raucous event that brought together 200 mountain men and 200 lodges of Nez Percé and Flathead Indians to trade over several days. According to one account, the valley was filled with "the motley populace connected with the fur trade." Driggs is quieter today and still a farming community of fewer than 1,000 residents in a postcard-pretty setting. It is also home to a major ski and summer resort, Targhee, known for snowcat skiing and snowfall that averages 500 inches a year, appealing to skiing's "powderhounds."

Information: **Teton Valley Chamber of Commerce** | 208/354–2500.

Attractions

Grand Targhee Ski and Summer Resort. The resort is nestled on the sunny west side of the Grand Tetons, and is known for uncrowded slopes and abundant powder snow, over 500 inches each year. Skiers are also treated to Grand Tetons scenery. There are two ski mountains with 3,000 total skiable acres. More than 1,500 acres are served by lifts, with 68 wide, groomed runs and 1,200 acres of skiable natural powder. The second 1,500-acre, 2,800-ft-vertical-drop mountain is reserved for snowcat skiing only. Facilities include a ski lodge, a ski school, rentals, on-site lodging, a restaurant, shops, downhill and cross-country skiing, snowboarding, snowcat skiing, and summer recreation. | Ski Hill Road, Alta, WY | 307/353–2300 or 800/443–8146 | www.grandtarghee.com | Skiing mid-Nov.–mid-Apr.; summer recreation, June–Aug.

Teton Valley Aviation You can get aerial views of the Tetons from a glider or small airplanes. Flights leave from Driggs-Reade Memorial Airport. | 675 Airport Rd. | 800/472–6382 | Gliders $135 per hour, airplane flightseeing $65–$115.

ON THE CALENDAR

JULY: *Teton Valley Hot-Air Balloon Festival.* A two-day festival featuring more than 30 hot-air balloons in a race in a picturesque setting overlooking the majestic Grand Tetons. Balloon rides, crafts and antiques fairs, games, parades, rodeo action, glider rides, golf tournament, bike races. | July 4th weekend | 208/354–2500.

Dining

Breakfast Shoppe. American. This small diner is where locals go to have breakfast and discuss the latest town gossip. Smoking permitted. | 95 Main St. | 208/354–8294 | $4–$9 | AE, D, MC, V.

Knight's British Rail. Eclectic. A menu with American, Italian, and Asian dishes makes this a good place to go if you're with an indecisive group. Housed in a charming building dating from 1916, this restaurant prides itself on its country charm and Old World feel. You'll find a variety of beers on tap. | 65 Depot St. | 208/354–8365 | $10–$13 | AE, D, MC, V.

O'Rourke's Sports Bar and Grill. American. There is a sports bar atmosphere at this pub where locals congregate to watch "the game" on one of the several large screen televisions. Enjoy the especially large portions of dishes such as steak and shrimp. | 42 E. Little Ave. | 208/354–8115 | $7–$15 | AE, DC, MC, V.

Lodging

Best Western Teton West. Only 30 mi from Grand Targhee resort, this is a good alternative to the high-priced resort-area accommodations. There's a ski-wax room on the premises. Rooms are furnished with dark-rose floral spreads and carpet and dark-wood furniture. Most have views of the Grand Tetons. Complimentary Continental breakfast. Cable TV. Indoor pool. Hot tub. Pets allowed (deposit). | 476 N. Main St. | 208/354–2363 | fax 208/354–2962 | 40 rooms | $48–$79 | AE, D, DC, MC, V | Closed Oct.–Dec.

Grand Targhee Resort Ski and Summer Resort. Designed as an all-season, family-oriented resort, the village complex includes 3 lodges, 5 restaurants, retail shops, a spa, and a fitness cabin. You can ski and hike and many other things in winter; in no-snow months, you can hike or whatever. The Teewinot Lodge and Conference Center has 48 conventional guest rooms and Western-inspired furnishings. Condominium-style lodging is available at the Sioux Lodge, where rooms have adobe walls and lodgepole pine balconies. 5 restaurants, bar (with entertainment), dining rooms, picnic area. Some kitchenettes. In-room VCRs (and movies) available. Pool. Hot tubs, massage, spa. Gym, exercise equipment. Tennis. Hiking, horseback riding. Cross-country and downhill skiing. Children's programs (ages 6–12). Laundry facilities. Business services. | Box SKI, Alta, WY; 12 mi east on Ski-Hill Rd. (lodge is accessible only from Idaho) | 307/353–2300 or 800/827–4433 | fax 307/353–8148 | 94 rooms in 3 lodges | $98 | AE, D, MC, V | Closed Apr.–June, Sept.–mid-Nov.

Intermountain Lodge. Modern, small, log cabins nestled in cottonwood trees, these lodges have kitchenettes and basic, comfortable furnishings. Complimentary Continental breakfast, picnic area. No air-conditioning, kitchenettes. Satellite TV. Outdoor hot tub. Volleyball. Laundry facilities. No pets allowed. No smoking. | 34 Ski Hill Rd. | 208/354–8153 | fax 208/354–2998 | www.tetonvalleychamber.org | 14 rooms (with shower only) in 7 cabins | $49–$69 | AE, D, MC, V.

★ **Pines Motel Guest Haus.** The big stucco and cedar-shingled cottage looks as though it would be right at home in the Bavarian Alps and is surrounded by 1 acre of shady lawn. Guest rooms are comfortable, with country-style furnishings and quilts. You're one block from the center of town and 12 mi from Grand Targhee. In-room phones. Cable TV. Hot tub. Pets allowed ($10 fee). | 105 S. Main | 208/354–2774 or 800/354–2778 | www.travelassist.com | 8 rooms | $40–$50 | AE, D, DC, MC, V.

Super 8 Teton West. The rooms are spacious and the setting is quiet in at this chain property. Many rooms have open views of the Grand Tetons. Complimentary Continental breakfast. Microwaves, refrigerators. Indoor pool, wading pool. Hot tub. Laundry facilities. No pets. | 133 Rte. 33 N | 208/354–8888 | fax 208/354–8853 | 46 rooms | $50–$70 | AE, D, DC, MC, V.

★ **Teton Ridge Ranch.** Built of lodgepole pine in 1984, this luxuriously rustic ranch lodge west of the Tetons accommodates just 12 guests. The 10,000-square-ft lodge has beamed cathedral ceilings, stone fireplaces, an inviting lounge, and a library with comfy sofas. Forty-five minutes from Grand Targhee resort, the lodge is on 4,000 acres atop a 6,800-ft knoll, with majestic views. Suites—five in the main lodge, two in a cabin—have woodstoves, hot tubs, and steam showers. You decide what you want to do with your time: hiking on 14 mi of marked trails, horseback riding with an experienced wrangler, fishing at two spring-fed stocked ponds, cycling, and shooting at two sporting clay courses. Sleigh rides are also offered. In-room hot tubs. TV in common area. Hiking, horseback riding. Fishing. Library. Laundry facilities. Kids over 6 only. Some pets allowed. | 200 Valley View Rd., Tetonia | 208/456–2650 | fax 208/456–2218 | www.ranchweb/teton | 7 suites | $450–$550 | MC, AE, V | Closed Nov.–Dec., Apr.–May | AP.

FORT HALL INDIAN
RESERVATION

INTRO
ATTRACTIONS
DINING
LODGING

FORT HALL INDIAN RESERVATION

MAP 3, E8

(Nearby towns also listed: Blackfoot, Pocatello)

The Shoshone-Bannock Indian tribe claims 3,000 enrolled members and is headquartered at the Fort Hall Indian Reservation, a 544,000-acre tract that is only a small portion of the area that the Shoshones and Bannocks once inhabited. The two tribes hunted, gathered, and fished for salmon in what is now Wyoming, Utah, Nevada, and Idaho. Horses were introduced in the early 1700s, allowing bands to hunt buffalo in Montana and Wyoming. Sacajawea, a Lemhi Shoshone woman, led Lewis and Clark on their famous expedition through the Northwest. A Presidential Executive Order established the 1.8-million-acre Reservation in 1867 and was confirmed by the Fort Bridger Treaty of 1868. The reservation was reduced to 1.2 million acres in 1872 owing to a survey error and was eventually whittled down to its present size. You can still see ruts of the Oregon Trail near the monument where the original Fort Hall once stood, a fur-trading post established in 1834 by Nathaniel Wyeth. Along with remnants of the trail are remains of buildings from the old Fort Hall Indian Agency and a re-created fur-trader's post known as Old Fort Hall Replica. Other popular stops are the "bottoms area" along the Snake where a protected herd of tribal buffalo roams, the tribal museum, and the Clothes Horse store with the tribe's colorful bead and quill work. One of the annual highlights is the Shoshone-Bannock Indian Festival held the second week in August. It is a top-drawing event with an all-Indian rodeo. The tribe operates as a sovereign government with a constitution and elections.

Information: Shoshone-Bannock Tribal Enterprises | Fort Hall, 83221 | 208/237–9791 | www.sho-ban.com/festival.htm.

ON THE CALENDAR
AUG.: *Shoshone-Bannock Indian Festival and Rodeo.* Held at the Fort Hall Rodeo Grounds, the festival features traditional Indian dancing, drumming, a rodeo, and an arts and crafts fair. 208/238–3700.

Attractions
Snake River Bottons Area. A protected herd of tribal buffalo roams here, and the Snake River offers excellent fishing. With a special permit from the Tribal Fish and Game Department you can fish and hunt ducks, geese, and pheasant in season.

Shoshone-Bannock Tribal Museum. The exhibits here include artifacts and historical photographs commemorating the tribal heritage. | I–15 Exit 80 | 208/237–9791 | Free | Daily 10–5.

Clothes Horse. The main outlet for the tribes' craftwork, this shop on the Ft. Hall reservation sells quill- and beadwork, tanned and smoked leather goods, and Native American artwork. | Ft. Hall Reservation | 208/237–8433.

Dining
Oregon Trail Restaurant. Try some traditional Native American dishes at this restaurant on the reservation. Specialties include buffalo steaks, buffalo burgers, buffalo stew, Indian tacos, and Indian fry bread. | Ft. Hall Indian Reservation | Daily 7 AM–9 PM.

GLENN'S FERRY

MAP 3, B8

(Nearby towns also listed: Bruneau, Mountain Home)

Now a bucolic community of 1,300 (many of them descendents of Oregon Trail pioneers), this town once had the most dangerous river crossing on the 2,000-mi trail. Those who made it this far had to decide whether to risk their lives crossing the fast-flowing Snake River here, which would give them a shorter, easier route on the north side, or plod through the barren, rocky desert south of the river, which offered little water and feed for livestock. Some 300,000 people are believed to have crossed the river here in a 30-year period beginning in the early 1840s. The first to try, two missionaries named Marcus Whitman and Henry Spalding, had their wagon break up in mid-crossing. They salvaged the pieces, constructed a cart, and continued on their way. The town is named for Gus Glenn, who in 1869 began offering pioneers a safe crossing 2 mi upriver.

Attractions

Glenn's Ferry Historical Museum. Housed in a native stone schoolhouse built in 1909, this small museum has artifacts from the Oregon Trail and ranch and railroad memorabilia. Check out the photographs of the horse teams dragging 1,000-pound sturgeon out of the Snake River. | 200 W. Cleveland St. | No phone | 12-5 Fri.-Sat., June–Sept. | Donations accepted.

Opera Theater. This newly restored theater was built as an opera house in 1914 and is now listed on the National Register of Historic Places. In its original incarnation, famous opera stars would perform while changing trains or waiting out a blizzard while they were en route from Salt Lake City to Seattle. During the summer, you can attend the mystery dinner theater on Friday and old-time melodramas on Saturday. Events such as the Christmas bazaar are held there the rest of the year. | 208/366–7408 | Mem. Day–Labor Day.

Three Island Crossing State Park. You can see wagon ruts from the Oregon Trail at this park 1 mi southwest of town, and also fish, picnic, and camp. From time to time, buffalo and longhorn cattle are pastured in the enclosure at the southeast corner of the park. | Take exit 120 off Business 84, go ½ mi southeast, into Glenn's Ferry, turn south on Commercial St. and go ½ mi to state park sign. The park entrance is just under a mile down the paved road | $2 per vehicle; fees for camping | 208/366–2394 | fax 208/366–2060 | thr@idpr.state.id.us | www.idahoparks.org.

Three Island Crossing Oregon Trail History and Education Center. Life-size dioramas, wagon replicas, diary entries, and interactive displays tell the pioneers' stories at this center, which opened in 2000. | $3 | At park entrance | 208/366–2394.

Attractions

Carmela Vineyard. This family-owned winery overlooks the Snake River near Three Mile Crossing. You can sample a variety of wines on the wine-tasting tour, then stop for lunch at the restaurant on the premises. There's also a nine-hole golf course and a pro shop. | 795 W. Madison Ave. | 208/366–2313 | 9 AM–9 PM, June–Aug. | Call to arrange tours.

Snake River Stage Line. You can take stagecoach and covered-wagon rides and tours that start from the visitor center, the winery, and other places. | Various venues | 208/366–2550 | Memorial Day–Labor Day.

ON THE CALENDAR

JULY: *Elmore County Fair.* Rides, livestock competitions, and other events are held at the county fairgrounds. 208/366–7375.

AUG.: *A Crossing in Time Festival and Three Island Crossing Re-enactment.* This annual event commemorates the hundreds of pioneers who lost their lives crossing the river. The festival includes a horse parade, cowboy poetry, a pioneer breakfast and barbecue, a mountain man rendezvous, and arts and crafts. 208/366–7375.

Dining

Carmela Vineyards Restaurant. American. A family-style restaurant that overlooks the river, this place has fresh seafood such as halibut and sturgeon, as well as hamburgers and other kid-friendly fare. | $6–$20 | 795 W. Madison Ave. | 208/366–2313 | 8 AM–8 PM | MC, V.

Hanson's Cafe. American. Solid fare at very reasonable prices is served at this downtown, down-home eatery. Try biscuits and gravy or chicken-fried steak. Daily specials. | $5.50–$11 | 201 E. First Ave. | 208/366–9983 | No dinner Sun. | No credit cards.

Oregon Trail Restaurant. Native American. Try traditional dishes at this restaurant on the reservation. Try buffalo steaks and fry bread. | $5–$11 | 110 E. Idaho Ave. | 208/366–2280.

Lodging

Cunningham's Bed & Breakfast. The large, sunny rooms in this wooden lodge are furnished with Western antiques and artifacts and named for ferries that cross the Snake River, and all have views of the river. Natural hot well water fills the hot tub on a patio at the back of the house. You can fish off the inn's dock. | 5 rooms. Full breakfast. Hot tub. Fishing. | $75–$85 | Box 760; on the road to Three Rivers State Park, south of town | 208/366–7342 | No credit cards.

Great Basin Bed & Breakfast. Built in 1917 as a boarding house for railroad workers and once the site of a bootleg whiskey operation, this downtown inn was refurbished and furnished with antiques in 2000. The theme rooms are named for local people and places: the Walker Ranch room commemorates a nearby state stop, and the Kitty Wilkins room is named for a horse trader. | 4 rooms, one with private bath | $65–$75; weekly rates available. Continental breakfast. TV in common area. | 319 E. First Ave. | 208/366–7406 | No credit cards.

Hanson's Motel. Downtown, this is a good place for families, with reasonable rates and a cafe on the premises. The rooms were remodeled in 2000 and are comfortable, if not fancy, with two double beds in each. Cable TV. Air-conditioning. | 7 rooms | $30–$45.

Redford Motel. Room sizes vary from small to large enough for two king-size beds here at this non-chain motel in the downtown area. Some have kitchens. Some kitchens. Cable TV, air-conditioning. Pets allowed. | 11 rooms | $28–$65.

GRANGEVILLE

MAP 3, B5

(Nearby towns also listed: Lewiston, Orofino)

Grangeville was first a supply town serving the mining districts in the Gospel Mountains and Buffalo Hump. When a Grange Hall was built in 1874, the building was the first in the fledgling town and is thought to have been the first local chapter of the National Grange of the Patrons of Husbandry, a secret fraternal organization for farmers, in the Northwest. The organization helped determine the town's name. In 1902, the town became the county seat of Idaho county. Today Grangeville is a town of 3,500 and the northern gateway to Hell's Canyon and four of the state's five wilderness areas. Fishing and hunting outfitters and river runners use the town as a base camp. The town sits at the foot of the 6,000- to 7,000-ft Bitterroot Mountains overlooking the Camas Prairie, a 200,000-acre stretch of rolling foothills bordered by the Clearwater and Snake rivers.

Information: Grangeville Chamber of Commerce | Box 212, Grangeville, 83530 | 208/983–0460 | fax 208/983–1429 | www.grangevilleidaho.com.

Attractions

Cottonwood Butte Ski Resort. The small resort is a family skiing spot with a vertical drop of 845 ft and 260 skiable acres. The ski area features downhill skiing, snowboarding, and night skiing. The base elevation is 4,280 ft, with crests reaching 5,565 ft. | 19 mi north of Grangeville | 208/962–3624 or 208/746–6397 | Mid-Dec.–Feb.

Hells Canyon National Recreation Area. The centerpiece of the 622,977-acre area is the 71½-mi long, steep-walled black basalt canyon of the Snake River. The deepest in North America, the canyon plunges several hundred feet deeper than the Grand Canyon. (At the mouth of Granite Creek, approximately 7 mi below Hells Canyon Dam, the river elevation is 1,480 ft and the canyon depth is 7,913 ft. On the west, the gorge is edged by Oregon's rim, which rises to an elevation of 6,982 ft at Hat Point Lookout.) The terrain and wildlife habitats range from desert at the canyon floor to alpine in the mountains. Idaho's Seven

Devils Mountains tower above one rim and Oregon's Wallowas on the other. Rapids such as Granite and Wild Sheep are Class III to Class IV. You can see the gorge two ways. Sight-seeing cruises originate in Lewiston at the northern end and from Hells Canyon dam at the southern end. Or you can take a raft or dory and float the central 34-mi section of the river designated Wild and Scenic. The two can be combined by float-boating down the river and jet-boating back to your starting point. In spring Hells Canyon is lush with wildflowers. Hot summers from June to August bring daytime temperatures of 80 to 100 degrees. Long Indian summers and fall are ideal for steelhead and sturgeon fishing. | 88401 Rte. 82, Enterprise | 541/426–4978, 509/758–0616, or 509/758–1957 (river info) | www.fs.fed.us/r6/w-w | Free | Daily.

Hells Canyon Creek. This is the primary launch point for float trips on the Snake River and is the only place in Hells Canyon where the Snake is accessible by a two-lane paved road. Pick up information at the staffed visitor center. | Forest Rd. 517; west of Riggins and HCNRA office | 208/628–3916 | Free | Daily.

Cache Creek Ranch. At the very northern end of the area, the ranch was historically part of the Dobbins and Huffman sheep ranch that flourished in the 1930s, and is now a rest stop for river trips and is reached via water only. The buildings are surrounded by lawns, a fruit orchard and a small visitor center that provides information about the river. | 208/628–3916 | Donations accepted | Visitor Center: June–Sept., daily dawn to dusk.

Pittsburg Landing. You reach the area via the only year-round public road leading to the Snake River. There is a concrete boat ramp and float apron for launching or takeout. | North of Riggins on U.S. 95, west on Forest Rd. 493 at White Bird | 208/628–3916 | Free | Daily dawn to dusk.

Kirkwood Historic Ranch. The historic ranch on Kirkwood Bar offers a glimpse of canyon life from the 1930s. Displays in the old bunkhouse contain historic and prehistoric artifacts. You can reach it by boat or trail only. Call ahead for road conditions. From the end of the road you hike 6 mi on the Snake River National Recreation Trail. | North of Riggins on U.S. 95, west on Forest Rd. 493 at White Bird, south on Forest Rd. 420, west on Forest Rd. 242, or drive to Pittsburg and hike | 208/628–3916 | Donations accepted | Daily dawn to dusk.

Nez Perce National Forest. Four rivers with the Wild and Scenic designation and several recreational rivers with deep canyons in mountainous terrain are within the forest property. Ogling the scenery and white-water boating are the primary activities. The terrain ranges from 1,000 to 9,000 ft in elevation, with a range of ecosystems, from alpine with cedar groves along the Selway River to arid with desert flora along the Snake and Salmon

GRANGEVILLE

INTRO
ATTRACTIONS
DINING
LODGING

KODAK'S TIPS FOR PHOTOGRAPHING WEATHER

Rainbows
- Find rainbows by facing away from the sun after a storm
- Use your auto-exposure mode
- With an SLR, use a polarizing filter to deepen colors

Fog and Mist
- Use bold shapes as focal points
- Add extra exposure manually or use exposure compensation
- Choose long lenses to heighten fog and mist effects

In the Rain
- Look for abstract designs in puddles and wet pavement
- Control rain-streaking with shutter speed
- Protect cameras with plastic bags or waterproof housings

Lightning
- Photograph from a safe location
- In daylight, expose for existing light
- At night, leave the shutter open during several flashes

From *Kodak Guide to Shooting Great Travel Pictures* © 2000 by Fodor's Travel Publications

rivers. In addition to impressive runs of steelhead salmon in the fall and winter, the forest is home to the largest trophy elk herd in the continental United States. The forest land is also rich in Nez Percé and gold-mining history. Chinook salmon and 15- to 20-pound steelhead are regularly hooked by anglers on the Clearwater and Salmon Rivers. | RR 2, Box 475 | 208/983–1950 | www.nezperce.fs.fed.uf | Free | Daily dawn to dusk.

Gospel Hump Wilderness Area. In the forest near Elk City is Idaho's newest wilderness area. The elevation ranges from 3,500 ft at the Salmon River to 8,940 ft at Buffalo Hump. You can hike at Oregon Butte and Buffalo Hump, and the Elk City Road provides a fascinating trip through Idaho's mining past. | RR 2, Box 475; 50 mi east on U.S. 14 to Crooked River Rd., 20 mi to Orogrande Summit | 208/983–1950 | www.nezperce.fs.fed.uf | Free | Daily dawn to dusk.

★ **Nez Perce National Historical Park.** For thousands of years, the prairies and plateaus of north-central Idaho, northeastern Oregon, and southeastern Washington have been home to the Nee-Me-Poo people, or Nez Percé. This park interprets Nez Percé culture and history. It includes 38 sites in Idaho, Montana, Oregon, and Washington. At the visitor center near Spalding, you can study interpretive exhibits, enjoy audio-visual programs, and attend daily talks in summer months. | Headquarters and Visitor Center, Spalding; 1 mi east on U.S. 12 | 208/843–2261 | www.nps.gov/nepe | Free | Spalding Visitor Center, June–Sept., daily 8–5:30; Nov.–May, 8–4:30.

White Bird Summit and Road. The Old White Bird Road can be seen en route to the summit on U.S. 95, south of Grangeville. This road was considered an engineering feat in its day, as its zigzags gained 4,429 ft in elevation within 14 mi. Paved in 1938, it is listed on the National Register of Historic Places. | 5 mi south on U.S. 95 | 208/843–2261 | Free | Daily.
White Bird Hill Battlefield Auto Tour. The first battle of the Nez Percé War was fought here on June 17, 1877. Thirty-four soldiers were killed while the Nez Percé lost none. The visitor center in Spalding has maps you can use for a tour of the battlefield. The White Bird Interpretive Shelter has exhibits that explain the sequence of the battle. | 12 mi south on U.S. 95 | 208/843–2261 | Free | Daily dawn to dusk.

River Trips—Idaho Outfitters and Guides Association. Information on river trips is available from the Idaho Outfitters and Guides Association (Box 95, Boise | 208/342–1919 | www.visitid.org/outdoor/Rivers), which lists more than 400 outfitters, guides, and related services.

Snake River Wild and Scenic River. The 31½-mi section of river between Hells Canyon Dam and Pittsburg Landing was designated Wild in 1975 under the Wild and Scenic Rivers Act. The 36-mi section downstream from Pittsburg Landing to Mile 180.2 is designated Scenic. An additional 4.2 mi of the river from Mile 180.2 north to the National Recreation Area boundary at the Oregon-Washington line is recommended for Scenic designation. (The river corridor itself is not wilderness, and wilderness regulations do not apply. Developed campsites and man-made structures are permitted and some motorized equipment is allowed.) | Box 699, Clarkston, WA 99403 | 509/758–0616 (general information); 509/758–1957 (float information); or 509/758–0270 (powerboat information) | Free | Daily dawn to dusk.

Dining
Oscar's Restaurant. American. The memorabilia and photos scattered throughout trace the town's history and make this almost as much a museum as a restaurant. The downtown eatery serves gourmet burgers and steaks and other basic fare. | 101 E. Main St. | 208/983–2106 | $6–$11 | MC, V.

Lodging
Meadow House. The Victorian-style house is surrounded by a rose garden. One mile from town, the house was built in 1905 and is furnished with period pieces. Complimentary breakfast. | 306 S. Meadow | 208/983–4350 | 3 rooms | $65–$75 | MC, V.

HAGERMAN

MAP 3, C8

(Nearby town also listed: Buhl)

The Shoshone Indians fished for migrating salmon here at Lower Salmon Falls (eliminated when a dam was built in 1947) and wintered in the Valley of the Thousand Springs because of its ready supply of thermal spring water. Hagerman later became a stop near the Oregon Trail and was established as a town in 1892. Today it is best known for the long-extinct Hagerman horse, the zebra-like horse that roamed these grasslands along the Snake more than 3 million years ago during the Pliocene epoch, before the Ice Age. The town is set back off the east rim of the Snake River on U.S. 30 and looks across to the west rim with its abundant fossil beds. The visitor center for Hagerman Fossil Beds National Monument is located in town and features fossil exhibits, a slide show, video, and programs. The Hagerman fossil beds are one of the top four such sites in the nation, and contain the largest concentration of *Equus simplicidens* (Hagerman horse) fossils in North America. Just east of town is the Thousand Springs area, where a curtain of spring water falls along the east side of the river (see Buhl). The valley's mild climate and plentiful water have sustained many trout farms in the area, making the Hagerman Valley the world's largest commercial producer of trout.

Information: Hagerman Valley Chamber of Commerce | Box 599, Hagerman, 83332 | 208/837–9131 | www.hagerman-idchamber.org.

Attractions

Hagerman Fossil Beds National Monument. One of the world's foremost fossil beds. Digs in this region have unearthed over 125 full skeletons of prehistoric zebralike horses from the Pliocene epoch and beavers as much as 3.5 million years old. | Off U.S. 30 | 208/837–4793 | Free | Tours only.

Dining

Snake River Grill. American. Decorated with stuffed animals, this restaurant strives for the exotic. The menu is strong on steaks and regional fare. | State St. and Hagerman Ave. | 208/837–6196 | $12–$17 | MC, V.

Lodging

Hagerman Valley Inn. An all-cedar, homey motel in the Frog's Landing retail and commercial complex has spacious guest rooms that open onto a grassy picnic area and two large decks. Restaurant nearby, picnic area. Cable TV. Pets allowed (fee). | 661 Frogs Landing | 208/837–6196 | www.northrim.net¢hvimotel | 16 rooms | $46 | AE, MC, V.

Rock Lodge Resort. Ernest Hemingway once stayed here. The setting is tranquil and the fishing is great. You can stay in the motel or guest cottages with full kitchens. Complimentary breakfast. Spa. | 17940 Hagerman Hwy. | 208/837–6227 | 8 rooms | $40–$79 | MC, V.

HAILEY

MAP 3, C7

(Nearby towns also listed: Ketchum, Sun Valley Area)

Hailey was one of the hub communities in the Wood River valley mining district and once had a booming Chinatown. The town was laid out in 1881 and two years later the Oregon Short Line laid track into it. It was also the first Idaho community to have a telephone exchange. Only 11 mi south of Ketchum and Sun Valley, this is where the valley's working class lives and shops. The tiny downtown has shady old-time neigh-

HAILEY

INTRO
ATTRACTIONS
DINING
LODGING

borhoods and a wide main street with handsome brick storefronts from the early 1900s, now filled with a handful of clothing shops and restaurants.

Information: **Hailey Chamber of Commerce** | 13 W. Carbonate, 83333 | 208/788–2700.

Attractions

The Rock Down Under. Rock climbers and the adventure minded can enjoy a 2,500-square-ft climbing gym in the Blaine County Fitness Center. | 21 E. Maple St. | 208/788–1155 | $9 | Daily.

Blaine County Museum. This charming museum is housed in a tan brick storefront on the north edge of downtown. Photographs, artifacts, and memorabilia from mining and railroading are showcased. | Main and Galena Sts. | 208/788–1801 | Free | Memorial Day–Labor Day, Mon., Wed.–Sat., 11–5, Sun. 1–5.

ON THE CALENDAR
JULY: *Days of the Old West.* Held at McKercher Park, this celebration has a rodeo, a barbecue, a street fair, a parade, and a fireworks finale. 208/788–2700.

Dining
Shorty's Diner. American. Fittings and all, Shorty's is a throwback to the 50s, complete with plush booths, mood lighting, and jukeboxes. It specializes in grand sandwiches and burger specials. | 126 S. Main St. | 208/788–6047 | $7–$12 | MC, V.

Lodging
Airport Inn. A half-mile from the airport, this inn offers both suites and kitchenettes with contemporary design and decor, as well as standard-size rooms. Complimentary breakfast. In-room phones. Hot Tub. | 409 Cedar St. | 208/788–2477 | 29 rooms | $70–$80 | MC, V.

HARRISON

MAP 3, A3

(Nearby town also listed: St. Maries)

In the early 1900s, the town of Harrison, on the quiet southeastern shore of Lake Coeur d'Alene, was a major port for lake steamers. The charming town of 350 retains its Victorian feel in old brick and wood buildings and is still quiet today although it's less than an hour from bustling Coeur d'Alene at the northern end of the lake.

Information: **Harrison Chamber of Commerce** | Box 222, Harrison, 83833 | 208/689–3711. .

ON THE CALENDAR
JULY: *Old Time Picnic.* A parade along the lake, also live entertainment and free potato salad and hot dogs. 208/689–3529.

Dining
Gateway Resort and Marina. American. This small restaurant is right on the water. You get nice views of the lake along with steaks, burgers, and other basic fare. | 208/689–3951 | $7–$12 | No credit cards.

Lodging
Hidden Creek Ranch. Unlike most western resorts, this one has mind, body, and spiritual wellness programs, including yoga, meditation, and relaxation classes. This secluded, luxuriously rustic-looking timber lodge sits in pine woods overlooking Hidden Creek. The 7,000-

square-ft lodge has a dining room with a rock fireplace. New cabins are furnished with modern log furniture, Native American artwork, and fabric motifs. In summer you can fish, hike, practice your archery and trap shooting, take boat tours, and get fly-fishing instruction. Mountain bikes are available upon request, and there are also guided nature awareness hikes. No in-room phones. No TV. 2 hot tubs, massage. Exercise equipment. Hiking, horseback riding. Fishing. Laundry facilities. No pets allowed. | 7600 E. Blue Lake Rd. | 208/689–3209 or 800/446–3833 | fax 208/689–9115 | hiddencreek@hiddencreek.com | www.hiddencreek.com | 16 units | $3,258–$3,900 6–day stay; includes all meals | AE, MC, V | AP.

Osprey Inn. A former boarding house for lumberjacks, built in 1915, this place retains a rustic atmosphere. Some rooms have full kitchens. The private dock in the rear of the building is perfect place to relax. Complimentary breakfast. Private dock. | 134 Fredrick St. | 208/689–9502 | 5 rooms | $85 | MC, V.

IDAHO CITY

MAP 3, B7

(Nearby town also listed: Boise)

Gold was found here in 1862, and the rush to the Boise Basin was the biggest since California's gold rush. In 1863, during the mining boom, Idaho City was Idaho's largest town, with a population of 6,275. At one time more than 200 buildings stood along the town's dusty streets. In 1898, the mining area surrounding the frontier town of Idaho City was overrun with dredging operations; the scars from these giant machines that raked the earth can be seen for miles today. Today the town is part historic mining ghost town and part thriving community at the confluence of More's and Elk creeks. You can see weathered wood-frames and other buildings from the town's heyday, including the oldest Masonic hall west of the Mississippi still in use, the former county courthouse, the Independent Order of Odd Fellows (IOOF) hall, and a Catholic church. The town publishes a walking-tour map and brochure that points out these and other sights.

Information: Idaho City Visitors Center | 511 Main St., 83631. | 208/392–6040 | www.idahocitychamber.com.

Attractions

Boise Basin Museum. Originally a post office, the brick building was built in 1867 and later became a stage-coach station. It also served at times as a private residence before it was turned into a museum. Mining boom days are illustrated with exhibits, and there is also a short movie on the gold rush. | 501 Montgomery St. | 208/392–4550 | www.idahocitychamber.com | $2 | Memorial Day–Labor Day, daily 11–4.

Pioneer Cemetery. Men carried guns in Idaho City's rough gold-mining days, and they used them when challenged. The losers are buried here, as well as many other people. The cemetery, ¼ mi northwest of town, provides a fascinating look at the area's colorful history. | 208/392–4550 | www.idahocitychamber.com | Free | Daily.

Gold Hill. Former mines and dredging areas are located on Gold Hill, about 1½ mi past the school. | Main St. | 208/392–4550 | www.idahocitychamber.com | Free | Daily.

ON THE CALENDAR
JUNE: *Idaho City Arts and Crafts Festival.* A 25-year-old arts and crafts fair with work by regional artists, live entertainment, and food vendors, held in John Brogan Park. 208/392–4553.
JULY: *Thousand Springs Festival.* Two days of music, locally made arts and crafts, antique dairy-barn tours, hiking, meals, and canoe outings. 208/726–3007.

IDAHO FALLS

(Nearby towns also listed: Blackfoot, Rexburg)

First named Taylor's Bridge, after J. M. Taylor, who built a toll bridge across the Snake River in 1865, the town later called itself Eagle Rock before settling on Idaho Falls in 1891. The low falls that span the river in the heart of town are the centerpiece of Idaho's third-largest city, population 50,000. A 14-mi Greenbelt lines the east side of the river a few blocks from the historic downtown, where old storefronts are filled with shops and eateries. A patchwork of rich farm fields, lava, and sagebrush flats surrounds the town, which is also home to the University of Idaho and is a gateway community to the Tetons and Yellowstone to the north and east. The Ridge Historic District borders the river in a triangular area north of 13th Street; the district includes more than 65 residential buildings dating from the late 1800s to the 1940s. Idaho Falls also tends 39 parks, from street-corner pocket gardens with inviting benches and picnic tables to expansive preserves like Tautphaus Park on the south side of town. The latter is home to a well-known zoo. The Snake River is an important spring stop for migrating water-fowl like trumpeter swans and brown pelicans, and both are often spotted along the Greenbelt.

Information: **Idaho Falls Chamber of Commerce** | 505 Lindsay Blvd. (Box 50498), 83405-0498 | 800/634–3246 or 208/523–1010 | fax 208/523–2255 | www.idahofallscham-ber.com.

Attractions

★ **Bonneville Museum.** The museum is housed in a Carnegie library built in 1916. Included in the exhibits are artifacts, photographs, and collections on natural history, early Native Americans, explorers, agriculture, mining, the military, and nuclear energy. Traveling exhibits are displayed on the second floor, as well as a replica of the room of an pioneer, Fred Keefer. The lower level contains a walk-through re-creation of Eagle Rock, a small 19th-century community that preceded Idaho Falls. | 200 N. Eastern Ave. | 208/522–1400 | $2 | Weekdays 10–5, Sat. 1–5.

Heise Hot Springs and Expeditions. The spa and resort built here in 1896 is now a huge pool fed by natural hot springs. In summer there's a 350-ft water slide, and in winter a heated mineral-water pool. You can also play golf and take river expeditions. There's a pic-nic area, and in the original log hotel, a pizza parlor and snack bar. | 5116 E. Heise Rd., Ririe | 208/538–7312 | fax 208/538–7466 | www.srv.net/~heise/heise.html | $6 | Swimming pool: May–Oct., daily 10–9; mineral pool: Nov.–Apr., daily 10–5.

Hell's Half Acre Lava Flows. The first travelers to cross this desolate stretch said it reminded them of hell, a place none had yet visited. Not quite as showy as Craters of the Moon, the 222-square-mi lava flow is still impressive. The centerpiece is a vent reaching 5,350 ft and measuring up to 200 ft wide and 730 ft long, with 13 pit craters. The park includes a rest area and interpretive signs. | 25 mi east on I–15 | 208/524–7500 | Free | Daily.

Idaho Falls. The town's namesake waterfalls cover a wide and low area in the center of town. There is a 2½-mi greenway along the river. | 208/523–1010 | Free | Daily dawn to dusk.

Kelly Canyon Ski Resort. The family-oriented ski area features intermediate terrain and a vertical drop of 938 ft across 740 skiable acres. Four double lifts and 1 rope tow access 26 runs. The base elevation is 5,600 ft. Facilities include a ski lodge, rentals, a ski school, downhill skiing, including night skiing, and snowboarding. | 420 West 4th St., Rexburg; 12 mi east of Wallace on Rte. 90 | 208/538–6261 | $20 | Dec.–mid-Mar.

Tautphaus Park Zoo. The main feature of the park is the zoo, home to more than 250 ani-mals from six continents. Large natural habitats have been created for such animals as

Bactrian camels, African lions, and debrazza guenon monkeys. There are also African penguins at the 16,000-gallon Penguin Cove exhibit. The children's zoo features a petting area. | 2725 Carnival Way | 208/528–5552 | www.netib.com/vcb/ifz10252 | $3.50 | Apr., Oct.–Nov., weekends 9–4:30; May, Sept., daily 9–4:40; Memorial Day–Labor Day, daily 9–6:30.

ON THE CALENDAR

APR.: *Snake River Fiber Fair.* A weeklong event at the Bonneville County Fairgrounds celebrates fiber arts with workshops, craft sales, demonstrations, animal exhibits, fleece competitions, and a gallery show. 208/529–3549.

JULY: *Sidewalk Art Show.* A 40-year-old fine-arts sidewalk art show is sponsored by the Eagle Rock Art Guild. In a pleasant space along the river on Memorial Drive. 208/524–2961.

Dining

Hawg Smoke Cafe. American. The casual setting at this minute five-table restaurant doesn't give much of a clue to the distinctive menu of chef's specialties. Whether it's squid tacos or Mongolian stir-fry, the French master chef delivers. | 475 Northgate Mile | 208/523–4804 | Reservations required | $13–$19 | No credit cards.

Jaker's. Contemporary. Redwood paneling and modern furnishings create a relaxed and refined setting for fresh fish, steaks, and creative Northwest cuisine. Kids' menu. | 851 Lindsay Blvd. | 208/524–5240 | $20–$50 | AE, D, MC, V | No lunch Sun.

Mama Inez. Mexican. The Idaho Falls outpost of this popular Mexican restaurant chain (other locations: Ketchum and Boise) is regarded as the best south-of-the-border home-style food in town. | 346 Park Ave. | 208/525–8968 | $10–$15 | MC, V.

Sandpiper. Contemporary. Here you'll find a nautical theme and a casual setting with views of the Snake River. On the menu is a variety of steak and seafood dishes. Try the prime rib or the Hawaiian crunch halibut grilled with macadamia nuts, chives, and lime herb butter. There is also an outdoor patio which is partially covered and offers a great view of the river. | 750 Lindsay Blvd. | 208/524–3344 | $7–$20 | AE, D, MC, V | No breakfast.

Smitty's Pancake and Steak House. American. A long-time casual eatery where the waitstaff make you feel at home. Dinner plate–size pancakes and breakfast are served all day, also steaks, burgers, and other basic fare in generous servings. | 645 W. Broadway | 208/523–6450 | Reservations not accepted | $5–$10 | AE, V.

Lodging

Ameritel Inn. Near the falls, off I–15, this hotel has a fireplace in the common area and freshly baked cookies every evening. Each room has a large desk, useful for business travelers. You're within walking distance of several restaurants and a five-minute drive of the mall. Complimentary Continental breakfast. In-room data ports, some kitchenettes, some microwaves. Cable TV. Indoor pool. Hot tub, spa. Exercise equipment. Business services. Airport shuttle. No pets allowed. | 645 Lindsay Blvd. | 208/523–1400 or 800/600–6001 (reservations) | fax 208/523–0004 | www.ameritelinns.com | 126 rooms, 43 suites | $75–$100, $199–$209 suites | AE, D, DC, MC, V.

Best Western Cottontree Inn. With newly remodeled rooms and conveniently located off I–15, this inn is within walking distance of both the falls and restaurants. Complimentary Continental breakfast. Some kitchenettes, some in-room hot tubs. Cable TV. Indoor pool. Hot tub. Exercise equipment. Laundry facilities. Business services. Airport shuttle. Pets allowed ($25 deposit). | 900 Lindsay Blvd.; I–15 Exit 119 | 208/523–6000 or 800/662–6886 | fax 208/523–0000 | 94 rooms | $74–$145 | AE, D, DC, MC, V.

Best Western Driftwood Inn. Landscaped with flower gardens and overlooking a grassy lawn, this hotel is 34 steps from the Snake River and the falls. Nicely renovated guest rooms have coffeemakers, and some rooms are actually fireplace suites. You're ¼ mi from downtown. Restaurant. Complimentary full breakfast. Some kitchenettes, microwaves, refrigerators. Cable TV. Pool. Hot tub. Fishing. Bicycles. Pets allowed ($10 fee). | 575 River Pkwy. | 208/523–2242 or 800/939–2242 | fax 208/523–0316 | 60 rooms | $55–$109 | AE, D, DC, MC, V.

Hampton Inn. Next to the Grand Teton Mall and Eastern Idaho Regional Medical Center, this lodging has spacious, comfortable rooms. Complimentary Continental breakfast. Microwaves (in suites), refrigerators (in suites). Cable TV. Indoor pool. Hot tub. Exercise equipment. Business services. | 2500 Channing Way | 208/529–9800 | fax 208/529–9455 | 70 rooms | $64 | AE, D, DC, MC, V.

Littletree Inn. An older, well-maintained motel with rooms that overlook a landscaped courtyard in a quiet setting across from a golf course. You can walk to some shops and department stores. Restaurant, complimentary Continental breakfast. Cable TV, VCRs on request. Pool. Hot tub, sauna. Gym. Laundry facilities. Pets allowed ($25 deposit). | 888 N. Holmes Ave. | 208/523–5993 or 800/521–5993 | fax 208/523–7104 | 92 rooms | $49–$59 | AE, D, DC, MC, V.

Quality Inn. This single-story modern motel-style inn has spacious rooms. It's less than ¼ mi from the falls and shopping. Complimentary Continental breakfast. Pool. Hot tub. | 850 Lindsay Blvd. | 800/228–5151 or 208/523–6260 | 127 rooms | $64–$84 | AE, D, DC, MC, V.

Shilo Inn. A big hotel that overlooks the Snake River and has spacious suites. It's close to Idaho Falls and to shopping areas. Restaurant, bar, complimentary breakfast, room service. In-room data ports, microwaves, refrigerators. Cable TV. Indoor pool. Hot tub. Exercise equipment. Laundry facilities. Business services. Airport shuttle. Some pets allowed. | 780 Lindsay Blvd. | 208/523–0088 or 800/222–2244 | fax 208/522–7420 | www.shiloinns.com | 161 suites | $69–$119 suites | AE, D, DC, MC, V.

Super 8. Along a stretch of road with several other chain motels, this one has the most reasonable rates and is close to the falls and shopping. Complimentary Continental breakfast, hot tub, sauna. | 705 Lindsay Blvd. | 208/522–8880 | 90 rooms | $50–$55 | AE, D, DC, MC, V.

Towne Lodge. The rates are reasonable at this basic motel, and you're right downtown. | 255 E St. | 208/523–2960 | 40 rooms | $40–$60 | AE, DC, MC, V.

West Coast Idaho Falls Hotel. Some of the rooms in this high-rise hotel overlook the Snake River, some are pool-side. Restaurant, lounge, complimentary full breakfast. Some refrigerators. Some microwaves. Cable TV. Pool. Hot tub, sauna. Gym. Pets allowed. | 475 River Pkwy. | 208/523–8000 or 800/325–4000 | fax 208/529–9610 | www.westcoasthotels.com | 138 rooms, 1 suite | $89–$109, $350 suite | AE, D, DC, MC, V.

JEROME

MAP 3, C8

(Nearby towns also listed: Buhl, Twin Falls)

The town of Jerome was platted in 1902, just before irrigation canals began to criss-cross the dry, scrubby, sagebrush-dotted flat of the Snake River Plain. It was named for Jerome Hill, one of the investors in the Twin Falls Canal Company, the enterprise that founded the town. Today it is surrounded by dairy farms and massive operations producing beans, sugar beets, alfalfa hay, and potatoes.

Information: **Jerome Chamber of Commerce** | 1731 S. Lincoln Ave., Suite A, 83338 | 208/324–2711 | fax 208/324–6881 | www.jchamber@northrim.net.

Attractions

Jerome County Historical Museum. Memorabilia and artifacts at the museum primarily pertain to the area's farming history. Included are an irrigation canal display and a research room with archival material. | 220 N. Lincoln Ave. | 208/324–5641 | Free | May–Sept., Mon.–Sat. 1–5; Oct.–Apr., Tues.–Sat. 1–5.

Malad Gorge State Park. The Malad River canyon is the main attraction of this 652-acre park. A 2-mi trail skirts the rim, offering views of Devils Washbowl and other features. Side trails lead to nearby fingers of the gorge where crystal-clear springs create ponds and streams. The historic Kelton Trail runs through the park, and wagon ruts and traces of the Kelton Stage Stop remain. The Malad Gorge lies on what was a northern alternate route of the Oregon Trail. | 26 mi west on I–84 to Exit 147 | 208/837–4505 | www.idahoparks.org | Free | Daily.

ON THE CALENDAR
JUNE *Live History Days*. A nostalgic dip into pioneer life has exhibits on weaving, spinning, and farming and a cookout. 208/324–2711.

Dining
Oop's City Market. American. Here you can find a meat counter, espresso bar, deli, and Rocket Bob's cap collection. | 628 S. Lincoln Ave. | 208/324–5952 | $3–$8 | No credit cards.

Lodging
Best Western Sawtooth Inn and Suites. River-rock details against tan siding make the exterior of this hotel distinctive. The interior is contemporary in style. Complimentary Continental breakfast. Microwaves (in suites), some refrigerators. Cable TV. Indoor pool. Hot tub. Exercise equipment. Laundry facilities. Business services. Some pets allowed ($50 deposit). | 2653 S. Lincoln Ave. | 208/324–9200 | fax 208/324–9292 | 57 rooms, 12 suites | $69–$79, $79–$100 suites | AE, D, MC, V MC.

Days Inn. Just off I–84 and U.S. 93, this three-story white inn is within walking distance of the town. In-room data ports. Cable TV, VCRs and movies. Hot tub. Laundry facilities. Business services. Pets allowed ($15 fee and $100 deposit). | 1200 Centennial Spur Rd. | 208/324–6400 | fax 208/324–9207 | 73 rooms | $49–$65 | AE, D, DC, MC, V.

Holiday Motel. Clean, comfortable budget rooms in a convenient downtown location. In-room TV. | 401 W. Main St. | 208/324–2361 | 23 rooms | $40–$50 | D, DC, MC, V.

KELLOGG

MAP 3, B3

(Nearby town also listed: Coeur d'Alene)

Like most communities in the Coeur d'Alene mining district known as Silver Valley, Kellogg was born a mining town and was one of the hub communities. In the 1880s, thick veins of lead, zinc, silver, and gold ores were discovered in Silver Valley, an area 23 mi long and 9 mi wide extending from the Montana border to Coeur d'Alene. A century later, the district led the nation in silver production, ringing up more than $3 billion in sales. Kellogg is in the middle of the Silver Valley, along the South Fork of the Coeur d'Alene River, and named after miner Noah Kellogg. Supposedly, Kellogg's mule Jimmy kicked over a rock that was covering the largest vein of silver ever seen in Idaho, and this event kicked off a rush that has been likened to the one in California. Soon, miners swarmed the community, and by the 1890s the town of Kellogg had been established. Today mining museums recall the district's colorful past, and vacationers flock to two ski resorts and more than 1,000 mi of snowmobile trails across two states in the winter. About 20 years ago, Kellogg reinvented itself and took on the look and feel of a Bavarian village, with neighboring Silver Mountain Ski and Summer Resort following suit. The resort has the world's longest single-span gondola, traveling from the interstate exit to a 6,000-ft peak 4 mi away.

Information: Greater Kellogg Area Chamber of Commerce | 608 Bunker Ave., Kellogg, 83837 | 208/784–0821 | www.nidlink.com/~kellogg.

Attractions

Kellogg Mining District Ghost Towns. Retrace a colorful era in the mining region by visiting the historic towns of Murray, Pritchard, and Enaville. Some still thrive while others are deserted shells of decaying wood. Maps and information are available at the Kellogg Chamber of Commerce. | 208/784–0821 | www.nidlink.com/~kellogg | Free | Daily dawn to dusk.

Old Mission State Park. The 18-acre park contains the oldest building in Idaho, the Mission of the Sacred Heart, which was built between 1850 and 1853. The mission walls are 1 ft thick and were built without nails. The structure was woven carefully of straw, mud, and wooden pegs. Inside, there are no pews because the Indians preferred to worship in an open room. Over 300 members of the Coeur d'Alene tribe labored on the building's construction. The recently restored parish house is next door, and a historic cemetery is nearby. You can picnic in a large grassy area. The visitor center includes an interpretive exhibit on the area and the Coeur d'Alene Indians. There is a short trail linking the mission to the visitor center. August 15 is the annual Coeur d'Alene Indian pilgrimage. | Box 30, Cataldo; Rte. 30 Exit 39 | 208/682–3814 | www.idahoparks.org | $3 per vehicle | Daily, call for hours.

Staff House Mining and Smelting Museum. Exhibits trace the history of the Bunker Hill Mining and Smelting Company, one of the oldest and largest mining companies in the Coeur d'Alene district. On display in the historic home are mineral and metallurgical exhibits, artifacts important to local history, a scale model of the Bunker Hill mine, and mining and smelting equipment. A pie social is held on the last Sunday of September. | 820 McKinley Ave. | 208/786–4141 | www.kellogg-id.org | $ | Late May–Sept., daily 10–5.

Sunshine Mine Disaster Memorial. Visible from I–90, the monument is a memorial to the 91 miners who perished in the 1972 Sunshine Mine Fire, the worst mining disaster in recent history. Set against the cliff, north of Big Creek Canyon, the memorial is a 12-ft-tall sculpture of a miner with his drill raised. It is surrounded by plaques listing the names of those who perished. A nearby local landmark is a building constructed in the shape of a miner's hat that was once a tavern and now houses a real-estate office. | I–90 Exit 54 | 208/784–0821 | www.nidlink.com/~kellogg | Free | Daily dawn to dusk.

ON THE CALENDAR

DEC.: *Dickens Christmas Festival.* Hundreds of community residents don Dickens-era costumes and, along with Dickens characters, engage in high tea, performances, and town sing-alongs. 208/784–0821.

Dining

Edelweiss. German. You get great views of the valley if you ask to be seated on the north side of this casual eatery. The menu is strong on well prepared fresh seafood and a variety of steaks. Smoking is permitted. | 210 McKinley Ave. | 208/783–0114 | $10–$16 | No credit cards.

Enaville Resort. American. Known also as Snakepit, Josies, and what the proprietors term a slew of other "unprintable names," this is definitely not a resort. The rustic, weathered, wood-frame house is at a fork of the Coeur d'Alene River and was built sometime in the 1880s. The Old West dominates the interior, too, with trophies above the rock fireplace and comfy twig and log furniture. The restaurant serves plates heaped high with buffalo burgers, barbecued ribs, steaks, and a Friday night seafood buffet and breakfast. Kids' menu. | Coeur d'Alene River Rd.; 1½ mi from I–90 Exit 43 | 208/682–3453 | $5–$15 | AE, D, MC, V.

Lodging

Silverhorn. This big multistory hotel has shutters and window boxes that make it resemble an Old World inn. And it's less than ½ mi from Silver Mountain base gondola. The gift shop features Native American crafts. Restaurant, room service. Cable TV. Hot tub. Cross-country and downhill skiing. Laundry facilities. Business services. Pets allowed. | 699 W. Cameron Ave.; I–90 Exit 49 | 208/783–1151 or 800/437–6437 | fax 208/784–5081 | sminn@rand.nidlink.com | 40 rooms | $48–$56 | AE, D, DC, MC, V.

KETCHUM

(Nearby towns also listed: Hailey, Sun Valley Area)

Long before Sun Valley was created just a mile away, Ketchum held a place of distinction in the Wood River Valley as the smelting center for the Warm Springs mining district. The town was first known as Leadville, then because the Postal Service objected to overuse of the name, it was changed to Ketchum after David Ketchum, who had staked a claim there in the late 1880s. From 1895 to 1930, the town was a major sheep-shipping center. Today the trailing of the sheep is still an annual event, when herds of sheep move through town en route to the high pastures in the Big Wood River valley to the north. When the Union Pacific railroad set up shop under the Sun Valley Company with plans to build the nation's first destination ski resort, the town was forever changed. Today, most Sun Valley area residents hail from Ketchum or nearby Hailey, a less pricey place to live. Although shops, galleries, and restaurants crowd two-block-long Main Street and surrounding streets, Ketchum still maintains its small-town character. The one-stoplight town was recently forced to add a second to deal with traffic crowding its streets.

Information: Sun Valley Ketchum Chamber of Commerce | Box 2420, Sun Valley, 83353 | 800/634–3347 | fax 208/726–4533 | www.visitsunvalley.com.

Attractions

Ernest Hemingway Memorial. The small memorial is a bust of Hemingway with a passage taken from an epitaph the novelist wrote for a friend who had died in a hunting accident during Hemingway's first visit to Idaho. Hemingway had a home in Ketchum and is buried in the local cemetery. | 2 mi east on Sun Valley Rd. | 208/726–4533 | www.visitsunvalley.com | Free | Daily.

Sun Valley Paragliding. Young and old alike can enjoy the thrill of this experience with tandem jumps off Bald Mountain. The company also offer courses in paragliding. | 260 1st Ave. N | 208/726–3332 | $110–$120.

ON THE CALENDAR

AUG.: *Sun Valley Music Festival.* Performers from around the world are brought into town in August. Past performers have included Branford Marsalis and Jimmy Cliff. | Sun Valley Center for the Arts and Humanities | 208/726–9491.

SEPT.: *Wagon Days.* A popular four-day event with Old West entertainment is held in both Sun Valley and Ketchum. A shootout, barbecues, live music, and the Big Hitch parade. There are also pancake breakfasts, evening Western dances, antiques shows, live entertainment, food, a rodeo, and a collectors' car auction. 208/726–3423.

OCT.: *Trailing of Sheep.* Events include a variety of cultural activities and programs relating to the history of sheep ranching in the Wood River valley. There are wool-carding demonstrations, spinning and weaving, shearing, herding sheep with stock dogs, storytelling, making sheepherder bread, a traditional Basque lamb dinner, music, and dancing. On Monday morning the "trailing" occurs, when hundreds of sheep move down Main Street and south through the valley alongside Route 75. 208/726–3423.

Dining

Evergreen Restaurant. Continental. This old house is now a restaurant filled with European antiques. Along with the great mountain view, there's good food. The menu includes venison, rack of lamb, and fresh fish. Don't miss the homemade ice cream. You can dine on the garden patio with a fountain in nice weather. | 171 1st Ave. | 208/726–3888 | Reservations essential | $20–$35 | AE, MC, V | Closed May, Nov. No lunch.

Globus. Pan-Asian. The menu borrows from the Asian portion of the map with inventive fare from Thai to Chinese and Indian. You can try the huge white porcelain bowls mounded with steaming Hunan chile beef, sizzling twice-cooked pork, and pungent vegetarian Thai green curry. Desserts such as five-spice ice cream cool the palate. Globus recently stepped out of its home base, the Wood River valley, by adding a second venue in Boise. | 291 6th St. | 208/726–1301 | $15–$25 | AE, D, MC, V | No lunch.

Ketchum Grill. Contemporary. A small wood-frame cottage, this restaurant serves inventive fare such as shrimp with pasta and lemon cream sauce, grilled salmon, and citrus salsa. End your meal with one of the rich and decadent desserts. You can dine indoors and look at all the old posters or outside on the covered patio garden. | 520 East Ave. | 208/726–4660 | $8–$18 | AE, D, DC, MC, V | No lunch.

Michel's Christiana. Continental. This is as old-line as Sun Valley gets. Hemingway had cocktails here during his final months. Michel Rudigoz, a former U.S. ski team coach, took over the restaurant in 1994, reinvigorating the menu with traditional French cuisine and maintaining its refined atmosphere on Ketchum's main thoroughfare. Idaho ruby red trout is sautéed then drizzled with cream and dusted with toasted hazelnuts. Ginger-infused cranberries and red wine sauce dress up venison chops. Patio dining, weather permitting. | Sun Valley Rd. and Walnut Ave. | 208/726–3388 | Reservations essential | $35–$45 | AE, D, DC, MC, V | Closed Sun.–Tues. No lunch.

Ore House. American. The only restaurant in town that gives you the option of fine dining or a more casual setting. The two-room restaurant offers a casual pub room and a fancier room with dark-wood booths, both rustic and elegant. | 271 Main St. | 208/726–2267 | $12–$25 | AE, MC, V.

Perry's. Cafe. The Belgian waffles in this café are prized by local skiers who want a carbohydrate and sugar rush. Hot oatmeal, cereals, fresh fruits, yogurts, and legendary cakelike muffins round out the breakfast menu, or they'll do you a cooked-to-order full breakfast. Hot and cold sandwiches, soups, and a selection of salads are offered for lunch. They bake their own bread. Eat-in and take-out service are available. The large patio is open for dining in nice weather. | 131 W. 4th St. | 208/726–7703 | $4–$7 | MC, V | No supper.

Warm Springs Ranch Restaurant. American. In an old ranch log cabin next to Warm Springs Creek, the best bet is the trout, or try the prime rib. Family-style service. Kids' menu. | 1801 Warm Springs Rd. | 208/726–2609 | $12–$24 | AE, MC, V | No lunch.

Lodging

Bald Mountain Lodge. On the National Register of Historic Places and right in the center of town, this 1929 single-story log hotel has tastefully decorated rooms, many in knotty pine. Apartments have several beds and full kitchens. Pool. | 151 S. Main St. | 208/726–9963 | fax 208/726–1854 | 10 rooms, 20 apartments | $65–$125 | AE, D, DC, MC, V.

Best Western Christiania Lodge. This two-story U-shape gray-wood motel near the center of town has rooms with contemporary decor; some have fireplaces. Pool. Hot tub. | 651 Sun Valley Rd. | 208/726–3351 or 800/535–3241 | fax 208/726–3055 | 38 rooms | $75 | AE, D, DC, MC, V.

Best Western Kentwood Lodge. A downtown Ketchum hotel on busy Main Street, built of river rock and timbers, with views of Bald Mountain, and near shops and restaurants. Refrigerators. Cable TV. Indoor pool. Hot tub. Exercise equipment. Laundry facilities. Business services. No smoking. | 180 S. Main St. | 208/726–4114 | fax 208/726–2417 | 57 rooms | $79–$159 | AE, D, DC, MC, V.

Best Western Tyrolean Lodge. Standard chain rooms at this lodge often frequented by skiers. Suites with kitchens available. Within walking distance of the River Run Lift. Complimentary Continental breakfast. Pool. Spa, sauna. | 260 Cottonwood | 208/726–5336 or 800/333–7912 | fax 208/726–2081 | 57 rooms | $90–$126 | AE, D, DC, MC, V.

Heidelberg Inn. An older hotel set back off the road about 1 mi from Ketchum on Warm Springs Road, en route to the Sun Valley base day lodge and lifts. Rooms have been updated and redecorated. Complimentary Continental breakfast, picnic area. Some kitchenettes, microwaves, refrigerators. Cable TV, in-room VCRs and movies. Pool. Hot tub, sauna. Laundry facilities. Pets allowed. | 1908 Warm Springs Rd. | 208/726–5361 or 800/284–4863 | fax 208/726–2084 | 30 rooms | $100–$150 | AE, D, DC, MC, V.

Ketchum Korral Motor Lodge. Clean, comfortable motel rooms and eight rustic cabins with fireplaces and full kitchens are in a tranquil setting with good views and reasonable rates. Complimentary Continental breakfast. In-room phones. Hot tub. | 310 S. Main St. | 800/657–2657 or 208/726–3510 | 17 rooms | $45–$125 | AE, DC, MC, V.

Knob Hill Inn. With lots of wood and log furnishings, the interior of this exclusive inn suits Ketchum's Western character. The building is brand new, though, so everything that should be modern is. All rooms have large tubs and mountain views. Intermediate rooms, suites, and penthouse suites have fireplaces. The intimate Felix at the Knob Hill Inn restaurant features a one-page menu with exquisitely prepared Continental cuisine with a Mediterranean flair. A full breakfast, afternoon snacks, and fresh baked goods are included. Restaurant, complimentary breakfast. Indoor-outdoor pool. Sauna. Gym. | 960 N. Main St. | 208/726–8010 or 800/526–8010 | fax 208/726–2712 | 22 rooms, 4 suites | $185–$240, $300–$375 suites | AE, MC, V.

Lift Tower Lodge. This modest motel sits beside the highway and takes its name from the genuine lift tower and chair in front. Budget-minded skiers make up the winter clientele, since the hotel is less than 3 blocks from the River Run lift. Complimentary Continental breakfast. Refrigerators. Cable TV. Outdoor hot tub. | 703 S. Main St. | 208/726–5163 or 800/462–8646 | fax 208/726–0945 | www.sunvalleylive.com | 14 rooms | $66–$90 | AE, D, DC, MC, V.

LAVA HOT SPRINGS

MAP 3, E8

(Nearby town also listed: Pocatello)

Native Americans were first attracted to the bubbly geothermal springs along the Portneuf River for their supposed curative powers. Later, in the early 1920s, the railroads started bringing scores of vacationers to the area. The main attraction in the town today is the sprawling complex of outdoor and indoor pools, all fed by the 3 million gallons of water that flow from the springs each day. Scientists think the pools have maintained a constant temperature of 110°F for at least 50 million years. The river is also popular for tubing, and the town serves as the gateway to Caribou National Forest. The quaint settlement seems like it's been caught in a time warp and features a handful of cozy cafés and shops.

Information: Lava Hot Springs State Foundation | Box 669, Lava Hot Springs, 83246 | 208/776–5221 or 800/423–8597 | fax 208/776–5273 | ci.lava-hot-springs.state.id.us.

Attractions
Lava Hot Springs. The town's prime natural resource fills a complex of five pools (private and public), ranging from whirlpool- to Olympic-size, open to the public year-round. One pool covers 1/3 acre on a 25-acre landscaped property. Suits, towels, and lockers are available for rent. The natural mineral water is free of sulphur, and geologists speculate that the water has been a consistent 110°F for at least 50 million years. The nearby Portneuf River is also popular for tubing (inner tube rentals are available in town). | East on U.S. 30 | 208/776–5221 | www.idoc.state.id.us/irti/Site | $4.50; special rates for seniors and children | Hot pools: daily 8 AM–11 PM; swimming complex: weekdays 11–9, weekends 10–9.

Portneuf River. A 1-mi-long stretch of river is popular with fans of inner-tubing. The run takes about fifteen minutes, depending on how fast the water is flowing. | Center St. Bridge | 208/776–5500 | Free | Daily.

South Bannock County Society and Museum. The museum focuses on the county's past, with exhibits illustrating its railroad history and the heritage of the area's Shoshone-Bannock tribes. | 110 Main St. | 208/776–5254 | www.ohwy.com/id/s/sbchcm.htm | $2 | Daily.

ON THE CALENDAR
JULY: *Pioneer Days Celebration.* This celebration of pioneer life features exhibits on weaving, spinning, and farming and a cookout. 208/776–5500.

Dining
Blue Moon Bar and Grill. American. No-frills bar with pool tables, low lights, big burgers, good fries—a locals' favorite. The chicken strips are good, too. Live music on the weekends. Bingo on Wednesday, Friday, and Sunday with a jackpot of $1,200. | 89 1st St. | 208/776–5327 | $3–$5 | MC, V.

Pizza Royal. Italian. The simple menu at this small downtown restaurant includes tasty gourmet pizzas and calzones made from scratch. You also get great people-watching from the floor-to-ceiling windows. | 11 E. Main St. | 208/776–5216 | $3–$9 | MC, V.

Lodging
Howard Johnson. Skiers on a limited budget get good value at this standard chain establishment with modest rooms. Pool. Laundry services. | 1716 Main St. | 208/743–9526 | 66 rooms | $66 | AE, DC, M, V.

Riverside Inn. This grand old hotel near the Portneuf River was built in 1914 and promptly labeled "the Honeymoon Hotel." Fully renovated with new baths, rooms are furnished with quilts, ceiling fans, antiques, and simple traditional furniture for a light and airy atmosphere. A roomy lobby features striking woodwork, and a small library and enclosed porch offer space for relaxation. The restaurant, Duke's Fine Dining and Lounge, serves dinner Wednesday through Sunday. Private hot mineral baths are located indoors and outdoors. Restaurant. Library. | 255 Portneuf Ave. | 208/776–5504 or 800/773–5504 | fax 208/776–5504 | 16 rooms (4 with shared baths) | $65–$105 | D, MC, V.

Royal Hotel B&B. This turn-of-the-20th-century house on the edge of town has been renovated to a modern design. Guests can choose suites with shared baths or private ones. Complimentary Continental Breakfast. In-room TV. | 11 E. Main | 208/766–5216 | 5 rooms | $99–$119 | No credit cards.

LEWISTON

MAP 3, A4

(Nearby towns also listed: Grangeville, Moscow)

At the confluence of the Snake and Clearwater rivers, Lewiston was founded in the early 1860s as a supply center for miners making the final leg of the trip to the goldfields to the northeast in the Clearwater River district. By 1863 it was the territorial capital. The town's name pays homage to Meriwether Lewis; its sister city, Clarkston, across the Snake in Washington, recognizes William Clark, the other half of the famous Corps of Discovery duo who trekked through the Clearwater River valley in 1805. They followed the valley from the Bitterroot Mountains near Montana to this point on the Snake River. Lewiston sits at 738 ft, the lowest point in the state and also the state's only port. Barges chug some 460 mi upriver, making the town a thriving center for commerce, agriculture, and industry. The 25-mi paved Clearwater and Snake River Recreation Trail skirts the rivers on levees throughout the two cities. One of the best views of the valley and the two cities is from atop Lewiston Hill, reached by the old Spiral Highway, which branches off U.S. 95 8 mi north of town. Along with shipping and industry, Lewiston thrives on a growing outfitter and guide industry for excursions into the Hell's Canyon area.

Information: Port of Lewiston | 1626 6th Ave., Lewiston, 83501 | 208/743–5531 | fax 208/743–4243 | www.lewiston.com.

Attractions

If you're an outdoor adventure lover, give **Beamers Hells Canyon Tours and Excursions** a try. Jet-boat tours include the one-day tour, which takes you 100 mi upriver to Rush Creek, just past the end of navigation on the Snake River. The historic mail-run tour is offered year-round; boaters help deliver the U.S. mail to rugged canyon reaches as it's been done since 1919. The overnight is at Beamers' Copper Creek Lodge, and includes private modern cabin accommodations. It departs at 9 AM every Wednesday year-round for a two-day, one-night tour. | 800/522–6966 | fax 509/758–3643 | www.hellscanyontours.com.

Hells Gate State Park. This park sits at an elevation of 738 ft along the Snake River. There are grassy open areas for picnicking, a large swimming beach, boating facilities, a volleyball area, 93 shady campsites within 100 yards of the Snake River, and trails. A campground trailhead follows a 2-mi trail along the river past basalt cliffs. The park connects with the Lewiston beltway bike path. The marina has over 100 slips available on a daily to annual basis. If you're an angler, try the famous steelhead runs of the Snake during the fall and winter. You can also see upland birds such as pheasants, quail, chukar, hawks, geese, ducks, and owls, as well as eagles, pelicans, herons, and swans. Keep your eyes open for cottontail rabbits, deer, and otters. | 3620-A Snake River Ave. | 208/799–5015 | www.idahoparks.org | $2 per car | Marina closed Dec.–Feb.

Nez Perce County Museum. Formerly known as the Luna House, this house-museum is devoted to the history of Nez Perce County and its surrounding area. It contains reproductions of a pioneer kitchen and a typical room setting. | 306 3rd St. | 208/743–2535 | Free; donation suggested | Mar.–mid-Dec., Tues.–Sat. 10–4.

Winchester State Park. More than one-fourth of the park's total area is water. A little more than 300 acres of land surround a 103-acre lake. The stands of ponderosa pine and Douglas fir that make up the forest are at 3,900 ft in elevation at the base of the Craig Mountains. You can camp, hike, and picnic in summer, and in winter, weather permitting, cross-country ski, ice-skate, and ice-fish. The park has two yurts for rent year-round. You can see white-tailed deer, beavers, raccoons, muskrats, and the painted turtle. Trails ring the lake, and there is an interpretive nature trail next to the park headquarters. | Off I–95 near Winchester, or follow signs from town | 208/924–7563 | www.idahoparks.org | $2 per car | Daily.

ON THE CALENDAR

APR.: *Lewiston Dogwood Festival.* A celebration of dogwood-blossom time with an art show and crafts fair, wine and beer tasting, garden tours, crafts, concerts, and plays. 208/799–2243.

SEPT.: *Lewiston Round-Up.* The area's largest and oldest community event, with three days of professional rodeo action. 208/743–3531.

Dining

Bojack's Broiler Pit. American. A small restaurant where casual dining and good food are the order of the day. The house favorites are the prime rib and the shrimp salad. | 311 Main St. | 208/746–9532 | $9–$17 | AE, D, DC, MC, V | Closed Sun.

Jonathan's. Contemporary. A new building holds this traditional restaurant with a solid mahogany bar. The menu is strong on Northwest-inspired dishes—fresh seafood and the highest-quality beef in the area, or so they say, and local produce. | 1516 Main St. | 208/746–3438 | $16–$30 | AE, MC, V | Closed Sun.

Zany's. Contemporary. This offbeat restaurant has '50s decor with jukeboxes, an old-fashioned soda counter, a carousel horse, a bathtub, and other miscellany hanging from the ceiling. They serve some Mexican dishes, as well as basic steaks, chicken, burgers, salads, and pasta. | 2006 19th Ave. | 208/746–8131 | $15–$20 | AE, D, MC, V.

Lodging

Howard Johnson. An older, low-slung motel with a small pool in downtown. Complimentary Continental breakfast. Some kitchenettes, refrigerators. Cable TV. Pool. Laundry facilities. Airport shuttle. Pets allowed. | 1716 Main St. | 208/743–9526 or 800/634–7669 | fax 208/746–6212 | 66 rooms | $55–$99 | AE, D, DC, MC, V.

Red Lion Hotel. Set on a hillside above the Clearwater River 1 mi from I–15, this hotel features a full-service athletic club, a sports bar, and its own microbrewery. Restaurant, bar, room service. Cable TV. 2 pools (1 indoor). Hot tub. Gym. Laundry facilities. Airport shuttle. | 621 21st St. | 208/799–1000 | fax 208/748–1050 | www.redlionlewiston.com | 136 rooms | $66–$99 | AE, D, DC, MC, V.

Riverview Hotel. A large, multistory hotel with newly decorated rooms 2 mi from I–95. Complimentary Continental breakfast. Cable TV. Pool. Pets allowed. | 1325 Main St. | 208/746–3311 or 800/806–7666 | fax 208/746–7955 | 75 rooms | $38–$48 | AE, D, DC, MC, V.

Sacajawea Select Inn. An older motel with well maintained rooms in a quiet setting 1mi from I–15 and near downtown. The motel's restaurant, the Helm, serves simple, well prepared food. Restaurant, bar. Refrigerators. Cable TV. Pool. Hot tub. Exercise equipment. Laundry facilities. Airport shuttle. Some pets allowed. | 1824 Main St. | 208/746–1393 or 800/333–1393 | fax 208/746–3625 | 90 rooms | $50 | AE, D, DC, MC, V.

Super 8. Just off I–95, this is a good choice if you're only stopping for the night. Refrigerators (in suites). Cable TV. Laundry facilities. Pets allowed ($25 deposit). | 3120 North-South Hwy. | 208/743–8808 | fax 208/743–8808 | 62 rooms | $39–$49 | AE, D, DC, MC, V.

MCCALL

MAP 3, B6

(Nearby town also listed: Riggins)

The quiet community of McCall sits at 5,021 ft and spreads along the southern tip of Payette Lake. The town was founded by the McCall family, who were part of a wagon train passing through the area and decided to camp there in 1899. Logging has always been important to McCall, although less so in recent years. McCall takes pride in its mammoth trees, like the century-old ponderosa pines that cover the mountain slopes. Signs reading WE SUPPORT THE TIMBER INDUSTRY can still be seen throughout the area. Today the village is a resort town with one of Idaho's oldest alpine ski areas, Brundage. Ponderosa State Park and the Payette Forest are also nearby, with dozens of trails for hiking and mountain biking that lead to mountain lakes. This is also a hot-springs area, with seven nearby. McCall also has a couple of city parks and Davis Beach along the east side of the lake.

Information: **McCall Area Chamber of Commerce** | Box D, McCall, 83638 | 208/634–7631 | fax 208/634–7752 | www.mccall-idchamber.org/toplay/lodging.html.

Attractions

Brundage Mountain Ski Resort. The ski resort has 1,300 acres of wide, groomed runs and powder glades, all in an area reporting 300 inches of snowfall each year. The vertical drop totals 1,800 ft, and skiers have access to 38 runs. The peak elevation at the area is 7,640 ft, with base operations at 5,840 ft. The big day lodge has a restaurant, a retail and rental shop, and a ski school. The Kids' Center offers day-care for children as young as eight weeks and ski programs for children through age 12. You can also do guided skiing by Sno-Cat on more than 19,000 acres of steep chutes and bowls of untracked snow. | 3890 Goose-lake Rd. | 208/634–4151 or 800/888–7544 | fax 208/634–4155 | www.brundage.com | $32 | Mid-Nov.–mid-Apr.

Cascade Reservoir. The 28,300-acre reservoir is one of southwestern Idaho's most popular places for boating and fishing. Cascade and the west side of the reservoir near Don-nelly have boat ramps. Fishing brings catches of brown trout, coho salmon, kokanee salmon, rainbow trout, white fish, and bullhead catfish. | 79 mi north of Boise on Rte. 55 | www.idahoparks.org | Free | Daily dawn to dusk.

Payette National Forest. The Payette includes some of the largest remaining blocks of unde-veloped land in the United States, including 800,000 acres of classified wilderness and approximately 650,000 acres of roadless land. You can reach another 850,000 acres by roads. The forest contains about 2,800 mi of roads and almost the same in trails. Elevations range from 1,500 ft in Hells Canyon to over 9,500 ft in the Frank Church–River of No Return Wilder-ness. Summer temperatures can exceed 100°F at the lower elevations, while winter tem-peratures can drop to –40°F. It is bordered on the north by the Salmon Wild and Scenic River, on the west by the Snake River, on the east by the Middle Fork of the Salmon River, and on the south by the Boise National Forest. The Payette includes a large portion of the Frank Church–River of No Return Wilderness. Approximately 24,000 acres of the Hells Canyon Wilderness is also within the forest boundary. | 800 W. Lake Side Ave. | 208/634–0700 | www.mccall.net/pnf | Free | Daily dawn to dusk.

Payette River. The rapids on this river range from Class I to Class V (*See* Grangeville). | Idaho Outfitters and Guides Association, Box 95, Boise | 208/342–1919 | www.ioga.org | Free | Daily.

Ponderosa State Park. The 1,470-acre park covers most of a peninsula in Payette Lake. At 5,050 ft, you'll find everything from arid sagebrush flats to dense woodlands. The North Beach Unit has a beach and picnic area. You can follow a self-guided nature trail or take guided walks with park naturalists and attend evening campfire programs. The scenic over-look at Porcupine Point offers a spectacular view of Payette Lake. Hiking and mountain-bike trails in the park include Lily Marsh and Meadow Marsh hiking trails, from which you'll often glimpse wildlife. The visitor center has park and trail maps, bird and plant check-lists, and wildlife notes. | 2 mi northeast, on Payette Lake | 208/634–2164 | www.ida-hoparks.org | $3 per car | Daily.

ON THE CALENDAR

JAN.–FEB.: *Winter Carnival.* The weeklong carnival takes over the whole town and fea-tures world-class ice sculptures, pyrotechnics, the Snowflake Ball, wine tasting, sled-dog races, a variety show, and a parade. 208/634–7631.

JULY: *Annual Blues Festival.* An evening of blues music featuring regional and area bands with food is held at the Brundage Mountain Ski Resort. 208/634–4151.

JULY: *Payette Apple Blossom Festival.* A celebration of apple-blossom time with an apple-bobbing competition, chamber breakfast, the Apple Core Open Golf Tournament, a talent show, an ice-cream social, a pretty baby contest, a pie-eating contest, arts and crafts, a carnival, and a parade. 208/642–2362.

Dining

McCall Brewing Company. American. A lake view adds a nice touch to this casual restau-rant. The menu includes vegetarian choices, steak, and fresh seafood. You can wash it all down with ales made on the premises. Dine outside on the deck if it's nice. | 807 N. 3rd St. | 208/634–2333 | $12–$25 | AE, D, MC, V.

Mill Steak and Spirits. American. This lively family-owned restaurant has a casual, rustic look and is popular for its steak and seafood. Kids' menu. | ½ mi south on Rte. 55 | 208/ 634–7683 | $10–$44 | AE, D, DC, MC, V | No lunch.

Sagebrush BBQ. Barbecue. In a 1938 building with an Old West storefront and seating in booths, the setting is perfect for the menu of beef brisket, pork ribs, and chicken barbecue. Ice-cream treats come from a 1930s soda fountain. | 210 Virginia Ave., New Meadows; 5 mi north on Rte. 55 | 208/347–2818 | $12–$20 | MC, V.

Lodging

Bear Creek Lodge. Among pine trees in a wooded mountain meadow, this rustic yet elegantly furnished lodge also has luxurious cabins, set on 65 acres next to Bear Creek, 4 mi west of town. Restaurant. In-room phones. Laundry facilities. Pets allowed ($100 deposit). | 3492 Rte. 55 | 208/634–3551 | fax 208/634–7699 | 9 lodge rooms, 4 cabins | $120, $125–$200 cabins | AE, D, DC, MC, V.

Best Western. A new hotel with light brick and white trim, this place is two blocks from Payette Lake and near downtown. In-room data ports, refrigerators, microwaves. Cable TV. Indoor pool. Hot tub. Exercise equipment. Laundry facilities. Business services. Some pets allowed. | 415 3rd St. | 208/634–6300 or 800/528–1234 | fax 208/634–2967 | 79 rooms | $74–$105 | AE, D, DC, MC, V.

Hotel McCall. Newly renovated, this lakeside hotel was built in 1939 in the center of town. The light and airy rooms have traditional and antique furnishings. Complimentary Continental breakfast. Cable TV. No smoking. | 1101 N. 3rd St. | 208/634–8105 | fax 208/634–8755 | 22 rooms (6 with shared bath) | $55–$110 | AE, D, MC, V.

Riverside Inn. Some of the rooms have kitchens at this reasonably priced, in-town motel that's near the lake. In-room TV. Hot tub. | 400 W. Lake St. | 800/326–5610 | 16 rooms | $45 | AE, MC, V.

MONTPELIER

MAP 3, F9

(Nearby town also listed: Lava Hot Springs)

Montpelier, a community of 3,000, has long been a rest stop for travelers, first those trudging the California and Oregon trails, which are nearby, and today those drawn to the intersection of two major highways, U.S. 89 and U.S. 30. A new Oregon/California Trail Visitor Center is the pride of Montpelier. The town is also the northern gateway to Bear Lake Valley, Minnetonka Cave, and the historic town of Paris. Originally settled in 1864, it got its name from Brigham Young, the Mormon leader, who was born in Montpelier, Vermont. The notorious outlaw Butch Cassidy once robbed the local bank of $7,165. Border Summit at 6,335-ft elevation offers a good view of an undisturbed portion of the Oregon Trail about 12 mi south of town off U.S. 30.

Information: **Bear Lake Regional Commission** | Box 26, Fish Haven, 83287 | 208/945–2333 or 800/448–BEAR.

Attractions

Bear Lake. Dubbed the Caribbean of the Rockies, the 120-square-mi Bear Lake is 20 mi south of Montpelier and dips down into Utah. Its color, which runs from bright turquoise to robin's-egg blue, is thought to be caused by high concentrations of carbonates suspended in the water. Other theories claim it's the sandy bottom. It's one of the state's most distinctive bodies of water. The surrounding area is either largely undeveloped or state park property. The lake is particularly picturesque when viewed from the summit of U.S. 89 at 7,800 ft in Garden City, Utah. | 2661 U.S. 89 | 208/847–1045 | www.bearlakechamber.org | Free | Daily dawn to dusk.

Bear Lake National Wildlife Refuge. The refuge occupies the north end of the park. The 17,600 acres of marsh, open water, and grasslands provide nesting habitat for ducks, such as mallard, pintail, and canvasback, as well as sandhill cranes, herons, egrets, Canada geese, and white pelicans. | 2661 U.S. 89 | 208/847–1045 | www.idoc.state.id.us/irti/stateparks | Free | Daily dawn to dusk.

Bear Lake State Park. The park covers 966 acres and is about 6,000 ft in elevation. The park's two units on the north and east end have 5 mi of sandy beaches where you can swim and go powerboating, waterskiing, sailing, and fishing. The gradual slope of the lake bottom provides a large swimming area. You can catch native cutthroat or lake trout in the summer and in the winter, come back with buckets and nets when the Bonneville Cisco run; this is the only place this species of fish is found. Nearby, Bear Lake Hot Springs is popular. | 2661 U.S. 89; 20 mi south on U.S. 89 | 208/847–1045 | www.idoc.state.id.us/irti/stateparks | $2 per car | Daily dawn to dusk.

Caribou National Forest. The 1-million-acre forest is mostly in southeastern Idaho, with small portions in Utah and Wyoming. The Caribou Forest takes its name from Jesse Fairchild, a gold miner nicknamed "Cariboo Jack"; there are no caribou herds in the forest. In 1870, Fairchild, known for telling tall tales of the Canadian caribou country, and two other miners discovered gold near what is now called Caribou Mountain. The resulting gold rush lasted 20 years and produced $50 million worth of placer gold. Remains of the mining era and settlement can still be found near Caribou Mountain. Several north–south mountain ranges run through the forest. Slopes are both forested and sagebrush-covered. The Curlew National Grasslands near Malad are also administered by the forest and are known for their upland game birds. You can hike on the 1,200 mi of trails. Pebble Creek ski area is on the west side of Mt. Bonneville, near Inkom, Idaho. The Caribou is also known for some of the best range and grazing lands in the intermountain West and about 22,000 cattle and 91,000 sheep graze there each year. | Montpelier Ranger District, 322 N. 4th St. | 208/847–0375 | Free | Daily dawn to dusk.

★ **Minnetonka Cave.** In 1907, a grouse hunter discovered the cave, which opened to the public in 1947. Guided tours take you to soda-straw formations, banded travertine, and helicites in nine chambers. The hour-long tours of the state's largest developed limestone cave climb more than 400 steps and travel 1,800 ft into the cave, which is at a constant, chilly 48°F. | St. Charles canyon | 208/847–0375 | $3 | Guided tours mid-June–Labor Day.

Paris Tabernacle Historical Site. The majestic Mormon tabernacle was built of red sandstone blocks in 1889, all hauled by sled through the snow from a quarry 18 mi away. The Romanesque-styled temple has intricately carved woodwork and a soaring sanctuary with balcony lofts. A small museum houses heirlooms and artwork left by the homesteaders. You can take guided tours. | U.S. 89, Paris | 208/945–2333 | Free; donations accepted | Memorial Day–Labor Day, daily 10–5.

Soda Springs Geyser. Although the eruptions are controlled, the geyser is a spectacle worth seeing. The four-inch stream of water that reaches 135 ft was created when drillers hit a pocket of carbonated water. Today it is turned on during regularly scheduled geyser shows. | 39 W. 1st S | 208/547–2600 | Free | Apr.–Nov.

ON THE CALENDAR

JUNE: *Great West Music Fest.* A series of classical music concerts features performers from throughout the intermountain West. 208/945–2333.

AUG.: *Bear Lake Raspberry Festival.* An annual raspberry celebration has a craft fair, a rodeo, dances, fireworks, and local entertainment. 208/945–2333.

Dining

Butch Cassidy's Restaurant and Saloon. American. Supposedly, Butch spent time in town, then robbed a bank, inspiring the restaurant's name. The spacious dining room serves prime rib and big steaks, sandwiches, and seafood, with dancing and live entertainment on weekends. | 230 N. 4th St. | 208/847–3501 | $15–$25 | AE, DC, D, MC, V.

Lodging

Best Western Clover Creek Inn. A nice redbrick hotel featuring wide windows for sunny guest rooms. There's a restaurant nearby. Complimentary Continental breakfast. In-room data ports, some refrigerators. Cable TV. Hot tub. Exercise equipment. Business services. Some pets allowed. | 243 N. 4th St. | 208/847–1782 | fax 208/847–3519 | 65 rooms | $62–$70 | AE, D, DC, MC, V.

Park Motel. Some rooms have kitchens at this reasonably priced standard motel. In-room TV. Hot tub. | 745 Washington St. | 208/847–1911 | 25 rooms | $40 | MC, V.

MOSCOW

MAP 3, A3

(Nearby town also listed: Lewiston)

The town's name is said to date from 1877, when Samuel Neff, one of the early settlers, filed for a postal permit under the name Moscow because the countryside reminded him of his hometown of Moscow, Pennsylvania. Before that, the town had been known as Paradise Valley and even Hog Heaven. Camas plants were prolific in the area when settlers first arrived. The bulb was a favorite food of the settlers' hogs, and the name Hog Heaven stuck, at least for a while. The railroad chugged into town in 1885, and two years later Moscow was incorporated as a town. It was selected as the site for a land grant institution, the University of Idaho. The Palouse Hills, a bumpy rolling landscape with extremely fertile soil, surround Moscow to the west, making the town of 20,000 the dry pea and lentil capital of the world. Moscow Mountain, a few miles northeast of town via Mountain View Road, offers a bird's-eye view of the town cradled by the Palouse Hills.

Information: **Moscow Chamber of Commerce** | 411 S. Main St. (Box 8936), 83843 | 208/882–1800 or 800/380–1801 | fax 208/882–6186 | www.moscowchamber.com.

Attractions

Appaloosa Museum and Heritage Center. This museum highlights the history of the Appaloosa horse, noted for its spotted markings. Regalia, saddles, and artifacts associated with the Appaloosa are on display, including Native American items. The Nez Percé tribes who lived in the area practiced selective horse breeding and produced large herds of high-quality horses, including Appaloosas. | 2720 W. Pullman Rd. | 208/882–5578 | www.appaloosa.com | Free | Tues., Fri. 10–5, Sat. 10–4.

Latah County Historical Society McConnell Mansion. Built in 1886 by Idaho's third governor, the house is a combination of Eastlake, Queen Anne, and Victorian Gothic styles. Period furnished rooms display artifacts and Victorian-style furniture from the early 1900s to 1930s. The mansion also houses the Latah County Historical Society, which presents changing exhibits on county history on the second floor. | 110 S. Adams St. | 208/882–1004 | www.moscow.com | $2 suggested admission | Tues.–Sat. 1–4.

Prichard Art Gallery. A downtown art gallery features the work of regional artists, with an emphasis on student work. | 414 S. Main St. | 208/885–3586 | Free | Daily.

University of Idaho. Established in 1889, the college was founded a year before Idaho became a state. As one of the state's largest institutions of higher learning, the school enrolls 10,000 and offers an agricultural extension service that reaches 42 of the state's counties. Colleges include architecture, art, agriculture, business, education, engineering, and forestry. | 208/885–6163 | Free | Daily.

ON THE CALENDAR

FEB.: *University of Idaho Lionel Hampton Jazz Festival.* An internationally known weeklong event featuring more than 50 of the world's great jazz artists with workshops and performances. 208/885–6765.

MAR.: *Mardi Gras and Beaux Arts Ball.* A festival that has parades and bands in East City Park. 208/882–1800.

JULY: *Rendezvous in the Park.* A wide range of music is performed and also children's events are featured during the weekend festival at East City Park. 208/882–8100.

Dining

Bacilio's. Italian. In the Moscow Hotel, this restaurant offers updated Italian cuisine in a bright dining room fitted with artwork from ceiling to floor. The menu has a good variety of pastas. | 313 S. Main St. | 208/892–3848 | $9–$16 | MC, V.

Casa de Oro. Mexican. This small Mexican restaurant is known for it massive margaritas and genuine south-of-the-border entrées at very reasonable prices. You can eat in the dining room or go for the tables outside. | 415 S. Main St. | 208/883–0536 | $4–$7 | AE, DC, MC, V.

Gambino's. Italian. The interior of this restaurant might be modeled after a set in *The Godfather.* With its variety of traditional Italian dishes such as spaghetti and meatballs, red and white checkered tables, and dim lighting, it's quite the authentic Italian dining experience. | 306 W. 6th St. | 208/882–4545 | $7–$15 | AE, DC, MC, V.

Lodging

Best Western—University Inn. This big, newer hotel on the Washington state line is at the west end of the University of Idaho campus. Rooms are decorated with light blue and tan floral spreads, light wood furniture, and tan walls. 2 restaurants, bar, room service. Some refrigerators. Cable TV. Indoor pool, wading pool. Hot tub, sauna. Business services. Laundry services. Airport shuttle. Pets allowed ($10 fee). | 1516 Pullman Rd. | 208/882–0550 | fax 208/883–3056 | 173 rooms | $85–$105 | AE, D, DC, MC, V.

Hillcrest. An older strip motel downtown has modest rooms that are well maintained. You're close to restaurants and shopping, and the rates are very modest. Some refrigerators. Cable TV. Business services. Laundry facilities. Pets allowed ($5 fee). | 706 N. Main St. | 208/882–7579 or 800/368–6564 | fax 208/882–0310 | hillcrest@moscow.com | 35 rooms | $36 | AE, MC, V.

Mark IV Motor Inn. Spacious rooms and traditional furnishings make this older, remodeled downtown hotel pleasant. Restaurant, bar, room service. Cable TV. Indoor pool. Hot tub. Business services. Airport shuttle. | 414 N. Main St. | 208/882–7557 | fax 208/883–0684 | 86 rooms | $49–$60 | AE, D, DC, MC, V.

Peacock Hill. At the base of Moscow Mountain, this inn has expansive views of the countryside and a casual cozy atmosphere. Each of three guest rooms has a private bath, one with a Jacuzzi. Horseback riding. | 1245 Joyce Mountain Rd. | 208/882–1423 | www.commquest.com/-lodging/peacock | 3 rooms | $95 | AE, DC, M, V.

Royal Motor Inn of Moscow. A central downtown location and low rates make this a good choice for budget travelers. In-room TV. | 120 W. 6th St. | 208/882–2581 | 38 rooms | $35 | AE, DC, M, V.

Super 8. A 14-year-old hotel with modest rates and just off I–95, this a good choice for overnight stops. Cable TV. | 175 Peterson Dr. | 208/883–1503 | fax 208/883–4769 | 60 rooms | $42–$75 | AE, D, DC, MC, V.

MOUNTAIN HOME

MAP 3, B8

(Nearby town also listed: Boise)

First known as Rattlesnake Station, the town got its start in 1864 as an Overland Stage stop. The stage line ran for another 20 years until the Union Pacific railroad came to town in 1883. The current name is a misnomer; the town sits on a sagebrush flat, with the mountains looming above the Oregon-Idaho state line about 60 mi away. It is perhaps best known as the home of Idaho's only active military installation, Mountain Home Air Force Base. The town is also a gateway to river-running excursions on the Owyhee, Jarbridge, and Snake rivers to the south. Head to Teapot Dome, 7 mi north, for a good view of the Boise Basin and Mountain Home. Oregon Trail travelers used the dome as a major landmark. You can hike up the 1,000-ft dome but there is no developed trail. Well-preserved ruts of the Oregon Trail are still visible here.

Information: **Mountain Home Chamber of Commerce** | 205 N. 3rd E | 208/587–4334 | www.mhchamber@mhicon.net.

Attractions

Bruneau and Jarbridge Rivers, Bruneau Canyon. Bruneau and Jarbridge are remote canyonland rivers that start in the mountains of northern Nevada and run through the remote high desert of the Owyhee Uplands to the Snake River in southern Idaho. The rivers can be run only for a few months each spring from April to June. The 40-mi-long Bruneau is a small river that squeezes through a narrow and deep basalt-walled canyon that is, at places, 800 ft deep and 1,300 ft wide from rim to rim. It offers generally Class III to Class IV rapids. Jarbridge is a Shoshone Indian word for monster, and probably refers to the Jarbridge Falls. Bruneau is two French words run together, meaning "brown water." The rapids include Five-Mile, which drops 22 ft per mile. The 29-mi-long Jarbridge is steep, and the rapids are boulder strewn. The surrounding backcountry is remote, with no signs of civilization and no hiking out. Both rivers provide a wilderness desert canyon experience. River runners camp in small juniper groves, and trips usually last four to five days. | 20 mi south on Rte. 51 to Bruneau, then southeast on local road | 208/384–3300 | Free; registration required | Daily.

Elmore County Historical Foundation Museum. The small museum displays artifacts, photographs, and documents relating to miners, immigrants, and ranchers from the area. | 180 S. 3rd E | 208/587–3951 | Donations accepted | Mar.–Dec., Fri., Sat., tours by appointment.

Soldier Mt. Ski Area. A family-oriented ski mountain is an affordable alternative to Sun Valley, about 70 mi away. The vertical drop is 1,500 ft and the top elevation is 7,150 ft. You can downhill ski, snowboard, and do Sno-Cat skiing. The day lodge has a snack bar and rentals as well as lessons. | 59 mi northeast on U.S. 20 to Fairfield, then 10 mi north | 208/764–2300 or 208/764–2626 | Mid-Nov.–early Apr.

ON THE CALENDAR

SEPT.: *Air Force Appreciation Days.* Honoring the service that has a nearby base, this features an air show, parade, barbecue, and other entertainment. 208/587–4334.

Dining

Stoney Desert Inn. American. Renowned for its homemade soups and pies, the restaurant offers a dinerlike, casual environment and modestly priced food. Its a local favorite, so be prepared to wait for a table. | 1500 Sunset Strip | 208/587–9931 | $4–$9 | AE, DC, MC, V.

Tacos El Tio Pancho. Mexican. This small Mexican restaurant is frequented by those who want great food at reasonable prices. The soft tacos are a great deal. Eat inside or on the outdoor patio. | 815 S. 3rd W | 208/587–2665 | $2–$7 | No credit cards.

Lodging

Best Western—Foothills Motor Inn. Just off I–84, this tan brick building has remodeled rooms and good amenities. Complimentary Continental breakfast. Cable TV. Pool. Hot tub. Fitness room. Business services. Laundry facilities. Pets allowed ($50 deposit). | 1080 U.S. 20; I–84 Exit 95 | 208/587–8477 | fax 208/587–5774 | 76 rooms | $65–$125 | AE, D, DC, MC, V.

Hilander Motel and Steak House. A small, older strip motel is 4 mi from I–84 near the center of town. Some rooms have kitchenettes, and the fee for pets is unusually low. Restaurant, bar, room service. Some kitchenettes. Cable TV. Pets allowed ($4 fee). | 615 S. 3rd W; I–84 Exit 90 | 208/587–3311 | fax 208/580–2152 | 34 rooms | $35–$39 | AE, D, DC, MC, V.

Sleep Inn. A newer motel near I–84, on a strip of highway with other chain motels. Complimentary Continental breakfast. In-room data ports, refrigerators. Cable TV, in-room VCRs. Business services. Pets allowed ($50 deposit). | 1180 U.S. 20 | 208/587–9743 | fax 208/587–7382 | 60 rooms (with shower only) | $53–$74 | AE, D, DC, MC, V.

Towne Center Motel. An excellent value, this small downtown motel is close to restaurants and shopping. In-room TV. Pool. | 410 N. 2nd E | 208/587–3373 | 32 rooms | $37 | AE, DC, MC, V.

NAMPA

MAP 3, A7

(Nearby towns also listed: Boise, Caldwell)

Today Nampa and its sister city to the west, Caldwell, are thriving agricultural communities that are practically suburbs of Boise. Named after a Shoshone chief Nampuh, whose name referred to his big feet, the town was founded in 1883 as a railroad town on the Oregon Short Line of the Union Pacific railroad. The stately Victorian train depot built of brick in 1903 with a tiled mansard roof and turret details is now a museum and one of the main attractions downtown. There are more than a dozen notable buildings dating from the 1900s included in a walking-tour map and brochure of the four-square-block downtown area. Surrounding Nampa are fields teeming with orchards and fragrant mint, and vineyards that spread across the sloping hillsides. During the summer, fruit ranches and produce stands in the countryside sell the harvest.

Information: Nampa Chamber of Commerce | 1305 3rd St., 83651 | 208/466–4641 | www.nampa.com.

NAMPA

INTRO
ATTRACTIONS
DINING
LODGING

Attractions

Canyon County Historical Society Museum. Housed in an early-1900s Union Pacific depot, the museum displays blacksmithing and farm tools, railroad artifacts, medical instruments, mustache cups, and other relics from the region's early settlement in the late 1800s. | 1200 Front St. | 208/467–7611 | $2 | Tues.–Sat. 1–5.

Deer Flat National Wildlife Refuge. The 11,585-acre refuge is in a vast region of rolling, sagebrush-covered hills that stretch to the Owyhee mountains in the southwestern corner of the state. The refuge area was a low swale with many springs that grew grasses, attracting deer and elk that migrated there from the mountains during the winter. The herds of deer temporarily gave rise to the name Deer Flat. The Oregon Trail passed to the north of the refuge, along the Boise River, and south, along the Snake River. Lake Lowell is a 9,000-acre reservoir created in the early 1900s that eventually supplied water to irrigate more than 200,000 acres of land. In addition to the lake, the refuge includes more than 107 islands in the Snake River and is known mainly for its resident and migratory waterfowl. | 13751 Upper Embankment Rd.; 5 mi southwest off I–84 | 208/467–9278 | fax 208/467–1019 | Free | Daily.

Givens Hot Springs. The natural hot springs along the Snake River first attracted Native American tribes who wintered here for about 5,000 years. Homesteaders built a pool in the 1880s, and it was also a popular stopping point on the Oregon Trail. The original pool building burned in 1939 and was rebuilt in 1952. Today the resort is still a popular place to swim and soak in the 95°F water. | 17 mi south on Rte. 45, 8 mi west on Rte. 78 | 208/495–2000 | Fee varies | Daily.

ON THE CALENDAR

JULY: *Snake River Stampede.* A huge event more than 20 years old has one of the top 20 rodeos in the nation, featuring leading cowboys and cowgirls, with bareback bronc riding, calf roping, saddle bronc riding, steer wrestling, team roping, barrel racing, and bull riding. Also a wrangler bullfight, mutton busting, and the Stampeders Night Light Drill. | 208/466–8497.

Dining

Tacos Jalisco. Mexican. A popular Mexican restaurant where traditional Mexican dishes taste the way they would in Mexico, and include some, like menudo, not regularly found in the U.S. Sombreros and crucifixes adorn the walls. | 219 11th Ave. N | 208/465–5788 | $4–$7 | No credit cards.

Lodging

Alpine Villa Motel. This motel offers cottagelike rooms for the budget minded. Continental breakfast. In-room phones. Cable TV. | 124 3rd St. S | 208/466–7819 | 11 rooms | $50 | AE, DC, MC, V.

Shilo Inn. The older of the two Shilo Inns, this is a basic motel with modest rooms that's convenient to downtown, ¾ mi from the Nampa physics center and 3 mi from the Idaho center. Complimentary Continental breakfast. Cable TV. Pool. Hot tub, sauna, steam room. Laundry facilities. Airport shuttle. Pets allowed ($7 fee). | 617 Nampa Blvd.; I–84 Exit 35 | 208/466–8993 | fax 208/465–3239 | www.shiloinns.com | 61 rooms | $69 | AE, D, DC, MC, V.

Shilo Inn Nampa Suites. The newer of the two Shilos, this multistory contemporary-styled hotel features minisuites with tan walls, blue, green, and burgundy print spreads, and framed prints. It's located just off I–84. Restaurant, room service. Some kitchenettes, refrigerators. Cable TV. Indoor pool. Hot tub. Exercise equipment. Laundry facilities. Airport shuttle. Pets allowed ($10 fee). | 1401 Shilo Dr.; I–84 Exit 36 | 208/465–3250 | fax 208/465–5929 | www.shiloinns.com | 83 suites | $79–$89 suites | AE, D, DC, MC, V.

OROFINO

MAP 3, B4

(Nearby towns also listed: Grangeville, Lewiston)

Meaning "fine gold" in Spanish, Orofino is a gold-rush town that was established in 1898. Miners were in the area by the 1870s, though, and Lewis and Clark passed by the town's later location when they made their trek in 1805. It sits near the Clearwater River in a valley of just 1,097 ft elevation, within the Nez Percé Indian Reservation land. With a long growing season and rather moderate climate, the wide open valleys and high prairies of north-central Idaho make the area an important agricultural center. Lumbering is also important to the economy, and the town is a gateway to the Dworshak Dam, Dworshak State Park, and the Nez Perce National Historical Park.

Information: Orofino Chamber of Commerce | 217 1st St. (Box 2346), 83544 | 208/476–4335 | www.orofinochamber@clearwater.net.

Attractions

Bald Mountain Ski Resort. At this small ski area run by the Idaho Parks and Recreation Department, the vertical drop is 975 ft. The lodge has a snack bar, rentals, and lessons. | 42 mi east, 6 mi north of Pierce on Rte. 11 | 208/464–2311 or 208/743–6397 | Dec.–mid-Mar.

Clearwater Historical Museum. A collection of artifacts from the Nez Percé, early exploration and settlement years, and the gold-rush era fill this downtown museum. | 315 College Way | 208/476–5033 | Free | Tues.–Sat. 1:30–4:30.

Clearwater National Forest. The varied forest terrain includes 1.8 million acres ranging from 1,600 ft to nearly 9,000 ft in elevation. Deep forested canyons with a mix of lofty rugged ridges are the main features of the forest. The climate features distinct seasons, and much of the property is snowbound from December through May. There are more than 1,700 mi of hiking trails, some easily reached trailheads in the White Pine Scenic Drive area along U.S. 12, Route 247, and Forest Road 250, next to the North Fork of the Clearwater River. You can see elk herds and there are black bears, mountain goats, white-tailed and mule deer, moose, and mountain lions. | 12730 U.S. 12 | 208/476–4541 | www.fs.fed.us/r1/clearwater | Free | Daily 24 hrs.

The **Lolo Pass Visitor Center** (Daily, 9–5), a refurbished log cabin, stands in a rest stop at the Idaho-Montana state line. Exhibits at the center trace the Lewis and Clark trail as it passed through Idaho. The backcountry **Lochsa Historical Ranger Station** (Donations accepted | June–Sept., daily 10–5), built in the early 1920s, was accessible only on foot until 1956, when the Lewis and Clark Highway (now U.S. 12) was constructed. The old station has been restored and is maintained as an example of early life in the Forest Service. Retired Forest Service employees operate the station as volunteers to greet visitors, answer questions, and guide tours.

Some of the natural highlights in the forest include the Selway-Bitterroot Wilderness, Mallard-Larkins Pioneer Area, and a number of buttes, lookouts, and waterfalls.

One-fourth of the **Selway-Bitterroot Wilderness** area is within the Clearwater National Forest. Elevations range from 1,800 ft on the Selway and Lochsa rivers to 8,800-ft mountain peaks along the Bitterroot Divide. Hundreds of miles of trails are maintained through the Wilderness. The Selway Bitterroot Wilderness encompasses 9,767 acres located on the Lolo, reachable on forest roads west off U.S. 93. Mechanized equipment, including bicycles, is not permitted in the wilderness or on trails leading into the wilderness.

The **Mallard-Larkins Pioneer Area** is a 33,000-acre roadless region encompassing rugged mountains between the St. Joe and Clearwater rivers. The area lies partly in the St. Joe National Forest and partly in the Clearwater Forest. A trail system provides access on both sides.

The **Weitas Butte, Austin Ridge, and Castle Butte Lookouts** are no longer used for fire detection and are available for rent by the public during the summer for overnight stays. The lookouts offer dramatic views but are not recommended for families with small children. The surrounding area features three waterfalls, **Elk Creek Falls,** and is a popular area for hiking, camping, and picnicking. There is a ½-mi trail leading to the falls. The **Lochsa River** (Lochsa means "rough water" in Nez Percé) originates in the Bitterroot Mountains and joins the Selway and Clearwater rivers after 26 mi. It includes 40 Class III to Class IV rapids. The river parallels U.S. 12 for much of its course. Most outfitters use paddle boats on the Lochsa to make it a participatory trip. The river-running season is short, from mid-May to late June. Most trips take from one to three days.

Dent Bridge. A 1,050-ft-long suspension bridge at Dworshak Reservoir is similar to San Francisco's Golden Gate Bridge, only smaller. 208/476–4335.

Dworshak Dam and Reservoir. Completed in 1972 and originally known as Bruce's Eddy Dam project, the dam is the largest straight-axis dam in North America, and it impounds a 54-mi-long reservoir. The visitor center is on top of the dam, and exhibits cover the dam's history and native wildlife. Tours are available through the interior of the structure. | 3 mi past Orofino bridge | 208/476–1255 | Free | Daily 10–4.

Orofino Scenic Golf and Country Club. A 5,415-yard 18-hole golf course plays a par 70. There's a snack bar and pro shop. | 3430 U.S. 12 | 208/476–3117 | $12 | Closed Nov.–Mar.

Selway River. The 46-mi river has a Class III to Class V rating with a rafting season from May to July for three- to five-day trips. With only one launch per day allowed, this is the state's most private Wild and Scenic river. The stream runs between banks lush with cedar, fir, huckleberries, and ferns. The water is always crystal clear. The rapids are all large and at high flows. Rapids such as Ladle and Double Drop can reach Class IV to Class V levels. Trips are popular and require reservations 8 to 12 months in advance. Catch-and-release fishing trips for native cutthroat trout are also available. | Bitterroot National Forest, West Fork Ranger Station, Darby, MT | 406/821–3269 | Free | Daily dawn to dusk.

ON THE CALENDAR

SEPT.: *Lumberjack Days.* An international event attracts loggers from all over the world for burling, axe-throwing, tree races, two-person handsaw, power saw races, and other competitions.208/476–4335.

Dining

Ponderosa Restaurant and Lounge. American. On the outskirts of town, this is a family establishment by day and a lounge in the evening. The house favorite is prime rib. | 220 Michigan Ave. | 208/476–4818 | $7–$17 | MC, V.

Lodging

Helgeson Place Hotel Suites. Some rooms have kitchenettes at this budget hotel in the heart of downtown. In-room phones, TV. | 125 Johnson Ave. | 800/404–5729 | 19 rooms | $50 | AE, DC, MC, V.

WHITE-WATER RUNNING

With roughly 3,100 mi of white water, more than any other western state, Idaho offers the ideal vacation activities of running the rapids or even just an easygoing float. Opportunities for river trips range from leisurely day floats to six-day excursions of almost non-stop rapids. Idaho's rivers are evenly distributed throughout the state, so you're never far from an outfitter. To plan a river trip:

First determine the destination and your priorities, then the type of watercraft desired. For example, there are river guides who run rafts, kayaks, canoes, dory and drift boats, and jet boats, providing everything from a leisurely float to a challenging adventure. (Rapids are ranked in difficulty from Class I to Class IV.) Calculate the length of your trip taking into account time of year. Water levels can vary significantly with the season.

River scenery ranges from the deep and narrow desert wilderness canyon of the Owyhee in Idaho's southwest corner to verdant pine forest along the Selway in northern Idaho.

Remember to account for lodging and travel time to the launch and take-out points. Some trips involve tent camping along the river bank; others feature rustic yet luxurious guest ranch lodging. Most river runners take pride in preparing sumptuous food, so boaters are almost always assured of great eats on their trips.

Check with the Idaho Outfitters and Guides Association (Box 95, Boise, 208/342–1919, www.ioga.org) for a list of licensed outfitters and guides.

© Corbis

POCATELLO

(Nearby towns also listed: American Falls, Blackfoot)

The town's melodic name comes from the name of a Shoshone chief who granted the railroad a right-of-way through the Fort Hall Indian Reservation. The Shoshone and Bannock tribes inhabited most of southeastern Idaho for centuries before Lewis and Clark and the Oregon Trail brought settlers to the area. The area was also an important center for fur trapping and trading, and the Hudson's Bay Company established one of the first permanent settlements at Fort Hall in 1834, a few miles northeast of Pocatello. After the fur-trading industry waned, Pocatello was a supply and rest stop along the Oregon Trail. The peak of activity came with the railroad, when "Pocatello Junction" was the largest rail hub west of the Mississippi. The prosperity the town enjoyed around the turn of the 20th century can be seen in its elegant mansions, downtown commercial buildings, and the majestic three-story train depot. After the railroad boom, the town became an agricultural center and continued to grow. Today it is the state's third largest city, with a population of more than 51,000. Modern irrigation networks drawing water from the Snake River have transformed the surrounding wide, flat valley into lush farmland. Pocatello is also home to Idaho State University.

Information: Bannock and Chubbuck Visitor Center | 2695 S. 5th St., Pocatello, 83201 | 208/233–1525 | fax 208/233–1527 | www.pocatelloidaho.com.

Attractions

City Creek. A popular local spot for for those who enjoy hiking and mountain biking. A trip up the trail will lead you to Kinport Peak, with an elevation of 7,222 ft. | City Creek Rd. | 208/233–1525 | Free.

Idaho State University. The state-supported institution enrolls more than 12,000 students in undergraduate and graduate programs in the arts and sciences, health professions, business, education, engineering, pharmacy, and applied technology. The university's outreach program takes classes and degree programs to students in Idaho Falls, Twin Falls, Boise, and Lewiston. | 741 S. 7th Ave. | 208/236–3532 | www.isu.edu | Daily.

Idaho State Arboretum. A large collection of labeled shrubs and trees is scattered across the grounds of the Museum of Natural History. Among them are plants indigenous to Idaho, including the state flower, syringa. Ask about guided tours. | S. 5th Ave. at E. Dillon St. | 208/ 236–3168 | Free.

★ **Idaho Museum of Natural History.** This museum is affiliated with Idaho State University, with a primary focus on education and research in the natural history of the state and region. Diverse exhibits display artifacts, including fossils, preserved plant-life specimens, animated replicas and skeletons of dinosaurs, a large rock collection, and Indian relics. The Discovery Room for children has hands-on displays of fossils, shells, and other specimens as well as games and puzzles about natural history. | 741 S. 7th Ave. | 208/282–3317 or 208/ 282–2262 | www.isu.edu/departments/museum.com | $2.50 | Mon.–Sat. 9–5.

Pebble Creek Ski Resort. The 50-year-old, 1,100-acre ski area includes a vertical drop of 2,000 ft with a base elevation at 6,300 ft. The runs cover all ability levels. You can snowboard, and there's night skiing, a ski lodge, and school. | 10 mi southeast on I–15 to Inkom, then 5 mi east on Green Canyon Rd. | 208/775–4452 | www.pebblecreekskiarea.com | Early Dec.– mid Apr.

Ross Park. The town's main municipal park includes the Ross Park Zoo, with cougars, black bears, deer, and other animals native to the northern Rockies. It also has an outdoor swimming pool with a water slide. | 2901 S. 2nd Ave. | 208/234–6196 | Free | Daily year-round.

The **Old Fort Hall Replica** is part museum and part living-history center with a re-creation of a fort built in the 1830s. The original fortress was a fur-trading outpost. The replica includes massive wooden gates and log cabins that house a trader's store, a dining hall, and a blacksmith shop. Other cabins are fully furnished. Displays also tell the story of the fort. You can watch the video *Fort Hall, Gateway to the Northwest*. | 208/234–1795 | poky.interspeed.net/forthall/ | $2.50 | Mid-Apr.–mid-June, Tues.–Sat. 10–2; mid-June–Labor Day, daily 10–6; Labor Day–late Sept., daily 10–2.

ON THE CALENDAR

MAR.: *Dodge National Finals Rodeo.* This second-largest points-qualifying rodeo in the United States features cowboys from 12 nationwide circuits, all on the campus of Idaho State University. 208/233–1525.

Dining

Continental Bistro. Continental. All meals are prepared to order here. The sleek interior has track lighting, and you can eat on the patio in nice weather. The menu favorites are lobster medallions and broiled chicken. | 140 S. Main St. | 208/233–4433 | $12–$23 | AE, D, DC, MC, V.

Remo's. Italian. With its castlelike interior, Remo's is unlike any other restaurant in town. Check out the bar on the patio on those hot summer afternoons. Locals consider it one of the best restaurants in town, with such signature dishes as fettuccine alfredo and New Zealand lamb. | 160 W. Cedar | 208/233–1710 | $10–$21 | AE, D, DC, MC, V.

Lodging

Ameritel Inn. A large, new, multistory hotel just off I–15 in the interstate lodging district. Some of the rooms are extra-large for families. Complimentary Continental breakfast. In-room data ports, some kitchenettes, some refrigerators. Cable TV. Indoor pool. Hot tub. Exercise equipment. Laundry facilities. Airport shuttle. | 1440 N. Bench Rd.; I–15 Exit 71 | 208/234–7500 or 800/600–6001 | fax 208/234–0000 | www.ameritelinns.com | 365 rooms | $69–$139 | AE, D, DC, MC, V.

Comfort Inn. The suites are a good value at this chain that's off I–15 in the lodging district and set back off an access road. Complimentary Continental breakfast. Cable TV. Indoor pool. Hot tub. Pets allowed. | 1333 Bench Rd.; I–15 Exit 71 | 208/237–8155 | fax 208/237–5695 | 52 rooms, 14 suites | $56, $66 suites | AE, D, DC, MC, V.

Days Inn. Standard chain rooms with modern furnishings and decor. Smoking rooms are available. In-room phones, TV. Pool. Hot tub. | 133 Burnside Ave. | 800/325–2525 or 208/237–0020 | 116 rooms | $55 | AE, DC, MC, V.

Hales' Half Acre Inn. Family hospitality is the order of the day at this down-on-the-farm bed-and-breakfast with good amenities for a modest price. Keep warm by the stone fireplace while the children play in the treehouse or maybe take a walk through the garden. No smoking. The rooms are spacious, with great views and contemporary furnishings. In-room phones, TVs. Pool. Hot tub. | Rte. 2, Box 26 | 208/237–7130 | 2 rooms | $45 | No credit cards.

Holiday Inn. This property is in the motel strip off I–15. Some rooms are poolside and overlook a putting green. Restaurant, bar, complimentary Continental breakfast, room service. Cable TV. Indoor pool. Hot tub. Putting green. Exercise equipment. Laundry facilities. Business services. Airport shuttle. Some pets allowed. | 1399 Bench Rd.; I–15 Exit 71 | 208/237–1400 | fax 208/238–0225 | 202 rooms | $79 | AE, D, DC, MC, V.

Super 8. A new multistory hotel in the lodging district just off I–15. Some rooms have hot tubs, microwaves, and refrigerators. The fee for pets is unusually low. Complimentary Continental breakfast. Cable TV, VCRs on request. Laundry services. Some pets allowed ($2 fee). | 1330 Bench Rd.; I–15 Exit 71 | 208/234–0888 | fax 208/232–0347 | 80 rooms | $56–$70 | AE, D, DC, MC, V.

West Coast Pocatello Hotel. This is one of the original hotels along the interstate lodging strip. It has a steak-house restaurant and 24-hour coffee shop in a redbrick Colonial-style building with white trim and traditional furnishings. Restaurant, bar, room service. Cable TV. Indoor pool, wading pool. Hot tub. Exercise equipment. Laundry facilities. Business services. Airport shuttle. Some pets allowed. | 1555 Pocatello Creek Rd.; I–15 Exit 71 | 208/233–2200 | fax 208/234–4524 | www.westcoasthotels.com | 150 rooms | $59–$89 | AE, D, DC, MC, V.

PRIEST LAKE AREA

(Nearby towns also listed: Bonners Ferry, Sandpoint)

The lake was first named Roothan, after his superior in Rome, by Jesuit priest Pierre DeSmet in 1846. Forty years later, in 1890, in a move to appeal to the Great Northern Pacific Railroad, which was courting the area, the name was changed to generic Priest Lake. Though it's the smallest of the top three northern Idaho lakes, the rugged, mountainous setting attracts scores of vacationers, fishers, and hunters. The 26,000-acre lake sits at 2,438 ft, while mountains along the eastern shore rise 7,000 ft. The lake consists of an upper lake (3½ mi long) and a larger lower lake (17½ mi long), connected by a 2-mi stretch of the Priest River called "the thoroughfare." A handful of rustic cabin resorts and more than 16 campgrounds rim the 70 mi of wooded shoreline, and four of the lake's seven islands have campsites, some of which are only accessible by boat. In 1972 a 57½ pound Mackinaw trout was hooked, one of the largest ever. The thick forests surrounding the lake include an ancient grove of cedars near Nordman. The climate is rather rainy, with 33 inches of rain and just 10 inches of snow falling each year. In summer vacationers are often rewarded with a show of the northern lights. Remote Priest Lake retains more of its backwoodsy character than popular lakes Coeur d'Alene and Pend Oreille, the latter less than 30 mi away.

Information: Priest Lake Chamber of Commerce | Box 174, Coolin, 83821 | 208/443–3191 or 888/774–3785 | www.priestlake.org.

Attractions

Albeni Falls Dam and Reservoir. The dam offers a scenic viewpoint over the Pend Oreille River and includes a picnic area and visitors center that offers one-hour tours of the powerhouse. | 40 mi south of Nordman on U.S. 57 to U.S. 2, then 3 mi west | 208/437–3133 | Free | Memorial Day–Labor Day, daily.

Priest Lake. The lake is actually two lakes connected by a river, and together they are 25 mi long, making them the third-largest lake in the Panhandle region. Anglers know the lake for its world-class Mackinaw trout and kokanee salmon. On the west shore is the Roosevelt Grove of Ancient Cedars, with trees more than 200 years old. | 4 mi east of Nordman | 208/267–5922 | Free | Daily dawn to dusk.

Priest Lake State Park. The lake is the highlight of the 755-acre park that spreads across forested rolling highlands at 2,400-ft elevation. The lake is noted for its clear water and the Selkirk Mountain Range, which rises nearby. Park trails thread through forests of giant cedars and hemlocks, passing by quiet streams. Rugged roadways originate at both park units and head east into the mountains, a habitat for white-tailed deer, moose, black bears, coyotes, and mountain goats, though rarely seen. There is a ½-mi hiking trail at the Lionhead Unit, a ½-mi trail at the Indian Creek Unit, and a ¾-mi trail at Viewpoint. | 38 mi north of Hwy 2 on East Shore Rd. | 208/443–2200 | www.idahoparks.org | $2 per car | Daily dawn to dusk.

Dining

Frizzy O' Leary. American. A small lounge and café where the locals go to have a quiet meal in an ultracasual atmosphere. | Luby Bay Rd. and Rte. 57 | 208/443–3043 | $7–$14 | DC, MC, V.

Lodging

Elkin's. A secluded rustic and elegant cabin resort at Reeder Bay on the west side of Priest Lake. Restaurant, bar, picnic area. No air-conditioning, kitchenettes. Cross-country skiing. Beach, boating. Pets allowed ($10 fee). | West shore of Priest Lake | 208/443–2432 | fax 208/443–2527 | 30 cottages | $75–$100 cottages | D, MC, V.

Grandview. Romantic, panoramic views of pristine Priest Lake. Cottages, lodge rooms, and lakeside suites in a quiet setting. Bar, dining room. No air-conditioning, kitchens (in cottages and suites). Pool, beach, water sports, boating. Cross-country skiing. Game room. Laundry facilities. Airport shuttle. | 3492 Reeder Bay Rd.; west shore of Priest Lake | 208/443–2433 | fax 208/443–3033 | Grandview@nidlink.com | www.gvr.com | 8 rooms, 10 suites, 10 cottages | $75–$85 rooms, $165 suites, $135–$175 cottages | MC, V.

Hill's Resort. A long-time resort with a central lodge and cabins spread along the shoreline and among the trees on Luby Bay. These are family-oriented lodgings with ample recreation options. Bar, dining room, picnic area. No air-conditioning, some kitchenettes. Driving range, putting green, tennis. Beach, water sports, boating. Bicycles. Cross-country skiing, snowmobiling, tobogganing. Game room. Laundry facilities. Business services. Pets allowed ($10 fee). | West shore of Priest Lake via Rte. 57 to Luby Bay Rd. | 208/443–2551 | fax 208/443–2363 | 30 cabins, 25 condos | $900–$2,500/wk, $1,200–$2,600/wk condos (7–day minimum stay in summer) | D, MC, V.

Inn at Priest Lake. The hexagonal stone structure a stone's throw away from the lake may not look like a inn at first but it houses a beautiful hotel with a restaurant and has with a landscaped backyard. In-room phone, TV. Pool. Hot tub. | Dickensheet and Cavenaugh Bay Rds | 208/443–4066 or 800/443–6240 | 23 rooms | $100 | AE, DC, MC, V.

Whispering Waters B&B. Friendly bed-and-breakfast with three elegantly decorated guest rooms, each with its own bath, pellet wood stove, and private entrance. There's a private dock and access to mountain bike trails. In-room phones, TV. | Outlet Bay Rd. | 208/443–3229 | 3 rooms | $85 | AE, DC, MC, V.

REXBURG

MAP 3, F7

(Nearby towns also listed: Idaho Falls, St. Anthony)

The town started out as a Mormon colony of only 13 settlers under the Bannock Ward in 1883. It took its name from Thomas Ricks, the newly ordained bishop of the ward. A year later, it had a population of 875 and 1,600 plowed acres. Ricks College, affiliated with the Church of Latter-day Saints, dates back to 1888. Today the town is the 12th-largest in the state, with a population of over 14,000. Food processing figures prominently in its economy. Among its most notable landmarks is the former LDS tabernacle, a majestic twin-towered stone building built in 1911 and designed to seat 1,400.

Information: Rexburg Chamber of Commerce | 420 W. 4th S, 83440 | 208/356–5700 | fax 208/356–5799 | www.rexcc.com.

Attractions

Porter Park Carousel. One of the last of its kind in the world, the carousel was built by the Spillman Engineering Co. around 1926. The amusement was restored in 1985, and reopened a few years later. It now goes around to the music of a new band organ. | 250 W. 2nd S | 208/359–3020 | 50¢ | June–Labor Day, daily.

Ricks College. Ricks College is a small private college of the Church of Jesus Christ of Latter-day Saints. It opened in 1888, when many other church academies were established in the Mormon communities of the western United States. The college has associate degree programs in arts and sciences and specialized disciplines and enrolls about 8,600 full-time students. | 525 S. Center St. | 208/356–2200 | www.ricks.edu | Daily.

Teton Flood Museum and the Old LDS Tabernacle. One of the main architectural attractions in town, the gray stone church is the old Latter-day Saints (LDS) Tabernacle. The twin-tower structure dates from 1911 and now houses the Teton Flood Museum. Exhibits tell of the disastrous flood that struck Rexburg on June 5, 1976, when the Teton Dam broke. There's a model of the dam before it broke and displays on the flood. Other exhibits show artifacts from the town's early settlement in a furnished log cabin setting. | 51 N. Center St. | 208/356–9101 | www.rexcc.com | Donations accepted | Weekdays 10–4.

ON THE CALENDAR
JULY–AUG.: *International Folkdance Festival.* Hundreds of dancers from around the world share their culture during a weeklong dance festival with showy opening and closing ceremonies, a street dance, parade, fireworks, and youth culture day. 208/356–5700.

Dining
Frontier Pies. American. A local landmark, this eatery is known for home-style meals and a dozen kinds of pies baked fresh daily, in a rustic setting with Western memorabilia and antiques. The Navajo taco is a scone with chili and traditional taco toppings. Locals also favor the longhorn tips—steak with peppers and onions and a special sauce. | 460 W. 4th S | 208/356–3600 | $8–$15 | AE, D, DC, MC, V.

Lodging
Best Western Cottontree. The motel is in the center of town at a main highway intersection. Some rooms have balconies, and all are well equipped for business travelers. Restaurant. In-room data ports, some microwaves, some refrigerators. Cable TV. Indoor pool. Hot tub. Health club privileges. Fitness center. Laundry facilities. Laundry services. Business services. Pets allowed. | 450 W. 4th S | 208/356–4646 or 800/662–6886 | fax 208/356–7461 | 99 rooms | $50–$70 | AE, D, DC, MC, V.

Comfort Inn. This mid-sized, family hotel is outside of town, in suburban surroundings. The suites are well equipped for families. Complimentary Continental breakfast. Microwaves (in suites), refrigerators (in suites). Cable TV. Indoor pool. Hot tub. Exercise equipment. Business services. Pets allowed. | 1565 W. Main St. | 208/359–1311 | fax 208/359–1387 | 52 rooms | $62–$120 | AE, D, DC, MC, V.

Super 8. The downtown location of this modest, modern chain is convenient to restaurants and shops. In-room phones, TV. | 215 W. Main St. | 208/356–8888 | 41 rooms | $40 | AE, DC, MC, V.

RIGGINS

MAP 3, B5

(Nearby towns also listed: Grangeville, McCall)

Named after a stage driver, Riggins was first known as Gouge-Eye. For years the town thrived on logging and the timber industry until a major lumber mill perished in a fire in 1970. Today the community has reinvented itself as a hub and base camp for excursions to Hells Canyon and river trips on the Salmon River. The town is situated where the Little Salmon flows into the main Salmon River, and is also at the start of the scenic Salmon River canyon via U.S. 95 north of town. The area looks west to the scenic Seven Devils Range, with 9,000-ft peaks.

RIGGINS

INTRO
ATTRACTIONS
DINING
LODGING

Information: **Riggins Area Chamber of Commerce** | Box 289, Riggins, 83549 | 208/628–3778.

APR.: *North Idaho Whitewater Races.* Featuring a kayak and jet-boat race on the Little Salmon River. It draws over 100 competitors. 208 628 3778.

Dining

Restaurant at Salmon River Inn. American. This spacious casual restaurant in the lobby of the Salmon River Inn offers a varied selection of homemade pizzas and gourmet sandwiches. A great place to take the family. | 129 S. Main St. | 208/628–3813 | $7–$14 | AE, MC, V.

Lodging

★ **Lodge at Riggins Hot Springs.** This lodge, named for hot springs that have been harnessed into pools on the bank of the Salmon River, is just over 10 mi upriver from Riggins along a narrow, winding road. Inside, Western antiques and Native American crafts abound, and a sitting room is dominated by a large rock fireplace. Rooms have pine paneling and wooden bed frames. Very romantic and great for couples. Dining room, complimentary meals (full breakfast, snack lunch, dinner). Complimentary beverages. Pool. Hot tub, sauna. Game room. Conference room. No kids under 12. | Box 1247; on the Salmon River, 9 mi east of Salmon River Rd. | 208/628–3785 | fax 208/628–4129 | rhslodge@cyberhighway.net | www.rhslodge.com | 10 rooms | $250–$350 | D, MC, V | AP.

Riggins Motel. In the middle of town, the Riggins Motel offers modest, modern accommodations at budget rates. In-room phones. Cable TV. | U.S. 95 | 800/669–6739 | 3 rooms | $43 | AE, DC, MC, V.

Shepp Ranch. The closest road is 15 mi from this this very remote backcountry lodge that can accommodate 14 guests. Once there—you arrive by air or by jet boat from Riggins—you can fish, hike, raft, boat, and do almost anything else outdoorsy. | Box 5446, Boise 83705; 43 mi upriver from Riggins | 208/343–7729 | $170 per person per day | AP.

ST. ANTHONY

MAP 3, E7

(Nearby town also listed: Rexburg)

The tiny town of St. Anthony sits astride Henry's Fork of the Snake River and is best known for the sand dunes that nudge the outskirts of town to the west. Roughly 5 mi from town, the shifting "live" dunes are the highest in the state and surpass those in Death Valley, California. They are particularly attractive to dune buggy enthusiasts.

Information: **South Fremont County Chamber of Commerce** | St. Anthony, 83445 | 208/624–4870.

Attractions

St. Anthony Sand Dunes. The dunes, made of quartz sand, are 35 mi long and 5 mi wide, formed by prevailing winds blowing across the Snake River Plain. Reaching 500 ft, they surpass in height those found in Death Valley, California. The 10,000-acre dunes region includes the Elgin Lakes Recreation Area, a 15-mi stretch suitable for all-terrain vehicles. The Sand Mountain Wilderness Study Area is off-limits to motorized travel and covers 10,000 acres of dunes, sagebrush, and juniper. | 1 mi north of town, left at sign | 208/524–7500 | Free | Daily dawn to dusk.

JULY: *Fremont County Pioneer Days.* A three-day festival has music, a rodeo, and a parade. 208/624–4870.

ST. MARIES

(Nearby town also listed: Coeur d'Alene)

The town grew up at the confluence of the St. Maries and St. Joseph rivers, considered an ideal site for a sawmill a century ago. Plentiful timber and transportation supported the sawmill in the early days, and for years logging operations sustained the community of 2,700. Following World War II, the demand for lumber rose. By 1961, however, after three recessions and the loss by fire of the St. Maries Lumber Company, the biggest mill in the area and its largest employer, the working-class community was struggling. Local residents rallied and formed the Benewah County Development Corporation, which used federal assistance to build a plywood mill on the site of the former lumber mill. Today St. Maries is still a timber town, with the plywood mill operating under the Potlatch Corporation as part of its St. Maries Complex, which manufactures plywood, lumber, and wood chips. Although the hard-working town is closely allied with the timber industry, it is also known for its wild rice, harvested at Heyburn State Park along the marshy southern end of Lake Coeur d'Alene, where three lakes—Benewah, Round, and Chatcolet—support the grain. The town is also a hub for river running on the St. Joe and excursions into the Panhandle National Forests. As the world's highest navigable river, the St. Joe still sees flotillas of logs trailing behind tug boats in "brails," headed for the sawmills.

Information: St. Maries Chamber of Commerce | 906 Main St. (Box 162), 83861 | 208/245–3563 | www.stmarieschamber.org.

Attractions

Heyburn State Park. This is one of the more popular state parks, spanning 5,505 acres near Chatcolet Lake. Water accounts for 2,300 of those acres. Herons and ospreys are especially common. Each fall a festival highlights the wild rice harvest. The Hawleys Landing Amphitheater presents lectures, slide shows, and other naturalist programs. There are six hiking trails for a total of 20 mi, most of them passing through stands of 400-year-old ponderosa pines. The trails are at the west end of the lake. The historic Mullan Trail starts at the Chatcolet area. | 7 mi west on Rte. 5 | 208/686–1308 | www.idoc.state.id.us/irti/stateparks | $2 per car | Daily.

St. Joe, Moyie, and Clearwater Rivers. The Moyie, St. Joe, and Clearwater rivers are popular for river trips that take only a single day but still give you a white-water experience. The picturesque St. Joe has blue-green water and its banks are covered with moss and dotted with cedars. Beginning rafters learn to paddle here. The Clearwater River is a quiet and scenic river with no rapids and is popular with families. | Just east of town on Rte. 5 | 208/476–4541 | Free | Daily.

ON THE CALENDAR

JULY: *smART Festival.* A weekend festival with food booths, entertainment, fine arts booths, and children's art is held at the Cherry Bend Boat Park on the St. Joe. | 208/245–3417.
SEPT.: *Paul Bunyan Days.* The Labor Day weekend sees logging displays, pool events, an auction, community booths, a carnival, a parade, and fireworks in the city park. | 208/245–3563.

SALMON

(Nearby town also listed: Challis)

The great outdoors is still the highlight of Salmon, a town established as a gold-mining center in 1867. With a population of 3,000, it stands on the Salmon River,

SALMON

INTRO
ATTRACTIONS
DINING
LODGING

surrounded by the 10,000-ft peaks of the Bitterroot, Beaverhead, and Salmon River ranges. It is a major hub for rafting trips on the Salmon and backpacking, fishing, and hunting outings into the 2.4-million-acre Frank Church–River of No Return Wilderness Area, 30 mi to the west. Set in a high mountain valley at 4,000 ft, it has earned the title Whitewater Capital of the World, owing to the legendary rapids on the Salmon River and its Middle Fork. Dozens of guides, outfitters, and guest ranches are based here. Mountain men like Jim Bridger and Kit Carson, miners, and loggers have all spent time here. Today the town retains a genuine Old West atmosphere. Salmon is also roughly 25 mi north of the famed Lemhi Pass, where Lewis and Clark crossed the Continental Divide in 1805. Their Corps of Discovery's Indian guide, Sacajawea, hailed from what is today Lemhi County.

Information: **Salmon Valley Chamber of Commerce** | 200 Main St., Suite 1, Salmon, 83467 | 208/756–2100 | fax 208/756–4840 | www.salmoninternet.com.

Attractions

Lemhi County Historical Museum. The museum displays a unique collection of Oriental artifacts relating to early Chinese settlers. Exhibits also include such Indian artifacts as headdresses and peace pipes. You'll learn about Elmer Keith, the notorious sharpshooter, from a display that includes his five-gallon hat, pistol, and boots. | 210 Main St. | 208/756–3342 | $1 | Mid-Apr.–Oct.

Salmon National Forest. The 2.4 million acres of forest are bordered by the Bitterroot Range of the Continental Divide on the east and include part of the Frank Church–River of No Return Wilderness on the west. It reaches to Gilmore Summit on the south and Lost Trail Pass on the north. Deer, elk, bears, bighorn sheep, mountain goats, and moose all inhabit the area. The earliest known inhabitants were the Sheepeaters, Shoshone Indians who lived along the Salmon River. Their name derives from the bighorn sheep, part of the tribe's diet. No known descendants of this tribe remain. The Flatheads and Nez Percé Indians spent winters in the Salmon River country. Lemhi Indian Reservation, established in 1875, was home to 700 Shoshone, Bannock, and Sheepeater Indians. Chief Tendoy was the leader of the reservation. The town of Salmon was also the birthplace of Sacajawea, the guide for the Lewis and Clark Expedition, which passed through here in 1805. Trappers, traders, and missionaries later appeared in the area between 1819 and 1865. Kit Carson and Jedediah Smith were among them. The discovery of gold in Napias Creek in 1866 finally brought permanent residents. | Rte. 2, Box 600; 1 mi south on U.S. 93 | 208/756–5100 | fsweb.r4.fs.fed.us | Free | Daily dawn to dusk.

Frank Church–River of No Return Wilderness. The wilderness is the largest such area in the lower 48 states. This 2.3-million-acre tract contains portions of four national forests, including the Nez Perce, Payette, and Boise national forests in Idaho and the Bitterroot National Forest in Montana. The name of Idaho senator Frank Church was added to the wilderness in 1983, one month before his death. Church was instrumental in the creation of the wilderness and in helping to enact the 1964 Wilderness Act and Wild and Scenic Rivers bill in 1968. Elevations in the area range from 2,000 to 10,000 ft, and trails can be very steep. The central features of the wilderness are the Middle Fork of the Salmon Wild and Scenic River, the Salmon itself, and the Selway. These are all famous white-water rivers, and some 8,000 kayakers, rafters, jet-boaters, and steelhead anglers converge on an 80-mi wilderness section of the Salmon River Gorge, the nation's second-deepest canyon at over 6,000 ft deep. About 10,500 visitors float the Middle Fork each year. The area is also known for mountain lions and was chosen as one of the two best areas in the nation to reintroduce the Rocky Mountain gray wolf. Among the other wildlife are bighorn sheep, mountain goats, elk, mules, whitetail deer, moose, martens, fishers, lynxes, coyotes, red foxes, wolverines, and numerous raptors. The terrain is primarily rugged conifer-forested mountains. There are 1,500 mi of trails. | Salmon National Forest, U.S. 93 south (Rte. 2, Box 600) | 208/756–5100 | Free | Daily.

Salmon River. The 79-mi Main Salmon threads through the Frank Church–River of No Return Wilderness Area. The Shoshoni called the river Tom-Agit-Pah, or "Big Fish Water." They camped along the river during the annual salmon run, yet considered the river too dangerous for canoe travel and developed an extensive trail system for canyon access. The Nez Percé used the lower section and the Sheepeater Shoshoni lived upstream. The Main Salmon features huge waves at Class III to Class IV, with sandy beach campsites along its course. River trips usually take from five to seven days. There are hiking trails up the side canyons. The river corridor is not part of the wilderness, and jet boats are permitted. | 10 mi north on U.S. 93 | 208/756–2100 | Free | Daily.

ON THE CALENDAR
AUG.: *Sacajawea Heritage Days/Balloon Fest.* Assorted hot-air balloon races are held during this celebration of Sacajawea. There are also replicas of all the objects taken on Lewis and Clark's journey, intertribal dancing, and period craft demonstrations—not to mention food. 208/756–2100.

Dining
Salmon River Coffee Shop. American. This family restaurant downtown in a historic building has home-style cooking, pies, and big breakfasts. The menu favorite is steak. Salad bar. Entertainment (weekends). Kids' menu. | 606 Main St. | 208/756–3521 | $7–$15 | AE, DC, MC, V.

Lodging
Salmon River Lodge. This wilderness guest ranch offers family-style meals, hunting, fishing, horseback riding, and water trips. Cozy rooms with a rustic cedar finish can sleep four or more. On the river, 70 mi from Salmon, the lodge is accessible only by the proprietors' boat. Buffet dinner, lounge with fireplace. Boating. Jet-boating. Fishing. | Box 927 | 208/756–6622 or 800/635–4717 | fax 208/756–3033 | 8 rooms | $60–$100 | AE, D, MC, V | Closed Nov.–Feb.

Stagecoach Inn. Overlooking the Salmon River, this quiet inn has some riverside rooms and some with balconies. Complimentary Continental breakfast. Cable TV. Pool. Laundry facilities. No pets. Children under 12 free. | 201 U.S. 93 N | 208/756–4251 | 100 rooms | $48–$75 | AE, DC, MC, V.

SANDPOINT

MAP 3, B2

(Nearby towns also listed: Bonners Ferry, Coeur d'Alene)

Sandpoint spreads along the forested shoreline of Lake Pend Oreille (pronounced pond-er-*ray*), the largest in Idaho at 94,600 acres. Aeons ago, a glacier scooped out the area where the lake sits. It reaches a depth of 1,200 ft and has 111 mi of shoreline. Fur traders first built a trading post, the first in the Northwest, on the sandy shore of the lake where the town sits today. It became a town in the 1880s and, like most others in the heavily forested Panhandle, Sandpoint saw its moments as a logging center and a railroad town. It led a quiet existence until the 1970s, when it was discovered as a vacation destination and Schweitzer, a major ski resort, was developed. By the end of the 1970s, the surrounding county counted a 55-percent increase in its population. Sandpoint itself numbers 5,000 year-round residents and swells during peak summer and winter tourist seasons. Timber continues to figure in the town's economy along with tourism. The lake is popular with anglers and is known for its hefty Kamloops rainbow trout, a species found only here, that can weigh in at more than 30 pounds. The city is still known for its pristine sand beach nearly ¼ mi long.

Information: **Greater Sandpoint Chamber of Commerce** | Box 928, Sandpoint, 83864 | 208/263–2161 | www.chamber@sandpoint.net.

Attractions

Bonner County Historical Society Museum. Lakeview Park is home to the museum whose exhibits detail the history and development of Bonner County. There are displays on Native Americans, fur traders, and the steamboat and railroad eras, as well as on the Farragut U.S. Naval Training Base. | 611 S. Ella St. | 208/263–2344 | bchsmuseum@nidlink.com | $1 | Tues.–Sat. 10–4.

Coldwater Creek on the Cedar St. Bridge. This is a huge strip of shops along a rustic timbered bridge. It's the only marketplace on a bridge in the United States, built with massive tamarack logs and passive-solar windows overlooking Sand Creek. There's the Coldwater Creek store, best known for women's and men's apparel, Northwestern-inspired gifts, and home furnishings, an espresso shop, and a deli. | Cedar St. and First Ave. | 208/263–2265 | www.thecreek.com | Free | Mon.–Sat. 9–9.

Lake Pend Oreille. Idaho's largest lake at 94,600 acres, with an astonishing depth of 1,200 ft, is a fisherman's paradise. Fourteen species of game fish inhabit its waters, including kokanee, largemouth bass, and bluegill. The world-record Kamloops trout and a 42-pound Mackinaw (also known as lake trout) came from this lake. The lake's name, Pend Oreille (pronounced pond-or-*ray*), comes from the term used by early French trappers to describe the pendent ornaments the local Indians wore in their earlobes. The lake is in Kootenai and Bonner counties, covers 180 square mi, and is 65 mi long and 15 mi wide. Its shoreline is 111 mi long. It formed when an ice dam broke 25,000 years ago. Warren Island, at 160 acres, is the largest in the lake. The chief tributary to the lake is the Clark Fork River and its chief outlet is the Pend Oreille River. | 208/263–2161 | www.sandpoint.com | Free | Daily dawn to dusk.

Round Lake State Park. The small state park of 142 acres surrounds 58-acre Round Lake, formed by glacial activity nearly 1 million years ago. The lake is only 37 ft deep, so it warms for comfortable swimming. Campsites are shaded by towering western red cedars, western hemlocks, ponderosa pines, Douglas firs, and western larch. A 2-mi "Trappers" nature trail around the lake wanders through stands of western white pine, Engelmann spruce, grand fir, lodgepole pine, black cottonwood, paper birch, red alder, and Rocky Mountain maple. You can see gophers, muskrats, mink, bobcats, black bears, and white-tailed deer. The self-guided botanical trail also gives you glimpses of the state flower, syringa, plentiful here, which blooms in late June. The visitor center has wildlife, botanical, and geological displays, as well as brochures and trail maps. | 10 mi south on U.S. 95, then 2 mi west on Dufort Rd., near Sagle | 208/263–3489 | www.idahoparks.org | $2 per car | Daily.

Sandpoint Public Beach. The city beach has several hundred feet of sand and a sweeping view of the Cabinet Mountains east across the lake. The surrounding park has beach volleyball, basketball, tennis, concessions, boat ramps, and docks. | Foot of Bridge St. from 1st Ave., along the eastern edge of downtown | 208/263–2161 | www.sandpoint.com | Free | Memorial Day–Labor Day, daily dawn to dusk.

Schweitzer Mountain Resort. With a sweeping view of Lake Pend Oreille, Schweitzer Mountain Resort rises to a top height of 6,389 ft in the Selkirk Mountains. More than 300 inches of snow fall each year, blanketing the resort's 2,350 acres. The vertical drop is 2,400 ft. The resort has day lodges, a general store, restaurants and cafés, a lounge, and a chapel as well as a ski school, day care, and special children's programs. You can also stay on the mountain. There are cross-country ski trails, snowmobile tours, and sleigh rides. | 10000 Schweitzer Mountain Rd.; 11 mi northwest off U.S. 2 and U.S. 95 | 208/263–9555 or 800/831–8810 | www.schweitzer.com | Nov.–Apr., daily.

ON THE CALENDAR

JAN.: _Winter Carnival._ Five days of festivities celebrate winter in the Panhandle region with a parade, snow sculptures, snowshoe softball, cross-country, and telemark races. 208/263–2161 or 800/800–2106.

AUG.: _Festival at Sandpoint._ A series of classical, ragtime, blues, country, pop, and jazz concerts under the stars with food—or bring a picnic—at War Memorial Field. 208/263–2161.

AUG.: _Lake Pend Oreille Arts and Crafts Fair._ A long-standing annual fair features fine art, photography, fiber arts, metal crafts, ceramics, woodworking, and jewelry. Craftsmen come from all over the Northwest to sell their work at the city beach. 208/263–2161.

Dining

Hydra. Contemporary. A trendy eatery with local artwork and contemporary decor specializes in creatively prepared pasta dishes, steaks, and fresh seafood. At one end of the restaurant is a large, stylish lounge with many plants. Sun. brunch. | 115 Lake St. | 208/263–7123 | $9–$20 | AE, D, DC, MC, V | No lunch Sat., no supper Sun.

Ivano's. Italian. Named one of the best restaurants in the Northwest, this place has Mediterranean furnishings and a cathedral ceiling in main dining room. You can eat the gourmet Italian fare by candlelight on linen or sit outside on the brick porch. Kids' menu. | 124 S. 2nd Ave. | 208/263–0211 | $10–$22 | AE, D, DC, MC, V | No lunch.

Swan's Landing. Contemporary. With waterfront dining, a fireplace, and a casual lodge atmosphere, this place is known for Northwest cuisine. Try the roast rack of Ellensburge lamb pressed in rosemary and garlic with a cabernet Dijon reduction with roasted garlic mashed potatoes. You can also dine on the patio, right on the Pend Oreille River—highly romantic. | U.S. 95 | 208/265–2000 | $15–$23 | AE, D, MC, V.

Lodging

Best Western Edgewater resort. An older, rambling hotel, this is beside the lake and only one block from downtown shopping. Every room has lake and mountain views. You can drive to the ski slopes in ½ hour. Restaurant, bar, room service. Cable TV. Hot tub, sauna. Beach. Weight room. Business services. | 56 Bridge St. | 208/263–3194 or 800/635–2534 | fax 208/263–3194 | www.keokee.com/sandida/home.html | 55 rooms | $69–$199 | AE, D, DC, MC, V.

★ **Hawthorne Inn and Suites.** Rooms are spotless and tastefully decorated, with special touches like marbled wallpaper. At Connie's Café, locals gather for breakfast at the counter, but the basic fare—pancakes, eggs, cereal, sandwiches (often big enough for two), steaks, and chicken—is also served in the café, cocktail lounge, or dining room with fireplace. You're six blocks from the lake and 9 mi from skiing and golfing. Restaurant, bar, dining room, room service. In-room data ports, microwaves and refrigerators available. Cable TV. Pool. Hot tub. Exercise room. Laundry services. Business services. | 415 Cedar St. | 208/263–9581 | fax 208/263–3395 | www.sandpoint.com | 70 rooms | $69–$99 | AE, D, DC, MC, V.

Lakeside Inn. Overlooking the lake, in a parklike wooded setting, this motel is one block from downtown. Picnic area, complimentary Continental breakfast. Some kitchenettes. Cable TV. Hot tub, sauna. Laundry facilities. Airport, RR station shuttles. Some pets allowed ($5 fee). | 106 Bridge St. | 208/263–3717 or 800/543–8126 | fax 208/265–4781 | 60 rooms | $54–$79 | AE, D, DC, MC, V.

Quality Inn. Rooms on the second floor have a lake view, and this is the only Sandpoint lodging with an indoor pool. You're close to both downhill and cross-country skiing. Restaurant, bar. Cable TV. Indoor pool. Hot tub. Cross-country and downhill skiing. Laundry facilities. Business services. | 807 N. 5th Ave. | 208/263–2111 | fax 208/263–3289 | quality1netw.com | www.keokee.com/sandida | 57 rooms | $69–$89 | AE, D, DC, MC, V.

Selkirk Lodge. Ski to your door with lifts just 50 yards away. The chalet-style lodge has the feel of an alpine country inn, and most rooms have a view of the lake or mountains. 2 restaurants. Pool. 3 hot tubs. Fitness room. No pets allowed. | 10000 Schweitzer Mountain Rd.; 11 mi northwest off U.S. 95 | 208/265–0257 or 800/831–8810 | fax 208/265–0257 | www.shweitzer.com | 82 rooms | $99–$499 | AE, D, MC, V.

Western Pleasure Guest Ranch. Secluded new cabins and a 10,000-square-ft timber lodge are set among towering pines on a 960-acre ranch. Horseback riding. | 1413 Upper Gold Creek Rd. | 208/263–9066 | fax 208/265–0138 | www.keokee.com/WPguestranch | 6 rooms in lodge, 3 cabins | $85–$95, $60–$120 cabins | MC, V.

SHOSHONE

MAP 3, C8

(Nearby towns also listed: Hailey, Twin Falls)

Shoshone was a pioneer town founded in the 1870s, set between arid sagebrush flats to the south and a wide band of craggy lava to the north. It served as the gateway to the Wood Rivers mines 45 mi north. When the railroad arrived in 1882, Shoshone became a wild town with several arrests a day, unlimited bad whiskey, and dance halls on every corner. It long since settled down, and today it depends on agriculture for its livelihood. Several of its buildings, including a quaint United Methodist church, reflect the masonry skills of the Basques and other southern Europeans who settled the area. Fitting together huge blocks of black lava stone blocks is now a lost art.

Information: **City of Shoshone** | City Hall (Box 208), 83352 | 208/886–2030.

Attractions
Mary L. Gooding Memorial Park. This large park has the little Wood River running through it. A playground, benches, and a pool make it a nice stop. Across the street from the Union Pacific depot. | 300 N. Rail St. | 208/886–2030 | Free | May–Sept., daily.

STANLEY

MAP 3, C7

(Nearby towns also listed: Challis, Ketchum)

The rough-and-tumble town is a three-square-block grid of dirt streets, a throwback to the Old West. The main street is named Ace of Diamonds. With its rustic wood buildings and the Sawtooths looming into the sky only a few miles away, it could be mistaken for a village in the Swiss Alps. But this town is pure cowboy, no pretense, and it relishes its no-frills frontier character. In the winter, the fewer than 100 full-time residents weather the lowest temperatures in the state, at times dipping to –50°F. In summer things heat up with the arrival of outfitters, guides, and river runners. On weekend nights the place usually hoots and hollers as the music starts up in its saloons and vacationers and river guides unwind in the two-step "Stanley Stomp."

Information: **Stanley-Sawtooth Chamber of Commerce** | Box 8, Stanley, 83278 | 208/774–3411 or 800/878–7950 | www.stanleycc.org.

Attractions
Sawtooth National Recreation Area (SNRA). Among the Recreation Area's 756,000 acres are 217,000 acres designated as the Sawtooth Wilderness Area. Galena summit overlooks the Sawtooth and White Cloud ranges and the 30-mi-long Sawtooth Valley. Two other moun-

tain ranges, the Boulders and Smokies, are also within the area. There are more than 50 major peaks over 10,000 ft, 300 lakes, and 750 mi of trails. The more than 1,000 high mountain lakes are popular destinations for hiking and backpacking trips. Central Idaho's major rivers, the Salmon, the South Fork of the Payette, the Boise, and the Big Wood, are also located within the property. An audio-tape tour describing U.S. Forest Service management of the SNRA, geology, and natural history can be borrowed at no charge at the Sawtooth National Recreation Area Headquarters visitor center, the Ketchum ranger station, or the Stanley ranger station.

The **Sawtooth Wilderness** (208/727–5000 | Free | Daily).

At the northern end of Redfish Lake, the **Redfish Lake Visitor Center** (5 mi south on Rte. 75, then 2 mi southwest | 208/774–3376 | Free | mid-June–Labor Day, daily 9–5) has information, interpretive programs, and summer evening campfire programs.

Galena Lodge (24 mi north of Ketchum on Rte. 75 | 726–4010 | Free | Daily), in the SNRA, is a rustic log lodge with winter cross-country trails that are regularly groomed and summer mountain bike rentals and trails nestled in the canyon just south of the ascent to the Galena summit. Once a mining camp, the lodge is surrounded by more than 20 mi of trails. A collection of mining and ski memorabilia hangs inside, and there's also a restaurant. | Star Rte., Ketchum; in Sawtooth National Forest | 208/727–5000 | www.idoc.state.id.us | Free | Mon.–Sat. 10–5, Sun. 12–4.

Sawtooth Valley and Stanley Basin. Roughly 30 mi north of Ketchum (just south of Stanley on Rte. 75) is the summit that marks the divide between the Wood River and Salmon River drainages. Completed in 1881, the road over the top was first a toll road called the Sawtooth Grade, built to serve the Sawtooth mines. The scenic overlook views the old road and Sawtooth Valley. | 208/727–5013 or 800/260–5970 | Free | Daily.

ON THE CALENDAR

JULY: *Sawtooth Mountain Mamas Arts and Crafts Fair.* A weekend art fair with 150 artists and craftsmen from throughout the Northwest, music, and food. Also a pancake breakfast Sunday morning. 208/774–3411.

SEPT.: *Sawtooth Quilt Festival.* A quilt and crafts fair with an auction. Quilt block contests, vendors prizes, all held in the Community Building. 208/774–3411.

Lodging

Diamond D Ranch. At the end of 28 mi of hair-raising dirt road near Stanley comes the payoff: snowcapped mountains all around, homey meals, cozy rooms with a Laura Ashley touch, and a big fireplace surrounded by overstuffed chairs. Pool. Hot tub, sauna. Horseback riding. | Box 1555, Boise; in Frank Church Wilderness Area | 208/336–9772 | 8 rooms in lodge, 4 cabins | $330 rooms and cabins | No credit cards | Closed Nov.–May; hunters only Oct.–Nov. | AP.

★ **Idaho Rocky Mountain Ranch.** Conveniently situated in the heart of the Sawtooth Valley just off Route 75, the 8,000-square-ft lodgepole-pine lodge and surrounding cabins were constructed in the 1930s for use as an invitation-only guest ranch by a New York businessman. The lodge, with its massive rock fireplace, remains much as it was 60 years ago, with period photographs on the walls, animal trophies, rustic artifacts, and even the original monogrammed white china. Lodge rooms and most of the duplex cabins have Oakley stone showers and handcrafted log furniture. Breakfast and dinner are served in the lodge dining room. Plan to end the day watching the sun set over the Sawtooths from the lodge's wide front porch. A natural hot springs pool is a short walk from the lodge and cabins. Dining room. No room phones. Pool. Hiking, horseback riding, volleyball. Bicycles. Cross-country skiing. No pets allowed. No smoking. | HC 64, Box 9934, Stanley; 9 mi south on Rte. 75 | 208/774–3544 | fax 208/774–3477 | www.idahorocky.com | 4 rooms in lodge, 17 cabins | $148–$248 rooms and cabins | D, MC, V | Closed May and Oct.

Mountain Village Lodge. At a highway intersection in the tiny town, the rustic wood-sided building resembles a strip motel but features recently remodeled guest rooms with contemporary decor in shades of brown, tan, and dark green. It has its own private hot springs. Restaurant, bar (with entertainment). Cable TV. Laundry facilities. Business services. Airport shuttle. Pets allowed ($12 fee and $25 deposit). | Rtes. 75 and 21 | 208/774–3661 or 800/843–5475 | fax 208/774–3761 | 60 rooms | $63–$74 | AE, D, DC, MC, V.

SUN VALLEY AREA

MAP 3, C7

(Nearby town also listed: Ketchum)

In central Idaho, where alpine and high desert climes converge, sunshine is ample and powdery snow is plentiful. The result was the creation 65 years ago of the grande dame of ski resorts, Sun Valley. In the early 1930s, when Union Pacific Railroad executive Averell Harriman sent his expert scout Count Felix Schaffgotsch out west to find the ideal location for a European-style ski resort, he struck gold. "Among the many spots I have visited, this combines more delightful features than any place I have seen in the United States, Switzerland, or Austria . . ." Today, a stroll through the center of Sun Valley still holds a special charm. Sun Valley Company was the first to build the ski chairlift, and today it has one of the largest computerized artificial snow-making systems in the world. The main attraction in the Sun Valley Area, which includes the quaint 1880s-era mining town of Ketchum a mile away, is the ski mountain and its operations. But the resort is now a four-season attraction as well, with summer recreation in addition to challenging skiing on Mount Baldy. The village of Sun Valley is basically a manufactured village of shops, restaurants, and lodgings. The village area, also called the "mall," is quaint and quiet, and a grassy green surrounds ponds where swans float in summer. Throughout the Ketchum and Sun Valley area, the paved 20-mi Wood River Trails system provides ample opportunity to see local sights on foot, by bicycle, or on horseback.

Information: Sun Valley/Ketchum Chamber of Commerce | Box 2420, 83353 | 800/634–3347 | www.visitsunvalley.com.

Attractions

Sun Valley Resort. The nation's first destination ski resort, dating from 1936, lies near the Sawtooth National Recreation Area. Its European-style village is world-famous. The challenging ski mountain with a 3,400-ft vertical drop also has expertly groomed runs, bowls, and new lodges at the top and base. There are 2,054 skiable acres, appealing primarily to intermediate and advanced skiers. Beginners use Dollar Mountain a few miles away, at the edge of Sun Valley village. The elevation at the top is 9,150 ft, and the area receives 220 inches of snowfall, supplemented by the world's largest snow-making operation. You can also take rail rides or sleigh rides, swim, golf, play tennis, or go mountain-biking and in-line skating on paved trails throughout the Sun Valley–Ketchum area. | North on U.S. 75, take left before entering Ketchum | 208/622–4111, 208/622–2231, or 800/635–8261 | www.sunvalley.com | Mid-Nov.–mid-Apr.

ON THE CALENDAR

JUNE–SEPT.: *Sun Valley Ice Show.* A summerlong series of ice shows with Olympic medalists and world-class performers skating on Saturday evenings in the outdoor rink. 208/622–2231.

JULY, AUG.: *Sun Valley Summer Symphony.* A 15-year-old series has 12 classical music concerts in a tent at the Sun Valley Lodge esplanade. 208/622–5607.

AUG.: *Sun Valley Arts and Crafts Festival.* A 30-year-old outdoor arts and crafts festival features a juried competition of artists from the Northwest. Food, beverages, and entertainment complete the event.

DEC.: *Christmas in Sun Valley.* A monthlong celebration with a variety of events includes a gingerbread decorating party, a torchlight parade, a tree lighting, and caroling parties all over town. 208/726–3423.

Dining

Gretchen's. American. A cozy, French-country atmosphere for family dining overlooks the outdoor ice-skating rink. The menu is strong on fresh salmon and trout, gourmet burgers, hazelnut-crusted elk loin, spicy farfalle pasta with roasted roma tomatoes, entrée salads, and raspberry chocolate mousse. | In Sun Valley Lodge | 208/622–2144 | $20–$30 | AE, D, DC, MC, V.

Sun Valley Lodge Dining Room. Continental. An elegant setting with crisp white linens and formal service also has inventive gourmet cuisine. Tables overlook the outdoor ice-skating rink. Sun. brunch. Kids' menu. | In Sun Valley Lodge | 208/622–2150 | Reservations essential | Jacket and tie | $30–$40 | AE, D, DC, MC, V | No lunch.

Lodging

Idaho Country Inn. Set on a knoll halfway between Ketchum and Sun Valley, this newly built inn features views of the ski mountain and spacious guest rooms, each decorated with a different theme. Log beams and river-rock fireplaces in the lounge and dining room give it a Western mountain-lodge atmosphere. Dining room, bar, complimentary full breakfast and afternoon snacks. No air-conditioning (in some rooms), refrigerators. Cable TV. Hot tub. Library. No pets allowed. No smoking. | 134 Latigo La.; ½ mi north on Rte. 75, right on Saddle Rd., left on Valleywood | 208/726–1019 or 800/250–8341 | fax 208/726–5718 | www.premeireresortsv.com | 11 rooms | $163–$205 | AE, MC, V.

River Street Inn Bed and Breakfast. A quiet 8-room B&B located on Trail Creek in Ketchum. Offering delectable breakfasts and private baths with Japanese soaking tubs. Complimentary breakfast and afternoon snacks. Refrigerators. Cable TV. Cross-country and downhill skiing. No smoking. | 100 Rivers St. W | 208/726–3611 or 800/954–8585 | fax 208/726–2439 | 8 rooms | $145–$175 | AE, D, MC, V.

Sun Valley's Elkhorn Resort and Golf Club. This is Sun Valley's "other" resort, a large hotel and restaurant complex nestled next to a sage-covered mountainside and surrounded by condominiums. The resort and top-ranked golf course are just over the mountain from the Sun Valley Resort. Elkhorn's hotel has fully appointed rooms with modern decor and refrigerators. Upgraded rooms have fireplaces, kitchens, and hot tubs. The resort offers a variety of year-round activities, including jazz concerts under the stars on the complex's center terrace and surrounding lawn area. The Robert Trent Jones–designed golf course challenges even the best golfers. 2 restaurants, 3 bars, dining rooms, room service. No air-conditioning, in-room data ports, some kitchenettes, some in-room hot tubs. Cable TV, in-room VCRs. 2 pools. Hot tub, massage. Driving range, 18-hole golf course, putting green, 18 tennis courts. Exercise equipment. Fishing. Bicycles. Downhill skiing. Shops. Children's programs (ages 6–12). Business services. Airport shuttle. Some pets allowed ($25 fee). | Elkhorn Rd. (Box 6009); 3 mi from Ketchum on Sun Valley Rd. to Dollar, then Elkhorn | 208/622–4511 or 800/355–4676 | fax 208/622–3261 | 124 rooms, 7 suites, 90 condos | $128–$228, $248–$299 suites, $120–$425 condos | AE, D, DC, MC, V.

★ **Sun Valley Lodge and Inn.** The lodge has been elegantly redecorated with European styling. Accommodations range from luxury suites to family units. The formal dining room features French cuisine. A sports director can guide you in planning river rafting, fishing, and hunting trips, or help you choose from entertainment including ice shows, movies, and trap and skeet shooting. 3 restaurants (*see* Gretchen's), 3 bars, dining rooms, picnic area. No air-conditioning, microwaves (in condos), some refrigerators. Cable TV. 3 pools, wading pool. Barbershop, beauty salon, massage, sauna. Driving range, 18-hole golf course, putting green, 18 tennis courts. Bowling, exercise equipment, horseback riding, boating. Fishing. Bicycles, ice-skating. Sleigh rides. Children's programs (ages vary). Business services. Airport shuttle. | 1 Sun Valley Rd. | 208/622–4111 or 800/786–8259 | fax 208/622–

2030 | www.sunvalley.com | 253 rooms, 8 suites in 2 buildings, 4 apartments in inn, 6 houses, 193 condos | $124–$419, $600–$1,000 houses, $139–$419 condos | AE, D, DC, MC, V.

★ **Tamarack Lodge.** A European-style lodge with luxury accommodations at affordable prices. Rooms vary from one-bedroom suites with fireplaces to singles. All rooms have coffeemakers. The building resembles a Tyrolean chalet, with warm pink stucco and decorative painting. Within walking distance of restaurants, nightlife, shopping, and art galleries. There is a shuttle to the ski slopes. Microwaves, refrigerators. Cable TV. Indoor pool. Hot tub. | 291 Walnut Ave.; 3 blocks east of Rte. 75 | 208/726–3344 or 800/521–5379 | fax 208/726–3347 | www.tamaracksunvalley.com | 21 rooms, 5 suites | $74–$99, $99–$149 suites | AE, D, DC, MC, V.

TWIN FALLS

MAP 3, C9

(Nearby town also listed: Buhl)

Most tourists head for Twin Falls in the spring to see Shoshone Falls—taller than Niagara—at its maximum flow before summertime agricultural use siphons off much of the water. The Oregon Trail passed near the present-day town site and wagon ruts can be seen near Milner Dam, at Massacre Rocks State Park near American Falls, and at Three Island Crossing State Park near Glenns Ferry. The town was established in 1904 in conjunction with an irrigation project, and was named the seat of the county by the same name in 1907. The Twin Falls are a smaller cascade about a mile upstream from Shoshone Falls. The area is also known as Magic Valley, because water gradually turned the arid sagebrush flats into one of the nation's most productive farming regions. At the time the Perrine Bridge was completed across the Snake River canyon in 1927, it was the highest cantilever bridge of its length in the world. The Snake River canyon is deepest at the north edge of Twin Falls. In 1976, the old span was replaced by a new bridge that is still the highest in Idaho. Today Twin, as locals call the town, is still an important agricultural center, with six of the city's 10 largest employers involved in food processing.

Information: Twin Falls Chamber of Commerce | 858 Blue Lakes Blvd. N, 83301 | 208/733–3974 or 800/255–8946 | www.twinfallschamber.com.

Attractions

Evel Knievel Jump Site. In 1974, daredevil Evel Knievel tried to jump across the Snake River Canyon on a rocket-powered motorcycle. Though he didn't make it across the divide, his parachute deployed and he landed safely. The launching site can be seen from the Buzz Langdon Visitor Center. | U.S. 93, to the right after crossing Perrine Bridge | 208/733–3974 | www.twinfallschamber.com | Free | Daily dawn to dusk.

Herrett Center for Arts and Science. On the College of Southern Idaho campus, the Herrett Museum contains a collection of artifacts ranging from 12,000-year-old relics to contemporary Hopi kachina dolls. On display are pre-Inca textiles, Mayan jade, and Peruvian pottery. In 1995 the Faulkner Planetarium, a 151-seat theater, was added to the museum. | 315 Falls Ave. | 208/733–9554, ext. 2655 | www.csi.cc.id.us/l3.cfm?herrett | Free | Tues.–Sat. 1–9.

Idaho Heritage Museum. The museum displays one of the largest private collections of Indian artifacts in the western United States and specimens of indigenous wildlife. Included in the collection are arrowheads, lance points, bone needles, and awls. There is also a 15,000-year-old bison skull that serves as the museum's logo. | 2390 U.S. 93 S; 20 mi south on U.S. 93 | 208/733–3974 or 208/655–4444 | www.twinfallschamber.com | Donations accepted | By appointment only.

Perrine Memorial Bridge. The bridge is a 1,500-ft span 486 ft above the Snake River. The first bridge, opened in 1927, was the highest bridge in the world at the time. | 1½ mi north on U.S. 93 | 208/733–3974 | www.twinfallschamber.com | Free | Daily.

Shoshone Falls Park. The 337-acre park is a prime falls viewing area along the southern rim. At 212 ft, Shoshone Falls are higher than Niagara Falls and have a comparable volume of water. The flow is heaviest in March and April, before summer irrigation season diverts it. | 3300 East Rd.; 3 mi east, on south bank of the Snake River | 208/736–2265 or 208/736–2266 | www.twinfallschamber.com | $3 per vehicle; free Oct–Apr. | Daily.

Twin Falls Park. The lower twin waterfalls are cataract falls that gave the town its name. The Twin Falls are upstream and east of famed Shoshone Falls. The park on the southern canyon rim includes a small viewing area and picnic tables. It is maintained by the Idaho Power Company. | 3500 East Rd.; 2 mi east of Shoshone Falls Park, south bank of the river | 208/773–3974 | www.twinfallschamber.com | Free | Daily dawn to dusk.

ON THE CALENDAR

MAY–JUNE: *Western Days*. A family-oriented event features a carnival, two days of music, an arts and crafts show, food booths, and a parade. 208/733–3974 or 800/255–8946.

JULY: *Kids' Art in the Park*. An annual arts and crafts for children festival in Twin Falls City Park. 208/733–3974 or 800/255–8946.

AUG.–SEPT.: *Twin Falls County Fair and Rodeo*. A junior rodeo, 4-H exhibits, events, and food at the county fairgrounds. 208/733–3974 or 800/255–8946.

Dining

A'roma. American. Opened in 1985, when the downtown area was struggling, this small Italian restaurant has become a local favorite by serving such standards as lasagna, ravioli, and pizza. Tablecloths are plastic and the decor simple in a storefront setting with friendly service. | 147 Shoshone St. N | 208/733–0167 | $15–$40 | MC, V | Closed Sun., Mon.

Buffalo Café. American. Ask anybody in town where to go for breakfast, and you'll get the same answer: this tiny café. The house specialty is the Buffalo Chip, a concoction of eggs, fried potatoes, cheese, bacon, peppers, and onion. | 218 4th Ave. W | $5–$15 | 208/734–0271 | No credit cards | No dinner.

Jaker's. American. One in a small chain of restaurants throughout south-central and southeast Idaho, this place serves well-prepared steaks and seafood in a relaxed family dining atmosphere with a children's menu. Try the prime rib or the seafood linguini. | 1598 Blue Lakes Blvd. | 208/733–8400 | $13–$50 | AE, D, DC, MC, V | No breakfast.

La Casita Restaurant. Mexican. Hand-cut meat and fresh tortillas go into made-to-order Mexican fare. The homey bright interior displays Mexican crafts and posters. | 111 S. Park Ave. | 208/734–7974 | $5–$10 | D, MC, V.

Rock Creek. American. A steak, prime-rib, and seafood house west of downtown with a dark-red interior and wide booths, known for its wide selection of single-malt whiskies and vintage ports. One of the most complete wine lists in town. Salad bar. | 200 Addison Ave. W | 208/734–4154 | $12–$38 | AE, MC, V.

Lodging

Ameritel Inn. The rooms have been remodeled here, and the accommodations expanded. The amenities are good considering the reasonable rates. Complimentary Continental breakfast. Cable TV. Indoor pool. Hot tub. Exercise equipment. Fitness room. Laundry facilities. Laundry services. Airport shuttle. no pets allowed. | 1377 Blue Lakes Blvd. | 208/736–8000 | fax 208/734–7777 | www.ameritelinns.com | 118 rooms | $65–$130 | AE, D, DC, MC, V.

Best Western Apollo Motor Inn. This smaller motel offers clean, reliable rooms but no restaurant or lounge. A breakfast is served in the lobby, and restaurants are a short walk away.

Complimentary Continental breakfast. In-room phones. Pool. Hot tub. Small pets allowed. | 296 Addison Ave. W | 208/733–2010 or 800/528–1234 | fax 208/734–0748 | www.best-westerninns.com | 50 rooms | $56–$85 | AE, D, DC, MC, V.

Best Western Cavanaughs Canyon Springs. Dark-brown stained-wood siding on units gives the hotel a residential feel. Diamondfield Jack's serves homestyle fare amid turn-of-the-century decor. Within walking distance of a mall and laundry facilities. Restaurant, bar, room service. Cable TV. Pool. Spa, sauna. Exercise equipment. Fitness center. Airport shuttle. Pets allowed. | 1357 Blue Lakes Blvd. N | 208/734–5000 | fax 208/733–3813 | 112 rooms | $60–$112 | AE, D, DC, MC, V.

Comfort Inn. Across from the Magic Valley Mall about 1 mi from I–84 and on the edge of town, this inn is also within walking distance of mall stores and restaurants. Complimentary Continental breakfast. Cable TV. Indoor pool. Hot tub. Health club privileges. Laundry services. Pets allowed. | 1893 Canyon Springs Rd. | 208/734–7494 | fax 208/735–9428 | www.choice-hotels.com | 52 rooms, 15 suites | $64–$79, $90–$130 suites | AE, D, DC, MC, V.

Shilo Inn. A big new multistory hotel with suites is off I–84 and popular with business travelers. You can walk to restaurants and the Valley Mall. Complimentary Continental breakfast. In-room data ports, microwaves, refrigerators. Cable TV, pay-per-view movies. Indoor pool. Hot tub. Exercise equipment. Laundry facilities. Business services. Some pets allowed ($10 fee). | 1586 Blue Lakes Blvd N | 208/733–7545 | fax 208/736–2019 | 128 suites | $75–$140 suites | AE, D, DC, MC, V.

WALLACE

MAP 3, B3

(Nearby town also listed: Kellogg)

Although a fire in 1910 reduced a third of the town to ashes, much of the gracious turn-of-the-century architecture created during Wallace's heyday as the capital of the Silver Valley mining area remains intact. The Old West town of 1,400 residents is known for its turreted and decorative storefronts that today house eateries and hotels. The town was named after Colonel W. R. Wallace, a cousin of Lew Wallace, author of *Ben Hur*, and was incorporated in 1888. It was a major supply center for the mines, and today a dozen museums recall its mining and railroad years.

Information: Wallace Chamber of Commerce | Box 1167, 83873 | 208/753–7151 | www.wallace-id.com.

Attractions

Historic Wallace Walking Tour. This self-guided tour of Wallace follows the route laid out in a brochure with a map and description of the town's historic buildings. The complete tour takes about one hour. | 10 River St. | 208/753–7151 | Free | Daily dawn to dusk.

Lookout Pass Ski and Recreation Area. Idaho's second-oldest ski area opened in 1938, and remains affordable for families, with downhill skiing on groomed and ungroomed Nordic ski trails. The area includes 150 skiable acres and 14 runs and the vertical drop is 850 ft. The double chairlift carries skiers to the top elevation of 5,650 ft, with skiing from there in St. Regis Basin. Also available are guided snowmobile trips into Montana. The annual snowfall is 389 inches, and there are 50 new acres of expert terrain for snowboarders and treed skiing. There are rentals, a cafeteria, and a ski lodge. | 12 mi east on I–90, in Idaho Panhandle National Forest | 208/744–1392 | fax 208/744–1227 | www.skilookout.com | Mid-Nov.–mid-Apr.

Northern Pacific Depot Railroad Museum. Exhibits trace the history of railroading in the Coeur d'Alene mining district and of the depot itself. On display is a rare 13-ft glass map of the Northern Pacific Railroad route. | 219 6th St. | 208/752–0111 | $2 | Apr.–mid-Oct.

Oasis Bordello Museum. The museum depicts the days of the Oasis Rooms, one of the town's bordellos. An accurate and tasteful tour is presented by proprietress Michelle Mayfield, who shares a 20-minute glimpse into the past, with details that range from poignant to hilarious. In addition to the second-floor brothel, the tour highlights an old wine press in the basement and the history of the Bi-Metallic Building, which began as a hotel and saloon in 1895. The building is one of the few structures to have survived the 1910 fire. Of particular interest are its mosaic floor tiles imported from China. The Oasis was one of five such establishments in town. The brothels operated until 1973, when a newspaper article charged a politician with agreeing to go easy on law enforcement in northern Idaho in exchange for a $25,000 campaign contribution. The brothels soon closed. At halftime during a University of Idaho football game, students unfurled a 40-ft-long banner inscribed GIVE WALLACE BACK ITS HOUSES. Each summer a melodrama is presented in the 80-seat theater. | 605 Cedar St. | 208/753–0801 | www.silver-country.com | Donations accepted; summer melodrama $7–$9 | May–Oct., daily; summer melodrama, July, Aug.

Sierra Silver Mine Tour. An open-air San Francisco–style trolley transports visitors from the tour office to the mine, where they are fitted with hard hats. Tours include a brief overview of the mine's history and early mineral discoveries in Wallace. Underground displays explain how minerals were extracted in the 19th century. Kids over 4 only. | 420 5th St. | 208/752–5151 | $8 | May–Sept. daily.

Wallace District Mining Museum. The museum opened in 1956, and since 1974 has been housed in the old Rice's Bakery building. It features exhibits on the history of mining methods and operations locally from the 1880s to the modern times, and includes lighting devices from old stearic candles and oil lamps to today's rechargeable electric cap lamps. In addition, the museum has the only complete steam-driven diamond drill known to have been preserved. The video *North Idaho's Silver Legacy* relates the history of the area from the 1850s to the present. | 509 Bank St. | 208/556–1592 | $2.

ON THE CALENDAR
AUG.: *Huckleberry Festival.* A 5K run and walk, plus a huckleberry pancake breakfast, a chili cook-off, a peddlers' fair, and a bake-off. 208/753–7151.

Dining
Albi's Steak House. American. The historic building that is home to this restaurant has an old-fashioned air. Steaks, fresh seafood, chicken dishes, and pastas dominate the menu; locals come for the prime rib. Open-air dining. | 220 6th St. | 208/753–3071 | $7–$15 | AE, D, MC, V.

Jameson Restaurant and Saloon. American. In a Victorian-era building, the polished brass and dark wood give the saloon and dining room a vintage elegance. The specialties are sandwiches, prime rib, and shrimp. This is relaxed family dining. | 304 6th St. | 208/556–1554 | $20–$30 | AE, D, MC, V | Closed Sun.–Wed. and Apr.–Oct.

Lodging
Best Western–Wallace Inn. A new hotel with spacious rooms and suites is in the center of town, near museums and other attractions. Restaurant, bar, room service. Minibars and refrigerators (in suites). Cable TV. Indoor pool. Hot tub. Exercise equipment. Business services. | 100 Front St. | 208/752–1252 or 800/643–2386 | fax 208/753–0981 | 59 rooms, 4 suites | $69–$82, $125–$175 suites | AE, D, DC, MC, V.

Historic Jameson. The three-story redbrick building was opened as a hostelry and saloon in 1908. It was restored roughly 70 years later, and now it's a hotel, saloon, and restaurant with lots of Victorian charm. Ceiling fans, bentwood chairs, polished brass, chandeliers, and Oriental carpets evoke the Old West at the turn of the 20th century. Although rooms are small, each has been carefully furnished with choice antiques appropriate for the space. Vintage photographs and prints hang above antique beds. Simple white woven bedspreads are a nice contrast to the rich dark oak and walnut headboards. Restaurant. Indoor pool. Hot tub, steam room. Gym. | 314 6th St. | 208/556–1554 | fax 208/753–0981 | 6 rooms (5 with shared bath) | $62 | MC, V.

Stardust. This economy lodging is well maintained and clean, in the center of town. No air-conditioning (in some rooms). Cable TV. Cross-country and downhill skiing. Airport shuttle. Pets allowed. | 410 Pine St. | 208/752–1213 | fax 208/753–0981 | 42 rooms | $47 | AE, D, DC, MC, V.

WEISER

MAP 3, A6

(Nearby towns also listed: Boise, Caldwell)

The history of Weiser reads like a romance novel. In 1863 William Logan and his sweetheart Nancy Harris, having passed through on the Oregon Trail, eloped and returned to the area to build a primitive home of willows, rocks, and mud. The home soon became a way station on the trail. A year later, a general store was opened, then a gristmill, and by 1870, the town along the Weiser River had taken root. Brick homes from the early 1900s and the castlelike Knights of Pythias Building can still be admired downtown. There are several theories regarding the origin of the town's name. One is that it bears the name of Peter Weiser, a Revolutionary War veteran who served as a cook on the Lewis and Clark expedition. The town is also a gateway to the Hells Canyon area and is best known as the nation's fiddling capital. The first of the fiddling contests that now draw hundreds of musicians from around the country was held in 1914.

Information: Weiser Chamber of Commerce | 8 E. Idaho St., 83672 | 208/549–0452 | fax 208/549–0255 | weisercc@cyberhighway.net | www.cyberhighway.net/~wcedc/weiser.htm.

ON THE CALENDAR

JUNE: *National Old Time Fiddlers Contest and Festival.* Fiddling has been associated with Weiser ever since the town's founders, the Logan family, provided entertainment for those passing through on the Oregon Trail. Approximately 347 contestants compete in the most prestigious fiddlers contest in the country. They compete in 8 divisions during the weeklong competition. 208/549–0450 or 208/549–0452.

JUNE: *Weiser Valley Round-Up.* Known for years as the "Best Show in Idaho," this professional rodeo was first held in 1916. 208/549–0452.

Eating Well is the Best Revenge

Start at the top By all means take in a really good restaurant or two while you're on the road. A trip is a time to kick back and savor the pleasures of the palate. Read up on the culinary scene before you leave home. Check out representative menus on the Web—some chefs have gone electronic. And ask friends who have just come back. For big-city dining, reserve a table as far in advance as you can, remembering that the best establishments book up months ahead. Remember that some good restaurants require you to reconfirm the day before or the day of your meal. Then again, some really good places will call you, so make sure to leave a number where you can be reached.

Adventures in eating A trip is the perfect opportunity to try food you can't get at home. So leave yourself open to try an ethnic food that's not represented where you live or to eat fruits and vegetables you've never heard of.

One of them may become your next favorite food.

Beyond guidebooks You can rely on the restaurants you find in these pages. But also look for restaurants on your own. When you're ready for lunch, ask people you meet where they eat. Look for tiny holes-in-the-wall with a loyal following and the best burgers or crispiest pizza crust. Find out about local chains whose fame rests upon a single memorable dish. There's hardly a food-lover who doesn't relish the chance to share a favorite place. It's fun to come up with your own special find—and asking about food is a great way to start a conversation.

Sample local flavors Do check out the specialties. Is there a special brand of ice cream or a special dish that you simply must try?

Have a picnic Every so often eat al fresco. Grocery shopping gives you a whole different view of a place.

Beyond T-Shirts and Key Chains

Budget for a major purchase If souvenirs are all about keeping the memories alive in the long haul, plan ahead to shop for something really special—a work of art, a rug or something else hand-crafted, or a major accessory for your home. One major purchase will stay with you far longer than a dozen tourist trinkets, and you'll have all the wonderful memories associated with shopping for it besides.

Add to your collection Whether antiques, used books, salt and pepper shakers, or ceramic frogs are your thing, start looking in the first day or two. Chances are you'll want to scout around and then go back to some of the first shops you visited before you hand over your credit card.

Get guarantees in writing Is the vendor making promises? Ask him to put them in writing.

Anticipate a shopping spree If you think you might buy breakables, bring along a length of bubble wrap. Pack a large tote bag in your suitcase in case you need extra space. Don't fill your suitcase to bursting before you leave home. Or include some old clothing that you can leave behind to make room for new acquisitions.

Know before you go Study prices at home on items you might consider buying while you're away. Otherwise you won't recognize a bargain when you see one.

Plastic, please Especially if your purchase is pricey and you're looking for authenticity, it's always smart to pay with a credit card. If a problem arises later on and the merchant can't or won't resolve it, the credit-card company may help you out.

© Artville

Montana

The name "Montana" conjures up majestic scenes of snowcapped mountain peaks, raging rivers, and weathered cowboys herding cattle over vast prairiescapes that have felt few footsteps over the course of mankind. Tens of thousands of people come to see this; some stay to learn about life amid the mountains and plains of this vast frontier.

Few states can rival Montana's scenic wonders and outdoor recreation. You can hike, bike, white-water raft, watch birds and animals, fish, hunt, and ride horses. A windswept plain covers the eastern two-thirds of the state, interrupted only occasionally by solitary mountain ranges. On the state's western edge, the towering Rocky Mountains dominate the skyline. High above these plains and peaks is an endless expanse of azure sky; hence the nickname "Big Sky Country."

Except for a few communities—Billings, Missoula, Helena, and Great Falls— Montana is decidedly rural, and its residents take great pride in their frontier heritage and yeoman attitudes. Farming and ranching, minerals, fuels, and timber are the state's major industries, although tourism has a significant impact on the economy of western Montana, home to Glacier and Yellowstone national parks, as well as millions of acres of national forest, state parks, and wilderness areas.

Within all this scenery are Montana's highways and backroads, which are lined with historic sites that tell of a past filled with legendary Native American warriors, gold seekers, fur traders, cavalry soldiers, and curious explorers. On weekends from May through September, you can stop for frontier celebrations and powwows.

In winter, you'll discover that Montanans don't suffer from cabin fever. You can join the locals in downhill and cross-country skiing, snowmobiling, and ice fishing. Faced with an often fickle, resource-based economy and a sometimes severe climate, Montanans have learned to treasure their space, way of life, and surroundings all year round.

CAPITAL: HELENA	POPULATION: 856,057	AREA: 147,138 SQUARE MI
BORDERS: ID, WY, SD, ND, CANADA	TIME ZONE: MOUNTAIN	POSTAL ABBREVIATION: MT
WEB SITE: VISITMT.COM		

History

As in much of the western United States, human habitation of Montana is believed to have begun 10,000 to 30,000 years ago, when Asian migrants crossed the Bering Strait land bridge and began to people North America. Some of these hunters wandered as far as South America, while others remained in the north, living on herbs, plants, and large game animals, including the now-extinct mammoth.

Around 2,000 to 3,000 BC, the last wave of prehistoric migrants arrived in Montana from the west and south, as evidenced by buffalo jumps and teepee rings still visible on the plains of eastern and central Montana. Historians believe that these "paleo Indians" were direct ancestors of today's Native American tribes.

The Flathead tribe entered the state in the early 1500s, followed a century later by the Plains tribes we know today. In the ensuing three centuries, several tribes flourished on the Great Plains and in the state's western valleys, before French fur traders and mountain men arrived on the scene. The Lewis and Clark Expedition traveled through Montana in 1805–06 and documented a land extremely rich in beaver and otter pelts. The explorers' journals unlocked the West for a wave of traders and trappers eager to cash in on the state's abundant natural resources.

By 1880, the virtual extinction of the buffalo caused by entrepreneurs changed the way of life and and culture of the Plains tribes forever. After the tribes were lured to reservations with the promise of meat and blankets, miners, loggers, stockmen, and sodbusters arrived. Although diluted by a half-dozen generations, the Old World names of Russian, Croatian, Scandinavian, Italian, and other European immigrants are still found in Montana neighborhoods and towns they founded, including Belgrade, Caledonia, Dublin Gulch, Finn Town, Frenchtown, Glasgow, and Scotch Coulee.

While Native Americans settled onto reservations, miners began settling the canyons and coulees, where they discovered deposits of gold, silver, and copper. The Mother Lode—a thick vein of copper—in 1882 at Butte dictated the development, politics, and media of the state for a century. The era ended only with ARCO's closure of operations in Anaconda, Butte, and Great Falls in the early 1980s.

The early decades of the 20th century witnessed methodical changes in Montana, with the establishment of Glacier National Park in 1910, construction of the park's spectacular Going-to-the-Sun Road in 1916, and the birth of the massive Fort Peck Dam in 1934. Electrification and better roadways arrived, but otherwise life for most Montanans changed very slowly through the remainder of the century. In 1951, discovery of a massive oil field beneath eastern Montana and neighboring North Dakota and Saskatchewan, although welcome, did little to affect the state's population base, which remains in western Montana.

With a tradition of uneven growth and decline and a state economy inseparably linked to the processing of raw minerals and the vagaries of the weather, Montana reached a peak population of 824,000 in 1985, then slipped to less than 800,000 by 1990. The state's largest employer, the Anaconda Company, abandoned its mining and

MT Timeline

30,000–10,000 BC	5000–4000 BC	3000–2000 BC	AD 1500
Asiatic peoples enter North America via the land bridge formed across the Bering Strait. Some venture into present-day Montana to hunt and scavenge.	Migrant foragers from the desert southwest inhabit the state's western valleys.	The "late hunters," the last wave of prehistoric visitors, enter Montana from the south and west.	The Flathead arrive in western Montana.

smelting operations in Montana, and a persistent drought hampered agricultural production. Both contributed to corresponding decreases in per capita income, which fell to 20 percent below the national average by 1987.

By the close of the century, though, Montanans faced a reenergized economy bolstered by adequate rainfall and a diversified mix of ranching, farming, mining, logging, tourism, and recreation. Today you'll discover an economy as varied as Montana's topography, and as rich as the history from which it is born.

INTRODUCTION
HISTORY
REGIONS
WHEN TO VISIT
STATE'S GREATS
RULES OF THE ROAD
DRIVING TOURS

Regions

1. GLACIER COUNTRY

This is as close as you'll get in the real world to a perfect, untamed wilderness. Crowned by Glacier National Park, flanked by the Bob Marshall Wilderness Area, and watered by a chain of lakes known as the Seely Swan, this wild realm encompasses nearly 3 million acres—roughly the size of Connecticut.

Add to this the National Bison Range, the Jewel Basin Hiking Area, the Flathead National Wild and Scenic River, and Flathead Lake—the largest body of fresh water in the West—and you'll see why Glacier Country is among the most popular tourist destinations in Montana.

Tucked between the peaks and forests are numerous farms that yield such traditional crops as barley, wheat, seed potatoes, oats, and hay. But the peculiar soil and climate of the Flathead Valley also yield outstanding cherries, peppermint, Christmas trees, and champagne grapes.

For more information about northwest Montana, contact Glacier Country, 836 Holt Dr., Bigfork 59911, or call 406/837-6211 or 800/338-5072.

Towns listed: Bigfork, Browning, Columbia Falls, East Glacier, Hamilton, Kalispell, Libby, Missoula, Polson, Whitefish

2. GOLD WEST COUNTRY

Montana's southwest corner was built on the promise of gold-rush riches. More than 30,000 miners and merchants arrived in the five years after the first news of gold strikes on Grasshopper Creek started circulating in 1862. The gold and silver did not last long, but the unexpected discovery of a massive vein of copper beneath Butte ushered in the greatest era of Montana's colorful mining history.

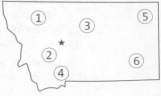

You'll find now that the southwest's real treasures are its untamed national forests, blue-ribbon trout streams, and state parks. The Gold West Country also has an ample supply of museums and art galleries, as well as numerous historic sites—the Big Hole National Battlefield, the Grant-Kohrs Ranch, and the stately restored gold camps of Bannack, Virginia City, and Helena's Last Chance Gulch.

1620	1803	1805–06	1807	1828
Plains tribes begin arriving in Montana.	United States purchases Louisiana Territory from France, including that part of Montana east of the Rocky Mountains, for three cents an acre.	Explorers Meriwether Lewis and William Clark travel through Montana on their transcontinental expedition. Their journals confirm the presence of beaver, otter, and other fur-bearing animals.	American fur trade begins with Manuel Lisa's construction of the Missouri Fur Company's trading post at the confluence of the Bighorn and Yellowstone rivers.	Fort Union Trading Post is established at the mouth of the Yellowstone River by John Jacob Astor's American Fur Co.

For more information about southwest Montana, contact Gold West Country, 1155 Main St., Deer Lodge 59722, or call 406/846–1943 or 800/879–1159.

Towns listed: Anaconda, Butte, Deer Lodge, Dillon, Ennis, Helena, Virginia City

3. RUSSELL COUNTRY

Named for cowboy artist Charles M. Russell, who captured the broad and beautiful landscape on canvas, this region remains much the same as it was when solitary Native American scouts, cavalry soldiers, and explorers first saw it. Lewis and Clark used the Missouri River as their highway through this region when they brought their Corps of Discovery through in 1805–06.

Encompassing the so-called "Hi-Line" along Montana's northern tier and stretching south past Great Falls to Lewistown and White Sulphur Springs, Russell Country is compellingly vast and tranquil. The resilient residents of the few communities and Native American reservations eke out a living off the land, amid a setting of river breaks, farmland, and cattle range, offset by the occasional change such as the Upper Missouri National Wild and Scenic River below Fort Benton.

For more information about north-central Montana, contact Russell Country, Box 3166, Great Falls 59403, or call 406/761–5036 or 800/527–5348.

Towns listed: Chinook, Fort Benton, Great Falls, Harlowtown, Havre, Lewistown, White Sulphur Springs

4. YELLOWSTONE COUNTRY

Wildlife, water, and wilderness are the hallmarks of this south-central region, bordered on the south by Yellowstone National Park. Here you'll find enough scenic vistas, ragged ridgelines, white-water rivers, and wildlife to impress even the most staid traveler.

Three of Yellowstone National Park's five entrances are here, as is the incredible Beartooth Highway, the Absaroka-Beartooth Wilderness, and the nation's longest free-flowing river. The region's communities, such as Bozeman, Livingston, Red Lodge, and West Yellowstone, sponsor year-round special events and facilities that make this one of the state's most popular tourist destinations.

For more information about south-central Montana, contact Yellowstone Country, Box 1107, Red Lodge 59068-1107, or phone 406/446–1005 or 800/736–5276.

Towns listed: Big Sky, Big Timber, Bozeman, Cooke City, Gardiner, Livingston, Red Lodge, Three Forks, West Yellowstone

5. MISSOURI RIVER COUNTRY

This region put the "Big" in Montana's "Big Sky." No man-made object interrupts the plains horizon in this rangeland country. Colossal Fort Peck Reservoir contains 1,500

1859	1862		1863	1864
The first steamboat from St. Louis arrives in Fort Benton, the farthest-inland port in the world.	Montana's first major gold strike occurs near the present-day town of Dillon. John Bozeman founds the Bozeman Trail, which will be abandoned in 1868 after frequent Sioux	attacks. Congress passes the Homestead Act, opening thousands of acres to pioneer settlers.	Gold is discovered near Virginia City and Nevada City, attracting thousands of prospectors seeking the new El Dorado.	Montana Territory is created on May 26, with the first capital at Bannack. John M. Bozeman leads first wagon train over Bozeman Trail.

mi of shoreline. The C. M. Russell Wildlife Refuge sprawls across a million acres of Missouri River Country.

With an average of one person per 3 square mi, this ranks among the West's most sparsely populated regions. But the folks you'll find here are both hearty and eager to please. In small towns like Glasgow and Malta, residents are friendly and accommodating, as glad to help you find a good restaurant or historic site as to take part in their next branding or wagon train.

For more information about northeast Montana, contact Missouri River Country, Box 387, Wolf Point 59201, or call 406/653–1319 or 800/653–1319.

Towns listed: Glasgow, Malta, Wolf Point

6. LITTLE BIGHORN COUNTRY

If you're hell-bent on reaching the snowcapped peaks and raging rivers of western Montana, you can easily overlook Little Bighorn Country. Indeed, while life is a bit slower here and the landscape somewhat less captivating, you can still see some outstanding sights and have some real-life Western experiences unavailable elsewhere.

From the wild cowboys and ornery rodeo stock of Miles City's annual Bucking Horse Sale to the eerie silence of the historic hillsides at the Little Bighorn National Monument (formerly Custer Battlefield), this region's past still lives in the present. You'll also find prehistoric fossil beds and pictographs. Pompeys Pillar preserves graffiti from the Lewis and Clark Expedition. Some of the best fishing in the state is at Bighorn Lake, Bighorn River, and Tongue River, supporting as many as 10,000 trout per mile.

Montana's largest city—Billings—is the region's retail, medical, educational, entertainment and cultural center. Bordered by distinctive rimrocks, the community has numerous theaters, museums, art galleries, and shops, as well as restaurants and hotels.

For more information about southeast Montana, contact Custer Country, Room 40, Rte. 1, Box 1206A, Hardin 59034, or call 800/346–1876 or 406/665–1671.

Towns listed: Billings, Glendive, Hardin, Miles City

When to Visit

There truly is no bad time to visit Montana. Your specific interests in sightseeing and outdoor sports may define when you want to come, but Montana's scenery, wildlife, and friendly local residents will usually surpass those of the place you left in any season.

Sure, it gets cold during a Montana winter (the record low stands at −70°F at Rogers Pass on January 20, 1954), but it's not the icebox you'll find in other areas of the country. Cold snaps are frequently interrupted by mild periods and warm Chinook winds. And although summers can certainly get hot (the highest temperature recorded was 117°F at Medicine Lake on July 5, 1937), Montana's low humidity means the weather is seldom stifling. Summer evenings are generally cool, especially in the western portion of the state, where a milder, Pacific weather pattern prevails.

INTRODUCTION
HISTORY
REGIONS
WHEN TO VISIT
STATE'S GREATS
RULES OF THE ROAD
DRIVING TOURS

1872	1875	1876	1877	1880
Congress establishes Yellowstone, overlapping Montana's southern border, as the world's first national park.	Helena becomes Montana's third Territorial capital (following Bannack and Virginia City, sites of the state's first two major gold strikes).	Lt. Col. George Armstrong Custer and his 7th Cavalry fall victim to Sioux and Cheyenne warriors at the Battle of the Little Bighorn.	The Nez Percé, led by Chief Joseph, surrender to the U.S. Army near present-day Chinook after leading troops on a six-month, 1,170-mi trek that included nearly a dozen battles.	Hide hunters shoot buffalo to near extinction.

Of course, the majority of Montana's visitors travel to the state during the summer months, when warm-weather travel reaches its peak and outdoor activities are at their optimum. Winter sports, including snowmobiling and skiing, continue to increase in popularity in Montana. The shoulder season of April–May is characterized by late spring storms, muddy or snowed-in backroads and trails, and high rivers. But the fall shoulder season, September and October, can often provide ideal visiting conditions without the crowds, including excellent fishing and hiking and prime colors for leaf-peepers.

CLIMATE CHART
Average High/Low Temperatures (°F) and Monthly Precipitation (in inches)

	JAN.	FEB.	MAR.	APR.	MAY	JUNE
BILLINGS	32/14	39/19	46/25	57/34	67/43	78/52
	.9	.64	1.2	1.7	2.6	2.
	JULY	AUG.	SEPT.	OCT.	NOV.	DEC.
	87/58	85/57	72/47	61/38	45/26	34/17
	.94	1.	1.4	1.1	.84	.8
	JAN.	FEB.	MAR.	APR.	MAY	JUNE
GLASGOW	20/1	27/8	40/19	57/32	67/43	78/51
	.37	.27	.41	.69	1.8	2.1
	JULY	AUG.	SEPT.	OCT.	NOV.	DEC.
	85/57	84/55	70/44	59/33	40/19	25/6
	1.7	1.4	1.	.61	.28	.38
	JAN.	FEB.	MAR.	APR.	MAY	JUNE
GREAT FALLS	31/12	38/17	44/23	55/32	65/41	75/49
	.91	.57	1.1	1.4	2.5	2.4
	JULY	AUG.	SEPT.	OCT.	NOV.	DEC.
	83/53	82/52	70/44	59/33	40/19	25/6
	1.2	1.5	1.2	.78	.66	.85
	JAN.	FEB.	MAR.	APR.	MAY	JUNE
HELENA	30/10	37/16	45/22	56/31	65/40	76/48
	.63	.41	.73	.97	1.8	1.9
	JULY	AUG.	SEPT.	OCT.	NOV.	DEC.
	85/53	83/52	70/41	59/32	42/21	31/11
	1.1	1.3	1.2	.6	.48	.59
	JAN.	FEB.	MAR.	APR.	MAY	JUNE
KALISPELL	28/13	35/18	43/24	55/31	64/38	72/44
	1.5	1.1	1.	1.1	1.9	2.2

1882	1888	1889	1894	1910
A thick vein of copper is discovered beneath the played-out gold-mining camp of Butte, the richest cache of copper ore in the world.	Sweetgrass Hills Treaty establishes boundaries for Fort Peck, Fort Belknap, and Blackfeet reservations.	Montana is admitted to the Union on November 8 as the 41st state.	Helena is selected as Montana's permanent state capital, in a run-off election against Anaconda following a $3 million campaign financed by rival copper barons.	Glacier National Park is established by act of Congress.

INTRODUCTION
HISTORY
REGIONS
WHEN TO VISIT
STATE'S GREATS
RULES OF THE ROAD
DRIVING TOURS

	JULY	AUG.	SEPT.	OCT.	NOV.	DEC.
	80/47	79/46	68/39	54/29	38/24	30/16
	1.1	1.4	1.3	.87	1.3	1.7
	JAN.	FEB.	MAR.	APR.	MAY	JUNE
MISSOULA	30/15	37/21	47/25	58/31	66/38	74/46
	1.2	.79	.97	.96	1.8	1.8
	JULY	AUG.	SEPT.	OCT.	NOV.	DEC.
	83/50	82/49	71/40	57/31	41/24	30/16
	.91	1.2	1.1	.74	.81	1.2

FESTIVALS AND SEASONAL EVENTS

WINTER

Feb. **Whitefish Winter Carnival.** An all-out celebration of winter wonders has parades, food, dance, and numerous winter activities. | 406/862–3501.

"Race to the Sky" Sled Dog Race. At 350 mi, this is one of the longest dogsled races in the lower 48 and commemorates the War Dog Training and Reception Center that was here during World War II. The race starts in Camp Rimini near Helena and ends in Missoula five days later. | 406/442–4008.

SPRING

Mar. **St. Patrick's Day Events** in Butte bring home the Irish and Irish wannabes for parades, concerts, food, the Blarney Stone Run, and other spirited—even rowdy—shenanigans. | 800/735–6814.

The **World Snowmobile Expo** in West Yellowstone attracts vendors, equipment, power pulls, drag racing, and all the newest sleds. | 406/646–7701.

SUMMER

June During **Little Big Horn Days and Custer's Last Stand Reenactment** in Hardin more than 250 participants relive the events that led to history's most famous battle between Native Americans and the U.S. Cavalry—Custer's Last Stand. A military ball and rodeo round out the celebration. | 406/665–3577 or 406/665–1672.

During the **Montana Traditional Dixieland Jazz Festival** in Helena, the 1920s come alive as Prohibition-era jazz resounds through the city for five nights and four days. | 800/847–4868.

1916	1934	1951	1959	1970
Construction begins on Glacier National Park's Going-to-the-Sun Road. The engineering marvel takes 16 years to complete. Rocky Boy's Indian reservation is established near Havre.	Construction begins on Fort Peck Dam, one of the world's largest earth-filled dams. At its peak in 1936, the project employs 11,000 workers. Its price tag: $156 million.	Geologists discover the Williston Basin—a massive underground oil field beneath eastern Montana, western North Dakota, and southern Saskatchewan.	An evening earthquake registering 7.1 on the Richter scale topples half a mountain into the Madison River canyon, dams the river, creates Quake Lake, and buries 28 campers in an unmarked grave.	Newsman Chet Huntley and Chrysler Corp. announce plans for the massive Big Sky resort complex north of Yellowstone National Park.

July   Red Lodge's **Mountain Man Rendezvous** is a reenactment of the pre-1840 Rocky Mountain fur-trade era popular with locals, traders, trappers, and those passing through. | 406/446–1718.

Lewis and Clark Festival. Share the excitement of the famed explorers' trek in Great Falls, with trips and tours, demonstrations, exhibits, site visits, and other events for children and adults. | 406/761–4434.

Great Falls is home to the **Montana State Fair and Rodeo,** eight days of concerts, rodeos, exhibits, horse racing, carnival, livestock shows, and free entertainment. | 406/727–8900.

North American Indian Days in Browning, the largest Blackfeet tribal event, welcomes Native Americans from every region of the United States and Canada for traditional drumming and dancing contests, the crowning of Miss Blackfeet, a parade, and a fun run. | 406/338–7276.

Aug.   With traditions a half-century old, the weeklong **Festival of Nations** in Red Lodge celebrates the community's diverse ethnic heritage with food, crafts, and dance. Each day a different group sponsors food sampling, exhibits, programs, and other activities. | 406/446–2445.

Lewistown goes all out for the **Montana Cowboy Poetry Gathering,** three days of cowboy poetry and music are combined with a cowboy art and gear show, workshops, kid's classes, and a jam session. | 406/538–5436.

More than 225,000 people attend the **Montana Fair** in Billings, the largest statewide event of the year. It features a carnival, top country music entertainers, rodeos, horse racing, and exhibits. | 406/256–2400 or 406/256–2422.

AUTUMN

Sept.   **Havre Festival Days** present parades, arts and crafts shows, quilt and doll shows, concerts, and a powwow. | 406/265–4383.

Malta's **Milk River Wagon Train** features the oldest continuous wagon train in the West in a five-day celebration packed with four-horse hitches, wagons, fireside chats, parades, and chuckwagon dinners. | 406/654–1796.

1977	1980	1983	1995	1996
Oil giant Atlantic Richfield Co. (ARCO) buys Anaconda Co.	ARCO closes Anaconda copper smelter and Great Falls refinery, putting more than 1,000 employees out of work.	After more than a century of mining operations and $4 billion in mineral production, ARCO closes all its Butte mines.	Wolves are reintroduced to Yellowstone National Park. As a result of changes in federal law, Montana becomes the only state without a specified daytime speed limit.	Theodore Kaczynski, suspected "Unabomber" serial bomber, is arrested at his remote Lincoln-area cabin. After an 81-day standoff near Jordan, a group of "Freemen" surrender to the FBI.

State's Greats

INTRODUCTION
HISTORY
REGIONS
WHEN TO VISIT
STATE'S GREATS
RULES OF THE ROAD
DRIVING TOURS

Mother Nature did some great work in Montana. On the rolling green plains of eastern Montana you can hunt, fish, and boat. In the mountains of the west, try whitewater rafting, hiking, rock climbing, and mountain biking.

Forest, Parks, and Wilderness Areas

Two million travelers venture to **Glacier National Park** each year, most in summer, when creeks are flowing, wildlife is roaming, and dry pavement prevails. But come in the other seasons, and you'll miss the summer crowds. In spring the animals in the million-acre park produce their young and magnificent streams swell with snow melt from the highest reaches of Glacier. With warm days and brisk nights, fall offers incredible colors and the annual migration of eagles through the park. Glacier's 52-mi **Going-to-the-Sun Road,** which crosses the crest of the Continental Divide and traverses the towering Garden Wall, is both an engineering marvel and a superb sight-seeing adventure.

Although Montana claims only a small part of **Yellowstone National Park** (most of it is in northwestern Wyoming), three of the 2.2-million-acre park's entrances are here. All told, Yellowstone and the national forests and wilderness areas, lakes, streams, wildlife refuges, and roadless areas that surround the park constitute nearly 14 million acres of wild country in the Rockies.

The landscape's ragged ridges, majestic mountain peaks, refreshing clear-water streams, and alpine lakes invite mountain biking, backcountry hiking, rafting, and horseback riding. Elk, grizzly and black bears, buffalo, geese, swans, and many other Yellowstone residents migrate freely in and out of the park; you'll see a lot.

The best of the many memorable sites in the park include the Grand Canyon of the Yellowstone and its incredible waterfall, the Upper Geyser Basin (the world's largest concentration of geysers), Old Faithful, and Yellowstone Lake. Most of the 3 million annual visitors arrive in summer and bring traffic jams, congestion, and the comforts of metropolitan life. Fewer people come in fall and spring, when there is less active wildlife. In winter, a welcome hush falls over Yellowstone's peaks and valleys, with only the occasional growl of snowmobiles.

Huge swaths of Montana designated as **wilderness areas** are just as wild and beautiful as the national parks. Together, the **Great Bear, Bob Marshall,** and **Scapegoat** wilderness areas preserve 1.5 million acres of roadless retreat south of Glacier National Park.

Encompassing 2,400 contiguous square mi and roughly 1,800 mi of backcountry trails, the "Bob" is the best of the nation's wilderness areas. You can reach it only by trail; once there, you can fish, hunt, hike, camp, horseback ride, and float on the river. Some 250 to 350 grizzly bears live there, too, as do many cutthroat trout.

1999
After the State Supreme Court declares Montana's lack of a speed limit unconstitutional, the state re-establishes speed limits on Montana roadways.

Culture, History, and the Arts

Montana's history is one of proud Native American tribes, pioneer spirit, and thousands of faceless miners, mule skinners, and madams who struggled to tame this rugged land. You can retrace the footsteps of legendary Native American warriors, determined soldiers, famed cross-country explorers, and countless sodbusters in numerous sites scattered across the state.

Maintained by the National Park Service, **Big Hole National Battlefield** is the site of the tragic engagement between the nontreaty bands of the Nez Percé and the 7th U.S. Cavalry led by Colonel John Gibbon on August 9–10, 1877. It has two self-guided trails, a visitor center, a museum, and daily ranger programs in the summer.

Fifteen miles south of Hardin and east of Interstate 90, **Little Bighorn Battlefield National Monument** represents one of the last armed efforts of the northern Plains Native Americans to retain their traditional way of life.

Sitting Bull, Crazy Horse, and Gall masterminded the conflict and led 10,000 Sioux, Cheyenne, and Arapaho on June 25–26, 1876. They annihilated the 263-member 7th Cavalry, among them Lieutenant Colonel George A. Custer, his two brothers, his brother-in-law, and a nephew. The Native Americans lost fewer than 50 men. They've changed the name from Custer Battlefield National Monument, but all the monuments on this battlefield are to the losers. You can stop at the visitors center, museum, Custer National Cemetery, 7th Cavalry Memorial, and Reno-Benteen Battlefield. Summer brings guided tours, an interpretive program, films, and one of the best battlefield reenactments anywhere.

In Billings the **Yellowstone Art Center** is the state's premier museum displaying Western and contemporary art from nationally and internationally acclaimed artists. The museum recently underwent a $10 million expansion.

Take a trek through 4 billion years of Rocky Mountain history in the **Museum of the Rockies,** adjacent to the campus of Montana State University at Bozeman. Highlighting this contemporary museum are a world-class dinosaur exhibit, the Taylor Planetarium, the Tinsley Homestead, Native American artifacts, and the Kirk Hill Nature Trail.

The **Lewis and Clark National Historic Trail Interpretive Center** is on the banks of the Missouri River overlooking Black Eagle Falls, at about the midpoint of the explorers' transcontinental trek. The center focuses on the relationships between the Corps of Discovery and the many Native American tribes it encountered, as well as its month-long portage around the five falls on the Missouri River near present-day Great Falls. The center's theater shows a film by noted documentary producer Ken Burns.

Constructed in 1890 by Irish immigrant Marcus Daly, one of Butte's legendary "copper kings," the 42-room, 24-bedroom, 15-bath **Daly Mansion** features five Italian marble fireplaces and 50 manicured acres in Montana's scenic Bitterroot Valley.

Sports and Recreation

More than 14,000 acres of Montana's slopes are dedicated to **downhill skiing.** With 15 downhill ski areas, 548 runs, and 65 lifts, you can definitely find a place to ski. Facilities range from day-use areas such as the **Bear Paw Ski Bowl** near Havre to full-fledged destination resorts such as **Big Sky** and **Bridger Bowl,** both near Bozeman.

On Continental Drive in Butte, the **U.S. High Altitude Sports Center** is a training facility for Olympic-class athletes and site of world-class speed-skating competitions.

You'll find some of the nation's best **cross-country skiing** in Montana, as well as resorts that give guided wilderness and wildlife tours and provide expert instruction on groomed trails. Hundreds of trails run through two national parks, nine national forests, and a dozen wilderness areas. Many lodges and resorts have private trail systems.

In **Yellowstone National Park** you ski past bubbling geysers and through thousands of acres of wilderness. Border towns offer guided ski tours, snowcoach tours, and

INTRODUCTION
HISTORY
REGIONS
WHEN TO VISIT
STATE'S GREATS
RULES OF THE ROAD
DRIVING TOURS

rentals. Contact Visitor Services, Box 168, Yellowstone National Park, WY 82190, call 307/344–7381, or visit their Web site at www.nps.gov/yell.

In **Glacier National Park** you can rent skis, take guided tours, and explore more than a million acres of beauty on a dozen ski trails. For maps and more information, contact: Superintendent, Glacier National Park, West Glacier, MT 59936, call 406/888–7800, or visit their Web site at www.nps.gov/glac.

There are nearly 17 million additional acres of public lands in Montana, and in winter they become a wonderland. You can stay anywhere from city motels and hotels and posh mountain resorts to secluded Forest Service cabins and backcountry lodges. For ski reports and additional travel information, call 800/847–4868 or visit Travel Montana's Web site at www.travel.state.mt.us/.

A half-dozen Montana companies offer **guided dogsled treks** into remote areas and state parks. You can tour by the hour or go on overnight excursions. For more information, call 800/847–4868 and ask for the "Montana Winter Guide" or visit Travel Montana's Web site at www.travel.state.mt.us/.

Among the most popular **snowmobiling** destinations in the country, Montana has 3,700 mi of groomed trails and hundreds of miles of backcountry open to sleds. Snow depths generally range from 1 to 3 feet at lower elevations to 6 to 15 feet higher up. The season extends from mid-December to April.

All motorized vehicles are prohibited from operating in federally designated wilderness areas. Snowmobiles on public lands must display a registration decal; machines registered in other states are not required to display a Montana registration. Unregistered snowmobiles must display a nonresident, temporary-use permit, which can be obtained from the Montana Fish, Wildlife and Parks Department.

For more information, contact the Montana Snowmobile Association, Box 4714, Missoula 59806, call 800/847–4868 and ask for the "Montana Winter Guide," or visit Travel Montana's Web site at www.travel.state.mt.us/.

Many **hunting, fishing, and backcountry tour operators, outfitters, and guide services** can help you with everything from solitary backcountry walks and activities for nonfishing companions to hunting and fishing trips, trail rides, white-water raft trips, scenic floats, stagecoach rides, wagon-train rides, wilderness bicycle tours, nature studies, and multiday boat trips.

You can get directories of licensed outfitters from the Montana Board of Outfitters, 1424 9th Ave., Helena 59620, 406/444–3738, and the Montana Outfitters and Guides Association, Box 1339, Townsend 59644, 406/266–5625.

Rodeo is probably Montana's third most popular sport. Throughout the summer and fall, rodeos are held in virtually every community in the state. For specific dates, ask for the "Calendar of Events" from Travel Montana, 1429 9th Ave. (Box 200533), Helena 59620-0533, call 800/847–4868, or visit their Web site at www.travel.state.mt.us.

For additional information, call the Montana Pro Rodeo Circuit at 406/454–1821 or contact the Northern Rodeo Association, Box 1122, Billings 59103, 406/252–1122.

Rock climbing is also popular. You can find indoor rock climbing and expert instruction for all ages and abilities through the Missoula Rock Garden, 406/728–0714. The company also has guided instruction in the mountain ranges around Missoula.

Other Points of Interest

One of America's most sophisticated small cities, **Missoula** retains a nice mix of Wild West boastfulness, youthful college vigor, artsy folk feeling, and independence. At the confluence of three mighty rivers and set in the peaceful confines of five scenic valleys, Missoula serves as western Montana's commercial and cultural hub. Still, a lazy trout stream that flows through town reminds everyone that they haven't wandered too far from nature.

As the state's third largest city, with 43,000 residents, Missoula home to the University of Montana, the outstanding Missoula Children's Theatre, the Garden City Ballet, the String Orchestra of the Rockies, the Montana Repertoire Theatre, the International Wildlife Film Festival, 140 restaurants, and many art galleries and museums. Three state parks are within 26 mi of town—Beavertail, Frenchtown Pond, and Council Grove.

Described by the late CBS correspondent Charles Kuralt as "the most beautiful road in America," the 69-mi, three-hour **Beartooth Highway** overlooks dizzying panoramas of snowcapped peaks, alpine lakes, glaciers, and plateaus from 11,000 feet. This drive begins at Red Lodge and climbs the glacially carved walls of Rock Creek Canyon en route to Yellowstone National Park. The route has many hairpin curves and mountain switchbacks.

Rules of the Road

Montana's snowy winters can make for hazardous driving, when sudden storms commonly block highways. You should prepare for the unexpected with winter survival kits of snow tires or chains, a shovel and window scraper, flares or a reflector, a blanket or sleeping bag, a first-aid kit, sand, gravel or traction mats, a flashlight with extra batteries, matches, a lighter and candles, paper, non-perishable foods, and a tow chain or rope. Check on weather and road conditions before you travel.

License Requirements: Montana recognizes valid driver's licenses from other states and countries. The minimum driving age is 15 with driver training or 16 without.

Right Turn on Red: Right turns on red are allowed unless otherwise posted.

Seat Belt and Helmet Laws: The driver and all passengers in motor vehicles on Montana roadways must wear seatbelts. Law-enforcement officers will not pull you over if you're not wearing a seat belt, but they will ticket you if you commit other infractions while unbelted. Children two and younger must be in a federally approved child restraint device. Children ages two to four who weigh no more than 40 pounds must also be secured in a child restraint device. All motorcycle riders under 18 years of age must wear a helmet in Montana. Those over 18 may choose whether or not to wear a helmet.

Speed Limits: The maximum speed on the state's interstate highways is 75 mph; non-interstate roadway limits are 70 mph daytime and 65 mph at night. Trucks over one-ton capacity have interstate speed limits of 65 mph and non-interstate limits of 60 mph daytime and 55 mph at night.

For More Information: contact the Montana Highway Patrol at 406/444–3780.

Beartooth Highway Drive
A DRIVE ALONG THE ROOF OF THE ROCKIES

Distance: 69 mi (111 km)   Time: 3 hours
Breaks: Frequent turnouts to look at scenery or take a quick hike. The community of Red Lodge is 8 mi from the byway's eastern start. The Top of the World Store is near Beartooth Pass.

This roadway is designated a National Forest Scenic Byway, but that doesn't begin to describe it. With mountain switchbacks and high-altitude views of Montana and Wyoming's snowcapped peaks, giant glaciers, and sprawling valleys with deep-blue alpine lakes, the Beartooth Highway ranks among North America's premier scenic byways. The route is impassable and closed to traffic for much of the year, open only from approximately June to September (depending on weather conditions).

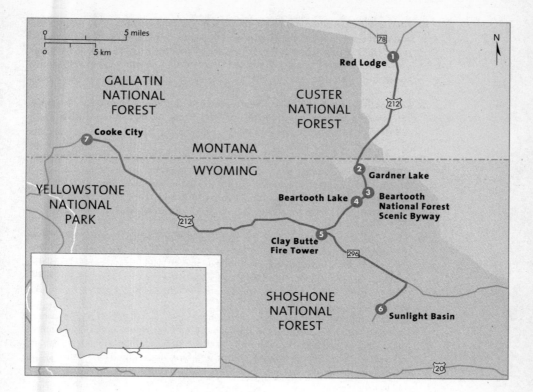

Driving from east to west means you'll have a long, steep uphill climb, but you'll save your brakes. To avoid glare, you may want to drive east to west in the morning and west to east in the afternoon. The towns of Red Lodge and Cooke City, at the east and west starting points, respectively, have full services, including lodging, gasoline, and food. The Beartooth Highway passes 10 National Forest campgrounds with picnic tables, fire grates, drinking water, and toilets, but no hookups. Daytime summer temperatures generally average in the 70s, but sudden snowstorms have been reported in every month of the year. Check road conditions.

❶ **Red Lodge** (U.S. 212 and Rte. 78) is a historic mining town in Rock Creek Valley at the base of the Beartooth Mountains. In winter it is a magnet for skiers; in summer you can hike, bike, golf, fish, and just look around. The **Beartooth Nature Center** (406/446–1133) has native North American animals and a children's petting zoo. Directly out of Red Lodge, the Beartooth Highway enters Custer National Forest, one of the three national forests it bisects as it skirts the Montana-Wyoming border adjacent to the eastern edge of Yellowstone National Park; the others are the Gallatin and Shoshone national forests.

❷ Continuing on U.S. 212, you'll enter the Beartooth Loop National Recreation Trail, which begins at **Gardner Lake** and traverses 10 mi of rolling alpine landscape typically found in the Arctic. Note how plants have adapted to this severe climate. View Sawtooth Mountain to the southwest; across the valley to the north, a black fang known locally as the Bear's Tooth juts up from the surrounding forest.

❸ From **Beartooth National Forest Scenic Byway** you get incredible vistas to the south and west—snowcapped peaks, glaciers and alpine lakes, colorful wildflowers, and far-reaching plateaus. Tiny patches of snow and ice remain up here much of the year, often tinted pink from algae. Winter can last into July. The summit air is invigorating and as fresh as it gets.

❹ **Beartooth Lake** is at the base of Beartooth Butte. Summer fishermen like its 21-site campground and boat launch. You'll find lots of good hiking and can reach the 100-ft Beartooth Falls on an easy ½-mi trail along a creek.

❺ **Clay Butte Fire Tower** is a beautiful 3-mi detour from the Beartooth. Its visitor information center is open in summer, and from the top of the tower you get a spectacular view of Granite Peak (Montana's highest at 12,799 feet) to the northwest, the North Absaroka Wilderness and Yellowstone National Park to the west, the Clarks Fork Valley and Absaroka Mountains to the southwest, and the Bighorn Mountains to the east.

❻ West of Beartooth Pass you leave the alpine vegetation and descend through a forest of spruce, fir, and lodgepole pine mixed with stands of aspen. To the south and west is the North Absaroka Wilderness; with the Beartooth Wilderness it blankets nearly a million acres. At the junction with Route 296 (also known as Chief Joseph Scenic High-way) you can take a side trip into the remote **Sunlight Basin** to sightsee, camp, hike, and fish.

Blackened north-facing slopes remain from the raging fires of 1988. The byway continues west, skirts the Clarks Fork of the Yellowstone River, climbs over the summit of Colter Pass, then travels through some of the 1988 burn areas. You can see steady regrowth, as well as new flowers, shrubs, and birds, including hawks, falcons, and eagles, and, at times, grizzly and black bears, bighorn sheep, mountain goats, moose, and marmots.

❼ Head back to the intersection of Route 296 and U.S. 212 and proceed west on U.S. 212, which will take you straight into **Cooke City** on the Montana-Wyoming border. This mining town with a colorful past is now a friendly, small resort community where you can hike, horseback ride, fish, climb, and ski in winter. After Cooke City, the byway drops through Silver Gate and ends at the Northeast Gate to Yellowstone National Park.

Bozeman Trail Driving Tour
FROM LITTLE BIGHORN NATIONAL BATTLEFIELD TO BOZEMAN

Distance: 200 mi (322 km)   Time: 2 days

Breaks: Frequent historical sites about the Lewis and Clark Expedition, Bozeman Trail, and Plains Indian War, as well as an excellent assortment of things to see, cultural events, and recreation make this an outstanding east-west route. U.S. highways, Interstates 90 and 94, and abundant visitor services make this among the most reliable routes through the state in any season. You can overnight in Billings, which has lots of museums, restaurants, hotels, and nightlife.

You'll go from the Little Bighorn Battlefield and Bighorn Canyon National Recreation Area in the southeast, northwest to Montana's largest city, then west to Bozeman, one of the state's most attractive communities. Weather permitting, you can drive through the Crow and Northern Cheyenne reservations and entrances to Yellowstone National Park, skirt the bank of the Yellowstone River and the fringes of the Gallatin National Forest, climb Bozeman Pass, then descend into Gallatin Valley. Particularly in mountain passes, roads can close suddenly because of sudden storms year-round. Check road conditions before you travel and be prepared for emergencies.

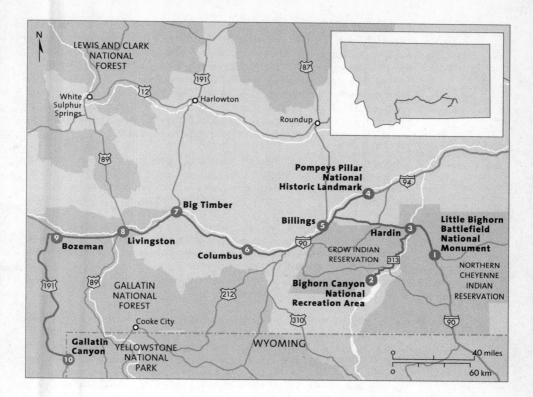

❶ Little Bighorn Battlefield National Monument, at the junction of I–90 and U.S. 212 near Crow Agency, memorializes one of the last armed efforts of the Northern Plains people to preserve their way of life, and illuminates the significance of what occurred here on June 25–26, 1876. An overconfident lieutenant colonel named Custer and his 7th Cavalry came face to face with the fiercest warriors of the Sioux, Cheyenne, and Arapaho. You can stop at the visitor center, museum, and interpretive exhibits; see programs and films; and take guided tours in summer.

❷ Bighorn Canyon National Recreation Area has stunning canyon scenery and trails where you can hike, plus interpretive programs, boating, fishing, and camping. Located on Route 313 south of Hardin, 525-ft-high Yellowtail Dam creates picturesque, 71-mi-long Bighorn Lake, surrounded by the canyon's spectacular limestone walls. Below the dam, the Bighorn River is one of Montana's best year-round trout streams.

❸ In **Hardin** you can stop for a full range of visitor services, restored buildings, picnic areas, and shops. Try the **Purple Cow** if you like heaping family-style helpings and super shakes and sandwiches. Off I–90 at Exit 497 is the Big Horn County Historical Museum and Visitor Information Center for regional history and interpretation.

❹ Pompeys Pillar National Historic Landmark is 28 mi east of Billings off I–94. In 1806, Captain William Clark carved his name on the sandstone butte—the only remaining physical evidence along the trail of the Lewis and Clark Expedition. In season, you can take interpretive tours along the Yellowstone River.

⑤ Billings is eastern Montana's cultural, medical, commercial, educational, and entertainment center. The town is surrounded by distinctive rock formations called the Rimrocks, and has many museums, art galleries, shopping, and theaters, as well as Rocky Mountain College and Montana State University–Billings. Billings Trolley Tours gives historic tours of town and Pompeys Pillar. The Visitor Center and Cattle Drive Monument on South 27th Street near I-90 commemorate Montana's centennial cattle drive; you can also get information on all area attractions. The Alberta Bair Theater at 2801 3rd Avenue North downtown, is the state's largest performing-arts center and one of its busiest—more than 100 events are scheduled annually.

⑥ Columbus, in the foothills of the scenic Beartooths, is good for outdoor recreation, fine shops, and cafes, and has three city parks, a public swimming pool, and tennis, basketball, and a walking path. You can camp and picnic for free at Itch-Ke-Pe, near the Yellowstone River.

⑦ Big Timber is off I-90 40 mi west of Columbus. There you get an impressive view of the Crazy Mountains, and can visit museums, galleries, antiques shops, historic sites, and the **Yellowstone River Fish Hatchery.** On Route 298, 27 mi south of Big Timber, and worth a detour, is the Natural Bridge, a spectacular falls and creek-carved canyon along the Boulder River. You can follow interpretive signs and trails, with fishing and access to the Absaroka-Beartooth Wilderness.

⑧ Continue roughly 32 mi west on I-90 to **Livingston.** This is the original gateway to Yellowstone National Park. The large historic district downtown is made up of 436 buildings. Surrounded by the Gallatin National Forest and granite peaks, Livingston is built on the banks of the scenic Yellowstone River. An angler's heaven, scenic Paradise Valley lies to the south. The 52-mi Paradise Valley Corridor leads to Yellowstone National Park and is bordered by the Absaroka Range and the Yellowstone, the longest free-flowing river in the United States and one of America's top trout streams. The town's **Firehouse 5 Playhouse** shows live community theater.

⑨ Bozeman may be Montana's most beautiful community. Nestled in the green cradle of the Gallatin Valley, surrounded by a half-dozen mountain ranges, Bozeman is a small town with big-city amenities. At the base of the Bridger Range, it is an ideal place from which to start exploring Yellowstone National Park, Big Sky, and numerous Lewis and Clark historic sites. Walk through the campus of Montana State University or the **South Wilson Historic District,** a residential area where houses range from stately mansions to small cottages. The **Museum of the Rockies,** on the south edge of the MSU campus, includes a planetarium, a world-class dinosaur exhibit, Native American artifacts, and exhibits about Montana history.

⑩ Gallatin Canyon is an 80-mi drive south of Bozeman on Route 191, following the Gallatin River as it skirts the snowcapped Spanish Peaks then enters the northeast corner of Yellowstone National Park. Along the route, you can fish, camp, watch wildlife, and go white-water rafting.

ANACONDA

MAP 6, D6

(Nearby towns also listed: Butte, Deer Lodge)

Founded in 1883, this small community exists because of Marcus Daly and the Anaconda Copper Company. The company stopped smelting operations in 1980, but "the Stack" building remains an important landmark and state park. Anaconda has a population of about 10,000. The Copper Village Museum and Arts Center has a copper smelter display and exhibits on area history. Self-guided walking and bus tours of the town's historic district begin at the Anaconda Visitor Center. From the 1.6-mi Upper Works Historic Trail, you can get an overview of Anaconda and the Old Works smelter site, now a Jack Nicklaus signature golf course.

Information: Anaconda Chamber of Commerce | 306 E. Park, Anaconda, 59711 | 406/563–2400 | www.anacondamt.org.

Attractions

Anaconda Visitor Center. This old railroad depot holds memorabilia of railroad and copper history. It also has tours, performances, and exhibits. | 306 E. Park | 406/563–2400 | www.anacondamt.org | Free | Daily.

Anaconda-Pintler Wilderness. Shared by three ranger districts of the Beaverhead-Deerlodge National Forest, the 159,000-acre Anaconda-Pintler extends more than 30 mi along the Continental Divide to the southwest of Anaconda. No motorized travel is permitted in the wilderness area. Popular access points include Moose Lake, Georgetown Lake, and the East Fork of the Bitterroot River. Elevations range from 5,400 feet near the Bitterroot River to 10,793 feet at the summit of West Goat Peak. Glaciation formed many spectacular cirques, U-shape valleys, and glacial moraines in the foothills. If you hike or ride horseback along the Continental Divide, at times you can view the Mission Mountains to the northwest and the mountains marking the Idaho-Montana border to the southwest. About 280 mi of Forest Service trails cross the area. If you want to explore the wilderness, you must obtain a detailed map and register your plans with a Forest Service office. Stock forage is scarce, so if you're riding a horse, you're encouraged to bring concentrated feed pellets. Wildlife is abundant, and the habitat supports mountain lions, deer, elk, moose, bears, and many smaller animals and birds. | Access to East Fork of Bitterroot River via U.S. 93 (there are more than 20 other access points) | 406/821–3201 | Free | Daily.

Anaconda Smoke Stack State Park. "The Stack" is a solid reminder of all that the Anaconda Copper Company and Marcus Daly did for the area. Smelting operations ceased 20 years ago. The park is not yet open to visitors. | Rte. 1 | 406/542–5500 | www.state.mt.us.

Beaverhead-Deerlodge National Forest, Philipsburg District. *See* Deer Lodge, *below.* | Philipsburg Ranger District: Box 805, Philipsburg | 406/859–3211. .

Copper Village Museum and Arts Center. You'll find displays on the area's history along with video presentations, music performances, and special events. | 401 E. Commercial St. | 406/563–2422 | Free | May–Sept., daily 10–4; Oct.–Apr., Tues.–Sat. 10–4.

Granite State Park. The abandoned buildings of the ghost town of Granite, about 4 mi east of town off Rte. 10A, still stand as examples of frontier architecture. | 406/542–5500 | www.state.mt.us | Free | May–Sept., daily.

Lost Creek Raceway. Stop here for drag, street car, and motor cross races. | Galen Rd.; Rte. 1 to Rte. 48 | 406/563–5161 or 406/949–DRAG | www.lostcreek-raceway.com | May–Sept., call for schedule.

Lost Creek State Park. The scenic recreation area has a short trail to Lost Creek Falls. Views of limestone cliffs rising 1,200 ft above the canyon floor, and frequent sightings of bighorn sheep and mountain goats. The 25-site campground has hiking trails and creek fishing. | 1½ mi east of Anaconda on Rte. 1, then 2 mi north on Rte. 273, then 6 mi west | 406/542–5500 | www.state.mt.us | Free | Daily.

Old Works Golf Course. Montana's only Jack Nicklaus course is public and designed around Anaconda's historic Old Works copper smelter. | 1205 Pizzini Way | 406/563–5989 | www.oldworks.org | $29–$38 | May–Oct., daily.

Washoe Park. Anaconda's favorite playground has flower gardens, tennis courts, picnic areas, an outdoor swimming pool, and the Montana State Fish Hatchery. | Park St. | 406/563–2400 | Free | Daily dawn to dusk.

Washoe Theatre. Built in 1931, this classic Art Deco theater was ranked by the Smithsonian as the fifth most-beautiful theater in the nation. | 305 Main St. | 406/563–6161 | Daily.

ON THE CALENDAR

FEB.: *Chocolate Festival.* Local merchants give away free chocolates to all customers—a constable fines them if they don't (with proceeds going to a local charity). The chocolate bake-off has prizes for winners. All entries are sold the following day. | 406/563–2422.

JULY: *Art in Washoe Park.* Juried art and crafts booths, ethnic foods, and professional entertainment make a good three-day show. | 406/563–2422.

Dining

Barclay II. American/Seafood. The classically elegant dining room at this restaurant just outside town has great mountain views. The specialties include prime rib and various kinds of fresh fish. | 1300 E. Commercial St.; 1 mi east on Rte. 10A | 406/563–5541 | $21–$28 | D, MC, V | Closed Mon. No lunch.

The Haufbrau. American. A family restaurant with a bright cheerful interior. Try one of the many specialty pizzas. | 111 Hwy. 1 W | 406/563–9982 | $7–$11 | AE, D, MC, V.

Jim & Clara's Dinner Club. American. This traditional supper club specializes in seafood dishes, plus steak and pasta. It also offers a full bar, which is open daily. | 509 E. Park, Anaconda | 406/563–9963 | Closed Tues. | $13–$42 | AE, D, MC, V.

Lodging

Celtic House and Harp & Thistle. A hotel in the traditional Irish fashion, with rooms upstairs and a pub featuring microbrews downstairs, housed in a 100-year-old former brothel. Rooms are antique-decorated and comfortable. Kitchenettes, Cable TV. | 23 Main St., Anaconda | 406/563–5072 | 10 rooms, 5 with kitchenettes | $35 | AE, D, MC, V.

Fairmont Hot Springs Resort. This is the place to come for both relaxation and recreation. The soaking pools are fed by 155°F natural hot springs, and there are two Olympic-size pools. You can also play golf, bicycle, or just relax in your spacious, bright room or suite. Restaurant, bar, room service. Cable TV, in-room VCRs (movies). 4 pools, 2 indoor. Driving range, 18-hole golf course, tennis. Exercise equipment. Bicycles. Video game room and game room with pool and Ping-Pong tables. Business services, convention center. Airport shuttle. | 1500 Fairmont Rd. | 406/797–3241 or 800/332–3272 (except MT), 800/332–3272 (MT) | fax 406/797–3337 | www.fairmontmontana.com | 152 rooms | $109, $129–$299 suites | AE, D, DC, MC, V.

Georgetown Lake Lodge. A large log cabin inn, situated 100 feet from the trout-laden Georgetown Lake; the dining room is highlighted by a 27-foot-high stone fireplace. Restaurant, lounge, satellite TV, video gambling, fishing, hiking trails. | Denton's Point Rd., Georgetown Lake, Anaconda | 406/563–7020 | fax 406/563–4292 | www.centric.net/montanarec/georgetownlakelodge.htm | 10 rooms | $49–$79 | D, MC, V.

Lodge at Skyhaven. Close to wilderness trails and fishing spots, this is a great base from which to venture afield. The rooms have views of the valley and mountains. No-smoking rooms. Cable TV. Pets allowed. | 1711 Rte. 48, next to airport | 406/563–8342 or 800/563–8089 | fax 406/563–3317 | www.skyhavenlodge.com | 10 rooms | $45 | AE, D, DC, MC, V.

Marcus Daly. A small, economy lodging, this place has basic modern, spacious rooms and is in the heart of downtown, with restaurants around the corner. Cable TV. Airport shuttle. | 119 W. Park St. | 406/563–3411 or 800/535–6528 (MT) | fax 406/563–2268 | 19 rooms | $48–$54 | AE, D, DC, MC, V.

Vagabond Lodge Motel. The rooms here are Early American style. There is a 24-hour restaurant across the street. Cable TV. | 1421 E. Park. St. | 406/563–5251 or 800/231–2660 | fax 406/563–3356 | www.vagabondmontana.com | 18 rooms | $54, $72 suites | MC, V.

BAKER

(Nearby towns also listed: Glendive, Miles City)

Old-fashioned hospitality is the hallmark of this 1,700-population town in the southeast corner of Montana at the junction of U.S. Highway 12 and Montana Highway 7. Just 12 mi from North Dakota, Baker is a bustling commercial center for area farmers. Residents here are proud of their history and community spirit. Travelers are invited to drop by the senior center for a game of cards, and everyone seems willing to share their tips for a great fishing spot or a bite to eat. Baker has an entertaining, informative Web site that focuses on the town's history. Fossil hunting is a popular pastime, and the pursuit of live game—from antelope to wild turkey—also draws many to Baker.

Information: Baker Chamber of Commerce and Agriculture | P.O. Box 849, Baker, MT 59313 | 406/778–2266 | www.bakermt.com.

Attractions

O'Fallon Historical Museum. Native American artifacts and perhaps the world's largest stuffed steer—a bovine brute that weighed in at 4,000 pounds—highlight the collections at this folksy local museum housed behind the courthouse complex in the original county jail. Two old homestead cabins are nearby. | 723 S. Main St. | 406/778–3265 | Free | 9 AM–noon and 1– 5 PM, Tues.–Fri., Sun. .

Dining

Sakelaris Kitchen. American. Chicken-fried steak and homemade pies are local favorites at this homey, cheerful place, which boasts "the best food you ever sunk your choppers into." Everything is homemade and homestyle. | Lakeside Shopping Center | 406/778–2202 | Casual | $4–$10 | D, MC, V.

Lodging

Roy's Motel. Clean rooms, a hot tub and information about local sights are offered at this affordable motel, which also has an RV campground. Whirlpool. RV camping. Pets allowed. | 327 W. Montana Ave. | 406/778–3321 or 800.552–3321 | fax 406/778–2180 | 22 | $40 | MC, V.

Sagebrush Inn. This attractive spot offers nicely decorated modern rooms and an older extension with lower prices. Pets allowed. | 518 W. Montana Ave. | 406/778–3341 or 800/638–3708 | fax 406/778–2753 | 40 | $40–$50 | MC, V.

BIG SKY

(Nearby town also listed: Bozeman)

Here at the home of Big Sky Ski and Summer Resort, outdoor enthusiasts won't get much closer to heaven. You can golf, play tennis, hike, horseback ride, fish, bike, go white-water rafting, and, in season, ski and snowmobile. Get an exceptional view from the summer gondola rides, and take a hike in the nearby Lee Metcalf Spanish Peaks Wilderness.

Information: Big Sky Chamber of Commerce | Box 160100, Big Sky, 59716 | 406/995–3000 or 800/943–4111 | www.bigskychamber.com.

Attractions

Big Sky Ski and Summer Resort. Play here any time of year if you'd rather be outdoors than in. The resort is a destination in itself, with golf, tennis, hiking, horseback riding, fishing, mountain biking, white-water rafting, skiing, and snowmobiling. For beautiful views, you can take a gondola ride in summer. Choose from the 75 trails on two mountains for winter skiing; you'll also find ski rentals, a ski school, day care, 15 restaurants, 11 night spots, and full accommodations on the mountain. | 1 Lone Mountain Trail | 406/995–5000 or 800/548–4486 | www.bigskyresort.com | Lift tickets $54 | Daily.

RIVER TRIPS

Yellowstone Raft Co. Try scenic and white-water rafting, fishing, and kayak instruction on three premier Montana rivers, ½ day on Gallatin River, full day on Madison River or Yellowstone River. | U.S. 191 | 406/995–4613 or 800/348–4376 | www.yellowstoneraft.com | May–Sept.

ON THE CALENDAR

JULY: *Big Sky Food Festival.* Local restaurants collaborate in presenting an unforgettable feast at Buck's T-4 Lodge. Music and dancing. | 406/995–4111.

Dining

Corral Steakhouse Cafe. American. Five miles out of Big Sky is this small restaurant with western-influenced furnishings. They specialize in all types of steak and prime rib dishes. | Hwy. 191 | 406/995–4249 | $7–13 | MC, V.

First Place. Continental. Game birds, steak, and chicken are the favorites here. You can also get vegetarian dishes. Kids' menu. | Meadow Village | 406/995–4244 | $22–$28 | AE, D, MC, V | Closed last 2 weeks of May. No lunch.

Lone Mountain Ranch Dining Room. Continental. This luxurious guest ranch has themed breakfast and lunch buffets including Cajun, Thai, French, and American cuisine. Two favorites are smoked bison and grilled swordfish. In winter, sleigh-ride dinners include entertainment. No smoking. | Off U.S. 191 | 406/995–2782 | Reservations essential for dinner | $27–$32 | D, MC, V | Closed Apr.–mid-June and Oct.–mid-Dec.

Lodging

Best Western–Buck's T-4 Lodge. Spacious rooms and a quiet mountain setting set this chain apart. Outdoor hot tubs add a touch of luxury. Restaurant, bar, complimentary Continental breakfast. No air-conditioning, some VCRs. Cable TV. Game room with pool and Ping-Pong. Laundry facilities. Business services. Pets allowed. | U.S. 191 | 406/995–4111 or 800/822–4484 | fax 406/995–2191 | www.buckst4.com | 75 rooms | $79–$154, $174–$214 suites | AE, D, DC, MC, V | Closed mid-Apr.–mid-May.

Big Sky Resort. This spacious all-season mountain resort complex has ski and sports shops, ski storage, and a ski school. You can play golf and tennis in summer. When you're ready to quit for the day, go for the complete massage, spa, and, energy permitting, health club—the only one on the mountain. Bar, dining room, picnic area, room service. No air-conditioning in some rooms, refrigerators. Cable TV. 2 pools. Hot tub. Driving range, 18-hole golf course, putting green, tennis. Exercise equipment. Downhill and cross-country skiing. Playground. Laundry facilities. Business services. Airport shuttle. | 1 Lone Mountain Rd. | 406/995–5000 or 800/548–4486 | fax 406/995–5001 | www.bigskyresort.com | 298 rooms | $194, $322 suites | AE, D, DC, MC, V.

Comfort Inn at Big Sky. A Western-style hotel only 30 yards from the Gallatin River and 9 mi from Lone Peak. You can take the ski shuttle in winter. The indoor 90-foot waterslide is very popular year-round. All public areas are non-smoking; smoking rooms are available. Cable TV, AC, pool, hot tub, laundry services, business services. Pets allowed in some rooms. | 47214 Gallatin Rd., Bigfork | 406–995–4552 | fax 406–995–2277 | 62 rooms, 1 with kitchen | $49–$129 | V, MC, AE, D.

Corral Bar, Café & Motel. A small motel with standard rooms, each offering two queen-size beds: worth special mention is the restaurant, an excellent steakhouse in an old log cabin by the side of the Gallatin River. | 42895 Gallatin, Big Sky | (406)995–4249 or (888)995–4249 | 8 rooms | $48–$78 | Closed the first week in Dec. and the week after Easter | V, MC, AE, D.

Lone Mountain Ranch. Secluded in a wooded spot near Yellowstone, the ranch puts you up in log cabins with fireplaces. The outdoor activities run year-round and include family adventures, fishing (with a professional guide, if you want), and great cross-country skiing. In winter, you can try a sleigh-ride dinner. Restaurant (*see* Lone Mountain Ranch Dining Room), bar, picnic area. No air-conditioning. Hot tub. Fishing. Cross-country skiing. Children's programs (June–Labor Day), playground. Laundry facilities. Airport shuttle. | Box 160069 | 406/995–4644 or 800/514–4644 | fax 406/9950–4670 | www.lmranch.com | 30 cabins | $3,235/wk 2 adults | D, MC, V | Closed Oct.–mid Dec. | AP.

Nine Quarter Circle Ranch. This working dude ranch set amid spectacular mountain scenery caters to families. Some cabins have fireplaces. Horse adventures include pack trips and wildlife-watching horseback trail rides. There's also an airstrip. Dining room. No air-conditioning. Pool. Horseback riding. Fishing. Children's programs (mid-June–mid-Sept.), playground. Laundry facilities. Airport shuttle. | 5000 Taylor Fork Rd., Gallatin Gateway | 406/995–4276 | www.ninequartercircle.com | 15 1-bedroom cabins, 8 2-bedroom cabins | $1,337/wk adult | No credit cards | Closed mid Sept.–mid May | AP.

Rainbow Ranch Lodge. At the base of Lone Mountain, away from Big Sky proper, this lodge has 16 rooms remodelled in the late 1990s, with private balconies overlooking the nearby river. You can ride, hike, fish, ski (in winter), and ride horses. Restaurant, hot tub. | 5 mi south of Big Sky on U.S. 191 | 406/995–4132 | www.rainbowranch.com | 16 rooms | $140–$250 | Closed May, Nov. | AE, D, MC, V.

River Rock Lodge. All of the spacious rooms feature down comforters, VCRs, and minibars; some have in-room data ports. Private shuttle and ski service. Complimentary Continental breakfast. Minibars, refrigerators. Cable TV, in-room VCRs (movies). Business services. Airport shuttle. No smoking. | 3080 Pine Dr. | 406/995–2295 or 800/995–9966 | fax 406/995–2727 | www.avicom.net/river-rock/ | 29 rooms | $115–$175, $215 suites | AE, D, DC, MC, V.

320 Guest Ranch. Luxurious log cabins are your accommodations here, some with fireplaces. The 320-acre ranch is close to Yellowstone. The staff includes professional fishing guides and wranglers. Chuckwagon barbecues and trail rides are popular. Restaurant, bar. Horseback riding. Fishing. Laundry facilities. | Mile Marker 36, U.S. 191 | 406/995–4283 or 800/243–0320 | fax 406/995–4694 | www.320ranch.com | 7 3-bedroom homes, 12 2-bedroom cabins, 40 1-bedroom cabins | $106–$121 cabins, $221–$290 2–bedroom cabins and 3–bedroom homes | MC, V.

BIGFORK

MAP 6, C3

(Nearby towns also listed: Columbia Falls, Kalispell)

Bigfork (population 3,000) is on a sheltered bay where the Swan River flows into Flathead Lake. The town is filled with art galleries, fine restaurants, specialty shops, and a challenging golf course; it also hosts special events each month. The Bigfork Summer Playhouse presents shows during the summer, and sports are good all year round.

Information: **Bigfork Chamber of Commerce** | Box 237, Bigfork, 59911 | 406/837–5888 | www.bigfork.org.

Attractions
Bigfork Art and Cultural Center. A nonprofit organization offering rotating exhibits of artists from western Montana. The center promotes the arts through lectures and performances.

The store sells local artists' work. The Bigfork Library is in the same building. The center is open in the off season, but hours are sporadic. | 535 Electric Ave. | 406/837–6927 | Free | Apr.–Dec., Tues.–Sat. 10–5.

Bigfork Summer Playhouse. One of the Northwest's finest repertory theaters is in this modern, air-conditioned, 450-seat facility. A showcase for local talent, the Bigfork Summer Playhouse starts each season in May with a comedy and follows with four musicals that run through August. | 526 Electric Ave. | 406/837–4886 | www.montanaweb.com/playhouse | Early season $15, regular season $18–$20 | May–Aug., Mon.–Sat. at 8 PM.

Flathead Lake Biological Station, University of Montana. Most of the year, you can tour this freshwater research lab that's halfway between Bigfork and Polson, although it restricts access June through August. | 311 Biostation La., at Yellowbay | 406/982–3301 | www.umt.edu/biology/flbs | Free | Weekdays 8–5.

Flathead National Forest, Swan Lake Ranger District. See Kalispell. | 406/837–7500.

Flathead State Park, Wayfarers Unit. This 68-acre state park has a 30-site campground, a boat dock, picnic tables, fishing, hiking trails, biking, and wildlife viewing. Look for it 5 mi south of Bigfork on Rte. 35. See also Kalispell for Flathead Lake State Park, West Shore Unit; Polson for East Shore units. | 406/752–5501 | www.state.mt.us | Day use $4, camping $12 | Daily.

Jewel Basin Hiking Area. These 35 mi of hiking trails take you through scenic meadows that offer great views of Flathead Lake and Valley. Trails can be used for day-trips and also for longer backbacking trips. | Echo Lake Rd (off Hwy. 33) | Free.

FLATHEAD LAKE TOURS

Questa. You can take a one- to two-hour cruise on Flathead Lake aboard a Q class racing sloop designed by L. Francis Herreshoff in 1929. Cruise length depends upon wind conditions. You need reservations; the craft holds only 18 persons. A shuttle boat departs from the Flathead Lake Lodge, 1 mi south of Bigfork, four times daily. | 150 Flathead Lake Lodge Rd. | 406/837–5569 | fax 406/837–5569 | Day cruise $20, sunset wine and cheese cruise $27 | May–Sept., daily at 10, 1, and 4; sunset cruise at 7 PM.

ON THE CALENDAR

MAY: *Bigfork Whitewater Festival.* International kayak racing on the "wild mile" of the Swan River through town. At the height of spring run-off, the stream is Class V white water. The event ends with a triathlon (mountain biking, canoeing, and running). | 406/837–9914.

MAY–AUG.: *Riverbend Concert Series.* Concerts are held in Everit L. Sliter Memorial Park every Sunday evening at 8. | 406/837–4848.

MAY–SEPT.: *Bigfork Summer Playhouse.* The repertory theater puts on five shows through August, four of them musicals. | 406/837–4886 or 837–6843 | www.montanaweb.com/playhouse.

Dining

Bigfork Inn. American. The old log cabin that houses this restaurant has a dance floor and bearskins on the wall. The menu is eclectic, all fresh and made to order. Local residents favor the prime ribs and fresh local fish. Try an emu steak. Kids' menu. | 604 Electric Ave. | 406/837–6680 | $12–$22 | AE, D, MC, V | No lunch.

Coyote Roadhouse. Contemporary. Just north of town you get a river view, silver service, and lots of antiques at this secluded restaurant. The veal and gumbo get high marks. Kids' menu. No smoking. | 602 Three Eagle La. | 406/837–4250 | $18–$22 | No credit cards | Closed Mon.–Tues. No lunch.

Showthyme. American. As its name suggests, it's close to where the shows are—right next door to Bigfork Summer Playhouse. Known for fresh seafood as well as beef, veal, and elk. Vegetarian meals are also available. You can dine outdoors on a patio that seats 40 at shaded tables with a view of the bay. Kids' menu. | 548 Electric Ave. | 406/837–0707 | $11–$21 | AE, D, MC, V | No lunch May–Sept.

Swan River Cafe and Dinner House. American. An elegant, comfortable restaurant that serves prime rib, seafood, and other fare. Dine on the terrace overlooking Bigfork Bay or indoors. Locals love the Sunday brunch and dinner buffets. | 360 Grand Ave. | 406/837–2220 | Reservations advised in summer | $12.95–$19.95 | AE, D, DC, MC, V.

Tuscany's. Italian. The local favorites are roasts and veal at this old converted farm house. You can dine inside in a rustic but elegant setting or choose the large deck with shaded tables and a view of the town, the river, and a lake. They have live jazz in summer. Kids' menu. No smoking. | 331 Bridge St. | 406/837–2505 | $12–$20 | AE, D, MC, V.

Lodging

Averill's Flathead Lake Lodge. This sprawling property has both log lodges and family cottages. You can choose to boat (motorboats, canoes, sailboats), take raft trips and lake cruises, water-ski, fly-fish (instruction available), or go white-water rafting. Dining room, picnic area. No air-conditioning. Pool. Tennis. Beach, boating, fishing. Business services. Airport shuttle. | 150 Flathead Lake Lodge Rd. | 406/837–4391 | fax 406/837–6977 | fll@digisys.net | www.averills.com/ | 19 rooms in lodge, 22 cottages | $2,063/wk adult all–inclusive | AE, MC, V | Closed Oct.–Apr.

Burggraf's Countrylane B & B. A modern 5,000-square-ft log house on seven acres bordering beautiful Swan Lake, seven miles south of Bigfork. All rooms have private baths and contemporary furnishings. Canoes, fishing. | Rainbow Dr., Bigfork | 406/837–4608 or 800/525–3344 | 5 rooms | $95–$130 | Closed Oct.–Apr. | No credit cards.

Marina Cay Resort. People come here for the water sports, but the accommodations are also a lure. Many of the rooms and suites have views of the water and mountains, and some have in-room Jacuzzis. The outdoor hot tub is open year-round. Bar, dining room, picnic area. Some microwaves, refrigerators. Cable TV, VCRs available. Pool. Boating. Fishing. Business services. | 180 Vista La. | 406/837–5861 or 800/433–6516 | fax 406/837–1118 | www.montanaweb.com/marinacay/ | 120 rooms | $109–$245 | AE, D, DC, MC, V.

O'Duach'ain Country Inn. In a quiet logdepole-pine forest near Flathead Lake and the Swan River, this lovely property has two log buildings. Rooms and common spaces are furnished with Old West antiques and Navajo rug wall hangings. Complimentary breakfast. No air-conditioning, no room phones, no TV in rooms. TV in common area, VCR available. Hot tub. Some pets allowed. No smoking. | 675 Ferndale Dr. | 406/837–6851, 800/837–7460 for reservations | fax 406/837–0778 | knollmc@aol.com | 5 rooms, 1 guest house | $89–$129 | AE, D, MC, V.

Schwartz's Bed and Breakfast. A half mile out of Bigfork, this charming bed and breakfast has a rural rustic setting and affordable rates. Take a dip in the private lake or use the communal canoe. The rooms are average size with shared baths. Canoes. Continental breakfast. | 890 McCaffrey Rd. | 406/837–5463 | 4 rooms | $45 | No credit cards.

Timbers. The rooms are contemporary and comfortable in this year-round establishment that's within walking distance of the village. Complimentary Continental breakfast. Cable TV. Pool. Hot tub, sauna. Laundry facilities. Pets allowed (fee). | 8540 Rte. 35 | 406/837–6200 or 800/821–4546 | fax 406/837–6203 | www.montanaweb.com/timbers | 40 rooms | $68 | AE, D, MC, V.

BIG TIMBER

MAP 6, G6

(Nearby town also listed: Livingston)

At the foot of the Crazy Mountains, this town of 1,750 is picturesque and lively. Explore the nearby Boulder Valley, fish in blue-ribbon trout streams, and stop by the Yellowstone River Trout Hatchery for an appreciation of cutthroat trout. The town has many

BIG TIMBER

INTRO
ATTRACTIONS
DINING
LODGING

museums, galleries, antiques shops, and historic sites, including the Crazy Mountain Museum.

Information: Big Timber Chamber of Commerce. | Box 1012, 59011 | 406/932–5131 | www.bigtimber.com.

Attractions

Box Canyon Trailhead. This trailhead, part of the 1-million-acre Absaroka Beartooth wilderness, leads to miles of spectacular wilderness hiking: be cautioned that the area is grizzly territory, so overnight stays require either a bear-proof food cannister or that all food be hung at least 10 feet off the ground. Phone for current trail conditions. | 50 mi south on Rte. 298 | 406/932–5155.

Crazy Mountain Museum. This beautiful building is filled with exhibits that represent Big Timber's history, its people, and the Crazy Mountains. Highlights include the Cramer Rodeo, sheep, and wool exhibits, and a room dedicated to pioneers with artifacts dating to the late 1890s. Other exhibits include a detailed miniature of Big Timber in 1907, the restored Sour Dough School House, and the "stabbur"—a reconstruction of an early Norwegian grain storehouse. | Cemetery Rd.; I–90 Exit 367 | 406/932–5126 | www.bigtimber.com/html/local_attractions.html | Donations accepted | Memorial Day–Labor Day, Tues.–Sun. 1–4, or by appointment.

Gallatin National Forest. *See* Bozeman. | U.S. 10 E | 406/932–5155. .

Greycliff Prairie Dog Town State Park. Ranchers don't like prairie dogs, but the animals are undeniably fascinating to observe. At this large prairie dog town, a preserved habitat, you can wander the trails for easy viewing. Watch for snakes. | Greycliff, I–90 Exit 377 | 406/247–2940 | www.bigtimber.com/html/local_attractions.html | $1 | May–Sept., daily dawn to dusk.

Natural Bridge State Park. The view of the 70-ft waterfall is spectacular from this river canyon along the Boulder River. The interpretive signs and trails are helpful, and you need good walking shoes. You can fish here and enter the Absaroka-Beartooth Wilderness. | 27 mi south of Big Timber via Rte. 298 | 406/247–2940 | www.lewisclark.org/m/mtparks.htm | Free | Daily dawn to dusk.

Yellowstone River Fish Hatchery. A biologist is usually on hand to explain the life cycle of the Yellowstone cutthroat trout. You can see all stages of the fish's development, from fingerlings to mature breeding stock. The hatchery is just a short stroll from downtown Big Timber. | ½ mi north on Fairgrounds Rd. | 406/932–4434 | www.bigtimber.com/html/local_attractions.html | Free | Daily 8–4:30.

ON THE CALENDAR

JUNE: *Big Timber Rodeo.* View an NRA-sanctioned rodeo with calf-roping, steer wrestling, bronc and bull riding, and barrel racing. | 406/932–6228.
JULY: *Yellowstone Boat Float.* The annual event begins at Livingston and ends at Laurel. | 406/248–7182.

Dining

The Grand. Continental. Built in 1890, this restaurant within a hotel has an elegant dark-green color scheme and antique paintings. The dining is casual, with a popular prime rib special on weekends and occasional exotic specials of antelope, ostrich, or buffalo. Locally raised lamb and beef are also popular, and the seafood is flown in fresh daily. Sun. brunch. Kids' menu. | 139 McLeod St. | 406/932–4459 | $14–$22 | D, MC, V.

Prospector Pizza. Italian. A favorite with locals who want good pizza and Italian fare in a casual setting with great prices. | 139 McLeod Street | 406/932–4846 | $3–7 | No credit cards.

Lodging

Grand Hotel. This historic brick bed-and-breakfast has been operating since 1890. The restored interior reflects that same ornate period. Though downtown, it has lovely views of the Crazy Mountains. Restaurant, complimentary breakfast. Cable TV. | 139 McLeod St. | 406/932–4459 | fax 406/932–4248 | www.thegrand-hotel.com | 10 rooms | $59–$145 | AE, D, DC, MC, V.

Lazy J. Right in the middle of town is the Lazy J, offering standard chain size rooms and modest, modern acommodations. | Hwy. 10 | 406/932–5532 | 20 | $55 | No credit cards.

Super 8. Spacious rooms and convenience to the interstate make this a good place to stop if you're passing through. Complimentary Continental breakfast. Cable TV. Laundry facilities. Pets allowed (fee). | I–90 Exit 367 (Rte. 10) | 406/932–8888 | fax 406/932–4103 | 39 rooms | $58–$81 | AE, D, DC, MC, V.

BILLINGS

(Nearby town also listed: Hardin)

Distinctive rock formations known as the Rimrocks surround Billings, the largest of Montana's cities, with 91,000 residents. As eastern Montana's retail, medical, cultural, and entertainment center, Billings is filled with museums, galleries, theaters, and shopping. You can take a historic town tour of Billings and Pompeys Pillar with Billings Trolley Tours. The University of Montana–Billings and Rocky Mountain College are here, too.

Information: Billings Chamber of Commerce | Box 31177, 59107 | 406/245–4111 or 800/735–2635 | www.billingscvb.visitmt.com.

Attractions

Alberta Bair Theater. The community fought to save this historic theater from demolition ten years ago. Now it is a cultural center, home to the Billings Symphony Orchestra and host to many other events. | 2801 3rd Ave. N | 406/256–6052 | www.albertabairtheater.org/.

Billings Area Visitor Center and Cattle Drive Monument. A heroic-size bronze sculpture of a cattle drover commemorates the "Great Montana Centennial Cattle Drive" of 1989 (which commemorated the drive of 1889). You can take guided tours of the center, study the exhibits, and gather all the information you'll need on area attractions. | 815 S. 27th St. | 406/252–4016 or 800/735–2635 | Free | Weekdays 8–5.

Boothill Swords Park Cemetery. H. M. Muggins Taylor was the army scout who carried word of Custer's defeat through 180 mi of hostile territory to Fort Ellis. He is only one of the many citizens and outlaws of early Billings buried here. | Airport and Main Sts.; north of Billings via Rte. 3 | 406/252–4016 | Free | Daily.

Chief Black Otter Trail. If you take this scenic trail atop the Rimrocks, you can visit the gravesite of famous frontier scout Yellowstone Kelly. The trail begins to the right of the Billings Logan International Airport. | 406/252–4016 | Free | Daily dawn to dusk.

Chief Plenty Coups State Park. The home and burial site mark the passing of the last chief of the Crow tribe. His log home and store remain as evidence of his efforts to lead his people to adapt to the white man's way of life. The site, with a visitor center and interpretive displays, is on the Crow Indian Reservation. Additional fees may be charged for special workshops or events. | 1 mi west of Pryor on Edger Rd. | 406/252–1289 | www.state.mt.us | $1 | May–Sept., daily 10–5.

Custer National Forest, Ashland and Sioux Districts. The rolling prairie, rock outcrops, and ponderosa pines of the Ashland and Sioux districts contrast dramatically with the western sections of the Custer National Forest. The Sioux District begins around Ekalaka at the far eastern edge of the state and extends into South Dakota; the Ashland spans the lands between Ashland and Broadus. You'll find good deer and turkey hunting in both places. *See* Red Lodge for information on the Beartooth Ranger District and Pryor Mountains Unit. | Custer Forest Supervisor's Office: 1310 Main St., Billings | 406/248–9885 or 406/784–2344 | www.fs.fed.us/r1/custer/main.html | Free | Daily.

Geyser Park. Go-carts, bumper boats, miniature golf, and laser tag give you an afternoon's diversion from sightseeing. | 4910 Southgate Dr.; I–90 Exit 447 | 406/254–2510 or 406/254–1563 | $4 per ride | Apr.–Oct., daily noon–11.

Lake Elmo State Park. Around a 64-acre reservoir in Billings Heights, the park is popular for hiking, swimming, fishing and other non-motorized boating. Concerts are occasionally held in the park. Site of the Beach Olympics. | U.S. 87 north to Pemberton La., then ½ mi west | 406/247–2940 | www.state.mt.us | $1 | Daily.

Peter Yegen, Jr—Yellowstone County Museum. Billings's first dental office—all of it—is one exhibit you'll see at this 1893 log cabin. The museum also has a chuckwagon, a barbed wire collection, clothing, and much more. Teddy Roosevelt attended meetings in this building and may have gazed out over the Yellowstone Valley, too, although the large veranda might not have been there in his day. | 1950 Terminal Circle; south of Billings Logan International Airport | 406/256–6811 | www.pyjrycm.com | Free | Weekdays 10:30–5, Sat. 10:30–3.

Pictograph Cave State Park. People who hunted woolly mammoths in the Yellowstone Valley documented their lives with paintings in caves that you can still explore. The pictographs, ¼ mi in from the park center, are almost 5,000 years old. Bring binoculars for the best view. Special workshops and events are conducted in the 23-acre park. Picnic area and hiking trails. | From Lockwood exit off I–90, 6 mi south on Coburn Rd. | 406/247–2940 | www.state.mt.us | $4 | May–Sept., daily.

Range Rider of the Yellowstone Museum. The museum displays a 400-piece gun collection, an 1880s-era Main Street scene, military and cowboy memorabilia, Native American artifacts, and pioneer photographs. | U.S. 10/12 W; from the Lockwood exit at Billings, 6 mi south on county road | 406/232–6146 | $3.50 | Apr.–Oct., daily 8–8.

Western Heritage Center. The main exhibit at this downtown museum, "Our Place in the West," is interactive and explores the social history of the Yellowstone region. In summer you can take tours to cultural sites. | 2822 Montana Ave. | 406/256–6809 | www.ohwy.com/mt/w/westhect.htm | Free | Tues.–Sun. 10–5; closed Sun. in Jan.

Yellowstone Art Center. The premier museum in a four-state region has Western and contemporary art from nationally and internationally known artists. | 401 N. 27th St. | 406/256–6804 | http://yellowstoneartmuseum.org | $5 | Tues.–Sun. 10–5; closed Jan.

ZooMontana. These zoological and botanical gardens specialize in northern-latitude temperate species. You can visit the children's zoo and see exotic and native animals and gardens. | 2100 S. Shiloh Rd. | 406/652–8100 | $5 | Daily 10–7.

TROLLEY TOURS

Billings Trolley. Ride on a replica of a 1930 trolley for a historic tour of Billings. You travel from Rimrock to the Yellowstone Valley with stops at local museums. On Wednesday evening ride ZooMontana and get a 3-hour expert tour with the zoo's director as your guide. The tour begins at 5:30, and you'll need reservations. | 888/618–4FUN | www.montana.net/funadventures/everything.html | Memorial Day–Labor Day.

ON THE CALENDAR

FEB.: *Northern Rodeo Association Finals.* Indoors at the MetraPark, the region's top 10 money winners compete on prime livestock in eight rodeo events for almost $60,000 in prize money. | 406/252–1122.

APR.–SEPT.: *Master's Series Concerts.* A series of seven concerts features varied composers and guest soloists. | 406/252–3610.

MAY: *Billings Micro Brew Festival.* There are more than 60 kegged microbrews, ciders, and root beers, with gourmet foods and 40 bottled wines. There's music and entertainment both days. | 406/675–2244.

MAY–DEC.: *Artwalk Downtown.* Established in 1994 to promote fine arts and crafts in Billings, this downtown event features artwork from participating galleries. | First Fri. in May, Aug., Oct., and Dec., 5–9 PM | 406/252–0122.

JUNE: *Big Sky Classic and Derby.* One of the largest horse shows in the Northwest attracts horses and riders from the West and Canada. | 406/494–3850.

JUNE: *Concert in the Park and Picnic on the Green.* One of the community favorites—an annual Billings Symphony Concert and picnic—draws more than 5,000 people for light classical music. | 406/252–3610.

JULY: *Summerfair.* Montana's finest juried arts and crafts festival gathers more than 100 artists from 20 states selling pottery, paintings, jewelry, stained glass, and more. There's ethnic and American food, as well as entertainment. | 406/256–6804.

JULY: *Big Skyfest.* Montana's premiere ballooning event also brings you a parade of balloons, fireworks show, laser shows, and more. | 406/255–0466 or 406/252–9355.

AUG.: *Montana Fair.* Attended by more than 200,000 people, this MetraPark event ranks as Montana's largest fair. You'll find concerts, rodeos, a carnival, food, animal exhibits, and many special events. | 406/256–2400 or 256–2422.

AUG.: *Billings Studio Theatre.* For more than 45 years, this community theater has dedicated itself to affordable quality entertainment—$7–$8. They also hold summer children's camps. | 1500 Rimrock Rd. | Weekends | 406/248–1141.

SEPT.: *Peaks to Prairies Triathlon.* The race begins with an 8.8-mi run south of Red Lodge, followed by a 43-mi bicycling leg from Red Lodge to Laurel, and finishes with a 22-mi boating leg on the Yellowstone River. | 406/245–1718.

OCT.: *Northern International Livestock Exposition.* A livestock show and sale also gives you a chance to see a farm and home trade show and five professional rodeo performances. | 406/256–2495.

Dining

Bruno's. Italian. Affordable Italian dishes are served in this casual family spot next to the fairgrounds. Housed in a 1920s building, the restaurant strives to keep the Art Deco look. They serve a good selection of pasta and veal. Kids' menu. | 1002 1st Ave. N | 406/248–4146 | $5–$15 | D, MC, V | Closed Sun. No lunch Sat.

Cafe Jones. Cafe. You get a wide range of coffee drinks and excellent homemade quiche in a 1950s-style bistro. | 2712 Second Ave. N., Billings | 406/259–7676 | $4–$9 | No credit cards.

Caramel Cookie Waffle. Cafe. Great soups and pastries. Home of the decadently delicious caramel cookie waffle. Closes at 5 p.m. | 1707 17th St., Billings | 406/252–1960 | Closed Sun. and Mon. | $2.25–$5.25 | MC, V.

CJ's Restaurant. Barbecue. Excellent mesquite grilled barbecue with a choice of three sauces, and a well-chosen wine list. | 2456 Central Ave., Billings | 406/656–1400 | $8.95–22.95 | AE, D, DC, MC, V.

El Burrito Cafeteria. Mexican. Burritos are the favorites at this downtown cafe that's popular with the local Hispanic community as well. The interior is standard Mexican kitsch. | 310 N. 29th St. | 406/256–5234 | Closed Sun. | $4–$8 | No credit cards.

George Henry's. Continental. Although the setting is elegant and Victorian, the atmosphere at this downtown restaurant is surprisingly laid-back. The favorites are prime rib, seafood pasta, and roasted crispy duck. Kids' menu. No smoking. | 404 N. 30th St. | 406/245–4570 | $21–$28 | AE, MC, V | Closed Sun. No lunch Sat.

Golden Belle. American. Billings's most elegant restaurant is downtown in the Radisson Northern Hotel. The specials are beef specially aged in-house, chicken, and seafood, including fresh catch specials. | 19 N. 28th St. | 406/245–2232 | Reservations essential for dinner | $24–$29 | AE, D, MC, V.

The Granary. Beef, seafood, chicken and a great salad bar, served in a restored flour mill. Outdoor seating in summer. Reservations advised. American. | 1500 Poly Dr., Billings | 406/259–3488 | Dinner only | $10–$30 | AE, D, MC, V.

Jake's. American. This more upscale downtown establishment is strong on steaks, seafood, and has an excellent salad bar. | 2701 First Ave. N, Billings | 406/259–9375 | Reservations advised | Dinner only on Saturday. Closed Sun. | $5.95–26.95 | AE, MC, V.

Juliano's. Contemporary. Seasonal, regional contemporary cuisine served in an intimate atmosphere. The menu is a mix of traditional Pacific Rim flavors blended with regional Montana cuisine. Try one of the fresh seafood entrées or the spit-roasted chicken. You can dine on a deck or patio with shaded tables and a view of the greenery beyond. No smoking. | 2912 7th Ave. N | 406/248–6400 | $24–$32 | AE, D, MC, V | Closed Sun. No dinner Mon.–Tues.

Matthew's Taste of Italy. Italian. The dining room's Romanesque furnishings match the cuisine at this casual family-style dining establishment. The local favorites are the diced grilled chicken and the pancetta. Kids' menu. | 1233 N. 27th St. | 406/254–8530 | $8–$15 | AE, D, MC, V.

Montana Brewing Company. American. Upscale pub menu with a beer for every taste, including its own specialty brews. It's popular for lunch and dinner; be prepared to wait. | 133 N. Broadway | 406/252–9200 | No reservations | $6–$13 | AE, D, MC, V.

Pug Mahon's. Irish. Good Irish stew, pasties, and other traditional Irish fare for lunch and dinner. Also a popular Sunday brunch, with more than a dozen specialty omelets and complimentary champagne. | 3011 First Ave. N | 406/259–4190 | Sunday brunch only | $4–$14 | MC, V.

Rex. American. Built in 1910 by Buffalo Bill Cody's chef, this restaurant was saved from the wrecking ball and restored in 1975. Now it's a Black Angus-certified steak house with plenty of seafood specials nightly. You can also try the Rex Patio Bar and Grill. Kids' menu. No smoking. | 2401 Montana Ave. | 406/245–7477 | $15–$29 | AE, D, DC, MC, V.

Torres Café. Mexican. The authentic Mexican food here reflects the influence of Montana's Hispanic population. | 6200 Frontage Rd. | 406/652–8426 | Closed Sun. and Mon. | $4.65–$12.95 | AE, D, MC, V.

Walkers Grill. American Bistro. Murals grace the walls, the furnishings are contemporary, and the atmosphere is casual here, although it's housed in the 100-year-old Chamber Building. Fresh fish and mountain lamb are the local favorites on a menu that also has pastas, salads, and Mediterranean pizza. Kids' menu. | 301 N. 27th St. | 406/245–9291 | $10–$21 | AE, D, MC, V | Closed Sun. No lunch.

The Windmill. American. A popular place with locals that specializes in chicken, steak, and shrimp. | 3921 1st Ave. S., Billings | 406/252–8100 | Reservations advised | $15–$24 | AE, D, MC, V.

Lodging

Best Western. A round-the-clock restaurant next door and proximity to I–90 make this a good stop for last-minute or late arrivals. Complimentary Continental breakfast. Cable TV. Indoor pool. Hot tub, sauna. Laundry facilities. Business services. Some pets allowed. | 5610 S. Frontage Rd. | 406/248–9800 or 800/528–1234 | fax 406/248–2500 | www.bestwestern.com | 80 rooms, 12 suites | $72–$87 | AE, D, DC, MC, V.

Best Western Ponderosa Inn. You'll find comfortable modern rooms at this hotel in downtown Billings. All rooms are done in pastels, and the courtyard is pleasant. Restaurant, bar. Cable TV. Pool. Sauna. Exercise equipment. Laundry facilities. Business services. Airport shuttle. Some pets allowed. | 2511 First Ave. N | 406/259–5511 or 800/628–9081 | fax 406/245–8004 | www.bestwestern.com | 130 rooms | $70–$78 | AE, D, DC, MC, V.

Billings Inn. Located in the downtown medical corridor, this inn has basic, comfortable rooms. Complimentary Continental breakfast. Some refrigerators, some microwaves. Cable TV. Laundry facilities. Airport shuttle. Some pets allowed (fee). | 880 N. 29th St. | 406/252–6800 or 800/231–7782 | fax 406/252–6800 | tbi@wtp.net | 60 rooms | $53, $59 suites | AE, D, DC, MC, V.

C'Mon Inn. The rooms are contemporary in design, spacious, and comfortable. You can splurge on a suite with an in-room Jacuzzi. The amenities are great. Complimentary Continental breakfast. Minibars, refrigerators (in suites). Cable TV. Indoor pool. Hot tub. Exercise equipment. Video games. Business services. | 2020 Overland Ave. | 406/655–1100 or 800/655–1170 | fax 406/652–7672 | 80 rooms, 8 suites | $68–$79, $104–$114 suites | AE, D, MC, V.

Comfort Inn. The rooms are modern and modest and equipped for the handicapped. Complimentary Continental breakfast. Some refrigerators. Cable TV. Indoor pool. Hot tub. Business services. Some pets allowed. | 2030 Overland Ave. | 406/652–5200 or 800/221–2222 | www.comfortinn.com | 60 rooms | $59–$90, $69 suites | AE, D, DC, MC, V.

Days Inn. The rooms have been refurbished, and some have spas. If you need a different kind of scenery, you're only 2½ mi from Montana's largest shopping center. Complimentary Continental breakfast. Cable TV. Hot tub. Laundry facilities. Some pets allowed. | 843 Parkway La. | 406/252–4007 or 800/329–7466 | fax 406/896–1147 | www.daysinn.com | 63 rooms | $60, $130 suites | AE, D, DC, MC, V.

Dude Rancher Lodge. This downtown institution is furnished in western style, and serves great breakfasts. Restaurant. | 415 N. 29th St. | 406/259–5561 or 800/221–3302 | 57 rooms | $50–$69 | AE, D, DC, MC, V.

Fairfield Inn By Marriott. The 63 rooms are specifically designed for the business traveler, and all have in-room data ports. The furnishings are contemporary. Complimentary Continental breakfast. Some refrigerators. Cable TV. Indoor pool. Hot tub. Game room. Business services. | 2026 Overland Ave. | 406/652–5330 or 800/228–2800 | fax 406/652–5330 | 63 rooms | $74 | AE, D, DC, MC, V.

Hilltop Inn. The Western look prevails in the lobby and halls, and the rooms are modest, modern, and comfortable. Complimentary Continental breakfast. Some refrigerators, some microwaves. Cable TV. Laundry facilities. Pets allowed. | 1116 N. 28th St. | 406/245–5000 or 800/878–9282 | fax 406/245–7851 | hilltop@wtp.net | 45 rooms | $53, $69 suites | AE, D, DC, MC, V.

Holiday Inn Billings Plaza. This place is convenient to everything—a mall, a water park, entertainment, and the airport. The traditional rooms were recently given a multimillion dollar face-lift. Some have whirlpools. Restaurant, lobby lounge. Some refrigerators, some microwaves. Cable TV, in-room VCRs. Indoor pool. Hot tub, sauna. Exercise equipment. Video game room. | 5500 Midland Rd.; I–90 Exit 446 | 406/248–7701 | fax 406/248–8954 | hi429sales@sagehotel.com | www.holiday-inn.com | 315 rooms and suites | $59–$69, $89–$225 suites | AE, D, DC, MC, V.

Howard Johnson Express. This is a new establishment with spacious rooms and contemporary design. Three conference rooms are available. Restaurant, bar. Cable TV. Laundry facilities. Business services. Airport shuttle. | 1001 S. 27th St. | 406/248–4656 or 800/654–2000 | fax 406/248–7268 | www.hojo.com | 173 rooms | $70, $89 suites | AE, D, DC, MC, V.

Josephine B & B. A lovely historic home within walking distance of downtown offering 5 themed rooms and a guest parlor with library, TV/VCR, and a piano, each room has a private bath. You get free guest passes to a local health club. | 514 N. 29th St., Billings | 406/248–5898 or 800/552–5898 | www.thejosephine.com | 5 rooms, all with private bath | $58–$140.

Quality Inn Homestead. A delightful outdoor sundeck and indoor swim center are the lures here. The rooms are contemporary in design and average in size. Restaurant, complimentary breakfast. Some refrigerators. Cable TV. Indoor pool. Hot tub, sauna. Laundry facilities. Airport shuttle. Pets allowed (fee). | 2036 Overland Ave. | 406/652–1320 or 800/228–5151 | fax 406/652–1320 | www.qualityinn.com | 119 rooms | $75–$79, $85 suites | AE, D, DC, MC, V.

Radisson Northern. The downtown location makes it easy for you to walk to shops, theaters, museums, and restaurants. The rooms are traditionally American in design and have recently been remodeled. Restaurant, bar. Some refrigerators. Cable TV. Exercise equipment. Business services. Airport shuttle. Some pets allowed. | 19 N 28th St. | 406/245–5121 or 800/

333–3333 | fax 406/259–9862 | www.radisson.com | 160 rooms | $79–$99, $119 suites | AE, D, DC, MC, V.

Ramada Limited. The fireplace in the lobby gives a touch of Western charm. Contemporary design best describes the rooms, and two-room Jacuzzi suites are also available. Complimentary Continental breakfast. Cable TV. Pool. Exercise equipment. Playground. Business services. Some pets allowed. | 1345 Mullowney La. | 406/252–2584 or 800/272–6232 | fax 406/252–2584 | www.ramada.com | 116 rooms | $50–$69, $150 suites | AE, D, DC, MC, V.

Rimview Inn. This clean, convenient motel boasts Montana's largest saltwater aquarium—a 1,000-gallon tank in the lobby. Free Continental breakfast is provided, and some rooms have hot tubs and full kitchens. | 1025 N. 27th St. | 406/248–2622 | fax 406/248–2622 | 34 rooms, 20 suites | $45–$60 | AE, D, DC, MC, V.

Scott B & B. Once a boarding house for miners, this modest bed and breakfast is now on the National Register of Historic Places. Restaurant (reservations required). Continental breakfast. | 15 W. Copper St. | 406/723–7030 | fax 406/782–1415 | www.butteamerica.com/scott.htm | 7 rooms | $75–$85 | AE, D, MC, V.

Sheraton. This high-rise encloses a pleasant and large central courtyard. The downtown location is convenient, and the contemporary rooms are spacious. Restaurant, bar. Some refrigerators. Cable TV. Indoor pool. Hot tub. Exercise equipment. Video game room. Business services. Airport shuttle. Some pets allowed. | 27 N. 27th St. | 406/252–7400 or 800/588–7666 | fax 406/252–2401 | www.sheraton.com/billings | 282 rooms | $99–$105, $145 suites | AE, D, DC, MC, V.

Sleep Inn. Standard modern design characterizes the rooms, and in-room data ports are a nice convenience for those who like to stay connected. The bathrooms have showers only, no bathtubs. Complimentary Continental breakfast. Cable TV. | 4904 Southgate Dr. | 406/254–0013 or 800/627–5337 | fax 406/254–9878 | www.hotelchoice.com | 75 rooms, shower only | $58–$61 | AE, D, DC, MC, V.

Super 8 Lodge. The rooms are standard and comfortable and rates are reasonable. Cable TV. Pets allowed (fee). | 5400 Southgate Dr. | 406/248–8842 or 800/800–8000 | fax 406/248–8842 | 115 rooms | $67–$75 | AE, D, DC, MC, V.

BOULDER

MAP 6, D6

(Nearby town also listed: Butte)

The Peace Valley derives its name from local American Indians, who designated this area between Helena and Butte as a sanctuary where no fighting was allowed. That peaceful spirit still lingers in Boulder with soothing mineral-spring baths and mind-clearing hikes in the surrounding mountains. With a population of about 1,600, Boulder offers a town center of historic red-brick buildings and the massive, gargoyle-bedecked Jefferson County Courthouse.

Information: Gold West Country Regional Tourism Office | 1155 Main St., Deer Lodge, MT 59722 | 406/846–1943 or 800/879–1159 | www.goldwest.visitmt.com.

Lodging

Boulder Hot Springs Hotel. Built in 1883, Boulder Hot Springs was the first permanent building in the area and one of Montana's earliest tourist bases, hosting various presidents and wealthy power brokers. It occupies 274 pine-filled acres bordering the Deer Lodge National Forest. The geothermal water is piped to indoor pools, with separate bathhouse facilities for men and women. The grand old hotel offers seven bed and breakfast rooms in Arts and Crafts style, plus five hotel rooms and 26 simpler rooms used to accommodate groups.

The Sunday brunch buffet is generous and popular. You can hike, fish and and ski, both cross-country and downhill, nearby. Hot springs pools. Cold swimming pool. Steam rooms. Massage. Fishing. | Box 930, Boulder; Off Hwy. 69 about 40 mi west of Helena | 406/225–4339 | fax 406/225–4345 | www.boulderhotsprings.com | 38 | $45–$90 | Full breakfast with B&B rooms | MC, V.

BOZEMAN

(Nearby towns also listed: Big Sky, Livingston, Three Forks, Virginia City)

Nestled in the scenic Gallatin Valley at the base of the Bridger Range, Bozeman combines a small-town atmosphere with big-city amenities. In this town of 32,000 you'll find art galleries, museums, a symphony, an opera, fly-fishing shops, and one-of-a-kind Western stores. The South Wilson Historic District, near the Montana State University campus, features homes ranging from stately mansions to small cottages. For area history and artifacts, visit the Gallatin County Pioneer Museum. For 4 billion years of Northern Rockies history and one of the best museums in the state, visit the Museum of the Rockies at the south edge of the MSU campus.

Information: Bozeman Chamber of Commerce | Box B, Bozeman, 59771 | 406/586–5421 or 800/228–4224 | www.bozemanchamber.com.

Attractions

American Computer Museum. This is only the second museum in the world dedicated entirely to the history of the computer. The design is geared for all ages. | 234 E. Babcock St. | 406/587–7545 | www.compustory.com | $3 | June–Aug., daily 10–4; May and Sept., Tues., Wed., Fri., Sat. noon–4; Oct.–Apr., Tues.–Sat. noon–4.

Bridger Bowl Ski Area. You will find everything a skier could want here, 16 mi northeast of Bozeman. More than 60 runs cover 2,000 acres of Gallatin National Forest. There's 2,000 vertical ft of lift-served terrain, with 500 additional vertical ft on nearly 400 acres. The average snowfall is 350 inches. There's skiing instruction, two cafeterias, a full-service bar, day

PACKING IDEAS FOR COLD WEATHER

- ❏ Driving gloves
- ❏ Earmuffs
- ❏ Fanny pack
- ❏ Fleece neck gaiter
- ❏ Fleece parka
- ❏ Hats
- ❏ Lip balm
- ❏ Long underwear
- ❏ Scarf
- ❏ Shoes to wear indoors
- ❏ Ski gloves or mittens
- ❏ Ski hat
- ❏ Ski parka
- ❏ Snow boots
- ❏ Snow goggles
- ❏ Snow pants
- ❏ Sweaters
- ❏ Thermal socks
- ❏ Tissues, handkerchief
- ❏ Turtlenecks
- ❏ Wool or corduroy pants

*Excerpted from *Fodor's: How to Pack: Experts Share Their Secrets*
© 1997, by Fodor's Travel Publications

care, and many events throughout the year. | 15795 Bridger Canyon Rd. | 406/586–1518 or 800/223–9609 | fax 406/587–1069 | www.bridgerbowl.com | $33 | Dec. 12–Apr. 4, daily 9–4.

Emerson Cultural Center. You can watch artists at work; take classes in conversational French, swing dancing, or cartooning; or attend a rock concert or civic forum. This historic building showcases all the visual and performing arts. The Cafe International is open for lunch, dinner, and Sunday brunch, and the menu is indeed international. | 111 S. Grand Ave. | 406/587–9797 | Free | Weekdays 10–5.

Gallatin County Pioneer Museum. The building served as the county jail for 70 years, the site for one man's hanging in 1924. The gallows and several jail cells remain. You'll also find hundreds of artifacts, automobiles, Northern Plains crafts, and a model of nearby Fort Ellis. | 317 W. Main St. | 406/522–8122 | www.pioneermuseum.org | Free | Oct.–May, Tues.–Fri. 11–4, Sat. 1–4; June–Sept., weekdays 10–4:30, Sat. 1–4.

Gallatin National Forest. The national forest includes the Absaroka Wilderness and part of the Beartooth Wilderness, and has 37 campgrounds. Tour scenic Gallatin Canyon, an 80-mi drive south of Bozeman on U.S. 191 along the Gallatin River. The road skirts the Spanish Peaks and enters the northwest corner of Yellowstone Park. You can fish, go white-water rafting, and watch wildlife. Additional ranger stations are in Big Timber, Gardiner, Hebgen, and Livingston. | Forest Supervisor's Office: 10 E. Babcock Ave.; Bozeman Ranger Station: 3710 Fallon St. | 406/587–6701 or 406/932–5155 | www.fs.fed.us/r1/gallatin | Most campgrounds are free; others $8–$9 per site per day plus $5 for each additional vehicle. Admission has gone up to from $10 to 20. | Daily.

Hyalite Canyon. Accessible to disabled people, this recreation area has hiking trails, waterfalls, fishing, picnicking, and camping areas. | 19th Ave. 4 mi south of Bozeman | 406/522–2520 | Free | Daily.

Montana State University. Founded in 1893 as Montana's land-grant institution, Montana State University–Bozeman is a comprehensive research university with approximately 12,000 students. | W. Kagy Blvd. | 406/994–6617 | www.montana.edu | Weekdays 8–5.
The university's **Museum of the Rockies** at the south edge of campus has lifelike displays and rooms full of flora and fauna as well as the Kirk Hill Nature Trail, a world-class dinosaur display, and a planetarium. The interactive exhibits provide a kid-friendly education. You can participate in dinosaur digs on the museum-sponsored summer field trips. | 600 W. Kagy Blvd. | 406/994–3466 | www.montana.edu/wwwmor/visit.html | $7; planetarium $3.50; laser shows $5 | Memorial Day–Labor Day, daily 8–8; Labor Day–Memorial Day, Mon.–Sat. 9–5, Sun. 12:30–5.
The university is the venue for large events such as rodeos, concerts, and home shows, held the **Fieldhouse.** | 11th Ave. and Grant St. | 406/994–7117.

ADVENTURE TRIPS

Backcountry Bicycle Tours. You'll get a different perspective on an inn-to-inn bicycle tour of Glacier, Yellowstone, and the Bozeman area. Most tours are on back roads. | Box 4029 | 406/586–3556 | May–Oct.

Montana Whitewater. Guided white-water raft trips will take you down the Gallatin or Yellowstone Rivers. Full-day, half-day, and dinner trips are available, as well as horseback/raft packages and kayak and canoe instruction. | 406/763–4465 or 800/799–4465 | www.montanawhitewater.com | May–Sept.

ON THE CALENDAR

JAN.: *Montana Winter Fair.* A winter county fair that's complete with livestock show and sale, food, photography, arts and crafts, exhibits, a Western rendezvous, and entertainment, all at the Gallatin County Fairgrounds. | 406/585–1397.

APR.: *MSU Indian Club Powwow.* A Native American festival at Montana State University features traditional dancing, foods, and arts and crafts. | 406/994–3751 or 406/994–4880.

JUNE–AUG.: *Shakespeare in the Parks.* For more than 25 years, this professional theater company in residence at Montana State University has brought classical theater to the parks and fields of Montana. For tour schedule and show information, call or write. | SUB Room 354, Montana State University, | June–Aug. | 406/994–3901.

JULY: *Gallatin County Fair.* Cows, sows, plows, computers, four-wheel-drive mud bog races, food, traditional livestock shows, carnival rides, arts and crafts, and music—all at the Gallatin County Fairgrounds | 406/582–3270.

AUG.: *Quilting the Country Outdoor Quilt Show.* As many as 500 quilts have been featured in past events, all displayed outdoors on the Quinn's farmstead buildings and fences. There are quilting demonstrations and trunk shows. | 406/587–8216.

AUG.: *Sweet Pea Festival.* An arts and crafts festival, this event held in Lindley Park, on the east end of town, also has food booths, bands, and theatrical performances. | 406/586–4003.

AUG.: *Taste of Bozeman.* A fun-filled dining experience downtown on Main Street is seasoned with music and entertainment. Seated dinners require reservations, but there's also snacking along the sidewalk. | 406/586–4003.

OCT.: *Bridger Mountain Raptor Festival.* Witness the biggest known migration of golden eagles in North America. Held at the Bridger Bowl Ski Area, the festival activities include slide shows on raptor identification and kid's programs. You can hike to the summit of Bridger Bowl to see as many as 17 different raptor species. | 406/586–1518.

Dining

Bacchus Pub. American. This downtown old German-style pub serves burgers, soups, salads, and daily specials for breakfast, lunch, and dinner. Try smoked chicken fettuccini. Kids' menu. | 105 W. Main St. | 406/586–1314 | $10–$15 | AE, D, MC, V.

Bistro. Eclectic. The Bistro offers a wide menu with an emphasis on seafood; also features Mexican dishes, stir fry, two-story omelets, and an award-winning wine list. | 242 E. Main St., Bozeman | 406/587–4100 | Reservations advised | Closed Sun. and Mon. | $16–26 | AE,D,MC,V.

Gallatin Gateway Inn. Continental. The food is great and elegantly presented, and you get to view the mountains, too. Try the prime rib or salmon. Kids' menu. Sun. brunch. | U.S. 191 | 406/763–4672 | Reservations essential | $24–$32 | AE, D, MC, V | No lunch.

John Bozeman Bistro. Eclectic. The menu is small, but one of the best in the state. Fresh seafood specials are flown in every day. You'll find Pacific Rim, Asian, and classical French entrées on the menu. The restaurant is downtown in the oldest brick building on the Historical Register. Kids' menu. No smoking. | 242 E. Main St. | 406/587–4100 | Reservations essential for dinner | $24–$29 | AE, D, MC, V | Closed Mon. No dinner Sun.

Leaf and Bean Coffee House. American. Stop here when you need a break from exploring downtown, and have a light meal or homemade pastries and desserts, plus a good selection of coffee and tea. You can also buy coffee in bulk. Thursday, Friday, and Saturday you can hear live music. No smoking. | 35 W. Main St. | 406/587–1580 | $6–$10 | MC, V.

Mackenzie River Pizza. Italian. The authentic Western atmosphere is great fun at this reasonably priced downtown eatery. Enjoy your pizza with salads, microbrew beers on tap, and specialty wines. | 232 E. Main St. | 406/587–0055 | $10–$15 | AE, D, MC, V.

Pickle Barrel. Delicatessen. Take-out deli sandwiches for lunch and dinner. Very popular with local college students. Picnic benches available for outdoor dining. Try the Philly cheese steak. | 809 W. College St.; 209 E. Main St., Bozeman | 406/587–2411 (College St. location) or 406/582–0020 | $4.50–$5 | No credit cards.

Spanish Peaks Brewery and Italian Cafe. Italian. This brewpub and restaurant has a large circular bar and separate dining area that's both spacious and uncrowded. The freshly brewed beers are good and so are the great desserts and breads that the pastry chef creates. The pasta is made fresh daily. Chef's specials include black pepper fettuccine with sausage and rotisserie chicken. No smoking. | 120 N. 19th St. | 406/585–2296 | $8–$27 | D, MC, V.

Lodging

Bozeman's Days Inn and Conference Center. The contemporary rooms have been refurbished, and all have in-room data ports, especially convenient if you're attending a convention. The Gallatin Valley setting offers good views of surrounding mountains and forest. Complimentary Continental breakfast. Cable TV. Hot tub, sauna. Business services. Pets allowed (fee). | 1321 N. 7th Ave. | 406/587–5251 or 800/987–3297 | fax 406/587–5351 | 80 rooms | $88–$99 | AE, D, DC, MC, V.

Bridger Inn B&B. Four rooms with western decor north of town in the Bridger foothills; full breakfast. | 3691 Bridger Canyon Rd., Bozeman | 406/586–6666 | fax 406/586–6666 | 4 rooms | $75 | MC, V.

Comfort Inn. In-room VCRs and data ports are nice extras, and the downtown location is convenient. In-room data ports, in-room VCRs. Cable TV. Indoor pool. Hot tub. Exercise equipment. Laundry facilities. Business services. | 1370 N. 7th Ave. | 406/587–2322 or 800/587–3833 | fax 406/587–2423 | www.comfortinn.com | 87 rooms | $80–$89, $98 suites | AE, D, DC, MC, V.

Fairfield Inn by Marriott. The rooms were designed with business travelers in mind and have spacious work areas and in-room data ports. There's one conference room. Complimentary Continental breakfast. Refrigerators (in suites). Cable TV. Indoor pool. Business services. | 828 Wheat Dr. | 406/587–2222 or 800/228–2800 | 57 rooms | $72–$84 | AE, D, DC, MC, V.

Fox Hollow Bed & Breakfast. You get a great combination of comfort, peace, and hospitality at this country-style home built in 1993. The country setting means panoramic views, with mountains and wide-open spaces. The hospitality is pure Montana; the atmosphere relaxed; the breakfasts terrific. Complimentary breakfast. TV in sitting room. Hot tub. No smoking. | 545 Mary Rd. | 406/582–9752 or 800/431–5010 | www.foxhollowbandb.com | 5 rooms | $79–$129 | AE, MC, V.

Gallatin Gateway. Built by the Milwaukee Railroad as a stopping-off point for visitors to Yellowstone, this sumptuous inn is conveniently situated in a great area for mountain biking (the hotel offers rentals). Restaurant (see Gallatin Gateway Inn), bar, complimentary Continental breakfast. No air-conditioning in some rooms. Cable TV. Pool. Hot tub. Tennis. Bicycles. Airport shuttle. | 76405 Gallatin Rd. (U.S. 191) | 406/763–4672 or 800/676–3522 | fax 406/763–4672 | www.gallatingatewayinn.com | 35 rooms | $120–$160 | AE, D, MC, V.

Holiday Inn. Bozeman's largest full-service hotel has quiet, spacious, comfortable rooms. Restaurant, bar, picnic area, room service. Some refrigerators. Cable TV. Indoor pool. Hot tub. Exercise equipment. Laundry facilities. Business services. Airport shuttle. Pets allowed. | 5 Baxter La. | 406/587–4561 or 800/366–5101 | fax 406/587–4413 | www.bznholinn.com/ | 178 rooms | $99, $129–$149 suites | AE, D, DC, MC, V.

Holiday Inn Express. You get beautiful mountain views and standard contemporary rooms here. Skiing is close by, and you can relax in the cozy lobby after a day on the slopes. In-room data ports. Cable TV. Hot tub. Pets allowed. No smoking. | 6261 Jackrabbit La. | 406/388–0800 or 800/542–6791 | fax 406/388–0804 | www.holiday-inn.com | 67 rooms | $72–$82 | AE, D, DC, MC, V.

Lehrkind Mansion B&B. A thoroughly restored 1897 Queen Anne–style mansion, plushly furnished with period antiques. The gourmet breakfasts are first-rate. Full breakfast. | 719 N. Wallace Ave. | 406/582–6932 or 800/992–6932 | www.bozemanbedandbreakfast.com | 5 rooms, 3 with bath | $78–$158 | AE, MC, V.

Lindley House Bed & Breakfast. The Joseph M. Lindley House was built in 1889 by one of Bozeman's early pioneers. The charming and distinctive Victorian manor is listed on the National Register of Historic Places. The house has been completely restored and now has dramatic French wall coverings, antique beds, fireplaces, stained-glass windows, a hot tub, and an enclosed English garden. You can walk to restaurants, shops, galleries, and theaters. Complimentary breakfast. No air-conditioning, some room phones. Cable TV. Kids over 10 only.| 202 Lindley Pl | 406/587–8403 | fax 406/582–8112 | www.avicom.net/lindley | 8 rooms (2 share bath, 4 with shower only) | $75–$350 (rate depends on room choice) | MC, V.

Mountain Sky Guest Ranch. Plenty of blue-ribbon trout fishing, children's programs, and gourmet meals make this a good place for the whole family. The atmosphere is relaxed, and the scenery is spectacular. Refrigerators, no room phones. Pool. Hot tub, sauna. Tennis. Fly-fishing. Hiking, boating. Playground, kids' programs. Business services. Airport shuttle. | Box 1128 | 406/333–4911 or 800/548–3392 | fax 406/587–3977 (winter) | mountainsky@mcn.net | 27 cabins, 1–3 bedrooms | $2,240 wk per person, including meals and activities, based on double occupancy | AE, D, MC, V | Closed Oct.–Apr. | AP.

Ramada Limited. A 40-ft water slide and great views of the mountains are the lures at this chain establishment. The reasonably priced suites make it a good choice for families. Complimentary Continental breakfast. Cable TV. Indoor pool. Hot tub. Pets allowed. | 2020 Wheat Dr. | 406/585–2626 | fax 406/585–2727 | 50 rooms, shower only | $84, $99 suites | AE, D, DC, MC, V.

Royal 7 Budget Inn. Small and homey, this inn has Western furnishings and several fireplaces. The staff is friendly, and you can walk to downtown and the university. Picnic area, complimentary Continental breakfast. Cable TV. Hot tub. Playground. Business services. Pets allowed. | 310 N. 7th Ave. | 406/587–3103 or 800/587–3103 | www.avicom.net/royal7 | 47 rooms | $51, $69 suites | AE, D, DC, MC, V.

Sleep Inn. Five suites, good for families, augment the comfortable, standard contemporary rooms. You can ski at the Bridger Bow ski area, a 15-minute drive. Downtown Bozeman is 2 mi away. Complimentary Continental breakfast. Some refrigerators. Cable TV. Indoor pool. Hot tub, sauna. Pets allowed. | 817 Wheat Dr. | 406/585–7888 or 800/377–8240 | fax 406/585–8842 | www.sleepinn.com/hotel/MT410 | 56 rooms, shower only | $79–$99 | AE, D, DC, MC, V.

TLC Inn. This two-story country lodging several miles outside town has a homey feel and a fireplace in the lobby. Some extra-large rooms are available. The inn has small but pleasant grounds surrounding it. Complimentary Continental breakfast. Cable TV. Hot tub, sauna. | 805 Wheat Dr. | 406/587–2100 or 877/466–7852 | www.tlc-inn.com | 42 rooms | $66–$68 | AE, D, DC, MC, V.

Torch & Toes Bed & Breakfast. This lovely, comfy inn has turn-of-the-20th-century furnishings, oak fixtures, and mountain views. Complimentary breakfast. No air-conditioning. No room phones. TV in common area. No smoking. | 309 S. 3rd Ave. | 406/586–7285 or 800/446–2138 (outside MT) | fax 406/585–2749 | www.avicom.net/torchntoes | 4 rooms in 2 buildings | $80 | MC, V.

Voss Inn. A restored 100-year-old brick mansion, the Voss Inn has six distinctive rooms, most furnished in Victorian style. Afternoon tea is served in the Victorian parlor, and the cottage perennial garden is lovely. Complimentary breakfast. TV in sitting room. No smoking. | 319 S. Willson Ave. | 406/587–0982 | fax 406/585–2964 | www.bozeman-vossinn.com | 6 rooms, (2 with air-conditioning) | $95–$115 | AE, MC, V.

Western Heritage. Five blocks from downtown, this hotel has some suites with fireplaces and full kitchens as well as standard rooms. Complimentary Continental breakfast. Some in-room hot tubs. Cable TV. Steam room. Exercise equipment. Laundry facilities. Business services. Pets allowed. | 1200 E. Main St. | 406/586–8534 or 800/877–1094 | fax 406/587–8729 | www.avicom.net/westernheritage | 38 rooms | $78, $115–$125 suites | AE, D, DC, MC, V.

BROWNING

MAP 6, D2

(Nearby town also listed: Columbia Falls)

Headquarters for the Blackfeet Nation, Montana's largest Native American tribe, Browning is just outside Glacier National Park. The town's premier event is its North

American Indian Days, held the second week of July. You can tour a tepee village and the reservation and go to a rodeo, as well as camp, fish, hunt, boat, horseback ride, and watch wildlife.

Information: **Blackfeet Nation** | Box 850, Browning, 59417 | 406/338–7406 | www.black-feetnation.com.

Attractions

Museum of Montana Wildlife and Hall of Bronze. Bob Scriver, Montana's best-known sculptor, combines his love of wildlife art and taxidermy in a studio with many works of art. | U.S. 2 and 89 | 406/338–5425 | www.lewisclark.org/s/scrmumwl.htm | Free | May–Sept., daily 9–7.

Museum of the Plains Indian. A comprehensive collection of artifacts from the tribes of the Northern Plains. | U.S. 2 and 89 | 406/338–2230 | $4 | June–Sept., daily 9–4:45; Oct.–May, weekdays 10–4:30.

ON THE CALENDAR

JULY: *North American Indian Days.* The largest Blackfeet tribal event hosts Native Americans from every region of the United States and Canada. You can watch traditional drumming and dancing contests, the crowning of Miss Blackfeet, and a parade, and take a fun run. | 406/338–7276.

Lodging

War Bonnet Lodge. Convenient to many local attractions, this small motel has few amenities but modest rates. Restaurant, bar. Cable TV. | U.S. 2 | 406/338–7610 | fax 406/338–2142 | 35 rooms | $59 | AE, MC, V.

BUTTE

MAP 6, D6

(Nearby towns also listed: Anaconda, Deer Lodge)

Steeped in century-old mining history, Butte became a melting pot of ethnic diversity as immigrants flocked to work here after the discovery of gold, silver, and a vast vein of copper. The Anselmo Mine Yard (open seasonally) in uptown Butte is the best surviving example of surface support facilities that once served the mines. Butte is home to Montana Tech and the free Mineral Museum, which displays 1,500 specimens, including a 27.5-ounce gold nugget. The population is 35,000. You can get walking tour brochures and information on this historic community at the Chamber of Commerce, or catch a tour of town on a vintage streetcar (June–Sept.).

Butte is also the closest major city to Big Hole National Battlefield, site of a tragic engagement between the nontreaty bands of the Nez Percé and the 7th Calvary led by Colonel John Gibbon on August 9–10, 1877. This battle was the turning point in the Nez Percé War of 1877. Today the National Park Service interprets and maintains the battlefield, which is open all year.

Information: **Butte–Silver Bow Chamber of Commerce** | 1000 George, Butte, 59701 | 406/723–3177 or 800/735–6814 | www.butteinfo.org.

Attractions

Arts Chateau Museum. This elegant 1898 four-story Victorian mansion was converted into gallery space and an interactive youth center. The collection includes 18th-and 19th-century furniture, textiles, and collectibles as well as art. | 321 W. Broadway | 406/723–7600 | www.artschateau.org | $3 | Tues.–Sat. 11–4.

Beaverhead-Deerlodge National Forest. *See* Deer Lodge. | Butte Ranger District: 1820 Meadowlark | 406/494–2147.

Big Hole Battlefield National Monument. The battle between Chief Joseph and the Nez Percé tribe and the U.S. Army was fought here. A visitor center explains the significance of the Nez Percé Indian War and includes exhibits on the Native American combatants and examples of military clothing and equipment. You can follow trails to historical reference points around the battlefield or take one of the scheduled ranger-guided tours conducted daily in summer. | Rte. 43, Wisdom | 406/689–3155 | www.nps.gov/biho/ | June–Aug. only, $2 per person, $4 per family | June–Aug., daily 8–6; Sept.–May, daily 9–5.

Copper King Mansion. Built in 1880 as the home for copper king William A. Clark, this 34-room mansion is lavishly furnished with antiques and also operates a bed-and-breakfast. Tours are available. | 219 W. Granite St. | 406/782–7580 | www.lewisclark.org/c/cokingma.htm | $5 | Apr.–Oct., daily 9–4, or by appointment.

Humbug Spires Primitive Area. You can go rock climbing and hiking, and investigate the geology of the unusual limestone rock formations. | 26 mi south off I–15 | 406/494–5059 | Free | Daily.

Montana Tech of the University of Montana. Undergrad and graduate degrees in engineering, science, and technology are granted here. | 1300 W. Park St. | 406/496–4266 | www.mtech.edu | Free | Daily.
The **Mineral Museum** on the campus of Montana Tech displays hundreds of objects, including a 27.5-ounce gold nugget. | 1300 W. Park St. | 406/496–4414 | www.mbmg-sun.mtech.edu | Free | Weekdays 9–4, and by appointment.

Our Lady of the Rockies. This tall statue stands above the city on the Continental Divide. You can tour it in summer. | 3100 Harrison Ave. | 406/782–1221 or 800/800–5239 | www.ourladyoftherockies.org | Tours $10 | June–Sept., daily, weather permitting; tours at 10 and 2, also at noon and 4 depending on demand.

Pioneer Mountains Scenic Byway. No highway number identifies this 41-mi stretch of backcountry road surrounded by a half-million acres of peaks, lakes, and headwaters in the Pioneer Mountains. You can drive straight through or stop to camp, hike the trails, fish, or visit the ghost town of Coolidge and remnants of the old Elkhorn Mill. | I–15 south to Divide/Wise River Exit, 23 mi to Wise River, south on national scenic byway | 406/683–3900 | skimt.com/other/scenicmontana.htm | Free | Apr.–Nov., daily; closed Dec.–May.

World Museum of Mining and 1899 Mining Camp. This turn-of-the-20th-century mining camp is a national historic site and has more than 36 structures on 12 acres. You can take a train ride around the museum on the *Orphan Girl Express*. | W. Park St. at Granite St. | www.lewisclark.org/w/womusmi.htm | $4 | Apr.–Oct., daily 9–6.

TOURS
Trolley Tour on Old No. 1. Take a 1½-hr tour through Butte (with two stops) on a one-of-a-kind old-time trolley. You sign up at the Chamber of Commerce office. | 1000 George St. | 800/735–6814 | www.lewisclark.org/t/trotouol.htm | $5 | June–Aug., weekdays 4 tours daily; Sept., weekdays 2 tours daily.

ON THE CALENDAR
MAR.: *St. Patrick's Day Events.* A legendary downtown St. Patrick's Day celebration starts March 16 with a concert, run, banquet, and the crowning of St. Urho (a fictional Finnish saint). The parade is on March 17 at noon. Bagpipers perform all over town. | 800/735–6814.
JULY: *4th of July Freedom Festival.* Concerts, a street dance, children's activities, patriotic ceremonies, fireworks, and a parade celebrate the holiday for several days. | 406/782–0742 or 491–3610.
JULY: *Vigilante Rodeo.* Professional riders compete in all events, including bronc riding, bull riding, bareback riding, barrel racing, and calf-roping. Lots of clowns. | 406/494–4867.

AUG.: *Butte–Silver Bow County Fair.* Butte's southwest Montana fair has arts and crafts, food booths, farm animals, a petting zoo, horse shows, a rodeo, and entertainment. | 406/723–8262.

AUG.: *Commemoration of the Battle of the Big Hole.* Ceremonies, demonstrations, traditional music, and park rangers help you understand this battle, which was fought August 9–10, 1877, between the U.S. military and the Nez Percé. The events are at Big Hole National Battlefield on Route 43. | 406/689–3155.

Dining

Lydia's. Continental. The menu at this traditional supper club favors meats, pasta, and seafood. The stained-glass windows give the place an Old World feel. Kids' menu. | 4915 Harrison Ave. | 406/494–2000 | $15–$60 | AE, D, MC, V | No lunch.

Spaghettini's. Italian. An authentic Italian restaurant—furnishings, music, and cuisine. The menu has many kinds of homemade pastas and sauces, in fact everything is made on the premises, including the breads. You can eat outside on the large deck overlooking the street. | 804 Utah Ave. | 406/782–8855 | $10–$22 | AE, D, MC, V.

Uptown Cafe. American. Here you'll find cafeteria-style lunches with choice of two soups, two entrées, and salads. Dinners are more dressed up, with four-course meals highlighting veal, poultry, and pastas. Decorative-art shows change monthly. | 47 E. Broadway | 406/723–4735 | $10–$23 | AE, D, MC, V | No lunch Sun.

Lodging

Comfort Inn. A TownHouse Inn of Montana, this place has some standard rooms equipped with the basics and some suites with microwaves, refrigerators, and hot tubs. Some rooms have in-room data ports. Complimentary Continental breakfast. Cable TV. Hot tubs. Exercise equipment. Laundry facilities. Business services. Airport shuttle. Pets allowed (fee). | 2777 Harrison Ave. | 406/494–8850 or 800/442–4667 | fax 406/494–2801 | 150 rooms | $80–$122 | AE, D, DC, MC, V.

Ramada Inn Copper King Park Hotel. You'll find lots of amenities here at the foot of the Rockies, as well as mountain views. Each room has a coffeemaker, direct-dial phone, data port, voice mail, an in-room safe, and heat and air conditioning controls. Restaurant, bar, room service. Cable TV. Indoor pool. Indoor tennis. Exercise equipment. Laundry facilities. Business services. Airport shuttle. Pets allowed. | 4655 Harrison Ave. S | 406/494–6666 or 800/332–8600 | fax 406/494–3274 | www.ramadainncopperking.com | 150 rooms | $89–$94, $175 suites | AE, D, DC, MC, V.

Super 8. The standard rooms here are reliably comfortable. Complimentary Continental breakfast. Cable TV. | 2929 Harrison Ave. | 406/494–6000 or 800/800–8000 | fax 406/494–6000 | 104 rooms | $60–$75 | AE, D, DC, MC, V.

War Bonnet Inn. This is a good place if you're here in the dead of winter—they have plug-in automobile block heaters. A newer facility, it also offers convention services. Room service. Cable TV. Indoor pool. Hot tub, sauna. Exercise equipment. Convention center. Airport shuttle. Pets allowed. | 2100 Cornell Ave. | 406/494–7800 or 800/443–1806 | fax 406/494–2875 | www.wbibutte.com | 131 rooms | $69, $99–$125 suites | AE, MC, V.

CHINOOK

MAP 6, G2

(Nearby town also listed: Havre)

A friendly small town of 1,200 on Montana's Hi-Line. A must-see while in Chinook is the Bear Paw Battlefield, 16 mi south of town, the site of Nez Percé Chief Joseph's surrender on October 5, 1877. Fox holes dug by Nez Percé warriors are still visible, as are the scars of bullets on rocks. A park ranger is available by appointment. For area history and artifacts, visit the Blaine County Museum.

Information: Chinook Chamber of Commerce | Box 744, Chinook, 59523 | 406/357–2100.

Attractions

Bear Paw Battleground. This is the site of the surrender of Chief Joseph and the Nez Percé tribe on October 5, 1877, after a 1,700-mi retreat. It is now a unit of the Nez Percé National Historic Park managed by the National Park Service. You can take self-guided walks and picnic, and there are rest rooms. | 15 mi south on Rte 240 | 406/357–3130 | www.havremt.com/bearpaw.htm | Free | Daily.

Blaine County Museum. You can see more of history at this museum filled with Native American artifacts from the Bear Paw Battlefield and other sites. | 501 Indiana St. | 406/357–2590 | Free | June–Aug., Tues.–Sat. 8–5; Sept.–May, weekdays 8–5.

ON THE CALENDAR

JULY: *Blaine County Fair.* Entertainment, agricultural exhibits and displays, rodeo performances, and a demolition derby are all held at the Blaine County Fairgrounds on the west edge of town. | 406/357–2100.
SEPT.: *Western Days.* Arts and crafts, food, wagon train rides, children's games, rodeo, cowboy poets, runs and walks, live music, wildlife museum open house, and a pet and doll parade, all downtown. | 406/357–3191.

Lodging

Bear Paw Court. There's nothing fancy at this small motel, but the rooms are clean and of average size, and the rates are hard to beat. Cable TV. | 114 Montana St. | 406/357–2221 or 888/357–2224 | 17 rooms | $43–$49 | D, MC, V.

Chinook Motor Inn. This two-story motel is on U.S. 2, the road to Glacier, a good place to stop if you want to take in some local history on your way to the park. Restaurant, bar. Cable TV. Pets allowed. | 100 Indiana Ave. | 406/357–2248 or 800/603–2864 | fax 406/357–2261 | www.chinookmotorinn.com | 38 rooms | $50–$60 | AE, D, MC, V.

CHOTEAU

MAP 6, D4

(Nearby town also listed: Great Falls)

Dramatic vistas and dinosaur bones are among the distinctions of this small town wedged between two distinct Montana regions—the Rocky Mountains to the West and flat rangeland to the east. This windswept country gave birth to the term "Big Sky" via native son novelist A. B. Guthrie. Named for a French fur trader, in recent years this community of about 1,700 has become a paleontological hot spot where researchers have pieced together revolutionary theories about dinosaurs based on bones and eggshells unearthed at Egg Mountain, an otherwise nondescript hill west of town.

Information: Choteau Chamber of Commerce | Box 897, Choteau, MT 59422 | 406–466–5316 or 800/823–3866.

Attractions

Old Trail Museum. Old West and prehistory mingle in this fascinating museum, set amid a cluster of frontier-period cabins loaded with artifacts in the heart of Choteau. Many exhibits focus on the area's dinosaur discoveries, and classes and two-day dinosaur workshops are available. | 823 N. Main Ave. | 406/466–5332 | $2 | Mid-May through mid-Sept., daily 9–6; late Sept.–early May, Tues.–Sat. 10–3.

Pine Butte Swamp Nature Conservancy Preserve. This brushy swamp provides rare wetland in this area and is home to fauna from grizzly bears to waterfowl. Afternoon tours can be coordinated with tours of nearby Egg Mountain. | South from Choteau on Hwy. 287; follow green DINOSAUR SCHOOL signs to Egg Mountain, and continue 5 mi to information center at Bellville Schoolhouse | 406/466–5526 | Free | Information center summer only.

ON THE CALENDAR

JULY: *Dinosaur Days.* This celebration of this area's prehistoric productivity features a parade, an open house at the Old Trail Museum, and tours of Egg Mountain and the Pine Butte Swamp. | Old Trail Museum, 823 N. Main Ave. | 406/466–5332.

Dining

Circle N. American. Burgers, steaks, hearty breakfasts, and a Sunday buffet draw locals and visitors to this reliable café. | 925 N. Main Ave. | 406/466–5531 | $5–$12 | MC, V.

Outpost Deli. Delicatessen. A good place to stop for a quick, reasonably priced lunch. You get ample sandwiches and typical deli side dishes at this small, tidy eatery. | 819 7th Ave. N | 406/466–5330 | $4–$8 | MC, V.

Lodging

Best Western Stage Stop Inn. This new, relatively luxurious entry in the local lodging competition has rooms with high ceilings and attractive, rustic decor. Some rooms have wet bars or whirlpools. Continental breakfast. Pool. Whirlpool. Cable TV. | 1005 Main Ave. N | 406/466–5900 | fax 406/466–5907 | 44 | $70–$85 | AE, D, MC, V.

Big Sky Motel. Small, cozy rooms and attentive management distinguish this clean downtown motel. Microwaves. Cable TV, Pets accepted (fee). | 209 S. Main Ave. | 406/466–5318 | fax 406/466–5866 | 13 | $44–$55 | AE, D, MC, V.

COLUMBIA FALLS

MAP 6, C3

(Nearby towns also listed: Hungry Horse, Kalispell, Whitefish)

One of the towns at the entrance of Glacier National Park, Columbia Falls, population 7,000, excels in outdoor recreation. You can enjoy championship golf, try the popular water slide, or go white-water rafting in summer. In winter you can go cross-country skiing, ice skating, and snowmobiling.

Information: **Columbia Falls Chamber of Commerce** | Box 312, Columbia Falls, 59912 | 406/892–2072.

Attractions

Big Sky Water Slide. An antique carousel is an added attraction here at the largest water park in Montana. The park has slides and an activity pool for kids, too. | U.S. 2; 1 mi east of junction with Rte. 206 | 406/892–5025 | www.bigskywaterslide.com | $14.95 | May–Sept., daily 10–8.

Flathead National Forest, Hungry Horse Ranger District, and Spotted Bear Ranger Districts. *See* Kalispell. | Box 340 (Hungry Horse) or Box 130 (Spotted Bear), Hungry Horse | 406/ 387–3800 (in summer, 406/758–5376 for Spotted Bear).

ON THE CALENDAR

JAN.: *Root Beer Classic.* A 60-mi staged run at the western border of Glacier National Park starts at the community of Polebridge. Teams run in two 30-mi heats. Fun and informal. | 406/881–2909.

JUNE: *Bitterroot Day.* A 20-year-old celebration of Montana's state flower, with blossoms, memorabilia, and arts and crafts. | 406/363–3338.

Dining

Glacier Highland Restaurant. American. Here's a place just outside Glacier Park if you want to fuel up for a hike. They serve a wide variety of family-style foods. Kids' menu. | U.S. 2 | 406/888–5427 | $12–$16 | MC, V | Closed Oct.–May.

Lodging

Bad Rock Country Bed & Breakfast. The favorite rooms at this B&B are in Bad Rock Bunny Junction, two new log buildings with two spacious rooms each. Each room has a private entrance and a fireplace. Lodgepole furniture adds to the rustic sophistication. Surrounded by 30 acres, the inn also has four rooms in the main house. All eight rooms have private baths and telephones. A 20-minute drive from Glacier Park. Complimentary breakfast. TV in common area. Hot tub. Business services. Airport shuttle. No smoking. | 480 Bad Rock Dr. | 406/892–2829, 800/422–3666 for reservations | fax 406/892–2930 | stay@badrock.com | www.badrock.com | 8 rooms | $120–$169 | AE, D, DC, MC, V.

Great Northern Chalets. Each log chalet sleeps six people at this family resort just a mile from the west gate of Glacier National Park. Fireplaces, kitchens, and a mountain view add to the charm. You can raft, fish, and ride horses here. Restaurant. No-smoking rooms. Indoor pool. Hot tubs. Horseback riding. Fishing. | 12127 U.S. 2 E | 406/387–5340 or 800/735–7897 | fax 406/387–9007 | www.gnwhitewater.com | 12 chalets | $175–$250 | AE, D, MC, V.

Izaak Walton. Four train cabooses have been renovated as cabin-style rooms next to the main building, originally built as a dormitory for railroad workers. As well as being a small piece of history, the inn is convenient for cross-country skiers, mountain bikers, and hikers. Bar, dining room, picnic area. No air-conditioning, no room phones. Sauna. Bicycles. Cross-country skiing. Game room with Ping-Pong and pool table. Laundry facilities. Business services. No smoking. | U.S. 2 | 406/888–5700 | fax 406/888–5200 | izaakw@digisys.net | www.izaakwaltoninn.com | 33 rooms | $98 | MC, V.

Meadow Lake Resort. Choose an inn room, a condo, or a vacation town house at this resort on the west side of Meadow Lake Golf Course. You can golf to your heart's content; if you don't golf, you can swim or play tennis. In winter, you can ice-skate and cross-country ski. Rooms have views of the water or golf course. Restaurant. Cable TV. 2 pools, 1 indoor. Hot tubs. Driving range, 18-hole golf course, putting green. Tennis. Exercise equipment. Ice skating. Cross-country skiing. Children's programs, playground. Business services. Airport shuttle. | 100 St. Andrews St. | 406/892–7601 or 800/321–4653 | fax 406/892–0330 | www.meadowlake.com | 114 units, 24 inn rooms, 60 condos, 30 town houses | $129, $139–$189 condos/suites | AE, D, DC, MC, V.

Plum Creek House. The late timber baron D. C. Dunham built this 5,000-square-ft ranch-style house along 600 feet of the wild and scenic Flathead River. With large windows throughout and decks and patio areas scattered around, you have great views of the Rocky Mountains and Glacier National Park. Complimentary breakfast. No air-conditioning. Cable TV, in-room VCRs (movies). Pool. Hot tub. Kids over 8 only. No smoking. | 985 Vans Ave. | 406/892–1816 or 800/682–1429 | fax 406/892–1876 | plumcreek@in-tch.com | www.wtp.net/go/plumcreek | 6 rooms (2 with shower only) | $105–$115 | AE, D, DC, MC, V.

West Glacier Motel. With the west side of Glacier National Park in one direction and shopping and restaurants in the other, you have a lot to choose from at this motel on the Flathead River. The Glacier View Golf Course is 1 mi away. Bar. | 200 Going-to-the-Sun Rd. | 406/888–5662 or 888/838–2363 | www.westglacier.com/motel,html | 32 motel and cabin units | $59–$68, $99 cabins | AE, D, MC, V | Closed Oct.–May.

Western Inns Glacier Mountain Shadows Resort. This mountain resort is within 2 mi of Flathead Lake and the Flathead River, where you can hike, boat, and fish. You can rent a tepee for the night if standard rooms don't appeal. Complimentary Continental breakfast.

Cable TV. Indoor pool. Hot tub. | 7285 U.S. 2 E | 406/892–7686 | fax 406/892–4575 | 24 rooms | $65, $150 suites | AE, MC, V.

COOKE CITY

(Nearby town also listed: Red Lodge)

With Yellowstone National Park and the Absaroka-Beartooth Wilderness at its back door, this tiny skytop community of 70 is a good starting place for hiking, fishing, horseback riding, pack trips, mountain climbing, snowmobiling, and more.

Information: **Cooke City Chamber of Commerce** | Box 1071, Cooke City, 59020 | 406/838–2495.

Lodging

High Country. In the Beartooth Mountains. Motel and cabins, some with kitchens and fireplaces. No air-conditioning, some refrigerators. Pets allowed. | U.S. 212 | 406/838–2272 | 15 rooms, 4 kitchenettes | $47–$49, $67 kitchen suites | AE, D, DC, MC, V.

Soda Butte Lodge. Rooms of varying sizes, a sunken lobby with large fireplace, and spectacular views. Restaurant, bar. Cable TV. Pool. Hot tub. Pets allowed. | 209 U.S. 212 | 406/838–2251 or 800/527–6462 | fax 406/838–2253 | 32 rooms | $65–$70, $100 suites | AE, D, MC, V.

DARBY

(Nearby town also listed: Hamilton)

Set in the scenic beauty of the Bitterroot Valley, this town of 900 lays claim to the Darby Pioneer Memorial Museum, Painted Rocks State Park, and Alta Ranger Station, the first USDA Forest Service ranger station.

Information: **Darby Chamber of Commerce** | 105 E. Main St., Hamilton 59840 | 406/363–2400 | www.bvchamber.com.

Attractions

Bitterroot National Forest, Darby, Sula, and West Fork Districts. *See* Hamilton. | Darby Ranger Station: 712 U.S. 93 N | 406/821–3913.

Darby Pioneer Museum. The museum was one of the first hand-hewn cabins in the area, built in 1886 on a homestead near the mouth of Tin Cup Creek. It now holds collections of home and business artifacts saved by many of the area's pioneer families. | Council Park | 406/821–3753 | www.lewisclark.org/d/darbypmm.htm | Free | June–Aug., weekdays 9–noon and 1–5.

Lost Trail Powder Mountain. A ski area known for reliable snowfall and consistently good snow conditions, Lost Trail straddles the Montana-Idaho border in the breathtaking Bitterroot National Forest. You get 18 runs and trails, full-service cafeteria, ski school, and a bed-and-breakfast. | 7674 U.S. 93 S, Sula | 406/821–3211 or 406/821–3508 | www.losttrail.com | $19 | Dec.–Apr., Thurs.–Sun. 9:30–4 (also holidays and every day through Christmas season).

Painted Rocks State Park. Tucked deep within the western bulge of Bitterroot National Forest is this 293-acre state park on Painted Rocks Reservoir. The park's name derives from the unusual yellow, green, and orange lichens covering the rocks and cliffs surrounding the park. You can swim, fish, boat, and camp at the 25-site campground. Get there by driving south on U.S. 93, then 23 mi southwest on Rte. 473. | 406/542–5500 | www.state.mt.us | Free | Daily.

Lodging

Rye Creek Lodge. Rustic and luxurious both, these hand-hewn log cabins have kitchens, stone fireplaces, and private outdoor hot tubs. The 120-acre site has two private ponds and a creek and is near the Selway-Bitterroot Wilderness Area. You can go white-water rafting and fish with a guide. Hot tubs. Horseback riding. Water sports. Fishing. Bicycles. Cross-country skiing, snowmobiling. | 458 Rye Creek Rd. | 406/821–3366 or 800 888/821–3366 | fax 406/821–3366 | www.ryecreeklodge.com | 3 cabins | $185–$210 | MC, V.

Triple Creek Ranch. Gourmet meals, box lunches for picnics, freshly baked cookies daily, and room service add to the charm of this resort, which already has almost every available amenity. The log or cedar cabins have fireplaces and steam showers and mountain views. Restaurant, bar, room service. In-room data ports, refrigerators. Cable TV, in-room VCRs. Pool. Massage. Putting green. Tennis. Hiking, horseback riding, fishing. Bicycles. Cross-country skiing, snowmobiling. Laundry service. Kids over 16 only. Business services. Airport shuttle. | 5551 W. Fork Stage Rd. | 406/821–4600 | fax 406/821–4666 | info@triplecreekranch.com | www.triplecreekranch.com | 18 cabins, 3 with shower only, 10 kitchenette cabins | $510–$995 per couple per night, depending upon cabin choice; includes all meals and beverages and most activities | AE, D, MC, V | AP.

DEER LODGE

MAP 6, D5

(Nearby towns also listed: Anaconda, Butte, Helena)

Home of the fabled Montana Prison, this is a Western town rooted in the state's cattle industry. On the outskirts of town is the Grant-Kohrs Ranch National Historic Site, once the headquarters of a cattle empire that spanned four states and a portion of Canada. A horse-drawn trolley (seasonally, Fri.–Mon.) takes visitors from the Old Montana Prison to the Grant-Kohrs Ranch. Deerlodge National Forest is nearby.

Information: Deer Lodge Chamber of Commerce | 406/846–2094.

Attractions

Beaverhead-Deerlodge National Forest. The combined and jointly managed national forests of Beaverhead and Deerlodge make the largest national forest in Montana at 3.32 million acres, covering eight southwestern Montana counties. Amid the spectacular mountains, you can hike, fish, camp at more than 50 campgrounds, snowmobile, cross-country and downhill ski, hunt, and watch wildlife. The mountains within the ranges in this national forest are among Montana's highest. | 1 Hollenback Rd. | 406/846–1770 | www.fs.fed.us/r1/b-d | Free; camping up to $17 per night per vehicle | Daily.

Frontier Montana. A bartender tells the story of the collection here, which has items owned and used by the Buffalo Bill Cody Wild West Show. Built in the early 1900s, the building was used as a mule barn and is now on the National Register of Historic Places. The wooden blocks in the floor were made by prisoners and covered with tar, and have been renovated to expose beautiful, unique wood flooring. This is one of four Old Montana museums. | 1153 Main St. | 406/846–0026 | www.state.mt.us | $7.95 includes admission to all 4 Old Montana museums; special rates for seniors and children | Memorial Day–Labor Day, daily 9–5.

Grant-Kohrs Ranch National Historic Site. A 19th-century cattle empire with herds that grazed in four states and Canada once occupied this land. You can take guided tours of the elegant ranch house, a bunkhouse, a blacksmith shop, and a wagon collection. On the second weekend in July, the ranch hosts a huge celebration of the Old West, with demonstrations of roping, branding, and blacksmithing and special kid's programs. | ½ mile off I–90 | 406/846–3388 | www.nps.gov/grko | May–Sept., $2 per person, $4 per car; Oct.–Apr., free | May–Sept. daily 8–5:30; Oct.–Apr, daily 9–4:30.

Montana Auto Museum. Another Old Montana museum holds a collection of 120 antique cars, from the early 1900s into the 1960s. Lots of old photos of the area, including shots of early Yellowstone campers, add to the sense of history. | 1106 Main St. | 406/846–3111 | $7.95 includes admission to all 4 Old Montana museums | Year-round.

Old Montana Prison Museum. The old Montana Territorial Prison was built in 1871 and vacated in 1979. It is now a downtown museum. Enter cells and learn about early Montana law. You can see the gallows taken from town to town in territorial days to hang convicted prisoners. Part of Old Montana museums. | 1106 Main St. | 406/846–3111 | $7.95 includes admission to all 4 Old Montana museums | Year-round.

Yesterday's Playthings. Whimsical old toys and dolls and a large and excellent clown collection live in an 1880s print shop. The building is on the National Register of Historic Places. Part of Old Montana museums. | 1017 Main St. | 406/846–1480 | $7.95 includes admission to all 4 Old Montana museums | Mid-May–Sept., daily 9–5.

ON THE CALENDAR

JUNE: *Prison Breakout Bluegrass Festival.* Bluegrass bands perform outdoors (weather permitting). Barbecue, vendors, and concessions. | 406/846–2094.

JUNE: *Territorial Days.* Street rods and a classic car show, barbecues, a parade, vendors, games, softball tourneys, and a dance round out this popular event. | 406/846–2090.

JULY: *Western Heritage Days.* For more than a quarter-century, this annual celebration has paid tribute to the cowboy and the cattleman's West with roping, branding, chuckwagon cooking, blacksmithing, and traditional cowboy music and poetry. | 406/846–2070.

JULY–AUG.: *Old Prison Summer Theater.* The Old Prison Players perform three plays during the summer season. | 406/846–3111.

AUG.: *Tri-County Fair and Rodeo.* Southwest Montana gets together at this old-fashioned county fair with four days of festivities, including livestock, exhibits, food, a rodeo, and a demolition derby. | 406/846–1477.

Lodging

Scharf Motor Inn. Modest rates and scenic views are matched with standard contemporary rooms at this in-town motel. Restaurant, bar. No-smoking rooms. Cable TV. | 819 Main St. | 406/846–2810 | fax 406/846–3412 | 44 rooms | $46–$52 | AE, D, MC, V.

Super 8. A convenient downtown location is the draw at this basic modern motel. Cable TV. Pets allowed. | 1150 N. Main St. | 406/846–2370 | fax 406/846–2373 | 54 rooms | $64–$70, $80 suites | AE, D, DC, MC, V.

DILLON

MAP 6, D7

(Nearby towns also listed: Butte, Ennis, Virginia City)

A diverse mix of culture, history, and recreation characterizes this town of 4,200, which is the trading center for the Big Hole and Beaverhead valleys. Western Montana College is here and has an an art gallery and the Seidensticker Wildlife Collection. You can also visit summer theater, museums, and historic sites on the Lewis and Clark Trail.

Information: **Dillon Chamber of Commerce** | 15 S. Montana St., 59725 | 406/683–5511 | www.chamber@bmt.net.

Attractions

Bannack State Park. The ghost town of Bannack once flourished where there is now a 1,100-acre state park at an elevation of 6,000 ft. Main Street is lined with historic log and frame buildings. A Bannack Days celebration is held every third weekend in July. Grasshopper

Creek winds through the park and its 28-site campground. You can rent a tepee, drop by the visitor center, hike the trails, fish, and attend summer lectures. | 4200 Bannack Rd., off Rte. 278 | 406/834–3413, 406/834–3413 for reservations | www.state.mt.us | Day use $4; camping $11 June–Aug., $9 Sept.–May; tepee rentals $25 | Daily.

Beaverhead County Museum. Southwest Montana history is displayed indoors and out, along with photos, and taxidermy. You can take a walking tour of the historic downtown. | 15 S. Montana St. | 406/683–9351 | Free | Apr.–Aug., weekdays 10–8, weekends 1–5; Sept.–Dec., daily 1–5.

Beaverhead-Deerlodge National Forest. *See* Deer Lodge. | Lima Work Center: Box 229, Lima | 406/276–3676.

Beaverhead Rock State Park. A historical landmark, this rock shaped like the head of a beaver was recognized by the Lewis and Clark's Shoshone guide, Sacajawea, in 1805. Undeveloped and unsigned, the primitive park is north of Dillon on Rte. 41. | 406/834–3413 | Free | Daily dawn to dusk.

Dillon Visitor Center. A statewide travel-information center located in an old railroad depot, the Dillon Visitor Center displays a diorama of the Lewis and Clark Expedition at Beavershead Rock. | 125 S. Montana St. | 406/683–5511 | June–Aug., daily 8–8; May and Sept., daily 8–5; Oct.–Apr., weekdays 8–5.

Maverick Mountain Ski Area. An 18-run downhill ski area with a top elevation of 8,620 ft and a vertical drop of 1,927 ft. Reserve ahead if you want to use the nursery. | Rte. 278 (Maverick Mountain Rd.) | 406/834–3454 | $19 | Nov.–Apr., Thurs.–Sun. 9:30–4:30.

ON THE CALENDAR

JULY: *Bannack Days.* At this celebration of mining and life in Montana's first territorial capital, you can enjoy stagecoach rides, candlemaking, a main street gunfight, old-time dancing, and music. | 406/834–3413.

AUG.–SEPT.: *Beaverhead County Fair.* Fair activities take place Tuesday through Friday, with rodeo performances on Saturday and Sunday. | 406/683–5511.

Lodging

Best Western Paradise Inn. The rooms are average in size, the furnishings are contemporary, the view is extraordinary. The reasonably priced suites are good for families. Restaurant, bar. Cable TV. Pool. Hot tub. Business services. Pets allowed. | 650 N. Montana St. | 406/683–4214 | fax 406/683–4216 | 65 rooms | $50–54, $73–$83 suites | AE, D, DC, MC, V.

Comfort Inn–Dillon. Suites with microkitchens and a recreation area set this standard contemporary hotel apart. You're only 2 mi from fishing. Bar, complimentary Continental breakfast. Cable TV. Indoor pool. Laundry facilities. | 450 N. Interchange | 406/683–6831 or 800/442–4667 | fax 406/683–2021 | 48 rooms | $61–$65, $71 suites | AE, D, DC, MC, V.

Super 8. Modern furnishings, queen-size beds, and the option of no-smoking rooms make this a pleasant basic accommodation. Cable TV. | 550 N. Montana St. | 406/683–4288 or 800/800–8000 | 46 rooms | $50–$55 | AE, D, DC, MC, V.

EAST GLACIER AREA

MAP 6, D3

(Nearby town also listed: Browning)

A gateway community to Glacier National Park, the town of 350 offers full visitor services. You get a nice sense of anticipation as you approach the nearby million-acre wilderness.

Information: East Glacier Chamber of Commerce | Box 260, East Glacier, 59434 | 406/226–4403.

Lodging

Bison Creek Ranch. The seven rustic cabins here are very close to Glacier National Park and have fantastic views of the mountains. Restaurant, complimentary Continental breakfast. No air-conditioning. Hiking. Pets allowed. | U.S. 2 | 406/226–4482 or 888/226–4482 | 7 rooms | $40–$60 | D, MC, V | Closed Oct.–June.

Glacier Park Lodge. The great hall of this lodge is one of the most majestic ever built. Twenty-four Douglas firs form a colonnade in the 200-by-100-ft soaring lobby flanked by galleries on either side. Each tree is 48 ft high and four ft thick. Great Northern Railway president Louis Hill built the lodge in 1913. Restaurant, bar. Indoor pool. Hiking. Nine-hole golf course. | U.S. 2 | 406/226–9311 or 602/207–6000 | www.glacierparkinc.com/gpl.htm | 161 rooms | $195–$375 | AE, D, MC, V | Closed Oct.–mid May.

Jacobson's Cottages. Very clean cottages just ½ mi from the Amtrak station in a wooded area. Picnic area. No air-conditioning, no room phones. Cable TV. | 1204 Rte. 49 | 406/226–4422 | 12 cottages, 1 kitchenette | $55–$59 | AE, D, MC, V | Closed Oct.–Apr.

Mountain Pine Motel. Convenience distinguishes this quiet, no-frills motel. You're less than a mile from the Amtrak station and also very close to the trails of Glacier Park. Picnic area. No air-conditioning. Cable TV. | Rte. 49 | 406/226–4403 | fax 406/226–9290 | 26 rooms | $55–$60 | AE, D, DC, MC, V | Closed Oct.–Apr.

St. Mary Lodge and Resort. Choice is the lure here, with accommodations that range from lodge rooms to cabins to six new luxury cabins with park views. All lodge rooms have pine furniture and some have air-conditioning units (the only ones in Glacier). The two-bedroom cabins have kitchens and fireplaces. Restaurant, bar. Some air-conditioning. Laundry facilities. Pets allowed (fee). No smoking. | U.S. 89, St. Mary | 406/732–4431 or 208/726–6279; 800/368–3689 for reservations | fax 406/732–9265 | www.glcpark.com | 80 rooms, 62 with shower only | $75–$285 | AE, D, MC, V | Closed Oct.–Apr.

ENNIS

MAP 6, E7

(Nearby towns also listed: Butte, Dillon)

A mix of ranching and fishing permeates the atmosphere of this small town of 1,000. A popular base camp for summer visitors, Ennis is surrounded by 3 million acres of national forest lands and close to one of Montana's best-known trout streams—the Madison River. Three special state parks are located north of Ennis—Missouri Headwaters, Madison Buffalo Jump, and Lewis and Clark Caverns. The Ennis Fish Hatchery on Varney Road propagates six strains of rainbow trout that produce 23 million eggs per year.

Information: Ennis Chamber of Commerce | Box 291, Ennis, 59729 | 406/682–4388 | www.ennischamber.com.

Attractions

Beartrap Canyon. In this part of the Lee Metcalf Wilderness northeast of Ennis, you can hike, fish, and go white-water rafting on the Madison River. A picnic area and access to Trail Creek are at the head of the canyon below Ennis Lake. This was the first site along Madison River designed for disabled access. To get here, drive north out of Ennis on U.S. 287 to McAllister, turn right down a bumpy dirt road (no number), which takes you around to the north side of lake across the dam; turn left after the dam on unmarked road and go across the river to Trail Creek access point. | 406/683–2337 | Free | Daily.

Beaverhead-Deerlodge National Forest. *See* Deer Lodge. | 5 Forest Service Rd. | 406/682–4253.

Ennis National Fish Hatchery. Six strains of rainbow trout produce 23 million eggs per year for stocking throughout the United States. Blaine Springs provides fresh, clean spring water

KODAK'S TIPS FOR PHOTOGRAPHING LANDSCAPES AND SCENERY

Landscape
- Tell a story
- Isolate the essence of a place
- Exploit mood, weather, and lighting

Panoramas
- Use panoramic cameras for sweeping vistas
- Don't restrict yourself to horizontal shots
- Keep the horizon level

Panorama Assemblage
- Use a wide-angle or normal lens
- Let edges of pictures overlap
- Keep exposure even
- Use a tripod

Placing the Horizon
- Use low horizon placement to accent sky or clouds
- Use high placement to emphasize distance and accent foreground elements
- Try eliminating the horizon

Mountain Scenery: Scale
- Include objects of known size
- Frame distant peaks with nearby objects
- Compress space with long lenses

Mountain Scenery: Lighting
- Shoot early or late; avoid midday
- Watch for dramatic color changes
- Use exposure compensation

Tropical Beaches
- Capture expansive views
- Don't let bright sand fool your meter
- Include people

Rocky Shorelines
- Vary shutter speeds to freeze or blur wave action
- Don't overlook sea life in tidal pools
- Protect your gear from sand and sea

In the Desert
- Look for shapes and textures
- Try visiting during peak bloom periods
- Don't forget safety

Canyons
- Research the natural and social history of a locale
- Focus on a theme or geologic feature
- Budget your shooting time

Rain Forests and the Tropics
- Go for mystique with close-ups and detail shots
- Battle low light with fast films and camera supports
- Protect cameras and film from moisture and humidity

Rivers and Waterfalls
- Use slow film and long shutter speeds to blur water
- When needed, use a neutral-density filter over the lens
- Shoot from water level to heighten drama

Autumn Colors
- Plan trips for peak foliage periods
- Mix wide and close views for visual variety
- Use lighting that accents colors or creates moods

Moonlit Landscapes
- Include the moon or use only its illumination
- Exaggerate the moon's relative size with long telephoto lenses
- Expose landscapes several seconds or longer

Close-Ups
- Look for interesting details
- Use macro lenses or close-up filters
- Minimize camera shake with fast films and high shutter speeds

Caves and Caverns
- Shoot with ISO 1000+ films
- Use existing light in tourist caves
- Paint with flash in wilderness caves

From *Kodak Guide to Shooting Great Travel Pictures* © 2000 by Fodor's Travel Publications

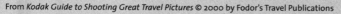

at a constant 54°F, ideal for nurturing trout. The 10-mi access road is bumpy. | 180 Fish Hatchery Rd. | 406/682–48477635 | fax 406/682–7635 | www.r6.fws.gov/HATCHERY/ENNIS/ENNIS.HTM | Free | Daily 8–5.

Madison River Canyon Earthquake Area. Some 42 mi south of Ennis, an August 1959 earthquake created a 21-cubic-meter slide of rock, soil, and trees from the steep sides of the Madison River Canyon that killed 28 campers. The landslide barrier completely blocked the gorge and the flow of the Madison River, creating a lake. *See* West Yellowstone. | U.S. 287 | 406/646–7369.

ON THE CALENDAR

JULY: *Rodeo*. Consistently among the most exciting and challenging rodeos in Montana, this NRA-sanctioned event attracts top cowboys, cowgirls, and rodeo stock. | 406/682–4700.

Dining

Continental Divide. Eclectic. The upscale fare here is part American, combined with French and regional cuisine. The intimate dining room seats 35, or you can dine outside. Favorite entrées use beef, salmon, halibut, and classic French sweetbreads. | U.S. 287 | 406/682–7600 | Reservations essential | $24–$32 | AE, MC, V | Closed Oct.–May. No lunch.

Lodging

El Western. Seventeen acres along a creek make this a fly-fisherman's heaven. Some of the hand-peeled, chinked log cabins have fireplaces, kitchenettes, or both. The pine interiors lend warmth. No air-conditioning, some kitchenettes. Cable TV. Hiking. Fishing. | ½ mi south on U.S. 287 | 406/682–4217 or 800/831–2773 | fax 406/682–5207 | www.elwe stern.com | 29 rooms, 18 with kitchenettes | $65, $95 kitchen suites | AE, D, MC, V | Most units closed mid-Oct–Apr.

Fan Mountain Inn. The lobby here looks like a homey living room, with a fireplace and television. The spacious and comfortable rooms include one extra-large suite that has a wet bar and refrigerator. You can walk the two blocks to downtown and also get to the Madison River on foot. No-smoking rooms. Cable TV. Conference room. | 204 N. Main St. | 406/682–5200 | fax 406/682–5266 | www.fanmountaininn.com | www.fanmtnin@3rivers.net | 28 rooms | $53–$61 | AE, D, DC, MC, V.

Rainbow Valley. Two cabins on Odell Spring Creek allow you to step out the front door and start fishing. Other rooms in the main lodge are unusually spacious, with pine interiors and contemporary furnishings. Some have kitchens. Picnic area. Cable TV. Pool. Laundry facilities. | 1 mi south on U.S. 287 | 406/682–4264 or 800/452–8254 | fax 406/682–5012 | www.rainbowvalley.com | 24 rooms, 6 kitchenettes | $65–$100 | AE, D, DC, MC, V.

FORT BENTON

MAP 6, F3

(Nearby town also listed: Great Falls)

Less than an hour downriver from Great Falls, Lewis and Clark first camped at this site in 1805. The first steamboat arrived here in 1859, and Fort Benton was once the farthest inland port in the world. In 1866, 2½ tons of gold dust were shipped downriver from here. Today, the town of 1,600 is the gateway to the wild and scenic Upper Missouri River, and reminders of its storied past are captured in the Museum of the Upper Missouri River and the Museum of the Northern Great Plains.

Information: Fort Benton Chamber of Commerce | Box 12, Fort Benton, 59442 | 406/622–3864 | www.fortbenton.com.

Attractions

Museum of the Northern Great Plains. The official museum of agriculture in Montana tells the story of three generations of farmers from 1908 until 1980. The 30,000 square ft of exhibition area hold a village of businesses from the homestead era. You can also see farm machinery outside. | 1205 20th St. | 406/622–5316 | www.fortbenton.com/museums/agmuseum.htm | $4; special rates for children | May, daily 11:30–4:30; June–Sept., daily 10–5; off-season by appointment only.

Museum of the Upper Missouri. Covering the era from 1800 to 1900, this museum highlights the importance of Fort Benton and the role it played as a trading post, military fort, and the head of steamboat navigation. Old Fort Benton is adjacent. Considered the birthplace of Montana, with its 1846 blockhouse, this is the oldest standing structure in Montana. | Old Fort Park | 406/622–5316 | www.fortbenton.com/museums/muminfo.htm | $4 | May, daily 11:30–4:30; June–Sept., daily 10–5; off-season by appointment only.

Upper Missouri National Wild and Scenic River. In 1805–06 Lewis and Clark explored this river and camped on its banks. Today the designated National Wild and Scenic stretch of the river runs 149 mi downriver from Fort Benton. Highlights include the scenic White Cliffs area, Citadel Rock, Hole in the Wall, Lewis and Clark Camp at Slaughter River, abandoned homesteads, and abundant wildlife. Commercial boat tours, shuttle service, and a variety of boat rentals—including rowboats, power boats, and canoes—are offered at Fort Benton and Virgelle. | Visitor Center, 1718 Front St. | 406/622–5185 | www.mt.blm.gov/ldo/umnwsr.html | Free | Daily (visitor center open May–Oct.).

ON THE CALENDAR

JUNE: *Summer Celebration*. Montana's "birthplace" community celebrates with a parade, arts, crafts, antiques, entertainment, a street dance, fireworks, Missouri River boat rides, and historical tours. | 406/622–3351.

AUG.: *Choteau County Fair*. Carnival rides, a rodeo, a dance, a concert, and a demolition derby are featured events at the fairgrounds here. Visitors also find artwork, photography, crafts, food, and livestock sales. | 406/622–5282.

Lodging

Grand Union Hotel. On the bank of the Missouri River, this is perhaps the oldest hotel in Montana, built to serve steamboat and stage travelers. Completely restored in 1999, the two-story building is as elegant as it ever was. Many of the spacious rooms have river views. Restaurant, bar. Cable TV. | 1 Grand Union Sq | 406/622–1882 | www.grandunionhotel.com | 27 rooms | $75–$120 | AE, D, MC, V.

Long's Landing Bed & Breakfast. This three-room bed and breakfast is almost like staying in someone's home. The furnishings are Western-style. Complimentary Continental breakfast. Cable TV. | 1011 17th St. | 406/622–3461 | fax 406/622–3455 | 3 rooms, 2 with shared bath | $50 | MC, V | Nov.–Apr.

GARDINER

(Nearby town also listed: Livingston)

The only year-round drive-in entrance to Yellowstone National Park, Gardiner is bustling in any season. The town's Roosevelt Arch has marked the north entrance to the park since 1903, when Theodore Roosevelt dedicated it. The Yellowstone River slices through town, beckoning fishermen and rafters. The town of 800 has quaint shops and good restaurants.

Information: **Gardiner Chamber of Commerce** | Box 81, Gardiner, 59030 | 406/848–7971 | www.gardinerchamber.com.

Attractions

Gallatin National Forest. *See* Bozeman. | Gardiner Ranger District: U.S. 89, Gardiner | 406/848–7485 | Daily.

RIVER TRIPS

Yellowstone Raft Co. This group will take you white-water rafting and on guided fishing trips as well as provide kayak instruction on the Yellowstone, Gallatin, and Madison Rivers. | 406 Scott St. | 406/848–7777 or 800/858–7781 | May–Sept.

ON THE CALENDAR

JUNE: *Gardiner Rodeo.* An annual rodeo on Father's Day weekend. A rodeo parade kicks off the event, which concludes with concessions and a dance. | 406/848–7971.

Dining

Four Wind. American. Formerly a vegetarian restaurant, this eatery now serves basic buffet-style lunches with a standard array of meat, potatoes, and vegetables. | U.S. 89; 7 mi north of town center | 406/848–7891 | $12–$16 | AE, D, DC, MC, V.

Yellowstone Mine. American. Spacious and furnished Western-style, this is a place for casual family-style dining. Town residents come in for the steaks and local fish. Kids' menu. No smoking. | U.S. 89 | 406/848–7336 | $12–$17 | AE, D, DC, MC, V | No lunch.

Lodging

Absaroka. The spacious grounds of this lodging are directly on the Yellowstone River, and the large rooms have excellent river views. You can walk to shops and restaurants, as well as to fishing spots. Some kitchenettes. Cable TV. Pets allowed (fee). | U.S. 89 | 406/848–7414 or 800/755–7414 | fax 406/848–7560 | www.yellowstonemotel.com | 41 rooms | $90–$100 | AE, D, DC, MC, V.

Best Western by Mammoth Hot Springs. On the banks of the Yellowstone River with both mountain and river views, this is an excellent place for wildlife viewing. Bar. Some kitchenettes, some microwaves, some refrigerators, some in-room hot tubs. Cable TV. Indoor pool. Hot tub, sauna. Business services. | U.S. 89 W | 406/848–7311 or 800/828–9080 | fax 406/848–7120 | www.bestwestern.com/mammothhotsprings | 85 rooms | $85–$96, $150–$165 suites | AE, D, DC, MC, V.

Comfort Inn. Family and honeymoon suites offer more spacious quarters, and they don't add a lot to the bill. The rooms are contemporary in style and comfortable. Complimentary Continental breakfast. Cable TV. Hot tubs. Laundry facilities. Business services. | 107 Hellroaring Rd. | 406/848–7536 or 800/228–5150 | fax 406/848–7062 | www.hotelchoice.com | 40 rooms | $99–$135, $145 suites | Closed Mar. and Dec. | AE, D, DC, MC, V.

Super 8. Some family rooms have kitchens at this hotel at north entrance to Yellowstone and across from the river. Complimentary Continental breakfast. Cable TV. Indoor pool. Some pets allowed (fee). | U.S. 89 | 406/848–7401 or 800/800–8000 | fax 406/848–9410 | super8.com | 66 rooms | $89, $165 suites | AE, D, DC, MC, V.

Westernaire. A covered porch and a spacious lobby lend charm to this small motel with mountain views. No air-conditioning. Cable TV. | U.S. 89 | 406/848–7397 | 11 rooms | $70–$75 | MC, V.

Yellowstone Village Inn. At the park's north entrance and within walking distance of shopping and restaurants, this inn has a comfortable lobby with a fireplace and mountain views. You can rent skis, tour the park, go rafting, and go on a trail ride. Complimentary Continental breakfast. Cable TV. Indoor pool. Sauna. Horseback riding. Laundry facilities. Business services. | U.S. 89 | 406/848–7417 or 800/228–8158 | fax 406/848–7418 | yellowstoneinn@gomontana.com | www.yellowstonevinn.com/ | 43 rooms, 3 condos | $69, $130–$155 suites and condos | AE, D, MC, V.

GLACIER NATIONAL PARK

(Nearby towns also listed: Columbia Falls, East Glacier, West Glacier)

Covering 1,500 square mi of spectacular, mountainous, glacier-carved terrain, Glacier National Park is, for the most part, a wholly undeveloped magnificent wilderness. Only one road—Going-to-the-Sun Road—traverses the park. Pristine lakes, snowcapped mountain ranges, and torrential waterfalls make the park a favorite travel destination. The park's 750 mi of hiking trails are enough for a lifetime of outdoor adventure.

Glacier adjoins Waterton Lakes National Park in Alberta, Canada. Together they create Waterton-Glacier International Peace Park World Heritage Site.

A permit is needed to camp overnight in backcountry anywhere in the park, and you may need to make a reservation for a permit. You do not need a permit for day hikes.

Glacier Park's magnificent 52-mi east–west highway, **Going-to-the-Sun Road,** cuts through the middle of the park from Lake McDonald to St. Mary Lake. It is an engineering masterpiece allowing travelers the opportunity to view the stunning mountain wilderness. The road is very slow going and not for the faint-hearted driver. Deep snows generally close the road in winter (call 406/888–7800 for current road conditions). The Road crosses the Continental Divide at **Logan Pass** and the **Garden Wall.** Views here are breathtaking, and it's a must-see area of Glacier Park. It is also the most easily accessible subalpine area of Glacier Park—which has the corollary effect of making it the most congested area of the park in July and August. Arrive early in the day to avoid the crowds. The geological formation of the Garden Wall stretches 20 to 30 mi north of the pass. A popular trail leaves from the parking lot and winds 7.5 mi to Granite Park Chalet. Climbing 500 ft to the Continental Divide and Hidden Lake, the Nature Trail overlooks Hidden Lake. You can't see this beautiful lake from the highway.

Some of the most popular lakes in the park are Avalanche Creek, Lake McDonald, St. Mary Lake, and Red Eagle Lake. One of Glacier's many mountain-ringed lakes, **Avalanche Creek/Lake** is also the the park's most accessible backcountry lake, with access right off Going-to-the-Sun Road. Take the 4-mi trail, a relatively easy walk, gaining 500 ft. This area is very crowded during July and August. **Trail of the Cedars** is a wheelchair-accessible ½-mi loop at Avalanche Campground. Ten-mile-long **Lake McDonald,** near the southwest entrance to the park, is surrounded by towering glacier-clad mountains. You can take boat rides and arrange horse trail rides at either end of the lake. Three drive-in campgrounds are near the lake; sites are first-come, first-served. You can fish for lake trout only from April 1 to December 31. You can catch one of Glacier Park's most popular views at **St. Mary Lake**— it acts as a reflecting pool mirroring the snowcapped granite peaks lining the valley. On the east side of Glacier Park, it is a great area for day hikes. St. Mary Lake's **Sun Point Nature Trail** follows the lake's shore, 1 mi each way. You can buy Park Service interpretive brochures at the trailhead for 50¢. Use it and drop it at the box at the other end of the trail. A small drive-in campground is accessible by a dirt road.

You can reach **Red Eagle Lake,** 8 mi from St. Mary Lake, by backcountry hiking trails only, but you'll find great fishing, beautiful scenery, and two campgrounds. You will need to reserve an overnight permit if you want to camp in backcountry.

Deep in the backcountry south of Going-to-the-Sun Road, the 8,020-ft **Triple Divide Peak** (midway across the park; backcountry access is from Cut Bank Campground on the west side of U.S. 89, between St. Mary and Kiowa Junction) straddles the Continental Divide, with snowmelt from its various flanks draining into the watersheds of the Pacific, Atlantic, and Arctic oceans. Hiking trails beginning at Cut Bank Campground and St. Mary traverse the pass.

About 10 mi west of Babb, or 20 mi northwest of St. Mary, the **Many Glacier Area** (Ranger Station: 406/732–7740 summer only) has several popular day-hiking trails, including a 3-mi nature trail that begins in front of the Many Glacier Hotel. The trail is easy

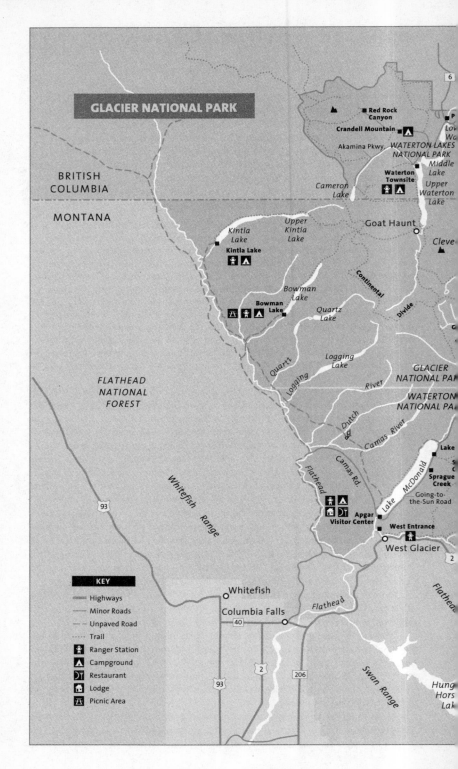

GLACIER NATIONAL PARK

BRITISH
COLUMBIA

MONTANA

Red Rock
Canyon

Crandell Mountain

Akamina Pkwy. WATERTON LAKES
NATIONAL PARK

Waterton
Townsite

Cameron
Lake

Middle
Lake

Upper
Waterton
Lake

Lov
Wa

P

Goat Haunt

Cleve

Kintla
Lake

Upper
Kintia
Lake

Kintla Lake

Bowman
Lake

Continental

Bowman
Lake

Quartz
Lake

Divide

Logging
Lake

FLATHEAD
NATIONAL
FOREST

Quartz

Logging

River

GLACIER
NATIONAL PAR

WATERTON
NATIONAL PA

Dutch

Camas River

Camas River

Lake

Sprague
Creek

Going-to-
the-Sun Road

Whitefish

Range

Camas Rd.

Flathead

Lake

McDonald

S
C

93

Flathead

Apgar
Visitor Center

West Entrance

West Glacier

2

KEY

Highways
Minor Roads
Unpaved Road
Trail
Ranger Station
Campground
Restaurant
Lodge
Picnic Area

Whitefish

Columbia Falls

40

Flathead

93

2

206

Swan Range

Flathead

Hung
Hors
Lak

6

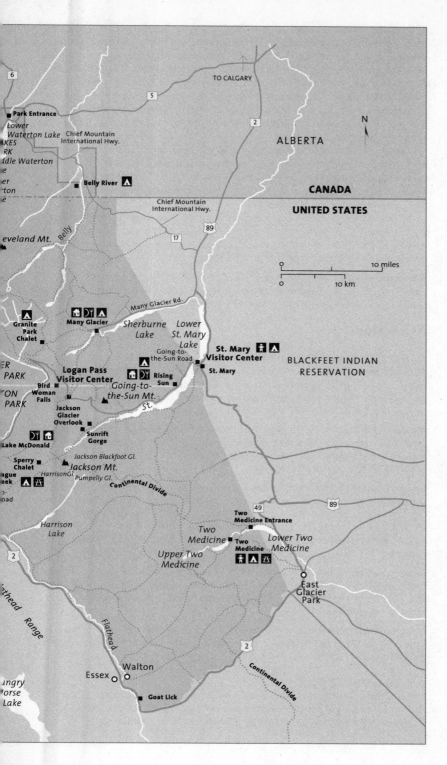

TO CALGARY

ALBERTA

N

CANADA

UNITED STATES

Park Entrance

*Lower
Waterton Lake*

Chief Mountain
International Hwy.

ddle Waterton

Belly River

eveland Mt.

Belly

Chief Mountain
International Hwy.

17

89

10 miles

10 km

Many Glacier Rd.

Granite
Park
Chalet

Many Glacier

*Sherburne
Lake*

*Lower
St. Mary
Lake*

St. Mary
Visitor Center

St. Mary

BLACKFEET INDIAN
RESERVATION

Logan Pass
Visitor Center

Bird
Woman
Falls

*Going-to-
the-Sun Mt.
St.*

Going-to-
the-Sun Road

Rising
Sun

Jackson
Glacier
Overlook

Sunrift
Gorge

Lake McDonald

Sperry
Chalet

Jackson Blackfoot Gl.

Jackson Mt.

Harrison Gl.

Pumpelly Gl.

*ague
eek*

*o-
oad*

Continental Divide

*Harrison
Lake*

2

49

**Two
Medicine Entrance**

89

*Two
Medicine*

Two
Medicine

*Lower Two
Medicine*

*Upper Two
Medicine*

East
Glacier
Park

*Flathead
Range*

Flathead

Essex

Walton

2

Continental Divide

Goat Lick

*ungry
orse
Lake*

6

5

2

PARK

ON
PARK

ER
PARK

GLACIER NATIONAL
PARK

INTRO
ATTRACTIONS
DINING
LODGING

and relatively level. One of the best trails leads to Grinnell Glacier, the park's most trail-accessible glacier. An 8-mi round-trip, it is well worth the effort to view one of the most spectacular and largest glaciers in the park. From July to mid-September, a ranger-led hike begins every morning from the Many Glacier Hotel boat dock at 8:30 AM. The hike is strenuous, and you should check with the ranger station to make sure the hike is scheduled for the morning you want to go. Another ranger-led hike to Iceberg Lake is a moderately strenuous 10 mi round-trip, easier than the hike to Grinnell Glacier. The trail is open from June to mid-September and begins at the Swift Current Motor Inn, where you meet the ranger.

Two Medicine Valley is a lovely area in the southeast corner of the park. You can drive in part of the way on a dirt road. This is a good place for day hikes and is one of the least-developed and least-visited parts of Glacier Park. A camp store that sells supplies and a campground are at Two Medicine Lake. You can make arrangements for a boat pick-up or drop-off across the lake.

With lots of campgrounds, large alpine lakes, and fabulous scenery, **Belly River Country,** in the northeast section of the park, is one of the most popular spots for back-country camping. The area has a nice mix of low meadows and spectacular high mountains. Call the park to get a map of trails and information.

Information: Glacier National Park | U.S. 2, West Glacier, 59936 | 406/888–7800 | www.nps.gov/glac/home.htm | $5 per person, $10 per car, $20 for one-year Glacier Pass | Daily dawn to dusk; Going-to-the-Sun Rd. generally closed Nov–May.

Attractions

TOURS AND ADVENTURES

Glacier Gateway Outfitters. On this working cattle and horse ranch, you can take a full- or half-day ride in the Two Medicine drainage area with Blackfeet cowboy guides. They have overnight camping and fishing, too, as well as a campground. | 435 Badger Creek, Valier; 1 mi east on U.S. 2 | 406/338–5560 | Varies with trip | May–Sept.

The Glacier Institute. This is the place to go if you would like a deeper understanding of the natural world. The educational organization has field seminars and programs for individuals and groups in and around Glacier Park. | 137 Main St., Kalispell | 406/755–1211 or 406/888–5215, summer only | Apr.–Oct.

Glacier Wilderness Guides/Montana Raft Co. You can attend fly-fishing school here first, then get a Montana fishing license (required) and take fishing trips from half-day to overnight. If you don't fish, you can take a rafting trip. Half-day trips are run on the Middle Fork River. Lunches are included in longer trips. | Box 535, West Glacier | 406/387–5555 or 800/521–7238 | www.glacierraftco.com | $195–$250 per person per day, 2-person minimum | Apr.–Oct.

Great Divide Guiding and Outfitters. For the longer haul, you can try five-day custom pack trips and high-country cow camps, scheduled for every weekday June–August in the Lewis and Clark National Forest. | Box 315, East Glacier | 406/226–4487 or 800/431–9687 | www.recworld.com/greatdivide | May–Sept.

Great Northern Whitewater. River outfitters since 1977, they offer trips of three hours to three days, guided fly-fishing, kayak and canoe trips, and horseback trips. | West Glacier | 406/387–5340 or 800/735–7897 (reservations) | www.gnwhitewater.com | Apr.–Oct.

ON THE CALENDAR

OCT.: *Glacier Golden Autumn Arts and Crafts Show.* The historic Izaak Walton Inn hosts this annual show and sale featuring outstanding crafts and artists. Shop and then visit Glacier National Park in the full golden color of fall. | 406/888–5700.

Lodging

Apgar Village Lodge. The cabins and motel units here have views of the lake, and most of the cabins have kitchens. The furnishings are Western-style, and you can also go Western with a picnic prepared at the barbecue pits on the grounds. Cable TV. Hiking, boating. | West Glacier | 406/888–5484 | fax 406/888–5273 | www.westglacier.com | 48 rooms and cabins | $59–$78, $89–$210 1-to 3-bedroom cabins | AE, D, MC, V | Closed mid-Oct.–Apr.

Granite Park Chalet. Built by the Great Northern Railroad in the early to mid-1900s, Granite Park Chalet was a de rigueur stop for early tourists, who rode horses through the park 7 to 9 mi each day and stayed at a different chalet each night. This and the Sperry Chalet are the only two chalets still standing. You can reach it only by hiking trails. A combination of public and private funds is being used to transform the chalet back into a full-service hotel, and Granite Park is now available from July through mid-September as a hikers' shelter for overnight stays; currently you still must bring sleeping bags and your own food, and you need a reservation. You can park at Logan Pass Visitor Center and the Loop Trailhead. | Box 535, West Glacier | 406/387–5555 or 800/521–RAFT | fax 406/387–5656 | glguides@cyberport.net | www.glacierguides.com | 12 rooms | $60 | Closed mid-Sept.–early June | AE, MC, V | EP.

Lake McDonald Lodge. Opened in 1914, Lake McDonald is one of the great lodges of the West, meticulously restored. A Swiss chalet in design, it has open stairways and burled newel posts and massive timbers surrounding stone fireplaces. You can hike and boat nearby. Restaurant, bar. No air-conditioning. Hiking, boating. No smoking (lodge). | Going-to-the-Sun Rd. | 602/207–6000 or 406/756–2444 | www.glacierinc.com | fax 406/888–5681 | 100 rooms in lodge, cabins, or motel-style complex | $87–$135 | AE, D, MC, V | Closed Oct.–May.

Many Glacier Hotel. This grand old Western lodge has a great hall that's pillared with massive peeled timbers. You can best enjoy the spectacular views from the vast veranda above the lake. Built in 1915 by Great Northern Railway president Louis Hill, this is the largest lodging in the park. Restaurant, bar. No air-conditioning. Hiking. | Box 147, East Glacier | 406/756–2444 or 602/207–6000 | fax 602/207–5589 | www.glacierinc.com | 210 rooms | $103–$135, 175–$190 suites | D, MC, V | Closed mid-Sept.–mid-May.

Prince of Wales Hotel. Over the border in Waterton, Canada, this historic hotel built in the 1920s overlooks Waterton Lake. The large windows in the lobby give grand mountain views. High tea served daily. Restaurant, lounge. | General Delivery, Waterton, Alberta, Canada T0K 2M0 | 403/859–2231 or 406/756–2444 | www.glacierparkinc.com | 87 rooms | $209–$255 US | AE, D, MC, V | Closed Sept.–Apr.

Sperry Chalet. One of the two surviving Great Northern Chalets, Sperry Chalet has been reconstructed over the past few years. You can now stay here from July through mid-September as a full-service hotel with small restaurant for backcountry hikers. A steep 6-mi trail from Lake McDonald Lodge on the west side of the park is the only way you'll get here, but the commanding views are worth the strenuous effort. You can park at Lake McDonald Lodge. Restaurant. | Box 188, West Glacier | 406/387–5654 or 888/345–2649 | www.ptinet.net/sperrychalet/menu | 17 | $50 room, $100 per person | AE, MC, V | Closed early Sept.–early July | AP.

GLASGOW

MAP 6, I3

(Nearby town also listed: Fort Peck)

North of the vast Fork Peck Lake and near the Charles M. Russell National Wildlife Refuge, Glasgow is rich in history. The 3,500-resident town has the Pioneer Museum, which displays Native American artifacts and fossils, as well as collections on railroads, early business, aviation, and wildlife.

Information: Glasgow Chamber of Commerce | Box 832, Glasgow, 59230 | 406/228–2222 | www.glasgow.com.

Attractions

Charles M. Russell Wildlife Refuge. This refuge covers a million acres of range around the reservoir, and is a sanctuary for at least 200 species of birds, 45 different mammals, and many kinds of reptiles. Bighorn sheep, deer, and elk roam the federally protected wilderness area. You'll find dinosaur bones, buffalo kill sites, abandoned homesteader's shacks, and wagon-wheel ruts. Road conditions vary; check before driving here. Over 1,520 mi of shoreline surrounds massive Fort Peck Lake. Best known for walleye fishing, the lake contains many game fish, including northern pike, perch, and salmon. You can stay at any of the many campgrounds and recreation areas that ring the lake and swim, fish, boat, and go horseback riding. | Visitor Center: U.S. 220, beside Airport Rd. | 406/228–3700 | Free | Daily.

Hell Creek State Park. You have good access for boating and fishing at this 172-acre state park on Fort Peck Reservoir's shoreline, and there's a swimming beach as well. The 52 undeveloped campsites have limited facilities, though you can buy groceries, gas, and bait from May through September. | Rte. 543 | 406/232–0900 | www.state.mt.us | Day use $4, camping $11 | Daily.

Pioneer Museum. Fossils and Native American artifacts are displayed here, as are collections on the railroad, early business, aviation, and wildlife. | 816 U.S. 2 | 406/228–8692 | Free | Memorial Day–Labor Day, daily 9–5; closed Labor Day–Memorial Day.

ON THE CALENDAR

JUNE: *Longest Dam Run.* The run/walk across the top of the historic Fort Peck Dam comes in several distances; 5K or 1-mi walks, and 5K or 10K runs. There's a pasta feed the night before the event. | 406/228–2222.

JULY: *Montana Governor's Cup Walleye Tournament.* Anglers from throughout Montana and a dozen other states vie for prizes in the largest walleye tourney in the West. Events include a fish fry, barbecue, guys and gals tournament, and youth fishing contests. | 406/228–2222.

AUG.: *Northeast Montana Fair and Rodeo.* Free entertainment with music, magic acts, clowns, a PRCA rodeo, a demo derby, and lawnmower races. Livestock and 4-H exhibits, arts and crafts, and more, all at the fairgrounds at the west edge of the city. | 406/228–8221.

JUNE–AUG.: *Fort Peck Summer Theater.* Professional actors join local thespians for three summer presentations set at a wonderful theater constructed for dam workers in the 1940s, 17 mi southeast of Glasgow. | Rte. 24, Fort Peck | 406/228–9219.

Lodging

Campbell Lodge. The rooms here are modest, with very reasonable rates, and you get downtown convenience. Complimentary Continental breakfast. Cable TV. Exercise equipment. | 534 3rd Ave. S | 406/228–9328 | fax 406/228–4962 | 31 rooms | $32–$36 | AE, D, MC, V.

Cottonwood Inn. Antiques and mounted hunting trophies greet you in the lobby. The spacious rooms are furnished in Western style, and if you're a business traveler, check out the executive suites with desks and in-room data ports. Restaurant, bar, room service. Some refrigerators. Cable TV. Indoor pool. Hot tub. Exercise equipment. Laundry facilities. Business services. Airport shuttle. | U.S. 2 | 406/228–8213 or 800/321–8213 | fax 406/228–8248 | 92 rooms | $56, $81 suites | AE, D, DC, MC, V.

GLENDIVE

MAP 6, K4

(Nearby town also listed: Sidney)

Home to Makoskika State Park, Glendive is also known as the "Paddlefish Caviar Capital" and is a great place to hunt for moss agates and fish. The town of 6,000 has the Bell Street Bridge, a historic district, the Frontier Gateway Museum displaying exhibits on Plains Native American and ranch history and culture, and a frontier main street in miniature. For a glimpse into the region's past, visit the Krug Mansion.

Information: Glendive Chamber of Commerce | 313 S. Merrill Ave., 59330 | 406/365–5601 | www.midrivers.com/~chamber.

Attractions

Frontier Gateway Museum. You can learn more about Plains Native American history and culture and farm and ranch history, and see a miniature frontier main street. | Belle Prairie Frontage Rd. | 406/377–8168 | www.lewisclark.org/f/frogatmu.htm | Free | June–Aug., daily 9–noon and 1–5; May and Sept., daily 1–5.

Hunting moss agates. Look for moss agates—multicolored, semiprecious stones—and other minerals along the Yellowstone River, with a guide in season. You can also take an agate-hunting float trip; contact **LeMar Schock** (406/365–2442); for a guide who'll help you hunt rocks and fossils call **Vaughn Russell** (406/377–7201). The agate-hunting season is March–October.

Krug Mansion. Built in 1906, the Krug Mansion is on the National Register of Historic Places. It retains 8,000 square ft of high ceilings, gleaming woodwork, and original family furnishings, and is now operated as the Charley Montana B&B (*see* Lodging, *below*). | 103 N. Douglas | 406/365–3207 | www.ohwy.com/mt/c/charmtbb.htm | Daily.

Makoshika State Park. Makoshika means "bad earth" in the Lakota language. Wind and water have created caprocks, pinnacles, and hogback ridges. Many fossils can be found throughout this 8,832-acre badlands park, including those of the tyrannosaurus. At the visitor center, you can see displays and find information on scenic drives, nature trails, picnic sites, and the 22 campsites. No digging, no removal of fossils, and no metal detectors are allowed. Watch for snakes. | Snyder Ave. | 406/365–6256 | www.state.mt.us | Day use $4 | Daily.

Paddlefish Fishing. The paddlefish fishing season on the Yellowstone River runs from May 15 to June 30. The Intake, a seasonal fishing shack 16 mi north of Glendive, sells supplies and will clean your fish for free in exchange for the roe, the females' eggs, which is then processed into caviar and sold. They give the proceeds to community groups—baseball leagues, schools, and Boy Scouts—in the form of grants. Old hands who fish all summer hang out here and will talk your ear off. For guide services and equipment rental, contact the Intake. | Rte. 16 | 406/365–5601 | May 15–June 30, daily.

ON THE CALENDAR

JUNE: *Badlands Drifters Classic Car Show.* This annual show displays classic and custom cars and street rods and stages a poker run, dancing, a barbecue, and a competition. | 406/365–5601.

JUNE: *Buzzard Day.* Mark the return of turkey buzzards to Makoshika State Park with nature walks, a pancake breakfast, runs, kite-flying, a badlands bike rodeo, and hikes. | Makoshika State Park | 406/365–6256.

AUG.: *Dawson County Fair and Rodeo.* The annual county fair includes 4-H and open-class exhibits, free stage acts, a PRCA rodeo, a country and western concert, food, displays, and a ranch rodeo. | 406/377–6781 or 406/365–5601.

Lodging

Best Western Jordan Inn. Walk to shops and restaurants from this contemporary-style motel that's 3 mi from Makoshika State Park. Restaurant, bar. Pool. | 223 N. Merrill St. | 406/377–5555 or 800 888/GLENDIVE | fax 406/365–6233 | www.bestwestern.com | 69 rooms | $68, $94 suites | AE, D, MC, V.

Charley Montana Bed & Breakfast. Built for millionaire Charles Krug in 1907, the structure is now on the National Register of Historic Places and became a bed-and-breakfast in 1997. The 9-ft doorways are made of mahogany, and the leaded-glass windows look onto great views. Reservations suggested. Complimentary breakfast. | 103 N. Douglas Ave. | 406/365–3207 | www.bbonline.com/mt/charley | 7 rooms, 2 with shared bath | $55–$70 | AE, D, MC, V.

Days Inn. The rooms are furnished in a contemporary style and are average in size. Complimentary Continental breakfast. Cable TV. | 2000 N. Merrill St. | 406/365–6011 or 800/325–2525 | fax 406/365–2876 | 59 rooms | $56 | AE, D, DC, MC, V.

GREAT FALLS

MAP 6, E4

(Nearby town also listed: Fort Benton)

The state's second-largest city, with 59,000 residents, Great Falls is north-central Montana's commercial and social hub. It is also the place where explorers Lewis and Clark encountered one of the most daunting obstacles of their entire expedition—the great falls that gave the town its name. For an overview of the city, stop at the Great Falls Visitor Center (406/771–0885) at Broadwater Overlook Park on Upper River Road. For narrated sightseeing tours, catch the Great Falls Historic Trolley at the Visitor Center. The C. M. Russell Museum Complex holds the world's most complete collection of cowboy artist Charles M. Russell's artwork.

Information: Great Falls Chamber of Commerce | 710 1st Ave. N, 59403 | 406/761–4434 | www.gfa-mtchamber.org.

Attractions

C. M. Russell Museum Complex and Original Log Cabin Studio. The museum holds the world's most complete collection of the original art and personal objects of cowboy artist C. M. Russell. Russell's log-cabin studio and home also contain art by Winold Reiss, O. C. Seltzer, E. E. Heikka, Joseph Henry Sharp, and others. There's also a large Browning firearms collection. | 400 13th St. N | 406/727–8787 | www.cmrussell.org | $4 | June–Sept., Mon.–Sat. 9–6, Sun. noon–5; Oct.–May, Tues.–Sat. 10–5.

Giant Springs State Park and State Trout Hatchery. The cold-water springs here feed a state trout hatchery that covers 400 acres of parkland. The springs qualify as the shortest river in the world, the Roe River. There's a visitor center, picnic grounds, and river drive. You can also attend educational programs and take tours. The park has hiking and biking trails, fishing, and a playground. | 4600 Giant Springs Rd. | 406/454–5840 | www.state.mt.us | $1 | Weekdays 8–4:30.

Lewis and Clark National Forest. The national forest has seven separate mountain ranges and spans almost 2 million acres from the Continental Divide eastward to the plains. On a map, the National Forest System lands look like islands of forest within oceans of prairie. Due to the land patterns, the forest is separated into two divisions: Rocky Mountain and Jefferson. The rest is managed primarily for recreational use. The six remaining mountain ranges are spread across the Jefferson Division of the forest. In Great Falls, you can get information on all units of the park at the Forest Headquarters; for specific units, you can get park maps, and lists of campgrounds and recreation areas at the following ranger station offices. *See* also White Sulphur Springs and Harlowton. | Lewis and Clark Forest Headquarters: 1101 15th St., North Great Falls; Augusta Ranger Station: 405 Main St., Augusta; Choteau Ranger Station: 1102 Main Ave., Choteau; Judith Ranger District: 109 Central Ave., Stanford; Belt Creek Information Station: 4234 U.S. 89, Neihart | Headquarters: 406/791–7700; Augusta Ranger Station: 406/562–3247; Choteau Ranger Station: 406/466–5341; Judith Ranger District: 406/566–2292; Belt Creek Information Station: 406/236–5511 | www.fs.fed.us/r1/lewisclark | Free; camping up to $17 per day per vehicle | Daily.

Lewis and Clark National Historic Trail Interpretive Center. The nation's newest Lewis and Clark interpretive center opened in late 1998 on the bank of the Missouri River overlooking Black Eagle Falls. The center's focus is on relations between the Corps of Discovery and the many Native American tribes they encountered. | 4201 Giant Springs Rd. | 406/727–

8733 | www.fs.fed.us/r1/lewisclark | $5 | Memorial Day–Labor Day, daily 9–8; Labor Day–Sept. 30, daily 9–5; Oct.–Memorial Day, Tues.–Sat. 9–5, Sun. noon–5.

Paris Gibson Square Museum of Art. Built in 1895 as the town's first high school, this building now houses the Cascade County Historical Museum, many art galleries and exhibits, a café, and a gift shop. | 1400 1st Ave. N | 406/727–8255 | Free | Sept.–May, Wed.–Fri. 10–5, weekends noon–5, Tues. 7 PM–9 PM; June–Aug., Mon. and Wed.–Fri. 10–5, weekends noon–5, Tues. 7 PM–9 PM.

Ulm Pishkun State Park. This prehistoric bison kill site consists of a mile-long buffalo jump believed to be the largest in the United States. The name "Pishkun" is derived from the Blackfeet word meaning "deep blood kettle." A new visitor center, opened in June 1999, has a gallery, bookstore, classroom, and storytelling area. The terrain is rough; watch for rattlesnakes. You may have to pay additional fees for special programs or workshops. | Ulm exit off I–15, 10 mi south | 406/454–5840 | www.fwp.state.mt.us/cgi-bin/parks.pl | Day use $4 | Visitor center June–Aug., daily 10–6; rest of year by appointment.

TOURS

Great Falls Historic Trolley. Tour the greater Great Falls area aboard a 21-seat, climate-controlled trolley. The cultural and historical ride takes you to the Charles M. Russell Museum, historic neighborhoods, Giant Springs, Paris Square, and the sites of lots of Lewis and Clark history, including the spot where a grizzly bear chased Captain Lewis into the river. The tour's one stop is at Rainbow Falls. Christmas luminary tours operate in mid-December. | Tours start at the visitor center at Broadwater Overlook Park, off 10th Ave. S on the west end of town | 406/771–1100 or 888/707–1100 | www.seemontana.com/greatfalls/tours | $10 | June–Sept., daily; rest of year by appointment only.

Tour de Great Falls. Tours of greater Great Falls and the surrounding area start at the visitor center and last 2½-hours and include the true Great Falls at Ryan Dam as named by Lewis and Clark, Hudderite colonies, Ulm Pishkin buffalo jump tours, and custom tours to Havre, Helena, and other destinations. | 406/771–1100 or 888/707–1100 | $15 | By reservation only.

ON THE CALENDAR

JAN.: *Montana Pro Rodeo Circuit Finals.* Montana's top 12 pro rodeo contestants travel to Great Falls to pit their abilities against Montana's finest rodeo stock. Auctions and a dance complete the event at the Four Seasons Arena. | 406/727–1481.

MAR.: *C. M. Russell Auction of Original Western Art.* One of the largest Western art auctions in the world. Proceeds benefit the C. M. Russell Museum Complex. It has a 30-year history of excellent art, a chuckwagon brunch, and more than 100 exhibitor rooms, as well as seminars, an artist autograph party, three receptions, and two Quick Draw auctions. | 800/803–3351.

APR.: *Ice Breaker Road Race.* One of the nation's top 100 road races, this annual event is geared toward families and experienced runners. Events include a 5-mi race, a 3-mi race/jog, and a 1-mi walk. About 4,000 runners participate. | 406/771–1265.

JUNE: *Lewis and Clark Festival.* The celebration highlights events of the Lewis and Clark Expedition's 1805 stay in Great Falls with re-enactments, tours of historic sites, demonstrations, seminars, and float trips. | 406/727–8733.

JULY–AUG.: *State Fair.* Superstars entertain at the state's largest carnival. There's also horse racing, PRCA rodeo action, food, and livestock shows. | State Fairgrounds | 406/727–8900.

Dining

Borrie's. American. The atmosphere is casual and the dining family-style here. Regulars favor the steaks, chicken, lobster, hamburgers, crab legs, and soups. Kids' menu. | 1800 Smelter Ave., Black Eagle | 406/761–0300 | $12–$18 | D, MC, V | No lunch.

Eddie's Supper Club. American. Campfire steak, lobster, prime rib, and shrimp are the entrées of choice here. The atmosphere is casual, and they have entertainment on weekends. | 3725 2nd Ave. N | 406/453–1616 | $22–$29 | D, MC, V.

Jaker's Steak, Rib & Fish House. American. You get fine dining and a good variety here in a relaxed atmosphere warmed by the cherry-wood interior. The wine list is extensive, and they have 16 microbrews on tap. The homemade Louisiana-style barbecue sauce is a local favorite, as are crab legs, lobster, and steak. There's a healthy choice menu and kids' menu. A bar and casino are adjacent. | 1501 10th Ave. S | 406/727–1033 | $24–$32 | AE, D, DC, MC, V | No lunch Sat.

Lodging

Best Western Heritage Inn. Balconies that overlook the indoor pool and poolside rooms distinguish this modern facility in a suburban area 3 mi from the airport. Restaurant, bar, room service. Cable TV. Indoor pool. Hot tub. Exercise equipment. Laundry facilities. Business services. Airport shuttle. | 1700 Fox Farm Rd. | 406/761–1900 or 800/548–8256 | fax 406/761–0136 | www.bwheritageinn.com | 239 rooms | $79–$89, $89–$129 suites | AE, D, DC, MC, V.

Budget Inn. Close to the airport and five minutes from shopping, this hotel has comfortable contemporary rooms. Complimentary Continental breakfast. Cable TV. Airport shuttle. | 2 Treasure State Dr. | 406/453–1602 or 800/362–4842 | 60 rooms | $55–$63 | AE, D, DC, MC, V.

Collins Mansion Bed & Breakfast. Newly renovated, the Victorian interior has private baths and spacious rooms. The master suite has a fireplace, too. Built in 1891, the building is on the National Register of Historic Places. The wraparound porch is a pleasant place to sit and enjoy the large grounds that surround the inn. Complimentary breakfast. No smoking. | 1003 2nd Ave. NW | 406/452–6798 | fax 406/452–6787 | www.mccc.net/collins | 5 rooms | $75–$85 | MC, V.

Comfort Inn. Across from the Holiday Village Mall, this three-story motel is convenient to shopping and restaurants. Complimentary Continental breakfast. Cable TV. Indoor pool. Hot tub. Business services. Pets allowed (fee). | 1120 Ninth St. S | 406/454–2727 or 800/228–5150 | www.comfortinn.com | 64 rooms | $64–$80, $90 suites | AE, D, DC, MC, V.

Days Inn. If you're here for the State Fair or anything on the fairgrounds, this is a convenient place to stay. The rooms are contemporary and of standard size, and the lobby has nice Western art. Shopping is close. Complimentary Continental breakfast. Cable TV. Laundry facilities. | 101 14th Ave. NW | 406/727–6565 or 800/329–7466 | fax 406/727–6308 | www.daysinn.com | 62 rooms | $59–$75 | AE, D, DC, MC, V.

Fairfield Inn by Marriott. This chain caters to business travelers, and rooms have ample work areas and in-room data ports. The inn is close to shopping and the C. M. Russell Museum Complex. Complimentary Continental breakfast. Microwaves and refrigerators (in suites). Cable TV. Indoor pool. Hot tub. | 1000 Ninth Ave. S | 406/454–3000 or 800/228–2800 | www.marriott.com/fairfieldinn | 63 rooms, 16 suites | $64–$89 | AE, D, DC, MC, V.

Holiday Inn. A seven-story atrium and indoor recreation facilities combine with contemporary furnishings to make this a good, standard hotel, which also has convention facilities. Restaurant, bar. Cable TV. Indoor pool. Hot tub, sauna. Business services. Airport shuttle. Some pets allowed. | 400 10th Ave. S | 406/727–7200 or 800/257–1998 | www.holiday-inn.com | 169 rooms | $71–$74, $100–$165 suites | AE, D, DC, MC, V.

Townhouse Inn. The indoor swim center is convenient for families who are on the road, and the small casino will give parents a little distraction, should they choose. The standard-sized rooms with contemporary furnishings have data ports. There are Ping-Pong and pool as well as video games. Restaurant, bar, room service. Cable TV. Indoor pool. Hot tub, sauna. Game room. Laundry facilities. Business services. Airport shuttle. | 1411 10th Ave. S | 406/761–4600 or 800/442–4667 | fax 406/761–7603 | www.townpump.com | 109 rooms | $78–$80, $120 suites | AE, D, DC, MC, V.

THE CORPS OF DISCOVERY: AMERICA'S GREAT ADVENTURE

As America relishes the new millennium and its attendant predictions, revelations, and astonishing, advanced technologies, it becomes even more apparent that a 28-month, 8,000-mi transcontinental trek two centuries ago may still rank as this nation's most incredible adventure.

The journey truly began when President Thomas Jefferson, in a single real-estate transaction with a cash-strapped France, doubled the size of the United States. His purchase of the vast Louisiana Territory added an unmapped and virtually unknown tract of land, which stretched from the Gulf of Mexico to the Canadian border and reached from the Mississippi River to the Rocky Mountains.

To understand what $16 million had wrought, the president appointed a secret "Corps of Discovery" to venture west, make contact with native peoples, chart the rugged landscape, and observe the growing British presence in the Pacific Northwest. The group would be headed by Jefferson's personal secretary—Meriwether Lewis—and another intrepid explorer named William Clark.

On May 14, 1804, Lewis and Clark set out from St. Louis on their grand expedition with a party of 45 seasoned soldiers, scouts, interpreters, and others, poling up the Missouri River in well-stocked flatboats and keelboats. After wintering with the Mandans in North Dakota, the corps continued upriver in canoes and keelboats as soon as ice jams had cleared the waterway.

They entered what is now Montana on April 27, 1805, and then followed the Missouri to its Montana headwaters—the confluence of the Jefferson, Madison and Gallatin rivers. After they reached the Continental Divide, Shoshone Indians helped them cross the Rockies. The party then followed the Snake, Clearwater, and Columbia Rivers, reaching the Pacific Ocean that fall. On the return eastbound trip, Lewis and Clark split the expedition into two groups in Montana and explored several rivers, including the Yellowstone.

On September 23, 1806, the expedition arrived back in St. Louis after traveling more than 8,000 mi on foot, on horseback, and by boat. More than a quarter of the expedition was spent in Montana, where much of the land the intrepid explorers observed, mapped, and pondered in their timeless journals remains unchanged today.

Contemporary Montana travelers may retrace Lewis and Clark's footsteps and come to understand more about this great adventure and the expedition's encounters with Indian tribes. The best place to start is the new Lewis and Clark National Historic Trail Interpretive Center in Great Falls, where the 200-year-old adventure unfolds before you. Nearby Giant Springs State Park marks the place where Clark discovered a large "fountain or spring" during an 18-mi portage around a series of waterfalls.

Missouri Headwaters State Park near Three Forks preserves the spot where the explorers traced the river to its birthplace. The Lolo Pass Visitor Center located on U.S. 12 at the Montana-Idaho border interprets the significance of the Lewis and Clark Expedition and the Nez Percé Indians in this area of the state.

Another memorable avenue of Lewis & Clark discovery for Montana visitors is a boat tour on the "Mighty Mo." Several commercial operators offer tours at Gates of the Mountains, north of Helena off I-15, and also at the White Cliffs area of the Upper Missouri National Wild and Scenic River below Fort Benton. A canoe rental and shuttle service on the Missouri near Loma affords visitors a self-guided option.

Lewis and Clark Trail signs allow visitors to follow the expedition's route along portions of many state, U.S., and interstate highways in Montana.

© Artville

HAMILTON

(Nearby towns also listed: Anaconda, Missoula)

In the heart of the Bitterroot Valley, this town of 5,000 is the gateway to the Selway-Bitterroot Wilderness and other good places to hike, swim, and fish or visit historic sites. Among them is the Ravalli County Museum.

Information: Hamilton Chamber of Commerce | 223 S. 2nd St., Hamilton, 59804 | 406/363–2400.

Attractions

Bitterroot National Forest. Hamilton stands at the center of this 1.6-million-acre national forest, made up of the Bitterroot Mountains, the Sapphire Mountains, and parts of the Selway-Bitterroot, Anaconda-Pintler, and Frank Church–River of No Return wildernesses. The forests are full of bears, elk, moose, bighorn sheep, songbirds, eagles, and many smaller woodland animals. Hiking, horseback riding, camping, fishing, downhill skiing and other backcountry pastimes are most popular. You'll find more than 1,600 mi of trails in this forest. The trail system contains portions of three nationally significant trails: the Continental Divide Scenic Trail, the Lewis and Clark Trail, and the Nez Percé Trail. The Salmon and Selway rivers flow through, both part of the National Wild and Scenic Rivers system. The 23 campgrounds range from primitive sites at road ends to more developed sites adjacent to highways. The region was hit hard by the wildfires of 2000, though, so be sure to call before heading for any particular destination. *See also* Darby. | 1801 North Ave. | 406/363–3131 or 406/777–5461 | www.fs.fed.us/recreation/forest_descr/mt_11_bitterroot.html | Free; camping up to $17 per vehicle per day | Daily.

Daly Mansion. Copper king Marcus Daly built this large mansion at the turn of the 20th century. It has 42 rooms, 24 bedrooms, 15 baths, and 5 Italian marble fireplaces and sits on 50 planted acres in the scenic Bitterroot Valley. Tours are available. | 251 Eastside Hwy. | 406/363–6004 | $9 | Apr. 15–Oct. 15, tours on the hr daily 11–4; Oct. 16–Apr. 14, by appointment only.

Fort Owen State Park. In 1850, Major John Owen established a trading post for grain and livestock and a store to supply nearby gold camps. You can take a self-guided tour through the remaining part of the fort, the East Barracks, and an on-site museum. | 3201 Spurgin Rd. | 406/542–5500 | www.fwp.state.mt.us/parks/parks.htm | Free; donations accepted | Daily 8 AM–10 PM.

Lee Metcalf National Wildlife Refuge. The refuge lies along the Bitterroot River, 30 mi north of Hamilton on U.S. 93. Here you can observe the distinctive relationship between tree-nesting geese and ospreys as well as abundant other wildlife. Public access to the refuge is limited, but you can still stop by the 140-acre picnic area on Wildfowl Lane, a country road that traverses the southern half of the refuge. A seasonal hiking trail with photographic/viewing blinds is open mid-July through mid-Sept. | Box 257, Stevensville; U.S. 93 | 406/777–5552 | Free | Daily dawn to dusk.

Ravalli County Museum. The former Ravalli County Courthouse houses this museum that gives you a cross-section of Montana history. Built by A. J. Gibson in 1900, it was the courthouse until 1979. The permanent collections include Native American articles, an antique kitchen, a miner-trapper display, and a display of military artifacts. | 205 Bedford St. | 406/363–3338 | www.artcom.com/museums/nv/mr/59840.htm | Free | Thurs.–Sat. and Mon. 10–4, Sun. 1–4.

ON THE CALENDAR

JUNE: *Bitterroot Day.* A 20-year-old celebration of Montana's state flower brings together blossoms, memorabilia, and arts and crafts. | 406/363–3338.
JULY: *Bitterroot Valley Bluegrass Festival.* Weekend-long jam sessions complement this nationally recognized family festival that offers free workshops on banjo, mandolin, fiddle, and guitar playing. | 406/363–5450.

JULY: *Good Nations Powwow.* A gathering of native and non-native peoples in celebration of life. Drummers, singers, and dancers perform in a traditional lodgepole pine arbor. | 406/726–3701.

JULY: *Senior Pro Rodeo.* One of the best in the United States, this senior rodeo at the Ravalli County Fairgrounds features more than 300 contestants, as well as a fine art show, cowboy poetry, crafts, and an excellent bluegrass festival. | 406/363–5676 | www.rodeomontana.com.

SEPT.: *Ravalli County Fair.* In the heart of the Bitterroot Valley, this fair offers a rodeo, a bull-a-rama, food, carnival, family entertainment, and exhibits at the Ravalli County Fairgrounds. | 406/363–3411.

OCT.: *Apple Days.* The biggest bake sale under the Big Sky has apple pies and apple cookies, and apple butter bubbling. | 406/363–3338.

Dining

Banque Club and Exchange. American. In the old Ravalli County Bank building, this place has fine dining as well as an bar and grill. White tablecloths and flowers are the setting for the dining room, which serves up specials like beef loin with a mushroom brandy bordelaise sauce, prime rib, and rack of lamb. Upstairs is the Exchange bar and grill, where an after-work crowd kicks back for drinks, a little music, and sometimes to watch sporting events. Historic photos of the Bitterroot Valley cover the walls of both areas. | 225 W. Main St. | 406/363–1955 | $6–$30 | AE, MC, V.

Spice of Life. Eclectic. The historic building is traditional, the atmosphere romantic, but the fare here is a real mix. You can try steaks, seafood, or pasta or more exotic Thai and Japanese dishes. Kids' menu. There's music on Friday night. | 163 2nd Ave. S | 406/363–4433 | $7–$19 | AE, MC, V | No dinner Sun.–Tues.

Lodging

Best Western Hamilton Inn. A choice of room sizes, all with contemporary furnishings, and a good downtown location distinguish this new hotel. There's a small picnic grounds on the property, and good restaurants are nearby. Complimentary Continental breakfast. Cable TV. Hot tub. | 409 S. 1st St. | 406/363–2142 or 800/426–4586 | www.bestwestern.com | 36 rooms | $59–$66, $85–$91 suites | AE, D, DC, MC, V.

Comfort Inn. Suites with kitchens are a convenient offering here. The rooms are modern and of standard size. Room service. Cable TV. Hot tub, sauna. Business services. Laundry facilities. | 1113 N. 1st St. | 406/363–6600 or 800/442–4667 | fax 406/363–5644 | www.comfortinn.com | 65 rooms | $64–$67 | AE, D, DC, MC, V.

Deer Crossing. This historic homestead cabin now houses four luxury suites with fireplaces, hot tubs, and Western furnishings. You can view the 25 surrounding acres, lush pastures, tall pines, and mountain views, from the sun room. Complimentary breakfast. No air-conditioning, no room phones. Hiking, horseback riding. Fishing. No smoking. | 396 Hayes Creek Rd. | 406/363–2232 or 800/763–2232 | www.wtp.net/go/deercrossing | 4 rooms | $75–$110 | MC, V.

Lost Horse Creek Lodge. These Western-style wood frame town houses lie 4 mi into the forest, within 1 mi of fishing and horseback riding trails. All rooms are suites with wooden porches and full kitchens, and some have private hot tubs. The restaurant menu ranges from burgers and steak to fish and lobster. Restaurant, bar. Kitchens. Volleyball. Playground. | 1000 Lost Horse Rd. | 406/363–1460 | www.montananet.com/lost/horse.htm | fax 406/363–6107 | 7 suites | $67–$78 | MC, V.

Trout Springs Bed & Breakfast. At this riverside B&B, trout is a regular part of the four-course breakfast—they'll cook up fish you've caught yourself if you'd like them to. In the garden you can play horseshoes or boccie. Some in-room TV, some in-room hot tubs, bicycles. | 721 Desta St. | 406/375–0911 or 406/375–0988 | www.troutsprings.com | 5 rooms | $80–$100 | AE, MC, V.

HARDIN

(Nearby town also listed: Billings)

This southeastern Montana community of 3,000 has its roots in cattle country and its history colored by the nearby Battle of the Little Bighorn. You can visit the nearby Little Bighorn Battlefield National Monument, Custer National Cemetery, and Bighorn Canyon National Recreation Area. The Big Horn County Historical Museum and Visitor Information Center have cultural exhibits, restored buildings, special events, a picnic area, gifts, and statewide travel information.

Information: Hardin Chamber of Commerce | 21 E. 4th St., 59034 | 406/665–1672 or 800/735–2635 | www.wtp.net/bacc.

Attractions

Bighorn Canyon National Recreation Area. Straddling the Montana–Wyoming border, Bighorn Canyon gives you stunning canyon scenery and a lake that stretches almost 75 mi. You can boat, swim, fish, hike trails, take naturalist-guided trips, and camp. At the Yellowtail visitor center, rangers present programs about the Bighorn Canyon area and its spectacular limestone canyon walls. | 25 mi south on Rte. 313 | 406/666–2412 | www.nps.gov | $5 per day per vehicle, including camping | Daily dawn to dusk.

Bighorn County Historical Museum and Visitor Information Center. The museum complex sits on 24 acres and includes 20 permanent buildings. The museum focuses on Native American and early homestead settlement. It also serves as an official Montana State Visitor Center. | I–90 Exit 497 | 406/665–1671 | Free | May–Sept., daily 8–8; Oct.–Apr., weekdays 9–5.

Custer National Forest. *See* Billings and Red Lodge.

Little Bighorn Battlefield National Monument and Custer National Cemetery. History comes alive in the summer here, when park personnel portray the soldiers and Native American warriors who fought here in the 1876 Battle of the Little Bighorn. Custer's 7th Cavalry was defeated by leaders Sitting Bull, Crazy Horse, and Gall and their Sioux and Cheyenne warriors. The site was named a national cemetery in 1879 to protect the graves of 7th Cavalry troopers buried there and in 1886 proclaimed a National Cemetery of Custer's Battlefield Reservation, with veterans of other campaigns also interred here. It was redesignated Custer Battlefield National Monument in 1946 and renamed December 10, 1991. An interpretive center and museum are on the premises, or you can take a guided tour. | U.S. 212 | 406/638–2622 | www.nps.gov/libi/ | $6 per vehicle; $3 per pedestrian | Memorial Day–Labor Day, daily 8 AM–9 PM; Labor Day–Nov., daily 8–6; Dec.–Apr., daily 8–4:30.

Pompeys Pillar National Historic Landmark. Captain William Clark carved his name on this sandstone butte in 1806, the only remaining evidence along the trail of the Lewis and Clark expedition. Stop at the visitor center or take interpretive tours. | Off I–94, along Yellowstone River | 406/896–5013 | www.mt.blm.gov/pompeys/index.html | Free | May–Sept., daily 8–8.

Rosebud Battlefield State Park. The undeveloped site of the 1876 battle between the Sioux and General Crook's infantry set the stage for an Indian victory eight days later at the Battle of the Little Bighorn. This park commemorates one of the largest battles between U.S. forces and Native Americans. The displays explain the battle. You can hike, but watch for rattlesnakes. | 20 mi south, off Rte. 314 | 406/232–0900 | www.state.mt.us | Free | Daily.

Tongue River Reservoir State Park. Summer is when you'd want to camp at one of the 106 campsites at this new recreational area on the Tongue Reservoir. You can rent boats (there's a boat ramp), the fishing and swimming are great, and you can buy groceries from May through August. | Off Rte. 314 6 mi north of Decker | 406/232–0900 | www.state.mt.us | Day use $4, camping $7 | Daily dawn to dusk.

JUNE: *Little Bighorn Days and Custer's Last Stand Reenactment.* More than 250 reenactors spend six days commemorating Custer's famous last stand. There's a period costume ball, arts, crafts, entertainment, a fair, a rodeo, parades, a carnival, and street dances. | 406/665–1672.

JULY–AUG.: *Little Bighorn Battlefield Summer Lecture Series.* Local and nationally known historians and experts on the Little Bighorn Battle and campaign, the Indian Wars, and cultural history present free programs at the museum. | Big Horn County Historical Museum | 406/638–2621.

AUG.: *Crow Fair and Rodeo.* Rodeo action, parades, Native American dancing, authentic costumes, all in the "Tepee Capital of the World," the Crow Reservation. | 406/638–2601.

Dining

Purple Cow. American. The shakes and steaks are good here at this family restaurant, or try beef, chicken, or salad. Kids' menu. | Rte. 1, off U.S. 212 at the north end of town | 406/665–3601 | $7–$16 | MC, V.

Lodging

Hotel Becker Bed & Breakfast. On the National Register of Historic Places, this Victorian house was renovated in 1997. It's convenient to Little Bighorn Battlefield and museums. Complimentary Continental breakfast. | 200 N Center St. | 406/665–2707 or 406/665–3074 | 7 rooms, 2 with shared bath | $60–$70 | MC, V.

Super 8. The museums are close to this modest, contemporary motel, and Little Bighorn Battlefield is about 13 mi away. Complimentary Continental breakfast. Cable TV. Laundry facilities. Pets allowed. | 201 14th St. W | 406/665–1700 or 800/800–8000 | fax 406/665–2746 | www.super8.com | 53 rooms | $52–$65 | AE, D, DC, MC, V.

HARLOWTON

MAP 6, G5

(Nearby towns also listed: Big Timber, Lewistown)

The pioneer bronze sculpture *And They Called the Land Montana* is the most striking sight in this town at the junction of U.S. 12 and U.S. 191. The Upper Mussellshell Museum includes a general store, Native American artifacts, a pioneer home, and a dinosaur display. At nearby Chief Joseph Park, off U.S. 12, you can camp, stroll the scenic walkways, fish, and enjoy the playground.

Information: Harlowton Chamber of Commerce | Box 694, Harlowton, 59036 | 406/632–4694.

Attractions

Lewis and Clark National Forest, Musselshell District. *See* Great Falls. The ranger station is on the west edge of town on U.S. 12. | 809 2nd, NW | 406/632–4391.

Upper Musselshell Museum. An 1809 limestone house turned museum holds artifacts of the people who lived in, worked, and developed the Upper Musselshell area. The collection includes fossils and bones, a 2,000-year-old buffalo skull, and dinosaur displays. | 11 S Central St. | 406/632–5519 | $1 per person suggested donation | May–Oct., Mon. 1–5, Tues.–Sat. 10–5, Sun. 1–5; closed Mon. Nov.–Apr.

JULY: *Rodeo.* This event in Chief Joseph Park includes the full range of rodeo action, as well as parades, fireworks, live music, and dances. | 406/632–4694.

Lodging

Corral Motel. Family units with separate bedrooms and a great supper club next door set this standard hotel with modern furnishings apart. Restaurant, bar. | U.S. 12 and U.S. 191 | 406/632–4331 or 800/392–4723 | fax 406/632–4748 | 18 rooms | $35–$45 | MC, V.

HAVRE

(Nearby towns also listed: Chinook, Fort Benton)

The trading center for a wide area of extreme north-central Montana and southern Alberta and Saskatchewan, Havre is between the Milk River and the Bear Paw Mountains. The town of 10,700 is home to Northern Montana College, Fort Assinniboine, and the H. Earl Clack Memorial Museum. The museum displays exhibits, dioramas, and collections of horse-drawn equipment. A 10,000-acre preserve known as Beaver Creek Park is south of town, where you can fish in the two lakes, camp, picnic, or stare at the view.

Information: Havre Chamber of Commerce | 518 1st St., 59501 | 406/265–7748 | www.havremt.com.

Attractions

Beaver Creek Park. The nation's largest county park has great fishing in two lakes, and you can also camp, picnic, and view the scenery. | 10 mi south on Rte. 234, in Bear Paw Mountains | 406/395–4565 | $5 per day | Daily.

Fort Assinniboine. Once the largest military fort west of the Mississippi, this is now a museum. Tours begin at H. Earl Clack Memorial Museum. | 306 3rd Ave. | 406/265–4000 | www.the-heritagecenter.com/fortassinniboine/index.html | $3; special rates for children | Tours daily May–Sept. only; call for hours.

H. Earl Clack Memorial Museum. Displays include murals, artifacts, and military and mining exhibits. | 306 3rd Ave. | 406/265–4000 | www.theheritagecenter.com/clackmuseum/index.html | $3 | Oct.–May, Tues.–Fri. 10–5, Sat. 1–5; June–Aug., daily 10–5.

Havre Beneath the Streets. A historic community hidden under the streets has a bordello, opium den, bakery, and more. You can tour it. | 100 3rd Ave. | 406/265–8888 | $6; special rates for seniors and children | Sept.–May, Mon.–Sat 10–4; June–Aug., daily 9–5.

Wahkpa Chu'gn Archaeology Site. Managed by the H. Earl Clack Museum, the site is the largest and best-preserved bison kill camp in the plains. You can sign up for guided tours and see artifacts at museum. | U.S. 2, behind Holiday Village Mall | 406/265–6417 | www.the-heritagecenter.com/wahkpa/index.html | $5 | June–Aug., daily 10–5 and 7 PM–8 PM; Sept.–May by appointment.

MAY: *Black Powder Shoot.* For 20 years, shooters of all kinds have competed in this annual event, which also has tomahawk-and knife-throwing competitions and a pancake race. Primitive dress is encouraged. | 406/265–2483.

AUG: *Great Northern Fair.* A 4-H fair, night shows, PRCA and youth rodeos, carnival, open talent stage, and food vendors. | 1676 U.S. 2 W | 406/265–7121.

AUG.: *Rocky Boy's Annual Powwow.* Beginning with a walk for sobriety, this powwow includes dance, colorful costumes, and drumming competitions for all ages that last all weekend. Excellent cultural demonstrations and traditional foods. | 406/395–4282.

SEPT.: *Havre Festival Days.* A northern Montana tradition is filled with community events including bed races, arts and crafts, a parade, food booths, a pancake feed, a classic car show, a demolition derby, dancing, and entertainment. | 406/265–4383.

Dining

Lunch Box. American. This family-style deli has daily specials of soup and sandwich; two soups are made fresh daily. The menu has a lot of healthy choices, with 70 sandwiches, as well as salads, nachos, baked potatoes, latte, and espresso. Kids' menu. | 213 3rd Ave. | 406/265–6588 | $10–$14 | No credit cards | Closed Sun.

Lodging

Best Western Great Northern Inn. Spacious and close to restaurants, this inn has contemporary furnishings. Restaurant, bar, complimentary Continental breakfast. In-room data ports. Cable TV. Indoor pool. Laundry facilities. Airport shuttle. Some pets allowed. | 1345 1st St. | 406/265–4200 or 888/530–4100 | 65 rooms | $69–$79 | AE, D, DC, MC, V.

El Toro Inn. The Spanish design reflects the inn's name. Rooms come in various sizes, but all are spacious. The Amtrak Station is two blocks away. Complimentary Continental breakfast. Cable TV. Some pets allowed. | 521 1st St. | 406/265–5414 or 800/422–5414 | 41 rooms | $45–$49 | MC, V.

Townhouse Inn. Some rooms have Jacuzzis and some have been remodeled. You can also ask for a poolside room or one with a balcony. All are contemporary and comfortable and within walking distance of restaurants. Cable TV. Indoor pool. Hot tub. Fitness center. Laundry facilities. Airport shuttle. Some pets allowed. | 629 W. 1st St. | 406/265–6711 or 800/442–4667 | fax 406/265–6213 | www.townpump.com | 104 rooms | $84–$86 | AE, D, DC, MC, V.

HELENA

MAP 6, D5

(Nearby towns also listed: Deer Lodge, Townsend)

Montana's capital city of 29,000 residents, Helena traces its history to the 1860s gold rush that attracted thousands of miners to the state. The city's main street retains its name of Last Chance Gulch as a reminder of the four down-and-out prospectors who designated this spot their "last chance" after they'd followed played-out gold strikes across the West. Their perseverance paid off when the quartet discovered the first of several gold deposits, which propelled Helena to the ranks of Montana's leading gold producers.

A decade later, the ramshackle huts, tents, and log cabins of prospectors had given way to mansions, merchants, and dozens of small businesses. By 1888 as many as 50 millionaires lived in the town, making it the richest community per capita in the country. In 1875, Helena became Montana's third territorial capital. In 1894, it became the state's permanent capital following a $3 million election campaign against Anaconda.

Helena is nestled along the eastern front of the Rocky Mountains, 12 mi from the Continental Divide and 4,000 feet above sea level. The town is at the intersection of I–15 and U.S. Highways 12 and 287, halfway between Yellowstone and Glacier National Parks.

NEIGHBORHOODS

Much of Helena's rough-and-tumble history has been preserved in its architecture, including the downtown district and adjacent residential neighborhoods. You can get brochures to take a self-guided tour of **Last Chance Gulch** at the Helena Chamber of Commerce or at the visitor center off I–15. Reflecting the community's late-19th-century origins, you will encounter a colorful collection of neo-Baroque, Gothic, Italianate, and Romanesque architecture. Many of the stone buildings that anchor the Gulch have arched windows, ornate pillars, masonry patterns, sculpted metal, and carved faces, flowers, and lions' heads, all reminders of the town's golden era. Century-old mansions dot the **Westside** neighborhoods of Helena, with an eclectic mix of designs and styles that include Tiffany windows, tile fireplaces, parquet floors, exquisitely handcrafted oak and cherry woodwork, high ceilings, spacious porches, gazebos, and carriage houses. This area is the home of the original Governor's Mansion. The town's magnificent Cathedral of St. Helena towers over the city, lending a European dignity to its skyline.

TRANSPORTATION

Airports: Helena Regional Airport, Montana's fifth-busiest, has 14 passenger flights per day with direct connections to Salt Lake City, Seattle, Spokane, and other West Coast cities.

Amtrak: Amtrak's *Empire Builder* parallels U.S. 2 across northern Montana as it travels from St. Paul to Seattle. The passenger train stops daily at Hi-Line communities.

Bus Lines: Greyhound Lines provides east–west service in Montana along I–90 and I–94, with stops in all major cities. Two local bus companies, Rimrock Stages and Intermountain Bus Co., go from Helena to Anaconda, Cut Bank, Dillon, Great Falls, Kalispell, Havre, Lewistown, and Shelby.

Other: Local transportation includes taxis and door-to-door bus service.

Information: **Helena Chamber of Commerce** | 225 Cruse Ave., | 406/442–4120 or 800/743–5362 | www.helenamt.com.

Attractions

ART AND ARCHITECTURE

Original Governor's Mansion. Governors lived in this Victorian mansion between 1913 and 1959. You can take a guided tour. | 304 N. Ewing St. | 406/444–4789 | Free | June–Aug., Tues.–Sun. tours at noon, 1, 2, 3, and 4; call for special tour times Sept.–Dec. and Apr.–May; closed Jan.–Mar.

Pioneer Cabin. Built in the 1860s, this historic cabin remains as it was then. | 200 S. Park Ave. | 406/443–7641 | Free | May–Oct., daily 9–5; closed Nov.–Apr.

State Capitol. A Renaissance-style building with interior murals depicting Montana's history. The Montana Historical Society directs the maintenance of the building, which was renovated in 2000. You can take guided tours. | Montana Ave. | 406/444–4789 | Free | Daily tours mid-June–Labor Day; call for specific tour times.

PARKS AND NATURAL SIGHTS

Black Sandy State Park. On the north end on Hauser Lake between the Big Belt Mountains and I–15, the park has a 33-site campground with a boat ramp and an interpretive center. You can swim at the beach. | Rte. 453, then 3 mi north on county road | 406/444–4720 | www.state.mt.us | Day use $4, camping $12 | Daily dawn to dusk.

Canyon Ferry Recreation Area. More than 75 mi of shoreline gives you a great place to fish, boat, sail, camp, and watch wildlife. If you're here in mid-November, look for bald eagles. | Rte. 284 | 406/475–3310 | Free | Daily dawn to dusk.

Gates of the Mountains Wilderness. The rock formations on either side of the Missouri River gave this site its name. They appeared to block Lewis and Clark from continuing their westward journey. It's now a federally designated wilderness area, and a like-named company offers boat tours of the route of the Corps of Discovery through the spectacular Missouri River Canyon. With the picturesque limestone cliffs and weathered rock formations behind you, you can hike, boat, and look for wildlife. | Off I–15 | 406/458–5241 | Free; tours $8.50 | Apr.–Nov.

Helena National Forest. The vast and mountainous Helena National Forest covers six counties and opens up some of the most vivid glimpses into Montana's history. Ranger offices are in Helena, Lincoln, and Townsend. Six cabins are available for rent for $20–$25 per night. | U.S. 12, U.S. 287, I–15, or Rte. 200 | 406/449–5201 or 406/449–5490 | www.fs.fed.us/r1/helena | Free; camping up to $17 per vehicle per night | Daily.

Hunting for Sapphires. You can dig for sapphires and other gems (or take home some dirt to sift through at your leisure) at Spokane Bar Mine (406/227–8989) or El Dorado Sapphire Mine (406/442–7960). Buy a bucket of concentrate for $25 or dig your own for $25 per day. Rental equipment available. The on-site campground at El Dorado has showers and electricity. You can find sapphires in various colors at the Spokane Mine. Blue is most common, and red is most prized. The largest known sapphire found here was 155 carats. People have also found diamonds, topaz, and rubies. | 5360 Castles Rd. | May–Oct., daily 7–5; closed Nov.–Apr.

Spring Meadow Lake State Park. If you visit this park on the city's west edge, you'll find educational programs, and can watch wildlife, hike, ice-skate in season, fish, picnic, and take a ride in a non-motorized boat. | 2715 Country Club Ave. | 406/444–4720 | www.state.mt.us | Day use $4 | Daily dawn to dusk.

CULTURE, EDUCATION, AND HISTORY

Archie Bray Foundation. Ceramic artists from around the world come here to work and study. The gallery includes pottery, ceramics, and sculpture. | 2915 Country Club Ave. | 406/443–3502 | www.archiebray.org | Free | Weekdays 9–5, weekends 12–5.

Reeder's Alley. Carefully restored, this area of old Helena has some distinctive shops, restaurants, and a visitor center. | Near south end of Last Chance Gulch | Daily.

MUSEUMS

Holter Museum of Art. Both contemporary and traditional art are displayed in this attractive downtown museum. | 12 E. Lawrence St. | 406/442–6400 | www.holtermuseum.org/ | Free | Tues.–Fri. 11:30–5, weekends noon–5.

Montana Historical Society Museum. The Montana Homeland exhibit traces 11,000 years of history under the Big Sky. The museum also houses the Macay Gallery with works by Charles M. Russell and the Haynes Gallery of photography. | 225 N. Roberts St. | 406/444–2694 | www.his.mt.gov/ | Free | June–Aug., daily 8–6; Sept.–May, daily 9–5.

RELIGION AND SPIRITUALITY

Cathedral of St. Helena. This replica of the Vienna's Votive Church was inspired by the cathedral in Cologne, Germany. | 530 N. Ewing St. | 406/442–5825 | Free; donations accepted | Daily 10–4; guided tour available with 1-day notice.

RAILROAD TOUR

Last Chance Tour Train. A one-hour narrated train tour of historic Helena begins at the corner of 6th and Roberts streets. Helena Unlimited, a nonprofit group, operates the tours. | 225 N. Roberts St. | 406/442–1023 | $5 | Call for tour schedule.

ON THE CALENDAR

FEB.: *"Race to the Sky" Dog Sled Race.* One of the longest dogsled races in the lower 48, this 350-mi cross-country endurance race starts at historic Camp Rimini and finishes near Missoula. | 406/442–4008.

APR.: *Annual Helena Railroad Fair.* The largest railroad hobby event in the state is divided into equal parts railroad memorabilia, tin plate and toy trains, and scale models. You'll find a complete range of cars, engines, structures, and accessories to buy, sell, swap, or just look at. | 406/442–0315.

APR: *Kite Festival and Spring Fling Runs.* Design and fly a kite, take wagon rides, enjoy music, concessions, kite making, and flying booths, or participate in runs. | Ryan Park | 406/443–4608.

JUNE: *Governor's Cup Marathon.* Montana's premier road event for serious runners and families. Marathon relay, 5K, 10K, and 20K races. Pre-race dinner, dancing, food, and arts and crafts show at the finish line. | 888/340–3724.

JUNE: *Montana Traditional Dixieland Jazz Festival.* The 1920s come alive as Dixieland jazz resounds through Helena for three days and four nights. Twelve great bands play in six locations, along with dancing, arts, crafts, gospel services, jazz masses, and a food fair. | 406/227–9711 or 888/229–1484.

JULY: *Last Chance Stampede and Fair.* A classic Western rodeo and fair comes complete with a carnival, parades, professional cowboys, livestock and fair exhibits, a trade show, food, children's activities, and live entertainment, all at the Lewis and Clark Fairgrounds. | 406/442–1098.

AUG.: *Western Rendezvous of Art.* Guest artists display their handiwork for public viewing and sale. | 406/442–4263 or 406/442–3256.

OCT.: *Annual Autumn Art and Craft Show.* Nearly 100 juried artists and craftspeople from the Northwest are featured at this show, where all items are handmade. | 406/449–4790.

OCT.–DEC.: *Bald Eagle Migration.* Every fall an estimated 1,000 migrating bald eagles stop at Canyon Ferry to feed on spawning salmon. At the lookout station at the Riverside Campground, spotting scopes and binoculars are set up on weekends, when volunteers are available to answer questions. | 406/475–3128.

WALKING TOUR

Helena's Historic District (approximately 3 hours)

Start this tour near the center of Old Helena, at the **Pioneer Cabin** at 208 S. Park Avenue. It is the oldest home still standing in Helena. Built in 1864, by Wilson Butts, this typical miner's hewn-log cabin is now a museum. Up the block, **Reeder's Alley** is a collection of small, modest buildings that represent Helena's transition from mining camp to capital city. Between 1872 and 1884, Lewis Reeder, a mason from Pennsylvania, built 30 one-room apartments, and his simple masonry protected against the fires that plagued wooden structures along the gulch. Today, those structures house unique shops and restaurants, and the narrow alleyway is the town's most complete remaining block from the era. Above Reeder's Alley, the stone pillars and wooden stringers of the **Morelli Bridge** span a dry gulch. A foundry first operated at the site of the **B. K. Tatem House,** 440 S. Park, prior to 1868. Benjamin K. Tatem built the house in 1875. Its low-pitch hip roof, wide eaves, and round-arch windows show the influence of Italianate architecture. Commanding a clear hilltop view of downtown Helena and its surrounding neighborhoods, the **Old Fire Tower,** 60 S. Warren Street, kept a silent watch against a recurring enemy. The first tower was built here in 1869, then replaced by this larger version in 1874. **The Bluestone House,** 80 S. Warren, was built in 1889, designed by James F. Stranahan, one of the city's early architects. He had planned to live here with his new wife, but tragically he became ill while on his honeymoon and died. Over the years, the house was abandoned and its hand-cut limestone walls began to crumble. In 1976, the structure was rebuilt and is now used as a law office. **The Colwell Building,** 62 S. Last Chance Gulch, stands just a stone's throw northwest of the site where the miners first found gold nuggets in the gulch. Helena's First National Bank, the first chartered in the territory, stood here from 1866 to 1886. The **Antique Block,** 17–19 S. Last Chance Gulch, and the **Boston Block,** 21–25 S. Last Chance Gulch, were home to much of the community's early commerce, ranging from newspaper offices, vaudeville houses, and bowling alleys to glassware shops, clothing stores, and "houses of ill repute." The **California Wine House,** 46 S. Last Chance Gulch, which became "Helena's No. 1 Saloon," was originally here. Next door at 40–42 S. Last Chance Gulch, the pioneer business of **Clarke, Conrad & Curtin** sold stoves, tinware and tools from 1869 to the turn of the 20th century. The **Dunphy Block,** 32 S. Last Chance Gulch, housed offices and the Helena Bowling Gymnasium by 1869. Originally a stone building, it was remodeled after 1887, when Thomas Cruse, an Irish miner-turned-millionaire, opened his savings bank here. **Raleigh and Clark,** 38 S. Last Chance Gulch, and **Sands Brothers,** 36 S. Last Chance Gulch, were two of the town's oldest dry goods stores, competing for many years. The Romanesque design of the Sands Brothers building was one of the finest in the territory, and lions' heads above the upper windows still stand as sentinels. George Herrmann opened the doors to **Herrmann's Furniture,** 201 Broadway, in 1869, and until it closed in 1988 it was the oldest business in Helena. Late in 1868, the Helena Herald reported that the finishing touches were being placed on "one of the most beautiful structures of its kind in the West"—the **C. W. Cannon House** at 303 Broadway Street. It is the best surviving example of Gothic Revival architecture in town. The **Lewis and Clark County Courthouse** at 228 Broadway was also the Territorial and state capitol until 1902, and combined Montana granite with Wisconsin brownstone. A large clock tower once shadowed the courthouse but was removed after the earthquake of 1935. Nearby, at the edge of what was once known as "Courthouse Square," stands the **Lewis and Clark County Jail,** 15 N. Ewing Street. Opened in 1891, the building now houses the **Myrna Loy Theatre,** a jewel in the crown of Helena's performing arts community. The **U.S. Assay Office,** 206 Broadway, was built in 1875, as one of only five such offices in the nation. For nearly six decades, miners brought their gold bullion to the office's melting rooms, where the gold was processed. The **Brown Block,** 11–21 N. Warren, is one of Helena's oldest commercial buildings. Built in 1879, it housed small shops, offices and lodgings. The **Parchen Block,** 106 Broadway, was celebrated on its opening in 1886 and features French Second Empire designs, including a mansard roof, large front gables, and an attic dormer. Built in 1885, the **Masonic Temple** at 104 Broadway served Masons from 1886 to 1942. Designed by local architects, the ornate facade was constructed of brick and stone, handsomely trimmed with native granite and an imposing cornice. Its ironwork was cast at a local foundry. Around the corner at 38–42 N. Last Chance Gulch stands the **Lalonde Building,** with its frosting-like facade. Although the name of its designer has been lost to history, today's visitor may take comfort in its **Parrot Confectionery,** which has satisfied many sweet tooths for over half a century. Several other nearby buildings, including the **Gold Block,** 50–56 N. Last Chance Gulch, the **New York Store,** 44–46 N. Last Chance Gulch, and the **Granite Building,** 34–36 N. Last Chance Gulch, were reconstructed immediately after the July 1928 blaze that consumed many of Helena's most outstanding business blocks. The **Power Block,** 58–62 N. Last Chance Gulch, designed by noted Chicago architects Willetts and Ashley, has been one of Helena's most prominent downtown landmarks since 1889. It was built as a monument to its original owner, T. C. Power, who eventually owned 95 corporations, including 26 stores, a steamboat line, a stage company, livestock, mines, and real estate. In 1903, fire destroyed the magnificent Gothic Revival building that housed the **Montana Club** at 24 W. 6th Street. Rising from the ashes in 1905, this exclusive club, founded by wealthy stockmen and the mining elite of Helena in 1885, still operates in the building today, making it the oldest private club in the Northwest. Just down the street, the **Diamond Block,** 40–52 W. 6th, another of T. C. Power's creations, features copper oriel windows with diamond and sunburst patterns and rusticated native granite. The building perches dramatically on a sloping street. Small shops occupy the street level while offices are upstairs, much as they were a century ago. The **Cathedral of St. Helena,** 530 N. Ewing, was started in 1908 and completed 16 years later. Modeled after Cologne's cathedral, this Gothic building features stained-glass windows from Bavaria. Two blocks away, the **Original Governor's Mansion,** 304 N. Ewing, was home to nine Montana governors. The Queen Anne–style home is now maintained as a museum by the **Montana Historical Society.**

Dining

On Broadway. Italian. Wooden booths, discreet lighting, and exposed brick make this a pleasant interior. The seafood is as good as the pasta, though, and it's a romantic place to relax. The excellent wine list is updated frequently. | 106 E. Broadway St. | 406/443–1929 | $10–$25 | AE, MC, V | Closed Sun. No lunch.

Stonehouse Restaurant. American. Housed in a pretty Victorian home, this restaurant was voted to have the best romantic dinner in Helena. The large back room seats 70. Regulars come for the great seafood. Kids' menu. No smoking. | 120 Reeder's Alley | 406/449–2552 | $11–$20 | AE, D, MC, V | Closed Sun. No lunch.

Windbag Grill. American. Big Dorothy's Bordello closed in 1973 and was replaced with this restaurant. It has a reputation for great hamburgers and the "Humble Ribs" served in a 24-ounce rack. Locals hang out here on Friday night—maybe because of the large selection of imported beers on tap and in bottles. Try the Cajun battered shrimp, Cajun chicken kebabs, and steaks. | 19 S. Last Chance Gulch | 406/443–9669 | $7–$22 | AE, D, MC, V.

Lodging

Barrister. Original antiques furnish the rooms of this Victorian-style house that has a large common area. Carved staircases, stained-glass windows, and five fireplaces add elegance. The wraparound porch is a nice place to sit and admire the garden. Complimentary breakfast, complimentary evening wine and cheese. No phones in rooms. Cable TV. Business services. Airport shuttle. Pets allowed. No smoking. | 416 N. Ewing St. | 406/443–7330 or 800/823–1148 | fax 406/442–7964 | 5 rooms | $90 | AE, MC, V.

Best Western Cavanaughs Colonial Hotel. Helena's largest hotel is a brick building with a Colonial theme. The rooms are spacious and modern, and there's a 15,000-square-ft meeting space. Restaurant, bar, room service. Some in-room hot tubs. Cable TV. 2 pools, 1 indoor. Barber shop, beauty salon. Laundry facilities. Business services. Airport shuttle. Pets allowed. | 2301 Colonial Dr. | 406/443–2100 or 800/422–1002 | fax 406/442–0301 | www.bestwestern.com | 149 rooms | $89–$99 | AE, D, DC, MC, V.

Comfort Inn. Mount Helena is only ½ mi from this freshly renovated hotel. Rooms are spacious and modern. Complimentary Continental breakfast. Cable TV. Indoor pool. Hot tub. Business services. | 750 Fee St. | 406/443–1000 or 800/228–5150 | 56 rooms, 14 suites | $65–$75 | AE, D, DC, MC, V.

Helena's Country Inn & Suites. Within walking distance of the Mall, State Capitol, and the Montana Historical Society Museum. Some of the comfortable rooms have fireplaces. The rates are extremely reasonable. Restaurant, bar, complimentary Continental breakfast. Cable TV. Indoor pool. Hot tub, sauna. Business services. Airport shuttle. Pets allowed. | 2101 11th Ave. | 406/443–2300 or 800/541–2743 in Montana | fax 406/442–7057 | 72 rooms | $49, $60–$70 suites | AE, D, DC, MC, V.

Holiday Inn Express. The reliably comfortable contemporary rooms are spacious and have in-room data ports for business travelers. Complimentary Continental breakfast. Some refrigerators. Cable TV. Exercise equipment. Business services. Some pets allowed. No smoking. | 701 Washington St. | 406/449–4000 or 800/465–4329 | fax 406/449–4522 | 75 rooms | $75 | AE, D, DC, MC, V.

Jorgenson's Inn and Suites. The Capitol Hill Mall is next door to this pleasant contemporary hotel. Restaurant, bar. Refrigerators (suites). Cable TV. Indoor pool. Business services. Airport shuttle. | 1714 11th Ave. | 406/442–1770 or 800/272–1770 in Montana | fax 406/449–0155 | 117 rooms | $64, $86 suites | AE, D, DC, MC, V.

Park Plaza. You can look out the window and see the gulch where the miners discovered gold. The renovated hotel is within walking distance from downtown, and the rooms are modern and of average size. Restaurant, bar. Cable TV. Business services, convention center. Airport shuttle. Pets allowed. | 22 N. Last Chance Gulch | 406/443–2200 or 800/332–2290 in Montana | fax 406/442–4030 | 71 rooms | $79–$89 | AE, D, DC, MC, V.

Sanders Bed & Breakfast. Built in 1875, this B&B is listed in the National Register of Historic Places, and it does exude old-fashioned charm. The furnishings are 19th-century, and the rooms are spacious, with good views. Complimentary breakfast. Guest refrigerator. Cable TV, in-room VCRs. No smoking. | 328 N. Ewing St. | 406/442–3309 | fax 406/443–2361 | thefolks@sandersbb.com | www.sandersbb.com | 7 rooms | $85–$105 | AE, D, MC, V.

Shilo Inn. A newly remodeled chain lodging with contemporary design and furnishings. Complimentary Continental breakfast. Refrigerators. Cable TV, in-room VCRs (movies). Indoor pool. Hot tub. Sauna, steam room. Laundry facilities. Airport shuttle. Pets allowed. | 2020 Prospect Ave. (U.S. 12) | 406/442–0320 or 800/222–2244 | fax 406/449–4426 | www.shiloinns.com | 47 rooms, 3 kitchenettes | $89 | AE, D, DC, MC, V.

Super 8. Convenience is the selling point at this motel that is close to the Capitol, downtown, and the airport. Complimentary Continental breakfast. Cable TV. Pets allowed. | 2200 11th Ave. | 406/443–2450 or 800/800–8000 | fax 406/443–2450 | 102 rooms | $54–$66 | AE, D, DC, MC, V.

HUNGRY HORSE

MAP 6, C2

(Nearby towns also listed: Columbia Falls, Kalispell, Whitefish)

This tiny town surrounded by massive mountains is best known for its proximity to Glacier National Park, 15 mi east, and the dam, 4 mi south, that bears its name. That name derives from two logging-camp draft horses that wandered off during the rough winter of 1900 and were later found, bony and famished. Hungry visitors now are treated to the area's famed huckleberries, sold at roadside stands in summer and featured on most local menus. If you want to pick your own, nearly any foray into the surrounding hillsides in late summer should yield the purple prize. But remember— bears like 'em, too.

Information: Glacier Country Regional Tourism Office | Box 1035, Big Fork, MT 59911-1035 | 406–837–6211 or 800/338–5072 | www.visitmt.com/glacier. .

Attractions

Hungry Horse Dam. This 564-ft-high structure, one of the tallest concrete dams in the world, holds back the 34-mi-long Hungry Horse Reservoir. You can take free guided tours on the hour during the summer and check out the interactive displays and informational videos at the visitor center. | 4 mi east of U.S. 2 | 406/387–5241 | Free | Visitor center Memorial Day– Labor Day, 9:30–6.

Dining

Huckleberry Patch. American. The name says it all. This seasonal restaurant caters to travelers with all things huckleberry. The pies and pancakes are particularly popular and tasty. If you want something a little less purple, they provide a hearty all-you-can-eat spaghetti dinner for about $5. | 8858 Hwy. 2 E | 406/387–5000 | Closed Oct.–Apr. | $5–$10 | AE, D, MC, V.

Lodging

Glacier Park Inn Bed & Breakfast. This distinctive B&B is housed in a contemporary octagonal house with breathtaking views of the Flathead River and surrounding mountains. The rooms are comfortable and all have private baths. Each floor has a lovely common area with cathedral ceilings and plenty of glass to let in the view. Two big decks are perfect for lounging and watching the abundant wildlife, including deer, bear, elk, eagles, and the occasional mountain lion. The friendly host takes guests fishing and has plenty of gear to lend. Full breakfast. Fishing. No smoking. No pets. | P.O. Box 190799, Highway 2 E | 406/387–5099 or 877–295–7417 | jchris@glacierparkinn.com | www.glacierparkinn.com | 4 rooms | $100; 2–night minimum | D, MC, V.

Mini Golden Inns Motel. This efficient, contemporary motel at the east end of town offers easy access for all travelers, with one level and at-door parking. Kitchenettes and two-bedroom units are available. Cable TV. Continental breakfast. Small pets only. Designated smoking areas. | 8955 U.S. 2 E | 406/387–4313 | fax 406/387–4317 | 38 | $86 | AE, D, MC, V.

Tamarack Lodge and Motel. A romantic, rustic setting distinguishes this log lodge, which offers at-door parking and mountain views. Cable TV. Continental breakfast. Nearby fishing, hiking and biking. No pets. | 9549 U.S. 2 E; 1.5 miles north of Hungry Horse on Highway 2 E | 406/387–4420 | fax 406/387–4450 | 8 rooms | $70–$105 | Open May 1–Sept. 30 | AE, D, MC, V.

KALISPELL

MAP 6, B3

(Nearby towns also listed: Columbia Falls, Hungry Horse, Libby, Polson, Whitefish)

Founded in 1891, Kalispell is a bustling town of 33,111 wrapped in natural beauty and notable for a pleasant way of life. A walking tour takes you through the town's historic district. You can explore regional culture at the Hockaday Center for the Arts.

Information: **Kalispell Chamber of Commerce** | 15 Depot Park, 59901 | 406/758–2800 | www.kalispellchamber.com.

Attractions

Bob Marshall Wilderness Area. This federally protected natural wilderness area is bordered on the west by the Swan Mountain Range, with more than 1 million acres of wildlands. The beauty of the vastness is highlighted by a huge escarpment known as the Chinese Wall. The wall averages 1,000 ft in height and extends 22 mi along the Continental Divide, which winds for more than 200 mi through the region. No access roads lead into the wilderness area; you can reach it only by trail. Trails originate from forest roads off major roads that encircle the area, including U.S. 2, Rte. 83, and U.S. 89. Any walk into these remote areas is a serious undertaking. If you want to explore the areas, contact a National Forest Ranger District office for a detailed map and up-to-date information about weather conditions and anything else you should be aware of. For safety you should register a travel plan with a ranger office. The wilderness is home to some of America's largest big-game animals, including 250–350 grizzly bears. If you do go, you can fish, hunt, hike, float down the river, and ride horses through the roughly 1,800 mi of trails. More than 50 outfitters offer guided trips into the area. | Flathead National Forest Supervisor's Office, 1935 3rd Ave. E; Trails accessible from U.S. 2, Rte. 83, and Rte. 89 | 406/755–5401; in summer, 406/387–5376 | www.gorp.com | Free | Daily dawn to dusk.

Conrad Mansion. The turn-of-the-20th-century home of C. E. Conrad, a Montana pioneer, Missouri River trader, freighter, and founder of the city, has been brought back to its state of Victorian elegance. | 313 4th St. E | 406/755–2166 | $7; special rates for children | May 15–June 14, daily 10–5:30; June 15–Sept. 15, daily 9–8; Sept. 16–Oct. 15, daily 10–5.

Flathead Lake State Park, West Shore Unit. If you follow U.S. 93 20 mi south of Kalispell, you encounter this 146-acre state park on Flathead Lake with a 26-site campground, a boat dock, and a picnic area. You can swim at the beach, study interpretive displays, fish (tribal license is not required), or use biking and hiking trails. *See also* Bigfork for Flathead Lake State Park, Wayfarers Unit; Polson for other east-shore units. | Montana Fish, Wildlife and Parks Office, 406/844–3901 | www.state.mt.us | Day use $4, camping $11 summer, $9 winter | Daily.

Flathead National Forest. The Flathead National Forest is bordered by Canada on the north, Glacier National Park to the north and east, and the Lolo National Forest to the south. The forest has 34 developed campgrounds and picnic areas. You can reach the numerous lakes by vehicle, horseback, or on foot. At the scenic Hungry Horse Reservoir, with roads on both sides of the reservoir, you can camp, hike, and boat. The Bob Marshall, Great Bear, and Mission Mountain wilderness areas are primarily within the forest. *See* Bigfork, Columbia Falls, and Whitefish for ranger stations in or near those towns. | Flathead

National Forest Supervisor's Office, 1935 3rd Ave. E | 406/755–5401 | Free; camping up $17 per vehicle per night | Daily.

Flathead National Wild and Scenic River. Kalispell is the logical staging area for an adventure on the Flathead National Wild and Scenic River, the nation's longest waterway so designated. The South, Middle, and North forks of the Flathead River stretch 219 mi across some of Montana's most rugged and beautiful backcountry, skirting Glacier National Park and running through designated wilderness. For outfitters leading trips on the river, *see* below and Glacier National Park and Polson sections. | 406/755–2706 | Free | Daily dawn to dusk, weather permitting.

Hockaday Center for the Arts. Kalispell's cultural center has art exhibits and educational programs for adults and children. | 302 2nd Ave. E | 406/755–5268 | $2 | Tues.–Sat. 10–6.

Jewel Basin Hiking Area. Specially designated for hiking, this area covers 15,349 acres with 38 mi of trails. Twenty-seven alpine lakes are all within a two-to-three-hour hike of the parking lot. One of the best views in western Montana is from the top of Mount Aeneus. You can see Glacier Park, Bob Marshall Wilderness, and the Swan and the Mission ranges from the peak. | North end of the Swan Range between Hungry Horse Reservoir and Flathead Lake | 406/755–5401 | Free | July–Sept., daily dawn to dusk.

Lawrence Park. A city park with walking trails. | N. Main St. | Free | Daily dawn to dusk.

Logan State Park. On the north shore of Middle Thompson Lake, with access to over 3,000 acres of recreational opportunities. Fishing access. Campground with 41 sites, boat ramp, swimming beach, and playground. | 45 mi west on U.S. 2 | 406/844–3901 | www.state.mt.us | Day use $4, camping $12 summer, $10 winter | Daily dawn to dusk.

Lone Pine State Park. A day-use area on Foys Lake Road has scenic views of the Flathead Valley. You can watch interpretive programs and wildlife, bike or hike on trails, then lunch in the picnic area. The visitor center meeting room may be rented for groups of fewer than 50. | 300 Lone Pine Rd.; 4 mi southwest on Foy Lake Rd. | 406/755–2706 | www.state.mt.us | Day use $4 | Mid-Apr.–Oct., daily 8–8; trails open until 10 PM.

Woodland Park. This is a city park with ice skating, a duck and geese pond, rose gardens, and walking trails. | 2nd St. E | Free | Daily dawn to dusk.

ADVENTURE TRIPS

A-Able Fishing Charters. You can rent covered boats and private facilities for fishing and floating charters. Half- to multi-day trips. | 63 Twin Acres Dr. | 406/257–5214 | May–Sept.

Wilderness River Outfitters. Flathead River rafting tours on the Middle and South forks include multi-day trips and shorter excursions. | 208/756–3959 or 800/252–6581 | May–Sept.

ON THE CALENDAR

JULY: *Artists and Craftsmen of the Flathead Summer Show.* Nearly 100 booths feature pottery, wood crafts, needlework, paintings, jewelry, and other handicrafts. | 406/881–4288.

AUG.: *Northwest Montana Fair and Rodeo.* A carnival, parade, exhibits, PRCA rodeo, horse racing, night shows, and demolition derby are part of the fair at the Flathead County Fairgrounds. | 406/758–5810.

OCT.: *Glacier Jazz Stampede.* This four-day festival features ragtime, Dixieland swing, modern, and big-band jazz at fun venues around Flathead Valley. Workshops for students, gospel services on Sunday, and costume contests complete the offerings. | 406/758–2800.

Dining

1st Avenue West. Continental. Relaxed and romantic, this restaurant is in one of Kalispell's oldest buildings, with hardwood floors and traditional Western style. It is known for filet mignon, alligator, calamari, salads, and steaks. Open-air dining is on a patio overlooking the street. Kids' menu. | 139 1st Ave. W | 406/755–4441 | $7–$32 | AE, MC, V | No lunch weekends.

Lodging

Angel Point. With 312 feet of private shoreline on Flathead Lake and views of six mountain ranges, it's hard to find a nicer setting. The rooms are spacious, and there are two suites. Complimentary breakfast, picnic area. No air-conditioning, refrigerators. Fishing. No smoking. | 829 Angel Point Rd., Lakeside | 406/844–2204 or 800/214–2204 | 2 suites | $100–$115 3–night minimum, additional $10 per day for breakfast | No credit cards.

Best Western Outlaw Inn. Close to Glacier National Park and Flathead Lake, this newer hotel is near eight golf courses. The furnishings are contemporary, and there's a large landscaped area around the motel. You can also raft, bicycle, and fish. Restaurant, bar, room service. Cable TV. 2 indoor pools. Barber shop, beauty salon, 4 hot tubs. Tennis. Exercise equipment, racquetball. Playground, laundry facilities. Business services. Pets allowed (fee). | 1701 U.S. 93 S | 406/755–6100 or 800/325–4000 | fax 406/756–8994 | www.cavanaughs.com | 220 rooms | $125 | AE, D, DC, MC, V.

Blue and White Motel. Basic and comfortable, the rooms here have modern furnishings. The Flathead Valley is the lure. Restaurant, bar, complimentary Continental breakfast. No-smoking rooms. Cable TV. Pool. Hot tub. Some pets allowed. | 640 E Idaho St. | 406/755–4311 or 800/382–3577 | fax 406/755–4330 | www.blu-white.com | 107 rooms | $52–$54 | MC, V.

Cavanaugh's at Kalispell Center. Attached to a downtown mall, this large, modern hotel has a strong Western style throughout. The location is convenient. Restaurant, bar, room service. Cable TV. Indoor pool. Barber shop, beauty salon, hot tubs. Exercise equipment. Busi-

AS CLEAR AS A GLACIER

It would be nice if life were as clear as a Glacier. Not the slow-moving bodies of ice travelers encounter on northerly slopes, which really aren't especially clear. Rather, as clear as everything appears in Glacier National Park.

If all the highways we traveled had the impact of Glacier's Going-to-the-Sun Road, for instance, few of us would ever stay home. If the water that flowed from the tap in our kitchen sink could capture one-tenth of the crystal-clear, creek-cold cascade of a Glacier stream, we'd drink far fewer diet sodas.

Each year, a couple of million visitors soak in the exquisite, ice-carved canyons, alpine meadows and turquoise lakes of Glacier—a 1,500-square-mi preserve tucked in Montana's northwest corner. Few walk away unaffected. Like an ocean sweeping to the horizon, the simple vastness and grandeur of Glacier has a way of stirring the soul and leaving something unsettling in its wake.

Hidden lakes are sheltered by granite peaks. Living glaciers lead past snowfields to cloud-covered mountain passes. Gushing waterfalls drop into cool, captivating canyons. Stoic bighorn sheep and curious marmots keep company with grizzlies and Rocky Mountain goats. In this place of pristine beauty and boundless energy, of proud peaks and quiet valleys, people often re-connect—with nature, with families, with themselves. It would be nice if life were as clear as a Glacier.

© Corbis

ness services. Some pets allowed. | 20 N. Main St. | 406/752–6660 or 800/325–4000 | fax 406/751–5051 | www.cavanaughs.com | 132 rooms, 14 suites | $135, $171–$205 suites | AE, D, DC, MC, V.

Days Inn. The reasonable rates are one reason to stop at this otherwise standard chain. For those traveling with a family or group, the suites don't raise the price much. Complimentary Continental breakfast. Cable TV. | 1550 U.S. 93 N | 406/756–3222 or 800/329–7466 | fax 406/756–3277 | 53 rooms | $69, $80–$85 suites | AE, D, DC, MC, V.

Hampton Inn. In-room hot tubs set this inn apart. The rooms have contemporary furnishings. Complimentary Continental breakfast. Cable TV, in-room VCRs. Indoor pool. Hot tub. Exercise equipment. Laundry facilities. Airport shuttle. Business services. Pets allowed. | 1140 U.S. 2 W | 406/755–7900 or 800/426–7866 | fax 406/755–5056 | www.hamptoninn.com | 120 rooms | $108 | AE, D, DC, MC, V.

Kalispell Grand. History is visible in the furnishings of this downtown hotel. The lobby ceiling is pressed tin and the staircase is golden oak. The walls are rich cherry-wood. Victorian in style, the rooms are spacious and comfortable. Restaurant, bar. Cable TV. Exercise equipment. Business services. Some pets allowed. | 100 Main St. | 406/755–8100 or 800/858–7422 | fax 406/752–8012 | www.kalispellgrand.com | 40 rooms, 38 with shower only | $75–$84, $115 suites | AE, D, DC, MC, V.

Stillwater Inn Bed & Breakfast. A historic home turned bed-and-breakfast was built at the turn of the century and retains furnishings from that period. The spacious guest rooms have private baths. You can walk to shop, dine, and go to art galleries and parks. Complimentary breakfast. | 206 4th Ave. E | 406/755–7080 or 800/398–7024 | fax 406/756–6564 | 4 rooms | $85 | AE, D, DC, MC, V.

LEWISTOWN

MAP 6, G4

(Nearby town also listed: Harlowton)

Lewistown began as a small trading post and evolved into a pleasant small town of 6,000 residents in the shadow of the low-lying Moccasin Mountains. Self-guided tour brochures are available for areas listed on the National Register of Historic Places, including the Silk Stocking and Central Business districts, Courthouse Square, Judith Place, and Stone Quarry. Area history and culture is explored at the Central Montana Museum and Lewistown Art Center.

Information: Lewistown Chamber of Commerce | 408 N.E. Main, 59457 | 406/538–5436 or 800/216–5436 | www.lewistown.net/~lewchamb.

Attractions

Ackley Lake State Park. Just to the north of the Little Belt Mountains, Ackley Lake has a 23-site campground, a boat ramp, and great fishing. | U.S. 87 to Rte. 400, then 2 mi southwest | 406/454–5840 | www.state.mt.us | Free | Daily dawn to dusk.

Big Spring Creek Trout Hatchery. The state's largest cold-water production station nurtures several species of trout and kokanee salmon. | Rte. 238 | 406/538–5588 | Free | Not gated; view during daylight hours, usually winter 9–4, summer 7 AM–9 PM.

Central Montana Museum. Pioneer relics, blacksmith and cowboy tools, guns, and Native American artifacts are displayed at this small museum. | 408 N.E. Main St. | 406/538–5436 | Free | Daily 10–6.

Crystal Lake. In the Big Snowy Mountains unit of the Lewis and Clark National Forest, you find excellent hiking and camping, plus fossil and ice-cave exploration. The ice cave is a 6-mi hike from the 28-site campground. June is the best time to see the 30-ft ice pillars formed over the winter. There's a cabin available for snowmobilers in winter. You can hike on both interpretive and wildflower trails. No motorized boats are allowed on the lake. | Rte. 238 | 406/566–2292 | $8 per night | Daily; automobile access June–late Nov., other times by snowmobile only.

Lewistown Art Center. A regional arts center showcases local talent. | 801 W. Broadway St. | 406/538–8278 | Free | Call for performance schedules.

War Horse National Wildlife Refuge. Established in 1958 as a refuge and breeding ground for migratory birds and other wildlife, the refuge has three units, War Horse Lake, Wild Horse Lake, and Yellow Water Reservoir. You can view waterfowl and other migratory birds. The three units are geographically separated, but all are part of the Charles M. Russell Wildlife Refuge, which encompasses more than 1 million acres along the Missouri River. You take gravel roads to reach fishing and wildlife areas. The Charles M. Russell Complex Headquarters is in Lewistown with substations at Ft. Peck, Jordan, and Roy. | 76 mi northeast of Lewistown on U.S. 191 | 406/538–8706 | Free | Refuge open daily; headquarters open weekdays 8–4.

RAILROAD TOUR

Charlie Russell Chew-Choo. Discover and enjoy the landscapes that inspired Western artist Charles M. Russell as you take a 3½-hr dinner tour aboard a 1950s vintage train. | 211 E. Main St. | 406/538–5436 | www.lewistownchamber.com | $75, including dinner | May–Sept., Sat.; call for departure times.

SELF-RELIANCE: A MONTANAN HALLMARK

Founded on the brute strength of Lewis and Clark, who helped bare-knuckle their keelboats upstream to the birthplace of the mighty Missouri, and on the rugged individualism of a thousand faceless miners, muleskinners, and madams who came to settle the West, Montana has always drawn a particularly rugged breed of individualist.

"... it is the resilience and diversity of its meager population that give Montana its fresh face and big heart," claims author Norma Tirrell. "Smoke rising from Crow Indian sweat lodges beside Interstate 90 and cornucopian displays of fresh produce at Montana's Hutterite colonies hint at the cultural mix. Full-tilt Western blowouts, like the Miles City Bucking Horse Sale and Lewistown's Cowboy Poetry Gathering, are brassy statements about Montana's overriding cowboy culture and its attendant mythology."

Jeannette Rankin was one of Montana's most celebrated individuals and the first woman elected to the U.S. House of Representatives. Four days after taking her seat in Congress, Rankin cast her first vote against the America's joining the Allies in their fight against Germany. Twenty-eight years later, on December 8, 1945, Rankin was the only member of Congress to vote against United States entry into World War II, saying "As a woman I can't go to war, and I refuse to send anyone else." The vote cost her re-election, but gained her the respect only history can give. More recently, in the wake of stand-offs between Freeman and FBI agents and the apprehension of the Unabomber in a remote cabin, Montanans jokingly refer to their state as "the last best place to hide." But in reality, state residents are proud of their past, and pleased that somehow they landed in a place where one man (or woman) can matter—in a place called Montana.

© Corbis

JULY: *Central Montana Horse Show, Fair, Rodeo.* A draft, open, and all-class horse show, plus three sessions of rodeo, a carnival, 4-H and open exhibits, night shows, and auto races, all at the Fergus County Fairgrounds. | 406/538–8841.

AUG.: *Montana Cowboy Poetry Gathering.* For cowboy poetry and Western music, this gathering tops them all. Daytime sessions and evening performances combine with a juried Western art and cowboy gear show, workshops, kid's classes, and a jam session to make this a special treat. | 406/538–5436.

SEPT.: *Montana State Chokecherry Festival.* Taste and judge jams, jellies, wines, and other chokecherry items, and have a pancake breakfast. Also races, a farmers' market, an arts festival, a 100-mi bike-a-thon, and a food fair. | 406/538–5436.

Dining

Whole Famdamily. Continental. Homemade family-style cooking on this menu includes dinner specials of stir-fry, Mexican entrées, or beef and chicken. It's known for soups and salads. Save room for the famous cream puffs and other desserts. Wooden tables and chairs and pictures of the Old West lend homey touches. Kids' menu. No smoking. | 206 W. Main St. (U.S. 87) | 406/538–5161 | $5–$14 | AE, D, MC, V | Closed Sun.

Lodging

Super 8. The economical rates make this a good stop for budget travelers who want comfortable and inexpensive lodging. Cable TV. Laundry facilities. | 102 Wendell Ave. | 406/538–2581 or 800/800–8000 | fax 406/538–2702 | 44 rooms | $47–$53 | AE, D, DC, MC, V.

Yogo Inn of Lewistown. The name comes from the yogo sapphires found nearby. This is where you pick up the Charlie Russell "Chew-Choo" dinner train. You can also take Western buggy rides, tours of historical ghost towns. Rooms are contemporary and comfortable, nothing fancy. Restaurant, bar. No-smoking rooms. Indoor-outdoor pool. Hot tub. Pets allowed. | 211 E Main St. | 406/538–8721 or 800/860–9646 | fax 406/538–8696 | www.yogo@lew.net | 122 rooms | $69–$79 | AE, D, MC, V.

LIBBY

MAP 6, A3

(Nearby town also listed: Kalispell)

Tucked deep in the timberlands of northwestern Montana, Libby is a small logging community of 10,724 that offers countless chances to hike, fish, and otherwise enjoy the Cabinet Mountain Wilderness, the Kootenai National Forest, and Kootenai River and Falls. The Heritage Museum explores area history.

Information: Libby Chamber of Commerce | 905 W. 9th St., 59923 | 406/293–4167 | www.libby.org/libbyacc.

Attractions

Heritage Museum. Explores area logging and mining history. | 1367 U.S. 2 | 406/293–4167 | Free | June–Aug., Mon.–Sat. 10–5, Sun. noon–5.

Kootenai National Forest. Libby is right in the heart of this national forest, which is made up of 2.25 million forested acres, the Cabinet Mountain Wilderness Area, several small rivers, more than 100 lakes, and two special management areas. Ten Lakes Scenic Area, just north of Eureka along U.S 93, is 15,700 acres with views of alpine glaciers and rim-rocked basins. Northwest Peaks Scenic Area has more than 19,000 acres in the very northwest corner of the state. You can reach it by forest roads extending from U.S. 2 and Route 508. Ross Creek Scenic Area is a grove of ancient western red cedar trees growing along the banks of Ross Creek. The area is just west of Route 56, 15 mi north of Route 200. The Kootenai Falls on the Kootenai River adjacent to U.S. 2 between Libby and Troy are a major scenic attraction. The placid river gathers momentum surging through China Rapids and then over Kootenai Falls, dropping 90 ft in less than a mile. You can hike, camp, watch wildlife, fish, and backpack. | Kootenai National Forest Supervisor's Office, 506 U.S. 2, West Libby | 406/293–6211 | Free; camping up to $17 per vehicle per night | Daily dawn to dusk.

Libby Dam/Lake Koocanusa. Stretching almost 100 mi through the Purcell Mountains, Lake Koocanusa crosses the Canadian border. A visitor center with an observation deck is at the dam; you can tour the dam and power house with the Army Corps of Engineers in the summer. Various campgrounds, boat ramps, and recreation areas abut the lake. | Rte. 37 | 406/293–5577 | www.nws.usace.army.mil/opdiv/libby/libby1.html | Free; camping fee to $6 per night | Visitor Center daily 9:30–6; tours daily Memorial–Labor Day.

Thompson Falls State Park. This quiet, primitive park is a good place to watch birds, fish, and picnic. There's a boat ramp and 17 campsites. | 406/752–5501 | www.state.mt.us | Free; camping $11 | May–Sept., daily dawn to dusk.

Turner Mountain Ski Area. Twenty-six runs and a 2,110-ft vertical drop. Seventy-five percent of the area's runs are for advanced skiers. A warming shack and snack bar are on site. You can rent equipment in Libby. | Pipe Creek Rd. | 406/293–4317 | www.libby.org/skiturner/ | $17 | Dec–Mar; weekends and holidays 9:30–3:30.

ON THE CALENDAR

JULY: *Logger Days.* A celebration of nature, history, and friendly competition in J. Neils Memorial County Park includes a parade, adult and youth events, karaoke and lip-synch contests, vendors, crafts, and a concert. | 406/293–4167.

SEPT.: *Nordicfest.* A huge celebration of the community's Scandinavian heritage has the International Fjord Horse Show, ethnic foods, costumes, music, dance, arts and crafts, as well as home tours and concerts. | 800/785–6541.

Lodging

Caboose Motel. Within walking distance of a shopping mall and a mile from the Amtrak Station, this motel has modest, modern furnishings and a very friendly staff. Complimentary Continental breakfast. No-smoking rooms. Pets allowed. | 714 W. 9th St. | 406/293–6201 or 800/627–0206 | fax 406/293–3621 | 28 rooms | $40–$60 | AE, MC, V.

Super 8. A good home base if you're going to explore the nearby Kootenai National Forest and within walking distance of the Kootenai River, this motel has standard-size rooms and contemporary furnishings. No-smoking rooms. Pool. Pets allowed. | 448 U.S. 2 W | 406/293–2771 or 800/800–8000 | fax 406/293–9871 | 42 rooms | $62–$74 | AE, D, MC, V.

Venture Motor Inn. A slight Nordic influence is evident at this motel at the base of the Cabinet Mountain Wilderness Area. The decor is modern and modest. Restaurant. No-smoking rooms. Cable TV. Pool. Hot tub. Gym, hiking. Boating. Fishing. Snowmobiling. | 443 U.S. 2 W | 406/293–7711 | fax 406/293–3326 | 72 rooms | $62–$75 | AE, D, MC, V.

LIVINGSTON

MAP 6, F6

(Nearby towns also listed: Big Timber, Bozeman)

Much of Livingston (population 7,500), one of Yellowstone's original gateway communities, is designated a Historic District on the National Register. The walkable district numbers 436 buildings. Built on the banks of the Yellowstone River, the town is a great place to fish and float. The Firehouse 5 Playhouse has live community theater. Several museums present the area's rich railroad, frontier, and natural history.

Information: Livingston Chamber of Commerce | 208 W. Park St., 59047 | 406/222–0850 | www.livingston.avicom.net.

Attractions

Depot Center. A restored Northern Pacific Railroad station, the museum houses railroad and Western history displays and artwork. | 200 W. Park St. (U.S. 89) | 406/222–2300 | $3 | May–Sept., Mon.–Sat. 9–5, Sun. 1–4.

Firehouse 5 Playhouse. The playhouse presents vaudeville and comedy during the summer and musical productions during the fall and winter. | U.S. 89 S | 406/222–1420 | $10 | Call for performance schedule.

Gallatin National Forest. *See* Bozeman. | Livingston Ranger District, 5242 U.S. 89, | 406/222–1892 | Free | Daily dawn to dusk.

Park County Museum. Occupying a turn-of-the-20th-century schoolhouse, this museum has displays on early settlers, Yellowstone National Park, and area railroad history. | 118 W. Chinook St. | 406/222–4184 | $3 | June–Labor Day, daily 10–5:30; Labor Day–May, by appointment only.

ON THE CALENDAR

MAY–SEPT.: *Firehouse 5 Playhouse.* Vaudeville theater. | 406/222–1420.
JUNE–JULY: *Western Days and Roundup Parade.* The city-wide Western celebration features one of the state's largest parades, a PRCA rodeo, fireworks, arts and crafts, music, and dance, all at the fairgrounds. | 406/222–0850.
OCT.: *Livingston Wind Festival.* The Wind Festival celebrates Livingston's most abundant "resource" with exhibits and presentations, an art show, a quilt display, entertainment, and performances for all ages. | 406/222–3793 or 406/222–8701.

Dining

Livingston Bar and Grille. Continental. Homey and rustic, this restaurant has lots of art depicting local history. The menu changes weekly and could include buffalo burgers, chicken sandwiches, and seafood. Large selection of desserts. Kids' menu. | 130 N. Main St. | 406/222–7909 | $14–$28 | AE, D, MC, V | No lunch.

Uncle Looie's. Italian. Across from the depot, this restaurant serves classic Italian cuisine with a French influence. Local favorites include catch-of-the-day specials, beef dish of day, tenderloin, or medallions. Buffet lunch. Kids' menu. No smoking. | 119 W. Park St. (U.S. 89) | 406/222–7177 | $7–$26 | AE, MC, V | No lunch weekends.

Lodging

Chico Hot Springs. Two open-air hot-spring mineral pools are a welcome find if you've been hiking all day. The accommodations range from lodge rooms to cabins, and the hotel is set on 150 acres 30 mi from Yellowstone, in the foothills of the Absaroka Beartooth Mountains. Bar, dining room, picnic area. No air-conditioning, some refrigerators, some room phones. Pool. Massage. Exercise equipment, hiking. Bicycles. Fishing. Children's activities (summer only). Business services. Pets allowed (fee). | Old Chico Rd., Pray | 406/333–4933 or 800/468–9232 | fax 406/333–4694 | www.chicohotsprings.com | 49 lodge rooms, 29 motel units, 16 cottages | $45–$85, $189 cottages | AE, D, MC, V.

Comfort Inn. With a game room that has video and other games plus an indoor pool, this standard chain lodging is a good bet for traveling families. The suites with refrigerators are moderately priced. Complimentary Continental breakfast. Refrigerators (suites). Cable TV. Indoor pool. Hot tub. Game room with video games and pinball. Laundry facilities. | 114 Loves La. | 406/222–4400 or 800/228–5150 | fax 406/222–7658 | 49 rooms | $80–$90, $100 suites | AE, D, DC, MC, V.

Jumping Rainbow Ranch. This secluded ranch on 300 acres along the Yellowstone River was the site for the movie *A River Runs Through It*. Besides the river, where you can go fly-fishing, the ranch has six private stocked ponds. You can also go bird-watching or take a pack trip. The dining is gourmet and ranch-style both; take your pick. Kitchenettes. Fly-fishing. Horseback riding. | 110 Jumping Rainbow Rd. | 406/222–5425 | www.jumpingrainbowranch.com | 24 units | $75–$100; meals $30 per person per day | MC, V | Closed mid Oct.– Mar.

Paradise Inn. An indoor pool and some suites make this good for families. The rooms are contemporary in style and average in size. Restaurant, bar. Cable TV. Indoor pool. Hot tub. Pets allowed. | Rogers La. | 406/222–6320 or 800/437–6291 | fax 406/222–2481 | 43 rooms | $89, $125 suites | AE, MC, V.

Super 8. Rooms here are reasonably priced and a good choice for travelers who don't like surprises. Cable TV. Laundry facilities. | 105 Centennial Dr. | 406/222–7711 or 800/800– 8000 | 36 rooms | $64 | AE, D, DC, MC, V.

LOLO

MAP 6, C5

(Nearby town also listed: Missoula)

The gateway to the Bitterroot Valley, Lolo marks the start of the Lolo Trail, which the Nez Percé used as a buffalo trail and Lewis and Clark traversed en route to the Pacific. The Lolo Pass Visitor Information Center is scheduled to reopen in 2002.

Attractions

Bitterroot National Forest, Stevensville District. *See* Hamilton. | 88 Main St., Stevensville | 406/777–5461 | Free | Daily dawn to dusk.

ADVENTURE TRIPS

Montana River Guides. A professional guide service will design a float trip down western Montana's rivers to match your interests, whether they be wildlife photography or learning river skills. Trip lengths run from ½ day to seven or more days. | 210 Red Fox Rd. | 406/ 273–4718 | www.montanariverguides.com | ½-day trips start at $35 | Apr.–Sept.

MALTA

MAP 6, H3

(Nearby towns also listed: Chinook, Glasgow, Zortman)

A friendly stop on the Hi-Line, Malta is a ranching community of 2,400 with a big heart. The Phillips County Historical Museum has history and dinosaur exhibits.

Information: **Malta Chamber of Commerce** | 406/654–1776 or 800/704–1776.

Attractions

Bowdoin National Wildlife Refuge. You'll find great wildlife-and bird-watching here, with deer, antelope, upland game, and more than 200 species of birds. The roads are undeveloped. | 7 mi east on U.S. 2 | 406/654–2863 | www.r6.fws.gov/refuges/bowdoin/bowdoin.htm | Free | Daily dawn to dusk.

Phillips County Historical Museum. Kid Curry and the Wild Bunch gang were local outlaws. You can see Kid's gun and other artifacts here, as well as photos of the gang and exhibits on area history and dinosaur fossils. | 431 U.S. 2 E | 406/654–1037 | Free | Memorial Day– Labor Day, daily 10–5; Labor Day–Memorial Day, by appointment only.

JULY: *Outlaw Days.* A wild weekend in town has a fast-draw Western gunslinging contest, Kid Curry Symposium, sidewalk sales, a golf tourney, and historic tours. | 406/654–1776.

SEPT.: *Milk River Wagon Train.* This event includes a top-notch wagon train loaded with fun-seekers and friendly locals who enjoy five days of outdoor fun with horses, teams, wagons, and people who love 'em all. | 406/654–1796.

Lodging

Great Northern Hotel. The downtown location makes for views of small-town street life. The comfortable rooms have modern furnishings, and you can eat at the steak house. Restaurant. Cable TV. Convention center. Pets allowed. | 2 1st Ave. E | 406/654–2100 or 888/234–0935 | fax 406/654–2622 | 29 rooms | $46 | AE, D, DC, MC, V.

Maltana. The downtown location is convenient, and the rooms are modest but modern. Cable TV. Airport shuttle. | 138 1st Ave. W | 406/654–2610 | fax 406/654–1663 | 19 rooms | $41–$46 | AE, D, DC, MC, V.

MILES CITY

MAP 6, J5

(Nearby town also listed: Glendive)

MILES CITY

INTRO
ATTRACTIONS
DINING
LODGING

A classic Western town has been made famous by its annual celebration of cowboy culture—the Miles City Bucking Horse Sale. The town of 8,700 has three districts listed on the National Register of Historic Places.

Information: Miles City Chamber of Commerce | 901 Main St., 59301 | 406/232–2890 | www.mcchamber.com.

Attractions

Custer County Art Center. The art center features the works of local, regional, and state artists. During the annual Western Art Roundup, it is the site of quick-draw contests, cowboy poetry, and an auction. | Water Plant Rd. | 406/232–0635 | www.lewisclark.org/y/ycustarc.htm | Free | Tues.–Sun. 9–5; closed Jan.

Fort Keogh. Some of the original buildings remain at what was Montana's largest army post from 1877 to 1908. | Main St. | 406/232–2890 | Free | Daily.

Medicine Rocks State Park. Wind and water have sculpted the sandstone into unusual shapes at this mystical place near Ekalaka on U.S 12. Native American hunting parties once conjured up spirits here. You can stay at the 12-site campground and hike the trails, but beware of rattlesnakes. | 406/232–4365 | www.state.mt.us | Free | Daily dawn to dusk.

Range Riders Museum and Pioneer Memorial Hall. This historic center includes the officers' quarters from 1876 Fort Keogh, a Pioneer Memorial Hall, Old Miles Main Street, Native American artifacts, and the 400-piece Bert Clark gun collection. | Main St. | 406/232–6146 | www.lewisclark.org/r/ranridmu.htm | $3 | Apr.–Oct., daily 9–6.

Wool House Gallery. A 1909 wool warehouse once owned by the Milwaukee Railroad features railroad artifacts and memorabilia. | 419 7th St. | 406/232–0769 | Free | Tues.–Sat. 1–5, or by appointment.

FEB.: *Cowtown Beef Breeders Show, Craft & Agriculture Trade Show.* Beef producers take over Main Street with portable corrals holding their prize yearling bulls. An arts and crafts show is held at the Elks Lodge. | 406/232–2890.

MAY: *Bucking Horse Sale.* Held at the fairgrounds, one of the West's most enduring events features a bucking horse auction, bareback and saddle bronc riding, bull riding, wild horse races, street dances, and a parade. | 406/232–2890.

JUNE: *5th Infantry Days Encampment.* Relive the 1870s and '80s with competitions using period guns and rifles, marching maneuvers, cannon shoots, and cooking over an open fire. | 406/232–2182.

AUG.: *Eastern Montana Fair.* Celebrated by seven counties, this fair features free entertainment, a rodeo, a bump-and-run car derby, a carnival, and exhibits, all at the fairgrounds. | 406/232–9554.

Lodging

Best Western War Bonnet Inn. Many amenities are included at this standard contemporary chain accommodation with reasonable rates. Complimentary Continental breakfast. No-smoking rooms. Cable TV. Indoor pool. Hot tub, sauna. Pets allowed. | 1015 S. Haynes St.

FIVE DAYS IN THE SADDLE

It was a decade-and-a-half ago when Montana's Milk River Wagon Train was half as old as it is now. Still, you know that some things never change.

We had a hundred horses and 25 wagons—two-horse hitches and a couple of four-horse rigs with brave pilots and prized percherons guarded by fearless outriders with well-worn hats. I was the greenhorn with the borrowed boots and the big grin. That is, until it started raining horizontally and I realized my saddle bags bore no slicker. Never knew just one side of a horse and rider could get wet, or that a sleeping bag could ever weigh as much as the person occupying it.

We rode south from the Canadian border, skirting the breaks and keeping an eye out for coyotes and the right river crossings. Of course, Doc Curtis and the veterans knew where those were. They'd had 15 years to figure it out without a map. We, as they say, were along for the ride.

At night, the wagons were circled and the fires burned nearly as brightly as our whiskey-filled bellies. Calico-clad Hutterite hosts shucked corn while we ate pork and beans and sipped campfire coffee from tin cups. The sweet twang of guitar-pickin' and lonely ballads slid across the darkened prairie, stealing the time between storytelling, outright lies, and lingering laughter.

Each morning, the sweet smell of fresh straw mixed with dew and sunshine, signaling the start of a new adventure in the Old West. Each day was made memorable by new horizons, new challenges and new-found friends. Sadly, the wagon train ended five days after it'd begun, slowly rolling into the ranching town of Malta, where we served as a decidedly dusty, quite sore and exceptionally tired Labor Day parade. Ice-cold refreshments soon replaced words lost on the prairie and with quenched thirsts and clasped hands we disbanded, promising frequent association in the future.

Sometimes in September when the first frost chases the color from the prairie grasses, I think about that wagon train—those five glorious days in the saddle some 15 years ago—and I wonder if I ever returned those boots.
—T. D. Griffith

© Corbis

| 406/232–4560 or 800/528–1234 | fax 406/232–0363 | www.bestwestern.com | 54 rooms | $75–$99 | AE, D, DC, MC, V.

Comfort Inn. An indoor pool and hot tub give you several ways to relax after a day of sightseeing. The rooms have modern furnishings. Complimentary Continental breakfast. Cable TV. Indoor pool. Hot tub. Laundry facilities. Business services. | 1615 S. Haynes Ave. | 406/232–3141 or 800/228–5150 | fax 406/232–2924 | www.choicehotel.com | 49 rooms | $63–$76 | AE, D, DC, MC, V.

Rodeway Inn and Historic Olive Hotel. Built in 1899, the Olive Hotel is on the National Register of Historic Places. The style is traditional Old World, with original oak woodwork, stained-glass windows, and leaded-glass doors. You can walk to museums and the art center. Restaurant, bar. Cable TV. Pets allowed. | 501 Main St. | 406/232–2450 | fax 406/232–5866 | 59 rooms | $39–$50 | MC, V.

MISSOULA

MAP 6, C5

(Nearby towns also listed: Hamilton, Lolo, Seeley Lake, Stevensville)

Missoula is both artsy and outdoorsy, a hip kind of town that retains its Western identity. The state's third-largest city, Missoula has super shops, galleries, and restaurants, as well as the University of Montana, the Missoula Children's Theatre, and the Montana Repertoire Theatre. At the head of five scenic valleys and the junction of three great rivers, the town is a great base for excursions. Kids and adults love the exquisite Carousel for Missoula in downtown Caras Park.

Information: Missoula Chamber of Commerce | Box 7577, 59807 | 406/543–6623 or 800/526–3465 | www.missoulachamber.com.

Attractions

PARKS AND NATURAL SIGHTS

Beavertail State Park. You can rent a tepee and camp at one of the 28 sites here on the Clark Fork River and go boating (carry-in) and swimming. There are park interpretive programs and a visitor center. You go ½ mi on the county road after taking Exit 130 off I–90. | 406/542–5500 | www.state.mt.us | Day use $4, camping $12, tepee rentals $25 | Daily.

Council Grove State Park. They signed the Hellgate Treaty here in 1855 and established the Flathead Indian Reservation. The park is 87 primitive acres, off Mullan Rd. | 406/542–5500 | www.state.mt.us | Free | Daily.

Frenchtown Pond State Park. At Frenchtown Pond, off Frontage Road, you can fish, swim, picnic, and boat in non-motorized boats. The interpretive kiosk gives you some background. | I–90 Exit 89 | 406/542–5500 | www.state.mt.us | Day use $1 | May–Sept.

Lolo National Forest. Missoula is surrounded by the 2.1 million acres of the Lolo National Forest, the spectacular mountainous country that follows the Montana-Idaho border from the Cabinet Mountains in the north to just south of U.S. 12. This highway takes you over the historic Lolo Trail into Idaho. Lewis and Clark followed the trail and camped at "Travelers Rest" near the junction of U.S. 93 and U.S. 12 at Lolo. The Forest Service operates a visitors center at Lolo Pass, which explains the significance of the trail. The forest is divided into five administrative districts. You can hike the trails, fish, ski, and watch wildlife, and visit historic sites. The forest is accessible from U.S. 10, U.S. 12, U.S. 93, Route 200, I–90 (Exit 89 to Reserve St.), and numerous county and forest-service roads; visit the Missoula ranger station for more information. | 406/329–3750 | www.fs.fed.us/r1/lolo | Free; camping up to $17 per night per vehicle | Daily.

Placid Lake State Park. Showers, a boat ramp, and a staffed kiosk make this a civilized place to camp. On the 32 acres you have excellent fishing, hiking, and boating, surrounded by the Lolo National Forest, 3 mi west on a county road off Rte. 83 | 406/542–5500 | www.state.mt.us | Day use $4, camping $12 | May–Nov., daily.

Salmon Lake State Park. Surrounded by Lolo National Forest, this pristine lake park off Route 83 has interpretive programs. You can camp (20 sites), boat (ramp), hike the trails, swim, and picnic. Special workshops or events held in the amphitheater may charge a fee. | Rte. 83 | 406/542–5500 | www.state.mt.us | Day use $4; camping $12 Memorial Day–Labor Day, $10 May and Sept.–Nov. | May–Nov.

CULTURE, EDUCATION, AND HISTORY

USDA Forest Service Aerial Fire Depot. You can stop here to see the displays, dioramas, and videos to get ready for firefighting guided tours. | 5775 U.S. 10 W | 406/329–4900 | Memorial Day–Labor Day, daily 9–4.

USDA Forest Service Smokejumper Visitors Center. Smokejumpers are highly trained specialists who parachute into remote areas of national forests to fight wildfires. This headquarters for the USDA Forest Service is the nation's largest training base for smokejumpers. You can tour the station. | 5765 U.S. 10 W | 406/329–4934 | www.smokejumpers.com | Free | Memorial Day–Labor Day, daily 8:30–5.

Northern Forest Fire Laboratory. The laboratory is the Rocky Mountain Research Station of the USDA Forest Service. It houses a huge wind tunnel, which is used to test different burns, as well labs that test different materials and how they burn, the effects of smoke, the benefits and drawbacks of prescribed burns, and how lightning starts fires. Tours are available by special request. | 5775 U.S. 10 W | 406/329–4934 | Free | By special request only.

Ninemile Remount Depot. From 1930 to 1953 the depot provided experienced packers and pack animals for firefighting and backcountry work projects throughout the northern Rockies. Self-guided tour. | 25 mi west on I–90 to Ninemile exit | 406/626–5201 | Free | Memorial Day–Labor Day, daily 9–5.

University of Montana. The University opened in 1895 with 50 students. Today it numbers nearly 10,600 students. MSU's 640 acres contain 47 buildings, including a performing arts center, tennis courts, swimming pool, track, stadium, and soccer fields. | University and Arthur Aves | 406/243–2522 | www.umt.edu.

MUSEUMS

Art Museum of Missoula. This is a museum of contemporary Western art with both rotating exhibits and a permanent collection. | 335 N. Pattee St. | 406/728–0447 | $2 | Tues.–Thurs. and Sat. noon–5, Fri. noon–9.

Historical Museum at Fort Missoula. Culture and history both make this worth a stop. The old fort is historic in itself, and you can explore it. It also houses the Fort Missoula Theater Company, with nightly musical performances. | Building 322 at Fort Missoula | 406/728–3476 | www.montana.com/ftmslamuseum/ | Free; performances $10.

Museum of Fine Arts and Henry Mellet Gallery. Both contemporary and historical visual arts are displayed at this University of Montana gallery. | Performing Arts Building, Arthur Ave. | 406/243–2019 | www.umt.edu | Free | Weekdays 8–noon and 1–5, Sat. noon–5.

Rocky Mountain Elk Foundation Wildlife Visitor Center. Natural history is the theme here, with displays of elk, a wildlife theater, and an art gallery. | 2291 W. Broadway | 406/523–4545 or 800/225–5355 | Free | Weekdays 8:30–5, weekends 11–4.

RELIGION AND SPIRITUALITY

St. Francis Xavier Church. Built in the late 1800s, the church is known for its graceful steeple, paintings, and stained glass. | 420 W. Pine St. | 406/542–0321 | Free | Variable hours; call.

SPORTS AND RECREATION

A Carousel for Missoula. The first fully hand-carved carousel built in America since the Great Depression is impressive indeed. Volunteers created the carousel, which is one of the fastest in the country. You can tour it or rent it privately. | 1 Caras Park | 406/549–8382 | www.ohwy.com/mt/c/caromiss.htm | $1 | June–Aug., daily 11–7; Sept.–May, daily 11–5:30.

Montana Snowbowl. Snowbowl is an extremist's dream with deep powdery bowls and 2,600 ft of continuous vertical drop. Along with more than 35 trails and groomed runs, open powder bowls, and tree skiing on 1,200 acres of Lolo National Forest, you'll find 700 acres of extreme skiing. You can rent equipment, and there's a cafe, chalet lodging, and a saloon. Snow Bowl Road will take you there. | Off I–90 | 406/549–9777 | www.montanasnowbowl.com | $27; beginner tow rope free | Late Nov.–early Apr., daily 9:30–4; early and late season, closed Tues.

Marshall Mountain Ski Area. With 22 runs and a 1,500-ft vertical drop, this area also has lessons, a snack bar, and a pub. Every so often on Friday night you can ski until midnight on lighted slopes. | 5250 Marshall Canyon Rd. | 406/258–6000 | www.marshallmountain.com | $19 | Dec.–Mar., Wed. 4:30–9:30, Thurs. and Fri. 9:30–9:30, weekends 9:30–4.

ADVENTURE TRIPS

Western Timberline Outfitters. Overnight big-game hunting trips on horseback give you a shot at elk, deer, bear, bighorn sheep, antelopes, and mountain lions. You can also take fly-fishing excursions. | 91 Hideaway La., Plains | 406/826–3874 | $300–$1,900 | May–Dec.

White Tail Ranch Outfitters, Inc. With a tent camp as a base, you can hunt elk, deer, and bear. | 520 Cooper Lake Rd., Ovando | 406/793–5666 or 800/987–5666 | www.wtroutfitters.com.

ON THE CALENDAR

APR.: *International Wildlife Film Festival.* The wildest film stars in the world gather for this week-long festival in downtown Missoula. Top winners are showcased at screenings all week. Seminars, panel discussions, a parade, and artwork are also part of the event. | 406/728–9380.

MAY: *Garden City Micro B.R.I.W. Fest.* Montana's largest brewfest lures more than 50 breweries and 80-plus brews, from light pilsners to barley wines. Live music, food, and cigars. | 406/721–6061.

JUNE–AUG: *Charlie Russell's Montana.* Held at rustic Fort Missoula and preceded by an authentic Western barbecue, this historical musical pageant celebrates the state through the artist's eyes. It's outdoor drama at its best. | 800/665–3871.

AUG.: *Western Montana Fair.* Horse racing, 4-H exhibits and sales, a demolition derby, free stage acts, antique engine displays, country and western concerts, fireworks, and a parade mark this annual celebration at the fairgrounds. | 406/721–3247.

Dining

MODERATE

Montana House. American. The interior is authentically German, with open rafters and a wood interior. Pizza, steak, seafood, pork, and pastas are all on the menu, and there's a large salad bar. Thursday is all-you-can-eat prime rib with salad bar $10.95. | 2620 Brooks St. | 406/543–3200 | $6–$13 | AE, D, MC, V.

Old Town Cafe. American. The locals come here for breakfast on weekends, drawn by the healthful, whole-grain cooking. Beef, chicken, pasta, and great milk shakes are also on the menu. Kids' menu. | 127 W. Alder St. | 406/728–7050 | $12–$18 | AE, D, MC, V.

The Shack. American. Great omelettes and huckleberry pancakes help explain why this is a local favorite, especially for breakfast. The interior is Old Victorian with Western antiques, brass chandeliers, swinging doors, and fresh flowers. They use fresh local mushrooms in season and serve hamburgers and fresh fish. In summer you can dine on the small patio. Kids' menu. No smoking. | 222 W. Main St. | 406/549–9903 | $12–$18 | MC, V.

EXPENSIVE

Depot. Seafood. This fully restored historic railroad depot offers fine or casual-at-the-bar dining. Two bars have more than 20 microbrews on tap. The menu features salmon, tuna, swordfish, shark, mahimahi, chicken, and great prime rib. Open-air dining. | 201 W. Railroad St. | 406/728–7007 | $24–$32 | AE, D, DC, MC, V | No lunch.

Lodging

MODERATE

Days Inn. The rooms are comfortable and the furnishings contemporary. Complimentary Continental breakfast. Cable TV. Hot tub. Laundry facilities. Airport shuttle. | 8600 Truckstop Rd. | 406/721–9776 or 800/329–7466 | fax 406/721–9781 | 69 rooms | $66 | AE, D, DC, MC, V.

4 B's Inn—North. Five miles from skiing and conveniently situated downtown, this inn has comfortable rooms and home-style dining. There are some suites that are ideal if you're traveling with a larger group. Refrigerators in suites. Cable TV. Hot tub. Laundry facilities. Pets allowed. | 4953 N. Reserve St. | 406/542–7550 or 800/272–9500 outside Montana | fax 406/721–5931 | www.bestinn.com | 67 rooms | $60 | AE, D, DC, MC, V.

4 B's Inn—South. This large convention facility has a convenient location and rooms with contemporary furnishings. Cable TV. Hot tub. Laundry facilities. Business services. Pets allowed. | 3803 Brooks St. | 406/251–2665 or 800/272–9500 | fax 406/251–5733 | www.bestinn.com | 91 rooms | $60–$63 | AE, D, DC, MC, V.

Orange Street Budget Motor Inn. The staff is pleasant, the rooms modest, and the location near downtown and restaurants. Complimentary Continental breakfast. Cable TV. Exercise equipment. Business services. Airport shuttle. Pets allowed. | 801 N. Orange St. | 406/721–3610 or 800/328–0801 | fax 406/721–8875 | 81 rooms | $53–$58 | AE, D, DC, MC, V.

Super 8. At the south edge of town, this motel has standard and economical accommodations. Complimentary Continental breakfast. Cable TV. Pets allowed. | 3901 S. Brooks St. | 406/251–2255 or 800/800–8000 | fax 406/251–2989 | www.super8.com/ | 104 rooms | $52 | AE, D, DC, MC, V.

Super 8. The rooms are basic and economical at this motel in the north end of town, and the amenities are good. Complimentary Continental breakfast. Cable TV. Hot tub. Laundry facilities. Airport shuttle. | 4703 N. Reserve St. | 406/549–1199 or 800/800–8000 | fax 406/549–0677 | www.super8.com/ | 58 rooms | $57–$62, $110 suites | AE, D, DC, MC, V.

Travelodge. Close to I–90, this unpretentious hotel has reliably comfortable rooms and modest rates—good for those who want a quick start in the morning. Restaurant. Cable TV. | 420 W. Broadway | 406/728–4500 or 800/578–7878 | fax 406/543–8118 | 60 rooms, no ground floor rooms | $59–$66, $76 suites | AE, D, DC, MC, V.

Val-U Inn. Southgate Mall is next door for shopping, restaurants, and lounges. Complimentary Continental breakfast. Cable TV. Hot tub, sauna. Laundry facilities. Business services. Airport shuttle. | 3001 Brooks St. | 406/721–9600 or 800/443–7777 in Montana | fax 406/721–7208 | 84 rooms | $60–$67, $85 suites | AE, D, DC, MC, V.

EXPENSIVE

Cougar Ranch Bed & Breakfast. This secluded, spacious home with scenic views is done in a rustic Western style. The open-beam home with floor-to-ceiling windows has wonderful views. A creek runs just outside the door. Complimentary breakfast. Cable TV. No smoking. | 19310 Rte. 93 N | 406/726–3745 | fax 406/542–9352 | 5 rooms | $60–$120 | Credit cards not accepted.

Doubletree Edgewater. Wood carvings and murals decorate the lobby, and the furnishings have a hint of Western style. On the Clark Fork River across from the university, this hotel also has most amenities you can think of and a good beef and seafood restaurant.

Restaurant, bar, room service. In-room data ports, some refrigerators. Cable TV. Pool. Beauty salon, hot tub. Exercise equipment. Business services. Airport shuttle. Pets allowed. | 100 Madison St. | 406/728–3100 or 800/222–8733 | fax 406/728–2530 | 171 rooms | $99–$105, $120–$185 suites | AE, D, DC, MC, V.

Hampton Inn. Beautiful views of Lolo Peak and Snowbowl distinguish this newish hotel. The rooms are modern and comfortable. Complimentary Continental breakfast. Cable TV. Indoor pool. Hot tub. Exercise equipment. Business services. Airport shuttle. Pets allowed. | 4805 N. Reserve St. | 406/549–1800 or 800/426–7866 | fax 406/549–1737 | 60 rooms | $85–$89 | AE, D, DC, MC, V.

Holiday Inn—Parkside. You get panoramic mountain views from the atrium balconies and rooms. The patios have shaded tables. With in-room data ports, this is a good choice for business travelers. Restaurant, bar, room service. Cable TV. Indoor pool. Hot tub. Exercise equipment. Business services. Airport shuttle. Pets allowed. | 200 S. Pattee St. | 406/721–8550 or 800/399–0408 | fax 406/721–7427 | www.montana.com/parkside | 200 rooms | $99–$109, $129 suites | AE, D, DC, MC, V.

Red Lion. The oversize rooms are useful if you're here for business. The design and furnishings are modern. Complimentary Continental breakfast. In-room data ports. Cable TV, in-room VCRs. Pool. Hot tub. Business services. Airport shuttle. Pets allowed. | 700 W. Broadway | 406/728–3300 or 800/547–8010 | fax 406/728–4441 | www.redlion.com | 76 rooms | $80–$84 | AE, D, DC, MC, V.

VERY EXPENSIVE

Goldsmith's Bed & Breakfast. Built in 1911, this charming Victorian house near downtown and the university was once occupied by the second president of the University of Montana. The rooms have nice views from the balconies, and some have fireplaces and sitting rooms. Complimentary breakfast, picnic area. Cable TV. No smoking. | 809 E. Front St. | 406/721–6732 | fax 406/543–0045 | www.goldsmithsinn.com | 7 rooms | $95–$129 | AE, DC, MC, V.

POLSON

MAP 6, C4

(Nearby town also listed: Kalispell)

Polson is known for its mild climate and good water sports on on Flathead Lake. Stop by the Polson Historical Museum on Main Street to learn about the town's history.

Information: Polson Chamber of Commerce | Box 667, 59860 | 406/883–5969 | www.polsonchamber.com.

Attractions

Flathead Lake State Park. Flathead Lake is the largest natural freshwater lake in the western United States. Studies by the Flathead Lake Biological Station concluded that the lake's water quality is among the best in the world. With its massive volume and the area's winds, the lake rarely freezes over. You can boat (sail or motor), swim, and try for a trophy mackinaw or lake trout. Expensive summer homes and vacation rental properties nestle in the forest by the lake. Seven state parks abut the lake, six with camping facilities and boat launches, and Wildhorse Island sprawls across the southwest arm of the lake. *See also* Bigfork for Flathead Lake State Park, Wayfarers Unit; Kalispell for Flathead Lake State Park, West Shore Unit. | 406/849–5255 | Fees vary | Daily dawn to dusk.

Flathead Boat Rentals allows you to explore Wildhorse Island and Flathead Lake by water. You can rent paddle boats, personal water craft, fishing boats, canoes, and kayaks by the hour, day, or even longer. | Kwa Taq Nuk Marina (Box 1161) | 406/883–3900 or 800/358–8046 | Memorial Day–Labor Day, daily 9–9.

Forget tepees and rent a yurt at the 55-acre **Big Arm Unit.** With access to Wildhorse Island, you can attend interpretive programs, hike, boat, bike, camp, and fish (tribal license required). The campground has 37 sites where you can put your circular domed tent made of skins or felt. | 15 mi north on U.S. 93 | 406/849–5255 or 406/751–4577 | www.state.mt.us | Day use $4, camping $12 | Daily dawn to dusk.

The 24-acre **Finley Point Unit,** set amid conifer forest, has a 16-site campground and boat dock, biking, and fishing (tribal license required). | 10 mi northeast on Rte. 35 | 406/887–2715 | www.state.mt.us | Day use $4, Camping $15 | May–Sept., daily dawn to dusk.

The **Wild Horse Island Unit** has 2,163 acres of primitive state park. You can view the bighorn sheep transplanted to the island park in 1940, as well as deer, coyotes, wild horses, raptors, and songbirds. Boats are the only way to get here (use Big Arm Unit boat ramp), but once you do you'll find a swimming beach, interpretive hiking trails, and fishing (tribal license required). | 15 mi north on U.S. 93 | 406/752–5501 | www.state.mt.us | Daily dawn to dusk.

The 10-acre **Yellow Bay Unit** features a very small five-site tent campground amid conifer forest and a boat dock. You need a tribal license to fish. | 15 mi northeast on Rte. 35 | 406/752–5501 | www.state.mt.us | Day use $4; camping $12 summer, $10 winter | Daily dawn to dusk.

Lake Mary Ronan State Park. Between Flathead Lake and part of the Flathead National Forest, Lake Mary Ronan has a secluded 27-site campground with a boat ramp, where you can picnic, swim, fish, and enjoy some great wildlife viewing. | 7 mi northwest of U.S. 93 on Rte. 352 | 406/752–5501 or 406/751–4577 | Day use $4, camping $11 | May–Feb., daily dawn to dusk.

Miracle of America Museum and Historic Village. Largest collection of antique artifacts in western Montana, including everything from toys to tractors. You can also visit a pioneer village with 26 historic buildings. | 58176 U.S. 93 | 406/883–6804 | $2.50 | Mon.–Sat. 8–5, Sun. 1:30–5.

National Bison Range. This area of 19,000 acres of natural grassland was established in 1908 to protect one of the most important remaining herds of American bison. Stop by the visitor center. | U.S. 212, in Moiese | 406/644–2211 | $4 per car | Daily 7–7; roads open May–Oct. only.

Ninepipe and Pablo National Wildlife Refuges. This is a good stop if you're a bird-watcher or wildlife photographer. The glacial potholes, ponds created by melting glacial ice, and

© Artville

BIG SKY, BIG SCREEN

Montana's wide open spaces and rugged mountains have provided many a moviegoing moment. Its most recent cinematic fame came with Robert Redford's 1991 *A River Runs Through It,* a saga set in Missoula but filmed around Bozeman and Livingston.

But many other movies have been made—at least in part—in Montana, from the groundbreaking Western *Little Big Man* to Michael Cimino's box-office bomb, *Heaven's Gate.* Other Westerns filmed in Big Sky country include *Return to Lonesome Dove, Son of the Morning Star* and *Missouri Breaks.* Further big screen samplings of Montana vistas include Steven Spielberg's smoke-jumper romance *Always;* the Robin Williams love-conquers-death flick *What Dreams May Come;* John Travolta's high-flying action film *Broken Arrow;* Meryl Streep's white-water action film *The River Wild;* and Redford's ranch-set romance *The Horse Whisperer.*

Like Montana itself, the films that are set there tend have themes of individualism, of people placed in extreme situations (as Meryl Streep saves her family from disaster on the river), and, as in *The Horse Whisperer,* of healing in part through the power of nature. Montana is also a natural place to set the cowboys-and-Indians flicks, which have changed in recent years—witness *Little Big Man* and *Son of the Morning Star.*

large reservoirs on both refuges are home to many birds, including bald eagles, herons, gulls, and pheasants. Ninepipe Refuge is between St. Ignatius and Ronan at the intersection of U.S. 212 and U.S. 93. Pablo Refuge is halfway between Pablo and Polson on County Road 354. You can fish in the reservoirs in season with a license. | 406/644–2211 | Free | Call for seasonal schedules.

The People's Cultural Center. The focus here is on the Salish and Kootenai tribes. You can do "Native Ed-Venture" programs that include guided heritage, culture, wildlife, and history tours through the Flathead Reservation Group and customized itineraries. | U.S. 93, Pablo | 406/675–0160 or 800/883–5344 | Varies according to tour | June–Aug., weekdays 9–5, weekends 11–6.

Polson-Flathead Historical Museum. Dedicated to the history of the Polson area, the exhibits here include steamboat memorabilia, photographs, and cowboy gear. | 708 Main St. | 406/883–3049 | www.montanacyberzine.com/POI/Museums/Polson.asp | Free | May–Sept., Mon.–Sat. 9–6, Sun noon–6.

RIVER TRIPS

Flathead Raft Co. Choose your white-water excursion on the lower Flathead River. | U.S. 93 on Flathead Lake | 406/883–5838 | June–Sept., daily at 10 and 2.

ON THE CALENDAR

JULY: *Kerr Country Rodeo.* Concessions, special events, a rodeo showcase, and clown acts make up this traditional event. | 406/883–5255.

JULY: *Montana State Fiddler's Contest.* Held the fourth full weekend in July, this two-day event has featured the state's finest fiddlers for more than 30 years. | 406/323–1198 or 406/883–3360.

OCT.: *Port Polson Annual Octoberfest.* Along with authentic German food, beer, music, and dances, Octoberfest costumes are welcome. | 406/883–4345.

Lodging

Best Western Kwataqnuk Resort at Flathead Bay. Proximity to Flathead Lake makes this a good choice if you fish. You can rent boats. The views are spectacular; the rooms are contemporary in furnishings and design. Restaurant, bar, room service. Cable TV. 2 pools, 1 indoor. Hot tub. Marina. Video game room. Business services. | 303 U.S. 93 E | 406/883–3636 or 800/882–6363 | fax 406/883–5392 | www.kwataqnuk.com | 112 rooms | $94–$124, $179 suites | AE, D, DC, MC, V.

Port Polson Inn. You can stay in a golf room, a log room, or various other theme rooms in this contemporary inn with nice views of nearby mountains. On the south shore of Flathead Lake, the inn strives for a lodge-like atmosphere. The hotel is surrounded by lush greenery. Complimentary Continental breakfast. Cable TV. Indoor hot tub. | 502 U.S. 93 | 406/883–5385 or 800/654–0682 | fax 406/883–3998 | www.imalodging.com/lodges/w154.html | 44 rooms | $79–$89, $135–$175 suites | AE, DC, MC, V.

RED LODGE

MAP 6, G7

(Nearby towns also listed: Big Timber, Laurel)

A historic mining town of about 2,300 at the base of the Beartooth Mountains, this is one of Montana's premier ski destinations in winter. In summer, you can golf, hike, mountain bike, fish, camp, and take scenic drives along the beautiful Beartooth Highway. The Beartooth Nature Center offers North American animals and a children's petting zoo, and the Peaks to Plains Museum explores area history.

Information: **Red Lodge Chamber of Commerce** | Box 988, 59068 | 406/446–1718 | www.redlodge.com.

Attractions

The Beartooth District, above the northeastern edge of Yellowstone National Park, is the most popular part of the 2.5-million-acre **Custer National Forest,** which sprawls across Montana, South Dakota, and North Dakota. Montana's highest point, Granite Peak, is about 10 mi north of Cooke City off the northeast corner of Yellowstone National Park. Most people visiting the Beartooth District stick close to the spectacular Beartooth National Forest Scenic Byway, but if you want to go into the wilderness areas, get trail information from the Forest Service (*see below*). The Beartooth Ranger District also contains the very different Pryor Mountain Unit, west of Bighorn Canyon National Recreation Area, with limestone caves, canyons incised into the landscape, archaeological sites, and a large wild horse herd. *See also* Billings. | South on U.S. 212 | 406/446–2103 | www.fs.fed.us/r1/custer/main.html | Free; camping up to $17 per vehicle per day | Daily dawn to dusk.

The late CBS correspondent Charles Kuralt described this as "the most beautiful road in America." The **Beartooth National Forest Scenic Byway** runs from Red Lodge to Cooke City, near Yellowstone National Park's northeast entrance. From start to finish a 69-mi and three-hour drive, the Beartooth runs through Custer and Shoshone national forests, and all the way you get skytop views of snowcapped mountains, glaciers, and alpine lakes. Several national forest campgrounds are along the route, as well as numerous trailheads leading into the mountains. | U.S. 212 | Late May–mid-Oct., daily.

Beartooth Nature Center. Animals that have been injured and cannot be released in the wild again live at this nonprofit educational organization. The native Montana wildlife on display includes bears, elk, mountain lions, and deer, as well as miscellaneous birds and other animals. They have year-round educational programs and a summer camp for children. | 2nd Ave. E, in Coal Miner's Park | 406/446–1133 | $5 | June–Sept., daily 10–5:30; Oct.–May, daily 10–2, weather permitting.

Cooney Reservoir State Park. You'll find great walleye and rainbow trout fishing in the reservoir here. The campground has 75 sites, with hiking trails, a boat ramp, and a swimming beach. Pets restricted. | Off U.S. 212 | 406/445–2326 | www.fwp.state.mt.us/parks/parks.htm | Day use $4, camping $12 | Daily.

Peaks to Plains Museum. The museum houses the Greenough Exhibit, the family heirlooms of the Greenough sisters, two lady bronc riders, and their brother, Turk, who was married to famous fan dancer Sally Rand. Exhibits on fur trading, a Finnish kitchen, and a large coal mine replica in the basement are other highlights. | 224 S. Broadway | 406/446–3667 | $3 | Weekdays 8–5, weekends 1–5.

Red Lodge Historic District. Built during the coal-mining boom between 1883 and 1910, Red Lodge still offers many traces of its ethnic roots. Neighborhoods bear names like Finn Town, Little Italy, and "Hi Bug"—a schoolyard tag invented by kids to describe where the English-speaking upper class lived. In August, the nine-day Festival of Nations takes over town. | Main St. | 406/446–1718 or 406/446–3914 | Daily.

Red Lodge Mountain Ski Area. Licensed day care and 30 acres of extreme chute skiing are two offerings that distinguish this facility, one of the Northern Rockies' top ski areas. It also has 70 trails and groomed slopes and 60 acres of tree skiing, plus rentals and a ski school. You can eat at two full-service restaurants and a cafeteria. | Off U.S. 212, in Custer National Forest | 800/444–8977 or 406/446–2610 | $33 | Early Nov.–Apr., daily 9–4.

ON THE CALENDAR

MAR.: *Winter Carnival.* A traditional parade downtown starts the carnival on Friday night, followed Saturday by snow events at Red Lodge Mountain, including a costume contest, cardboard classic race, fire-hose race, obstacle course, and treasure hunt for the kids, also held downtown. Nighttime brings a spaghetti feed and torchlight parade. | 406/446–1718.

JUNE: *Annual Beartooth Run.* Runners start at 7,000 ft and finish at 9,000 ft, traveling 8.2 mi along the beautiful Beartooth Highway. | 406/446–1718.

JUNE: *Music Festival.* Nearly 200 high-school students from a five-state region perform live concerts of classical music. During the nine-day festival at the Red Lodge Civic Center, there are also five recitals for the teachers when 30 professional musicians perform. | 406/446–1905.

JULY: *Home of Champions Rodeo and Parade.* Part of the PRCA circuit, this event brings nearly all the national champs to Red Lodge. A parade runs each day at noon downtown. | 406/446–1718.

JULY: *Mountain Man Rendezvous.* The reenactment of the Rocky Mountain fur-trade era before 1840 is a favorite of locals, traders, and tourists, who explore more than 130 camps, each with one or more tepees. More than 5,000 people attend. | 406/446–1718.

AUG.: *Fat Tire Frenzy.* Red Lodge hosts this NORBA-sanctioned mountain-bike race in the scenic Beartooth Mountains. The four events: downhill, cross-country, trails, and a free kid's race. | Silver Run, off West Fork Rd. | 406/446–1600 or 888/281–0625.

AUG.: *Festival of Nations.* For a half-century, the Festival of Nations has honored the diverse ethnic groups that worked and settled here. Each day, on Main Street, you can sample foods and programs prepared by different nationalities. | 406/446–4960.

Dining

Greenlee's at the Pollard. American. Fresh flowers decorate this elegant restaurant in a beautiful, restored 19th-century hotel. It has an excellent import and domestic wine cellar, microbrews, and bottled beers, as well as a full bar. Try sage-smoked chicken, grilled gulf shrimp, and garlic mashed potatoes. Kids' menu. No smoking. | 102 N. Broadway | 406/446–0001 | $13–$23 | AE, D, MC, V.

Old Piney Dell. American. This small restaurant with Western style and design has good Sunday brunch specials. Kids' menu. It's part of the Rock Creek Resort. | Rock Creek Rd. | 406/446–1196 | $16–$23 | AE, D, DC, MC, V | No lunch Mon.–Sat.

Lodging

Best Western Lupine Inn. Six blocks from downtown, this convenient hotel has standard contemporary rooms and some in-room hot tubs. Complimentary Continental breakfast. Some in-room hot tubs. Cable TV. Indoor pool. Hot tub. Exercise equipment. Video game room. Playground. Laundry facilities. Business services. Some pets allowed. | 702 S. Hauser St. | 406/446–1321 or 888/567–1321 | fax 406/446–1465 | www.bestwestern.com | 46 rooms | $79, $85 suites | AE, D, DC, MC, V.

Chateau Rouge. These deluxe condos come with one or two bedrooms, full kitchens, and some fireplaces. The common area has a huge natural stone fireplace. Cable TV, in-room VCRs. Pool. Hot tub. Pets allowed. No smoking. | 1505 S. Broadway | 406/446–1601 or 800/926–1601 | fax 406/446–1602 | www.wtp.net/chateaurouge/ | 24 1-and 2-bedroom units | $68–$85 | AE, D, MC, V.

Comfort Inn. Mountain oak furniture lends warmth to this newer facility with family suites. Complimentary Continental breakfast. Cable TV. Indoor pool. Hot tub. Business services. Pets allowed (fee). | 612 N. Broadway | 406/446–4469 or 888/733–4661 | fax 406/446–4669 | www.wtp.net/comfortinn | 55 rooms | $80, $100–$129 suites | AE, D, DC, MC, V.

Pollard. The turn-of-the-century hotel that served Buffalo Bill, Calamity Jane, and other Western legends reopened in 1994 after a complete restoration. The rooms have balconies overlooking the gallery and fireplace, and some have mountain views. Restaurant, complimentary breakfast. Some in-room hot tubs. Cable TV. Hot tub. Gym. Business services. No smoking. | 2 N. Broadway | 406/446–0001 or 800/765–5273 | fax 406/446–0002 | www.pollardhotel.com | 38 rooms, 5 with shower only, 4 suites | $95–$225 | AE, D, MC, V.

Rock Creek. This spacious cedar-lodge resort just south of town along Rock Creek and beneath Beartooth Pass can host family reunions, business retreats, or banquets. Restaurant (*see* Old Piney Dell, *above*). No air-conditioning, some in-room hot tubs. Cable TV. Indoor pool.

Hot tub. Tennis. Exercise equipment. Playground. Laundry facilities. Business services. | Rock Creek Rd. | 406/446–1111 or 800/667–1119 | fax 406/446–3688 | rcresort@wtp.net | www.rcresort.com | 90 rooms, 39 kitchenettes | $88–$100, $125–$245 suites | AE, D, DC, MC, V.

Super 8. You're only 1 mi from the Red Lodge Mountain ski area at this contemporary hotel with modern furnishings. It's on the Beartooth Highway (U.S. 212). Complimentary Continental breakfast. Some refrigerators, some in-room hot tubs. Cable TV. Indoor pool. Hot tub. Video game room. Laundry facilities. Some pets allowed. | 1223 S. Broadway | 406/446–2288 or 800/813–8335 | fax 406/446–3162 | 50 rooms | $70–$90 | AE, D, DC, MC, V.

SEELEY LAKE

MAP 6, C4

(Nearby town also listed: Missoula)

Here in the water-loving Seeley-Swan Valley, this town of about 900 offers a full complement of tourist services and stunning views of the Mission and Swan mountain ranges. You can hike, camp, and do almost anything else outdoorsy.

Information: Seeley Lake Chamber of Commerce | Box 516, Seeley Lake, MT 59868 | 406/677–2880.

Attractions

Clearwater Canoe Trail. On this combination floating and hiking trail, you get 3 mi of lovely paddling among the loons on the Clearwater River, followed by a 1-mi hike back to the launch spot. The Double Arrow Lodge runs an outfitting service. | 4 miles north of Seeley Lake | Outfitting, 406/677–2411 or 677–2317 | Free | Late spring through fall.

Morrell Mountain Lookout. This 18-mi trek can be tough on vehicles, but when you get there, the views across mountain and valley are worth it. It's a good idea to check with the ranger station for current road conditions. | Head east from Hwy. 83 on Cottonwood Lakes Rd., then continue on Rte. 4365 | Road conditions, 406/677–2233 | Free | Spring through fall.

Dining

Lindey's Prime Steak House. Steaks. Tender slabs of aged, flavorful beef are the big attraction at this popular lakeside spot. Thick, juicy "Bay Burgers" offer a lighter option. You can dine outdoors, overlooking the lake, in summer. Those who don't like red meat should probably dine elsewhere. | Just south of town on Highway 83 | 406/677–9229 | No lunch in winter. Closed Tues. and Wed. October through mid-April | $14–$20 | No credit cards.

Seasons Restaurant. Eclectic. This elegant, well-run restaurant overlooking the valley is a centerpiece of the Double Arrow Resort, which describes the cuisine as "classic country." Ingredients are fresh and often prepared with an Asian flair. You'll find plenty of Montana staples—bison, venison, trout, and huckleberries—with creative touches. Sample dishes include pan-seared sea scallops with wasabi cream and huckleberry Szechwan sauce, and roasted duckling with lingonberry and blackberry brandy. The Sunday brunch is ample and very popular. | 2 miles south of Seeley Lake at Double Arrow Resort | 406/677–2777 | $12–$25 | AE, D, MC, V.

Lodging

Double Arrow Resort. You can stay in the lovely main lodge, rent a cabin, or have an entire 3- or 4-bedroom house to yourself at this sprawling 200-acre resort. The more adventurous or short on cash can opt to sleep in a tipi or a sheepherder's wagon. Views are outstanding, service is first-rate, and you can do everything from fly fishing to taking sleigh rides (weather permitting). Restaurant. Golf. Hiking. Fishing. Horseback riding. Cross-country skiing. Outfitting. | 2 miles south of Seeley Lake off Highway 83 | 406/677–2777 or 800/468–0777 | info@doublearrowresort.com | www.doublearrowresort.com | 3 lodge rooms, 14 cabin units, 3 houses | $115–$155 | AE, D, MC, V.

Emily A. If you want a classic Montana B&B experience, try this massive log lodge, with only 6 rooms in an 11,000-square-ft structure. A two-story stone fireplace, luxurious furnishings, and collections of Western art and sports memorabilia create a welcoming, spacious atmosphere. You can also stay in the original homestead cabin. The lovely grounds and private lake make this a popular wedding spot. Ducks, geese and deer like it, too. The proprietors are a doctor and a dietitian, so you can count on healthful but delicious breakfasts. Full breakfast. Canoeing. Fishing. Hiking trails. No smoking. Pets allowed with advance notice. | 5 miles north of town on Highway 83, just past mile marker 20 | 406/677–3474 or 800/977–4639 | fax 406/377–6474 | slk3340@blackfoot.net | www.theemilya.com | 6 plus cabin | $115 | MC, V.

Wilderness Gateway Inn. This attractive, well-maintained motel lies at the south end of town and derives its name from the three nearby wilderness areas. Hot tub. Designated smoking areas. Pets allowed with fee. | Highway 83, south end of town | 406/677–2095 | fax 406/677–2095 | 19 | $56–$59 | D, MC, V.

SIDNEY

(Nearby town also listed: Glendive)

This rural ranching community of 5,200 on the banks of the Yellowstone River is just a few miles west of the North Dakota border. Stop at the MonDak Heritage Center if you're a history buff; it has extensive displays of area history and art, plus a research library.

Information: Sidney Chamber of Commerce | 909 S. Central Ave., 59270 | 406/482–1916 | www.sidneymt.com. .

Attractions

Fort Union Trading Post National Historic Site. Established in 1820 as a fur-trading post, this place on the Montana–North Dakota border operated until the Civil War. In its heyday, it was a gathering point for riverboaters, fur traders, Plains tribes, and frontier capitalists. Bourgeois House, once the setting of elegant dinners for distinguished guests, is now a visitor center. In summer you can take guided tours and see living-history programs and exhibits. The bookstore is good. | 15550 Rte. 1804, Williston, ND | 701/572–9083 | Free | June–Aug., daily 8–8; Sept.–May, daily 9–5:30.

MonDak Heritage Center. Exhibits on area history are the focus here. | 120 3rd Ave. SE | 406/482–3500 | $2.50 | June–Aug., weekdays 9–6, weekends noon–4; Sept.–May, Tues.–Sun. 1–5.

ON THE CALENDAR

APR.: *Peter Paddlefish Day and Kite Festival.* Run or cycle in the opening 27-mi Paddlefish Run 'n' Ride, then enjoy a family picnic, kite festival, model airplane dogfights, a pinewood derby, and static displays of models airplanes and trains. | 406/482–1916.
JULY: *Sunrise Festival of the Arts.* Enjoy artists and crafts booths under colorful canopies, pottery demonstrations, a food fair, children's activities, and live entertainment, as well as Shakespeare in the Park in the evening. | 406/482–1916.
AUG.: *Richland County Fair and Rodeo.* Eastern Montana's showcase summer event has as its highlights the motorsports on Wednesday, PRCA rodeo on Thursday and Friday, and big-name entertainment Saturday. | 406/482–2801.

Dining

South 40. American. Locals come here for homemade soups, prime rib, and the Mexican dishes on the menu. There's a salad bar. Kids' menu. | 207 2nd Ave. NW | 406/482–4999 | $8–$17 | AE, DC, MC, V.

SIDNEY

INTRO
ATTRACTIONS
DINING
LODGING

STEVENSVILLE

MAP 6, C5

(Nearby towns also listed: Lolo, Missoula)

Residents call it "Stevi"—prounounced "Steve-eye." The state's first white settlement, St. Mary's Mission, is a restored treasure that dates back to 1841. But the 1,200-population town that grew around it is a casual blend of beautiful old homes and haphazard modern construction. Venerable yet low key, Stevensville is a nickname kind of place.

Information: Bitterroot Valley Chamber of Commerce | 105 E. Main St., Hamilton, MT 59840 | 406–363–2400.

Attractions

St. Mary's Mission. The landmark memorializes the relationship between the Catholics and the Flathead tribe. The church was established in 1841 by the Jesuit Father Pierre DeSmet as the first in the Northwest. It was closed in 1850, and the building that still stands was built in 1866 by the Italian Jesuit Father Anthony Ravalli. You can visit the museum and cemetery. | West end of 4th St., Stevensville | 406/777–5734 | $3 | Seasonal schedule.

Lee Metcalf Wilderness Area. Crowned by the snowcapped Spanish Peaks, this wilderness area is part of the Greater Yellowstone ecosystem. Steep, rugged, knifelike ridges topped with snow edge the alpine meadows dotted with pristine lakes in the upper reaches of the area. The wilderness has four separate units in the Madison Range, the Spanish Peaks, Taylor Hilgard, Monument Mountain, and Bear Trap Canyon and extends into the Beaverhead and Gallatin national forests. Grizzly bears are not usually seen in the Spanish Peaks, but they frequent other parts of the area. Access is extremely limited. You can get in at several points along U.S. 191, a narrow, twisting highway that follows the Gallatin River between Yellowstone National Park and Bozeman. | U.S. 191 | 406/682–4253 | Free | Daily dawn to dusk.

Dining

Frontier Cafe. American. This bustling, basic cafe offers solid, homestyle fare to a loyal crowd of locals. | 3954 Highway 93 N | 406/777–4228 | $5–$10 | MC, V.

Stevi Cafe. American. Homemade bread, pies, and hearty breakfasts available all day long are the staples of this friendly local eatery in the heart of town. | 202 Main St. | 406/777–2171 | $4–$10 | No credit cards.

Lodging

Big Creek Pines Bed & Breakfast. Each room is distinctive and has a ceiling fan in this relaxed B&B by Big Creek in a scenic rural setting with views of the Bitterroot Mountains. Ample, inventive breakfasts are just part of the sincere hospitality. | 2986 U.S. 93 N; 4.5 miles south of Stevensville on Hwy. 93 between mile markers 62 and 63 | 406/642–6475 | bcp@cybernet1.com | www.bigcreekpines.com | 4 rooms | $80 | Full breakfast | MC, V.

Haus Rustica. Nestled in the countryside 8 mi from town, this remodeled home offers a tranquil setting and 20 acres to wander. A small creek has a waterfall, and a nature trail winds through the pines. Comfortable rooms are decorated with finds from the owners' extensive travels. Breakfast is free, and tasty lunches and dinners are available for a fee. Or guests can cook in the small kitchenette. Each room has a sink, but guests share a bathroom and shower. Three porches offer plenty of opportunity to drink in the view and the country quiet. Kitchenette. | 396 Dry Gulch Rd. | 406/777–2291 | rustika@marsweb.com | 4 | $60 | Full breakfast; other meals by arrangement | MC, V.

THREE FORKS

(Nearby town also listed: Bozeman)

Just off I–90 northwest of Bozeman, the small town of Three Forks (population 1,700) is near Missouri Headwaters State Park and Madison Buffalo Jump State Park. For area history, check out the Headwaters Heritage Museum.

Information: Three Forks Chamber of Commerce | 15 E. Cedar St., 59752 | 406/285–6743 | www.threeforksmontana.com.

Attractions

Elkhorn State Park. A ghost town that stands as a reminder of Montana's 1880s silver boom. Excellent examples of frontier architecture. Great photo spot. No facilities. | Rte. 69 north, then 11 mi on County Rd. | 406/444–4720 | www.state.mt.us | Free | Daily.

Headwaters Heritage Museum. A gem off the well-traveled highway, the museum contains thousands of local historical artifacts. The largest brown trout caught in Montana is displayed, as well as a small anvil, all that is left of a trading post established in 1810. | Main and Cedar Sts. | 406/285–4778 | Free | June–mid-Sept., Mon.–Sat. 9–5, Sun. 1–5, or by appointment.

Lewis and Clark Caverns State Park. Lewis and Clark passed the caverns while traveling down the Jefferson River. You can tour the beautifully decorative caves from May through September. The visitor center has displays and programs. You can hike the trails that run through the 3,034-acre park and swim and fish in the Jefferson River. The 40-site campground has a shower house. | Rte. 2, Milepost 271 | 406/287–3541 | www.state.mt.us | Walk-in fee $1, day use $4, camping $12, cabin rentals $39 | May–Sept., daily.

Madison Buffalo Jump State Monument. Ancient Native Americans killed Buffalo by stampeding them over a cliff. The visitor center has interpretive displays and historical information on the practice and the history of the site. | Off I–90, on Buffalo Jump Rd. | 406/994–4042 | www.state.mt.us | Free | Daily dawn to dusk.

Missouri River Headwaters State Park. Lewis and Clark found the confluence of the Jefferson, Gallatin, and Madison rivers here, the headwaters of the Missouri River. The 530-acre park has 23 campsites, and you can hike, fish, and boat. There's a visitor center here, four miles northeast of Three Forks off Rte. 287. | 406/994–4042 | www.state.mt.us | Free, camping $4–$11 | Daily dawn to dusk.

ON THE CALENDAR

JULY: *Rodeo Weekend.* Real rodeo action in a small-town setting. Music, food, bull and bronc riding, a flea market and crafts show, as well as a hometown parade. | 406/285–4556.
AUG.: *Montanan Antique Aircraft Association Fly-in and Air Show.* The skies above town buzz with the sounds of antique aircraft flying in for this event. You can see the vintage planes up close. | 406/285–4880.

Dining

Land of Magic. American. Rustic barn wood, brands on the walls, and a basic menu of steak and seafood makes this a good bet. The chef uses a secret recipe for the twice-baked potatoes. Kids' menu. | I–90 | 406/284–3794 | $12–$18 | AE, MC, V.

Sacajawea Inn. Continental. Once a railroad hotel, this restaurant now has lots of rustic pine and wooden tables. The locals favor the prime rib, Montana beef, and pasta dishes. Kids' menu. Sunday brunch. No smoking. | 5 N. Main St. | 406/285–6515 | $10–$23 | AE, D, MC, V | No lunch.

THREE FORKS

INTRO
ATTRACTIONS
DINING
LODGING

Lodging

Fort Three Forks. This newer hotel has Western-style furnishings, a friendly staff, and balconies that overlook the mountains. Complimentary Continental breakfast. Cable TV. Hot tub. Laundry facilities. Business services. Pets allowed (fee). | 10776 U.S. 287 | 406/285–3233 or 800/477–5690 | fax 406/285–4362 | www.fortthreeforks.com | 24 rooms | $50–$54 | AE, D, DC, MC, V.

Sacajawea. Built in 1872, this hotel was later rolled on logs to higher ground before the main building was added. The interior lobby and rooms retain the 19th-century style, and the front porch has rockers where you can meditate on the view. You're close to places where you can golf, swim, and hike. Restaurant, bar, room service. Cable TV. | 5 N. Main St. | 406/285–6515 or 800/821–7326 | fax 406/285–4210 | www.sacajaweahotel.com | 31 rooms | $75–$105 | AE, D, MC, V.

VIRGINIA CITY

MAP 6, E7

(Nearby towns also listed: Bozeman, Dillon)

You can still stroll the boardwalks in this town of 150 residents that's in one of the West's richest and most colorful mining districts. News of the 1863 gold strike spread like wildfire, turning Virginia City into an overnight mining camp. It grew to 10,000 residents and was the state's second territorial capital from 1865 to 1875. Restored gold-rush buildings and shops greet you today. The Virginia City Players, one of Montana's premier summer theater troupes, performs 19th-century melodramas each night at the Virginia City Opera House.

Information: Virginia City Chamber of Commerce | Box 218, 59755 | 406/843–5555 or 800/829–2969 | www.virginiacitychamber.com.

Attractions

Beaverhead-Deerlodge National Forest. *See* Deer Lodge. | Sheridan Work Center, Box 428, Sheridan | 406/842–5434.

Boot Hill. Out on the point, with a beautiful view of the town and surrounding mountains, lie the marked graves of five hanged outlaws. You turn left at the Thomas Hickman Building, go to the top of the hill, and turn left again. | 406/843–5555 | Free | Daily.

H. S. Gilbert Brewery. At the brewery, you'll find the original fixtures, including the vats, boilers, and hoppers. The Brewery Follies (suitable for ages 12 and up) takes place every night but Tuesday. Beer, wine, and soft drinks are served during the show. | E. Cover St. | 406/843–5218 | $12.50 | Memorial Day–Labor Day, Wed.–Mon. at 4:30 and 8:30.

Nevada City. Built in 1863 along Adler Gulch after news of a gold strike made its way east, these structures were brought to Nevada City, 1 mi west of Virginia City on Rte. 287. They were restored during the 1950s and 1960s. You can visit 20–30 buildings today. *Little Big Man, Lonesome Dove,* and *Missouri Breaks* were all filmed here. | 800/648–7588 | $5 | Memorial Day–mid-Sept., daily 9–7.

St. Paul's Episcopal Church. Originally built of wood in the 1860s, the church was later rebuilt out of locally quarried stone. The beautiful building is open daily for tours, and services are held Sunday in summer at 9 AM. It's in LaRae on Sheridan exchange. | Idaho St. | Free | Memorial Day–Labor Day, Mon.–Sat. 8–5.

Thompson-Hickman Memorial Museum. This is your chance to see a petrified wedding cake, the club foot of Club Foot George Lane, rifles, and many photos. The historic collection is made up of heirlooms of three local families from 1860 to 1900. | Wallace St. (U.S. 287) | 406/843–5238 | Donations accepted | May–Sept., daily 10–5.

Virginia City Players. The longest-running summer stock theater in America, the Virginia City Players began performing in 1949. The old-time melodrama is performed nightly in the historic opera house, formerly Old Livery Stable. | Wallace St. | 406/843–5314 | www.vcplayers.com | $12.50 | Reservations recommended | Mid-June–Labor Day, Tues.–Fri. at 8, Sat. at 4 and 8, Sun. at 4.

Virginia City–Madison County Historical Museum. The pharmacy from Ranks' Mercantile, a very nice collection of historic clothing, local families' memorabilia, and family photos are the core exhibits here. The privately run museum is in an old building, and also has displays on the history of Ruby Valley and Alder Gulch. | Wallace St. (U.S. 287) | 406/843–5500 | $3 | May–June, daily 11–4; July–Sept., daily 10–5.

A RAILROAD TOUR
Nevada City Depot. The *Alder Gulch Short Line* steam locomotive runs from Memorial Day to Labor Day, making the 3 mi round-trip from Nevada City to Virginia City and back again seven times daily. | 406/843–5247 | $7 | Memorial Day–Labor Day, daily at 10:30, 11:30, 12:30, 2, 3, 4, and 5.

ON THE CALENDAR
MAY–SEPT.: *H. S. Gilbert Brewery.* Check out these cabaret-style theater presentations at the local Opera House. Reservations recommended. | Wallace St. | May–Sept., Sun., Mon., and Wed.–Fri. at 8:30, Sat. at 6 and 9; closed Tues. | 406/843–5218 or 800/648–7588.

MAY–SEPT.: *Virginia City Players.* Family entertainment is performed in a historic opera house. Reservations strongly recommended. | Wallace St. | Tues.–Fri. at 8, Sat. at 4 and 8, Sun. at 4 | 406/843–5314.

AUG.: *Annual Arts Festival.* For 25 years, this festival has been a highlight of Virginia City summers. The displays include quality Western and wildlife artwork, as well as popular quick-draw contests and an auction. | 406/843–5555.

WEST YELLOWSTONE

MAP 6, E8

(Nearby town also listed: Big Sky)

Affectionately known among winter recreationists as the "snowmobile capital of the world," this town of 1,000 is Yellowstone National Park's busiest gateway. You can go fly-fishing, river rafting, and cross-country skiing. Learn about the bears of Yellowstone and the fire of 1988 at the Museum of the Yellowstone. For a night of comedy, variety and melodrama, don't miss the Playmill Theatre.

Information: **West Yellowstone Chamber of Commerce** | 30 Yellowstone Ave., 59758 | 406/646–7701 | www.westyellowstonechamber.com.

Attractions
Gallatin National Forest. *See* Bozeman. | Hebgen Lake Ranger District, U.S. 287 | 406/646–7369.

Grizzly Discovery Center. This center is devoted to protecting threatened bears and wolves. Eight bears and ten grey wolves live here. The staff will answer questions on the self-guided tour. | 201 S. Canyon, at west entrance of Yellowstone National Park | 406/646–7001 or 800/257–2570 | www.grizzlydiscoveryctr.com | $7.50 | Oct.–Apr., daily 8:30–dusk; May–Sept., daily 8:30–8:30.

Madison Canyon Earthquake Lake Visitors Center. About 40 years ago, an earthquake slid half of a mountain into this canyon 22 mi west of Yellowstone. The result was a giant natural dam and Quake Lake—eerie reminders of nature's random violence. A visitor center documents the event, which killed people camped along the river. | U.S. 287, in Gallatin National Forest | 406/823–6961 | Free | May–Sept., daily 8:30–6.

Museum of the Yellowstone. If you're interested in natural disasters, this is a good stopping place. A film on the 1988 fires repeats continuously all day, and a room is dedicated to the earthquake of 1959. You'll also find mounted wildlife, information on bears, Plains Native American artifacts, and a history of the town of West Yellowstone. The old Union Pacific Railroad Depot houses the museum. | 124 Yellowstone Ave. | 406/406–646–7814 (summer only) | $5.95 | Mid-May–mid-Oct., daily 8 AM–10 PM.

The Playmill Theater. The Playmill, dedicated to providing fun-filled family summer entertainment, opened its doors in June 1964. The old building has been refitted with new seats. | 29 Madison Ave. | 406/646–7757 | www.playmill.com | $10–$11 | Reservations recommended | Memorial Day–Labor Day.

Yellowstone IMAX Theatre. This IMAX theater at the park's west entrance shows three films exploring the grandeur of Yellowstone, its wildlife, and its geothermic activity. | 101 S. Canyon St. | 406/646–4100 | $7.50; special rates for seniors and children | Daily, shows on the hour.

Yellowstone National Park Visitors Center. Here at the park's west entrance, you can get statewide travel information and visit the West Yellowstone Chamber of Commerce. | 30 Yellowstone Ave. | 406/646–4403 | Weekdays 8–6.

TOURS AND ADVENTURES

Buffalo Bus Lines. Choose between two loop tours of Yellowstone National Park: the upper loop takes in Mammoth Springs and the Grand Canyon of Yellowstone, the lower loop passes Old Faithful, the Fishing Bridge, and the Grand Canyon of Yellowstone. Call for pickup locations at area hotels and campgrounds. | 406/646–9564 or 800/426–7669 | www.yellowstonevaction.com | $34.95; $65 for both tours | Mid-Apr.–early Nov., daily at 8 AM.

Geyser Whitewater Expeditions. Whether you're looking for white-water excitement or a gentler outdoor experience for younger children, this outfitter should be able to accommodate you. Options include half- and full-day rafting, kayak trips, scenic floats, and white-water trips on the Gallatin River, and horseback riding. | 406/995–4989 or 800/922–7238 | www.raftmontana.com | From $37 | May–Sept.

Gray Line Bus Tours. You can pick from six one-day tours in comfortable motorcoaches. The tour areas include Yellowstone, the Tetons, and the surrounding area. The knowledgeable guides can answer your questions. Call for pick-up locations at area motels and campgrounds. | 406/646–9374 | www.greylineyellowstone.com | From $38 | Apr.–mid-Oct.

Madison River Outfitters. The store offers fly-fishing tackle and gear as well as backpacking and hiking equipment. Fly-fishing guides take anglers to the Madison River for half-day to 7-day float or walking trips. Prices start at $285 per day per angler. You can also take guided wildlife and nature walks into Yellowstone National Park starting at $200 for two people. | 117 Canyon St. | 406/646–9644 | www.flyfishingyellowstone.com | May–Sept., daily.

ON THE CALENDAR

MAR.: *World Snowmobile Expo.* Top-notch racing is combined with a first look at the upcoming season's new sleds and after-market products. The SnowWest SnoCross is the season closer for the RMXCRC and attracts racers from throughout the snowbelt, as well as the sport's top pro riders. | 406/646–7701.

MAY–SEPT.: *Playmill Theater.* This theater has been providing solid summer entertainment for more than three decades. | 29 Madison Ave. | Memorial Day–Labor Day, Mon.–Sat. at 6 and 8:30 | 406/646–7757.

AUG.: *Burnt Hole Rendezvous/Historical Reenactment.* At a primitive camp, traders sell and demonstrate pre-1840s crafts. Events include a black-powder shoot, tomahawk and knife throwing, a living-history reenactment, and Native American dancers. | 406/646–7110.

Dining

Three Bears. American. Remodeled with a Montana theme, this place looks like a log cabin and retains the rustic style inside. It's a good place for family dining. The old photographs trace Yellowstone's history. Try the prime rib or roasted chicken. Kids' menu. No smoking. | 205 Yellowstone Rd. | 406/646–7811 | $12–$22 | D, DC, MC, V | Closed mid-Mar.–early May and mid-Oct.–mid-Dec. No lunch.

Lodging

Best Western Pine Motel. Some of these standard, comfortable rooms have kitchenettes. The furnishings are modern. Restaurant, bar. Cable TV. Pool. Hot tubs, sauna. Laundry facilities. | 234 Firehole Ave. | 406/646–7622 or 800/646–7622 | fax 406/646–9443 | 46 rooms | $75–$85 | AE, D, DC, MC, V.

Comfort Inn. The rooms have been remodeled in this comfortable, contemporary motel. Complimentary Continental breakfast. Microwaves (suites). Cable TV. Indoor pool. Hot tub. Exercise equipment. Laundry facilities. Business services. | 638 Madison Ave. | 406/646–4212, 800/228–5150, or 888/264–2466 | www.comfortinn.com | 78 rooms, 7 suites | $129, $179 suites | AE, D, DC, MC, V.

Days Inn. On the very quiet edge of town, this modest but modern motel is a good choice if you want to stay a bit away from the center of action. Complimentary Continental breakfast. Some refrigerators. Cable TV. Indoor pool. Hot tub. Business services. Pets allowed. | 301 Madison Ave. | 406/646–7656 or 800/548–9551 | fax 406/646–7965 | 45 rooms | $89–$110 | AE, D, DC, MC, V.

Firehole Ranch. This Orvis-endorsed fly-fishing guest ranch is rustically elegant, with a very friendly staff. The cabins have fireplaces, carpeting, individual baths, and cozy sitting areas. Some are adjoining if you're traveling with a large family or group. The 20-guest maximum keeps the ranch small and personal. Hiking, horseback riding, fishing, bicycles. | 11500 Hebgen Lake Rd. | 406/646–7294 | fax 406/646–4728 | www.fireholeranch.com | 10 cabins | $270–$300 per person per night, 3–night minimum; includes all meals and beverages | No credit cards | Closed Oct.–May | AP.

Gray Wolf Inn and Suites. The rooms are oversized in this 1998 inn, and the underground parking is nice in winter. The style is modern in the lobby and the rooms. Complimentary Continental breakfast. Refrigerators, microwaves (suites). Cable TV. Indoor pool. Hot tub. Laundry facilities. Business services. | 250 S. Canyon St. | 406/646–0000 or 800/852–8602 | fax 406/646–4232 | www.greywolf-inn.com | 102 rooms, 16 suites | $89–$189, $289 suites | AE, D, DC, MC, V.

Holiday Inn. Three blocks from Yellowstone is about as close as you'll get. The spacious rooms all have minifridges, microwaves, and in-room data ports. This is a popular place for conventions. Restaurant, bar. Microwaves, refrigerators, some in-room hot tubs. Cable TV. Indoor pool. Hot tub. Exercise equipment. Laundry facilities. Business services. | 315 Yellowstone Ave. | 406/646–7365 or 800/646–7365 | fax 406/646–4433 | wyconferencehotel@wyellowstone.com | www.yellowstone-conf-hotel.com | 123 rooms | $139–$149, $175–$200 suites | AE, D, DC, MC, V.

Kelly Inn. Large rooms, a lobby fireplace, and a Western-style interior make this newer hotel a pleasant place to stay. Complimentary Continental breakfast. Some refrigerators, microwaves. Cable TV. Indoor pool. Hot tub. Laundry facilities. Business services. Pets allowed. | 104 S. Canyon St. | 406/646–4544 or 800/259–4672 (reservations) | fax 406/646–9838 | www.wyellowstone.com/kellyinn | 78 rooms | $95–$109, $149 suites | AE, D, DC, MC, V.

Parade Rest Guest Ranch. Slightly north of Yellowstone, this informal ranch has modern log cabins set on Grayling Creek. The rooms are furnished in Western style. The chuckwagon cookouts are fun. Hot tub. Hiking, horseback riding. Fishing. Bicycles. Game room. | 7979 Grayling Creek Rd. | 406/646–7217 or 800/753–5934 | www.Parade-Rest-Ranch.com | 13 cabins | $109 per person per night; includes meals and horseback riding | MC, V | Closed Oct.–Apr. | AP.

Stage Coach Inn. Just outside Yellowstone, this has room choices ranging from deluxe to economy, but all are air-conditioned. The style is casual Western, with a spacious lobby. Restaurant, bar. Cable TV. Hot tubs, sauna. Laundry facilities. | 209 Madison Ave. | 406/646–7381 or 800/842–2882 | fax 406/646–9575 | sci@yellowstoneinn.com | www.yellowstoneinn.com | 80 rooms | $55–$125 | AE, D, DC, MC, V.

Super 8 Lionshead Resort. The fresh trout served in the restaurant here is a touch that distinguishes the motel. The modern rooms are comfortable, and you're less than 10 mi from the park. In winter, you can use the snowmobile trails. Restaurant, bar. Cable TV. Hot tub, sauna. Playground, laundry facilities. | 1545 Targhee Pass Hwy. (U.S 20) | 406/646–9584 or 800/800–8000 | fax 406/646–7404 | 44 rooms | $90–$104, $135–$145 suites | AE, D, DC, MC, V.

WHITEFISH

MAP 6, B3

(Nearby towns also listed: Columbia Falls, Hungry Horse, Kalispell)

One of Montana's most popular destinations, this is the ideal place from which to explore Glacier National Park, swim in Whitefish Lake, or try the state's only 36-hole championship golf course. Big Mountain has world-class skiing, and the town of 6,000 has award-winning restaurants, shops, and galleries, as well as exceptional nightlife. The town's I. A. O'Shaughnessy Cultural Arts Center has theater, music, and dance year-round. At Whitefish Lake State Park, you can camp, boat, fish, and swim.

Information: **Whitefish Chamber of Commerce** | Box 1120, 59937 | 406/862–3501 | www.whitefishchamber.com.

Attractions

Big Mountain Ski and Summer Resort. Big Mountain has three ski areas: Big Mountain Resort, Hellroaring Basin, and the North Side. These combine to give skiers 67 world-class marked runs on 3,500 acres of the Flathead National Forest, with a vertical drop of 2,400 ft. Ski-in lodging, several restaurants, saloons, and day care are offered on the mountain. You can also take a four-hour guided snowcat skiing trip that ventures into territory normally only accessible by hiking. | 8 mi north on Big Mt. Rd. | 406/862–1900 or 800/858–3913 | www.bigmtn.com | $40.

Flathead National Forest, Tally Lake Ranger District. *See* Kalispell. | 1335 U.S. 93 | 406/863–5400.

I. A. O'Shaughnessy Cultural Arts Center. The center houses the Whitefish Theater Company, which produces or sponsors musical events and theater throughout the year. | 1 Central Ave. | 406/862–5371 | wtc@bigsky.net.

Whitefish Lake State Park. The 25-site campground has showers, and the park is only 2 mi from Whitefish. You can lounge on a sandy beach, fish, and boat. | U.S. 93 to State Park Rd. | 406/862–3991 | www.state.mt.us | Day use $4, camping $12 | Daily dawn to dusk.

ON THE CALENDAR

FEB.: *Winter Carnival.* For forty years now, outstanding winter fun, including a parade, a pancake feed, and activities for young and old. | 406/862–3501.
APR.: *Annual Furniture Race.* Competitors attach skis or sleds to a piece of furniture and race down Hope Slope wearing a helmet. | Big Mountain Resort | 406/862–2900.

MAY: *Stumptown Days.* Founders Day celebration highlights the town's logging and railroading heritage. There are historic window displays and walking tours, wagon rides, fiddlers, storytelling, and a period costume contest. | 406/862–3501.

Lodging

Best Western Rocky Mountain Lodge. A stone fireplace warms the lobby of this comfortable lodge within walking distance of restaurants, shops, and galleries. Complimentary Continental breakfast. Some in-room hot tubs. Cable TV. Pool. Hot tub. Exercise equipment. Laundry facilities. | 6510 U.S. 93 S | 406/862–2569 or 800/862–2569 | fax 406/862–1154 | bwrml@fcva.org | www.rockymtnlodge.com | 79 rooms | $119, $159 suites | AE, D, DC, MC, V.

Duck Inn Lodge. The lodge is small but the views are large, and you can soak in the deep tubs after a day of hiking or fishing on the Whitefish River. Complimentary Continental breakfast. Hot tub. | 1305 Columbia Ave. | 406/862–3825 or 800/344–2377 | www.duckinn.com | 10 rooms | $79 | AE, D, MC, V.

Good Medicine Lodge. Vaulted wood ceilings and lodgepole beds stand out in these spacious rooms, most with mountain views and balconies. A Western motif prevails: solid wood furniture and fabrics influenced by Native American designs. The largest suite sleeps five. Complimentary breakfast. No air-conditioning in some rooms. Outdoor hot tub. Laundry facilities. No smoking. | 537 Wisconsin Ave. | 406/862–5488 or 800/860–5488 | fax 406/862–5489 | goodrx@digisys.net | www.wtp.net/go/goodrx | 9 rooms, 2 with shower only | $95–$145 | AE, D, MC, V.

Grouse Mountain Lodge. The spacious rooms of the log building have views, and you can also sit on the sun porch to watch nature. Shopping and fine dining are both nearby. The golf course doubles as ski trails in winter. Bar, dining room, room service. Some refrigerators, some in-room hot tubs. Cable TV. Indoor pool. Hot tubs, sauna. Driving range, 36-hole golf course, putting green, tennis. Game room; no video games. Business services. Airport and ski shuttles. | 1205 U.S. 93 W | 406/862–3000 or 800/321–8822 | fax 406/862–0326 | gmlodge@digisys.net | www.grmtlodge.com | 144 rooms, 10 kitchenettes | $159, $209 suites | AE, D, DC, MC, V.

Hidden Moose Lodge. Built into the side of a hill, the lodge evokes the rugged, rustic history of the state. Each of the guest rooms has a private bath and deck and French doors. The furnishings are in Montana-lodge style. You can go many directions on the nature trails: to Whitefish Lake, through gardens, deep into the forest, or just around the property. You can also go rafting. Complimentary breakfast. Cable TV. Hot tub. Hiking, horseback riding, water sports. Fishing. Bicycles. No smoking. | 1735 East Lakeshore Dr. | 406/862–6516 or 888/733–6667 | fax 406/862–6514 | www.wtp.net/go/hiddenmoose | 8 rooms | $99–$125 | AE, D, MC, V.

Kandahar. A sunken lobby containing an immense rock fireplace is furnished with period antiques, original art, and comfortable sofas and chairs. The rooms are furnished in comfortably rustic Montana style. The entrance to the lodge has window arches and side panels of etched glass that display mountain and forest scenes by local Whitefish artist Myni Fergeson. Restaurant, bar. No air-conditioning. Cable TV. Hot tub, massage, sauna. Laundry facilities. Business services. | Big Mountain Rd. | 406/862–6098 or 800/862–6094 | fax 406/862–6095 | www.kandaharlodge.com | 50 rooms, 16 kitchenettes | $135–$147, $209 suites | AE, D, MC, V.

Quality Inn Pine Lodge. The rustic log structure has Western-style furnishings and is less than 10 mi from Big Mountain. The in-room data ports are convenient for business travelers. Complimentary Continental breakfast. Microwaves, refrigerators (suites). Cable TV. Indoor pool. Hot tub. Exercise equipment. Laundry facilities. Business services. Airport shuttle. Some pets allowed. | 920 Spokane Ave. | 406/862–7600 or 800/305–7463 | fax 406/862–7616 | www.thepinelodge.com | 76 rooms, 25 suites | $100–$180 | AE, D, DC, MC, V.

Super 8. Proximity to both the Whitefish River and downtown make this modest and modern motel convenient. Cable TV. Hot tub. Some pets allowed (fee). | 800 Spokane Ave. | 406/862–8255 or 800/800–8000 | 40 rooms | $80 | AE, D, DC, MC, V.

WHITE SULPHUR SPRINGS

MAP 6, F5

(Nearby towns also listed: Harlowton, Helena)

The springs that gave the town of 970 its name are still popular with visitors to the Spa Hot Springs. The Castle Museum, an imposing 1892 mansion, houses the Meagher County Museum (open seasonally), and weathered homes and outbuildings are all that remain of the nearby ghost town of Castle, which flourished with the silver-mining boom of the 1880s.

Information: **White Sulphur Springs Chamber of Commerce** | Box 356, 59645 | 406/547–3366.

Attractions

Castle. The ghost town of Castle was probably named after the castlelike rocks adorning Castle Mountain near White Sulpher Springs. The little mining community was one of the richest camps in the state in 1884, with a school, 80 homes, a jail, 14 saloons, and 7 broth-els. By the early 1890s the town, at the junction of U.S. 89 and U.S. 12, was almost deserted, and by 1927 abandoned claims were sold for taxes. | 406/547–2324 | Free | Daily.

The Castle Museum. The museum is housed in a Victorian home built in 1890–92 at a cost of $36,000. At the time, no other Montana home had a central-heat furnace (the owners had coal shipped in from Pennsylvania), indoor plumbing, and bathrooms. Electricity was installed in 1893. Furnishings include the original sofa and the bar from the Ringling House. | 310 2nd Ave. NE | 406/547–2324 | $3 | May 14–Sept. 14, daily 10–5:30.

Kings Hills National Scenic Byway. The 71-mi scenic section of U.S. 89 bisects the Little Belt Mountains and provides spectacular scenery, bits of history, and hiking trails. | 406/547–3361 | Free | May–Oct., daily.

Lewis and Clark National Forest, Kings Hill Ranger District. *See* Great Falls. | 204 W. Folsom; Off U.S. 89 | 406/547–3361.

Showdown Ski Area. You'll find some of best skiing in central Montana, with 34 runs of tree-lined trails, open slopes, and a 1,400-ft vertical drop. A restaurant and saloon, ski school, and special kids' programs add to the fun. You can also navigate the more than 200 mi of groomed snowmobile trails. Day use only. | U.S. 89 | 406/236–5522 or 800/433–0022 | www.travelbase.com.activies.skiing.showdown | $25 | Dec.–Apr., Wed.–Sun. 9–4:30.

Spa Hot Springs. The two pools here are drained and refilled nightly from the hot springs. The larger outdoor pool has a water temperature of 98°F and a smaller indoor pool measures 104 to 106°F. The pools contain no chemicals. The attached clinic uses the pools for hydrotherapy. You can stay at the hotel next door. | 202 W Main St. (U.S. 89) | 406/547–3366 | $4.50 | Daily 7 AM–11 PM.

ON THE CALENDAR
JULY: *Annual Ranch Rodeo and Fireworks.* Celebrate the Fourth of July with a ranch rodeo and fireworks in a small town. | 406/547–3932.

WOLF POINT

MAP 6, J3

(Nearby town also listed: Fort Peck)

In this small community of 3,600 on the edge of the Fort Peck Indian Reservation, you can make an appointment to see the John Deere Tractor Collection or check out regional history at the Wolf Point Area Historical Society and Museum. Nearby Fort Peck, home of the Fort Peck Dam, caters to outdoor enthusiasts. From a scenic overlook east of the dam on Rte. 24 you have views of the lake and and can hear interpretations of Lewis and Clark's journey through northeast Montana. In the summer, lively musicals and dramas are presented at the lovely Fort Peck Theatre. See *Fort Peck.*

Information: Wolf Point Chamber of Commerce | 218 3rd Ave. S, Suite B, 59201 | 406/653-2012.

Attractions

John Deere Tractor Collection. Owned by Louis Toavs, the collection contains more than 500 tractors, including every one built from 1923 to 1953. They are displayed on his farm north of Wolf Point. Some of the tractors date from as early as 1892. You reach the farm by going 1 mi west then 15 mi north on Rte. 250. | 406/392-5224 | Hours vary; call ahead.

Wolf Point Area Historical Society and Museum. Opened in 1972, the museum displays artifacts and belongings of the first settlers and homesteaders who arrived in Wolf Point in the late 1880s, as well as Native American artifacts. The building also houses the public library. | Fort Peck Indian Reservation, 220 Second Ave. S | 406/653-1912.

ON THE CALENDAR
JULY: *Wild Horse Stampede.* This three-day event includes a PRCA-sanctioned rodeo that attracts some of the best rodeo cowboys. A carnival, parades, street dances, and a legendary wild horse race round out the event. | 406/653-2220.
AUG.: *Wadopana Powwow.* The Wadopana Band—also known as the Canoe Paddlers—invite the public to join in this traditional powwow celebration of thanks and sharing. | 406/768-5131 or 406/653-2012.

Dining
Old Town Grill. Mexican. Known for the Mexican entrées, this friendly spot also serves steaks, pork chops, burgers, and the like. Kids' menu. | 400 U.S. 2 W | 406/653-1031 | $6-$12 | No credit cards.

Nevada

Most people picture Nevada in one of two ways: a barren desert landscape or Las Vegas. These two images are indeed part of the Nevada experience, though they couldn't be farther apart.

The surprise lies in just how much variety you'll find in between.

Nevada is the seventh-largest state in the country; you could fit more than two New Yorks inside of it. One county in Nevada is almost as large as northern New England. The state's boundaries are ruler straight; it's 500 mi down the eastern edge of the state, and 400 mi across the north. Within them there's every kind of ecology except rain forest and ocean.

Nevada has 250 named mountain ranges. Two peaks are higher than 13,000 ft, six more than 12,000 ft, and another 25 more than 10,000 ft. All the biggest mountain ranges are well watered, lush in the upper elevations with juniper, four kinds of pine, cedar, fir, and spruce, and topped by bristlecone pine, the oldest living organisms on earth. Streams and springs send water down to the equally verdant valley floors or "basins." Ranches, corporate and family-owned, grow alfalfa, run livestock, and string fence in and around them. These basins are some of the most beautiful country in Nevada—ranch houses, barns, white picket fences, and tree breaks backed by 10,000-ft peaks and underlain by a rich green carpet.

Big rivers flow through, including the Colorado, the longest in the West. You can boat at more than two dozen sites and fish at thousands. Lake Mead is one of the world's largest man-made lakes, spreading big water across southern Nevada, and Lake Tahoe is the dazzling crown of western Nevada.

But the rest of Nevada that isn't Las Vegas (and a handful of other towns) are deserts, three of them. The Great Basin occupies roughly 75% of the state, the wide northern portion; this is the high desert, from 4,500 to 6,200 ft in elevation. Sagebrush is nearly

CAPITAL: CARSON CITY	POPULATION: 1,800,000	AREA: 110,000 SQUARE MI
BORDERS: CA, AZ, UT, ID, OR	TIME ZONE: PACIFIC	POSTAL ABBREVIATION: NV
WEB SITE: WWW.TRAVELNEVADA.COM		

a monoculture in the Great Basin. The Mojave Desert occupies the southern wedge of the state. This is the low desert, which supports mostly creosote, mesquite, yucca, and the haunting native Joshua tree. At the tip of the wedge is the fierce Sonoran Desert, which extends through Arizona and California all the way down the Baja Peninsula and deep into mainland Mexico.

Which leaves the bright lights of the cities and towns scattered across Nevada. Astronauts agree that Las Vegas is Earth's most identifiable city from high orbit; they can also outline the state by the lights of the boomtowns on the borders. Las Vegas is the biggest boomtown this country has ever seen, growing by leaps and bounds for the past 75 years. Sin City now attracts more than 30 million annual visitors bent on partaking of all the games people play. And Reno was offering that kind of action for 50 years before. Carson City, Elko, Winnemucca, Ely, Tonopah, Boulder City—only a few towns have enough people to be worth remembering.

That's Nevada—a vast desert, Las Vegas, and some diversions in between.

History

Nevada was one of the last sections of the continent to be explored. The first Europeans arrived in 1776—two Spanish friars surveying a traders' trail from Santa Fe to the southern California coast. In fact, a treaty with Mexico in 1819 ceded Nevada (along with New Mexico, Arizona, and southern California) to the Spanish. The United States didn't win Nevada until 1848, in the treaty that ended the Mexican-American War.

Emigrants were already wagon-training west to California when gold, discovered in 1849, started a stampede. Most fortune seekers passed through Nevada without noticing it, but a handful of hardy prospectors drifted back across the Sierra to look for gold in the east-facing creeks. They didn't find a lot, just enough for gold fever to keep these desert rats interested. For 10 years they swished pans across Gold Flats and up Gold Creek to its source on Sun Mountain. There, one intuitive prospector sunk his shovel into the mountain itself—and struck the richest body of ore ever discovered in the Lower 48.

The Comstock Lode launched Nevada with a bang in 1859. By 1864, it had become the 36th state in the Union. Virginia City, directly above the mines of the Comstock on Sun Mountain, was the Las Vegas of its day, with a boom that lasted a full 20 years—an eternity in mining-town lore. For a time, Virginia City rivaled San Francisco; indeed, Comstock precious metals inaugurated the Golden Age of San Francisco.

But then, like all great booms, it busted, and in a few years Virginia City was a semi-ghost town. Reno emerged from Virginia City's shadow and soon made a name for itself for a different kind of gold mine: divorce. Thanks to the most liberal divorce laws of the time, Reno basked in the glow of marital dissolution from 1905 through the 1930s, reveling in its reputation as the naughtiest town in the country.

That was before gambling, legalized in 1931, caught on as a legitimate leisure activity. The 1920s and 1930s were Reno's heyday, and only a force as strong as Las Vegas could have made a louder boom.

NV Timeline

1100s	1200s	1776	1826
The area is colonized by Anasazi, southwestern Pueblo Indians.	The Lost City colony is suddenly abandoned for unknown reasons.	Two Spanish missionaries travel through southern Nevada.	Jedediah Smith leads a party of fur trappers on the Spanish Trail.

INTRODUCTION
HISTORY
REGIONS
WHEN TO VISIT
STATE'S GREATS
RULES OF THE ROAD
DRIVING TOURS

Also in 1931 Hoover Dam was completed. This gave the fledgling gambling town of Las Vegas so much electricity and water that it's been growing brighter and wetter ever since! The '40s and '50s were Las Vegas's wildcat years, with mob cash building the early oasis legally. Then the feds, the state, not even the county had any regulations or taxes. But when the power of the federal government began to grow in the 1960s, Vegas's freewheeling days were over, and the mob was ready and willing to sell out to the politically correct masters of the game, the corporations. The stock-market boom of the '80s and '90s has fueled the growth of the gambling corporations to an extreme: Bellagio, which opened in October 1998, is the most expensive hotel ever built.

Regions

1. LAS VEGAS AND VICINITY

Out of 10 Nevada visitors, 9 go to Las Vegas. It's in the remote and inhospitable eastern Mojave Desert, 40 mi from the electrical power of Hoover Dam and the abundant water of Lake Mead. Las Vegas equals non-stop action: games of chance that excite the greedy; extravagant and at times risque stage shows; and Bacchanalian yet inexpensive feasts. Las Vegas goes year-round; you barely notice the slowdown during the hot, hot months of July and August, when temperatures can reach 115.

Las Vegans are now 1.2 million strong, most of them having arrived in the past 10 years. This is a second-chance town, where people come to start over, rebuild, and get in on the good life.

But go a few minutes from the lights, and you're in a different world, the desert at the edge of the city. A mighty Nevada mountain range rims western Las Vegas Valley; red rock erupts in scattered locations. Lakes Mead and Mojave and the Colorado River hug the edge of it all, never more than a couple of hours away.

Towns listed: Boulder City, Goodsprings, Henderson, Las Vegas, Laughlin, Overton

2. EASTERN NEVADA

U.S. 93 enters Nevada when it crosses the two-lane road atop Hoover Dam. It travels roughly 500 mi in a straight line up the eastern side of the state, paralleling mighty north–south mountain ranges, running up vast valleys with little elevation change. Out here, it's known as "going with the grain." It crosses great swaths of country without any civilization; there are only six towns of noticeable size and another half-dozen minor ones.

The road starts out 40 mi east of Vegas and follows the route surveyed by the Salt Lake–Los Angeles railroad in the early 1900s. The tracks were built along a well-watered strip known as the Meadow Valley Wash. The towns of Alamo, Ash Spring, Caliente, and Panaca also take advantage of this high water table in the desert.

1829	1830	1841	1844	1848
Peter Skene Ogden discovers the Humboldt River.	Antonio Armijo discovers a shortcut on the Spanish Trail via Big Spring; he names it Las Vegas, the Meadows. Joseph Walker blazes a trail through northern and western Nevada.	The Bidwell-Bartleson party is the first to emigrate from Missouri to California following Walker's route.	John C. Fremont explores, maps, and names large sections of Nevada.	the Treaty of Guadeloupe-Hidalgo cedes the Southwest, including Nevada, to the United States.

From there, the narrow ribbon of road stretches 90 mi north to Ely, parallel to the big Schell Creek Range on the west and the mighty Snake Range on the east, home to Great Basin National Park, the only one in the state. Ely is an old copper-mining center and crossroads town, where east–west U.S. 6 and U.S. 50 intersect U.S. 93. Then it's another 140 mi to Wells, again cruising a flat valley hemmed by a dozen small mountain ranges. Wells is a small railroad town in which U.S. 93 intersects east–west I-80. Finally, it's another 60 mi of basins and ranges to Jackpot, the border boomtown on the Idaho state line.

Towns listed: Caliente, Ely, Jackpot, Panaca, Pioche

3. CENTRAL NEVADA

Just as U.S. 93 slices off eastern Nevada, U.S. 50 bisects the state, cutting right through the heart of it and defining central Nevada. U.S. 50 is known far and wide as the loneliest highway in the country, and a state marketing campaign will remind you of it all along the way. However, U.S. 50 is positively jammed with traffic compared to U.S. 93. Furthermore, if you know a little history of the area, you'll have 160 years of stories to keep you company. Finally, the road "goes against the grain," struggling up a dozen mountain ranges, cresting a dozen passes, and coasting down to a dozen basins.

The central Nevada route to California was blazed in the 1820s, and emigrants were traveling it regularly by the late 1840s. Coming from the east, it skirts Great Basin National Park and climbs the Schell Creeks to get into Ely. From there it crosses the Egan, White Pine, and Fish Creek ranges and the intervening basins to reach Eureka, founded in 1864. Then it hugs the northern edge of three of the mightiest ranges in the state: the Monitors, Toquimas, and Toiyabes. South of the road there are hundreds of miles of wilderness, some of the most popular in the state for local hikers and climbers.

Austin, the first town settled in central Nevada, is at 6,200 ft in the Toiyabes; don't blink as you drive through on U.S. 50. From there the road meanders around the bases of the ranges into western Nevada.

Towns listed: Austin, Eureka, Ely, Goldfield, Lunar Crater, Tonopah

4. WESTERN NEVADA

U.S. 50 continues into the other urban area of Nevada, also the oldest part of the state. It passes Dayton, site of the original Gold Creek at the base of Virginia City's Sun Mountain, and cruises by the state capital, Carson City, nestled in the big Carson Valley at the base of the Sierra Nevada. Then it's up and over Spooner Summit at 7,200 ft and into California at South Lake Tahoe.

In Carson City it intersects U.S. 395, which runs north through the scenic Washoe Valley and into Reno, the third-largest population center in the state (Henderson, a suburb of Las Vegas, is second). Just north of Reno, western Nevada is a great untracked

1851	1855	1858	1859	1860
Latter-Day Saints from three-year-old Salt Lake City build a trading post at Mormon Station (now Genoa).	Nevada is officially designated Carson County of the Utah Territory.	The number of prospectors panning gold out of Gold Creek (now Dayton) swells to 20.	Two Irish gold miners dig a hole near a spring high up on Sun Mountain and discover the Comstock Lode.	A frenzied rush back across the Sierra by boomtowners; the first wave carves Virginia City into the mountainside and digs the Comstock out of the mountain.

INTRODUCTION
HISTORY
REGIONS
WHEN TO VISIT
STATE'S GREATS
RULES OF THE ROAD
DRIVING TOURS

wilderness, sprawling all the way to the Oregon border. Pyramid Lake, the forbidding Smoke Creek and Black Rock deserts, the mighty Granite Range, High Rock Canyon, and the Charles Sheldon National Wildlife Refuge, home to a large herd of pronghorn, are served by three main roads, only one of them partly paved. A mere 90-minute drive from Reno puts you in some of the most rugged and remote country in the state.

Towns listed: Carson City, Crystal Bay, Fallon, Genoa, Hawthorne, Incline Village, Lake Tahoe, Minden-Gardnerville, Pyramid Lake, Reno, Sparks, Stateline, Virginia City, Yerington

5. NORTHERN NEVADA

Like eastern and central Nevada, the northern section of the state is defined by a road, I–80. For most of the trip east and west through the state, I–80 follows the Humboldt River, the longest waterway in the state. The river route was blazed by Peter Skene Ogden in the 1820s, and followed by the emigrants, the transcontinental railroad, transcontinental U.S. 40 (the Victory Highway), and finally rendered high-speed as I–80. The railroad might have transported people into northern Nevada, but mining settled it.

Elko, Battle Mountain, and Winnemucca are located near some of the richest mineral deposits in the world. Pockets of the country are scarred with the signs of men battling mountains, wresting precious metals from the reluctant earth.

Of course, northern Nevada also has more than its fair share of mountains and basins and dirt roads and tiny towns. It claims the mighty Ruby, Jarbidge, Santa Rosa, and East Humboldt mountains, along with gorgeous Independence Valley, the Idaho-like Owyhee Gorge and Wildhorse Reservoir, and Ruby Marsh, a bird sanctuary.

Towns listed: Battle Mountain, Elko, Lovelock, Winnemucca

When to Visit

Nevada's climate is delineated by the two main deserts. Weather in the Great Basin, the high desert, is typically mild in summer and harsh in winter. In the Mojave, the low desert, it's mild in winter and harsh in summer. Most people like to go to the Las Vegas area between October and May, avoiding the June–September heat of 105 and above for weeks on end. Temperatures rarely fall below 30 degrees in Las Vegas in winter; days often peak out above 60.

Many also choose summer for northern Nevada, where, depending on the altitude, temperatures rarely exceed 90–95. Plenty of people like northern Nevada in the winter as well for its abundant skiing, but conditions can be severe. Blizzards can shut down even the main roads for days at a time; temperatures regularly drop below 20 degrees.

1861	1864	1869	1872	1878
Nevada becomes a United States territory; Samuel Clemens, 20, travels to Carson City with his brother Orion, personal secretary to Governor James Nye.	Nevada becomes the nation's 36th state.	The transcontinental railroad is laid across northern Nevada.	The Big Bonanza discovered, the Comstock's richest ore body.	From 15,000 people six years earlier, Virginia City shrinks to a mere 4,000.

CLIMATE CHART
Average High/Low Temperatures (°F) and Monthly Precipitation (in inches)

	JAN.	FEB.	MAR.	APR.	MAY	JUNE
ELKO	37/13	43/20	50/25	59/30	69/37	80/45
	.98	.8	.96	.82	1.	.91
	JULY	AUG.	SEPT.	OCT.	NOV.	DEC.
	91/50	89/49	78/39	66/30	49/23	37/14
	.33	.65	.62	.65	1.1	1.1
	JAN.	FEB.	MAR.	APR.	MAY	JUNE
ELY	40/9	44/15	48/21	57/26	67/34	78/41
	.7	.65	.96	1.	1.15	.88
	JULY	AUG.	SEPT.	OCT.	NOV.	DEC.
	87/48	84/47	75/37	64/28	49/19	41/11
	.69	.83	1.01	.89	.67	.7
	JAN.	FEB.	MAR.	APR.	MAY	JUNE
LAS VEGAS	57/34	63/39	69/44	76/51	88/60	100/70
	.48	.48	.42	.21	.28	.12
	JULY	AUG.	SEPT.	OCT.	NOV.	DEC.
	106/76	103/74	95/66	82/54	67/43	58/34
	.35	.49	.28	.21	.43	.38
	JAN.	FEB.	MAR.	APR.	MAY	JUNE
RENO	45/21	52/24	56/30	64/33	73/40	83/47
	1.07	.99	.71	.38	.69	.46
	JULY	AUG.	SEPT.	OCT.	NOV.	DEC.
	92/51	90/50	80/41	69/33	54/27	46/20
	.28	.32	.39	.38	.87	.99
	JAN.	FEB.	MAR.	APR.	MAY	JUNE
WINNEMUCCA	42/17	49/23	55/25	63/30	73/38	83/46
	.74	.62	.78	.84	.83	.86
	JULY	AUG.	SEPT.	OCT.	NOV.	DEC.
	93/51	91/49	80/39	68/29	52/23	43/17
	.27	.45	.4	.62	.94	.88

FESTIVALS AND SEASONAL EVENTS
WINTER

Dec. **National Finals Rodeo** in Las Vegas. At the Super Bowl of the rodeo circuit, more than 120 top rodeo athletes vie for $2.5 million in prize money. | 702/731–2115.

1880
The beginning of the 20-year bust, when most of Nevada is deserted.

1900
Jim Butler discovers silver at Tonopah, launching a 20-year boom that spreads to Goldfield, Manhattan, Beatty, and Ely.

1905
Las Vegas becomes a stop on the Salt Lake–Los Angeles railroad.

1906
Reno first makes the headlines as a divorce haven.

1917
A big fire in Goldfield signals the end of Nevada's second mining boom.

INTRODUCTION
HISTORY
REGIONS
WHEN TO VISIT
STATE'S GREATS
RULES OF THE ROAD
DRIVING TOURS

Jan.   The **Cowboy Poetry Gathering** in Elko is one of the largest cowboy poetry and music festivals in the country; five days of poetry readings, yodeling, concerts, art exhibits, and serious partying. | 775/738–7508 or 888/880–5885.

SPRING

Mar.   The **NASCAR Winston Cup 400 Race** in Las Vegas is the largest event of the year in Nevada; 120,000 racing fans converge on Las Vegas for the top race sponsored by the top racing organization. | 702/644–4443.

June   **Kit Carson Rendezvous** in Carson City is a variety of mountain-man events, including musket demonstrations, battle reenactments, storytelling, Western music, arts and crafts, and food. | 775/687–7410 or 800/638–2321.

Reno Rodeo is one of the largest, oldest, and richest rodeos in the country. | 775/329–3877.

SUMMER

July   **Jim Butler Days** in Tonopah is one of Nevada's most popular pioneer festivals, attracting participants from all over the state for a parade, car races, a summit run, a barbecue and chili cook-off, an arts and crafts fair, a dance, and the state's biggest pancake breakfast. | 775/482–3878.

National Basque Festival in Elko features Basque costumes, dancing, music, bota-drinking, strength and endurance competitions, sheep hooking, bread baking, and a public dance. | 775/738–7135.

Aug.   **Hot August Nights** in Reno is the biggest classic-car congregation in the country; a four-day blow-out with events citywide. | 775/356–1956.

AUTUMN

Sept. **Candy Dance Fair** in Genoa is the oldest annual event in Nevada (1919) selling two tons of candy, plus arts, crafts, food, and a formal ball. | 775/782–8696.

Oct.   **Nevada Day Celebration** in Carson City celebrates statehood with Nevada's largest parade, arts and crafts, a carnival, concerts, fireworks, and a grand ball. | 775/882–2600.

1930	**1931**	**1935**	**1941**	**1942**
The Bureau of Reclamations starts building Hoover Dam.	Wide-open casino gambling is legalized for good.	Harold Smith opens Harold's Club in Reno and begins to popularize gambling for the masses; Hoover Dam completed.	The first resort–motor inns are built on the Las Vegas Strip.	Soldiers arrive at Las Vegas Aerial Gunnery Range.

State's Greats

Las Vegas is one of the world's greats. There's no place on earth like the **Las Vegas Strip**, God's own miniature golf course. The top 18 of the world's largest 21 hotels are here; 30 million visitors leave $20 billion behind. That's a lot.

The rest of Nevada has its share of boastables. **Lake Mead** is practically an inland waterway in the middle of the desert. And it's within a stone's throw of Nellis Air Force Base and the Nevada Test Site, an area the size of New Hampshire; this whole big chunk of south-central Nevada is off-limits by order of the federal government, which has blown up a couple of hundred nuclear weapons inside it.

Tahoe's no slouch for scenic beauty, surrounding wilderness, top resorts, and varied recreation. **Pyramid Lake** is no less awe-inspiring, but utterly unknown, and it's only 110 mi away as the river flows.

Great Basin National Park has a 12,000-ft peak, complete with the southernmost permanent icefield on the continent. The road travels above 10,000 ft, some of the highest pavement in the West. Lehman Cave is a bonus.

A dozen major mountain ranges, another dozen spectacular canyons, vast salt flats and cracked playa, hot springs and crystal-clear air—all recommend Nevada as a place to explore, as long as you're going to Las Vegas anyway.

Beaches, Forests, and Parks

Contrary to popular misconception, Nevada has several beaches worth visiting. **Boulder Beach** and **Echo Bay** on **Lake Mead**, **Nevada Beach** and **Sand Harbor** on **Lake Tahoe**, **Pelican** and **Warrior** points on **Pyramid Lake**, and little sandy spots on another half-dozen reservoirs have all the swimming, splashing, mud mucking, rock diving, snorkeling, and lounging of beaches everywhere.

Unlike most of the rest of the country, trees in Nevada grow only in the higher elevations. No trees are indigenous to the low **Mojave Desert** (no higher than 4,000 ft); even the palms are imported. The closest you come is a Joshua "tree," which is actually a yucca cactus. Trees don't get going until much farther north and another couple of thousand feet in elevation. If you drew a line from Caliente to Goldfield, that's where the trees would begin.

At about 5,500 ft, you start to get juniper and piñon pine. Though some piñon can grow "tall," both are little more than shrubs. Not until you get to around 7,000 or 8,000 ft, always wetter than below, do you encounter the bigger pines and spruce and cedar. Growth is thick all the way up to 10,000 ft: the forests of Nevada. Above that, the winds keep the trees compact.

Nevada has one national park—**Great Basin National Park,** near the Utah border—23 state recreation and historic sites, and another dozen large areas patrolled by the U.S. Park and Forest services and the Bureau of Land Management. Places like **Lake Tahoe-Nevada, Valley of Fire,** and **Berlin-Ichthyosaur** have visitors centers, camping,

1958	**1966**	**1968**	**1979**	**1989**
The Stardust, the last of eight mob-built casinos, opens on the Strip.	Howard Hughes moves to Las Vegas and buys out the mob.	Circus Circus opens, one of five hotels built in the '60s.	The Year of the Crane in Reno; eight hotels are built.	The Mirage opens in Las Vegas, launching the current boom.

and running water. Nevada also has 13 national wilderness areas, where whole mountain ranges are the parks, but there are no facilities, often including roads.

INTRODUCTION
HISTORY
REGIONS
WHEN TO VISIT
STATE'S GREATS
RULES OF THE ROAD
DRIVING TOURS

Culture, History, and the Arts

Strange things pass for culture and the arts in Nevada. The **Liberace Museum,** for example. It would impress an urban sophisticate by horrifying him. Two of the largest collections in the state are of automobiles; if your great American love affair is not with the automobile, you might as well be touring a museum of vacuum cleaners or oil burners.

Theater is another case in point. Las Vegas theater consists of $50 million extravaganzas, overwhelming spectacles of high-tech wizardry and bodies galore, but little of cultural value. And the off-Strip theater is confined to illusionists, superstar imitators, female impersonators, jugglers, comics, daredevils, musclemen, marionetteers, and indescribable gimmicksters.

And the art is all gambling-inspired. Signs (especially neon), casino architecture, faux landscapes, themed reproductions—they're all surface images. There's no depth to them, nothing that grabs hold of your imagination and wrestles with it for more than a minute at a time.

But all that, of course, is in the city. The real culture is in the country. It's a rural culture, a cowboy culture, a libertarian culture. In the city, where physical distances are so small, psychic distances are correspondingly large. In the country, where physical distances are so large, psychic distances are correspondingly small. The people stick together with Western music, cowboy poetry, a common live-and-let-live attitude, and a nearly universal distaste for central government.

Sports

Las Vegans are nuts about Jet Skis, speed boats, sailboats, houseboats, riverboats, even inflatable boats. Luckily, **Lake Mead** is big enough to absorb all the **water sports,** even on a summer holiday weekend. The water sports at **Lake Tahoe** somehow don't seem so fast, with sternwheelers plying back and forth amid an armada of sailboats. At **Pyramid and Walker lakes,** along with a dozen reservoirs, the pace could be considered dead: anglers sit in silent contemplation of the denizens of the deep.

Red Rock Canyon, outside Las Vegas, is Nevada's best-known **rock climbing** destination, attracting international climbers year-round; countless routes (no trails) penetrate and ascend the nearby Spring Mountains. **Lake Tahoe,** again, has **car camping, hiking, backpacking, mountain biking,** and **hang gliding** to spare. But you can do the same things at the dozens of lesser-known mountain-lake areas in Nevada.

Downhill skiing is world-class around the **Tahoe Basin** (though most of it is in California). There's a downhill ski resort on **Mt. Charleston,** an hour from Vegas, with a base elevation of 8,400 ft. People come even from Switzerland to helicopter-ski the Ruby Mountains.

1999
The Mandalay Bay, Venetian, Regents at Summerlin, Paris, and the Hyatt at Lake Las Vegas open, sending the boom into the next millennium.

Throughout the state, **golf** is huge. A couple of dozen golf courses dot **Las Vegas,** another half-dozen, the **Reno** area. You find golf courses in some unlikely places in Nevada. The **Sandy Bottom Golf Course,** for example, is a nine-holer outside the barren mining town of Gabbs, where you're given a piece of green carpet for the tee and green; the Black Rock Desert, as well, has seen many a makeshift golf course with thousand-yard fairways and 20-ft hole posts.

Oddball sports such as **landsailing** (a cross between windsurfing and sailing on land) and **flyawaying** (indoor aerobatics on a cushion of air created by a giant fan) have sprung up hereabouts. Both Reno and Las Vegas have major **water parks. Thrill rides** are all the rage in Las Vegas, both the actual and virtual kind; there's even a bungee jump into a pool at Circus Circus.

Spectator sports include the popular **UNR Wolf Pack football** and **UNLV Runnin' Rebels basketball** teams. The **Las Vegas Stars** is a Triple-A San Diego Padres farm team. **Rodeos** are rampant in every population center in the state. Even the new **roller derby** league has a Nevada team.

Rules of the Road

License Requirements: To drive in Nevada you must be at least 16 years of age and have a valid driver's license. You also have to have your wits about you when you're driving near a casino. Free booze at the games is bad for drivers and pedestrians alike.

Right Turn on Red: Allowed everywhere. Also left turn on red onto a one-way street.

Seat Belt and Helmet Laws: All drivers and front-seat passengers must wear seat belts. Children under 10 must wear a seat belt at all times; children under four must ride in child seats. Motorcyclists are required to wear helmets at all times.

Speed Limits: Some places on I–80 and I–15 you can drive legally at 75 mph. Other places, and on the U.S. highways, the speed limit is 70. It's a quick 65 mph on the interstates in the heart of Las Vegas and Reno. Nevada isn't known for speed traps.

For More Information: Contact the Nevada Department of Motor Vehicles at | 702/ 486–4368.

Into the Desert Driving Tour
LAS VEGAS TO PIOCHE ON I–15 AND U.S. 93

Distance: 175 mi   Time: 2 days
Breaks: You can stop overnight at Caliente Hot Springs Motel, where a soak in the large Roman tubs will soothe your stiff muscles and rinse off the road dust.

This tour takes you on a little-traveled and scenically varied stretch of country northeast of Las Vegas. After 75 mi of barren desert, you enter a well-watered strip of southeastern Nevada: green valleys lush with grass and towering cottonwoods, a string of lakes and springs, alfalfa fields backed by rugged and bare mountains, washes carved by time, and a handful of small towns for gassing up the car.

❶ **Pahranagat National Wildlife Refuge** (22 mi northeast on I–15, 60 mi north on U.S. 93). Two unexpected lakes, improbably in the desert, cover 700 acres and preserve a habitat for hundreds of species of migrating and resident birds. Follow the old road at Upper Lake to the lakeside campgrounds.

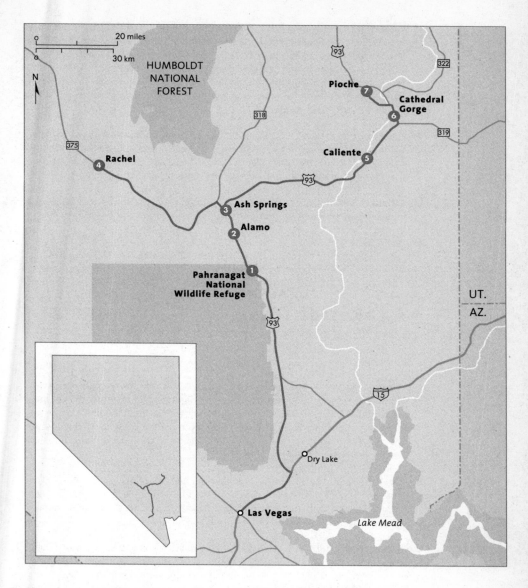

❷ **Alamo** (15 mi north of Upper Pahranagat Lake on U.S. 93) is a small and somewhat remote farming and ranching center that went its own quiet way from the 1880s 'til the 1950s— when the Atomic Energy Commission began above-ground nuclear testing at the Nevada Test Site just on the other side of the Pahranagat Range. The explosions rocked the town, and the residents were required to wear radiation badges. But since the Test Ban Treaty of the early 1990s, peace has returned to Alamo.

❸ **Ash Springs** (7 mi north of Alamo) is another small settlement with two gas stations, a mini-market, an on-again, off-again eatery, and a primitive public warm spring: take a right across from R Place Texaco (ignore the No Trespassing sign if it's still there) and park under the big cottonwood.

❹ **Rachel** (5 mi north to Rte. 375, then 36 mi northwest). This tiny hamlet of no more than 100 residents has achieved international notoriety as the closest town to Groom Lake, also known as Area 51. Reportedly, this top-secret Air Force research facility has hosted extraterrestrial aircraft and, some believe, extraterrestrials themselves. UFO enthusiasts from all over converge for get-togethers at the Little A'Le'Inn, Rachel's bar and grill (775/729–2515). Route 375 has been designated the Extraterrestrial Highway by the Nevada Department of Transportation.

❺ **Caliente** (43 mi east on U.S. 93 from Rte. 375) is a small railroad town with a big Spanish mission–style depot. A 20-mi side trip to the end of scenic Rainbow Canyon (turn on Rte. 317 at the south end of Caliente) travels along sheer polychrome canyon walls, past many railroad trestles and bridges, and by idyllic ranches.

❻ **Cathedral Gorge** (15 mi north on U.S. 93, then right ½ mi) is a simple desert wash that time and erosion have transformed into a gorgeous gorge (775/728–4467).

❼ **Pioche** (12 mi north on U.S. 93, then right ½ mi). A 150-year-old mining community that has one of the most colorful and sordid histories in the state. The Million Dollar Courthouse and Boot Hill cemetery tell the tale.

A Lakeside Drive

STATELINE TO CRYSTAL BAY

Distance: 27 mi   Time: 1 day

This exhilarating ride up the east shore of Lake Tahoe begins at the high-rise casinos of Stateline, but quickly leaves behind the neon lights and noisy slot machines. Unlike the west (California) shore of the lake, with more than a dozen towns along the way, this ride is mostly undeveloped, with forested mountainsides, rocky coves, sandy beaches, alpine lakes, and small marinas. And just about the time you're ready for civilization again, the glittering casinos of Crystal Bay appear.

❶ **Stateline** (starting north on U.S. 50). Four major and two minor casinos make up the action in Stateline, clustered on the flats a short hike from the lake. A small residential area hugs the hills above the high-rises, chalets, and condos, close to the sprawling Heavenly Valley Ski Resort (Ski Run Blvd., Stateline | 800/243–2836).

❷ **Nevada Beach** (3 mi north on U.S. 50; turn left onto Elk Point Rd.). The nearest public lake access to Stateline on the Nevada side, this large Forest Service facility has a sandy beach, picnic areas, and a 54-site campground (reservations 800/280–2267; information 530/573–2600).

❸ **Zephyr Cove** (4 mi north on U.S. 50) is the largest settlement between Stateline and Incline Village, though it's a tiny resort, with a beach, marina, campground and RV park, riding stables, and lodge (775/588–6644). The 550-passenger sternwheeler MS *Dixie II* (775/588–3508) and the 20-passenger trimaran *Woodwind* (775/588–3000) sail from Zephyr Cove.

❹ **Cave Rock** (4 mi north on U.S. 50) is 25 yards of solid stone; U.S. 50 passes through it via one of Nevada's few tunnels. This monolith towers over a parking lot, with a lakefront picnic area and a boat launch.

❺ **Lake Tahoe-Nevada State Park** (8 mi northeast on U.S. 50, then 2 mi north on Rte. 28)

INTRODUCTION
HISTORY
REGIONS
WHEN TO VISIT
STATE'S GREATS
RULES OF THE ROAD
DRIVING TOURS

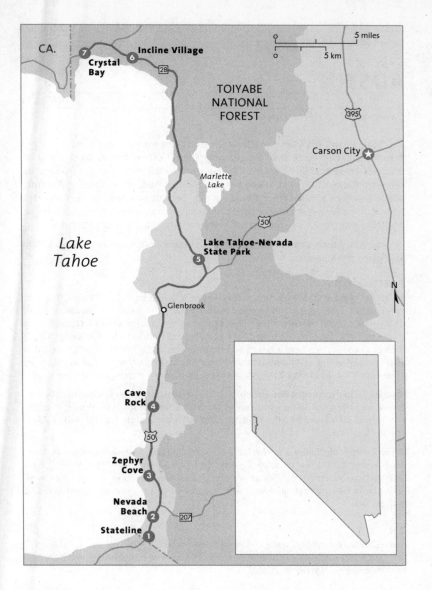

preserves 3 mi of shoreline and a 10-mi by 5-mi clump of the Carson Range rising from the lake. Spooner Lake (just north of the junction) has a nature trail and the trailhead for a 5-mi hike through North Canyon to Marlette Lake. Sand Harbor (8 mi north on Rte. 28 | 775/588–7230) is the focal point of the park; it has a sandy beach, rocky cove, and nature trail, and gets very crowded by noon in summer.

○ **Incline Village** (4 mi north on Rte. 28) is one of Nevada's few master-planned towns, dating back to the early 1960s; it's still privately owned. Check out Lakeshore Drive to see some of the most expensive real estate in the state. Ponderosa Ranch is a Western theme park open during the summer (775/831–0691).

❼ Crystal Bay (3 mi north on Rte. 28) has a cluster of low-rise casinos. The historic Cal-Neva is bisected by the state line.

AUSTIN

MAP 10, C4

(Nearby town also listed: Eureka)

This town of 300 souls lies 12 mi from the exact center of the state, and its history demonstrates that Austin lived up to its geographical responsibilities. When silver was discovered here in 1863, it became the first offspring boomtown of Virginia City, the second settlement in what would become Nevada. Prospectors fanning out from Austin launched a dozen other Nevada mining boomtowns over the next 20 years. Today, Austin claims numerous original buildings (including a hotel, county courthouse, and three churches), three motels, two restaurants, and a chamber of commerce.

Information: **Austin Chamber of Commerce.** | Lander County Courthouse, 100 Main St., 89310 | 775/964–2200.

Attractions

Berlin-Ichthyosaur State Park. Fifty miles southwest in Toiyabe National Forest, this state park combines the small, well-preserved town of Berlin, with an archaeological exhibit of ichthyosaurs. Berlin consists of the ruins of shops, offices, homes, a cemetery, and the big stamp mill of a silver-mining town that had its heyday from 1900 to 1907. Under a fossil shed you can see the site of a quarry where the remains of 40 ichthyosaurs, believed to be the largest prehistoric marine creatures, were unearthed between 1928 and 1954. | 23 miles east of Gabbs, via Rte. 844 | 775/964–2440 | www.state.nv.us/stparks/ | Free | Daily.

Hickison Petroglyph Recreation Site. An easy ½-mi trail passes through sagebrush, by Ponderosa pine trees, and along an outcrop of sandstone. You can study the dozens of petroglyphs (rock art) carved into the sandstone. Many are prehistoric. | Off U.S. 50 | 775/635–4000 | Free | Daily.

Lander County Courthouse. This wood-and-brick building was constructed in the mid-1860s, when Austin was the seat of Lander County (Battle Mountain wrested the county administration from Austin in 1980). Pick up some brochures from the rack in the foyer. The Chamber of Commerce, upstairs, is open most weekdays. | 12 Main St. | 775/964–2447 | Free | Weekdays 9–noon, 1–4.

ON THE CALENDAR

JUNE: *Gridley Days.* Local, state, and Western events include the Gridley Sack of Flour foot race, the Nevada State Fiddler's Championship, mining competitions, and a Civil War encampment. | 775/964–2200.

Lodging

Lincoln Motel. This is the largest hotel in Austin. The rooms are small and spartan but have satellite TV. | 17 rooms | 60 Main St. | 775/964–2698 | $29–$43 | MC, V.

Pony Express House. This extremely small facility gives you the choice of renting one or both of its rooms. You make your own breakfast. | 2 rooms | 115 N.W. Main St. | 775/964–2306 | fax 775/964–2447 | $35–$70 | MC, V.

BATTLE MOUNTAIN

MAP 10, C3

(Nearby town also listed: Elko)

One of the largest deposits of gold, precious metals, and minerals in the world under-lies an area in northern Nevada between Winnemucca and Elko. Battle Mountain, within the boundaries, has reaped the benefits of the mining on and off since 1870, most recently in the early 1990s, when two large mines operated south of town. Battle Mountain is the quintessential dusty and drab outback desert town, little more than a rest stop on the interstate, and home to several thousand residents.

Information: Battle Mountain Chamber of Commerce. | Civic Center, 625 S. Broad St., 89820 | 775/635–8245.

Attractions
Trail of the '49ers Interpretive Center. This small museum packs a historic punch, with displays of artifacts from the days of the Humboldt or Overland Trail that the gold-rush-ers followed through northern Nevada. You can see exhibits on Native American culture, antique firearms, covered wagons, and stock animals (ask the docent to describe the mechanics of the Conestoga wagon centerpiece). | 453 N. 2nd St. | 775/635–5720 | Dona-tions accepted | Weekdays 10–5, Sat noon–4.

Lodging
Best Western–Big Chief Motel. The largest and most modern motel in town, renovated, offers standard contemporary rooms. Some kitchenettes with microwaves, some refrig-erators. Rooms for guests with disabilities. Cable TV. Pool. Guest laundry. Pets allowed. | 58 rooms | 434 W. Front St. | 775/635–2416 or 800/528–1234 | fax 775/635–2418 | www.best-western.com | $37–$66 | AE, D, MC, V.

Colt Service Center. The first motel on the west side is more than a motel; it's a travelers' complex with mini-mart, truck stop, repair shops, and an RV park. In room spas. Cable TV. Exercise room. Business services. | 70 rooms | 650 W. Front St. | 775/635–5424 or 800/343–0085 | fax 775/635–5699 | $39–$59 | AE, D, DC, MC, V.

Comfort Inn. The rooms are standard and the amenities good. Complimentary Conti-nental breakfast. Some refrigerators. Cable TV. Pool. Hot tub. Laundry facilities. Business services. Pets allowed (fee). | 72 rooms | 521 E. Front St. | 775/635–5880 | fax 775/635–5788 | $38–$54 | AE, D, DC, MC, V.

Owl Hotel. In this old hotel in the heart of downtown, the rooms are small and comfort-able. Restaurant. No-smoking rooms. Cable TV. | 18 rooms | 8 E. Front St. | 775/635–5155 | fax 775/635–2444 | $30 | AE, D, MC, V.

BOULDER CITY

MAP 6, E8

(Nearby towns also listed: Henderson, Las Vegas)

Hoover Dam is one of the man-made wonders of the world, toured by millions of visi-tors every year. But diverting the mighty Colorado and erecting the colossal river-block weren't the only major construction projects in the area in the early 1930s. An entire town had to be built to house the workers and officials. Boulder City was one of the first master-planned communities in the United States, laid out entirely by a govern-ment planner, and was government owned and operated (both gambling and alco-hol were prohibited). A 1960 act of Congress established Boulder City as an independent

BOULDER CITY

INTRO
ATTRACTIONS
DINING
LODGING

municipality. Today, Boulder City retains the town plan (including the gambling ban—Nevada's only town with no casinos) and many of the original buildings. The Boulder Dam Hotel remains in its original configuration, and a row of 70-year-old worker bungalows still lines Cherry Street.

Information: **Boulder City Chamber of Commerce.** | 1305 Arizona St., 89109 | 702/737–4300.

Attractions

Boulder City/Hoover Dam Museum. This is primarily a photographic museum but the exhibits of black-and-white images of the construction of colossal Hoover Dam are worth a look. You can also see a 30-minute documentary, *The Story of Hoover Dam*. | 444 Hotel Plaza | 702/294–1988 | www.nvohwy.com/b/bldhovmu.htm | bcmuseum@anv.net | Donations accepted | Daily 10–4.

Hoover Dam. Construction of this amazing project began in 1931 and was completed in 1935, 7 million tons of concrete later. The dam, 660 ft thick at the base, 726 ft high, and 1,244 ft across, holds back the mighty Colorado River in Lake Mead, the largest man-made lake in North America. You can stop at the visitors center and take a popular tour, which takes you into the guts of the dam. | Off of U.S. 93 | 702/293–8321 or 702/294–3523 | www.hooverdam.com | $8 | Daily 8:30–5:20.

Lake Mead National Recreation Area. Lake Mead is more than 100 mi long and has 822 mi of shoreline. Three long, skinny arms extend north to Overton Beach, east to the west rim of the Grand Canyon, and south past Lake Mojave and Davis Dam. The Nevada side has six major beach resorts where you can swim, camp, stay in your RV, and launch your boat. Weekends, a veritable Vegas flotilla takes to the lakes, everything from sailboards to sailboats, from Jet Skis to houseboats; a tourist sternwheeler plies the lake year-round. You can fish for bass, crappie, catfish, and trout; dive to explore ruins, caves, even the Tennis Shoe Graveyard; and follow the many hiking routes (few actual trails in the desert). | 601 Nevada Hwy. | 702/293–8906 | www.nps.gov/lame/ | Free | Daily; visitors center, Memorial Day–Labor Day, daily 8:30–5:30, Labor Day–Memorial Day, daily 8:30–4:30.

LAKE MEAD CRUISES

Desert Princess. This old-time two-deck 250-passenger sternwheeler plies the lake from Lake Mead Marina to the dam and back on a variety of cruises offering sightseeing and brunch to dinner and dancing. The captain narrates; you can also join him on the bridge and take a turn at steering. You can get snacks on board. | Off Hwy. SSR166 on Lakeshore Rd., 3 mi north of the Alan Bible visitor center | 702/293–6180 | www.lakemeadcruises.com | $16–$43 | Daily except Dec. 25.

ON THE CALENDAR

JULY: *Boulder Damboree*. Big parade, food stands, craft sale, and organized games for kids are all in Central Park. | 5th St. and Ave. B | July 4 | 702/293–9256.

OCT.: *Art in the Park*. One of the largest art shows in the West brings together more than 300 exhibitors, who display and sell fine art, crafts, and collectibles under the trees of Wilbur Square in downtown Boulder City. | 702/293–1611.

Lodging

El Rancho Boulder. A cut above the neighboring chain motels, this place has standard contemporary decor. No-smoking rooms, refrigerators. Cable TV. Pool. Airport shuttle. | 39 rooms | 725 Nevada Hwy. | 702/293–1085 | fax 702/293–6685 | $60–$150 | AE, D, DC, MC, V.

Super 8. The design and furnishings are typical modern. You're close to downtown and not far from Las Vegas. McCarren and Boulder City airports are close by. Restaurant, bar, picnic area. No-smoking rooms. Cable TV. Indoor pool. Hot tub. Game room. *Airport shuttle.* | 114 rooms | 704 Nevada Hwy. | 702/294–8888 | fax 702/293–4344 | $43–$225 | AE, D, DC, MC, V.

CALIENTE

(Nearby towns also listed: Panaca, Pioche)

Meadow Valley Wash is a well-watered stretch of southeastern Nevada, along which the Salt Lake–Los Angeles railroad built its tracks. The railroad founded the town of Caliente in 1905 as a watering stop for its steam engines and named the town for its hot springs. The focal point of Caliente is the original 1923 Union Pacific depot, which houses all the town offices. Schools, the post office, bungalows, even apartment buildings all date back to the earliest years. Rainbow Canyon, just outside town, is one of the most spectacular scenic drives in Nevada.

Information: Caliente Chamber of Commerce. | 100 Depot La., 89008 | 775/726–3129. **Regional Development Authority of Lincoln County.** | 100 Depot Ave., Suite 6, 89008 | 775/726–3209 | mccrosky@juno.com | www.tradecon.com/lincoln.

Attractions

Beaver Dam State Park. Remotest of the 22 Nevada state parks, Beaver Dam is right on the Utah state line, 7 mi southwest of Carlinville. You get hiking trails, cliffs, canyons, a trout-stocked reservoir, and an idyllic campground, not to mention the long dusty drive. | Off U.S. 93 | 775/728–4460 | www.state.nv.us/stparks/ | $3 | Apr.–Oct.

Caliente Railroad Depot & Boxcar Museum. The chamber of commerce, city hall, and the library all use this space, and most of the walls are covered with local artwork. The Boxcar Museum is in an old boxcar, and covers the history of Lincoln County from prehistoric times through the railroad (which founded the town) and nuclear fallout (from the Nevada Test Site next door). To see the museum, make arrangements by calling 775/726–3199. | 100 Depot St. | 775/726–3129 | Depot, free; museum, $1 | Weekdays 10–2.

Cathedral Gorge State Park. This unusual desert wash, a million years old and a state park since 1935, has walls made of soft clay, carved by time and weather into some wondrous shapes. Paths pass through tight canyons and secondary washes; you can also take a 4-mi nature trail from the walls to the campground. | U.S. 93, Panaca | 775/728–4460 | www.state.nv.us/stparks/ | $3 | Daily.

Echo Canyon State Park. This park is in the verdant Meadow Valley Wash, around a small earthen dam and reservoir 12 mi east of Pioche. The campground is usually full of anglers fishing for rainbow trout. | Rte. 323 | 775/962–5103 | www.state.nv.us/stparks/ | $3 | Daily.

Spring Valley State Park. This park, 20 mi east of Pioche, is much like Echo Canyon, though it's larger and not as lush. The reservoir is stocked with rainbow and cutthroat trout. | Rte. 322 | 775/962–5102 | www.state.nv.us/stparks/ | $3 | Daily.

ON THE CALENDAR

MAY: *Lincoln County Homecoming.* An annual Memorial Day weekend celebration for the community, this has been going on for 50 years. Picnics, dances, baseball tournaments, and a demolition derby are scheduled. | 775/726–3129.

SEPT.: *Meadow Valley Western Days.* A pioneer and railroad festival are combined with games and contests, food booths, and a parade. | 775/726–3205.

Lodging

Caliente Hot Springs Motel. Ordinary rooms, a little frayed around the edges. But it's worth it for the use of the hot baths: private rooms with Roman hot tubs 5 ft square and 3 ft deep; fire-hydrant faucets fill them with sulfur-free 105-degree water in minutes flat. Hot tubs in some rooms. Cable TV. | 18 rooms | U.S. 93 N | 775/726–3777 | fax 775/726–3513 | $45–$55 | MC, V.

CALIENTE

INTRO
ATTRACTIONS
DINING
LODGING

CARSON CITY

MAP 10, A4

(Nearby towns also listed: Fallon, Reno, Virginia City)

Carson City is Nevada's capital, one of the smallest in the nation, and one of the only state capitals that doesn't have scheduled air service. Named for famed Western explorer Kit Carson, it has been the seat of state government since October 31, 1864, the day Nevada entered the Union as the 36th state. It was also the seat of territorial government for five years prior to statehood; in fact, it was the "capital" from the day it was founded, by Abraham Curry.

Abraham Curry was one of Nevada's true visionaries. A New York businessman who caught gold fever, Curry immigrated as far as Carson Valley, in the shadow of the sheer eastern scarp of the Sierra Nevada, and had a vision of destiny. He foresaw a state capital where there wasn't a state yet. There wasn't even a territory. There was barely a settlement within 200 mi. But Curry laid out a town site for the capital, with wide downtown streets, a government plaza, and small lots for homes (he tried to pay the surveyor with prime "downtown" property, but the man refused, accepting a horse and two pounds of butter instead). Five years later, the Comstock Lode had given rise to the state of Nevada, with "Curry's Folly" as the capital.

Curry started up a business quarrying the local sandstone and built the Carson City Mint (now the Nevada State Museum), the Ormsby Hotel, the legislative building, and the Supreme Court (all still standing). Carson grew apace with the state, and today it's an expanding town of 75,000.

Carson City is full of historic buildings and houses shaded by 150-year-old trees. It has the Capitol (with an excellent Nevadiana collection in the old legislative hall). The State Museum boasts the most extensive exhibits of any such facility in Nevada—a good place to start or end a visit to the state. You can also visit railroad, fire, and Native American museums, a commercial hot springs, two major casinos (and several minor ones), and two commercial strips with plentiful traveler facilities.

Information: Carson City Area Chamber of Commerce. | 1900 S. Carson St., Suite 100, 89701 | 775/882–1565. **Carson City Convention and Visitors Bureau.** | 1900 S. Carson St., Suite 200, 89701 | 775/687–7410 | www.virtualtahoe.com.

NEIGHBORHOODS

Carson Street. Carson City's main drag is Carson Street (a.k.a. U.S. 395 Business), which runs north–south for 3 mi right through the heart of town. All the historic sandstone buildings are lined up in a three-block stretch on Carson Street; the two main casinos and the railroad museum are on Carson Street as well.

Governor's Mansion Area. Carson City's historic residential neighborhood is a few blocks west of the downtown, centered on the Governor's Mansion. Some of the houses (and trees) are more than 125 years old.

William Street. William Street (U.S. 50) runs into town from the east, joins U.S. 395 (south) for 2 mi, then continues west straight up into the Sierra Nevada to and around Lake Tahoe. Centennial Park is just off U.S. 50 a little east of town; one of the largest municipal parks in Nevada, it has several baseball and soccer fields, along with tennis courts, a public golf course, and picnic sites. Mills Park is also off William Street closer into town, with tennis courts, picnic sites, a 1-mi kiddie choo-choo ride, and indoor and outdoor pools next door at the community center.

TRANSPORTATION INFORMATION

Airports: Carson City Airport. Unless you have a private plane, you won't need this information: no regularly scheduled aircraft fly in or out of the Nevada state capital. | 2600 E. Graves La.; Hot Springs Rd. off U.S. 395.

Bus Lines: Greyhound. Several buses a day run north (to Reno) and west (to Sacramento via South Lake Tahoe). **K-T** buses pass through twice a day, once north to Reno and once south to Las Vegas. | 1718 N. Carson St.; At the Frontier Motel | 775/882–3375.

Attractions

ART AND ARCHITECTURE

Bowers Mansion. This 16-room house, 10 mi north in Washoe Valley, was built in 1867 by Sandy and Eilley Bowers, who made a fortune in the early days of the Comstock Lode. It was restored, stocked with donated period pieces, and reopened as a museum in 1968. You can take one of the tours conducted every half hour in summer and see the small historical exhibit in the original root cellar. | U.S. 395 | 775/849–0201 | $3 | Memorial Day–Labor Day, daily 11–4:30; May, Sept., Oct., weekends 11–4:30.

BEACHES, PARKS, AND NATURAL SIGHTS

Humboldt-Toiyabe National Forest. The Carson District of the largest national forest in the Lower 48 (538,000 acres) has 75,000 acres in western Nevada west of Carson City. The Forest Service manages an excellent campground with 24 campsites near the summit of Mt. Rose and another at Nevada Beach (see Lake Tahoe). | 1536 S. Carson St. (administrative offices with a lobby for visitor info) | 775/882–2766 | www.fs.fed.us/toiyabe | Mt. Rose campground $9 | Memorial Day–Labor Day.

CULTURE, EDUCATION, AND HISTORY

State Capitol. Completed in 1871, the entire building was renovated 107 years later. You can see a unique collection of Nevada memorabilia displayed in a small museum on the second floor. The old Assembly Chamber down the hall generally has an exhibit or two. Portraits of Nevada's governors hang from the walls. | N. Carson and Musser Sts. | 775/687–5000 | www.carsoncity.nv.us/ | Free | Daily 8–5.

MUSEUMS

Nevada State Museum. The largest collection of Nevadiana is housed in the old Carson City Mint, built in 1870. You'll see extensive exhibits that focus on the history of the mint, flora and fauna, archaeology, Native Americans, and geology. There is also an underground mine. The museum shop sells Nevada books and gifts. | 600 N. Carson St. | 775/687–4810 | $3 | Daily 8:30–4:30 in winter, 9–5:30 in summer.

Nevada State Railroad Museum. If you're a railroad buff, you'll thrill to the beautifully restored steam engine, passenger car, caboose, and boxcar; check out the photo exhibit of the restoration process. During the summer, you can hop on one of two trains, one with a steam engine, that loop around the grounds. | 2180 S. Carson St. | 775/687–6953 | www.nsrm-friends.org | $2 | Daily 8:30–4:30.

Warren Engine Company No. 1 Fire Museum. Carson City claims the oldest volunteer fire department in the West, operating continuously since 1863. The museum displays 140 years of gear used by the squad, including a 1913 Seagrave, Nevada's first motorized fire engine. | 777 S. Stewart St. | 775/887–2210 | Donations accepted | Daily on request.

ON THE CALENDAR

JUNE: *Kit Carson Rendezvous.* This big mountain-man fair has musket loading and shooting demonstrations, battle reenactments, Native American storytelling and teepee decorating, and Western music. | Mills Park | 775/687–7410 or 800/638–2321.
OCT.: *Nevada Day Celebration.* The Silver State celebrates its statehood on October 31

with the largest parade in Nevada, an arts and crafts fair, a carnival, concerts, fireworks, and a grand ball. | 775/882–2600.

WALKING TOUR
HISTORIC DOWNTOWN (approximately 60 minutes)
Begin at the corner of Carson and Musser streets, in front of the **State Capitol,** built in 1871 with local sandstone (quarried by inmates at the state prison nearby). Walk two blocks north to Telegraph Street and the **Commission on Tourism building,** which dates back to 1891, the first federal office building in Nevada (and the post office). Head two blocks west (toward the mountains) to the corner of Telegraph and Nevada streets and the **Abe Curry House,** built of inmate-quarried sandstone in 1871 by the founder of Carson City (Curry was also the warden of the prison). Another block west on Telegraph and Division is **St. Peter's Episcopal Church,** dating back to 1868, when it was completed for $5,500; this church is an exceptionally fine example of the Gothic Revival style popular in the 19th century. A block and a half north at 502 N. Division Street is the **Orion Clemens Home,** built in 1864 for the first and only secretary of the Nevada Territory. Orion's brother Samuel visited the territory and got a job as a reporter at the Virginia City daily newspaper, where he took the pseudonym Mark Twain; the whole hilarious story is told in *Roughing It.* Up the block at 512 North Division is the **Henry Yerington House,** built in 1869 for the general manager of the Virginia & Truckee Railroad. The arched windows of the solarium were designed in the style of a railroad observation car. Take a left on Robinson Street; at 503 West Robinson is the **William Stewart House,** built in 1887 for Nevada's first U.S. senator. Three blocks west is the **Governor's Mansion,** built in 1909 in the Southern Colonial style and refurbished in the 1960s. A block south at 500 North Mountain Street is the **Krebs-Peterson House,** built in 1914. This home's claim to fame is that it served as the location for *The Shootist,* John Wayne's last and possibly best movie (also starring Lauren Bacall, Jimmy Stewart, Ron Howard, and Richard Boone). Now stroll several blocks to King Street and take a left. At 449 West King is the **Carson Brewery Co.** (1864), which brewed Tahoe Beer for nearly 100 years and is now owned by the Nevada Arts Alliance. Take a right on Minnesota and a left on 3rd Street for the **George Ferris House** (1869; 311 W. 3rd). George Ferris II invented the Ferris wheel. Continue on 3rd back to Carson Street; at the corner is the **St. Charles-Muller Hotel.** Built in 1862, it's one of the oldest commercial buildings in town. It was renovated in the mid-1990s, and you can rent rooms with period furnishings.

Dining

MODERATE
Adele's. Continental. In a Victorian house with period furnishings, this favorite features local lamb dishes; filet mignon stuffed with lobster, crab, shrimp, and cognac sauce and topped with poached oysters; and Australian lobster tails stuffed with prosciutto. Dinner includes a salad, a vegetable, and your choice of pasta, rice, or a potato. Heart-healthy menu items and a full bar are available. | 1112 N. Carson St. | 775/882–3353 | $15–$35 | AE, MC, V | Closed Sun.

Silvana's. Italian. Intimate and friendly Old World charm envelops this restaurant, which features authentic Venetian dishes. The menu includes 25 homemade pastas, chicken marsala, pasta primavera, and New York rib-eye steak. Complete dinners are served with soup or salad and garlic bread. | 1301 N. Carson St. | 775/883–5100 | $17 | AE, DC, MC, V | Closed Sun. No lunch Mon.

EXPENSIVE
Carson Nugget Steak House. Steak. The Western-style interior matches the basic Western menu, which is strong on steak, prime rib, and seafood. You can also try the buffet dining room and a coffee shop open 24 hours. Kids' menu. | 507 N. Carson St. | 775/882–1626 | $24 | AE, D, DC, MC, V | No lunch.

Lodging

INEXPENSIVE

Carson Nugget. This downtown motel has spacious rooms, a casino, and a sundeck with great views. Restaurant. Casino. Kids' lounge. Business services. Cable TV. | 60 rooms | 651 N. Stewart St. | 775/882–7711 | fax 775/882–7801 | $35–$75 | AE, D, MC, V.

Carson Station Hotel Casino. The weekend entertainment and the casino lend excitement to this basic, well run small hotel. Restaurant, bars. No-smoking rooms, some refrigerators. Cable TV. Pool. Hot tub. Game room. Business services. | 92 rooms | 900 S. Carson St. | 775/883–0900 or 800/528–1234 | fax 775/887–3981 | $54–$90 | AE, D, DC, MC, V.

MODERATE

Hardman House Motor Inn. Right downtown, this three-story motel has spacious rooms and is within easy walking distance to everything. No-smoking rooms, some refrigerators. Cable TV. Business services. Parking garage. | 62 rooms | 917 N. Carson St. | 775/882–7744 | fax 775/887–0321 | $50–$110 | AE, D, DC, MC, V.

Mill House Inn. The rooms are quiet and large at this small inn. Quiet, oversize units with king- and queen-size beds. Picnic area. Cable TV. Pool (seasonal). | 24 rooms | 3251 S. Carson St. | 775/882–2715 | $32–$80 | AE, D, MC, V.

EXPENSIVE

Deer Run Bed & Breakfast. A working alfalfa ranch with a natural pond, gardens, an orchard, and a potter's studio, this very small B&B has views of Washoe Lake, area ranches, and the Sierra Nevada. Complimentary breakfast. Cable TV. Pool. Ice-skating. Tobogganing. | 2 rooms | 5440 Eastlake Blvd., Washoe Valley | 775/883–3643 | $80–$95 | MC, V.

CRYSTAL BAY

MAP 10, A4

(Nearby towns also listed: Carson City, Reno)

A typical Nevada border town, one of a dozen scattered around four state lines. The casinos are all on the east side of the population center, while most of the residents live on the west side (California, in this case), King's Beach. Crystal Bay is little more than a post office, a handful of houses and apartments, two major casinos and one minor one, and a couple of restaurants. The state line runs right through the middle of the Cal-Neva Lodge-Casino, also a historic Tahoe property (1927). The Tahoe Biltmore is the low-roller joint, while Jim Kelley's is the slot emporium, as well as Nevada's only brick casino and the only one that ever closes (late October through late April).

Gambling is just one of many things to do around Lake Tahoe; for a discussion of outdoor recreation opportunities and other area attractions, see the Carson City, Incline Village, and Lake Tahoe sections.

Information: Lake Tahoe Visitors Bureau at Incline Village and Crystal Bay. | 969 Tahoe Blvd., 89451 | 775/832–1606 or 800/GO–TAHOE | gotahoe@sierra.net | www.tahoeguide.com/go.vcb.

ON THE CALENDAR

DEC.: *Northern Lights Festival.* A street dance, a formal gala and ball, free skiing (Diamond Peak), and an arts and crafts fair celebrate the shortest days of the year. | Cal-Neva, Tahoe Biltmore, Hyatt in Incline | 775/831–4440.

Lodging

Cal-Neva Resort. Bisected by the California-Nevada border, at the edge of the Crystal Bay isthmus, this place gives you a fantastic view from every room. Built in the 1920s, this is the oldest lodging on the Nevada side. The stunning lodge lobby is in California, and the casino in Nevada. As well as the casino, it has both a showroom and lounge entertainment. Restaurant, bars. No-smoking rooms, some refrigerators. Cable TV. Pool. Hot tub. Barber-shop, beauty salon, massage. Tennis. Exercise equipment. Business services. | 220 rooms | 2 Stateline Rd. | 775/832–4000 or 800/CAL–NEVA | fax 775/831–9007 | www.calnevaresort.com | $69–$289 | AE, D, DC, MC, V.

Tahoe Biltmore. The rooms are basic and contemporary in furnishing and style, but the prices are good. You can't do much better than the $1.99 breakfast and the lunch specials. You can spend time at the casino, too, and they also have entertainment. Restaurant, bars, complimentary breakfast. No-smoking rooms, some microwaves, some refrigerators. Cable

BASQUE FOOD

Basque adventurers left their homeland in the Pyrenees mountain provinces between France and Spain in the 1850s and 1860s and traveled to the American West to work as miners and shepherds. Northern Nevada, in particular, lent itself to the Basque brand of pastoralism, and for nearly 50 years Basque ranchers in Nevada managed the largest herds of sheep in the country. They imported relatives, friends, and townspeople from the old country to run the sheep; lone herders tended flocks in the backcountry throughout the summer. The herders were laid off till spring, and many passed the winter at Basque boarding houses in nearby towns, such as Reno, Gardnerville, Winnemucca, Elko, and Ely.

The "Basque hotel" is something of an institution in Nevada to this day. Most have public restaurants on the main floor, where hungry boarders and diners flock (so to speak) to partake of more food than you'll ever see piled up on a restaurant table other than a buffet. At the authentic Basque restaurants, guests are seated at long banquet tables and served family-style. First comes the red wine, three or four bottles for the table, accompanied by baskets of French bread. Then big tureens of soup arrive, followed by big bowls of salad; diners help themselves to as much as they want (if anything runs out, it's quickly replenished).

You still haven't seen a menu, because there aren't any. The waitress recites the entrées: lamb chops, lamb steak, lamb stew, T-bone, fried chicken, and garlic shrimp. You choose, the waitress disappears, and when she returns, she brings beans, pasta, french fries, sliced tongue, more wine, more bread, more wine, and then the entrées.

No one cooks lamb better than a Basque.

There's usually ice cream or cake for dessert, and then it's time for the favored after-dinner drink, known as picon punch. It's made from Amer (a liqueur), grenadine, and a shot of brandy. (It's also good before dinner, and during dinner, and during lunch.) To toast the house, the chef, the waitress, and your companions, you say, "Oso garria!"

© Artville

TV. Pool. Hot tub. Business services. | 92 rooms | 5 Stateline Rd. | 775/832–4000 or 800/BILT-MOR | fax 775/833–6715 | www.tahoebiltmore.com | $29–$129 | AE, D, DC, MC, V.

ELKO

(Nearby town also listed: Battle Mountain)

Elko started life in 1869 the same way that Reno, Winnemucca, Battle Mountain, and Carlin did, as a railroad town. The origin's of the town's name remain unknown. It soon became the major supply center for all the mines and ranches within 200 mi in every direction. Gambling arrived as soon as it was legalized in 1931, and a resurgence of gold mining along the world-class Carlin Trend just north of town gave Elko a major boost in the early 1990s.

The town has a fine museum, old hotel-casinos, a well-known saddle shop, and the Western Folklore Center, which sponsors popular cowboy poetry (January) and cowboy music (June) gatherings.

The country south of Elko is well worth an overnight visit. So few people ever pause to experience Lamoille Valley, Lamoille Canyon, and the mighty Ruby Mountains that they beg to be explored. You'll find 50-mi hiking trails, alpine lakes and forests, climbing peaks, vast vistas, and blessed solitude.

Information: Elko Chamber of Commerce. | 1405 Idaho St., 89801 | 775/738–7135 or 800/428–7143 | ecva@elko.com | www.cattle-log.com/elkocc.htm. **Elko Convention and Visitors Authority.** | 700 Moren Way, 89801 | 775/738–4091 or 800/428–7143 | ecva@elko.com | www.cattle-log.com/ecva.htm.

ELKO

INTRO
ATTRACTIONS
DINING
LODGING

Attractions

Humboldt-Toiyabe National Forest. The Elko district of the national forest administers 763,000 acres and encompasses the Independence and Jarbidge ranges, as well as the 93,000-acre Jarbidge National Wilderness Area, with eight peaks over 10,000 ft high. You'll find organized campgrounds just outside of Jarbidge town. The Ruby District is 450,000 acres of wilderness, with a procession of 10,000-ft peaks and the greatest stretch of alpine tundra in Nevada. You can camp at Thomas Canyon. The Ruby Mountain section is 20 mi southeast on Rte. 228. | 2035 Last Chance Rd. (administrative offices with lobby with visitor information) | 775/738–5171 | www.fs.fed.us/htnf/ | Free; $10 to camp | May–Oct.

Lamoille Canyon. Nevada has upward of 250 mountain ranges, of which the Ruby Mountains and their main canyon, the Lamoille, are the most spectacular. The 12-mi road up Lamoille Canyon is lined on both sides with solid metamorphic-rock ridges. At the end of the road you reach a picnic area and trails that lead deep into the rugged and remote Rubies. | 775/738–5717 | www.fs.fed.us/htnf | Free | Apr.–Nov.

Northeastern Nevada Museum. Your first stop in northeastern Nevada should be this fine museum dedicated to the history, industry, and cultural tapestry of this vast underpopulated corner of the state. Here you can learn about the local Basque ranching heritage, railroad history, the gold-mining business (Elko is the center of one of the largest gold-producing regions on earth), and a varied ecology. | 1515 Idaho St. | 775/738–3418 | www.nenv-museum.org | Free | Mon.–Sat. 9–5, Sun. 1–5.

ON THE CALENDAR

JAN.: *Cowboy Poetry Gathering.* One of the largest cowboy poetry and music festivals in the country, this is sponsored by the Western Folklife Center, which is responsible for the resurgence in popularity of this folk art. Five days of poetry readings, yodeling, concerts, art exhibits, and serious partying. | Elko Convention Center | 775/738–7508 or 888/880–5885.

JULY: *National Basque Festival.* The largest of many Basque festivals throughout northern Nevada, the Elko national festival centers around a parade of colorful costumes, with dancing, music, bota-drinking, strength and endurance competitions, bread baking, and a public dance. | City Park, Convention Center, Basque House | 775/738–7135.

SEPT.: *County Fair and Livestock Show.* A typical county fair, this one has a 4-H show and sale, horse races, livestock judging, flower and vegetable competitions, team penning and roping, carnival rides, a buckaroo breakfast, a parade, and dancing. | County Fairgrounds | Labor Day weekend | 775/738–7135.

OCT.: *Elko Te-Moak Powwow.* Native American drums, dance, song, arts and crafts, and games are all part of this powwow. | Indian Colony Gym | 775/738–7464.

Lodging

Best Western Ameritel Inn Elko. The rooms are modern and comfortable, and the gym makes a nice extra. Complimentary Continental breakfast. No-smoking rooms. Cable TV. 2 pools, 1 indoor. Hot tub. Gym. Business services. | 110 rooms | 837 Idaho St. | 775/738–8787 or 800/600–6001 | fax 775/753–7910 | $67–$150 | AE, D, DC, MC, V.

Centre Motel. This is your basic, small downtown motel, with modest rooms and prices. You see more than you hear of downtown's neon because the room is a block off a main street. No-smoking rooms. Cable TV. Pool. | 22 rooms | 475 3rd St. | 775/738–3226 | fax 775/753–8497 | $30–$62 | AE, D, DC, MC, V.

Holiday Inn. The second-largest lodging in Elko has standard rooms and good amenities, plus a casino. Restaurant, bar, room service. No-smoking rooms. Cable TV. Indoor pool. Hot tub. Exercise equipment. Laundry facilities. Airport shuttle. Pets allowed. | 170 rooms | 3015 E. Idaho St. | 775/738–8425 or 800/HOLIDAY | fax 775/753–7906 | $64–$99 | AE, D, DC, MC, V.

Red Lion Inn & Casino. The largest and fanciest hotel in town has big rooms, a showroom, and lounge entertainment. Restaurant, bar. No-smoking rooms. Cable TV. Pool. Barbershop, beauty salon. Business services. Airport shuttle. Pets allowed. | 223 rooms | 2065 E. Idaho St. | 775/738–2111 or 800/545–0044 | fax 775/753–9859 | $79–$259 | AE, D, DC, MC, V.

Shilo Inn. Some of the accommodations here, the only all-suite lodging in Elko, have kitchenettes. Complimentary Continental breakfast. In-room data ports, some microwaves, no-smoking rooms, some refrigerators. Cable TV. Indoor pool. Hot tub, steam room. Exercise equipment. Laundry facilities. Business services, meeting room. Airport shuttle. Pets allowed (fee). | 70 suites, 16 kitchenette units | 2401 Mountain City Hwy. | 775/738–5522 or 800/222–2244 | fax 775/738–6247 | $65–$125 | AE, D, DC, MC, V.

ELY

MAP 10, E4

(Nearby towns also listed: Austin, Eureka)

Ely grew in the second wave of the early Nevada mining boom, right at the optimistic turn of the 20th century. And it wasn't the usual gold, silver, lead, barite, or mercury. It was copper—unimaginable gazillions of tons of ore to smelt out hundreds of millions of tons of copper at a few bucks each. Ely became the headquarters for the open-pit mines (5 mi west in Ruth), the giant mill (5 mi north in McGill), and the railroad (1 mi east in East Ely). For 70 years, copper kept the town in action, but then it ran out in the early 1980s, and Ely declined fast. But only for a few years.

Since then, it has been rebuilt and revitalized. The entire Nevada Northern Railroad, from the depot and administrative offices to the rolling stock and track, has been turned into a working museum. Ely is also the county seat and the intersection of three U.S. highways, and has a great old hotel-casino. When the National Park Service designated Great Basin National Park 60 mi east (1986), Ely got a boost from the increased traffic.

Information: **White Pine Chamber of Commerce.** | 636 Aultman St., 89301 | 775/289–8877. **Ely Bristlecone Convention Center.** | 150 6th St., 89301 | 775/289–3720 or 800/496–9350.

Attractions

Cave Lake State Recreation Area. High in the pine and juniper forest of the big Schell Creek Mountains that hem in Ely to the east, this is an idyllic spot, where you can spend a day fishing for rainbow and brown trout in the reservoir, a night sleeping under the stars—and a morning begun with a piping hot shower. Arrive early; it gets crowded. | 20 mi east on U.S. 93 | 775/728–4467 | www.state.nv.us/stparks/ | $3 | Daily; access may be restricted in winter.

Nevada Northern Railway Museum. The Nevada Northern Railroad ran from its yard in east Ely to the copper mines in nearby Ruth to the smelter in nearby McGill and up to the main transcontinental line in the northeast corner of the state. When the mines and mill shut down in the early 1980s, the railroad followed suit, abandoning a $50 million operation. Eight years later, the townspeople turned the whole operation into the most authentic museum in Nevada. You can tour the depot, offices, warehouses, yard, roundhouses, and repair shops and catch a ride on one of the trains in the summer. | 1100 Ave. A | 775/289–2085 | pages.prodigy.com/NevadaNorthern/index.htm | $3–$18 | Memorial Day–Labor Day, daily 9:30–4.

Ward Charcoal Ovens Historic State Monument. You can see this row of ovens, the largest in one spot in Nevada, in the desert south of Ely. They were used to turn piñon and juniper into charcoal, used for refining silver and copper from the local ore. It's worth the 12 mi drive to take in this well-preserved piece of Nevada mining history. | U.S. 6/50 | www.state.nv.us/stparks/ | Free | Daily.

White Pine County Museum. A typical small-town museum packed with an eclectic collection of local memorabilia, here you can see photos, minerals, dolls, pioneer furniture, maps, and some Nevada Northern rolling stock outside. | 2000 Aultman St. | 775/289–4710 | white-pine.areaguide.net/ | Donations accepted | Daily 9–3.

ON THE CALENDAR

SEPT.: *Silver State Classic Challenge.* The largest (and longest) open-road race for amateur fast-car enthusiasts in the country features street-legal muscle cars that reach a top speed of 200 mph. The race runs from Preston to Hiko. | South on Rte. 318 | 775/289–8877.

SEPT.: *White Pine County Fair.* Hay contest, livestock, flower, and vegetable-growing competitions, carnival rides and midway, food booths, dance, and a buckaroo breakfast make this fair the real thing. | County Fairgrounds | Labor Day weekend | 775/289–8877.

Lodging

Holiday Inn & Prospector Casino of Ely. Built in 1994, this establishment has standard contemporary style and furnishings and remains the newest lodging in town. Restaurant. No-smoking rooms. Cable TV. Pool. Health club. | 61 rooms | 1501 Ave. F | 775/289–8900 or 800–HOLIDAY | fax 775/289–4607 | www.holiday/inn.com | $52–$79 | AE, D, DC, MC, V.

Hotel Nevada. One of the oldest hotel buildings in the state, the Nevada is in excellent shape. The hotel was built in 1908 at the main intersection downtown, and the rooms were renovated in 1997. You also get a casino and entertainment. Restaurant, bars, complimentary Continental breakfast. No-smoking rooms. Cable TV. Business services. Pets allowed. | 65 rooms | 501 Aultman St. | 775/289–6665 or 800/406–3055 | fax 775/289–4715 | $20–$69 | AE, D, DC, MC, V.

Jailhouse Motel & Casino. This modern motel at the main downtown intersection has a curious jailhouse theme: the rooms are referred to as "cells." Restaurant. No-smoking rooms. Cable TV. Pets allowed. | 47 rooms | 211 5th St. | 775/289–3033 or 800/841–5430 | fax 775/289–8709 | $40–$49 | AE, D, DC, MC, V.

Motel 6. The largest lodging in Ely is attractive because of its contemporary-style rooms with modern furnishing and its modest prices. Complimentary Continental breakfast. No-smoking rooms. Cable TV. Pool. Hot tub. Pets allowed. | 122 rooms | 770 Ave. O | 775/289–6671 or 800/466–8356 | fax 775/289–4803 | $28–$42 | AE, D, MC, V.

Ramada Inn Copper Queen & Casino. The casino encircles the pool here, and it is the only lodging in Nevada with this particular configuration that allows you to feed the slots to the odor of chlorine. Restaurant, bar, complimentary Continental breakfast. No-smoking rooms, some refrigerators. Cable TV. Indoor pool. Hot tub. Business services. Airport shuttle. | 65 rooms | 701 Ave. I | 775/289–4884 or 800/851–9526 | fax 775/289–1492 | $50–$84 | AE, D, DC, MC, V.

EUREKA

MAP 10, D4

(Nearby towns also listed: Austin, Ely)

Only 70 mi east of Austin, Eureka was its first offspring boomtown, founded in 1864 when silver was discovered here. The ore had a high lead content, however, and the smelting process was very dirty. A pall hung over Eureka for 15 years until the boom went bust. But Eureka has remained the county seat, a supply center for surrounding ranches, and a rest stop on U.S. 50. Today you can visit the fine brick County Courthouse (1880), the Eureka Opera House, and the Jackson House, both restored, all right downtown. Several artists have settled in this small desert community and have shops along Main Street.

Information: Eureka Chamber of Commerce. | Monroe and Bateman Sts. (Box 14), 89316 | 775/237–5484.

Attractions

Eureka Opera House. Built in 1880, this structure remained the focal point of entertainment in Eureka for 100 years, as the movie theater for 45 of them. It was completely renovated and reopened in 1994. Once again the pride of downtown Eureka, it has a horseshoe balcony and a grand hall. | 100 Main St. | 775/237–6006 | Free | Weekdays 8–noon and 1–5.

Lodging

Jackson House Bed and Breakfast. Built in 1877, this venerable and still lovely downtown landmark was restored in 1994 with heavy wood, heavy quilts, and funky floors. You can see all the downtown action from the balcony. Bar. Pets allowed. | 9 rooms | 251 N. Main St. | 775/237–5577 | fax 775/237–5155 | $39–$59 | D, MC, V.

Sundown Lodge. A standard motel right downtown, this lodge is popular, and the rooms fill up fast. Reserve as far in advance as you can. Pets allowed. | 27 rooms | 60 N. Main St. | 775/237–5334 | fax 775/237–6932 | $31–$45 | MC, V.

FALLON

MAP 10, B4

(Nearby towns also listed: Carson City, Reno)

The U.S. Bureau of Reclamations was established in 1902, and Fallon was its first project. Reclamation engineers built their first dam on the Truckee River, diverting water out to the Fallon agricultural project in 1903. It's remained a desert farm town for nearly a century. There's a Naval Air Station just outside of town, which has hosted the Top Gun air combat school since 1986 and contributes greatly to the local economy. Stillwater National Wildlife Refuge is a large marsh 5 mi or so east of Fallon, providing a habitat for hundreds of species of birds. In years of plentiful water, the marsh is a stunning oasis in the desert.

Information: Greater Fallon Area Chamber of Commerce. | 379 W. Williams Ave., 89406 | 775/423–2544.

Attractions

Churchill County Museum and Archives. Fallon's old Safeway building has been converted into the town museum and a gift shop, jam packed with Falloniana. You can see exhibits on local Native American culture, including an archaeological excavation, the agricultural history of Fallon, which was one of the first projects of the U.S. Bureau of Reclamations in the early 1900s, along with quilts, bottles, and pioneer dioramas. | 1050 S. Main St. | 775/423–3677 | fax 775/423–3662 | www.ccmuseum.org/aboutus.htm | Donations accepted | Mon.–Sat. 10–5, Sun. noon–5.

Lahontan State Recreation Area. One of the largest reservoirs in Nevada, Lahontan was created by the damming of the Carson River, impounding 10,000 acres of water for the Fallon irrigation district. The reservoir also provides swimming, boating, fishing, camping, and RVing. | U.S. 50 | 775/867–3500 | www.state.nv.us/stparks | $3–$7 | Daily.

ON THE CALENDAR

JULY: *All Indian Stampede and Pioneer Days.* A rodeo goes along with Native American dance, song, crafts, food, and a Wild West parade. | Fallon Regional Park | 775/423–2544.
SEPT.: *Hearts of Gold Cantaloupe Festival.* Harvest celebration for Fallon agriculture; Fallon is locally famous for its cantaloupes. There are farmer's markets, music, games, and an arts and crafts show at the Fairgrounds. | 775/423–4556.

Lodging

Best Inn and Suites. A bit further away from the heart of downtown, this chain is nevertheless convenient, with spacious rooms and good amenities. Complimentary Continental breakfast. No-smoking rooms. Cable TV. Pool. Business services. | 84 rooms | 1830 W. Williams Ave. | 775/423–5554 | fax 775/423–0663 | $50–$80 | AE, D, DC, MC, V.

Bonanza Inn & Casino. This is where you stay if you want to be in the heart of the action, right downtown. Rooms can get noisy on the weekends. Restaurant, bar. Cable TV. Business services. Pets allowed (fee). | 74 rooms | 855 W. Williams Ave. | 775/423–6031 | fax 775/423–6282 | $40–$50 | AE, D, DC, MC, V.

GENOA

MAP 10, A4

(Nearby town also listed: Carson City)

Only two years after gold was discovered in California, Mormon settlers from Salt Lake City established a trading post in this lush valley at the foot of the sheer eastern wall of the Sierra Nevada. Genoa (pronounced juh-*noa*) is the oldest town in Nevada, thus claims many Nevada firsts, including the first house, first public meeting, and first newspaper. Genoa was quickly eclipsed by Virginia City, Carson City, and Reno, but its scenic beauty and historic significance have kept it alive over the years.

Genoa boasts the oldest continuously operating bar in the state, the Genoa Bar (1863), the Courthouse Museum, the Mormon Station State Park, buildings dating back to the 1860s and 1870s, and a handful of bed-and-breakfasts and restaurants.

Information: Greater Genoa Business Association. | c/o Genoa Country Store, Box 571, 89411 | 775/782–5974. **Carson Valley Chamber of Commerce.** | 1512 U.S. 395, Suite 1, 89410 | 775/782–8144 or 800/727–7677 | info@cvchamber.gardnerville.nv.us.

Attractions

Mormon Station State Historic Park. The oldest town in Nevada, Genoa was founded by Latter-Day Saints who settled in lush Jack's Valley in the early 1850s to supply the gold-rushers. They built a stockade and trading post, which are re-created at this small historic park. There's a good exhibit relating to the *Territorial Enterprise,* Nevada's first newspaper. | Main St. and Genoa La. | 775/782–2590 | www.state.nv.us/stparks/ | Free | May–Oct., daily 8–5.

ON THE CALENDAR

SEPT.: *Candy Dance Fair.* One of the oldest annual events in Nevada (1919), this fundraiser held downtown and at Mormon Station provides most of the annual revenues for the town: 300-plus vendors set up booths selling two tons of candy, plus arts, crafts, and food; a formal ball follows. | 775/782–8696.

Lodging

Genoa House Inn Bed and Breakfast. Built in 1872 and listed on the National Register of Historic Places, the house has been lovingly restored by the current proprietors. The three rooms are furnished in Victorian style, and each has a private bath, one with a Jacuzzi. You can also enjoy the commercial hot springs 2 mi away. Complimentary breakfast. Hot tub. No smoking. | 3 rooms | 180 Nixon St. | 775/782–7075 | fax 775/782–7998 | $103–$130 | MC, V.

GOLDFIELD

MAP 10, C6

(Nearby town also listed: Tonopah)

Shortly after Tonopah became a silver boomtown in 1900, a couple of prospectors located metal of a more precious variety, and within a couple of years Goldfield had become the largest city in Nevada. Large stone buildings rose out of the desert and bank vaults bulged with gold and cash; in 1910, the population peaked at 20,000, and gold production at $11 million. It's been downhill ever since, and today Goldfield claims a mere 400 residents. But the county courthouse is open (with 1,300 residents, Esmeralda County is one of the smallest in the country); the old high school, telephone company, and Goldfield Hotel are shut down, but interesting to see from the outside. Follow the signs down 5th Avenue to the Santa Fe Saloon for some real local color.

Information: **Goldfield Chamber of Commerce.** | Box 219, 89013 | 775/485–3560.

GOODSPRINGS

MAP 10, E8

(Nearby towns also listed: Boulder City, Henderson, Las Vegas)

Joseph Good operated a lead mine here in the late 1860s, but it wasn't until gold was discovered in the 1890s that a town grew up around the mines. The Goodsprings district produced $31 million in gold all told. At its peak in 1917–18 (spurred by World War I demand for lead and zinc), Goodsprings had 800 residents. Today it's a semi-ghost town, with some ruins, old buildings, old-timers, and Las Vegas commuters who appreciate the peace and quiet.

Information: **Jean Visitors Center.** | Box 19470, 89019 | 702/874–1360.

GREAT BASIN NATIONAL PARK

MAP 10, F4

This is one of the newest and smallest national parks in the country, and preserves the second-highest mountain peak in Nevada. It also has the state's only permanent icefield, an extensive network of eroded-granite caves, a large forest of 3,000- to 4,000-year-old bristlecone pine trees, and about 77,000 acres of Great Basin wilderness. The visitors center has exhibits on the flora, fauna, and geology of the park, plus books, videos, and souvenirs for sale; a coffee shop is attached. You can tour Lehman Cave on tours that leave from here.

The park road ascends to 10,000 ft (highest pavement in the state), where there's a thin-air campground. The hiking trails will lead you to alpine lakes, the bristlecone forest, and the icefield. Spur roads lead to other camping areas, hiking trails, and four-wheel-drive tracks.

The nearest town to the national park is Baker, at the bottom of the park entrance road, which has a couple of motels and eateries.

Information: Great Basin National Park. | Rte. 488, Baker 89311 | 775/234–7331.

Attractions

Lehman Caves. An extensive network of underground caves underlies Great Basin National Park. They eroded from a minor intrusion of granite in the primarily limestone Snake Mountains. On the Park Service tour, you can see countless stalactites, stalagmites, and other odd subterranean shapes. The tour covers several "rooms" in the network. | 775/234–7331 | www.great.basin.national-park.com/ | $4 adults, kids 11 and under free | Memorial Day–Labor Day, daily.

HAWTHORNE

MAP 10, B5

(Nearby towns also listed: Fallon, Tonopah)

In a state where most of the population centers have a strange story behind them, Hawthorne's story is probably the strangest. It started life in the 1880s as a whistle-stop on the Carson and Colorado Railroad from Carson City, but by the 1920s, after the tracks were rerouted to bypass the town, Hawthorne nearly became a ghost town. In 1926 it was selected to serve as the site of a major ammunition dump for the military, and today thousands of concrete bunkers dot the desert around the town, storing everything from small-caliber handgun rounds and hand grenades to depth charges and missiles. The town also has one major casino, a string of travelers' services along the main drag, and an eclectic museum. Walker Lake, a gorgeous desert body of water, is 10 mi north.

Information: Mineral County Chamber of Commerce. | 932 E St., 89415 | 775/945–5896. **Hawthorne Convention Center.** | 932 E St., 89415 | 775/945–5854.

Attractions

Mineral County Historical Museum. Here's another small-town museum with historical and mining equipment and local color, such as Spanish mission bells and the "Cecil the (Walker Lake) Serpent" parade float. Check out the post-office display, as well as the exhibit on the ordnance that's stored around Hawthorne in a thousand bunkers that make up one of the largest ammunition dumps in the country. | 400 10th St. | 775/945–5142 | www.greatbasin.net/~mcmuseum/page2.html | Donations accepted | Tues.–Sat. 11–5.

HAWTHORNE

INTRO
ATTRACTIONS
DINING
LODGING

Walker Lake. Like Pyramid Lake 100 miles north, Walker Lake was once part of a monster lake that covered much of western Nevada during the last Ice Age, roughly 15,000 years ago. The East and West forks of the Walker River feed Walker Lake, where you can swim, boat, and the like. The north end of the lake is within the Walker River Paiute Reservation. The Bureau of Land Management manages Sportsman's Beach, which has picnic tables, outhouses, and campsites; the Tamarack picnic area and boat launch is 2 mi south. | 15 mi north on U.S. 95 | 775/885–6000 | www.state.nv.us/stparks/ | Free | Daily.

ON THE CALENDAR

FEB.: *Walker Lake Fish Derby.* Besides the fishing competition for the biggest cut-throat trout, you can also go to a hobo dinner and a liar's contest. | Cliff House, Walker Lake | 775/945–5896.

Dining

El Capitan. American. The 24-hour casino coffee shop serves typical road food—bacon and eggs, burgers, sandwiches, and steaks. | 540 F St. | 775/945–3321 | $10 | AE, D, DC, MC, V.

Maggie's Bakery. American. Maggie's serves three meals, with nearly everything made from scratch. The salad bar is reliable. | 758 E. Main St. | 775/945–3908 | $10–$20 | D, MC, V.

Lodging

El Capitan Resort & Casino. Right in the center of downtown and across the street from the casino, this standard model is the place to stay to be in the middle of the action. Restaurant, bar. No-smoking rooms, refrigerators. Pool. Game room. Pets allowed. | 103 rooms | 540 F St. | 775/945–3321 | fax 775/324–6229 | $41 | AE, D, DC, MC, V.

Sand n Sage Lodge. One of the nicer hotels in Hawthorne. Some refrigerators. Cable TV. Some pets allowed. | 37 rooms | 1301 E. 5th St. | 775/945–3352 | $25–$40 | AE, D, MC, V.

HENDERSON

MAP 10, E8

(Nearby town also listed: Las Vegas)

Like its next-door neighbor Boulder City, Henderson was virtually built in a day. In the late 1930s, magnesium was being mined in huge quantities from a site in central Nevada, but a giant production plant was needed to process the metal into war materiel. Henderson was selected for its proximity to the unlimited electricity supplied by Hoover Dam, and a town site for 10,000 workers was built alongside the plant.

Today the magnesium plant has been subdivided into smaller industrial and chemical factories, but like its other next-door neighbor Las Vegas, Henderson is thriving, thanks to the economic boom in southern Nevada over the past decade. Now a vast bedroom community for Vegas, Henderson has in fact overtaken Reno as the second-largest city in Nevada. It has a small downtown, a fine local museum, and a handful of small casinos.

Information: **Henderson Chamber of Commerce.** | 500 S. Boulder Hwy., 89015 | 702/945–5896.

Attractions

Clark County Heritage Museum. In a metropolitan area that seems so eager to suffocate its past, the Clark County Heritage Museum is a breath of fresh air. The highlight here is Heritage Street: a row of four historic buildings, including a home built in downtown Vegas in 1912. The main building houses exhibits covering the Southern Paiute, the railroad that founded Las Vegas, the construction of Hoover Dam, gambling, and the unusual story of the founding of Henderson. | 1830 S. Boulder Hwy. | 702/455–7955 | www.co.clark.nv.us/parkrec/heritage.htm | $1.50 | Daily 9–4:30.

ON THE CALENDAR
APR.: *Heritage Days.* A big local celebration includes a parade, carnival, talent show, barbecue, chili cook-off, street dance, antique car show, beauty pageant, and softball tournament. | Henderson Convention Center | 702/565–8951.

Dining
Carver's. Steakhouse. An upscale steak house with a soft and sophisticated decor and an ambitious menu. As you'd guess, any beef dish is a good bet. | 2061 W. Sunset Rd. | 702/433–5801 | $25 | AE, D, DC, MC, V | No lunch.

Rainbow Club. Coffee Shop. Inside the Rainbow Club casino in downtown Henderson, this is truly a local joint with great basic food and round-the-clock service. | 122 Water St. | 702/565–9777 | $5–$8 | MC, V.

Lodging
Best Western–Lake Mead. If you're headed for Lake Mead, 7 mi away, and Hoover Dam, this is a good place to stay. The rooms are standard modern in style, and the park across the street is nice for a stroll. Complimentary Continental breakfast. No-smoking rooms, refrigerators. Cable TV. Pool. | 59 rooms | 85 W. Lake Mead Dr. | 702/564–1712 or 800/528–1234 | fax 702/564–7642 | $48–$58 | AE, D, DC, MC, V.

Sunset Station. Locals outnumber hotel guests 100 to one in the casino here in the heart of downtown. The rooms are secondary to the casino, although many guests get complimentary rooms through the "slot club." With several restaurants on the premises, you never have to leave. 6 restaurants, bars, room service. No-smoking floors. Cable TV. Pool. Barbershop, beauty salon. Business services. | 450 rooms, 52 suites | 1301 W. Sunset Rd. | 702/547–7777 or 888/786–7389 (reservations) | $50–$119 | AE, D, DC, MC, V.

INCLINE VILLAGE

MAP 10, A4

(Nearby towns also listed: Carson City, Reno)

In 1960, a developer from Oklahoma bought 9,000 acres of prime property on the north shore of Lake Tahoe, including 3 mi of lakefront, and laid out a master-planned community for 10,000. Today the town is still privately owned; the "General Improvement District" company manages the public beaches, golf courses, ski resort, recreation center, and unimproved land. Incline is one of the most exclusive settlements in Nevada, with multi-million-dollar mansions on the lake, million-dollar chalets on the mountain, and posh condos in the village. It's a year-round resort, with snow sports in winter and lake and mountain sports in summer. There's one casino (upscale), the Ponderosa Ranch tourist attraction, and more outdoor stores per linear foot than anywhere else in the state.

Information: **Lake Tahoe Visitors Bureau at Incline Village and Crystal Bay.** | 969 Tahoe Blvd., 89451 | 775/832–1606 or 800/GO–TAHOE | gotahoe@sierra.net | www.tahoeguide.com/go.vcb.

Attractions
Diamond Peak Ski Resort. Diamond Peak has a fun family atmosphere, and is smaller and less crowded than many of the super ski resorts nearby. The 1-mi Crystal chairlift rewards you with the best views of the lake of any local ski area. There's a half-pipe run for snowboarders and 22 mi of cross-country skiing. The vertical drop is 1,840 feet. Free shuttles run

continuously from the ski area around Incline Village and Crystal Bay. | 1210 Ski Way | 775/831–3211 (24–hr snow phone) or 775/832–1177 | www.diamondpeak.com | $15–$38.

Lake Tahoe–Nevada State Park. Unlike the California side of Lake Tahoe, which is so developed that there's barely a park, a long stretch of Nevada lakefront is a state park. Preserving a full 3 mi of shoreline and 22 square mi of prime Sierra wilderness, the focus of the park is Sand Harbor Beach State Recreation Area, one of the largest and most popular sandy beaches on the lake. You can follow the short nature trail to explore Sandy Point and have a lesson in Tahoe ecology. The park runs along most of Rte. 28, near Sand Harbor. | 775/831–0494 | www.state.nv.us/stparks/ | $5 | Daily.

Mount Rose Ski Area. This is one of the highest ski areas around Tahoe, with a vertical drop of 1,440 feet; as such, it's geared toward intermediate and advanced (though beginners will find plenty of gentle slopes and an excellent first-timer ski package). It's also the closest skiing to Reno, so it's a popular resort and the parking lots fill up fast. Snowboarders have their own terrain park. Ski shuttles run from downtown Reno. | 22222 Mount Rose Hwy. | 775/849–0704 or 800/SKI–ROSE (outside NV) | www.skirose.com | $13–$42.

Ponderosa Ranch and Western Theme Park. No, the popular 1960s television series *Bonanza* was not based on this ranch at the south end of town off Rte. 28. It's the other way around: the Ponderosa is a theme park based on the television show. It centers on the Cartwright ranch house; you'll also find a petting zoo and a collection of antique vehicles. Take a wagon ride, have a chuck-wagon breakfast, and watch a melodrama with a shoot-out. The Ponderosa is one of Tahoe's top commercial attractions, always crowded during the season. | 100 Ponderosa Ranch Rd. | 775/831–0691 | www.ponderosaranch.com/ | Adults $9.50, kids free | May–Oct., daily 9:30–6.

ON THE CALENDAR
AUG.: *Shakespeare Festival*. An award-winning summer festival of Shakespeare plays performed on a temporary stage on the beach, with the lake and sunset as backdrops. | Sand Harbor | 775/832–1606 or 800/747–4697.
OCT.: *Native American Snow Dance*. A powwow, Native American dancing, an arts fair, and food booths are part of this festival that kicks off ski season. | Preston Field | 775/832–1606.

Dining

Lone Eagle Grille. American. A cozy place that's great for pre- or après-ski drinking or dining. The restaurant is a cabin with 2 fireplaces and the open-air dining is right on the beach. Dungeness crab cakes, spit-roasted duck, and braised lamb shank are among the favorites. Entertainment weekends. Kids' menu. Sun. brunch. No smoking. | Country Club Dr. at Lakeshore | 775/832–3250 | $25–$60 | AE, D, DC, MC, V.

Lodging

Hyatt Regency Lake Tahoe. A self-contained resort half a block from its own beach, this place has virtually everything. The large rooms are both rustic and sophisticated, and you can also relax in the spa. The children's programs for kids 3–12 are a nice extra. 3 restaurants, bars. Minibars, some microwaves, some refrigerators, no-smoking floors. Cable TV. Pool, hot tub, massage. Tennis, gym, beach, bicycles. Game room. Business services. | 458 rooms | 111 Country Club Dr. | 775/832–1234 | fax 775/831–7508 | $79–$685 | AE, D, DC, MC, V.

Inn at Incline. Book early here. It's one of the only motels in a town full of condos. Complimentary Continental breakfast. No air-conditioning, no-smoking rooms. Cable TV. Indoor pool. Hot tub, sauna. Business services. | 38 rooms | 1003 Tahoe Blvd. | 775/831–1052 or 800/824–6391 | fax 775/831–3016 | $69–$135 | AE, D, MC, V.

JACKPOT

(Nearby town also listed: Elko)

Jackpot is a border town in the middle of nowhere, with big Las Vegas–style casinos and a strictly Idaho clientele. Jackpot is also on Idaho (Mountain) time, has mostly Idaho-based suppliers and employees, and is powered by Idaho utilities. What does Jackpot have that Idaho wants? Gambling. And it has since Jackpot was founded in 1956, two years after Idaho banned most forms of gambling. Five casinos line U.S. 93 for a half-mile, the length of the town. Cactus Pete's is the lodestar, with a 10-story tower and bright lights visible for miles around, a full-scale casino, restaurants, lounge, showroom, convention center, golf course, and RV park. The rest of Jackpot consists of four-plexes and mobile homes—and a school zone.

Information: Jackpot Recreation and Tourism Center. | 2395 Progressive Rd., 89825 | 775/755–2653 or 800/411–2052 | jrc@cyberhighway.net.

Lodging

Barton's Club 93. The old Hillside wing rooms are a bargain. Newer Sandstone wing rooms are larger and more luxurious. | 125 rooms. Casino, restaurants, cable TV. | U.s. 93 | 775/755–2341 or 800/258–2937 | fax 775/755–2397 | $41–$56 | DC, MC, V.

Cactus Pete's Hotel-Casino. This is the highest-rise hotel within several hundred miles in every direction. The casino has every amenity imaginable, including a restaurant and showroom. | 420 rooms. Restaurants, room service, cable TV, VCRs, pool, hot tub, free parking. | 1385 US 93 | 775/755–2321 or 800/821–1103 | fax 775/755–2740 | $59–$69 | AE, D, MC, V.

LAKE TAHOE

(Nearby towns also listed: Carson City, Incline Village, Reno)

Lake Tahoe—12 mi wide, 22 mi long, 72 mi of shoreline, and more than 1,000 ft deep—is stunning. The clarity of its water is legendary throughout the West; the bi-state Tahoe Basin is one of the most environmentally restricted areas in the country. The lake has hundreds of inlets and one outlet, the Truckee River, which flows 50 mi north to Truckee, then 60 mi east through Reno, and empties into Pyramid Lake. The top 6 ft, controlled by a dam at the source of the river, is a reservoir, providing water for much of western Nevada.

The California side is heavily populated; only a handful of small state parks have not been developed. The Nevada side stretches between two border towns, Stateline and Crystal Bay, with their bright lights, resort-casinos, and parking lots. Lake Tahoe–Nevada State Park takes up most of the middle.

Recreation abounds. In the surrounding mountains you can choose from a dozen world-class ski resorts in winter, and venture into the endless wilderness to hike, backpack, mountain bike, and climb the rest of the year. At the lake, you can swim, boat, fish, and dive. Two big sternwheelers, a large trimaran, and cabin cruisers ply the lake commercially. A hot-air balloon floats overhead and lands on a barge on the water (it's easier to steer the barge than the balloon!).

Information: Lake Tahoe Visitors Authority. | 1156 Ski Run Blvd., South Lake Tahoe, CA 96150 | 530/544–5050 or 800/AT–TAHOE | www.virtualtahoe.com. **Lake Tahoe Visitors Bureau at Incline Village and Crystal Bay.** | 969 Tahoe Blvd., 89451 | 775/832–1606 or 800/GO–TAHOE | gotahoe@sierra.net | www.tahoeguide.com/go.vcb.

LAKE TAHOE

INTRO
ATTRACTIONS
DINING
LODGING

Attractions

Nevada Beach. The nearest public lake access to Stateline on the Nevada side—3 mi north on U.S. 50—this large Forest Service facility has a sandy beach, picnic areas, and a 54-site campground. Make camping reservations as far ahead as possible (up to 120 days in advance). | Left on Elk Point Rd. | 530/573–2600 or 800/280–2267 | $3 day use; $16 campsites | May–Oct.

Zephyr Cove Resort. This is the only major lakeside resort between Stateline and Incline Village. The main lodge building, constructed in 1900, retains its original rustic charm, and the log cabins are charming and more private. You can swim, boat, camp, ride, and rent all kinds of water equipment. In addition, the 550-passenger sternwheeler MS *Dixie II* and the 20-passenger trimaran *Woodwind* sail from Zephyr Cove. You can take a dinner cruise on the *Dixie II*. | 6 lodge rooms, 28 cabins | 760 U.S. 50; 7 mi north of Stateline | 775/588–6644 | www.tahoedixie2.com/ | $50–$100 lodge rooms, $80–$295 cabins.

LAS VEGAS

MAP 10, E8

(Suburb also listed: Henderson)

Las Vegas is one of a kind. It's proof of the old (paraphrased) adage "Nothing succeeds like excess." You will encounter 18 of the world's 21 largest hotels here, several of which cost more than a billion bucks to build. The tallest building west of the Mississippi is here, along with a 2,500-room pyramid, a mini-skyline of New York, a half-size Eiffel Tower, the world's largest electric sign, thousands of miles of neon, $6 buffets that are veritable mini food cities, free booze, and more pounds of exposed showgirl flesh than anywhere. And it's all lighted by a spotlight so bright it can be seen from everywhere in the world.

Las Vegas, which means "the meadows," was the site of a desert oasis known to the Anasazi (12th century), Southern Paiute (17th–19th centuries), and the Salt Lake–Los Angeles Railroad Company, which founded the town in 1905 to serve as a watering stop for its steam-powered trains. Gambling was legalized in 1931; Hoover Dam was built 40 mi away between 1931 and 1935, and tens of thousands of soldiers were trained at the Las Vegas Aerial Gunnery School during World War II. The mob built the original Strip resorts after the war. Howard Hughes bought out the mob in the 1960s, and the big hotel corporations have been opening bigger and better mousetraps ever since, culminating in the $1.8 billion Bellagio, the most expensive hotel ever built.

And that's all you need to know about Las Vegas through the ages. Las Vegas isn't about history. It's possible that no other city in the world is less devoted to its past and less mindful of its future. To Las Vegas, history is something that might've happened, written by someone who wasn't there. And to Las Vegas, the future spirals outward into an infinity of alternative possibilities.

What Las Vegas is really about is the present, the now. Las Vegas's now, in fact, is the consummate now. All its life, Las Vegas has pursued the perfection of the present, the moment, that twitch in time when the card turns, the ball falls, the dice stop, the reels freeze, and fate itself hangs in the balance. The next moment materializes, and existence is reduced to the simple result of win or lose: life is kind or life is cruel. An instant later the cards fly, the ball spins, the dice roll, the reels whir, and the previous moment is in the past, forgotten, as fate again is on the line and life reverts to either/or. String enough of these moments together and each twitch elongates endlessly, transcending time and according an intimation of eternity.

Information: Las Vegas Chamber of Commerce. | 3720 Howard Hughes Pkwy., 89109 | 702/735–1616 | fax (702) 735–2011 | info@lvchamber.com | www.lvchamber.com. **Las**

Vegas Convention and Visitors Authority. | 3150 Paradise Rd., 89109 | 702/892–0711 or 800/332–5333 | www.lasvegas24hours.com.

NEIGHBORHOODS

Downtown. Downtown is "Old Las Vegas," the 40-block grid laid out by the railroad. Several buildings around downtown date back 80 or 90 years, and though most are more recent, the original grid remains mostly intact. Fremont Street from Main to 4th streets is known as Glitter Gulch; it's contained by the Fremont Street Experience, a four-block-long, 100-ft-tall canopy, lined with 2 million polychromatic bulbs programmed for a light and sound show after dark.

The North Strip. Las Vegas Boulevard South, south of Sahara Avenue (which marks the northern boundary of the unincorporated "county"), is the beginning of the famed Las Vegas Strip. The North Strip has the Sahara, Circus Circus, the Riviera, Westward Ho, the Stardust, the New Frontier, and the Desert Inn. None of these hotel-casinos is less than around 30 years old: the North Strip has benefited the least from the recent megaresort development. The mostly second-tier casinos are the best on the Strip for bargain rooms and good gambling.

The Center Strip. The Center Strip, which huddles around the intersection of Las Vegas Boulevard South and Flamingo Road, is home to Treasure Island, the Venetian, the Mirage, Harrah's, Imperial Palace, Caesars Palace, Flamingo Hilton, Barbary Coast, Bally's, Paris, and Bellagio. This is Las Vegas's "Old Four Corners," launched by Bugsy Siegel in the late 1940s with his Fabulous Flamingo, and completed in the late 1990s by the Bellagio and Paris. This corner boasts 27,000 rooms, 80 restaurants, 14 showrooms, five spectacular pools, two free spectacles, and a half-size Eiffel Tower—along with some of the city's highest prices for rooms, food, and shows.

The South Strip. The South Strip, on and near the intersection of Las Vegas Boulevard South and Tropicana Avenue, is Las Vegas's "New Four Corners." Only the Tropicana is more than 10 years old; the Excalibur, MGM Grand, Luxor, Monte Carlo, New York–New York, and Mandalay Bay were all built in the 1990s. This corner has 25,000 rooms, 70 restaurants, 10 showrooms and two arenas, 10 top-of-the-line pool areas, and a half-size Statue of Liberty. It is the choice of families, with its two roller coasters, state-of-the-art arcades (including Spielberg's GameWorks), movie theater, and amusement park.

East of the Strip. Las Vegas residential neighborhoods fall on either side of the Strip. The east side developed first, since most commuters wanted to be driving west toward the Strip and downtown in the morning and east toward home in the evening, with the sun at their backs both ways. The east side also has the University of Nevada–Las Vegas, the Liberace Museum, the Las Vegas Country Club, and a handful of locals' casinos.

West of the Strip. The west side is bounded by the Strip on the east and the mighty Spring Mountains on the west. Its development probably won't stop until there's not a home site left in between. It is home to huge master-planned communities with names like The Lakes, Desert Shores (both built around man-made lakes and canals), and Tahoe. It has the local zoo, Siegfried and Roy's house, a handful of locals' casinos, and Red Rock Canyon.

Summerlin. Summerlin is the largest master-planned community in the country, occupying 22,000 acres in the northwest suburbs. Howard Hughes bought the property from the federal government in the early 1950s; his Summa Corporation began developing Summerlin (named after Hughes's grandmother) in the 1980s. When it's completed in the year 2020, it will contain 80,000 houses spread over seven separate "neighborhoods." Three of the seven are nearly completed, including Del Webb's 2,000-acre Sun City retirement community.

Henderson. Henderson is actually a separate town southeast of Las Vegas, though it's contiguous to Las Vegas and considered a part of the greater metropolitan area. Henderson has been doubling in population every few years. It's now the second-largest city in Nevada, having eclipsed Reno in mid-1999. It's little more than a vast bedroom community of new (and slightly used) houses that feeds Las Vegas's insatiable appetite for workers and home buyers.

SOUTHERN NEVADA

The favorite vacation destination in Nevada isn't hard to guess. It's the small wedge at the very bottom of the state that the rest of Nevada rests on. Seventy-five major casinos, upscale shopping malls, amusement parks with monster thrill rides, a massive dam and one of the the largest man-made lakes in the world, an 11,000-ft mountain peak with a downhill ski resort, and a large chunk of haunting desert interspersed with flaming red rock, are all within a two-hour drive of each other in this compact section of southern Nevada.

This vacation destination is favored by almost everyone: gamblers, thrill seekers, sightseers, families with children, shoppers, bargain hunters, gourmets and gourmands, showgoers, hikers, rock climbers, skiers, divers, and anglers.

Gamblers have nearly four score places to play, everything from the largest (MGM Grand) and costliest (Bellagio) hotels on earth to tiny grind joints (Gold Spike, Golden Gate) with dollar blackjack and $20 rooms. The hotel-casinos are attractions in themselves: the Stratosphere is the tallest building west of the Mississippi, New York–New York is built in the shape of a mini-skyline, Luxor is a 2,500-room pyramid, Mirage has an entire dolphin habitat, to name only a few.

Also lining the Las Vegas Strip and downtown are four roller coasters, three gravity rides, an extensive water park, and dozens of simulators; two dozen stage shows, including some of the most high-tech and highly produced productions anywhere; hundreds of restaurants, from $3 all-you-can-eat buffets and $4.95 complete steak dinners to $100 entrées and $1,000 bottles of wine; and world-class shopping outlets such as the Forum Shops at Caesars, the most successful mall in history.

In the vicinity of Las Vegas are plentiful day trips. A 20-minute drive from city center is Red Rock Canyon, a stunning multicolored palisade of sandstone, a favorite of bikers, hikers, and rock climbers. Forty-five minutes north is the Mt. Charleston recreation area, with campgrounds, a downhill ski resort, and two lodges, and crisscrossed with hundreds of miles of hiking trails. Forty minutes east is the historic town of Boulder City, with its Depression-era bungalows and proximity to Hoover Dam, one of the man-made wonders of the world. Lake Mead, 10 minutes from Boulder City, provides all the water sports—swimming, speed boating, houseboating, jet-skiing, fishing, and diving—that can be imagined in the middle of a barren desert landscape. And 90 minutes south is the border boomtown of Laughlin, with its major casinos lined up on the Colorado River and water sports right out the hotel back doors.

Towns listed: Las Vegas, Henderson, Boulder City, and Laughlin are the towns in the vacation destination, while Red Rock Canyon, Hoover Dam, Lake Mead, and the Spring Mountains are the outdoor attractions.

© Corbis

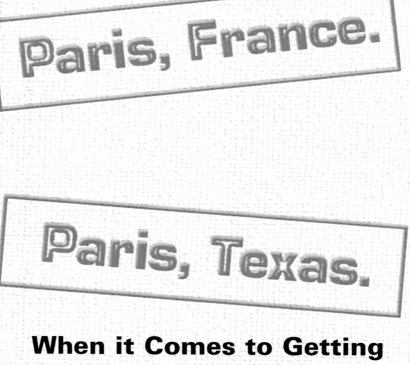

Paris, France.

Paris, Texas.

When it Comes to Getting Cash at an ATM,

Same Thing.

Whether you're in Yosemite or Yemen, using your Visa® card or ATM card with the PLUS symbol is the easiest and most convenient way to get cash. Even if your bank is in Minneapolis and you're in Miami, Visa/PLUS ATMs make getting cash so easy, you'll feel right at home. After all, Visa/PLUS ATMs are open 24 hours a day, 7 days a week, rain or shine. And if you need help finding one of Visa's 627,000 ATMs in 127 countries worldwide, visit **visa.com/pd/atm**. We'll make finding an ATM as easy as finding the Eiffel Tower, the Pyramids or even the Grand Canyon.

It's Everywhere You Want To Be.®

Find America *with a Compass*

Written by local authors and illustrated throughout with images from regional photographers, Compass American Guides reveal the character and culture of America's most spectacular destinations. Covering more than 35 states and regions across the country, Compass guides are perfect for residents who want to explore their own backyards, and for visitors seeking an insider's perspective on all there is to see and do.

Fodor's Compass American Guides

At bookstores everywhere.

Attractions

BEACHES, PARKS, AND NATURAL SIGHTS

Floyd Lamb State Park. Originally called Tule Springs, this state park has been a desert oasis for nearly 15,000 years—and can prove it. An extensive archaeological dig around the springs has turned up bones and remains that date back to the last Ice Age. The springs were first developed in 1915; in the 1940s a dude ranch was opened. (Most of the buildings that remain are from that period.) Besides casting for catfish and rainbow trout here, you can picnic and play volleyball. | 9200 Tule Springs Rd. | 702/486–5413 | www.state.nv.us/stparks/ | $5 | Daily 8–7.

Red Rock Canyon National Conservation Area. The towering and massive Spring Mountains hem in Las Vegas Valley on the west. The centerpiece of the Spring Mountains is Red Rock Canyon, a small patch of the red sandstone found throughout the American Southwest. A scenic 13-mi loop road circles the canyon, with trails and attractions along the way. A mere 20-minute drive from downtown Las Vegas, Red Rock is the closest wilderness to the neon beast. | W. Charleston Blvd. | 702/363–1921 | www.grouptravels.com/usa_can/blm/redrock.htm | $5 | Daily 7–8.

Spring Mountain Ranch State Park. Three miles down Route 159 from Red Rock Canyon is this lush and scenic park at the base of thousand-foot cliffs. Add to that a red ranch house, white picket fences, green, green grass, and open vistas in every direction, and you've got one of the best places for a picnic in southern Nevada. | Blue Diamond Rd. and W. Charleston Blvd. | 702/875–4141 | www.state.nv.us/stparks/ | $5 | Daily 8–7.

CULTURE, EDUCATION, AND HISTORY

Old Mormon Fort. Southern Nevada's oldest historical site was built by Mormons in 1855 as an agricultural mission to supply travelers and traders along the Old Mormon Trail. Abandoned for a decade, the fort was resettled and later turned into a resort, with Las Vegas's first swimming hole. Today, a tiny remnant of the fort remains; inside you can see historical displays and antiques. | 500 E. Washington Ave. | 702/486–3511 | www.state.nv.us/stparks/ | Free | Daily 8:30–3:30.

University of Nevada–Las Vegas. This center of higher learning, though one of the largest universities in the West, disappears as an attraction into the maw of the resort industry. But it's an attractive campus, 1½ mi east of the Strip, with an extensive greenbelt, architecturally interesting buildings, and plenty of local culture. Lectures, music, dance, and film festivals continually fill the Judy Bayley Theater and the University Dance Theater; large events, especially local-favorite Runnin' Rebels basketball games, are held in the 15,000-seat Thomas and Mack Arena. The Donna Beam Fine Arts Gallery, displaying student and professional works, is one of the largest in town. Ten tennis courts are open to the public. | 4505 Maryland Pkwy. | 702/895–3011 or 702/895–3443 | www.unlv.edu | Free.

The roomy **Donna Beam Fine Art Gallery** displays artwork by UNLV students and other artists from around the country. An upstairs gallery looks over the main floor. | Alta Ham Fine Arts Building, 4505 S. Maryland Pkwy. | 702/895–3893 | Free | Weekdays 9–5.

The **James Dickinson Library,** a strange building with one round and one square wing, with tubes connecting the two—houses the largest collection of books in the state. It also has a huge periodicals department, video, audio, and computer labs, and a Special Collections archive. Within Special Collections is the Gaming Research Center, the largest repository of gambling media in the world. | 4505 Maryland Pkwy. | 702/895–3285 | library.nevada.edu/info/jdl.html | Free | Hours vary; call ahead.

The **Marjorie Barrick Museum of Natural History** is jam-packed with desert fauna, from gila monsters to cockroaches to an ichthyosaur skeleton (there's also plenty of decidedly un-desert fauna, like the 10-ft polar bear). A comprehensive display features southern Nevada history, and a gallery shows changing art exhibits. Also be sure to visit the Xeric desert garden near the front entrance, the focal point of UNLV's campus arboretum. | 4505 Maryland Pkwy. | 702/895–3381 | gigueta@nevada.edu | hrcweb.lv-hrc.nevada.edu/mbm/mbm-main.htm | Free | Weekdays 8–4:45, Sat. 10–2.

The university's **Thomas and Mack Center** is a multi-purpose building that hosts UNLV Runnin' Rebels basketball games, the National Finals Rodeo, rock concerts, tennis matches, conventions and trade shows, and other big events. | 4505 S. Maryland Pkwy. | 702/895–3761 or 702/895–3900 (tickets) | fax 702/895–1099 | www.thomasandmack.com/index.html.

MUSEUMS

Guinness World of Records Museum. If you've ever been curious about oddball world records, this is the museum for you: the world's tallest, fattest, oldest, and shortest men, top-selling cookie (Oreos) and candy (LifeSavers), smallest bicycle, longest domino-toppling line, greatest engineering projects, tallest buildings, and on and on. A small exhibit displays Las Vegas's fun statistics. | 2780 Las Vegas Blvd. S | 702/792–0640 | $4.95 | Daily 9–5:30.

Imperial Palace Auto Collection. Every city has to have a collection of antique automobiles, but the one on the fifth floor of the Imperial Palace's parking garage is one of the world's best. From horseless carriages and Hitler's 1939 armored Mercedes parade car to a 1910 Thomas Flyer and $50 million worth of Duesenbergs, this car museum is a fascinating diversion from the other attraction on the Las Vegas Strip. | 3535 Las Vegas Blvd. | 702/731–3311 or 702/794–3174 | www.imperialpalace.com/index.html. | $6.95 (but look for free-entry coupons everywhere) | info@autocollections.com | Daily 9:30 AM–11:30 PM.

Las Vegas Art Museum. Three galleries are within this small but vital art museum: the main gallery, the Southwest gallery, and a mini gallery. Most exhibits feature the work of local artists and change monthly. The museum gift shop sells art at reasonable prices. | 9600 W. Sahara Ave. | 702/360–8000 | lvam@earthlink.net | www.lastplace.com/exhibits/lvam/index.htm | $7 residents, $10 nonresidents | Tues.–Sat. 10–5, Sun. 1–5.

Las Vegas Natural History Museum. This little-known attraction is home to displays of stuffed mammals from Alaska to Africa and has rooms full of sharks (including live ones, fed publicly), birds, dinosaur fossils, and hands-on exhibits. | 900 Las Vegas Blvd. N | 702/384–3466 | www.vegaswebworld.com/lvnathistory/nevada.html | $5.50 | Daily 9–4.

Liberace Museum. Costumes, cars, pianos, photographs, even mannequins of the late entertainer make this the kitschiest place in town. Lee's collection of pianos is here, one played by Chopin; another owned by George Gershwin; a third is covered with 50,000 rhinestones. You can see his Czar Nicholas uniform and a blue-velvet cape styled after the coronation robes of King George V. | 1775 E. Tropicana Ave. | 702/798–5595 | www.liberace.org/museum.html | $6.95 | Tues.–Sat. 10–5, Sun. 1–5.

Lied Children's Discovery Museum. Across the street from the Natural History Museum is one of the nation's largest children's museums. The Lied (pronounced *leed*) contains more than 100 hands-on exhibits on the sciences, arts, and humanities. Children can pilot a space shuttle, perform on stage, or stand in a giant bubble. Kids under 11 must be accompanied by an adult. | 833 Las Vegas Blvd. N | 702/383–5437 | www.vegaswebworld.com/lied/more-info.html | $5.00 | Tues.–Sun. 10–5; closed Mon.

Nevada State Museum and Historical Society. Here's where you find out about the building of Las Vegas after World War II and the growth of the American Southwest (particularly southern Nevada). Lorenzi Park surrounds the museum and has some of the oldest plants and trees in town, from the 1920s. | 700 Twin Lakes Dr. | 702/486–5205 | $2 | Daily 9–5.

SHOPPING

Forum Shops at Caesars Palace. Next door to Caesars Palace, this is the most commercially successful mall in the world. Sales per square foot are quadruple the average mall. The three wings with 70 stores go from FAO Schwartz and the Virgin Megastore to Gucci and Victoria's Secret. The Palm, Spago, Stage Deli, Cheesecake Factory, Caviarteria, and Bertolini's are among the restaurants. And two animatronic performances take place on the hour. |

3500 Las Vegas Blvd. S | 702/893–4800 | www.las-vegas-guide.com/forum-shops-cae-sars.htm | Free | Daily 10 AM–11 PM.

SPORTS AND RECREATION

Bonnie Springs Old Nevada. A commercial attraction that has stood the test of time in Las Vegas, Bonnie Springs Old Nevada combines a theme-park village with a zoo, horse-back riding, and a bar and coffee shop fronted by a spring-fed duck pond. A little railroad shuttles between the lower parking lot and the entrance, where there's a saloon, opera house, jail, and a frontier reenactment. | 1 Gunfighter La. | 702/875–4191 | www.nvohwy.com/b/bonnranc.htm | $6 adults | Daily 10:30–5.

Las Vegas Motor Speedway. This is not just a 107,000-seat car-racing stadium that hosts one of the prestigious NASCAR Winston Cup races every March (and sets yearly attendance records for the biggest sporting event in Nevada). The sprawling complex 7 mi from down-town also has many smaller tracks, auto-racing clubs, race-car storage and repair facilities, and even manufacturing (legendary Carrol Shelby builds race cars on the premises). | 7000 Las Vegas Blvd. N | 702/644–4444 | www.na-motorsports.com/tracks/lasvegasms.html | Daily.

Mount Charleston Recreation Area. For a mountain retreat, head for Mount Charleston, fifth-highest mountain in Nevada (11,988 ft). During the summer you'll find the campgrounds, hiking trails, bristlecone forest, and lodges a welcome relief from the sizzling valley heat; it's at least 30 degrees cooler here. During the winter, you can ski, cross-country and down-hill both, on the higher parts of the mountain | Rte. 157 to Kyle Canyon | 702/873–8800 | Free | Daily.

★ **Wet 'n Wild.** A town where summer lasts for at least six months, temperatures reaching 115°F for three of them, needs a big central water park. This one fits the bill. Right on the North Strip, it has a half-dozen thrills, including a 300-ft water slide and a wave pool with 5-ft surf, as well as kids' swimming and splash pools. | 2601 Las Vegas Blvd. | 702/737–3819 | www.wetnwild.com/ | $25.95 | May–Oct., daily 10–8.

SIGHTSEEING TOURS/TOURS COMPANIES

Eagle Canyon Airlines. The largest of several flightseeing companies flies small planes from Las Vegas to the Grand Canyon. You can choose from a quick fly-by to a long day trip with ground transportation around the South Rim. | 2705 Airport Dr. | 702/736–3333 or 800/446–4584 | www.scenic.com/ | $129–$249 | Daily.

Gray Line bus tours. Ubiquitous Gray Line offers bus tours throughout southern Nevada. Luxury coaches take you on an eight-hour city tour, and to Hoover Dam, Red Rock Canyon, Valley of Fire, Laughlin, and Death Valley and Bryce Canyon national parks. You can also take a Gray Line Colorado River rafting trip and tours to the Grand Canyon, including motorcoach and flightseeing trips. | 702/384–1234 or 800/634–6579 | www.grayline.com/ | $25–$215.

OTHER POINTS OF INTEREST

★ **Fremont Street Experience.** Stretched along Fremont Street, a.k.a. Glitter Gulch, in down-town Las Vegas is a four-block long, 100-ft-high arched canopy. Lining the underside is the largest electric sign in the world, with 2 million lightbulbs programmed and controlled by 31 computers with 100 gigabytes of memory, along with half a million watts of sound broadcast via 200 concert-quality speakers. You can catch the seven-minute light-and-sound shows that are presented on the hour after dark. | Fremont St. between Main and 4th Sts. | 702/678–5600 | www.vegasexperience.com | Free | Daily.

Southern Nevada Zoological Park. Five minutes from downtown, the hot desert air keeps a Bengal tiger, an Asian spotted leopard, and African green monkeys happy in their cages. You can also see a large collection of exotic birds, a rare and endangered species breed-ing program, and a petting zoo. | 1775 N. Rancho Dr. | 702/647–4685 | $5.95 | Daily 9–5.

The Strip. What's to say that hasn't been said before? The Las Vegas Strip, south of town, is the most famous and most visited 5-mi stretch of urban boulevard in the world. The

Strip has more attractions, restaurants, showrooms, boutiques, and spectacles per linear foot than anywhere else. And then there are the rooms and games. See it once, anyway. | Las Vegas Blvd.

ON THE CALENDAR

MAR.: *NASCAR Winston Cup Race.* The largest event of the year in Nevada brings 120,000 racing fans to Las Vegas for the grueling 400-mi race on the 1½-mi Las Vegas Motor Speedway, with top national drivers competing for $3 million in prize money. | 702/644–4443.

MAY OR JUNE: *Helldorado Festival.* A pioneer festival and rodeo established in 1935 has Las Vegas's biggest parade of the year, an art exhibit, an arts and crafts fair, and a grand ball. | 702/870–1221.

OCT.: *Pro Bull Riders Finals.* The two-day Super Bowl of the bull-riders circuit has the top 50 riders compete for a $1 million purse. | Thomas and Mack Center | 702/891–7272 or 800/929–1111.

OCT.: *Las Vegas Invitational.* Top PGA golfers compete for high stakes at three golf courses around the city. Nationally televised. | Desert Inn, Las Vegas Country Club, and Spanish Trails | 702/734–1122.

DEC.: *National Finals Rodeo.* The biggest draw of the rodeo circuit, more than 120 top rodeo athletes vie for $2½ million in prize money. Las Vegas goes country and western for 10 days in early December, with top musicians performing nonstop and big parties at all the casinos. | Thomas and Mack Center | 702/731–2115.

WALKING TOURS

DOWNTOWN (approximately 90 minutes)

Start your walking tour where Las Vegas itself started: at **Jackie Gaughan's Plaza,** at the corner of Main and Fremont streets. The original land auction held by the railroad that founded Las Vegas was held here; the train depot was built on this site a few months later (the Amtrak depot is still here, though Amtrak doesn't service Las Vegas). The four-block stretch of Fremont Street known as Glitter Gulch and the Fremont Street Experience starts across Main Street from the Plaza; when the high-tech Experience canopy went up in 1996, these four blocks were turned into a pedestrian mall.

On the southeast corner of Fremont and Main is the **Golden Gate,** known for its 99¢ shrimp cocktail (served 24 hours). The **Victory Hotel,** a block south of the Gate on Main Street, was built in 1910 and retains its original balcony and veranda. Up Fremont Street at the corner of 1st Street, atop the Fremont Street Experience logo shop, stands **Vegas Vic,** Las Vegas's most famous neon cowboy; across Fremont is Vegas Vickie, Las Vegas's most famous neon cowgirl.

Across 1st is the **Golden Nugget,** the classiest joint downtown, with white marble floors, gold-plated slots, and a display of the world's largest gold nuggets. Across Casino Center Drive is the **Four Queens,** serving downtown low rollers since 1965. Next up is **Fitzgeralds,** which has the only outdoor overlook of Glitter Gulch, complete with lounge furniture!

Walk three blocks east to 6th Street and cross on Fremont Street to the venerable **El Cortez,** which opened in 1941 and retains the original casino (the oldest continuously operating casino building in town, which also means in the country). From there, head over one block to Ogden Street and the **Gold Spike,** where rooms are $22 year-round and the blackjack minimums are $2. West two blocks on Ogden, you'll come to the **Lady Luck,** which, with its big picture windows, is the brightest and airiest casino downtown.

Another two blocks west, on the corner of Ogden and 1st, is the **California,** which has a distinct aloha vibration, since the majority of its clientele hails from the islands. A pedestrian bridge across Main Street connects the California with **Main Street Station,** one of the most aesthetically interesting casinos in town, full of antiques, stained glass, and woodwork.

From there, recross Main Street, head a block down to Fremont, and walk another block east to the last stop, **Binion's Horseshoe.** This is the quintessential old-time gambling hall, with rompin'-stompin' action and a display of a cool million dollars in cash (a hundred rare $10,000 bills).

SOUTH STRIP (approximately 3 hours)

Start your walk at **Mandalay Bay,** near the corner of Las Vegas Boulevard and the Strip, which opened in March 1999. Check out the vodka locker at Red Square, the food belt that circles the bar at China Grill Cafe, the folk art at House of Blues, and the Treasures of Mandalay Bay, a small museum with an interesting display of rare currency and coins. From there, walk (or take the monorail) to **Luxor** next door, a perfect pyramid with 2,500 rooms and the largest atrium in the world (29 million cubic ft). And next to Luxor is **Excalibur,** a pink-and-blue, towers-and-turrets, medieval-themed castle-casino. All three are owned by Circus Circus, which also runs the monorail.

Across Tropicana Avenue is **New York–New York,** the most monumental piece of pop art the world has ever seen. Stroll across the Brooklyn Bridge into the Art Deco lobby, then take in Central Park (the casino) and Greenwich Village (the restaurant area) before boarding Manhattan Express, the Coney Island-like roller coaster that runs around the place. Next door to the little Big Apple is **Monte Carlo,** whose lobby overlooks the pool area with big picture windows. Stop in for some liquid refreshment at the microbrewery.

Across the Strip is the **MGM Grand,** the largest hotel in the world with 5,005 rooms. Allow at least an hour to explore this gargantuan gambler gobbler, with its huge casino and race and sports book, long restaurant row, lush pool area, and big amusement park out back, where you can watch thrill seekers defy death on the monster SkyScreamer ride. (To extend this walk, take the monorail from the MGM to Bally's and explore the Center Strip.)

Cross Tropicana again to get to the **Tropicana,** which has anchored this corner since 1958; it was 32 years before another resort showed up here. The Trop's main attractions are the 4,000-square-ft leaded-glass dome over the main pit and the Casino Legends Museum, with the largest and most fascinating collection of Nevada casino memorabilia in existence.

Dining

INEXPENSIVE

Chapala. Mexican. The interior is done in run-of-the-mill south-of-the-border style, but this place is very popular with locals. The large booths and seating areas make this convenient for large groups. The favorites are standards: salsa, burritos, fajitas, and quesadillas. | 2101 S. Decatur Blvd. | 702/871–7805 | $14 | MC, V.

Cheesecake Factory. American. The cheesecake is so good (over 30 different kinds), they'll ship it anywhere in the United States for you, but dessert is not the only thing at this restaurant in the Forum Shops at Caesars Palace. Try the pastas, seafood, and steaks, as well as salads and sandwiches. | 3500 Las Vegas Blvd. S | 702/792–6888 | $12 | AE, D, DC, MC, V.

Country Inn. American. Spacious and casual, this family restaurant caters to large groups and people on budgets. You can get solid fare for every meal. Dinner favorites are meat loaf and pork chops. | 1401 Rainbow Blvd. | 702/254–0520 | 2425 E. Desert Inn Rd. | 702/731–5035 | 1990 W. Sunset Rd. | 702/898–8183 | $12 | AE, D, DC, MC, V.

Dive! American. A wild and wacky sub shop in the Fashion Show Mall, here you get video monitors, sound effects, and lots of funky models who take you and the kids on a funny simulated submersible voyage as you await your order. Try the subs, of course, along with some flavorful French fries. | 3200 Las Vegas Blvd. S | 702/369–DIVE | $14 | AE, D, DC, MC, V.

Fasolini's Pizza Cafe. Italian. In a diner-like setting, you can have good Italian food and some of the best pizzas in town. | 222 Decatur Blvd. | 702/877–0071 | $8–$15 | AE, MC, V | Closed Sun.

Garduno's. Mexican. Garduno's brings an Albuquerque institution to Las Vegas, within the Fiesta Hotel. Huge variety of salsas (over 20 at last count at the salsa bar) and a serious nod to authenticity have made this a hugely popular spot with locals. Best bets include a killer chili verde (with huge chunks of pork and pepper), chili Colorado (beef), and massive chimichangas. You'll be glad for the large microbrew selection after a sprinkle of habanero-pineapple salsa. | 2400 N. Rancho Dr. | 702/631–7000 | $9–$20 | AE, D, DC, MC, V.

Gordon Biersch. Eclectic. One of the leading microbreweries in Las Vegas, this restaurant in the Hughes Center also has a varied menu, from American dishes to Asian delicacies such as sushi. The lagers brewed on premises are smooth and very potable. There is live entertainment some nights. | 3987 Paradise Rd. | 702/312–5247 | $10–$25 | AE, D, DC, MC, V.

Habib's. Middle Eastern. This small and friendly establishment offers such rich and authentic Middle Eastern dishes as hummus, tabouleh, and filet mignon kebabs. | 4750 W. Sahara Ave. | 702/870–0860 | $12–$20 | AE, MC, V | Closed Sun.

Hard Rock Cafe. American. Loud, loud, loud, but still fun for rock aficionados of all ages. The kids will want to stay and soak up the music and rock and roll memorabilia while most adults will be looking for the exits after less than an hour. It's known for chicken and ribs. It's next to the Hard Rock Hotel. | 4475 Paradise Rd. | 702/733–7625 | $12–$20 | AE, DC, MC, V.

Il Fornaio. Italian. This quaint eatery in the New York–New York Hotel bakes its own bread and imports a special olive oil from Europe. The pizzas are great. | 3790 Las Vegas Blvd. S | 702/740–6969 | $12–$27 | AE, D, DC, MC, V.

Landry's. Seafood. A large neighborhood seafood restaurant with a contemporary look, this restaurant is very popular with the locals. The specialties include stuffed broiled flounder or herbed, seared red snapper, and whatever the catch of the day is. Try the pecan-crusted chicken breast if you're not in the mood for seafood. | 2610 W. Sahara Ave. | 702/251–0101 | $10–$28 | AE, D, DC, MC, V.

Laredo Del Mar. Mexican. The chef at this popular restaurant uses traditional Mexican cooking techniques in interesting ways: swordfish fillet wrapped in cornhusks and wolf fish baked in parchment with, among other things, poblano chiles. The standard fare is good, too—enciladas, burritos, and fajitas. | In the Texas Station Hotel-Casino, 2101 Texas La. | 702/631–1000 | $10–$20 | AE, D, DC, MC, V | Closed Tues.

Lindo Michoacan. Mexican. If you're looking for the real thing, try this place, the best Mexican restaurant in town. The numerous regional specialties are favorites, such as *birra de chivo*—roasted goat meat served with huge tortillas in a rich and mild red sauce, and the *mole rojo,* a chicken breast smothered in piquant dark-red mole sauce. | 2655 E. Desert Inn Rd.; 2 mi east of Las Vegas Blvd. | 702/735–6828 | $12–$40 | AE, D, DC, MC, V.

Macaroni Grill. Italian. Noisy, crowded, and large, this place has some distinctive specialty pizzas such as thin crust pizza with ricotta, pancetta, Gruyère, smoked mozzarella, and sun-dried tomatoes. They also serve standard entrées like chicken marsala. | 2400 W. Sahara Ave. and other locations | 702/248–9500 | $9–$20 | AE, D, DC, MC, V.

Motown Cafe. American. Firehouse meat loaf, chicken and waffles, strawberry shortcake, and even s'mores cake make this an artery hardener if ever there was one. Once the house R&B group begins its act, all will be forgiven. If you must take in the "theme scene," make this the one, within the New York–New York Hotel. Open-air dining, facing the Las Vegas strip, right on the sidewalk. Entertainment. | 3790 Las Vegas Blvd. S | 702/740–6969 | $12–$22 | AE, D, DC, MC, V.

North Beach Cafe. Italian. One of Las Vegas's most popular neighborhood restaurants, this Italian place is big with the business crowd at both lunch and dinner. Friendly and cozy, it also offers some Spanish and Mediterranean dishes. Open-air dining. Pianist Wed.–Sun. evenings. | 2605 S. Decatur Blvd.; I–15 Sahara exit | 702/247–9530 | $10–$30 | AE, D, DC, MC, V.

Planet Hollywood. American. This is the place that Sylvester built, right in the Forum Shops of Caesars Palace! You can also get your own Planet Hollywood souvenirs and be very cool. A few distinctive offerings stand out amidst the burgers, such as Captain's Chicken, an appetizer that's chicken fingers coated in pulverized Captain Crunch cereal. | 3500 Las Vegas Blvd. S | 702/791–7827 | fax 702/791–7828 | $14–$19 | AE, D, DC, MC, V.

Ricardo's. Mexican. Mariachis stroll among the big, comfortable tables and booths in the three dining rooms here, east of the Strip, each a different take on south of the border. All of the traditional dishes are good, but the locals favor the fajitas. | 2380 E. Tropicana Ave. | 702/798–4515 | $12–$18 | AE, D, DC, MC, V.

Saigon. Vietnamese. If you wish to experience what Saigon does best, stick with Vietnamese items and avoid the Chinese-sounding ones. What it truly excels in are its *pho* dishes— hearty, huge bowls of noodle soups—sometimes very hot and spicy, sometimes not, but always full of thick rice noodles and made with deeply flavored broth. | 4251 W. Sahara Ave. | 702/362–9978 | $10–$24 | AE, D, DC, MC, V.

Sam Woo BBQ. Chinese. A simple place in Chinatown Mall, it's always crowded here with Asian tourists who come for the barbecued meats. This is not a place for the tofu and bean sprout crowd. With whole barbecued pigs, ducks, and chickens hanging in the front window, you have no doubt where this kitchen does its best work. The combination plate is huge and enough for four. | 4215 Spring Mountain Rd. | 702/368–7628 | $7–$15 | AE, D, DC, MC, V.

Sfuzzi. Northern Italian. Pronounced "Foozi," this restaurant fronts the Strip and backs into the ultra-classy Fashion Show Mall. It couldn't have a better location, and that plus good service and a fun atmosphere all make for a lively experience. Go for the Sfuzzi (a Bellini-like cocktail), the nice bar atmosphere, or the northern Italian specialties. Open-air dining. | 3200 Las Vegas Blvd. S | 702/699–5777 | $8–$20 | AE, D, DC, MC, V.

Shalimar. Northern Indian. Comfortable, friendly, and almost never crowded, this Indian restaurant in a shopping mall east of the Strip has a generic menu that's spiced for the milder taste buds and features a bargain all-you-can-eat buffet lunch. Favorites include a fiery lamb vindaloo, Goan chicken, and saag paneer. The cardamom-spiced rice pudding provides just the right cool-down. | 3900 Paradise Rd. | 702/796–0302 | $10–$22 | AE, D, DC, MC, V | No lunch Sun.

Stage Deli. Deli. The side-by-side seating is reminiscent of the namesake 7th Avenue joint at this locally popular deli in the Forum Shops at Caesars Palace. The huge sandwiches, half-sour pickles, tomatoes, bagels, and blintzes fill the bill without breaking your wallet. Sandwiches are best shared, but the kreplach is so good you'll want a whole bowl for yourself. Even the egg creams taste authentic. This is as good as it gets for a New Yorker needing a kosher fix. | 3500 Las Vegas Blvd. S | 702/893–4045 | $10–$12 | AE, D, DC, MC, V.

Thai BBQ. Thai. Although it's hard to get to and hard to get a seat, it's also hard not to go crazy over. Inside this tiny well-kept dining room lies a meat-oriented Thai kitchen that turns out hearty and huge portions of classic Thai dishes along with such fetching menu items as Wings of Angel (two huge boneless and stuffed chicken legs) and Dearest Crab, and the best Thai beef saté in town. Soups and hot pots like the hot-and-spicy beef noodle soup pack a wallop and demonstrate that pain/pleasure, hot/sweet phenomenon that Thai cuisine does so well. You'll see more Asians than gringoes here. | 1424 S. 4th St. | 702/383–1128 | $12–$14 | AE, D, DC, MC, V.

Viva Mercado's. Mexican. A solid Mexican standout, huge burritos, steak azata, and lobster and fish tacos are among its specialties. Locally owned and very popular with people who live here, Mercado's is one of the few Mexican restaurants in town that attempts to cook and serve authentic Mexican food. | 6182 W. Flamingo Rd. | 702/871–8826 | Reservations accepted (dinner) | $8–$16 | AE, D, DC, MC, V.

Xinh-Xinh. Vietnamese. This restaurant has a minimalist Southeast Asian interior design and some of the city's best Vietnamese food. | 220 W. Sahara Ave. | 702/471–1572 | $10–$14 | MC, V.

MODERATE

Aqua. Seafood. Clean lines and a smart casual look provide the perfect backdrop at this establishment in the Bellagio Hotel. Pristine tastes and impeccable ingredients are the order of the day here, with starters like Dungeness crab cakes on chopped tomatoes. The signature dish of ahi tuna with seared foie gras in a pinot noir wine sauce is exceptional. | 3600 Las Vegas Blvd. S | 702/693–7223 | Reservations essential | $11–$34 | AE, D, DC, MC, V | No lunch.

Aureole. Continental. Within the Mandalay Bay Hotel you'll find the world's largest wine vault/refrigerator spanning a 42-ft ceiling, and holding 9,000 bottles of wine. The menu is short. Start with a light and fresh salad of seasonal lettuce and herbs. First course choices include breast of capon "saltimbocca" with sweet garlic, oak-smoked salmon with tiny corn blinis and a tasting of mallard duck with country bread, pan-roasted lobster with caramelized fennel. | 3950 Las Vegas Blvd. S | 702/632–7777 | Reservations essential | $20–$36 | AE, D, DC, MC, V | No lunch.

Bamboleo. Latin. With South American specialties and exotic drinks, this restaurant in the Rio Hotel serves traditional flavors of Mexico, Brazil, and Argentina. Try the tortilla soup, pollo asado, and the grilled prawns. | 3700 W. Flamingo Rd. | 702/247–7923 | $18–$22 | AE, D, DC, MC, V.

Battista's Hole In The Wall. Italian. A genuine hoot right off the Strip serving Italian in a kitschy setting. You get one-price meals—including pasta, seafood, or veal, with unlimited red and white house wine. The fresh pasta and the cioppino are worth a try. | 4041 Audrie St. | 702/732–1424 | $15–$20 | AE, D, DC, MC, V | No lunch.

Bertolini's. Italian. Solid, consistent, Italian food here under the rotating sky at Caesars Forum Shops. Pastas and pizzas are the safest bet, but getting a table never is. And don't miss the gelato or the tiramisu. One of the best spots in town to watch the parade of worldwide humanity that fills the Forum Shops daily. | 3500 Las Vegas Blvd. S | 702/735–4663 | $25–$30 | AE, DC, MC, V.

Cafe Nicolle. Greek-Italian. A beautiful setting with al fresco dining, very big with the power lunch crowd. Open-air dining. A Mediterranean fountain trickles in the intense sun as customers dine under large umbrellas. Fragrant jasmine perfumes the air while misters keep the desert heat at bay. For lunch, try the Caesar salad or spinach pie. For dinner, try any of the lamb, steak, or seafood dishes. Entertainment. | 4760 W. Sahara Ave. | 702/870–7675 | $18–$25 | AE, DC, MC, V | Closed Sun.

Cathay House. Chinese. Close to the center of town, this restaurant draws both locals and Asian tourists. The menu is Cantonese and the dim sum is popular, too. | 5300 W. Spring Mountain Rd. | 702/876–3838 | fax 702/876–8208 | $20–$25 | AE, D, DC, MC, V.

Chinois. Eclectic. This establishment in Caesars Forum Shops is more Chinese than its sister restaurant, Chinois on Main in Santa Monica, California. The standouts include whole fried fish, whole roasted Shanghai lobster, fried rice, and vegetable dishes, with the dry fried string beans a must. Pot stickers, dim sum, and sushi all shine, both in the downstairs (slightly less expensive and less formal) café, and as appetizers in the open-kitchen second-floor dining area. Desserts are flights of French fancy interwoven with the seasonings and flavors of the Far East. The wine list is good. Lunch and dinner in the café seven days a week. | 3500 Las Vegas Blvd. S | 702/737–9700 | Reservations essential | $25–$50 | AE, D, DC, MC, V.

Circo. Continental. Officially the name is Osteria del Circo or "House of the Circus." Unofficially this establishment in the Bellagio Hotel is the best Italian restaurant in Las Vegas, as convivial as the original restaurant in New York, and with French touches. Some favorites are the zuppa de pesce, the ethereally light gnocchi in a truffle cream sauce, or basil and ricotta-stuffed homemade ravioli. | 3600 Las Vegas Blvd. S | 702/693–8150 | Reservations essential | $28–$38 | AE, D, DC, MC, V | No lunch.

Coyote Café. Mexican. This trend-setting offshoot of the Santa Fe original gives Las Vegas one of its best restaurants, one that consistently impresses with nouvelle southwestern, chili-inspired creations. The Grill Room features different entrées every month, however the "cowboy" rib steak is a permanent fixture. No meal is complete here without one of the many fresh-fruit margaritas or custom-blended pineapple rum daiquiris. The Coyote Café received a 1999 Award of Excellence by *Wine Spectator* for its wine list. | In the MGM Grand Hotel, 3799 Las Vegas Blvd. S | 702/891–7349 | $15 | AE, D, DC, MC, V.

Delmonico's. American. The menu has a Cajun twist with such dishes as Cajun rib eye, and the steaks are simple but exquisite at this steakhouse in the Venetian Hotel. Other favorites include a tender lamb shank on a bed of risotto, and a chateaubriand that melts in your mouth. Seafood offerings are also strong, with shrimp and crab given the full and exotic New American/Cajun treatment. The bread pudding is outstanding. | 3355 Las Vegas Blvd. S | 702/414–3737 | Reservations essential | $25–$50 | AE, D, DC, MC, V.

★ **Emeril's New Orleans.** Cajun/Seafood. The French Quarter restaurant's Vegas outpost in the MGM Grand Hotel retains the same terrific food and atmosphere. Signature dishes include Fall River clam chowder and barbecued shrimp, as well as the "study of Maine lobster" served with tempura-fried claws, lobster potato salad, and lobster relish. You can also try a "degustation," five or six savory courses for which the sommelier pairs food and wine. | 3799 Las Vegas Blvd. S | 702/891–7374 | $28 | AE, D, DC, MC, V.

Ferraro's. Italian. Art Deco in style, this establishment highlights northern Italian classics, with osso buco a standout. The menu also has a selection of seafood and pastas and a sophisticated wine list. You can eat in the enclosed patio/atrium area. | 5900 W. Flamingo Rd. | 702/364–5300 | In the Stratosphere Tower, 2000 Las Vegas Blvd. S | 702/382–9090 | $20 | AE, D, DC, MC, V | Closed for lunch.

Francesco's. Italian. The Treasure Island Hotel that houses this place should not mislead you about the menu, which offers some of the most authentic and best-priced Italian food in town. The restaurant's interior is spacious and charming. *Sgombro ai ferri su couscous funghi orientali* (grilled Escolar fish with large Israeli couscous and mushrooms in a red wine reduction sauce) is genuine Tuscany. | 3300 Las Vegas Blvd. S | 702/894–7111 | $25 | AE, D, DC, MC, V.

Golden Steer Steak House. Steak. Las Vegas's oldest steakhouse and its third-oldest restaurant looks like a cross between a Gay Nineties bordello and a Dodge City saloon. Portions are large, and the menu includes prime rib, steak, and seafood, as well as some game dishes. | 308 W. Sahara Ave. | 702/384–4470 | Reservations recommended | $28 | AE, D, DC, MC, V | No lunch.

Hamada of Japan. Japanese. In its several locations, including the Flamingo Hilton, the restaurant has separate rooms—including a sushi bar—that feature highlights of Japanese cooking. The main dining room menu includes shabu-shabu and seafood yosenabe; the Teppan Room has knife-wielding chefs who prepare steak, shrimp, lobster, and marinated chicken. Good for large groups. | 598 E. Flamingo Rd. | 702/733–3005 | In the Flamingo Hilton, 3555 Las Vegas Blvd. S | 702/737–0031 | 3743 Las Vegas Blvd. S | 702/736–1984 | www.hamadaofjapan.com | $18 | AE, D, DC, MC, V | Closed for lunch.

Lillie Langtry's. Chinese. The Szechuan and Cantonese offerings here will satisfy both those who crave spicy food and those who do not. The specialties at this establishment housed in the Golden Nugget include Mongolian beef, lobster Cantonese, and stir-fried lobster. You can also try the mesquite-broiled steaks. | 129 Fremont St. | 702/385–7111 | Reservations suggested | $22 | AE, D, DC, MC, V | No lunch.

Manhattan of Las Vegas. Italian. The closest thing in town to the Vegas of old. If the Rat Pack were intact, this is where they would hang out. Plush booths, tuxedoed waiters, and old-time elegance are matched with a menu that has almost everything: steak, veal, chicken, lamb, and Italian dishes such as canneloni. | 2600 E. Flamingo Rd. | 702/737–5000 | $22 | AE, D, DC, MC, V | No lunch.

Marrakech. Moroccan. While you consume a hugely satisfying six-course meal, you will be entertained by the dancers at this venerable belly dancing venue. Sit in the low-lying booths, sip some retsina, and allow yourself to be transported. The six-course fixed menu begins with shrimp scampi sautéed in a lemon, wine and garlic sauce. Next is harira soup, which consists of lentils, rice, lemon and a perfect blend of spices. That's followed by salade Marrakech made of vegetables, olive oil, lemon, and seasoning. Then comes back-to-back entrées: lamb shish kebab followed by game hen in a light lemon sauce. For dessert, pastilla, is a light, crispy capper to the meal. | 3900 Paradise Rd. | 702/737–5611 | $24.95 | http://marrakech-lv.com/ | AE, MC, V | Closed for lunch.

Mayflower Cuisinier. Eclectic. The streamlined modern interior is paired with ingenious fare that includes some distinctive hybrids. Mongolian grilled lamb chops come with a creamy cilantro-mint sauce and blackened rare ahi tuna salad is also popular. The seafood ravioli appetizer is another favorite. You can also get traditional Chinese dishes. Open-air dining with mist cooling. A patio seats another 60 people in mist-cooled comfort. No smoking. | 4950 W. Sahara Ave. | 702/870–8432 | http://www.mayflowercuisinier.com/ | $15–$30 | AE, D, DC, MC, V | Closed Sun. No lunch Sat.

McCormick and Schmick's. Seafood. Fresh fish, flown in daily, is the mainstay of this menu, and it is served in a wood-paneled dining room. A private dining room, with fireplace, seats 80. Open-air dining. | 335 Hughes Center Dr. | 702/836–9000 | www.mccormickand-schmicks.com/ | $17–$27 | AE, D, DC, MC, V.

Mortoni's. Italian. Northern Italian food and walls lined with pictures of the Rat Pack are the distinguishing factors here within the Hard Rock Hotel. Servings are large. Open-air dining. | 4455 Paradise Rd. | 702/693–5000 | $20–$36 | AE, D, DC, MC, V | No lunch.

Palm Restaurant. Steak. Clubby, masculine, and brightly lit, from the opening bread basket to the prime steaks and huge grilled lobsters, Palm gets the nod for best steak house in Las Vegas. The only drawbacks are an excessive noise level and uncomfortable booths. | 3500 Las Vegas Blvd. S | 702/732–7256 | $15–$48 | AE, DC, MC, V.

Pamplemousse. French. Here's an elegantly casual French-style bistro that's known for poultry, duck, and veal. The wine cellar is interesting. | 400 E. Sahara Ave. | 702/733–2066 | fax 702/733–9139 | www.pamplemousserestaurant.com | Reservations essential | $22 | AE, D, DC, MC, V.

Papyrus. Chinese. There are many Chinese restaurants in town, but few that try to encompass most of the Pacific Rim. This one in the Luxor Hotel has a Polynesian flair along with the traditional Cantonese and Szechuan cuisine. | 3900 Las Vegas Blvd. S | 702/262–4774 | $24 | AE, D, DC, MC, V.

Philips Supper House. Italian. Popular with locals, this old home turned restaurant features Italian specialties as well as beef and fresh seafood. | 4545 W. Sahara | 702/873–5222 | www.philipssupperhouse.com/ | $26 | AE, D, DC, MC, V | No lunch.

Sacred Sea. Seafood. This gourmet room at the Luxor serves saltwater seafood and freshwater fish shipped in daily. Murals and reproduction low-relief carvings of fishing on the Nile line the walls, and a wavelike blue ceiling mosaic with matching plates make this a most interesting dining room. | 3900 Las Vegas Blvd. S | 702/262–4772 | $27 | AE, D, DC, MC, V | No lunch.

Samba Grill. Brazilian. The chef has been chef de cuisine for Four Seasons as well as for Ritz-Carlton properties. Here he parlays his experience into a New Brazilian restaurant. | In the Mirage Hotel, 3400 Las Vegas Blvd. S | 702/791–7223 | $26 | AE, D, DC, MC, V.

Sir Galahad's. Steak. The medieval theme park and Tudor style of this restaurant in the Excalibur Hotel indicate a bit of historical confusion, but the fare is very solid. Prime rib is prime, served with creamed spinach and Yorkshire pudding. | 3850 Las Vegas Blvd. S | 702/597–7777 | http://www.excalibur-casino.com/dining.html | $26 | AE, D, DC, MC, V | No lunch.

★ **Spago.** Eclectic. The food at this branch in the Forum Shops is fairly close to that at the original. Pizzas gave Spago its original cachet, and are still the most popular items on the menu. The dinner menu is divided into appetizers, pastas, and entrées, including the elegant thin corn blinis with the familiar dill cream and golden caviar. Prices are generally high, though, and portions of the appetizers very small. If you want volume, stick with the pizzas, pastas, and salads. Nothing misses on the dessert menu. | In the Forum Shops, Caesars Palace, 3500 Las Vegas Blvd. S | 702/369–6300 | $20–$54 | AE, D, DC, MC, V.

Star Canyon. Mexican. In the Venetian Hotel, this may be one of the few restaurants that uses barbed wire as a decorative accessory, along with cowboy boots. The menu is intriguing, with such dishes as spicy rock shrimp taquitos with a killer guacamole, tamale tart with savory egg custard and Gulf Coast crab meat, and vegetable plate with wood-roasted corn, or some of the best roasted chicken imaginable. | 3355 Las Vegas Blvd. S | 702/414–3772 | $15–$28 | AE, D, DC, MC, V.

Stefano's. Italian. You'll get mostly standard Italian dishes here; what sets it apart is the singing waiters. If you ask, they'll serenade you, solo or in groups. This restaurant in the Golden Nugget Hotel is a great place to go if you want a romantic serenade for your sweetheart, but may drive you mad if you do not mix music and mozzarella. | 129 Fremont St. | 702/385–7111 | $14–$35 | AE, D, DC, MC, V.

Wolfgang Puck's Cafe. Eclectic. Pizza and Austrian classics are the mainstays at California Chef Wolfgang Puck's circular establishment in the MGM Grand Hotel. Austrian dishes include Weiner schnitzel, veal cutlet, and rib eye. | 3799 Las Vegas Blvd. S | 702/895–9653 | $15 | AE, DC, MC, V.

Yolie's Churrascaria. Brazilian. If you're a carnivore, this is your kind of place. Meat is served as an appetizer, followed by a main course of rotisserie-grilled, marinated poultry and other meat. The waiter slices this "Rodizio" directly onto your plate. Open-air dining. Kids' menu. | 3900 Paradise Rd., Suite Z | 702/794–0700 | www.yolies.com/ | Reservations essential | $23 | AE, D, DC, MC, V | No lunch weekends.

Z'Tejas Grill. Southwestern. A hot and happening bar scene has kept this place going despite food that is neither as bad as it could be nor as good as it should be. The gumbo specials are usually good, though, as is a pork roast with a spicy tomato-based sauce. Simpler fare includes Jamaican jerk chicken and crunchy fried catfish. No smoking. | 3824 Paradise Rd. | 702/732–1660 | $16 | AE, D, DC, MC, V.

EXPENSIVE

Andre's. French. The downtown Andre's is rustic and friendly, whereas on the Strip (in the Monte Carlo Hotel), a more formal and elegant setting surrounds the haute and bourgeois French cuisine that has kept Andre's at the forefront of local restaurants for more than 15 years. Popular with the high-roller and business crowd. Regular patrons swear by the classic renditions of sole meunière; seared foie gras with apple puree, balsamic glaze, and roasted hazelnuts; rack of lamb; and some killer soufflés. Also, a world-class wine cellar. | 401 S. 6th St. or 3770 Las Vegas Blvd. S | 702/385–5016 | Reservations essential | $38–$48 | AE, D, DC, MC, V | No lunch.

Antonio's. Italian. Enjoy fine Italian cuisine with lobster specialties. Consistently great food, a beautiful room, and fun waiters are the recipe for success at this splendid Italian spot in the Rio; though a few carp about the strict dress code (collared shirt and slacks required), most agree that the festive atmosphere at this very elegant place makes the extra sartorial effort worth it. | In the Rio Hotel, 3700 W. Flamingo Rd. | 702/252–7777 | Reservations essential | $37 | AE, D, DC, MC, V | No lunch.

Aristocrat. Continental/French. This cozy spot serves both lunch and dinner and is a local favorite. The gourmet cuisine with hints of a French flair is consistently good. Specialties include angel-hair pasta and fresh seafood, but for heartier appetites the best bets are the filet mignon and osso buco. | 850 S. Rancho Dr. | 702/870–1977 | $30 | AE, D, DC, MC, V.

Buccaneer Bay Club. American. Given its location in the Treasure Island Hotel, this is the best spot on the Strip to view the pirate battle, though the cannon blasts can be distracting.

LAS VEGAS

INTRO
ATTRACTIONS
DINING
LODGING

The chef can also impress with unusual fare such as pheasant and buffalo prime rib. The more traditional specialties include smoked salmon Napoleon and salmon pommery. For dessert, go for the soufflés. | In the Treasure Island Hotel, 3300 Las Vegas Blvd. S | 702/894–7223 | $35 | AE, D, DC, MC, V | No lunch.

Drai's. French. Leopard-skin fabric predominates on the overstuffed chairs and the banquettes lining the walls. In other words, its intentionally dated look, straight from an ultra-glamorous 1930s movie set, is very cool indeed. Drai's makes its mark with the pungent scents of Mediterranean cooking, especially fish, chicken, and lamb with a Provençal flavor. If you desire heavier fare, try the grilled free-range chicken served with roasted garlic and perfect French fries or the seven-hour leg of lamb, stewed in red wine and succulent as a good stew. Of the desserts, the orange crème brûlée is consistently fine. | In the Barbary Coast Hotel, 3595 Las Vegas Blvd. S | 702/737–0555 | www.barbarycoastcasino.com/drais.html | Reservations essential | $40 | AE, D, DC, MC, V | No lunch.

Hugo's Cellar. Continental. This restaurant is popular with locals who are having a special night out. Despite the fact that Hugo's Cellar is below ground-level, it can be quite romantic. A small bar is the entrance to a dark-wood and brick interior. The dim lighting sets the mood and each female guest is given a single red rose. The meals are expensive, but include some nice touches. For example, salads that come with the entrées are mixed right at the table. The food itself is basically a selection of fish and chops that are pretty good. As at some other restaurants in Las Vegas, you're paying for the evening, not just the food. | In the Four Queens Hotel, 202 Fremont St. | 702/385–4011 | Jacket | $35 | AE, D, DC, MC, V | No lunch.

Lawry's The Prime Rib. Steakhouse. For over five decades, Lawry's The Prime Rib has been internationally recognized for serving the finest quality beef available. Every standing rib roast is specially selected, then aged and roasted for natural tenderness. | 4043 Howard Hughes Pkwy. | 702/893–2223 | fax 702/731–6668 | $30 | AE, D, DC, MC, V | No lunch.

Le Cirque. French. Le Cirque brings a slice of Big Apple sophistication to the ersatz shores of Lake Como. The chef pushes the envelope nightly with such succulent offerings as "Black Tie" scallops tied with black truffles, consommé de boeuf with foie gras ravioli, salade mesclun, roasted duck with honey spice glaze with figs, and roasted lobster in a port wine sauce. Follow these with ethereal desserts like a trio of crème brûlées, bomboloni (Italian doughnuts filled with vanilla cream), or a dense and warm chocolate fondant with the richest oozing center imaginable. | In the Bellagio Hotel, 3600 Las Vegas Blvd. S | 702/693–8100 | Reservations essential | Jacket required | $28–$45 | AE, D, DC, MC, V | No lunch.

Michael's. Continental. The highlights are specialties such as fresh Dover sole, rack of lamb, and chateaubriand for two. The wine list is lengthy and the desserts are extraordinary. Two separate seatings are available. | In the Barbary Coast Hotel, 3595 Las Vegas Blvd. S | 702/737–7111 | Reservations essential | $40 | AE, D, DC, MC, V.

Rosewood Grille. Seafood. This Las Vegas favorite offers steaks and seafood, lobster being its specialty. Judging from the quality of service and food, you might think the Rosewood Grille is pretentious, but it's far from it—the atmosphere is warm and inviting. | 3399 Las Vegas Blvd. S | 702/792–9099 | $40 | AE, D, DC, MC, V.

Ruth's Chris Steak House. Steakhouse. In addition to steak, the menu includes select fresh seafood and other meat entrées. A variety of fresh-cooked vegetables, including seven kinds of potatoes, salads with dressings made fresh daily, and homemade desserts such as chocolate mousse cheesecake complete the offerings. The menu varies slightly from location to location to meet local tastes and to take advantage of fresh products. An extensive wine list complements the meal. | 3900 Paradise Rd., Suite 121 | 702/791–7011 | fax 702/731–2605 | 4561 W. Flamingo Rd. | 702/248–7011 | fax 702/248–8032 | www.ruthschris.com/main.htm | $40 | AE, D, DC, MC, V | No lunch Fri., Sat.

Seasons. Continental. No matter what time of year, you'll enjoy a superb menu of Continental cuisine and delicious seasonal specialties; served in an elegant setting with impeccable service. | In Bally's Hotel, 3645 Las Vegas Blvd. S | 702/739–4111 | Reservations required | $44 | AE, D, DC, MC, V | No lunch.

Tillerman. Seafood. Its nickname is the "Mighty Tillerman," and it's well deserved. The seafood offerings compete with the best in town. Puck, Lagasse, and the invading hordes of celebrity chefs have nothing on the Tillerman's planked salmon, roasted halibut, or sautéed scallops, and all should sit up and take notice of the superior Dungeness crab cakes offered here. The wine list has been excellent for 20 years, just like the steaks and the atmosphere. | 2245 E. Flamingo Rd. | 702/731–4036 | $33 | AE, D, DC, MC, V | No lunch.

Top of the World. Continental. Even if they served nachos and pizza, this sky-high rotating room would rate near the top of the city's most romantic and impressive spots. Instead, expect traditional Continental fare mixed with some New Wave touches that keep 300-plus diners a night satisfied. Start with an onion or mushroom soup followed by an upscale mesclun salad, then enjoy some roasted duck or perfectly seared sea bass, and you'll know you're not in Kansas anymore—if the 108th-story view hasn't already convinced you. (For the best effect, go right before sunset.) Wine lovers should check out the bargains in the French, Alsatian, and German sections of the list, where the mark-ups are lowest. No smoking. | In the Stratosphere Tower, 2000 Las Vegas Blvd. S | 702/382–4446 | Reservations essential | $36 | AE, D, DC, MC, V | No lunch.

Voodoo Cafe and Lounge. Cajun/Creole. With one of the best views in town, Voodoo has a mystical style. The Cajun/Creole entrées are impressive and beautifully presented. There's also a great selection of martinis. | In the Rio Hotel, 3700 W. Flamingo Rd. | 702/247–7800 | $30 | AE, D, DC, MC, V.

VERY EXPENSIVE

Empress Court. Chinese. Overlooking the spectacular Garden of the Gods swimming pools and gardens, the Empress Court was inspired by the superb dining destinations in Hong Kong. Order à la carte, or select one of two multicourse feasts. The menu also spotlights varied Asian fare, including Malay, Thai and Indonesian delicacies—meticulously prepared and beautifully presented. Giant kitchen fresh-water and saltwater aquariums house daily shipments that can include live rock cod, Dungeness crab, and lobster. Open for dinner Thursday through Monday. Reservations suggested. | In the Caesars Palace Hotel, 3570 Las Vegas Blvd. S | 702/731–7110 | Jacket required | $55 | AE, DC, MC, V | No lunch.

Gatsby's. French. Gatsby's is an intimate 86-seat restaurant decorated in the Biedermeier style. It offers the finest of signature Chef Terence Fong's classical cuisine with Pacific Rim flair. The chef's table allows guests to view the kitchen operation. Gatsby's presents a fine collection of 600 different wine selections, where bottles are housed in three separate climate-controlled cellars to ensure perfect serving temperature. Signature dishes include: macadamia nut escolar, imported Japanese Kobe beef, sautéed Dover sole, and kapalua soufflé. | In the MGM Grand Hotel, 3799 Las Vegas Blvd. S | 702/891–7337 | $65 | AE, D, DC, MC, V | Closed Sun., Mon. No lunch.

Monte Carlo. French. Very classy, very French, and very expensive. The traditional haute-cuisine fare such as striped bass en croute, tournedos Rossini, and duck à l'orange explain why this remains a big favorite. From the beautiful wall murals to the flattering lighting and views of the Desert Inn's pool, this French, over-the-top setting whispers "quality and romance" as soon as the maître d' leads you to your table. | In the Desert Inn Hotel, 3145 Las Vegas Blvd. S | 702/733–4444 | Jacket required | $50 | AE, D, DC, MC, V | Closed Tues., Wed. No lunch.

★ **Napa.** French. Nouvelle cuisine finally comes to Las Vegas (20 years after it was big news in Europe, New York, and California). The service is formal yet relaxed, and the prices are way up there where they should be for ingredients and cooking this good. The incredible wine list and by-the-glass selection is unmatched by any establishment in Las Vegas, or maybe even the United States. | In the Rio Hotel, 3700 W. Flamingo Rd. | 702/252–7777 | $60 | AE, D, DC, MC, V | No lunch.

Palace Court. French/Continental. Gorgeous, formal, beautifully lighted dining room that is consistently one of the best in town. It remains the prettiest dining room in Las Vegas. Open, circular, and surrounded on three sides by floor-to-ceiling windows. | In the Caesars Palace Hotel, 3570 Las Vegas Boulevard S | 702/731–7110 | Jacket required | $52 | AE, DC, MC, V | No lunch.

Prime. Steakhouse. Sophisticated cuisine in a striking royal-blue and brown decor that's at eye level for the spectacular fountain shows of Lake Bellagio. Prime steaks are the highlights, but don't overlook the roasted free-range chicken, seared ahi tuna, or wood-grilled veal chop, or one of the 10 potato or side dishes. Our favorite is the mélange of 27 vegetables that might make you swear off top-quality steer meat (not likely). What also takes the chophouse to a new level are the 11 sauces complementing the meat and the seven mustards for those who can't make up their mind. | In the Bellagio Hotel, 3600 Las Vegas Blvd. S | 702/693–7111 | $18–$54 | AE, D, DC, MC, V.

Sterling Brunch. Buffet/Brunch. Bally's Sterling Brunch is one of Las Vegas's best restaurants, even though it is open only for one meal a week. That meal, of course, is Sunday brunch. Everything, from the breads to the sushi to the pastries, is made in-house, specifically for this day alone. This is Vegas as it used to be: upscale food, tuxedoed waiters, flowing champagne, all lapped up by swellegantly dressed guys and dolls. | In the Bally's Grand Hotel, 3645 Las Vegas Blvd. S | 702/739–4111 | $50 | AE, D, DC, MC, V | Closed Mon.–Sat.

Lodging

INEXPENSIVE

Arizona Charlie's. Popular locals' (off-Strip) casino in a west-side commercial district opened in 1990. Rooms are often available when the town is crowded; when it's uncrowded, rooms are often a bargain. Lounge and showroom entertainment. 4 restaurants, bar. No-smoking rooms. Pool. Business services. Airport shuttle. | 258 rooms | 740 S. Decatur Blvd. | 702/258–5200 or 800/342–2695 | fax 702/258–5192 | www.azcharlies.com | $38–$65 | AE, D, DC, MC, V.

Best Western McCarran Inn. Very close to the airport; convenient for overnighters. Complimentary breakfast. Pool. Laundry facilities. Business services. Airport shuttle. | 99 rooms | 4970 Paradise Rd. | 702/798–5530 or 800/626–7575 | fax 702/798–7627 | www.bestwestern.com/thisco/bw/29058/29058b.html | $49–$125 | AE, D, DC, MC, V.

Binion's Horseshoe. The quintessential old-time downtown Las Vegas gambling hall, home of the prestigious World Series of Poker (winner takes a mil) and the legendary $3 late-night complete steak dinner. The 69 rooms in the old wing, built in 1950, are all comped to players. The new wing, built in 1965 (the old Mint), is available to the public. There's a glass elevator to the top of the tower. 3 restaurants, bar. No-smoking rooms. Cable TV. Pool. Casino. | 370 rooms | 128 Fremont St. | 702/382–1600 or 800/622–6468 | fax 702/384–1574 | $45–$60, $150 suites | AE, D, DC, MC, V.

Circus Circus. Original Vegas family resort, opened in 1968. Many expansions, the most recent of which added 1,000 rooms in 1996, have created a maze. This is kid central, low-roller heaven. Its buffet is the busiest restaurant in the world. Circus area with performances and games, 5-acre indoor amusement park, world's largest indoor roller coaster, and flume ride. 7 restaurants, bar. In-room data ports, some in-room safes, no-smoking floors. Cable TV. 3 pools. Barbershop, beauty salon. Business services. | 3,800 rooms | 2880 Las Vegas Blvd. | 702/734–0410 or 800/634–3450 | fax 702/734–5897 | www.circuscircus-lasvegas.com | $49–$129 | AE, D, DC, MC, V.

Comfort Inn. Right next to I–15 and very close to McCarran airport. Complimentary Continental breakfast. No-smoking rooms. Cable TV. Pool. | 121 rooms | 211 E. Flamingo Rd. | 702/733–7800 | fax 702/733–7353 | www.hotelchoice.com | $55–$75 | AE, D, DC, MC, V.

Comfort Inn–Airport. Near both the strip and the airport, this cozy inn provides a lot of high-class amenities, but at affordable prices. Complimentary Continental breakfast. No-smoking rooms. Cable TV. Pool. Business services. | 106 rooms | 5075 Koval La. | 702/736–3600 | fax 702/736–0726 | www.hotelchoice.com | $57–$150 | AE, D, DC, MC, V.

Days Inn. Tennis and golf are nearby if you need a respite from the casino area and the Fremont Street Experience. The rooms are spacious and simple. Restaurant. No-smoking rooms, TVs. Pool. | 147 rooms | 707 E. Fremont St. | 702/388–1400 or 800/325–2344 | fax 702/388–9622 | $35–$100. | AE, D, DC, MC, V.

El Cortez. Downtown's original high-class resort opened in 1940 and is now as modest a lodging as you'll find. Its 300-room tower was built in the early 1980s. The dinners at the steak house are a great value. 2 restaurants, bar, room service. Cable TV. | 308 rooms | 600 E. Fremont St. | 702/385–5200 or 800/634–6703 (reservations) | fax 702/385–9765 | $23–$40 | AE, D, DC, MC, V.

Excalibur. This is a medieval theme park that happens to have 4,000 rooms and a giant casino attached. The hotel is ultra family-friendly, and has a midway with Renaissance carnie games and strolling minstrels. Adults have lounge and showroom entertainment. 6 restaurants, bars. In-room data ports, no-smoking floors, in-room hot tubs in suites. Cable TV. 2 pools. Barbershop, beauty salon. Business services. | 4,008 rooms | 3850 Las Vegas Blvd. S | 702/597–7777 or 800/937–7777 | fax 702/597–7040 | www.excalibur-casino.com | $49–$125 | AE, D, DC, MC, V.

Fairfield Inn by Marriott. Designed for business travelers, this chain hotel is within walking distance of the Convention Center, close to the airport, and has ample work areas with in-room data ports. Complimentary Continental breakfast. In-room data ports, no-smoking rooms. Cable TV. Pool. Hot tub. Airport shuttle. | 129 rooms | 3850 Paradise Rd. | 702/791–0899 or 800/228–2800 | fax 702/791–0899 | $56–$70 | AE, D, DC, MC, V.

Fiesta. Reserve early at this super-popular locals' casino serving the northwest suburbs—rooms go fast. The place bills itself as the "Royal Flush Capital of the World" (excellent video poker). The buffet is fantastic. 4 restaurants, bar. No-smoking rooms. Cable TV, game room. | 100 rooms | 2400 North Rancho Dr., North Las Vegas | 702/631–7000 or 800/731–7333 | fax 702/631–6588 | $59–$109 | AE, D, DC, MC, V.

Fitzgeralds. The tallest building in Nevada for 15 years opened in 1984. Rooms are a little rough around the edges, but usually available when the town is crowded, and a bargain when it's not. 4 restaurants, bar, room service. No-smoking floors. Cable TV. Laundry facilities. Business services. | 638 rooms, 14 suites | 301 Fremont St. | 702/388–2400 or 800/274–5825 | fax 702/388–2181 | $29–$69 | AE, D, DC, MC, V.

Fremont. This downtown hotel opened in 1956. It is generally nondescript, except for the Second Street Grill, one of the best restaurants in town. 3 restaurants, bar. No-smoking rooms. Cable TV. | 452 rooms | 200 E. Fremont St. | 702/385–3232 or 800/634–6182 | fax 702/385–6270 | $40–$85 | AE, D, DC, MC, V.

Gold Coast. One of the most popular locals' hotels in town, known for its breakfast meal deal, slot club, entertainment, bowling alley, movie theaters, Western dance hall, and many amenities. 5 restaurants, bar. Some refrigerators, no-smoking floors. Cable TV. Pool. Game room. Children's programs. Business services. | 711 rooms | 4000 W. Flamingo Rd. | 702/367–7111 or 888/402–6278 (reservations) | fax 702/367–8419 | $45–$85 | AE, D, DC, MC, V.

★ **Gold Spike.** A little-known haven for rock-bottom bargain hunters; rough around the edges but worth the slight bother for the savings. Restaurant. No-smoking rooms. Cable TV. Business services. | 110 rooms | 400 E. Ogden Ave. | 702/384–8444 or 800/634–6703 (reservations) | http://www.goldspikehotelcasino.com/ | $22–$33 | AE, D, DC, MC, V.

★ **Golden Gate.** The rooms here were upgraded in the early 1990s, but they retain their historic downtown hotel feel. The first lodging in Las Vegas, the hotel was built in 1906. The rooms are small but very comfortable, and an excellent value. 2 restaurants, bar. No-smoking rooms. Cable TV. | 106 rooms | 1 E. Fremont St. | 702/385–1906 or 800/426–1906 (outside NV) | fax 702/382–5349 | $29–$49 | AE, D, DC, MC, V.

Holiday Inn Boardwalk. A relatively small, homey hotel-casino with a Coney Island theme is dwarfed by its next-door neighbors Monte Carlo and Bellagio. The location is good. 2 restaurants, bar. No-smoking rooms, some refrigerators. Cable TV. Pool. Hot tub. Exercise equipment. | 654 units, 140 suites | 3750 Las Vegas Blvd. S | 702/735–2400 | fax 702/739–8152 | $39–$99 | AE, D, DC, MC, V.

La Quinta. The location makes this motel popular with budget business travelers and university visitors. It's convenient to the airport, rental car companies, the Convention Center, and the university. Complimentary Continental breakfast. In-room data ports, no-smoking rooms, refrigerators, in-room hot tubs, cable TV. Pool. Laundry facilities. Business services. Airport and Strip shuttle. | 228 units, 171 kitchenettes | 3970 S. Paradise Rd. | 702/796–9000 | fax 702/796–3537 | $65–$109. | AE, D, DC, MC, V.

La Quinta Motor Inn. Standard motel literally squashed between New York–New York and Monte Carlo. Fine once you're there, but tough getting in and out. No-smoking rooms. Cable TV. Pool. Business services. Airport shuttle. | 114 rooms | 3782 Las Vegas Blvd. S | 702/739–7457 | fax 702/736–1129 | $55–$85 | AE, D, DC, MC, V.

Main Street Station. A little-known downtown hotel-casino that could be the most aesthetically pleasing and sophisticated in Las Vegas; it abounds with antiques, art, and expensive wood, brass, bronze, and stained glass. The rooms were renovated in 1997. 3 restaurants, bar. In-room data ports, in-room safes, no-smoking rooms. Cable TV. Business services. | 406 rooms | 200 N. Main St. | 702/387–1896 or 800/634–6255 (reservations) | fax 702/386–4421 | $39–$59 | AE, D, DC, MC, V.

Maxim. A compact and quiet hotel-casino two blocks from the Strip, good-value rooms for the slightly inconvenient location. 2 restaurants. No-smoking rooms. Pool. Barbershop, beauty salon. Business services. | 798 rooms | 160 E. Flamingo Rd. | 702/731–4300 or 800/634–6987 | fax 702/735–3252 | maxim@anu.net | www.maximhotel.com | $39–$109 | AE, D, DC, MC, V.

New Frontier. The oldest casino on the Strip was built first in 1942, then torn down and rebuilt three times. Lodging is utilitarian and unthemed; the Atrium Tower, built in 1990, is all mini-suites. 4 restaurants, bar. In-room data ports, some in-room safes, no-smoking rooms. Cable TV. Pool. Barbershop, beauty salon, hot tub. Tennis courts. Game room. Business services. | 987 rooms, 384 suites | 3120 Las Vegas Blvd. S | 702/794–8200 or 800/634–6966 (reservations) | fax 702/794–8230 | $35–$69 | AE, D, DC, MC, V.

Orleans. Opened in late 1996, this locals' casino has a huge following. Some of the best video poker schedules in town are found here, combined with an excellent slot club. Bargain rooms, a great view of the Strip from east-facing side, a child-care facility, a 12-plex movie theater, swinging lounge entertainment, and a giant bowling alley upstairs make this a place with something for everyone. 5 restaurants, bar. No-smoking rooms. Cable TV. Pool. Barbershop, beauty salon. Game room. Baby-sitting. Business services. | 840 rooms | 4500 W. Tropicana Ave. | 702/365–7111 or 800/675–3267 (reservations) | fax 702/365–7499 | $49–$199 | AE, D, DC, MC, V.

Palace Station Hotel and Casino. The original locals' casino, this place launched the concept in the late '80s. It's off-Strip, with plenty of parking, great cheap food (including the first super buffet), lots of slots and video poker, easy comps, promotion-intensive. It's been eclipsed in the past few years by sister resorts (Boulder, Texas, and Sunset Stations), along with Orleans and Arizona Charlie's, but it still draws the local crowds. 5 restaurants, bar. No-smoking rooms. Cable TV. 2 pools. Hot tubs. Game room. Business services. | 1,029 rooms | 2411 W. Sahara Ave. | 702/367–2411 or 800/634–3101 (outside NV) | fax 702/367–2478 | $99–$149 | AE, D, DC, MC, V.

Plaza. The anchor of downtown, this place opened in 1970 and is probably the most photographed resort in town. Cheap rooms are always available. Its Centerstage is one of Vegas's best bargain steak houses with what is definitely the greatest view: right down Glitter Gulch. You get lounge and showroom entertainment as well as a wedding chapel. 3 restaurants, bar. No-smoking rooms. Cable TV. Pool, wading pool. Tennis. Laundry facilities. Business services. | 1,037 rooms | 1 Main St. | 702/386–2110 or 800/634–6575 | fax 702/382–8281 | http://www.plazahotelcasino.com/ | $25–$75 | AE, D, DC, MC, V.

Santa Fe Station Hotel & Casino. Highly popular locals' hotel-casino in the far northern suburbs. Mostly comped players and relatives of locals stay here. Ice-skating, bowling, bingo, and promotions galore. 5 restaurants, bar. No-smoking rooms. Cable TV. Bowling. Ice-skating. Game room. Children's programs. Business services, meeting room. | 200 rooms | 4949 N. Rancho Dr. | 702/658–4900 or 800/872–6823 | fax 702/658–4919 | $39–$99 | AE, D, DC, MC, V.

Showboat. The largest bowling alley in the country lies within this first hotel-casino to be built outside of downtown and the Strip. It's popular with locals and loyal visitors. Many of the bowling tournaments are televised. 5 restaurants, bar. No-smoking rooms. Cable TV. Pool. Bowling. Game room. Business services. Airport shuttle. | 451 rooms | 2800 E. Fremont St. | 702/385–9123 or 800/826–2800 (outside NV) | fax 702/383–9238 | $39–$125 | AE, D, DC, MC, V.

Silverton. Formerly known as Boomtown, this small locals' hotel is 4 mi south of the Strip. 2 restaurants. No-smoking rooms. Cable TV. 2 pools, wading pool. Hot tub. Laundry facilities. Business services. | 300 rooms | 3333 Blue Diamond Rd. | 702/263–7777 or 800/588–7711 | fax 702/896–5635 | feedback@silvertoncasino.com | http://www.silvertoncasino.com/ | $35–$75 | AE, D, DC, MC, V.

Texas Station. This is the fourth of four great Station casinos in the neighborhoods of Vegas. Restaurant, bars. Cable TV. Pool. | 200 rooms | 2101 Texas Star La., North Las Vegas | 702/631–1000 or 800/654–8888 | fax 702/631–8120 | $49 | AE, D, DC, MC, V.

Travelodge–Downtown. The name notwithstanding, this small, standard chain motel is not within walking distance of downtown. No-smoking rooms. Cable TV. Pool. Pets allowed. | 58 rooms | 2028 E. Fremont St. | 702/384–7540 | fax 702/384–0408 | $35–$85 | AE, D, DC, MC, V.

Travelodge–Las Vegas Strip. With a great location right next to Circus Circus and easy in and out and parking right at the room, the motel also has comfortable, standard rooms. Complimentary Continental breakfast. No-smoking rooms. Cable TV. Pool. Business services. | 100 rooms | 2830 Las Vegas Blvd. | 702/735–4222 | fax 702/733–7695 | $50–$125 | AE, D, DC, MC, V.

Westward Ho Hotel & Casino. The largest motel in the world is a sprawling low-rise Strip resort-casino. You can get good deals on suites, some of which sleep six, and parking is close to the rooms. There's a lounge and showroom. 2 restaurants, bar. Some microwaves, no-smoking rooms, some refrigerators. Cable TV. 4 pools. Hot tubs. Airport shuttle. | 777 rooms | 2900 Las Vegas Blvd. S | 702/731–2900 or 800/634–6803 (outside NV) | fax 702/731–6154 | www.westwardho.com | $36–$89 | AE, MC, V.

MODERATE

Bally's. Originally the MGM Grand, built in 1973, this became Bally's in 1986. The location is fabulous, and the rooms are large and were recently renovated. The parking garage is some distance from the room tower elevators, but shuttles run between them. 6 restaurants, bar. In-room data ports, some in-room safes, no-smoking floors, some refrigerators. Cable TV. Pool. Barbershop, beauty salon, hot tub. Tennis courts. Exercise equipment. Business services. | 2,814 rooms | 3645 Las Vegas Blvd. S | 702/739–4111 or 800/634–3434 | fax 702/739–3848 | www.ballyslv.com | $99–$430 | AE, D, DC, MC, V.

Barbary Coast. A tiny Strip hotel-casino with a huge Strip location across from Bally's, Caesars, Bellagio, and Flamingo Hilton. 2 restaurants, bar. No-smoking rooms. Cable TV. Free parking. | 200 rooms | 3595 Las Vegas Blvd. S | 702/737–7111 or 800/634–6755 (outside NV) | fax 702/894–9954 | www.barbarycoastcasino.com | $75–$205 | AE, D, DC, MC, V.

Boulder Station. This classy locals' casino on Boulder Strip opened in 1994. Known for good food at great prices. There's a Kid's Quest child-care facility and a 12-plex movie theater. 5 restaurants, bars. In-room data ports, no-smoking rooms. Cable TV. Pool. Business services. | 300 rooms | 4111 Boulder Hwy. | 702/432–7777 or 800/683–7777 | fax 702/432–7744 | www.stationcasinos.com | $50–$140 | AE, D, DC, MC, V.

California. Downtown hotel-casino that caters primarily to Hawaiian package tours and has a strong aloha vibration. An enclosed pedestrian overpass connects the hotel to Main Street Station. 3 restaurants, bar. No-smoking rooms, some refrigerators. Cable TV. Pool. Hot tub. | 781 rooms | 12 Ogden Ave. | 702/385–1222 or 800/634–6255 | fax 702/388–2660 | www.thecal.com/ | $35–$110 | AE, D, DC, MC, V.

Carriage House. Small off-Strip, all-suite, non-casino hotel. Its west-facing rooms and restaurant/bar on the 9th floor have great views of south Strip. Restaurant, bar. In-room data ports, microwaves, no-smoking rooms, refrigerators. Cable TV. Pool. Hot tub. Tennis.

KODAK'S TIPS FOR PHOTOGRAPHING THE CITY

Streets
- Take a bus or walking tour to get acclimated
- Explore markets, streets, and parks
- Travel light so you can shoot quickly

City Vistas
- Find high vantage points to reveal city views
- Shoot early or late in the day, for best light
- At twilight, use fast films and bracket exposures

Formal Gardens
- Exploit high angles to show garden design
- Use wide-angle lenses to exaggerate depth and distance
- Arrive early to beat crowds

Landmarks and Monuments
- Review postcard racks for traditional views
- Seek out distant or unusual views
- Look for interesting vignettes or details

Museums
- Call in advance regarding photo restrictions
- Match film to light source when color is critical
- Bring several lenses or a zoom

Houses of Worship
- Shoot exteriors from nearby with a wide-angle lens
- Move away and include surroundings
- Switch to a very fast film indoors

Stained-Glass Windows
- Bright indirect sunlight yields saturated colors
- Expose for the glass not the surroundings
- Switch off flash to avoid glare

Architectural Details
- Move close to isolate details
- For distant vignettes, use a telephoto lens
- Use side light to accent form and texture

In the Marketplace
- Get up early to catch peak activity
- Search out colorful displays and colorful characters
- Don't scrimp on film

Stage Shows and Events
- Never use flash
- Shoot with fast (ISO 400 to 1000) film
- Use telephoto lenses
- Focus manually if necessary

From *Kodak Guide to Shooting Great Travel Pictures* © 2000 by Fodor's Travel Publications

Laundry facilities. Business services. Airport shuttle. | 155 kitchen suites | 105 E. Harmon Ave. | 702/798–1020 or 800/221–2301 | fax 702/798–1020 | $99–$525 | AE, D, DC, MC, V.

Courtyard by Marriott. This lower-priced Marriott opened in 1989 with gorgeous grounds and king-size beds. Restaurant, bar. In-room data ports, no-smoking rooms, some refrigerators. Cable TV. Pool. Hot tub. Exercise equipment. Laundry facilities. Business services. Airport shuttle. | 149 rooms | 3275 Paradise Rd. | 702/791–3600 or 800/321–2211 | fax 702/796–7981 | www.marriot.com | $99–$169 | AE, D, DC, MC, V.

Flamingo Hilton. The house that Bugsy built in 1946, though he wouldn't recognize a bit of it. It's been expanded a dozen times in the past 53 years, and now has the best water park in town, complete with African penguins. 7 restaurants, bar. In-room data ports, some refrigerators, some in-room safes, no-smoking floors. Cable TV. 5 pools. Barbershop, beauty salon, hot tubs. Exercise equipment. Business services, convention center. | 3,642 rooms | 3555 Las Vegas Blvd. S | 702/733–3111 or 800/732–2111 (outside NV) | fax 702/733–3353 | $69–$700. | AE, D, DC, MC, V.

Four Queens. A major downtown hotel-casino, this opened in 1965. Reserve early if you want a big room; they go quickly. 2 restaurants, bar. No-smoking rooms. Cable TV. Business services. | 730 rooms | 202 Fremont St. | 702/385–4011 or 800/634–6045 | fax 702/387–5122 | $29–$150. | AE, D, DC, MC, V.

Golden Nugget. The classiest and largest hotel-casino downtown is also one of the few with a pool. There's also a lounge and showroom. 5 restaurants, bar. In-room data ports, in-room safes, no-smoking rooms, some refrigerators. Cable TV. Pool. Hot tub, massage. Gym. Business services. | 1,907 rooms | 129 E. Fremont St. | 702/385–7111 or 800/634–3454 (outside NV) | fax 702/386–8362 | $49–$279 | AE, D, DC, MC, V.

Hard Rock. The world's only Hard Rock casino-hotel, a mecca for hip young brand loyalists, opened in 1994. The rock 'n' roll theme is set with tons of memorabilia, continuous live concerts, and some of Las Vegas's friendliest employees. No lounge entertainment, though. The rooms are great—and hard to get. 3 restaurants. No-smoking rooms. Cable TV. Pool. Gym. Business services. | 340 rooms | 4455 Paradise Rd. | 702/693–5000 or 800/473–7625 | fax 702/693–5021 | www.hardrock.com | $95–$185 | AE, D, DC, MC, V.

Harrah's. Another Strip megaresort opened in 1970, expanded several times, and recently renovated. The latest expansion added 700 rooms in 1997. A great location, with lounge and showroom. Restaurant, bars. No-smoking floors. Cable TV. Pool. Barbershop, beauty salon, hot tub, massage. Exercise equipment. Game room. Business services. | 2,699 rooms | 3475 Las Vegas Blvd. S | 702/369–5000 or 800/427–7247 (reservations) | fax 702/733–6724 | $89–$500 | AE, D, DC, MC, V.

Holiday Inn Crowne Plaza Suites. This non-casino hotel is a good place to stay if you're here on business other than gambling. The suites are large, and it's close to both the airport and the Convention Center. Restaurant, bar. In-room data ports, in-room safes, mini-bars, no-smoking floors. Cable TV. Pool. Hot tub. Exercise equipment. Business services. Airport shuttle. Pets allowed. | 201 suites | 4255 Paradise Rd. | 702/369–4400 or 800/2CROWNE | fax 702/369–3770 | www.crowneplaza.com | $145–$185 | AE, D, DC, MC, V.

Imperial Palace. An Asian-themed Strip megaresort is scrunched into a small lot, so it built up instead of out. The coffee shop is on the second floor, a theater on the third, restaurants on the fourth, an auto museum on the fifth floor of the parking garage, etc. Most of the rooms are standard chain quality; some are original (1970s) and shabby. Lounge and showroom. 6 restaurants, bar. In-room data ports, no-smoking rooms, some refrigerators. Cable TV. Pool. Barbershop, beauty salon, hot tub. Exercise equipment. Business services. Free self-parking or valet parking. | 2,700 rooms | 3535 Las Vegas Blvd. S | 702/731–3311 or 800/634–6441 (outside NV), 800/351–7400 (in NV) | fax 702/735–8578 | www.imperial-palace.com | $49–$499 | AE, D, DC, MC, V.

Lady Luck Casino. A popular downtown casino slightly off the beaten gulch. Big picture windows brighten the casino. Rooms and mini-suites are a great deal. 4 restaurants, bar. No-smoking rooms, refrigerators. Cable TV. Pool. Airport shuttle. | 792 rooms | 206 N. 3rd St. | 702/477–3000 or 800/523–9582 | fax 702/477–7021 | www.ladyluck.com/lasvegas/index.html | $39–$105 | AE, D, DC, MC, V.

Las Vegas Club. One of the oldest hotels in town doubled its size in 1996 with a new hotel tower. Sports memorabilia cover the walls. The rooms are a good value. 3 restaurants. Some in-room safes, no-smoking rooms. Cable TV. Business services. | 418 rooms | 18 E. Fremont St. | 702/385–1664 or 800/634–6532 (reservations) | $45–$350 | AE, D, DC, MC, V.

Luxor. One of the world's most unusual hotels and the second-largest in Las Vegas, this 2,500-room pyramid opened in 1993 (with a 2,000-room expansion completed in 1996). Inside is the world's largest atrium. "Inclinators" (elevators) run up the 30 floors at a 39-degree angle. The shape is disorienting, though; finding your room can be an adventure. 6 restaurants, bar. In-room safes, no-smoking floors. Cable TV. 5 pools, wading pool. Barbershop, beauty salon, massage. Exercise equipment. Business services. | 4,474 rooms, 473 suites | 3900 Las Vegas Blvd. S | 702/262–4000 or 800/288–1000 | fax 702/262–4452 | www.luxor.com | $69–$309 | AE, D, DC, MC, V.

MGM Grand. Largest hotel in the world—largest casino, largest porte cochere, largest parking garage, largest video wall. Checking in and out for a weekend stay can cause the world's largest headache: come early Friday and leave late Sunday. Once you're in, though, you don't have to leave. Everything is here from an events arena to an amusement park to a wedding chapel. 9 restaurants, bar. In-room data ports, in-room safes, no-smoking floors. Cable TV. Pool, wading pool. Barbershop, beauty salon, spa. Tennis courts. Gym. Game room. Children's programs (ages 3–12). Business services, convention facilities. | 5,005

KODAK'S TIPS FOR PHOTOGRAPHING PEOPLE

Friends' Faces
- Pose subjects informally to keep the mood relaxed
- Try to work in shady areas to avoid squints
- Let kids pick their own poses

Strangers' Faces
- In crowds, work from a distance with a telephoto lens
- Try posing cooperative subjects
- Stick with gentle lighting—it's most flattering to faces

Group Portraits
- Keep the mood informal
- Use soft, diffuse lighting
- Try using a panoramic camera

People at Work
- Capture destination-specific occupations
- Use tools for props
- Avoid flash if possible

Sports
- Fill the frame with action
- Include identifying background
- Use fast shutter speeds to stop action

Silly Pictures
- Look for or create light-hearted situations
- Don't be inhibited
- Try a funny prop

Parades and Ceremonies
- Stake out a shooting spot early
- Show distinctive costumes
- Isolate crowd reactions
- Be flexible: content first, technique second

From Kodak Guide to Shooting Great Travel Pictures © 2000 by Fodor's Travel Publications

rooms, 751 suites | 3799 Las Vegas Blvd. S | 702/891–1111 or 800/929–1111 | fax 702/891–1030 | www.mgmgrand.com | $89–$549 | AE, D, DC, MC, V.

Monte Carlo. Built in a record 14 months, the Monte Carlo opened in 1996. It combines European elegance and American informality with a great location. It offers frequent good deals on rooms. It does not have much by way of a theme, which is a plus if what you're looking for is a good hotel. It does have a water park. 6 restaurants, bars. In-room data ports, no-smoking floors. Cable TV. Pool. Tennis. Gym. Game room. Business services. | 3,002 rooms | Las Vegas Blvd. S | 702/730–7777 or 800/311–8999 (reservations) | fax 702/730–7200 | www.montecarlo.com | $69–$269 | AE, D, DC, MC, V.

New York–New York. Most highly themed hotel-casino in town: mini–New York skyline; Brooklyn Bridge; Coney Island-like roller coaster; Central Park casino; Greenwich Village food court; cramped and crowded and claustrophobic. Gawkers abound; gridlock is common. Rooms are (sub)standard. Lounge and showroom. 5 restaurants, bar. In-room data ports, in-room safes, no-smoking floors, some refrigerators. Cable TV. Pool. Barbershop, beauty salon, hot tub. Business services. | 2,034 rooms | 3790 Las Vegas Blvd. S | 702/740–6969 or 800/695–8284 (reservations) | fax 702/740–6920 | $89–$499 | AE, D, DC, MC, V.

Residence Inn by Marriott. Great for business travelers and families, these apartmentlike rooms all have eat-in kitchens and some have working fireplaces, in condolike units. The grounds and gardens are lush. Complimentary Continental breakfast. No-smoking rooms. Cable TV, VCRs and movies. Pool. Hot tub. Laundry facilities. Business services. Airport shuttle. Some pets allowed (fee). | 192 kitchenette suites | 3225 Paradise Rd. | 702/796–9300 | fax 702/796–9562 | $79–$500 | AE, D, DC, MC, V.

Riviera. One of a handful of '50s hotel-casinos left on the Strip, the Riviera has been expanded numerous times and is a typical maze of elevators and room towers. It's the only joint that fronts the Strip and backs up almost to the Convention Center. It has four showrooms and a fast-food court. Most of the rooms have been renovated. 5 restaurants, bar. No-smoking floors, some refrigerators. Cable TV. Pool. Barbershop, beauty salon, hot tub. Tennis courts. Exercise equipment. Business services. | 2,100 rooms | 2901 Las Vegas Blvd. S | 702/734–5110 or 800/634–6753 (outside NV) | fax 702/794–9663 | $29–$239 | AE, D, DC, MC, V.

Sahara. Like the Riviera, the Sahara was built in the early 1950s, though nothing remains of the original joint. It was recently remodeled. It's a 10-minute walk to the Convention Center. There's a large virtual-reality racing area called Speedworld. Lounge and showroom entertainment. 5 restaurants, bar. No-smoking floors, some refrigerators. Cable TV. Pool. Business services. | 1,716 rooms | 2535 Las Vegas Blvd. S | 702/737–2111 or 800/695–8284 | fax 702/791–2027 | $29–$350 | AE, D, DC, MC, V.

Sam's Town. Large locals' hotel 20 minutes from the Strip on Boulder Highway; a country-and-western theme with biggest Western-wear store in town. There's a large parklike indoor atrium and dancing-waters spectacle, along with Vegas's best sports bar with half-court basketball. Newer rooms are spacious. 8 restaurants. No-smoking rooms. Cable TV. Pool. Laundry facilities. Business services. | 648 rooms | 5111 Boulder Hwy. | 702/456–7777 or 800/634–6371 | fax 702/454–8014 | roomres@samstown.boydnet | $39–$199 | AE, D, DC, MC, V.

San Remo. A medium-sized hotel-casino in an excellent location, a three-minute walk from the Tropicana-Strip Four Corners intersection and a $5 cab ride from the airport. 3 restaurants, bar. No-smoking rooms. Cable TV. Pool. Business services. | 711 rooms | 115 E. Tropicana Ave. | 702/739–9000 or 800/522–7366 | fax 702/736–1120 | $39–$229 | AE, D, DC, MC, V.

Stardust Resort & Casino. This was the largest hotel in the world when it opened in 1958. It is a typical sprawling '50s casino; the original "garden" rooms (renovated many times) are a good deal. 6 restaurants, bar. No-smoking rooms, some refrigerators. Cable TV. 2 pools. Barbershop, beauty salon. Game room. Business services. | 2,341 rooms | 3000 Las Vegas Blvd. S | 702/732–6111 or 800/634–6757 | fax 702/732–6296 | roomres@stardust.com | www.vegas.com | $36–$350 | AE, D, DC, MC, V.

Stratosphere Tower. The tallest building west of the Mississippi offers two thrill rides at the top of the tower and a big shopping mall at the bottom. Its casino and hotel rooms are unremarkable, however, and its tough location three blocks north of the Strip accounts for its frequent bargains on rooms. Lounge and showroom. 5 restaurants, bar. No-smoking rooms. Cable TV. Pool. | 1,500 rooms | 2000 Las Vegas Blvd. S | 702/380–7777 or 800/998–6937 | fax 702/380–7732 | www.grandcasinos.com | $29–$450 | AE, D, DC, MC, V.

Treasure Island. This themed megaresort opened in 1993 next to the Mirage. It presents a Buccaneer Bay pirate battle out front, the greatest free spectacle in town. The game arcade is big; the hotel rooms are small. Lounge and showroom. 7 restaurants, bar. In-room data ports, in-room safes, no-smoking rooms, some refrigerators. Cable TV. 2 pools, wading pool. Barbershop, beauty salon. Exercise equipment. Business services. | 2,679 rooms | 3300 Las Vegas Blvd. S | 702/894–7111 or 800/944–7444 | fax 702/894–7414 | www.treasureislandlasvegas.com | $69–$299 | AE, D, DC, MC, V.

★ **Tropicana.** This is a '50s hotel-casino with some original bungalow rooms and the lushest pool area in town, complete with water slides and swim-up blackjack (heaters dry wet money). There's a Wildlife Walk in the tunnel between towers. The rooms have been renovated many times. Its location right at Four Corners is fabulous. Lounge and showroom. 6 restaurants, bar. No-smoking rooms, some refrigerators. Cable TV. Pool. Barbershop, beauty salon, hot tub. Exercise equipment. Business services. | 1,875 rooms | 3801 Las Vegas Blvd. S | 702/739–2222 or 800/634–4000 (outside NV) | fax 702/739–2469 | $69–$169 | AE, D, DC, MC, V.

EXPENSIVE

★ **Bellagio.** Opened in October 1998, Bellagio is the most expensive hotel ever built ($1.6 billion, not including $300 million for fine art). You enter via the 11-acre Lago di Bellagio; the lobby holds a $10 million glass-flower chandelier, the largest glass sculpture in the world. Next to the lobby is a 12,500-square-ft conservatory supplied by a 2-acre greenhouse and managed by the 115-employee garden department (the hotel's floral decor and aromas change with the seasons). The Gallery of Fine Art contains one of the finest collections of artwork in the world. The shopping is the most exclusive in town, and the restaurants are attractions in and of themselves (Picasso's has several of the painter's works on display). No children are allowed. Lounge and showroom. 11 restaurants, bar. In-room data ports, no-smoking floors, refrigerators in suites. Cable TV. Pool. Barbershop, beauty salon, massage. Gym. Business services. | 3,025 rooms | Las Vegas Blvd. S | 702/693–8771 or 888/987–6667 (reservations) | fax 702/693–8778 | www.bellagio.com | $159–$499 | AE, D, DC, MC, V.

Caesars Palace. One of the most famous hotels in the world opened in 1966. A half-dozen major expansions have turned it into a maze; the last one, in 1997, added 1,000 rooms. Caesars has everything; you never have to leave. Three lounges with entertainment; showroom. 19 restaurants, bar. In-room data ports, no-smoking floors, some refrigerators, some in-room hot tubs. Cable TV. 4 pools, 2 hot tubs. Barbershop, beauty salon, massage. Gym. Racquetball. Game room. Business services. Parking garage. | 2,750 rooms | 3570 Las Vegas Blvd. S | 702/731–7110 or 800/634–6001 (outside NV) | fax 702/731–6636 | www.caesarspalace.com | $59–$2,500 | AE, D, DC, MC, V.

Desert Inn. The smallest and most exclusive resort-casino on the Strip, opened in 1950. It has a country-club atmosphere and gorgeous, expansive grounds. It offers a high-limit casino and gourmet dining with a dress code. The structure was completely renovated in 1998 and given a new facade. 4 restaurants, bars, room service. In-room data ports, no-smoking rooms, refrigerators in suites. Cable TV. Pool. Hot tub. Driving range, 18-hole golf course, putting green, tennis courts. Gym. Business services. | 3,025 rooms | 3145 Las Vegas Blvd. S | 702/733–4444 or 800/634–6906 | fax 702/733–4676 | www.thedesertinn.com | $220–$500 | AE, D, DC, MC, V.

Las Vegas Hilton. Next door to the Las Vegas Convention Center (10–15 minutes' walk from the Strip), the Hilton mostly caters to a business clientele. Also to Star Trekkies: Paramount's $70 million Star Trek museum and thrill ride The Experience is here. Biggest sports book in town. 8 restaurants, bar. In-room data ports, in-room safes, no-smoking floors, some refrigerators. Cable TV. Pool. Barbershop, beauty salon, hot tub, massage. Putting green, tennis courts. Gym. Game room. Business services. | 3,174 rooms | 3000 Paradise Rd. | 702/732–5111 | fax 702/794–3611 | www.lv/hilton.com | $99–$1,540 | AE, D, DC, MC, V.

Mirage. A South Seas fantasy atmosphere prevails here, but the service and room amenities are down to earth. Marble and palms, a 100-ft-high glass dome, and an immense aquarium, exclusive shopping, home of *Siegfried and Roy* and California Pizza Kitchen, a man-made volcano, and peel-and-eat-shrimp buffet—the Mirage launched the era of the megaresort and still sets the standard. 6 restaurants, bar. In-room data ports, in-room safes, no-smoking floors, refrigerators in suites. Cable TV. Pool. Barbershop, beauty salon, massage. Gym. Business services. | 3,044 rooms | 3400 Las Vegas Blvd. S | 702/791–7111 or 800/723–1723 (reservations) | fax 702/791–7446 | www.mirage.com | $79–$1,100 | AE, D, DC, MC, V.

★ **Rio Suite Hotel & Casino.** One of the great resorts in Las Vegas opened in 1990 and has been under continuous expansion ever since (the latest 1,000-room tower was completed in early 1997). All rooms are suites with big picture windows and sitting areas. There are a bunch of restaurants, including two buffets (one is an excellent daily seafood buffet). There's an extensive pool area, upscale shopping mall, Parade in the Sky spectacle, and excellent service. 13 restaurants, 2 bars. No-smoking floors, refrigerators. Cable TV. 3 pools. Barbershop, beauty salon, massage, hot tubs. Exercise equipment. Business services. | 2,563 suites | 3700 W. Flamingo Rd. | 702/252–7777 or 800/752–9746 | fax 702/252–7670 | www.playrio.com | $95–$149; mid–wk rates | AE, D, DC, MC, V.

St. Tropez. St. Tropez, across the street from the Hard Rock Cafe/Casino, features newly decorated suites in a two-story stucco hotel. Bar. In-room data ports, minibars, no-smoking rooms, refrigerators. Cable TV, in-room VCRs. Pool. Exercise equipment. Business services. Airport and Strip shuttle. | 149 suites | 455 E. Harmon Ave. | 702/369–5400 or 800/666–5400 | fax 702/369–5400 | $95–$250; family rates | AE, D, DC, MC, V.

VERY EXPENSIVE

Alexis Park Resort. This sprawling, upscale low-rise business hotel is minutes from the airport and the Convention Center. All rooms are mini-suites, and there's no casino (an attractive feature to some). Restaurant, bar. In-room data ports, minibars, refrigerators, no-smoking rooms, some in-room hot tubs. Cable TV. 3 pools. Barbershop, beauty salon, hot tub. Putting green. Exercise equipment. Business services. Some pets allowed (fee). | 500 suites | 375 E. Harmon Ave. | 702/796–3300 or 800/582–2228 (outside NV) | fax 702/796–4334 | $99–$500 1–bedroom, $475–$1,000 2–bedroom; under 12 free | AE, D, DC, MC, V.

★ **Four Seasons.** On the top floors of the Mandalay Bay complex, with its own private entrance, elevators, and pool and recreation area, this is one of the finest hotels in Las Vegas. It's also one of the only places in town with no slot machines or gaming tables. Rooms have views of the mountains, desert, and the Strip. Afternoon tea is served daily in the lobby lounge. The deluxe guest rooms have hair dryers, irons, robes, and two phone lines with voice mail. | 338 rooms, 86 suites. Restaurants, bar, in-room data ports, in-room safes, no-smoking rooms, refrigerators, room service, pool, hot tub, massage, sauna, steam room, exercise room, laundry facilities, concierge, business services, airport shuttle, valet parking. | 3950 Las Vegas Blvd. S | 702/632–5000 | fax 702/632–5222 | $225–$450 | AE, D, DC, MC, V.

LAUGHLIN

MAP 10, F9

(Nearby town also listed: Boulder City)

Nevada's biggest border town, drawing from southern California and northwestern Arizona, Laughlin was founded in the late 1960s by Don Laughlin, the local latter-day pioneer and owner of the Riverside Resort-Casino, the first joint you pass coming into town from the north. Eight other casinos (seven major and one minor) are strung along Casino Drive. Their back doors hug the west bank of the Colorado River. They all arrived in the 1980s, when Laughlin was at its peak in terms of commercial and population growth.

Maybe Laughlin is overbuilt, since its revenues have been flat throughout the '90s. No matter. Competition for customers is so intense that rooms are as good as free and food prices are rock-bottom. Also, the river is right at hand, providing abundant recreation and blessed relief from the blistering heat in the summer—regularly 4 to 7 degrees hotter than Vegas and often the hottest spot in the country.

Another thing that recommends Laughlin: the casinos are airy and bright, with big picture windows overlooking the river.

Information: **Laughlin Chamber of Commerce.** | 1725 S. Casino Dr., 89125 | 702/298–2214 or 800/227–5245. **Laughlin Visitors Bureau.** | 1555 S. Casino Dr., 89125 | 702/298–3022 or 800/4–LAUGHLIN.

Attractions

Davis Dam. Completed in 1953, Davis Dam impounds the lower Colorado in Lake Mojave, which stretches in a long thin line almost all the way to Hoover Dam. The dam produces electricity and controls the river flow; the lake irrigates southern Nevada and northwestern Arizona and provides boaters and anglers with abundant recreation. You can take a self-guided tour. | www.enjoylaughlin.com/visitor/davisdam.htm | Free | Daily 7:30–3:30 (Mountain Time).

Lake Mead National Recreation Area. *See* Boulder City.

Public Beach. Commercial water sports are plentiful in Laughlin, which hugs the Colorado River; you can find Jet Skis, waterskiing, boat rides, and the like at the kiosks lining the strand that runs along the back sides of the resorts. Amazingly, however, there's only one public beach in the Laughlin casino core. It's on Harrah's property, just south of the hotel. Park in the lot and mosey down to the river. There's a concession renting beach equipment and selling drinks, suntan lotion, and T-shirts. | 2900 S. Casino Dr. | 702/298–4600 | Free | Daily.

ON THE CALENDAR

MAY: *Laughlin Riverdays.* Twenty-five Pro Racing Outboard Performance teams compete in Formula One boat races on the Colorado River for $1 million in prize money. A classic rock festival and water-oriented games and contests are also featured. | 702/298–2214.

OCT.: *River Flight.* A hot-air balloon rally with more than 100 balloons launching before dawn over the Colorado River. Pilots compete in touching-down contests and dropping bean bags onto targets. Celebrity headliners, street fair. | 702/298–2214.

Lodging

Colorado Belle. An anomaly in Nevada: a riverboat casino actually on a river. This is a huge casino with a Mississippi riverboat theme and bargain rooms and food. 3 restaurants, bar, room service. No-smoking floors. Cable TV. 2 pools. Hot tub. Business services. Airport shuttle. | 1,230 rooms | 2100 Casino Dr. | 702/298–4000 or 800/477–4837 | fax 702/298–2597 | www.coloradobelle.com/main.htm | $19–$40 | AE, D, DC, MC, V.

Cottonwood Cove Resort And Marina. This is a full-scale resort facility right on Lake Mojave. The standard one-story motel is surrounded by pleasant grassy grounds. Restaurant, bar, picnic area. No-smoking rooms, some refrigerators. Cable TV. Beach, boating, jet skiing, waterskiing. Fishing. Pets allowed. | 24 rooms | 1000 Cottonwood Cove Rd. | 702/297–1464 | fax 702/297–1464 | $55–$95 | AE, D, MC, V.

Don Laughlin's Riverside Resort. This was the first joint in Laughlin, owned by the town's founder and namesake. It has been repeatedly expanded in the last 30 years, most recently with the addition of a 1,000-room tower. Lounge and showroom. 4 restaurants, bar. No-smoking rooms. Cable TV. 2 pools. Business services. Airport shuttle. | 1,404 rooms | 1650 Casino Dr. | 702/298–2535 or 800/227–3849 | fax 702/298–2231 | www.riversideresort.com | $18–$109 | AE, D, DC, MC, V.

Edgewater Hotel/Casino. Like the Colorado Belle, its sister hotel next door, the Edgewater is a sprawling affair. A 1,000-room tower opened in 1992. 3 restaurants, bar. No-smoking floors. Cable TV. Pool. Hot tub. Airport shuttle. | 1,452 rooms | 2020 Casino Dr. | 702/298–2453 or 800/677–4837 | fax 702/298–8165 | www.edgewater-casino.com/ | $19–$80 | AE, D, DC, MC, V.

Flamingo Hilton–Laughlin. The largest and newest hotel-casino in Laughlin opened in 1990. It offers large rooms and an airy casino. 5 restaurants, bar, room service. Some in-room safes, no-smoking rooms. Cable TV. Pool. Tennis courts. Business services. Airport shuttle. | 1,971 rooms | 1900 S. Casino Dr. | 702/298–5111 | fax 702/298–5129 | www.laughlinflamingo.com/ | $17–$189 | AE, D, DC, MC, V.

Golden Nugget. This is the smallest hotel in town, reminiscent of the Las Vegas Mirage, with a tropical atrium and classy casino. 3 restaurants, bar. No-smoking rooms. Cable TV. Pool. Hot tub. Business services. Airport shuttle. | 300 rooms | 2300 Casino Dr. | 702/298–7111 or 800/950–7700 | fax 702/298–7122 | www.gnlaughlin.com/ | $21–$99 | AE, D, MC, V.

Harrah's. A gorgeous south-of-the-border-themed resort, this is the only hotel-casino with a public beach on the river. 4 restaurants, bars. No-smoking floors. Cable TV. Pool. Barber. Exercise equipment. Beach. Airport shuttle. | 1,652 rooms. | 2300 S. Casino Dr. | 702/298–4600 or 800/427–7247 | fax 702/298–6855 | $19–$74 | AE, D, DC, MC, V.

Pioneer Hotel & Casino. A cramped and crowded low-rise hotel-casino right on the river. Frequent bargain room specials; they're nearly given away. 2 restaurants, bar. No-smoking rooms, some refrigerators. Cable TV. Pool. Business services. Airport shuttle. | 415 rooms | 2200 S. Casino Dr. | 702/298–2442 or 800/634–3469 | fax 702/298–5256 | $17–$55 | AE, D, MC, V.

Ramada Express. A mini-train that runs around the hotel shuttles guests to the parking lots. This is the only resort on the non-river side of Casino Drive. 3 restaurants, bar. No-smoking floors, refrigerators in suites. Cable TV. Pool. Game room. Business services. Airport shuttle. | 1,501 rooms | 2121 Casino Dr. | 702/298–4200 | fax 702/298–6403 | www.ramadaexpress.com | $16–$49 | AE, D, DC, MC, V.

River Palms Resort & Casino. Formerly the Gold River, this is a four-level casino, with one of the few balconies overlooking the action in the state. 4 restaurants, bar. No-smoking rooms. Cable TV. Pool. Hot tub. Exercise equipment. Children's programs. Business services. Airport shuttle. | 1,003 rooms | 2700 S. Casino Dr. | 702/298–2242 or 800/835–7903 | fax 702/298–2117 | www.rvrpalm.com/hotel.html | $18–$200 | AE, D, DC, MC, V.

LOVELOCK

MAP 10, B3

(Nearby town also listed: Fallon)

George Lovelock homesteaded Lovelock Valley, well watered by the Humboldt River, in the 1860s. A few farmers and ranchers eked out a living in the area until the 1930s, when the Humboldt was dammed, creating Rye Patch Reservoir and stabilizing the flow of irrigation water over a 40,000-acre reclamation district. The farms grow livestock grain; several specialize in alfalfa seed. Lovelock is also the seat of Pershing County, twice the size of Connecticut; the county courthouse is one of only two round courthouses in the country. The town has a museum, a string of motels, and a medium-size casino.

Information: Lovelock/Pershing County Chamber of Commerce. | W. Marzen La., 89419 | 775/273–7213.

Attractions

Pershing County Museum. The restored Marzen House, from a local 3,400-acre 19th-century ranch, is home to the mostly agricultural heritage of the Lovelock area. Check out the big map of Lake Lahontan, which covered most of western Nevada only 15,000 years ago, and the wide-angle photograph of Lovelock from 1913, when it was bigger than it is today. | 2 W. Marzen La. | 775/273-7213. | Donations accepted | Tues.-Sun. 1:30-4.

Rye Patch State Recreation Area. Though Nevada has the image of being a desolate desert wasteland, it has 27 bodies of water large enough for boating. Rye Patch Dam impounds Humboldt River water in the 22-mi-long Rye Patch Reservoir for irrigating the Lovelock area's alfalfa farms and cattle ranches. You can boat, fish (for cutthroat trout, walleye, and bass), swim, and camp here. | 2505 Rye Patch Reservoir Rd. | 775/538-7321 | www.state.nv.us/stparks/ | $8 | 8-4.

ON THE CALENDAR

JULY: *Frontier Days.* This annual event held in the town's park has all sorts of competitions, such as weightlifting, arm wrestling, and a triathlon, plus a parade, street dances, and a carnival. | 775/273-7213.

AUG.: *World Fast-Draw Championship.* Contestants come from all over the world to compete in drawing single-action.45 revolvers in one of the most exciting and politically incorrect events of Nevada's year. | 775/575-5748.

Lodging

Lovelock Inn. A modern motel right off the I-80 west exit, next to the museum and Chamber of Commerce, No-smoking rooms. Pool. Pets allowed. | 37 rooms | 55 Cornell Ave. | 775/273-2937 | fax 775/273-2242 | $42-$59 | MC, V.

Sturgeon's Ramada Inn. This is the largest lodging in Lovelock, right at the east I-80 exit. It offers a big casino (for Lovelock), a coffee shop and steakhouse, and remodeled rooms. Restaurant. No-smoking rooms. Pool. Pets allowed. | 74 rooms | 1420 Cornell Ave. | 775/273-2971 or 888/298-2054 | fax 775/273-2278 | $39-$105 | AE, D, MC, V.

MINDEN-GARDNERVILLE

MAP 10, A5

(Nearby towns also listed: Carson City, Stateline)

The big Carson Valley was originally settled in the 1860s by John Gardner, who founded Gardnerville to serve as the supply center for the extensive valley ranches. The area was especially conducive to sheep ranching, and Basque shepherds gravitated to Gardnerville in the early 1900s. To this day the percentage of Basques in the town's population is greater than anywhere else in Nevada.

The Virginia and Truckee Railroad was extended from Carson City to the area in 1905, but the depot was built a little south of Gardnerville. The railroad town of Minden grew up around the depot.

The towns are contiguous, though each has its own history and flavor. Starting from the north, Minden's old buildings are industrial: a flour mill, a butter company, and the oldest operating car dealership in the state, with a garage dating back to 1910. Heading south, Gardnerville centers on the Overland, a Basque hotel dating back to 1909.

Information: Carson Valley Chamber of Commerce. | 1512 U.S. 395, Suite 1, 89410 | 775/782-8144 or 800/727-7677 | info@cvchamber.gardnerville.nv.us.

ON THE CALENDAR

JUNE: *Carson Valley Days.* The pioneer weekend festival has food booths, softball games, rodeo events, and a dance, all in downtown Lampe Park. | 775/782-1280 or 775/265-2021.

AUG.: *Carson Valley Fine Arts & Crafts Street Celebration.* Arts, crafts, food, music, and dance mark this street fair on Esmerelda Street in Minden. | 775/782–8144.

Lodging

Carson Valley Inn. The main action in town has expanded continually over the past decade and offers big, modern hotel rooms. 2 restaurants, bar, room service. No-smoking rooms, some refrigerators. Hot tub. Game room. Children's programs (ages 4–12). Business services. | 154 rooms | 1627 U.S. 395, Minden | 775/782–9711 or 800/321–6983 | fax 775/782–7472 | $49–$79 | AE, D, DC, MC, V.

Carson Valley Motor Lodge. A modest motel right next to the larger Carson Valley Inn. No-smoking rooms. Cable TV. | 76 rooms | 1643 U.S. 395, Minden | 775/782–9711 or 800/321–6983 | fax 775/782–7472 | www.cvn.com | $39–$59 | AE, D, DC, MC, V.

Nenzel Mansion. A Southern Colonial–style house with 12-ft ceilings and a huge great room. The guest rooms are up a 25-step staircase. The hosts live on the third floor. Complimentary breakfast. No room phones. Cable TV in sitting room. Pets allowed. | 4 rooms, 2 share bath | 1431 Ezell St. | 775/782–7644 | $80–$110 | MC, V.

OVERTON

MAP 10, F7

(Nearby towns also listed: Las Vegas)

Overton is a small farm town in Moapa Valley on the Muddy River. It's a fertile delta area, with the Virgin River on the other side of the valley a few miles east; both empty into the north end of Lake Mead. The northernmost outpost of the Anasazi Pueblo Indians was located hereabouts from around AD 1000 to 1250, and the area is rich in archaeological treasures. The Lost City Museum preserves and displays an extensive collection of them. Mormons began farming the valley in the 1860s, and many still do. The riverine habitat is great for waterfowl and trout.

Information: Moapa Valley Chamber of Commerce. | Box 361, 89040 | 702/397–2160 | www.moapavalley.com.

Attractions

Lake Mead National Recreation Area. *See* Boulder City for overall description.

Lost City Museum of Archaeology. Lost City is the site of a major outpost of Pueblo, or Anasazi, Indians dating back to the 13th century. Black-and-white photographs record the excavation in 1924. So many artifacts were unearthed that this museum claims one of the most complete collections of early Pueblo remains in the world. Other exhibits relate to the Mormon farmers who settled the rich delta area in the 1860s, and the filling up of Lake Mead in the 1930s and '40s. | 721 S. Moapa Valley Blvd. | 702/397–2193 | http://enos.comnett.net/~kolson/ | $2; under 18 free | Daily 8:30–4:30.

Overton Beach. Lake Mead stretches nearly 50 mi from Hoover Dam to the Overton Arm, at the mouth of the Muddy River. Overton Beach is a few miles downstream, the last of three small resorts along Route 167, also known as Northshore Road. There's a marina, complete with gas dock, grocery store, and laundry; an RV park and swimming beach are also on the premises. The Overton Beach area boasts the best fishing on Lake Mead, since the Muddy and nearby Virgin rivers deliver plenty of fish food. | Rte. 167 | 702/394–4040 | Free | Daily.

Valley of Fire State Park. Nevada's oldest state park, Valley of Fire is 46,000 acres of stunning red-rock formations. Arches, sheer walls, jagged pinnacles, beehives, red sand, petrified wood, petroglyphs, and natural erosion keep your eyes popping from start to finish. Elephant Rock, Seven Sisters, Mouse's Tank, and Rainbow Vista are a few of the attractions; Atlatl Rock is a large flat sandstone bulletin board for prehistoric graffiti; Nevada's tallest

a,

a slot-
k, and an
ld-class sk
and Pyramic
also only a sho
nearly year-roun

5 Marsh Ave., 8950
no-sparkschamber.c
rginia St., 89502 | 775/8

(a.k.a. U.S. 395 Business), which
n. Downtown hosts a dozen majo
al Automobile Museum and Neva
nearly 2 mi along the Truckee River

s is the historic residential neighborhoo
rich Nevadans, flush from the mining boo
atial homes. Frederic de Longchamps, Neva
any of them.
iversity District is north of downtown on Virgi
tes back to the 1880s, when four-story Morrill Hal
e school). In the early 1900s, noted New York archite
buildings that surround the central quadrangle in th
cho San Rafael, a 408-acre municipal park, sprawls

d/Smithridge. The Meadowwood and Smithridge area, 4 mi s
d the intersection of South Virginia Street and McCarran Bo
main commercial district, with the Meadowwood Mall, Smithri
, and several new retail centers on all sides.

RANSPORTATION INFORMATION
Airport: Reno-Tahoe International Airport. This bustling airport serve
Nevada (and much of eastern California and southern Oregon). | 2001
exit off U.S. 395 S.
Amtrak: Two trains a day pass through downtown (blocking South \
10 minutes in the process), one eastbound, the other westbound.
Row | 775/329–8638.

outdoor staircase gives you a direct view of the petroglyphs. A visitor center orients you to the geology, ecology, and archaeology of the park. | ⬚⬚⬚ | 702/397–2088 | www.state.nv.us/stparks/ | $5 | Daily.

ON THE CALENDAR

APR.: *Clark County Fair.* Livestock show and sale, rode⬚ and crafts, and extensive food booths, all at the Logan⬚ you're in the same county with Las Vegas. | 702/398–⬚

Lodging

Echo Bay Resort and Marina. A bit of a trip from⬚ right on the best beach on Lake Mead. It is a sm⬚ away from Las Vegas to be relatively private and qu⬚ and jet-ski. The motel is right at marina. Rest⬚ some refrigerators. Cable TV. Beach, boating, ⬚ | 52 rooms | Northshore Rd. (Rte. 167) | 702/394⬚ | $69–$74 | AE, D, DC, MC, V.

PANACA

(Nearby town also listed: Pioche)

Panaca is perhaps the most orderly ⬚ a small settlement in the heart of ⬚ Valley Wash. It was settled by ⬚ the past 140 years. When th⬚ will be in the school parki⬚ some old houses, and a ⬚ about a mile from the ⬚

Information: Region⬚ 6, Caliente 8900⬚ coln/lincoln.htm⬚

ON THE ⬚

AUG.: *Linc⬚* racing), alo⬚ Rodeo Grounds. ⬚

PIOCHE

(Nearby town also listed: Panaca)

Gold was discovered in the hills around Pioche (pronounced ⬚ boomtown sprang up immediately. But it wasn't any ordinary boom⬚ tion of Bodie, California, and Tombstone, Arizona, Pioche gained a reputatio⬚ one of the most rough-and-tumble Old West mining communities; it's said that upw⬚ of 50 men died violently here before anyone succumbed to natural causes. In addi⬚ an unusual amount of political corruption gripped Pioche, evidenced by the "mi⬚ dollar courthouse" (which cost $26,000 to build in 1871 and was finally paid off in 1⬚ The usual boom-bust economy defined the fortunes of the town up through World⬚ II, and Pioche has had a population of hard-core small-towners since.

[Overlapping torn page — NEVADA | RENO:]

⬚⬚ed a "red line" to contain gambling in a tight core downtown, which gave Reno nearly a dozen new casinos within a couple of years. Meanwhile, Reno was busy diversifying: the university, light industry, warehousing, and outdoor recreation ⬚ much faster than Reno wanted to grow. So the city controlled the proliferation of casinos through the 1970s. A building boom ensued that ensure that gambling doesn't monopolize the economy.

Still a dozen major resorts deliver all the cheap casinos. The 120-year-old tainment that can be subsidized by immensely profitable casinos. The 120-year-old campus of the University of Nevada–Reno sits on a scenic bluff just north of down⬚ town and offers a planetarium, historical and mining museums, a stadium, an aren⬚ and the largest library in the state.

The compact metropolitan area has an auto museum, an art museum, even ⬚ machine museum, a number of large parks. Bowling and golf are big here, and a dozen wor⬚ amusement park with rides. Lake sports are split between Tahoe ⬚ resorts are all within an hour's drive. Historic Virginia City and Carson City are both a mere 45 minutes away. And a nonstop series of events keeps the excitement u⬚ drive away. And a nonstop series of events keeps the excitement u⬚

Information: Greater Reno-Sparks Chamber of Commerce. | 4⬚ 775/686–3030 | info@reno-sparkschamber.org | www.re⬚ **Reno/Sparks Convention and Visitor Authority.** | 4950 S. V⬚ RENO or 800/FOR–RENO | www.playreno.com.

NEIGHBORHOODS

Virginia Street. Reno's main drag is Virginia Stree⬚ north-south for 3 mi through the heart of tow⬚ nos (and a handful of minor ones), the Nati⬚ Museum, and a string of parks extendi⬚ runs right through it.
Newlands Heights. Newlands Heig⬚ of downtown and the river, wher⬚ turn of the century, built their p⬚ famous architect, designed ⬚
University District. The U⬚ The 200-acre campus d⬚ (and housed the entir⬚ White designed the ⬚ Revival style. Ra⬚ campus.
Meadowwoo⬚ town aro⬚ Cent⬚

[lower fragment:] mills a⬚ eno gained a mea⬚ ⬚vered Nevada's liberal divor⬚ ⬚bling arrived in 1931, furthering Reno's repu⬚ ⬚nuch more than a dot on the map. By the early 193⬚

DIVORCE, RENO-STYLE

In drawing up statutes for the new state government, the first Nevada legislators called for a relatively short (six-month) requirement for residency, which encouraged population growth and eased the complications created by a highly mobile citizenry. A logical outgrowth of the residency requirement was the waiting period in state for the dissolution of a marriage: as soon as a man or woman became a resident of Nevada, he or she could be granted a divorce.

In the late 19th and early 20th centuries, it was next to impossible to be granted a divorce in most American states. In many, the only grounds were adultery or desertion; in some, it required an individual act of the legislature; and a few states disallowed divorce for any reason.

Nevada not only had a short residency requirement, it also had a traditional tendency of conforming the law to fit the person rather than conforming the person to fit the law. Reno, Nevada's largest town, was a divorce haven waiting to happen.

In 1905, a scandal that had raged in the tabloids for three years reached its climax—in Reno. William B. Corey, president of U.S. Steel, at the time the world's largest corporation, had been married to his wife, Laura, for 20 years, and had a strapping teenage son, Allan, when he initiated a highly public affair with actress and chorus girl Maybelle Gillman. Public opinion weighed in heavily on the side of Laura Corey, the jilted wife and virtuous mother.

A savvy lawyer, familiar with the benefits of Nevada's divorce laws, sent her to Reno to wait out the six months. A society-page editor for a Pittsburgh newspaper got a tip as to Mrs. Corey's whereabouts, and from then on, every mention of the most notorious divorce in the country included the name Reno.

Laura Corey was granted her divorce in June 1906. In January 1907, William H. Schnitzer, a New York attorney, moved to Reno, opened a law office, and published a 24-page booklet, "Nevada Divorce Practice and Procedure." In it, Schnitzer extolled the virtues of Nevada as a divorce haven. It not only had the shortest residency requirement in the nation, but it also provided seven grounds for divorce, including an ambiguous and omnibus "cruelty" clause. There was no bar to immediate remarriage. And Nevada's remoteness proved a benefit for privacy. Schnitzer advertised his booklet in East Coast newspapers and San Francisco theater programs, which spread the word fast and far.

In the early years, only socialites were able able to afford marital surgery in the Reno clinic. The cost of the train ride, the Reno lawyers, and six months of room and board were within the reach of only the upper-crust of unhappy couples. But by 1926 a few other states had passed their own six-month divorces, so Nevada legislators reduced the residency requirement to three months. Finally, in 1931, the particularly libertarian legislature that legalized wide-open gambling also again cut the residency requirement in half—to a scandalous six weeks. That was the peak year for divorce Reno-style: nearly 5,000 were granted, upward of 20 every working day of the year.

At the time, Reno had all of 15,000 residents.

Bus Lines: Greyhound. The Dog runs continuously east and west. **K-T buses** run once a day south through Nevada to Las Vegas. | 155 Stevenson St. | 775/322–2970.

Attractions

NATURAL SIGHTS

Oxbow Nature Study Area. An unusual city park on the Truckee River awaits explorers in need of air and water. A series of paths meanders through and around an oxbow of the river that runs through downtown Reno. Decks, overlooks, narrative signs, and an interpretive center make this a great place for learning about Reno's river and water system. | Dickerson Rd. off W. 2nd St. | 775/785–4319 | Free | Daily.

CULTURE, EDUCATION, AND HISTORY

University of Nevada–Reno. UNR was established in 1864 as part of the Nevada Statehood Act. The campus has been in Reno since 1885; much of the landscaping and some of the buildings on the idyllic 200-acre campus, situated on a bluff over downtown, are more than 100 years old. The university has excellent schools of medicine, mining, journalism, and agriculture. Wolf Pack football is the local rage; large concerts and events are held in the Lawlor Events Center. | 1664 N. Virginia St. | 775/784–1110 | www.unr.edu.

The **Fleischmann Planetarium** has a 6-ft-diameter model of the earth and moon, computerized exhibits, an observatory, a telescope, and science quiz games. In the meteorite collection is one space rock that you can handle. The planetarium programs special shows that change periodically. | 1650 S. Virginia St. | 775/784–4811 | www.scs.unr.edu/planet/ | $6 | Weekdays 8 AM–9 PM, weekends 11–9.

The oldest museum in Nevada (circa 1904), the **Nevada Historical Society Museum** was completely renovated in 1998. Permanent exhibits survey the local ecology and Native Americans, mining, gambling, and tourism. Photography and fine arts exhibits change regularly. A library attached to the museum is open to the public, and a bookstore stocks a wide variety of books of local interest. | 1650 N. Virginia St. | 775/688–1190 | $2 | Mon.–Sat. 10–5.

The **W. M. Keck Minerals Museum,** formerly known as the Mackay School of Mines Museum, houses the largest collection of minerals and rocks in a state founded and built on mining. In the John Mackay School of Mines (Mackay was a bonanza king of the Comstock Lode), the museum displays hundreds of specimens from Nevada mining operations; Mackay's own vault houses authentic Comstock ore. Historical black-and-whites, fossils, and mining tools and machines round out the exhibits. | 1650 N. Virginia St. | 775/784–6052 | Free | Weekdays 9–5.

MUSEUMS

National Automobile Museum. Reno's biggest downtown museum attraction, this large collection of antique and classic automobiles is displayed in clever era-appropriate settings. Among them are Elvis's 1973 Cadillac Eldorado, John Wayne's 1953 Corvette, and Al Jolson's 1933 V-16 Cadillac. Don't miss the 22-minute multimedia theater presentation; a café on the Truckee River and a gift shop complete the complex. | 10 S. Lake St. | 775/333–9300 | fax 775/333–9309 | www.automuseum.org | $7.50 | Mon.–Sat. 9:30–5:30, Sun. 10–4.

Nevada Museum of Art. This fine arts museum, one of the few in Nevada, presents an array of permanent exhibits of Native American baskets, sculpture, and paintings. It also hosts traveling exhibits, from Old Masters to Rodin sculptures. | 160 W. Liberty St. | 775/329–3333 | fax 775/329–1541 | $5 adults | Tues., Wed., Fri. 10–4, Thurs. 10–7, weekends noon–4.

Wilbur May Museum. Wilbur May, the heir to the May Department Store fortune, was an international traveler, hunter, and collector. He settled in Reno and donated his collection in his will. This museum has a fine display of wild animals and exotic artifacts from around the world. Changing exhibits cover everything from insects to dinosaurs. There's an arboretum outside, and next door is Great Basin Adventure, a commercial kids' park with a flume ride and horseback riding. | 1502 Washington St. | 775/785–5961 | www.co.washoe.nv.us/parks/great.htm | $2.50 | Tues.–Sat. 10–5, Sun. noon–5.

SIGHTSEEING TOURS/TOUR COMPANIES

Gray Line bus tours. Ubiquitous Gray Line dispatches luxury motor coaches on a variety of tours around the Reno–Lake Tahoe area. There's a seven-hour Reno–Carson City–Virginia City tour (a nine-hour tour includes Lake Tahoe). There are also three tours, ranging from seven to nine hours, of Lake Tahoe, and in the winter you can take one-day and overnight ski trips. | 775/329–1147 or 800/634–6579 | fax 775/359–9774 | www.grayline.com/.

ON THE CALENDAR

JUNE: Reno Rodeo. One of the largest, oldest, and richest rodeos in the country, the Reno Rodeo has been coming to town in June since 1919; 85,000 fans and hundreds of world-class cowboys compete for more than $500,000 in prizes in the Reno Livestock Events Center. Buckaroo breakfasts, barrel races, horse sales, bronc riders, steer wrestlers, calf ropers, even a cattle drive of 300 head right down Virginia Street fill the nine days of festivities; there's also a parade, carnival, Western wear market, and country music concerts. | 775/329–3877.

AUG.: Nevada State Fair. Big carnival and midway, livestock exhibits and judging, entertainment, crafts, and big crowds fill the Reno Livestock Events Center. | 775/329–3877.

AUG.: Hot August Nights. More than 4,000 classic cars and 100,000 classic-car enthusiasts cruise into Reno for the most popular classic-car congregation in the country. The four-day blow-out kicks off with a formal prom, then it's perpetual parades, concerts, and sock hops, a massive automobile swap meet, the largest classic-car auction around, and "show 'n' shine" car displays held in parking lots all over town. | 775/356–1956 | www.hotaugustnights.com.

SEPT.: National Championship Air Races. The world's largest and longest-running air-race event, since 1968. It's the only event of its kind, featuring all four race classes: biplanes, Formula Ones, AT-6s, and the big Unlimiteds. Modern military aircraft fly-bys, aerobatics, skywriters, and skydivers entertain the up to 150,000 spectators at Stead Air Field, 12 mi north of downtown. | 775/972–6663.

SEPT.: Street Vibrations. A downtown motorcycle event for thousands of Harley Davidsons and custom tour bikes with rock 'n' roll, crafts, a parade, and a 300-decibel "burn-off." | 775/329–7469.

WALKING TOUR

DOWNTOWN (approximately 90 minutes)
Park at the Circus Circus high-rise garage at the corner of 6th and West streets and take the monorail to the main building. The **Circus Midway** on the Circus Circus mezzanine features all manner of carnival games and circus acts; it's also the entrance to Nevada's first (and only) "casino mall." This mall covers five city blocks and contains three casinos connected by two wide enclosed pedestrian walkways; between the wide passageways and almost seamless interior design, you never quite know where one casino ends and another begins. From the Circus Midway, stroll into the **Silver Legacy,** Reno's newest megaresort. This casino boasts Reno's only free spectacle: a 120-ft-tall mining rig. Also check out its attractive Victorian lobby; don't miss the exhibit of Tiffany silver tableware commissioned by John Mackay, one of the Comstock's bonanza kings. The Legacy connects to the **Eldorado,** which has a good coffee shop, buffet, and food court. Walk outside at the north end of the Eldorado and cross the railroad tracks; see if a little luck o' the Irish rubs off on you at **Fitzgeralds,** sister hotel to the one in downtown Las Vegas. At the **Reno Nugget** just down the street is an old-fashioned diner (not retro, but opened in the 1950s and little changed since); try the Awful Awful burger.

Now walk two blocks to the **Truckee River,** which connects Lake Tahoe in the Sierra Nevada to Pyramid Lake in the Great Basin Desert and supplies all the water for the city and surrounding communities. **The Riverwalk** is an attractive urban park along the river that you can follow to **Wingfield Park,** with its green lawns and afternoon concerts in the Wingfield Amphitheater in the summer. For a long stroll (extends the walk an hour round-trip), continue along the river to 70-year-old **Idlewild Park,** which has a a community pool, a rose garden, a kiddie playground, and a small amusement park.

At the South Virginia Street bridge over the Truckee, head east two blocks to the corner of Mill and Lake streets for the **National Automobile Museum** to see its collection of vintage and specialty cars displayed along four period "streets." Now walk back to South Virginia Street and go right one block to the **Cal-Neva,** with its low minimums and cheap food, including northern Nevada's most renowned 24-hour, 99¢ breakfast. Across 2nd Street is **Harrah's,** Nevada's first carpet joint (fancy casino), founded in the 1930s by Bill Harrah, the original of two dozen Harrah's around the country.

Continue two blocks north of Virginia Street to East Plaza, then right one block to the **National Bowling Stadium,** a gorgeous 80-lane tournament facility; there's a visitor center in the lobby, a '50s diner, and an Omnimax movie theater, plus the lanes (admission charge when a tournament is in progress, free when not). From there, walk back and cross Virginia Street, enter the Eldorado, and retrace your steps through the casino mall to the Circus Circus parking garage.

Dining

INEXPENSIVE

Glory Hole. Steak House. A quaint little steak house outside downtown Reno. | 4201 W. 4th St. | 775/786–1323 | $15 | AE, D, DC, MC, V | No lunch.

Palais De Jade. Chinese. Chinese silk paintings hang from the walls and green plants line the backs of the booths at this storefront restaurant in a shopping center. The menu features standard Chinese dishes at extremely reasonable prices, and many entrées include soup, egg roll, and a fortune cookie. | 960 W. Moana La. | 775/827–5233 | $5–$10 | AE, MC, V.

Rapscallion. Seafood. The atmosphere here is more typical of turn-of-the-century San Francisco restaurants than Reno. The menu has up to 20 varieties of fresh fish daily. | 1555 S. Wells Ave. | 775/323–1211 | www.rapscallion.com/ | $15–$21 | AE, MC, V.

MODERATE

Bricks Restaurant and Wine Bar. Continental. Close to Reno's casino strip, this restaurant is as well known locally for its large selection of wines by the glass and single-malt Scotches as for its food. | 1695 S. Virginia St. | 775/786–2277 | $24 | AE, D, DC, MC, V | Closed Sun. No lunch Sat.

Famous Murphys. American. The Irish logo belies the cuisine here, which tends toward steak and chicken. You can get corned beef and cabbage, though. The interior is standard pub style. The specialties include coconut-breaded prawns, and chicken with Portobello mushrooms, pine nuts, fresh tomatoes, and cheese-filled tortellini. You can order on-line and have your food delivered. | 3127 S. Virginia St. | 775/827-4111 | www.famousmurphys.com | $18–$25 | AE, D, DC, MC, V.

Ichiban. Japanese. The interior is designed to resemble a Japanese garden, with fountains and little bridges. On the second floor of a building that houses Eddie's Fabulous '50s Casino, this restaurant has a sushi bar and a steak house, with chefs preparing the food at your table. Kids' menu. | 210 N. Sierra | 775/323–5550 | $18–$25 | AE, D, DC, MC, V.

EXPENSIVE

Atlantis. Continental. One of the seven restaurants at Reno's Atlantis Resort and Casino, this one specializes in seafood and steaks, with other entrées such as veal medallions with morel mushrooms in Cognac sauce. The underwater theme is enhanced by an 1,100-gallon aquarium. | 3800 S. Virginia St. | 775/825–4700 | $29–$34 | AE, D, DC, MC, V | No lunch.

Fourth Street Bistro. French. In a converted house off the beaten track, the bistro specializes in French provincial cuisine. Two miles west of downtown, it's a local favorite for special occasions. | 3065 W. 4th St. | 775/323–3200 | $30–$50 | AE, MC, V | Closed Sun., Mon. No lunch.

Steak House. Steakhouse. This English Tudor–style dining room in the Reno Hilton specializes in steak, prime rib, pork chops, and the freshest seafood entrées. | 2500 E. 2nd St. | 775/789–2270 | $30–$45 | AE, MC, V | No lunch.

Lodging

INEXPENSIVE

Atlantis. Full-scale Caribbean-theme resort-casino outside of the downtown core. The resort is the result of the continual expansion on a 1960s motel; the latest (fall 1999) added 600 rooms. The "garden" rooms are often a good deal. 4 restaurants, bar. No-smoking rooms. Cable TV. Pool. Hot tub. Exercise equipment. Business services. Airport shuttle. | 1,192 rooms | 3800 S. Virginia St. | 775/825–4700 or 800/723–6500 | fax 775/826–7860 | mkt@atlantis.reno.nv.us | www.atlantiscasino.com | $50–$159 | AE, D, DC, MC, V.

Boomtown. Ten miles west of Reno, this major resort-casino on the California-Nevada line has a big casino, a new buffet, a large kids' play center, a theater, a merry-go-round, a Ferris wheel, indoor miniature golf, and arcade games. 3 restaurants, bar. No-smoking rooms. Cable TV. Business services. | 294 rooms | I–80 at Garson Rd. | 775/345–6000 or 800/648–3790 | fax 775/345–2327 | www.boomtowncasinos.com | $40–$99 | AE, D, DC, MC, V.

Circus Circus. A miniature version of the sister hotel in Las Vegas. This is a popular tourist attraction, with crowded facilities, a mezzanine midway and circus games, and a hopping buffet. Book well in advance for rooms. Connected to Silver Legacy via skywalk. A mini-monorail runs to the parking garage. 4 restaurants, bar. No-smoking floors. Cable TV. Game room. Business services. Airport shuttle. | 1,572 rooms | 500 N. Sierra St. | 775/329–0711 or 800/648–5010 | fax 775/329–0599 | circus@circus.reno.nv.us | www.circuscircus.org | $49–$159 | AE, D, DC, MC, V.

Comstock. A medium-size downtown hotel-casino with a stunning display of neon fireworks on two outside walls. The casino is dark and smoky; the rooms are light and airy. Restaurant, bar. Hot tubs in some suites. Cable TV. Pool. Hot tub. Exercise equipment. Business services. Airport shuttle. | 310 rooms | 200 W. 2nd St. | 775/329–1880 or 800/266–7862 | fax 775/329–7267 | www.thecomstock.com | $29–$230 | AE, D, DC, MC, V.

Fitzgeralds. A luck of the Irish theme (green!), a rockin' two-level casino, and frequent bargains on rooms. 2 restaurants, bar. No-smoking rooms. Cable TV. Valet parking. | 351 rooms | 255 N. Virginia St. | 775/785–3300 or 800/648–5022 (outside NV) | fax 775/786–7180 | www.fitzgeralds.com | $28–$200 | AE, D, DC, MC, V.

Hampton Inn. One of the newer downtown high-rise hotels without a casino opened in 1996. It's connected to Harrah's casino, though. The rooms are modern, the location great, and the amenities the same as at the megaresort-casinos. Bar, complimentary Continental breakfast. In-room data ports, in-room safes, no-smoking rooms. Cable TV. Pool. Barbershop, beauty salon. Exercise equipment. Business services. Airport shuttle. Pets allowed. | 408 rooms | 175 E. 2nd St. | 775/788–2300 | fax 775/788–2301 | $62–$94 | AE, D, DC, MC, V.

La Quinta Inn–Airport. You're close to the airport and the interstate both at this standard motel, making it a good choice for those who don't plan a long stay in town. Complimentary Continental breakfast. No-smoking rooms. Cable TV. Pool. Business services. Airport shuttle. Pets allowed. | 130 rooms | 4001 Market St. | 775/348–6100 | fax 775/348–8794 | www.laquinta.com | $59–$85 | AE, D, DC, MC, V.

Rodeway Inn. Standard Travelodge motel, convenient for business travelers. Complimentary Continental breakfast. Microwaves in kitchenette units, no-smoking rooms. Cable TV. Pool. Hot tub, sauna. Laundry facilities. Business services. Airport shuttle. Pets allowed ($8 fee). | 210 rooms | 2050 Market St. | 775/786–2500 | fax 775/786–3884 | $39–$127 | AE, D, DC, MC, V.

Silver Legacy. Opened in 1995, this was the first wholly new hotel-casino to be built in Reno since the early '80s. Squeezed into two blocks downtown, it's the tallest building in northern Nevada, and it's the classiest joint downtown, with a tourist-attraction lobby (antiques displays), up-to-date rooms, a restaurant row, and an incongruous Las Vegas–style spectacle that has to be seen to be believed. 5 restaurants, bar. No-smoking rooms. Cable TV. Pool. Hot tub. Gym. Business services. Airport shuttle. Free Parking. | 1,720 rooms | 407 N. Virginia St. | 775/329–4777 or 800/687–8733 | fax 775/325–7340 | resv@silverlegacy.com | www.silverlegacy.com | $49–$99 | AE, D, DC, MC, V.

Vagabond Inn. This motel at the south end of South Virginia Street is distinguished by its lack of a casino. Complimentary Continental breakfast. No-smoking rooms. Cable TV. Pool. Business services. Airport shuttle. Some pets allowed (fee). | 129 rooms | 3131 S. Virginia St. | 775/825–7134 | fax 775/825–3096 | www.vagabondinns.com | $50–$145 | AE, D, DC, MC, V.

MODERATE

Adventure Inn. Highly themed rooms and suites: jungle, bridal, Roman, Adam and Eve, tropical, bordello, cave, and space. All come with round or heart-shaped beds, "rain forest" showers, free limo rides within 10 mi, complimentary champagne, and more. No-smoking rooms. Cable TV. Pool. Hot tub. | 45 rooms | 3575 S. Virginia St. | 775/828–9000 or 800/937–1436 | fax 775/825–8333 | www.adventureinn.com | $50–$249 | AE, D, DC, MC, V.

Best Western Airport Plaza. A low-rise casino-motel directly across from the entrance to the airport and a 7-minute walk from the terminal building. Restaurant, bar, room service. No-smoking rooms, some refrigerators. Cable TV. Pool. Putting green. Exercise equipment. Business services. Airport shuttle. | 270 rooms | 1981 Terminal Way | 775/348–6370 | fax 775/348–9722 | applaza@worldnet.att.net | $65–$300 | AE, D, DC, MC, V.

Flamingo Hilton. Familiar pink-plumage neon fronts this high-rise hotel-casino on Sierra Street, one block from Virginia Street. It's connected to a small slot casino on Virginia Street via skywalk. Most noteworthy characteristic: it has the highest restaurant and bar in town (23rd floor). Lounge and showroom. 3 restaurants, bar. In-room data ports, no-smoking rooms. Cable TV. Exercise equipment. Game room. Business services. Airport shuttle. | 604 rooms | 255 N. Sierra St. | 775/322–1111 | fax 775/785–7086 | $59–$219 | AE, D, DC, MC, V.

Peppermill Hotel Casino. Playing Pepsi to the Atlantis's Coke, the Peppermill has been expanded and remodeled many times over the decades, most recently in 1997. Known for friendly service, excellent gourmet food, a good fast-food court, an attractive pool area, and a gamut of rooms from bargain-basement to top-shelf. It's also very close to the airport. 4 restaurants, bar. Minibars, no-smoking rooms. Cable TV. 2 pools. Hot tub. Exercise equipment. Business services. Airport shuttle. | 1,070 rooms | 2707 S. Virginia St. | 775/826–2121 or 800/282–2444 | fax 775/826–5205 | www.peppermillcasinos.com | $59–$500 | AE, D, DC, MC, V.

Reno Hilton. The big boy on the block, the largest hotel-casino in the state outside of Vegas and the only place in town you never have to leave. It is literally a monument in the middle of the valley, so big it has two exits off the freeway. You can spend a weekend doing everything the Hilton offers, but unlike other megaresorts, this one will never make you feel lost. Lounge and showroom. 6 restaurants, bar. In-rooms safes, no-smoking floors, some refrigerators. Cable TV. Pool. Barbershop, beauty salon, hot tub, massage. Driving range, tennis courts. Bowling, gym. Game room. Business services. Airport shuttle. | 2,001 rooms | 2500 E. 2nd St. | 775/789–2000 | fax 775/789–1678 | $69–$149 | AE, D, DC, MC, V.

EXPENSIVE

★ **Eldorado.** A large, classy resort-casino owned by the local Carano family. The rooms run from basic to ultra-deluxe. It is renowned for good food (the Caranos own a winery in Sonoma, California) and for its microbrewery. 5 restaurants, bar. In-room data ports, some in-room safes, no-smoking rooms, some refrigerators. Cable TV. Pool. Hot tub. Business services. Airport shuttle. | 817 rooms | 345 N. Virginia St. | 775/786–5700 or 800/648–5966 (outside NV) | fax 775/322–7124 | www.eldoradoreno.com | $59–$750 | AE, D, DC, MC, V.

Harrah's. Opened in 1937, this is the oldest casino in Reno and one of the oldest in the state. The snazzy joint covers nearly two blocks with three casinos and two hotel towers. New sports book, great buffet, and one of the few kids' arcades downtown. 4 restaurants, bar. No-smoking rooms. Cable TV. Pool. Hot tub, massage. Gym. Game room. Business services. Airport shuttle. Some pets allowed. | 958 rooms | 219 N. Center St. | 775/786–3232 or 800/427–7247 | fax 775/788–3274 | $54–$299 | AE, D, DC, MC, V.

SPARKS

(Nearby town also listed: Reno)

Reno's smaller and younger sister city Sparks was founded in 1905 when the Southern Pacific Railroad built a switching yard and maintenance plants in the marshy valley east of Reno. Sparks quickly grew into a solid family-oriented company town, aloof from the licentious ways of the big city next door. It wasn't until a boom period in the 1970s that Reno and Sparks began to merge physically; still, to this day they're separate cities with individual characteristics.

Sparks is more industrial, with one of the largest warehousing and trans-shipment districts in the western United States, taking advantage of Nevada's freeport laws. Downtown surrounds John Ascuaga's Nugget and Victorian Square, which hosts numerous street events throughout the year. Along Victorian Boulevard are a small museum, a stone amphitheater, and a park with rolling stock and an 1860s schoolhouse.

Information: Greater Reno-Sparks Chamber of Commerce. | 405 Marsh Ave., 89505 | 775/686–3030 | info@reno-sparkschamber.org | www. reno-sparkschamber.org. **Reno/Sparks Convention and Visitor Authority.** | 4950 S. Virginia St., 89502 | 775/827–RENO or 800/FOR RENO | www.playreno.com.

Attractions

Sparks Museum. Interesting artifacts from the railroad history of Reno's sister town; ask for a "Story of Sparks" brochure, with a driving tour of the town's historical buildings | 820 Victorian Ave. | 775/355–1144 | Donations accepted | Tues.–Sun. 1–4.

ON THE CALENDAR

DEC.: *Hometowne Christmas.* Parade, tree-lighting ceremony, big crafts fair, food booths, street entertainment, and caroling bring out the holiday spirit. | 775/353–2291.

Lodging

★ **John Ascuaga's Nugget.** Three miles east of town, John A's is the largest employer in Sparks. It opened in 1956 and has continually expanded ever since—even the interstate was built over it. The full-scale resort has seven restaurants, the best indoor pool in the state, and great food. The place is promotion intensive. Lounge and showroom. 7 restaurants, 2 bars. Some microwaves, no-smoking floors, some refrigerators. Cable TV. Indoor/outdoor pool. Beauty salon, hot tub, massage. Exercise equipment. Business services. Airport shuttle. | 1,998 rooms | 1100 Nugget Ave. | 775/356–3300 or 800/648–1177 (outside NV) | fax 775/356–4298 | www.janugget.com | $35–$160 | AE, D, DC, MC, V.

STATELINE

MAP 10, A5

(Nearby towns also listed: Carson City, Minden-Gardnerville)

Like Crystal Bay/King's Beach on the north shore of Lake Tahoe, Stateline is the Nevada casino town with high-rise hotel-casinos, while South Lake Tahoe next door is the California service town with low-rise support facilities. There are four major and two minor casinos in Stateline, with a small residential area hugging the hills above the main drag on the lakeshore flats. Heavenly Valley Ski Resort also overlooks the border-town flats, with skiing on both sides of the California-Nevada state line. The nearest beach on the Nevada side is Nevada Beach, 2 mi north of the casinos on U.S. 50, a large Forest Service beach, picnic area, and campground.

Information: Lake Tahoe Visitors Authority. | 1156 Ski Run Blvd., South Lake Tahoe, CA 96150 | 530/544–5050 or 800/AT–TAHOE | ltva@sierra.net | www.virtualtahoe.com. **Tahoe-Douglas Chamber of Commerce and Visitors Center.** | 195 U.S. 50 at Roundhill (Box 7139), 89449 | 775/588–4591 | tdcc@sierra.net | www.virtualtahoe.com.

Attractions

Cave Rock. A towering slab of solid granite, this rock is sacred to the Washoe Indians. U.S. 50 passes through it via one of Nevada's few tunnels. It looms over a parking lot, with a lakefront picnic area and a boat launch. | 11 mi north on U.S. 50 | Free | Daily 10:30–5.

Nevada Beach. *See* Lake Tahoe.

ON THE CALENDAR

JULY: *Jim Butler Days.* One of Nevada's most popular pioneer festivals attracts participants from all over the state for a parade, car races, a summit run, a barbecue and chili cook-off, horseshoe and volleyball tournaments, an arts and crafts fair, a dance, and the state's biggest pancake breakfast. | 775/482–3878.

Dining

Chart House. Steakhouse. A lake view and nautical decor with lots of wood paneling now match the menu, which has added a lot of fresh fish and seafood. Sesame-crusted salmon, seared, peppered ahi tuna, and grilled swordfish are specialties. Serious steaks are still served, as well. Kids' menu. | 392 Kingsbury Grade (Rte 28); 2 mi east off U.S. 50 | 775/588–6276 | www.chart-house.com | $18–$25 | AE, D, DC, MC, V | No lunch.

Friday's Station. American. The food is second to the view of Lake Tahoe—one of the best you'll find in the state. Steaks are the most popular item on the menu, with seafood following. At Harrah's. | U.S. 50, Harrah's, 18th floor | 775/588–6611 | www.harrahstahoe.com/restaurants/fridays.html | $26–$49 | AE, D, DC, MC, V | No lunch.

Llewellyn's. Continental. High atop Harveys on the 19th floor, Llewellyn's offers a spectacular view and a beautiful presentation. Lunch, dinner and Sunday champagne brunch year-round. No smoking. | In Harvey's Hotel & Casino | 775/588–2411 | $18–$35 | AE, D, DC, MC, V.

Sage Room. American. Steak and other beef cuts top the menu here. Opened in 1947, the place retains its Old West furnishings and style. The favorite dessert is bananas Foster. | 775/588–2411 | $16–$40 | AE, D, DC, MC, V | No lunch.

Summit. Continental. Harrah's Lake Tahoe's crown jewel restaurant looks out over the landscape from the sixteenth floor. The chef has a nightly special, but regular entrées include roasted rack of lamb, wild mushroom saute with fettuccine, grilled New Zealand venison, and many beef and seafood dishes. No smoking. | U.S. 50 | 775/588–6611, ext. 2196 | $20–$40 | AE, D, DC, MC, V | No lunch.

Lodging

Caesars Tahoe. Most of the rooms and suites at Caesars, across U.S. 50 from the lake, have Roman tubs, king-size beds, two telephones, and a view of the lake or mountains. An opulent casino and fancy restaurants keep you from spending too much time in the room. The indoor pool has a restaurant surrounding it. 5 restaurants, bar. In-room safes, some microwaves, no-smoking rooms, some refrigerators. Indoor pool. Barbershop, beauty salon, hot tub, massage. Tennis court. Exercise equipment, racquetball. Game room. Business services. | 440 rooms | 55 U.S. 50 | 775/588–3515 or 800/648–3353 | fax 775/586–2068 | www.caesars.com | $105–$195 | AE, D, DC, MC, V.

★ **Harrah's.** The luxurious guest rooms here have private bars and two full bathrooms, each with a television and telephone. The 16th-floor Summit Restaurant is one of the best in the state. Lounge and showroom. 6 restaurants, bar, room service. No-smoking floors. Cable TV. Indoor pool. Barbershop, beauty salon, hot tub, massage. Exercise equipment. Game room. Business services. Pets allowed. | 532 rooms | U.S. 50 | 775/588–6611 or 800/648–3773 | fax 775/586–6607 | www.harrahstahoe.com | $169–$350 | AE, D, DC, MC, V.

Harvey's. The oldest casino on the lake, opened in the early 1940s, was expanded and remodeled continually through the early '90s, so that it is now the largest resort on the lake. Rooms have custom furnishings, oversized marble baths, and minibars. 8 restaurants, 6 bars, complimentary Continental breakfast, room service. Minibars, no-smoking floors, room service. Cable TV. Pool. Barbershop, beauty salon, hot tub, massage. Gym. Game room. Business services. Airport shuttle. | 740 rooms | U.S. 50 | 775/588–2411 or 800/427–8397 | fax 775/588–6643 | www.harveys.com/reservations.html | $99–$199 | AE, D, DC, MC, V.

Lake Tahoe Horizon. This is the smallest of the high-risers at Stateline, so a little less expensive. It has standard rooms, a cookie-cutter casino, and average food. 3 restaurants, bar. No-smoking rooms. Cable TV. Pool, wading pool. Hot tubs, massage. Exercise equipment. Game room. Business services. | 539 rooms | 50 U.S. 50 | 775/588–6211 or 800/648–3322 | fax 775/588–1344 | horizoncasino@oakweb | www.horizoncasino.com | $79–$159 | AE, D, DC, MC, V.

Lakeside Inn. A long walk from the main Stateline action, the Lakeside is the only low-rise resort in town. Standard motel rooms and a small but nice casino. The least-expensive hotel-casino at Stateline. Restaurant, bars. No-smoking rooms. Cable TV. Pool. Game room. Business services. | 124 rooms | 168 U.S. 50 | 775/588–7777 or 800/624–7980 | fax 775/588–4092 | www.lakesideinn.com | $79–$129 | AE, D, DC, MC, V.

TONOPAH

MAP 10, C6

(Nearby town also listed: Hawthorne)

TONOPAH

INTRO
ATTRACTIONS
DINING
LODGING

Nevada experienced a 20-year bust between 1880 and 1900, when the original mines across the state had been exhausted and no new ones were being discovered. That all changed in the fall of 1900, when Jim Butler staked several claims on Mizpah Hill in central Nevada and dug out ore containing a large percentage of high-grade gold and silver. Immediately, Tonopah erupted onto the scene, launching another 20-year mining boom that extended as far as Beatty in southwest Nevada and Ely in east-central, with such small boomtowns as Goldfield, Manhattan, and Round Mountain in between.

Tonopah's fortunes rode high for 15 years, then rose and fell with the mining cycles through the 1980s. It's also the closest town to the Tonopah Test Range, an Air Force base that tests top-secret aircraft. And Tonopah is a crossroads town, where U.S. 95 and U.S. 6 intersect, with plenty of travelers' facilities, a big museum, a historic mining park, and many original buildings and houses.

Information: Tonopah Chamber of Commerce. | 301 Brougher Ave., 89049 | 775/482–3859. **Tonopah Convention Center.** | 301 Brougher Ave., 89049 | 775/482–3558.

Attractions

Central Nevada Museum. An excellent and extensive collection of items from all over central Nevada. The outdoor exhibit contains big mining machinery and a replica town site; inside are Shoshone artifacts, a purple bottle collection, aerial photographs, and an exhibit on the Tonopah Army Air Force Base. | Logan Field Rd. | 775/482–9676 | Donations accepted | Summer, daily 9–5; winter, daily 11–5.

Tonopah Mining Park. A 70-acre collection of silver mines just as they were left when they closed. A one-hour guided tour, which starts from the Central Nevada Museum, takes you through the Top and Mizpah mines: hoistworks, warehouses, stopes, and a 100-ft-deep glory hole. There's an excellent view of downtown Tonopah from the park. | 775/482–9676 | fax 775/482–5423 | www.tonopahnevada.com/tonopahhistoricminingpark.htm | $3 | May–Sept., daily, 10–5; Oct.–May, Tues.– Sat., 11–4.

Lodging

Best Western Hi Desert Inn. The most modern and most expensive motel in town, and one of the few with a pool. No-smoking rooms. Cable TV. Pool. Hot tub. Pets allowed. | 62 rooms | 320 Main St. (U.S. 95) | 775/482–3511 or 800/528–1234 | fax 775/482–3300 | $49–$65 | AE, D, DC, MC, V.

Jim Butler. Named after the founder of Tonopah in 1900, the Butler is a standard motel in the heart of downtown. No-smoking rooms. Cable TV. | 24 rooms | 100 S. Main St. | 775/482–3577 or 800/635–9455 | fax 775/482–5240 | $30–$39 | AE, D, DC, MC, V.

Silver Queen. The rooms at this downtown hotel are spacious and modestly priced, and you're in the heart of the historic mining town and within walking distance from the Convention Center. The staff is very friendly and will help guide you to the best local attractions. Restaurant, bar. No-smoking rooms. Cable TV. Pool. Pets allowed. | 85 rooms | 255 S. Main St. (U.S. 95) | 775/482–6291 | fax 775/482–3190 | $30–$40 | AE, D, DC, MC, V.

Station House. The most extensive lodging in Tonopah, built in 1982, has a full-scale casino, a 24-hr restaurant, a drug store, a supermarket next door, and a great snack bar. Inside is a display of antique slot machines. Rooms are large and quiet, and there's a McDonald's across the street. Restaurant, bar. No-smoking rooms. Cable TV. Barbershop, beauty salon. | 75 rooms | 1100 Erie Main St. | 775/482–9777 | fax 775/482–8762 | $33–$80 | AE, D, DC, MC, V.

VIRGINIA CITY

MAP 10, A4

(Nearby towns also listed: Carson City, Reno)

Prospectors had been working the creeks at the bottom of Sun Mountain for nearly a decade before a couple of them climbed up the steep eastern slope, stuck a shovel into the ground, and discovered the richest lode of silver and gold in the history of the continental United States. The lode was named after another prospector, Henry Comstock, who claimed that the land on the mountain was part of his "ranch." A few months later, the Comstock Lode had attracted upward of 10,000 fortune seekers and the town of Virginia City had mushroomed up from the hillside.

The Comstock boom raged for 20 years, during which time Virginia City was one of the largest cities in the country. Roughly $750 million (in 1880 dollars) in silver and gold was wrestled from the underground hard-rock mines below the streets of Virginia City, worth a conservative $10 billion today; the boom supported upward of 25,000 residents at its peak. But even a boomtown the size of Virginia City must bust eventually, and it remained a has-been for more than 100 years.

Today Virginia City is a typical Old West mining-town tourist trap, with enough gift, candy, jewelry, craft, leather, candle, glass, cigar, mineral, book, and old-time photo shops to make the eyes of even the most determined shoppers roll right into the back of their heads. Add the museums, mansions, mine tours, churches, cemeteries, saloons, railroad ride, and back streets, and Virginia City will keep you busy for a whole holiday weekend.

Information: Virginia City Chamber of Commerce. | Box 464, 89440 | 775/847–0311. **Virginia City Convention and Tourism Authority.** | Box 920, 89440 | 775/847–7500.

Attractions

The Castle. The best original mansion in Nevada, the Castle was never restored. It was built in 1868 by a mine superintendent and only sold twice, with all of its furnishings included. The museum part of the house has a fascinating collection of the original European antiques, such as crystal chandeliers, Carrara marble fireplaces, furniture, mirrors, lamps, even wallpaper. Your guide will give you a lesson on the Italian hanging staircase. | 70 South B St. | 775/847–0275 | $3 | Daily 10–5.

Fourth Ward School. Built in 1876, the Fourth Ward is one of the nation's few schools of this size and type still standing. The four-story building was built to accommodate 1,000 students and it remained a school until 1936. Several classrooms have been restored to their original state; the museum part contains some Comstock history. Restoration efforts are ongoing; a meeting room on the top floor is used for history lectures and slide shows. | C St. | 775/847–0975 | Donations accepted | Mid-May–Oct., daily 10–5.

Virginia and Truckee Railroad. One of the most celebrated and profitable short-line railroads in American history, the VT was completed in 1869 and hauled millions of dollars in gold and silver ore from the Comstock mines to the mills in Carson City. Today the steam-powered train makes 35-minute rail trips nine times daily down the hill to Gold Hill, Virginia City's bedroom community, passing through Tunnel No. 4. You can ride in either open or covered cars. | Washington and F Sts. | 775/847–0380 | $4.75 | Late Apr.–Sept., daily 10:30–5:45.

The Way It Was Museum. For insight into local history, spend some time at this venerable museum. Check out the mining artifacts, including a working model of an early water-powered stamp mill. Costumed mannequins, mining equipment, pioneer tools, and a blacksmith shop round out the exhibits. There's also a 16-minute video on Comstock history. | C St. and Sutton Dr. | 775/847–0766 | $2.50 | Daily 10–6.

ON THE CALENDAR

SEPT.: *International Camel Races.* Camel races were all the rage in the 1870s at the height of Virginia City's heyday, and camels are brought from Australia to re-create the pursuit. Local celebrities ride the camels in a hilarious dash to the finish line. A parade and headline entertainers round out the activities. | 775/847–0311 or 775/329–7469.

Lodging

Gold Hill Hotel. The oldest lodging house in the state and the second-oldest building is 1 mi south and down the hill from Virginia City. The four rooms in the original wing are authentic (two share a bath); the new-wing rooms are luxurious; four suites have fireplaces. The original great room is now the lounge, with stone floors and rock walls. Restaurant, complimentary Continental breakfast. No-smoking rooms. Cable TV. | 14 rooms | 1540 Main St., Gold Hill | 775/847–0111 | $40–$135 | AE, D, MC, V.

WINNEMUCCA

MAP 10, C2

(Nearby town also listed: Elko)

Winnemucca was a great Paiute chief who in the 1860s made a lasting peace between the Northern Paiute and white settlers in northern Nevada. The town named after him

WINNEMUCCA

INTRO
ATTRACTIONS
DINING
LODGING

grew up around a ferry service across the river for immigrants turning north into Oregon. The transcontinental railroad established a station at the settlement, which ensured its survival; Winnemucca's population didn't crack 3,000 for the next 100 years. But the deregulation of gold in the late '70s prompted a huge modern-day rush, centered on an area that included the vicinity of Winnemucca, which experienced a major boom, culminating in upward of 10,000 residents, enough for a Wal-Mart.

Winnemucca has a couple of museums, a couple of casinos, a couple of Basque restaurants, and the Winnemucca Hotel, one of the oldest in the state.

Information: Winnemucca Chamber of Commerce. | 30 Winnemucca Blvd., 89445 | 775/623–2225 or 800/962–2638. **Winnemucca Convention and Visitors Bureau.** | 50 W. Winnemucca Blvd., 89445 | 775/623–5071 or 800/962–2638 | winnemucca@desertlinc.com.

Attractions

Humboldt Museum. A church built in 1907 now houses Native American and early Winnemucca items (including the town's first piano), and local movie posters (a Gary Cooper movie was filmed nearby in 1926). A newer building contains more memorabilia, including a car collection and a wall-length mural of turn-of-the-century Winnemucca. | Jungo Rd. and Maple Ave. | 775/623–2912 | www.humboldt-county-nv.net/ | Donations accepted | Weekdays 10–noon, 1–4, Sat. 1–4.

ON THE CALENDAR

JUNE: *Basque Festival*. A major ethnic festival, with a parade, folk music and dancing, wood-chopping, weight-carrying, and yelling contests, and a barbecue | 775/623–5071 or 800/962–2638.

Dining

Ormachea's. Basque/American. Family-style dinners, with a choice of entrée and complimentary house wine and ice cream included. No smoking. | 180 Melarky St. | 775/623–3455 | $12–$25 | AE, D, MC, V | Closed Mon., Oct.–Mar. No lunch.

Lodging

Best Western Gold Country Inn. The rooms are spacious here at the fanciest motel in town, and the most expensive. No-smoking rooms. Cable TV. Pool. Business services. Airport shuttle. Some pets allowed. | 71 rooms | 921 W. Winnemucca Blvd. | 775/623–6999 | fax 775/623–9190 | $75–$115 | AE, D, DC, MC, V.

Days Inn. Downtown, with modest rates, this motel is comfortable and predictable. No-smoking rooms. Cable TV. Pool. Pets allowed. | 50 rooms | 511 W. Winnemucca Blvd. | 775/623–3661 or 800/DAYSINN | fax 775/623–4234 | $59–$69 | AE, D, DC, MC, V.

Parker's Model T. A casino and truck stop at the west end of town have a standard motel attached. Restaurant, bar, complimentary breakfast. No-smoking rooms. Cable TV. Pool. Laundry facilities. | 75 rooms | 1122 Winnemucca Blvd. | 775/623–0222 or 800/645–5658 | fax 775/623–8987 | $50–$85 | AE, D, MC, V.

Red Lion Inn. This big motel is fronted by a mini-casino. the cutest little joint in town. Restaurant, bar. No-smoking rooms. Cable TV. Pool. Game room. Business services. Some pets allowed (fee). | 105 units | 741 W. Winnemucca Blvd. | 775/623–2565 or 800/633–6435 | fax 775/623–2527 | $79–$165 | AE, D, DC, MC, V.

Val-U Inn. This motel in the heart of downtown has modest rates and is one of the few with a sauna and steam room. Continental breakfast in lobby. No-smoking rooms. Cable TV. Pool. Sauna, steam room. Business services. Pets allowed (fee). | 80 rooms | 125 E. Winnemucca Blvd. | 775/623–5248 or 800/443–7777 | fax 775/623–4722 | $44–$75 | AE, D, DC, MC, V.

YERINGTON

(Nearby towns also listed: Carson City, Hawthorne)

Yerington is a small supply town for the Smith and Mason valleys, some of the richest agricultural land in Nevada, watered by the Walker River. Yerington also has some recent mining history: a large open-pit copper mine sits in the hills just outside of town, from which Anaconda Copper mined hundreds of million tons of copper from the 1950s into the 1970s. You can see an interesting exhibit on copper technology and products in the excellent museum downtown. Yerington has one major casino and a smaller one and a very slow pace.

Information: Mason Valley Chamber of Commerce. | 227 S. Main St., 89447 | 775/463–2245.

Attractions

Fort Churchill State Historic Park. Fort Churchill was the first and largest army fort built in Nevada, in 1860, to protect travelers and miners. The 700-acre park, 32 mi north of Yerington proper, contains extensive ruins of the fort buildings, along with a visitor center; exhibits impart the history, which includes the Pony Express, the Civil War, and the telegraph. A beautiful campground is near the Carson River under towering cottonwoods. | U.S. 95A | 775/577–2345 | www.state.nv.us/stparks | Free. | Daily 10–4.

Lyon County Museum. This museum overflows with items of local interest: Paiute baskets and cradleboards, Chinese carved walnuts, a sheriff's office, a pioneer kitchen, a barber shop, a large copper-mining exhibit, even George Washington's personal strongbox. Outside is a good desert wildlife exhibit. | 215 S. Main St. | 775/463–6576 | Donations accepted | Fri. noon–4, Sat. 10–4, Sun. 1–4, and by appointment.

ON THE CALENDAR

AUG.: *Spirit of Wovoka Days Powwow.* A small spiritual powwow in honor of Wovoka, who started the Ghost Dance movement that culminated in the massacre at Wounded Knee. The powwow is held on the Yerington Paiute Reservation; Wovoka was from the Yerington area. | 775/463–2350.
SEPT.: *Sundae in the Park.* Entertainment, food, and ice-cream sundaes are all featured at Pool Park. | 775/463–3066.

Lodging

Casino West. Considering the size of the town, this is a big motel. There's a casino across the street and bowling is one of the amenities. Restaurant, complimentary Continental breakfast. No-smoking rooms. Cable TV. Pool. Bowling. Game room. Pets allowed. | 79 rooms | 11 N. Main St. | 775/463–2481 or 800/227–4661 | fax 775/463–5733 | $40–$55 | AE, D, DC, MC, V.

YERINGTON

INTRO
ATTRACTIONS
DINING
LODGING

Utah

There are 10 other states with more area than Utah, but it's not likely that any of them exceed the diversity and breadth of Utah's topography, or the wild variation of its climate zones. Majestic mountains in the north can be covered with snow, yet in the central valleys crocuses are in bloom and in the southern desert reaches it can be uncomfortably warm for a heavy-laden hiker. Around virtually every bend, mountains jut skyward. Acres of sagebrush roll toward the horizon. Canyons score the earth. Compacted salt flats shimmer like a desert mirage. Evergreen forests blend seamlessly into aspen-rimmed meadows, and hundreds of mountain lakes and streams sparkle in the sun.

There's more to Utah than first meets the eye. This is a state where cultural and heritage sites are tended with loving care by citizens from many ethnic backgrounds. Interpretive panels and historic markers attest to the legacy of Pueblo cultures, along with rock-art panels and the scattered remnants of the places where Utah's first residents lived out their lives. A predominantly Mormon population cherishes the stories of its ancestors and is willing to share them in many church-related sites state-wide.

The story of the Mormon exodus from the Midwest to the Salt Lake valley is well known. The impact of Mormon culture is felt in politics, community planning, and those infamous liquor laws. But it also contributes greatly to volunteerism and civic pride.

Salt Lake City may have been given the honor of hosting the 2002 Olympic Winter Games, but event sites are flung along the urban corridor for nearly 100 miles. Residents of communities that hardly ever get snow are planning ways to share their own stories with the world.

CAPITAL: SALT LAKE CITY	POPULATION: 2,135,200	AREA: 84,990 SQUARE MI
BORDERS: NV, ID, WY, CO, NM, AZ	TIME ZONE: MOUNTAIN	POSTAL ABBREVIATION: UT
WEB SITE: UTAH.COM		

History

Ancient Pueblo cultures known as the Anasazi and Fremont Indians raised corn in southern Utah from about AD 1 to 1300. Utes and Navajos roamed the region for centuries before the arrival of outsiders. At the time the eastern seaboard was struggling to gain independence from England, Spanish explorers and Mexican traders were documenting Utah's terrain and making notes on its plant and animal life. In the 1820s, fur trappers like Jedediah Smith, William Ashley, and Jim Bridger discovered northern Utah's abundant trapping opportunities. In 1847, 1,637 Mormons migrated to the Salt Lake valley seeking religious freedom. By 1869, when the first transcontinental railroad was completed at Promontory, Utah, more than 60,000 Mormons had come to Utah by covered wagon or handcart.

All of this history—Pueblo peoples, Native American tribes, explorers, pioneers, Mormon settlers—is important to Utah's modern-day residents, all of whom share a sense that the state's past is an important part of its future.

Regions

1. THE WASATCH FRONT

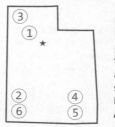

Named for the Wasatch Mountains towering along its eastern border, the Wasatch Front is Utah's urban corridor, extending from Brigham City in the north to Payson in the south. Utah's early pioneers settled this narrow strip of land to take advantage of the rich soil washed down from the mountains and all the water available for irrigating their fields. Interstate 15 runs north and south along this corridor following the paths of early explorers. It is the major route from northern Utah to Las Vegas and Los Angeles, encouraging commerce along its sweep.

Towns listed: Brigham City, Ogden, Park City, Provo, Salt Lake City

2. THE GREAT BASIN

The western edge of the Wasatch Front meets the Great Basin and Range Province. Small mountain ranges parade across farmland on the north and a huge desert stretches south to central Utah. There are a few rivers, but their waters evaporate in the dry air or eventually sink into the soil. The Great Basin's history is one of arduous crossings in search of more favorable terrain beyond the desert. The wagon ruts of the Donner Party are still visible. Pony Express riders galloped across this barren landscape. Railroad builders met, linking their rails across the continent, at a lonely spot north of Great Salt Lake. The basin can be beautiful, in a stark and wild way; however, it's still thought of as a region to pass through on the way to somewhere else.

Towns listed: Fillmore, Nephi, Wendover

UT Timeline

230–65 million years ago (Mesozoic Era)	16,000–11,000 years ago		12,000–700 years ago
Dinosaurs of many types flourish then become extinct in the eastern portion of what is now Utah.	Lake Bonneville covers nearly 20,000 square miles, filling the entire Great Basin in western Utah and vast areas of Nevada and Idaho as well. The lake is 1,000 ft deep	and filled with fish. By 11,000 years ago this inland sea has dropped to roughly the same level as its modern remnant, Great Salt Lake.	The area's first human habitants evolve with the changing landscape. Paleo-Indians who follow North America's last ice age hunt big game. People of the

INTRODUCTION
HISTORY
REGIONS
WHEN TO VISIT
STATE'S GREATS
RULES OF THE ROAD
DRIVING TOURS

3. THE MOUNTAIN PROVINCE

In Utah the Rocky Mountain Province shapes the northeastern portion of the state. It includes the Wasatch Mountains and the Uinta Range. This is a land of craggy peaks, high mountain lakes, and rivers that can seem both calm and dangerous as they are fed by melting snows. The Green River crosses the area on its way to meet the Colorado deep within Canyonlands National Park. Fertile farm valleys and grazing lands seem to stretch forever, but when winter comes it brings the deep powder snow Utah's ski-industry boosters call "The Greatest Snow on Earth"—and plenty of skiers agree. The High Uintas Wilderness is the state's largest and caps the eastern edge of the province. The history here echoes the perception of the Wild West—a stomping ground for traders and mountain men, explorers and outlaws.

Towns listed: Garden City, Heber, Logan, Park City, Roosevelt, Vernal

4. CENTRAL UTAH

Cutting a wide swath west to east, central Utah jumbles desert and forest with the brief spines of mountain ranges in the middle of the state. Then come sheltered valley locations where Mormon pioneers stopped briefly then moved on, creating one settlement after another. In the eastern portion of this region, cataclysmic forces have pushed and compressed the earth, leaving strange fields of stone, coal mines, and prehistoric swamps now layered with plant and animal fossils.

Towns listed: Ephraim, Manti, Payson, Price, Richfield, Salina

5. CANYON COUNTRY

The vibrant red rock of the Colorado Plateau characterizes the southeastern part of Utah. The cities and towns here were the last to be settled. Some of them are barely learning the meaning of economic development. The land here will never be settled. There are broad, rolling hummocks of sandstone known as "slickrock" and high, snow-capped mountains rising like a verdant mirage above the desert. Mile after mile of sagebrush flats may suddenly drop away into deep and narrow slot canyons. Mesas stretch, level and unbroken, or stacked one next to the other like giant step stools. The people of southeastern Utah, like the ancient inhabitants of the region, are resilient and inventive. They understand the elements of water, desert, and stone, and the need to carefully manage what surrounds them.

Towns listed: Blanding, Bluff, Green River, Moab, Monticello

6. UTAH'S DIXIE

The southwestern corner of the state is referred to as Color Country, and sometimes, as Utah's Dixie. The settlers here gave it this name, and politically correct or not, Dixie it is. These days it's retirees rather than pioneers who populate the area. St. George is a regional hub for shopping, dining, and cultural events. This portion of the state has

		1300s	**1765**	**1776**
Archaic stage (7,000–1,500 years ago) gather plants and seeds to supplement their diets. The Anasazi (2,000–700 years ago) are a farming culture in southern and southeastern Utah.	The roughly contemporary agricultural Fremont Culture (15,000–700 years ago) lives north and west of the Anasazi.	The Ute, Paiute, and later Navajo cultures develop. All three survive today.	Juan Maria Rivera explores southeastern Utah.	Franciscan priests Fathers Dominguez and Escalante and a 10-man team explore portions of northeastern and north-central Utah, keeping detailed maps and descriptions of plant and

three of Utah's five national parks (Bryce Canyon, Capitol Reef, and Zion), so tourism is a major industry year-round. Sweaters are needed all winter long. When summer brings on the heat, there's always someplace shaded and cool if you're willing to walk a little way into a canyon edged with giant cliffs or drive until the desert rises and becomes a forest.

Towns listed: Beaver, Boulder, Cedar City, Escalante, Kanab, Loa, Panguitch, St. George, Springdale, Torrey

When to Visit

Most visitors to Utah come either in summer or in winter. Summer visitors use Salt Lake City as a jumping-off point for adventures into northern, central, or southern Utah. If they travel north or into mountain communities they find a pleasant drop in temperature and green landscapes. Summer visits to central Utah are a fairly good bet. This section of the state has a large number of heritage and cultural tourism opportunities that most people speed through on their way to southern Utah. Southern Utah summers are hot and dry. Both southeastern and southwestern Utah have higher-elevation attractions, mountains, and forests, but it takes a real effort to break away from the well-worn travel patterns to access them.

In winter, skiers come for the deep, dry powder of their dreams—"The Greatest Snow on Earth." Utah mountain resorts (primarily found in northern Utah) can be cold,

© Corbis

LIQUOR LAWS

Utah repealed Prohibition in February 1933. In fact, Utah can be considered the state responsible for ending national prohibition because it was the 36th, and final, state to ratify the 21st Amendment. Still, the rumor persists that it's impossible to get a "drink" in Utah. Not so. It just requires a little information.

State-operated liquor stores are the only places where bottled liquor can be purchased. Beer is available at most grocery and convenience stores. Mixed drinks are served in "non-exclusive private clubs." Their designation aside, visitors are most welcome at these clubs with temporary memberships available for a small fee.

If you want to have an alcoholic beverage with a restaurant meal (particularly in rural areas of the state) it's best to call ahead to make sure they are able to serve you. Once you're seated, ask your server for a beverage menu. In some places, liquor is not available, and in others, your server can bring you a drink but can't ask you if you'd like to have one.

| animal life and the lifestyles of the Utes and Paiutes. | **1820s** Mountain men and fur trappers explore most of Utah's rivers and valleys. Trapper Jim Bridger reports sighting the Great Salt Lake in 1824. | **1844** Miles Goodyear establishes Fort Buenaventura on the Ogden River, the first permanent stockade and trading post in the area. | **1846** The Donner Party breaks a trail into the Salt Lake Valley from the north. | **1847** Brigham Young and the first party of Mormon Emigrants arrive in the Salt Lake Valley following the Donner Party's route. |

particularly at night. Central Utah experiences snowy, quiet winters and its historic attractions don't lose their appeal. Southeastern Utah has cool days and cooler nights. Winter is a growing season for mountain bikers who don't want to compete with the summer crowds. As there are plenty of accommodations, they can count on outdoor fun on sunny days and a motel to hole up in at night. In southwestern Utah, Dixie residents play golf and tennis all winter. Days are pleasant and nights are cool. Zion and Bryce Canyon national parks are both at higher elevations. Winter days in either location are cold, but the incredible mix of snow and the native red rock is unforgettable.

More and more visitors are scheduling their Utah vacations in the spring and fall. They may be harder to plan, but the rewards, in terms of scenery, weather, and lower cost, make it worth the extra effort.

INTRODUCTION
HISTORY
REGIONS
WHEN TO VISIT
STATE'S GREATS
RULES OF THE ROAD
DRIVING TOURS

CLIMATE CHART
Average High/Low Temperatures (*F) and Monthly Precipitation (in inches)

	JAN.	FEB.	MAR.	APR.	MAY	JUNE
BLANDING	38/16	44/22	52/27	62/34	72/42	83/50
	1.36	1.18	1.04	.85	.73	.46
	JULY	**AUG.**	**SEPT.**	**OCT.**	**NOV.**	**DEC.**
	88/57	86/56	78/56	66/37	51/26	41/19
	1.18	1.39	1.39	1.42	1.03	1.38

	JAN.	FEB.	MAR.	APR.	MAY	JUNE
LOGAN	30/11	37/16	48/25	59/41	69/48	80/48
	1.08	1.2	1.73	1.74	1.77	1.39
	JULY	**AUG.**	**SEPT.**	**OCT.**	**NOV.**	**DEC.**
	89/54	88/52	77/43	64/33	46/24	34/15
	.73	.88	1.43	1.59	1.45	1.25

	JAN.	FEB.	MAR.	APR.	MAY	JUNE
MOAB	42/18	51/24	62/33	72/41	82/48	92/56
	.66	.6	.83	.81	.73	.42
	JULY	**AUG.**	**SEPT.**	**OCT.**	**NOV.**	**DEC.**
	98/62	95/61	86/51	73/39	57/28	44/20
	.76	.83	.85	1.02	0.7	.77

	JAN.	FEB.	MAR.	APR.	MAY	JUNE
PARK CITY	32/12	36/15	41/20	53/28	63/36	74/44
	2.37	2.1	2.39	1.58	1.2	0.79
	JULY	**AUG.**	**SEPT.**	**OCT.**	**NOV.**	**DEC.**
	82/50	79/49	70/41	58/32	43/21	34/15
	1.31	1.46	1.21	1.41	1.58	2.07

1848
The treaty of Guadalupe Hidalgo ends the Mexican War, giving the United States title to much of the Southwest, including Utah.

1849
Mormons form a political government and Brigham Young proposes the creation of the State of Deseret, with boundaries encompassing all of present-day Utah and large portions of Nevada, California, Idaho, Oregon, Wyoming, Colorado, New Mexico, and Arizona—an astonishing 480,000 square mi.

1850
As part of the Missouri Compromise, Utah is given territorial status at a greatly reduced size. Deseret is disregarded as a name, and Utah, derived from a Spanish reference to the Ute Indians, is chosen instead.

	JAN.	FEB.	MAR.	APR.	MAY	JUNE
ST. GEORGE	53/25	60/30	67/36	77/43	86/50	96/58
	1.06	.98	.97	.51	.4	.19

	JULY	AUG.	SEPT.	OCT.	NOV.	DEC.
	101/66	99/65	93/55	80/43	65/31	54/25
	.68	.77	.59	.67	.62	.8

	JAN.	FEB.	MAR.	APR.	MAY	JUNE
SALT LAKE CITY	36/19	43/24	52/31	62/38	72/45	82/53
	1.29	1.22	1.7	1.96	1.66	.92

	JULY	AUG.	SEPT.	OCT.	NOV.	DEC.
	92/62	90/60	79/50	66/40	50/29	34/22
	.67	.86	.94	1.33	1.31	1.26

FESTIVALS AND SEASONAL EVENTS
WINTER

Dec.   **Temple Square Lights.** The day after Thanksgiving, Salt Lake City turns on the lights that will brighten evenings until after New Year's. For sheer elegance, the display of more than 250,000 twinkling, colored lights adorning 10-acre Temple Square is the undisputed champion. A month-long concert series offers concurrent nightly performances in the Assembly Hall, the Tabernacle, the Joseph Smith Memorial Building, and each of the two visitors centers on the square. These concerts mingle community choirs and professional musicians, giving many residents a chance to perform. | 801/240–4390.

Jan.   **The Sundance Film Festival.** For ten days in January, Park City turns into Hollywood Central as actors, producers, and directors gather for Robert Redford's film festival, where the spotlight is on independent filmmakers from all over the world. There are awards, tributes, workshops, and, of course, film screenings. Packages of film and event passes go on sale in the late fall and sell out quickly. However, tickets for individual screenings are often available right up to show time. As the festival has grown, films are now screened in Salt Lake City and Ogden as well as in Park City. | 801/328–3456.

SPRING

May   **Golden Spike Reenactment.** Each year on May 10, railroad and history buffs are joined by hundreds of regular folks at Golden Spike National Historic Site to watch a precise reen-

---

1857
In response to reports that Utahns were in rebellion against the federal government, President James Buchanan sends troops to the territory.

1861
The overland telegraph connecting Omaha, Nebraska, and San Francisco is completed in Salt Lake City.

1863–early 1900s
Silver, gold, lead, and copper mining take a firm hold on Utah's economy. Those connected with the mines—primarily non-Mormons—impact business, politics, and social life.

1869
The Union Pacific and Central Pacific Railroads meet at Promontory, Utah, completing the transcontinental railroad and uniting the nation by rail.

1869 and 1871
John Wesley Powell explores the Green and Colorado rivers. His vivid descriptions published in Eastern newspapers capture the country's imagination.

actment of the 1869 ceremony marking the completion of the first transcontinental railroad. Promontory, on a sagebrush flat north of Great Salt Lake, may not have been a spot well suited to pomp and circumstance, but officials of the Union Pacific and Central Pacific Railroads did their best. | 435/471–2209.

INTRODUCTION
HISTORY
REGIONS
WHEN TO VISIT
STATE'S GREATS
RULES OF THE ROAD
DRIVING TOURS

SUMMER

June–July **America's Freedom Festival.** A month-long patriotic celebration that involves much of Provo City. Along with parades, pancake breakfasts, running races, talent competitions, and an essay contest, the Freedom Festival sponsors concerts, forums with nationally recognized political and religious leaders, and the largest 4th of July fireworks display in the state. | 801/370–8013.

June–Sept. **Utah Shakespearean Festival.** This summer-long event transforms Cedar City with bawdy skits, strolling musicians, Royal Feastes, and professionally staged productions. Shakespeare's plays are performed in a replica of the Globe Theater nightly, but as the festival's popularity has grown, matinee performances have been added in a lovely indoor theater. In the mid-1990s, the seasonal repertoire was expanded to include "works of today's Shakespeares." The festival now includes four of Shakespeare's plays and two or three modern works each season. | 800/752–9849.

July **Days of '47 Celebration.** July 24 is a designated Utah state holiday honoring the day that the first group of Mormon pioneers entered the Salt Lake valley in 1847. Pioneer Day celebrations are held in nearly every city and town in the state, but Salt Lake City's Days of '47 is the largest and longest. For the two weeks preceding July 24, the state's biggest rodeo is held nightly. In the week before the 24th there are parades, races, carnivals, and fireworks across the valley, including a children's parade and a horse parade. Spectators set up camp along the parade route a full 24 hours before the parade on the 24th. | 801/560–0047.

Aug. **Festival of the American West.** Based at Jensen Historical Farm in Wellsville, the Festival of the American West is a 2-week encampment of soldiers, cowboys, peddlers, and other types from the Wild West era. There are craft and skill demonstrations, ax throwing, black-powder rifle competitions, story

1877	1890	1894	1896	1900
Brigham Young dies and Wilford Woodruff assumes leadership of the Mormon Church.	Wilford Woodruff issues a statement forbidding the practice of polygamy.	President Grover Cleveland signs Utah's Enabling Act, satisfied that it has met the criteria for statehood.	Utah becomes the 45th state.	An explosion in the Winter Quarters Mine in Scofield kills 200 coal miners. The event leads to the organization of labor unions in the state.

tellers, and more. The "world championship" dutch oven cook-off is held during this event, as well as a quilting show. The pageant *The West: America's Odyssey,* with a cast of more than 200, is performed each night in an outdoor amphitheater. | 435/797–1143.

AUTUMN

Sept.   **Utah State Fair.** For ten days the Utah State Fair draws residents from all over Utah to see and display award-winning livestock, flowers, vegetables, preserves, sewing projects, quilts, and paintings and other works of art. Several stages are kept busy days and evenings with local performers, talent contests, and other entertainment. The fair also has a nightly rodeo and outdoor country music concerts. | 801/538–3247.

Oct.   **Bison Round-Up on Antelope Island.** There are antelope on this island in Great Salt Lake, but during the bison round-up they head for the hills. 250 volunteers on horseback round up the island's herd of about 600 bison and drive them to holding pens on the north end of the island to be counted and given medical care. Watching this galloping spectacle, it's hard to believe that the current free-roaming herd is descended from a group of six animals placed on the island in the late 1800s by a pioneer stockman "just to see how they'd do." | 801/773–2941.

State's Greats

Utah's wide-open spaces provide a tapestry of recreation, scenery, and history. Nearly 80% of the state is public land administered by the federal or state government for recreation.

Utah cities have come of age. The art scenes in Salt Lake, Ogden, and Provo are diverse and professional. Park City has emerged as a year-round sports and arts destination.

Perhaps Utah's greatest treasures are simply the state's residents. The population base is younger than the national average, but Utah culture honors families and the older generations who have important stories to tell.

Forests and Parks

In Utah, six **national forests** protect nine million acres of spectacular woodlands, meadows, and mountains. Within these forests are 13 designated wilderness areas set aside for solitary and primitive recreational pursuits. More than any other topographic designation, Utah's forests attest to the geologic mayhem that shaped the state's landscapes and climate zones.

1914	1929	1942–45	1948	1964
Auto racing begins on the Bonneville Salt Flats.	First radio broadcast of the Mormon Tabernacle Choir's weekly program *Music and the Spoken Word,* which continues today.	Topaz, a Japanese-American relocation camp with a population of 3,000, operates in west-central Utah.	Reva Beck Bosone, a democrat from Utah, becomes the first woman elected to Congress.	The Flaming Gorge Dam on the Green River is dedicated and Arizona's Glen Canyon Dam on the Colorado River, completed the year before, creates Lake Powell.

INTRODUCTION
HISTORY
REGIONS
WHEN TO VISIT
STATE'S GREATS
RULES OF THE ROAD
DRIVING TOURS

In northern Utah, the **Wasatch-Cache,** the **Ashley,** and the **Uinta** forests are known for giant, craggy mountains made of ancient granite and silt-layered limestone that's been gouged by glaciers and carved by rivers. Yet each of these northern forests is also marked by strange bands and protrusions of ruddy stone like that associated with the famed red rock of southern Utah.

The forests and mountains of central and southern Utah—the **Fishlake,** the **Dixie,** and the **Manti-La Sal**—are strewn with volcanic rock. Their slopes are softened a bit, rounded with time and shifted along primal fault lines to reveal slices of layered sediments in colors and mineral types most typical of northern Utah.

In Utah the term "parks" includes everything from municipal recreation sites—of which every city and town has its fair share—to every variety of public land designated for specific uses by the state and federal governments. In fact, there are five national parks, seven national monuments, two national recreation areas, a national historic site, and 45 state parks focusing on heritage, scenic beauty, mountain and desert recreation, and waterfront facilities.

Culture, History, and the Arts

To be accurate, a description of Utah's history and heritage needs to reach way back to the age when dinosaurs rumbled across eastern Utah, leaving behind a wealth of fossils and other clues to prehistory. **Dinosaur National Monument,** the **Cleveland-Lloyd Quarry,** the **Blanding Dinosaur Museum,** and the natural-history museums at the **University of Utah, Brigham Young University,** and the **College of Eastern Utah** are excellent Jurassic jaunts.

Next are the mysteries of the Puebloan cultures that left artifacts scattered across the state in ruins of their homes and places of worship, like those preserved at **Anasazi State Park Museum** in Boulder, **Fremont Indian State Park and Museum** near Richfield, and **Edge of the Cedars State Park Museum** in Blanding.

There are historic towns like **Bluff** and **Spring City,** where the Mormon pioneer heritage is preserved as a celebration of the days when men and women commonly aimed at far horizons and were strong enough and determined enough to get there.

From settlement days forward, Utahns have upheld a tradition of active support for the arts. **Ballet West,** the **Utah Opera Company,** and the **Utah Symphony** perform throughout the state, and the **Utah Shakespearean Festival** has put Cedar City on the cultural map.

Sports

Nearly every type of outdoor adventure can be experienced in Utah. At northern Utah ski resorts, **Deer Valley, The Canyons,** and **Powder Mountain,** it's possible to ski the exact runs that will challenge Olympic athletes in 2002. For hikers, the state is crisscrossed by trails, from a casual stroll through the **Fruita Campground** at Capitol Reef to serious explorations of Canyonlands' **Maze District.**

1976
At his own insistence, despite numerous court appeals on his behalf, convicted murderer Gary Gilmore is executed by firing squad at the Utah State Prison near Salt Lake City. It is the first exercise of the death penalty in the United States for 10 years.

1983
Due to excess runoff from record-breaking winter snows, the Great Salt Lake overflows, inundating I-80. Water from City Creek is diverted down Salt Lake City's State Street, creating a virtual river.

1985
Utah Republican Jake Garn is the first U.S. Senator to fly in space.

1995
More than 30 years after its first bid, and with several tries in between, Salt Lake City is named the site of the 2002 Olympic Winter Games.

For what's generally considered a desert state, Utah has a lot of water! Lakes, reservoirs, and rivers place Utah in the nation's top-ten list for surface acres of boatable waters. The sport of white-water rafting was created in Utah when John C. Powell set off into the unknown to chart the **Green and Colorado Rivers.** Experienced tour operators still follow his routes.

Moab is a mecca for mountain bikers, drawn to the slickrock routes and inspiring scenery. Rock climbers head for **Logan** and **Provo Canyons** in northern Utah and the cliffs framing the **Colorado River** in southeastern Utah; there is guided climbing and mountaineering in **Zion National Park.**

Rules of the Road

License Requirements: The minimum driving age in Utah is 16. All drivers must have a valid driver's license. Visitors from other states or countries may drive in Utah as long as they have a current driver's license and are at least 16 years old.

Speed Limits: On major highways the speed limit is 55 miles per hour, particularly in urban areas. Speed limits increase to 65 or 75 miles per hour on interstate highways in rural areas. But watch out. "Rural areas" are determined by census boundaries, and sometimes seem to make little sense. Increased speeds are allowed only where they are clearly posted. Transition zones from one speed limit to another are indicated with pavement markings and additional signs. Fines are automatically doubled for speeding in highway work zones. Since portions of I–15 north and south of Salt Lake City will be under major construction until 2001, this is an important thing to remember. In some areas, double fines also apply to citations issued for speeding in a school zone.

Right Turn on Red: Generally, right turns are allowed on a red light after the vehicle has come to a complete stop. Right turns on red are prohibited in some areas, but these are signed accordingly.

Seat Belt and Helmet Laws: Utah law requires seatbelt use for drivers, front-seat passengers, and all children under 10. Children under the age of two are required to be in federally approved safety seats. Helmet use is mandatory for motorcyclists and passengers under the age of 18.

For More Information: Contact the Utah Department of Motor Vehicles (801/965–4518) or the Utah Highway Patrol (801/297–7780).

1996
President Bill Clinton announces the creation of the Grand Staircase–Escalante National Monument in southern Utah. It is the first national monument to be administered by the

Bureau of Land Management.

2002
Olympic Winter Games scheduled to take place in Salt Lake City.

From Salt Lake
into the Mountains Drive

*PARK CITY TO THE MIRROR LAKE HIGHWAY THROUGH THE WASATCH-CACHE
NATIONAL FOREST ON ROUTE 150*

INTRODUCTION
HISTORY
REGIONS
WHEN TO VISIT
STATE'S GREATS
RULES OF THE ROAD
DRIVING TOURS

Distance: 90 miles   Time: 2 days

Breaks: In late spring to fall, after the skiers have packed it in, Park City is an excellent place to
while away an afternoon with shopping, hiking, or just enjoying the scenery. Overnight here in
one of the city's fine bed-and-breakfast inns (at off-season rates), and enjoy some of Utah's best
dining and nightlife.

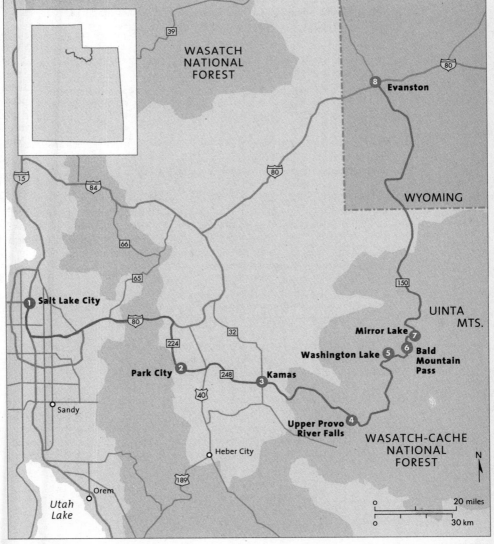

This tour will lead you from Salt Lake City to Park City, northern Utah's premier year-round resort town. From Park City it leads across the Heber Valley and into the pristine beauty of the Wasatch-Cache National Forest. In spring and fall, Park City provides local color and the forest promises vibrant bursts of natural color in its meadows, lakes, and mountains. Don't plan to take this tour in winter. Route 150 may be closed due to snow, and some of Park City's dining and lodging rates double during ski season.

❶ From **Salt Lake,** I–80 runs through Parley's Canyon toward Park City. This is Utah's original toll road, devised by enterprising Mormon settler Parley P. Pratt; he stationed his home midway in the canyon and charged settlers a fee to pass through the canyon, the easiest route into the Salt Lake valley.

❷ Proceed 20 mi east on I–80, then south for approximately 5 mi on Route 224 into Park City. Main Street in **Park City** (435/649–6100) is an easy up-and-down walk of less than a mile. Window shopping is its chief interest, but take a few minutes to enjoy the art galleries on both sides of the street and decide which of several restaurants looks best for dinner.

❸ Leaving Park City, head east on Route 248 approximately 7 mi to the **Kamas** Ranger District Office (435/783–4338) to find out about road conditions and gather interpretive information before heading into the **Wasatch-Cache National Forest.**
   The **Uinta Mountains** will be visible to the east for the remainder of this tour. They are one of only a few mountain ranges in North America running on an east–west axis.

❹ The Provo River parallels the road along much of this drive. **Upper Provo River Falls** (22 mi east of Kamas on Route 150) is a lovely place to stretch your legs. Walkways near the road follow the river past a series of small cascades.

❺ As the highway continues to climb in elevation, there are several signed turnoffs leading to small lakes. Some of these roads may be suitable only for high-clearance vehicles, but a couple of them are maintained gravel with developed picnic and camping areas and short hikes to lakes nestled in thick pine forest. **Washington Lake** (approx. 27 mi northeast of Kamas on the west side of Route 150) is particularly beautiful in summer when wildflowers are in bloom.

❻ Continue along Route 150 for another 5 mi or so to **Bald Mountain Pass,** where the road climbs to 10,687 ft, an elevation close to the timberline. Watch during the climb as tree stands begin to thin out and meadow areas are strewn with boulders.

❼ Another mile on Route 150 will take you to **Mirror Lake,** on the northeastern descent from Bald Mountain, about 1 mi from the top of the pass. This alpine lake's tranquil waters beautifully reflect the sky and the ring of pine trees surrounding the lake's shore.

❽ To finish this drive, you can either continue north to Evanston, Wyoming (32 mi north on Route 150), then take I–80 back into the Heber Valley (approximately 40 mi southwest), or go back the way you came (33 mi southwest to Kamas). If you choose to return via Kamas, try the family-owned fast-food place on the north side of Route 150 (just west of the national forest boundary); it serves extremely thick, fresh-fruit milk shakes.

A Color-Country Drive

ZION, BRYCE, AND GRAND STAIRCASE–ESCALANTE NATIONAL MONUMENTS

INTRODUCTION
HISTORY
REGIONS
WHEN TO VISIT
STATE'S GREATS
RULES OF THE ROAD
DRIVING TOURS

Distance: Approx. 140 miles   Time: 3 days
Breaks: Overnight in Springdale at the southern entrance to Zion National Park; overnight at Bryce Canyon Lodge inside the national park; overnight in Escalante.

This driving tour winds across southern Utah, through the finest examples of the beauty and variety of red-rock terrain. It visits three vastly different landscapes and incorporates pieces of three designated scenic byway roads.

1 It's easy to spend a full day in the western portion of **Zion National Park.** A stop at the Visitor Center (Zion Park Blvd./Rte. 9, 435/772–3256) should be the first item of business. A sign lists any ranger-guided hikes or lectures for the day and indicates any trails that may be closed due to weather or poor trail conditions. Three-dimensional topographic maps lying on tables help orient visitors and get them ready for the scope of Zion Canyon. For example, note how deeply the Virgin River has cut through the rock.

In the spring of 2000 Zion launched a major **Visitor Transit System,** which basically limits traffic in Zion Canyon on the 8-mi Park Service road north of Route 9 to hikers, bicyclists, and a fleet of 21 propane-fueled shuttle vehicles. The shuttles will stop at all of the canyon's trailheads.

2 The first thing you'll notice as you enter Zion Canyon is **The Watchman,** a formation carved, like the canyon's other dramatic features, from layers of the Markagunt

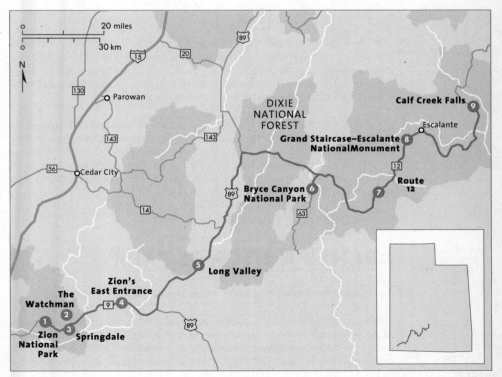

Plateau—Navajo sandstone and sedimentary rock cemented by iron, silica, and lime. There are many other soaring formations in the park, and a variety of walks and hikes.

❸ Spend the night in **Springdale** (just south of the park on Route 9), where there are numerous hotels, motels, restaurants, and bed-and-breakfast properties.

❹ After breakfast, head east on gradual switchbacks and pass through two tunnels cut through the massive canyon walls in the late 1920s. East of the tunnels, petrified sand dunes roll along the roadside to **Zion's East Entrance.** From Springdale east to the park entrance is approximately 12 mi on Route 9.

❺ Turn north onto U.S. 89 at Mt. Carmel Junction and drive through verdant **Long Valley,** which is naturally irrigated by the Virgin River and bordered by yellow-, red-, and white-banded cliffs. After 44 mi, turn east on Route 12 toward

❻ **Bryce Canyon National Park** (435/834–5322). Fifteen miles on Route 12 brings you to the junction with Route 63, which leads to the park boundary 3 mi south.

Tour **Bryce Canyon**'s rim or amphitheater trails and enjoy the park's **Scenic Drive** (the Park Service road running south from the park entrance for 37 mi). Stay the night at the historic **Bryce Canyon Lodge or Cabins** (435/834–5361 or 303/297–2757 for reservations). These rustic structures were built between 1920 and 1930, and are listed on the National Register of Historic Places.

❼ In the morning, watch how the rising sun makes the formations of Bryce seem to shift shape and color. Spend a couple of hours exploring the park. When you're ready, return to **Route 12** and head east. *Car and Driver* has called Route 12 one of the country's most enjoyable drives. So, enjoy as you travel through the towns of Tropic, Boulder, Cannonville, and Henrieville.

❽ Enter **Grand Staircase–Escalante National Monument** (435/865–5100). Everything you can see is part of this enormous park. Many of the monument's most incredible landscapes and features—slot canyons, rock-art panels, ancient ruins, twisted river courses—are deep inside these formidable mesas. Continue to the town of **Escalante** (30 mi northeast on Route 12) to eat, gas up, and fill your water bottles.

❾ From Escalante, travel north to the signed parking area for **Calf Creek Falls** (20 mi north on Route 12). If you're so inclined, take the 2½-mi hike to the falls. (Don't forget to carry plenty of water.) A brochure at the trailhead locates more than 20 points of interest along this level path, including Anasazi ruins, interesting petroglyphs, some abandoned late-19th-century farming equipment, and lots of wildlife. At the canyon's end, an impressive waterfall plunges from the top of a high sandstone cliff.

After hiking back to the trailhead, take a moment to rest and replenish your water supply before returning to Escalante to spend the night.

ARCHES NATIONAL PARK

MAP 14, E7

(Nearby towns also listed: Green River, Moab, Monticello)

Arches has a remarkable concentration of natural stone arches—more than 2,000 within its 114 square mi—and other bizarre geological features, all sculpted through the aeons by water and windblown sand. A scenic drive winds through the landscape, but stop the car: this is a park for hiking. At least a dozen trails are accessible from the main road, some as short as ½ mi. Other areas have longer loop trails, guided hikes, and acres of sagebrush flats punctuated with sandstone "fins" inviting exploration.

Information: **Arches National Park** | Box 907, Moab, 84532 | 435/259–8161 | fax 435/259–8341 | www.nps.gov/arch. **Grand County Travel Council** | Box 550, Moab, UT 84532 | 435/259–8825 or 800/635–6622.

Attractions

Delicate Arch and Wolfe Ranch. A 3-mi hike across greasewood flats and rolling slickrock terrain leads to Delicate Arch, the most famous span in the park. To get to the trailhead parking area, drive 8½ mi east of the visitor center to the Balanced Rock and Windows section turnoff; take this side road for 2½ mi to a signed road. At the trailhead parking area you'll find directions for a brief exploration of the remnants of the Wolfe Ranch, now a National Historic Site. Just east of the ranch area, a short trail branches off to a panel of Ute pictographs showing riders on horseback, bighorn sheep, and some odd animals that could be dogs. From here, the Delicate Arch Trail climbs gradually to an elevation gain of 580 ft from the parking area. At the top, the trail slips around a sandstone fin and suddenly there is Delicate Arch, stunningly perched above a slickrock basin with the dark shadow of the La Sal Mountains as its backdrop.

Devil's Garden. You can hike a 1½-mi loop that winds to Landscape Arch, over 100 ft high and 306 ft wide. But the Devil's Garden trail system, whose trailhead is 18 mi east of the visitor center, also has well-signed paths to several other impressive arches. A thorough exploration of Devil's Garden requires about 7 mi round-trip, a full day's adventure. Take plenty of water, food, and sun protection.

The Fiery Furnace. You can see this jumbled collection of flame-colored sandstone fins, 14 mi east of the park entrance on Route 153, from several places in the park. But nothing

ARCHES NATIONAL
PARK

INTRO
ATTRACTIONS
DINING
LODGING

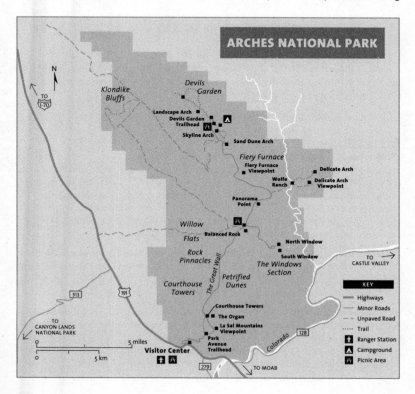

ARCHES NATIONAL PARK

compares with exploring the furnace up-close. The geology of this area is so complex that a ranger takes small groups of hikers on explorations to explain it, describe the plant and animal life, and give help and encouragement when the hike requires squeezing through narrow slots, jumping down from ledges, or scrambling over boulders. Sign up for the hike at the visitors center, generally for the next day.

Scenic Drive. An 18-mi road winds from the visitors center to the parking area at Devil's Garden. From this paved road most of the park's formations are easily accessible. You'll find both road guides and hiking brochures at the visitor center. | Begin at visitor center, 5 mi north of Moab off U.S. 191.

ON THE CALENDAR
APR.–OCT.: *Fiery Furnace Walks.* Wander through the mazelike sandstone canyons during the summer on these daily, guided, 2½- to 3-hour walks. There is no trail, and the terrain occasionally requires hands as well as feet: be prepared. These tours are popular; they start about 14 mi north or at the visitors center, where you can reserve space a few days in advance. | 435/259–8161.

Lodging
Devil's Garden Campground. This is the only campground in Arches, 18 mi north of the park entrance on the main park road. It operates on a first-come, first-served basis; at times it's full before noon. Arrive early, too, so you have lots of time to view the red rock and arches. Tables, grills, water, flush toilets. | 54 sites | 435/259–4351 | fax 435/259–4285 | $10 | Mid-Mar.–Oct.

BEAVER

MAP 14, B7

(Nearby towns also listed: Cedar City, Panguitch, Richfield)

When it was settled in the mid-1800s, Beaver was a welcome bit of civilization in the middle of the uninhabited territory south of Fillmore. More than 150 years later, I–15 neatly slices through what is still wild, unbroken country, but Beaver, now with about 2,000 residents, remains a lovely respite.

Information: **Beaver County Travel Council** | 40 S. Main St., Beaver, 84713 | 435/438–2975.

Attractions
Elk Meadows Ski and Summer Resort. Elk Meadows is kind of a sleeper among Utah ski areas. It's out of the way, yet still easy to get to. It's never really crowded, and skiers from Las Vegas, Phoenix, and Los Angeles often know more about it than those from northern Utah. The vertical drop of 1,350 ft can be experienced on 37 runs on two mountains—Elk Meadows and Mt. Holly. You'll find beginner to expert terrain, snowmobiling, cross-country skiing, and snowshoeing. | 150 S.W. Village Circle, Rte. 153 | 435/438–5433 or 888/881–7669 | www.elkmeadows.com | $25 Mon.–Thurs., $33 Fri.–Sun. | Dec.–Mar.

Fishlake National Forest. Beaver is a gateway to the Tushar Mountains, which dominate the area's skyline. The southern end of one of four distinct blocks of the Fishlake National Forest, east on Route 153, is best for recreation. | 150 E. 900 N | 435/896–9233 | www.fishlake.r4.fs.fed.us | Free day use; camping fees | Daily.

Historic Homes. More than 100 historic homes remain in Beaver, many on the National Register of Historic Places. Some are early log cabins and one-story stuccoed adobe houses built in the 1860s. More common are homes constructed of black basalt, pink tufa, or ruddy brick in the 1870s and 1880s. All are private homes and not open for tours, but a walk or drive around town is diverting. You can get more information at the Beaver County Travel

Council office in the County Courthouse on Main Street. | 435/438–2975 or 435/438–2808 | www.dced.state.ut.us/history.

ON THE CALENDAR

JULY: *Pioneer Days*. Horse races, a parade with more than 100 floats, and contests, including a tricycle race for children, all celebrate the area's settlement by Mormon pioneers in 1847. | 435/438–2975 | July 23–24.

Dining

Arshel's. American. A friendly, small-town sort of place that opened as a gas station and grill in the 1930s but finally dropped the gas station to concentrate on the restaurant. Specialties include chicken dishes, potato soup, and lemon meringue pie. | 711 N. Main St. | 435/438–2977 | $7–$15 | AE, MC, V.

Kan Kun. Mexican. This restaurant has a cheerful interior with colorful serapes and hats hanging on the walls. The specialties are carnitas asadas, fajitas, and tangy salsa. | 1474 S. 450 W | 435/438–5908 | $8–$14 | MC, V.

Kelly's Garden of Eat'n. American. This classic eatery, complete with booths and a full-length counter, serves hearty rib-eye steaks, sirloin tips over noodles, smoked pork chops, and local specials like Utah red trout and the Western hamburger with green chiles and guacamole. | 314 W. 1450 N | 435/438–5464 | $14–$23 | AE, D, MC, V.

Lodging

Aspen Lodge Motel. A central location and some of the best rates in the area distinguish this small, local motel. Service is especially friendly, amenities are few. Cable TV. | 14 rooms | 265 S. Main St. | 435/438–5160 | $35 | D, MC, V.

Best Western Butch Cassidy Inn. Brick, with white trim and surrounded by flowers and shrubbery, this downtown, one-story motel has better-than-average services and amenities. Restaurant. In-room data ports. Cable TV. Pool. Hot tub, sauna. Business services. Some pets allowed. | 24 rooms | 161 S. Main St. | 435/438–2438 | fax 435/438–1053 | $45–$55 | AE, D, DC, MC, V.

SWEET THINGS—UTAHNS, JELL-O, AND ICE CREAM

Utahns love Jell-O. They eat four times as much of it as the rest of the country. Over 4 million boxes of sugared and sugar-free Jell-O are sold every year to about a million Utah households. Lime Jell-O, which is a vivid green, is the top-selling flavor.

Utahns also love ice cream. Depending on the source, Utah ice-cream fans rank between first and fifth for the highest per capita consumption in the United States.

Is this sweet tooth socially significant, with long-term ramifications for Utah's future? No. But it might be interpreted as a cultural curiosity. Although it is completely unproven, the accepted explanation for Utahns' love affair with sweet desserts is that it has to have something to do with the fact that 70% of Utah's populace are members of The Church of Jesus Christ of Latter-day Saints, more simply known as Mormons. The Mormon faith encourages members to refrain from indulging in alcohol, tobacco, and caffeine . . . making ice cream and Jell-O the logical alternatives.

© Corbis

Best Western Paradise Inn Large family suites are available at this one-story motel, and the location, right off I–15, is convenient for stopovers. Cable TV. Indoor pool. Hot tub, exercise room. Some pets allowed. | 50 rooms, 3 suites | 300 W. 1451 N | 435/438–2455 or 877/233–9330 | fax 435/438–2455 | $59, $77 suites | AE, D, DC, MC, V.

Days Inn. Location makes this a good choice for an I–15 stopover. Some kitchenettes. In-room data ports. Cable TV. | 51 rooms | 645 N. Main St. | 435/438–2409 | fax 435/438–3248 | www.daysinn.com | $55–$70 | AE, D, DC, MC, V.

Quality Inn. Away from the interstate and off Main Street, this is a quiet, restful place to stop, just 2 mi from the national forest. Rooms are comfortable, with desks. Cable TV. Indoor pool. Hot tub. Business services. | 52 rooms | 781 W. 1800 S. | 435/438–5426 | fax 435/438–2493 | www.qualityinn.com | $50–$65 | AE, D, DC, MC, V.

BLANDING

MAP 14, F8

(Nearby towns also listed: Bluff, Monticello)

Plenty of evidence indicates that the mesa on which Blanding sits has been a favored living site for centuries. It's been said that the archaeological sites in this vicinity ought to be counted by the acre if not the square mile. Thousands of ancient Pueblo ruins are scattered across the area, and Blanding offers some excellent museums as windows to the past. Blanding is also the commercial hub for a huge swath of southeastern Utah, and as such a starting point for visits to sights from Natural Bridges National Monument and Lake Powell to Monument Valley, Hovenweep National Monument, and the Navajo Nation.

One thing Blanding does not offer is alcohol. There is no state liquor store here, and no beer is sold in grocery or convenience stores. Stock up in Monticello, 20 mi north on U.S. 191.

Information: San Juan County Community Development and Visitor Services | 117 S. Main St., Monticello, 84535 | 435/587–3235 or 800/574–4386 | fax 435/587–2425 | jrbryan@state.ut.us | www.canyonlands-utah.com.

Attractions

Dinosaur Museum. The private collections of a family of working paleontologists make this small-town museum a world-class attraction. Fossils from all over the world are neatly displayed. Some specimens, including rare petrified wood, are found nowhere else in the world. An expert in dinosaur skin, who believes that these ancient creatures were very brightly colored, displays his works here as well. | 754 S. 200 W | 435/678–3454 | www.moab-utah.com/dinosaur/museum.html | $2 | Mid-Apr.–mid-Oct., Mon.–Sat. 8–8.

Edge of the Cedars State Park. The stabilized remains of an ancient Anasazi pueblo and its ceremonial kiva dominate the park, one of six clusters of ruins within the park boundaries. You can see pottery and the only known metal implements from the Anasazi era in Utah in the interpretive center and museum. Navajo, Ute, and early Hispanic and Anglo artifacts are also on view. | 660 W. 400 N | 435/678–2238 | www.utah.com | $5 per vehicle | Daily 9–5.

Hovenweep National Monument. Hovenweep is a group of six well-preserved village ruins on the Utah/Colorado border, on County Road 212. The residents of this area may have come from Mesa Verde some time in the late 1200s and lived an agricultural life at Hovenweep until drought or a need for better food sources caused them to abandon the villages and press southward. The towers and ruins are linked by short hiking trails and a network of dirt roads. | 970/562–4282 | www.nps.gov/hove | $6 per vehicle | Daily.

Lake Powell. Lake Powell is definitely the recreation area's most famous feature. The second-largest man-made reservoir in the world, it begins at the Glen Canyon Dam and is about 200 mi long with nearly 2,000 mi of serpentine coast. It has hundreds of side canyons, coves, and inlets. Its striking combination of water lapping steep, multi-hued canyon walls and jutting sandstone formations is found nowhere else in the world. The best points of access are the Hite Marina, which has a ferry service to Bullfrog Resorts, across the lake. The headquarters is in Page, AZ. | Glen Canyon National Recreation Area: 520/608–6404; Bullfrog: 435/684–3000; Halls Crossing: 435/684–7000 | www.nps.gov/glca | $5 per car; use fees vary | Daily.

Running on the hour between Halls Crossing and Bullfrog, the 245-ton **John Atlantic Burr Ferry** can carry eight cars and two tour buses per trip, displacing 100 tons of water. The crossing takes approximately 20 minutes. | 435/684–7000 | www.canyon-country.com | $10 per car | Daily; reduced hours in winter.

If you're interested in a **boat trip,** you can rent boats and watercraft of all sizes and shapes at either marina or arrange guided tours. | Bullfrog or Halls Crossing Marina | 800/528–6154 | www.visitlakepowell.com | Daily.

Rainbow Bridge National Monument is on Navajo Nation land, most readily accessed from Forbidding Canyon, a winding channel on the south side of Lake Powell. The featured sight is the largest and most symmetrical natural bridge in the world. Carved from ruddy Navajo sandstone, the bridge is 290 ft tall and 270 ft across. Its narrowest section is 230 ft thick. Behind Rainbow Bridge is Navajo Mountain, a brooding backdrop to the vividly colored span. Both Rainbow Bridge and Navajo Mountain are considered sacred in Navajo culture. Visitors to the monument come by private boat or on tour boats that embark from Bullfrog, Halls Crossing, or Wahweap Marina in Arizona. You can also reach Rainbow Bridge on foot or horseback, but these arduous routes require a permit from the Navajo Nation (520/608–6404). | Navajo Nation Tourism Dept | 520/871–6636 or 520/871–6647 | www.nps.gov/rabr | Free. Admission included in fees charged at Lake Powell | Daily.

The Nations of the Four Corners Cultural Center. This center celebrates the Ute, Navajo, Hispanic, and Anglo cultures that coexist in southeastern Utah. A ½-mi trail leads to a Navajo hogan, a Ute tepee, a hacienda, and a pioneer log cabin. There's also an observation tower, and regular outdoor performances honoring all four cultures are presented. | 707 W. 500 S | 435/678–2072 | Free | Mon.–Sat., dawn–dusk.

Natural Bridges National Monument. Nowhere but in Natural Bridges National Monument are three large river-carved bridges found so close together. Sipapu is the second-largest natural bridge in the world. Kachina is the most massive in the monument. It was named for pictographs near its base that resemble kachina dolls. At 106 ft high and 9 ft thick, Owachomo Bridge is the smallest of the three. A 9-mi loop drive connects pull-outs and overlooks with excellent views of each bridge. You can also get close views of each bridge from the moderate hiking trails, some with wooden ladders or metal stairs. The visitor facilities at Natural Bridges are solar powered. | 42 mi west on Rte. 95, then northwest on Rte. 275 | 435/692–1234 | www.nps.gov/nabr | $6 per car | Daily.

ON THE CALENDAR

JULY: *Folk Fair Festival.* This Fourth of July celebration has folk singers and other musicians, ethnic dancing, and a marketplace featuring local craftsmen. | 435/678–2791.

DEC.: *Lake Powell Festival of Lights Parade.* A parade of private and tour boats led by the paddlewheeler *Canyon King* and decorated with colored lights makes its way up and down the lake. | Wahweap Marina, south end of the lake via U.S. 89 | 800/528–6154 | www.visitlakepowell.com | 1st Sat. in Sept.

Dining

Fry Canyon Lodge Cafe. American. Plain but good is the best way to describe the simple fare in the restaurant at this lonely outpost in Fry Canyon, some 50 mi west of Blanding, north of the Natural Bridges National Monument. The interior is stainless steel, with tables bedecked with blue-and-white checked cloths, booths, stools at a fountain, and an upright piano. | Rte. 95 | 435/259–5334 | $11–$23 | MC, V.

Kenny's Restaurant. American. This small-town diner on the city's main strip specializes in hand-breaded chicken-fried steak and fresh mashed potatoes. | N. U.S. 191 | 435/678–3604 | $10–$18 | MC, V.

Patio Drive-In. American. A typical southern Utah hamburger joint—small, eclectic, and right on the highway—whose shakes make it worth a stop; they're thick and all ice cream. | 95 N. U.S. 191 | 435/678–2177 | $4–$6 | No credit cards.

Old Tymer. American. Large, hearty breakfasts, burgers for lunch, and steak for dinner are the local favorites at this family restaurant, although some Mexican dishes are also on the menu. | 733 S. Main St. | 435/678–2122 | www.mokee_ent.com | $4–$16 | D, MC, V.

Lodging

Best Western Gateway Inn. The downtown location is convenient and you get free movies in every room here. Cable TV. Pool. Pets allowed. | 60 rooms | 86 E. Center St. | 435/678–2278 | fax 435/678–224 | $60–$85 | AE, MC, V.

Blanding Super 8 Motel. A hot tub and larger-than-average rooms set this two-story downtown motel apart from the handful of other places off U.S. 191. It has a three-bed-room family suite and a deluxe Jacuzzi suite. Continental breakfast. In-room data ports. Cable TV. Indoor pool. Laundry facilities. | 58 rooms, 2 suites | 755 S. Main St. | 435/678–3880 or 800/800–8000 | fax 435/678–3790 | super8@mokee-ent.com | www.mokee-ent.com | $60–$67, $87 suites | AE, D, DC, MC, V.

Comfort Inn of Blanding. This downtown establishment is next door to one of the most popular restaurants in Blanding. The rooms are standard. Restaurant, bar. Cable TV. Pool. No pets. | 52 rooms | 711 S. Main St. | 435/622–3271 or 800/622–3250 | fax 435/678–3219 | comfortinn@mokee-ent.com | www.mokee-ent.com | $74 | AE, D, DC, MC, V.

Defiance House. The double queen rooms that sleep five are a good deal at this Lake Powell lodge at Bullfrog Marina. Some rooms have lake views, some mountain views. The deluxe king rooms have been redone with southwestern furnishings. Bar, restaurant. Cable TV. Many room phones. Playground. Laundry facilities. | 56 units, 8 cottages | Bullfrog | 435/684–2233 or 800/528–6154 | fax 435/684–2312 | www.visitlakepowell.com | $75–$110 | AE, D, DC, MC, V.

Four Corners Inn. The rooms are spacious, and one suite is available at this locally owned and operated mom-and-pop motel. Continental breakfast. Cable TV. | 31 rooms, 1 suite | 131 E. Center St. | 435/678–3257 or 800/574–3150 | fax 435/678–3186 | $60, $70 suite | AE, D, DC, MC, V.

Fry Canyon Lodge. This is the only building in the 120 miles between Hanksville and Blanding on Rte. 95, and the only relic of what was once a town built by the uranium boom. Built in 1955 and remodeled, with rooms added, in 1999, the lodge has deluxe, standard, and economy rooms, depending on size. Deluxe rooms have desks and Native American wall hangings; all rooms have lovely quilts on the beds and simple wooden furniture. The 2,500-ft airstrip—the only way to get here until the highway was finished in 1976—is an artifact of the uranium boom, but handy if you plan to fly in. Stop at the small general store to restock if you're not staying the night. Café. Pool table. Piano. Airstrip. | 10 rooms | Rte. 95 | 435/259–5334 | fax 435/259–4101 | $68–$89 | D, MC, V.

Grayson Country Inn. Each of the rooms in this reasonably priced, lovely Victorian inn is individually furnished with antiques. The house is nestled in a quiet neighborhood, and the small, shaded yard has a play area for children. Full breakfast. Cable TV. | 8 rooms, 3-room cottage | 118 E. 300 S | 435/678–2388 or 800/365–0868 | fax 435/678–2000 | $70–$100 | AE, MC, V.

Rogers House Bed & Breakfast. With a large lawn, large, bright flower beds, and a white picket fence, this cheerful, gabled house does not look like it's in the middle of the desert. The rooms are individually decorated and spacious. Complimentary breakfast. Cable TV. |

5 rooms | 412 S. Main St. | 435/678–3932 or 800/355–3932 | fax 435/678–3276 | hosts@roger-shouse.com | www.rogershouse.com | $55–$90 | MC, V.

Ticaboo Resort. The lobby is airy with a high ceiling, and the rooms, redone in 2000, have white walls with southwestern furnishings and fabric. The family suite has a queen-size bed and a double bed with a single bunk above it. On Lake Powell, the resort is 10 mi north of Bullfrog Marina. Restaurant, bar. Cable TV. | 72 rooms | Rte. 276, Ticaboo, | 435/788–2110 or 800/987–5253 | fax 435/788–2118 | $49–$95 | AE, D, DC, MC, V.

BLUFF

(Nearby towns also listed: Blanding, Monticello)

Bluff is near the San Juan River, making it the put-in spot for float trips on this smooth but fast waterway. In the town's center are the sandstone-block homes of the first Anglo settlers from the late 1800s, Mormons who decided to stop there after an arduous six-month journey. The town has a population of 300. The surrounding desert shelters kivas, cliff dwellings, and the rock art of the Anasazi, or ancient Pueblo Indians.

Information: San Juan County Community Development and Visitor Services. | 117 S. Main St., Monticello, 84535 | 435/587–3235 or 800/574–4386 | fax 435/587–2425 | jrbryan@state.ut.us | www.canyonlands-utah.com.

Attractions

Bluff Walking Tour. You can get the free brochure "Historic Bluff by Bicycle and on Foot" at any business in town, then take a walk past the historic homes it describes. About 2 mi east of Bluff on U.S. 163 is St. Christopher's Episcopal Mission (801/672–2244 or 800/422–7654), established in 1943 by Father Harold Lieber. For decades, Navajo children crossed the San Juan River on a swinging bridge to attend school here. The bridge, which is still sound, is about 2 mi east of the mission, with the Navajo Nation on the other side of the river. The mission and the bridge are discussed in the Historic Bluff brochure, as is the windswept Bluff Cemetery, located on a nearby hill. | www.bluff-utah.org | Free | Daily.

Monument Valley Navajo Tribal Park. You may get a sense of déjà vu at your first glimpse of Monument Valley. The valley and formations have been the setting for hundreds of commercials, dozens of movies, and print ads selling everything from cigarettes to shampoo and designer fashions. Many of the most famous formations are recognizable from the highway approach to the actual boundary of the park. There is a self-guided 17-mi scenic drive on a maintained dirt road, with excellent views of The Mittens, Three Sisters, Elephant, Camel, and many other eroded stone formations. Monument Valley is sacred to the Navajo Nation, or Dine (stress on the second syllable), as they refer to themselves. Any exploration of the valley beyond the scenic drive must be accompanied by a Navajo guide. | 435/727–3287 | www.desertusa.com/monvalley | $2.50; prices vary for Navajo-guided tours | Daily.
Goulding's Trading Post and Lodge was established in the 1920s. The original two-story red sandstone building is now a museum. Out back is a reconstructed movie set from John Ford's *She Wore a Yellow Ribbon*, filmed in Monument Valley in 1949. The Anasazi Theater has three shows nightly of the multimedia presentation *Earth Spirit: A Celebration of Monument Valley.* | 435/727–3231 | fax 435/727–3344 | www.gouldings.com | Museum free, admission for film | Daily.
Monument Valley was designated a Navajo Tribal Park in 1959. The **Monument Valley Visitor Center** was built the next year, offering exhibits, a Navajo crafts store, and an information desk. On arrival at the visitors center, you are likely to be approached in the parking lot by guides offering **tours of Monument Valley.** Monument Valley Navajo Tribal Park has approved about a dozen tour operators, and you can get information on them inside the center. Whether you choose an approved company guide or a freelance guide, ask about

prices and specific details of the tours before making a selection. | 435/727–3287 | www.desertusa.com/monvalley | Admission may be charged | Mid-Apr.–Oct., daily 7 AM–8 PM; late Oct.–early Apr., daily 8–5.

San Juan River. The San Juan River is known for spectacular scenery and rapids with enough ripple to add excitement but not danger. The portion of the river between Bluff and Mexican Hat makes an unforgettable two-day trip, with plenty of time to view pictograph panels and other remnants of the history of this isolated corner of the state. You can take extended trips, too. | Bureau of Land Management–Moab District, 82 E. Dogwood, Moab | 435/259–2100 | Fees for river use | Apr.–Oct.

Bluff-based **Wild Rivers Expeditions** has been rafting the San Juan longer than any other company. The professional river guides are well versed in archaeology, history, and geology along the river, and it's the company's policy to share that wealth of knowledge on every trip. | 101 Main St. | 435/672–2244 or 800/422–7654 | fax 435/672–2365 | www.riversandruins.com | Mar.–mid Nov.

ON THE CALENDAR

SEPT.: *Bear Dance.* Traditional Ute ceremonial dances, contests of skill, games, and cooking demonstrations sponsored by the White Mesa Ute Council in a three-day celebration held Labor Day weekend. | 435/678–3397.

SEPT.: *Utah Navajo Fair.* Rodeo and powwow with Navajo foods and dances. | 520/871–6478.

Dining

Cow Canyon Trading Post. Eclectic. The building is an old trading post, with a sandstone block exterior. The small dining room feels like an old house, with southwestern furnishings. The menu ranges from Navajo to Italian to Greek, depending on the week and the season. Navajo specialties include squash-blossom soup and ash bread. The glassed-in porch overlooking a restored farm has a spectacular view. | U.S. 163 | 435/672–2208 | $10–$16 | MC, V.

Stagecoach Restaurant. Southwestern. Picture windows frame views of Monument Valley's northern formations at this restaurant that's part of Goulding's Trading Post and Lodge. The breakfast offerings make for some tough choices: huevos rancheros, granola, and breakfast sandwiches stuffed with eggs, meat, and cheeses. The dinner menu has a pasta of the day and fresh stir-fried vegetables. | U.S. 163 | 435/727–3231 | $12–$25 | AE, D, DC, MC, V.

Twin Rocks Cafe. American. Views of the sandstone cliffs are stunning from the large log-beamed porch at this cozy restaurant. You'll find such specials as beef stew with Navajo fry bread and flavorful prime ribs au jus. Vegetarians options include Navajo tacos (fry bread stuffed with chili). | 913 E. Navaho Twins Dr. | 435/672–2341 | $10–$18 | AE, D, DC, MC, V.

Lodging

Desert Rose Lodge. This alpine-style, two-story lodge surrounded by cliffs is homey with handmade quilts and lamps and log headboards. Sunsets from the picture windows are spectacular. The cabins are paneled in light pine. In-room data ports. Cable TV. No-smoking rooms. Conference room. | 30 rooms, 6 log cabins | 701 W. Main St. | 435/672–2303 or 888/475–7673 | fax 435/672–2303 | $69–$89, $85–$125 cabins | AE, D, MC, V.

Goulding's Lodge. Near the 1923 Trading Post, the two-story lodge has a private balcony for each room, giving you a great close-up of nearby landforms and panoramic views of the valley. Restaurant. Some kitchenettes, refrigerators. Cable TV, VCRs. Pool. Small fitness room. | 62 rooms | 1000 Main St. | 435/727–3231 or 800/874–0902 | fax 435/727–3344 | gouldings@gouldings.com | www.gouldings.com | $140 | AE, D, DC, MC, V.

Kokopelli Inn. Convenient to restaurants and laundry facilities, with reasonable rates, this single-story brick motel is just ½ mi from the San Juan River. Cable TV, room phones. | 26 rooms | U.S. 191 | 435/672–2322 or 800/541–8854 | fax 801/672–2385 | office@kokoinn.com | $40–$50 | AE, D, DC, MC, V.

Pioneer House Inn. Every suite in this elegant, two-story Victorian family home in Bluff's historic district, built in 1898, has a private entrance with a porch and sitting area. Rooms are contemporary, hung with photographs and paintings by local artists, and the fruit trees in the yard offer much-needed shade in summer. The owners offer tours of archeological and ecological interest under the name Bluff Expeditions. Full breakfast, dining room, picnic area. | 5 1–3 bedroom suites | 189 N. 3rd East St. | 435/672–2446 or 888/637–2582 | fax 435/672–2446 | www.pioneerhouseinn.com | $56–$70 | MC, V.

BOULDER

MAP 14, D8

(Nearby towns also listed: Escalante, Panguitch, Torrey)

This town is remote enough to have received its mail by horse and mule until 1940. It was founded by cattle ranchers, and ranching continues to be the primary occupation of its residents. Just as its location once kept Boulder out of the limelight, its position on scenic byway Rte. 12, just over the mountain from Capitol Reef National Park and between the Dixie National Forest and the northern boundary of the Grand Staircase–Escalante National Monument, now ensures it a place on the map.

Information: Garfield County Travel Council. | 55 S. Main St., Panguitch, 84759 | 435/676–8826 | www.brycecanyoncountry.com.

Attractions
Anasazi State Park Museum. A modern museum dedicated in 1997 deals with aspects of Native American cultures and traditions, including an exhibit honoring the role of oral history and storytelling in preserving tribal identities. The museum is part of the stabilized excavation of an 87-room Anasazi pueblo built in approximately AD 1075. The complex includes living quarters, storage areas, rooms used for religious ceremonies, and some burial chambers. Interpretive information is provided. | Rte. 12 | 435/335–7308 | www.utah.com | $5 | Daily.

Dining
Burr Trail Cafe. American. Local cowboys still ride up to the back porch for meals at this quaint restaurant and trading post, which serves such contemporary fare as smoked trout on bagels and pesto pizza. The outdoor seating area has views of Boulder Mountain and the Aquarius Plateau. | Rte. 12 and Burr Trail Rd. | 435/335–7500 | $12–$20 | AE, MC, V.

Hell's Backbone Grill. American. Large windows overlook an herb garden, the floor is saltillo tiles, and the glass-topped bar is filled with rock samples. Specialties include lime-marinated grilled chicken and vegetable pastas. | Hell's Backbone Rd., off Rte. 12 | 435/335–7480 | www.boulderutah.com/bmr | $12–$25 | D, MC, V.

Lodging
Boulder Mountain Lodge. A large wooden balcony and many of the rooms overlook an 11-acre bird sanctuary at this unusual lodge. Vaulted ceilings with exposed beams, craftsman furniture, and traditional quilts make the rooms bright and comfortable. Some kitchenettes, microwaves, and refrigerators. TV in some rooms. Laundry facilities. | 18 rooms, 2 suites | 20 N. Rte. 12 | 435/335–7460 or 800/556–3446 | fax 435/335–7461 | $79–$124, $149 suites | D, MC, V.

BRIGHAM CITY

MAP 14, C3

(Nearby towns also listed: Logan, Ogden, Salt Lake City)

For many Utahns, Brigham City is synonymous with the sweetest peaches known to humanity. Brigham also has some century-old buildings grand enough to be striking in this small-town setting. From Brigham, population 16,000, you can head west for outstanding bird-watching in an ecosystem heavily influenced by the Great Salt Lake or step back to the railroad era at Golden Spike National Historic Site.

Information: Box Elder County Economic Development | 102 W. Forest St., Brigham, 84302 | 435/734–2634 | www.box-elder.com. **Golden Spike Empire Travel Region** | 2501 Wall Ave., Odgen, 84401 | 801/627–8288 or 800/255–8824 | www.odgencvb.org | fax 801/399–0783.

Attractions

Brigham City Museum-Gallery. This museum combines community history with art-gallery space housing regional art collections and touring regional and national shows. | 24 N. 300 W | 801/723–6769 | Free | Tues.–Fri 11–6, Sat. afternoon.

Bear River Migratory Bird Refuge. This 65,000-acre refuge is at the mouth of the Bear River. Because it's beneath two of North America's major migratory waterfowl flyways, you may spot any of more than 200 species of birds. Get a birding checklist and take the 12-mi auto and bicycle loop. | 58 S. 950 W | 435/723–5887 | www.npwrc.usgs.gov | Free | Daily dawn–dusk. Closed Jan.–mid-Mar.

Golden Spike National Historic Site. Thirty miles west on Rte. 83, down a rural road, this site recalls one of the most important accomplishments of the 19th century. In 1869 officials of the Union Pacific Railroad and the Central Pacific Railroad met here to drive four symbolic spikes—two gold, one silver, and one a combination of iron, silver, and gold—into a laurel-wood tie in celebration of the completion of the first transcontinental railroad. You can get an intriguing look at this bit of history in the visitor center, which displays working reproductions of original steam engines. | Promontory Rd. | 435/471–2209 | www.nps.gov/gosp | $7 per vehicle, $3.50 per person | June–early Oct., daily 8–6; late Oct–Apr., daily 8–4:30.

ON THE CALENDAR

MAY: *Bear River Bird Refuge Festival.* An annual one-day festival at this 65,000-acre refuge, 15 mi east of Brigham City via Forest Street, starts off with a big breakfast. Tours follow, along with an outdoor photography walk, an outdoor sketching walk, conservation talks, and children's activities. | 435/723–5887.

MAY: *Driving of Golden Spike.* Held May 10, this is the annual commemoration of the linking of the Atlantic and Pacific coasts by railroad at this site, 30 mi west off Rte. 83, in 1869. | 435/471–2209 | $7 per vehicle, $3.50 per person.

AUG.: *Railroaders Festival.* This annual gathering has bluegrass music and contests like buffalo "chip" throwing, boiler stoking, a greased pole climb, rail walking, and hand-car races. Held at the Golden Spike National Historic Site, there's also a baseball tournament with rules, equipment, and uniforms styled after those of the 1880s. | 435/471–2209 | 2nd Sat. in Aug.

SEPT.: *Peach Days Celebration.* For nearly 100 years, the community has held this annual festival in the Brigham City Center in honor of this prolific local crop. There's a Peach Queen pageant, a parade, an art show, and freshly baked peach cobbler. | 435/723–3931.

Dining

Idle Isle. American. Built in 1921, the cafe maintains its wooden booths and player piano, and the old menus feature home-style dishes like beef pot roast and halibut steak, with memorable desserts. | 24 S. Main St. | 435/734–2468 | $8–$15 | AE, D, MC, V.

Maddox Ranch House. American. This family-owned establishment 1 mi south of town has Western-style furnishings and several dining areas. Locals come here for the chicken, beef, and seafood. Kids' menu. | 1900 S. U.S. 89, Perry | 435/723–8545 | $9–$23 | AE, D, DC, MC, V | Closed Sun.–Mon.

Lodging

Crystal Inn. The spacious rooms of this two-story motel have comfortable sitting areas with desks. There are mountain views from the swimming pool. Complimentary Continental breakfast. In-room data ports, microwaves, refrigerators. Cable TV. Indoor pool. Hot tub. Business services. | 52 rooms | 480 Westland Dr. | 435/723–0440 or 800/408–0440 | fax 435/723–0446 | www.crystalinns.com | $55–$79 | AE, D, DC, MC, V.

Galaxie Motel. Reasonable rates and some rooms with kitchen facilities attract students and senior citizens to this standard motel. Some kitchenettes and full kitchens. Cable TV. | 29 rooms | 740 S. Main St. | 435/723–3439 or 800/577–4315 | $33.95 | AE, D, DC, MC, V.

Howard Johnson Inn. You're not far from the I–15/U.S. 89 split, and within walking distance to restaurants and historic buildings. Complimentary Continental breakfast. Cable TV. Indoor pool. Hot tub. Business services. Some pets allowed. | 44 rooms | 1167 S. Main St. | 435/723–8511 | fax 435/723–8511 | www.hojo.com | $50–$65 | AE, D, DC, MC, V.

BRYCE CANYON NATIONAL PARK

MAP 14, B8

(Nearby towns also listed: Cedar City, Escalante, Kanab, Panguitch)

BRYCE CANYON
NATIONAL PARK

INTRO
ATTRACTIONS
DINING
LODGING

Bryce Canyon is not really a canyon. It's actually the eastern escarpment of the vast Paunsaguant Plateau, sculptured by uplift, wind, water, and gravity into thousands of pillars, columns, windows, and hoodoos. A Paiute Indian story explains Bryce as the home of the Legend People, fantastic animals and birds who angered the god Coyote and were turned to stone in their beautiful basin home. Pioneer cattleman Ebenezer Bryce, for whom the canyon was named, explained the rugged amphitheaters simply as "a hell of a place to lose a cow." These days the park is known for incredible viewpoints along its rim trails and for awe-inspiring hikes through the wilderness of its depths.

Information: **Bryce Canyon National Park** | Bryce Canyon, 84717 | 435/834–5322 | fax 435/834–4102 | www.nps.gov/brca. **Garfield County Travel Council** | 55 S. Main St., Panguitch, 84759 | 435/676–1160 | www.brycecanyoncountry.com.

Attractions

Bristlecone Loop. At the southernmost edge of the park, right off Rainbow Point, this short 1.5-mi trail enters briefly into Bryce Canyon's conifer forest, and, in places, offers spectacular 270-degree views of the surrounding canyon country. | Daily, most of year.

Navajo Loop Trail. The Navajo Loop is actually a "down, and then back up the way you came." It is short, only 1½ mi round-trip, but from the trail's beginning at Sunset Point to the turn-around deep in the canyon, it's a drop of 520 ft. You get the best view of many of Bryce's most famous formations—Thor's Hammer, The Pope, and Temple of Osiris among them—from this trail. Rangers lead guided trips on the Navajo Loop at least twice a day. | Daily, except when icy or snow-packed.

Queen's Garden Trail. Considered the "easiest" trail into Bryce Canyon, the Queen's Garden hike begins at Sunrise Point. Round-trip, this jaunt is 1½ mi, and its 320-ft descent is more gradual than that of most of the park's other trails. The route is marked with signs offering geological information on the pillars, hoodoos, balanced rocks, and spires on every side. Stories of the origin of formation names, like Gulliver's Castle and Queen Victoria, also make interesting reading. | Daily, except when icy or snow-packed.

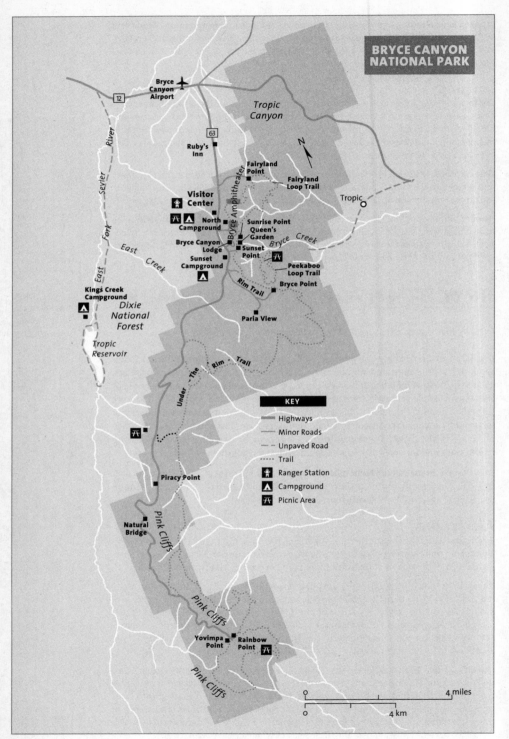

BRYCE CANYON
NATIONAL PARK

Tropic
Canyon

Bryce
Canyon
Airport

12

63

Ruby's
Inn

Fairyland
Point

Fairyland
Loop Trail

Tropic

Sevier River

East Fork Sevier River

Visitor
Center

North
Campground

Sunrise Point
Queen's
Garden

Bryce Amphitheater

Bryce Creek

Bryce Canyon
Lodge

Sunset
Point

East Creek

Sunset
Campground

Peekaboo
Loop Trail

Bryce Point

Kings Creek
Campground

Dixie
National
Forest

Rim Trail

Paria View

Tropic
Reservoir

Under — The — Rim — Trail

KEY

Highways

Minor Roads

Unpaved Road

Trail

Ranger Station

Campground

Picnic Area

Piracy Point

Pink Cliffs

Natural
Bridge

Pink Cliffs

Yovimpa
Point

Rainbow
Point

Pink Cliffs

0   4 miles

0   4 km

Rim Trail. Skirting the edge of Bryce Canyon for 5½ mi, this trail is probably the most complete way to see and enjoy the bizarre and beautiful geology of Bryce. Though the distance may sound a bit daunting (particularly if you don't arrange for a shuttle or someone with a car to meet you at the trail's end), the path is fairly level and rated easy to moderate. The ½-mi stretch between Sunrise and Sunset Points (*see below*) sees the most traffic, but there are amazing vistas all along the way. Plenty of benches are nicely positioned for resting and enjoying the views. | Daily, most of year.

Sunrise and Sunset Points. The ½-mi stretch between these two overlooks is paved and level, well adapted for wheelchairs or strollers. These viewpoints are two of the park's most impressive, with sweeping panoramas of the colors, erosional forms, and mysterious landscapes for which Bryce Canyon is known. | Daily.

Attractions

Canyon Trailrides. This concessionaire offers 2-hour and half-day trips into the depths of Bryce Canyon. Children 5 years and older are allowed on the shorter ride. Eight is the minimum age for the longer trip. You sign up for these rides in the lobby of Bryce Canyon Lodge, but it's best to have advance reservations. | Box 128 | 435/679–8665 | www.homepages.com/canyonrides | 2-hr trip, $30; half-day trip, $40 | May–Oct.

ON THE CALENDAR
FEB.: *Winter Festival.* Cross-country skiing and other cold-weather recreation, including snow sculpting and ski archery, take place at Ruby's Inn, 3 mi west of the park boundary. | 435/834–5341 or 800/468–8660.

Dining
Bryce Canyon Lodge. American. In the middle of the historic lodge built in 1924, this restaurant is a long room with native stone fireplaces. The specialties are mountain red trout and wagon-wheel pasta with marinara sauce. | 435/834–5361 | www.amfac.com | $8–$20 | AE, D, DC, MC, V | Closed Nov.–Mar.

Bryce Canyon Pines Restaurant. American. Known for homemade soups like tomato broccoli and corn chowder, and for fresh berry and cream pies, this homey, antiques-filled restaurant 6 mi northwest of the park entrance dishes up quality comfort food. | Rte. 12 | 435/834–5441 | $5–$16 | AE, D, DC, MC, V.

Lodging
Best Western Ruby's Inn. The closest accommodation outside the park, this large two-story inn has spacious rooms and a comfortable lobby. It's a good place to stay if you like organized activities such as chuckwagon cookouts, trail rides, and helicopter and ATV tours. Restaurant, picnic area. Cable TV, in-room VCRs and movies. 2 indoor pools. Cross-country skiing. Laundry facilities. Business services. Pets allowed (fee). | 368 rooms | Rte. 63, 1 mi off Rte. 12 | 435/834–5341 or 800/468–8660 | fax 435/834–5265 | jean@rubysinn.com | www.rubysinn.com | $65–$95 | AE, D, DC, MC, V.

Bryce Canyon Lodge. Built in 1925, this lodge has been named a National Historic Landmark. With no television, it's a great place to come for peace and quiet. You can stay in the spacious motel rooms or the cabins, which have southwestern furnishings, and walk to the canyon rim. Restaurant. Room phones. Laundry facilities. Business services. | 40 cabins, 70 motel units, 3 suites, 1 studio | 1 Bryce Canyon | 435/834–5361 or 303/297–2757 (reservations) | fax 435/834–5464 | www.amfac.com | $88 rooms, $98 cabins, $119 suites | Closed Nov.–mid-Apr. | AE, D, DC, MC, V.

Bryce Canyon Pines. Some of the pine-paneled rooms in this motel have fireplaces and kitchens. Six miles from Bryce Canyon, the establishment has a campground, too, and horseback riding. Restaurant. Cable TV. Pool. Business services. | 50 rooms | Box 43, Bryce | 435/834–5441 or 800/892–7623 | fax 435/834–5330 | www.color-country.net/~bcpines | $75 | D, DC, MC, V.

BRYCE CANYON
NATIONAL PARK

INTRO
ATTRACTIONS
DINING
LODGING

Bryce Canyon Resort. Renovated and remodeled, this rustic lodge is across from the local airport and 3 mi from the park entrance. Restaurant. In-room data ports. Cable TV. Indoor pool. Laundry facilities. | 57 rooms, 2 suites | 13500 E. Rte. 12 | 435/834–5351 or 800/834–0043 | fax 435/834–5256 | $85, $95 suites | MC, V.

Bryce View Lodge. Next to the Bryce Canyon National Park entrance, this motel has reasonable rates, and you can use the pool and other amenities at the mammoth Ruby's Inn next door. 2 restaurants. Cable TV. Pool access. Laundry facilities. Pets allowed. | 160 rooms | Rte. 63 | 435/834–5180 or 888/279–2304 | fax 435/834–5181 | $55 | AE, D, DC, MC, V.

CANYONLANDS NATIONAL PARK

MAP 14, E7

(Nearby towns also listed: Blanding, Green River, Moab, Monticello)

Divided into three distinct districts, Canyonlands has as its heart the confluence of the Green and Colorado rivers. The park is well known for hiking, white-water rafting, four-wheel-drive terrain, and mountain biking on designated trails, but Canyonlands remains the most mysterious of Utah's national parks by virtue of its rugged landscapes. Backcountry permits, detailed maps, extra drinking water, and professional guides are de rigueur for much of the park.

© Artville

HOODOOS, AND BRIDGES, AND ARCHES. OH MY!

After a while, the fantastically eroded landscapes and formations found in southern Utah can all begin to look the same. Don't worry. It happens to everyone. A brief course in the geology of the Colorado Plateau can get your vacation back on track and clear up any confusion while you're busy making memories.

An arch is an opening created primarily by the ceaseless erosional powers of wind and weather. Airborne sand constantly scours cliff faces; tiny and huge chunks of stone are pried away by minuscule pockets of water freezing, expanding, then thawing, again and again. Arches are found in all stages, from cave-like openings that haven't finished cutting through a stone fin or wall to gigantic stone ribbons shaped by an erosional persistence that defies imagination.

Bridges are the product of stream, or river erosion. They span what at some time was a water source powerful enough to wear away softer layers of sedimentary stone through constant force and motion. As softer stone is washed away, the harder capstone layers remain in the form of natural bridges.

The most bizarrely shaped formations have the strangest name. Hoodoos are chunks of rock already chiseled through time into columns or pinnacles. Like all rock formations, hoodoos are constructed of layers and layers of horizontal bands. Each band or stratum has its own composition. When wind or water, particularly in the form of heavy, sporadic rainstorms, goes to work on these pillars, the eventual result is a hoodoo—an eccentric and grotesque formation usually found in the company of other hoodoos.

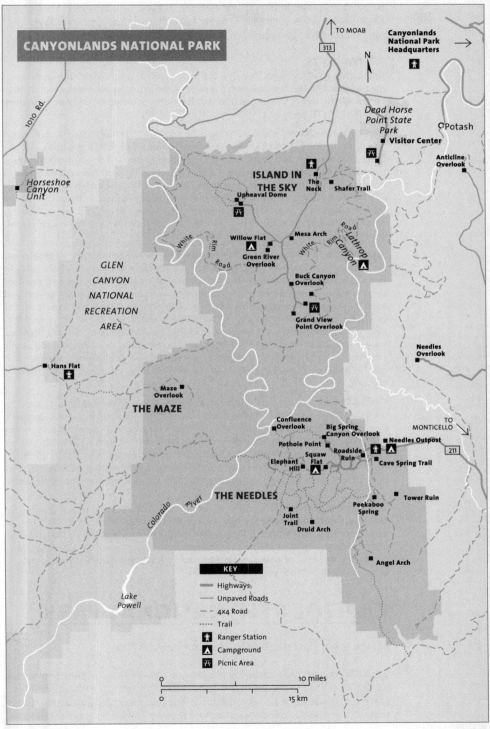

CANYONLANDS NATIONAL PARK

TO MOAB

313

N

Canyonlands National Park Headquarters

○ Potash

1010 Rd.

Dead Horse Point State Park

Visitor Center

Anticline Overlook

Horseshoe Canyon Unit

ISLAND IN THE SKY

Upheaval Dome

The Neck

Shafer Trail

GLEN

Willow Flat

Mesa Arch

White Rim Road

Canyon

Lathrop

Road

CANYON

White Rim Road

Green River Overlook

NATIONAL

Buck Canyon Overlook

RECREATION

AREA

Grand View Point Overlook

Needles Overlook

Hans Flat

Maze Overlook

THE MAZE

Confluence Overlook

TO MONTICELLO

Big Spring Canyon Overlook

Needles Outpost

211

Pothole Point

Roadside Ruin

Elephant Hill

Squaw Flat

Cave Spring Trail

THE NEEDLES

Colorado River

Peekaboo Spring

Tower Ruin

Joint Trail

Druid Arch

Angel Arch

Lake Powell

KEY

▬▬	Highways
──	Unpaved Roads
─ ─	4x4 Road
⋯⋯	Trail
🛉	Ranger Station
⛺	Campground
⛱	Picnic Area

0   10 miles

0   15 km

Information: Canyonlands National Park | Moab, 84532 | 435/259–7164 | fax 435/259–8628 | www.nps.gov/cany. **Grand County Travel Council** | Box 550, Moab, 84532 | 435/259–8825 or 800/635–6622.

Attractions

Grand View Point Overlook Trail. One of the best and most accessible vantage points in the park, the 1-mi trail from the overlook offers stunning views of three major mountain ranges–the Henrys, La Sals, and Abajos–and the surrounding desert and canyon country. | 435/259–7164 | Daily, most of year.

Island in the Sky District. Island in the Sky is the northern section of Canyonlands National Park, 10 mi north of Moab off U.S 191. Here, from a mesa 6,000 ft high, you can look down to the Colorado River to the east and the Green River to the west. The "island's" northern tip overlooks the rivers' confluence. A scenic road runs through the park leading to a dozen trailheads. The Mesa Arch Loop leads ½ mi to a photogenic arch perched on the lip of a cliff. From Grand View Trail more than 100 mi of desert, mesas, canyons, rivers, and distant mountain ranges form an incredible panorama. You can get brochures with details of specific hikes at the visitor center near the park entrance. | Rte. 313 | Visitor Center, mid-Mar.–mid-Nov., daily 8–6; mid-Nov.–mid-Mar., daily 8–4:30.

Maze District. From Island in the Sky or overlooks in the Needles District, it's easy to pick out The Maze's convoluted stone playground. From a distance its 30-square-mi sprawl looks jumbled but benign. In fact, The Maze is Canyonlands' most primitive and least explored area—a place where one needs to bring topographic maps, extra water, equipment, and food. The Maze can be reached only with four-wheel-drive vehicles or on hiking trails. You need a backcountry permit for any exploration here, and they are issued in limited numbers. Some professional tour companies lead trips into The Maze, and though there are no facilities, a few unforgettable hiking routes are marked by rock cairns or rough trails (see Moab, below). | From Rte. 24, approx. 25 mi south of I–70, an unpaved road runs 46 mi east to Hans Flat Ranger Station, then approx. 20 mi south past the Flint Trail to the Maze overlook.

Needles District. Canyonlands' southeastern district is dubbed The Needles because of its profusion of red-rock spires and fins. You can hike and bicycle or drive in your four-wheel-drive vehicle. A 7-mi trip on the Colorado River Overlook Road offers beautiful scenery and ends with a view of the Colorado more than 1,000 ft below. There is a campground at Squaw Flat. From this point, a trailhead accesses four different day hikes from 7½ to 11 mi round-trip. Each of these trails finds its way into the colorful needle formations. | Rte. 211, 22 mi north of Monticello (or 50 mi south of Moab) on U.S. 191, then 35 mi west to visitor center.

ON THE CALENDAR

MAY: *Indian Arts and Crafts Festival.* Held on Memorial Day weekend, this is a demonstration and sale of traditional Indian jewelry, pottery, beading, and folk-art decorations, along with Native American dance performances. You can try Western barbecue, Navajo fry bread, mutton stew, and Hispanic specialties, including menudo and tamales. | 435/587–2300.

CAPITOL REEF NATIONAL PARK

MAP 14, D7

(Nearby towns also listed: Boulder, Escalante, Richfield, Torrey)

Capitol Reef's most distinctive geological feature is an enormous upthrust bulge that runs for more than 100 mi north and south through the park. The Waterpocket Fold, as it is called, was named for the millions of indentations eroded into the sandstone that catch and hold rain from desert storms. The park's hiking trails explore the soaring cliffs and canyons. Below this "reef" of stone is a grassy valley watered by the Fremont River and its tributary Sulphur Creek. The park's main campground lies in this verdant corridor in orchards originally planted by Mormon settlers in the 1800s.

Information: **Capitol Reef National Park, HC-70** | Box 15, Torrey, 84775 | 435/425–3791 | fax 435/425–3026 | www.nps.gov.care. **Capitol Reef Country** | Box 7, Teasdale, 84773 | 800/858–7951 | capreef@xmission.com | www.xmission.com/~capreef/.

Attractions

Capitol Gorge. It's just about 2 mi round-trip up this ancient river gorge as it winds between two sheer-wall cliffs. In hot summer the cliffs create delicious shade in the morning and late afternoon. There are two "destinations" on this hike. The first is a rock face known as the Pioneer Register because of the names and dates carved into the wall in the late 1800s. Just beyond the next curve, sunk into a small mesa, are pool-sized pockets known as the Tanks, where early settlers reportedly swam and bathed. | Daily.

CAPITOL REEF
NATIONAL PARK

INTRO
ATTRACTIONS
DINING
LODGING

Cohab Canyon. This hike begins near the Fruita Campground and starts with a formidable set of switchbacks climbing a steep bentonite slope. Once you complete this ¼-mi stretch, you are rewarded with a broad view from a narrow canyon entrance high on the towering reef of the Waterpocket Fold. From here, the hike continues 1½ mi on a level sandy route, following stream beds and stretches of undulating sandstone. From this trail you can take several turnoffs to more arduous routes with more dramatic viewpoints, but there is much to enjoy in this canyon's simple course: narrow slots that are cool on even the hottest day, hanging gardens of desert plants growing from tiny cracks in the canyon walls, piles of velvety coral sand tucked under ledges, and alcoves peppered with eroded pockets. | Daily, unless switchbacks are muddy or slick.

Fruita. In the late 1800s, Mormon settlers chose this spot watered by the Fremont River to establish a desert oasis. They planted hundreds of fruit trees and named their township Fruita. The original pioneer orchards are now maintained by the National Park Service, and if you visit the park, you can pick fruit in season. A few of the buildings from Fruita have also been preserved, including a blacksmith's shop, a hay barn, and the Gifford family farmhouse, which is now a museum. At the one-room schoolhouse, built in the 1890s and used until the 1940s, you can peer through the windows while listening to an oral history recorded by one of the school's original teachers. | Daily.

Grand Wash. You can enter Grand Wash from a parking area off Rte. 24, about 4 mi east of the park visitors center, or from a signed access point on the scenic drive. The hike is about 2½ mi long in a corridor created by an ancient river. You won't do any climbing, but the hike does pass through the depths of the Waterpocket Fold, sometimes narrowing to passages only a few yards wide with canyon walls soaring hundreds of feet above. If there's any possibility of rain, choose another hike! Flash flooding can occur, sweeping away anything in its path. It's a good idea to have someone waiting with a vehicle at the end of this hike to avoid having to backtrack on foot. | Daily.

Hickman Bridge Trail. There's a gradual upward slope for much of the 1-mi hike to the river-carved natural bridge. Don't turn around once you've sighted Hickman Bridge. Follow the trail around the back side of the formation for views of Fruita and the confluence of Sulphur Creek and the Fremont River far below. At the visitors center, and generally at the trailhead, you can get a pamphlet explaining 18 interpretive markers along this moderate trail. | 2 mi east of visitor center on north side of Rte. 24 | Daily.

ON THE CALENDAR

SEPT.: *Harvest Homecoming Days.* Held on the Fruita Campground, about 1 mi from the visitors center, this celebration generally coincides with the apple harvest in the park's historic orchards. You can see demonstrations of quilting, jerky-making, and other pioneer-era skills. | 435/425–3791.

Camping

Fruita Campground. Situated alongside the Fremont river, the campground 1 mi southeast of the visitors center gets its name from the surrounding fruit orchards, some planted in the 1880s. This is the only developed camping in the park; several other no-fee sites are available but lack water. | 70 sites | 435/425–3791 | $10.

CEDAR CITY

MAP 14, B8

(Nearby towns also listed: Beaver, Panguitch, St. George, Springdale)

Cedar City has dubbed itself "The Festival City." Its 13,500 residents and businesses seem hospitable enough to support the title. The city's major event, the Utah Shakespearean Festival, has been stretching its season a little farther into the summer—and now the fall—as its reputation has grown, a process that the residents have embraced wholeheartedly. Many Cedar City families can trace their ancestry back to the original Mormon families sent to settle this area in 1851. This pioneer heritage is also a strong part of Cedar City's allure, expressed in architecture and attractions.

Information: Iron County Travel Council | Box 1007, Cedar City, 84721 | 435/586–5124 or 800/354–4849 | fax 435/586–4022 | www.utahsplayground.org.

Attractions

Brian Head–Panguitch Lake Scenic Byway. This 55-mi scenic road starting at Parowan, about 12 mi northeast of Cedar City, east off I–15, is especially wonderful during the fall. You pass Parowan's Vermillion Cliffs, Parowan Canyon, and Brian Head Peak on Rte. 143. It rises to 10,000-ft forests before ending in the small town of Panguitch *(below)*. | Rte. 143 at Parowan | 435/586–5124 | Free | Daily.

Brian Head Ski Resort. In the red-rock country of southwestern Utah, Brian Head is known for its mix of great skiing, unique family and group programs, and the unbridled enthusiasm that seems to be shared by the resort staff and skiers of all abilities. You get 500 acres of skiable terrain plus snowcat service to 11,307 ft and 53 trails. The vertical drop is 1,329 ft, or 1,707 if you take the peak express to the very top. | 3 mi north of Cedar Breaks National Monument on Rte. 143 | 435/677–2035 | www.brianhead.com | $35 | Nov.–Apr.

Cedar Breaks National Monument. From the hiking trails on the rim of Cedar Breaks, a natural amphitheater plunges 2,000 ft into the Markagunt Plateau, 29 mi north of Cedar City. Inside this colorful bowl are hundreds of limestone formations. The pillars, columns, hoodoos, and other geologic oddities here are particularly vivid because they are concentrated in a small area, and the surrounding alpine vegetation is lush and green. | Rte. 14 | 435/586–945 | www.nps.gov/cebr | $4 per vehicle | Visitor facilities, May–Oct., daily; accessible in winter for cross-country skiing and snowmobiling.

Dixie National Forest. The Dixie is Utah's largest national forest. The forest area outside of Cedar City is popular for day use, and its scenery is marked by scattered outcrops of red rock bursting through large stands of pines. | 74 N. 100 E | 801/865–3200 | www.fs.fed.us/dxnf/ | Day use free; camping fees | Daily.

Iron Mission State Park Museum. Iron Mission is more museum than park. Its unique collection includes surreys, sleighs, and an authentic bullet-scarred stagecoach that ran between southwest Utah communities around the turn of the century. The museum also chronicles the development of the iron industry in this area. Outside is a log cabin built in 1851, the oldest remaining home in southern Utah. | 585 N. Main St. | 435/586–9290 | www.utah.com | $4 | Daily.

Kolob Canyons of Zion National Park. This is the northernmost section of Zion National Park and provides one of the most stunning drives in the state. From a visitors center just off I–15, a paved road climbs several switchbacks on its 5-mi ascent, with more of the spectacular Kolob Canyons revealed at each turn. Nicknamed the "Finger Canyons," these fissures are rugged and narrow and colored vibrant shades of red. There are pull-outs with splendid overlooks and geological information all along the route, as well as access to several backcountry hiking trails. | 25 mi south of Cedar City off I–15 | 435/772–3256 | $10 entry and day use, fees for backcountry permits and camping | Daily.

Parowan Gap Petroglyphs. A rock formation called a wind gap is the natural canvas for this 1,000-year-old collection of Native American art and writing. You'll see a gravel road with a sign PAROWAN PETROGLYPHS after you drive almost 13 mi northeast on Rte. 130. Follow the newly paved road for about 2 ½ mi. | 435/586–5124 | Free | Daily.

Southern Utah University. Southern Utah University began as a branch normal school in 1897. It functioned as a branch agricultural college, a junior college, and a four-year college before earning university status in 1990. SUU anchors the social, recreational, and cultural life of Cedar City and environs. Its best-known event is the annual Utah Shakespearean Festival. The two original school buildings dating from 1898 and 1899 are still in use. | 351 W. Center St. | 801/586–7700 | www.suu.edu | Free | Mon.–Sat.

ON THE CALENDAR

JUNE: *Utah Summer Games.* More than 7,000 Utahns compete in everything from archery to horseshoes, arm wrestling, basketball, and gymnastics at Southern Utah University. | 435/865–8421.

JUNE: *Paiute Restoration Gathering and Powwow.* Parade, queen and princess contests, talent night, and powwows are part of this event held in the Municipal Park. | 435/586–1112.

JUNE–SEPT.: *Utah Shakespearean Festival.* Each year, the university selects both well-known and more obscure plays by Shakespeare, and stages them in a replica of the Globe Theatre on the Southern Utah University campus. Each evening, you can see outdoor "greenshows," with jugglers, musicians, dancers, and strolling food vendors. There's also a seven-course Renaissance Feaste with entertainment, seminars, pre-performance lectures, and backstage tours. | 435/586–7880 or 800/PLAYTIX.

JULY: *Mid-Summer Renaissance Faire.* Held in Municipal Park during the peak of the Utah Shakespearean Festival, the faire provides entertainment from fencing demonstrations to belly-dancing, games, crafts, and a large assortment of food choices. | 435/586–4484 or 435/586–5124.

AUG.: *Brian Head Bash.* This mountain-bike festival held at Brian Head Resort has guided bicycle tours, games for children, live entertainment, and nightly barbecues. | 435/677–2035.

Dining

Adriana's. Continental. A bungalow-style building has been decorated to resemble an English country inn, with pewter dishes and lace tablecloths. The specialties include fish-and-chips, chateaubriand, and tenderloin of pork. | 164 S. 100 W | 435/865–1234 | $7–$21 | AE, D, DC, MC, V.

Club Edge and Restaurant. American. At the south end of Brian Head Resort, this restaurant has rustic decor, a large fireplace, and a 50-inch TV. Specialties are prime rib and chicken Angelo. The view of 11,307-ft Brian Head Peak is stunning. | 406 S. Utah Hwy.; 3 mi north of monument on Rte. 143 | 435/677–3343 | $15–$30 | AE, D, DC, MC, V | No lunch in winter.

Market Grill. American. A ranch-style building next to the Cedar City stockyard, this place has vinyl-bench booths and a rutted dirt parking area. The fare is also basic: burgers, barbecued ribs, salad bar. | 2290 W. 400 N | 435/586–9325 | $6–$13 | MC, V | Closed Sun.

Milt's Stage Stop. American. This family restaurant with Western-style furnishings 5 mi east of Cedar City is known locally for prime rib, jumbo shrimp, lobster, and crab. | Rte. 14 | 435/586–9344 | $13–$42 | AE, D, DC, MC, V | No lunch.

Rusty's Ranch House. American. You drive 2 mi east of Cedar City, up through the Cedar Canyon on Rte. 14, to reach this Old West–style steak house nestled under the cliffs. The specialties include petit filet mignon with coconut shrimp, creamy chicken pasta, and homemade bread pudding. | Cedar Canyon | 435/586–3839 | $22–$26 | AE, D, MC, V.

Lodging

Abbey Inn. Less than a decade old, this two-story property has spacious rooms with balconies. Some suites have kitchens, and the elegant honeymoon suite has an in-room spa. You can walk to six nearby restaurants and the Utah Shakespearean Festival. Complimentary Continental breakfast. In-room data ports, refrigerators. Cable TV. Indoor pool. Hot tub. Laundry facilities. Business services. Airport shuttle. | 81 rooms | 940 W. 200 N | 435/586–9966 or 800/325–5411 | fax 435/586–6522 | www.abbeyinncedar.com | $60–$85 | AE, D, DC, MC, V.

Baker House Bed and Breakfast. Burnished wood floors, a huge wraparound porch with ceiling fans, in-room fireplaces, and exquisite details like Victorian china and stained-glass windows give this Queen Anne–style Victorian mansion a refined beauty. As it sits atop a hill, you can see Cedar City Valley and the surrounding mountain ranges from many rooms. Full breakfast, dining room. Some microwaves and refrigerators, in-room Jacuzzis. In-room VCRs. | 5 rooms, 1 suite | 1800 Royal Hunte Dr. | 435/867–5695 or 888/611–8181 | fax 435/867–5695 | $99–$149, $159 suite | AE, D, MC, V.

Best Western El Ray Inn. The closest accommodations to the Shakespearean Festival, this motel is popular for its convenience and numerous amenities. Restaurant. Microwaves, refrigerators. Cable TV. Pool. Hot tub, sauna, exercise room. Game room. | 78 rooms | 80 S. Main St. | 435/586–6518 or 800/528–1234 | fax 435/586–7257 | $99–$119 | AE, D, DC, MC, V.

Best Western Town & Country Inn. Actually two buildings directly across the street from each other, this one-story motel has good amenities and a friendly staff. You can walk to the Shakespearean Festival. Restaurant. Cable TV. 2 pools, 1 indoor. Hot tub. Laundry facilities. Business services. Airport shuttle. | 160 rooms | 189 N. Main St. | 435/586–9900 | fax 435/586–1664 | tcinn@tcd.net | www.bestwestern.com | $75–$100 | AE, D, DC, MC, V.

Cedar Breaks Lodge. One suite here sleeps 10, useful if you're traveling with a large group. The lodge, built in the 1980s and renovated in 1997, also has studios and suites with sleeper sofas in the sitting areas. You can ski, sightsee, hike, and bike. Restaurant. Some kitchenettes. Pool. Hot tub, sauna. Exercise equipment. Downhill and cross-country skiing. Business services. | 128 rooms | 223 Hunter Ridge Rd., Brian Head | 435/677–3000 or 888/282–3327 | fax 435/677–2211 | www.cedarbreakslodge.com | $70–$100 | AE, D, DC, MC, V.

Holiday Inn. Very spacious rooms with pull-out sofa beds make this two-story inn a good stopping place for families. Just west of I-15, it is also handy for late-night check-in or early departures. Restaurant, room service. Cable TV. Pool. Hot tub. Exercise equipment. Laundry facilities. Business services. Airport shuttle. | 100 rooms | 1575 W. 200 N | 435/586–8888 | fax 435/586–1010 | www.holiday-inn.com | $65–$95 | AE, D, DC, MC, V.

Quality Inn Downtown. Contemporary furnishings and a convenient downtown location characterize this hotel. Complimentary Continental breakfast. Cable TV. Pool. Airport shuttle. | 50 rooms | 18 S. Main St. | 435/586–2433 | www.qualityinn.com | $89 | AE, D, DC, MC, V.

Rodeway Inn. Downtown and within walking distance of the Utah Shakespearean Festival, this is a convenient place whose rates are lower than those of other chains. Cable TV. Pool. Sauna. Business services. Airport shuttle. Pets allowed. | 48 rooms | 281 S. Main St. | 435/586–9916 | www.hotelchoice.com | $60–$75 | AE, D, DC, MC, V.

Willow Glen Inn Staying on this 10-acre farm on the city outskirts is like staying at grandma's. Rooms are individually furnished and have homey details like flowered bed cozies and wall hangings. The sitting areas in the gardens invite you to relax. Full breakfast, dining room, picnic area. Library, conference room. | 8 rooms, 2 suites | 3808 N. Bulldog Rd. | 435/586–3275 | fax 435/586–3275 | $50–$75, $90–$100 suites | MC, V.

EPHRAIM

MAP 14, D6

(Nearby towns also listed: Manti, Nephi, Salina)

Ephraim was settled in the 1850s by a group of Mormon families. During their first years, their farms were plagued by everything from grasshoppers to devastating early frosts. Eventually, they mastered the climate and set about becoming a prosperous community. Today Ephraim is quiet, with side streets that indicate the town's success in the character and architecture of the homes. The present-day inhabitants, of whom there are 3,363, take great pride in their forebears' efforts.

Information: Sanpete County Chamber of Commerce | Box 59, Ephraim, 84627 | 435/283–4321 or 800/281–4346.

Attractions

Ephraim Co-Op Building. Mormon settlers built this impressive Greek Revival building from native oolite limestone in 1872. It functioned as a cooperative retail store, with a second story used for meetings, community theater, and dances. In 1990 the building was restored and reopened as an arts and crafts cooperative, the Sanpete Sampler. Next door, an old mill now houses an art gallery. | 96 N. Main St. | 435/283–6654 | www.utahreach.usu.edu/sanpete | Free | Sanpete Sampler: Mon.–Sat. 10–6; art gallery: Mon.–Sat. noon–5.

Snow College. Snow College is a two-year institution with about 3,000 students. It was founded as a Mormon academy in 1888 and became a state college in 1932. Many of its students come from larger cities, attracted to the school because of its small-town setting. Snow College's theater and sports programs receive major community support. | 150 E. 100 N | 435/283–4631 | www.snow.edu | Daily.

Spring City Historic Building Tour. During Heritage Days (*see* On the Calendar, *below*), many private homes are open and guided tours are given of public buildings and some artists' studios. At any business in town you can get a pamphlet that details 60 historic homes and buildings in Spring City and covers the town's history. | 187 N. Main St. | 435/462–2211 | www.utahreach.usu.edu/sanpete | Free.

ON THE CALENDAR

MAY: *Scandinavian Festival.* This two-day bash celebrates the traditions of the Scandinavian settlers who came to this area in the late 1800s. Scandinavian foods, Old World crafts, and an Ugly Troll Contest are combined with purely American pastimes, including a tennis tournament and a rodeo. | 435/283–6654.
MAY: *Spring City Heritage Days.* You can tour historic homes and visit art-studio open houses, and try the turkey barbecue dinner. | 435/462–2708.

Dining

The Satisfied Ewe. American. The home-style cooking at this local downtown coffee shop and diner includes huge traditional breakfasts and dinner specials like battered halibut, home-style roast beef, and, of course, lamb chops. | 350 N. Main St. | 435/283–6364 | $8–$20 | MC, V.

Lodging

Ephraim Homestead Bed & Breakfast. An 1880s cottage and Scandinavian cabin form this antiques-filled "homestead," which has both wood- and coal-burning stoves. Complimentary breakfast. No smoking. | 2 rooms with bath, 1 with shower only; 1 cabin with full bath and kitchen | 135 W. 100 N | 435/283–6367 | www.sanpete.com | $55–$95 | No credit cards.

W. Pherson House Bed & Breakfast. This landmark turn-of-the-century, eclectic Victorian-style inn with a shared bath is a good choice for groups or families. Complimentary

EPHRAIM

INTRO
ATTRACTIONS
DINING
LODGING

Continental breakfast. TV in common area and rooms. | 3 rooms share 1 bath | 244 S. Main St. | 435/283–4197 | karen@minti.com | $55 | D, MC, V.

Willow Creek Inn. One of the largest and newest facilities in Ephraim, this downtown motel has numerous amenities and super-sized showers. In-room data ports. Cable TV. Outdoor hot tub. Laundry facilities. Conference rooms. No pets allowed. No-smoking rooms. | 56 rooms, 2 suites | 450 Main St. | 435/283–4566 or 877/283–4566 | fax 435/283–4566 | $55–$95, $85–$115 suites | AE, D, DC, MC, V.

ESCALANTE

MAP 14, D8

(Nearby towns also listed: Boulder, Panguitch, Torrey)

Though the Dominguez and Escalante expedition of 1776 came nowhere near this area, the town's name does honor the Spanish explorer. It was bestowed nearly a century later by a member of a survey party led by John Wesley Powell, charged with mapping this remote area. These days, Escalante has modern amenities and a state park like nothing else in the state, and is a western gateway to the Grand Staircase–Escalante National Monument.

Information: Garfield County Travel Council | 55 S. Main St., Panguitch, 84759 | 435/676–8826 | www.brycecanyoncountry.com.

Attractions

Escalante State Park. The park was created to protect a huge repository of fossilized wood and dinosaur bones. It takes very little time on either of the two brief interpretive trails before you start to feel like an expert on things petrified. Wood especially becomes easy to spot in twisted pieces, partially buried pieces, and entire fallen forests. Another feature of the park is Wide Hollow Reservoir, with its associated wetlands. You can fish for trout in the reservoir, and go birding at the wetlands, one of the few bird-watching sites in southern Utah. | 710 N. Reservoir Rd. | 435/826–4466 | www.utah.com | $4 | Daily.

Grand Staircase–Escalante National Monument. At 1.7 million acres, the state's newest national monument dominates any map of southern Utah, stretching west from Glen Canyon National Recreation Area and Capitol Reef National Park to Bryce Canyon. Its southern boundary is U.S. 89 and the Utah/Arizona border. Rte. 12 and a block of the Dixie National Forest serve as a rough northern boundary. There are three major sections, the Escalante Canyons, the Kaiparowits Plateau, and the Paria River. Any one of these sections alone is larger than most national parks. If it sounds formidable, it is. Only a few roads go into the depths of the monument, none of which you should try to negotiate in a standard passenger car. Nevertheless, you can still experience and enjoy these fabulous landscapes; guided tours, including bicycle, four-wheel-drive, and backcountry hiking trips, are readily available in Escalante and other monument border towns. The BLM maintains a list of guides and outfitters permitted to operate inside the monument. Advance reservations are suggested. | 337 S. Main St., Suite 10, Cedar City | 435/865–5100 | fax 435/865–5170 | www.ut.blm.gov/monument | Free for drive-through and day use; fees for camping and backcountry permits | Daily.

Kodachrome Basin State Park. Within a single day, the sandstone chimney formations of Kodachrome Basin may appear gray, buff, or any of a huge palette of reds and oranges, all depending on the moods of sunlight and weather. On-site rangers will tell you the story behind the park's name. | 9 mi SE of Cannonville | 435/679–8562 | www.utah.com | $5 | Daily.

Lower Escalante River. Some of the best backcountry hiking in the area lies 15 mi east of Escalante on Rte. 12, where the river carves through striking sandstone canyons and gulches. You can camp at numerous sites along the river for extended trips, or you can spend a little time in the small park where the highway crosses the river. | 435/865–5100 | Free | Daily.

JULY: *Escalante Pioneer Day Celebration.* An annual day-long celebration commemorates the original settlers of the area and includes a parade, rodeo, and dance. | 435/826–4205.

Dining

Circle D Restaurant. Eclectic. Low-key and downtown, this place has nothing pseudo-Western about it. Try Navajo tacos, trout, or the house specialty, a chili verde from a Mexican sheepherder's recipe. | 425 E. Main St. | 435/826–4251 | $10–$17 | MC, V.

Ponderosa Restaurant. European. The Old World meets the Old West at this log cabin restaurant where the Hungarian chefs prepare creative and contemporary cuisines. The goulash soup, chicken paprika, shrimp scampi, and rack of lamb are favorites. | 45 N. 400 W | 435/826–4658 | $20–$30 | MC, V.

Lodging

Escalante Outfitters. This is the place to stay if you're on a budget and don't care about amenities. The seven log bunkhouses/cabins have a common bath house. Barbecues. | 7 double-occupancy cabins, 3 with double beds, 4 with bunk beds | 310 W. Main St. | 435/826–4266 | fax 435/826–4388 | www.arof.net/~slickroc/escout | $30 | MC, V.

Escalante's Grand Staircase Bed & Breakfast Inn. Rooms in this in-town inn have skylights, tile floors, log furniture, and murals reproducing area petroglyphs. You can relax on the outdoor porches or in the library, or make use of the on-premises bike-rental shop and explore the adjacent national monument. Full breakfast, dining room. Cable TV. Hot tub. | 5 rooms | 280 W. Main St. | 435/826–4890 | fax 435/826–4889 | $80 | MC, V.

Prospector Inn. A large, square, three-story brick building on Main Street, this is the largest hotel in town, and the rates are reasonable. Restaurant. Cable TV. Business services. | 50 rooms | 380 W. Main St. | 435/826–4653 | fax 435/826–4285 | $50–$70 | AE, MC, V.

FILLMORE

MAP 14, C6

(Nearby towns also listed: Nephi, Richfield, Salina)

Fillmore was intended to be Utah's capital. Mormon colonizer Brigham Young chose the settlement to be the seat of the territorial government practically before there were any settlers in the area. It seems he liked the geographic location and envisioned a state with cities radiating in a spoked pattern from its capital. The Territorial Statehouse had barely been completed when it was judged impractical to have a capital city 150 mi south of the territory's major population center. Fillmore still has great civic pride in its status as Utah's first capital, and a graceful capitol building and museum to show for it.

Information: Millard County Tourism | 80 N. Main St., Delta, 84624 | 435/864–4316 or 800/864–0345 | dacc@millardcounty.com | www.millardcounty.com.

Attractions

Clearlake Waterfowl Refuge. An oasis in the middle of a salt desert, this marsh attracts waterfowl and various other bird species year-round. You can stop at the numerous viewing areas along the marked gravel road that starts about 12 mi south of Delta on Rte. 257. | I–15 north to Holden, then U.S. 50 north to Delta | 435/865–6100 | Free.

Fishlake National Forest. From Fillmore you can access the Paiute Trail, a 200-mi loop over three mountain ranges and through desert canyons. The trail is unique because it's set aside for all-terrain-vehicles and cyclists. | Enter Fishlake National Forest trails from the

FILLMORE

INTRO
ATTRACTIONS
DINING
LODGING

junction of I–15 and I–70 | 435/896–9233 | www.fs.fed.us.recreation/forest_descr/ut_r4_fish-lake | Fees for camping and use of the Paiute ATV trail | Daily.

Territorial Statehouse State Park Museum. The Territorial Statehouse is the oldest exist-ing government building in the state. The territorial legislature met in the building only once, in December of 1855. A museum of territorial-era artifacts opened in 1930 and is still growing. The statehouse and surrounding grounds became Utah's first state park in 1957. | 50 W. Capitol Ave. | 435/743–5316 | www.utah.com | $3 | Daily.

ON THE CALENDAR
SEPT.: *Old Capital Art Festival.* Local arts and crafts, music, children's games, and tours of the statehouse museum and surrounding rose gardens are part of this early fall event held in the Territorial Statehouse Museum. | 435/743–5316.

Dining
Caleb's Country Grill. American. Large windows, a 50-gallon fish tank, and a multitude of plants make this home-style, downtown restaurant inviting. The country breakfasts and grilled sandwiches are always a good bet, and the steak dinners are local favorites. | 590 N. Main St. | 435/743–6876 | $12–$18 | MC, V.

Deano's Pizza. Pizza. Fresh homemade crusts make for tasty pizza. Salad bar. Kids' menu. | 90 S. Main St. | 435/743–6385 | $8–$16 | D, MC, V | Closed Sun.

Lodging
Best Inn Fillmore. Family suites are ample at this inn, the newest accommodation in Fill-more, and they have jetted tubs, too. Continental breakfast. In-room data ports. Indoor heated pool. Hot tub. Laundry facilities. | 48 rooms, 6 suites | 940 S. Rte. 99 | 435/743–4334 | fax 435/743–4054 | $59, $59–$79 suites | AE, D, DC, MC, V.

Best Western Paradise Inn. The largest property in town also has good amenities and a downtown location. Restaurant. Cable TV. Pool. Hot tub. Business services. Pets allowed. | 80 rooms | 1025 N. Main St. | 435/743–6895 | fax 435/743–6892 | www.bestwestern.com | $50–$60 | AE, D, DC, MC, V.

GARDEN CITY

MAP 14, D2

(Nearby town also listed: Logan)

Garden City sits at the junction of U.S. 89 and Rte. 30, on Bear Lake. Most of the perma-nent residents here are farmers who wait out the cold winters just as farmers do every-where. Warm weather adds to the population with summer-home residents and water-sports enthusiasts drawn to the lake's beaches.

Information: **Bridgeland Travel Region** | 160 N. Main St., Logan, 84321 | 435/752–2161 or 800/882–4433 | fax 435/753–5825 | btr@sunrem.com. **Bear Lake Convention and Vis-itors Bureau** | 800/448–2327.

Attractions
Bear Lake State Park. Bear Lake straddles the Utah–Idaho border, with recreation sites in both states. The state park has a marina, camping and picnicking areas, and boat rentals on the Utah side. | U.S. 89 | 435/946–3343 | www.utah.com | $5 | Daily.

Bear Lake Loop Bicycle Trail. On a bicycle, you can see Bear Lake from every angle on this easy 45-mi loop. Interpretive materials are being developed and placed along the route. Watch for the Bear Lake National Wildlife Preserve on the north end of the lake. | From Gar-den City, ride south and east on Rte. 30; at Laketown, turn north onto an unnumbered improved county road skirting the east side of the lake; a paved road follows the northern shoreline then joins U.S. 89 at St. Charles, Idaho; follow U.S. 89 back to Garden City | 800/448–BEAR | www.utah.com | Free | May–early Oct., daily.

Beaver Mountain Ski Area. Owned and operated by the same family since 1939, the resort has 26 runs on 525 acres and a 1,600-ft vertical drop. | 1045½ N. Main St. | 435/753–0921 or 435/753–4822 | fax 435/753–0975 | www.utah.com or www.skiutah.com | $24 | Dec.–early Apr., daily.

Garden City Boardwalk. Follow this ¼-mi boardwalk, which passes through a small wetlands preserve, from Garden City Park to Bear Lake. | 420 S. Bear Lake Blvd. | 435/946–2901 | Free | Daily.

Garden City Park. This small-town 3-acre park has plenty of shade, picnic tables, and play areas for children. It's a nice place to take a break from sunning on the lake. | 420 S. Bear Lake Blvd. | 435/946–2901 | Free | Daily.

Naomi Peak Trail. At 9,980 ft, Naomi Peak is the highest point of the Bear River Range in Cache National Forest. This 3.2-mi trail starts in the parking lot of the Tony Grove Campground and gains almost 2,000 ft in elevation. You hike through conifer forests and open meadows and along subalpine basins and rocky ledges. A shorter hike to White Pine Lake, which begins on the same trail and splits after a quarter of a mile, is also lovely. | From Garden City, take U.S. 89 southwest from Garden City Logan approx 15 mi | 435/755–3620 | Free | July–Nov., depending on snow.

Old Ephraim's Grave. A northern Utah legend, Old Ephraim was the last grizzly bear known to roam and terrorize livestock around Garden City and Logan. His huge skull is now exhibited at the Smithsonian Institution in Washington, D.C., and the rest of his 1,100 pound body was buried in 1923 under this 11-ft stone monument in his old stomping grounds, 21 mi from Garden City on U.S. 89. You're close when you see the signs at Temple Flats. | 435/755–3620 | Free | Daily.

Pickleville Playhouse. A local favorite, this lively summertime dinner-theater show features musical-comedy performances and a huge Western cookout. | 2049 S. Bear Lake Blvd. | 435/946–2918 | Jun.–Sept.

Rendezvous Beach. This was the site of many historic mountain-man rendezvous in the 1800s, hence its name. Actually a part of Bear Lake State Park, Rendezvous Beach is on the southern shore of the lake. It has wide, sandy beaches, showers, and a concessionaire that rents every water toy imaginable, from Jet Skis and sailboats to canoes and "water weenies" to be pulled behind speedboats. A modern mountain-man rendezvous convenes on the beach each September. | 10 mi south of Garden City on Rte. 30 | 435/946–3343 | www.utah.com | $5 | Daily.

Round Valley Ghost Town. At the south end of Bear Lake, this small town holds all that remains of a pioneer village. A small wood-frame schoolhouse and an old pioneer mansion have endured. | From Garden City, take Rte. 30 southeast to Laketown; follow signs to Round Valley | 800/448–2327 | Free | Daily.

Wasatch-Cache National Forest, Logan Canyon. *See* Logan. | 435/755–3620 | Free | Daily.

ON THE CALENDAR

AUG.: *Raspberry Days.* A parade, a craft fair, and entertainment are almost eclipsed by the main event: sampling myriad raspberry concoctions. | 800/448–BEAR.

SEPT.: *Mountain Man Rendezvous.* Held at Rendezvous Beach in Bear Lake State Park, site of many actual mountain-man rendezvous in the 1800s. There are cooking demonstrations, light-hearted "trading," storytelling, and cannon and rifle shooting competitions. | 435/946–3343.

Dining

Harbor Village Restaurant. American. One of the only restaurants in town that stays open year-round, this comfortable eatery serves basic, well-made steak, seafood, and sandwich platters, and is right across from Bear Lake. | 900 N. Bear Lake Blvd. | 435/946–3448 | $5–$15 | AE, D, DC, MC, V.

LeBeau's Drive-in. American. Old-fashioned fast food. No drive-up window, no microwaved food. The classic order would be a raspberry shake and a burger topped with ham, cheese, onions, and the homemade sauce. | 69 N. Bear Lake Blvd. | 435/946–8821 | $5–$8 | MC, V | Closed Sun. and winter.

Lodging

Harbor Village Resort. Condo sizes vary at this pleasant resort, which is across the street from Bear Lake and has access to 300 mi of snowmobile trails. All two-bedroom condos have jetted tubs, and most have private decks or patios. Restaurant. Pool. Hot tub, sauna. 2 tennis courts, exercise room. Game room. | 42 condos | 900 N. Bear Lake Blvd. | 435/946–3448 | fax 435/946–2819 | $119–$199 | AE, D, DC, MC, V.

Ideal Beach Resort. At this family resort on the shore of Bear Lake you can swim and boat, as well as play tennis and miniature golf. Restaurant. 2 pools. Hot tub, saunas. Miniature golf, tennis courts. Business services. | 2176 S. Bear Lake Blvd. | 36 condos | 435/946–3364 or 800/634–1018 | fax 435/946–8519 | $100–$190 | AE, DC, MC, V.

GREEN RIVER

MAP 14, E6

(Nearby towns also listed: Moab, Price)

Green River City gets its name from the river that runs through the middle of town. The town is on the site of a centuries-old river crossing along the historic Spanish Trail. It is famed for several varieties of melons grown in fields irrigated with water diverted from the river. This is the terminus for river trips on the Upper Green through Desolation and Gray canyons. It's also the launch point for adventures on calm and wild water down to the Green River's confluence with the Colorado in Canyonlands National Park, or longer trips south through infamous Cataract Canyon to Hite, at the north end of Lake Powell.

Information: Castle Country Travel Region | 90 N. 100 E. #2, Price, 84501 | 435/637–3009 or 800/842–0789 | fax 435/637–7010 | www.castlecountry.com.

Attractions

Arches National Park. See Arches National Park, *above*. | 5 mi north of Moab on U.S. 191 | 800/635–6622.

Goblin Valley State Park. This isolated park is "hoodoo headquarters," with hundreds of intricately eroded gnarled sandstone knobs and pillars. From the covered observation area above the formation-filled basin you can see the entire valley. There are many off-road vehicle trails. | Rte. 24 south to Temple Junction, then 14 mi southwest on gravel road | 435/564–3633 | www.utah.com | $4 | Daily.

John Wesley Powell River History Museum. With its grounds right on the Green River, the museum makes a lovely picnic spot. The facility is dedicated to the history of John Wesley Powell's explorations of the Green and Colorado rivers in 1869 and 1871. Powell, who had lost his right arm at the battle of Shiloh, led a 10-man scientific expedition that explored the unknown river canyons in four wooden boats. The displays include artifacts and panel displays, and in the small auditorium you can watch a presentation that combines dramatic slides of the rivers with narrative drawn from Powell's journals. The museum also functions as a visitor information center. | 885 E. Main St. | 435/564–3427 | $2 | Daily 8–8.

RUNNING THE GREEN AND YAMPA RIVERS

Adrift Adventures Dinosaur. Take a one-day rafting trip or four- to five-day white-water trips on the Green and Yampa rivers. Family trips are also offered. | Box 192, Jensen, | 800/824-0150 | info@adrift.com | www.adrift.com | May–Sept.

Dinosaur River Expeditions. This outfit has scenic daily trips on the Green River and two-.to five-day white-water trips. | Box 3387, Park City, | 435/649-8092 or 800/247-6197 | fax 435/649-8092 | dinoadv@xmission.com | www.dinoadv.com | May–Sept.

Hatch River Expeditions. For more than 60 years these outfitters have offered trips to Dinosaur National Monument and on the Green and Yampa rivers, both one- and multi-day trips and family trips. | Box 1150, Vernal, | 435/789-4316 or 800/342-8243 | fax 435/789-8513 | info@hatchriver.com | www.hatchriver.com | May–Sept.

Moki Mac River Expeditions. If you want a longer trip or more choices of craft, this outfit can give you Green River trips through Desolation, Gray, and Stillwater/Labyrinth canyons of from 1 to 14 days, traveling by paddle boats, kayaks, or canoes. | Box 71242, Salt Lake City, | 801/268-6667 or 800/284-7280 | fax 801/262-0935 | www.mokimac.com | May–Sept.

Western River Expeditions. River trips combined with guest-ranch stays, horseback riding, and hiking; single or multiday trips on the Green River. | 7258 Racquet Club Dr., Salt Lake City, | 801/259-7019 or 800/453-7450 | fax 801/942-8514 | www.westernriver.com | May–Sept.

ON THE CALENDAR

MAY: *San Rafael Swell Mountain Bike Festival.* Gear up your mountain bike for this three-day event that features rides of varying difficulty throughout the red-rock wilderness of the San Rafael Swell. Some of the overnight rides have live entertainment out on the desert; you can also choose a series of day-long rides, returning to Green River each night. You register at the John Wesley Powell Museum, and the $45 registration fee includes meals on Friday and Saturday. | 435/381-5620 or 888/214-1922.

SEPT.: *Melon Days.* In celebration of the famed melons grown in this area, the festivities in and around Green River State Park include square dancing, a city fair, melons for sale, and plenty of free samples. | 435/564-3526 or 888/564-3600.

Dining

Ben's Cafe. Mexican. At the local hot spot for homemade enchiladas you can also get porterhouse steak. This unpretentious restaurant on Green River's main thoroughfare offers plenty of choices at reasonable prices. | 115 W. Main St. | 435/564-3352 | $6–$16 | AE, D, DC, MC, V.

Tamarisk. American. Named for the bush that grows wild along the Green River, this place has great omelettes and local melons in season. Salad bar. Dinner buffet. Kids' menu. No smoking. | 870 E. Main St. | 435/564-8109 | $7–$17 | AE, D, DC, MC, V.

Lodging

Book Cliff Lodge. Rooms at this basic downtown motor inn are larger than average, and children can try the on-site mini-golf course. Restaurant. Cable TV. Outdoor heated pool. Pets allowed. | 99 rooms | 395 E. Main St. | 435/564-3406 | fax 435/564-8359 | $60–$70 | AE, D, DC, MC, V.

Best Western River Terrace. On the east bank of the Green River, this motel is known for its interesting views and the soothing sounds of the river. Restaurant. Cable TV. Pool. Hot tub. | 51 rooms | 880 E. Main St. | 435/564-3401 | fax 435-564-3403 | $69–$120 | AE, D, DC, MC, V.

Green River Comfort Inn. Right off I-70, this reliable inn is convenient if you're only stopping for the night. Continental breakfast. Pool. Hot tub. Exercise room. Laundry facilities. No pets. | 55 rooms, 3 suites | 1065 E. Main St. | 435/564-3300 | fax 435/564-3299 | $68–$76, $80.95 suites | AE, D, DC, MC, V.

Westwinds Rodeway Inn. This inn on the business loop next to I-70 is great for those eager to get an early start on the river or on the road. Restaurant. Cable TV. Laundry facilities. |

42 rooms | 525 E. Main St. | 435/564–3421 | fax 435–564–8162 | www.hotelchoice.com | $50–$75 | AE, D, DC, MC, V.

HEBER CITY

MAP 14, D4

(Nearby towns also listed: Park City, Provo)

Bounded by the Wasatch Mountains on the west and the rolling foothills of the Uinta Mountains on the east, the Heber Valley is well supplied with snow in the winter for cross-country skiing, snowmobiling, and other snow sports. Summers are cool and green, so Heber City and vicinity enjoy steady, but not overwhelming, tourism year-round. A miles-long string of fast-food places indicates that Heber also profits from its position on U.S. 40.

Information: **Heber Valley Chamber of Commerce** | 475 N. Main St., Heber City, 84032 | 435/654–3666 | www.hebervalleycc.org.

Attractions

Deer Creek State Park. Consistently good fishing, mild canyon winds, and water warmer than you'd expect are responsible for the Deer Creek Reservoir's popularity with windsurfers, sailboaters, swimmers, and those just kicking back in the mountain sunshine. | 5 mi south of Heber on U.S. 189 | 435/654–0171 | www.utah.com | $6 | Daily.

Jordanelle State Park. Two distinct facilities are associated with Jordanelle Reservoir. Hailstone on the western shore is known for fishing and boating. It has beach cabanas for day use, three large camping areas, a children's playground, and a trail system for mountain-biking and hiking. Rock Cliff is at the southern end, next to the Provo River. The focus here is wildlife-watching and environmental education. A nature center and a series of boardwalks help display this unique semi-wetland zone. The 50-site campground is for walk-in use only. | Approx. 10 mi north on U.S. 40, then State Rd. 319 | Hailstone: 435/649–9540; Rock Cliff: 435/783–3030 | www.utah.com | $6 | Daily.

Wasatch Mountain State Park. Wasatch Mountain, 3 mi from Heber City, is easily Utah's most developed state park. You can play the 36-hole golf course, hike trails, go horseback riding, camp, and picnic, and use the buildings for group gatherings. During the 2002 Olympic Winter Games, the park's Soldier Hollow area will host the biathlon events. | 1281 Warm Springs Rd., Midway | 435/654–1791 or 435/654–0532 for golf information | www.utah.com | $4 day use; camping and golf fees | Daily.

PACKING IDEAS FOR HOT WEATHER

- ☐ Antifungal foot powder
- ☐ Bandanna
- ☐ Cooler
- ☐ Cotton clothing
- ☐ Day pack
- ☐ Film
- ☐ Hiking boots
- ☐ Insect repellent
- ☐ Rain jacket
- ☐ Sport sandals
- ☐ Sun hat
- ☐ Sunblock
- ☐ Synthetic ice
- ☐ Umbrella
- ☐ Water bottle

*Excerpted from *Fodor's: How to Pack: Experts Share Their Secrets*
© 1997, by Fodor's Travel Publications

JULY: *Oakley Rodeo.* One of the state's longest-running small-town rodeos, this one in Oakley, 20 mi northeast of Heber City, has a parade, outdoor dances, fireworks, and a patriotic program. | 435/649–8561.

AUG.: *Wasatch County Fair.* A 60-car demolition derby is the odd, but popular, kickoff for this week-long fair. A rodeo caps the action at the week's end. | 435/654–1661.

SEPT.: *Swiss Days.* Entertainment and contests themed to honor the town of Midway's original Swiss settlers. More than 300 gallons of sauerkraut are consumed during the two-day event, held 4 mi west of Heber City. | 435/654–3666.

Dining

Blue Boar Inn. European. High ceilings and white linens give this inn's bright, airy restaurant an understated elegance. The weekly menu is based on the freshest available ingredients and often includes sesame salmon, Chilean sea bass, tenderloin steak, and grilled caribou. Leave room for the warm chocolate cake. | 1235 Warm Springs Rd., Midway | 435/654–1400 | $30–$45 | AE, D, MC, V.

Simon's Fine Dining. Contemporary. Part of the Homestead Resort, this dining establishment overlooks the Heber Valley. The crisp linens and china place settings lend elegance. Two prix-fixe, five-course dinners are offered each evening, including such entrées as rack of lamb and salmon. Open-air dining on the patio in warm weather. | 700 N. Homestead Dr. | 435/654–1102 | www.homesteadresort.com | Reservations recommended | $18–$34 | AE, D, DC, MC, V | No lunch.

Snake Creek Grill. Eclectic. In a refurbished train depot in the quaint downtown area, this popular restaurant serves comfort food with a twist. Jamaican pork medallion, ten-spice salmon with Japanese noodles, and barbecued baby back ribs are local favorites, and the homemade pastas and raviolis and fresh fish specials are arranged nicely and well prepared. | 650 W. 100 S | 435/654–2133 | $18–$32 | MC, V.

Lodging

Danish Viking Lodge. A simple but solid favorite for families and Park City skiers more interested in value than resort-town atmosphere. | 34 rooms, 3 kitchenettes. Microwaves, refrigerators. Cable TV. Pool. Hot tub, sauna. Playground. Laundry facilities. Some pets allowed. | 989 S. Main St. | 435/654–2202 or 800/544–4066 (except Utah) | fax 435/654–2770 | $50–$65 | AE, D, DC, MC, V.

Homestead Resort. Several choices of lodging are available here. The rooms are furnished in southwestern style, and the Virginia House bed and breakfast has more traditional furnishings. The suites and condos are very spacious, with fireplaces. 2 restaurants, bar. Cable TV. 2 pools, 1 indoor. Hot tub, massage. 18-hole golf course, tennis courts. Exercise equipment, horseback riding. Business services. | 150 rooms, 18 executive rooms, 9 2-room suites | 700 N. Homestead Dr., Midway | 435/654–1102 or 800/327–7220 | fax 435/654–5087 | info@homesteadresort.com | www.homesteadresort.com | $119–$269 | AE, D, DC, MC, V.

Inn on the Creek. A luxurious Swiss chalet–inspired inn that sprawls along the base of the Wasatch Mountains. Gas-lit fireplaces and jetted tubs are available in all of the individually decorated rooms, and most have balconies with exceptional views. Restaurant, complementary Continental breakfast (full breakfast on Sat.), dining room. Some kitchens and kitchenettes. In-room VCRs. Conference rooms. | 48 rooms | 375 Rainbow La., Midway | 435/654–0892 | fax 435/654–5871 | $130–$150 | AE, D, DC, MC, V.

Ivo's K-Motel. This funky 1950s-style roadside motel has pleasant renovated rooms and a festive yard with flower boxes and a Jacuzzi-gazebo. Restaurant. Cable TV. Outdoor pool. Hot tub. | 23 rooms | 330 S. 100 E | 435/644–2611 or 800/644–2611 | fax 435/644–2788 | $55 | MC, V.

Johnson Mill Bed & Breakfast. This historic inn, a converted flour mill, has restful rooms decorated in soft colors. The 25 beautiful acres that surround the property include streams, fields, a pond, and, next to the house, a 30-ft waterfall. Dining room, full breakfast. In-room VCRs and movies. | 5 rooms | 100 Johnson Mill Rd., Midway | 435/654–4333 or 888/272–0030 | fax 435/657–1454 | $125 | AE, D, MC, V.

National 9 High Country Inn. The downtown location and modest rates make this one-story motel a good value. Complimentary Continental breakfast, picnic area. Microwaves, refrigerators. Cable TV. Pool. Hot tub. Playground. Laundry facilities. | 38 rooms | 1000 S. Main St. | 435/654–0201 or 800/345–9198 (except Utah) | $60 | AE, D, MC, V.

KANAB

MAP 14, C9

(Nearby towns also listed: Cedar City, St. George)

Conjure up Hollywood's vision of the American West, and you have Kanab. Soaring vermilion sandstone cliffs and sagebrush flats with seemingly endless vistas as their backdrop have lured filmmakers to this area for more than 75 years. Abandoned film sets have become tourist attractions, and old movie posters or still photographs are a decorating staple. In addition to a movie-star past, Kanab has an ideal location. With major roads radiating in four directions, it offers easy access to three national parks, three national monuments, state parks, and historic sites.

Information: Kane County Travel Council | 78 S. 100 E (U.S. 89), Kanab, 84741 | 435/644–5033 | fax 435/644–5923 | kanetrav@xpress web.com | www.kaneutah.com.

Attractions

Best Friends Animal Sanctuary. The nation's largest sanctuary for homeless animals has cabin accommodations, Anasazi ruins, and rock art on the property. | Angel Canyon Ranch, 5001 Angel Canyon Dr. | 435/644–2001 | www.bestfriends.org | Daily.

Coral Pink Sand Dunes State Park. The sand here is an amazing coral color, the product of millions of years of erosion from the surrounding sandstone cliffs. Off-highway vehicle use is a big thing here, but you can get away from the noise and enjoy an undisturbed look at the vegetation, rocky hummocks, and all that sand. | 20 mi north of Kanab on Highway 89 | 435/648–2800 | www.utah.com | $4 | Daily.

Grand Canyon National Park–North Rim. The viewpoints of the forested North Rim of the Grand Canyon, 83 mi south of Kanab, are 1,200 ft higher than those of the South Rim. They are also less crowded, and facilities are more primitive. The whole atmosphere is much more leisurely. | Rte. 67 | 520/638–7888 | www.nps.gov/grca or www.thecanyon.com/NPS/trip-planner/northrim | $20 per vehicle | Mid-May–Oct., until roads are closed by snow.

Pipe Spring National Monument. Native Americans used this site as a water source for thousands of years. It was the first place where Mormon ranchers were more than marginally successful in the cattle business. The monument, 21 mi south of Kanab, does a nice job of re-creating a slice of ranch life in the late 1800s. You can see demonstrations of skills like cattle branding and quilting and learn about desert gardening techniques. | 401 West Pipe Springs Rd., off Rte. 389 | 602/643–7105 | www.nps.gov/pisp | $2 | June–Sept., daily 7:30–5:30; Oct.–May, daily 8–4.

Zion National Park. *See* Zion National Park, *below*. | Rte. 9.

ON THE CALENDAR
JULY: *Red Mesa Bluegrass Festival.* Join bluegrass lovers from the Four Corners and beyond for this annual three-day jamboree, which includes fiddle, mandolin, and flat-pick guitar performances and contests, quilt shows, arts and crafts booths, and a street fair. | 435/644–3497.

Dining

Chef's Palace. American. Rib-eye steaks, prime rib, and seafood specialties are favorites at this old-style cowboy steak house; the Dude Room, full of saddles and cowboy hats, is straight out of a Western. | 151 W. Center St. | 435/644–5052 | $8.50–$15 | AE, D, DC, MC, V.

Houston's Trail's End. American. Servers wear cowboy shirts, denim, and holstered six-shooters (replicas, presumably) at this downtown eatery. Locals come for the steaks and other basics. Tasty country potatoes with onions and peppers are served with breakfast entrées. Kids' menu. | 32 E. Center St. | 435/644–2488 | $9–$14 | AE, D, MC, V | Closed Jan.–Feb.

Nedra's, Too. Mexican. The first Nedra's restaurant was in Fredonia, Arizona, hence the name of this place. Booths and tables, friendly service, and authentic Mexican specialties make this a nice stop for a meal at a reasonable price. The menu also has sandwiches, soups, and desserts. | 310 S. 100 E | 435/644–2030 | $10–$15 | D, MC, V.

Lodging

Best Western Red Hills. This is one of Kanab's larger properties, and it has a hearty dose of cowboy flavor accenting its city-style amenities. Refrigerators. Cable TV, VCRs (movies). Pool. Hot tub. Business services. | 75 rooms | 125 W. Center St. | 435/644–2675 | www.bestwestern.com | $60–$75 | AE, D, DC, MC, V.

Four Seasons Inn. Close to shopping, strolling, or people-watching, this downtown motel is basic and convenient. Restaurant. Cable TV. Pool, wading pool. Business services. | 41 rooms | 36 N. 300 W | 435/644–2635 | $60–$90 | AE, D, DC, MC, V.

Holiday Inn Express. The spacious rooms here have views of the coral cliffs right behind the inn. Numerous conveniences like in-room ironing boards, curling irons, dryers, and work desks with lamps are nice pluses. Continental breakfast. In-room data ports. Cable TV. Outdoor heated pool. Hot tub. Laundry facilities. Pets allowed in some rooms. | 71 rooms | 815 E. U.S. 89 | 435/644–8888 or 800/574–4061 | fax 435/644–8880 | $89 | AE, D, DC, MC, V.

Parry Lodge. The lobby of this Colonial-style building, constructed in 1929, is lined with photos of movie stars who stayed here while filming in the area, including Ronald Reagan and Barbara Stanwyk. Some of the spacious rooms have plaques over the doors to tell you who stayed here before you. The lodge barn, which housed Victor Mature's camels during the making of *Timbuktu*, is now a playhouse, where old-time Western melodramas are performed in summer. Restaurant. Cable TV. Pool. Laundry facilities. Business services. Pets allowed. | 89 rooms | 89 E. Center St. | 435/644–2601 or 800/748–4104 | fax 435/644–2605 | $45–$75 | AE, D, MC, V.

Shilo Inn. On the outskirts of town, this two-story western chain has rooms done in soft pastels. The largest property in town also offers in-room Nintendo. Complimentary Continental breakfast. Microwaves. Movie rentals available. Pool. Hot tub. Laundry facilities. Business services. Airport shuttle. | 118 rooms | 296 W. 100 N | 435/644–2562 | fax 435/644–5333 | www.shiloinns.com | $70–$95 | AE, D, DC, MC, V.

LOA

(Nearby towns also listed: Richfield, Torrey)

Loa is at the northern end of the Fremont River valley, one of several small towns you pass through when approaching Capitol Reef National Park from the northwest on Rte. 24, a designated scenic byway. Because it is the county seat in Wayne County, Loa may be a bit more sophisticated than neighboring towns, but not too much. It remains charmingly quiet and serene.

Information: **Capitol Reef Country** | Box 7, Teasdale, 84773 | 800/858–7951 | info@capitolreef.org | www.capitolreef.org.

Attractions

Capitol Reef National Park. *See* Capitol Reef National Park, *above; see also* Torrey, *below.* | 5 mi east of Torrey on Rte. 24.

Chappell Cheese Company. From the upstairs viewing room, you can watch the entire process of cheesemaking. Several varieties of local cheese are sold in the factory store. | 982 W. Rte. 24 | 435/836–2821 | Free | Mon.–Sat. 8–6.

ON THE CALENDAR

AUG.: *Wayne County Fair.* Horse shows, turkey shoots, and the tilt-a-whirl are all standards at this small town fair, which also schedules a rodeo, a parade, and plenty of food and entertainment. | 435/836–2731.

Dining

Road Creek Inn. American. This hotel dining room is in the renovated Loa General Store, built in 1912. Known for local trout cooked eight different ways, including charbroiled, smoked, sautéed, or in a sandwich. They also serve steak and trout combos. | 90 S. Main St. | 435/836–2485 | www.roadcreekranch.com | $12–$20 | AE, D, DC, MC, V | No lunch.

Wanda's American. This old-fashioned drive-through cafe along Loa's main strip serves grilled burgers and has more than 40 flavors of shakes. | 193 E. 300 S | 435/836–2760 | $5–$7 | No credit cards.

Lodging

Road Creek Inn. The inn is part of the Road Creek Ranch. Right on Main Street in Kanab, the three-story square brick building retains the look of a country store. The elegant stairway leads from the high-ceilinged lobby to the very spacious rooms. The nearby Family Barn has more lodging, including a former hayloft that contains eight double beds, as well as six private rooms. A good choice for families, the barn also has volleyball, horseshoes, and a playground. Restaurant. Cable TV. Fishing and hunting guides. Business services. No smoking. | 22 rooms, 3 suites | 90 S. Main St. | 435/836–2485 or 800/388–7688 | fax 435/836–2489 | www.roadcreekranch.com | $75–$100 | AE, D, MC, V.

LOGAN

MAP 14, C3

(Nearby towns also listed: Brigham, Garden City)

As the largest city north of Ogden, Logan is a practical stop for people on their way through northern Utah to Yellowstone National Park. However, Logan is more than a wide spot in the road. Utah State University, originally a land-grant college, is a leader in such diverse fields as agriculture, natural resources, and space technology. The university also contributes to a growing arts community. And Logan has managed to make the most of the elegant architecture and historic Mormon landmarks found off its main drag.

Information: **Bridgeland Travel Region** | 160 N. Main St., Logan, 84321 | 435/752–2161 or 800/882–4433 | www.cachechamber.com | btr@sunrem.com.

Attractions

American West Heritage Center. This farm was created to represent a typical 1917 Mormon farm. It is staffed by costumed volunteers and graduate students from Utah State University studying outdoor museum management, folklore, or history. This is a "working museum," and on any given day you can watch them shearing sheep, harvesting grain, churning butter, or gathering eggs. Special events are held throughout the year, celebrating holidays as they would have been celebrated in the early 1900s. The farm, 6 mi south of Logan in Wellsville, also hosts the Festival of the American West each summer. | 4025 S. U.S. 89/91, Wellsville | 435/245–4064 | www.americanwestcenter.org | $5 | Apr.–Oct., Tues.–Sat. 10–5.

Daughters of the Utah Pioneers Museum. In the same building as a well-stocked visitors information center, this small museum is an informative summer stop. The collection has musical instruments, furniture, clothing, and other artifacts from the 1850s to the early 1900s. | 160 N. Main St. | 435/752–5139 | Free | Summer only, Tues.–Sat. 10–4.

Hyrum State Park. The lake contrasts vividly with the farmland that stretches nearly to its sandy shore. You can take boats of all sorts on the lake, but still-water canoeing is particularly satisfying. | 405 W. 300 S | 435/245–6866 | www.utah.com | $4 | Boating Apr.–Oct.; fishing daily.

Mormon Tabernacle. The Logan Tabernacle is a striking building constructed of gray granite in the late 1800s. Although this was, and is, a Mormon church building, its purpose has always been to serve as a community meeting place. You can tour the building and use a genealogical research facility. | 100 N. Main St. | 435/755–5598 | Weekdays.

Mormon Temple. High on a hill on Logan's east side, the Mormon Temple can be seen from almost any place in the Cache Valley. The temple's design is very Gothic, with battlements, towers, and buttresses built of the same granite used for the tabernacle. Only active members of the Mormon Church may go inside. The view from Temple Hill is exquisite. | 175 N. 300 E | 435/752–3611.

Nora Eccles Harrison Art Museum. The permanent collection of this museum on the Utah State University campus focuses on 20th-century American artists from the western states, and includes a gallery of ceramics and Native American Indian pottery. Rotating exhibits change every few months, and include traditional paintings from estate collections as well as works of contemporary artists. | 650 N. 1100 E | 435/797–0163 | Free | Tues., Thurs., Fri. 10:30–4:30, Wed. 10:30–8, weekends 2–5.

Utah State University. USU opened as Utah Agricultural College in the late 1800s. It achieved university status in the late 1950s. Many of the school's areas of specialty are related to agriculture and environmental studies. It also has strong humanities and science programs and offers theatrical and musical entertainments for the community. | Old Main Hill | 435/797–1129 | www.usu.edu | Free | Mon–Fri; closed all holidays and Dec. 22–Jan. 2.

Wasatch-Cache National Forest, Logan Canyon. U.S. 89 slides northeast through the national forest for 41 mi between Logan and the Utah/Idaho border. Logan Canyon is one of Utah's 27 designated scenic byways. Climbing through the striated limestone of the Bear River Mountains from an elevation of 4,700 ft to 7,800 ft at the canyon's summit, you pass several signed hiking trailheads and excellent national forest campgrounds. | U.S. 89 northeast to Rte. 30, near Bear Lake | 435/755–3620 (Logan Ranger District) | www.fs.fed.us/wcnf | $10–$12 camping fees | Daily.

ON THE CALENDAR

JUNE: *Summerfest.* An arts and crafts festival with music, folk dancing, and other cultural events, this one takes place on the grounds of the Tabernacle in Logan's historic downtown. | 435/752–2161.

JULY–AUG.: *Utah Festival Opera.* Three operas are performed in repertory on the stage of the historic Ellen Eccles Theatre, which was built in the early 1900s and recently restored. | 435/750–0300 or 435/752–0026 for tickets | Evening and matinee performances.

JULY–AUG.: *Festival of the American West.* An event at Jensen Historic Farm, with demonstrations of traditional crafts, including blacksmithing, quilting, and woodcarving; historic games; Western music and dancing; "world championship" dutch-oven cooking contest; and nightly performances of *The West: America's Odyssey,* a musical pageant with a cast of more than 200 actors, singers, and dancers. | 801/797–1143 or 800/225–3378.

AUG.: *Cache County Fair.* The Cache County Fairgrounds host agricultural and culinary competitions and demonstrations, with a nightly rodeo. | 435/752–2161 or 800/882–4433.

Dining

The Bluebird Cafe. American. Opened in 1914 as a soda fountain, this downtown establishment retains its old-time atmosphere. Meals run to meat—roast beef, ham, turkey—and mashed potatoes. For dessert, try the ice-cream specialties and hand-dipped chocolates. Kids' menu. | 19 N. Main St. | 435/752–3155 | $8–$14 | AE, D, MC, V.

Café Habanero. Mexican. The high ceilings and intricate woodwork are memorable at this restored train-depot restaurant, which serves steak and lobster as well as traditional Mexican food. The carnita, slowly simmered pork on a corn tortilla, and the seafood enchiladas are house specialties. | 600 W. Center St. | 435/753–8880 | $16–$30 | AE, DC, MC, V.

Gia's. Italian. The dining rooms upstairs are more formal; the basement pizzeria is fun with sawdust on the floor, a big-screen TV, and, generally, students from Utah State University. The restaurant's menu is strong on chicken, seafood, and veal dishes. Kids' menu. | 119 S. Main St. | 435/752–8384 | $7–$16 | AE, D, DC, MC, V.

The Grapevine. Continental. In a remodeled Victorian home, the dining areas are dressed with fresh flowers and linen tablecloths. In warm weather, patio dining is popular. The menu changes to take advantage of fresh ingredients. Inspiration for entrées comes from the culinary traditions of several European countries. | 129 N. 100 E | 435/752–1977 | Reservations essential | $24–$45 | AE, D, MC, V | Closed Sun., no lunch.

Lodging

Anniversary Inn. Rooms at this bed and breakfast mansion range from more traditional bridal suites to wildly colorful, even kitschy, theme rooms with names like Space Odyssey (with a silver spaceship bathroom), Aphrodite's Court (marble goddesses and a canopied jet tub), and Jesse James Hideout (not for everyone). All rooms have jetted tubs, and many have fireplaces. Continental breakfast. Cable TV, in-room VCRs. | 21 rooms | 169 E. Center St. | 435/752–3443 or 800/574–7605 | fax 435/752–8550 | $99–$199 | AE, D, MC, V.

Best Western Baugh Motel. A cluster of five redbrick, Colonial-style buildings makes up this downtown motel with standard rooms. The outdoor pool is heated. Restaurant. Cable TV. Pool. Hot tub. Business services. | 77 rooms | 153 S. Main St. | 435/752–5220 or 800/462–4154 | fax 435/752–3251 | www.bestwestern.com | $58–$68 | AE, D, DC, MC, V.

Comfort Inn. In the newer, northern commercial district, this centrally located establishment is near several restaurants and grocery stores. The rooms were renovated in the late 1990s. Complimentary Continental breakfast. In-room data ports, refrigerators in suites. Cable TV. Indoor pool. Hot tub. Exercise equipment. Laundry facilities. Business services. | 83 rooms | 447 N. Main St. | 435/752–9141 | fax 435/752–9723 | www.comfortinn.com | $55–$70 | AE, D, DC, MC, V.

Days Inn. A quiet property between Logan's downtown and verdant farmland to the south, the inn is 2 mi from a mall and 2 mi from Utah State University. The rooms were renovated in 2000, and some have kitchenettes. Complimentary Continental breakfast. Refrigerators, some in-room hot tubs, Cable TV. Indoor pool. Laundry facilities. | 64 rooms, 19 with kitchenettes | 364 S. Main St. | 435/753–5623 | www.daysinn.com | $60–$80 | AE, D, DC, MC, V.

Logan House Inn. Built in 1895, this bed and breakfast features an interior furnished in keeping with the period. The Colonial-style inn has nice grounds, too. Complimentary breakfast and afternoon snacks. In-room data ports, in-room hot tubs. Cable TV, VCRs (movies). Guest laundry. Business services. No smoking. | 6 rooms | 168 N. 100 E | 435/752–

7727 or 800/478–7459 (reservations) | fax 435/752–0092 | www.loganhouseinn.com | $95–$110 | AE, D, DC, MC, V.

Providence Inn. The stone part of the three-story stone and cream-brick inn was once the Old Rock Church, built in 1889. With Palladian windows and other nice architectural touches, the property is elegant, with ample grounds and individually decorated rooms, some Colonial style, some Georgian, and some Victorian. Complimentary breakfast, picnic area. In-room data ports, in-room hot tubs. Cable TV, VCRs (movies). Laundry facilities. Business services. No smoking. | 15 rooms, 3 suites | 10 S. Main St., Providence | 435/752–3432 or 800/480–4943 (reservations) | fax 435/752–3482 | provinn@cache.net | www.providenceinn.com | $119–$139 | AE, D, DC, MC, V.

University Inn. This well-maintained property on the edge of the Utah State University campus offers basic, comfortable rooms. Suites have in-room data ports, work desks, and comfortable arm chairs. The inn is part of the university. Cable TV. Conference rooms, business services. | 60 rooms, 14 suites | 4300 Old Main Hill | 435/797–0016 or 800/231–5634 | fax 435/797–1580 | $53, $57–$69 suites | AE, D, DC, MC, V.

MANTI

(Nearby town also listed: Ephraim)

Manti was one of the first five towns settled and incorporated in Brigham Young's "State of Deseret." The most prominent feature of the town is its Mormon Temple. The impressive structure was built of creamy oolite limestone on a hill overlooking the city. Its financing and construction were a great sacrifice for the people of the town, who worked from 1877 to 1888 to finish it at a cost of more than a million dollars. An often repeated, but unproven, anecdote is that the women of Manti gave up their fine china to be crushed and added to the exterior mortar.

Information: Sanpete County Chamber of Commerce | Box 59, Ephraim, 84627 | 435/283–4321 or 800/281–4346.

Attractions

Mormon Temple and Grounds. The Manti Temple dominates the view of Manti from U.S. 89 and many spots in the Sanpete Valley. Certainly the town of Manti is oriented to its landmark. The temple has been called "the crowning achievement of 19th-century Mormon architecture." Like other Mormon temples, this building is open only to active members of the Mormon church. You can learn more about it at the adjacent visitor center. The surrounding hillside grounds bloom with bright colors from spring through fall. | 500 N. and U.S. 89 | 435/835–8888 | www.utahreach.usu.edu/sanpete.

ON THE CALENDAR

JUNE: *Mormon Miracle Pageant.* This outdoor pageant on the grounds of the Mormon Temple portrays the early history of the Mormon Church. It draws up to 30,000 spectators nightly during its two-week run and involves performers and volunteers from all over the Sanpete Valley. | 435/835–3000.

Dining

Don's Gallery Cafe. American. The homemade scones, onion rings, and fresh mashed potatoes and gravy (served with most meals) are favorites at this quaint Main Street restaurant. The interior is hung with paintings by local artists and photographs depicting Sanpete County history. | 115 N. Main St. | 435/835–3663 | $5–$15 | AE, D, MC, V.

The Manti Country Village Restaurant. American. This is both a restaurant and a friendly local gathering place. The specialties are mainly comfort foods—scrambled eggs with cheese;

big burgers with lettuce, onions, pickles and tomatoes on the side; real mashed potatoes. | 145 N. Main St. | 435/826–4251 | $10–$17 | MC, V.

Miller's Bakery. American. A fast-food joint that has been popular with the locals for more than 20 years, this one is famed for its homemade donuts, pies, and rolls, and serves hamburgers, sandwiches, and pizza at great prices. | 227 N. Main St. | 435/835–4931 | $3–$5 | No credit cards.

Lodging

Legacy Inn. This white Victorian-style inn with a turret and porch is filled with personal touches—chocolate truffles in the rooms, evening "snacks" like crepes and pesto pizza, a wide array of great old books, and lovely antique furniture. The front porch and some of the rooms offer views of the Manti Temple, only ½ block away. A comfortable family suite sleeps six. Full breakfast, dining room. TV in common area. | 3 rooms, 1 suite | 337 N. 100 E | 435/835–8352 | fax 435/835–8342 | $75–$95 | MC, V.

Manti Country Village Inn. On the main street of Manti, this quiet inn is nicely located for walks around town. Cable TV, room phones. Hot tub. | 23 rooms | 145 N. Main St. | 435/835–9300 or 800/452–0787 | fax 435/835–6286 | $55–$70 | AE, D, DC, MC, V.

Manti House Inn. This building was erected in 1880 as housing for workers who came from throughout the area to construct the Manti Temple. It's built of the same oolite limestone as the temple and many other Sanpete Valley buildings. It was renovated in the early 1990s to function as a bed and breakfast. Complimentary breakfast. Cable TV, VCRs. No smoking. | 5 rooms, 1 suite with hot tub | 401 N. Main St. | 435/835–0161 or 800/835–7512. | www.mantihouse.com | $59–$109 | MC, V.

Temple View Lodge. The sports facilities make this homey, local motel a good stop for families. It is surrounded by a large grassy park and is across the street from the Manti Temple. Basketball, volleyball, playground. | 12 rooms | 269 E. 400 N | 435/835–9300 or 888/505–7566 | $35–$40 | AE, D, MC, V.

Yardley Inn. A turn-of-the-century Victorian house with a remodeled interior. All rooms have private baths, and suites feature wood-burning fireplaces and large jetted tubs. Dinners by arrangement. Complimentary breakfast. Cable TV, VCRs. Hot tub. No smoking. | 2 rooms, 2 suites | 190 S. 200 W | 435/835–1861 or 800/858–6634 | fax 435/835–1863. | www.virtualcities.com/ut/yardleyinn.htm | $50–$100 | AE, D, MC, V.

MOAB

MAP 14, E7

(Nearby towns also listed: Green River, Monticello)

Moab was a Mormon farming community when it was established in the late 1800s. Its residents were fairly quiet and devout until uranium was discovered in the early 1950s and an influx of prospectors tripled the town's population. When the boom went bust, Moab became a haven for outdoors enthusiasts drawn by opportunities for rafting, hiking, four-wheel-drive vehicle travel, and rock climbing. All of these sports continue to attract visitors today, as do Arches and Canyonlands national parks and many scenic drives in the area. All-terrain bicycles and the thousands of acres of rolling, asphalt-smooth sandstone or slickrock that surround Moab were an inevitable match. It was mountain biking that brought sufficient outsiders to support a winery and a brew pub and to entice McDonald's and national-chain motels to Moab. While some savvy travelers look farther south to Monticello, Blanding, or Bluff as a base for their adventures, Moab remains "the" southeastern Utah destination.

Information: **Grand County Travel Council** | Box 550, Moab, 84532 | 435/259–8825 or 800/635–6622 | gctc@sisna.com | www.canyonlands-utah.com.

THE SANPETE VALLEY

Visitors to Utah are generally curious about Mormons. Particularly curious it seems, about the earliest Mormons, pioneers who practiced polygamy, made their own laws, and minted their own money. Interestingly, a more lasting impression was made on Utah's culture by the second wave of emigrants, hundreds of Europeans who converted to Mormonism in the mid-1800s and left their home countries to travel to "Zion" in Utah.

More than any other place in the state, the Sanpete Valley gives visitors a glimpse of this history, and the ways European converts integrated their diverse cultures into the body of the Church. Today, a strong Mormon legacy remains, making the area a perfect destination for learning about early Mormon culture and heritage.

Sanpete County is centered geographically in the state. The first residents were Mormons from the eastern United States sent from Salt Lake City to function as "place markers" in the expanding territory. Then in the 1850s an influx of Danish, Swedish, and Norwegian Mormons began to build closely knit communities here; first Manti, then Ephraim and Spring City. They followed church founder Joseph Smith's plan for the city of Zion. Brigham Young employed the same design in Salt Lake City, but it remains much more obvious with these towns' smaller scale.

The designs of many homes and commercial buildings from this era reflect Scandinavian influences. Then asymmetrical Victorian designs appeared in the 1890s. Between 1910 and 1930, bungalows were in vogue. All of these home styles retain a place in Sanpete Valley, with some of the finest examples operating as bed and breakfast inns.

Typical of preservation efforts common to Sanpete, in 1980 the entire town of Spring City was placed on the National Register of Historic Places as a pristine example of an agrarian Mormon village. The city has since become an arts colony of sorts, but its historic designation remains intact.

The Manti Mormon temple, designed by architect William Folsom, blends Gothic Revival, French Renaissance Revival, and French Second Empire styles. It was considered the finest religious building in the state when it was completed in 1888. The temple is still in use today, and is still viewed as an icon of the faith shown by the Scandinavian families who financed and built it.

The Sanpete Valley is considered by historians to reflect "a distinctive Mormon landscape heritage"; square fields separated by unpainted posts and barbed-wire strands, cattle and sheep grazing in the same pastures, and functioning roadside irrigation ditches dug by the families who farmed this land in the last century. Original unpainted barns remain, as well as "inside-out granaries," with their studs on the outside to better support the weight of grain pushing against interior walls.

The fact that this area was bypassed by the interstate highway system probably accounts for some of its rural preservation. However U.S. 89 offers easy access, so cultural pride is the real reason Sanpete Valley has become Utah's most accurate reflection of its Mormon roots.

Related Towns: Ephraim, Manti, Spring City

© Artville

Attractions

Arches National Park. *See* Arches National Park, *above*. | Off U.S. 191, 5 mi north of Moab.

Arches Vineyard. This is Utah's only commercial winery, producing about 80,000 bottles annually. You can take a free ½-hr tour (call ahead for times), and the winery, at the south end of town, has a tasting room. | 420 Kane Creek Blvd.; ½ mi west of U.S. 191 | 435/259–5397 or 800/797–6702 | Free | Mon.–Sat. 12–8.

Canyonlands Field Institute. You can take outdoor learning seminars, writers' workshops, elderhostels, and customized study programs at this school in southeastern Utah. | 1320 S. U.S. 191 | 435/259–7750 or 800/860–5262 | fax 435/259–2335 | www.canyonlandsfieldinst.org | Mon.–Fri. 9–12 and 1–5.

Canyonlands National Park. *See* Canyonlands National Park, *above*. | Rte. 313, 35 mi southwest of Moab.

Dan O'Laurie Museum. Collections here focus on the history and prehistory of the Moab area. The forces that formed the geology of the area, the Spanish Trail, and the uranium boom of the 1950s are among the themes explored. Visit the art gallery on the second floor, which has works by local artists. | 118 E. Center St. | 435/259–7985 | www.4x4now.com/mbdom.htm | Free; donations accepted | Nov.–Mar., Mon.–Thurs. 3–7, Fri.–Sat. 1–7; Apr.–Oct., Mon.–Sat. 1–8.

Dead Horse Point State Park. From here, you get a sweeping view of the multicolored, upside-down geography of Canyonlands National Park's Island in the Sky and a steep look down to the Colorado River. An excellent museum and visitors center does a good job of demystifying the enormous erosional forces that have carved and scoured this upthrust corner of the state. The park was named for a band of wild horses once stranded on this isolated peninsula. | Rte. 313 | 435/259–2614 | www.utah.com | $6 per car | Daily.

Hole 'n the Rock. Albert Christensen spent more than 20 years blasting, chiseling, and sculpting this 14-room "hole" inside a solid sandstone ridge. The Christensen family actually lived here for many years. The indestructible home is a curiosity that particularly appeals to kids. | 11037 U.S. 191, 15 mi south of Moab | 435/686–2250 | www.roadsideamerica.com/attract/UTMOAhole.html | $3 | Daily.

Manti–La Sal National Forest, La Sal Division. The La Sal Mountain Loop Road enters the national forest just as the dominant red-rock cliffs east of Moab begin to alternate with sage-brush and juniper flats. The road passes through the cool heights of the La Sal Mountains, winding north to Castle Valley and an intersection with Rte. 128. This road is paved, except for a couple of gravel sections, but it does have steep switchbacks, and the portion running through the national forest is typically closed by snow each winter. | 62 E. 100 N | 435/259–7155 or 435/637–2817 | www.fs.fed.us/r4/mantilasal | Day use free; camping fees | Daily; parts closed by snow Nov.–Apr.

Matheson Wetlands. This 875-acre preserve is the only high-quality wetlands along the Colorado River. The La Sal Mountains, not the river, are the main water source. Melting snow runs through underground channels then seeps to the surface, forming a sort of oasis. You'll often see river otters, mule deer, and beavers here. Hundreds of birds, including great blue herons, also make the fertile slough their home. Paths and walkways make it easy to explore the area, and on Saturday at 8 AM, from March to October, you can take one of the Nature Conservancy's guided nature walks. The wetlands are named for the late Scott M. Matheson. The former Utah governor was an advocate of conservation and responsible land use. | Off Kane Creek Blvd. near the south end of town, turn northwest off U.S. 191 at Kane Creek Blvd. and continue northwest approximately 2 mi | gctc@sisna.com | Free | Daily.

Slickrock Trail. Motorcyclists originated this trail in 1969, but conquering the 10-mi roller-coaster route marked only by dashes of paint on raw rock has become a rite of passage for mountain bikers. A 2-mi practice loop near the parking area introduces most of the terrain challenges found on the actual trail. The area is administered by the Bureau of Land

Management. | Sand Flats Rd.; east on 300 S. to 400 E., then south to Mill Creek Dr., then east to Sand Flats Rd. and north to the trailhead | 435/259–6111 | www.blm.gov/utah/moab | User fee | Daily.

ADVENTURE TOURS

Lake Powell Air. See the countryside from above on these tours. | Canyonlands Field; 18 mi north on U.S. 191 | 435/259–7421 | fax 435/259–4032 | www.moab-utah.com/redtail/ | Daily.

Adventure Bound River Expeditions. One- to five-day Colorado River trips; white-water rafts and inflatable kayak instruction. | 2392 H Rd., Grand Junction, CO | 970/245–5428 or 800/423–4668 | fax 970/241–5633 | www.raft-utah.com | Rates vary | Apr.–Oct.

Canyonlands By Night. Evening float trips on a section of the Colorado are accompanied by music, storytelling, and special effects. | 1861 N. U.S. 191 | 435/259–5261 | www.moab.net/canyonlandsbynight | $38 includes dinner | May–mid-Oct., daily at sundown, weather permitting.

Colorado River & Trail Expeditions, Inc. Individual, family, and group trips may be from one day to three weeks long. | 5058 S. 300 W, Salt Lake City, | 801/261–1789 or 800/253–7328 | www.crateinc.com | Mid-Apr.–Oct.

Lin Ottinger's Scenic Tours. Four-wheel-drive-vehicle tours take you through the deserts and mountains of southeastern Utah, with some trips in Canyonlands and Arches National Parks. | Moab Rock Shop, 600 N. Main St. | 435/259–7312.

Pack Creek Ranch. Guided horseback adventures go through the La Sal Mountains and into the desert. | La Sal Pass Rd. (Box 1270) | 435/259–5505 | fax 435/259–8879 | www.pack-creekranch.com | Mar.–Oct., depending on availability.

Rim Tours. Half-day to six-day backcountry mountain-biking tours on beginner to advanced routes. | 1233 S. U.S. 191 | 435/259–5223 or 800/626–7335 | fax 435/259–3349 | www.rimtours.com.

Sheri Griffith River Expeditions. Personalized two- to six-day trips give you a choice of rowboats, paddleboats, or kayaks; bilingual guides by request. You can also put together a custom combination river, biking, and hiking trip. | 2231 S. U.S. 191 | 435/259–8229 or 800/332–2439 | fax 435/259–2226 | www.GriffithExp.com | May–Sept.

Tag-A-Long Expeditions. One- to eight-day adventures with four-wheel-drive vehicles, bicycles, rafts, or any combination. | 452 N. Main St. | 435/259–8946 or 800/453–3292 | www.tagalong.com | tagalong@tagalong.com | Nov.–Feb. and Apr.–mid-Oct.

ON THE CALENDAR

MAR.–APR.: *Canyonlands Film Festival.* This international film festival is heading into its seventh year, and offers a week of screenings, new wave and abstract short films, and feature-length independent movies. The festival operations are Web-based, so consult the Web site for more information. | www.moab-utah.com/film.

MAR.–APR.: *Jeep Safari.* Four-wheel-drive enthusiasts have been coming here each spring since 1966 for organized events and rides on more than 25 different trails. | 435/259–7625.

MAY: *Moab Art Festival.* Artists from across the West gather at the Moab Arts and Recreation Center to show their wares, including pottery, photography, and paintings. Live music, varied food options. | 435/259–2742.

SEPT.: *Moab Music Festival.* Chamber music is performed in a natural amphitheater along the Colorado River, with both indoor performances and a family picnic concert. | 435/259–8431.

OCT.: *Fat Tire Festival.* A week-long celebration of the mountain bike has hill climbs, guided group rides, archaeology tours, and evening entertainment. | 435/375–3231.

Dining

Center Cafe. Eclectic. The work of local artists decorates the walls of this sleek, no-smoking eatery. The menu includes such dishes as crab cakes with fresh tomatoes, Asian barbecue chicken, and ginger basmati rice. | 92 E. Center St. | 435/259–4295 | $23–$40 | D, MC, V | Closed Jan. No lunch.

Eddie McStiff's Brew Pub. American. The tavern and patio of this establishment serve liquor. A dining room opposite is designed for families with children. The brewery's unusual stock of beers and ales can be enjoyed in either setting. Menu items include pizza, salads, burgers, pastas, and southwestern dishes. Raspberry wheat is McStiff's most popular beer. Others include amber ale, a spruce beer made with roots, bark, and needles, and a jalapeño beer that only burns a little on the way down. You can eat in the garden room, which is enclosed and cooled, but opens onto the outdoor dining section. | 57 S. Main St. | 435/259–2337 | www.moabbrewery.com | $10–$19 | AE, D, MC, V.

Jail House Café. American. The people who ate here originally didn't do so voluntarily; they were prisoners in the county courthouse. This popular breakfast restaurant serves some of the best omelettes in town. Specialties like eggs Benedict, eggs Florentine, and Grand Marnier–flavored French toast are filling and flavorful. | 101 N. Main St. | 435/259–3900 | $5–$10 | MC, V | Breakfast only | Closed Nov.–Feb.

La Hacienda. Mexican. Although this restaurant next to a motel may not have much in the way of Mexican-style furnishings, the large portions of good south-of-the-border food, tasty margaritas, and friendly service lend authenticity. | 574 N. Main St. | 435/259–6319 | $10–$22 | AE, D, MC, V.

Poplar Place. American. A two-story adobe house built over 100 years ago shelters this eatery, known for fun, lively dining, and excellent pizzas, pastas, and sandwiches. Appetizers like the Poplar Hot Wings are a great mid-day snack. | 11 E. 100 N. Main St. | 435/259–6018 | $14–$17 | MC, V.

Slickrock Cafe. American. A two-story brick business building constructed in 1906 is the front-and-center location for this popular restaurant. The menu favorites are the uranium burger with fresh garlic and chunks of blue cheese, shrimp and chicken jambalaya, and grilled vegetable skewers. | Center and Main Sts. | 453/259–8004 | $12–$22 | AE, D, MC, V | Closed Sun.

Lodging

Archway Inn. Only two mi from Arches National Park, this inn is good for longer stays with its large suites, numerous amenities, and outdoor grills. The immaculate property is surrounded by red-rock cliffs and the greenery of a wetlands preserve. Continental breakfast. Refrigerators, some kitchenettes. Pool. Hot tub. Exercise room. Conference rooms. | 80 rooms, 15 suites, 2 apartments | 1551 N. U.S. 191 | 435/259–2599 or 800/341–9359 | fax 435/259–2270 | $94, $115–$150 suites, $175 apartments | AE, D, DC, MC, V.

Best Western Canyonlands Inn. Here you're close to the Colorado River and north of downtown Moab, but can still easily walk to several restaurants. Complimentary breakfast. Refrigerators, coffeemakers. Cable TV. Indoor/outdoor pool. Exercise equipment. Laundry facilities. Business services. | 77 rooms, 46 suites | 16 S. Main St. | 435/259–2300 | fax 435/259–2301 | www.bestwestern.com | $75–$120 | AE, D, DC, MC, V.

Best Western Green Well. A mid-size property in downtown Moab, with a long-standing reputation as a good value, close to restaurants, shopping, and attractions. Restaurant. Cable TV. Pool. | 72 rooms | 105 S. Main St. | 435/259–6151 | fax 435/259–4397 | www.bestwestern.com | $99 | AE, D, DC, MC, V.

Castle Valley Inn Bed & Breakfast. A quiet setting with a 360-degree view of sandstone buttes makes for a pleasant stay, especially if you like wildlife-watching. Deer pass through the yard daily, and many kinds of birds visit the feeders. Complimentary breakfast, afternoon snacks. Refrigerators, no room phones. Hot tub. Kids over 15 only. | 8 rooms | 424 Amber La., Castle Valley | 435/259–6012 | fax 435/259–1501 | www.castlevalleyinn.com | $95–$135 | D, MC, V.

Comfort Suites. You get a lot for the price of a night's lodging here, with comfortable, spacious, and nicely decorated suites. A handsome lobby and modern fitness facilities are nice pluses. Continental breakfast. Microwaves, refrigerators. Indoor pool. Hot tub. Exercise room. | 75 suites | 800 S. Main St. | 435/259–5252 or 800/228–5150 | fax 435/259–7110 | $99 | AE, D, DC, MC, V.

Gonzo Inn. One of Moab's newer properties, this is the place to stay if you're here to bike. It offers bike storage and a bike wash and repair station. The rooms are done in vibrant colors with a desert theme, and there's a large private courtyard. Microwaves and refrigerators in suites. Cable TV, some VCRs in suites. Pool. Hot tub. | 43 rooms, 21 suites | 100 W. 200 S | 435/259–2515 or 800/791–4044 | www.gonzoinn.com | $95–$135 | AE, D, DC, MC, V.

Landmark Motel. A true Moab landmark, this 1960s-style motor inn has been around for decades. The eclectic, retro rooms here are comfortable, and you're close to downtown restaurants and shops. Continental breakfast. Pool. Hot tub. Laundry facilities. | 36 rooms | 168 N. Main St. | 435/259–6147 or 800/441–6147 | fax 435/259–5556 | $94 | AE, D, DC, MC, V.

Pack Creek Ranch. With neither in-room telephones nor televisions, peace and quiet are the lures here. The log building has open-beamed ceilings inside. Some of the spacious, one- to four-bedroom cottages have kitchens. Restaurant, picnic area. No room phones. Pool. Hot tub, sauna, massage. Hiking. Cross-country skiing. Pets allowed. | 10 1-, 2-, 3-, and 4-bedroom cottages | La Sal Mountain Loop Rd. | 435/259–5505 | fax 435/259–8879 | www.packcreekranch.com | Apr.–Oct., $135–300 per cabin (with breakfast); Nov.–Mar., $100–$200 (no meals) | AE, D, MC, V | AP.

Sorrel River Ranch. This is the only property in Moab's vicinity—17 mi north—that's directly on the Colorado River. You can choose between several kinds of lodgings, from motel-style to cabins and lodge rooms. Most have river views. The impressive food service includes two restaurants open to the public. Restaurant. Some room phones. Cable TV. Hot tub. | 9 rooms, 10 suites | Rte. 128, 17 mi north of Moab | 435/259–4642 or 877/359–2725 | fax 435/259–3016 | info@sorelriver.com | www.sorrelriver.com | $179–$250 | MC, V.

Sunflower Hill Bed & Breakfast. On a quiet residential side street three blocks from downtown Moab, this establishment is both tranquil and convenient. The deluxe rooms have jetted tubs and French doors that lead to private balconies or patios. All have antique furniture and are light and spacious. The two-building, two-story inn is surrounded by vibrant perennial gardens. Rooms run from simple to very elegant. Complimentary breakfast, afternoon snacks. Cable TV. Hot tub. No kids under 8. No smoking. | 11 rooms, 6 suites | 185 N. 300 E | 435/259–2974 | fax 435/259–3065 | innkeeper@sunflowerhill.com | www.sunflowerhill.com | $105–$170 | MC, V.

MONTICELLO

MAP 14, F8

(Nearby towns also listed: Blanding, Moab)

Beneath the Abajo Mountains, at an elevation of 7,000 ft, Monticello offers a welcome break from summer desert heat and easy access to mountain recreation in the Manti–La Sal National Forest. It's actually the city closest to the Needles District, the most accessible part of Canyonlands National Park. Tourism has caused some recent growth here, but for the most part Monticello remains a quiet, mostly Mormon community.

Information: San Juan County Community Development and Visitor Services | 117 S. Main St., Monticello, 84535 | 435/587–3235 or 800/574–4386 | jrbryan@state.ut.us | www.canyonlands-utah.com.

Attractions

Canyon Rims Recreation Area. The Bureau of Land Management administers this area adjacent to the Needles District of Canyonlands National Park. A paved road leads across a narrow peninsula to Needles Overlook, where the picnic area offers incredible views. The recreation area also has hundreds of 4-wheel-drive-vehicle routes and hiking trails. | 82 E. Dogwood | 435/587–2141 | www.ut.blm.gov/monticello/play.html | Free | Daily.

Canyonlands National Park. *See* Canyonlands National Park, *above.* | Needles District: U.S. 191 to Rte. 211 to Squaw Flats Campground.

Horse Head Peak. More than a century ago, Monticello cowboys noticed a horse's head and ears formed by the shadows, trees, and terrain on the eastern side of the Abajo Mountains. Since then the horse head has become a distinctive southeastern Utah landmark. With imagination, you can spot if from most anyplace in Monticello, but for a little help, find the carefully placed viewing pipes in the city park at Main and Center Streets. | Free | Daily.

Manti–La Sal National Forest, La Sal Division. The Abajo Mountains are wedded to the red rock of the desert floor. There is a quiet transition from sandstone and juniper foothills to forests of Ponderosa pine at almost 11,000 ft. From this section of the national forest, impressive panoramas unfold of Canyonlands National Park to the north. | Forest Road 105, then approximately 18 mi north to Forest Road 079, which meets U.S. 191 near Blanding. Traveling this entire loop may require a high-clearance vehicle | 62 E. 100 N | 435/587–2041 or 435/637–2817 | www.fs.fed.us/r4/mantilasal | Day use free; overnight fees | Daily; higher elevations closed Oct.–May.

Newspaper Rock. One of the finest examples of rock art to be found in the southwest, Newspaper Rock is a panel of hundreds of figures and designs incised on a southwest-facing cliff. The stone "bulletin board" includes over 350 distinct petroglyphs carved more than 800 years ago. Figures riding horses and shooting arrows are considered a portrayal of the Ute Indians, who first had horses in the 1600s. Other images attributed to the Ute culture probably date from the 19th century. | 14 mi north on U.S. 191, then 12 mi west on Rte. 211 | 435/587–2141 | www.ut.blm.gov | Free | Daily.

ON THE CALENDAR

JULY: *Monticello Pioneer Days.* A softball tournament and other activities for all ages take place in the Monticello City Park, fueled by snacks such as Navajo tacos. | 435/587–3235 or 800/574–4386.

AUG.: *San Juan County Fair and Rodeo.* Experience local culture at this traditional week-long county fair that includes garden produce and flower judging, junior livestock shows, performances and rides, and a southwestern-style rodeo with bronco and bull riding, barrel racing, and team roping. | 800/574–4386.

Dining

Houston's. Southwestern. The lunch crowd almost fills this mid-size diner. The blue-corn piñon pancakes are a delicious breakfast. Burritos and sandwiches are the locals' lunch choices. | 296 N. Main St. | 435/587–2531 | $10–$15 | MC, V | Closed Tues. No dinner.

Lamplight Restaurant. American. Antique furniture gives a Victorian look to this quiet steak house at the center of town. You can get fresh salmon and halibut, as well as the various steak dinners, and all dinners are served with homemade soup, salad, and dessert. | 665 E. Central St. | 435/587–2170 | $9–$16 | MC, V | Closed Sun.–Tues.

Los Tachos. Mexican. This small adobe restaurant has a festive, low-key dining area, and is a local favorite for authentic, homemade, south-of-the border dishes. The Tres Amigos platter gives you a sampling of the enchiladas, tacos, and burritos. | 280 E. Central St. | 435/587–3094 | $6–$11 | V.

Lodging

Best Western Wayside Inn. A large yard and a fenced pool surrounded by bright flower beds make this one-story brick motel a nice family stopover. The staff is helpful about suggesting the best things to do in the area. Cable TV. Pool. | 38 rooms | 195 E. Central (U.S. 666) | 435/587–2261 | www.bestwestern.com | $64–$95 | AE, D, DC, MC, V.

Canyonlands Motor Inn. Quiet, local, and in the central part of town, the inn has newly remodeled rooms that are clean and rates that are modest. Some microwaves and refrigerators. Cable TV. Pool. Hot tub. Playground. Laundry facilities. | 32 rooms | 197 N. Main St. | 435/587–2266 or 800/952–6212 | fax 435/587–2883 | $35–$55 | AE, D, MC, V.

Grist Mill Inn Bed & Breakfast. A restored flour mill built in the 1930s is now a picturesque inn that still resembles a mill. The rooms are individually decorated. Complimentary breakfast. TV in common area. | 10 rooms | 64 S. 300 E | 435/587–2597 or 800/645–3762 | fax 435/587–2580 | gristmill@sisna.com | www.moabutah.com/gristmillinn | $60–$85 | AE, DC, MC, V.

Monticello Days Inn. One of the largest properties in town, this chain motel is right off U.S. 191 and offers numerous amenities and a sparkling poolside area. Continental breakfast. Some microwaves and refrigerators. Cable TV. Indoor pool. Hot tub. | 43 rooms | 549 N. Main St. | 435/587–2458 or 800/329–7466 | fax 435/587–2191 | $70–$85 | AE, D, DC, MC, V.

Triangle Hotel. Built in 1965, this is one of Monticello's older properties. The moderate prices make it a good stopover if you're on a limited budget. Cable TV. Room phones. | 26 rooms | Rte. 666 E | 435/587–2274 or 800/657–6622 | fax 435/587–2175 | $45–$60 | AE, D, DC, MC, V.

NEPHI

MAP 14, C5

(Nearby towns also listed: Ephraim, Payson)

Nephi is a well-supplied stop for travelers heading south from the Provo area on I–15. It is also the southern end of the Nebo Loop Scenic Byway, which winds its way through a section of the Uinta National Forest (*see also* Payson, *below*). Nephi was briefly called "Little Chicago" before being named after a prophet in The Book of Mormon.

Information: Panoramaland Travel Region | Box 427, Nephi, 84648 | 435/623–5203 or 800/748–4361 | fax 435/623–4609.

Attractions

Yuba State Park. A boat-in camping area with docking facilities right at the campsites is the novel feature at this park, 30 mi south of Nephi on I–15. You can catch walleye and yellow perch year-round, but from spring to fall Yuba Lake is for swimming and boating. | Exit 202 off I–15 | 435/758–2611 | www.utah.com | $5 | Daily.

ON THE CALENDAR

JULY: *Ute Stampede.* Street dances, foot races, and a golf tournament are held, in addition to one of Utah's largest rodeos. | 435/623–4407 or 435/623–0643.

Dining

Mickelson's. Jay Mickelson was a traveling salesman who retired with the goal of providing the kind of home-cooked meals he had missed on the road. Try the pot roast or baked chicken with rice, with fresh fruit pies in season for dessert. Salad bar. Kids' menu. | 793 N. Main St. | 435/623–0152 | Closed Sun. | $10–$16 | D, MC, V.

My Rancherito. Mexican. Piñatas and Mexican tiles fill the inside of this cozy restaurant. The friendly staff serves authentic tacos, burritos, and fajitas, all with homemade rice and beans. | 390 S. Main St. | 435/623–4391 | $5–$10 | AE, MC, V.

Lodging

Nephi Super 8. Convenient to town and 3 mi from hunting and fishing, a no-frills chain motel offers reasonable, comfortable lodging. Cable TV. | 41 rooms | 1901 S. Main St. | 435/623–0888 | fax 435–623–5024 | www.super8.com | $50–$65 | AE, D, DC, MC, V.

Starlite Motel. This locally owned motel mixes echoes of a past generation with modern conveniences. The location is nice for strolls in the town. Some kitchenettes. Cable TV. Pool. | 24 rooms | 675 S. Main St. | 435/623–4000 | $50–$75 | D, MC, V.

Whitmore Mansion Bed & Breakfast. Listed on the National Register of Historic Places, this Queen Anne–style home built in 1898 offers Nephi's most formal accommodations. Rooms are filled with antiques, fine woodwork, and much lace and velvet. Full breakfast, dining room. No smoking. | 8 rooms | 110 S. Main St. | 435/623–2047 or 877/709–8073 | fax 435/623–2436 | $75–$115 | AE, D, MC, V.

OGDEN

MAP 14, C3

(Nearby towns also listed: Brigham, Salt Lake City)

The city of Ogden marks the northern end of the Wasatch Front, Utah's urban corridor. The city has grown up around the site where mountain man Miles Goodyear built a stockade and trading post in the early 1800s. Ogden's personality is reflected in its raucous history, which includes mountain men and women, culturally diverse workers who laid hundreds of miles of railroad track, the railroad magnates who profited from their labor, and a strong military presence dating back to World War II. More than any other Utah city, Ogden celebrates its whole past.

Information: Golden Spike Empire Travel Region | 2501 Wall Ave., Odgen, 84401 | 801/627–8288 or 800/255–8824 | fax 801/399–0783 | www.ogdencvb.org.

Attractions

Antelope Island State Park on the Great Salt Lake. The Great Salt Lake is truly a curiosity. Water flows into it but there is no outlet other than evaporation. Consequently, minerals and salts are trapped, creating the most saline body of water on earth except for the Dead Sea. Antelope Island, south of Ogden, is the most developed and most scenic spot in which to experience the lake. You can go saltwater bathing at several beach areas, with hot showers to remove the chill and the salt. The island has historic sites, hiking and biking trails, and wildlife and birds in their natural habitat. If you're there to boat, you can use the small marina. Kite-flying is particularly exciting here. With no trees, power lines, or other obstacles, the length of a kite's string is the only limit to the heights it can reach. | 15 mi south on I–15, then west on a 7½-mi causeway across the lake | 801/773–2941 | www.utah.com | $7 per vehicle, including a causeway fee | Daily.

Daughters of Utah Pioneers Museum. Housed in an elegant, brick, turn-of-the-century courthouse, this museum displays artifacts from pioneers who settled the area in 1853. You can see 19th-century pioneer furniture, tools, clothing, and shoes, as well as old cameras and photographs. The Old Territorial Prison, which was used as a jail until 1974, is also on the property. | 4 S. Main St. | 435/623–5202 | Free; donations accepted | Weekdays 1–5.

Eccles Dinosaur Park. Five acres of land near the mouth of Ogden Canyon are the stomping grounds for about 100 dinosaur models and the delighted children who come to see them. The park opened in 1993. The dinosaurs are made of a mixture of concrete and fiberglass and painted in colorful and distinctive designs. Easy-to-read interpretive signs help make visits educational. Be prepared for realism, in the form of the bloody teeth of a tyrannosaurus and the remains of its dinner on the ground. A playground with dinosaurs to crawl all over is a lure for children. | 1544 Park Blvd. | 801/393–3466 | www.dinopark.org | $3.50 | Mar.–Oct., daily.

Fort Buenaventura State Park. Fort Buenaventura was established by Miles Goodyear in the early 1840s, a time that marks the end of trapping, trading, and exploration in the West. It was the first permanent Anglo settlement in the Great Basin. The state park includes stockade and log-cabin replicas on their original sites. | 2450 A Ave. | 801/621–4808 | www.utah.com | $4 | Apr.–Nov.

Hill Aero Space Museum. Hill Air Force Base is home to F-16 squadrons today, often heard booming overhead. In the affiliated museum are dozens of World War II–vintage aircraft, also a P-38 fighter bomber, one of only 21 remaining of the more than 10,000 built in the 1940s. The hangar has some sleek, modern additions, too, including a Lockheed Blackbird spy plane. Often, tours of the museum, hangar, and grounds are conducted by retired Air Force pilots. | 7961 Wardleigh Rd. | 801/777–6868 | www.ogdencvb.org | Free | Tues.–Fri. 9–3, Sat. 9–5, Sun. 11–5.

Nordic Valley. The 85 skiable acres at this small ski area have a 1,000 vertical drop, 50% intermediate slopes, 18 runs. It's a good place to go if you're not quite ready for the high-powered resorts. | 3567 Nordic Way Valley | 801/745–3511 | www.skiutah.com | $20 | Dec.–Apr., daily.

Ogden Nature Center. As one of very few wildlife sanctuaries set within a city, this 127-acre nature center is bounded by a huge Internal Revenue Service center on the west and the army's Ogden Defense Depot on the east. In between are thousands of trees, marshlands, and ponds, with nature trails used for cross-country skiing in the winter. You can see Canadian geese, great blue herons, red-tailed hawks, and snowy egrets, as well as red foxes, mule deer, porcupines, and more. The nature center museum has activities for children. | 966 W. 12th St. | 801/621–7595 | www.ogdencvb.org | $2 | Mon.–Sat. 10–4.

Pineview Reservoir. You can fish at Pineview, at the east end of Ogden Canyon, year-round for practically anything with gills. Crappie and tiger muskellunge are most common, but bluegill, perch, black bullhead, and bass are also reeled in regularly. Trout are a prized catch because fewer live in the reservoir. Boat in summer, and use the forest service roads in the vicinity for bike riding or cross-country skiing. | Exit 347 off I–15 and head east through the Wasatch-Cache National Forest | 801/625–5306 | www.fs.fed.us/wcnf | $5 | Daily.

Powder Mountain. A new lift has eliminated the need for Snowcat access to the 2,000 vertical drop here. There are 70 designated runs in packed and powder snow areas. | East on Rte. 39, then north on Rte. 158 | 801/745–3772 | powdermtn@aol.com | www.powder-mountain.net | $33 | Mid-Nov.–Apr., daily.

Snowbasin. Downhill and Super G races will be held here during the 2002 Winter Olympic Games. The resort, 17 mi east of Ogden, has 39 designated runs, powder bowls, tree and glade skiing, and a vertical drop of 3,400 ft. | Rte. 226 in Wasatch-Cache National Forest | 801/399–1135 | fax 801/399–1138 | www.snowbasin.com | $30 | Late Nov.–Apr.

Treehouse Children's Museum. Although it's in a shopping mall, this museum is not a drop-off point for kids whose parents want to browse; adults are also charmed by the programs and activities. Most focus on literature, the environment, and imagination. One of the most popular features is a small theater where trunks of costumes tempt children and adults to take part in spontaneous performances called "participlays." | North end of Ogden City Mall, 22nd St. and Washington Blvd. | 801/394–9663 | www.ogdencvb.org | $2 | Mon.–Sat. 10–6, Fri. until 9.

Twenty-Fifth Street. In the late 1800s, Ogden was the major connecting point for transcontinental railroad travel between Chicago and San Francisco. Directly east of the railroad depot was 25th Street, infamous for its bars and bordellos. These days, 25th Street is a shopping district. Antiques stores, restaurants, and boutiques fill the historic buildings, making the street almost, but not quite, as lively as in the past. | East of Union Station | 801/627–8288 | www.ogdencvb.org | Free | Daily.

OGDEN

INTRO
ATTRACTIONS
DINING
LODGING

Union Station. Union Station served as a train depot until 1966. The Spanish Colonial–style station now houses a visitor information center with several museums: the Browning firearms collection, a large display room filled with vintage cars, the Utah State Railroad Museum, and a natural history museum focusing particularly on gems and minerals. If you're a railroad buff, check out the diorama of the transcontinental railroad route between Ogden and the Sierra Mountains. Twelve miniature trains run along the tracks winding from room to room. Union Station also has an art gallery and a gift shop. | 2501 Wall Ave. | 801/629-8444 | www.ogdencvb.org | $3 for all 4 museums | Daily 10–6.

Weber State University. Weber State is on the east side of the Ogden Valley with the Wasatch Mountains towering over the campus. It began as the Weber Academy in 1889, and is now a central part of the community. An indoor ice rink (4390 Harrison Blvd., 801/399-8750) offers open skating daily. The university also has a planetarium, an art gallery, and a museum of natural history. | 3700 Harrison Blvd. | 801/626-6000 | www.weber.edu | Daily.

Willard Bay State Park. Willard Bay is a 10,000-acre fresh-water arm of the Great Salt Lake. Boating and waterskiing are the favorite activities here, with year-round fishing for crappie, walleye, wiper, and catfish coming in a close second. | 900 W. 650 N | 435/734-9494 | www.utah.com | $5 | Daily.

ON THE CALENDAR

MAY: *A Taste of Ogden.* Diverse entertainments, from Thai, Native American, and Middle Eastern dancers to polka bands, Latin musicians, and African American storytellers combine with Japanese, Greek, Tongan, and Thai food in this fest held on the Ogden Municipal Building grounds. | Grant Ave. and 25th St. | 801/479-6503.

OCT.: *Buffalo Round-Up.* More than 250 volunteers on horseback round up Antelope Island's more than 600 head of free-roaming bison and herd them to the island's north end to be counted. | 801/773-2941.

Dining

Bavarian Chalet. German. Old World collectibles create a distinctive German atmosphere, with candlelight and white tablecloths. The menu features traditional German dishes like Wiener schnitzel and sauerbraten, with strudels for dessert, as well as vegetarian entrées. In summer you can eat outside, where there's a nice mountain view. Kids' menu. No smoking. | 4387 Harrison Blvd. | 801/479-7561 | $11–$20 | AE, DC, MC, V | Closed Sun.–Mon. and July. No lunch.

Cajun Skillet. Cajun. It's not unusual to see alligator or frogs' legs accompanying the fresh fish specials chalked on the north wall of this lively spot. They are occasionally flown in by air express from Baton Rouge, where the owner's brothers raise catfish, frogs, and turtles. Locals come for gumbo, hush puppies, sweet-potato pie, and Cajun-style breakfasts. | 2550 Washington Blvd. | 801/393-7702 | $10–$23 | AE, MC, V.

Gray Cliff Lodge. American. Built in 1912 as the summer home of a Mormon pioneer from Wales, this white clapboard building 5 mi up Ogden Canyon has a dining room lined with windows and furnished with lace-covered tables. The house specialties are prime rib, mountain trout, and roasted leg of lamb. Kids' menu. No smoking. | 508 Ogden Canyon | 801/392-6775 | www.grayclifflodgerestaurant.com | Reservations essential on holidays | $14–$30 | AE, D, DC, MC, V | Closed Mon. No lunch.

Lee's Mongolian Barbeque. Mongolian. Choose from a variety of fresh vegetables, meats, and sauces, and then watch the chef stir-fry your hand-picked meal in front of you. Although the simple restaurant at the center of town is not much to look at, the exotic and flavorful fare make it worth a visit. | 2866 Washington Blvd. | 801/621-9120 | $4–$8 | MC, V.

Prairie Schooner. American. Desert sand covers the floor, and each table is enclosed in a covered wagon at this Western-style steak house. Although the setting may be a bit much for some, the basic steak and seafood specialties are good. | 445 Park Blvd. | 801/392–2712 | $18–$35 | AE, D, DC, MC, V.

Rooster's 25th Street Brewing Company. American. Ogden residents voted this the best place to bring a first date. The two-story redbrick building was built in 1892. It's been a liquor store, a Chinese laundry, and a Salvation Army store. The local favorites are soups, barbecue platters, and a cheese, artichoke, and crab appetizer called "what a crock." Brewed on-site are Junction City Chocolate Stout and Bees Knees Honey Wheat, as well as an excellent non-alcoholic root beer. | 253 25th St. | 801/627–6171 | $11–$18 | AE, D, MC, V.

Shooting Star Saloon. American. The oldest saloon in Utah, this tavern has operated for 121 years and serves what many consider the best burgers in the country, worth the 17 mi trip from Ogden. The Star Burger with Polish sausage is a favorite. The stuffed St. Bernard's head on the wall and the dollar bill-lined ceiling add to the saloon's quirky appeal. | 7350 E. South St., Huntsville | 801/745–2002 | $3–$6 | No credit cards.

Lodging

Best Western High Country Inn. Near I–15, this inn has nicely decorated rooms done in maroons and greens, and more amenities than most of the chain motels in the area. Restaurant, room service. In-room data ports, refrigerators. Cable TV. Pool. Hot tub. Exercise room. Laundry facilities. | 111 rooms | 1335 W. 12th St. | 801/394–9474 or 800/594–8979 | fax 801/392–6589 | $69 | AE, D, DC, MC, V.

Days Inn. Many amenities and a downtown location near restaurants and shopping, plus modest rates, are the distinguishing characteristics of this chain property. Complimentary Continental breakfast. In-room data ports. Cable TV. Indoor pool. Hot tub. Exercise equipment. Laundry facilities. Business services. Some pets allowed. | 108 rooms | 3306 Washington Blvd. | 801/399–5671 | fax 801/621–0321 | www.daysinn.com | $69–$79 | AE, D, DC, MC, V.

Ogden Marriott. Ogden's largest lodging facility is downtown, close to government offices and corporate headquarters for the aerospace industry and within walking distance of the Ogden City Mall. Restaurant. Refrigerators in suites. Cable TV. Indoor pool. Hot tub. Exercise equipment. Laundry facilities. Business services. | 292 rooms, 4 suites | 247 24th St. | 801/627–1190 or 800/421–7599 | fax 801/394–6312 | www.ogdenmarriott.com | $75–$125 | AE, D, DC, MC, V.

Radisson Suite Hotel. Totally restored, this downtown historic building was once the Hotel Ben Lomond and is on the National Register of Historic Places. Now part of the Radisson group, it has spacious and elegantly appointed rooms and suites furnished with reproductions of antiques. It's close to stores, offices, and restaurants. Restaurant, complimentary breakfast buffet. Refrigerators, microwaves in suites. Cable TV. Exercise equipment. Laundry facilities. Business services. Some pets allowed. | 144 rooms, 122 suites | 2510 Washington Blvd. | 801/627–1900 | fax 801/393–1258 | $150–$175 | AE, D, DC, MC, V.

Snowberry Inn This quiet, rustic, log-cabin inn overlooks the Pineview Reservoir in the Wasatch mountains above Ogden. The small rooms are cozy, with lovely bedspreads and unique furnishings. You can get to area ski resorts and hiking trails in minutes. Dining room, full breakfast. TV in common area. Hot tub. Laundry facilities. | 5 rooms | 1315 Rte. 158, Eden | 801/745–2634 | fax 801/745–0585 | $115 | AE, D, MC, V.

PANGUITCH

MAP 14, C8

(Nearby town also listed: Cedar City)

In Panguitch, according to a local joke, "there are nine months of winter and three months of darn cold weather." An elevation of 6,650 ft makes Panguitch one of Utah's highest towns and one of its coldest. Despite the cold, Panguitch has around 1,500 residents, making it the "big city" for this part of the state. Good amenities and an excellent location 24 mi north and west of Bryce Canyon National Park at the junction of U.S. 89 and two scenic byways make Panguitch a comfortable launching pad for the varied recreation in the area.

Information: Garfield County Travel Council | 55 S. Main St., Panguitch, 84759 | 435/676–8826 | fax 435/676–8239 | www.brycecanyoncountry.com.

Attractions

Bryce Canyon National Park. *See* Bryce Canyon National Park, *above*. | Rte. 12.

Cedar Breaks National Monument. *See* Cedar City, *above*. | Rte. 148.

Panguitch Lake. Reportedly, this mountain lake takes its name from a Paiute Indian word meaning "big fish." They may not all be big, but several types of trout are plentiful in the lake, and it's a favored choice for ice-fishing. | In Dixie National Forest | 435/676–2649 | www.fs.fed.us/dxnf | Free day use; Forest Service camping fees | Daily.

Paunsagaunt Wildlife Museum. The old Panguitch High School, built in 1936, is still a place of learning. The collection has stuffed animals (as in taxidermy) in tableaus representing actual terrain and animal behavior. Exhibit explanations are well researched and written. The animals and birds come from all parts of the food chain. An African room has baboons, bush pigs, Cape buffalo, and a lion. | 205 E. Center St. | 435/676–2500 | $2 | May–Nov., daily 9 AM–10 PM.

ON THE CALENDAR

JUNE: *Quilt Walk Festival.* In their initial attempt to settle Panguitch in 1864, the starving and winter-weary settlers had to lay quilts over snow pits to complete a trip to gather provisions. This festival commemorates them with quilting classes, a quilt walk dinner theater, a pioneer home tour, craft shows, and a cowboy action shoot. | 800/444–6689.

Dining

Cowboy's Smokehouse. Barbecue. Operated by two transplanted Texans and a rancher's son from southern Colorado, this smokehouse has hospitality, great food, and Western music (even cowboy-song sing-alongs on the weekends). Mesquite-smoked beef, pork, turkey, and chicken; no fewer than 15 secret ingredients in the barbecue sauce; and peach, apricot, or cherry cobbler. | 95 N. Main St. | 435/676–8030 | $7–$16 | AE, D, MC, V.

Grandma Tina's Spaghetti House. Italian. A rare treat in meat-and-potatoes country, this family-run eatery serves homemade Italian and vegetarian food. The spaghetti with vegetable sauce, made with mushrooms, olives, green peppers, onions, garlic, and wine, is fresh, as is the seasonal strawberry pie. | 523 N. Main St. | 435/676–2377 | $6–$18 | MC, V.

Lodging

Best Western New Western Motel. In a town where accommodations run to tiny bed and breakfasts and locally owned motels, this reliable chain is a predictable option. Some refrigerators. Cable TV. Pool. | 55 rooms | 200 E. Center St. | 435/676–8876 | www.bestwestern.com | $65 | AE, D, DC, MC, V.

Panguitch Inn. This motel, housed in a 100-year-old, two-story, Old West–style building, has newly renovated rooms and is within walking distance of downtown restaurants and shops. Cable TV. Conference room. | 25 rooms | 50 N. Main St. | 435/676–8871 or 800/331–7407 | fax 435/676–8340 | $60–$75 | AE, D, DC, MC, V.

PARK CITY

(Nearby towns also listed: Heber, Salt Lake City)

From Salt Lake, Park City is over the mountain on the east side of the Wasatch Range but only a half-hour's drive away via I–80 through Parley's Canyon. The Park City area was once the province of a few hardy farmers and some small-scale cattle ranches. Dramatic change came in the 1880s and 1890s when silver mining brought a huge and sometimes rowdy population. The start of the 20th century saw a sharp decline in mining fortunes, and Park City returned to its rural roots until the second half of the century, when its ski industry was born. The sport of snow skiing, probably first enjoyed by Scandinavian silver miners nearly a hundred years ago, has made Park City Utah's premier resort town. It is the permanent headquarters of the U.S. Ski Team and will be the site of several events during the 2002 Olympic Winter Games. Skiing aside, Park City actually bustles year-round, with three all-season resorts and some of Utah's best restaurants.

Information: Park City Chamber/Bureau | Box 1630, Park City, 84060 | 435/649–6100 or 800/453–1360 | fax 435/649–4132 | www.parkcityinfo.com.

Attractions

Alpine Slide, Gorgoza Skate Park, and Little Miners' Park. In summer, the resort center at Park City Mountain Resort transforms ski operations into facilities for other sports. The Alpine Slide begins with a chairlift ride about halfway up the mountain, then special "sleighs" carry sliders down 3,000 ft of winding concrete and fiberglass track at a breathtaking pace. In winter, the Gorgoza Skate Park is the snow tubing course; you can take a skate course or just test your skills. The Little Miners' Park has children's rides: a mini Ferris wheel, a slow-moving train, and an airplane ride. There's also a miniature golf course. | Park City Mountain Resort | 435/647–5333 | www.parkcitymountain.com | June–Sept., weekdays 2–9, weekends 11–9.

The Canyons. Now the fifth-largest ski resort in the country, this establishment is also open year-round for hiking, biking, and horseback riding. In winter, snowboarders remain loyal to the place, one of the first in Utah open to them. With 3,625 acres, though, the mountain has plenty of room for everyone to co-exist peacefully. The vertical drop is 3,190 ft, and there are 13 lifts, including an eight-passenger gondola and five high-speed quads. | 4000 The Canyons Dr.; north on Rte. 224 | 435/649–5400 or 888/CANYONS | fax 435/649–7374 | www.thecanyons.com.

Deer Valley Resort. Considered Utah's most upscale resort—and proud of it. Now year-round, the resort has lift-assisted mountain biking in summer, as well as hiking and riding. During the 2002 Olympics, Deer Valley will host the alpine slalom, aerial free-style, and mogul events. The vertical drop is 3,000 ft, serviced by 18 lifts including a gondola, and six high speed quads. The 84 runs and six powder bowls yield a total of 50% intermediate terrain. | 2250 Deer Valley Dr. S | 435/649–1000; 435/649–2000 snow report | www.deervalley.com.

Egyptian Theatre. This Art Deco theater built in 1926 is an architectural standout on historic Main Street. It's now used to stage musicals, comedies, and dramas, and screenings are scheduled here during the Sundance Film Festival each January. | 328 Main St. | 435/649–9371 | www.ditell.com/~egyptian | Thurs.–Sat.; some performances other days.

Factory Stores at Park City. Fifty factory outlet stores, including Nike, Brooks Brothers, Bose Sound Systems, Carter's Children's Wear, and Guess Jeans. There are also a wonderful children's playground and two restaurants. | 6699 N. Landmark Dr. | 435/645–7078 | www.shopparkcity.com | Mon.–Sat. 10–9, Sun. 11–6.

Hangtime Climbing Gym. If you need to take a day off from traveling and work off excess energy, consider a stop at this gym, where you can climb the walls for real. They offer private and group lessons. | 1490 Munchkin Rd. | 435/649–8701 | info@whitepinetouring.com | www.whitetouring.com | Day pass $9.

Kimball Art Center. One of more than a dozen art galleries in Park City, this center combines exhibit space with traveling shows and arts and crafts workshops. | 638 Park Ave. | 435/649–8882 | www.kimball-art.org.com | Free; fees for classes | Mon., Wed.–Sat. 10–6, Sun. 12–6.

Park City Mountain Resort. The resort's summit is at 10,000 ft, with a total vertical drop of 3,100 ft. Only 16 of 97 runs are designed for beginners, but the ski school here is one of the best. The runs here range from $\frac{1}{4}$ to $3\frac{1}{2}$ mi long. There's 750 acres of bowl skiing for powder fans. The Olympic alpine giant slalom and snowboard events will be run at this resort. | 1310 Lowell Ave.; in town, off Rte. 224 | 435/649–8111 or 435/647–5449 (snow report) | fax 435/647–5374 | www.parkcitymountain.com | $60.

Rockport State Park. Swimming and fishing areas still leave plenty of room on this reservoir for sailboating and windsurfing. There are eight campgrounds, some developed and some more rustic. | 9040 N. Rte. 302; off I–80 | 435/336–2241 | www.utah.com | $5 day use, $7–$14 camping | Daily.

Utah Winter Sports Park. If you have an itch to take flight, take a two-hour ski-jumping lesson here at the official training site for the U.S. nordic and free-style ski teams. Choose the 18- or 38-m hill, and use your own equipment or rent it from the park. At the 2002 Olympics, nordic ski jumping, bobsled, and luge events will be held here. There are public recreational rides on the bobsled/luge track. After the snow melts, you can watch the free-style skiers train on an artificial slope, landing in a huge splash pool. | 3000 Bear Hollow Dr., off Rte. 224 | 435/658–4200 | fax 435/647–9650 | www.saltlake2002.com | Tours $3.50–$6 | Daily.

White Pine Touring Center. Guided day and overnight trips are offered here, as well as independent skiing on 12 mi of trails. Rentals and lessons are offered. With 60% beginner terrain, this is a good place to try cross-country skiing. | 1541 Thaynes Canyon Dr. | 435/649–8710 or 435/649–8701 (winter) | www.whitepinetouring.com | $10 | Nov.–Apr., daily.

ADVENTURE TOURS

Interconnect Adventure Tour. Advanced skiers: this is a guided full day of skiing as many as five resorts (Park City, Brighton, Solitude, Alta, and Snowbird), all connected by backcountry ski routes with unparalleled views of the Wasatch Mountains. The tour leaves from Park City Mountain Resort. | 150 W. 500 S, Salt Lake City | 801/534–1907 | fax 801/521–3722 | www.skiutah.com | $150 | Dec.–Mar.

White Pine Touring. Experienced guides lead you on mountain-biking tours on area trails. You can rent all equipment. | 210 Heber St. | 435/649–8710 or 435/649–8701 | info@whitepinetouring.com | www.whitepinetouring.com.

ON THE CALENDAR

JAN.: *Sundance Film Festival.* Sponsored by Robert Redford's Sundance Institute, the festival is ten days of seminars, tributes, and film screenings at various venues in Park City and Salt Lake City. | 801/328–FILM.

FEB.: *Winterfest and Snow Sculpture Contest.* Competitors meet for outdoor games, sports demonstrations, and huge snow sculptures in City Park. | 435/649–6100.

AUG.: *Art Festival.* Historic Main Street is closed to traffic the first weekend of August during this yearly gathering of local and national artists. Live music, upscale food, and local micro-brewery beers. | Main St. | 435/649–8882.

AUG.: *Park City International Jazz Festival.* Artists like George Benson, Bela Fleck and the Flecktones, and the Ramsey Lewis Trio have performed at this annual three-day festival dedicated to jazz music. Daily workshops and clinics for jazz musicians are offered, and the nightly performances feature many kinds of jazz groups and styles. | 435/649–6100 or 800/453–1360.

Dining

Baja Cantina. Mexican. Western artifacts and ski memorabilia are everywhere, and a sign on the door reads IF YOU HAVE RESERVATIONS, YOU ARE IN THE WRONG PLACE. In the Park City Mountain Resort Center, it's known for burritos with anything and everything from pork chili verde to snow crab and black tiger prawns. | 1284 Empire Ave. | 435/649–2252 | $12–$19 | AE, MC, V.

Burgies. American. Large-screen TV, pool tables, and football upstairs. The menu lists more than twelve different burgers, including buffalo, lamb, and bratwurst, as well as veggie sandwiches and Olympic Onion Rings. | 570 Main St. | 435/649–0011 | $9–$14 | AE, D, MC, V.

Café Terigo. Continental. A pleasant, airy, two-level café in the center of town serves trendy dishes like smoked chicken fettuccine, grilled flank steak with garlic mashed potatoes, pesto pizza with artichoke and shrimp, and almond-encrusted salmon. The outdoor patio is nice in summer, and the bread pudding is delicious. | 424 Main St. | 435/645–9555 | $20–$35 | AE, MC, V.

Chimayo. Southwestern. Designed after the Chimayo mission in Mexico, this attractive restaurant with fawn-colored stone walls, tiles, and wooden ceiling trusses offers innovative dishes like crab-stuffed grouper steamed in a banana leaf, avocado slaw, and seared elk burritos. The wine list is eclectic, with Spanish and South American varietals. | 368 Main St. | 435/649–6222 | $35–$50 | AE, D, MC, V | Closed May.

Claimjumper. American. Standing at the center of historic Old Town, this lively restaurant is pure Americana, from its hardwood floors, green drapes, and grand stone fireplace to its emphasis on steaks, prime rib, and burgers. All the beef is aged, and cooked to your request. | 573 Main St. | 435/649–8051 | $12–$29 | AE, D, DC, MC, V.

Eating Establishment. American. Near the top of Main Street, this affordable local favorite is known for its hearty keep-you-skiing-all-morning breakfasts and its barbecue dinner specials. Dine on the patio in summer; the glass roof, atrium, fireplaces, and plants make winter seem warm and bright. | 317 Main St. | 435/649–8284 | $6–$20 | AE, D, MC, V.

Gamekeeper's Grille. American. Large portions of innovative game dishes like pan-seared elk, smoked buffalo ravioli, and wild-game chili are served at this cozy restaurant housed in a historic downtown building. You can also get fish and lamb dishes. | 508 Main St. | 435/647–0327 | $15–$30 | AE, MC, V | Closed May.

★ **Glitretind.** Continental. Self-described as "a European mountain bistro," it's really more of a grand lodge. The menu highlights wild game dishes like grilled buffalo and venison, but also offers lunch sandwiches on thick, crusty bread, dinners of Asian duck, baked salmon, or tender steaks. In warm weather, you can eat on the deck, with a view of the Heber and Deer valleys. Kids' menu. | 7700 Stein Way, in the Stein Eriksen Lodge | 435/649–3700 | $29–$36 | AE, D, DC, MC, V.

Grappa. Italian. Hand-painted ceramic tiles and Tuscan motifs of grape leaves and vines decorate the dining room of one of the most upscale Italian restaurants in town. The tasty food is cooked over wood-fired grills or in ovens burning cherry, apple, and oak. It's known for osso buco and such specialties as risotto-stuffed chicken. Try one of the gourmet pizzas, seafood, or soups. Open-air dining in tiered gardens. Kids' menu. No smoking. | 151 Main St. | 435/645–0636 | $22–$36 | AE, D, MC, V | Closed mid-Apr.–mid-May. No lunch.

Main Street Deli. American. For a quick bite, this basic deli serves well-made classics like reubens and Philly cheese steaks, as well as interesting vegetarian combos, hearty omelettes, and homemade granola. | 525 Main St. | 435/649–1110 | $6–$11 | D, MC, V.

Main Street Pizza & Noodle. Italian. Huge windows, a bright, airy dining area, good no-frills food, and reasonable prices make this a family favorite. The pizzas are made California style, and the pastas and calzones are filling. | 530 Main St. | 435/645–8878 | $10–$20 | AE, D, DC, MC, V.

PARK CITY

INTRO
ATTRACTIONS
DINING
LODGING

Morning Ray Café & Bakery. American. The Continental crowd favors this bakery café that serves specialty breads, bagels, pastries, and substantial omelettes, pancakes, and quiches. Wooden chairs and tables and yellow-toned walls hung with local art make the space inviting. | 268 Main St. | 435/649–5686 | $8–$12 | AE, MC, V | No dinner.

Mt. Air Café. American. Outside the Main Street hub, this country diner with booths and an old-fashioned counter serves large portions of familiar dishes. Ground sirloin, country-fried steak, and fish-and-chips are favorites. Breakfasts are hearty, and the fresh strawberry pie is a good finish to any meal. | Rtes. 248 and 224E | 435/649–9868 | $10–$12 | AE, MC, V.

Riverhorse Cafe. Contemporary. This cafe occupies two high-ceilinged rooms on the upper floor of the turn-of-the-century wood-framed Masonic Hall. It serves specialties such as Alaskan halibut, seared tuna, steaks, and pastas. In warm weather, dine on the deck that overlooks Main Street. The atrium room has live entertainment weekends. Kids' menu. No smoking. Wine list. | 540 Main St. | 435/649–3536 | www.riverhorsecafe.com | $19.50–$27 | AE, D, MC, V | No lunch.

Texas Red's Pit Barbecue and Chili Parlor. Barbecue. Tables are crowded together in a friendly way in the southwestern-style dining room of this downtown eatery. Try catfish fillets or barbecued anything—ribs, beef brisket, pork, turkey, or chicken. Kids' menu. | 440 Main St. | 435/649–7337 | $10–$19 | AE, D, MC, V.

350 Main. Seafood. Known for its fresh oysters, mussels, and shellfish, as well as tuna and sea bass specials, this Old Town restaurant has copper verdi-gilded furniture and a rust-tinted ceiling. It's warm and inviting after a day on the slopes. | 350 Main St. | 435/649–3140 | $30–$35 | AE, D, MC, V.

Zoom Roadhouse Grill. Contemporary. The Union Pacific Railway station at the bottom of historic Main Street houses this establishment. The room is decorated with antiques, art, and some tongue-in-cheek Western touches. The menu runs from southern catfish to a stew of polenta with wild mushrooms. Dine outside on the patio at umbrella-shaded tables. | 660 Main St. | 435/649–9108 | $12–$27 | AE, D, DC, MC, V.

Lodging

All Seasons. These deluxe condominiums next to the Park City Golf Course have spectacular views of the mountain and full kitchens with state-of-the-art appliances, jetted tubs, sleeper sofas, fireplaces, hardwood floors, and other such comforts. Condos vary in size, and can be rented for longer periods. TVs, in-room VCRs. Pool. Laundry facilities. | 16 condos | 1585 Empire Ave. | 435/649–5500 or 800/331–8652 | fax 435/649–6647 | $550–$750 | AE, D, MC, V.

Best Western Landmark Inn. Right off I–80, near a cluster of popular factory outlet stores, this inn is a little less pricey than most Park City hotels. Pleasantly furnished rooms, a relaxing poolside area, and a recreation area make this a good bet for stopovers and families. Restaurant, Continental breakfast. In-room data ports, refrigerators. Cable TV. Indoor pool. Hot tub. Exercise room. Laundry facilities. | 92 rooms, 14 suites | 6560 N. Landmark Dr. | 435/649–7300 or 800/548–8824 | fax 435/649–1760 | $169, $199–$375 suites | AE, D, DC, MC, V.

Edelweiss Haus. About 200 yards from the Park City Mountain Resort lifts and a pleasant walk from historic Main Street, these condos are spacious and up to date. They vary in size. Microwaves, kitchens. Cable TV. Pool. Hot tub, sauna. Exercise equipment. Laundry facilities. Business services. | 54 condos | 1482 Empire Ave. | 435/649–9342 or 800/438–3855 | fax 435/649–4049 | identity@pclodge.com | www.pclodge.com | $380–$395 | AE, D, MC, V.

Inn at Prospector Square. An all-condo property has accommodations that range from studios to three bedrooms. Standard rooms, furnished in pastels, have a queen-size bed and sleeper sofa. The two-story inn has grocery stores nearby, and kitchen areas are stocked with equipment and spices. Restaurant, bar. In-room data ports, microwaves, refrigerators. Cable TV. Pool. Some hot tubs. Business services. | 230 units, 125 kitchenettes | 2200 Sidewinder Dr. | 435/649–7100 or 800/453–3812 (except Utah) | fax 435/649–8377 |

www.thelodgingcompany.com | $95–$110 standard rooms, $167–$187 studio rooms with kitchenettes, $175–$400 1–, 2–, and 3–bedroom condos with full kitchens | AE, D, DC, MC, V.

Lodge at Mountain Village. Rooms are spacious, modern, and bright at this deluxe wood-and-stone villa at the base of the Park City lifts. You can ski in and ski out, too. The condos have fireplaces, kitchenettes, floor-to-ceiling windows, stucco walls, and luxury carpets. TV. Indoor-outdoor pool. Hot tub, sauna, steam room. | 20 rooms, 125 condos | 1415 Lowell Ave. | 435/649–0800 or 800/824–5331 | fax 435/645–9132 | $240 rooms, $315–$1,500 condos | AE, D, DC, MC, V.

1904 Imperial Hotel. Built in 1904 as a boarding house for miners and travelers, the hotel has been restored to a more upscale turn-of-the century Western Victorian style. Complimentary breakfast. No air-conditioning. Cable TV. Hot tub. | 10 rooms, 2 suites | 221 Main St. | 435/649–1904 or 800/669–8824 | fax 435/645–7421 | www.1904imperial.com | $140–$220 | AE, D, MC, V.

Old Miners' Lodge. Built in 1893, the lodge is one block off Main Street, with individually decorated rooms named for locally famous and infamous people. The "Black Jack" Murphy room has an entry designed to look like the portal to a mine and is furnished in a rustic Victorian style. You can walk to the town lift, which services Park City Mountain Resort. Complimentary breakfast. No air-conditioning. Hot tub. Business services. No smoking. | 12 rooms, most with baths; 3 suites | 615 Woodside Ave. | 435/645–8068 or 800/648–8068 | fax 435/645–7420 | stay@oldminerslodge.com. | www.oldminerslodge.com | $130–$270 | AE, D, DC, MC, V.

Park City Marriott. The contemporary condos come in various sizes, each individually decorated. Restaurant, bar, room service. In-room data ports. Cable TV. Indoor pool. Hot tub. Exercise equipment. Business services. | 199 units | 1895 Sidewinder Dr. | 435/649–2900 or 800/234–9003 | fax 435/649–4852 | www.parkcityutah.com | $89–$399 | AE, D, DC, MC, V.

Shadow Ridge. The basic hotel rooms here have the same amenities as the lavish suites, making them a good value for a modest price. At the base of the Park City Mountain Village. Restaurant. Some microwaves. Cable TV. Pool. Hot tub. Exercise equipment. Laundry facilities. Business services. | 150 rooms, 50 suites | 50 Shadow Ridge Dr. | 435/649–4300 or 800/451–3031 | fax 435/649–5951 | david@holland.com | www.davidholland.com | $85–$250 | AE, D, DC, MC, V.

Silver King Hotel. Minutes from the ski lifts, this modern, luxurious condominium hotel has an expansive atrium lobby with fireplace and plush sofas, huge windows, and exposed beams. Units vary in size, from studio to three bedrooms, and are made cozy with handmade furniture, pastel colors, and woven rugs. TV, in-room VCRs. Pool. Laundry facilities. | 62 rooms | 1485 Empire Ave. | 435/649–5500 or 800/331–8652 | fax 435/649–6647 | www.silverkinghotel.com | $160–$575 | AE, D, MC, V.

Silver Queen. This brick building in historic Old Town blends Old World elegance with modern convenience. Rooms are individually decorated with antique furnishings, brass beds, cushioned chairs, and richly colored rugs. They have full kitchens, jetted tubs, fireplaces, and washer/dryer units. You can ski close by, and ski lockers are available. Cable TV. Laundry facilities. | 12 rooms | 632 Main St. | 435/649–5986 or 800/447–6423 | fax 435/649–3572 | $310–$395 | D, MC, V.

Snow Flower. A four-building wooden complex at the side of a hill, this place is known more for its ski-in/ski-out convenience, varied rooms, and comparatively affordable rates than for its design. Because each unit is individually owned, rooms vary considerably in size, furnishings, and style. All the condos have kitchens, fireplaces, and single-person jetted tubs. In-room data ports. TV, VCRs. 2 outdoor pools. Laundry facilities. | 142 condos | 401 Silver King Dr. | 435/649–6400 or 800/852–3101 | fax 435/649–6049 | $270 | AE, MC, V.

Snowed Inn. A pleasant Victorian-style inn whose opulent parlor with a huge fireplace invites relaxing. High ceilings, large windows, bright wall coverings, and goose-down comforters make the rooms as cozy as the rest of the inn. In winter you can take afternoon and evening horse-drawn sleigh rides. Continental breakfast. TV, in-room VCRs. Hot tub. | 10 rooms | 3770 N. Rte. 224 | 435/649–5713 or 800/545–7669 | fax 435/645–7672 | $225–$325 | AE, D, MC, V.

Stein Eriksen Lodge. This upscale lodge at mid-mountain has every imaginable amenity in the spacious rooms and suites. Everything is done in light colors with a lot of unstained wood in woodwork and furniture. 2 restaurants, bar, room service, complimentary Continental breakfast in winter. In-room data ports, refrigerators, many in-room hot tubs. Cable TV, VCRs (movies). Pool. Hot tub, massage. Exercise equipment. Mountain bikes. Downhill skiing. Sleigh rides, snowmobiling. Business services. | 81 rooms, 50 suites | 7700 Stein Way | 435/649–3700 or 800/453–1302 | fax 435/649–5825 | info@steinlodge.com | www.stein-lodge.com | $300–$700 | AE, D, DC, MC, V.

Washington School Inn. The bell tower with a flag attests to the history of this building, originally a school house one block from Main Street. Built in 1889, it was renovated in 1985 with rooms named for the teachers who taught in them. The furnishings are turn of the century, with striped wallpaper and brass lamps. The living room has a cathedral ceiling and a fireplace. No kids under 9. Complimentary breakfast. No air-conditioning. Cable TV in some rooms. Exercise equipment. Business services. | 12 rooms, 3 suites | 543 Park Ave. | 435/649–3800 or 800/824–1672 | fax 435/649–3802 | www.washingtonschoolinn.com | $115–$350 | AE, D, DC, MC, V.

Yarrow Resort Hotel & Conference Center. Easy access to all three Park City resorts and a golf course across the street are principal attractions here. Some rooms have fireplaces. Restaurant, bar, room service. Microwaves. Cable TV. Pool. Hot tubs. Exercise equipment. Laundry facilities. Business services. | 181 rooms and suites | 1800 Park Ave. | 435/649–7000 or 800/927–7694 | fax 435/649–4819 | $269–$589 | AE, D, DC, MC, V.

PAYSON

MAP 14, C5

(Nearby towns also listed: Nephi, Provo)

Payson is easily accessed from I-15. A short drive around town offers the chance to see some carefully tended Victorian-style homes from the settlement era. Payson is best known as the northern access to the Nebo Loop Scenic Byway, one of only 27 roads nationwide to have received scenic byway designation from the Federal Highways Administration. The byway is Forest Service Road 015, edging through the Uinta National Forest east of the Mount Nebo Wilderness. It ends 38 miles south in Nephi.

Information: **Mountainland Travel Region** | 586 E. 800 N, Orem, 84097 | 801/229–3800 | fax 801/229–3801 | www.mountainland.org.

Attractions

Mt. Nebo Loop National Scenic Byway. Locally, this road is known simply as the Nebo Loop. It's part of the National Forest Service's scenic roads program, and in 1999 was recognized by the Federal Highway Administration. The 38-mi-long road loops around 12,000-ft Mt. Nebo, between the towns of Payson and Nephi. Part of what makes this route outstanding are magnificent views of the Mt. Nebo Wilderness, the Wasatch Mountains, and the Utah Valley. You see a lot of wildlife year-round, and the road has long been considered one of the most beautiful fall color drives anywhere. A side trip leads to Devil's Kitchen, a gulch filled with red gravel and silt spires that have eroded from the mountainside. | Southeast on an unnumbered but well-signed Uinta National Forest road | 435/623–2735 | www.fs.fed.us/rf/uinta | Day use free; camping fees charged | Daily; closed in winter by deep snow.

Payson Lake Recreation Area. An appealing setting for group gatherings, with paved hiking trails, shady picnic and camping areas, and fishing on a small lake. | On the Nebo Loop

Byway, in Payson Canyon, within the Uinta National Forest | 435/623–2735 | www.fs.fed.us/rf/uinta | Camping fees | Daily.

Peteetneet Academy and Museum. Built in 1901 as the area's first multiclassroom elementary school, this beautiful adobe and redbrick building now houses a historical museum. The Utah Historical Society and the Daughters of the Utah Pioneers have galleries with exhibits on local and Utah history, and in the Freedom Room you can see displays on the Mormon battalion during the Civil War. Another exhibit shows typewriters, printing presses, and various objects dealing with the advance of printing, and an genie-like oil lamp that dates from 1000 BC. | 10 S. 600 E | 801/465–9427 | Free | Weekdays 10–4.

ON THE CALENDAR
JULY: *Scottish Festival.* Bagpipe music and scents of traditional Scottish cooking fill the air during this lively annual festival, which showcases pipe bands, Scottish athletic events, vendors, and members of more than 20 clans. | 801/465–5200.

Dining
Dalton's Fine Dining. American. Notice the ironwork on the chairs, light fixtures, and candlesticks at this cabinlike rustic eatery, known for its hand-battered fish-and-chips, onion rings, and homemade cheescake. The prime rib, chicken, and steak dinners are also popular. You can catch live performances on the grand piano most nights. | 20 S. 100 W | 435/465–9182 | $15–$30 | MC, V.

Lodging
Comfort Inn. Right on Main Street, this inn gives you easy access to the Mt. Nebo Scenic Byway and the Uinta National Forest. Complimentary Continental breakfast. Cable TV. Indoor pool. Hot tub. Exercise equipment. Laundry facilities. Business services. Pets allowed (fee). | 62 rooms, 6 kitchenettes (no equipment) | 830 N. Main St. | 801/465–4861 | fax 801/465–4861 | www.comfortinn.com | $70–$85 | AE, D, DC, MC, V.

Western Inn Spanish Fork. A great stopover motel, this new property is off I–15 6 mi north of Payson and offers numerous amenities at reasonable rates. Continental breakfast. In-room data ports. Cable TV. Laundry facilities. Conference room. | 45 rooms, 2 suites | 632 Kirby La. (I–15 Exit 260) | 801/798–9400 or 888/700–5335 | fax 801/798–9400 | $59, $70–$80 suites | AE, D, DC, MC, V.

PRICE

MAP 14, D5

(Nearby town also listed: Provo)

Like many Utah towns, Price began as a Mormon farming settlement in the late 1800s. In 1883 the railroad arrived, bringing immigrants from around the world to mine coal reserves that had barely been acknowledged up until that point. Mining became the town's primary industry, and still is. Where there's coal or oil there were generally dinosaurs. Thousands of visitors annually come to Price to take a look at the prehistoric past in the specialized setting of the College of Eastern Utah Prehistoric Museum.

Information: Castle Country Travel Region–Carbon County Visitors Bureau | 90 N. 100 E, #2, Price, 84501 | 435/637–3009 or 800/842–0789 | fax 435/637–7010 | www.castle-country.com.

Attractions
Cleveland-Lloyd Dinosaur Quarry. This quarry has been designated a national natural landmark because of the many dinosaur bones that have been found here. The visitor center near the quarry has skeletons of a stegosaurus and an allosaurus. This is a working site,

with paleontologists excavating throughout the open season. There's also a guided nature trail and a campground. | 25 mi south of Price off Rte. 10 | 435/636–3600 | www-a.blm.gov/utah/price/quarry.htm | $3 | Memorial Day—Labor Day, daily 10–5; Easter–Memorial Day, weekends 10–5.

College of Eastern Utah Prehistoric Museum. Coal beds throughout this area have proven ideal for preserving ancient fossils. This museum shows off some of the finds, including full-size dinosaur skeletons and a Columbian Mammoth. One exhibit tells about the discovery of the Utahraptor, as bad as the clawed villain from *Jurassic Park*, which was filming in Utah when paleontologists found the bones. In the Hall of Archeology, you can see exhibits on ancient human inhabitants of this area. | 155 E. Main St. | 435/637–5060 | www.ceu.edu/MUSEUM | Donations accepted | Apr.–Sept., daily 9–6; Oct.–May, Mon.–Sat. 9–5.

Manti–La Sal National Forest, Manti Division. Skyline Drive, locally known as Huntington Canyon Road, runs through the Manti division of the national forest. The entire route is on paved state roads winding over the Wasatch Plateau at elevations of 5,000 to 10,000 ft. You can stop at several high-elevation lakes with developed areas for fishing and camping. Acres of aspen forest mingled with vertical cliffs and escarpments make this a stunning autumn drive. | Rte. 31 | 435/637–2817 | www.fs.fed.us | Day use free; camping fees | Daily.

Nine Mile Canyon. This corridor is actually 40 mi long, and with time for frequent stops, hiking, and picnics, plan a minimum of 6 hours to explore it thoroughly. Dilapidated ranch houses were once way-stations for travelers, but the canyon is known for over 1,000 rock-art and habitation sites from the Fremont Indian culture. The rock art depicts birds, snakes, humans, and other animals. | 7½ mi east on U.S. 6, then 12 mi north on a paved road, then 25 mi of maintained gravel road | 435/636–3600 | fax 435/636–3657 | www-a.blm.gov/utah/price/9mile.htm | Free | Daily.

Price Canyon Recreation Area. Off U.S. 6 and 18 mi northwest of Price, this area on a ridge above Price Canyon is shaded by stands of Ponderosa pines. A short nature trail focuses on the plant life of the area. The campground and day use area has barbecue grills. | Off U.S. 6 | 435/636–3600 | fax 435/636–3657 | www-a.blm.gov/utah/price | Camping fee | May–mid-Oct., daily.

Scofield State Park. A large lake high in the forests of the Manti–La Sal Mountains offers boating and year-round fishing; however, facilities close in late October. In winter the area is a base for snowmobiling and cross-country skiing. | Rte. 96 | 435/448–9449 | www.utah.com | $5 | May–Oct.

ON THE CALENDAR

MAY: *Utah Prehistory and Heritage Week.* Various activities and tours focus on this area's unique past—everything from dinosaurs to ancient Pueblo cultures and the traditions of the many nationalities that mingled here during the peak of coal-mining activity in the early 1900s. | 435/637–5060 or 800/842–0789.

Dining

Greek Streak. Greek. On the site of a Greek coffee house from the early 1900s, this café is a reminder of the strong Greek heritage in this area of the state. The menu includes traditional recipes from Crete: gyros, dolmades, lemon rice soup, and such. The baklava, kataifi, koulourakia, and honey-nut cookies made and served here are considered the best Greek pastries in the state. | 84 S. Carbon Ave. | 435/637–1930 | $12–$20 | D, MC, V | Closed Sun., Mon.

Ricardo's. Eclectic. If everyone in the group is craving something different, the vast menu here will accommodate all. This popular local diner-style restaurant at the center of town serves the standard enchiladas, burritos, and tacos, as well as sandwiches and steak and seafood dishes. | 655 E. Main St. | 435/637–2020 | $7–$20 | AE, MC, V.

Lodging

Best Western Carriage House Inn. Behind a white, Colonial-style facade, the soft-hued rooms are restful. You can walk to restaurants and shops. Cable TV. Indoor pool. Hot tub. Airport shuttle. | 41 rooms | 590 E. Main St. | 435/637–5660 or 800/228–5732 | fax 435/637–5660 | www.bestwestern.com | $60–$75 | AE, D, DC, MC, V.

Holiday Inn Hotel and Suites. The only full-service accommodations in Price, this one has a friendly staff, is well-maintained, and is convenient both to U.S. 6 and downtown. Rooms are spacious, and suites have jetted tubs and kitchenettes. Restaurant. In-room data ports. Cable TV. Indoor pool. Meeting rooms. | 137 rooms, 14 suites | 838 Westwood Blvd. | 435/637–8880 or 800/465–4329 | fax 435/637–7707 | $74–$89, $99–$119 suites | AE, D, DC, MC, V.

PROVO

(Nearby towns also listed: Heber, Payson, Salt Lake City)

Provo is best known for Brigham Young University, one of the largest church-affiliated universities in the world. It's the Mormon university's programs and attractions that bring most people to this area. Provo and its northern neighbor Orem are so closely connected that they are generally referred to as "Provo-Orem." The cities spread from Utah Lake in the west into the foothills of the Wasatch Mountains to the east.

Information: Utah County Travel Council | 51 S. University Ave., Suite 110, Provo, 84601 | 801/370–8390 or 800/222–8824 | fax 801/370–8050 | www.utahvalley.org/cvb.

PROVO

INTRO
ATTRACTIONS
DINING
LODGING

Attractions

Brigham Young University. The Mormon Church–owned BYU has policies and curriculum generally perceived to be a reflection of Mormon values. BYU has a dress code, mostly involving guidelines about the wearing of shorts and other summer clothing. Students and faculty are expected to refrain from alcohol and tobacco use. | 1230 N. Provo Canyon Rd. | 801/378–4636 | fax 801/378–4264 | www.byu.edu/home2.html | Free | Mon.–Fri.

Besides providing performance spaces for school and community events, the **Harris Fine Arts Center** has a fine display of contemporary visual arts. | East campus | 801/378–2881 | www.byu.edu/cfac/events | Free | Mon.-Sat. 10–5.

When it opened in 1993, the lovely 100,000-square-ft **Museum of Art**—with more than 14,000 pieces in its collection—was the biggest art museum between Denver and San Francisco. The museum debuted with a temporary show on the Etruscan civilization from the Gregorian Etruscan Museum of the Vatican Museums. It has been the site of several other touring exhibits, including "The Imperial Tombs of China," the "Masada Exhibit from Israel," and a collection of Rodin sculptures. | East campus | 801/378–2787 | www.byu.edu/moa | Free, except for special shows | Tue., Wed., Fri. 10–6, Mon., Thurs. 10–9, Sat. 12–5.

BYU's dinosaur museum is the **Earth Science Museum.** Allosaurus and camptosaurus skeletons quarried in eastern Utah form an impressive exhibit. A popular display outlines the numerous ways that fossils are formed, and a giant mural depicts the relative sizes of various dinosaurs. | 1683 Canyon Rd. | 801/378–3680 | www.cpms.byu.edu/ESM/index.html | Free | Mon. 9–9, Tues.–Fri. 9–5, Sat. 12–4.

The **Monte L. Bean Life Science Museum** is a treasure trove of mounted or preserved animals and plants. Two full floors hold examples of everything from pronghorn antelope to about a million preserved insects, an emperor penguin, snakes, lions, a tiger, and five different types of bears. There's also a hands-on Children's Discovery Room and a gift shop. | East campus, just north of the Museum of Art | 801/378–5051 | www.bioag.byu.edu/mlbean | Free | Weekdays 10–9, Sat. 10–5.

The **Museum of Peoples and Cultures** is the university's anthropology museum, with comprehensive displays of ancient artifacts from all over the globe. | 710 N. 100 E | 801/378–6112 | www.nauvoo.byu.edu/neighbors/People/Museum/underside2.cfm | Free | Weekdays 9–5.

Camp Floyd, Stagecoach Inn State Park and Museum. From 1858 to 1861, this was a military post that housed 3,500 troops sent to Utah to suppress an anticipated Mormon uprising. The soldiers spent a great deal of their time prospecting for gold and silver in the mountains west of the encampment, then left at the start of the Civil War in 1861. The Stagecoach Inn, now a museum, was an overnight stop on the overland stage and Pony Express route. | On Rte. 73 | 801/768–8932 | www.utah.com | $4 | Apr.–Oct.

John Hutchings Museum. One of Utah's oldest museums, this collection is a labor of love undertaken by the Hutchings family in 1913. It has no particular theme, but that makes the resulting combination all the more interesting. You find a variety of artworks, Native American artifacts, pioneer farming equipment, rare rocks, and marine exhibits. | 55 N. Center St., Lehi | 801/768–7180 | $2.50 | Mon.–Sat. 9:30–5.

McCurdy Historical Doll Museum. Two turn-of-the-century carriage houses joined by a large exhibit room house a charming collection of thousands of dolls, which began with Laura McCurdy Clark's personal collection of 800 dolls from all over the world. They've been joined by kachinas, Japanese dolls, ballerinas, Shirley Temple dolls, and on and on. One grouping of more than 200 dolls focuses on the history of military uniforms from ancient times to the present. Injured dolls can come to the doll hospital for repairs. | 246 N. 100 E | 801/377–9935 | $2 | Tues.–Sat. 1–5.

Springville Museum of Art. A white stucco Spanish Mission–style building constructed in the 1930s holds Utah's first and oldest museum of art. The collection has about 1,300 works by 250 artists from Utah and across the United States. Special events are held annually and include the Spring Salon, a showcase for living Utah artists. | 126 E. 400 S, Springville | 801/489–2727 | www.shs.nebo.edu/museum/museum.html | Free. Donations accepted | Tues.–Sat. 10–5, Wed. until 9, Sun. 3–6.

Sundance. In 1969, Robert Redford opened Sundance with the goal of creating a community devoted to recreation, the environment, and the arts. The Sundance Institute, Sundance Film Festival, and Summer Theater have had a significant impact on the arts in Utah and beyond. But it may be the result of Redford's environmental commitment—careful resort management focused on improving the quality of existing facilities instead of targeting growth potential—that has contributed most to Sundance's cachet. | North Fork Provo Canyon on Rte. 92 | 801/225–4100 or 800/892–1600 (except Utah) | www.sundance-utah.com.

The **Sundance Ski Area** on the slopes of 12,000-ft Mt. Timpanogos has been recognized by *Ski* magazine as one of the best "smaller" resorts in the country. The 41 trails on 450 acres include several long, groomed runs serviced by one quad and two triple chair lifts. | $39 | Dec.–Apr., daily.

Each summer, two or three professional productions are staged outdoors against the magnificent backdrop of Mt. Timpanogos at the **Sundance Summer Theater.** A Children's Theatre does two plays in repertory with matinee and evening performances. | Ticket prices vary | Mid-June–Aug., Mon.–Sat. 8:00 PM; children's productions, July–Aug., matinees Wed.–Sat. at 11 AM and 1 PM.

Timpanogos Cave National Monument. On the north slope of Mt. Timpanogos (over the mountain from Sundance Resort), three limestone caverns connected by man-made tunnels form Timpanogos Cave National Monument. The first cave entrance is 1,000 ft above the parking and interpretive areas, a strenuous 1½-mi hike. Temperatures inside the caves are about 45°F during the monument's open season. Stalactites, stalagmites, dripstone, flowstone, and other odd textures that you see inside the caves are the result of calcium carbonate and other minerals deposited by evaporation. | American Fork Canyon (Rte. 92) | 801-756–5238 | www.nps.gov/tica | $3 per vehicle for 3 days | Mid-May–mid-Oct.

Uinta National Forest. The Uinta National Forest covers almost a million acres of north-central Utah. Both American Fork Canyon and Provo Canyon have beautiful riverside campgrounds with a mix of aspen and pine. Between the two canyons lies the 10,750-acre Timpanogos Wilderness. | 88 W. 100 N | 801/377–5780 | www.fs.fed.us/r4/uinta | Day use free; camping fees | Daily.

Utah Lake State Park. Fishing is popular on Utah Lake, the state's largest freshwater lake. You can also come here for boating—power boats to canoes—and in winter skate at the Olympic-size ice rink. | 4400 W. Center St. | 801/375–0731 or 801/375–0733 | www.utah.com | $6 | Daily.

ON THE CALENDAR
JUNE–JULY: *Freedom Festival.* A month-long series of patriotic activities and contests peaks with a hot-air balloon festival and the state's biggest Independence Day parade. A gathering in 65,000-seat Cougar Stadium on the Brigham Young University campus closes the festival with live entertainment and an enormous fireworks display. | 801/370–8019 or 801/370–8052.

JUNE–AUG.: *Sundance Summer Theater.* Towering mountains form a backdrop for outdoor performances of two or more productions each season; Children's Theater July–Aug. | 801/225–4100 | Mon.–Sat.

AUG.: *Timpanogos Storytelling Festival.* Nationally and regionally known storytellers join local performers in Orem to weave tales gathered from around the world. | 801/229–7436.

Dining

Foundry Grill. Eclectic. Rough-hewn logs and southwestern art fill the dining room at this Sundance Resort restaurant. Three meals a day of basic fare are accompanied by organically grown vegetables, fruits, and herbs. Specialties vary with the seasons, but uniquely seasoned fish, poultry, beef, and lamb are standards. Breads are baked in a wood-burning oven. | Sundance Resort; North Fork Provo Canyon | 801/225–4107 | www.sundance-utah.com | $17–$36 | AE, D, DC, MC, V.

Gandolfo's Delicatessen. Delicatessen. In a basement location, just odd enough to be interesting, you get a good variety of thick sandwiches, all named after New York City locations. No smoking. | 18 N. University St. | 801/375–3354 | $7–$12 | MC, V | Closed Sun.

Magelby's. American. Many of the locals have been coming to this restaurant for years, not only for the well-prepared steak, seafood, and chicken dishes, but also for the the mammoth list of nearly three dozen homemade desserts, prepared daily. Although part of a one-level business complex, the restaurant's interior is made distinctive with displays of works of local sculptors and artists. | 1675 N. 200 W | 801/374–6249 | $20–$30 | AE, D, MC, V | Closed Sun.

Osaka. Japanese. An interior with simple, clean lines, Japanese calligraphy on the walls, and the gentle light of lanterns over each table is a fine setting for a meal here. Three tatami rooms are available. Specialties include sashimi, gyoza, katsu, and tempura dishes, and the always safe chicken donburi. No smoking. | 46 W. Center St. | 801/373–1060 | $5–$12 | MC, V | Closed Sun.

The Restaurant Roy. Continental. Two outside towers and 150-year-old stained-glass windows give a distinctly European style to this restaurant right outside of Provo. Freshly made pastas, steaks, and seafood are served—the pepper steak and Macadamia-encrusted halibut are recommended. Both the antiques-filled dining area and the outdoor patio offer wonderful views of the Wasatch Front. | 2005 S. State St., Orem | 801/235–9111 | $25–$32 | AE, D, DC, MC, V.

The Tree Room. Eclectic. This Sundance Resort restaurant was built around a large tree. The soaring trunk remains a central feature. The Western look is made more interesting since it's made up of memorabilia collected by Robert Redford. Among the steak, chicken, and fish dishes, the pepper steak with mango and chutney sauce is a favorite. Open-air dining in warm weather. | Sundance Resort; North Fork Provo Canyon | 801/225–4107 | www.sundance-utah.com | $22–$41 | AE, D, DC, MC, V | No lunch.

Lodging

Best Inn & Suites. Next to the BYU campus, this chain inn is convenient to museums and shopping. Complimentary Continental breakfast. In-room data ports, some microwaves, refrigerators. Cable TV. Indoor pool. Hot tub. Laundry facilities. Business services. Some pets allowed. | 101 rooms, 6 suites | 1555 N. Canyon Rd. | 801/374–6020 | fax 801/374–0015 | www.comfortinn.com | $69–$129 | AE, D, DC, MC, V.

Best Western Cottontree Inn. Midway between downtown and Brigham Young University, this is a good place to stay if you are interested in seeing both. The rates are reasonable and the amenities better than average. Complimentary Continental breakfast. Cable TV, VCRs (movies). 2 pools, 1 indoor. Hot tub, beauty salon. Business services. | 80 rooms | 2230 N. University Pkwy. | 801/373–7044 | fax 801/375–5240 | www.bestwestern.com | $55–$80 | AE, D, DC, MC, V.

Days Inn. Close to three major shopping areas, this chain property offers comfortable, contemporary rooms. Restaurant, complimentary Continental breakfast. Some in-room data ports, some microwaves, refrigerators. Cable TV. Pool. Business services. Some pets allowed. | 49 rooms | 1675 N. 200 W | 801/375–8600 | fax 801/374–6654 | www.daysinn.com | $50–$75 | AE, D, DC, MC, V.

Hines Mansion Bed & Breakfast Much of the original woodwork, brick, and stained glass has been left intact at this beautiful 105-year-old historic mansion. Rooms are decorated around various themes, and have period furniture, two-person Jacuzzis, and plenty of light. Full breakfast. In-room data ports. Cable TV. | 9 rooms | 383 W. 100 S | 801/374–8400 or 800/428–5636 | fax 801/374–0823 | $99–$199 | AE, D, DC, MC, V.

Holiday Inn. Proximity to U.S. 89 makes this a good place to stop if you're not lingering for a long time, although the rooms are comfortable and the amenities good. Restaurant, complimentary Continental breakfast, room service. Cable TV. Pool. Exercise equipment. Business services. | 78 rooms | 1460 S. University Ave. | 801/374–9750 | fax 801/377–1615 | www.holiday-inn.com | $79–$89 | AE, D, DC, MC, V.

Hotel Roberts. Basic, eclectic rooms for incredibly low prices characterize this historic hotel, built in 1883 and remodeled in the 1920s. The lobby has a lot of woodwork, and some lovely old dressers and mirrors in the rooms date back to the early 1900s. Not all rooms have private baths, so ask ahead about your accommodations. Cable TV, no TV in some rooms. | 54 rooms | 192 S. University Ave. | 801/373–3400 | $14–$25 | MC, V.

Howard Johnson. A good on-and-off stopover, this is easy to reach from I–15, but away from high-traffic areas. Restaurant. Cable TV. Pool. Hot tub. Exercise equipment. Laundry facilities. Business services. | 116 rooms | 1292 S. University Ave. | 801/374–2500 | fax 801/373–4510 | www.hojo.com | $55–$75 | AE, D, DC, MC, V.

Provo Courtyard by Marriott. Situated in front of the Wasatch Range near Brigham Young University, some rooms have mountain views. Friendly service, comfortable common areas, and touches like fresh fruit and warm cookies in the evening give this chain a personal touch. Restaurant, room service. In-room data ports. Cable TV. Indoor pool. Hot tub. Exercise room. Conference room, business services. | 94 rooms, 6 suites | 1600 N. Freedom Blvd. | 801/373–2222 or 800/321–2211 | fax 801/374–2207 | $64–$109, $109–$129 suites | AE, D, DC, MC, V.

Provo Marriott. Provo's most upscale lodging has a central location. The amenities are better than average, and the surrounding area is nice for walking. Restaurant. In-room data ports, microwaves, some refrigerators. Cable TV. Pool. Hot tub. Exercise equipment. Business services. Airport shuttle. | 331 rooms | 101 W. 100 N | 801/377–4700 or 800/777–7144 | fax 801/377–4708 | www.marriott.com | $80–$150 | AE, D, DC, MC, V.

Sundance Cottages. Featured in *Architectural Digest*, the cottages are a collection of suites of various sizes decorated with a simple Western elegance. Restaurant. Cable TV. Exercise equipment. Bicycles. Downhill and cross-country skiing. Children's programs (ages 6–12).

Business services. | 93 kitchenette units | North Fork Provo Canyon | 801/225–4107 or 800/892–1600 | fax 801/226–1937 | www.sundance-utah.com | $195–$250 | AE, D, DC, MC, V.

RICHFIELD

(Nearby towns also listed: Fillmore, Salina)

If you forgot to pack something important, it's a pretty good bet you can find a replacement in Richfield, central Utah's business hub. Richfield also serves as a gateway to Fish Lake in the Fishlake National Forest, and to Fremont Indian State Park, the largest Fremont habitation site in the state.

Information: **Sevier County Travel Council** | 220 N. 600 W, Richfield, 84701 | 435/896–8898 or 800/662–8898. **Panoramaland Travel Region** | 4 S. Main St. (Box 71), Nephi, 84648 | 435/623–5203 or 800/748–4361.

Attractions

Big Rock Candy Mountain. Minerals have colored this distinctive mountain green, tan, brown, orange, yellow, and gray. In 1897 a railroad brakeman who frequently traveled through the canyon, "Haywire Mac" McClintock, immortalized the mountain in the song "In the Big Rock Candy Mountain," later recorded by Burl Ives and Tex Ritter. The lodging facilities near the mountain have been renovated. You can also fish and bicycle, as well as go on rafting trips on the Sevier River. | U.S. 89, in Marysvale Canyon | 888/560–7625 | Activity fees | Daily; river trips May–Sept.

Capitol Reef National Park. *See* Capitol Reef National Park, *above.* | Rte. 24.

Fishlake National Forest. Immediately west of Richfield, forest service roads form a jagged "Y." These unnumbered but maintained roads meander to the north and south, through wooded areas of aspen, spruce, and fir. | 115 E. 900 N | 435/896–9233 | www.fishlake.r4.fs.fed.us | Day use free, camping fees | Daily.

Fremont Indian State Park and Museum. Twelve interpretive trails lead to rock art and archaeological sites clustered in Clear Creek Canyon. The state park was developed to preserve the art and artifacts uncovered during construction on I–70 in 1983. | 11550 W. Clear Creek Canyon Rd., Sevier | 435/527–4631 | www.utah.com | $5 per vehicle, $3 per person | Daily.

Kimberly Ghost Town. Only the foundations remain of this once-thriving turn-of-the-century mining town, 7 mi up a mountain. You can still see doors in the flat rocks that led to storage spaces and mines. The drive along the dirt road can be a bit rough, but offers nice vistas. | From Richfield, west on I–70 to Exit 17, then left on first dirt road | 435/896–8898 | Free | Daily.

ON THE CALENDAR

JULY: *A Field of Stars Pageant.* Part of the city's Independence Day celebrations, this production dramatizes famous events from the American Revolution, including the Boston Tea Party, Paul Revere's ride, and the Battle of Bunker Hill. | 435/896–5120 or 800/662–8898.

Dining

El Mexicano. Mexican. Always packed, this restaurant on Richfield's main strip looks standard but is not. The authentically Mexican meals are freshly prepared each day and include specialties like shrimp enchiladas, vegetarian chiles rellenos, and various egg dishes. The friendly staff make sure the atmosphere stays lively. | 499 S. Main St. | 435/896–9358 | $10–$18 | AE, D, DC, MC, V | Closed Sun.

The Little Wonder Cafe. American. The huge portions at this comfy home-style diner with booths and large windows keep locals and visitors coming back regularly. Tempura cod, steak and shrimp, and prime rib are particularly popular, as are the freshly made desserts. | 101 N. Main St. | 435/896–8960 | $5–$12 | AE, D, MC, V.

Steve's Steakhouse. American. Previously the Topsfield Lodge Steakhouse, known as one of central Utah's finest, the favored restaurant now has a new name, look, and location, but the same owners and the same high-quality prime rib and steaks. Boots and spurs adorn the walls in the southwestern-style dining area, now adjacent to a motel. | 647 S. Main St. | 435/893–8880 | $12–$22 | AE, MC, V | Closed Sun.

Lodging

Best Western Apple Tree Inn. The trees around this motel create a shady spot in the city center, but you're still close to restaurants and shopping. Complimentary Continental breakfast. Cable TV. Pool. Hot tub. Business services. | 62 rooms | 145 S. Main St. | 435/896–5481 | fax 435/896–9465 | www.bestwestern.com | $55–$129 | AE, D, DC, MC, V.

Budget Host Night's Inn. At the heart of the city, this standard, locally owned motel is clean and affordable. Restaurant. Microwaves, refrigerators. Cable TV. Pool. | 50 rooms | 69 S. Main St. | 435/896–8228 or 800/525–9024 | fax No fax | $60 | AE, D, DC, MC, V.

Days Inn. This member of the chain has a popular coffee shop and good mountain views and is convenient to downtown shops and offices. Restaurant. In-room data ports, refrigerators. Cable TV. Pool. Hot tub, sauna. Business services. | 51 rooms | 333 N. Main St. | 435/896–6476 | www.daysinn.com | $55–$70 | AE, D, DC, MC, V.

Quality Inn. The rooms here are furnished in the soft rose and beige colors of the desert. A pleasant pool area offers a nice counterpoint to the downtown. In-room hot tubs (suites). Cable TV. Pool. Exercise equipment. Business services. | 79 rooms | 540 S. Main St. | 435/896–5465 | www.hotelchoice.com | $60–$80 | AE, D, DC, MC, V.

Richfield Travel Lodge. Centrally located, this facility is within walking distance of many shops and restaurants. The newly renovated property has more amenities than most lodgings in town, basic rooms, and a friendly staff. Restaurant, Continental breakfast. Cable TV. Indoor pool. Hot tub. | 40 rooms | 647 S. Main St. | 435/896–9271 or 800/549–8208 | fax 435/896–6864 | $52–$56 | AE, D, MC, V.

Romanico Inn. Some of the spacious rooms here have three beds, some have refrigerators and microwaves, and there's a lawn with picnic tables. In a quiet area on the outskirts of town, this is a good place to stay if you're traveling with children or pets. Some microwaves and refrigerators. Cable TV. Hot tub. Laundry facilities. Pets allowed. | 29 rooms | 1170 S. Main St. | 435/896–8471 | $50–$65 | AE, D, DC, MC, V.

ROOSEVELT

MAP 14, E5

(Nearby town also listed: Vernal)

Roosevelt lies between blocks of the sovereign land of the Uinta and Ouray Indian Reservation. It's a fair-sized town, with a population just over 4,000, named for President Theodore Roosevelt, and is 30 mi southwest of Vernal, the major center for accommodations in northeastern Utah.

Information: **Dinosaurland Travel Region** | 25 E. Main St., Vernal, 84078 | 435/789–6932 or 800/477–5558 | dinoland@easilink.com | www.dinoland.com.

Attractions

Uinta and Ouray Indian Reservation. Sprawling across almost one million acres on the Uinta Basin and portions of northeast Utah, the border of this sovereign land mass lies right outside Roosevelt, about 6 mi northeast of town on U.S. 40. Although you're asked to stay on the main roads, you can purchase camping and fishing licenses for some of the lakes, streams, and mountain areas on the reservation. The Ute Plaza Supermart sells the licenses issued by the Department of Fish and Wildlife. | 435/722–5141 | Free; camping $10 a day up to six people, fishing $10 a day per person | Daily.

ON THE CALENDAR

JULY: *Northern Ute Powwow.* Drumming, dancing, and singing competitions, a rodeo, and an arts and crafts fair take place at the Ute tribal headquarters at Fort Duchesne, 8 mi east of Roosevelt. | 435/722–5141 or 435/722–4598.

Dining

Frontier Grill. American. A bustling country-style restaurant at the center of town, this place has old photographs on the walls and comfortable booths. The large menu includes soups, salads, sandwiches, steaks, seafood, and prime rib dinners, plus local favorites like Navajo tacos, hot breaded veal, and homemade apple pie. | 65 S. 200 E | 435/722–3669 | $7–$18 | AE, D, DC, MC, V.

Lodging

Best Western Inn. Three miles east of Roosevelt proper, this is a good base for area day trips. There's a convenience store on the premises. Restaurant. Cable TV. Pool. Hot tub. Exercise equipment. Business services. No-smoking rooms. | 40 rooms | E. U.S. 40 | 435/722–4644 | fax 435/722–0179 | www.bestwestern.com | $60 | AE, D, DC, MC, V.

Frontier Motel. The restaurant at this downtown motel is the most popular in town, and you're close to shops. A golf course is ½ mi away. Restaurant. Cable TV. Pool. Hot tub. Some kitchens. Conference room. Business services. Pets allowed. | 54 units, 2 kitchenettes | 75 S. 200 E | 435/722–2201 | fax 435/722–2212 | $50–$75 | AE, D, DC, MC, V.

Western Hills Motel. This small mom-and-pop motel has some of the best prices around, and the service is friendly. The rooms are basic, but have been renovated. Amenities are few. Cable TV. | 22 rooms | 737 E. 200 N | 435/722–5115 | $35–$40 | AE, D, MC, V.

ST. GEORGE

MAP 14, A9

(Nearby towns also listed: Cedar City, Springdale)

The first Anglo residents of St. George were 300 Mormons who, based on reports of the area's mild year-round weather, located here planning to establish a textile industry by growing cotton and raising silkworms. Neither endeavor was successful, but since they found the desert climate preferable to northern Utah's snow, the settlers stayed on. It is still enormously popular. Exceptional scenery, access to national parks and many other recreational areas, well-preserved historic sites, and year-round tennis and golf have made St. George a tourist destination and retirement haven.

Information: **St. George Area Chamber of Commerce** | 97 E. St. George Blvd., St. George, 84770 | 435/628–1658 | www.stgeorgechamber.com. **Washington County Travel and Convention Bureau** | 425 S. 700 E, St. George, 84770 | 435/634–5747 or 800/869–6635 | fax 435/628–1619 | www.utahszionandbryce.com.

Attractions

Brigham Young Winter Home. Mormon leader Brigham Young lived out the end of his life in St. George. His home, built of adobe on a sandstone and basalt foundation, has been carefully restored; you can take guided tours that begin in the one-room office next door. | 200 N. 100 W | 435/673–2517 or 435/673–5181 | www.infowest.com/Utah/colorcountry/History/brigham.html | Free | Daily 9–dusk.

Golf Courses. There are golf courses all over Utah in mountainous and desert settings, but St. George is the state's only true golf "destination." Golfers come to St. George year-round to enjoy well-designed and exceptionally beautiful courses.

Bloomington offers a striking combination of manicured fairways and greens beneath sandstone cliffs. 18 holes/par 72/6,948 yards. | 3174 E. Bloomington Dr. | 435/673–2029 | www.uga.com | Daily.

Pockets of red sandstone and mature trees accent the **Dixie Red Hills** course. 9 holes/par 34/2,564 yards. | 1000 N. 700 W | 435–634–5852 | www.uga.com | Daily.

Designed by Johnny Miller, **Entrada at Snow Canyon** is known for its rolling dunes, winding arroyos, and ancient black lava beds. 18 holes/par 72/7,200 yards. | 2511 W. Entrada Trail | 435/674–7500 | www.golfentrada.com | Daily.

Green Spring offers spectacular views from a course filled with natural obstacles—gorges, hills, and ravines. 18 holes/par 71/6,717 yards. | 588 N. Green Spring Dr. | 435/673–7888 | www.uga.com | Daily.

Long fairways and new tees and greens have made **St. George Golf Club,** an old favorite, a whole new course. 18 holes/par 73/6,765 yards. | 2190 S. 1400 E | 435/634–5854 | www.uga.com | Daily.

Water provides challenges at **Southgate Golf Club,** with several holes bordering ponds or crossing the Santa Clara River. 18 holes/par 70/6,093 yards. | 1975 S. Tonaquint Dr. | 435/628–0000 | www.uga.com | Daily.

Sunbrook was rated by *Golf Digest* as Utah's finest course for 1997–98. Designed by Ted Robinson, fairway features include rock walls, lakes, and waterfalls. 27 holes/par 72/6,800 yards. | 2240 W. Sunbrook Dr. | 435/634–5866 | www.uga.com | Daily.

At **Sky Mountain Golf Course,** natural black lava outcroppings have been left in place throughout the course's rolling terrain. 18 holes/par 72/6,312 yards. | 1030 N. 2600 W., Hurricane; 15 mi east via Rte. 9 | 435/635–7888 | www.uga.com | Daily.

A small, picturesque course, **Twin Lakes** has a devoted following. 9 holes/par 27/1,001 yards. | 660 N. Twin Lakes Dr. (1500 E.) | 435/673–4441 | www.uga.com | Rates are subject to change. Call for tee times and current fees | Daily.

Gunlock State Park. The desert scenery is exceptional, although aside from a boat ramp and chemical toilets, the facilities here are minimal. You can boat, swim, and fish in Gunlock Reservoir. | On Old Rte. 91 | 435/628–2255 | www.utah.com | Free | Daily.

Jacob Hamblin Home. Jacob Hamblin came to southwestern Utah in 1854 as a missionary from the Mormon church to the Paiute, Navajo, and Zuni Indians. He became best known to the tribes not as a religious zealot but as a negotiator and a fair man. Tour his sandstone home for interesting look at Hamblin's life and insight into the curiosities of the Mormons of Utah's Dixie. | 3386 Santa Clara Dr., Santa Clara | 435/673–2161 or 435/673–5181 | www.infowest.com/Utah/colorcountry/History/JHHome | Free | Daily 9–dusk.

Pine Valley Chapel. This symmetrical two-story, white church is the oldest Mormon chapel still in use. It was supposedly designed and constructed by Ebenezer Bryce (Bryce Canyon's namesake), who had worked as a shipmaker in Australia. The chapel was made using shipbuilding techniques. | 30 mi north via Rte. 18, central exit, in Dixie National Forest | 435/673–3431 | Free | Daily 9–dusk.

Snow Canyon State Park. Red Navajo sandstone mesas and formations are crowned with black lava rock, creating high-contrast vistas from either end of the canyon. From the campground you can scramble up huge sandstone mounds and overlook the entire valley. A moderate climate makes this park especially popular for spring and fall camping. Horseback riding. | 1002 Snow Canyon Dr., Ivins | 435/628–2255 | www.utah.com | $5 | Daily.

Tabernacle. Mormon settlers began work on this building in June 1863, just a few months after St. George was established. The building was dedicated by Brigham Young 13 years later. The tabernacle was built of sandstone, and its clock tower is 140 ft tall. This is one of the best-preserved pioneer buildings in the entire state. It's still used for public meetings and community programs. | Main and Tabernacle Sts. | 435/628–4072 | Daily 9–6.

St. George Temple and Visitor Center. Made of native sandstone covered in white stucco, this temple was dedicated in 1877. Though it was not the first to be planned or started, it was the first temple to be opened after the Mormons came to Utah in 1847. Only members of the Church are allowed inside Mormon temples, but a visitors center is open to the public, where you can find information on the construction of this historic building. The temple, visitors center, and gardens fill an entire city block. | 490 S. 300 E | 435/673–5181 | www.infowest.com/Utah/colorcountry/History/Temple/temple.html | Daily 9–9.

Zion National Park. *See* Zion National Park, *below.*

ON THE CALENDAR
APR.–MAY: *St. George Arts Festival.* Artisan booths, food, children's activities, and entertainment, including "cowboy poets," are all part of this celebration. | 435/634–5850.
OCT.: *World Senior Games.* Athletes age 50 and over compete in sporting activities ranging from tennis, golf, and race walking to swimming, running, and bowling. | 435/674–0550 or 800/562–1268.

Dining
Cafe Basîlas. Greek. Greek instrumental music adds color in this intimate dining room. Imported spices add zest to the specialty Greek combination platter—dolmades, spanakopita, shish kebab, carrots, and Arabic-style rice with raisins and almonds. Open-air dining on the patio. | 2 W. St. George Blvd. | 435/673–7671 | $12–$25 | AE, D, DC MC, V | Closed Sun.–Mon.

J. J. Hunan Chinese Restaurant. Chinese. Enter through the phoenix- and dragon-adorned archways into this pleasant restaurant near the center of town. The tablecloths and candles come out for dinner, and entrées like orange-flavored shrimp, sesame beef, and clams in black bean sauce keep the locals returning. Plenty of vegetarian options are available. | Ancestor Sq., 2 W. St. George Blvd., #14 | 435/628–7219 | $8–$20 | AE, D, DC, MC, V.

Pancho & Lefty's. Mexican. Locals come to this lively, authentic restaurant hung with sombreros and colorful blankets for the *flautas* (rolled, fried tortillas stuffed with various meats and vegetables), chimichangas, sizzling fajitas, and ice-cold margaritas. | 1050 S. Bluff St. | 435/628–4772 | $7–$16 | AE, D, MC, V.

Sullivan's Rococo. American. Tables have linens, candles, and fresh flowers, and plants and rock formations fill the interior of this establishment that looks out over the city from Airport Hill. Known for prime rib and fresh salmon dinners, this is a good place for a quiet or romantic dinner. | 511 Airport Rd. | 435/628–3671 or 435/673–3305 | $25–$35 | AE, D, DC, MC, V.

Tom's Deli. Delicatessen. No-nonsense decor with lots of take-out business describes this deli that opened in 1978. The menu includes 35 kinds and combinations of sandwiches, and they make the potato salad fresh daily. | 175 W. 900 S, Bluff | 435/628–1822 | $4–$6.50 | AE, D, MC, V.

Lodging
Best Western Coral Hills. Across from the Old Courthouse on the edge of a historic district, this motel is close to many restaurants. The town's historic walking tour of pioneer buildings begins a block from here. Restaurant, complimentary Continental breakfast. Refrigerators. Cable TV. 2 pools, 1 indoor, wading pool. Hot tub. Exercise equipment. Business services. | 98 rooms | 125 E. St. George Blvd. | 435/673–4844 | fax 435/673–5352 | www.bestwestern.com | $75–$90 | AE, D, DC, MC, V.

Comfort Suites. Two blocks from the Dixie Convention Center, this hotel's "minisuites" have comfortable sitting areas and large TVs. The shaded outdoor common areas offer additional space in nice weather. Heated outdoor pool open year-round. Complimentary Continental breakfast. Microwaves, refrigerators. Cable TV. Pool. Hot tub. Business services. | 122 units | 1239 S. Main St. | 435/673–7000 | fax 435/628–4340 | www.comfortinn.com | $65–$80 | AE, D, DC, MC, V.

The Coyote Inn at Green Valley Spa & Tennis Resort. Minutes from downtown but in a world of its own, this serene, luxurious resort and inn is one of the best in the country. Here you can arrange your days around morning hikes in the surrounding red-rock canyon parks, golf or tennis lessons, exercise classes, massage therapy, facials, and excellent low-calorie gourmet meals. All meals, and some spa services, are included in the weekly rate. Dining room. In-room safes, refrigerators. 4 pools, 3 indoor, 1 outdoor. Spa. 4 indoor lighted tennis courts, 15 outdoor tennis courts. 2 exercise rooms. Hiking. Laundry service, Meeting rooms. Airport shuttle. No-smoking rooms. | 35 rooms | 1871 W. Canyon View Dr. | 435/628–8060 or 800/237–1068 | fax 435/673–4084 | $2,950 per week per person; $450 nightly rate per person available most times | AE, D, MC, V.

Greene Gate Village. The nine houses that make up this establishment are furnished in turn-of-the-century style, in keeping with their age. You can rent rooms or suites or the whole Greene House, which sleeps 22. The houses supposedly all had green gates after Brigham Young, head of the Mormon church, had the temple gates painted green, then gave the rest of the paint to the nearby households. Only one of those gates remains, displayed in the hotel's garden. Restaurant, picnic areas, complimentary breakfast. Cable TV. Pool. Hot tub. Business services. No smoking. | 19 rooms, 7 suites, 1 full house, 3 kitchenette units | 76 W. Tabernacle St. | 435/628–6999 or 800/350–6999 | fax 435/628–6989 | www.greenegate.com | $80–$125 | AE, DC, MC, V.

Holiday Inn Resort. Tennis courts, a putting green, and a playground in addition to the pool, Ping-Pong tables, and video games make this an attractive place to stop on vacation. The suites have extra-large baths with heart-shaped tubs. Restaurant, room service. In-room data ports, some refrigerators. Cable TV. Indoor-outdoor pool. Hot tub. Putting green. Tennis courts. Exercise equipment. Game room. Laundry facilities. Business services. Airport shuttle. | 164 rooms | 850 S. Bluff St. | 435/628–4235 | fax 435/628–8157 | www.holiday-inn.com | $90–$120 | AE, D, DC, MC, V.

Ramada Inn. Close to St. George's historic district, shops, and restaurants, this convenient property has modern, larger-than-average rooms, numerous amenities, and extras like in-room coffeemakers and hair dryers. Restaurant, full breakfast. Cable TV. Pool. Hot tub. Conference rooms. | 126 rooms, 10 suites | 1440 E. St. George Blvd. | 435/628–2828 or 800/713–9435 | fax 435/628–0505 | $65, $85–$135 suites | AE, D, DC MC, V.

Seven Wives Inn. This historic inn at the center of town consists of two wooden homes and a cottage. The larger structure, built in 1873, was used to hide polygamists after the practice was prohibited, and Brigham Young supposedly slept here. The rooms are furnished with antiques, and many have balconies, fireplaces, and/or Jacuzzis. They're named for the wives of a former owner's great-great-grandfather. An on-site massage therapist, a five-course dinner, and high tea are available for an extra charge. Dining room, full breakfast. Cable TV, some VCRs. Pool. | 13 rooms | 217 N. 100 W | 435/628–3737 or 800/600–3737 | fax 435/628–5646 | $60–$125 | AE, D, DC MC, V.

Sun Time Inn. Family suites are available at this downtown, locally owned, two-story motel. The rooms are away from the street, built around an inner courtyard that encloses the pool and parking lot. Some refrigerators. Cable TV. Pool. | 46 rooms | 420 E. St. George Blvd. | 435/673–6181 or 800/237–6253 | $55 | AE, D, MC, V.

Travelodge Motel. This modest-sized chain establishment has red-rock views from most rooms and is very close to golf. Some refrigerators. Cable TV. Pool. Business services. Pets allowed. | 40 rooms | 175 N. 1000 E | 435/673–4621 | fax 435/674–2635 | www.travelodge.com | $60–$75 | AE, D, DC, MC, V.

SALINA

(Nearby towns also listed: Ephraim, Richfield)

Since it stands at the intersection of I–70, U.S. 89, and U.S. 50, you'd expect Salina to be either a "drive through" or a tourist trap. Actually, it's neither. It's a simple ranching town, where the residents' attitude—expressed in the vernacular—is: "Hey, you're welcome to stop. But if you're just passin' through . . . well, hell. That's all right too."

Information: Sevier County Travel Council | 220 N. 600 W, Richfield, 84701 | 435/896–8898 or 800/662–8898. **Panoramaland Travel Region** | 4 S. Main St. (Box 71), Nephi, 84648 | 435/623–5203 or 800/748–4361.

Attractions

Burn's Saddlery. This is possibly the best place in Utah to buy cowboy boots. Experienced clerks can even determine a proper fit on squirming children. The store's huge variety of farm and ranch equipment has to be seen to be believed. | 79 W. Main St. | 435/529–7484 | Mon.–Sat. 9–6; closed Sun. and most holidays.

Palisade State Park. Palisade Reservoir is one of the few state park facilities closed to motorized boats or watercraft. Because of this it has a reputation for being a quiet place to swim, fish, kayak, or canoe. The park's 18-hole golf course is over the hill and out of sight. | 2200 E. Palisade Rd. | 435/835–7275 or 435/835–4653 | www.utah.com | $5, with additional fees for golfing | Daily.

ON THE CALENDAR

JULY: *Salina Riding Club Rodeo.* Watch modern-day gladiators wrangle bulls and broncos at this two-day rodeo hosted every Fourth of July weekend by the Professional Rodeo Cowboys Association. | 435/896–8898.

Dining

John's Mad House Cafe. American. Look for the 1950s-style wood and brick building with a sign that says WASATCH CAFE out front—the locals know the "Mad House" regardless—to find this hometown eatery. You'll find the usual burgers, sandwiches, salads, and spuds, along with weekend specials like prime rib, baked orange roughie, and filet mignon. The portions are huge, so a half-platter is usually enough for most appetites. | 430 W. Main St. | 435/529–4123 | $6–$12 | D, DC, MC, V.

Mom's Cafe. American. A cozy place with booths or tables and lots of customers that the waitresses know by name. Specialties include spare ribs, scones with honey butter, and other freshly made baked goods. Salad bar. | 10 E. Main St. | 435/529–3921 | $8–$16 | D, MC, V.

Lodging

Scenic Hills Motel. Simple, economic lodging off the highway. Restaurant. Air-conditioning. Cable TV, some room phones. Pool. Business services. Pets allowed. | 67 rooms | 75 E. 1500 S | 435/529–7483 | fax 435/529–3616 | $52 | AE, D, DC, MC, V.

The Victorian Inn. Built in 1896 by an area forestry chief, this Queen Anne–style home in the center of town has beautiful, high-quality woodwork and some of the original stained-glass windows. Cozy rooms have king-size beds with down comforters and old-fashioned tubs, and a landscaped yard with a rose garden courtyard surrounds the property. Full breakfast. | 3 rooms | 190 W. Main St. | 435/529–7342 | fax No fax | $75–$90 | MC, V.

SALT LAKE CITY

MAP 14, C4

(Nearby towns also listed: Ogden, Provo)

When Brigham Young led the first party of Mormon pioneers to the Salt Lake Valley, he had a mission statement of sorts: "If there's a place on this earth that nobody else wants, that's the place I am hunting for." So on July 24, 1847, when Young gazed across the vast and somewhat desolate valley of the Great Salt Lake and reportedly announced "This is the place," it would have been understandable if his followers had some mixed feelings. If they did, they must have kept them to themselves, for they continued down the mountain and began to build a home.

Salt Lake City is the heart of the Church of Jesus Christ of Latter-day Saints, as the Mormon faith is officially called. It is also an important western center for business, medicine, education, and culture.

Salt Lake City proper is really only a small piece of the Salt Lake Valley, which runs 25 mi north and south and 20 mi east to west. There are 250,000 people living in Salt Lake City. Another 600,000 live in widening rings of suburbia outside the city limits (*see* Neighborhoods, *below*). The Wasatch Mountains, on the east, border the entire length of the valley—and beyond—providing one of the most scenic backdrops in the country.

Modern Salt Lake City is a study in change. Salt Lakers have learned to deal with both victory and defeat while enthusiastically supporting their NBA team, the Utah Jazz. Increased commitment to the arts from the public and private sectors has created a cultural scene as prodigious as you'd expect in a city twice Salt Lake's size. Recent media attention touting Salt Lake City as an excellent environment for business has helped create an influx of new industries. Interstate 15 is under major reconstruction. A $312 million light rail system has been constructed.

The announcement that Salt Lake City is to be the site of the 2002 Olympic Winter Games focused well-deserved attention on little-known winter sports sites, but weathering Olympic-related scandals has contributed to the city's coming of age. Despite ups and downs, citizens continue to live up to their reputation as a down-to-earth, friendly, and resilient bunch. In fact, these days most Salt Lake residents would tell you "change is good."

Information: Salt Lake Convention and Visitors Bureau | 90 S. West Temple, Salt Lake City, 84101 | 801/521–2822 or 800/541–4955 | fax 801/534–4927 | www.visitsaltlake.com.

NEIGHBORHOODS

Capitol Hill/Marmalade District. Northwest of the capitol building, several streets crisscross the slope of Capitol Hill. This area is known as the Marmalade District because its streets were named after fruit trees. The architectural integrity of the small Victorian homes along these steep and narrow avenues has, for the most part, been maintained. Northeast of Capitol Hill, small, expensive housing developments, some of them closed-gate communities, are beginning to creep up the hillside.

The Gateway. The Gateway is a section of downtown Salt Lake City loosely bounded by Main Street on the east, I–15 on the west, and North Temple Street and 900 South on the north and south. As a neighborhood, its identity is still in a formative stage—a stage that's been going on for over 15 years, as this area has been considered for everything from an NFL stadium to a giant auto mall. Oddly enough, while the movers and shakers have been making plans, the Gateway has seen a persistent influx of eclectic shops, restaurants, and visual-arts facilities. The best example of this is Pierpont Avenue (240 South, between 200 and 400 West), with a handful of purveyors of the antique and unique, a couple of well-established restaurants, and ArtSpace (801/531–9378) a nonprofit organization that provides housing and studio space for more than 25 artists.

The Avenues. Tall trees, quaint and varied architecture, and a neighborhood identity separate this part of Salt Lake City from many other residential areas in the valley. The historic avenues are numbered from First to Ninth, running west to east between State Street and the University of Utah, and from A to S Streets, climbing north up the hillside beginning one block north of South Temple Street. There are some commercial entities in this area—bed-and-breakfasts, a hospital, a supermarket, two or three low-key eateries, and an art gallery. Still, as a visitor attraction, the main appeal here is driving slowly up and down streets lined with well-tended homes in modes from Victorian to Prairie Style.

Sugar House. This area was named in 1853 for a soon-to-be-completed sugar mill. Not a cube of sugar ever materialized, but the name stuck. Present-day Sugar House is primarily a shopping district located between 17th (1700 South) and 33rd (3300 South), from 5th (500 East) to 20th (2000 East). Sugar House Commons is a recently developed retail and office conglomerate at 21st (2100 South) and 13th (1300 East). It's attractive, in a two-story Barnes and Noble Booksellers sort of way, but not nearly as interesting as the area between 21st (2100 South) and 23rd (2300 South) and 9th (900 East) to 12th (1200 East). In this five-block area there are three family-run furniture businesses, Salt Lake's only hip-hop store, a café with an affiliated adult lingerie boutique, a drum and guitar shop, several places selling antiques and vintage clothing, and a large thrift store.

The Suburbs. Ask residents of the Salt Lake Valley where they live, and the most common reply will be "Salt Lake." It's a much simpler answer than the truth, which is that the majority of the people who work in Salt Lake City live in bedroom communities south or west of the city boundaries. South of Salt Lake are Murray, Midvale, Sandy, Draper, and Riverton. To the west are West Valley City, Taylorsville, Kearns, and South Jordan. These are all incorporated cities with amenities, lodging, and shopping galore. It's just a Utah quirk that their residents are unable to acknowledge their true origins.

TRANSPORTATION INFORMATION

Airport: Salt Lake City International Airport is the nation's 23rd-largest airport. It serves more than 21 million passengers annually. Eleven airlines, including Delta (which makes Salt Lake City a western hub), offer over 350 departures daily. | 7 mi west of downtown via I–80 | www.ci.slc.ut.us/services/airport/index.html.

Intra-area Transit: Utah Transit Authority provides mass transit throughout the entire Salt Lake area, including to the airport and ski resorts. | 801/262–5626 or 801/266–1187.

Driving Around Town

Like many major cities in the Midwest and Southwest, Salt Lake is predominantly a car culture. Because driving is the principal mode of transportation for the locals, the city is car friendly, with wide, well-marked streets and plenty of parking lots and spaces, even in the downtown area.

The massive Mormon Temple is the center of the city's system of streets, which follows a grid that was planned by Brigham Young in the 19th century. Streets with "North" or "South" in their names run parallel to South Temple Street, which is the southern border of Temple Square. South Temple is considered the main east-west thoroughfare through town. Main Street, which is the eastern boundary of Temple Square, is the main north-south thoroughfare; "East" and "West" streets run parallel to Main Street.

Street numbers indicate distances from these two main axes. For example, 200 South Street is 2 blocks south of South Temple, and 400 West Street is 4 blocks west of Main Street. (The numbers can get a bit confusing and overwhelming, as street names go into the 10,000s—10,600 South Street, for example, is in the suburbs, but still refers back to the center of town.) North Temple Street and West Temple Street form the other two boundaries of Temple Square. State Street, one block east of Main Street, is another major north-south thoroughfare.

Two major interstates intersect in Salt Lake City: I–15 runs north and south through the city; I–80 runs east and west. At the center of town I–15 and I–80 merge in a north-south direction for approximately three miles before I–80 continues east and west. I–215 loops around the outskirts of the city, and is divided into the West Side Belt and the East Side Belt. I–215 links I–15 with I–80, and is a good option if you want to avoid the downtown area.

The majority of the streets in Salt Lake are two-way streets; the only major one-way street is 5th South Street, which runs from the downtown area west to I–15. The main thoroughfare into downtown from I–15, 6th South Street, runs two ways. Except for 5th South, you will not have to worry about encountering one-way streets.

Rush hour in Salt Lake tends to hit its peak between 4:30 and 5:30 PM, but even during this time, unless there are major street repairs or accidents, traffic flow remains fairly steady. The downtown area, around Temple Square, is the only place that might suffer bottlenecks, but even here you would most likely not wait in traffic for longer than a few minutes. If you can avoid traveling until after six, you should not run into traffic at all.

Street parking outside the downtown area is free and plentiful; if you plan to be in the city center, there are many lots and parking areas, most of which charge approximately $2 an hour, or $10 a day. The ZCMI Mall, which is in the city center at South Temple and State Streets, has ample parking that is free to shoppers; if you are not shopping there, it will also run about $10 a day. From ZCMI Mall a trolley system takes you to all the major area sights for a $2 fee (this is actually one of the best ways to tour Salt Lake's attractions). The downtown area subway system, called the Track, is also an easy and affordable alternative to driving. Tickets are $1.

In Salt Lake City you can turn right on red lights. The speed limit is 30 mph on most city streets, 65 mph on area highways. State Street has areas that have a 40 mph limit, and school zones have a 20 mph speed limit (again, all speed limits are well posted). Speeding and parking penalties are strictly enforced. Remember that you can be fined for carrying alcohol in your vehicle (open container or not), and there is a $35 fine for driving without a seatbelt.

Attractions

ART AND ARCHITECTURE

Beehive House and Lion House. The Beehive House was Brigham Young's home when he was territorial governor; you can take a tour. The Lion House next door was built in 1855 to house Young's large family. The Lion House is used for wedding receptions and other group gatherings. No formal tours are offered, but The Pantry Restaurant on the lower level is open to the public weekdays for lunch and dinner and Saturday for brunch. | 63 and 67 E. South Temple | 801/363–5466 (Lion House) or 801/240–2671 (Beehive House) | Free | Daily.

PARKS

Liberty Park. This park is one of the city's largest and oldest open spaces. Several playgrounds are scattered around, and you can run or walk on the jogging path year-round. In summer, a few carnival-type rides are open near an outdoor swimming pool. Paddleboats can be rented to cruise around a small, shallow lake. A favorite summer feature is a creative fountain that echoes the topography of the Wasatch Mountains, including the paths that rivers and streams take from the mountains down canyons and into the valley lakes. Sixteen acres of the park are devoted to an aviary, with more than 1,000 birds from all over the world. In free-flying demonstrations, hawks, eagles, and other birds follow their trainer's cues and commands in an open-air setting. | 1300 S. 600 E | 801/596–8500 (Aviary); 801/972–7800 | www.tracyaviary.org | Park use free; aviary $3 | Daily.

Abravanel Hall. A beautiful angular structure with a two-story wall of windows on its east side, this concert hall was named for the late Maurice Abravanel, beloved conductor of the Utah Symphony Orchestra. The symphony performs about 200 concerts annually in this acoustically excellent hall. The building also hosts other musical events. | 123 W. South Temple | 801/533–6683 or 801/533–5626 | fax 801/521–6634 | www.utahsymphony.org/ | Daily.

Ballet West. Under the artistic direction of Jonas Cage, Ballet West performs a repertoire of full-length classical and modern ballets, as well as original works. The company's home stage is the historic Capitol Theatre, built in 1912 to host touring vaudeville shows. | 50 W. 200 S | 801/323–6901 or 801/355–2787 (box office) | fax 801/359–3504 | www.balletwest.org | Ticket prices vary.

Brigham Young Monument. A larger-than-life-size statue honoring the Mormon pioneer leader is surrounded by others of the Indians and mountain men who lived in the state before Mormon settlement. | Main and South Temple Sts.

Family History Library. The Mormon church has amassed the largest collection of genealogical information in the world, and that collection is open to the public. Library staff recommends that you take an orientation session before you start. | 35 N. West Temple | 801/249–2331 | www.utah.com.

Governor's Mansion. This impressive mansion was built in 1900 by silver-mining magnate Thomas Kearns. It has served as the residence of Utah's governors since the 1980s. In 1993 a Christmas tree fire damaged much of the interior. However, all the damage has now been repaired and some areas restored to their original design and color schemes. | 603 E. South Temple | 801/538–1005 | www.utahgovernorsmansion.com | Free | Apr.–Nov., Tues. and Thurs. afternoon.

State Capitol. On a hill at the north end of State Street, the capitol building is in Renaissance Revival style. It was completed in 1915. Depression-era murals in the rotunda depict events from Utah's past. Knowledgeable volunteer guides lead free hourly tours. | 300 N. State St. | 801/538–1563 or 801/538–3000 | Free | Mon.–Fri., hours vary.

This Is the Place Heritage Park. On the eastern bench of the Salt Lake Valley, this park details the trek of Mormon pioneers and re-creates an 1850s township, complete with cooking, crafts, and blacksmithing demonstrations. | 2601 Sunnyside Ave. | 801/582–1847 | www.utah.com | $6 | Memorial Day–Labor Day., Mon.–Sat. 11–5; special seasonal events.

University of Utah. Overlooking Salt Lake City from its East Valley location, the U of U is the state's oldest and largest public university. | 200 S | 801/581–6515 | www.utah.edu/.

The permanent collection at the small **Utah Museum of Fine Arts** includes art forms from throughout the world—paintings, sculpture, tribal arts, and furniture from Africa, Asia, Europe, and the Americas. The museum often hosts traveling exhibits as well. | Art and Architecture Center, 370 S. 1530 E; southeast side of campus | 801/581–7332 | www.utah.edu/umfa | Free | Weekdays 10–5, weekends 12–5.

The **Utah Museum of Natural History's** largest hall holds the skeletons of dinosaurs and other prehistoric creatures. An exhibit on rocks and minerals includes information on mining in Utah. The many hands-on science adventures for children change often. A recently donated collection of more than 1,000 pieces of Indian art, including jewelry and elaborate masks, has doubled the number of the museum's Native American artifacts. | 200 S. 1390 E. President's Circle | 801/581–4303 | www.umnh.utah.edu | $4 | Daily.

The professional **Pioneer Theatre Company** has a seven-production season; generally two musicals and five plays. Although it's an independent entity, the company works cooperatively with the university's theater department. | University and 300 S | 801/581–6961 | www.ptc.utah.edu | Ticket prices vary | Sept.–May.

Red Butte Garden and Arboretum has trees, shrubs, herbs, wildflowers, and stream-fed pools tucked into a private canyon in the Wasatch foothills. A large garden area is geared to children. A concert series is held each summer. | 300 Wakara Way; west edge of campus, through Research Park on Wakara Way to the mouth of Red Butte Canyon | 801/581–4747 | www.redbutte.utah.edu | $5 | Mon.–Sat. 9–8, Sun. 9–5.

Utah Opera Company. Utah Opera's season includes five or six productions a year, always a mix of old favorites and lesser-known modern operas, performed at the Capitol Theatre. Clever advertising, English supertitles, and nationally-known singers have helped make going to the opera a popular, mainstream entertainment. | 50 W. 200 S | 801/736–6868 or 801/355–2787 (box office) | www.utahopera.org.

MUSEUMS

Pioneer Memorial Museum. Thousands of artifacts are displayed here, including tools and carriages from the late 1800s and a doll and toy collection. Some of the more bizarre items in the collection are Maori masks, silkworm cocoons, and a two-headed lamb. Hundreds of paintings and photographs fill the stairwells between floors. | 300 N. Main St. | 801/538–1050 | Donations accepted | Mon.–Sat. 9–5 year-round; June–Aug., also Sun. 1–5.

Salt Lake Art Center. Contemporary visual arts in rotating exhibits and Kidspace, with art activities for children. The Art Center School has photography and ceramics classes. | 20 S. West Temple | 801/328–4201 | Suggested donation $2 | Tues.–Sat. 10–5, Fri. until 9, Sun. 1–5.

RELIGION AND SPIRITUALITY

Cathedral of the Madeleine. Built in 1909, this Rhenish Gothic church was completely restored in 1993. The process earned an award from the National Heritage Foundation. The cathedral's interior is distinguished by vibrant stained-glass windows and elaborate artwork and carvings. Guided tours are offered twice a week. | 331 E. South Temple | 801/328–8941 | www.madeleinechoirschool.org | Daily 7:30–9; tours Fri. at 1 and Sun. at 12:30.

Temple Square. This 10-acre plot is the very center of Mormonism. The square blooms with bright gardens in spring, summer, and fall. Thousands of colored lights illuminate the buildings and trees during the holiday season. In addition to the buildings detailed below, two visitors centers house exhibits and art with religious themes. | Bordered by Main St. and North, South, and West Temple Sts.; North Visitors' Center, 50 W. North Temple | 801/240–2534 | www.lds.org or www.saltlake.org | Free | Daily.
The Mormon Tabernacle Choir performs on Thursdays and Sundays in the squat, oval-shape, domed **Tabernacle.** You can also attend the extra rehearsals scheduled weekly. | Temple Square | 801/240–4872 | Free | Thurs. evening, Sun. morning.
The six-spired Gothic **Temple** is open only to active church members, but the public may enter (free of charge) the other buildings and monuments on the beautifully landscaped grounds.
The **Assembly Hall** is a Victorian Gothic–style chapel on the southwest corner of Temple Square. Open to the public, it's also used for small religious meetings and a weekend concert series. | 801/240–4872 | Free | Daily.
The **Seagull Monument,** just east of the Assembly Hall, is dedicated to "the miracle of the gulls," which occurred during the early days of Mormon settlement, when seagulls saved crops from infestation by crickets. | 801/240–4872.
The **Museum of Church History and Art** displays Mormon artifacts, paintings, fabric art, and sculptures. | 45 N. West Temple | 801/240–3310 | Free | Daily.
The **Family History Library** provides free public access to the Mormons' huge collection of genealogical records. | 35 N. West Temple | 801/240–2331 | www.familysearch.org | Free | Mon. 7:30–5, Tues.–Sat. 7:30–10.

The **Joseph Smith Memorial Building,** east of Temple Square, is a Mormon community center where visitors can learn how to do computerized genealogical research. It also shows an hour-long film on early Mormon history and the migration of Mormons to the Salt Lake

Valley in the mid-19th century. | 15 E. South Temple | 801/240–1266 or 800/537–9703 | Free | Mon.–Sat. 9–9.

SHOPPING

Simon's Trolley Square. The three sand-blasted redbrick car barns of Trolley Square once housed Salt Lake City's electric trolleys. Today they offer diverse shopping, as well as restaurants and movie theaters. The square is upscale enough to have attracted a Hard Rock Cafe and Salt Lake's only Nicole Miller and Williams Sonoma stores. | Between 500 and 600 S. and 600 and 700 E | 801/521–9877 | www.simon.com | Daily.

ZCMI Mall. This modern department store is a true Utah original. The store was founded in the late 1800s as Zion's Cooperative Mercantile Association, an attempt to provide everything required by a Mormon family and eliminate the need to trade with non-Mormon companies. These days there are no restrictions on Mormon commerce, and ZCMI stores are found in Utah, Idaho, and Arizona—there are actually five in the Salt Lake Valley alone. The modern ZCMI stores have come a long way from their roots. They now carry such "non-essentials" as designer clothing, fine jewelry, and major lines of cosmetics and fragrances. Nordstrom and Dillard's are their main competition. | 40 E. South Temple | 801/321–8745 | www.zsc.com | Mon.–Fri. 7–9, Sat 10–7.

SPORTS AND RECREATION

★ **Alta Ski Area.** Alta is the perennial favorite of serious local skiers. There's no glitz, no fancy cuisine, and no fashion show on the slopes, just an excellent ski school, incredible powder snow, and a mountain that some consider a sort of monument to the sanctity of skiing. Alta limits the uphill capacity of its lifts per hour, thus limiting the number of skiers on the mountain so as to "protect the skiing experience." 2,020 vertical drop, more than 40 runs. | Big Cottonwood Canyon; east on Rte. 152 | 801/359–1078 or 801/742–3333 | www.altaskiarea.com | $31 | Mid-Nov.–mid-Apr.

Brighton Ski Resort. Set in the Wasatch-Cache National Forest, Brighton has a vertical drop of 1,745 ft. The longest of the 64 runs is 3 mi. The lifts go to all terrains—beginner to advanced—so it's easy to regroup after a run if you are skiing with people with different levels of expertise. | Big Cottonwood Canyon; 25 mi southeast on Rte. 190 | 801/532–4731 or 800/873–5512 | fax 435/649–1787 | www.skibrighton.com | $35 | Early Nov.–Apr.

Delta Center. This arena is home to both the NBA's Utah Jazz, the Western Conference champions and enormously popular here, and the upstart WNBA's Utah Starzz. | 301 South Temple | 801/355–3865 | www.utahjazz.com | Jazz: Nov.–Apr.; Starzz: June–Aug.

"E" Center. This arena houses the Utah Grizzlies, a minor-league (IHL) hockey team. | 3200 S. Decker Lake Dr. | 801/988–8035 | www.utahgrizz.com | Oct.–Apr.

Franklin Covey Field. This is the home diamond of the Salt Lake Buzz, AAA baseball affiliate of the Minnesota Twins. | West Temple and 1300 S | 801/485–3800 | www.buzzbaseball.com | Apr.–Sept.

Lagoon Amusement Park, Pioneer Village, and Water Park. Beautifully landscaped grounds, enthusiastic staff, and exciting rides are elements that never seem to change. New rides and attractions open annually. The Lagoon-A-Beach Water Park is Utah's largest combo of pools, slides, and other water fun. Pioneer Village is a shady combination of mini-museums, actual turn-of-the-century structures, and Wild West–style amusements like shooting galleries and a log flume ride. | 375 North Lagoon Dr., Farmington; Exit 325 off I–15 | 801/451–8000 or 800/748–5246 | fax 801/451–8016 | www.lagoonpark.com | $30 all-day pass allows access to every area of the park | June–Aug., daily; late Apr.–Memorial Day and Labor Day–Oct., weekends.

★ **Snowbird Ski and Summer Resort.** When it opened in the 1970s, Snowbird was on the cutting edge of ski trends, and it's managed to stay there. Snowbird has the highest elevations, the greatest vertical drop, and black diamond runs all over the mountain. A gondola that holds 125 people takes you to deep powder bowls. At the base, several angular buildings provide upscale lodging, fine dining, and amenities such as swimming pools, tennis courts, and a full-service spa, all of which are open throughout the year. | Little Cottonwood Canyon; east on Rte. 210 | 801/742–2222 or 800/385–2002 | fax 801/947–8227 | www.snowbird.com | $45 chair lifts only, $54 including tram | Mid Nov.–late Apr.

Solitude Mountain Resort. Solitude is a good, solid choice for relaxed skiing. The resort has varied lesson options, great food, brand-new lodging, 63 runs and bowls, 7 lifts, and a 2,047-ft vertical drop. | 1200 Big Cottonwood Canyon, Solitude; I–215 and Rte. 190 | 801/534–1400 or 800/748–4754 | fax 435/649–5276 | www.skisolitude.com | $39 | Late Nov.–late Apr.

Solitude Nordic Center. Twenty kilometers of groomed trails—60% intermediate terrain. Cross-country ski tours, rentals, lessons, and good advice. | Rte. 190 at Solitude Resort | 801/534–1400 or 800/748–4754 | fax 435/649–5276 | www.skisolitude.com | $10 | Late Nov.–late Apr.

Utah Fun Dome. A new "extreme sports" area has opened here, adjacent to the bungee jumping tower, with such lures as the "Horizontal Terrorizer," which launches a cage and two riders 80 ft straight up at 70 mph. There's laser tag, a skating rink, batting cages, badminton, a three-dimensional theater, a maze of video games, and more. | 4998 S. 360 W; South on I–15 to 5300 S. exit, then west to 700 West, then north, in Murray | 801/263–8769 | www.fundome.com | Daily.

OTHER POINTS OF INTEREST

Council Hall. This two-story red sandstone building has a visitors information center and bookstore on the first floor, as well as some exhibits about regional history. The offices of the Utah Travel Council fill the second floor. | Capitol Hill | 801/538–1479 or 800/200–1160 | fax 801/538–1399 | www.utah.com | Free | Daily.

Hansen Planetarium. Star shows are offered daily in a domed theater, changing every month or so. Laser-light shows set to music of various types are a weekend favorite. Museum exhibits are free. | 15 S. State St. | 801/538–2104 | www.utah.edu/planetarium | Daily.

Hogle Zoo. You can see more than 1,300 animals here. Be sure to bring walking shoes and a hat—exhibits are spread out, and shade is at a premium. | 2600 E. Sunnyside Ave. | 801/582–1631 | www.hoglezoo.org | $6 | Daily 9–5.

Kennecott Bingham Canyon Mine. The indoor visitors center has a video show on the geology, history, and daily operations of this open-pit mine, one of the largest and most productive in the country. An outdoor overlook of the mine gives you a real sense of the enormous size of the excavation. | I–15 west to 8400 W., then south to 9000 S | 801/252–3234 | www.citysearchslc.com | $3 per vehicle | Apr.–mid-Oct., daily.

Wheeler Historic Farm. A sprawling farm surrounds the original brick and adobe farmhouse built in 1898, 12 mi south of Salt Lake City. The fields, pastures, woods, and outbuildings—chicken coop, icehouse, and more—are all part of the farm experience. You can tour both the house and animal facilities hourly, and milk the cows (for a modest fee) at 5 PM. Hayrides are held throughout the day (except Sundays), and seasonal events add to the fun. | 6351 S. 900 E; Exit 9 off I–215 | 801/264–2241 | www.co.slc.ut.us/wh/wheeler.htm | Free; fees for tour and activities | Daily.

ON THE CALENDAR

MAY: *Living Traditions Festival.* Nearly 20 countries and cultures are represented through food booths, demonstrations, crafts, and music and dance performances, all on the grounds of the historic City and County Building. | State St. between 400 and 500 S | 801/533–5760.

JUNE: *Utah Arts Festival.* Utah's largest and longest-running arts festival. Visual-arts shows and marketplace, book fair and book signings, indoor and outdoor music, dance, and performance art featuring local and nationally known performers. Interactive and children's arts areas. | State Fair Park | 801/322–2428 | $5 | www.uaf.org.

JULY: *"Days of '47" Celebration.* Celebrate the arrival of the first Mormon settlers in the Salt Lake Valley, July 24, 1847. Festivities are held statewide, but the Salt Lake City events are the largest. A horse parade, children's parade, and pioneer parade, one of the largest and oldest in the United States, are held downtown. There are also marathon and 10K races, an 8-day-long world championship rodeo, and a lavish fireworks display. | 801/521–2822.

SEPT.: *Utah State Fair.* The 10-day fair held at the State Fair Park has exhibits, contests, livestock auctions, produce displays, nightly concerts, carnival rides, a horse show, and a rodeo. | 801/538–8440 | $5.

SEPT.–OCT.: *Snowbird Oktoberfest.* Polka bands, yodeling, dancing, and German food and beer appear weekends at the Snowbird Resort. There are children's activities and crafts, and Alpenhorn performances on 11,000-ft Hidden Peak, accessed by the Snowbird tram. | 801/521–6040 | Labor Day–mid-October, weekends.

DEC.: *Alta Holiday Torchlight Parades on Christmas Eve and New Year's Eve.* Simply observe or participate with 200 to 300 light-bearing skiers on the resort's lower slopes. | 801/742–3333 or 801/359–1078.

DEC.: *Temple Square Christmas.* Thousands of tiny colored lights decorate the trees and buildings of Temple Square. Concerts are held nightly throughout the month. | 801/ 240–2534 | Thanksgiving–New Year's Day.

DEC.: *First Night.* The New Year's Eve celebration has myriad activities in dozens of indoor and outdoor locations. Last Dance Masquerade Ball, ice skating, children's activities. | 801/359–5118.

WALKING TOURS

Capitol Hill and Vicinity (2 to 3 hours)

Begin at the **Social Hall Heritage Museum,** between South Temple Street and 100 South Street. This small glass structure displays artifacts and wall remnants of the first public building constructed by early Mormon settlers. Directly across State Street, or under State Street via a pedestrian tunnel, is the **ZCMI Center Mall,** the sophisticated heir to Zion's Cooperative Mercantile Institution, a pioneer-era coop. Back on State Street, head north a quarter of a block to the **Hansen Planetarium.** The planetarium, in a historic building, has a free, hands-on space science museum and daily star shows. Just north of the planetarium, the **Eagle Gate,** which once marked the entrance to Mormon colonizer Brigham Young's property, spans State Street at the north side of its intersection with South Temple. Proceed one block north on State Street to **Brigham Young Memorial Park.** This small open space is accented by life-size sculptures of early settlers gardening and performing other outdoor tasks. Cross North Temple Street to **City Creek Park.** This small plaza is marked by a rock-strewn stream and pedestrian paths crisscrossing the area. Follow the paths and stream briefly north and east to the corner of the park, and continue along the sidewalk north into **Memory Grove,** dedicated to Utah's veterans. There are a number of small monuments here. On the west (right) slope are zig-zag paths. Follow these for a moderate climb to Capitol Hill. At the top of the pathway on the left are **The White Chapel,** a former Mormon church building now used primarily for weddings, and **Council Hall,** once housing city and territorial government functions and today a visitors information center and bookstore. On the right (north) are the **State Capitol Building** and grounds. The young trees in Memory Grove, on Capitol Hill, were planted after a freak tornado in August 1999 uprooted literally hundreds of trees in this area, some of them nearly a century old. The grounds and interior of the State Capitol building are scattered with plaques and statues. You can take guided tours of the Capitol. West of the Capitol at 300 North and Main Streets is the **Pioneer Memorial Museum,** an eclectic repository of items related to the period between 1847 and 1947, operated by the Daughters of the Utah Pioneers. It's open Monday–Saturday. Beyond the museum, a series of narrow streets runs north and south down the western slope of Capitol Hill. Filled with some of the oldest homes in the city, the streets are all named for types of fruit or nuts, hence the area's name, **Marmalade Historic District.** Return to the ZCMI Center Mall by following either State Street or Main Street down the hill.

The Wasatch Foothills (3–5 hours)

At 2601 East Sunnyside Avenue (800 South), near the mouth of Emigration Canyon, **This Is the Place Heritage Park** is a tribute to the spot where Brigham Young and the first party of Mormon settlers entered the Salt Lake Valley from the foothills of the Wasatch Mountains. The original portion of the park is built around a granite monument erected in 1947 in honor of the centennial of permanent settlement in the valley. If you walk around the monument, you see bronze figures and frieze panels of the many people and cultures who were part of the taming of the Wild West. A newer portion of the park is called **Old Deseret Village,** and is a living-history museum with authentic and reproduction buildings typical of a community in the mid-to-late 1800s. You can tour all of it, including a guided jaunt through Brigham Young's Forest Farmhouse. Across from Old Deseret, on the south side of Sunnyside Avenue, is the **Hogle Zoo,** which has imaginative activities for children. From Old Deseret or the zoo, follow Sunnyside Avenue west for about three blocks to Foothill Boulevard, then follow Foothill north two blocks to Wakara Way and the entrance to **Research Park,** an enclave of high-tech industries. Three blocks east on Wakara Way is the entrance to **Red Butte Gardens and Arboretum,** which has acres of planned and naturalized gardens, children's discovery areas, ponds, waterfalls, interpretive activities, and miles of mountain trails. The gardens and associated gift shop are open year-round. Leave Red Butte Gardens from the northwestern gate, then follow Red Butte Canyon Road approximately two blocks until the road becomes Stover Street. Continuing west on Stover Street, enter **Fort Douglas,** established in 1862. It was closed as a military installation in 1991 and given to the University of Utah. The fort's red sandstone buildings were made from rock quarried in Red Butte Canyon. On the grounds are a military museum and a cemetery with graves dating from the Civil War era on up through World Wars I and II. From the western side of Fort Douglas, go west three blocks, across the campus of the University of Utah, to the **Utah Museum of Fine Arts,** and enjoy its diverse collection. Follow campus walkways angling northwest about the equivalent of a block to the **Utah Museum of Natural History** in Presidents Circle (roughly 1400 East and 220 South). After studying 200 million years of history in the museum's collection, either retrace your route or inquire at the museum about when and where to catch a public bus to return you to This Is the Place Park.

Dining

INEXPENSIVE

Baba Afghan. Afghan. This small downtown restaurant has a store-front exterior. Inside, Afghani textiles add color to the walls. Specialties include poushtee kebab—grilled lamb marinated in a purée of garlic, onion, and sun-dried grapes, served with balsamic rice caramelized in spices. Try the 20-item buffet lunch (Mon.–Fri.). No smoking. | 55 E. 400 S | 801/596–0786 | $7.95–$14.95 | AE, D, DC, MC, V.

Buffalo Joe's Smokehouse. Barbecue. The right kind of place for barbecue: a little raucous with colorful linens and plenty of napkins. Open-air dining. Kids' menu. No smoking. | 5927 S. State St. | 801/261–3537 | $12–$23 | AE, D, MC, V.

Cowboy Grub. American. Cowboy paraphernalia—lariats, a mounted buffalo head, spurs, etc.—decorates the room and gets you in the mood for the grub: mostly grilled chicken and steaks. Salad bar. Kids' menu. | 2350½ Foothill Blvd.; I–80 to Foothill Dr. | 801/466–8334 | $11–$15 | AE, D, DC, MC, V | Closed Sun.

Cuchina. Continental. This popular eatery is part bakery, part Italian deli, part coffee shop, and part candy store. Scones are a breakfast specialty. Lunch and dinner means ready-to-eat entrées like meat loaf with garlic potatoes, chicken orzo salad with feta cheese and raisins, or salmon fillets stuffed with cheeses and herbs. Fresh soups daily. You can dine on the porch with a view of the garden. | 1026 E. 2nd Ave. | 801/322–3055 | www.cuchina.com | $10–$21 | MC, V.

Desert Edge Brewery. Contemporary. This lively microbrewery has brass-topped tables, loft seating, and lots of music and noise. The favorites include coconut rice with grilled chicken, pasta, and salmon. You can eat on the covered patio. | 273 Trolley Sq | 801/521–8917 | $8–$12 | AE, D, MC, V.

Ginza. Japanese. In a building that once housed a seedy beer bar, this small downtown restaurant is clean and bright, with colorful place settings and fresh flowers year-round. A good choice for sushi novices. Other favorites are the miso soup and chicken donburi. | 209 W. 200 S | 801/322–2224 | $11–$19 | AE, D, DC, MC, V.

Lamb's Restaurant. American. Claiming to be Utah's oldest restaurant (in operation since 1919), this historic building in the heart of downtown draws locals and tourists alike. The original interior and furniture from 1939 remain. Specials include beef tenderloin Stroganoff, baby beef liver, fresh trout and halibut, and a variety of lamb dishes. | 169 S. Main St. | 801/364–7166 | $15–$25 | AE, D, DC, MC, V | Closed Sun.

Litza's For Pizza. Italian. Small dining room with busy take-out pizza business. | 716 E. 400 S | 801/359–5352 | $8–$13 | AE, MC, V | Closed Sun.

Market Street Broiler. Seafood. Sleek black and white tiles with a lot of stainless steel accompany the equally sleek menu here. The signature item is Australian lobster tail, but any fresh seafood grilled over mesquite is also worth a try. The seating is at a counter and tables or, in nice weather, outside on a patio. | 258 S. 1300 E | 801/583–8808 | $13–$43 | AE, D, DC, MC, V.

Mikado. Japanese. The plain elegance of Japanese decorating prevails here, with long uncovered wooden tables adorned only by fresh flowers. The specials include seared ahi tuna and shichimi salmon, as well as soba noodles sautéed with Asian vegetables. Kids' menu. | 67 W. 100 S | 801/328–0929 | $10–$16 | AE, D, DC, MC, V | No lunch.

The Old Spaghetti Factory. Italian. Inside the festive Trolley Square Mall, this familiar chain restaurant serves huge portions of pasta at good prices, which makes it a favorite with groups, students, and families. The dining area is filled with antiques, and eating in the authentic trolley car may appeal to kids. | 600 S. 700 E | 801/521–0424 | $7–$14 | AE, D, DC, MC, V.

Pierpont Cantina. Mexican. You walk through a cactus just inside the revolving doors here. Seating is on three levels; the embossed tin ceiling is striking. The menu includes such Mexican standards as enchiladas and chimichangas, in substantial portions. Kids' menu. No smoking. | 122 W. Pierpont Ave. | 801/364–1222 | $14–$20 | AE, D, DC, MC, V.

Porcupine Pub and Grille. Eclectic. The decor is modern southwestern chic, but the menu really gets around; cherry-barbecue salmon, Thai chicken, a Portobello mushroom sandwich, tequila lime pasta. Dessert lovers go wild for the Chocolate Porcupine: a small chocolate cake (shaped like a porcupine, of course) filled with German chocolate mousse then dipped in milk chocolate, with vanilla-bean ice cream on the side. | 3698 E. Fort Union Blvd.; south of downtown at the mouth of Big Cottonwood Canyon | 801/942–5555 | $9–$22 | AE, D, MC, V.

Rafael's. Mexican. Away from downtown, this modest restaurant is furnished with Native American reproductions, and has wide windows and quiet corner tables. Favorites include chile verde (pork in green chile sauce) and various types of enchiladas. | 889 E. 9400 S, Sandy | 801/561–4545 | $6–$11 | D, MC, V | Closed Sun.

Red Butte Cafe. American. The street is busy outside, and on the inside, windows here are positioned to maximize views of the Wasatch Mountains. The menu is known for salads, sandwiches, and pastas, with a few southwestern dishes. You can also eat at the picnic tables on the patio. | 1414 S. Foothill Blvd. | 801/581–9498 | $7.95–$13 | AE, D, DC, MC, V.

Rio Grande Cafe. Mexican. A local artist's work decorates the walls and funky music plays on the jukebox here. Favorites are the cheese enchiladas, chimichangas, and carnitas. In nice weather, eat outside on the patio. Kids' menu. No smoking. | 270 S. Rio Grande St. | 801/364–3302 | www.riograndecafe.citysearch.com | $4.50–$8.50 | AE, D, MC, V.

Rodizio Grill. Brazilian. The servers sing here when they're not carrying huge slabs of marinated meat to slice and serve at the tables. The lively atmosphere at this Trolley Square establishment also includes music and percussion. Grilled pineapple is a surprise treat. Brazilian and American salad bars. No smoking. | 459 Trolley Sq | 801/220–0500 | www.rodizio.com | $12–$17 | AE, D, DC, MC, V.

Squatter's Pub Brewery. American. An oasis in dry country, here you can sample eight types of home-brewed ales, from pales to stouts, that are made fresh on the premises. The large wooden bar, spacious dining area, and huge windows make the brewery open and comfortable. Try the popular Squatterburger, Margherita pizza, fish-and-chips, and for dessert, homemade bread pudding. | 147 W. Broadway | 801/363–2739 | $12–$24 | AE, D, DC, MC, V.

The Sugar House Barbeque Company. Barbecue. You place your order at the counter and pick it up there, then eat it on paper plates with plastic utensils. The food is the real thing, though, at this restaurant formerly called Redbones. Authentic Memphis-style dry-rubbed ribs, a wide array of smoked meats including pulled pork, beef brisket, and turkey breast. Eat outside at the picnic tables on the patio in nice weather. No smoking. | 2207 S. 700 E | 801/463–4800 | www.redbones.com | $7–$17 | AE, D, DC, MC, V.

Xiao Li. Chinese. Plain wooden tables, white cloth placemats, oriental screens, and Chinese wall hangings decorate the interior here, inside the historic Crane Building. Specialties include shrimp and scallops with wood-ear mushrooms and garlic sauce. | 307 W. 200 S | 801/328–8688 | $7.95–$12.95 | DC, MC, V.

MODERATE

Absolute! Restaurant and Brasserie. Scandinavian. An indoor waterfall sculpture is the backdrop for small tables set on three levels. Specialties include Alaskan salmon chowder, halibut with creamy chardonnay sauce, and lingonberry mousse for desert. | 52 W. 200 S | 801/359–0899 | $20–$30 | AE, MC, V.

Argentine Grill. Continental. Set back from the road with herb and flower gardens spring, summer, and fall, this comfortable place serves such specialties as Milanese chicken, salmon with Dijon sauce, double-cut pork chops, and halibut with apricot brandy sauce. You dine in a glass-enclosed garden room, or eat at the tables on the adjoining patio. Sun. brunch. No smoking. | 6055 S. 900 E | 801/265–0205 | www.argentinegrill.citysearch.com | $14–$22 | AE, D, DC, MC, V.

Baci Trattoria. Italian. A sleek design with a black marble wraparound bar and tiered table arrangement is the setting for the upscale, Italian-inspired food on the menu. The specialties include blackened shrimp, scallop and crab fettuccini, and roasted duck in Grand Marnier and orange sauce. The small patio seats 10. | 134 W. Pierpont Ave. | 801/328–1500 | $10–$35 | AE, D, DC, MC, V.

Bangkok Thai. Thai. For authentic Eastern cuisine with a wide variety of vegetarian and meat dishes, this restaurant is a local favorite. The curry seafood and vegetable dishes are fresh and spicy, and the *padhinmaparn*, stir-fried meat and cashews, is extremely popular. | 1400 S. Foothill Dr. | 801/582–8424 | $14–$25 | AE, D, DC, MC, V | No lunch Sun.

Creekside. Continental. A fireplace and wood-burning pizza ovens contribute to the sensory experience. At the Solitude Ski Resort, the casual restaurant specializes in pizzas and pastas. In nice weather you can dine on the sundeck. Kids' menu. No smoking. | Solitude Resort; Big Cottonwood Canyon, Rte. 152 | 801/536–5787 | $15–$30 | AE, D, DC, MC, V | Closed Mon.–Tues. in summer.

Diamond Lil's. American. Once a brewery, it's been re-created to resemble an old country jail. The favorites are also old-fashioned: prime rib, chicken, and fish. Kids' menu. No smoking. | 460 S. 1000 E | 801/359–6090 | $10.95–$32 | AE, D, DC, MC, V | No lunch.

Market Street Grill. American. Like its offspring the Market Street Broiler, this place has stylish black-and-white decor and simple tables. It also serves a wide selection of seafood, including swordfish and trout, as well as pastas and salads. | 48 W. Market St. | 801/322–4668 | $13–$52 | AE, D, DC, MC, V.

Oasis Cafe. Vegetarian. An adjacent bookstore, rosy floor tiles, and wide, uncurtained windows create a welcoming environment. Specialties are the pastas and sandwiches. A large beverage selection includes teas, coffees, fresh juices, but no carbonation. | 151 S. 500 E | 801/322–0404 | $15–$27 | AE, D, DC, MC, V.

Santa Fe Restaurant. Southwestern. This establishment in scenic Emigration Canyon is well known for inventive entrées like seared Atlantic salmon roulade, tequila-lime glazed shrimp, and chili-spiced duck breast. The dining room is elegant with table linens, candles, windows, and skylights. Views of the surrounding mountains, from inside and from the outdoor patio, are worth the drive. | 2100 Emigration Canyon | 801/582–5888 | $24–$37 | MC, V | No lunch Sat. No dinner Sun.

EXPENSIVE

★ **The Aerie.** French/Continental. Elegant dining and breathtaking views unite here on the 10th floor of the Cliff Lodge at Snowbird, at the base of the mountain. The dining room is decorated with Chinese art from the owner's collection. The specialties include rabbit ravioli and duck breast with fresh seasonal fruit sauce. There's a sushi bar in winter. Kids' menu. Sun. brunch. No smoking. | Rte. 210 | 801/742–2222, ext. 550 | www.snowbird.com | Reservations essential | $14–$26 | AE, D, DC, MC, V | No lunch. Breakfast in winter only.

La Caille. French. Peacocks on the lawn and swans on the pond add to the already strong country estate atmosphere. The château-style building is surrounded by 22 acres of gardens and vineyards, with a pond. You can pick your view—the top floor has a mountain view, the main floor the pond and vineyards, and the ground floor, with a glass-ceilinged garden room, a close-up view of the garden. Specialties include duck à l'orange and rack of lamb. Sun. brunch. | 9565 S. Wasatch Blvd. | 801/942–1751 | www.lacaille.com | Reservations preferred | $40–$60 | AE, D, DC, MC, V | No lunch.

Log Haven. Contemporary. Built in 1920 and restored as a restaurant in 1994, this log mansion is simple and spacious, with a large, uncrowded patio for outdoor dining. The award-winning menu's signature dishes include lemon lacquered duck confit and coriander-rubbed ahi tuna. The vegetarian entrées are tasty and imaginative, like fresh calamata olive linguini. Kids' menu. | 6451 E. Millcreek Canyon; Exit 3900 S. off I–215 to Millcreek Canyon, east of downtown | 801/272–8255 | www.log-haven.com | $13–$30 | AE, D, DC, MC, V | No lunch.

The New Yorker and the Café at the New Yorker. Continental. In the basement of what used to be the New York Hotel, built in 1906, this café and dining room has backlit skylights and mirrors to good effect. Palm trees are scattered throughout. Seafood is prominent on the menu, which changes according to what is flown in fresh daily. They are also known for game, such as elk, and beef, simply prepared and of high quality. Seating is in booths and tables; the café section is more casual. | 60 W. Market St. | 801/363–0166 | Reservations recommended for dining room | $12–$33 | AE, D, DC, MC, V | Closed Sun. No lunch Sat.

The Shallow Shaft. Southwestern. At the only restaurant at Alta not affiliated with a lodge, you can wear a casual attitude and casual dress both. The views down the canyon are good. Specialties include crab-stuffed mushroom caps, smoked salmon quesadilla, and rack of lamb with an ancho chili sauce. | Alta; 8 mi east via Rte. 210, in Little Cottonwood Canyon | 801/742–2177 | $26–$50 | AE, MC, V.

Steak Pit. American. Views and food take precedence over interior design at this Snowbird ski area steak house. The dining room is warm and unpretentious, with some wood paneling and an expanse of glass. The menu offers well-prepared steak, chicken, baked potatoes, and fish. | Snowbird Plaza Ctr., Rte. 210 | 801/742–2222 | $14–$39 | AE, D, DC, MC, V | No lunch.

Tuscany. Italian. The dining room in this out-of-town restaurant has high ceilings, plaster walls, dark woodwork, and a Tuscan style. Favorites include "hearthbreads," which are essentially pizzas. You can also dine on the patio. Sun. brunch. | 2832 E. 6200 S; I–215 to Holladay, east of downtown | 801/277–9919 | $20–$45; brunch $14 | AE, DC, MC, V.

Lodging

INEXPENSIVE

Alta Lodge. In Little Cottonwood Canyon, this is the original lodge at Alta Ski Area, built in 1939. Wings were added later with wall-wide windows or two walls of glass in corner rooms to make excellent views. It remains a good value for the money. Restaurant, bar. No TV in rooms, cable TV in common area. Hot tub, sauna. Downhill and cross-country skiing. Children's programs (ages 3–12). Laundry facilities. Business services. | 57 rooms, 7 with shower only | Rte. 210 | 801/742–3500 or 800/707–2582 | fax 801/742–3504 | info@altalodge.com | www.altalodge.com | $75–$300 | D, MC, V | Closed May and Oct. | AP.

Anton Boxrud Bed & Breakfast. This historic three-story Victorian home is ½ block from the Governor's Mansion. You can walk to museums and other cultural sites. The amenities include chocolates and fresh flowers in each room. Complimentary breakfast. Hot tub. Airport shuttle. No smoking. | 7 rooms | 57 S. 600 E | 801/363–8035 or 800/524–5511 | fax 801/596–1316 | www.netoriginals.com/antonboxrud/index.html | $80–$150 | MC, V.

Best Western-Salt Lake Plaza. Within walking distance of shopping, restaurants, Temple Square, and the Delta Center, this is a good place to stay if you are interested in the city's history and culture. Restaurant, room service. In-room data ports, some refrigerators. Cable TV. Pool. Hot tub. Exercise equipment. Laundry facilities. Business services. Airport shuttle. Pets allowed (fee). | 226 rooms | 122 W. South Temple St. | 801/521–0130 | fax 801/322–5057 | sales@plaza-hotel.com | www.plaza-hotel.com | $80–$125 | AE, D, DC, MC, V.

Brighton Ski Resort. Situated slope-side, the lodge boasts a tradition of friendliness, comfort, and affordability. Rooms are basic and comfortable, with no frills. Bar. Refrigerators, TV in common room. Pool. Hot tub. Downhill and cross-country skiing. | 22 rooms | Star Route, Brighton | 801/532–4731 or 800/873–5512 | fax 801/649–1787 | www.skibrighton.com | $90–$125 | AE, D, MC, V.

Cavanaugh's Olympus Hotel. Close to I–15 exits and refurbished in 1999, this downtown high-rise is within walking distance of the Salt Palace convention center and Delta Center. The restaurant on the top floors is popular locally. Restaurant. Cable TV. Pool. Barbershop, hot tub. Exercise equipment. Business services. Airport shuttle. | 393 rooms | 161 W. 600 S | 801/521–7373 | fax 801/524–0378 | www.cavanaughs.com | $75–$95 | AE, D, DC, MC, V.

Comfort Inn. With easy freeway and resort access, this offers a good location to take advantage of the southward movement of business and shopping in the valley. Complimentary Continental breakfast. In-room data ports. Cable TV, VCRs (movies). Indoor pool. Hot tub. Business services. | 97 rooms | 8955 S. 255 W., Sandy | 801/255–4919 | fax 801/255–4998 | www.comfortinn.com | $80–$100 | AE, D, DC, MC, V.

Comfort Inn Airport. The furnishings make this new facility a more upscale property than many in this chain. Restaurant. Some microwaves, refrigerators. Cable TV. Pool. Hot tub. Business services. Airport shuttle. Pets allowed (fee). | 154 rooms | 200 N. Admiral Byrd Rd. | 801/537–7444 or 800/535–8742 | fax 801/532–4721 | www.comfortinn.com | $85–$130 | AE, D, MC, V.

Courtyard by Marriott. The large desks with data ports and spacious work areas were designed for business travelers. The hotel is a standout in a cluster of properties just off I–15 and next to a factory outlet mall. Restaurant, bar, room service. In-room data ports.

Cable TV. Indoor pool. Hot tub. Exercise equipment. Laundry facilities. Business services. | 124 rooms | 10701 Holiday Park Dr., Sandy | 801/571–3600 | fax 801/572–1383 | www.courtyard.com | $90 | AE, D, DC, MC, V.

Crystal Inn. Two blocks from Temple Square, this four-story property is close to restaurants and offices. The spacious rooms include sitting and work areas, and you can get a second phone line if you need one. Complimentary breakfast. In-room data ports, microwaves, refrigerators. Cable TV. Indoor pool. Hot tub. Exercise equipment. Laundry facilities. Business services. Airport shuttle. | 175 rooms | 230 W. 500 S | 801/328–4466 or 800/366–4466 | fax 801/328–4072 | www.crystalinns.com | $85–$100 | AE, D, DC, MC, V.

Days Inn Airport. Halfway between downtown and the airport, this renovated hotel has good amenities for both families and business travelers. Complimentary Continental breakfast. In-room data ports, some refrigerators and microwaves. Cable TV. Indoor pool. Business services. Airport shuttle. Pets allowed. | 110 rooms | 1900 W. North Temple | 801/539–8538 | www.daysinn.com | $75 | AE, D, DC, MC, V.

Hampton Inn Sandy. Within walking distance of South Towne Mall and 1 mi from the Jordan Temple, the inn is 15 mi south of Salt Lake City. Ski resorts are an easy drive, and there are restaurants nearby. Complimentary Continental breakfast. In-room data ports. Cable TV. Indoor pool. Hot tub. Laundry facilities. Business services. | 131 rooms | 10690 S. Holiday Park Dr., Sandy | 801/571–0800 | www.hamptoninn.com | $75–$100 | AE, D, DC, MC, V.

Hampton Inn Salt Lake City–North. This is a good alternative to pricier downtown lodgings yet still within easy reach of Salt Lake City. Eight miles north of downtown, the five-story hotel is close to businesses and restaurants. Complimentary Continental breakfast. In-room data ports. Cable TV. Indoor pool. Hot tub. Laundry facilities. Business services. Airport shuttle. Pets allowed. | 60 rooms | 2393 S. 800 W., Woods Cross | 801/296–1211 | fax 801/296–1222 | www.cottontree.net/hampton | $75–$95 | AE, D, DC, MC, V.

Hilton Salt Lake Center. Formerly the Doubletree, this property changed names and was completely renovated in 2000. Excellent location. The rooms are spacious and done in jewel tones decor. Restaurants, room service. In-room data ports, some refrigerators. Cable TV. Indoor pool. Hot tub. Exercise equipment. Business services. Airport shuttle. | 500 rooms | 255 S. West Temple St. | 801/328–2000 | fax 801/359–2938 | www.hilton.com | $90–$125 | AE, D, DC, MC, V.

Holiday Inn–Downtown. The tennis court, putting green, and playground are nice extras if you want to stay downtown but still be active. Just south of the major business district, this hotel is convenient to everything and has a lot of restaurants nearby. Restaurant, bar. Some refrigerators. Cable TV. Indoor-outdoor pool. Hot tub. Putting green, tennis. Exercise equipment. Playground. Laundry facilities. Business services. Airport shuttle. | 292 rooms, 14 suites | 999 S. Main St. | 801/359–8600 | fax 801/359–7186 | www.holiday-inn.com/hotel/slcdn/welcome.html | $75–$119 | AE, D, DC, MC, V.

Holiday Inn Express Airport. Between the airport and downtown, this convenient no-frills motel costs less and has more amenities than many area lodgings. Restaurant, Continental breakfast. In-room data ports. Cable TV. Pool. Airport shuttle. | 93 rooms | 2080 W. North Temple St. | 801/355–0088 or 800/465–4329 | fax 801/355–0099 | $99 | AE, D, DC, MC, V.

Inn at Temple Square. A nice alternative to the chains, this 1930, seven-story, downtown brick hotel has rooms with a 1930s style. The wallpaper is flowered, and some rooms have chaises longues. The high-ceilinged lobby has a chandelier and fireplace. The Salt Palace Convention Center is across the street. Restaurant, complimentary Continental breakfast, room service. Refrigerators. Cable TV. Business services. Airport shuttle. No smoking. | 90 rooms, 10 suites | 71 W. South Temple St. | 801/531–1000 or 800/843–4668 | fax 801/536–7272 | www.theinn.com | $90–$150 | AE, D, DC, MC, V.

La Quinta. A bit south of the city, this is one of the first South Valley motels, although remodeling and new furnishings keep it fresh. The building has a Spanish Mission look, with a red-tile roof over the entry. Rooms are spacious, with large TVs and desks with data ports.

Continental breakfast. In-room data ports. Cable TV. Pool. Hot tub. Laundry facilities. Business services. Pets allowed. | 121 rooms | 7231 S. Catalpa Rd., Midvale | 801/566–3291 | fax 801/562–5943 | www.laquinta.com | $60 | AE, D, DC, MC, V.

Little America Hotel and Towers. This is a pleasant low-rise, spread-out property with large, comfortable rooms at reasonable prices. Lots of amenities, including a great daily breakfast buffet. Restaurant. Some refrigerators. Cable TV. 2 pools, 1 indoor, wading pool. Barbershop, beauty salon, hot tub. Gym. Business services. Airport shuttle. | 850 rooms | 500 S. Main St. | 801/363–6781 | fax 801/596–5910 | lahinfo@lamerica.com | www.lamerica.com | $85–$174 | AE, D, DC, MC, V.

Peery Hotel. A turn-of-the-century hotel with some furnishings harkening back to that era in every room. Restaurant, bar, complimentary Continental breakfast. Cable TV. Hot tub. Exercise equipment. Business services. Airport shuttle. | 77 rooms | 110 W. 300 S | 801/521–4300 or 800/331–0073 | fax 801/575–5014 | www.citysearchslc.peery | $85–$140 | AE, D, DC, MC, V.

Quality Inn–Midvalley. Affordable and nicely appointed but not posh. The two-story motel has large rooms with desks. You're about 15 minutes from downtown, and the interstate is within easy reach. Complimentary Continental breakfast. In-room data ports. Cable TV. Pool. Hot tub. Laundry facilities. Business services. Airport shuttle. | 132 rooms | 4465 Century Dr. | 801/268–2533 | fax 801/266–6206 | www.qualityinn.com | $80–$95 | AE, D, DC, MC, V.

Radisson Airport. Close to the airport but only ten minutes from downtown, this is a good choice for business travelers. The outdoor pool is open year-round. Restaurant, room service, complimentary Continental breakfast. Cable TV. Pool. Exercise equipment. Business services. Airport shuttle. | 127 rooms, 46 suites | 2177 W. North Temple St. | 801/364–5800 | fax 801/364–5823 | said@radisson.com | www.radisson.com | $95–$160 | AE, D, DC, MC, V.

Ramada Inn–Downtown. The spacious rooms with work areas, a large pool in a courtyard, proximity to the convention center, and modest rates make this a good value. Restaurant, room service. In-room data ports. Cable TV. Indoor pool. Hot tub. Exercise equipment. Laundry facilities. Business services. Airport shuttle. Some pets allowed. | 160 rooms | 230 W. 600 S | 801/364–5200 | fax 801/364–0974 | www.ramadainnslc.com | $60–$85 | AE, D, DC, MC, V.

Reston Hotel. Corner rooms have king-size beds and couches, and some of the rooms have refrigerators. The hotel is close to the city's corporate areas. Continental breakfast, room service. Cable TV. Indoor pool. Hot tub. Conference rooms. | 96 rooms, 2 suites | 5335 College Dr. | 801/264–1054 or 800/231–9710 | fax 801/264–1054 | $71–$79, $130 suites | AE, D, DC, MC, V.

Rustler Lodge. The six-bed dorm rooms are good for families or groups on a budget. If you're not on a budget, the deluxe corner rooms have spacious sitting areas and sofa beds, along with mountain views. You can ski in and ski out to the Alta Ski Resort. The amenities are the same for everyone and include an early morning stretch class. Spa services like massages, facials, and aromatherapy are also available. Restaurant. No air-conditioning. Some cable TV in rooms. Common room with cable TV. Pool. Hot tub. Downhill and cross-country skiing. Laundry facilities. | 85 rooms | Rte. 210 | 801/733–0190 or 800/451–5223 | fax 801/742–3832 | www.rustlerlodge.com | $118–$569 | No credit cards | Closed May and Oct. | AP.

Saltair Bed & Breakfast. In a quiet residential neighborhood that's close to downtown, the inn was built in 1903 and is furnished in keeping with the period. You can also stay in the bungalow, the two Alpine cottages, or one of the five suites. On the Utah historic register, it is close to downtown. Complimentary breakfast, afternoon snacks. Some microwaves, refrigerators. Cable TV in some rooms, some room phones. Hot tub. No smoking. | 8 rooms, 3 share baths, 2 with shower only, 5 suites | 164 S. 900 E | 801/533–8184 or 800/733–8184 (reservations) | fax 801/595–0332 | saltair@saltlakebandb.com | www.saltlakebandb.com | $79–$149 | AE, D, MC, V.

Shilo Inn. Across the street from the Salt Palace Convention Center, this 12-story property has spacious rooms and shuttles to the ski resorts. Restaurant, complimentary breakfast. Microwaves, refrigerators. Cable TV, VCRs (movies). Pool. Hot tub. Exercise equipment.

Laundry facilities. Free parking. Business services. Airport shuttle. | 200 rooms | 206 S. West Temple St. | 801/521–9500 | fax 801/359–6527 | $80–$110 | AE, D, DC, MC, V.

Sleep Inn. In the quiet southwest end of the valley near the Mormon Jordan River Temple, the inn has modest rates that make it a good alternative to pricier resorts or downtown accommodations. The rooms have comfortable sitting areas and supersized showers. Complimentary Continental breakfast. In-room data ports. Cable TV, VCRs (movies). Indoor pool. Laundry facilities. Business services. | 68 rooms, shower only | 10676 S. 300 W, South Jordan | 801/572–2020 | fax 801/572–2459 | sleep-saltlake@travelbase.com | $70–$85 | AE, D, DC, MC, V.

Travelodge City Center. The rooms were renovated in 2000, and the rates are modest given the convenient downtown location, just off an I–15 exit. Rooms are plain but comfortable. Cable TV. Pool. Hot tub. Business services. | 60 rooms | 524 S. West Temple St. | 801/531–7100 | fax 801/359–3814 | www.travelodge.com | $55–$75 | AE, D, DC, MC, V.

University Park Marriott. Proximity to the Red Butte Gardens Arboretum makes this a good stopping place if you're a garden lover. The University of Utah campus is also close, as are restaurants and downtown attractions. Restaurant, bar. Microwaves, refrigerators in suites. Cable TV. Indoor pool. Hot tub. Exercise equipment. Business services. Airport shuttle. | 218 rooms, 28 suites | 480 Wakara Way | 801/581–1000 | fax 801/584–3321 | www.marriott.com | $89–$159 | AE, D, DC, MC, V.

Wildflowers Bed & Breakfast. An elegant "painted lady" Victorian house with a quiet, private yard, the inn was built in 1891. The interior has been renovated to bring in more light. The rooms are furnished in keeping with the period. If you're traveling with a group, you can also reserve the full-floor suite that has a full kitchen and dining room. Complimentary full breakfast. No smoking. | 5 rooms | 936 E. 1700 S | 801/466–0600 or 800/569–0009 (reservations) | fax 801/466–4728 | lark2spur@aol.com | www.wildflowersbb.com | $85–$145 | AE, D, MC, V.

Wyndham Hotel. You're minutes from two malls and Temple Square, close to the Delta Center and Abravanel Hall, and 30 minutes from ski resorts. The rooms are comfortable and have work areas. Restaurant, bar. In-room data ports. Cable TV. Indoor pool. Hot tub. Exercise equipment. Laundry facilities. Business services. Airport shuttle. | 381 rooms | 215 W. South Temple St. | 801/531–7500 | fax 801/531–9282 | www.travelweb.com | $95–$125 | AE, D, DC, MC, V.

MODERATE

The Anniversary Inn at Kahn Mansion. This Victorian-style mansion is famed for its unusual and at times over-the-top theme rooms. The Kahn Mansion and Country Villa suites are among the more traditional ones. The more adventurous can try the Tom Sawyer Room (the bed is on a log raft), the Jackson Hole Suite (the bed is in a covered wagon), and the Fisherman's Wharf Suite (with extensive murals, a ship bed, and a cavelike bathroom). All rooms have jetted two-person tubs. Continental breakfast. TV, VCRs. | 13 rooms | 678 E. South Temple St. | 801/363–4900 | fax 801/328–9955 | $119–$249 | AE, D, DC, MC, V.

Armstrong Mansion. The theme rooms are named for the months and decorated in a subtly seasonal style that's in keeping with the 1893 Victorian mansion's origins. The brick inn is set back from the street, with a front yard, trees, and hedges. December Dreams has dark green and dark red walls, a brass bed, and a fireplace, while the March room is all fresh and elegant whites, down to the gauze hung over the all-white bed. Restaurants, shopping, and Temple Square are close. Complimentary breakfast. Cable TV, VCRs. No smoking. | 13 rooms, 4 with shower only | 667 E. 100 S | 801/531–1333 or 800/708–1333 | fax 801/531–0282 | armstrong@vii.mail.com | www.armstrong-bb.com | $99–$229 | AE, D, DC, MC, V.

Brigham Street Inn. Built in 1898, this downtown two-story brick mansion has rooms that range from one twin bed to a suite with a sleep sofa, full kitchen, and private garden entrance. Each room is different; one is done in dark blue, with an elaborately carved fireplace mantel, another is airy, done in white and mauve. Some rooms connect. Many restaurants are nearby. Complimentary Continental breakfast. Cable TV. Business services. | 9 rooms | 1135

E. South Temple St. | 801/364–4461 | fax 801/521–3201 | www.brighamstreetinn.citysearch.com | $125–$185 | AE, D, DC MC, V.

Chase Suite Hotel. These airy and spacious suites have vaulted ceilings, fireplaces, full kitchens, and sitting areas. Each suite has two telephones, two TVs, plus high-speed Internet access and free videos. Only 30 minutes from most ski facilities, the hotel can be an alternative to pricey all-suite lodging at the resorts. Full breakfast. Microwaves. Cable TV, VCRs. Outdoor pool. Hot tub. Conference rooms. Airport shuttle. Pets allowed. | 150 suites | 765 E. 400 S | 801/532–5511 | fax 801/531–0416 | $159 | AE, D, DC, MC, V.

★ **Cliff Lodge.** This angular gray ski lodge next to Snowbird Ski Area echoes the craggy mountains at its front door. The rooms range from basic to deluxe, and suites are available. Appointments at the full-service spa are highly sought-after year-round. Restaurant. Some refrigerators. Cable TV. 2 pools, 1 rooftop. Hot tub. Barbershop, beauty salon, spa. Tennis. Gym. Downhill skiing. Supervised children's programs (ages infant–13). Laundry facilities. Business services. Airport shuttle. | 370 rooms | Rte. 210 | 801/742–2222 or 800/453–3000 | fax 801/742–3204 | www.snowbird.com | $160–$210 | AE, D, DC, MC, V.

Embassy Suites. The entrance strikes a cool, relaxing note, and the suites are spacious. You are close to restaurants, shopping, and church facilities. Restaurant, complimentary breakfast. In-room data ports. Microwaves, refrigerators. Cable TV. Indoor pool. Hot tub. Exercise equipment. Laundry facilities. Business services. Airport shuttle. | 241 suites | 110 W. 600 S | 801/359–7800 | fax 801/359–3753 | www.embassysuites.com | $130–$200 | AE, D, DC, MC, V.

Iron Blossam Lodge. One of the several lodging choices at Snowbird, this condominium lodging has studios, bedrooms with lofts, and one-bedroom suites. Many have fireplaces and balconies. Restaurant. Cable TV. 2 pools. Hot tub. Tennis. Exercise equipment. Downhill skiing. Children's programs (May–Oct.). Laundry facilities. Business services. Airport shuttle. | 159 rooms, 125 kitchenettes | Rte. 210 | 801/742–2222 or 800/453–3000 | fax 801/742–3445 | www.snowbird.com | $109–$769 | AE, D, DC, MC, V | Closed 1 week Nov., 1 week May.

La Europa Royale. Lawns surround this elegant mansion 5 mi south of the Salt Lake City. The mauve and blue rooms have three-sided glassed-in fireplaces separating them from the oversize whirlpool baths. Dine in the airy atrium or outside on the patio surrounded by gardens. The ZCMI and other stores are 1½-mi away, and at least 20 restaurants are within a mile. You can hear waterfalls from the walking path. Picnic area, complimentary breakfast. Business services. No smoking. | 9 rooms | 1135 E. Vine St. | 801/263–7999 | fax 801/263–8090 | www.laeuropa.com | $129–$250 | AE, D, DC, MC, V.

Sheraton Salt Lake City. A full-service hotel and convention center at the center of town, the Sheraton has completed a total renovation of the rooms and common areas. The huge lobby, with oversize chairs and fireplace, is elegant and comfortable, and the rooms are spacious, with numerous perks like balconies, morning newspaper, and coffee. Convenient to both the airport and downtown Salt Lake. Restaurant, bar. In-room data ports. Cable TV. Outdoor pool. Beauty salon, hot tub, sauna, Exercise room. Conference rooms. Business services. | 270 rooms, 50 suites | 150 W. 500 S | 801/532–3344 or 800/421–7602 | fax 801/531–0705 | $119–$178 rooms, $129–$189 suites | AE, D, DC, MC, V.

EXPENSIVE

Hotel Monaco Salt Lake City. The hip place to stay in downtown Salt Lake, this full-service hotel in the old Continental Bank Building evokes the plush style of 1940s Hollywood. The early Art Deco–inspired rooms, with green-and-cream striped wallpaper and mahogany furniture, feel luxurious, and have extra comfort details like terry-cloth robes and essential oils. You can even adopt a goldfish for your room during your stay. Room service. In-room data ports. Health club. Laundry service. Conference rooms. Business services. | 193 rooms, 32 suites | 15 W. 200 S | 801/595–0000 or 877/294–9710 | fax 801/532–8500 | $225, $265–$340 suites | AE, D, DC, MC, V.

Marriott Hotel. Large and convenient, this chain hotel has spacious rooms and a lovely indoor pool. You are close to the Salt Palace Convention Center and Crossroads Mall and ½ block from

Temple Square. Restaurant. In-room data ports. Cable TV. Indoor-outdoor pool. Hot tub. Exercise equipment. Laundry facilities. Business services. Airport shuttle. | 515 rooms | 75 S. West Temple St. | 801/531–0800 | fax 801/532–4127 | www.marriott.com | $205 | AE, D, DC, MC, V.

Wolfe Krest Bed & Breakfast. One of the landmarks of Capitol Hill, this stately Georgian Revival manor stands across the street from the Capitol Building in downtown Salt Lake. The individually decorated rooms are all elegant; some have fourposters and window seats in the bay windows. All have fireplaces and Jacuzzis. The patio gives you a good view of the sunrise. You can relax in the many lounge and patio areas. Dining room, full breakfast. Cable TV, VCRs. Conference room. | 13 rooms | 273 N. E. Capitol Blvd. | 801/521–8710 or 800/669–4525 | fax 801/531–0522 | $150–$300 | AE, D, DC, MC, V.

SPRINGDALE

MAP 14, B9

(Nearby towns also listed: Cedar City, Kanab, St. George)

Springdale is only a mile from the official entrance to Zion National Park, but a mile makes a huge difference in perspective. From Springdale's position at the mouth of Zion Canyon, soaring cliffs and massive formations spread out like the perfect set of postcards. As is the case in many gateway towns, Springdale's main road is lined with motels, souvenir shops, and restaurants, but look up from virtually any place in town and you'll be reminded why you made the trip.

SPRINGDALE

INTRO
ATTRACTIONS
DINING
LODGING

Information: Washington County Travel and Convention Bureau | 425 S. 700 E, St. George, 84770 | 435/634–5747 or 800/869–6635 | fax 435/628–1619.

Attractions

O. C. Tanner Amphitheater. This performance venue is set amid huge sandstone boulders at the base of the enormous red cliffs spilling south from Zion National Park. *The Grand Circle* is a multimedia presentation on the Southwest that shows nightly at dusk from Memorial Day to Labor Day. Also in summer, live concerts are held at the amphitheater each weekend, and could be anything from local country-music bands to the Utah Symphony Orchestra. | Lion Blvd. | 435/652–7994 | www.dixie.edu/community/ | Varies depending on program | May–Oct., daily.

Springdale Fruit Company. Surrounded by apple orchards, this small market is an interesting and healthy stop. The store carries freshly squeezed juices, organic fruit and vegetables, a huge variety of trail mix concoctions, and bakery items. A picnic area is behind the market. | 2491 Zion Park Blvd. | 435/772–3222 | Daily 8–dusk.

Zion Canyon Theatre. A 37-minute film, *Zion, Treasure of the Gods*, is shown once an hour in a 500-seat auditorium on a screen 80 ft wide and 6 stories high. Though it doesn't portray the history of this area in an altogether accurate way, it is a spectacular visual experience. | 145 Zion Park Blvd. (Rte. 9) | 435/772–2400 or 888/256–FILM | www.ziontheatre.com | $7.50 | Apr.–Oct., daily 9–9; Nov.– Mar., daily 11–7.

Zion National Park. *See* Zion National Park, *below.* | North of Springdale.

ON THE CALENDAR

MAR.: *St. Patrick's Day Celebration.* An eclectic parade led by a bagpipe band, a green Jell-O "bake-off" and sculpting contest, children's activities, and evening concert. | Zion Park Blvd. | 435/772–3244.

SEPT.: *Southern Utah Folklife Festival.* A three-day event highlights southern Utah's culture, traditional arts, and folkways with storytelling, a crafts market, quilting, music and dance, and demonstrations of historic methods of food preparation. | 435/673–6290 or 800/809–6635.

Dining

The Bit and Spur. Southwestern. Informal, with two small dining rooms; favorites run from the taco, enchilada, and pinto bean combo to chili-seared scallops with Asian dumplings. Open-air dining on a wraparound porch. There's live music Friday and Saturday. | 1212 Zion Park Blvd. | 435/772–3498 | $12–$21 | AE, D, MC, V.

Bumbleberry Inn. American. Famous for its homemade, one-of-a-kind bumbleberry pie (a combination of burple and binkle berries) and bumbleberry specials like pancakes and stuffed French toast, this local favorite is convenient to the park and area lodging. The salmon fish-and-chips, burgers, marinated chicken breast, fresh trout, and steak specials are also popular. | 897 Zion Park Blvd. | 435/772–3611 | $10–$20 | D, MC, V.

Flannigan's. American. An intimate restaurant at the center of town, this establishment is done in southwestern pastels with old photographs of Utah and has views of nearby Zion Canyon. Mesquite-roasted chicken, Road Creek trout, rabbit, and pork medallions are specialties of the house. A full range of wines is available from the wine cellar. | 428 Zion Park Blvd. | 435/772–3244 | $15–$30 | AE, D, MC, V.

Log House Restaurant. American. This attractive log-cabin restaurant has picture windows that look out over the canyons, a massive copper roof, and Native American–style furnishings. Although basically a meat and potatoes establishment, its newly expanded vegetarian menu offers fresh vegetable and pasta dishes as well. | 2400 Zion Park Blvd. | 435/772–3000 | $10–$25 | AE, DC, MC, V.

Pioneer Lodge and Restaurant. American. A good place to take the family, this rustic country diner with log walls and a fireplace serves meat and potatoes dishes, fish, and pasta, and has a full salad bar and homemade rolls. Try the homemade ice-cream pie for dessert. | 828 Zion Park Blvd. | 435/772–3009 | $8–$20 | AE, D, MC, V.

The Switchback Grille and Trading Company. Contemporary. Crowded with locals and visitors alike, this restaurant is one of the best in the area for wood-fired pizzas, ribs, and vegetarian dishes. The vaulted ceilings make the dining room open and comfortable. Try the excellent Portobello sandwich for lunch, and don't miss the smoothies, which are rare in Utah. | 1149 S. Zion Park Blvd. | 435/772–3777 | $15–$30 | AE, D, MC, V.

Zion Pizza and Noodle Company. Italian. Housed in the former Springdale LDS (Mormon) church, this is one of the town's most intriguing eating places. Tables are on an outside patio, a covered porch of sorts, in the main restaurant, and on the front apron overlooking Zion Park Blvd. Beer and ale are on tap. House specialties are pastas, salads, calzones, and pizzas baked in slate ovens for the perfect crisp crust. | 868 Zion Park Blvd. | 435/772–3815 | www.southernutah.com | $8–$13 | AE, D, MC, V | Closed Dec.

Lodging

Canyon Ranch Motel. These small cottage facilities tucked away from the highway are peaceful and well appointed. Rooms are basic and bright, and the lawn area is nice with large shade trees, picnic tables, and swings. Picnic area. TV in rooms. Pool. Hot tub. | 22 rooms in cottages | 668 Zion Park Blvd. | 435/772–3357 | fax 435/772–3057 | $58–$88 | AE, D, MC, V.

Cliffrose Lodge & Gardens. A riverfront property on five acres of landscaped lawns and gardens with views of Zion Canyon, the lodge has contemporary rooms and a lot of space for children to run around in. Cable TV. Pool. Playground. Pets allowed (fee). | 36 rooms | 281 Zion Park Blvd. | 435/772–3234 or 800/243–8824 | fax 435/772–3900 | clifrose@infowest.com | www.cliffrose.com | $109–$145 | AE, D, MC, V.

Flanigan's Inn. Close to the park with canyon views, this rustic country inn has contemporary furnishings. You can catch a shuttle to Zion on the property and walk to the visitors center. Restaurant, complimentary Continental breakfast. Cable TV. Heated pool. Business services. | 33 rooms | 428 Zion Park Blvd. | 435/772–3244 or 800/765–7787 | fax 435/772–3396 | www.flanigans.com | $39–$169 | AE, D, MC, V.

The Harvest House. A half-mile from the park entrance, this attractive pioneer-house inn with large wraparound porch caters to hikers and peace-and-quiet seekers. You can relax on the deck overlooking the koi pond or in the hot tub, which has a view of Watchman Peak, or spend time in the quiet, tasteful rooms, none of which has a telephone or television. Full breakfast. Hot tub. | 4 rooms | 29 Canyon View Dr. | 435/772–3880 | fax 435/772–3327 | $90–$110 | MC, V.

O'Toole's Under the Eaves Guest House. Built in 1929, this exquisite sandstone guest house is one of the nicest properties in Springdale. Rooms are bright with warm tones and antiques, and the grounds are beautifully landscaped with native plants and flowers. Two rooms in the main house share a bathroom, and the large room, which takes up the second floor of the house, has a gorgeous cathedral window and antique tub. Full breakfast. | 6 rooms, 4 with bath | 980 Zion Park Blvd. | 435/772–3457 | $69–$125 | D, MC, V.

Pioneer Lodge. About a mile from the park's south entrance, this Western-style two-story motel has some family apartments with full kitchens and sitting areas. The rooms are spacious if a bit dated, and the views of the Zion cliffs are wonderful. Restaurant. Cable TV. Pool. Hot tub. | 39 rooms, 2 apartments | 838 Zion Park Blvd. | 435/772–3233 | fax 435/772–3165 | $69, $129–$159 apartments | AE, D, DC, MC, V.

Snow Family Guest Ranch. This working horse ranch, on 12 acres of pastureland adjacent to Zion National Park, has comfortable ranch-style guest rooms with log furniture and inviting common areas. You can take trail rides on the property for an extra fee. Full breakfast. TV in common area. Pool. Hot tub. | 9 rooms | 633 E. Rte. 9, Virgin | 435/635–2500 or 877/655–7669 | fax 435/635–2758 | $89–$109 | AE, D, MC, V.

Terrace Brook Lodge. A mile from Zion's west entrance, the lodge has panoramic views and is close to restaurants and shopping, but away from the commercial district. Family rooms available. Picnic area. Cable TV. Heated pool. | 27 rooms | 990 Zion Park Blvd. | 435/772–3932 or 800/342–6779 | $39–$79 | D, MC, V.

Zion Canyon Campground Cabins and Motel. Nestled under a red-rock canyon and adjacent to the Virgin River, this private RV campground has cabins and a small motel on the premises. One family cabin sleeps up to four people, and river access and shade trees make it a great place during the summer. Pizzeria, picnic area. Cable TV. Pool. Recreation room. Laundry facilities. | 6 rooms, 12 cabins | 479 Zion Park Blvd. | 435/772–3237 | fax 435/772–3844 | $65–$75 rooms, $40–$60 cabins | MC, V.

Zion Park Inn. Springdale's largest property, with sophisticated amenities, including a liquor store. Restaurant, picnic area. Cable TV. Heated pool. Hot tub. Playground. | 120 rooms | 1215 Zion Park Blvd. | 435/772–3200 | www.zionparkinn.com | $65–$99 | AE, D, MC, V.

Zion Park Motel. In the center of Springdale, this convenient motor inn with views of the Zion area canyons has some family units that can accommodate up to six people. The adjacent general market is an added convenience. Picnic area. Cable TV. Pool. Laundry facilities. | 23 rooms | 865 Zion Park Blvd. | 435/772–3251 | $56–$99 | AE, D, MC, V.

TORREY

MAP 14, C7

(Nearby towns also listed: Boulder, Escalante, Loa)

At the junction of two of Utah's most scenic roads, Rte. 12 and Rte. 24, Torrey is the primary gateway for Capitol Reef National Park. Tall cottonwood and poplar trees shade irrigation ditches along the highway, providing some visual distraction from the town's rapidly-growing commercial district. Scattered here and there are the small homes of longtime residents and newer vacation homes built by city-dwellers from northern Utah. In the 11-mi drive from Torrey east to the national park boundary, Rte. 24 passes through landscapes that become increasingly colorful and geologically varied. The road almost seems to have been designed specifically to prepare visitors gradually for the awesome scope of Capitol Reef's formations, canyons, and domes.

Information: **Capitol Reef Country Information Center** | Box 7, Teasdale, 84773 | 800/ 858–7951 | info@capitolreef.org | www.capitolreef.org.

Attractions

Capitol Reef National Park. *See* Capitol Reef National Park, *above.* | 11 mi east via Rte. 24.

The Robbers' Roost. "The Roost" is part coffee bar, part bookstore, and part performance space, all contained in the late Ward Roylance's practically pyramid-shaped house. Roylance was a writer and naturalist who chronicled Utah's natural and cultural history in books and articles that were always methodically researched yet filled with emotion and a passion for Utah's landscapes. The Roost is an excellent place to stop to browse, talk about trails, or find out what's going on around town. | Rte. 24 | 435/425–3265 | www.xmission.com~capreef/index.html | Apr.–Oct.

The Torrey Gallery. There are no T-shirts, magnets, or post cards at this lovely little gallery. Several exhibits each summer fill two display areas. Art shown and sold here ranges from oil paintings, photographs, and Navajo rugs to eccentric batiks and barbed-wire sculptures. | Rte. 24 | 435/425–3909 | www.xmission.com~capreef/index.html.

ADVENTURE TOURS

Hondoo Rivers and Trails. This company has rapidly built a reputation for innovative adventures on horseback or via four-wheel-drive vehicle in the mountains and deserts surrounding Capitol Reef National Park. Its trademark is the ability to take visitors' uninformed or uncertain ideas and turn them into specialty tours never to be forgotten. | Rte. 24 (Box 98) | 435/425–3519 or 800/332–2696 | www.hondoo.com | May–Oct.

ON THE CALENDAR

JULY: *Big Apple Days.* Parade, kids' games area, flea market, outdoor dinner, and dancing. | Main St. (Rte. 24) | 435/425–3721 | Saturday closest to July 4.
JULY: *Bicknell International Film Festival.* A tongue-in-cheek weekend event centers around films of different genres each year. Past favorites: "UFO Flicks," "Japanese Monster Movies," and "Viva! Elvis." | Wayne Theater, Bicknell, 8 mi west on Rte. 24 | 435/425–3123.

Dining

Cafe Diablo. Southwestern. Saltillo-tile floors and matte plaster white walls are a perfect setting for the southwestern art that crops up here and there in this intimate establishment. Among the winners turned out by this nontraditional southwestern kitchen are prawns in three-pepper sauce, eggplant enchiladas, and trout fillets coated in pumpkin seeds. | 599 W. Main St. | 435/425–3070 | $10–$19 | AE, D, MC, V | Closed mid-Oct.–mid-Apr. No lunch.

Capitol Reef Cafe. Vegetarian. This spot has an unassuming exterior. Most dining tables are on an enclosed porch. Vegetarian spaghetti, mushroom lasagna, and stir-fried vegetables with brown and wild rice are the specialties, but a few non-vegan dishes are also on the menu—sweet and sour shrimp, barbecued chicken, and local trout. Live entertainment. Beer and wine. | 360 W. Main St. | 435/425–3271 | $9–$17 | AE, D, MC, V.

Rabbit Valley Bakery and Cafe. Contemporary American. This modernized version of a cozy café is known for breakfasts of build-it-yourself quiche, house pastries, and assorted coffees. Boxed lunches are available, and dinner offerings include nut-crusted Chilean sea bass, stuffed Portobello mushrooms, and comfort foods like pot roast with vegetables piled on a generous portion of garlic mashed potatoes. Red-onion vinaigrette is the house salad dressing. | 374 S. 300 E, Bicknell; north on Rte. 12 | 435/425–3953 | $15–$23 | AE, D, MC, V | No lunch.

Lodging

Best Western Capitol Reef Resort. Surrounded by red-rock desert along scenic byway Rte. 24, the facility has kitchenettes and is good for families. Restaurant. Kitchenettes. Cable TV. Pool. Hot tub. Tennis. Horseback riding. | 100 rooms | 2600 E. Rte. 24 | 435/425–3761 | fax 435/425–3300 | capreef@colorcountry.net | www.bestwestern.com/thisco/bw/45068.html | $99–$139 | AE, D, DC, MC, V.

Boulder View Inn. The motel-style lodging with casual basic decor is fine, and you're close to Capitol Reef National Park. Complimentary Continental breakfast. Room phones. Cable TV. | 12 rooms | 385 W. Main St. | 435/425–3800 | fax 435/425–3366 | cptlreef@colorcountry.net | www.ourworld.compuserve.com/homepages/tyler-albrecht/ | $50–$65 | D, MC, V.

Hidden Falls Resort–Holiday Inn Express. Comfortable, larger-than-average guest rooms are decorated with warm southwestern tones and have views of the surrounding mountain country. You can hike the ½ mi to area trails. The friendly staff can help answer questions about area attractions, and a three-tier waterfall and pond with paddle boats are favorites with children. Dining room, Continental breakfast. In-room data ports, microwaves, refrigerators. Cable TV. Outdoor pool. Hot tub. Exercise room. Laundry facilities. Conference room. | 36 rooms, 3 suites | 2424 E. Rte. 24 | 435/425–3866 or 888/232–4082 | $79–$89, $99 suites | AE, D, DC, MC, V.

★ **Sky Ridge Bed & Breakfast.** Light and airy, this inn has 75 windows, all with views of Capitol Reef or the surrounding mountains and valley. The interior is colorful and artistic. VCRs. No smoking. | 6 rooms, 1 with jetted indoor Jacuzzi, 2 with private outdoor hot tubs | 950 E. Rte. 24 | 435/425–3222 | fax 435/425–3222 | www.bbiu.org/skyridge | $95–$170 | MC, V.

Wonderland Inn. Sitting atop a hill overlooking Torrey Valley and the Capitol Reef cliffs, this motor inn is only 3 mi from the Capitol Reef National Park main entrance, at the junction of Routes 12 and 24. The grounds are nicely landscaped, the rooms standard. Restaurant. TV. Indoor-outdoor pool. Beauty salon, hot tub. Conference rooms. | 50 rooms | Junction Rtes. 12 and 24 | 435/425–3775 or 800/458–0216 | fax 435/425–3212 | $58–$76 | AE, D, DC, MC, V.

VERNAL

(Nearby town also listed: Roosevelt)

Vernal functions as a hub for visitors to what is proudly termed "Dinosaurland." Trying to count the number of dinosaurs pictured on billboards and businesses around town is an amusing, and somewhat difficult, task. But dinosaurs aren't the only things they're proud of in Vernal. The town can, and does, claim the ancient Fremont Indians, a rowdy ranching past, and more than a passing acquaintance with outlaw Butch Cassidy, who frequented the area whenever he felt it was safe to be seen around town.

Information: Dinosaurland Travel Region | 25 E. Main St., Vernal, 84078 | 435/789–6932 or 800/477–5558 | dinoland@easilink.com | www.dinoland.com.

Attractions

Ashley National Forest. The forest virtually covers northeastern Utah. Its major attractions are the High Uintas Wilderness and Flaming Gorge National Recreation Area. The southern slopes of the Uinta Mountains meet the northern border of the Uinta and Ouray Indian Reservation. Several guest ranches operate in the area. | 355 N. Vernal Ave.; 15 mi north on U.S. 191 | 435/789–1181 | www.fs.fed.us/r4/ashley | Free; camping fees apply | Daily.

Dinosaur National Monument and Quarry Visitor Center. Dinosaur National Monument takes its name from a strange cache of paleontological treasures discovered by Earl Douglass in the early 1900s—an ancient river sandbar 200 ft long, from which Douglass and his crew excavated many tons of fossils, including full skeletons and remains of some dinosaur species previously unknown. The site is now sheltered by the monument's Quarry Visitor Center. There are other fossil sites in the monument, some unexcavated, but also within its boundaries (which run east into Colorado) are hikes through mountains, plateaus, and deserts, scenic drives, and the white-water thrills of the Green and Yampa Rivers. | Quarry Visitor Center: Rte. 149 (Box 128), Jensen Monument Headquarters: 4545 U.S. 40, Dinosaur, CO | 435/789–2115 (Quarry Visitor Center); 970/374–3000 (Monument Headquarters) | www.nps.gov.dino | $10 per vehicle | Daily.

Flaming Gorge Dam and National Recreation Area. The recreation area is north of Dinosaur National Monument. Flaming Gorge Lake stretches north from the dam for 90 mi between twisting red-rock canyon walls. The lake is popular for boating, camping, and trophy trout fishing. Just south of the dam, the Green River is known for excellent fishing and calm-water rafting. | Junction Rtes. 43 and 44, north on U.S. 191, in Ashley National Forest | 435/784–3445 | www.fs.fed.us/r4/ashley | $2 for day pass, $5 for 16-day pass, $20 for year pass | Daily.

Ouray National Wildlife Refuge. This refuge established in 1961 consists of 12,467 acres of land along the Green River. An information kiosk at the refuge has several brochures, including an auto-tour guide and a bird checklist. The auto tour travels a 13-mi loop through feeding areas and marshlands to points overlooking the rest of the refuge. You can see more than 200 species of migratory birds in the spring and fall, mule deer and golden eagles year-round, and bald eagles in the early winter. | 19001 E. Wildlife Refuge Rd., Rendlett; 15 mi west on U.S. 40, then 15 mi south on Rte. 88 | 435/789–0351 | www.fwf.dov | Free | Daily.

Uinta Basin. This is Utah's land of lore. Dinosaurs rumbled through the area and left their remnants to be discovered millions of years later. According to local legends, Butch Cassidy and other outlaws often left caches of "loot" behind as they galloped through northeastern Utah's mountains and the canyons of the Green River. A Wild West feeling is still alive here in the sheep- and cattle-ranching operations scattered across the basin. If you want a taste of ranch culture, plenty of working ranches offer adventures from horseback riding in the Uinta Mountains to full-fledged cattle drives. | West via U.S. 191, Rte. 121, and paved local roads | 435/789–1352 for information | Daily.

Utah Field House of Natural History State Park Museum and Dinosaur Gardens. The natural and cultural history of the Uinta Mountains and the flatlands known as the Uinta Basin are the focus of the museum. If you can get them past the gift shop, kids love the outdoor dinosaur gardens, home to 18 life-size replicas of prehistoric animals. | 235 Main St. | 435/789–3799 | www.utah.com | $5 | Daily.

Western Heritage Museum. Inside a big, open building, this museum's collection is a good historical interpretation of the varied life-styles in this part of the state. There are examples of Fremont and Ute Indian artifacts. The baskets, water jugs, and intricate bead-work pieces are particularly beautiful. Another area has Western carriages, rifles, revolvers, and hand-tooled saddles. Farm implements, children's toys from the turn-of-the-century, and World War I memorabilia are also displayed. | 302 E. 200 S | 435/789–7399 | Donations accepted | Weekdays 9–6, Sat. 10–2.

RIVER TRIPS

Dinosaur River Expeditions. Take one of the scenic daily trips on the Green River or a two- to five-day white-water expedition. | Box 3387, Park City, | 435/649–8092 or 800/345–7238 | fax 435/649–8126 | www.dinoadv.com | Rates vary | May–Sept.

Hatch River Expeditions. These outfitters have been in business more 60 years. They'll take you through Dinosaur National Monument and on the Green and Yampa Rivers for one- to six-day trips, including family packages. | 55 E. Main St. (Box 1150), Vernal, | 435/789–4316 or 800/342–8243 | fax 435/789–8513 | www.hatchriver.com | May–Sept.

Holiday River and Bike Expeditions. Trip lengths range from a weekend to 8 days. You can raft through Dinosaur National Monument and beyond and take combination bike/rafting trips. | 544 E. 3900 S., Suite U, Salt Lake City, | 801/266–2087 or 800/554–7238 | fax 801/266–1448 | www.bikeraft.com | Late Apr.–early Oct.

ON THE CALENDAR

JUNE–JULY: *Outlaw Trail Festival.* Folk arts, a women's .22 rifle-shooting competition, guided horseback trail rides, and a rodeo are among the main events. There is also a nightly performance of a musical based on the exploits of Butch Cassidy in this corner of the state. | Western Park Arena | 435/789–6932 or 800/477–5558 | $6.

NOV.–DEC. *The Lighting of the Dinosaur Gardens.* A family tradition, this month-long display of more than 50,000 lights in the dinosaur garden attracts about 70,000 visitors. It takes the staff more than a month to wind the lights in and around the small garden area at the Utah Field House of the Natural History State Park Museum. The garden holds 18 life-size replicas of various dinosaur species. The lighting starts the Friday after Thanksgiving and stays up until New Year's. | Utah Field House of Natural History State Park Museum | 435/789–6932.

Dining

Casa Rios. Mexican. On the outskirts of town, this popular restaurant is in an old 1950s-style KOA campground pitched-roof building. The authentic south-of-the-border food is tasty, and specials include pork tamales, seafood enchiladas with rice and beans, and chimichangas. | 2015 W. Rte. 40 | 435/789–0103 | $6–$12 | AE, MC, V | Closed Sun.

Curry Manor. Varied. This turn-of-the-century home has been turned into an intimate restaurant and Vernal's most upscale dining room. The menu features creatively prepared steak, pasta, seafood, and prime rib. No smoking. | 189 S. Vernal Ave. | 435/789–2289 | $11–$32 | D, MC, V | Closed Sun. No lunch Sat.

7-11 Ranch. American. Most of the people who come here are ranchers. The furnishings are Western, as is the home-style cooking at this family restaurant. Kids' menu. No smoking. | 77 E. Main St. (U.S. 40) | 435/789–1170 | $5–$10 | MC, V | Closed Sun.

Lodging

Best Western Antlers Motel. Generally the first place suggested by locals, this basic motel has a nice playground for those traveling with children. Cable TV. Pool. Hot tub. Exercise equipment. Playground. | 144 rooms | 423 W. Main St. | 435/789–1202 | fax 435–789–4979 | www.bestwestern.com | $55–$80 | AE, D, DC, MC, V.

Best Western Dinosaur Inn. A classic U-shape motel broken up by the restaurant, this one-story property in downtown has comfortable rooms and is close to the Speedway Museum. Restaurant. Cable TV. Pool. Hot tub. Business services. | 60 rooms | 251 E. Main St. | 435/789–2660 | fax 435/789–2467 | www.bestwestern.com | $75 | AE, D, DC, MC, V.

Weston Lamplighter Inn The simply furnished rooms are larger than average, and the family suites accommodate groups of up to six. In central Vernal, the motel is within walking distance of area shops, theaters, restaurants, and attractions. Restaurant. Some microwaves and refrigerators. Cable TV. Pool. Some pets allowed. | 88 rooms, 6 suites | 120 E. Main St. | 435/789–0312 | fax 435/781–1480 | $40–$50 | AE, DC, MC, V.

WENDOVER

MAP 14, A4

(Nearby town also listed: Salt Lake City)

This border town originated as a gas station and small slot-machine operation in the late 1920s when U.S. 40 (now I-80) was built across the Bonneville Salt Flats and into Nevada. Wendover has two claims to fame: world speed records and the old Wendover Air Force Base. Speedsters from all over the world have set land-speed records on the salt flats; the first car to break the 600-mph mark did so right outside of town. The Air Force base, created in 1940 to train pilots heading for the Pacific, was one of the largest in the world (3.5 million acres); here the 509th Composite Group prepared to drop two nuclear bombs on Japan in 1945.

Four major and two minor resort-casinos are on the Nevada side; the Utah side has most of the homes, the Speedway Museum, a giant airport (nearly four miles of concrete runways), and salt flats.

Information: **Wendover USA Visitor and Convention Bureau** | 735 Wendover Blvd. | 775/664–3414.

Attractions

Bonneville Speedway Museum. A big car museum, with a collection of antique cars and hood ornaments, plus a large display of photographs, media clippings, and trophies from the speed trials and races out on the salt flats just east of town. | 300 Wendover Blvd. | 435/665–7721 | $2 | June–Sept., daily 10–6; Oct.–May, weekends 10–6.

ON THE CALENDAR

OCT.: *Bonneville Salt Flats World Finals.* See jet-engine cars hurtle at more than 600 mph across the famous salt-covered plains, where the expansive flatness has lured racers from around the world hoping to set speed records at the week-long event. Signs from Exit 4 off I–80 east direct you to the flats. | 775/664–3414.

Lodging

Best Western Salt Flat Inn. On the Utah side of Wendover, this small, fairly quiet motel with larger-than-average rooms is convenient to I–80 and local attractions. Continental breakfast. Cable TV. Pool. Hot tub, sauna. | 24 rooms | 895 E. Wendover Blvd. | 435/665–7811 | fax 435/665–2383 | $60–$65 | AE, D, DC, MC, V.

State Line Inn/Silver Smith Hotel-Casino. This is the oldest continuously operating casino in Nevada; it's been open since the early 1930s. The State Line and Silver Smith are two separate facilities on either side of Wendover Blvd., connected by a skywalk. Both have classy casinos, restaurants, and rooms; the Silver Smith has a small showroom. The State Line Inn has added 241 rooms, all furnished in southwestern style. Restaurant, bars. Cable TV. 2 pools. Spa. Health club. No-smoking rooms. | 840 rooms | 100 Wendover Blvd. | 775/664–2221 or 800/848–7300 | fax 801/531–4099 | www.statelinenv.com | $45–$200.

ZION NATIONAL PARK

MAP 14, B8

(Nearby towns also listed: Kanab, St. George, Springdale)

Zion National Park has a quiet grandeur all its own. In spring, wildflowers appear first at the bases of cliffs facing south into the warmth of the sun. Summer draws visitors deeper into the park to cool canyons and hanging gardens of flowers and herbs growing from cracks in sheer stone. Autumn is stunning with the blaze of leaves changing color against the deeper colors of the park's monoliths. In winter a dusting of snow lends dignity to nearly barren trees, and accents the contours of talus slopes and constantly eroding landscapes.

Zion is Utah's oldest national park. It was designated as a monument in 1909 and became a national park in 1919. With nearly three million visitors a year, it's also Utah's most heavily used park. Still, Zion offers an almost spiritual magnificence, evident even in the names given to its formations, such as Great White Throne, Watchman, Court of the Patriarchs, and Angels Landing. Zion has several easy self-guiding trails and more strenuous hikes with switchbacks carved by hand into sandstone walls graduated from cream to a deep purple. Popular in the park are the open-air shuttles that allow you to enjoy the scenery with nothing to obstruct your view, and a wide, level hiking and biking trail that winds gently along the Virgin River. Both of these features were created to reduce traffic inside the park.

Information: **Zion National Park** | Box 1099, Springdale, 84767 | 435/772–3256 | fax 435/772–3426 | www.nps.gov/zion. **Washington County Travel and Convention Bureau** | 425 S. 700 E, St. George, 84770 | 435/634–5747 or 800/869–6635 | fax 435/628–1619 | www.zionpark.com or www.zioncanyon.com.

Attractions

Bicycling. The 3½-mi Pa'rus Trail is a paved ride winding along the Virgin River in Zion Canyon. You can take guided tours both in the park and on BLM land south of the park. Electric bikes, tandem bikes, mountain bikes, children's bikes, and helmets for all ages can be rented by the hour, the half day, or all day in Springdale, just south of Zion Canyon. | Bike Zion, 1458 Zion Park Blvd. (Rte. 9) | 435/772–3929 | Rental and tour costs vary | Scenic Cycles, 205 Zion Park Blvd. (Rte. 9) | 435/772–2453 | Rental and tour costs vary.

Emerald Pools Trail. The trailhead for an easy to moderate hike to this series of pools and waterfalls lies across the street from the Zion Park Lodge, about 6 mi north of the park's main south entrance. You can walk to the Lower Emerald Pools in about an hour to see waterfalls cascading off the red cliffs into a series of pools. Getting to the Upper Pools is a bit more difficult, and takes about an hour longer, but the 1,000-ft sheer sandstone cliffs harboring other pools are worth the hike. | Zion Canyon Rd. | 435/772–3256 | Daily.

Hiking. Zion has hikes for every ability, and hiking is highly recommended if you want to better understand the size and environment of the park. You can get hiking brochures and sound advice at the visitor center or at Zion Lodge. | 435/772–3256.

Kolob Canyons. The Kolob Canyons are the northern primitive section of Zion National Park. A scenic drive enters the area, but backcountry exploration requires a permit issued at the Kolob Canyons visitors center. *See also* Cedar City, *above.*

Zion Nature Center. The Zion Nature Center has a neat program that's geared to children under 12 years old. It focuses on the geology, flora, and fauna of the park through expla-

KODAK'S TIPS FOR NIGHT PHOTOGRAPHY

Lights at Night
· Move in close on neon signs
· Capture lights from unusual van- tage points

Fireworks
· Shoot individual bursts using a handheld camera
· Capture several explosions with a time exposure
· Include an interesting foreground

Fill-In Flash
· Set the fill-in light a stop darker than the ambient light

Around the Campfire
· Keep flames out of the frame when reading the meter
· For portraits, take spot readings of faces
· Use a tripod, or rest your camera on something solid

Using Flash
· Stay within the recommended dis- tance range
· Buy a flash with the red-eye reduc- tion mode

From *Kodak Guide to Shooting Great Travel Pictures* © 2000 by Fodor's Travel Publications

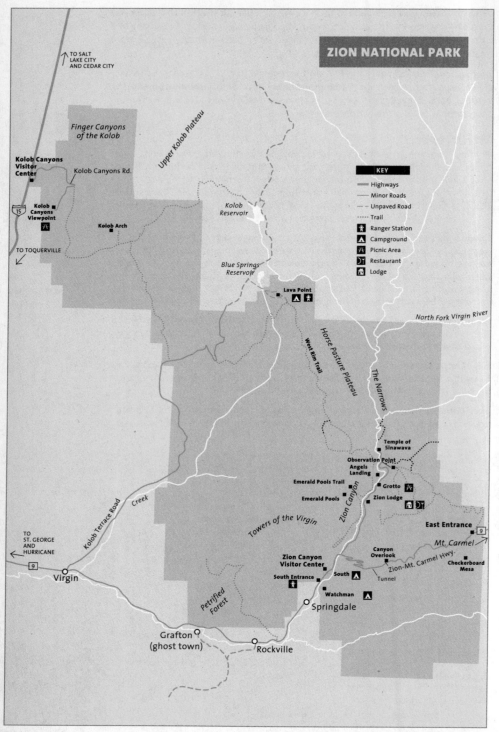

ZION NATIONAL PARK

TO SALT
LAKE CITY
AND CEDAR CITY

Finger Canyons
of the Kolob

Upper Kolob Plateau

Kolob Canyons
Visitor
Center

Kolob Canyons Rd.

Kolob Reservoir

KEY

Highways
Minor Roads
Unpaved Road
Trail
Ranger Station
Campground
Picnic Area
Restaurant
Lodge

Kolob
Canyons
Viewpoint

Kolob Arch

TO TOQUERVILLE

Blue Springs
Reservoir

Lava Point

North Fork Virgin River

Horse Pasture Plateau

West Rim Trail

The Narrows

Temple of
Sinawava

Observation Point

Angels
Landing

Emerald Pools Trail

Grotto

Zion Canyon

Emerald Pools

Zion Lodge

Creek

Kolob Terrace Road

Towers of the Virgin

East Entrance

Mt. Carmel

TO
ST. GEORGE
AND
HURRICANE

Canyon
Overlook

Checkerboard
Mesa

Zion Canyon
Visitor Center

Zion-Mt. Carmel Hwy.

Virgin

Petrified
Forest

South Entrance

South

Tunnel

Watchman

Springdale

Grafton
(ghost town)

Rockville

nations and activities. | Next to South Campground | 435/772–3256 | Programs generally free | Daily, but activities may not be scheduled every day.

Dining

The Golden Hills Restaurant. American. A funky little pink-and-blue roadside diner 12 mi east of the park's east entrance serves good, basic country-style fare like chicken-fried steak, liver and onions, and homemade breads and pies. It's quieter and less crowded than many other Zion-area establishments. | Mt. Carmel Junction, U.S. 89 and Rte. 9 | 435/648–2602 | $5–$12 | AE, MC, V.

Zion Lodge Restaurant. American. Photographs relating to the early days of this national park make interesting study while waiting for a table in the dining room. Casual lunch cuisine—sandwiches, burgers, and sack lunches for hikers. Dinners are traditional steaks, pastas, chicken-fried steak, and some seafood. You can eat at tables on the porch for a good view. Buffet breakfast. No smoking. | Zion Canyon Rd., off Rte. 9 | 435/772–3213 | Reservations essential June–Aug. | $14–$25 | MC, V.

Lodging

Best Western Thunderbird Resort. Set on a lush golf course surrounded by the Zion Mountains, this resort has spacious and bright rooms. About 15 minutes from the park's east entrance, it's a good place to stay if you want something a little less busy than the populated south entrance options. Restaurant. Pool. Hot tub. 9-hole golf course. | 61 rooms | Mt. Carmel Junction, U.S. 89 and Rte. 9 | 435/648–2203 or 888/848–6358 | fax 435/648–2239 | $79–$93 | AE, D, DC, MC, V.

Zion Lodge. There are spectacular views from these beautiful grounds. Restaurant. Hiking. Business services. | 75 rooms in lodge, 40 cabins | Zion National Park, Springdale | 435/772–3213 | fax 435/732–2001 | $95–$111 | AE, D, DC, MC, V.

Wyoming

Wyomingites take ornery pride in being specks on an uncluttered landscape. They know they have something that is fast disappearing elsewhere in the world—and yet most are willing to share it.

With only five people per square mile, Wyoming is the nation's least populated state. It's also the second highest, with an average elevation of 8,452 ft. Half of the state's 97,914 square mi is federally owned, and of that land 2.39 million acres are designated national parkland.

What these numbers mean is that Wyoming truly is "high, wide, and lonesome." Much of the state is substantially untouched by the development of the past century and a half. It has some of the nation's most spectacular scenery and attractions, from Yellowstone National Park—the first national park developed in the United States—to natural and historical sites like Devils Tower National Monument. It is an outdoor-sports mecca, with major mountain ranges and sweeping high plateaus in which to hike, hunt, ride horses, photograph, ski, or snowmobile. Numerous linchpins of Old West history are here as well, such as the Fort Laramie National Historic Site and some of the pioneer trails of the mid-19th century.

Every so often a town interrupts Wyoming's wide-open expanses. Only two towns are classified as metropolises: the capital city of Cheyenne and the economic hub of Casper; neither has even 70,000 residents. But the smaller cities and even smaller towns have their own distinctive characters. The two major resort areas are Jackson Hole and Cody, but several other communities are fast developing into tourist destinations, including Sheridan, Dubois, and Saratoga.

You won't find eclectic places to eat and stay in all Wyoming's communities, though you will in some. But you will experience a way of life in which it's more important to check your winter survival gear than to see if your lipstick has faded or if your shoes are scuffed. Casual and hardy best describe Wyoming's people. They are

CAPITAL: CHEYENNE	POPULATION: 480,797	AREA: 97,914 SQUARE MI
BORDERS: CO, UT, ID, MO, SD, NE	TIME ZONE: MOUNTAIN	POSTAL ABBREVIATION: WY
WEB SITE: WWW.STATE.WY.US/STATE/TOURISM/TOURISM.HTM		

generally an independent lot, who say what they mean and mean what they say. And they will almost always take the time to share their history and heritage, or guide you to your destination.

Wyoming calls itself the Equality State and earned that distinction when it was just barely a territory. Officials on December 10, 1869, granted women the right to vote, to serve on juries, and to hold office. Esther Hobart Morris became the first woman justice of the peace in the nation in 1870, the same year the first women served on a jury in Albany County. In 1924 Wyoming became the first state in the nation to have a female governor, when Nellie Tayloe Ross was appointed to fill the term left vacant by the death of her husband.

History

The earliest people to live in Wyoming arrived probably 25,000 years ago. They were hunters and gatherers. Later people built pit houses, where they might have lived while finding and preserving food to sustain them through the long winters. In historic times, say the last few hundred years, various tribes of Native Americans lived in Wyoming: Comanche, Shoshone, Arapaho, Lakota, Cheyenne, Crow, and occasionally Ute and Blackfoot. Today two of the tribes remain: the Shoshone and Arapaho, who share the Wind River Reservation in central Wyoming.

European-American contact came in 1807 when John Colter, a member of the Lewis & Clark Corps of Discovery, turned back at the Mandan Villages in present-day North Dakota to return to the West. He made a circuitous route through north-western Wyoming, seeing spouting geysers and sulfurous bubbling hot springs at a place later dubbed "Colter's Hell," just west of the what is now Cody. Then he criss-crossed mountain ranges, traveling into Jackson Hole and the regions that now are the Grand Teton and Yellowstone national parks. Other explorers followed in 1811, with the biggest influx after 1822 when fur trappers started their quest for beaver in the West's clear mountain streams and rivers. The first mountain-man rendezvous took place in 1825 on the Black Fork of the Green River, southeast of the present city of Green River.

By that time many other mountain men, later legendary in the development of the West, had followed Colter into the area. They included Jim Bridger, Thomas Fitz-patrick, Hugh Glass, David Jackson, William Pickney, Milton Sublette, James Beck-wourth, and dozens more. These men explored throughout the region, leaving their names on many of the state's streams, mountains, and other physical features.

They followed routes the Indians told them about and forged a path later followed by more than 400,000 immigrants headed toward Oregon, California, and Utah. During its 18-month existence, riders of the Pony Express raced across Wyoming and that same trail corridor linking the East with the West, but the Pony Boys lost their jobs when the transcontinental telegraph—also located in the same overland trail corridor—began working in October 1861.

WY Timeline

8,300 BC	AD 1500	1743	1803
Prehistoric people live in the Bighorn Basin.	Modern Indian tribes first establish homes and territories.	The Verendrye brothers are the first white men to visit Wyoming when they reach the Bighorn Mountains on an exploratory trip.	The United States concludes the Louisiana Purchase, which includes what will eventually be Wyoming.

INTRODUCTION
HISTORY
REGIONS
WHEN TO VISIT
STATE'S GREATS
RULES OF THE ROAD
DRIVING TOURS

Today travelers come from the world over to see Wyoming, but it is still for many people chiefly a highway from the East to the West. In 1849 Cherokee Indians crossed the region where the railroad would later lie, forging the Cherokee Trail as they headed toward California's gold fields. In 1865 wagons and stagecoaches started rolling across the landscape on the Overland Trail, established by the freighting firm of Ben Holladay.

The Union Pacific Railroad went in later that decade, across the southern portion of the present-day state. As workers laid rail from east to west, across what is now Wyoming, a string of rowdy, lawless boom towns sprang up; they became known as the hell-on-wheels towns, and included Cheyenne, Laramie City, Carbon, Benton, Rawlins, Rock Springs, Green River, Bear River City, Evanston, and several others. About half of these tent cities lived and died in short, dramatic episodes, and they are now only ghosts. But others hung on to become governmental seats for the five original counties: Laramie, Albany, Carbon, Sweetwater, and Uinta, which extended in vertical rectangles from Colorado Territory to Montana Territory. These five original counties were later split into the 23 that exist today. The southern Wyoming region continued its legacy as a transportation corridor in 1913 when the Lincoln Highway—U.S. 30—was completed. Decades later Interstate 80 cut across the same portion of Wyoming, along most of the old Lincoln Route.

Except for Native Americans, few people lived permanently in Wyoming until after the Union Pacific was established. But subsequent mineral discoveries—including coal in southern Wyoming and gold at South Pass—spurred growth, the establishment of the territory (July 25, 1868), and eventually statehood (July 10, 1890).

By the mid-1870s, cattlemen had brought Texas longhorns up such cattle trails as the Texas Trail and the Goodnight-Loving Trail to turn them loose on Wyoming's high-plains grassland. Sheep ranchers also began using the vast open spaces, creating conflicts over the range—some of which continued through most of the 20th century. Homesteaders also staked claims, building homes and sometimes raising crops.

Development coincided with the demise of traditional ways of life for the Native Americans, some of whom were involved in violent battles with the U.S. Army, particularly in Wyoming's Powder River Basin.

By 1880 the Indians had been forced onto reservations, and homesteaders were moving into all areas of the state. Wyoming achieved statehood in July 1890, but the state's rowdiness lingered, and, in 1892, powerful cattlemen squared off against smaller livestock operators and homesteaders in a conflict over cattle range. The cattlemen hired an "army" and invaded Johnson County, only to be surrounded by townspeople. Subsequently, the U.S. Army rescued the cattlemen and their "invaders." Though charged with various crimes, including the deaths of two homesteaders, the cattlemen and their associates never went to trial.

Mining and mineral development marked the early years of the 20th century, with copper-mine development near Encampment and coal mining continuing in the Hanna Basin. Tie hacks, who had prepared timbers for railroad projects as early as the 1870s, continued working in the timber industry, and eventually their horse and

1807–08
John Colter, a member of Lewis and Clark's Corps of Discovery, explores Wyoming, seeing the area later dubbed "Colter's Hell"; he is the first European to lay eyes on the geyser basins of the Yellowstone National Park ecosystem.

1811
Wilson Price Hunt's Astorians head east from Fort Astoria, crossing through Wyoming on a route that later becomes the Oregon Trail.

1825
The first trappers' rendezvous is held on Black Fork of the Green River

1834
The first permanent white settlement develops at Fort William near the confluence of the Laramie and North Platte rivers; it is eventually renamed Fort Laramie.

mule operations and annual tie drives, in which they floated timber down streams and rivers to loading docks, gave way to transportation by trucks. The mineral industry got a boost—and a bit of a federal black eye—in the 1920s when U.S. naval oil reserves were illegally leased at the Teapot Dome north of Casper. But the industry continued to make inroads into Wyoming in part because of the huge mineral reserves underlying the state—ranging from coal and oil to gas and trona (which is used in the manufacture of baking soda and glass).

The Wyoming economy boomed and then declined through the decades, with the most recent big boom starting in the late 1960s and continuing through the mid-1980s. The minerals industry then started a downward slide, although miners continue to dig coal and develop trona and oil and gas reserves. Throughout the 20th century, agriculture remained an economic mainstay in Wyoming. Family ranches, in many cases operated by the fourth or fifth generation, shared Wyoming's land with corporate holdings. The ranchers continue to raise beef and sheep, and some ranchers in the 1990s began running bison.

People have routinely visited Wyoming as tourists. They wanted to see its wide open spaces and such scenic attractions as Yellowstone National Park, Grand Teton National Park, Devils Tower National Monument, and various national historic sites and monuments such as Fort Laramie, Fossil Butte, and the Oregon-California-Mormon Pioneer National Historic Trails. The first dude ranch in the West started near Sheridan, and the cowboy lifestyle is alive and well, as much of the landscape remains virtually untouched. The state's mountain ranges and wilderness areas attract those who want to experience nature. And with its sparse population, plenty of elbow room remains.

Regions

1. SOUTHERN WYOMING/UNION PACIFIC COUNTRY

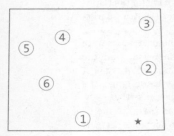

Early permanent development in Wyoming occurred primarily along the southern border, in the region crossed by the Union Pacific Railroad in 1867–69 and today defined by Interstate 80. This highway cuts across the entire 400-mi width of Wyoming between Evanston and Pine Bluffs. The terrain varies from rolling grassland to the mountains of the Laramie, Medicine Bow, and Sierra Madre ranges, and the desert landscape of the Great Divide Basin and Red Desert—complete with badlands and basins from which no water runs toward the oceans. The area is bordered on the east by Nebraska, on the south by Colorado, on the west by Utah, and to the north by an imaginary line slicing across the state about 80 mi north of its border with Colorado. Here you will find the primary state institutions, including the state capital (Cheyenne), the state university (Laramie), the state penitentiary (Rawlins), and the state mental hospital (Evanston).

1843	**1847**	**1849**	**1860–61**	**1861**
Migration begins over the Oregon Trail.	Brigham Young forges the Mormon Trail.	Goldseekers head to California over the California Trail.	The Pony Express delivers the mail by horseback courier.	The Creighton Telegraph begins operation in October, bringing to an end the need for the Pony Express.

INTRODUCTION
HISTORY
REGIONS
WHEN TO VISIT
STATE'S GREATS
RULES OF THE ROAD
DRIVING TOURS

There's a reason for this. When the Wyoming Territory was organized, the population was in this part of the state, and it was decided to divide up the necessary institutions somewhat equally among the counties. Only Sweetwater County failed to land a major state institution; it has always been a mining center, with coal operations dating back to the 1870s.

Towns listed: Cheyenne, Encampment, Evanston, Green River, Kemmerer, Laramie, Medicine Bow, Pinedale, Rawlins, Rock Springs, Saratoga

2. IMMIGRANT TRAIL COUNTRY

From the Nebraska border to the Continental Divide, central Wyoming is marked with the ruts of wagons carrying the 400,000 people bound for Oregon, California, and Utah between 1841 and 1869. The region today includes Goshen, Platte, Converse, Natrona, and Fremont counties, the communities of Torrington, Wheatland, Douglas, and Casper, and the courses of the North Platte and Sweetwater Rivers. The trail heritage is rich and carefully marked, with ruts and graves mingled with new trail interpretive centers.

Towns listed: Casper, Douglas, Lander, Lusk, Riverton, Torrington, Wheatland

3. DEVILS TOWER/POWDER RIVER

Northeast Wyoming—the Powder River Basin—is the traditional homeland of the Lakota (Sioux), and has a rich layer of mineral deposits, including oil, gas, and coal. Although it is primarily rolling grassland, a few rough breaks show at the edge of the Black Hills. The region is bordered by South Dakota on the east, Montana on the north, the Bighorn Mountains to the west, and the North Platte river to the south.

Towns listed: Buffalo, Gillette, Newcastle, Sheridan, Sundance

4. THE BIGHORN BASIN

Settled by the Crow, Arapaho, and Shoshone Indians, the Big Horn Basin is an almost circular area in northwest Wyoming that is bordered by the Bighorn Mountains to the south and east, Montana to the north, the Wind River Range to the southwest, and the Owl Creek and Absaroka mountains and Yellowstone on the west. It is the region first known to be inhabited by Native people in Wyoming and has a legacy of Indian spiritual sites, including pictographs and petroglyphs. Developed by Mormon settlers in the 1870s, the region is one of Wyoming's most productive agricultural areas, where sugar beets and malt barley are among the primary crops.

Towns listed: Cody, Greybull, Lovell, Powell, Thermopolis, Worland

5. YELLOWSTONE COUNTRY

Yellowstone's appeal is as strong today as it was in 1872, when the region became the first national park. The number of visitors to Yellowstone continues to increase in both

1865	**1868**	**1869**	**1872**	**1874**
Trail travel shifts south from the Oregon-Mormon-California corridor to the Overland Trail in southern Wyoming.	Wyoming Territory is established on July 25.	On Dec. 10 Wyoming grants women the right to vote, hold office, and serve on juries.	Congress designates Yellowstone as the first national park.	An army expedition led by Lt. Col. George A. Custer finds gold in the Black Hills, leading to a rush to the region with a primary route from Cheyenne to Deadwood, South Dakota.

summer and winter, leading park officials to consider future limits. The lure for the more than 3 million people who visit annually is the park's natural features: bubbling mud pots, spouting geysers, rushing rivers, spectacular waterfalls, and most of all, diversity of wildlife. Long known for its elk and buffalo herds, in 1995 Yellowstone again became home to North American wolves in an expensive, experimental repopulation program. The federal court system is still reviewing the program to see whether the wolves will stay or go. The last wild wolves to roam the region were killed by hunters in the 1930s, so the return of the carnivore drew worldwide attention. Although some of the wolves left the park and were subsequently killed either illegally or by wildlife officials, the majority remained and have formed new packs and had new litters. By late 1998 the wolves had moved into neighboring Grand Teton National Park as well. The Yellowstone region is bordered by Montana on the north, Idaho on the west, the Bighorn Basin to the east, and the open country of the Little Colorado Desert on the south.

Towns listed: Cody, Dubois, Jackson

6. GREEN RIVER/RENDEZVOUS COUNTRY

Mountain men trapped beaver on the river known to Native Americans as the Seedskadee Agie or Prairie Hen, to the French-Canadians as the Rio Verde (Colorado River), and to modern mapmakers as the Green. From the mountain peaks that separate this area of Wyoming from Jackson Hole, Green River/Rendezvous Country extends south to the Little Colorado Desert, including Big Piney, Pinedale, and Farson, and then west to Idaho, encompassing the Star Valley, with its small communities of Afton and Alpine Junction. The first white people known to have been in the area were Astorians headed east from Fort Astoria, Oregon, in 1812. Narcissa Whitman and Eliza Spalding accompanied their missionary husbands to a rendezvous here in 1835, and Jesuit priest Father Pierre De Smet gave the first Catholic service at Rendezvous in 1841.

Towns listed: Afton, Alpine, Pinedale

When to Visit

The best times to tour Wyoming are summer and fall, because the high mountain country gets lots of snow in the winter and spring is barely noticeable. July and August are your best bets for a chance to see any particular location without fear of driving through a snowstorm, but even then be aware that it can and does snow every month of the year in the mountains. Fall can be the perfect time to visit Wyoming; summer crowds have diminished, and days are warm and nights are cool. Mid-September usually brings the first snowstorm of the season, followed by an Indian summer of calm days and cool temperatures. Some mountain passes, such as the Snowy Range Scenic Byway, close in the winter. Many of Wyoming's museums also close or have limited hours in winter. Roads in Yellowstone National Park are generally closed by early October and don't reopen until late April or early May. Winter activities on snowmobiles,

1870		**1880**	**1886–87**	**1890**
Cowboys begin trailing cattle to the northern ranges over the Texas, Goodnight-Loving, and other trails, bringing them into and through Wyoming. Some herds are kept in	the state, beginning an industry that remains strong more than a century later.	Wealthy cattlemen form the Cactus Club in Cheyenne. It later becomes the Cheyenne Club and is a base where anti-rustling activities are planned.	A severe winter kills thousands of head of cattle. It becomes known as "The Great Die-Up."	Wyoming becomes a state on July 10.

snow coaches, and cross-country skis are generally allowed in Yellowstone from December through February. Grand Teton National Park also closes by late fall and doesn't reopen until April. Before Memorial Day, services in both parks are limited.

INTRODUCTION
HISTORY
REGIONS
WHEN TO VISIT
STATE'S GREATS
RULES OF THE ROAD
DRIVING TOURS

CLIMATE CHART

Average High/Low Temperatures (deg F) and Monthly precipitation (in inches)

	JAN.	FEB.	MAR.	APR.	MAY	JUNE
CASPER	37/16	41/20	46/23	58/30	69/40	80/48
	.49	.51	.91	1.66	2.37	1.66
	JULY	AUG.	SEPT.	OCT.	NOV.	DEC.
	89/55	87/53	75/43	54/34	47/24	39/19
	1.08	.76	.89	.98	.75	.49

	JAN.	FEB.	MAR.	APR.	MAY	JUNE
CHEYENNE	38/15	41/8	45/27	55/30	65/39	74/48
	.4	.39	1.03	1.37	2.39	2.08
	JULY	AUG.	SEPT.	OCT.	NOV.	DEC.
	82/55	80/53	71/44	60/34	47/24	39/17
	2.09	1.69	1.27	0.74	.53	.42

	JAN.	FEB.	MAR.	APR.	MAY	JUNE
EVANSTON	32/6	35/8	40/14	51/23	63/32	73/38
	.75	.63	.85	1.19	1.17	.98
	JULY	AUG.	SEPT.	OCT.	NOV.	DEC.
	83/44	80/42	72/34	60/25	43/15	34/8
	.73	.91	.91	1.03	.76	.76

	JAN.	FEB.	MAR.	APR.	MAY	JUNE
GILLETTE	31/9	37/15	43/20	55/30	66/40	76/48
	.58	.6	.77	1.76	2.72	3.11
	JULY	AUG.	SEPT.	OCT.	NOV.	DEC.
	87/55	85/53	74/43	62/34	44/21	36/14
	1.35	1.32	1.24	1.05	.69	.58

	JAN.	FEB.	MAR.	APR.	MAY	JUNE
JACKSON	27/16	32/8.4	39/14	51/24	62/30	72/37
	1.72	1.63	1	1.03	1.08	1.72
	JULY	AUG.	SEPT.	OCT.	NOV.	DEC.
	82/40	79/38	71/31	59/23	40/16	28/7
	.84	1.15	1.16	1.09	1.13	1.65

1892
A cattlemen's army invades Johnson County, killing two men before the army itself is surrounded and must be "rescued" by the U.S. Army. Although charges are filed, the case never goes to trial. The incident becomes known as the Johnson County Invasion or Johnson County War.

1903
Shoshone National Forest, the nation's first, is created in northwestern Wyoming.

1906
Devils Tower becomes the first national monument.

1913
The Lincoln Highway—the first trans-Continental road in the nation—opens across southern Wyoming; it is later replaced by Interstate 80.

FESTIVALS AND SEASONAL EVENTS

WINTER

Dec.–Feb. **Cutter/Chariot Races.** Horse-drawn chariots or cutters (small sleighs) compete in drag races held every weekend in Afton. | 307/883–2759, 307/777–7777, or 800/426–8833.

Jan. **Saratoga Lake Ice Fishing Derby.** Anglers compete for prizes in categories ranging from biggest fish to best ice hut. | Saratoga Lake, 1 mi north of Saratoga | 307/326–8855.

Jan.–Feb. **Wyoming State Winter Fair.** Horse and cattle shows, trade exhibits, livestock sales, and entertainment are part of the only winter fair in the state. | Fairgrounds, Lander | 307/332–3892 or 800/433–0662.

International Rocky Mountain Stage Stop Sled Dog Race. Dogsled racers, including many former Iditarod champions, compete in this multiday race throughout western Wyoming with stops at various towns. Known as the Race to Immunize, it is held to further the awareness of immunization for children. | 307/777–7777.

Feb. **Wild West Winter Carnival.** Two weeks of events, including tethered hot-air balloon rides, a "snodeo," and snow-cross races for snowmobilers, motorcycle and ATV races on ice, ice sculpting, casino night, ice-fishing derby, bowling and golf on ice, dances, a parade, and chariot races. The events are held at various venues in Riverton, Shoshoni, and Boysen Reservoir. | 102 S. 1st St., Riverton | 800/325–2732 or 800/645–6233.

Cowboy State Games Winter Sports Festival. The events in this Olympic-style sports competition are held at several venues in the Casper area. | 307/577–1125.

SPRING

Mar. **World Championship Snowmobile Hill Climb.** Snowmobilers put their machines to the test to see who can climb straight up the mountain farthest and fastest. Sponsored by Jackson Hole Snow Devils. | Snow King Mountain, Jackson | 307/734–9653 or 307/733–5200.

Apr. **Cowboy Songs and Range Ballads.** Performances and a symposium on cowboy music. Nightly programs are held at the Cody Auditorium and other Cody venues. | 307/587–4771.

1922
Scandal erupts in the oilfields when the Teapot Dome federal naval reserve is leased without competitive bids.

1929
The Colorado River Compact determines ownership of water in the Colorado River drainage by six states: Wyoming, Colorado, Utah, Nevada, Arizona, and California.

1929
Congress establishes Grand Teton National Park; it is expanded in 1950 to its present size.

1936
The silhouette of a cowboy riding a bucking horse first appears on Wyoming's license plates; the logo is subsequently copyrighted.

1942
Federal officials develop Heart Mountain Relocation Center between Powell and Cody, an internment camp for people of Japanese ancestry used throughout World War II.

INTRODUCTION
HISTORY
REGIONS
WHEN TO VISIT
STATE'S GREATS
RULES OF THE ROAD
DRIVING TOURS

Pole-Pedal-Paddle. In this wacky race, Jackson's annual rite of spring, participants ski downhill and cross-country, canoe, and bicycle. The course begins at Jackson Hole Mountain Resort and ends at Astoria Hot Spring. Some winners are serious competitors who race each other and the clock, while others are just out to have fun and wear zany costumes. | 307/733–6433.

May **Pack Horse Races.** On Memorial Day weekend in Dubois, teams of packers break camp, pack it, load their pack horses, and complete a several-mile course before they set up camp again in a timed event. | 307/455–2556 or 307/455–2174.

State Championship Old-Time Fiddle Contest. Wyoming's best fiddlers come to Shoshoni High School and make the strings sing at this annual competition. | 800/325–2732 or 800/645–6233.

Yellow Calf Memorial Powwow. Native American traditional dancing is a part of Ethete's annual powwow. | 307/856–7566 or 800/433–0662.

SUMMER

June **Bozeman Trail Days.** All the events and programs, held in Story, relate to the development and use of the Bozeman Trail. | 307/684–7687 or 684–7629.

Chugwater Chili Cook-off. Chili cooks prepare their own special blends as musicians and cowboy poets entertain, all at the Diamond Guest Ranch in Chugwater. | 307/322–2322.

Cowboy State Summer Games. Wyoming residents compete in an Olympic-style sports competition at various venues around Casper. | 307/577–1125.

Flaming Gorge Days Celebration. Several days of activities take place in various venues around Green River, from a battle of the bands to a basketball tournament, golf scramble, arm wrestling, horseshoes, and children's entertainment. | 307/875–5711.

1982
The world's largest wind turbine goes into operation near Medicine Bow.

1998
A new wind-energy project is developed east of Elk Mountain; it provides power throughout the Pacific Northwest.

Fort Caspar Mountain Man Rendezvous and Primitive Skills Contest. Buckskinners set up camp at Fort Caspar, and there are living-history demonstrations, a primitive-skills crafts fair, and the world open atlatl competition. (An atlatl is a spear-throwing device used by early hunters.) | 307/235–8462.

National Finals College Rodeo. The top collegiate rodeo teams and individual competitors gather for their national finals rodeo. This event runs in Casper for five years, starting in 2000. | Casper Events Center | 307/234–5311 or 800/852–1889.

Plains Indian Powwow. Plains Indians perform traditional dances, with fancy dancers, hoop dancers, traditional dancers, and jingle dancers from various tribes, at the Buffalo Bill Historical Center in Cody. | 307/587–4771.

Shoshone Indian Days. The events at Fort Washakie include an all-Indian rodeo, powwow, and a reenactment of Shoshone Indian treaty sessions. | 307/332–3532 or 800/433–0662.

Woodchopper's Jamboree and Rodeo. Loggers test their skills at felling trees, handsawing, axe chopping, and power-saw log cutting while rodeo cowboys compete in traditional events. Other activities include a parade, a barbecue, and a melodrama, all at the Riverside Lions Club in Encampment. | 307/327–5155, 307/327–5576 (rodeo), or 800/592–4309.

July   **Central Wyoming Fair and Rodeo.** Livestock exhibits, rodeos, a carnival, entertainment, and other activities are part of the Central Wyoming Fair and rodeo in Casper. | 307/235–5775.

Cheyenne Frontier Days. The biggest event in Cheyenne each year takes place during the last full week in July and involves four parades, top country entertainers performing nightly, nine PRCA rodeos, Plains Indian dancers, three free pancake breakfasts, and the Old West Governor's Art Show and Sale. | 307/778–7200 or 800/227–6336.

Cody Stampede. The Annual Fourth of July rodeo includes parades and fireworks in Cody's aptly named Stampede Park. | 307/587–5155.

1838 Mountain Man Rendezvous. Buckskinners gather on the Wind River at Riverton for black-powder shooting, tomahawk throwing, and even frying pan–throwing contests. At the trader's fair, you can buy a buckskin dress or coonskin cap. | 307/856–7306, 800/325–2732, or 800/645–6233.

Green River Rendezvous. Buckskinners congregate on the rodeo grounds in Pinedale for a rendezvous of several days like those of the fur trappers between 1825 and 1843. Parade, crafts booths, rodeo. | 307/367–4101.

Lander Pioneer Days. An annual celebration on the Fourth of July has events all over town, including a parade, a rodeo, a buffalo barbecue, and entertainment. | 307/332–3892 or 800/433–0662.

Laramie Jubilee Days. Rodeos, a carnival, parades, and a Western art show are part of the weeklong celebration that's partly at the Albany County Fairgrounds and partly in downtown Laramie. | 307/745–7339 or 800/445–5303.

Legend of Rawhide. A living-history reenactment in Lusk of the old legend about a man who, when traveling West more than a century ago, killed an Indian girl and was ultimately skinned alive by Indians. | 307/334–2950 or 800/223–LUSK.

Rendezvous Balloon Rally. Multicolored balloons free-float or give tethered rides over Riverton in this gathering of balloonists—the largest event of its kind in Wyoming. It is a part of the month-long Riverton Rendezvous celebration. Other events include an antique car and bike show, demolition derbies, rodeos, dances, fireworks, and cowboy poetry. | 307/856–4285.

Saratoga Arts Festival. Held over the Fourth of July weekend, the events in Saratoga include music, art shows and sales, food, crafts, author readings, cowboy poetry, and melodrama. | 307/326–8855.

July–Aug.   **Grand Teton Music Festival.** Regular symphony orchestra performances are held either at Walk Festival Hall or outdoors near Jackson Hole. There is also a winter concert schedule. | 12 mi northwest of town in Teton Village | 307/733–1128 or 800/959–4863.

Aug.   **Gift of the Waters Pageant.** A recreation of Shoshone Chief Washakie's gift of the waters, when he agreed to cede the land with the mineral springs, now Hot Springs State Park in Thermopolis, to the federal government. | 307/864–3192.

Wyoming Microbrewery Competition. Wyoming breweries come to Veteran's Island in Saratoga to compete for prizes. Brew tasting, food, music. | 307/326–8855.

AUTUMN

Sept.   **American Heritage Center Fall Symposium.** A different topic, ranging from water rights to education, is chosen for discussion each year at the American Heritage Center in Laramie. | 2111 Willett Dr. | 307/766–4114.

Buffalo Bill Art Show, Quick Draw, and Sale. Western artists come to Cody's Buffalo Bill Historical Center to create original pieces with live and silent auctions of artwork. | 307/587–5002.

Deke Latham PRCA Rodeo. Held in honor of a local professional rodeo cowboy who was killed in an accident, this small-town rodeo in Kaycee draws some of the biggest names on the PRCA circuit. | 307/738–2444.

INTRODUCTION
HISTORY
REGIONS
WHEN TO VISIT
STATE'S GREATS
RULES OF THE ROAD
DRIVING TOURS

Fort Bridger Mountain Man Rendezvous. The largest gathering of buckskinners, traders, and Indians in Wyoming meets at Fort Bridger State Historic Site, with traders selling period objects, and an Indian powwow. | 307/782–3842.

Platte Bridge Station Stage Race. Top cyclists from throughout the country compete in this stage race based in Casper. | 307/235–0262.

Western Design Conference. Cody's furniture exhibition, fashion show, and seminars are all on Western design and are held in the Buffalo Bill Historical Center. | 888/685–0574.

Sept.–Oct. **Jackson Hole Fall Arts Festival.** Artists in various mediums show and sell their work. Several special events include poetry and dance. Jackson's many art galleries have special exhibits and programs. | 307/733–3316.

State's Greats

In most people's minds, wild Wyoming is synonymous with its northwest section and its cluster of parks, forests, and ski resorts. Wyoming is really much more. The other most visited regions, the northeast and southeast, blend mountain and plain, mine and ranch, and country towns and small Western cities. In the southeast, the museums, festivals, and parks of Cheyenne and Laramie ensure that Wyoming's heritage as a frontier territory has a place in contemporary life. The Bighorn Mountains in the north central region attract hikers and fishermen.

Wyoming's slogan is "Like No Place on Earth," and indeed some sites, such as the geyser basins of Yellowstone National Park and the uplifted volcanic core of Devils Tower, are unlike any you'll find elsewhere. Miles of open spaces populated with free-ranging antelope and covered with sagebrush or native grasses are a part of the scenery. The ancient history of the earth is reflected in Wyoming as well, from the dinosaurs and fossils of southwest Wyoming—which you can see at **Western Wyoming College** in Rock Springs or at **Fossil Butte National Monument**—to dinosaur tracks and dig sites in the **Bighorn Basin** near Thermopolis and Greybull.

Forests and Parks

Wyoming's greatest attraction is **Yellowstone National Park,** closely followed by its neighbor to the south, **Grand Teton National Park.** Other top outdoor draws in the Cowboy State include **Devils Tower National Monument, Fort Laramie National Historic Site,** and the four national forests—**Bridger-Teton, Shoshone, Bighorn,** and **Medicine Bow–Routt.** The forests offer hunting and fishing, camping, and hiking. In wilderness areas such as **Cloud Peak** in the Bighorn Mountains west of Buffalo and the **Absaroka** west of Cody nature is preserved as it has been for centuries.

Culture, History, and the Arts

Much of Wyoming's culture is tied to the land. Native Americans have made this place their home for centuries, and cultural sites depicting their way of life remain on the **Wind River Reservation** in Fremont County. Among the sites commemorating the great western migration through the state are the **Mormon Trail/Martin's Cove Visitors Center** in central Wyoming, **Fort Laramie National Historic Site,** and **Fort Bridger.**

Learn more about the history of mountain men at the **Museum of the Mountain Man** in Pinedale, and explore cowboy culture and general Western history at the **Buffalo Bill Historical Center** in Cody, which has museums devoted to Western art, Plains

Indians, Buffalo Bill, and firearms. The **Jim Gatchell Museum** in Buffalo has displays relating to the 1892 Johnson County Invasion and Native Americans. The **Old West Museum** in Cheyenne has the largest collection of horse-drawn carriages in the region and displays related to the history of Cheyenne's frontier days. The museum also has public programs and hosts the Governor's Art Show every July.

Other top cultural attractions in Wyoming include the **National Wildlife Art Museum** in Jackson, with its permanent and rotating exhibits of wildlife paintings and sculpture, and a view of the National Wildlife Refuge. The **Nicolaysen Art Museum** in Casper has a permanent display devoted to Wyoming artist Conrad Schweiring, a children's discovery center, and revolving exhibits.

INTRODUCTION
HISTORY
REGIONS
WHEN TO VISIT
STATE'S GREATS
RULES OF THE ROAD
DRIVING TOURS

Sports

Wyoming has no professional sports teams, but sports abound, including the Cowboy State sport of choice—**rodeo.** You can see a rodeo with all the traditional events—saddle bronc riding, bareback bronc riding, bull riding, calf roping, and barrel racing—somewhere in Wyoming every day during the summer. Cody has a nightly rodeo, and Cheyenne and Laramie have periodic nightly events. The biggest rodeo is held during **Cheyenne Frontier Days** the last full week of July. **Laramie Jubilee Days** in early July include the King Merritt Steer Roping and other events.

Wyoming's **trout fishing** is famed far beyond its borders. Try casting a fly in the water in the Jackson Hole area, or look for your trout in the North Platte upstream from Saratoga or in the Miracle Mile Area (so named because of the large numbers of big fish caught there) near Casper.

Big game hunting flourishes statewide. Elk hunters can find trophy bulls in northeastern Wyoming near Cody and Dubois or in south central Wyoming in the Saratoga area. Antelope hunters might have their best luck around Rawlins, while white-tailed deer hunting is best in the Powder River Basin near Sundance and Gillette. Bird hunting is popular in eastern Wyoming.

All of the mountain areas and national forests are prime spots for **hiking, mountain biking,** and **horseback riding.** At **dude ranches** and **working cattle ranches**—primarily in northwestern Wyoming near Jackson, Dubois, Cody, and Sheridan—activities range from barbecues to overnight horseback trips and organized outings to such locations as Yellowstone National Park. At most dude ranches you stay in a comfortable private cabin, eat meals with other guests in the main lodge, and have structured daily activities in addition to swimming and tennis. At working cattle ranches, you actually experience ranch life. You might move cattle to summer pasture or spend time setting up water tanks or fixing fences. Either way, you'll quickly learn what everyday life is like for Wyoming ranchers and their families.

Wyoming has more months of winter than of the other three seasons combined. Luckily there is plenty to do when the ground is covered with snow. The state has several areas with groomed **snowmobiling trails,** including the Continental Divide National Scenic Snowmobile Trail in the Lander, Dubois, and Jackson areas, and trails in the Bighorn Mountains around Buffalo and Sheridan. Trails in the Black Hills near Sundance and Newcastle tie in with routes from South Dakota.

There are **downhill ski areas** near Jackson, Cody, Lovell, Casper, and Laramie, as well as cross-country ski trails, which are also in national forests. Gillette and Casper have indoor ice-skating rinks, and many smaller communities have outdoor rinks or ponds for skating.

Other Points of Interest

Some of Wyoming's small towns have outstanding sights either in town or nearby. **Guernsey** has ruts from the Oregon Trail only 3 mi west and Register Cliff 1 mi farther. The best small museum in the state is the **Grand Encampment Museum,** where the authentic buildings range from a stage station and one-room school house to a tie hack cabin, blacksmith shop, and two-story outhouse (the latter needed by settlers living in deep snow country). The best places to see wildlife (outside of Yellowstone) are from either the North Fork or South Fork highways west of Cody, on the **Whiskey Mountain** winter range for bighorn sheep near Dubois, or on a sleigh ride through the **National Elk Refuge** in Jackson Hole. The **Yellowstone Drug** in Shoshoni makes the best malts in the state, and you'll find the top steaks in Hudson at **Svilars** or **El Toro**. You're unlikely to run into crowds in any of the state's smaller towns unless you happen to show up during some annual celebration.

Every community in Wyoming has some annual event honoring its history and heritage. **Mustang Days** in Lovell are so named for the herds of wild horses that still roam on the Pryor Mountain Range north of town, and at the **Green River Rendezvous** in Pinedale, mountain men and Native Americans gather to barter, compete in various skills, and exchange lore.

Rules of the Road

License Requirements: To drive in Wyoming you must be at least age 16 and have a valid driver's license, unless you are age 15 and have a valid learner's permit and a licensed driver over age 18 is in the front passenger's seat to instruct you. Youth under age 15 can obtain "hardship permits" that allow them to drive to work or to school.

Speed Limit: Wyoming was one of the first states to adopt higher speed limits when federal authorities allowed it in 1995. Present limits are 65 mph on state highways and 75 mph on interstate highways for all vehicles.

Right Turn on Red: Allowed throughout the state unless posted otherwise.

Seatbelt and Helmet Laws: Drivers must wear seatbelts; carseats are required for infants and young/small children.

Road and Travel Reports: Available from WYDOT October–April, the regularly updated reports provide the most up-to-date road conditions. Call 800/WYO–ROAD.

For More Information: Contact the Wyoming Department of Transportation at 307/777–4484 or wydot@missc.state.wy.us.

From the Powder River to the Parks Driving Tour

SUNDANCE TO JACKSON HOLE

Distance: 488 mi   Time: Minimum 5 days
Breaks: Overnight stops in Buffalo, Sheridan, Cody, Yellowstone National Park, and Jackson.

On this tour you can see Wyoming's premier attractions, including Devils Tower, the first national monument; Yellowstone, the first national park; and other outstanding sites, from Grand Teton National Park to the world-class Buffalo Bill Historical Center, the Medicine Wheel, an ancient Native American ruin, and spectacular mountains, basins, and plains. You can't make this entire tour by automobile in winter as some of the roads— particularly those in Yellowstone—close. For the best conditions, travel either in September and early October or late May and early June, when you'll encounter less traffic and fewer people.

INTRODUCTION
HISTORY
REGIONS
WHEN TO VISIT
STATE'S GREATS
RULES OF THE ROAD
DRIVING TOURS

❶ Begin at **Sundance** (I–90, Exit 187 or 189, 19 mi east of South Dakota) which introduces you to the region's Native American culture; the town is named not for the robber-bandit of movie fame, but for the Indian ritual held each summer. The Sundance Kid did spend time in jail in the town, which is where he earned his nickname.

❷ Take I–90 north for approximately 21 mi to **Devils Tower** (Exit 185 off I–90 onto U.S. 14 and Route 24), which rises from the Belle Fourche River valley and is a sacred site for Native Americans. Popular with climbers, the tower has 7 mi of hiking trails, camping, picnicking, and a visitor center.

❸ Following U.S. 14 south to I–90, proceed west approximately 60 mi into **Gillette** (Exit 132). This is a coal-mining town with a high tax base, so it has great public facilities, from a recreation center to the Cam-Plex, where the town holds anything from craft shows to rodeos. Explore Devils Tower for the morning, then eat lunch in Gillette. Continue your drive across the rolling grasslands of the Powder River Basin.

❹ Nearly 70 mi west of Gillette at the intersection of I–90 and I–25 is **Buffalo,** which became nationally known in 1892 when cattlemen raised an "army" and invaded Johnson County in an attempt to eliminate rustlers. The cattlemen killed two cowboys before Buffalo townspeople surrounded the invaders, who were subsequently rescued by the U.S. Army. Visit the Jim Gatchell Museum for an interpretation of the invasion.

❺ When you're finished exploring Buffalo, continue on I–90 for about 12 mi to **Fort Phil Kearny** (Exit 44), a military post on the Bozeman Trail from 1864 to 1866. Nearby are the sites of the 1866 Fetterman Massacre and the 1867 Wagon Box battle. The fort has an interpretive center, and guides can direct you to the battle sites on Route 193 and U.S. 87. Take the latter to Big Horn and the Bradford Britton Memorial, which displays works by Charles Russell and Frederic Remington.

❻ From the battle sites, continue on U.S. 87 along the east face of the Bighorn Mountains for about 23 mi to **Sheridan** (I–90 Exit 20). Visit the King Museum and enjoy walking around the historic town center.

❼ From Sheridan, head north on I–90 to Exit 14. Get onto U.S. 14 and cross the Bighorn Mountains through the **Bighorn National Forest.** At Burgess Junction continue west on U.S. 14A to **Medicine Wheel,** where a short hike takes you to the Native American site. Then follow U.S. 14A down into the Bighorn Basin. The road is steep and curvy, so take it slow and enjoy the incredible view. **Bighorn Canyon National Recreation Area** (307/548–2251) is at the bottom of the mountain; there you can boat and fish, or take drives and hikes on which you may see wild mustangs in the Pryor Mountain herd.

❽ Continue west on U.S. 14A for approximately 40 mi to **Cody** (U.S. 14A and U.S. 14/16/20). Cody is named for Wild West scout and showman Buffalo Bill Cody. One of the four major museums at the **Buffalo Bill Historical Center** focuses on his life. The four museums—the Plains Indian Museum, the Buffalo Bill Museum, the Cody Firearms Museum, and the Whitney Gallery of Western Art—are in the same complex and have outstanding collections and diverse activities. Other Cody attractions are **Trail Town and the Museum of the Old West; Cody Nite Rodeo; Tecumseh's Old West Miniature Village & Museum;** and the **Irma Hotel,** built by Cody and named for his daughter. The rest of this tour will take you through Yellowstone National Park and Grand Teton National Park and into the town of Jackson. The drive is approximately 177 mi.

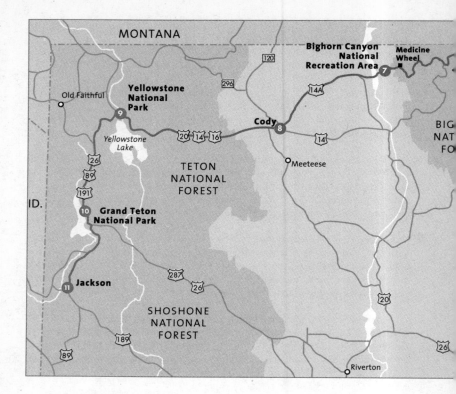

Yellowstone National Park (52 mi west of Cody on U.S. 14/16/20 or Routes 120 and 296) was America's first national park and has a deserved reputation as one of the best, with its boiling mud pots, steaming and spouting geysers, spectacular waterfalls, and diverse wildlife. The Yellowstone roads range from very good, with new pavement, to very poor, with potholes. Plan to travel slowly on the basic figure-eight system. Key places to stop include Grand Canyon of the Yellowstone, Old Faithful, Mammoth, and Yellowstone Lake. Visitor centers are situated throughout the park, as are hiking trails, boardwalk systems through geyser basins, and opportunities to ride horses or a stage-coach at Roosevelt. You almost certainly will see elk, bison, ducks, deer, squirrels, and coyotes. You'll also likely see foxes, bald eagles, trumpeter swans, Canada geese, and antelope. If you travel early in the morning or late in the evening, you may see black or grizzly bears or wolves. Remember that all the animals in Yellowstone are wild. Never approach or feed any animal. Keep your distance and give them their space.

Grand Teton National Park (south of Yellowstone National Park, north of Jackson on Route 26/89/191) encompasses the spectacular Grand Teton Mountain range and much of broad Jackson Hole. From any of the roads crossing the valley you can see the majestic Tetons, and you will often catch glimpses of the Snake River. You can hike, bike, fish, boat, ride horses, camp or, picnic. You may want to climb these mountains, but such excursions are only for skilled climbers. Companies in Jackson Hole can teach you the ropes—literally.

Continue south on Route 26/81/191 to **Jackson** (U.S. 189 and Route 22), a small Western town of about 4,000 people who play host to some 3 million visitors annually. It's compact, so you can park and walk to most hotels, motels, restaurants, and downtown

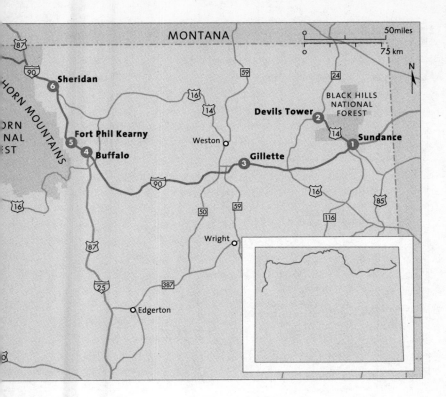

INTRODUCTION
HISTORY
REGIONS
WHEN TO VISIT
STATE'S GREATS
RULES OF THE ROAD
DRIVING TOURS

attractions. The town has a western flair and manages to maintain a folksy feeling most of the time, but you can both shop and have other kinds of fun. The fun around here might be a white-water trip on the Snake River or a walking tour of historic sites led by the **Jackson Hole Museum.** Art galleries abound, and the National **Wildlife Art Museum** has a good collection of sculpture and paintings. In the winter, view thousands of elk—and coyotes, bald eagles, or possibly a wolf—on a sleigh ride through the **National Elk Refuge.**

The quickest way back to Sundance is to retrace your route.

Historic Trails Trek Driving Tour

TORRINGTON TO EVANSTON

Distance: 390 mi   Time: Minimum of 4 days
Breaks: Casper, Lander, Rawlins

On this tour you can cross the same ground pioneers did when they traveled to Oregon, Utah, or California 150 years ago. In many ways the landscape has changed little in the intervening years. Follow the North Platte River, just as the pioneers did, and cross at Casper, then traverse the Sweetwater River valley and South Pass before trekking across the Red Desert country of western Wyoming, as you make your way between Fort Laramie and Fort Bridger. These were the only two provisioning points on the entire route at the time the emigrants walked or drove wagons over the trail. As an option, once you visit the Mormon Trail/Martin's Cove Visitors Center, you can

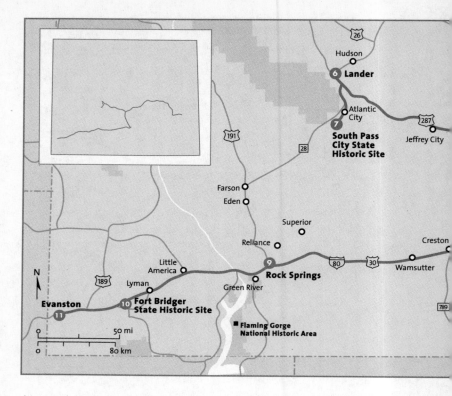

drive south to Rawlins and then continue west along the route of the Overland and Cherokee trails. Either trip will give you a real appreciation for the determination and spirit of the pioneers (especially if you turn off the air-conditioner in your car on a hot July or August day). You can make this trip at any time, but spring, summer, and fall are best because visitors centers are all open then, and you'll be less likely to run into a snowstorm on South Pass. Bear in mind, though, that the pass is 7,550 ft high, so you could hit snow even in July or August.

❶ Begin at **Fort Laramie National Historic Site** (U.S. 26, 20 mi west of Torrington), which became the most important site on the Oregon-California-Mormon trail route because it was a provisioning point and, after 1849, a U.S. Army post. Many of the fort's original buildings remain, and during the summer costumed interpreters illustrate life there. Actual ruts of the historic emigrant trails cross the fort grounds.

❷ Continuing west on U.S. 26, you'll come to Register Cliff and the Guernsey Ruts, both near **Guernsey.**

❸ From Guernsey continue west on U.S. 20/26 for 15 mi to I–25, then head north on I–25 to **Ayres Natural Bridge,** off the interstate between Douglas and Glenrock.

❹ After taking in the beauty of the bridge and its surroundings, head west on I–25 for approximately 40 mi to **Casper** (I–25, U.S. 20/26, and Rte. 220). This town is proud of its position on the national historic emigrant trails system. Several major trails converged here as emigrants crossed the North Platte River and continued west along the Oregon-California-Mormon routes to the Sweetwater River valley or headed north to Montana's

INTRODUCTION
HISTORY
REGIONS
WHEN TO VISIT
STATE'S GREATS
RULES OF THE ROAD
DRIVING TOURS

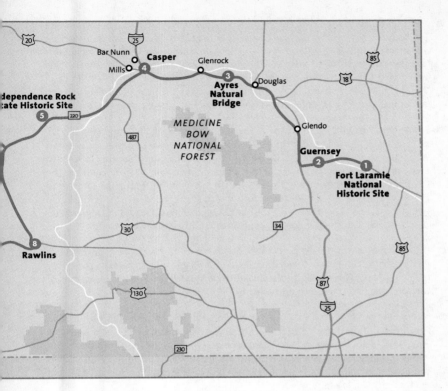

gold fields over the Bozeman or Bridger trails. No community existed here during the migration period, but **Fort Caspar,** which originally went by the name Platte Bridge Station, was a military installation during the later years of overland travel. You can do much in Casper that is not related to overland trails, including hiking, biking, and skiing in the winter on **Casper Mountain,** visiting such sites as the **Nicolaysen Art Museum & Discovery Center** and the **Casper Planetarium,** or walking along the **Platte River Parkway.** Plans are underway for a new National Frontier Trails Center—a joint project of the U.S. Bureau of Land Management, the City of Casper, and the State of Wyoming.

⑤ Independence Rock State Historic Site (60 mi west of Casper on Route 220) is one of the best-known of all trail sites along the entire 2,000-mi corridor from Missouri to Oregon or California, and pioneers almost always mentioned it in their journals. You can stretch your legs at a rest area, perhaps by climbing to the top of the rock, where you'll see some of the emigrant names carved in the granite. Then continue west on Route 220 to the **Mormon Trail/Martin's Cove Visitors Center** at the Sun Ranch, a site that interprets the Mormon migration to Utah and other emigrant stories as well. You can pick up a hand-cart and pull it along the trail route to get a real sense of what the travelers endured. From this point on, you can continue following the route of the Oregon-California-Mormon Trail to Lander, South Pass City, and eventually Fort Bridger, or you can travel south to Rawlins and follow the route of the Overland and Cherokee trails to Fort Bridger.

⑥ Leaving Independence Rock, continue west on Rte. 220/U.S. 287 to **Lander** (U.S. 287). Lander is off the main emigrant trail route, but it is a good place to hang your hat for the night and learn about the Shoshone and Arapaho Indian tribes, who have a reservation just to the northeast.

➐ Head south out of Lander on U.S. 287 to Route 28. **South Pass City State Historic Site** (off Route 28 between Lander and Farson) is only a few mi from the most important site of the entire route—South Pass—the long, low pass over the Rocky Mountains used by early travelers to cross the Continental Divide. South Pass City, meanwhile, was a gold town established in 1869 and is the birthplace of women's suffrage in Wyoming. A collection of historic buildings still marks the townsite, where you can sometimes pan for gold or hike trails used by miners of yesteryear.

➑ From South Pass City, backtrack to U.S. 287 and head southeast for approximately 125 mi to **Rawlins** (I–80 Exit 220 and U.S. 287), in the Great Divide Basin, a depression between two branches of the Continental Divide. Visit the **Carbon County Museum** to see artifacts from outlaw George Parrott, or take a tour of the Wyoming Frontier Prison. The Overland and Cherokee trails crossed southern Wyoming from near Laramie to Evanston. The Cherokees made their route in 1849 as they headed to California's gold fields; the Overland Route became the main stagecoach road across the region after 1865. I–80 parallels the two, which are generally south of today's highway.

➒ From Rawlins proceed west on I–80 for about 110 mi to **Rock Springs** (Exit 104), a historic coal-mining town. **Green River** (I–80 Exits 89 and 91) also owes its prosperity to mining. At the **Flaming Gorge National Historic Area** (south on U.S. 191 or Route 530) you can boat, fish, camp, bike, and hike.

➓ After you've explored Rock Springs, head west on I–80 for approximately 60 mi to the **Fort Bridger State Historic Site** (I–80 Exit 48 westbound or Exit 34 eastbound), the emigrants' major trading and provisioning point—the first they had seen since leaving Fort Laramie. Mountain man Jim Bridger and his partner Louis Vasquez established Fort Bridger "in the path of the emigrants" in 1841. It later became a military fort, and many original buildings remain.

⓫ Continue west out of the Fort on I–80 to **Evanston** (Exit 3), a town that got its start as a Union Pacific hell-on-wheels town. It had a significant Chinese population in its early years.

To return to Fort Laramie, head east on I–80 to Rawlins, north on U.S. 287/Route 789 to Route 220, then east into Casper. From Casper, follow I–25 east and south back to U.S. 26, which leads east into Fort Laramie.

AFTON

MAP 9, B4

(Nearby town also listed: Alpine)

With a population of 1,700, Afton is the largest town in the Star Valley, a remote mountain region in extreme western Wyoming, sometimes called "Little Switzerland of America." Other beautiful mountain valleys in the West make that same claim, but Afton has another unusual feature. The Periodic or Intermittent Spring—5 mi from town— is one of only three known fluctuating springs in the world. Native Americans called it "the spring that breathes." It doesn't flow all the time; instead, it gushes a large amount of water for a time then produces almost no flow at all.

Settled initially by Mormon families, Afton and its valley became widely known for dairy farms. In 1889 valley farmers established a cooperative creamery. Subsequently, cheesemaking became a big industry, and they produced even hard-to-make Swiss cheese. Although dairy production has declined in recent years, the dairy cows in this mountain valley still give it the look of a European countryside.

Information: **Star Valley Chamber of Commerce** | Box 1097, Afton 83110 | 307/883–2759 or 800/426–8833 | fax 307/883–2758 | svcc@silverstar.com.

Attractions

Big-Game Hunting. Trophy elk inhabit the Greys River area, and you can see a lot of them in this scenic valley in the summer or hunt them in the fall—elk season is generally in October. Numerous outfitters arrange anything from full-scale outings to more limited excursions. | Star Valley Chamber of Commerce, Box 1097 | 307/883–2759 or 800/426–8833 | fax 307/883–2758 | svccom@silverstar.com | www.starvalleychamber.com.

Bridger-Teton National Forest. Nearly half a million acres make up the Greys River Ranger District of the Bridger-Teton National Forest, where you'll find seven developed campgrounds, 448 mi of hiking and horseback trails, more than 100 mi of snowmobile trails, and 3 mi of cross-country ski trails. | Greys River Ranger District, 125 Washington St. | 307/886–3166 | www.fs.fed.us/btnf/ | Developed campgrounds: fee varies | Daily.

Periodic Spring. When the water level of an underground reservoir fills above a certain level, water is pulled up and out of the spring; when the spring lowers the reservoir's level below the siphon intake, the spring dies and the reservoir begins to fill again. Five mi east, up Swift Creek Canyon Rd., it is the largest of only three true fluctuating springs known in the world. | 307/886–3166 | Free | Daily.

ON THE CALENDAR

FEB.: *International Rocky Mountain Stage Stop Sled Dog Race.* This is one stop of a multiday race that includes many Iditarod champions. The race is held to increase awareness of the need for childhood immunization. | 307/777–7777 or 800/426–8833.
DEC.–FEB.: *Cutter/Chariot Races.* Horse-drawn chariots or cutters (small sleighs) compete in drag races held weekends at the racegrounds. | Allred Rd., 1 mi northwest of Afton | 307/883–2759 or 800/426–8833.

Dining

Gunnar's Pizza. Italian. Get your pizza, salads, or sub and dine either inside or on the deck that overlooks the street, or take out. | 845 S. Washington St. | 307/885–9795 | $3–$18 | No credit cards.

Homestead Restaurant. American. A coffee shop and a family dining area make this a good place to stop for lunch or a snack when you're driving U.S 89. | 84506 U.S. 89 | 307/885–5558 | $12–$14 | MC, V.

Timberline Steakhouse. American. In Colter's Lodge, this steak house has a rustic setting that includes a wildlife exhibit. You can get breakfast as well at the Valleon Cafe, also within the lodge, and buffet, family-style lunch and dinner. | 355 N. Washington St. | 307/886–9891 | $11–$21 | AE, D, DC, MC, V.

Lodging

Best Western Hi Country Inn. You get the convenience of downtown and are only 2 mi from the Periodic Spring. In winter, you can cross-country ski nearby. No air-conditioning. Cable TV. Pool in summer. Hot tub. Some pets allowed. | 689 S. Washington St. | 307/886–3856 | fax 307/885–9318 | 30 rooms | $50–$65 | AE, D, DC, MC, V.

Colters Lodge. This adobe-and-wood four-story lodge is straight out of the Old West. Rooms have wood panelling and log beds, and stuffed deer heads gaze out over the gift shop and common areas. The large suites sleep up to 8 people. You can rent snowmobiles in winter. 2 restaurants, bar. Cable TV. Hot tub. Business services. | 355 Washington St. (U.S. 89) | fax 307/885–2658 | 15 rooms, 3 suites | $40, $60 suites | AE, D, DC, MC, V.

Corral. The large backyard doubles as a children's play area, and the individual log cabins in downtown Afton let you have both rustic touches and downtown convenience. Picnic area. No air-conditioning, some refrigerators. Cable TV. Some pets allowed. | 161 Washington St. (U.S. 89) | 307/886–5424 | 15 rooms (2 with kitchenettes) | $40–$80 | Closed winter | AE, D, DC, MC, V.

Lazy B Motel. Not every motel offers lodgings for your horse. This is one of them. The 1960s style roadside motel has large grassy common areas with deer statuettes, and wonderful views of the surrounding mountains. Picnic area, grill. Cable TV. Playground. Pets allowed. | 219 Washington St. (U.S. 89) | 307/885–3187 | fax 307/885–3035 | 24 rooms, 1 suite | $53.50, $100 suite | AE, D, DC, MC, V.

Three Rivers Motel. Families may appreciate the kitchenettes in every room of this downtown motel, which has contemporary, L-shaped rooms. Pets allowed. | 60 Main St. | 307/654–7551 | threeriv@cyberhighway.net | www.wy-biz.com/3riversmotel/ | 23 rooms with kitchenettes | $50–$60 | AE, D, MC, V.

ALPINE

MAP 9, B3

(Nearby towns also listed: Afton, Jackson)

Known for its fishing on the Greys and Salt rivers and on Palisades Reservoir, Alpine is one of the small (pop. 480), attractive communities in the Star Valley. A third river, the Snake, flows nearby and is widely used during the summer floating season.

Information: Star Valley Chamber of Commerce | Box 1097, Afton 83110 | 307/883–2759 or 800/426–8833 | fax 307/883–2758 | svcc@silverstar.com.

Attractions

Fishing. Three major rivers—the Salt, Greys, and Snake—are filled with cutthroat and brown trout just waiting for you to land them. | 307/883–2759 or 800/426–8833.

ON THE CALENDAR
MAR.: *Alpine Fishing Derby.* Anglers compete for fun and prizes in this annual event. | 307/883–2759 or 800/426–8833.
NOV.: *Holiday Flea Market.* Arts, crafts, and food are all part of this holiday sale. | 307/883–2759 or 800/426–8833.

Dining

Frenchy's Outpost. Cafe. At this bakery and coffee shop you can get donuts, snacks, hamburgers, and ice cream. | U.S. 89 | 307/654–7629 | $1–$5 | No credit cards | Closed winter.

Gunnar's Pizza. Italian. Pizza, salads, and sub sandwiches; you can dine here or take out. | U.S. 89 | 307/654–7778 | $10 | No credit cards.

Roal Ridge Restaurant. American. In the Alpen Haus Hotel, this restaurant serves pasta, steak, seafood, chicken, and daily specials, including elk. | U.S. 26 and 89 | 307/654–7508 | $14.50–$25 | AE, D, DC, MC, V | Closed Sun.–Wed.

Lodging

Alpine Inn. Privacy and beautiful views distinguish these individual cabins tucked back from the highway in a large grassy yard. The six cabin suites have two rooms and kitchenettes, a plus for traveling families. TV. Hot tub. | 1180 U.S. 26 | 307/654–7644 | fax 307/654–7646 | 12 cabin rooms, 6 cabin suites | $50–$60 cabin rooms, $70 cabin suites | AE, D, MC, V.

Best Western Flying Saddle Lodge. Each individual cottage suite has a deck, and all are soundproofed. The furnishings in the spacious rooms are contemporary-elegant and comfortable. Restaurant, bar. In-room hot tubs, some refrigerators. Cable TV. Pool. Tennis. Business services. | U.S. 26 | 307/654–7561 | fax 307/654–7563 | 20 rooms, 6 cottages | $80 | AE, D, DC, MC, V | Closed winter.

Royal Resort. Only 8 mi from the Snake River, this resort makes a great headquarters for virtually any outdoor sport. The design and furnishings, both in the lobby and in the rooms, may remind you of a Bavarian lodge. The small market also has a gas station. Restaurant, bar, ice-cream parlor. Some minibars, some refrigerators. Cable TV, some VCRs. Hot tub. Exercise room. Horseback riding, white-water rafting. Cross-country skiing, snowmobiling. RV spaces. Playground. Small pets allowed. | U.S. 26 and 89 | 307/654–7545, ext. 331; 800/343–6755 (outside WY) | fax 307/654–7546 | www.royal-resort.com | 45 rooms | $50–$100 | AE, D, DC, MC, V.

BUFFALO

(Nearby town also listed: Sheridan)

BUFFALO

INTRO
ATTRACTIONS
DINING
LODGING

The Bighorn Mountains are the backdrop for Buffalo, a community of 3,800 that has twice made national headlines. The 1892 Johnson County invasion brought a force of Texas gunmen hired by Wyoming cattle barons to "clean out" rustlers and renegades. Nearly a century later, a 737 landed at the airport (which is not designed for 737s) when the pilot thought he was landing at Sheridan's much larger airport. Both incidents attracted nationwide media coverage.

The first entrepreneur in the community was likely Capt. H. E. Palmer, who took four wagon loads of goods to the region in 1855 and set up a trading establishment. But at that time the Lakota Indians had a treaty right to the region, and they wanted Palmer to leave. Palmer, facing bows and arrows, packed his goods and headed north to the Tongue River where he traded successfully for several years.

Following two different periods of conflict between the frontier army and the Plains Indians, European-Americans began to settle here, and Buffalo was established in 1879. The region quickly became a sheep and cattle area, and the ranching tradition continues. Many of the early settlers were Basque sheepmen whose families still raise sheep on the Powder River grasslands. Butch Cassidy and other members of outlaw gangs periodically passed through the vicinity, particularly when attempting to elude a posse by riding into the Hole-in-the-Wall country, southwest of Buffalo. Western novelist Owen Wister also visited such community hangouts as the Occidental Hotel, which still stands on Buffalo's winding main street.

Information: Buffalo Chamber of Commerce | 55 N. Main St., 82834 | 307/684–5544 or 800/227–5122 | nadgross@wyoming.com | www.buffalowyo.org.

Attractions

Bighorn National Forest. The Bighorn Mountains—roughly in between Buffalo and Tensleep in the south and Sheridan and Lovell in the north—are one of the many huge areas of public land in north-central Wyoming. You can camp (at 19 managed campgrounds and uncounted backcountry sites) and hike, ride horseback or fish. In the winter you can snowmobile. The Cloud Peak Wilderness Area, with 189,000 acres, has enough room for backpacking and horsepacking. Elevations range from 8,500 to 13,165 ft. | Buffalo Ranger District, 1425 Fort St., Buffalo | 307/864–1100 | www.fs.fed.us/r2bighorn/ | Daily.

Clear Creek Trail. Signs bearing a buffalo symbol mark the Clear Creek Trail, which includes about 11 mi of trails following Clear Creek through Buffalo and past historic areas. The trail has both paved and unpaved sections. Along it you see the Occidental Hotel (made famous by Owen Wister in *The Virginian*), a brewery and mill site, and the site of Fort McKinney, now the Veterans' Home of Wyoming. You can traverse the trail walking, jogging, bicycling, or skateboarding. You can also use the trail for wildlife viewing, photography, and access to fishing. | 307/684–5544 or 800/227–5122 | Free.

Fort Phil Kearny Site. In 1866 the army established several forts along the trail from central Wyoming to Montana's gold fields. Named the Bozeman Trail for one of the men who forged the route, it became better known as the Bloody Bozeman when the military clashed with Native Americans who considered this their territory. The region had been set aside for the tribes, including the Lakota (Sioux), in earlier treaties with the United States. Fort Phil Kearny became one of the posts established along the Bozeman Trail to protect travelers. The Native Americans opposed it fiercely, raided routinely, and won several decisive battles before forcing the military to withdraw from the region in 1868. Although the Indians promptly burned the fort, the site is now marked and the original foundations are still visible. There is a new, small visitor center. | 528 Wagon Box Rd. | 307/684–7629 | Mid-May–Sept., daily 8–6.

Jim Gatchell Museum of the West. You'll see detailed dioramas of the Powder River Basin Indian conflicts and the Johnson County Invasion of 1892 at this museum, which started as the private collection of a local resident. | 100 Fort St. | 307/684–9331 | www.wilderwest.com/wyoming/buffalo/gallery/gatchell.shi | $2 | May–Oct., Mon.–Sat. 9–8.

ON THE CALENDAR

MAY: *Memorial Day Weekend Lions Club Fishing Derby.* Anglers compete for prizes based on the size and type of fish they catch. | 800/227–5122.
JUNE: *Bozeman Trail Days.* Events and programs held in nearby Story are related to the development and use of the Bozeman Trail. | 307/684–7687 or 307/684–7629.
JUNE: *Powder River Roundup.* Rodeo action and entertainment at the Johnson County Fairgrounds include the Wyoming Country Music Festival. Downtown are a wildflower festival and crafts fair. | 307/738–2303.
JULY: *Living History Days.* Costumed interpreters provide information about pioneer life and events at the Jim Gatchell Museum. | 100 Fort St. | 307/684–9331.
AUG.: *Johnson County Fair & Rodeo.* 4-H and FFA projects are on display as well as open-class exhibits ranging from livestock to arts and crafts. | 307/684–7357.
DEC.: *Christmas Parade.* One of the best Christmas parades in Wyoming, this one winds its way through downtown Buffalo in early December. | 307/684–5544.

Dining

Art Works Too & Cowgirl Coffee Cafe American. In an 1890s stone-front building in historic downtown Buffalo, this funky coffee house–café is a favored local hangout, with backyard sitting area, sculpture garden, regional art work, and live acoustic music on the weekends. Try the organic coffee or tea, bagel sandwiches, biscotti, and brownies for a quick lunch; weekend barbecues feature homemade meals and live folk music. | 94 S. Main St. | 307/684–1299 | $5–$10 | D, MC, V.

Colonel Bozeman's. Southwestern. Literally on the Bozeman Trail, Colonel Bozeman's serves good food amid Western memorabilia. Local favorites include buffalo steak and prime rib. You can also dine outdoors on the deck. Kids' menu. | 675 E. Hart St. | 307/684–5555 | $8–$16 | AE, D, MC, V.

Deerfield Boutique and Espresso Bar. Contemporary. For a change from steak and potatoes, try this deli-style café next to Clear Creek, on a quiet side street in downtown Buffalo. In a renovated historic theater, with high ceilings and old wallpaper, the place offers a wide range of tortilla wraps and specialty sandwiches like lemon-ginger chicken pita and turkey and Swiss on foccacia. Chilled summer soups might be tomato wine, cream of canteloupe, or spinach cucumber. The Polynesian and mandarin orange salads are equally refreshing. | 7 N. Main St. | 307/684–2788 | $5–$12 | MC, V.

Stagecoach Inn. American. On the edge of town, this restaurant specializes in prime rib, steak, and seafood dishes, and is filled with Western antiques and memorabilia. | 845 Fort St. | 307/684–0713 | $9–$17 | MC, V.

Wagon Box Restaurant. American. This bright, spacious cabin restaurant in the Bighorn Mountains 15 mi northwest of Buffalo on I–90 is surrounded by ponderosa pines. It serves well-prepared steak, seafood, burgers, and sandwiches. Prime rib is the specialty, and the huge wine selection is unmatched in the area. | 108 N. Piney Rd., Story | 307/683–2444 | $18 | AE, D, DC, MC, V.

Lodging

Blue Gables Motel. Clustered like a small group of cabins, this U-shaped motel is a homey place with Old West collectibles and quilts that give it a comfortable feeling. No room phones. Pool. No-smoking rooms. | 662 N. Main St. | 307/684–2574 or 800/684–2574 | jakse@trip.com | 17 rooms | $55–$59 | D, MC, V.

Canyon Motel. An airport shuttle and three rooms with kitchenettes are added conveniences at this contemporary motel on the west side of Buffalo on U.S. 16, near the Bighorn Mountains. Picnic area. Cable TV. Airport shuttle. Pets allowed. | 997 Fort St. | 307/684–2957 or 800/231–0742 | 18 rooms, 3 with kitchenettes | $50–$80 | AE, D, MC, V.

Clear Creek Bed & Breakfast. Built in 1883, this historic family home near downtown Buffalo has a wraparound porch and shaded yard. Rooms are individually decorated with handmade quilts, needle and lace work, and antiques. The numerous sitting areas, including the parlor with the fossilized stone fireplace, invite relaxation. Full breakfast, dining room. TV in common area. No pets. | 330 S. Main St. | 307/684–2317 or 888/865–6789 | 4 rooms | $65–$85 | MC, V.

Cloud Peak Inn. Built during the early 1900s as the "in-town place" for a wealthy rancher and his family, this inn has a graceful staircase and elegant parlor complete with late 19th-century details and antiques. Complimentary breakfast. Hot tub. Cross-country skiing. No smoking. | 590 N. Burritt | 307/684–5794 | fax 307/684–7653 | 5 rooms, 1 with shower only, 2 share bath | $60–$80 | AE, MC, V.

Comfort Inn. Several blocks from downtown, this hotel was built in 1995 and has rooms priced to fit any budget. Complimentary Continental breakfast. Cable TV. Hot tub. Some pets allowed. | 65 U.S. 16 E | 307/684–9564 or 800/228–5150 | fax 307/684–9564 | 41 rooms | $39–$119 | AE, D, DC, MC, V.

CowboyTown Motel. The individual cabin units have front porches, and the bright rooms have king-size beds and Western-style furnishings. Cable TV. Outdoor hot tub. Pets allowed. No-smoking rooms. | 181 U.S. 16 E | 307/684–0603 or 888/323–2865 | fax 307/684–0605 | 4 rooms, 8 cabins, 2 kitchenettes | $62 rooms and cabins, $58–$88 kitchenettes | D, MC, V.

Crossroads HoJo Inn. Near the Bighorn Mountains and I–25, this large, modern hotel has spacious rooms and convenient access to the interstate. Restaurant, bar, complimentary breakfast. Pool. Hot tub. Pets allowed (fee). | 75 N. Bypass | 307/684–2256 | fax 307/684–2256 | 60 rooms | $79–$104 | AE, D, DC, MC, V.

Paradise Guest Ranch. Each room has a kitchenette and some have fireplaces, while the dining hall is a separate cabin. You can go horseback riding, take pack trips, and fly-fish. The children's programs are a nice amenity. Restaurant, bar, picnic area. Pool. Hot tub. Fishing. Children's programs, playground. Airport shuttle. | Hunter Creek Rd. (Box 790), off U.S. 16 | 307/684–7876 | fax 307/684–9054 | fun@paradiseranch.com | www.paradiseranch.com | 18 cabins with kitchenettes | $1,450 wk | No credit cards | AP | Closed May and Sept.

Ranch at Ucross. This converted old ranch home is a good place for business retreats, with full meeting facilities and cabins that have great views. Restaurant, bar, complimentary breakfast. Pool. Tennis. Fishing. Cross-country skiing, snowmobiling. Business services. Pets allowed. | 2673 U.S. 14 E, Ucross | 307/737–2281 or 800/447–0194 | fax 307/737–2211 |

blair@wavecom.net | www.innsite.com/inns/A002021.html | 31 rooms, 4 suites | $109–$159 | MC, V.

Wyoming Motel. Some extra-large rooms and some with kitchenettes make this a good stopping place for families on the road. The motel is near the intersection of I–90, I–25, and U.S. 16. Restaurant, picnic area. Cable TV. Pool. Hot tub. Pets allowed. | 610 E. Hart St. | 800/666–5505 | fax 307/684–5442 | wyomotel@vcn.com | 27 rooms, 5 with kitchenettes | $62–$67, $129–$145 large family rooms | AE, D, DC, MC, V.

Z-Bar Motel. At the base of the Bighorn Mountains, these clean, quiet cabins sit in a huge shaded yard with tables and barbecue grills. Some kitchenettes are available—ideal if you are traveling with pets or children. Picnic area. Refrigerators. Cable TV. Pets allowed. | 626 Fort St. | 307/684–5535 or 888/313–1227 | fax 307/684–5538 | 4 rooms, 22 cabins | $50–$63 rooms and cabins | AE, D, DC, MC, V.

CASPER

MAP 9, G4

(Nearby town also listed: Douglas)

A raucous boom-and-bust kind of city, Casper can rightfully claim that it's one of the oldest permanent crossroads in the state. The first white people to establish a winter home in Wyoming were probably Robert Stuart and his companions, who were headed east from Fort Astoria in 1811. But these early travelers identified the route that later became the Oregon-Mormon-California Trail. During almost all subsequent overland travel, people crossed the North Platte River around present-day Casper.

The town took its name from Lt. Caspar Collins, who, along with several companions, lost a fight with Sioux and Cheyenne Indians on July 26, 1865, as the soldiers rode toward a wagon train that was being threatened. The Indians subsequently killed all the people in the train. Originally known as a ferry crossing (Mormons built the first ferry in the region in 1847) and site of several bridges over the North Platte, the frontier army station went by the name Platte Bridge, later becoming Fort Caspar. When the town was founded, somebody misspelled the name, and the spelling with an "e" has been used ever since.

Permanence came with cattle and sheep ranching, but prosperity came with mining. Oil and gas development—along with coal, bentonite, and uranium—drives or has driven Casper's economy, which alternately soars on high prices and struggles with low ones.

Situated at the foot of Casper Mountain, with the North Platte River running through it, Casper is also near the geographical center of Wyoming. The city has the state's largest newspaper (the *Star-Tribune*), a symphony orchestra, art galleries, an assortment of restaurants, and the remarkable distinction of sitting where five of the major overland trails converged. Casper intends to cash in on that fact, and construction has begun on a new National Frontier Trails Center that will interpret the Oregon, California, Mormon, Bozeman, Bridger, and Pony Express trails. A joint project involving funding from the U.S. Bureau of Land Management, the State of Wyoming, the City of Casper, and private donors, it is not expected to open before summer 2001.

Information: Casper Chamber of Commerce | 500 N. Center St., 82601 | 307/234–5311 or 800/852–1889 | fax fax 307/265–2643 | visitors@trib.com | www.trib.com/ads/casper.

Attractions

Casper Mountain and Beartrap Meadow Parks. Rising to the east of the city, Casper Mountain is a recreational paradise where you can hike and fish in summer and cross-country and downhill ski in winter. The Crimson Dawn Museum is the original log-cabin home of Neal and Jim Forsling, who settled in the area with their daughters in 1915. Neal held her first Midsummer Night's Eve Celebration on June 21, 1929, and the event continues. She and her daughters and their friends built the first trails in the woods around Crimson Dawn Park. Today those same trails are marked with shrines and plaques commemorating the mythical "Enchanted Witches and Elves of Casper Mountain." | Casper Mountain Rd. | 307/235–9325 | Free | Daily; museum, mid-June–mid-Oct., Sat.–Thurs. 11–7.

In Skunk Hollow along Elkhorn Creek, 8 mi south of Rte. 251, the **Lee McCune Braille Trail** is a 1/3-mi route with rope handrails and 37 stops with print and Braille markers describing the scenery. Built in 1975 by the Casper Mountain Lions Club and Casper Field Services students, the Braille Trail is part of the National Trails System. | Casper Mountain Rd. | 307/235–9325 | June–Sept., depending on snowfall.

Casper Mountain is rated a premier **bird-watching** area, and the local Murie Audubon Society offers both a hot line and guides to 13 local birding areas. | 307/265–2473.

Casper Planetarium. Watch multimedia programs on astronomy and space subjects. | 904 N. Poplar St. | 307/577–0310 | fax 307/235–9611 | stars@trib.com | www.trib.com/WYOMING/NCSD/planetarium.html | $2 | Sept.–May, Thurs. at 7 PM, and 1st and 2nd Sat. of each month; June–Aug., daily at 4, 7, 8 PM.

Edness K. Wilkins State Park. At this state park along the North Platte River, you can swim, fish, picnic, and use the 3-mi bicycle and walking/jogging trail. | 8700 E. U.S. 20/26 | 307/577–5150 | $2 per vehicle residents, $5 per vehicle nonresidents | Daily 7 AM–10 PM; Centennial Group area closed Nov.–Apr.

Fort Caspar Museum. A small museum re-creates the post at Platte Bridge, which became Fort Caspar after the July 1865 battle that claimed the lives of several soldiers, including Lt. Caspar Collins. A post depicts life at a frontier station in the 1860s, and sometimes soldier reenactors go about their tasks. Museum exhibits show the migration trails, and the fort bookstore has an excellent selection of Western history titles. | 4001 Fort Caspar Rd. | 307/235–8462 | Free | Closed Sat.

Hogadon Ski Area. Just 9 mi south of downtown Casper, you can both downhill and cross-country ski on 60 acres, with 15 mi of cross-country trails, some lit for night skiing. You can rent equipment, and there's a ski school and food services. | Casper Mountain Rd. | 307/235–8499 or 307/235–8281 (summer); 307/235–8369 for snow conditions | $23 | Nov. 26–mid-Apr., daily 9–4.

Independence Rock. This turtle-shaped granite outcrop became an important site on the Oregon-California-Mormon trails. Pioneers carved their names in the rock, and many are still legible 150 years later. The rock, midway between Casper and Rawlins, is now a state historic site. A state rest area here has rest rooms and picnic tables. | Rte. 220 | 307/577–5150 | commerce.state.wy.us | Free | Daily.

Mormon Trail Handcart Visitor Center. Opened for the 1997 sesquicentennial of the Mormon Trail, this visitor center at the Sun Ranch interprets general trail travel, and particularly the plight of the handcart pioneers in the Willie and Martin Companies, who became stranded in this area of Wyoming in 1856. You can walk the Mormon Trail, and handcarts are available. There's a picnic area, but no food is sold. | 50 mi southwest of Casper on Rte. 220 | 307/324–5218 | Free | Daily.

Nicolaysen Art Museum and Discovery Center. Known locally as The Nic, this art museum has a permanent collection with works by Conrad Schweiring, as well as traveling exhibits. The Discovery Center is an interactive arts and crafts area for children. | 400 E. Collins Dr. | 307/235–5247 | www.thenic.org | $2 | Tues.–Sun. 9–5.

Pathfinder-Alcova Recreation Area. Alcova and Pathfinder reservoirs on the North Platte River store water for hydroelectric production and irrigation. On both, you can jet- or water-ski, boat, and fish. You can also camp in the reservoir area. The Miracle Mile—a stretch of the North Platte River between the Pathfinder and Seminoe reservoirs that actually ranges in length from 1 to 7 mi (depending on Pathfinder's fill level)—is one of the greatest fisheries in Wyoming. Fremont Canyon, between Pathfinder and Alcova, is good for rock climbing. | 4025 Lakeshore Dr., off Rte. 220 | 307/234–6821 or 800/852–1889 | $5 for camping | Daily.

Platte River Parkway. The natural beauty and historic significance of the North Platte River are preserved along this 4-mi paved trail with access points at Amoco Park at 1st and Poplar Streets, at the Historic Trails Overlook east of the Casper Events Center, and between Morad Park and Fort Caspar. Eventually the trail will cover 11½ mi. You can use it for walking, jogging, and wheeled-vehicles that are "user-powered," such as roller blades, bicycles, and skateboards. | Rte. 220 | 307/577–1206 | Free | Daily.

Tate Geological Museum. Fossils and minerals are part of the Tate display. Included are remains of Bertha, a 30-ton brontosaurus, and Sniffles, a newly identified dinosaur. At the fossil preparation lab, professionals work on fossil remains of various types. | 125 College Dr. | 307/268–2447 | www.cc.whecn.edu/tate/webpage.html | Free | Weekdays 9–4, Sat. 10–3.

Werner Wildlife Museum. The displays feature birds and animals indigenous to Wyoming, though animals of other countries are also part of the collection. | 405 E. 15th St. | 307/235–2108 | Free | June–Aug., Mon.–Sat. 10–5; Sept.–May, weekdays 10–5.

TOURS

Historic Tours. Five major trails pass through the Casper area, including the Oregon-California-Mormon Pioneer, Pony Express, and Bozeman trails. Morris Carter of Historic Trails Expeditions gives you a chance to travel them. You ride in specially designed Conestoga-style wagons (used by Carter for a 1993 six-month traversal of the Oregon Trail from Independence, Missouri, to Independence, Oregon) and sleep in tepees or military-style tents. Trips range from four hours to six days. | Box 428, Mills | 307/266–4868 | fax 307/266–2746 | www.historictrailsexpeditions.com | wgntrn@aol.com | $35–$1,195.

ON THE CALENDAR

FEB.: _Cowboy State Games Winter Sports Festival._ An Olympic-style sports competition with various categories. | 307/577–1125.

APR.: _Bullriders Only Rodeo._ This rodeo has only one contest—bull riding. Some of the best cowboys in the country are on hand. | 307/235–8441.

MAY: _Platte Bridge Station Stage Race._ Top cyclists from throughout the country take part in this stage race. | 307/235–0262.

JUNE: _Cowboy State Summer Games._ Wyoming residents compete in this Olympic-style sports event. | 307/577–1125.

JUNE: _Fort Caspar Mountain Man Rendezvous and Primitive Skills Contest._ Buckskinners set up camp at Fort Caspar, with living history demonstrations, a primitive-skills crafts fair, and the world open atlatl competition. (An atlatl is a spear-throwing device used by early hunters.) | 307/235–8462.

JUNE: _Midsummer Night's Eve._ A celebration of the summer solstice on Casper Mountain. | 307/234–5311.

JUNE: _National Finals College Rodeo._ The top collegiate rodeo teams and individual competitors gather for their national finals. This event will be in Casper from 2000 to 2005. | 307/234–5311 or 800/852–1889.

JUNE: _Platte Bridge Cavalry Encampment._ This encampment at Fort Caspar is a historic reenactment commemorating the July 1865 battle at Platte Bridge in which Lt. Caspar Collins was killed. | 307/235–8462.

JULY: _Beartrap Summer Festival._ Bluegrass is a part of this music festival, as is a mountain-bike race on Casper Mountain. | Beartrap Meadow, off Casper Mountain Rd. | 307/235–9325.

JULY: _Central Wyoming Fair & Rodeo._ Livestock exhibits, rodeos, a carnival, entertainment, and other activities are scheduled at the Central Wyoming Fairgrounds. | 307/235–5775.

JULY: _Powder River Sheepherders Fair._ Held in the small community of Powder River, 24 mi west of Casper, this fair includes a sheep ranchers' rodeo where kids ride sheep and dogs demonstrate their herding skills. There is also a lamb recipe cook-off. | U.S. 20/26 | 307/472–7055 or 307/876–2778.

DEC.: *Christmas with the Frontier Soldiers.* Candlelight provides the setting for this early December reenactment of a frontier Christmas at Fort Caspar. | 13th St. and Wyoming Blvd., Rte. 220 Exit 188b | 307/235–8462.

Dining

Armor's. American. Quiet, with cozy booths, this place also has views of Casper Mountain. Some of the local favorites are spare ribs and steaks. Kids' menu. | 3422 S. Energy La. | 307/235–3000 | $5–$20 | AE, D, DC, MC, V.

Chef's Coop. American. With country decorations and modest prices, this is a place to take a big family or someone with a big appetite. It's a local favorite for breakfast and lunch and has daily specials. | 1040 N. Center St. | 307/237–1132 | $5–$20 | No credit cards.

El Jarro. Mexican. Usually crowded and always noisy, this place has Mexican style and good food and margaritas. The local favorite is the green chili. | 500 W. F St. | 307/577–0538 | $4–$10 | D, MC, V.

Paisley Shawl. American. The turn-of-the-century interior is far more elegant than the exterior of this 1916 building, which also houses the Hotel Higgins. The favorites are steak and prime rib, and they have five-course meals with daily specials. You can also eat outside on the deck. | 416 W. Birch, Glenrock | 307/436–9212 | $12–$28 | DC, MC, V | Closed Sun.–Mon.

Poor Boy's Steakhouse. American. Reminiscent of a frontier mining camp, this steak house at the Parkway Plaza has blue-and-white-checked tablecloths and chair backs, quick service, and large portions of steak, seafood, or chicken, plus bread and salad. Local favorites are the Moonshine Mama (grilled chicken breast with mushrooms and Monterey Jack and cheddar cheeses) and the filet mignon and shrimp. For dessert: Ashley's Avalanche—a huge plate of ice cream, white-chocolate brownie, cherry-pie filling, chocolate sauce, and whipped cream. | 123 W. E St. | 307/235–1777 | fax 307/235–8068 | $11–$31 | AE, D, DC, MC, V.

Lodging

Best Western Casper. Convenient to both I–25 and downtown restaurants and attractions, this reliable lodging has spacious rooms and friendly service. Continental breakfast. Cable TV. Indoor pool. No-smoking rooms. | 2325 E. Yellowstone Hwy. | 307/234–3541 or 800/675–4242 | fax 307/266–5850 | 41 rooms | $59–$80 | AE, D, DC, MC, V.

Econolodge. Formerly the Kelly Inn, this contemporary hotel is near I–25 and the Casper Events Center. Cable TV. Hot tub. Laundry facilities. Pets allowed. | 821 N. Poplar | 307/266–2400 or 800/635–3559 | fax 307/266–1146 | 103 rooms | $46–$65 | AE, D, DC, MC, V.

Hampton Inn. Business travelers will appreciate the in-room data ports and other business services at this modern and comfortable hotel near I–25 and the Casper Events Center. Complimentary Continental breakfast. In-room data ports. Cable TV. Pool. Sauna. Business services. Airport shuttle. Pets allowed (fee). | 400 W. F St. | 307/235–6668 | fax 307/235–2027 | 122 rooms | $75–$95 | AE, D, DC, MC, V.

Holiday Inn. On the river, next to I–25 and several blocks from downtown Casper, this circular hotel has a lot of greenery in the public spaces and contemporary rooms, plus a terraced room that faces the river. Restaurant, bar, picnic area, room service. In-room data ports. Cable TV. Indoor pool. Hot tub. Exercise equipment. Game rooms, one with video games, one with pool tables. Laundry facilities. Business services. Airport shuttle. Some pets allowed. | 300 W. F St. | 307/235–2531 | fax 307/473–3400 | 200 rooms | $89–$109 | AE, D, DC, MC, V.

Hotel Higgins. This 1916 building looks a little questionable on the outside, but the interior is a delight. Rooms are furnished in Victorian style. Restaurant, bar, complimentary breakfast. Some air-conditioning. | 416 W. Birch, Glenrock; I–25 Exit 165 | 307/436–9212 or 800/458–0144 (outside WY) | fax 307/436–9213 | 8 rooms | $46–$70 | D, DC, MC, V.

Parkway Plaza. Guest rooms are large and quiet, with double vanities, one inside the bathroom and one outside. The public areas have Western furnishings. Restaurant, bar. Pool. Hot tub. Game room. Business services, convention center. | 123 W. E St. | 307/235–1777 | fax 307/235–8068 | 272 rooms | $60–$70 | AE, D, MC, V.

Radisson. This large facility has everything under one roof. The rooms are large and decorated in muted blue, green, and mauve. Restaurant, bar, coffee shop, room service. Some in-room hot tubs. Cable TV. Indoor pool. Beauty salon, hot tub. Cross-country and downhill skiing. Airport shuttle. Pets allowed. | 800 N. Poplar St. | 307/266–6000 | fax 307/473–1010 | 228 rooms | $69–$79 | AE, D, DC, MC, V.

Royal Inn. On-site car rental, some rooms with kitchenettes, and affordable rates distinguish this locally owned motel. Cable TV. Outdoor pool. | 440 E. A St. | 307/234–3501 or 877/234–3501 | fax 307/234–7340 | 37 rooms | $38–$42 | AE, D, DC, MC, V.

Sand & Sage Motel. Most rooms are newly remodeled at this small, local hotel, close to downtown and within walking distance of restaurants. Some rooms have kitchenettes. The parking space accommodates larger vehicles. Cable TV. | 901 W. Yellowstone Hwy. | 307/237–2088 | 27 rooms | $32.10, $45 kitchenettes | MC, V.

CHEYENNE

MAP 9, H6

(Nearby town also listed: Laramie)

Cheyenne became a wild Western town overnight when the Union Pacific Railroad pushed its way over the landscape in 1867. The first permanent residents included six men and three women who established camp here on July 9, 1867. Lots began selling almost immediately, and the first home was in place by July 25. The city was a vibrant place with little order and less law, so vigilantes organized to establish some type of control. The military then moved in when authorities established Fort D. A. Russell. Camp Carlin, also established by the military, brought a modicum of order to the raucous community.

Unlike some renegade railroad tent cities, which disappeared as the railroad tracks pushed further west, Cheyenne established itself as a permanent city, becoming the territorial capital in 1868. Its wild beginnings also gave way to respectability with the coming of the cattle barons, wealthy ranch owners who built fine homes—considered mansions in that era—on 17th Street, which became known as Cattleman's Row. The cattle barons had a gathering place, initially called the Cactus Club and later the Cheyenne Club (but never the Cheyenne Social Club as the Hollywood version of the establishment dubbed it). There the cattlemen ate fine meals and drank fine wine as they socialized and conducted business. It was at the Cheyenne Club that the cattlemen planned the 1892 invasion of Johnson County (some called it the Johnson County War).

Cheyenne became the state capital in 1890, at a time when the rule of the cattle barons was beginning to weaken after harsh winter storms in the late 1880s and financial downturns in the national economy. But Cheyenne's link to ranching didn't fade, for the community launched its first Cheyenne Frontier Day in 1897, an event involving ranching skills such as bronc riding. It captured the city's attention that first year, and in spite of press reports that the activities sought to "perpetuate the spirit of Western rowdyism through which the West is passing," organizers planned another Frontier Day celebration the following year. Thus was born the rodeo known by its trademark name "Daddy of 'em all." Cheyenne Frontier Days expanded over the decades to include nine days of rodeo competitions, night shows, and other events.

The business of state government stabilized Cheyenne as a community, now with 56,000 residents, and the military presence remains as well, centered at the Francis

E. Warren Air Force Base, a wing of the Strategic Air Command (SAC). In 1963 the SAC 90th Strategic Wing took control of the new Minuteman Missile, and soon 200 missile sites operated within a 150-mi radius of the Cheyenne base. Those sites are in Wyoming, Colorado, and Nebraska.

Information: **Cheyenne Convention and Visitor's Bureau** | Box 765 | 307/778–3133.

TRANSPORTATION
Airlines: Cheyenne Airport (200 E. 8th Ave. | 307/634–7071) is served by Horizon Air. You can also fly into Denver International Airport and drive the 90 mi north to Cheyenne.
Automobile: Cheyenne is at the intersection of I–80 and I–25.
Bus: Greyhound Lines (1503 Capitol Ave. | 307/634–7744 or 800/231–2222).

Attractions

ART AND ARCHITECTURE
State Capitol. Stately pine trees and a larger-than-life-size statue of Esther Hobart Morris greet you at the Wyoming State Capitol, with its broad staircase leading up to the oversize entrance doors. (There is a side entrance just north of the massive staircase for those unable to negotiate it.) You can visit the state legislature when it is in session: 40 days starting mid-January in odd-numbered years, 20 days in even-numbered years. Tours are available. | Capitol Ave. and 24th St. | 307/777–7220 | www.state.wy.us | Free | Weekdays 8:30–4:30.

WYOMING'S COWBOY SYMBOL

Ask an old-timer in Pinedale, Lander, Laramie, or Cheyenne who the cowboy is on the Wyoming license plate's bucking-horse symbol, and you'll probably get four different answers. The state's residents have regional favorites about the rider, depending on what candidates come from their area. Artist Allen True once said he had no particular rider in mind, though several well-known cowboys are often mentioned, including Stub Farlow of Lander and Guy Holt of Cheyenne (who later ranched near Pinedale).

During World War I, George Ostrem, a member of the Wyoming National Guard serving in Germany, had a bucking horse and rider design painted on a bass drum. His 148th Field Artillery unit soon had the logo on its vehicles as well, and it became known as the Bucking Bronco Regiment from Wyoming. And which horse was the symbol modeled after? In the case of the Wyoming National Guard logo, the horse was Ostrem's own mount, Red Wing.

In 1921, the University of Wyoming first used a bucking horse and cowboy as a logo on its sports uniforms, with that design modeled after a 1903 photograph by UW professor B. C. Buffum of Guy Holt riding Steamboat, one of the five horses recognized as the worst bucking horses of all time. The State of Wyoming first put the bucking bronco on its license plate in 1936, and the trademarked symbol has been there ever since.

© Artville

Wyoming Arts Council Gallery. The gallery displays rotating exhibits of work by Wyoming artists. | 2320 Capitol Ave. | 307/777–7742 | fax 307/777–5499 | www.state.wy.com/ | Free | Weekdays 8–5.

PARKS AND NATURAL SIGHTS

Cheyenne Botanic Gardens. The greenhouse conservatory at Cheyenne Botanic Gardens has a vegetable garden, a variety of flowers, roses, cactuses, and both perennial and annual plants. | 710 S. Lions Park Dr. | 307/637–6458 | fax 307/637–6453 | Free, donations accepted | Weekdays 8–4:30, weekends and most holidays 11–3:30; outside gardens open day and evening.

Curt Gowdy State Park. The park is named after Wyoming's most famous sportscaster, who got his start at local radio stations. You can fish, boat, hike, and camp. | 1351 Hyndslodge Rd. | 307/632–7946 | commerce.state.wy.us | $2 resident vehicles, $3 nonresident vehicles; $4 overnight | Daily 7–3:30.

Holliday Park. This is the place to see "Big Boy," the largest of all Union Pacific steam engines. Within Holliday Park you can also use the tennis, basketball, and volleyball courts, walking and bike paths, children's playgrounds, picnic areas, and fishing. | 520 W. 8th Ave. | 307/637–6429 | Free | Daily.

Lions Park. In one of Cheyenne's large parks, you can bike on paths, boat, fish, play miniature golf or softball, swim, and more. You can also visit the Cheyenne Botanic Gardens and wildlife exhibits. | Carey and 8th Aves | 307/637–6429 | Daily.

Veedauwoo. In the Medicine Bow National Forest, midway between Cheyenne and Laramie on Rte. 210, this natural area has huge granite formations in a forest setting. You can climb the rocks, or if you're not a rock climber, you can pull up a chair and watch. You can also hike and cross-country ski on trails in winter. | Rte. 210 | 307/745–2300 | www.fs.fed.us/mrnf.

CULTURE, EDUCATION, AND HISTORY

Warren Air Force Base. Home of the Tomahawk cruise missile and a branch of the Strategic Air Command, Warren started as Fort Warren. The place goes on high alert whenever there's any threat of military action or terrorism. The best way to really see the base is to take the Cheyenne Street Railway tour. The F. E. Warren Museum has exhibits about Fort D. A. Russell and life in Cheyenne in the late 1800s. | Randall Ave. W | 307/775–3381 | Free | Weekdays 8–4.

MUSEUMS

Cheyenne Frontier Days Old West Museum. Displays about early rodeo, Cheyenne Frontier Days, and ranching, as well as more than 125 carriages, are part of this vast collection of Western artifacts. Guided tours. | 4501 N. Carey Ave. | 307/778–7290 | $4 | Weekdays 9–5, weekends 10–5; during Cheyenne Frontier Days, 8–8.

Historic Governor's Mansion. Once the home of Wyoming's governor, this Colonial Revival mansion is now a museum with period furnishings, the original fleur-de-lis stained-glass windows over the door, and the children's room, arranged so they could hear their pet pony. | 300 E. 21st St. | 307/777–7878 | commerce.state.wy.us/sphs/govern.htm | Free | Tues.–Sat. 9–12, 1–5.

Wyoming State Museum. Ten gallery exhibits cover everything from energy to wildlife, giving you a sense of Wyoming's history and heritage. There is a special room for children and occasional speakers and programs. | 2301 Central Ave. | 307/777–7022 | fax 307/777–5375 | www.state.wy.us/cr/wsm/index.html | Free | Tues.–Sat. 9–4:30.

Wyoming Transportation Museum. Anchoring the downtown, down the street from the capitol, the old Union Pacific Depot is being transformed into the Wyoming Transportation Museum and Learning Center. The exterior is worth seeing, built in Romanesque style from yellow sandstone. The displays will show historic trails, railroads, highways, and air transportation. | 115 W. 15th St. | 307/637–3376 | www.wtmlc.org.

SPORTS AND RECREATION

Cheyenne Greenway. Winding paved pathways in both north and south Cheyenne are where you walk, ride your bike, rollerblade, push the babystroller, or maneuver your wheelchair. The Crow Creek trail runs through South Cheyenne, and the Dry Creek Trail in North Cheyenne is accessible at several locations along Dell Range Avenue or near the airport. | 307/637–6285 | Daily.

SIGHTSEEING TOURS/TOUR COMPANIES

Cheyenne Street Railway. Tours of Cheyenne describe local ghosts, the Union Pacific Railroad, and early society. Wheelchair accessible (for up to two wheelchairs at a time). | Convention and Visitors Bureau, 309 W. Lincolnway | 307/778–3133 | $8 adults, $4 children | May–Sept., tours daily; special holiday tours.

Terry Bison Ranch. Help move a herd of buffalo or just watch them from the vantage point of a wagon ride at this one-of-a-kind ranch. It has an RV park, a full-service restaurant, chuck-wagon cookouts, a saloon, horseback rides, fishing on a private lake, and horse-drawn wagon tours as well as five-day bison drives. | 51 I–25 Service Road E | 307/634–4171 | Chuckwagon dinners $14.95, trail rides $17, wagon rides through the buffalo herd $12.50 | Daily.

OTHER POINTS OF INTEREST

Wyoming Game and Fish Visitors Center. Displays of Wyoming wildlife include grizzly bears and Rocky Mountain bighorn sheep. | 5400 Bishop Blvd. | 307/777–4554 | gf.state.wy.us | Free | Winter, weekdays 8–5; Memorial Day–Labor Day, weekdays 8–5, weekends 9–5.

ON THE CALENDAR

MAY: *Cinco de Mayo.* Celebration of the Mexican holiday with food and music. | Wyoming Transportation Museum and Learning Center | 307/635–5608.

JUNE: *Brewer's Festival.* Regional brewers gather at the Wyoming Transportation Museum and Learning Center, where you can sample microbrews and also listen to music or dance. | 115 W. 15th St. | 307/637–3376.

JUNE: *Cheyenne Motor Sports Shoot-Out.* A street race goes down Cheyenne's historic avenues. | 800/464–5042.

JUNE: *Super Day at Lions Park.* Games, carnival, food, entertainment, and an arts and crafts show. | 307/637–6423.

JUNE–JULY: *Cheyenne Gunslinger Gunfights.* Gunfight reenactments and Old West activities take place weekdays at 6 PM and Saturday at noon. | Old Town Square | 307/778–3133.

JULY: *Cheyenne Frontier Days.* The biggest event in Cheyenne each year, this festival takes place the last week in July, and involves four parades, top country entertainers performing at night, nine PRCA rodeos, Plains Indian dancers, three free pancake breakfasts, and the Old West Governor's Art Show and Sale. | Frontier Park Arena, at 8th Ave. and Hines | 307/778–7200 or 800/227–6336.

JULY–MID-AUG.: *Atlas Theater Melodrama.* Local players from the Cheyenne Little Theater present melodramas, during which the audience routinely roots for the hero, cheers the heroine, and boos and hisses the villain. | 2706 E. Pershing Ave. | 307/638–6543.

AUG.: *Laramie County Fair and Rodeo.* Rodeos and 4-H and FFA projects are part of this county fair. | Frontier Park | 307/632–2634.

SEPT.: *Cheyenne Western Film Festival.* Classic Western films are shown, and screenwriters and actors discuss them. | 307/635–4646 or 800/250–1878.

OCT.: *Ghost Trolley Tours.* Learn about Cheyenne's ghosts (and the places they supposedly haunt) on these narrated tours. | 307/778–3133.

OCT.: *Shawn Dubie Memorial Rodeo.* This rodeo features top collegiate competitors. | 307/778–1291.

DEC.: *Christmas Light Trolley Tours.* Take a trolley ride to see the best of Cheyenne's Christmas lighting displays. | 307/778–3133.

Dining

INEXPENSIVE

Los Amigos. Tex-Mex. With Mexican sombreros, serapes, and artwork on the walls, this place is a traditional, family-owned Mexican restaurant. The portions are big and the food is good Tex-Mex. The favorites are deep-fried tacos and green chili. | 620 Central Ave. | 307/638–8591 | $2.50–$10 | MC, V | Closed Sun.

MODERATE

The Albany. American. Historic photos of early Cheyenne set the tone at this downtown icon, a place that seems as old as the city itself. It's a bit dark, and the booths are a bit shabby, but the food is solid. Cheyenne's movers and shakers used to meet here, and some still do to enjoy the steak and prime rib. | 1506 Capitol Ave. | 307/638–3507 | $11–$21.

Lexie's Cafe. Continental. In the oldest home in Cheyenne, a brick building more than a century old, Lexie's has delightful breakfast and lunch menus and offers heaping platters of Mexican, Italian, and American food. The breakfasts are big and excellent, as are the burgers. Locals voted it "best lunch" three years in a row. | 216 E. 17th St. | 307/638–8712 | $9–$15 | AE, D, DC, MC, V | Closed Sun. No dinner.

Little America. American. The coffee shop is quick and serves the same hearty portions you'll find in the more elegant dining room (at lower cost). This place has the best turkey dinner in the state, with real mashed potatoes, lots of gravy, dressing, and cranberry sauce. The hot turkey sandwich is also a winner. Live music evenings in the dining room. Kids' menu. Sun. brunch. | 2800 W. Lincolnway (U.S. 30) | 307/775–8400 or 800/445–6945 | $12–$35 | AE, D, DC, MC, V.

EXPENSIVE

Cheyenne Cattle Company. American. The name says it all. This is a fine restaurant located in the Hitching Post Inn; the decor is sophisticated, with dark wood, candlelight, and soft music. Known for beef, primarily steak, though you'll also find prime rib. | 1700 W. Lincolnway (U.S. 30) | 307/638–3301 | $15–$43 | AE, D, DC, MC, V.

Little Bear Inn. American. Locals rave about this classic American steak house, which also serves seafood. | 1700 Little Bear Rd. | 307/634–3684 | $17–$34 | D, MC, V.

Poor Richard's. American. Dark wood and stained glass give this place a rich feeling. The menu includes prime rib, formula-fed veal, pasta, chicken, and fish. The signature dish is champagne veal. It also serves buffalo and Cheyenne's only Saturday brunch. Open-air dining. Salad bar. Kids' menu. Sat. brunch. | 2233 E. Lincolnway (U.S. 30) | 307/635–5114 | $7–$30 | AE, D, DC, MC, V.

Lodging

MODERATE

Best Western Hitching Post Inn. State legislators frequent this hotel near the capitol. The Hitch, as locals call it, books country-western performers in its lounge. It has dark-wood walls and an elegance not found in many of the lodging properties in Wyoming. Restaurants, bar with entertainment, room service. In-room data ports, refrigerators. Cable TV. 2 pools (1 indoor). Hot tub. Exercise equipment, gym. Game room. Playground. Laundry facilities. Business services. Airport shuttle. Pets allowed. | 1700 W. Lincolnway (U.S. 30) | 307/638–3301 | fax 307/778–7194 | 166 rooms | $63–$179 | AE, D, DC, MC, V.

Comfort Inn. This modern hotel is on the west side of town near I–80 and I–25. The rooms have contemporary furnishings and handicapped facilities. Complimentary Continental breakfast. Cable TV. Pool. Laundry facilities. Business services. Pets allowed. | 2245 Etchepare Dr. | 307/638–7202 | fax 307/635–8560 | 77 rooms | $79–$99 | AE, D, DC, MC, V.

Days Inn. Mood lighting lends a touch of elegance to these contemporary rooms. The hotel is convenient to the I–25 and I–80 interchange. Complimentary Continental breakfast. In-room data ports. Cable TV. Hot tub. Exercise equipment. Business services. | 2360 W. Lin-colnway (U.S. 30) | 307/778–8877 | fax 307/778–8697 | 72 rooms | $74–$89 | AE, D, DC, MC, V.

Fairfield Inn by Marriott. Near the busy shopping district on Dell Range Avenue, this new motel has spacious rooms and interior hallways. Complimentary Continental breakfast. Refrigerators in suites. Cable TV. Indoor pool. Hot tub. Business services. | 1415 Stillwater Ave. | 307/637–4070 | fax 307/637–4070 | 62 rooms, 8 suites | $63–$69 | AE, D, DC, MC, V.

Historic Plains Hotel. Built in 1910, this old-fashioned brick hotel in the heart of downtown Cheyenne recalls a bygone era. Although accommodations are basic, the charming lobby has huge chandeliers, and the facilities include a flower shop and jewelry store. Some of the suites have hot tubs. Restaurant, bar. Cable TV. | 1600 Central Ave. | 307/638–3311 | 116 rooms, 24 suites | $42.95 rooms, $54.95–$95.95 suites | AE, D, MC, V.

La Quinta. The design and furnishings are Spanish style and the hotel is near the I–80 and I–25 interchange. You can rent video games. Complimentary Continental breakfast. In-room data ports. Cable TV. Pool. Some pets allowed. | 2410 W. Lincolnway (U.S. 30) | 307/632–7117 | fax 307/638–7807 | 105 rooms | $69–$72 | AE, D, DC, MC, V.

Porch Swing Bed and Breakfast. A lovely registered historic home (1907) in a quiet neigh-borhood near downtown, this bed-and-breakfast is homey with front and back porches, a garden, an old wood-burning kitchen stove and a pond in the back yard. Rooms are cozy, have hand-painted borders, and are individually furnished with cherry-wood antiques. Full breakfast. No smoking. | 712 E. 20th St. | 307/778–7182 | porchswing@juno.com | www.cruis-ing-america.com/porcbed.html | 3 rooms share bath | $43–$66 | MC, V.

Rainsford Inn. Built in 1903, this house now has five large rooms with whirlpool tubs and two suites. The patio is pleasant for unwinding. Complimentary breakfast. Cable TV. Air-port shuttle. Kids over 13 yrs only. No smoking. | 219 E. 18th St. | 307/638–2337 | fax 307/634–4506 | 5 rooms, 2 suites (2 with shower only, 2 share bath) | $75–$85 | AE, D, DC, MC, V.

Super 8. Comfortable and contemporary, this motel has a breakfast area and modern fur-nishings. Cable TV. | 1900 W. Lincolnway (U.S. 30) | 307/635–8741 | fax 307/635–8741, ext 401 | 61 rooms | $52–$54 | AE, D, MC, V.

EXPENSIVE

A. Drummond's Ranch. This English farm house has a secluded setting with High Plains atmosphere, flower gardens, near Curt Gowdy State Park. You can see for miles over the Wyoming landscape. Complimentary breakfast. No air-conditioning. Hot tub. Cross-coun-try skiing. Playground. Business services. No smoking. | 399 Happy Jack Rd.; I–25 Exit 10 | 307/634–6042 | adrummond@juno.com | www.cruising-america.com/drummond.html | 4 rooms (2 share bath) | $65–$200 | MC, V.

Holding's Little America. Stately pine trees mark the boundaries of this complex. The rooms are spread over a fairly large area of landscaped grounds and are in separate build-ings, with some closer to the pool. Some rooms are connected by a breezeway to the main lodge building with its restaurant, coffee shop, and bar. The rooms are large and done in pastels, with lots of extra pillows and double vanities. Restaurants, bar with entertainment, room service. Some refrigerators. Cable TV. Pool. 9-hole golf course, putting green. Exer-cise equipment. Laundry facilities. Convention center. Airport shuttle. | 2800 W. Lincolnway (U.S. 30) | 307/775–8400 or 800/445–6945 | fax 307/775–8425 | www.littleamerica.com | 188 rooms | $85–$135 | AE, D, DC, MC, V.

Nagle Warren Mansion. This historic mansion built in 1888 has gorgeous woodwork, ornate staircases, period furniture and wallpaper, and lavish rooms decorated with antiques. Close to downtown, within walking distance of area stores, shops, and restau-rants. Full breakfast, dining room. In-room data ports. Cable TV. Hot tub. Exercise room. Library. Business services, meeting room. No smoking. | 222 E. 17th St. | 307/637–3333 or 800/811–2610 | fax 307/638–6879 | 12 rooms | $98–$115 | AE, MC, V.

CODY

MAP 9, D2

(Nearby town also listed: Powell)

Founded in 1896, and named for William F. "Buffalo Bill" Cody, Pony Express rider, army scout, and Wild West show entertainer, Cody is the eastern gateway community to Yellowstone National Park. But this town has much to offer even without the big park in its backyard. It is home to one of the finest museums in the West: the Buffalo Bill Historical Center, sometimes called the Smithsonian of the West. The center houses four museums. The Whitney Gallery of Western Art has works by such artists as Charles M. Russell, Frederic Remington, James Bama (who lives near Cody), and Harry Jackson (also a Cody resident). The Buffalo Bill Museum's displays relate to the great Westerner's life. The Plains Indian Museum houses art and artifacts of the Plains tribes. The Cody Firearms Museum has the world's largest collection of American firearms, including the Winchester Arms Collection.

Situated at the mouth of the Shoshone Canyon (where the north and south forks of the Shoshone River join), Cody is becoming a prime place for people who want to experience a Western lifestyle with amenities. Cattle ranches share space with dude ranches up both forks of the river, and there is oil and gas development in the region as well. The shopping is a mixture of new and trendy, along with classic Western (compare the Cody Rodeo Company to Wayne's Boot Shop, for example). Cody is home to Wyoming's longest-running nightly rodeo, which is a regular event during the summer. You can do a lot outdoors here, too—hike or camp in nearby Shoshone National Forest, windsurf on Buffalo Bill Reservoir, or watch mountain sheep and other wildlife from either the South Fork or North Fork highway. Cody also makes a good base for a Wyoming river journey; the North Fork of the Shoshone River, the Shoshone River, and the Clarks Fork of the Yellowstone all have both white-water runs and scenic float trips from mid-May through early September.

Information: **Cody Country Chamber of Commerce** | 836 Sheridan Ave., 82414 | 307/587–2297 | fax 307/527–6228 | cody@codychamber.org | www.codychamber.org.

Attractions

Buffalo Bill Historical Center. One of the West's finest museums, this is actually four museums rolled into one, with art, firearms, the Wild West of Buffalo Bill Cody, and Plains Indians. The center also has educational courses and presentations. Plan to spend at least four hours, perhaps a couple of days or more if you're really interested in the West. Admission is good for two days. | 720 Sheridan Ave. | 307/587–4771 | bbhc@wavecom.net | www.TrueWest.com/BBHC | $10 adults, $4 children, children under 5 free | Apr., daily 10–5; May, daily 8–8; June–Sept., daily 7–8; Oct., daily 8–5; Nov.–Mar., Thurs.–Mon. 10–2.

The **Buffalo Bill Museum** is dedicated to the incredible life of William F. "Buffalo Bill" Cody. Shortly after Cody's death, some of his friends took mementos of the famous scout, Indian fighter, and Wild West showman and opened the Buffalo Bill Museum in a small log building. It is now in the BBHC and includes huge posters from the original Buffalo Bill Wild West and Congress of Rough Riders shows.

Started as the Winchester Museum, the **Cody Firearms Museum** was rededicated in 1991; it is comprehensive, tracing the history of firearms through thousands of models on display, from European blunderbusses to Gatling guns and modern weapons. Included are examples of Winchester and Browning arms, as well as a replica of an arms manufacturing plant.

The West's greatest artists are a part of the BBHC's **Whitney Gallery of Western Art.** The wing has artworks by such masters as Frederic Remington, Charles M. Russell, Albert Bierstadt, George Catlin, and Thomas Moran, and contemporary artists such as Harry Jackson, James Bama, and Peter Fillerup.

The history of the Plains Indians is showcased in the **Plains Indian Museum,** with information about the Sioux, Blackfeet, Cheyenne, Crow, Shoshone, and Nez Percé tribes.

Buffalo Bill State Park. The Buffalo Bill Reservoir is the focus of the park, and you can indulge in all sorts of water sports here, as well as hike and camp and picnic nearby. | 47 Lakeside Rd. | 307/587–9227 | commerce.state.wy.us | Day use $2 resident vehicles, $5 nonresident vehicles; camping $4 | Daily (campground May–Sept.).

Bricks with the names of local residents form the sidewalk in front of the **Buffalo Bill Dam and Visitor Center.** People bought them to help fund the center. You can walk across the actual dam, peering over to see the lake to the west or the outflow to the east. | East end of reservoir | 307/527–6076 | Free | May–Sept., daily 8–8.

Cody Nite Rodeo. Some towns have intermittent nightly rodeos. Cody has one every night and has since 1938. It's a training ground for tomorrow's world-champion cowboys and a competition arena for some of today's best rodeo hands. | Stampede Park, 1143 Sheridan Ave. | 307/587–5155 | cathyi@trib.com | www.comp-unltd.com/~rodeo/rodeo.html | $10 grandstand, $12 Buzzard's Roost (behind the chutes), special rates for children | Memorial Day-Labor Day.

North Fork Nordic Trails. At the east entrance to Yellowstone National Park, there is a 25-mi groomed cross-country trail system that connects Pahaska Teepee Resort and Sleeping Giant Ski Area. You can rent equipment at both. | 307/527–7701 | Free | Dec.–mid-Apr.

Olive Glenn Golf and Country Club. An 18-hole PGA championship course. | 802 Meadow La. | 307/587–5551.

Shoshone National Forest. The first national forest to be established. Here you can hunt, fish, hike, mountain bike, and ride horses in non-snowy weather and snowmobile and cross-country ski the trails after snow falls. There are picnic areas and campgrounds. | U.S. 14/16/20 | 307/527–6241 | www.fs.fed.us/r2/shoshone/ | Free; fee varies at developed campgrounds | Daily.

Sleeping Giant Ski Area. This is a family ski area with both downhill and nordic trails. There's a chairlift and a lodge, and you can rent both types of skis, boots, and snowboards. | 349 Yellowstone Hwy. | 307/587–4044 | $20, special rates for children | Dec.–mid-Apr., Fri.–Sun. 9–4.

Tecumseh's Wyoming Territory Old West Miniature Village and Museum. Dioramas depict early Wyoming Territorial and Native American history and Western events. | 140 W. Yellowstone Hwy. | 307/587–5362 | $3 | June–Aug., daily 8–9; May and Sept., daily 10–6.

Trail Town and the Museum of the Old West. Started by a local archaeologist, Trail Town is a collection of historic cabins, homes, and buildings including one that served as a hideout for Butch Cassidy and the Sundance Kid. There is a cemetery with seven relocated graves, including that of Jeremiah "liver-eatin" Johnson. | 1831 Demaris Dr. | 307/587–5302 | $4 | Mid-May–Sept., daily 8–7.

Wood River Valley Ski Touring Park. This cross-country ski park has 20 mi of trails that take you around the Wood River Valley near Meeteetse. You can get trail maps and rent skis in Meeteetse. | 349 Yellowstone Hwy. | 307/868–2603 | Free | Dec.–mid-Apr.

Wyoming Vietnam Veteran's Memorial. A small-scale version of the Vietnam Wall in Washington, D.C., this memorial recognizes the Wyoming residents who died during that conflict. | U.S. 16/20 | No phone | Free | Daily.

NIGHTLIFE

Angie's Silver Dollar Bar. Listen to live rock 'n roll music at this establishment that includes outdoor seating in the summer. | 1313 Sheridan Ave. | 307/587–3554 | Mon.–Sat. until 2 AM, Sun. until 11.

Cassie's Supper Club and Dance Hall. A trip to Cody wouldn't be complete without the opportunity to scoot your boots at Cassie's, the city's best Western bar and dance hall. (You can get a meal here, too.) Music is country, most often by the local band called West, which blends its own tunes with classics and today's hits. | 214 Yellowstone Ave. | 307/527–5500 | www.wavecom.net/~cassies/ | $5 cover summer | Mon.–Sat. 11–2, Sun. noon–10.

TOURS AND ADVENTURES

Grub Steak Expeditions and Tours. These personalized tours let you decide what interest to indulge, offering photography, geology, history, fishing, wildlife, nature walks, and day hikes in the region around Cody and Yellowstone National Park. They're led by a former Yellowstone park ranger, professional photographer, and retired teacher. Half-day, full day, or multi-day tours. | Box 1013, Cody | 307/527–6316 or 800/527–6316 | $300 for one or two people, $75 per person thereafter | Daily.

Red Canyon River Trips. You can take a two-hour float on the North Fork of the Shoshone, an evening white-water trip down the Clarks Fork of the Yellowstone, or find something between these two extremes. | 1220 Sheridan Ave. | 307/587–6988 or 800/293–0148 | $20–$50 | Mid-May–mid-Sept., daily.

Wyoming River Trips. Shoshone River floats last from 2 hours to a half-day. | 1701 Sheridan Ave. | 307/587–6661 or 800/586–6661 | fax 307/587–9430 | wrt@wave.park.wy.us | www.wyomingrivertrips.com | $20–$50.

ON THE CALENDAR

FEB.: *Buffalo Bill Birthday Ball.* Dancing, food, shooting exhibitions, and 19th-century costumes all are a part of this celebration of Buffalo Bill's birthday. | Cody Auditorium | 307/587–2297.
APR.: *Cowboy Songs and Range Ballads.* Performances and a symposium related to cowboy music. Buffalo Bill Historical Center, with nightly programs at the Cody Auditorium and various venues around town. | 307/587–4771.
JUNE: *Frontier Festival.* Pioneer skills are presented, from blacksmithing to spinning. | Buffalo Bill Historical Center | 307/587–4771.
JUNE: *Old West Show and Auction.* Cowboy collectibles and memorabilia are displayed and auctioned. | Wynona Thompson Auditorium | 307/587–9014.
JUNE: *Plains Indian Powwow.* Plains Indian dances bring together fancy dancers, hoop dancers, traditional dancers, and jingle dancers from various tribes. | Buffalo Bill Historical Center | 307/587–4771.
JULY: *Cody Stampede.* Fireworks and parades are part of this annual Fourth of July rodeo. | Stampede Park | 307/587–5155.
JULY: *Yellowstone Jazz Festival.* Jazz musicians play in concert in an outdoor setting. | Elks Club lawn | 307/587–966.
JUNE–AUG.: *Cody Nite Rodeo.* The nightly rodeo action includes bronc and bull riding, roping, and barrel racing. | Stampede Park | 307/587–5155.
SEPT.: *Buffalo Bill Art Show, Quick Draw and Sale.* Western artists create original pieces with live and silent auctions of artwork. | Buffalo Bill Historical Center | 307/587–2797.
SEPT.: *Western Design Conference.* A furniture exhibition, fashion show, and seminars all relate to Western design in furniture, fashion, and accessories. | Buffalo Bill Historical Center and Cody Auditorium | 888/685–0574.

Dining

Black Sheep. Greek/American. Murals of vine-strung trellises and a blue sky that fills the vaulted ceiling evoke a Grecian summer at this unusual restaurant off Cody's main strip. The steak Aegean is broiled with tomatoes, onions, and feta cheese, the shrimp Mykonos is sauteed with garlic and served over fettuccini, and a Greek platter includes favorites like *dolmades* (stuffed grape leaves) and hummus, a rare find in these parts. | 1901 Mountain View Dr. | 307/527–5895 | $9–$18 | MC, V.

Cassie's Supper Club. American. Steaks, prime rib, and hamburgers are the mainstays—along with seafood and chicken. The hometown favorite is stuffed mushrooms. Early in the evening the atmosphere is low-key, but at about 9 the band warms up and the dancing begins. Cassie's, a former house of prostitution just a mile from the rodeo, gets downright rowdy; it's certainly the best place in Cody to do some boot-scooting. Entertainment nightly. | 214 Yellowstone Ave. | 307/527–5500 | www.cassies.com | $4.50–$26 | AE, MC, V.

Cody Coffee Company and Eatery. American. This cozy, laid-back sandwich and coffee shop serves excellent Italian grilled sandwiches like chicken pesto and turkey artichoke, and prepares its own muffins, cinnamon rolls, freshly squeezed juices, smoothies and coffee drinks. In downtown Cody but off the main tourist strip, this is a great place to grab lunch, relax, and take in the views of Spirit and Rattlesnake mountains. | 1702 Sheridan Ave. | 307/527–7879 | $3–$6 | No credit cards | Closed Sun. No dinner.

Franca's. Northern Italian. This quiet, attractive place is known for its good pasta dishes. No smoking. | 1421 Rumsey Ave. | 307/587–5354 | $13–$25 | No credit cards | Closed Mon., Tues., and mid-Mar.–mid-May.

Hong Kong Restaurant. Chinese. Authentic homemade Mandarin and Cantonese-style dishes are served at this popular restaurant, whose huge menu includes the usual suspects. Silkscreens, plants, and Chinese portraits add a traditional touch to the contemporary building. | 1201 17th St. | 307/527–6420 | $6–$15 | D, MC, V | Closed Sun. Oct.–Apr.

Irma Hotel. American. No place in Cody truly compares with the Irma. This is Buffalo Bill Cody's original hotel, named for his daughter. With an elaborate cherry-wood bar, it retains the charm from Buffalo Bill's era. The favorites are steak, seafood, and chicken. There's a salad bar. Kids' menu. | 1192 Sheridan Ave. | 307/587–4221 or 800/587–4221 | fax 307/587–1775 | $14–$27.50 | AE, D, DC, MC, V.

La Comida. Mexican. Mexican wall hangings lend authenticity to this place, as does the food. The regulars go for the fajitas, tacoritos, and spinach enchiladas, and finish with the unique desserts. You can dine on a shaded patio in season. In winter, it closes at 8:30; in summer, it stays open until everyone leaves. Kids' menu. | 1385 Sheridan Ave. | 307/587–9556 | Reservations accepted | $3.25–$18.50 | AE, D, MC, V.

Maxwell's. Italian/American. A turn-of-the century Victorian house with huge windows and a porch is home to this upscale contemporary restaurant that serves homemade soups, breads, pastas, and sandwiches. The California chicken fettuccini with a sun-dried tomato alfredo is a favorite, as are the hand-cut steaks and fresh seafood. In the summer, find a table on the large wooden deck surrounded by flowers. | 937 Sheridan Ave. | 307/527–7749 | $6–$20 | AE, D, MC, V.

Proud Cut. American. This downtown eatery and watering hole has a Western look, complete with photos of cowboys and ranch work from the Charles Belden Collection (he used to own the huge TA Ranch near Meeteetse). Owner Del Nose claims to serve "kick-ass cowboy cuisine": steaks, prime rib, shrimp, fish, and chicken. You can always get Rocky Mountain oysters (calves' testicles). The prime rib is a sure thing. | 1227 Sheridan Ave. | 307/527–6905 | $4.95–$18.50 | AE, D, DC, MC, V.

Royal Palace. American. Only three blocks from the rodeo grounds, and on the thoroughfare that leads to Yellowstone, this Old West–style wood-and-banisters restaurant with Billy the Kid paraphernalia and red chandeliers serves standard steak and potatoes fare. Popular with tourists, be prepared for crowds, noise, and a good, hearty pork-chop dinner. | 103 Yellowstone Ave. | 307/587–5751 | Breakfast also available | $6–$15 | MC, V.

Stephan's. Contemporary. This intimate restaurant adorned with palm plants, tablecloths, and earth-toned Western art is a Cody favorite. Specialties include filet mignon stuffed with Gorgonzola, sun-dried tomatoes, and Portobello mushrooms, Southwest shrimp kebab grilled and scored with jalapeños and pepper jack cheese, and a penne pasta with artichoke hearts and prosciutto in a lemon caper sauce. Save rooms for the homemade chocolate cake or strawberries Napoleon. | 1367 Sheridan Ave. | 307/587–8511 | $10–$25 | AE, MC, V.

Tuscany. Italian. Recently opened, this unpretentious but classy eatery at the center of town is already a hit with the locals. Try the rigatoni with Italian sausage or the cod, crab, and shrimp over angel-hair pasta; other specialties include filet mignon and rib-eye steak. | 1244 Sheridan Ave. | 307/527–7744 | $8–$16 | MC, V.

Zapatas. Mexican. Fajitas, tamales, chimichangas, and homemade chips and salsa are the specialties at this restaurant in one of Cody's older redbrick buildings. Inside, adobe walls and hand painted murals depict Old Mexico, and the upstairs indoor patio with plate-glass window offers views of downtown Cody. The fried banana with vanilla ice cream and caramel, and the huge homemade pies (you'll need to share them!) are good finishes. | 1362 Sheridan Ave. | 307/527–7181 | $8–$16 | AE, D, DC, MC, V.

Lodging

Absaroka Mountain Lodge. About 10 mi from Yellowstone, this 1910 lodge is set in a canyon. Each Western-style log cabin along Gunbarrel Creek has a private bath. You dine in the lodge, where two fireplaces keep it cozy. Restaurant, bar, picnic area. No air-conditioning. Horseback riding. Playground. Airport shuttle. | 1231 E. Yellowstone Hwy., Wapiti | 307/587–3963 | fax 307/527–9628 | www.absarokamtlodge.com | 16 cabins | $76–$142, or $125 per person per day for lodging, 3 meals, 4–hr horseback ride | D, MC, V | Closed Sept.–May.

Best Western Sunset Motor Inn. This inn sits on a large grassy property with shade trees and has an enclosed play area for children. Numerous amenities, clean rooms, a downtown location, and a quiet and relaxed atmosphere make this a favorite with families. Restaurant. Cable TV. 2 pools. Hot tub. Exercise room. Playground. Coin laundry. Some pets allowed. | 1601 8th St. | 307/587–4265 or 800/624–2727 | fax 307/587–9029 | 116 rooms, 4 suites | $119, $145–$165 suites | AE, D, DC, MC, V.

Bill Cody's Ranch Resort. The original ranch of the Western scout, this resort is beside a stream and has rustic pine cabins furnished in southwestern style. You can go river rafting and have chuck-wagon cookouts and visit Yellowstone, just 30 minutes away. Restaurant, bar, picnic area. No air-conditioning. Horseback riding. Airport shuttle. | 2604 Yellowstone Hwy. | 307/587–2097 or 800/615–2934 | fax 307/587–6272 | billcody@cody.wtp.net | www.billcodyranch.com | 14 cabins | $105 (AP $125) | D, MC, V | Closed Sept.–May.

Blackwater Creek Ranch. On the North Fork of the Shoshone River, these 15 Western cabins are vintage 1930s. Some have fireplaces, some are by the creek, and all have covered porches. You can take pack trips, raft, hike, and ride horses. Restaurant, bar, picnic area. No air-conditioning. Pool. Hot tub. Airport shuttle. | 1516 North Fork Hwy. | 307/587–5201 | www.wyo.net/blackwater/ | 15 cabins | $1,050–$1,200 wk | MC, V | Closed Oct.–Apr. | AP.

Breteche Creek. In a remote mountain valley about 20 mi west of Cody, Breteche Creek is one of the area's most unusual lodgings because of where it is and also what it is: a school in the wilderness. You can study, among other things, horsemanship, ecology, writing, ornithology, and astronomy. The accommodations are rustic—tent cabins with wood frames and floors, no electricity, telephones, or water (though the dining room is modern, and there's a shower house). Each week a naturalist leads a trip to Yellowstone National Park. Minimum stay 3 nights. Dining room. Hot tub. Horseback riding. | 269 Rd. 6FU | 307/587–3844 | fax 307/527–7032 | breteche@wavecom.net | 9 tent-cabins | $200 per night, $1,100 wk | No credit cards | Closed mid-Sept.–May | AP.

Buffalo Bill Village. This downtown development has three lodgings, which share facilities. Most noteworthy are the Buffalo Bill Village Resort, with log cabins with modern interiors, and the Holiday Inn Convention Center, a typical two-story brick hotel. Shuttle to Cody Nite Rodeo. Restaurant, bar. Pool. | 1701 Sheridan Ave. | 307/587–5544 or 800/527–5544 | blair@wave.park.wy.us | 83 resort cabins, 184 inn rooms | $85–$100 | AE, D, DC, MC, V.

Casual Cove Bed and Breakfast. Quiet and relaxed, this historic cottage-style home sits in a shaded yard on a residential street near downtown Cody. Rooms are small and homey, service is friendly, and the prices are reasonable. Full breakfast, dining room. Cable TV. | 1431 Salsbury Ave. | 307/587–3622 | 3 rooms | $56–$66 | AE, D, MC, V.

Cody Guest Houses. Lovingly restored and elegantly decorated, the Victorian guest house has lace curtains, antique furniture, and ornate decorations. The Western Lodge, with four bedrooms, has traditional Western decor, a fireplace, a furnished kitchen, and a yard with a barbecue area. The Annie Oakley and Buffalo Bill Western cottages are each one room with a furnished kitchen and a yard with picnic table. The Garden and Executive Suite deluxe apartments have a furnished kitchen with laundry facilities, carport, and yard with gazebo. The Carriage House is a small one-bedroom with a living room and a furnished kitchen. Yellowstone is 50 miles away. | 1525 Beck Ave. | 307/587–6000 or 800/587–6560 | fax 307/587–8048 | www.wtponet/cghouses | 8 rooms, 1 suite (in separate buildings) | $110–$450 | AE, D, MC, V.

Comfort Inn. With a convenient downtown location, the inn has contemporary furnishings, in-room data ports, and a pool shared with an adjacent hotel. Complimentary Continental breakfast. Cable TV. Business services. Airport shuttle. | 1601 Sheridan Ave. | 307/587–5556 or 800/527–5544 | fax 307/587–8727 | 75 rooms | $90–$129 | AE, D, DC, MC, V.

Days Inn. Built in 1995, this motel is southwestern in style both inside and out. The furnishings are modern and comfortable. Complimentary Continental breakfast. Cable TV. Indoor pool. Hot tub. Laundry facilities. | 524 Yellowstone Ave. | 307/527–6604 | fax 307/527–7341 | 52 rooms | $90–$125 | AE, D, DC, MC, V.

Double Diamond X. Spectacular views of the upper South Fork region are right outside your door, and Yellowstone is only 40 miles away. The main lodge is spacious and has a Western look; the grounds are carefully tended with huge cottonwood and pine trees, flowers, and picnic tables in shady areas. Specialty vacations only are available from mid-October to May 1. The lodge organizes pack trips and excursions to Cody for rodeos, the Buffalo Bill Historical Center, and Old Trail Town. Indoor pool. Hot tub. Hiking, horseback riding. Fishing. Game room. Children's programs (June–Sept.). Airport shuttle. | 3453 Southfork Rd. | 307/527–6276 or 800/833–7262 | fax 307/587–2708 | www.ddxranch.com | 12 units, 5 cabins, 7 rooms in lodge | $1,460 wk | MC, V | Closed except for specialty vacations mid-Oct.–May | AP.

Elephant Head. Buffalo Bill's niece built these cabins, which have been modernized but retain their original charm. The resort is only 11 mi from Yellowstone, and is convenient to the Buffalo Bill Reservoir. You get to watch Western movies nightly. Restaurant, bar, picnic area. No air-conditioning. Playground. Pets allowed. | 1170 Yellowstone Hwy., Wapiti | 307/587–3980 | fax 307/527–7922 | www.elephantheadlodge.com | 12 cabins | $75–$150 | AE, D, MC, V | Closed Sept.–May.

Gateway Motel and Campground. Reasonable rates, friendly service, and a large shaded yard with mountain vistas keep people coming back. Accommodations are basic—cabins are smaller than the hotel rooms, but are separate. Convenient to Cody attractions, and good for those wanting to get an earlier start for Yellowstone. No phones. Cable TV. Playground. Coin laundry. | 203 Yellowstone Ave. | 307/587–2561 | fax 307/587–4862 | 6 rooms, 4 cabins, 37 campsites | $60–$65 rooms, $50–$55 cabins, $12–$18 campsites | AE, MC, V.

Goff Creek Lodge. Once a hunting lodge, this resort still has much wildlife to watch and is very close to Buffalo Bill Reservoir. The lodge was built in 1906; guest accommodations now are individual cabins. You can arrange trail rides. Yellowstone is 8 mi away. Restaurant, bar, picnic area. No air-conditioning, cable TV. | 995 E. Yellowstone Hwy. | 307/587–3753 or 800/859–3985 | fax 307/587–9370 | www.goffcreek.com | 14 cabins | $95–$125 | MC, V.

Holiday Inn. This Holiday Inn has perhaps the longest hallway of rooms in the state. In the same building are the Bottoms Up Lounge and QT's Restaurant. There is an outdoor courtyard with pool. Restaurant, bar, room service. In-room data ports. Cable TV. Pool. Business services, convention center. Airport shuttle. | 1701 Sheridan Ave. | 307/587–5555 | fax 307/527–7757 | blair@wave.park.wy.us | wave.park.wy.us/~blair/village.html | 184 rooms | $90–$100 | AE, D, DC, MC, V.

Irma Hotel. An ornate cherry-wood bar sent by the Queen of England in 1904 is one of the highlights of this hostelry, which is named for Buffalo Bill's daughter. The hotel was built in 1902, and some rooms have an early 20th-century Western style, with brass beds and period furniture. During the summer, locals stage a gunfight on the porch Tuesday–Saturday at 7 PM (using blank bullets, of course). Restaurant, bar. | 1192 Sheridan Ave. | 307/587–4221 | fax 307/587–4221 | www.irmahotel.com | 40 rooms | $69–$96 | AE, D, DC, MC, V.

Kelly Inn. The handcrafted wooden bears that inhabit the entrance and the lobby are one eye-catching element at this inn. The view from the rooms is another. On the hill above Cody's main business district and near the airport, the place has southwestern-style furnishings. Cable TV. Hot tub. Laundry facilities. Business services. Pets allowed. | 2513 Greybull Hwy. | 307/527–5505 or 800/635–3559 | fax 307/527–5001 | 50 rooms | $99–$105 | AE, D, DC, MC, V.

Lockhart Inn. Soak up to your neck in the large claw-footed tubs at this historic inn, which was the former home of Cody author Caroline Lockhart. Rooms are named after her characters and books, and are filled with Western antiques. On the main western strip of Cody, which is convenient to Yellowstone and area attractions. Full breakfast, dining room. No smoking. | 109 W. Yellowstone Ave. | 307/587–6074 or 800/377–7255 | 7 rooms | $82–$135 | D, MC, V.

Mayor's Inn. You can rent one room or the entire historic house, which was Cody's first "mansion." It has been carefully restored and features three rooms, the Meadowlark with a double shower, the Yellowstone with a hot tub, and the elegant Hart Mountain Suite with a double spa. Complimentary breakfast. | 1413 Rumsey Ave. | 307/587–6000 or 800/587–6560 | fax 307/587–8048 | 3 rooms | $95–$195 | AE, D, MC, V.

Pahaska Teepee Resort. Buffalo Bill's original getaway in the high country is 2 mi east of Yellowstone's east entrance. Reunion Lodge has seven bedrooms, eight baths, kitchen, deck, and Jacuzzi and is ideal for large groups or families. A condo is available by the week. Some of the cabins are at elevations of 6,000 ft. You can take pack trips, and the fishing is great in the nearby river. Restaurant, bar. No air-conditioning, no room phones. Horseback riding. Cross-country skiing, snowmobiling. | 183 Yellowstone Hwy. | 307/527–7701 or 800/628–7791 | fax 307/527–4019 | pahaska@pahaska.com | www.pahaska.com | 52 cabins | Cabins $90–150; condo $2,500 wk; Reunion Lodge $895 per night (2–night minimum) or $4,475 wk | D, MC, V.

Parson's Pillow Bed & Breakfast. Housed in a turn-of-the-century Methodist-Episcopal church whose bell was bought by Buffalo Bill's sister, this unique inn has a lovely steeple, intimate common areas, and theme rooms, all individually decorated with antique and Western-style wood furniture. Full breakfast, dining room. TV in common area, library. Laundry facilities. | 1202 14th St. | 307/587–2382 or 800/377–2348 | fax 307/587–2382 | 4 rooms | $75–$85 | AE, D, MC, V.

Rimrock Dude Ranch. One of the oldest guest ranches on the North Fork of the Shoshone River, Rimrock offers both summer and winter accommodations and activities, from winter snowmobile trips to Yellowstone National Park to guided big-game hunts and pack trips. Excursions to the Cody rodeo and Buffalo Bill Historical Center. Restaurant. No air-conditioning, refrigerators. Pool. Airport shuttle. | 2728 North Fork Hwy. | 307/587–3970 or 800/208–7468 | fax 307/527–5014 | rimrock@wyoming.com | www.rimrockranch.com | 9 1–2 bedroom cabins | $1,500 per week per person summer, double occupancy; $325 in winter. Snowmobile rental included | MC, V | AP.

Shoshone Lodge. The cabins are basic, but the location is scenic, on Grinnell Creek about 5 mi east of Yellowstone National Park. Restaurant. No air-conditioning, no room phones. Cross-country and downhill skiing. Laundry facilities. Pets allowed. | 349 Yellowstone Hwy. | 307/587–4044 | fax 307/587–2681 | 16 cabins, 3 kitchenettes (no equipment) | $80 | AE, D, MC, V.

Streamside Inn. Surrounded by mountain and canyon land, this basic motor inn has its own private trout stream and pond, and offers horseback riding, fishing, and river rafting. The extra-large pool and wide, open grassy areas are favorites with kids. Continental breakfast, picnic area. TV. Pool. | 3656 Yellowstone Park Hwy. | 307/587–8242 or 800/285–1282 | fax 307/587–8246 | 21 rooms | $64–$74 | AE, D, MC, V.

Uxu Ranch. The newest cabin is a historic stage stop moved to the site and decorated with Molesworth-style furnishings made by New West of Cody. You have to stay at least a week here. Pack trips. Restaurant, bar with entertainment. No air-conditioning, no room phones. Hot tub. Horseback riding, water sports. Children's programs, playground. | 1710 North Fork Hwy., Wapiti | 307/587–2143 or 800/373–9027 | fax 307/587–8307 | uxuranch@aol.com | www.uxuranch.com | 10 cabins, 11 1- to 3-bedroom cabins | $995–$1,425 wk per person, including activities | MC, V | Closed Oct.–May | AP.

Yellowstone Valley Inn. Only 32 mi from Yellowstone's main east entrance, this sprawling and peaceful property offers basic accommodations in a mountain setting. Campsites are also available, and some of the rooms are in duplex cabins. Restaurant, bar, picnic area. No phones, TV. Coin laundry. Meeting room. Pets allowed. | 3324 Yellowstone Park Hwy., 18 mi west of Cody | 307/587–3961 or 877/587–3961 | fax 307/587–4656 | 18 rooms, 18 cabin rooms | $83–$85 | AE, D, MC, V.

DOUGLAS

MAP 9, H4

(Nearby town also listed: Casper)

Surveyors kept a step head of the Fremont, Elkhorn, and Missouri Valley Railroad as it laid tracks into this area in 1886. They plotted a town, but the railroad, which owned the townsite, refused to let anyone settle here before the rails themselves arrived. Some people, wanting to jump-start the town's development, pitched tentlike structures on Antelope Creek, just outside the official boundaries. When the railroad arrived on August 22 they put their structures on wheels and moved them to the new city, named for Stephen A. Douglas, the presidential candidate who sparred with Abe Lincoln in the famous Lincoln-Douglas debates.

Now Douglas is best known for two things, the Wyoming State Fair, which has been held here annually since 1905, and the jackalope, a mythical animal that is a cross between a jack rabbit and an antelope. There's a large replica of the species in downtown Douglas, and many local businesses sell a smaller model.

Information: Douglas Chamber of Commerce | 121 Brownfield, 82729 | 307/358–2950 | fax 307/358–2972.

Attractions

Ayres Natural Bridge. Overland emigrants sometimes visited this rock outcrop that spans LaPrele Creek, and now it's a popular small picnic area and campsite where you can wade in the creek or simply enjoy the quiet. | Off I–25 | 307/358–2950 | Free.

Fort Fetterman State Historic Site. This fort dates from the 1860s Indian War period. | Rte. 93 | 307/358–2864 or 307/777–7629 | sphs@missc.state.wy.us | $1 residents, $2 nonresidents | Memorial Day–Labor Day, daily 9–5.

Medicine Bow National Forest, Douglas District. Forest lands southwest of Douglas in the Laramie Peak area include four campgrounds and areas where you can hunt, fish, and hike. | Douglas Ranger District, 2250 E. Richards St. | 307/358–4690 | www.fs.fed.us/r2/mbr/ | Campgrounds $5 per day | Campgrounds closed in winter.

Thunder Basin National Grassland. Between the Bighorn Mountains and the Black Hills in the Powder River Basin, this preserve encompasses 572,211 acres. The grasslands begin just north of town and extend almost to the Montana border. Although there are no developed campgrounds, you can still camp, as well as hike, hunt, and fish. | Douglas Ranger District, 2250 E. Richards St. | 307/358–4690 | www.fs.fed.us/mrnf/dgls/dgwel.html | Free.

Wyoming Pioneer Memorial Museum. The emphasis is on the Wyoming pioneer settlers and overland emigrants, but this small state-operated museum on the state fairgrounds also has displays on Native Americans and the frontier military. | 400 W. Center St. | 307/358–9288 | commerce.state.wy.us | Free | June–Aug., weekdays 8–5, Sat. 1–5; Sept.–May, by appointment.

ON THE CALENDAR

APR.: *High Plains Old Time Country Music Show & Contest.* Entertainment from singing to yodeling. | Douglas High School Auditorium | 307/358–2950.

JUNE: *Jackalope Days.* This local celebration has food and lots of events, including a kids parade. | 307/358–2950.

AUG.: *Wyoming State Fair.* The best from Wyoming's 23 county fairs comes together at the Wyoming State Fair, which also has country entertainers. | State Fairgrounds, west end of Center St. | 307/358–2398.

DEC.: *Holiday Winter Fest* Locals gather for the annual decorating of Jackalope Square during this city-wide month-long festival, which also includes a house lighting contest, caroling, a cookie night at participating businesses, and on given years, a light display at the Wyoming State Fairgrounds. | 307/358–2950.

Dining

Best Western Douglas Inn. American. The menu in this Best Western restaurant ranges from American to exotic, including buffalo and ostrich. Try a buffalo steak. Kids' menu. | 1450 Riverbend Dr. | 307/358–9790 | $12–$28 | D, MC, V.

Brights Cafe. American. Serving breakfast and lunch, this place is known for its burgers and fries. The fries are unusual, since each curly fry is made from a whole potato. | 3rd St. | 307/358–3509 | $8–$15 | MC, V.

Plains Trading Post. American. Antique furnishings and portions of old bank buildings are part of the scenario at this restaurant, where the menu is diverse but basic—chicken, burgers, steaks—and the portions large. It's open 24 hours a day. | 628 Richards St. | 307/358–4484 | $14–$22.25 | MC, V.

Lodging

Best Western Douglas Inn. The atrium lobby with a cathedral ceiling and fireplace makes for an impressive entrance. The location is convenient, next to I–25 on the north side of town and close to the Wyoming State Fairgrounds and the main tourist attractions. Restaurant, bar, room service. Cable TV. Indoor pool. Hot tub. Exercise equipment. Video game room. Laundry facilities. Business services. Some pets allowed. | 1450 Riverbend Dr. | 307/358–9790 | fax 307/358–6251 | 116 rooms | $79 | AE, D, DC, MC, V.

Morton Mansion Bed & Breakfast. Built in 1903 in the Victorian Queen Anne style, the inn is on a quiet, residential street and has a huge covered wraparound porch perfect for relaxing on. The attic suite has two bedrooms, a private living room, and a full kitchen. No kids under 10. Continental breakfast, dining room. Cable TV. | 425 E. Center St. | 307/358–2129 | fax 307/358–6590 | www.mortonmansion.com | 3 rooms, 1 suite | $60–$100 | AE, D, MC, V.

DUBOIS

MAP 9, D3

(Nearby town also listed: Grand Teton National Park)

The mountains around Dubois attracted explorers as early as 1811, when members of the Wilson Price Hunt party crossed through the region en route to Fort Astoria. Subsequently, fur trappers and hunters sought their quarry beneath the ramparts of the peak named the Ramshorn by one trapper. The first white family came to the area in 1866, and others followed. By the early 1900s, tie hacks had arrived. They lived in the mountain camps cutting timber and making ties to maintain and expand the railroad. Lumbering remained a stable industry for the community until the last quarter of the 20th century, when mills either closed or scaled back, and Dubois turned its attention toward promoting its distinctive location and attractions.

Just east and south of Grand Teton and Yellowstone national parks, Dubois is the least well known of the "gateway" communities to the parks. This brings some real benefits for travelers, who will find all the services they might want in this town of 1,000 without the crowds of Jackson or Cody. In Dubois you can still get a room for the night during the peak summer travel period without making a reservation weeks or months in advance, though it is a good idea to call a week or so before you intend to arrive. Dubois's other real treasure is its vast amount of nearby public land, including national forest and state-owned property where you can camp and hike in summer and snowmobile and race dogsleds in winter. The largest herd of free-ranging bighorn sheep in the country lives here, roaming the high country in summer and wintering just above town on Whiskey Mountain.

Information: Dubois Chamber of Commerce | Box 632 | 307/455–2556 | fax 307/455–3168 | duboiscc@wyoming.com.

Attractions

Big-Game Hunting. Hunters seek elk and Rocky Mountain bighorn sheep, among other species, when they come to this area. Many outfitters provide services. | 307/455–2556 (Chamber of Commerce) | gf.state.wy.us (Wyoming Game and Fish Dept.).

Fishing. High mountain lakes and streams are good for fishing, and multiple outfitters can help you find the best places to wet a line. | 307/455–2556 (Chamber of Commerce) | gf.state.wy.us (Wyoming Game and Fish Dept.).

National Bighorn Sheep Interpretive Center. Learn about all bighorn sheep, including the local variety, the Rocky Mountain bighorn, in this center that has mounted specimens and hands-on exhibits that illustrate a bighorn's body language, habitat, and characteristics. Winter tours. | 907 Ramshorn Ave. | 307/455–3429 or 888/209–2795 | $2; special rates for children | Memorial Day–Labor Day, daily 9–8; Labor Day–Memorial Day, daily (hours subject to change); wildlife viewing tours mid-Nov.–Mar.

Wind River Historical Center. Displays related to the Wind River tie hacks, local geology, and the archaeology of the Mountain Shoshone or Sheep Eater Indians are part of what you'll see at the Dubois museum. The Sheep Eater exhibit includes soapstone or steatite pots and information about the unique hunting bows the tribe made from the horns of bighorn rams. Tie hacks were the men and women who worked in mountain camps cutting trees and shaping them into railroad ties during the period after 1880. Outbuildings include the town's first schoolhouse, a saddle shop, a homestead, and a bunkhouse. The museum is renovating a historic lodge once visited by Clark Gable and Carole Lombard. Elderhostel programs. | 909 W. Ramshorn Ave. | 307/455–2284 | June, Mon.–Sat. 10–7; July–Aug., weekdays 9–7, weekends 10–5; call ahead to use collections of historical photographs, oral history tapes, and library.

ON THE CALENDAR

FEB.: *International Rocky Mountain Stage Stop Sled Dog Race.* Many former Iditarod champions compete in this multiday race throughout western Wyoming with stops at various towns. The Race to Immunize is held to advance awareness of the importance of immunization for children. | 307/777–7777 or 307/455–2556.

MAY: *Pack Horse Races.* In this timed event held on Memorial Day weekend, teams of packers break camp, pack it, load their pack horses, and complete a several-mile course before they set up camp again. | 307/455–2556 or 307/455–2174.

AUG.: *Wind River Rendezvous.* Buckskinners recreate a camp like those used during the fur trapping era. | 307/455–2556.

Dining

Ramshorn Bagel and Deli. American. This spot serves breakfast and lunch, including bagels, soup, and sandwiches. | 202 E. Ramshorn Ave. | 307/455–2400 | $4–$6.50 | No credit cards | No dinner.

Rustic Pine Steakhouse. American. The bar here is one of Wyoming's more memorable spots, where locals and visitors congregate to share news about hunting or hiking, and the steak house serves mouth-watering steak and seafood in a quiet atmosphere. Salad bar. | 123 E. Ramshorn Ave. | 307/455–2772 | $6.95–$26 | MC, V | No lunch.

Wild Bunch Cafe. American. This small, cozy log-cabin restaurant outside Dubois on the way to Yellowstone serves homemade comfort food like bread-bowl stews and chicken and dumplings. During the summer, flavorful roast beef, ribs, and pork roast are prepared outside in a Dutch oven. | 3577 U.S. 26, 20 mi west of Dubois | 307/455–3873 | $7–$15 | D, MC, V | Closed Nov., mid-April–mid.-May.

Lodging

Absaroka Ranch. Traditional guest-ranch activities and amenities in a mountain setting. Five Mile Creek runs through the property. Restaurant. Hiking, horseback riding. Game room. Children's programs. No smoking. | Box 929 | 307/455–2275 | fax 307/455–2275 | 4 cabins | $1,050 wk per person (1 week min) mid–June–mid–Sept.; lower rates early June–mid–June | No credit cards | Closed mid-Sept.–June | AP.

Black Bear Country Inn. The Wind River runs behind this eclectic redwood cabin-style motel, which has clean, basic rooms at reasonable rates. Each room has an outdoor patio with a table, and a large five-person apartment with a full kitchen is ideal for large groups and families. Picnic area. Refrigerators, microwaves. Cable TV. | 505 W. Ramshorn St. | 307/455–2344 or 800/873–2327 | fax 307/455–2626 | 16 rooms | $45–$60, $75 apartment | AE, D, DC, MC, V.

Brooks Lake Lodge. This mountain resort and sporting lodge in the Wind River Range on Brooks Lake gives you scenery and service. Each of the six lodge bedrooms and six cabins features handcrafted lodgepole furniture. For an extra fee, you can take dogsled rides with outfitters. Restaurant, bar with entertainment, picnic area, complimentary breakfast. Some minibars, refrigerators. Hot tub. Hiking, horseback riding, boating. Cross-country skiing, snowmobiling, tobogganing. Business services. | 458 Brooks Lake Rd. | 307/455–2121 | fax 307/455–2121 | info@brookslake.com | 6 rooms in main building, 6 1- and 2-bedroom cabins | Winter: $150 per person per day in Lodge, $175 in cabins; summer: $195–$215, includes meals and activities | AE, MC, V | AP.

Lazy L and B Ranch. Covering a whopping 2,000 acres, this ranch has comfortably furnished log cabins furnished in casual Western style. All have small refrigerators, private baths or showers, electric heat, and porches. Some have views of the Absaroka and Wind River mountain ranges. | 1072 E. Fork Rd. | 307/455–2839 or 800/453–9488 | fax 307/455–2634 | lazylb@aol.com | www.lazylb.com | 12 cabins | $975 wk per person | No credit cards | Closed Oct.–May | AP.

Stagecoach Motor Inn. Most of the rooms are newly remodeled at this locally owned motel, which has a huge backyard area and is bordered by Pretty Horse Creek. Rooms are standard and come in various sizes; some have full kitchens. Picnic area. Cable TV. Pool. Playground. Coin laundry. Airport shuttle. | 103 E. Ramshorn St. | 307/455–2303 or 800/455–5090 | fax 307/455–3903 | 42 rooms, 6 suites | $64 rooms, $75–$95 suites | AE, D, MC, V.

Super 8. On the north side of town, this motel was renovated in 1998 and has modern furnishings. It is near the National Bighorn Sheep Interpretive Center. Cable TV. Hot tub. Pets allowed. | 1414 Warm Springs Dr. | 307/455–3694 | fax 307/455–3640 | 32 rooms | $70 | AE, D, DC, MC, V.

ENCAMPMENT

(Nearby town also listed: Saratoga)

Trappers in 1838 held a rendezvous on a stream flowing from the Sierra Madre range, calling the site Camp le Grande. The name stuck, and when copper miners struck it rich in 1897 the community that sprang up became Grand Encampment. But the copper boom went bust by 1910 and the town dropped the "Grand," even though it survived as an agricultural and logging center. Agriculture is the mainstay, though recreation in the nearby Medicine Bow National Forest and logging and mining operations also are a part of the economy. This is the gateway community to the Continental Divide National Scenic Trail, accessed at Battle Pass, 15 mi west on Rte. 70.

Information: Saratoga-Platte Valley Chamber of Commerce | Box 1095, Saratoga 82331 | 307/326–8855 | fax 307/326–8855.

Attractions

Bottle Creek Ski Trails. A network of cross-country trails in Medicine Bow–Routt National Forest, these include several backcountry trails suitable only for expert skiers. Others are easy routes for skiers of all levels. Some trails double as snowmobile trails. For more information in town, go to the Trading Post. | Rte. 70, 6 mi southwest of Encampment | 307/327–5720 | Free | Nov.–Apr.

Grand Encampment Museum. A modern interpretive center displays exhibits about the history of the Grand Encampment copper district and logging and mining. A pioneer town of original buildings includes the Lake Creek stage station, the Big Creek tie hack cabin, the Peryam homestead, the Palace Bakery and Ice-Cream Shop, the Weber Springs guard station, the Slash Ridge fire tower, a blacksmith shop, a doctor's office, a transportation barn, and an outhouse. Other relics include three original towers from a 16-mi-long aerial tramway built in 1903 to transport copper ore from mines in the Sierra Madres. You can take guided tours, and there is a research area. The living-history program and Mountain Man Rendezvous is the third weekend in July. | 817 Barnett | 307/327–5308 | www.trib.com/ENCAMPMENT/GEMuseum.html | Free; donations accepted | Memorial Day–Labor Day, Mon.–Sat. 10–5, Sun. 1–5.

Green Mountain Ski Cabin. Cross-country ski or snowmobile to this small log cabin in the Medicine Bow–Routt National Forest, then spend the night or the week. A wood stove serves for cooking and heating; some utensils are provided. You sleep in the second-story sleeping loft. Supply your own sleeping gear and food; snowmobile shuttle drops are available for gear. You can also stay here in summer. | Rte. 70 to Rd. 550 | 307/327–5720 | www.fs.fed.us/mrnf/bch/bchwel.html | $25 per night.

Medicine Bow–Routt National Forest, Hayden District. The local Forest Service office has a lot of information about hiking trails, the Continental Divide National Scenic Trail, 14 campgrounds, the Grand Encampment, Huston Park, Savage Run, and Platte River wilderness areas, and cross-country skiing and snowmobiling trails. | 204 W. 9th St. | 307/327–5481 | www.fs.fed.us/mrnf/bch/bchwel.html | Fees for developed campgrounds vary | Weekdays.

TOURS AND ADVENTURES

Renegade Rides. Horseback trips by the hour or day include tours to Green Mountain Falls, the Encampment River Trail, Huston Park/Continental Divide National Scenic Trail, mines, and ghost towns. | 15 Hwy. 436, Ten Sleep | 307/327–5373 or 307/329–8279 | jpaxton@union-tel.com | $65 half day, $125 full day | Summer.

ENCAMPMENT

INTRO
ATTRACTIONS
DINING
LODGING

ON THE CALENDAR

JUNE: *Woodchopper's Jamboree and Rodeo.* Loggers test their skills at felling trees, handsawing, axe chopping, and power-saw log cutting while rodeo cowboys participate in traditional events. There's also a parade, barbecue, and a melodrama. | 307/327–5155, 307/327–5576 (rodeo), or 800/592–4309.

Dining

Bear Trap. American. This log building has the look and feel of a Western hunting lodge. You get large portions of basic food. The menu is strong on chicken, steak, and seafood, with lobster and crab on selected nights. | 120 E. Riverside Ave., Riverside | 307/327–5277 | $8–$19 | MC, V | Closed Mon.

Pine Lodge Bar. American. Old photographs of area back roads, mountain ranges, and sawmills give this steak-and-potatoes restaurant a rustic, local flavor. Standard fare includes burgers, sandwiches, chicken-fried steak, and, on the weekends, prime rib. The breakfast buffet is cheap and filling. | 520 McCaffrey Ave. | 307/327–5203 | $6–$14 | No credit cards | Closed Mon.–Tues.

Sugar Bowl. American. Old oak and copper cashier booths from the original 1904 bank still adorn this delightful old-fashioned soda fountain and eatery. The burgers are homemade, the lemonade is freshly squeezed, and the wide array of malts, shakes, splits, and sundaes will satisfy any sweet tooth. | 706 Freeman St. | 307/327–5270 | $5–$10 | AE, MC, V.

Lodging

Bighorn Lodge. Southwestern is the style at this motel, which has small but carefully furnished rooms. Cable TV. Hot tub. | 508 McCaffrey Ave. | 307/327–5110 | 12 rooms | $40–$47 | MC, V.

Grand and Sierra Bed & Breakfast Lodge. Hunting outfitter Glenn Knotwell handcrafted this lodge that has Western furnishings and a quiet location at the edge of town. Non-smoking rooms. Hot tub. | 1016 Lomax Ave. | 307/327–5200 | 5 rooms, 2 with private bath | $60 | MC, V.

Lazy Acres Campground and Motel. Location and camping facilities, not the tiny motel, are the lures here at what is considered the best campground in the area. Next to the Grand Encampment River, the one camping cabin has electricity, and sites are equipped for tents and RVs and have fire rings. Picnic area. Cable TV. Showers. Laundry facilities. | Rte. 230 | 307/327–5968 | 4 rooms, 31 campsites both tent and RV, 1 camping cabin | $32 motel, $13–$18 campsites, $20 camping cabin | MC, V | Closed Nov.–May.

Old Depot Bed & Breakfast. Once the Encampment depot for the Saratoga and Encampment Railway Company, known locally as the Slow and Easy, this large building was moved to a new site in Riverside, a block from Rick Martin Memorial Park. Remodeled, it has three guest rooms. You can rent the complete set or just one room. No room phones. Cable TV. Hot tub. Exercise equipment. | 201 N. 1st St. | 307/327–5277 | fax 307/327–5230 | www.wyoming-carboncounty.com/olddepot.htm | 3 rooms, 1 with Jacuzzi | $80 | MC, V.

Riverside Garage and Cabins. These modern, woodsy log cabins are close to the river, and a garage and gas station with food and drinks are also on the property. Cabins vary in size. Pets allowed. | 108 E. Riverside Ave., Riverside | 307/327–5361 | 8 cabins | $32–$85 | AE, D, MC, V.

Rustic Mountain Lodge. On one of the oldest ranches in this area, the place is still owned by the family that homesteaded the land. The log lodge has great views of the Sierra Madre, four guest rooms, and a large common area furnished Western style. You can take guided hunting, fishing, photography, and pack trips, also writing and outdoor workshops, eco-tours, and wild-horse tours. No room phones, no TV in rooms. | Rte. 230, 12 mi south of Riverside | 307/327–5539 | www.plattoutfitting.com | maplatt@union-tel.com | 4 rooms, 1 cabin | $45–$65 for bed and breakfast, $1,000–$1,500 wk for guest ranch/tour packages.

EVANSTON

(Nearby town also listed: Kemmerer)

Like other raucous towns established as the Union Pacific laid track across southern Wyoming, Evanston started as a tent city. Although rail workers were from all backgrounds, many who came to Evanston were Chinese. They established a Chinatown, a huddle of shanties and tarpaper shacks north of the railroad tracks. Some of the shacks became opium dens and gambling houses, but the Chinese residents helped develop the community by diverting water from the Bear River to raise crops. They also built a joss house, where they could practice their native religion, which succeeded in attracting others. Also settling in the area were a large number of Mormons, who saw opportunity in the Bear River Valley and in the Bridger Valley to the east, neither too far from church headquarters in Salt Lake City, Utah.

Evanston today pays homage to those roots, with evidence of the Mormon presence and a reconstructed Chinese joss house. The community has also seen its ups and downs from energy development in the Overthrust Belt, a huge area in southwest Wyoming that has some of the world's greatest reserves of oil, natural gas, and trona.

Information: Evanston Chamber of Commerce | Box 365, 82931 | 307/783–0370 or 800/328–9708 | fax 307/789–4807 | www.etownchamber.com.

Attractions

Bear River State Park. Wildlife, from ducks and Canada geese to herds of bison and elk, is abundant in the park, and you can hike and ski on the park's trails, which have picnic shelters. The park connects to Evanston's Bear Pathway, a paved trail that for much of its length is fully accessible to people with disabilities. | 601 Bear River Dr. | 307/789–6547 | www.state.wy.us | Free | Daily; closed evenings.

Fort Bridger State Historic Site. Started in 1842 as a trading post by mountain man Jim Bridger, Fort Bridger was owned by Bridger and his partner Louis Vasquez until 1853, when Mormons got control of it. The Mormons deserted the area and burned the original Bridger post as the U.S. Army approached during the so-called Mormon War of 1857. The site then became a frontier military post until it was abandoned in 1890. It is now a state historic site. Many of the original military-era buildings remain and have been restored; you can attend interpretive programs and living-history presentations in the summer. The largest mountain-man rendezvous in the intermountain West occurs annually at Fort Bridger over Labor Day weekend, attracting hundreds of buckskinners and Native Americans and thousands of visitors. | 37000 Business Loop I–80 | 307/782–3842 | fax 307/782–7181 | www.state.wy.us | sphs@missc.state.wy.us | $2 | Mar.–Apr., weekends 9–4:30; May–Sept., daily 9–5:30; Oct.–Nov., daily 9–4:30; closed Dec.–Feb. | Bridger/Vasquez Trading Co.: May–Sept., daily 9–5:30; closed Oct.–Apr.

Uinta County Historical Museum. Local history displays include antique photographs, historic books, and artifacts related to Chinese settlement in the area. | 36 10th St. | 307/783–0370 | Free | Memorial Day–Labor Day, weekdays 9–5, weekends 10–4; Labor Day–Memorial Day, Mon–Fri. 9–5.

ON THE CALENDAR

FEB.: *International Rocky Mountain Stage Stop Sled Dog Race.* Many former Iditarod champions compete in this multi-day race that stops in western Wyoming to promote awareness of childhood immunization. | 307/777–7777 or 307/789–2757.

JULY–SEPT.: *Horse Racing.* Races are held regularly at Wyoming Downs. | 10180 Rte. 89 N | 307/789–0511 | $5.

JUNE: *Chili Cook-Off.* Competitors vie for the honor of being named best chili chef., | 800/328–9708 | www.etownchamber.com.

AUG.: *Uinta County Fair.* Young people and adults exhibit crafts and livestock, with entertainment and a rodeo. | 800/328–9708 | www.etownchamber.com.

AUG.: *Bear River Mountain Man Rendezvous.* Buckskinners set up camp for a rendezvous re-creation on the Bear River in Bear River State Park, on the business loop of I–80. Events include shooting competitions and a traders' fair. | I–80 Exit 34 | 800/328–9708 | www.etownchamber.com.

SEPT.: *Cowboy Days.* Labor Day weekend features rodeo action and entertainment. | 800/328–9708 | www.etownchamber.com.

SEPT.: *Fort Bridger Mountain Man Rendezvous.* Held on Labor Day weekend at the Fort Bridger State Historic Site, this is the largest gathering of buckskinners, traders, and Indians in Wyoming. Traders sell period items, and there's an Indian powwow. | 37000 Business Loop I–80 | 307/782–3842.

Dining

Don Pedro's Last Outpost. Mexican. You can't get more authentic than this small, family owned and operated restaurant that's always packed. Try the sizzling fajitas, or the special *molcajete,* a stew of beef and chicken. | 205 Bear River Dr. | 307/789–3322 | $6–$12 | MC, V.

Legal Tender. American. In the Best Western Dunmar Inn, this restaurant is quiet, with good service. Salad bar. Kids' menu. Sun. brunch. | 1601 Harrison Dr. | 307/789–3770 | $12–$23 | AE, D, DC, MC, V.

Main Street Artisans Cafe & Gallery. Contemporary. The only place in town where you can get espresso, this cozy eatery and art gallery occupies one of the older downtown buildings, filled with paintings, pottery, and antiques. The homemade muffins and cakes are favorites, as are the pasta salad, the mesquite chicken sandwich, and the fresh tomato-basil soup. | 927 Main St. | 307/789–4991 | $5–$10 | MC, V | Closed Sun. and Oct.–May. No dinner.

Lodging

Best Western Dunmar Inn. The rooms are spread over a large area, but they are well appointed, and the public areas are casual and inviting. Restaurant, bar. Some refrigerators. Cable TV. Pool. Exercise equipment. | 1601 Harrison Dr. | 307/789–3770 | fax 307/789–3758 | 166 rooms | $75 | AE, D, DC, MC, V.

Pine Gables Inn B&B. In a quiet neighborhood, the building that houses this bed-and-breakfast is listed on the National Register of Historic Places. Each of the four rooms has a private bath, antique furnishings, hand-painted murals, and marbled walls. The homemade breakfast is the all-you-can-eat variety. | 1049 Center St. | 307/789–2069 or 800/789–2069 | pinegabl@allwest.net | www.cruising-america.com/pinegables | 4 rooms | $50–$70 | AE, MC, V.

Prairie Inn. No frills and modest furnishings and rates characterize this inn. Complimentary Continental breakfast. Cable TV. | 264 Bear River Dr. | 307/789–2920 | 31 rooms | $41–$45 | AE, D, DC, MC, V.

Super Budget Inn. Right off I–80, the clean rooms, reasonable rates, and basic amenities make this a great place for a stopover. Bar, dining room. Pool. Pets allowed. | 1936 Harrison Dr. | 307/789–2810 | fax 307/789–5506 | 115 rooms | $65 | AE, D, DC, MC, V.

Weston Plaza Hotel. Numerous amenities make for a comfortable stay at this basic but attractive 3-story hotel-style inn. Most of the rooms have new furniture, and some have microwaves and refrigerators. On the first I–80 exit east of Utah. Restaurant, bar, Continental breakfast, dining room. Pool. Hot tub. Laundry facilities. Pets allowed. | 1983 Harrison Dr. | 307/789–0783 | fax 307/789–3353 | 101 rooms | $55 | AE, D, DC, MC, V.

GILLETTE

(Nearby town also listed: Buffalo)

Gillette started as a livestock center where ranchers could ship cattle and sheep to eastern markets. The Burlington Railroad once shipped thousands of head of cattle and sheep from the livestock yards here every year. Charles Lindbergh once landed near the town, too.

But coal is the primary commodity, and millions of tons are mined and shipped out each year to coal-fired power plants. The Powder River Basin coal is not as low in sulfur or as high in BTU output as that mined in southern Wyoming operations. It can be mined more easily than southern Wyoming coal, though, because the coal beds are not covered by as much soil.

Huge coal mines operate throughout the Powder River Basin, and Gillette is the main city, with 25,000 residents. It is one of Wyoming's wealthiest cities as a result, and therefore has an excellent community infrastructure ranging from the Campbell County Public Library to the Cam-Plex, a multi-use center for everything from craft bazaars and indoor rodeos to concerts and fine-arts exhibits. Gillette is also a gateway town for Devils Tower National Monument, the volcanic plug that is one of the nation's most distinctive geological features and a mecca for rock climbers.

Information: Campbell County Chamber of Commerce | 314 S. Gillette Ave., 82716 | 307/682–3673 | fax 307/682–0538 | ccchamber@bcn.com | www.Gillette.com.

GILLETTE

INTRO
ATTRACTIONS
DINING
LODGING

Attractions

Campbell County Recreation Center and Pool. An indoor track, gymnasium, five racquetball/handball courts, squash court, free-weight room, golf driving range, locker rooms, and steam rooms are part of this facility that also includes a junior Olympic pool with a water slide (summer only). You can also try the Campbell County ice arena, the Bell Nob golf course, and the Cam-Plex picnic area. | 1000 Douglas Hwy. | 307/682–7406 | fax 307/682–7050 | ccg.co.campbell.wy.us/parkrec/ | Recreation center/pool $2.75; ice arena $2; golf course $18 (18 holes), $12 (9 holes) | Daily 5 AM–9 PM.

Cam-Plex. You have to check out what's going on at this multi-use facility; it could be anything from a rodeo to a concert to a craft show. | 1635 Reata Dr. | 307/682–0552, 307/682–8802 (tickets) | fax 307/682–8418 | www.cam-plex.com | $8–$30.

Devils Tower National Monument. Native American legend has it that the corrugated Devils Tower was formed when a tree stump turned into granite and grew taller to protect some stranded children from a clawing bear. Geologists say that the rock tower, rising 1,280 ft above the Belle Fourche River, is the core of a defunct volcano. Seventy miles northeast of Gillette (I–90 east, then U.S. 14 and Rte 24 north), it was a tourist magnet long before a spaceship landed on top of it in the movie *Close Encounters of the Third Kind,* and it is still a significant site for Native Americans. During June, rock climbers have agreed to stay away so that Natives Americans can conduct spiritual rites. You'll find 7 mi of hiking trails, a campground, a picnic area, and a visitor center. Hulett, a few miles northeast of the monument, is the closest town with services. | Rte 24 | 307/467–5430 (Hulett Chamber of Commerce) | www.nps.gov/deto/ | $8 per car, campsites $12 | Daily (visitor center Apr.–Oct., daily 8–7:30; Oct.–Apr., daily 8:30–4:30) | Campground closed Nov.–Mar.

Keyhole State Park. You can fish, boat, and swim at this state park. Camping and picnic areas are available, and the marina has a shower house and restaurant. | 353 McKean Rd. | 307/756–3596, marina info 307/756–9529 | fax 307/756–3534 | sphs@missc.state.wy.us | www.state.wy.us | Day use $2 resident vehicle, $5 nonresident vehicle; camping $4 resident vehicle, $9 nonresident vehicle | Daily.

Rockpile Museum. Local historical artifacts, from bits and brands to rifles and sheep wagons, make up the collection at this county museum. | 900 W. 2nd St. | 307/682–5723 | Free | June–Aug., Mon.–Sat. 9–8, Sun. 12:30–6:30; Sept.–May, Mon.–Sat. 9–5.

ON THE CALENDAR

JUNE–JULY: *Concerts in the Park.* The evening concerts in the city park Thursdays at 7 PM are free. | 307/686–0040.

JUNE–AUG.: *Coal Mine Tours.* Take a tour of the Campbell County coal mines. Tours depart from 1810 S. Douglas Hwy. | 307/686–0040.

SEPT.–OCT.: *Wyoming Cutting Horse Events.* Several events at the Cam-Plex involve cutting horse competitions. | 1635 Reata Dr. | 307/682–0552.

YEAR-ROUND: *Levi's and Lace Square Dance Club.* Square dancing takes place every first and third Saturday, 7:30 PM, at the Rockpile Community Center. | 912 W. 2nd St. | 307/682–0632.

Dining

Bailey's Bar and Grill. Eclectic. With an interior that evokes an English pub, this handsome restaurant in an old brick building serves delicious sandwiches at lunch and has some Mexican dishes on the dinner menu. | 301 S. Gillette Ave. | 307/686–7678 | $4–$13 | AE, MC, V.

Hong Kong. Chinese. A typical Chinese restaurant, both in furnishings and menu. The big banquet room seats 75. | 1612 W. 2nd St. | 307/682–5829 | $6–$14 | AE, D, MC, V.

Packard's Grill. American. Families are welcomed at this large, airy, casual, no-smoking establishment. The favorites include prime rib and Southern-style dishes. Kids' menu. | 408 S. Douglas Hwy. | 307/686–5149 | $6–$16 | AE, D, DC, MC, V | No dinner Sun.

Lodging

Best Western Tower West Lodge. The biggest hotel in town is also an excellent value, with large, comfortable rooms done in beige and teal. Most have cable TV and coffeemakers, and there is a 24-hr convenience store. Restaurant, bar with entertainment, room service. In-room data ports. Cable TV. Indoor pool. Hot tub. Exercise equipment. Video game room. Laundry facilities. Business services. Airport shuttle. | 109 N. U.S. 14/16 | 307/686–2210 | fax 307/682–5105 | 188 rooms | $58–$68 | AE, D, DC, MC, V.

Days Inn. Area shops and restaurants are within walking distance of this nondescript but reasonably priced motor inn with a pleasant sitting area. Continental breakfast. Cable TV. Business services, conference rooms. No pets. | 910 E. Boxelder Rd. | 307/682–3999 or 800/325–2525 | fax 307/682–9151 | 130 rooms | $65–$80 | AE, D, DC, MC, V.

Quality Inn. Right off I–90, this motel has large rooms and a breakfast room, but no frills. Complimentary Continental breakfast. | 1004 E. U.S. 14/16 | 307/682–2616 or 800/621–2182 | fax 307/687–7002 | 80 rooms | $70–$150 | AE, D, DC, MC, V.

Ramada Limited. Minutes from downtown and area attractions, rooms at this clean, dependable motor inn are spacious and comfortable. Continental breakfast. Cable TV. Outdoor pool. Hot tub. Pets allowed (fee). | 608 East 2nd St. | 307/682–9341 or 888/298–2054 | fax 307/682–9341 | 76 rooms | $75 | AE, D, DC, MC, V.

Thunder Basin Hotel. Travelers with a yen for exercise will appreciate the gym and the indoor pool big enough for swimming. Rooms at this former Holiday Inn are decorated in soft teal and mauve. Some have in-room data ports. Restaurant, bar with entertainment, room service. Cable TV. Indoor pool. Hot tub. Gym. Game room with pool table and video games. Laundry facilities. Business services. Airport shuttle. Pets allowed. | 2009 S. Douglas Hwy. | 307/686–3000 | fax 307/686–4018 | 158 rooms | $90–$94 | AE, D, DC, MC, V.

GRAND TETON NATIONAL PARK

(Nearby towns also listed: Dubois, Jackson, Yellowstone National Park)

This smaller park with a shorter history might be dwarfed by its northern neighbor Yellowstone, but nothing overshadows peaks like these. Mt. Moran, Teewinot Mountain, Mt. Owen, Grand Teton, and Middle Teton all form a magnificent and dramatic front along the west side of the Teton Valley. Large and small lakes are strung at the range's base, draining north into Jackson Lake, which flows into the Snake River.

The Teton Range itself formed the nucleus of Grand Teton National Park when it was set aside in 1929. In 1950 it expanded to include most of the area in Jackson Hole east of the Snake River, including former ranches that had been purchased during the 1930s by John D. Rockefeller, Jr., who ultimately donated the land to the federal government. A few oddities lie within the park's borders, including a commercial airport and the Jackson Lake Dam, which holds water for use in Idaho. Nevertheless, the region is hard to beat for fishing, hiking, climbing, boating, wildlife-watching, and pure rugged beauty.

Information: Grand Teton National Park | National Park Service, Box 170, Moose 83012 | 307/739–3300 or TTY 307/733–2053 | www.nps.gov/grte/ | 7-day pass good for both Yellowstone and Grand Teton national parks; $20 per motor vehicle, $10 non-motorized entry permit, $15 motorcycle or snowmobile; $40 annual permit; Golden Age and Golden Eagle permits accepted.

GRAND TETON
NATIONAL PARK

INTRO
ATTRACTIONS
DINING
LODGING

Attractions

Chapel of the Transfiguration. Scenes for the movie *Spencer's Mountain* were shot at this tiny mountain chapel—still a functioning house of worship. The chapel attracts couples who want to exchange vows with the Tetons as a backdrop.

Hiking Trails. Much of this park known for its spectacular mountains is best seen by hiking. You can get trail maps and information about hiking conditions from rangers at the park visitor centers at Moose or Colter Bay. Popular trails are those in the Jenny Lake area, the Leigh and String lakes area, and the Taggart Lake Trail, with views of Avalanche Canyon. You may see moose, but keep your distance.

Jackson Lake. The biggest of the Grand Teton Park's glacier-scooped lakes, Jackson Lake, in the northern reaches of the park, was enlarged by construction of the Jackson Lake Dam built in 1909. You can fish, sail, and windsurf and stay at the campgrounds and lodges that dot the shoreline. | U.S. 89/191/287 and Teton Park Rd.

Jenny Lake. Named for the Indian wife of mountain man Beaver Dick Leigh, this pristine mountain lake south of Jackson Lake draws boaters and hikers. You can use the trails surrounding the lake. | Teton Park Rd.

Menor's Ferry. The ferry on display is not the original, but it is an accurate re-creation of the craft built by Bill Menor in the 1890s, and it demonstrates how people crossed the Snake River before bridges were built. Several cabins, including the home and store used by Bill Menor, who also operated the ferry, remain at the site. You can see a historic photo collection in one of the cabins. | Signal Mountain Summit Rd.

Moose Visitors Center. At the park's south entrance, this is a good place to start any visit to Grand Teton National Park. You'll find information about all activities, a decent resource room where you can purchase maps, books, and the like, and knowledgeable people who can tell you what to expect on trails and lakes.

★ **Signal Mountain.** North of Moose and midway between Moose and Moran, Signal Mountain got its name when a valley resident was overdue and other people launched a search

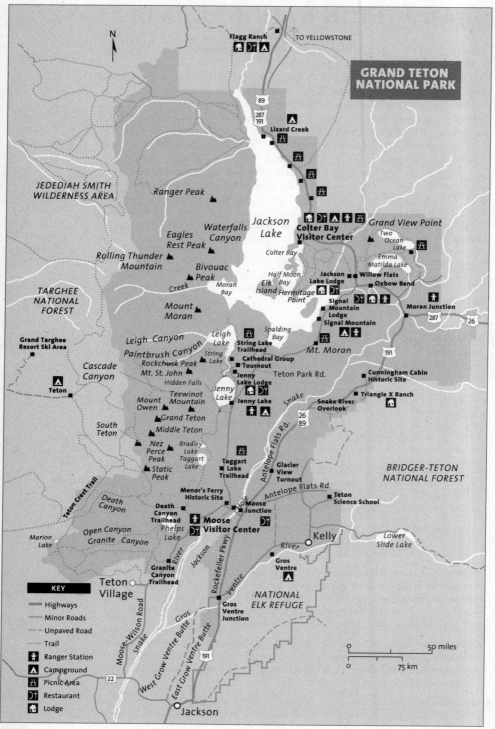

N

**GRAND TETON
NATIONAL PARK**

Flagg Ranch

TO YELLOWSTONE

89
287
191

Lizard Creek

*JEDEDIAH SMITH
WILDERNESS AREA*

Ranger Peak

*Jackson
Lake*

Grand View Point

Colter Bay
Visitor Center

Two
Ocean
Lake

*Waterfalls
Canyon*

Colter Bay

*Eagles
Rest Peak*

*Emma
Matilda Lake*

*Rolling Thunder
Mountain*

*Bivouac
Peak*

Half Moon
Bay

Elk
Island

Willow Flats

Jackson
Lake Lodge

Oxbow Bend

*TARGHEE
NATIONAL
FOREST*

*Moran
Bay*

Creek

Hermitage
Point

Signal
Mountain
Lodge

Moran Junction

*Mount
Moran*

Signal Mountain

287

26

Grand Targhee
Resort Ski Area

Leigh Canyon

*Leigh
Lake*

*Spalding
Bay*

191

Paintbrush Canyon

String Lake
Trailhead

*String
Lake*

Cathedral Group
Tournout

Mt. Moran

Teton Park Rd.

*Cascade
Canyon*

Rockchuck Peak

Cunningham Cabin
Historic Site

Teton

Mt. St. John

Hidden Falls

Jenny
Lake Lodge

Triangle X Ranch

*Teewinot
Mountain*

*Jenny
Lake*

Jenny Lake

Snake River
Overlook

*Mount
Owen*

Snake

26
89

Grand Teton

*South
Teton*

Middle Teton

*Nez
Perce
Peak*

*Bradley
Lake*

*Taggart
Lake*

*BRIDGER-TETON
NATIONAL FOREST*

*Static
Peak*

Taggart
Lake
Trailhead

Glacier
View
Turnout

Teton Crest Trail

*Death
Canyon*

Menor's Ferry
Historic Site

Moose
Junction

Antelope Flats Rd.

Teton
Science School

Death
Canyon
Trailhead

Moose
Visitor Center

Antelope Flats Rd.

Open Canyon

*Phelps
Lake*

Kelly

*Lower
Slide Lake*

*Marion
Lake*

Granite Canyon

River

Granite
Canyon
Trailhead

Jackson

Ventre

River

Gros
Ventre

KEY

**Teton
Village**

*NATIONAL
ELK REFUGE*

Highways

Gros
Ventre
Junction

Minor Roads

Unpaved Road

Trail

Ranger Station

Moose-Wilson Road

Snake

Gros

Campground

Ventre

Picnic Area

West Grow Ventre Butte

East Grow Ventre Butte

Rockefeller Pkwy.

50 miles

Restaurant

Lodge

191

75 km

22

Jackson

for him. They agreed that whoever found him would light a signal fire atop the mountain, which would be visible throughout Jackson Hole. Though the missing man was dead by the time he was found, nevertheless the signal fire burned and the mountain got a name. The narrow road (not suitable for RVs) leads to an overlook with spectacular views of Jackson Hole. | Teton Park Rd.

GRAND TETON
NATIONAL PARK

INTRO
ATTRACTIONS
DINING
LODGING

ON THE CALENDAR

JAN.–MAR.: *Teton Science School Winter Speaker Series*. The Teton Science School hosts this popular seven-program series at the National Museum of Wildlife Art. Speakers from around the United States lecture on the ecology, wildlife, science, natural history, and geology of the Grand Teton and Yellowstone areas. | 2820 Rungius Rd., Jackson | 307/733–4765.

Dining

Chuckwagon Restaurant at Colter Bay. American. In Colter Bay Village, this is a good place to take the family. It serves lasagna, trout, and barbecued spareribs, as well as wild game. | Off U.S. 89 | 307/543–3100 | $14–$24 | AE, D, DC, MC, V | Closed Sept.–May.

Dornan's. Barbecue. Hearty portions of beef, beans, potatoes, stew, and hot coffee or lemonade are the standbys at Dornan's, which is easily identified by its tepees. Locals know it for the beef and barbecue cooked over wood fires. You can eat inside the tepees if it happens to be raining or windy; otherwise, enjoy your meal at outdoor picnic tables with views of the Snake River and the Tetons. Buffet dinner. | 10 Moose Rd. | 307/733–2415 | $3–$25 | MC, V.

The Granary. American. Gourmet nouvelle Western cuisine and views of the Tetons make this outstanding restaurant in the Spring Creek Resort one of the glitziest, priciest, and most exotic in the area. The specialties include roast elk tenderloin with five-grain pilaf, green peppercorn orange marmalade, and blackberry cassis sauce, and cedar-planked wild Copper River salmon with chilled pearl onions and fingerling potato and leek melange. Find a seat on the outdoor deck in the summer. | 1800 Spirit Dance Rd., Jackson | 307/733–8833 | $35–$70 | AE, D, DC, MC, V.

Jackson Lake Lodge Dining Room. American. The stunning view of Jackson Lake through huge windows is the chief attraction here. There are four dinner menus in rotation in the Mural Room, often featuring buffalo and local game dishes. | U.S. 89 N | 307/543–3100 | fax 307/543–3143 | $5–$27 | AE, D, DC, MC, V | Closed late Oct.–mid-May.

Jackson Lake Lodge Pioneer Grill. American. Seat yourself at the 86-person continuous, winding counter at this homey luncheonette. They serve great comfort dishes like bacon and eggs, vegetable lasagna, and rotisserie chicken. Huckleberry pancakes and anything from the old-fashioned soda fountain are real treats. | U.S. 89 N | 307/543–2811, ext. 1911 | $7–$15 | AE, DC, MC, V | Closed early Oct.–late May.

Jenny Lake Lodge Dining Room. Continental. Elegant yet rustic, this is Grand Teton National Park's finest dining establishment. The breakfast and dinner menus are offered prix-fixe; lunch is à la carte. The wine list is extensive. House favorites are prime rib and steaks. Be aware that this is one of the few places where you're asked to dress for dinner. Kids' menu. No smoking. | Jenny Lake Rd. | 307/733–4647 | Dinner reservations essential | Jacket required | $38 | AE, DC, MC, V | Closed Oct.–May.

The Peaks. American. The enormous picture windows at this restaurant in Signal Mountain Lodge offer breathtaking views of Jackson Lake and the Tetons. Salmon and grilled Rocky Mountain trout, prepared differently each day, are specialties, as are the elk medallions and chicken Szechuan. | Teton Park Rd., Moran | 307/543–2831 | $20–$30 | AE, D, MC, V | Closed mid-Oct.–mid-May.

Lodging

Colter Bay Village. On Jackson Lake at Colter Bay, this is one of the park's cheaper lodgings, with cabins, tent cabins, and an RV park. The views are outstanding. Tent cabins have woodburning stoves, picnic tables, fee showers, and double-decker bunks (no bedding). You can rent sleeping bags, cots, and blankets. 2 restaurants, picnic area, snack bar. No air-conditioning, no room phones. Horseback riding, boating. Shops. Airport shuttle. Some pets allowed. | U.S. 89/191/287 | 307/543–3100 or 800/628–9988 (reservations) | fax 307/543–3046 | www.gtlc.com | 166 cabins, some with shower only, some share bath; 66 tent cabins; 113 RV spaces | $66–$120 | AE, DC, MC, V | Closed early Oct.–late May.

Cowboy Village Resort at Togwotee. High on the Togwotee Pass, 17 mi east of Moran, this is a great headquarters for trips to Yellowstone and Grand Teton national parks. In winter you can snowmobile or cross-country ski in a huge area that includes the Continental Divide National Scenic Trail. The cabins are small but have kitchens and fireplaces. The lodge is spacious with Western furnishings. Winter packages include lodging and snowmobiling. Restaurant, bar, picnic area, room service. No air-conditioning. Cable TV. Hot tubs. Cross-country skiing, snowmobiling. Laundry facilities. Airport shuttle (except in winter). | U.S. 26/287, Moran | 307/543–2847 or 800/543–2847 | fax 307/543–2391 | bcarson@wyoming.com | www.cowboyvillage.com | 89 units, 54 cabins with kitchens | $99 rooms; $88–$149 cabins | AE, D, MC, V | Closed mid-Oct.–mid-Nov.

Dornan's Spur Ranch Cabins. Near the park's southern visitors center and in Dornan's all-in-one shopping/dining/recreation development, this no-smoking facility has spacious duplexes with private baths. The log cabin–style structures have great views of the Tetons and the Snake River. Each has a full kitchen as well as generously sized living/dining room and porches with porch furniture and Weber grills in summer. No smoking. | 10 Moose La., Moose | 307/733–2522 | fax 307/739–9098 | spur@dornans.com | www.dornans.com | 12 cottages with kitchens | $125–$200 | D, MC, V.

Flagg Ranch. Just inside Grand Teton National Park, near the south entrance to Yellowstone National Park, the ranch is on the river and has cabins and RV sites. You can take snow coach rides to Yellowstone, hike, and snowmobile. Restaurant, bar. No air-conditioning. Business services. Airport shuttle. | U.S. 89, Moran | 307/543–2861 or 800/443–2311 (reservations) | fax 307/543–2484 | info@flaggranch.com | www.flaggranch.com | 92 2- and 4-room cabins | $99–$135 cabins, $33 full–hookup RV sites | MC, V.

Gros Ventre River Ranch. Along the Gros Ventre River, this 160-acre ranch is surrounded by national park and forest lands. You stay in lodges and log cabins, some with wood-burning stoves and doors that open onto decks, as well as kitchenettes and laundry facilities. You can take float trips down the river and go hiking, horseback riding, biking, and fishing. Restaurant. No air-conditioning, TVs, VCRs, or room phones. Playground. Airport shuttle. | Box 151, Moose | 307/733–4138 | fax 307/733–4272 | grosventre ranch@compuserve.com | www.ranchweb.com/grosventre | 4 cabins, 4 lodges | $1,188–$1,608 wk | No credit cards | Closed Apr. and Nov. | AP.

Hatchet Resort. Some units sleep up to 12 at this log-style motel about 10 mi south of the south gate to Grand Teton and 35 mi from Yellowstone. Ownership changed in 1999. Restaurant, picnic area. No air-conditioning. Pets allowed (fee). No smoking. | 19980 E. U.S. 89 | 307/543–2413 | fax 307/543–2034 | www.hatchetresort.com | $90–$99 | D, MC, V.

Jackson Lake Lodge. This large establishment is on a bluff with spectacular views across Jackson Lake to the Tetons. The upper lobby has 60-ft picture windows and a collection of Native American artifacts and Western art. Restaurants, bar with entertainment. Pool. Business services. Airport shuttle. | U.S. 89 | 307/543–3100 or 800/628–9988 (reservations) | fax 307/543–3143 | www.gtlc.com | 385 rooms | $110–$180 | AE, DC, MC, V | Closed late Oct.–mid-May.

Jenny Lake Campground. Tents-only sites in the woods near the water make this one of the more peaceful and desirable camping areas in the park. Sites are distributed on a first-come, first-served basis, and the campground, 8 mi north of Moose, can fill up by 8 AM in the summer, so arrive early. Picnic area. Phones. Boat access. Rest rooms. | Teton Park Rd. | 307/739–3300 | www.nps.gov/grte | 48 sites | $12 per site | No credit cards | Closed Oct.–late May.

Jenny Lake Lodge. Founded in the 1920s, this very pleasant and pricey establishment has Old West–style cabins with down comforters and handmade quilts, but no radios or televisions. You get a great view of the mountains from the main lodge, and can hike on nearby trails and walk easily to three lakes. Restaurant, bar. No air-conditioning, some refrigerators, room phones on request, no TV in rooms. Horseback riding, boating. Bicycles. Airport shuttle. | Jenny Lake Rd., Moran | 307/733–4647 | fax 307/543–0324 | www.gtlc.com | 37 duplex-style cabins | $318–$560 | AE, DC, MC, V | Closed mid-Oct.–early June | MAP.

Lizard Creek Campground. Views of Jackson Lake, wooded sites, and the relative isolation make a trip to this campground worthwhile. On the northern edge of the park, 18 mi north of Moran Junction, Lizard Creek is only 10 mi south of Yellowstone's south entrance, so this is a good bet for those who want to take in both parks. Picnic area, rest rooms, water. | U.S. 89/287 | 307/739–3300 | www.nps.gov/grte | 60 sites | $12 per site | No credit cards | Closed early Sept.–early June.

Lost Creek Ranch. Upscale, Old World, and luxurious, this dude ranch 8 mi north of Moose has large, well-furnished rooms with unsurpassed views. You get entertainment in the evening, and can hike in Grand Teton National Park, take one of the weekly trips to a rodeo, or tour Yellowstone. Restaurant, picnic area. No air-conditioning, refrigerators, some kitchens. Pool. Hot tub. Gym. Tennis. Game room. Children's programs (June-Aug.). Laundry service. Business services. Airport shuttle. | U.S. 89 | 307/733–3435 | fax 307/733–1954 | ranch@lostcreek.com | www.lostcreek.com | 10 cabins, 7 with kitchens | $4,298–$9,620 wk 1–4 persons, with early summer and fall specials | AE | Closed Oct.–May | AP.

Luton's Teton Cabins. These new, attractive duplex log cabins are nestled on a ranch property 4 mi east of Moran surrounded by the striking Teton mountains. Cabins are simple and immaculate, with hardwood floors, handcrafted furniture, one or two bedrooms, full kitchens, and front porches. No in-room phones or TVs. Laundry facilities. No pets. | U.S. 26 | 307/543–2489 | 105600.504@compuserve.com | www.tetoncabins.com | 11 cabins | $148 | D, MC, V.

McReynolds Blacktail Cabins. Spacious, charming, and private, these guest houses, on six acres at the foot of the Tetons, are great for groups who want to have a home base while exploring the area. Both cabins have two bedrooms, full kitchens, custom-made furniture, and beautifully designed common areas. Reservations are essential. Microwaves, refrigerators, TVs. Laundry facilities. | Antelope Flats Rd., ½ mi east of U.S. 89 | 307/733–4653 | fax 307/733–4653 | mcreynolds@blissnet.com | www.wyoming.com/~jacksonhole/blacktail-cabins | 2 guest houses | $250 (5–night minimum) | MC, V.

Moose Head Ranch. Completely surrounded by Grand Teton National Park, the spacious log cabins make this ranch a good bet for families. You can take supervised horseback rides, photograph wildlife, and fish in the stocked trout ponds. The Snake River flows just below the ranch, and you can take rafting trips. The dining room is a large lodge. No air-conditioning, refrigerators, no room phones. Hiking, horseback riding. Library. Airport shuttle. | Box 214, Moose | 307/733–3141 or 850/877–1431 (reservations off–season) | fax 307/739–9097 | 14 1- and 2-bedroom cabins | $225 per person per day (5 night minimum) | No credit cards | Closed Aug. 21–June 13 | AP.

Signal Mountain Lodge. The lodge-style cabins have a sofa bed in the living room, useful if you're traveling with a family. One-room units have refrigerators and fireplaces and are on the waterfront. Two-room units have kitchenettes. All have views of the Grand Tetons and some of Jackson Lake. Bring your own utensils. Restaurant, bar. No air-conditioning, some microwaves. Marina, boating. Fishing. Some pets allowed. | Teton Park Rd., Moran | 307/543–2831 | fax 307/543–2569 | www.signalmtnlodge.com | 79 cabins, 30 with kitchenettes | $80–$175 | AE, D, MC, V.

Split Creek Ranch. A charming log-cabin lodge only 6 mi from the park's south entrance, this family-friendly inn offers plenty of wildlife. You can fish in the two stocked trout ponds and take the short walk to the Snake River. Western-style rooms have wood furniture and warm hues. A deluxe cabin apart from the lodge is private and comfortable. Con-

GRAND TETON
NATIONAL PARK

INTRO
ATTRACTIONS
DINING
LODGING

tinental breakfast. Microwaves, refrigerators, no phones, TVs, some kitchenettes. Playground. Laundry facilities. | 240 West Zenith Dr. | 307/733–7522 | fax 307/734–2869 | www.splitcreekranch.com | 8 rooms, 1 cabin | $95–$110 rooms, $300 cabin | MC, V.

GREEN RIVER

MAP 9, D5

(Nearby towns also listed: Evanston, Kemmerer, Rock Springs)

Of all the towns along the Union Pacific Railroad, Green River is the only one that was already there by the time the railroad arrived in the late 1860s. Now with a population of about 13,000, it began as a Pony Express and stage station on the Overland Trail and settled in as a real town with the coming of the railroad. Green River remained a railroad town for many years—the shift workers led the town to ban door-to-door salesmen because so many workers slept in the day. Other Wyoming towns subsequently adopted the ordinance. Green River is now a community of miners who work in nearby coal and trona mines. The city is near the Green River, known to the Indians as the Seedskadee and to early explorers as either the Rio Verde or Spanish River.

In 1869 and again in 1871, John Wesley Powell launched expeditions down the Green and Colorado rivers to explore those waterways. Though it's not certain where Powell and his men put in to the river for the first trip, they set out on the second one from Expedition Island, near the town, which by that time had grown to number some 2,000 residents.

Information: Green River Chamber of Commerce | 1450 Uinta Dr., 82935 | 307/875–5711 or 800/354–6743 | fax 307/875–1646 | parobbin@wyoming.com | www.grchamber.com.

Attractions

Flaming Gorge National Recreation Area. The Flaming Gorge Reservoir straddles the border between Wyoming and Utah, though most of the park's visitors facilities are in Utah. The water flow comes from the Green River and is held back by Flaming Gorge Dam. You can boat and fish, as well as spot wildlife. The area is as rich in history as it is spectacularly beautiful. Mountain men and outlaws have found haven here, and in 1869, on his first exploration down the Green River, John Wesley Powell named many local landmarks: Flaming Gorge, Horseshoe Canyon, Red Canyon and the Gates of Lodore. Butch Cassidy and Jim Bridger made reputations around here, as did "Queen Ann" Bassett, a Colorado rancher's daughter who became a rancher in her own right. You'll find marinas, lodging, food, and campgrounds, places to rent horses and snowmobiles, and trails for mountain bikes as well. | 20 mi south on Rte. 530 or U.S. 191 | 801/784–3445, 800/277–7571 (for information on reservoir elevations and river flows), or 877/444–6677 or TDD 877/833–6777 (for campground reservations) | internet@ReserveUSA.com (campground reservations only) | www.gorp.com/gorp/resource/us_nra/ut_flame.htm | Free | Daily.

Seedskadee National Wildlife Refuge. Birds love Seedskadee National Wildlife Refuge, 14,000 prime acres inhabited by prairie falcons, peregrine falcons, Canada geese, and various species of hawks and owls. Trumpeter swans occasionally use the area as well. Within or near the refuge, you'll find homestead and ranch sites, Oregon Trail crossings, and ferry sites over the Green River, as well as the place where Jim Bridger and Henry Fraeb built a trading post in 1839. | 37 mi north of Green River on Rte. 372 | 307/875–2187 | Free | Daily.

Sweetwater County Historical Museum. The museum houses documents and other items related to the cultural heritage of southwestern Wyoming. | 80 W. Flaming Gorge Way | 307/872–6411 | Free | Weekdays 9–5, Sat. 1–5; July–Aug.

MAY: *Lake Flaming Gorge Fishing Derby.* Anglers compete for fun and prizes. | 435/784–3483.

JUNE: *Flaming Gorge Days Celebration.* The celebration includes a battle of the bands, a basketball tournament, a golf scramble, arm wrestling, horseshoes, and children's entertainment, and is held at various venues, including Expedition Island, the rodeo grounds, and Evers Park. | 307/875–5711.

Dining

Denali Grill and Bakery. American. The Mt. Denali theme is evident in this down-home restaurant with artificial pine trees galore, twig curtain rods, pictures of moose and bears, and iron caribou silhouettes on the walls. The owners pride themselves in their homemade breads, soups, and sandwiches. Local favorites include the baby back barbecued ribs and salmon fillet. Bread pudding, pecan torte, and lemon crunch pie are on the list of homemade desserts. | 375 Uinta Dr. | 307/875–4654 | $5–$15 | AE, D, MC, V.

Penny's Diner. American. The name pretty much says it all—a 1950s-style 24-hour diner with a bright shiny look reminiscent of a rail car and flashing neon lights. Try a burger, fries, and a milk shake. The diner is part of the Oak Tree Inn. | $8–$15 | 1172 W. Flaming Gorge Way | 307/875–3500 | AE, D, DC, MC, V.

Lodging

Little America. This one-stop facility 20 mi from Green River sits alone in the Little Colorado Desert, because the owner once became stranded here while sheep herding. Not wanting others to find themselves in the same predicament, he built the hotel. The rooms are large and comfortable, and some have in-room data ports. Restaurant, bar. Some refrigerators. Cable TV. Pool. Exercise equipment. Playground. Laundry facilities. Business services. | I–80 | 307/875–2400 or 800/634–2401 | fax 307/872–2666 | 140 rooms, 18 with shower only | $65–$95 | AE, D, DC, MC, V.

Oak Tree Inn. A completely no-smoking facility, this two-story inn was built in 1997. If you're a photographer, you can shoot the distinctive surrounding rock formations. Flaming Gorge is 20 mi away. Restaurant. Some refrigerators. Cable TV. Pets allowed. No smoking. | 1170 W. Flaming Gorge Way | 307/875–3500 | fax 307/875–4889 | 192 rooms | $65–$100 | AE, D, DC, MC, V.

Sweet Dream Inn. Some large suite-style rooms will sleep up to five people at this locally owned motel. The larger rooms have microwaves, refrigerators, and Jacuzzis. Restaurant, bar. Meeting rooms. Pets allowed. | 1416 Uinta Dr. | 307/875–7554 | 30 rooms | $68–$89 | AE, D, MC, V.

GREYBULL

INTRO
ATTRACTIONS
DINING
LODGING

GREYBULL

MAP 9, E2

(Nearby town also listed: Lovell)

A metal sculpture of a bison bull here is a constant reminder of how this Bighorn Basin town of about 1,800 got its name. Legend has it that an albino bull buffalo, likely either white or gray, roamed near the Bighorn River. Native Americans consider any white or gray bison to be sacred, and they began to call the river that flowed into the Bighorn from the west the Greybull. The town later adopted the name.

Some of Wyoming's greatest Jurassic Era artifacts have been found near Greybull, including a dozen large sauropods and the world's largest allosaurus. The dinosaur beds are on Bureau of Land Management land 10 mi north of the tiny town of Shell (15 mi east of Greybull). There are other dinosaur sites nearby, including the Red Gulch Dinosaur Tracksite, which has thousands of dinosaur tracks preserved in what was once mud and is now rock. Other geological features nearby include the Devil's Kitchen with its valuable fossils—including ammonites—and spectacular Shell Canyon with Shell Falls, named for the ancient shells embedded in the granite and sandstone cliffs over which thousands of gallons of water tumble every second.

Greybull is also home to the Wyoming Interagency Hotshot Crew, 20 elite firefighters who respond to wildfires throughout the United States and sometimes Canada.

Information: Greybull Chamber of Commerce | 333 Greybull Ave., 82426 | 307/765–2100 | fax 307/765–2100 | chamber@greybull.com | www.greybull.com.

Attractions

Antelope Butte Ski Area. You can downhill and cross-country ski in this small ski area 35 mi east of Greybull, in the Bighorn National Forest. You can also rent equipment, and there's a ski school as well as a lodge with food. | U.S. 14, Bighorn Mountain | 307/655–9530 | fax 307/655–9529 | $20 | Mid-Dec.–early Apr., Wed.–Sun. and holidays 9:30–4.

Greybull Museum. The collection here ranges from historical objects used by early pioneers to ammonites and other fossils. | 325 Greybull Ave. | 307/765–2444 | Free | June–Labor Day, weekdays 10–8, Sat. 10–6; Labor Day–Oct., weekdays 1–5; Nov.–Apr., Mon., Wed., Fri. 1–4; Apr.–May, weekdays 1–4.

Medicine Lodge State Archaeological Site. Petroglyphs and pictographs are the reason to stop here, 6 mi northeast of Hyattville. The more than 60 cultural levels span 10,000 years of human occupation. There are public corrals and footpaths and a visitor center. | 307/469–2234 | fax 307/469–2264 | sphs@missc.state.wy.us | Free | May–Labor Day, 8–dusk; visitor center May–Nov., daily 8–dusk.

Medicine Wheel National Historic Landmark. *See* Lovell. | 56 mi north on U.S. 310, then east on U.S. 14A.

Museum of Flight and Aerial Fire Fighting. Dozens of the last remaining examples of World War II bombers form part of the fleet of planes at the Hawkins and Powers Museum of Flight and Aerial Fire Fighting. This company's planes still drop fire retardant on forest fires throughout the West. | 2441 W. U.S. 20 | 307/765–4482 | fax 307/765–2535 | $2 | Summer, weekdays 8–6, weekends 10–6; winter, weekdays 8–5.

Shell Falls. The falls in Shell Canyon shoot about 3,600 gallons of water every second out over 3-billion-year-old granite. The gray and pink granite is some of the oldest rock on earth. Atop the granite is softer Flathead sandstone, which is about 550 million years old and contains fossils of hard-shelled creatures, hence the name. There is a visitors center at the Shell Falls overlook. | U.S. 14 | 307/765–2100 | fax 307/765–2100 | Free | Daily.

ON THE CALENDAR

JUNE: *Days of '49 Celebration.* This local festival has a variety of entertainment. | 307/765–2100.

DEC: *Greybull Craft Fair.* Hundreds of local artisans gather at the huge log Greybull Recreation Hall in the center of town to sell and trade their holiday wares. Usually held during the first weekend in December. | 527 1st Ave. S | 307/765–9575.

Dining

Lisa's Fine Foods. Southwestern. Locals recommend Lisa's for its fine food as well as its southwestern style, stucco walls, Indian memorabilia, and antiques. | 200 Greybull Ave. | 307/765–4765 | $8–$16 | D, MC, V | Closed Sun. No dinner.

Uptown Cafe. American. Biscuits and gravy, chicken-fried steak, and prime rib distinguish this hometown restaurant in the center of Greybull. | 536 Greybull Ave. | 307/765–2152 | $5–$15 | No credit cards.

Lodging

Greybull Motel. In a quiet residential neighborhood, this small motel has rooms remodeled in 1998 with Western-style furnishings. Picnic area. Cable TV. | 300 N. 6th St. | 307/765–2628 | fax 307/765–2933 | 13 rooms | $55–$66 | AE, MC, V.

Wheels Motel. One of the newest properties in Greybull, near the center of town, this motel has modern, larger than average rooms and friendly service. Restaurant. In-room data ports, refrigerators. Cable TV. | 1324 N. 6th St. | 307/765–2105 or 800/676–2973 | fax 307/765–4735 | www.tctwest.net/~wheelsmotel/ | 22 rooms | $50–$75 | AE, D, MC, V.

Yellowstone Motel. The motel is small but rooms are large, with colorful furnishings. Cable TV. Pool. Pets allowed. | 247 Greybull Ave. | 307/765–4456 | fax 307/765–2108 | 35 rooms | $63 | AE, D, MC, V.

JACKSON

MAP 9, C3

(Nearby towns also listed: Alpine, Grand Teton National Park, Pinedale)

JACKSON

INTRO
ATTRACTIONS
DINING
LODGING

Visitors to this area often mistakenly refer to the county seat of Teton County as Jackson Hole. Actually, the town is Jackson, while the mountain-ringed valley is Jackson Hole. Both get their name from mountain man David Jackson, who operated the Rocky Mountain Fur Company with his partners Jedediah Smith and William Sublette back in the 1820s and early 1830s. The region along the Snake River at the foot of the mountains—early explorers called them the Pilot Knobs or Les Tres Tetons—was Davy Jackson's favorite haunt. It later became a hangout—and hideout—for horse thieves and others on the dodge, in part because of its isolation.

No matter how you enter Jackson Hole, you have to cross a mountain range. That and the cold harsh winters kept lawmen out, making it the ideal spot for bad men to hole up. In the 1880s the first permanent homesteaders claimed land, and by 1919 it had become Wyoming's best playground. It hasn't lost that status over the years, and is the busiest region of the state year-round. In winter you can ski, downhill and cross-country; in all seasons, you can watch wildlife and enjoy the beauty.

With its raised wooden sidewalks and old-fashioned storefronts—some being replaced with more modern styles—the town of Jackson still looks a bit like a Western movie set, and it also manages to maintain at least part of its true Western atmosphere. Bear in mind this is a community of roughly 7,000 permanent residents, who play host annually to more than 3 million visitors. Residents hotly debate whether and how much to control development. For the time being the town remains folksy and compact, a place where genuine cowboys rub shoulders with the store-bought variety and where the antler-arched square, the whoop-it-up nightlife, and the surrounding wilderness are pretty much intact.

There's a lot to do here: museums, art galleries, good restaurants, dancing in Western bars, as well as hiking, climbing, and floating down the Snake River.

Information: Jackson Chamber of Commerce. | Box E, 83001 | 307/733–3316 | fax 307/733–5585 | wwwjacksonholeinfo.com.

Attractions

Bridger-Teton National Forest. In the hundreds of thousands of acres of forest, some wilderness, you'll find both developed and back-country campsites, and can hike, fish, hunt, and study nature. | 340 N. Cache St. | 307/739–5500 | fax 307/739–5010 | www.fs.fed.us/btnf/ | Camping fees at some sites, $8–$14 | Daily.

Grand Targhee Ski and Summer Resort. Just one hour from Jackson, Grand Targhee gets more than 500 inches of snow annually. The mountain village has five restaurants, shopping, lodging, and skiing. You can get there on the Targhee Express, daily round-trip coaches, from Jackson and Teton Village mid-December through late March ($51 including lift ticket). The vertical rise is 2,200 ft and there are two quads; 10 percent beginner, 70 percent intermediate, 20 percent advanced. | Follow Rte. 22 over Teton Pass and turn right onto Rte. 33; in Driggs, ID, turn right and follow Little Avenue 6 blocks to a fork; bear left onto Ski Hill Road and follow to Grand Targhee | 307/353–2300 or snow reports at 800–TARGHEE | info@grandtarghee.com | www.grandtarghee.com | $51 for adults; special rates for children; multiday passes available | Dec.–early-Apr., daily 9:30–4.

Grand Teton National Park. *See above.* | 13 mi north of Jackson on U.S. 191.

Granite Hot Springs. You can soak in the small pools of the hot springs or go hiking and mountain biking in non-snowy months, staying at shady creekside campgrounds. There's a changing room if you just want to stop in for a soak. In winter you might get there via snowmobile or dogsled. | U.S. 189/191 south to Granite Creek Rd., then east | 307/739–5500 | Free | Daily.

Jackson Historical Society and Museum. You'll find displays that illuminate local history. | 105 Mercill Ave. | 307/733–9605 | Free | Daily.

Jackson Hole Mountain Ski Resort. *See* Teton Village, *below.* | 12 mi northwest at Teton Village.

Jackson Hole Museum. Learn how Deadwood Bar got its name, or the story of Jackson's all-female town government. Historic photos, artifacts, and displays are part of the museum exhibits. You can also take walking tours of downtown and historic sites. | 105 N. Glenwood St. | 307/733–2414 (summer only) or 307/733–9605 | fax 307/739–9019 | jhhsm@sisna.com | $3 | Late May–early Sept., Mon.–Sat. 9:30–6, Sun., 10–5.

National Elk Refuge. More than 7,000 elk spend the winter in the National Elk Refuge, which was established in 1912 to save starving herds. The animals migrate to the refuge grounds in late fall and remain until early spring. The bulls tend to congregate together while the cows and calves remain in their own separate groups. Trumpeter swans live here, too, as do bald eagles, coyotes, and wolves, who moved in during the winter of 1998–99. In winter, you can take one of the regular wagon and sleigh rides through the herd; the sleigh rides leave from the National Wildlife Art Museum. | Visitors Center, 532 N. Cash St. | 307/733–9212 | www.r6.fws.gov/REFUGES/natlelk/ | $8 | Visitors Center, daily 8–5; National Wildlife Art Museum, 2820 Rungius Rd., mid-Dec.–early Apr., daily 10–4 (reservations not accepted).

National Wildlife Art Museum. A collection of wildlife art—most of it devoted to North American species—is displayed in the 12 galleries that have both permanent and traveling exhibits. Among the artists represented are Karl Bodmer, Albert Bierstadt, Charles Russell, John Clymer, Robert Bateman, and Carl Rungius. You can also look outward, using one of the spotting scopes set up in areas overlooking the National Elk Refuge to watch wildlife in its native habitat. | 2820 Rungius Rd. | 307/733–5771 | fax 307/733–5787 | www.wildlifeart.org | $6 | Summer and winter, daily 9–5; spring and fall, Mon.–Sat. 9–5, Sun. 1–5.

Snow King Ski Resort. At the western edge of Jackson, Snow King Resort has 400 acres of ski runs in the daytime and 110 acres for night skiing, plus an extensive snowmaking system. You can also use the snowboard and half-pipe and snowtubing parks. | 400 E. Snow King Ave. | 307/733–5200 or 800/522–5464 | $30 ($20 half-day, $14 night); snowtubing $6 1 hr, $10 2 hrs | Dec.–Apr., daily; snowtubing park weekdays 4–8, weekends noon–8.

TOURS AND ADVENTURES

Gray Line Bus Tours. Gray Line has regularly scheduled bus tours of Grand Teton and Yellowstone national parks. | 680 W. Martin La. | 307/733–4325 or 800/443–6133 | fax 307/733–2689 | www.jacksonholenet.com/grayline/ | $60 Grand Teton; $65 Yellowstone, plus park entrance fees | Memorial Day–Sept.

Snake River Rafting. The Snake River is a busy place for rafting and kayaking, with stretches of calm waters or white water up to Class III rapids. You have a lot of choice: most companies offer half-day trips. Some gear trips to wildlife viewing; others are truly white-water excursions. River running begins in May and extends through September, with the peak season during June, July, and August, when the river gets pretty crowded. The highest water is in late May and June.

Barker-Ewing Float Trips. For a gentler ride, try a 10-mi non-white-water excursion on the Snake River through Grand Teton National Park. It takes about 2½ hours. | Box 100, Moose; float trip parking lot is is next to park headquarters in Moose | 307/733–1800 or 800/365–1800 | $40 half-day | May–Sept.

Lewis and Clark Expeditions. Take your choice of white-water and tamer floats on the Snake River. | 335 N. Cache Dr. | 307/733–4022 or 800/824–5375 | fax 307/733–0345 | www.lewisand-clarkexpeds.com | $33 half-day white-water; $30 float | Mid-May–mid-Sept., daily.

Mad River Boat Trips, Inc. Special dinner trips distinguish this outfitter, which also does other trips on the Snake, including half-day white-water outings. | 1255 S. U.S. 89 | 307/733–6203 or 800/458–7238 | fax 307/733–7626 | www.mad-river.com | $33–$69 | Mid-May–mid-Sept., daily.

Solitude Float Trips. Tranquillity is the theme here; you can take sunrise, wildlife, and evening 10-mi float trips in Grand Teton National Park from mid-June. The standard floats are offered May–September. | 110 E. Carnes Ave., at Buckrail Lodge | 307/733–2871 | www.soli-tudefloat.com | $37 adults | May–Sept.

Teton Wagon Train & Horse Adventure. Your wagon guide will pick you up in Jackson and transport you to the wagon camp, where you can board a replica prairie schooner for a four day/three night trip into the Targhee National Forest with wagon rides, horseback riding, nature hikes, canoeing and swimming, campfire entertainment, and food cooked in a dutch oven. They provide all you need except clothing and personal gear. | Box 10307, Jackson | 307/734–6101 or 888/734–6101 | www.JacksonHoleNet.com/tetonwagon/ | $745; no kids under 4.

Teton Mountain Bike Tours. If you're a mountain biker, you can do guided tours into both Grand Teton and Yellowstone national parks, as well as the Bridger-Teton National Forest. | 800/733–0788 | www.tetonbike.com.

ON THE CALENDAR

FEB.: *International Rocky Mountain Stage Stop Sled Dog Race.* This race takes dogsled racers, some champions, through western Wyoming. They stop at various towns, with the aim of raising awareness of the need for children to be immunized. | 307/777–7777 or 307/733–3316.

MAR.: *Celebrity Winter Extravaganza.* At the Jackson Hole Mountain Resort, celebrities perform in events including skiing and tennis to benefit adults with disabilities. | 307/733–2770 or 307/734–2878.

MAR.: *World Championship Snowmobile Hill Climb.* Snowmobilers put their machines to the test to see who can climb straight up Snow King Mountain the farthest and fastest. The Jackson Hole Snow Devils sponsor the event. | 307/734–9653 or 307/733–5200.

APR.: *Pole-Pedal-Paddle.* This wacky race is a rite of spring. Entrants ski, downhill and nordic, canoe, and bicycle. The course begins at Jackson Hole Mountain Resort and ends at Astoria Hot Spring. Some serious competitors race each other and the clock, others have fun and wear silly costumes. | 307/733–6433.

MAY–AUG.: *Jackson Hole Rodeo.* Traditional rodeo events, including entertainment and food, are staged from Memorial Day to August 31. | 307/733–2805.

MAY–SEPT.: *The Shootout.* Between Memorial Day and Labor Day, gunslingers have regular daily shootouts in the town square. Don't worry, the bullets aren't real. | 307/733–3316 or 800/782–0011.

JULY–AUG.: *Grand Teton Music Festival.* Some of these regular symphony orchestra performances are at Walk Festival Hall, others outside, all at Teton Village. There is also a winter concert schedule. | 307/733–1128 or 800/959–4863.

SEPT.–OCT.: *Jackson Hole Fall Arts Festival.* Artists in a variety of mediums show and sell their work, and several special events are staged, including art, poetry, and dance. Jackson's many art galleries have special exhibits and programs. | 307/733–3316.

DEC.–JAN.: *Torchlight Parades.* Skiers celebrate Christmas and New Year's Eve with torchlight parades at Snow King Mountain in Jackson and at Jackson Hole Mountain Resort. | 307/739–2770 or 307/733–5200.

Dining

Anthony's. Italian. The Art Deco interior reveals that the owner is a collector of 1920s objects at this establishment just off the town square, but some 1950s memorabilia are thrown in, too. The classic Northern Italian food has a New Age twist; try such dishes as the chicken breast and fresh tomatoes roasted in white wine. The menu also includes a good selection of pasta, veal, and seafood dishes. Kids' menu. No smoking. | 62 S. Glenwood St. | 307/733–3717 | $14–$25 | AE, MC, V | No lunch.

Bar J. Barbecue. This may be the best value in Jackson Hole. You get a full ranch-style meal, served outdoors, plus a complete Western show featuring singing, stories, and even cowboy poetry. The Bar J Wranglers not only serve your food, they also sing to you and are well known for their talent. The dinner and show take place inside if necessary, so don't let the weather keep you away. | Teton Village Rd. | 307/733–3370 or 800/905–2275 | Reservations recommended | $14 | AE, MC, V | Closed Oct.–Memorial Day.

Billy's Giant Hamburgers. American. Sharing an entrance with the Cadillac Grille, Billy's is 1950s-style, whereas the Cadillac is contemporary. There are a few booths, and more tall tables with high stools. Though you can choose from a variety of sandwiches, Billy's specialties are big—really big—burgers that are really really good. | 55 N. Cache Dr. | 307/733–3279 | $15–$29 | AE, MC, V.

Blue Lion. Continental. This blue-clapboard house has been serving distinctive food in Jackson Hole for many years. The atmosphere is elegant but casual; in the summer you can dine outside on the patio. Favorites include rack of lamb, steak, and trout and other fresh fish. Open-air dining. No smoking. | 160 N. Millward St. | 307/733–3912 | $14–$27 | AE, D, MC, V | No lunch.

Bubba's Bar-B-Que. American. The succulent baby back ribs and spare ribs are specialties at this local barbecue joint, which evokes the Old West with its large wooden porch, wood booths, Western paintings, and antique signs. Homemade pies of the chocolate-buttermilk and fudge-pecan variety are popular. The huge salad bar has plenty of non-meat choices. | 515 W. Broadway | 307/733–2288 | $8–$18 | AE, D, MC, V.

★ **The Bunnery.** American. Tucked into a tiny spot in the Hole-in-the-Wall Mall, this is where locals go for breakfast. It's usually busy, so there may be a short wait, but the food's worth it. All the breads are made here, mostly of a combined grain known as OSM (oats, sunflower, millet), and they've been known to sell and ship the bread to customers throughout the world. Open-air dining. Kids' menu. | 130 N. Cache St. | 307/733–5474 | $8–$11 | MC, V.

Cadillac Grille. Contemporary. You'll be sure you've left the Western style of Jackson for someplace else when you step into the contemporary atmosphere of the Cadillac Grille. The menu features steaks, elk, and lamb, and a choice of pasta, pizza baked in a wood-fired oven, seafood, chicken, and duck. Kids menu. | 55 N. Cache Dr. | 307/733–3279 | $12–$28 | AE, MC, V.

Calico. Italian. On the road between Jackson and Teton Village, this former pizza place now also serves pastas and rotisserie chicken, prime rib, and Italian sausage. The bar occupies what used to be the Mormon Church at Grovont, now a ghost town. Open-air dining and a kids' playground outside. | 2650 Teton Village Rd. | 307/733–2460 | $16–$31 | AE, MC, V | No lunch.

Jedediah's. American. Friendly, noisy, and elbow-knocking, this restaurant a block east of the town square in a historic Jackson home caters to the big appetite. Try the sourdough pancakes, called sourjacks, or Teton taters and eggs. Kids' menu. | 135 E. Broadway | 307/733–5671 | $11–$16 | AE, D, MC, V.

Lame Duck. Pan-Asian. The furnishings are Chinese style—lighting, Chinese characters— and the menu more geographically diverse, with sushi and sashimi and Indonesian dishes as well as Szechuan offerings. Favorites include samurai chicken and ginger prawns. Open-air dining on a deck. Kids' menu. No smoking. | 680 E. Broadway | 307/733–4311 | $8–19 | AE, MC, V | No lunch.

Million Dollar Cowboy Steak House. American. Affiliated with the Million Dollar Cowboy Bar, this steak house serves steak, seafood, pork, and lamb. The atmosphere is appropriately Western with artwork by Charles Russell and Frederic Remington. Salad bar. | 25 N. Cache St. | 307/733–4790 | $15–$35 | AE, D, MC, V | No lunch.

Nani's Genuine Pasta House. Italian. The ever-changing menu at this cozy, almost cramped, restaurant may include braised veal shanks with saffron risotto or other regional Italian cooking. The place is almost hidden behind a motel and is designed to attract gourmets, not tourists. The menu changes nightly. | 240 N. Glenwood St. | 307/733–3888 | $19–$31 | MC, V.

Off Broadway. Eclectic. After the bustle of the square, this restaurant—set back from King Street—is quiet and peaceful. The food ranges from pasta to Thai dishes. Open-air dining. Kids' menu. No smoking. | 30 S. King St. | 307/733–9777 | Reservations accepted | $12–$22 | AE, MC, V | No lunch.

The Range. Continental. The menu at one of Jackson's finest restaurants varies seasonally but always has nightly fish and game specials. Try linguine with roma tomatoes and the fresh artichoke pâté. Kids' menu. | 225 N. Cache St. | 307/733–5481 | $20–$45 | AE, MC, V | No lunch.

Snake River Grill. American. The favorites are free-range veal chops, grilled venison, or grilled Idaho red-rainbow trout. Open-air dining. Kids' menu. No smoking. | 84 E. Broadway | 307/733–0557 | Reservations accepted | $18–$48 | AE, MC, V | Closed Apr. and Nov. No lunch.

Strutting Grouse. American. With stunning Teton scenery, this is an elegant place to enjoy a meal. The menu is known for the mesquite-grilled meats and seafood. Open-air dining at lunch on a deck. | 5000 Spring Gulch Rd. | 307/733–7788 | $20–$40 | AE, DC, MC, V | Closed Oct.–mid-May.

Sweetwater. Continental. Antique oak furnishings in this log building make the Sweetwater one of Jackson's truly unusual eateries. Though the surroundings are very Western, the menu is a combination of American and Greek dishes. Lavender roast of pork is one favorite. Open-air dining at picnic tables. Kids' menu. No smoking. | Pearl and King Sts. | 307/733–3553 | $21–$30 | AE, D, DC, MC, V.

Vista Grande. Mexican. Midway between Jackson and Teton Village you find this establishment that offers traditional Mexican dishes as well as innovative variations on same. Blackened chicken tostada salad is a favorite, as are the fresh veggie burritos and the crab chimichangas. Dine by the fireplace in winter. Open-air dining on a deck. Kids' menu. | 2550 Teton Village Rd. | 307/733–6964 | $8–$15 | AE, MC, V | No lunch.

Lodging

Alpine House. Run by two former Olympic athletes, this immaculate bed-and-breakfast near the town square is both refined and comfortable. Scandinavian design gives the rooms an elegant purity, with simple pale-wood furniture and muted blue and white wall hangings and quilts. Most rooms have fireplaces. Hosts will arrange for, or lead, skiing and winter mountaineering trips. A minimum two-night stay is required July through September. Full breakfast, dining room. No TV in some rooms. Outdoor hot tub, sauna. Library. No pets.

No smoking. | 285 N. Glenwood St. | 307/739–1570 or 800/753–1421 | fax 307/734–2850 | alpine-house@compuserve.com | www.alpinehouse.com | 21 rooms | $140–$265 | MC, V.

Amangani. Exquisite architecture and flawless design make this "peaceful home" on a cliff edge on Gros Ventre Butte pure luxury. Huge two-story windows in the simple yet magnificent lobby overlook the Teton valley, and a generous use of redwood, sandstone, and cedar complements the natural setting. You won't find more amenities or more understated elegance anywhere in the valley. You can go horseback riding, play tennis, cross-country ski, and take winter sleigh rides. Restaurant, bar, lounge, room service. In-room data ports, in-room safes, refrigerators, TVs, VCRs. Outdoor pool. Hot tub, sauna, spa. Health club. 2 tennis courts. Library. Laundry facilities. Conference room. Airport shuttle. | 1535 N.E. Butte Rd. | 307/734–7333 or 877/734–7333 | fax 307/734–7332 | www.amangani.com | 40 suites | $600–$800 | AE, D, DC, MC, V.

Anvil Motel. This two-story motor inn with a red wood exterior is steps from Old Town, and is one of the nicer mid-priced inns in the central Jackson area. Old West porches and banisters and family-friendly innkeepers contribute to the casual tone here. Rooms have Western-style pine furniture, and are clean and comfortable. Refrigerators, microwaves. Cable TV. Hot tub. No pets allowed. | 215 N. Cache St. | 307/733–3668 or 800/234–4507 | fax 307/733–3957 | anvilmotel@wyoming.com. | www.anvilmotel.com | 27 rooms, 2 suites | $80–$119, $149–$215 suites | MC, V.

Best Western Lodge at Jackson Hole. This lodge is a massive log construction where the mini-suites have sleeping, living, and kitchenette areas and sofa beds. Each has three telephones with a data port. Some have Jacuzzis and fireplaces. In winter, a nightly shuttle runs from the town square to the Jackson Hole ski area. Restaurant, bar, complimentary Continental breakfast. In-room data ports, minibars, microwaves, refrigerators. Cable TV, VCRs (movies). Indoor pool. Hot tubs. Laundry facilities. Business services. | 80 Scott La. | 307/739–9703 or 800/458–3866 | fax 307/739–9168 | 1030346@compuserve.com | www.lodgeatjh.com | 154 rooms | $79–$159 | AE, D, DC, MC, V.

Buckrail Lodge. At the base of Snow King mountain, these beautifully appointed, spacious cedar log rooms have cathedral ceilings and Western-style furnishings. Although the town square is just a short walk away, this is a quiet place to stay. Picnic area. No air-conditioning, no room phones. Cable TV. Hot tub. No smoking. | 110 E. Karns Ave. | 307/733–2079 | fax 307/734–1663 | www.buckraillodge.com | 12 rooms | $90–$110 | AE, D, MC, V | Closed winter.

Davy Jackson Inn. Convenience and charm both figure into the attraction of this bed-and-breakfast. The Victorian-style building is within walking distance of shops and restaurants. The lobby, dining room, and some guest rooms are furnished with antiques, although the rooms also have in-room data ports. Breakfast might include homemade cinnamon buns or sourdough buckwheat cakes. For greater privacy, check out the two-bedroom cottage. Complimentary full breakfast. Some in-room hot tubs. Cable TV. Hot tub. | 85 Perry Ave. | 307/739–2294 or 800/584–0532 | fax 307/733–9704 | davyjackson@wyoming.com | www.davy-jackson.com | 12 rooms | $179–$239 | AE, D, MC, V.

Days Inn. At the south end of town, this place has a Western look, complete with fireplaces. Complimentary Continental breakfast. Some in-room hot tubs, microwaves. Cable TV. Hot tub. | 350 S. U.S. 89 | 307/733–9010 | fax 307/733–0044 | 91 rooms | $159–$219 | AE, D, DC, MC, V.

El Rancho Motel. Close to downtown and with an intimate and hard-to-find gourmet Italian restaurant on the property, this facility was built in 1947 and has basic rooms with reasonable rates. Restaurant. Cable TV. Hot tub. No pets. | 215 N. Cache St. | 307/733–3668 or 800/234–4507 | fax 307/733–3957 | anvilmotel@wyoming.com | www.anvilmotel.com | 22 rooms | $65–$107 | MC, V.

Flat Creek. Every room has a view of the National Elk Refuge, where you can watch the elk, trumpeter swans, coyotes, eagles, and perhaps even wolves. Microwaves, refrigerators. Cable TV (movie channels). Hot tub. Exercise equipment. Laundry facilities. | 1935 N. U.S. 89 | 307/

733–5276 or 800/438–9338 | fax 307/733–0374 | fltcrkmotel@blissnet.com | www.flat-creekmotel.com | 75 rooms, 14 with kitchenettes, 2 suites | $91.50 | AE, D, DC, MC, V.

4 Winds. This hotel is 1½ blocks from the downtown square, where you can see the elk-horn arches and the longest-running Western shoot-out, shop, and dine. The rooms are contemporary and quiet. The basketball and tennis courts are a nice extra. Picnic tables. Cable TV. Playground. | 150 N. Millward St. | 307/733–2474 or 800/228–6461 | www.jack-sonholefourwinds.com | 21 rooms | $105 | AE, D, MC, V | Closed winter.

Friendship Inn-Antler Inn. Just one block from the town square, this inn is basic and contemporary in style. Cable TV. Hot tub. Exercise equipment. Some pets allowed. | 43 W. Pearl St. | 307/733–2535 or 800/522–2406 | fax 307/733–4158 | 104 rooms, 2 suites | $66–$110 | AE, D, DC, MC, V.

Hitching Post Lodge. Built in the early 1900s, these renovated cedar lodges each hold two units with refrigerators and microwaves. Some have kitchenettes. They're within walking distance of the town square. Picnic area, complimentary Continental breakfast. No air-conditioning, microwaves, refrigerators. Cable TV. Pool (summer). Hot tub (winter). Laundry facilities. | 460 E. Broadway | 307/733–2606 or 800/821–8351 | fax 307/733–8221 | hitching-post@jacksonhole.net | 33 rooms in cabins, 16 with kitchenettes | $78–$149 | D, MC, V.

Huff House Inn. Now a bed-and-breakfast, this Victorian house was built in 1917 and was one of the finest homes in Jackson. Five rooms are in the main house; four are in cottages and have fireplaces and whirlpools. You're midway between the town square and Snow King Ski Area, where you can downhill and cross-country ski. Complimentary breakfast. Some in-room hot tubs, some air-conditioning. Cable TV. No smoking. | 240 E. Deloney | 307/733–4164 | fax 307/739–9091 | huffhousebnb@blissnet.com | www.cruising-america.com/huff.html | 9 rooms, 2 with shower only | $103–$205 | D, MC, V.

Jackson Hole Racquet Club. Ideal for groups, this resort has everything from studios to four-bedroom units. The facility is 4 mi from the ski area and 8 mi from downtown, and has a golf course next door. Restaurant, bar. No air-conditioning, microwaves, refrigerators. Cable TV. Pool. Beauty salon, hot tub. Gym. | 3535 N. Moose–Wilson Rd. | 307/733–3990 or 800/443–8616 | fax 307/733–5551 | jhcondos@wyoming.com | jhresortlodging.com | 130 condo units | $97–$359 | AE, D, MC, V.

Nowlin Creek Inn. The handcrafted furnishings harmonize with the woodsy setting and Western style of this bed-and-breakfast. The rooms have fireplaces. Complimentary breakfast. Hot tub. No smoking. | 660 E. Broadway | 307/733–0882 | fax 307/733–0106 | www.jack-son-hole-lodging.com | 5 rooms | $180–$210 | AE, D, MC, V.

Painted Porch Bed and Breakfast. Built in 1901, this red-and-white wooden farmhouse sits on 3½ acres filled with pine and aspen and is surrounded by a white picket fence. It is ideal if you want space and privacy. Each room is different, with a blend of Western-style furniture, antiques, and designer linens. The Japanese soaking tubs are ultimately relaxing. Full breakfast. TVs, VCRs. No pets. No smoking. | 3680 N. Moose–Wilson Rd. | 307/733–1981 or 800/542–2632 | res@jacksonholebedandbreakfast.com | www.jacksonholebedand-breakfast.com | 2 rooms | $195–$295 | AE, D, MC, V.

Parkway Inn. Each room has a distinctive look, with oak or wicker, and all are filled with antiques, from 19th-century pieces onward. The overall effect is homey and delightful—especially appealing if you plan to stay several days or longer. Complimentary Continental breakfast. No-smoking rooms. Indoor pool. Hot tub. Gym. | 125 N. Jackson St. | 307/733–3143 | fax 307/733–0955 | info@parkwayinn.com | www.parkwayinn.com | 37 rooms, 12 suites | $99–$167 | AE, D, DC, MC, V.

Pony Express. A standard locally owned and operated motel on the west side of town, this is good for those who want to get an early start for the Tetons. South-facing rooms have mountain views, and service is friendly. Cable TV. Outdoor pool. Pets allowed. | 1075 W. Broadway | 307/733–2658 or 800/526–2658 | fax 307/733–2658 | 24 rooms | $70–$125 | D, MC, V.

Quality 49er. Suitable for families or business travelers, this hotel has 30 new fireplace suites, several conference rooms, and a 40-person outdoor hot tub. Near the town square, it's within easy walking distance of shopping and restaurants. Complimentary Continental breakfast. Some in-room hot tubs, microwaves, refrigerators. Cable TV. Hot tub. Exercise equipment. Some pets allowed. | 330 W. Pearl St. | 307/733–7550 or 800/451–2980 | fax 307/733–2002 | townsquareinns@wyoming.com | www.townsquareinns.com | 148 rooms | $70–$225 | AE, D, DC, MC, V.

Rusty Parrot. An imposing river-rock fireplace in the cathedral lounge lends warmth to this timber inn in the center of Jackson. You can walk to shops, galleries, and restaurants of the main town square. The rooms have handcrafted furnishings, and some have fireplaces and oversize whirlpools. An on-premise spa (massages, facials, other special treatments) is a nice plus. Complimentary breakfast, room service. Cable TV. Hot tub. Library. Business services. No smoking. | 175 N. Jackson St. | 307/733–2000 or 800/458–2004 (reservations) | fax 307/733–5566 | mail@rustyparrot.com | www.rustyparrot.com | 31 rooms | $250–$500 | AE, D, DC, MC, V.

Snow King Resort. Ski-in, ski-out to Snow King Mountain, which rises above this resort. The layout is multilevel and widely spread out, with many steps and ramps for people with disabilities. A free shuttle takes you to the Jackson Hole ski area. Restaurant, bar, room service. Cable TV. Pool. Barbershop, beauty salon, hot tubs. Exercise equipment. Cross-country and downhill skiing. Video game room. Laundry facilities. Business services. Airport shuttle. Some pets allowed. | 400 E. Snow King Ave. | 307/733–5200 or 800/522–5464 | fax 307/733–4086 | snowking@wyoming.com | www.snowking.com | 204 rooms | $90–$200 | AE, D, DC, MC, V.

Spring Creek Resort Hotel and Conference Center. You can see much of the Jackson Hole area from this mountaintop resort. The condominiums have large stone fireplaces, fully equipped kitchens, and lodge-pole pine furnishings. Restaurant, bar, room service, picnic area. Refrigerators. Cable TV. Pool. Hot tub. 2 tennis courts. Cross-country skiing. Business services. Airport shuttle. | 1800 Spirit Dance Rd. | 307/733–8833 or 800/443–6139 (outside WY) | fax 307/733–1524 | info@springcreekresort.com | www.springcreekresort.com | 117 rooms, some kitchenettes | $140–$250 | AE, D, DC, MC, V.

Teton Tree House. Surrounded by trees and mountains, this is a real retreat. Ninety-five steps lead up into this cozy lodgepole-pine bed-and-breakfast tucked in a sloping forest grove. Decks abound, rooms are full of wood furniture and warm southwestern colors, and an inviting common area has a two-story old-fashioned adobe fireplace. Full breakfast, dining room. Hot tub. No pets allowed. No smoking. | 6175 Heck of a Hill Rd., Wilson | 307/733–3233 | fax 307/733–3233 | dbecker@rmisp.com | 6 rooms | $145–$180 | D, MC, V.

Trapper Inn. This motel is within walking distance of the town square and has some of the best-appointed rooms for people with disabilities in Jackson. Some microwaves, refrigerators. Cable TV. Hot tubs. Laundry facilities. | 235 N. Cache St. | 307/733–2648 | fax 307/739–9351 | trapperinn@compuserve.com | www.trapperinn.com | 54 rooms | $98–$129 | AE, D, DC, MC, V.

Wildflower. The log inn has handmade log beds made up with down comforters. The private baths have pedestal sinks. The views are great. Complimentary breakfast. No air-conditioning. Cable TV. Hot tub. No smoking. | 3725 Teton Village Rd. | 307/733–4710 | fax 307/739–0914 | www.jacksonholewildflower.com | 5 rooms | $180–$260 | MC, V.

★ **Wort Hotel.** The locals have been gathering at this Jackson landmark half a block from the town square since the early 1940s, and you can view the history of Jackson through the photos and clippings posted in the lobby. Completely renovated after a fire in the 1980s, the spacious rooms now have lodgepole furniture and comfortable armchairs. Junior suites have large sitting areas. Restaurant, bar. Room service, cable TV. Hot tubs. Exercise equipment. Business services. | 50 N. Glenwood | 307/733–2190 or 800/322–2727 | fax 307/733–2067 | info@worthotel.com | www.worthotel.com | 60 rooms | $161–$220 rooms, $275–$485 junior suites and Governor's suite | AE, D, DC, MC, V.

Wyoming Inn. The reception desk in the lobby of this inn, one of the finest in Jackson, has a carving of two large bighorn sheep facing off. The rooms, done in soft blues and greens, have comfortable sitting areas, desks, and in-room data ports. Some have gas fireplaces and Jacuzzis. You can raft, go horseback riding, and hike in summer and snowmobile in winter. Complimentary Continental breakfast. Some refrigerators. Cable TV. Hot tubs. Business services. Airport shuttle. Pets allowed. No smoking. | 930 W. Broadway | 307/734–0035 or 800/844–0035 | fax 307/734–0037 | 73 rooms, 4 with kitchenettes | $249–$259 | AE, D, MC, V.

KEMMERER

MAP 9, C5

(Nearby towns also listed: Evanston, Green River)

Probably the most important person in Kemmerer's history was James Cash Penney, who in 1902 started the Golden Rule chain of stores. He later used the name J. C. Penney Company, which by 1929 had 1,395 outlets. Penney revolutionized merchandising in western Wyoming when he opened his store. The region was dominated by the coal-mining industry and miners were used to working for the company and purchasing their supplies at the company store—which often charged whatever it wanted, managing to keep employees in debt. But when Penney opened his Golden Rule, he set one price for each item and stuck to it. Later he developed a catalog, selling to people unable to get to town easily.

Kemmerer is named for M. S. Kemmerer, president of the Kemmerer Coal Company, and mining has been the main industry here since the town's inception. But oil and gas exploration are now part of the economy of this town of 4,000 as well, with many different companies involved.

Information: Kemmerer Chamber of Commerce | 800 Pine Ave., 83101 | 307/877–9761 | fax 307/877–9762.

KEMMERER

INTRO
ATTRACTIONS
DINING
LODGING

Attractions

Fossil Butte National Monument. A unique concentration of creatures is embedded in this natural outcrop, indicating clearly that this area was once an inland sea. The monument was established on October 23, 1972. You can hike the fossil trails. Picnic area. | 15 mi west on U.S. 30 | 307/877–4455 | fax 307/877–4457 | www.nps.gov/fobu/ | Free | Visitors center, June–Aug., daily 8–7; Sept.–May, daily 8–4:30.

Fossil Country Frontier Museum. This museum has fossils and displays related to early settlement in the area. | 400 Pine Ave. | 307/877–6551 | Free | Daily 10–4; June–Aug., 9–5.

Ulrich's Fossil Gallery. Participate in quarrying for fossils and view fossils from around the world. | U.S. 30 | 307/877–6466 | fax 307/877–3289 | Free | Daily 8–6.

ON THE CALENDAR

FEB.: *International Rocky Mountain Stage Stop Sled Dog Race.* This race goes across western Wyoming, and competitors include many former Iditarod champions. The goal is to increase awareness of the need for childhood immunization. | 307/777–7777 or 307/877–9761.

JULY: *Chamber Barbecue and Fireworks.* A barbecue and fireworks display are part of the local celebration on the Fourth of July. | 307/877–9761.

JULY: *Turn-of-the-Century Days.* Events include a carnival and a golf tournament. | 307/877–9761.

Dining

Busy Bee. American. This local favorite on the main street of town serves standard, hearty homemade fare like chicken-fried steak, chicken dinners, hamburgers, and omelettes. The theme is cows, with cow pictures and ceramic heifers dotting the walls and counters. The cream of broccoli soup deserves high marks. | 919 Pine St. | 307/877–6820 | $5–$10 | No credit cards.

Lodging

Bon Rico. Nothing fancy, but the motel rooms here, 12 mi south of Kemmerer on U.S. 189, are available throughout the summer at budget rates. The restaurant and bar are open year-round. Restaurant, bar. Cable TV. Pets allowed. | U.S. 189 | 307/877–4503 | 24 rooms | $25–$39 | Closed Nov.–Mar. | MC, V.

Energy Inn. The pleasant, basic rooms here in one of the nicer properties on the main thoroughfare in town are done in southwestern colors, and some have kitchenettes. A fax and microwave are available in the lobby, and you won't have trouble finding a parking spot on the 2-acre lot. In-room data ports, refrigerators, some kitchenettes. Cable TV. | 3 Rte. 30, Diamondville | 307/877–6901 | fax 307/877–6901 | 42 rooms | $48 | AE, D, DC, MC, V.

Fairview Motel. The rooms here are exceptionally large and comfortable, with good views. The film star Mel Gibson once spent several nights here while in the area fishing. In-room data ports, some microwaves, refrigerators. Cable TV. Airport shuttle. Business services. Pets allowed. | 61 Rte. 30 | 307/877–3938 or 800/247–3938 | fax 307/877–3938, ext. 2 | www.wy-biz.com/fairviewmotel.com | 61 rooms | $44–$50 | AE, D, MC, V.

LANDER

(Nearby town also listed: Riverton)

Frederick West Lander engineered the first government-financed road built in Wyoming when he laid out a route from South Pass to Fort Hall, Idaho, in 1857. The crew that built the Lander Road spent the winter of 1857–58 camped in the Wind River Valley along the Popo Agie (pronounced po-po-sha) River, building the first permanent house at a place they called Camp McGraw. Native Americans called the area Push Root, because warm winds in the spring would cause the plants to grow quickly or "push roots." In 1875, when the present town was established, it took the name Lander after the government engineer.

At the southwestern edge of the Wind River Indian Reservation and in the heart of country held dear by Shoshone Chief Washakie and his people, Lander has always had a strong tie with the Native American community. The small city is also known for its sculptures, which are placed throughout the main business district.

Information: Lander Chamber of Commerce | 160 N. 1st St., 82520 | 307/332–3892 or 800/433–0662 | fax 307/332–3893 | landerchamber@rmisp.com | www.landerchamber.org. **Wind River Visitors Council** | Box 1449, Riverton 82501 | 307/856–7566 or 800/645–6233 | info@wind-river.org | www.wind-river.org.

Attractions

Arapaho Cultural Center Museum and Heritage Center. Art and artifacts related to the Arapaho tribe are included in the collection of this museum, which is off Rte. 137. The center is also the site of the historic St. Michael's Episcopal Mission. The Heritage Center has displays of beadwork, crafts, and clothing. | St. Stephens | 307/332–3040 | Free; donations accepted | Weekdays 9–5.

Fremont County Pioneer Museum. You'll find information about the first oil well in Wyoming, early settlers, Native Americans, and mining and farming at this local museum established in 1915. | 630 Lincoln St. | 307/332–4137 | Free; donations accepted | Weekdays 9–5, Sat. noon–5.

National Outdoor Leadership School. This internationally known school will instruct you in all aspects of mountaineering, from low-impact camping and hiking to horsepacking. Courses are held locally and at international locations ranging from Patagonia to Alaska. | 228 Main St. | 307/332–6973 | www.nols.edu | Daily.

Oregon-Mormon-California Trails and The Pony Express. One of the best things to do in the Lander area is explore the historic wagon trails, evidence of which remains on the ground. | 307/332–3892 or 800/433–0662 | www.landerchamber.org/TRAILFRM.HTML.

Sinks Canyon State Park. A rushing river—the Popo Agie—combines with the unique formation known as the Sinks, where the river flows into a limestone cavern only to resurface ¼ mi downstream. There, at the Rise, huge fish swim in the still pool. Watch for Rocky Mountain bighorn sheep and other wildlife in this park, 8 mi south of Lander, that also has camping and picnic areas and hiking trails. | Rte. 131 | 307/332–6333 | www.state.wy.us/sphs/sinks1.html | Free; camping $4 | Daily; visitors center, Memorial Day–Labor Day.

Shoshone National Forest, Washakie District (Wind River Mountains). Known simply as the Winds, this is Wyoming's most rugged mountain range, with peaks sweeping up to 13,804 ft (Gannett Peak, the highest point in Wyoming). It's a great place to do almost anything outdoors, from mountain biking and hiking to climbing, dog sledding, cross-country skiing, and snowmobiling. The Continental Divide National Scenic Trail crosses the backbone of these mountains, and is a popular snowmobile trail in the winter. Lander is one of the gateway communities to this vast area that includes national forest and wilderness lands. A number of outfitters can help make your trip enjoyable; some specialize in guided hikes, others in horsepacking and treks with goats or llamas. Contact the Wind River Visitors Council or Shoshone National Forest for information. | Wind River Visitors Council, 337 E. Main St., Riverton | 307/856–7566 or 800/645–6233 | info@wind-river.org | www.wind-river.org | Shoshone National Forest, Lander District Office | 307/332–5460 | Free; campground fees vary | Daily.

Shoshone Tribal Cultural Center. Shoshone art and artifacts are part of the collections at this center that also has information about the two most famous Shoshones: Chief Washakie and Sacajawea, guide to Lewis and Clark. A small gift shop sells authentic Shoshone crafts and beadwork. | 31 Black Cove Rd., Fort Washakie | 307/332–9106 or 307/332–3040 | Free; donations accepted | Weekdays 9–5.

South Pass City State Historic Site. Established during the South Pass Gold Rush of 1868, South Pass City was the birthplace of women's suffrage in Wyoming. Julia Bright and Esther Hobart Morris are two of the women from the community who firmly believed in getting the vote. They no doubt expressed their opinions to Horace Bright, Julia's husband, who ultimately introduced the bill in the Wyoming Territorial Legislature that gave it to them. But South Pass City is also a model mining community. Many of the original buildings survive and have been restored. The small museum gives an overview of the South Pass gold district, and at certain times during the summer season you can try your hand at panning for gold in the cold stream that runs through town, which is off Hwy. 137. | South Pass City Rd. | 307/332–3684 | www.state.wy.us/sphs/south1.htm | $1 | Mid-May–early-Sept., daily 9–5:30.

Willie Handcart Monument. In 1856 Mormon emigrants from England and Scandinavia made their way to Salt Lake City pulling handcarts. They left their winter quarters in Omaha, Nebraska, too late in the year to make it across the Continental Divide before snow swept the landscape. In central Wyoming, the handcart company, led by Capt. James Grey Willie, was stranded by October blizzards along Rock Creek, just shy of South Pass and about 30 mi from Lander. Brigham Young sent relief parties, but the weather was too extreme, the food too sparse, and 15 died. They are buried in two graves. To Mormons this is sacred ground. The site is now owned by the Church of Latter-day Saints and may be visited by those interested in the tragic story of the Willie Company and in trail migration. There is a trail along the creek and the church holds periodic programs in an outdoor amphitheater. | Atlantic City Rd. | 307/856–7566 or 800/645–6233 | info@wind-river.org | www.wind-river.org | www.handcart.com.

TOURS AND ADVENTURES

Outfitting and Big Game Hunting. The variety of mountain terrain and public lands in this area of Wyoming invites exploration, whether you want to hike in to a camp that is already set up, ride a horse, take a goat or llama to pack your gear, or even go big-game hunting. On any trip you are likely to see deer, elk, Rocky Mountain sheep, many different birds and small animals, and possibly bears or wolves. Many outfitters can help you plan your trip.

Allen Brothers Wilderness Ranch and Outfitting. Mountain horse-packing trips and hunting trips are among your choices here, as well as drop camp services. Kids should be at least 7–8 years old to go on extended pack trips. Some trips originate at the ranch, and you stay in cabins and take day rides. | 307/332–2995 | fax 307/332–7902 | www.wyoming.com/~dmndfour | Drop camps $400 per person; guided trips $200 per day. Cabins $795 wk.

Rocky Mountain Horseback Adventures. Ride the Oregon Trail, take a pack trip into the high country, or participate in an "outlaw ride" in Hole-in-the-Wall Country. | 307/332–8535 or 800/408–9149 | fax 307/335–8626 | edabney@rmisp.com.

Lander Llama Company. You can take high-country pack trips with llamas to haul the heavy stuff. | 307/332–5624 or 800/582–5262 | fax 307/332–5624 | www.landerllama.com. /$825 per person, 5-day trip.

Taylor Outfitting. Pack and hunting trips take you into the Wind River Mountains. | 307/455–2161 | fax 307/455–3169 | metaylor@wyoming.com. /200 per person per day.

Wind River Pack Goats. Let the goats haul the weightiest stuff on your pack trip into the Wind Rivers. | 307/455–2410.

ON THE CALENDAR

JAN.–FEB.: *Wyoming State Winter Fair.* Horse and cattle shows, trade exhibits, livestock sale, and entertainment are part of the only winter fair in the state. | 307/332–3892 or 800/433–0662.

FEB.: *International Rocky Mountain Stage Stop Sled Dog Race.* The Race to Immunize, as it is known, is held to increase awareness of children's immunization needs. Dogsled racers, some Iditarod champions, compete in this multi-day race that stops at towns across western Wyoming. | 307/777–7777, 307/332–3892, or 800/443–0662.

MAY: *Yellow Calf Memorial Powwow.* Native American traditional dancing is a part of this annual powwow in Ethete. | 307/856–7566 or 800/433–0662.

JUNE: *Shoshone Indian Days.* The events, held at Fort Washakie, include an all-Indian rodeo, a powwow, and a reenactment of Shoshone Indian treaty sessions. | 307/856–7566 or 800/433–0662.

JUNE–AUG.: *Native American Cultural Program.* This is held on Mondays throughout the summer in Lander Jaycee Park beginning at 7 PM. | 307/856–7566 or 800/433–0662.

JULY: *Lander Pioneer Days.* The annual celebration on the Fourth of July includes a parade, a rodeo, a buffalo barbecue, and entertainment. | 307/332–3892 or 800/433–0662.

NOV.: *Native American Craft Fair.* Art and crafts created by Native Americans are shown and sold at the Lander Community Center. | 307/856–7566 or 800/433–0662.

Dining

Atlantic City Mercantile. American. You'll feel as if you've stepped directly into *Gunsmoke* when you enter this old building downtown, with its long mirrored back bar and great collection of mismatched tables and chairs. At times a honky-tonk piano player is on hand. In summer, steaks are cooked on an open-flame grill in the back of the building—

you can watch yours being cooked Thursday through Sunday. If you're there the fourth Wednesday of the month, try the seven-course Basque dinner. The menu has steak, chicken, seafood, and sandwiches. | 100 E. Main St., Atlantic City | 307/332–5143 | fax 307/332–9376 | $15–$47 | D, MC, V.

Club El Toro. Steak. Wyoming's two best steak houses (*See also* Svilars, *below*) sit across the street from each other in one of the state's tiniest towns. Odd but true, and people drive many miles to partake of the Club El Toro's huge portions of steak and prime rib. | 132 S. Main St., Hudson | 307/332–4627 | $12–$48 | MC, V.

Hitching Rack. American. Steaks, seafood, pasta, microbrews, and a huge salad bar are among the offerings at this casual downtown eatery. | 75 E. Main St. | 307/332–4322 | $10–$20 | MC, V.

Ranch Barbecue. Barbecue. This is the only microbrewery in Lander, and in summer you'll also hear live music, including jazz, blues, and country and western on the weekends. Try the barbecued ribs. They also serve smoked turkey and pork loin. | 148 Main St. | 307/332–7388 | $11–$22 | MC, V.

Svilars. American. Inside this small, dark restaurant you'll find what many natives say is the best food in all of Wyoming. It's rivaled only by the Club El Toro across the street. At this family-owned operation a meal begins with *sarma* (cabbage rolls) and other appetizers. You'll then have placed before you one of the biggest, if not *the* biggest, and best steaks you've ever seen. | 175 S. Main St., Hudson | 307/332–4516 | $20–$39 | No credit cards | Closed Sun. and every other Mon. No lunch.

Lodging

Best Western Inn at Lander. This cabin-style motel sits on the hill overlooking Lander. Some rooms have refrigerators, and the small outdoor area has picnic tables where you can eat your sandwiches. Complimentary Continental breakfast. Some refrigerators. Cable TV. Pool. Hot tub. Exercise equipment. Airport shuttle. | 260 Grandview Dr. | 307/332–2847 | fax 307/332–2760 | 46 rooms | $74 | AE, D, MC, V.

Blue Spruce Inn. Named after the five enormous spruce trees on the property, this 1920s brick home features a huge front porch with swing, interior design from the early 20th-century Arts and Crafts period, hardwood floors, and beautiful gardens. Theme rooms are cozy and individually decorated. In a residential area within walking distance of downtown, this is good for those who want both peace and convenience. Full breakfast. No TV in some rooms. Recreation room. Library. No pets. No smoking. | 677 S. 3rd St. | 307/332–8253 or 888/503–3311 | fax 307/332–1386 | bluespruce@rmisp.com | www.bluespruceinn.com | 4 rooms | $70–$80 | AE, D, MC, V.

Budget Host Pronghorn. The sculpture garden that spreads through Lander starts at this convenient downtown motel. Some rooms have kitchens. Restaurant, complimentary Continental breakfast. Some refrigerators. Cable TV. Hot tub. Laundry facilities. Some pets allowed. | 150 E. Main St. | 307/332–3940 | fax 307/332–2651 | pronghorn@wyoming.com | www.wyoming.com/~thepronghorn | 54 rooms | $55–$79 | AE, D, DC, MC, V.

LARAMIE

MAP 9, H6

(Nearby town also listed: Cheyenne)

Overland travelers started migrating through the Laramie Valley—named for trapper Jacques La Ramee—in 1849, when Cherokees from Oklahoma made their way to the California gold fields over a route that extended across Oklahoma, Kansas, Colorado, southern Wyoming, Utah, and Nevada. The Cherokee Trail entered Wyoming south of present-day Laramie, and the main branch followed a route now roughly marked by U.S. 287 from Virginia Dale to Laramie, then by Interstate 80 across the state to the west.

The Overland Trail followed a similar track beginning in 1865, as overland traffic moved south from the better-known Oregon-California-Mormon trails to avoid confrontation with Native Americans. By the time the Union Pacific Railroad arrived in the Laramie Valley in 1867, Ft. John Buford had already been established to protect travelers and railroad workers. The fort was soon renamed Fort Sanders, for Brig. Gen. William P. Sanders.

When the railroad crews arrived, Laramie City was born. It developed into a busy railroad division headquarters, and the railroad retains a strong presence. Early on, crime was rampant, and the community organized vigilante forces. But by 1873 Laramie City had a new structure on the bank of the Little Laramie River—the Wyoming Territorial Prison, which housed the likes of Butch Cassidy. The city's population is now about 30,000.

Eventually, Wyoming leaders decided to spread the primary state institutions across the state, so the territorial prison closed and a new facility was built in Rawlins, 100 mi to the west. At the same time, the University of Wyoming was established in Laramie. It remains the only university in the state.

Information: **Laramie Chamber of Commerce** | 800 S. 3rd St., 82070 | 307/745–7339 or 800/445–5303 | fax 307/745–4624. **Albany County Tourism Board** (800 S. 3rd St., 82070 | 307/745–4195 or 800/445–5303 | fax 307/721–2926 | info@laramie-tourism.org | www.laramie-tourism.org.

Attractions

Historic Downtown Laramie Walking Tour. Don't miss the charming, quaint buildings in the historic downtown area, some of which date back to 1868. You can get brochures from the Laramie Chamber of Commerce for a self-guided tour featuring late-19th-century Victorian architecture. Also available is an Architectural Walking Tour that focuses on the historic residences in the downtown area, and a guide to the Laramie Antique Trail, with locations of antiques shops in and around downtown. | 307/745–7339 or 800/445–5303 | Free | Daily.

UPPER NORTH PLATTE RIVER VALLEY SCENIC DRIVES

This is a big state, and distances between towns can be vast. This means that any vacation to Wyoming will involve a certain amount of driving. With that in mind, consider a driving trip to the upper North Platte River valley, which includes two spectacular mountain drives: the Snowy Range Scenic Byway (Rte. 130 between Laramie and Saratoga) and the Battle Highway (Rte. 70 west of Encampment). Both are high mountain passes reaching elevations in excess of 9,500 ft; they close in mid-October and don't reopen until late May or early June. But during that short summer/fall season, the views are breathtaking, with glacial mountains in the Snowies, and immense pine forests in both areas.

The region is full of history as well, since tie hacks worked in these mountains cutting ties (the crossbeams that underlie old railroad tracks) for the railroad in the late 1800s and early 1900s. And miners seeking both gold and copper worked the mountains during that same era. When hiking any of the many trails in the Medicine Bow National Forest, you are likely to come across abandoned cabins that are testament to that early period.

Wildflowers are usually in vibrant color, though in the fall the aspens paint the scenery, particularly on the Battle Highway.

© Artville

Laramie Plains Museum. Historical items from the Laramie Valley are displayed in the Ivinson Mansion, which is on the National Register of Historic Places. You can take guided tours. | 603 Ivinson Ave. | 307/742–4448 | $4 | Mid-June–late Aug., Mon.–Sat. 9–6, Sun. 1–4; Late Aug.–Dec. 15 and Feb.–mid-June, Mon.–Sat. 1–4.

Lincoln Monument. You can see this much larger than life-size bust of President Abraham Lincoln clearly from I–80, and the site, 9 mi east of the city, has a rest area and visitors information center. The monument commemorates the Lincoln Highway—U.S. 30—overlaid by I–80 in this area. It was the first transcontinental highway, completed across Wyoming in 1913. | Free | Daily.

Medicine Bow National Forest, Laramie District. You can hike, picnic, hunt, fish, ski, snowmobile, and take photographs in the million-acre Medicine Bow National Forest, and that's the short list. The Laramie District has 19 developed campgrounds; dispersed camping also allowed. | Laramie Ranger District Office, 2468 Jackson St., West Laramie | 307/745–2300, reservations 877/444–6777 | www.fs.fed.us/r2/mbr/ | Free; campground fee $10 | Daily.

Snowy Range Ski Area. Try the half-pipe for snowboarding, or snowmobile and cross-country ski. This small ski area is about 30 mi west of Laramie. You can rent equipment, and there's a ski school and lounge. | 6416 Mountain Mist Ct; Rte. 130 | 307/745–5750 or 800/Go–2–SNOW | fax 307/745–4113 | www.snowrange.com | $29 | Thanksgiving–Dec. 11, weekends 9–4; Dec. 11–Easter, daily 9–4.

University of Wyoming. Wyoming's only university has year-round events, from concerts to football games. The visitors center is at 14th St. and Grand Ave. | 307/766–4075 or 307/766–1121 | www.uwyo.edu.

American Heritage Center and Art Museum. Permanent and traveling art displays fill the art museum's space, and the American Heritage Center collections contain more than 10,000 photographs, rare books, and papers and memorabilia on such subjects as American and Western history, the petroleum industry, conservation movements, transportation, and the performing arts. Check out the annual fall symposium if you're around then. | 2111 Willet Dr. | 307/766–6622 (art museum), 307/766–4114 (Heritage Center) | www.uwyo.edu/ahc | Free | Winter, weekdays 8–5, Sat. 11–5; summer, weekdays 7:30–4:30, Sat. 11–5.

Wyoming Children's Museum and Nature Center. Here children are encouraged to explore, make noise, experiment, play, imagine, discover, and invent. | 412 S. 2nd St. | 307/745–6332 | $1 | Tues.–Thurs. 9–5, Sat., 10–4; in summer also Fri. 1–5.

Geological Museum. The dinosaur statue is out front and inside you'll find the skeleton of an apatosaurus 15 ft high and 75 ft long at this university museum in the Knight Geology Building. It likely weighed 30 tons. Other exhibits explore the dinosaur family tree, meteorites, fossils, and earthquakes. | 307/766–4246 | Free | Weekdays 8–5, weekends 10–3.

Wyoming Territorial Prison and Old West Park. The centerpiece of this park off I–80 is the prison, built in the 1870s. Also included are a re-created frontier or "hell-on-wheels" town and the U.S. Marshal's Museum. Regular entertainment takes place in the Horse Barn dinner theater. | 975 Snowy Range Rd. | 307/745–6161, ext. 5, or 800/845–2287, ext. 5 | fax 307/745–8620 | prison@lariat.org | www.wyoprisonpark.org | $2 Old West Frontier Town; $5.50 Territorial Prison and U.S. Marshal's Museum tour; $23.95 Horse Barn dinner theater | May–Sept., daily 9–5; dinner theater 6–9 (dark Sun.–Mon.).

ON THE CALENDAR

FEB.: *Sweethearts Territorial Ball.* Dancing is the highlight of this annual event held at the Wyoming Territorial Prison Park. | 307/745–6161 or 800/845–2287.

MAR.: *Keepers of the Light UW Spring Powwow.* Native American students and others participate in this annual powwow at the University of Wyoming. | 307/745–7339 or 800/445–5303.

JUNE: *Old West Territorial Park Festival.* Programs and demonstrations display frontier skills, with entertainment, at the Old West Territorial Park. | 307/745–6161 or 800/845–2287.

JULY: *Fire in the Sky.* A Fourth of July country music concert and fireworks display is held at the UW stadium. | 307/745–7339 or 800/445–5303.

JULY: *Laramie Jubilee Days.* Rodeos, a carnival, parades, and a Western art show are part of the week-long celebration at the Albany County Fairgrounds and downtown. | 307/745–7339 or 800/445–5303.

AUG.: *Albany County Fair.* Youth livestock and craft exhibits are part of the county fair, along with a demolition derby, all at the Albany County Fairgrounds. | 307/745–7339 or 800/445–5303.

SEPT.: *American Heritage Center Fall Symposium.* A different topic, from water rights to education, is chosen for discussion each year in this lecture series at the American Heritage Center. | 307/766–4114.

NOV.: *Olde-Fashioned Christmas Celebration.* At the Old West Territorial Park are displays of crafts that would have been practiced in the 19th century, along with entertainment and programs. | 307/745–6161 or 800/845–2287.

Dining

Cafe Jacques. American. A bar and grill that offers sandwiches and more than 70 beers, including domestic and imported brands, as well as microbrews and two on tap. | 220 Grand Ave. | 307/742–5522 | $5–$10 | AE, D, DC, MC, V.

Cavalryman Supper Club. American. At the site of the first military fort in this area, this place is a local favorite that serves steak, prime rib, and seafood. Salad bar. | 4425 S. 3rd St. | 307/745–5551 | $15–$32 | AE, DC, MC, V | No lunch.

Longhorn Restaurant. American. Built in the 1950s, about 18 mi east of Medicine Bow, this quaint log cabin restaurant is decked out in antiques, including an old Victrola. Everything is homemade, from the soups and pies to the salad dressing; the chicken-fried steak and the huge chili-burger platter are favorites, as is the fresh four-berry pie. | 362 N. 4th St., Rock River | 307/378–2567 | $6–$18 | MC, V | Closed Sun.

Overland Restaurant. Contemporary. Next to the Union Pacific Railroad tracks, in the heart of the downtown historic district, this place combines the traditional with the innovative. Pasta, chicken, quiche, beef, and seafood are on the menu, but for Sunday breakfast you might find yellowfin tuna and eggs, a buffalo chili omelette, or avocados Benedict. Open-air dining on a patio with a large mural. Good wine list. Sun. brunch. | 100 E. Ivanson | 307/721–2800 | $8–$14 | AE, D, MC, V.

The Rancher. American. A former dance hall, this ranch-style restaurant adorned with saddles and wagon wheels serves up Western fare like porterhouse steak, ribs, and a spicy Cajun chicken. Friday nights, you can join the locals who pack the place for the all-you-can-eat barbecue rib special. | 309 S. 3rd St. | 307/742–3141 | $7–$15 | V.

Lodging

Best Western Foster's Country Inn. At the intersection of I–80 and Rtes. 130/230, this hotel has full services, including a convenience store, filling station, restaurant, and bar. The lobby and halls are rustic Western knotty pine, and the rooms are standard contemporary. Restaurant, bar. Cable TV. Indoor pool. Hot tub. Airport shuttle. Pets allowed. | 1561 Snowy Range Rd. | 307/742–8371 | fax 307/742–0884 | 112 rooms | $64–$96 | AE, D, DC, MC, V.

Camelot. Near I–80, this motel has basic rooms and decent rates. Cable TV. Laundry facilities. | 523 Adams | 307/721–8860 or 800/659–7915 | 33 rooms | $50–$75 | AE, D, DC, MC, V.

Econo Lodge. The rooms are both extra-large and cozy, with burgundy and forest-green comforters. Some have coffeemakers. Some refrigerators. Cable TV. Indoor pool. Pets allowed. | 1370 McCue St. | 307/745–8900 | fax 307/745–5806 | econol@trib.com | 51 rooms | $54–$100 | AE, D, DC, MC, V.

First Inn Gold. Right off I–80, this standard motel has appealing, spacious rooms, numerous amenities, and efficient service at reasonable rates. Great if you want to get an early start.

Restaurant, bar, Continental breakfast. Cable TV. Pool. Hot tub. Pets allowed (fee). | 421 Boswell St. | 307/742–3721 or 800/642–4212 | fax 307/742–5473 | 80 rooms | $69 | AE, D, DC, MC, V.

Holiday Inn. Some of the rooms have in-room data ports in this standard contemporary hotel. An enclosed wing houses 32 of the rooms. Restaurant, bar, room service. Cable TV. Indoor pool. Hot tub. Laundry facilities. Airport shuttle. Pets allowed. | 2313 Soldier Springs Rd. | 307/742–6611 | fax 307/745–8371 | 100 rooms | $75–$85 | AE, D, DC, MC, V.

Laramie Comfort Inn. Laramie's newest motel has an indoor pool and spa, fitness room, and a fully equipped handicapped room with the only roll-in shower in the city. Of the three suites, one has a hot tub, and there's also an efficiency apartment. Continental breakfast. Indoor pool. Spa. Gym. | 3420 Grand Ave. | 307/721–8856 or 800–228–5150 | 55 rooms, 3 suites, 1 efficiency apartment | $70–$90 | AE, D, DC, MC, V.

Vee-Bar Guest Ranch. This historic guest ranch and bed-and-breakfast outside Laramie rests next to the Little Laramie River, and offers both cabins and rooms in the main lodge. The attractive log cabins are filled with Western antiques, wood furniture, quilts, and warm tones, and are primarily heated with wood-burning stoves. Nightly rates are available, but with weekly rates you get riding lessons (on your own "horse for the week"), fishing, meals, and an overnight camping trip. Full breakfast. Hot tub. No pets allowed. No smoking. | 2091 Rte. 130 | 307/745–7036 or 800/483–3227 | fax 307/745–7433 | VeeBar@Lariat.org | www.vee-bar.com | 9 cabins, 3 rooms | $150 bed and breakfast, ranch $2,895 wk for two | MC, V.

LOVELL

MAP 9, E1

(Nearby town also listed: Greybull)

Originally from Michigan, Henry Clay Lovell migrated to Texas, where he learned the cattle business. In 1879 he brought some of the first cattle into the Bighorn Basin, where he established three different ranches financed by Anthony L. Mason of Kansas City, Missouri. Mason had the money and Lovell had the expertise with which to form the Mason-Lovell cattle kingdom, which eventually numbered 25,000 head roaming the Bighorn Basin. When postal deliveries started at Cook's Road Ranch in 1888, the post office was named Lovell, for the cattle rancher.

The town didn't reach any size until after 1900, when Mormon colonists led by Abraham O. Woodruff moved into the region. They established farms and dug canals to irrigate crops. Lovell, which calls itself the Rose City of Wyoming because of the many roses that thrive in its mild climate, retains close ties to farming, particularly sugar beets, and a strong Mormon presence remains. Lovell is a gateway community to the northern Bighorn Mountains, to the Bighorn Canyon Recreation area, and to the Medicine Wheel, a Native American spiritual site high in the Bighorns.

Information: Lovell Chamber of Commerce | Box 245, 82431 | 307/548–7552 | fax 307/548–7614.

Attractions

Bighorn Canyon National Recreation Area. Geologic upheaval combined with natural forces of wind and water carved the Bighorn Canyon, with steep walls too rugged for easy access. Although early people in the area traveled and lived near the canyon, they spent little or no time on the river until the Yellowtail Dam was built near Fort Smith, Montana. Completed in 1968, the dam made Bighorn Lake, now a major recreation area that straddles the Wyoming-Montana border and lets you get to Devil Canyon and other previously almost inaccessible places. The Bighorn Canyon National Recreation Area includes part of the Yellowtail Wildlife Habitat and the Pryor Mountain Wild Horse Range, so the landscape you see has changed little in hundreds of years. | 20 U.S. 14A E | 307/548–2251 or 406/ 666–2412 | www.nps.gov/bica/ | Free | Daily.

The solar-heated **Bighorn Canyon Visitors Center** has information about boating, camping, fishing, and hiking in the park, as well as exhibits on the canyon's history and natural features. | 20 U.S. 14A E | 307/548–2251 | Free | Memorial Day–Labor Day, daily 8–6; Labor Day–Memorial Day, daily 8:30–5.

Medicine Wheel National Historic Landmark. Approximately 80 ft in diameter, the Medicine Wheel is a National Historic Landmark of uncertain origin. It is sacred to Native Americans. It was probably built between AD 1200 and 1700 and has a central cairn with 28 radiating spokes made of rocks. Now protected by a fence, the Medicine Wheel site is high in the Bighorn Mountains. From it you can see the entire Bighorn Basin. Visitors must park away from the site and walk 1½ mi to the actual wheel (people with disabilities are allowed vehicle access). The site, 30 mi east of Lovell on Rte. 14A, may be closed at times for Native American ceremonies. The narrow access road is not suitable for trailer traffic. | 307/548–6541.

Pryo Mountain National Wild Horse Range. Little more than 30,000 acres, this wild horse range is the first of its kind in the United States. A road system—usable only by those driving 4x4 vehicles—circles the primary Prior Mountain wilderness study area and allows you to view the horses, believed to be descendants of the first Spanish horses introduced to North America. Coat colors such as grulla, blue roan, dun, and sabino indicate Spanish lineage, as do markings such as a dorsal stripe, zebra stripes on the legs, and a stripe over the withers. The horse herd—generally broken into small family groupings—numbers between 120 and 160 animals, including about 20–30 new foals each year that repopulate the herd and keep it from becoming inbred. To maintain the health of the herd, the U.S. Bureau of Land Management captures and removes some of the animals every two to three years and allows those animals to be adopted by new owners. To view the wild horses you can drive Bad Pass Highway (Rte. 37) through the Bighorn Canyon National Recreation Area, where horses are usually visible in the Mustang Flat area. Or you can take a four-wheel-drive vehicle on other roads in the range and hike throughout the region, which lacks developed hiking trails. | Lovell Chamber of Commerce/Pryor Mountain Mustang Association, 287 E. Main St., Lovell | 307/548–7552; Britton Springs Administrative Site 307/548–2706 (seasonal) | www.webcom.com/~ladyhawk/breeding.html | Free | Daily.

Yellowtail Wildlife Habitat Management Area. More than 155 species of birds, including white pelicans, bald eagles, and great blue herons, inhabit the 19,424-acre Yellowtail area, as do a variety of other animal species—red foxes, mule deer, cottontail rabbits, and others. The management area, on Rte. 37 southwest of Bighorn Canyon National Recreation Area, includes sections along both the Bighorn and Shoshone rivers. | Wyoming Game and Fish District Office, 2820 State Highway 120, Cody | 307/527–7125 or 800/654–1187 (in Wyoming) | Free | Daily.

ON THE CALENDAR

JUNE: *Mustang Days.* A local celebration features food and special events. | 307/548–7552.

JULY: *Pioneer Day.* Commemorating the first settlers to the area, this event features an old-fashioned parade down Main Street, a rodeo, family activities, and a evening dance. | 307/548–7552.

Dining

Bighorn. American. Family owned and operated in downtown Lovell, this diner also caters to the entire family. The interior is southwestern in style. They serve breakfast all day. Kids' menu. | 605 E. Main St. | 307/548–6811 | Daily; 6 AM–9 PM | $6–$16 | AE, D, DC, MC, V.

Horseshoe Bend Marina. American. Stop here for fast food and snacks. | 12 mi northeast on Rte. 37 | No phone | $5–$10 | No credit cards | Closed Labor Day–Apr. 15.

Lange's Kitchen. American. Everything from biscuits and pies to omelettes and French dip sandwiches are made from scratch at this local downtown restaurant specializing in plain home cooking. Dinner specials include halibut and chicken-fried steak. The interior has antique kitchen memorabilia like butter churns, old recipes, and a wood-burning stove. | 483 Shoshone Ave. | 307/548–9370 | $5–$15 | MC, V.

Lodging

Cattleman Motel. Clean, simple Western-style rooms have lodgepole furniture at this basic one-story motel near the center of town. The rates are reasonable and the service is good. Continental breakfast. Cable TV. Hot tub. Pets allowed. | 470 Montana Ave. | 307/548–2296 or 888/548–2296 | fax 307/548–2483 | 13 rooms | $46 | AE, D, MC, V.

Horseshoe Bend Motel. Western-style and contemporary Western furnishings characterize this small in-town motel with modest rates. Cable TV. Pool. Pets allowed. | 375 E. Main St. | 307/548–2221 | fax 307/548–2131 | hsbmotelja@tctwest.net | 22 rooms, 5 with kitchenettes | $39–$49 | AE, D, DC, MC, V.

Super 8. You can walk around the lobby and look at the photographs of the sights you might want to see or things you can do. On the east side of Lovell, the motel has Western furnishings and small rooms. Cable TV. Laundry facilities. | 595 E. Main St. | 307/548–2725 | fax 307/548–2725 | 35 rooms | $50–$59 | AE, D, DC, MC, V.

LUSK

MAP 9, I4

(Nearby town also listed: Douglas)

The Cheyenne-Deadwood Stage Line, which operated between Wyoming's Territorial capital and the Black Hills gold town after the discovery of gold in 1875, gave rise to a number of stations, including one at Silver Cliff. When the Wyoming Central Railroad started moving into the area, officials attempted to purchase land from Ellis Johnson, who had a store, saloon, and hotel at Silver Cliff. Johnson, thinking he had a sure deal, held out for a better price for his land and nearby rancher Frank S. Lusk cut his own deal with the railroad. That meant the rail line bypassed Silver Cliff and instead went through the new area—named Lusk.

Once situated on a pioneering route that led to development of the Black Hills, Lusk became a different sort of pioneering town in the 1990s, when it was wired. Town leaders led the state of Wyoming into the 21st century when they installed fiber optic cable lines and subsequently obtained computers for schools, public facilities, and homes, making Lusk a "computer literate" population on the cutting edge of technology when other small Wyoming towns barely knew what the Internet was. The community of 2,000 was written up in national magazines and newspapers and was the subject of an advertising campaign conducted by Microsoft.

Information: **Niobrara-Lusk Chamber of Commerce** | Box 457, Lusk 82225 | 307/334–2950 or 800/223–5875.

Attractions

Stagecoach Museum. Artifacts from early settlement days and the period when the Cheyenne-Deadwood stage route was in full swing (1875) are some of the displays at this museum. You can also get information about the Texas Cattle Trail. | 322 S. Main St. | 800/223–LUSK | $2 | May–Aug., weekdays 10–6; Sept.–Oct., weekdays 10–4.

Historic Hat Creek Stage Station. The Cheyenne and Black Hills Stage Line ran through the area in the 1870s; you can still see the remains of the small Hat Creek stagecoach station, as well as an old schoolhouse and post office, in the tall grass plains about 15 mi north of Lusk off U.S. 85. | Follow marked gravel road 2 mi east | 307/334–2950 | Free | Daily.

ON THE CALENDAR

JULY: *Legend of Rawhide.* A living-history re-enactment depicts the legend of a man who killed an Indian girl when traveling West more than a century ago and was ultimately skinned alive by Native Americans. | 307/334–2950 or 800/223–5875.

JULY: *Charlie Chamber Days.* A festive community event features basketball tournaments, sidewalk sales at local businesses, and food and crafts booths. | 307/334–2950.

SEPT.: *Senior Pro Rodeo.* On Labor Day weekend, older rodeo contestants show they still have the right stuff as they rope and ride in traditional events. | 307/334–2950 or 800/223–LUSK.

Dining

El Jarros. Mexican/American. At the center of town, this festive restaurant is filled with DeGrazia paintings, strung with lights, and decked in bright, warm colors. Try the fajitas, barbecue ribs, or spicy shrimp stir-fry, and complement your meal with an icy margarita. | 625 S. Main St. | 307/334–5004 | $7.50–$18 | MC, V | Closed Sun. and on weekdays and Saturdays 2–5.

Pizza Place. Italian. A casual atmosphere and good food come together here at this downtown eatery. You can have homemade pizza, calzones, and sub sandwiches with homemade bread. Salad bar. | 218 S. Main St. | 307/334–3000 | $3–$23 | No credit cards.

Lodging

Best Western Pioneer Court. Near downtown and the Stagecoach Museum, this hotel has some extra-large rooms. Cable TV. Pool. | 731 S. Main St. | 307/334–2640 | fax 307/334–2642 | 30 rooms | $51–$89 | AE, D, DC, MC, V.

Covered Wagon. With a covered wagon on the front portico, an indoor pool, and an outdoor playground, this U-shape hotel is an inviting place for families with kids. Cable TV. Indoor pool. Hot tub, sauna. Playground, laundry facilities. | 730 S. Main St. | 307/334–2836 or 800/341–8000 | fax 307/334–2977 | 51 rooms | $73 | AE, D, DC, MC, V.

Rawhide Motel. The standard-size rooms are newly remodeled, and service is friendly at this affordable, locally owned motel in downtown Lusk. It's within walking distance of area restaurants. Cable TV. Pets allowed. | 805 S. Main St. | 307/334–2440 or 888/679–2558 | fax 307/334–2440 | ludoug@coffey.com | www.rawhidemotel.net | 19 rooms | $32–$42 | AE, D, MC, V.

MEDICINE BOW

MAP 9, G5

(Nearby town also listed: Laramie)

When novelist Owen Wister first visited Medicine Bow, he said the community looked "as if strewn there by the wind." He immortalized the place in his classic Western tale *The Virginian,* published in 1902. Today the town still looks somewhat windblown, though the small business district is anchored by the Virginian Hotel, built in the early 1900s and commemorating the book of the same name. This is a community of 320 struggling for survival, with an economy based on the vagaries of agriculture and mining. Although it sits at the intersection of U.S. 30 (Lincoln Highway) and Wyoming Route 487, you'll seldom encounter much traffic here, except during the fall hunting season— this area is particularly noted for its antelope-hunting opportunities—and when there are football or basketball games at the University of Wyoming. On those days, expect a crowd on the road and fans talking of sports at the Virginian Hotel.

Information: **Town of Medicine Bow** | Box 156, 82329 | 307/379–2225 | www.medicinebow.org.

Attractions

Medicine Bow Museum. You can learn about the history of this small town, made famous by Owen Wister in *The Virginian*. | 405 Lincoln Pl | 307/379–2225, tour appointments 307/379–2581 | Free | Memorial Day–Sept., weekdays 10–5 and by appointment.

ON THE CALENDAR
JUNE: *Medicine Bow Days.* A rodeo and special activities highlight this event. | 307/379–2225 or 307/379–2571.

Dining

Dip Diner. American. The Dip Diner (short for diplodocus, because there are major dinosaur diggings not far outside of town) has a Western look that includes wood carvings done by the owner. The menu is basic: burgers, steaks, and chicken. | 202 Lincoln Hwy. | 307/379–2312 | $3–$12 | No credit cards | Closed Sun.

Virginian Hotel. American. The historic hotel serves basic American fare—chicken-fried steak, meat loaf, and steak—in the formal Owen Wister dining room, complete with Victorian antique chairs and buffets. The less formal coffee shop has large, brightly colored murals. Salad bar. | 404 LincolnHwy. | 307/379–2377 | $4–$15 | MC, V.

Lodging

Loghorn Lodge. Off the beaten path, about 18 mi east of Medicine Bow, this is a quiet and cozy place to stay. In the spring, lilac bushes bloom around these rustic, individual cabin-style rooms, which are basic, comfortable, clean, and affordable. Restaurant. TVs. Pets allowed. | 362 N. 4th St., Rock River | 307/378–2567 | fax 307/378–2567 | 8 rooms | $34 | D, MC, V.

Trampas Lodge. Rooms at this motel have no fancy decorations but are clean and affordable. Pets allowed. | Lincoln Hwy. | 307/379–2280 | 20 rooms | $31–$36 | MC, V.

Virginian Hotel. Inspired by the Owen Wister novel *The Virginian*, this sandstone hotel was built in 1909 and has been operating nearly continuously ever since. The rooms are Victorian, with claw-footed tubs, tulip-shaped lights, and high beds with comforters. The historic photos on the walls include one of Owen Wister in the Owen Wister Suite. The Scott suite has a small bath, sitting room, and bedroom. None of the rooms in the main hotel has a telephone, radio, or TV, and most don't even have electrical outlets. But the atmosphere more than makes up for the lack of such amenities. Only the suites have bathrooms; other rooms use the water closet down the hall. Rooms in the annex do have TVs and bathrooms. Restaurant, bar. | 404 Lincoln Hwy. | 307/379–2377 | 33 rooms | $20–$48 | MC, V.

NEWCASTLE

MAP 9, H2

(Nearby town also listed: Gillette)

Newcastle was shaken in December 1998 when an early-morning fire destroyed much of its downtown business district. But this community of 3,000 is as tenacious now as it was when coal miners settled it in the late 1880s. Cambria Coal Company superintendent J. H. Hemingway named it for Newcastle-on-Tyne, a coal-mining town in England. Though coal mining gave the town its start, the development of oil production and ranching has stabilized it through the years.

Information: Newcastle Chamber of Commerce | Box 68, 82701 | 307/746–2739 or 800/835–0157.

NEWCASTLE

INTRO
ATTRACTIONS
DINING
LODGING

Attractions

Anna Miller Museum. You'll find local historical relics and information here. | 401 Delaware St., at Washington Park | 307/746–4188 | Free | Sept.–May, weekdays 9–5; June–Aug., Mon.–Sat. 9–noon.

Snowmobiling. A large network of snowmobile trails threads through the Black Hills National Forest near Newcastle. | 307/746–2739 or 800/835–0157 | www.fs.fed.us/r2/black-hills/index.htm.

Thunder Basin National Grassland. Between the Bighorn Mountains and the Black Hills lies the 572,211-acre Thunder Basin National Grassland. You can hike, hunt, fish, and camp, though it lacks developed campgrounds. | Elk Mountain Ranger District Office, 1225 Washington Blvd. | 307/746–2739 or 307/283–1361 | www.fs.fed.us/bhnf/.

ON THE CALENDAR

JUNE: *Sagebrush Festival.* Crafts booths, a watermelon feed, a street dance, a carnival, and sagebrush-seed packets are part of this annual celebration. It even has a Sagebrush Queen and King. | 307/746–2739 or 800/835–0157.

JULY: *Gymkhanas.* Young people participate in horse events, from pole bending to goat tying. | 307/746–2739 or 800/835–0157.

JUNE–AUG.: *Mini-Sprint Races.* National Organized Mini-Sprint Association races are held throughout the summer on the track at the Weston County Fairgrounds. | 307/746–2739 or 800/835–0157.

Dining

Hi-16 Cafe. American. A good, substantial breakfast is one selling point at this all-American style cafe. | 2951 W. Main St. | 307/746–4055 | $6–$20 | No credit cards.

Main Street Diner. American. At the center of town you can feed the entire family for under $30. The walls are decked with antlers at this classic, small-town eatery that serves home-style fare. Specialties include the Daisy Mae, a roast beef sandwich on a French bun with grilled onions and peppers, chicken-fried steak, and homemade pies and cinnamon rolls. | 207 W. Main St. | 307/746–2905 | $4–$8 | No credit cards.

Old Mill Inn. American. You'll get excellent breakfasts in this historic mill. At lunch and dinner you can choose from 100 domestic and imported beers and microbrews. Try the local game and fish; locals also like the prime rib. | 500 W. Main St. | 307/746–2711 | $7–$14 | MC, V.

Lodging

Flying V Cambria Inn. Completed in 1928, this European manor-style inn began as a resort for the then-booming mining town of Cambria. The mine went bust, and the inn was used as a Bible school, cattle ranch, and casino before evolving into this bed-and-breakfast with individually decorated rooms and spacious common areas. Nestled in the Black Hills 8 mi north of Newcastle, the inn is quiet, down-home, and relaxed. Full breakfast, restaurant, bar, dining area. Some shared baths. Some pets allowed. | 23726 U.S. 85 | 307/746–2096 | www.trib.com/~flyingv | 7 rooms | $78.50 | D, MC, V.

Fountain Motor Inn. Ponds and fountains on the 20 landscaped acres around this inn set it apart, as does the pool. Apartment-style accommodations and campsites are also available. Restaurant. Some rooms with kitchenettes. Cable TV. Pool. Some pets allowed. | 2 Fountain Plaza | 307/746–4426 or 800/882–8858 | fax 307/746–3206 | 80 rooms | $70 | AE, D, DC, MC, V.

Four Corners Store, Diner & Country Inn. Four Corners serves as the diner, general store, inn, and church. It's a popular spot with rooms for all budgets. Restaurant. Pets allowed. | 24713 U.S. 85 N, Four Corners | 307/746–4776 | 9 rooms | $35–$100.

PINEDALE

(Nearby town also listed: Jackson)

Trappers found the icy streams of the Green River watershed to be among the best places to capture beaver and even better for holding a summer rendezvous during the fur-trading era of 1825–43. They held seven such meetings near what is now Pinedale. The short-lived fort here was officially called Fort Bonneville, after Capt. Benjamin Bonneville, but more commonly folks referred to it as Fort Nonsense, because the harsh winters on the upper Green made it utter nonsense to maintain a year-round fort in the area. Once the fur trade declined, the region saw little traffic until the late 1870s, when cattlemen and sheepherders started moving their stock into the area. Pinedale now has 1,200 residents and continues to be a ranching center, though its proximity to the Wind River Range to the east gives you lots of things to do.

Information: Pinedale Chamber of Commerce | Box 176, 82941 | 307/367–2242 | fax 307/367–6830 | www.pinedaleonline.com.

Attractions

Bridger-Teton National Forest, Pinedale District. Encompassing parts of the Wind River Range, the Bridger-Teton National Forest gives you millions of acres to explore. The peaks reach higher than 13,000 ft, and the area is liberally sprinkled with more than a thousand

PINEDALE

INTRO
ATTRACTIONS
DINING
LODGING

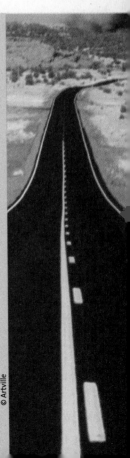

© Artville

LET'S RENDEZVOUS

In 1825 Andrew Henry met beaver trappers on the Black Fork of the Green River for the first mountain-man rendezvous. For the next 18 years, trappers and traders (along with Indians and even a few missionaries) gathered annually to exchange goods. The trappers sold or exchanged the furs they'd harvested during the previous winter for goods the traders had, such as weapons, ammunition, food, clothing, and other supplies they would need for another year of trapping beaver.

Though the first rendezvous was a quiet affair and simply an opportunity to exchange beaver pelts (called plews) for supplies, subsequent gatherings were raucous with a lot of whiskey. At least seven rendezvous took place on the Upper Green River near present-day Pinedale; two took place on the Wind River near present-day Riverton, and one small rendezvous convened on "Potter's Fork," a stream that became the Grand Encampment River, near present-day Encampment.

Fort Laramie started as a fur trader's post, and Fort Bridger was built "in the path of the emigrants" by Jim Bridger, one of the legendary mountain men.

The fur trade petered out by 1843 because many streams had been nearly denuded of beaver, and beaver hats had gone out of style, but the era isn't forgotten. Each summer, present-day buckskinners load up their tepees, put on their skins, and take their black-powder guns to rendezvous held at or near some of the historic sites: Pinedale, Riverton, Encampment, and Fort Bridger. There they have shooting contests, throw axes and frying pans, or barter with traders for skins, beads, pots, or kettles.

high mountain lakes where the fishing is generally excellent. You can also hike, snowmobile, camp, picnic, and hunt. | Pinedale Ranger District, 29 E. Fremont Lake Rd. | 307/367–4326 | www.fs.fed.us/btnf/.

Bridger Wilderness. In 1964 Congress set aside this section of the Wind River Range with pristine mountain lakes and high peaks. You can hike and horseback ride on more than 600 mi of trails.

Museum of the Mountain Man. Tucked away in northwestern Wyoming, this museum is primarily dedicated to depicting the era of the mountain man. The basement section is devoted to Sublette County pioneer and ranch history. | 700 E. Hennick Rd. | 307/367–4101 | fax 307/367–6768 | www.museumofthemountainman.com | $4 | May–Sept., daily 10–6; call for winter hours.

ON THE CALENDAR

FEB.: *International Rocky Mountain Stage Stop Sled Dog Race.* This multi-day race goes through many towns in western Wyoming. The competitors include Iditarod champions. Known as the Race to Immunize, it is held to improve awareness children's immunization needs. | 307/777–7777 or 307/367–2242.

JULY: *Green River Rendezvous.* Buckskinners gather for a rendezvous on the rodeo grounds that lasts several days, in commemoration of the get-togethers the fur trappers staged between 1825 and 1843. There's a parade, craft booths, black-powder demonstrations, and rodeo. | 307/367–4101.

AUG.: *Sublette County Fair.* Youngsters show and sell livestock, and there are exhibits of crafts, clothing, and other projects at the Sublette County Fairgrounds. | 307/367–2242.

Dining

McGregors Pub. American. Built in 1905, this converted hotel has a classic Western interior. Local favorites are steaks and seafood, but they also serve some Italian dishes. Open-air dining. Kids' menu. | 21 N. Franklin St. | 307/367–4443 | $7–$60 | D, DC, MC, V | Closed weekends. No lunch.

Moose Creek Trading Company. American. As the name suggests, the theme here is moose, from the wrought-iron bar tables with carvings of moose to the stuffed animals in the gift shop. Upbeat and eclectic, this downtown restaurant does well with the basic prime rib, seafood, and lobster dishes, as well as the homemade pies and desserts. Try the chunky chicken salad for a refreshing summer meal. | 44 W. Pine St. | 307/367–4616 | $6–$18 | AE, D, DC, MC, V.

Lodging

Best Western Pinedale Inn. The inn is on the north side of town, within walking distance of shops and restaurants. The rooms are modest and contemporary. Complimentary Continental breakfast. Some refrigerators. Cable TV. Indoor pool. Hot tub. Exercise equipment. Pets allowed. | 850 W. Pine St. | 307/367–6869 | fax 307/367–6897 | 58 rooms | $99 | AE, D, DC, MC, V.

Wagon Wheel. Contemporary design and large rooms are the standard at this small, new motel on the north side of town. No air-conditioning. Cable TV. | 407 S. Pine St. | 307/367–2871 | fax 307/367–2872 | 15 rooms | $55–$80 | AE, D, DC, MC, V.

Window on the Winds B&B. This comfortable log home gets its name from huge windows that offer stunning views of the Gros Ventre Range, the Wind River Mountains, and Gannett Peak, the state's highest point. All of the rooms have lodgepole-pine beds, jewel- or earth-toned southwestern quilts and rugs, and mountain views. Children and pets are welcome at this family-oriented, homey place. Full breakfast, dining room. 2 bedrooms have shared bath. Hot tub. Pets allowed. | 10151 U.S. 191 | 307/367–2600 or 888/367–1345 | fax 307/367–2395 | www.windowonthewinds.com | 4 rooms | $75–$95 | AE, D, DC, MC, V.

POWELL

(Nearby towns also listed: Cody, Lovell)

John Wesley Powell explored the Green and Colorado rivers and was one of the first people to endorse the idea of reclaiming arid lands by building dams for irrigation. It's fitting, then, that the community of Powell is named for him, because the small city came into being as the result of such endeavors. The Shoshone Reclamation Project, brainchild of Col. William F. Cody and his partners George Beck and Horace Alger, included construction of the Buffalo Bill Dam and Reservoir west of Cody. The first town in the region was Camp Coulter, subsequently renamed Powell. It was established in 1894, two years earlier than the town of Cody. Irrigated fields of sugar beets and malt barley provide its economic base, but Powell, with a population of 5,500, is also the home of Northwest College, one of the state's seven community colleges.

Information: Powell Chamber of Commerce | Box 841, 82435 | 307/754–3494 or 800/ 325–4278 | fax 307/754–3483 | powell@wave.park.wy.us | wave.park.wy.us/~powell/pvcc.html.

Attractions

Heart Mountain Relocation Center. During World War II, Japanese-Americans were interned at various relocation centers, including one at Heart Mountain, west of Powell on Rte. 19. The center became a thriving community, with a hospital, school, and newspaper. The internees labored in area farms throughout the war. The site is now deteriorating, but a monument stands to commemorate the Issei and Nissei who spent the war years here. | 307/754–2272 | Free | Daily.

Homesteader Museum. Local history, including the development of the Shoshone and Bighorn Basin irrigation projects, is featured at this museum. | 1st St., off Coulter Ave. | 307/ 754–9481 | Free | Tues.–Fri. 1–5.

ON THE CALENDAR

AUG.: *Park County Fair.* Livestock and craft exhibitions, a carnival, and entertainment make up the fair at the Park County Fairgrounds. | 307/754–5421.
SEPT.: *Happy Days.* An all-American antique quilt show also has a street dance and entertainment. | 307/754–3494.
OCT.: *Oktoberfest.* The German heritage is celebrated with bratwurst and beer, polka dancing, and other music. | 307/754–3494.
DEC.: *Country Christmas.* Entertainment and other Christmas activities. | 307/754– 3494.

Dining

Hansel & Gretel's Restaurant. German. On the main street of town, with a dark-wood interior with pictures from the fairy tale, this brick restaurant has a Bavarian air. Try the Black Forest sandwich, with German sausage and sauerkraut on dark rye, or "Your Sandwich"— ham, tomato, and fresh broccoli covered with Hollandaise sauce on an English muffin. Lobster and steak dishes are also popular. | 113 S. Bent St. | 307/754–2191 | $8–$20 | MC, V | Closed Sun.

Lamplighter Inn. American. The relaxed service gives this place a bit of style—you'll be tempted to linger a bit and soak it up after you've finished your meal. | 234 E. 1st St. | 307/ 754–2226 | $16–$44 | AE, D, DC, MC, V.

Time Out. American. You can have a sandwich while cheering for your favorite team at this sports bar. | 124 N. Bent Ave. | 307/754–9778 | $9.50–$17.50 | MC, V.

Lodging

Best Western Kings Inn. Blocks from Powell's business district, this basic motor inn has standard rooms decorated in neutral tones. Restaurant, bar. Cable TV. Outdoor pool. Conference rooms. | 777 E. 2nd St. | 307/754–5117 or 800/441–7778 | fax 307/754–2198 | www.best-western.com | 49 rooms | $72–$77 | AE, D, DC, MC, V.

Lamplighter Inn. Near downtown and renovated in 1999, this hotel has reasonably priced rooms done in blue, mauve, rose, and cream. Many are no-smoking. Restaurant, bar. Pets allowed. | 234 E. 1st St. | 307/754–2226 | fax 307/754–2229 | 20 rooms | $49 | AE, D, DC, MC, V.

Super 8. This standard Super 8 is close to downtown and caters to varied budgets. Cable TV. Pets allowed. | 845 E. Coulter Dr. | 307/754–7231 | 35 rooms | $40–$73 | AE, D, DC, MC, V.

RAWLINS

MAP 9, F5

(Nearby town also listed: Saratoga)

Started as one of the Union Pacific's hell-on-wheels towns, Rawlins became a large sheep-raising center in the late 1800s and early 1900s. Kingpins in the sheep industry, such as George Ferris and Robert Deal, also became involved in the development of the Grand Encampment Copper Mining District, when miner Ed Haggarty discovered copper there in 1897, and they backed mine development. Rawlins was an important transportation center as early as 1868, when miners heading for the gold fields at South Pass to the north rode the Union Pacific to Rawlins or points nearby, then went overland to the gold diggings.

Recent declines in sheep growing, long Rawlins's mainstay industry, have hurt the community economically, as have downturns in regional mineral production. But the city of 10,000 still has many railroad workers based here and can rely on the operation of the Wyoming State Penitentiary just outside of town—a facility that underwent a major expansion in 1999 that led to the creation of hundreds of new jobs.

Information: Rawlins-Carbon County Chamber of Commerce | Box 1331, 82301 | 307/324–4111 or 800/228–3547 | fax 307/324–5078 | rcccoc@trib.com.

Attractions

Carbon County Museum. Here and only here you can see a pair of shoes made from the skin of Big Nose George Parrott. Parrott was an outlaw who was lynched in 1881 after he attempted to escape from the county jail, where he was being held awaiting execution for his role in the murder of two law enforcement officers, the first officers to die in the line of duty in Wyoming. After his death Parrott's body was used for "medical study," and he was ultimately skinned (which is how they made the shoes). Other more traditional articles illuminate the area's settlement. | 9th and Walnut Sts. | 307/328–2740 | Free | Oct. 1–April 30, Mon., Wed., and Sat. 1–5; May–Oct., weekdays, 10–12 and 1–5; tours by appointment.

Independence Rock. Called the "Register of the Desert" by pioneer travelers, this turtle-shaped granite outcrop on Rte. 220 became an important landmark on the Oregon-California-Mormon trails. Emigrants carved their names in the rock, and many remain legible more than 150 years later. The rock is now a state historic site, located midway between Casper and Rawlins. Stop to stretch your legs by climbing the rock face, which looks steep but is actually easy to climb without any special equipment. A state rest area at the site has restrooms and picnic tables. | 307/577–5150 | www.state.wy.us | Free | Daily.

Mormon Trail Handcart Visitor Center. *See* Casper, *above.* | 60 mi north on U.S. 287/Rte. 220.

Seminoe State Park. The Seminoe Reservoir is the primary attraction here, and you can fish, boat, and waterski, as well as camp and picnic. It's on a Bureau of Land Management backcountry byway, County Road 351, linking Sinclair with Alcova. | 307/328–0115 or 307/320–3013 | sphs@missc.state.wy.us | www.state.wy.us | Day use $2 resident vehicle, $3 non-resident vehicle; camping $4 | Daily.

Wyoming Frontier Prison. Cold steel and concrete, the Death House, and the Yard are all part of the tour of the Wyoming Frontier Prison, which remained in use as the state's penitentiary until about two decades ago. Now you can tour it, perhaps on a special midnight or Halloween tour. | 5th and Walnut Sts. | 307/324–4422 | $4.25 | April–Sept., daily 8:30–5:30; other months by appt.

ON THE CALENDAR

FEB.: *Winterfest.* Come for the craft fair, carnival, and sporting events at the Rawlins Recreation Center. | 307/324–3411 or 800/228–3547.

MAR.: *Stars of Tomorrow Talent Show.* Local youth compete in a talent show at the Fine Arts Auditorium in Rawlins High School. | 307/324–7947.

JULY: *Carbon County Gathering of Cowboy Poets.* Cowboy poets gather at the Wyoming Frontier Prison to share stories of working cattle, cowdogs, and ranch life. Past headliners have included Waddie Mitchell. | 307/324–2251.

JULY: *Fiesta Days.* Events and activities recognize the area's Hispanic heritage. | 307/324–4111.

AUG.: *Carbon County Fair and Rodeo.* A traditional fair has livestock, crafts, food, a rodeo, country entertainers, and a parade. | 307/324–6866.

AUG.: *Old West Summerfest.* Entertainment and events take place at the Frontier Prison. | 307/324–4025.

OCT.: *Halloween Night Tours.* It's a frightening experience to tour the Wyoming Frontier Prison—known locally as the Old Pen—made even scarier on Halloween night. | 307/324–4422.

OCT.: *Oktoberfest Antiques and Collectibles Fair.* At the Jeffrey Center, you'll find dances and a beer garden as well as displays and sales of antiques and collectibles. | 307/324–4111.

DEC.: *Christmas in the Big House Craft Fair.* Arts and crafts are on display and for sale at the Frontier Prison. | 307/324–4422.

DEC.: *Holiday Art Fair.* Local and visiting artists and crafters display and sell their work. | 307/328–1988.

Dining

Hungry Miner. American. The Cottontree Inn houses this place with a quiet atmosphere and both tables and booths to relax in. The menu mainstays are steak, seafood, and chicken. Kids' menu. | 2300 W. Spruce St. | 307/324–2737 | fax 307/324–5011 | $12–$22 | AE, D, DC, MC, V.

The Pantry. American. The original rooms of a historic house provide a quiet setting for your meal, which may include homemade soup and bread. | 221 W. Cedar St. | 307/324–7860 | $12–$18 | D, MC, V.

Rose's Lariat. Mexican. You absolutely will not find better Mexican food in Wyoming than at Rose's, a tiny place that serves authentic meals. If you can't handle it hot and spicy, have a sandwich, hamburger, or one of the Italian dishes on the menu. | 410 E. Cedar St. | 307/324–5261 | $8–$12 | No credit cards | Closed Sun.–Mon.

Su Casa. Mexican. Rivaling Rose's Lariat for great Mexican foods is Su Casa, another small place, this one in Sinclair. The menu includes shrimp, beef, and chicken fajitas, green chili, enchiladas, and even Navajo tacos. Hamburgers are also on the menu. Try the enchiladas or the chiles rellenos. Take out available. | 705 E. Lincoln Ave., Sinclair | 307/328–1745 | Tues.–Sun. | $8–$15 | No credit cards.

Lodging

Bit o' Country Bed & Breakfast. This rose-colored mansion, built in 1903 and restored in 1992, sits on a shady street in the historic Sheep Hill district. Antiques-filled rooms and common areas, friendly hosts, and quiet afternoon lemonade breaks on the huge wrap-around porch are reminders of earlier times. Continental breakfast, dining room. No pets. | 221 W. Spruce St. | 307/328–2111 or 888/328–2111 | www.bbonline.com/wy/country/ | 2 rooms | $60 | MC, V.

Cottontree Inn. This is Rawlins's finest motel, with spacious guest rooms and inviting public areas where you'll find easy chairs to relax in. Restaurant, bar. In-room data ports. Cable TV. Indoor pool. Hot tub, sauna. Business services. Pets allowed. | 23rd and Spruce | 307/324–2737 | fax 307/324–5011 | cotton@trib.com | 122 rooms | $74 | AE, D, DC, MC, V.

Days Inn. On the east side of town near the junction of I–80 and U.S. 287, you'll find average-size, contemporary rooms, some equipped for the handicapped. Restaurant, bar, room service. In-room data ports. Cable TV. Pool. Laundry facilities. Business services. Pets allowed. | 2222 E. Cedar St. | 307/324–6615 | fax 307/324–6615 | 118 rooms | $66 | AE, D, DC, MC, V.

Sleep Inn. Next to I–80 at the Rip Griffin Truck Stop, this is a basic modern motel with some nice amenities and good rates. Complimentary Continental breakfast. In-room data ports. Cable TV. Sauna. Business services. | 1400 Higley Blvd. | 307/328–1732 | fax 307/328–0412 | 81 rooms, many with shower only | $59–$61 | AE, D, DC, MC, V.

Super 8. Modern, basic, and on the west side of town, this place has rooms equipped for the handicapped. Cable TV. Exercise equipment. Laundry facilities. | 47 rooms | 2338 Wagon Circle Rd. | 307/328–0630 | fax 307/328–1814 | AE, D, MC, V.

Weston Inn. At the eastern edge of town, off I–80, this standard motel has affordable rooms that come in a variety of sizes, and is a good place for stopovers. Continental breakfast, bar. Cable TV. Pool. Small pets allowed. | 1801 E. Cedar St. | 307/324–2783 | fax 307/328–1011 | 132 rooms | $54 | AE, D, DC, MC, V.

RIVERTON

MAP 9, E3

(Nearby towns also listed: Lander, Thermopolis)

Riverton calls itself the "Rendezvous City," and legitimately so. The 1830 and 1838 rendezvous of mountain men and traders occurred on the Wind River in what is now on the outskirts of town. The city was founded in August 1906, when the federal government opened to homesteading some lands within the boundaries of the Wind River Indian Reservation—the only Indian reservation in Wyoming, and one set aside for the Shoshone and Arapaho tribes. The original tent city went by the name Wadsworth, but the town later became Riverton owing to its proximity to four rivers.

Two "long-drag" business districts, both along U.S. 26, which makes a 90-degree turn in the heart of the community, characterize the city of 10,060. Riverton is also the home of Central Wyoming College. The town gets less wind than most spots in Wyoming and so attracts hot-air balloonists. The surrounding landscape is dominated by alfalfa fields and specialized crops like sunflowers.

Information: **Riverton Chamber of Commerce** | 1st and Main Sts., 82051 | 307/856–4801 or 800/325–2732 | fax 307/856–4802. **Wind River Visitors Council** | Box 1449, 82501 | 307/856–7566 or 800/645–6233 | info@wind-river.org | www.wind-river.org.

Attractions

Boysen State Park. Boysen Reservoir was created by a U.S. Bureau of Reclamation dam at the head of the Wind River Canyon. You can fish and boat, and the park has camping, boat-launch ramps, marinas, cabins, and trailer parks. | 15 Ash Boyen Rte | 307/876–2796 | fax 307/876–9305 | sphs@missc.state.wy.us | www.state.wy.us | Camping $4 | Daily.

Riverton Museum. A replica of an early school room, a general store, and a post office share space with local Native American artifacts. | 700 E. Park Ave. | 307/856–2665 | Free | Tues.– Sat. 10–4.

Yellowstone Drug Store. People drive for miles for a malt or a milk shake at the Yellowstone Drug Store in Shoshoni. The store is old-fashioned, with a traditional soda-fountain counter and gift items ranging from homemade products to boots and saddles. In 1998 they served 63,872 malts and shakes, with a one-day record of 662 malts on July 5. | 127 Main St. | 307/876–2539 | Daily 10–7.

TOUR

Rendezvous Trail/Castle Gardens Self-Guided Driving Tour. The Wind River Visitors Council has developed full-day driving tours in the Wind River Basin, including one that visits the site of the 1838 rendezvous and Castle Gardens, an Indian petroglyph site. The tour takes most of a day, and and you drive on both paved and dirt roads; in wet weather you may find it impossible to reach Castle Gardens. | Box 1449, Riverton | 307/856–7566 or 800/ 645–6233 | info@wind-river.org | www.wind-river.org.

ON THE CALENDAR

FEB.: *Wild West Winter Carnival.* Two weeks of events include tethered hot-air balloon rides, a "snodeo," and snow-cross races for snowmobilers, motorcycle, and ATV races on ice, ice sculpting, casino night, an ice-fishing derby, bowling and golf on ice, dances, a parade, and chariot races. | 800/325–2732 or 800/645–6233.
MAY: *State Championship Old-Time Fiddle Contest.* Wyoming's best fiddlers get together at Shoshoni High School to make the strings sing at this annual competition. | 800/325–2732 or 800/645–6233.
MAY–SEPT.: *Powwows.* Native Americans perform traditional dances at various venues through the spring and summer. | 800/325–2732 or 800/645–6233.
JULY: *1838 Mountain Man Rendezvous.* Black-powder shooting, tomahawk throwing, and even frying-pan throwing contests characterize this gathering of mountain men at Riverton's Rendezvous Grounds. There is a traders' fair where you can buy a buckskin dress or coonskin cap. | 307/856–7306, 800/325–2732, or 800/645–6233.
JULY: *Rendezvous Balloon Rally.* You can free-float or take a tethered ride over the city in a multi-colored balloon in this gathering of balloonists—the largest event of its kind in Wyoming and part of the month-long Riverton Rendezvous celebration. Other events include an antique car and bike show, demolition derbies, rodeos, dances, fireworks, and cowboy poetry. | 307/856–4285.
AUG.: *Fremont County Fair and Rodeo.* Young people exhibit livestock and crafts, and there's entertainment. | 800/325–2732 or 800/645–6233.
OCT.: *Wyoming Cowboy Poetry Roundup.* Wyoming's best cowboy poets (including cowgirls and even some from out-of-state) present their work, sharing stories of ranch life. | 800/325–2732 or 800/645–6233.

Dining

Broker Restaurant. American. Housed in the historic La Pere Hotel, this restaurant offers both atmosphere and fine food. The menu is strong on steak, seafood, and chicken. | 203 E. Main St. | 307/856–0555 | $15–$26 | AE, MC, V | Closed Sun.

The Depot. Mexican. A model train still runs on the tracks inside this turn-of-the-century train depot, home to one of Riverton's best Mexican restaurants. The homemade sauces make a difference—a green chili sauce spices up the beef and chicken chimichangas, and the popular chicken verde enchiladas are enhanced by a creamy white sauce. Finish with the flan or *helado,* ice cream with shaved Mexican chocolate, roasted almonds, and Kahlua. | 110 S. 1st St. | 307/856–2221 | $8–$12 | MC, V | Closed Sun.

Lodging

Holiday Inn. Blue, green, and mauve carpets and bedspreads furnish the rooms here, and the walls are hung with Western and Native American paintings. Restaurant, bar, room service. Cable TV. Indoor pool. Beauty salon, hot tub. Game room. Laundry facilities. Airport shuttle. Pets allowed. | 900 E. Sunset | 307/856–8100 | fax 307/856–0266 | 121 rooms | $69–$89 | AE, D, DC, MC, V.

Roomers. This quaint motor inn is housed in an older, restored brick building on Riverton's main thoroughfare. The Early American–style rooms, although smaller than average, are filled with personal touches like quilts, extra pillows, and wallpaper borders. Most rooms have refrigerators and microwaves. Cable TV. Pets allowed (fee). | 319 N. Federal Blvd. | 307/857–1735 or 888/857–4097 | 13 rooms | $35–$40 | AE, D, DC, MC, V.

Sundowner Station. The furnishings are modern and the rooms of average size, but this hotel strives for a home away from home style. The courtyard and waterfall are soothing, and shopping centers are close on the east side of the city. Restaurant, bar. Cable TV. Sauna. Airport shuttle. Pets allowed. | 1616 N. Federal | 307/856–6503 or 800/874–1116 | fax 307/856–6503 | 60 rooms | $55–$60 | AE, D, DC, MC, V.

ROCK SPRINGS

(Nearby town also listed: Green River)

Coal mining has always defined the community of Rock Springs, established when the Union Pacific Railroad pushed through in the late 1860s. Coal mining started soon after the railroad arrived, and mines remain open in the region. Early miners worked in underground operations. When the white workers struck for higher pay in the early 1880s, the railroad imported Chinese. Tensions rose, even though the initial strike was resolved. But in 1885 the white miners revolted, attacking and killing some of their Chinese co-workers. Eventually most of the Chinese were forced to leave their jobs and their homes in the Rock Springs area. Other immigrant miners eventually moved into the community to dig coal for the Union Pacific Railroad, which used it to power trains and to sell to utility companies.

Sprawled at the base of White Mountain, Rock Springs has long struggled to soften its image. The town of 24,000 is now the site of Western Wyoming Community College, a facility known for its paleontological resources.

Information: Rock Springs Chamber of Commerce | Box 398, 82902 | 307/362–3771 or 800/463–8637.

Attractions

Flaming Gorge National Recreation Area. *See* Green River.

Western Wyoming Community College Natural History Museum. Dinosaurs are among the prehistoric animal and plant specimens on display, ranging from 180 million to 67 million years old. | 2500 College Dr. | 307/382–1600 | Free | Daily 8–7; self-guided tours available.

ON THE CALENDAR

MAY–AUG.: *Stock Car Races.* Races are held weekly at the Rock Springs Speedway. | 307/362–3771 or 800/463–8637.
JULY: *Red Desert Round-Up.* Traditional rodeo events range from barrel racing and calf roping to bull riding, all at the Sweetwater County Fairgrounds. | 307/362–3771 or 800/463–8637.

AUG.: *Great Wyoming Polka and Heritage Festival.* At the Sweetwater County Fairgrounds, polka bands provide music for listening and dancing; there are also food and exhibits. | 307/362–3771 or 800/463–8637.

NOV.: *Horse Show and Wagon Auction.* Horse and mule teams and wagons—ranging from stagecoaches and chuckwagons to Conestogas and even sleighs—are part of this annual sale at the Sweetwater County Fairgrounds. Cowboy collectibles and antiques are also sold. | 307/362–3771 or 800/463–8637.

NOV.: *Wasatch Gun Show.* Guns of all sorts are shown and sold at the county fairgrounds. | 307/362–3771 or 800/463–8637.

Dining

Sand's Cafe. Chinese. Specialties at this standard highway-side restaurant include the Sand's Singapore chow mein (chicken, beef, and vegetables served over noodles) and sweet and sour chicken. Fast and convenient for those just stopping in town to eat. | 1549 9th St. | 307/362–5633 | $5–$10 | MC, V.

Lodging

Comfort Inn. On the west side of the city, near the shopping mall and Western Wyoming Community College, this hostelry offers good amenities and varied furnishings. Complimentary Continental breakfast. In-room data ports. Cable TV. Pool. Hot tub. Exercise equipment. Playground. Laundry facilities. Business services. Pets allowed (fee). | 1670 Sunset Dr. | 307/382–9490 | fax 307/382–7333 | 103 rooms | $62–$68 | AE, D, DC, MC, V.

Days Inn. This standard chain motel is right off I–80 and hosts a bright lobby and breakfast nook area. Rooms have modern amenities, and an otherwise neutral color scheme is splashed with bright pinks, mauves, and teals. Continental breakfast. In-room data ports, microwave, refrigerator. Cable TV. Outdoor pool. Laundry facilities. Pets allowed. | 1545 Elk St. | 307/362–5646or 800/544–8313 | fax 307/382–9440 | www.daysinn.com | 107 rooms | $50–$70 | AE, D, DC, MC, V.

Elk Street Motel. An older mom-and-pop establishment, this eclectic motor inn is convenient to I–80 and has rooms with microwaves and refrigerators. The decor is Early American. Rates are affordable and the service is friendly and casual. Microwaves, refrigerators. Cable TV. Some pets allowed. | 1100 Elk St. | 307/362–3705 | 18 rooms | $36 | MC, V.

Holiday Inn. A good place for a convention, this hotel is on the west side of town near a shopping mall and I–80. Rooms have coffeemakers and two-line phones with modems. Convention facilities can handle up to 600 people. Restaurant, bar, room service. Cable TV. Indoor pool, wading pool. Hot tub. Laundry facilities. Business services. Airport shuttle. Pets allowed. | 1675 Sunset Dr. | 307/382–9200 | fax 307/362–1064 | 114 rooms | $75–$79 | AE, D, DC, MC, V.

Inn at Rock Springs. This establishment is near Western Wyoming Community College. The rooms are large, and the lobby is spacious. Restaurant, bar. In-room data ports, some minibars. Cable TV. Indoor pool. Hot tub. Game room. Business services. Airport shuttle. | 2518 Foothill Blvd. | 307/362–9600 or 800/442–9692 | fax 307/362–8846 | 150 rooms | $54–$75 | AE, D, DC, MC, V.

Ramada Limited. The basic rooms are decorated in soft tones in this hotel on the western side of the city. The rooms are large, and there is a lot of space outside for children to play in. Complimentary Continental breakfast. In-room data ports. Cable TV. Pool. Fitness center. Business services. Pets allowed. | 2717 Dewar Dr. | 307/362–1770 | fax 307/362–2830 | 130 rooms | $70–$75 | AE, D, DC, MC, V.

SARATOGA

(Nearby towns also listed: Encampment, Medicine Bow, Rawlins)

When Native Americans gathered at the hot mineral springs here they considered this ground neutral territory. The first settlers to claim homesteads and begin ranching in the area called the community Warm Springs, but in 1884 they wanted a new, more sophisticated name, so it became Saratoga, after Saratoga Springs, New York. And this small town has been trying to become more sophisticated ever since. In an agricultural area along the North Platte River, the town of 1,800 people has a lumber mill and a small, vibrant business district. Locals say this is "where the trout leap in Main Street," and there's some truth to that because the North Platte River runs right through town. The free hot mineral pool is open year-round, along with a commercial swimming pool open in summer. The Bridge Street business district got a facelift in 1998 and 1999 with new pavement, curbs and gutters, and—get this—heated sidewalks, which will make snow removal less of a chore during the cold winter.

Information: **Saratoga-Platte Valley Chamber of Commerce** | Box 1095, 82331 | 307/326–8855 | fax 307/326–8855.

Attractions

Saratoga Historical and Cultural Association Museum. The main museum building used to be the local railroad depot. You can now see displays about local history. A sheep wagon, a railroad car, and a small cabin are on the grounds. In summer, you can attend concerts and performances at a nearby gazebo. | 104 Constitution Ave. | 307/326–5511 | www.members.xoom.com/kaiken/welcome/ | $2; free on Mon. | Memorial Day–Labor Day, daily 1–5.

Saratoga Hobo Pool. Hot mineral water flows freely through this small pool in which people have soaked for generations. Initially, the hot springs attracted Native Americans, who considered it neutral ground. Since settlement in the 1880s, the community has promoted the pool for relaxation. | 201 S. River St. | Free | Daily.

Saratoga Lake. The fishing is almost always good on Saratoga Lake, where you can also boat in summer. In the winter it becomes a city of ice huts; you drill holes in the ice to fish for trout. | Saratoga Lake Rd. | 307/632–0761 | Free; $10 for power boats, $7 for non-power boats | Daily.

TOURS AND ADVENTURES

North Platte River Trips. The upper reach of the North Platte River—from the Colorado state line to Seminoe Reservoir—is a blue-ribbon trout fishery, the best of the best. You can also take a spectacular float, with everything from the Class V rapids of Northgate Canyon to scenic floating to choose from. | 307/326–8855.

Great Rocky Mountain Outfitters. Great Rocky Mountain Outfitters have been in the business here longer than anyone, and their guides know the river like the backs of their hands. Your choices go from scenic and fishing floats to exhilarating white-water rafting. They also have canoe and drift-boat rentals, a shuttle service, and multi-day lodging/floating/fishing packages. | 216 E. Walnut | 307/326–8570 | fax 307/326–5390 | GRMO@union-tel.com | www.grmo.com/main.html | Full-day trips, 2 people per boat, $325; ½-day trips, 2 people per boat, $225.

Medicine Bow Drifters. They do guided wild trout fishing on the North Platte and Encampment rivers. | 307/326–8802 | jdobson@union-tel.com | www.medbow.com/ | June–Oct.

Platte Valley Outfitters. Guided fishing and scenic or white-water floating trips on the North Platte River are custom designed for families or groups by this company 1 mi west of Saratoga on Bridge Rd. In winter they rent snowmobiles. | 112 S. 1st St. | 307/326–5750 | www.plattevalleyoutfitters.com | Float fishing trips $320 full-day, $220 half-day; scenic trips, $150 for three people, ½-day plus $50 per additional person; full-day white-water $280 per boat | May–Sept.

ON THE CALENDAR

JAN.: *Saratoga Lake Ice Fishing Derby.* Anglers compete for prizes in categories ranging from biggest fish to best ice hut. | 307/326–8855.

FEB.: *Donald Erickson Memorial Chariot Races.* Horses pulling chariots (small contraptions on two wheels) race down a ¼-mi track at the Buck Springs Arena. A draft-horse pull and mule races are also a part of the weekend event, which takes place 7 mi north of Saratoga. | 307/326–8855.

JULY: *River Festival and Rodeo.* Bet on which rubber duck will float fastest between two set points or attend a rodeo at this annual festival. | 307/326–8855.

JULY: *Saratoga Arts Festival.* Held over the Fourth of July weekend, events include music, art shows and sales, food, crafts, author readings, cowboy poetry, melodrama. | 307/326–8855.

AUG.: *Wyoming Microbrewery Competition.* Wyoming breweries compete for prizes. Brew tasting, food, music, all on Veteran's Island. | 307/326–8855.

Dining

Hotel Wolf. American. The Victorian elegance of the dining room at this downtown hotel is matched by the exceptional food. Prime rib is the specialty (with Wednesday deals in winter) but the teriyaki beef kebabs and chicken are also good. The Wolf burger is hard to beat, and they have daily lunch specials. If you prefer a smaller sandwich, ask for a half order. Salad bar. Kids' menu. | 101 E. Bridge Ave. | 307/326–5525 | $10–$19 | AE, MC, V | Closed Sun. in winter. No lunch Sun. in summer.

Lazy River Cantina. Mexican. Decent Mexican food is the order of the day in this small downtown restaurant that has a south-of-the-border interior to match. | 110 E. Bridge Ave. | 307/326–8472 | $7–$20 | MC, V.

Lollipops. American. This bright, old-fashioned ice-cream parlor at the center of town boasts wrought-iron chairs and tables and a soda fountain. Gourmet coffee and espresso drinks complement light fare like croissant sandwiches and omelettes, and the homemade ice cream is some of the best in town. | 107 E. Bridge St. | 307/326–5020 | $3–$10 | MC, V | Closed Jan.–Mar. No dinner.

Saratoga Inn. Contemporary. Candlelight, rich dark-wood furnishings, and Western style add to the elegance of the Saratoga Inn dining room. Entrées include beef, chicken, and seafood, with occasional barbecues and buffets. | E. Pic Pike Rd. | 307/326–5261 | $14–$25 | AE, DC, MC, V.

Lodging

Brush Creek Ranch. At this working cattle ranch you can help with livestock handling and branding or spend your time fly fishing private waters. Barbecues and barn dances keep things lively. Horseback riding. Fishing. Cross-country skiing, snowmobiling. Children's programs. | Star Rte. Box 10 | 307/327–5241 or 800/726–2499 | fax 307/327–5384 | kblumenthal@csn.net | www.brushcreek.com | 6 rooms in lodge, 5 cabins | $1,050 wk; 6–day fishing pkg, $2,000 double occupancy; 3–day fishing pkg., $1,175 double occupancy | MC, V | AP.

Far Out West Bed & Breakfast. The owners have lovingly decorated every room at this B&B, which is really more like a great Western lodge. Two rooms are in the main house. The Hole-in-the-Wall is a play room, and it's filled with toys, games, and books. Other rooms outside the main house sleep from two to six. Each has a bench by the front door, a place to remove hunting or fishing boots or to just sit outside and enjoy the quiet. The Hideout is a one-bedroom house with a full kitchen. Full complimentary breakfast. Spa (fee). Exercise equipment. Library. No smoking. | 304 N. 2nd St. | 307/326–5869 | fax 307/326–9864 | fowbnnb@union-tel.com | www.cruising-america.com/farout.html | 6 rooms | $95–$100 | No credit cards.

Hacienda Motel. A two-story adobe motor inn at the southern edge of Saratoga, this one has larger-than-average rooms and a lobby adorned with Native American crafts and blankets. Kitchenettes are available. In-room data ports. Cable TV. Pets allowed. | Rte. 130 S | 307/326–5751 | 32 rooms | $64 | AE, D, DC, MC, V.

Hotel Wolf. This downtown hotel, on the National Register of Historic Places, is well maintained. All rooms are on the second and third floors and are small, but all have Victorian charm. Some share bathrooms, and there is no elevator. The renovated downstairs dining room, bar, and lounge have Victorian furnishings, including antique oak tables, crystal chandeliers, and lacy drapes. Restaurant, bar. | 101 E. Bridge Ave. | 307/326–5525 | 5 rooms, 3 suites | $64–$85 | AE, D, MC, V.

Riviera Lodge. On the North Platte River and two blocks north of downtown businesses, shops, and restaurants, this standard motor inn sits in a shaded park. Some rooms have balconies that overlook the river, and condominiums come with full kitchens. Picnic area. Cable TV. Conference room. Pets allowed. | 104 E. Saratoga St. | 307/326–5651 | fax 307/326–5651 | 29 rooms, 2 condos | $42–$90, $150 condos | AE, D, MC, V.

Saratoga Inn. This is a rustic 1950s fishing, hunting, and golfing lodge that has been completely renovated. The classic Western style includes pole-frame beds, lush leather couches, and artwork that carries out the theme. On a nine-hole public golf course, you'll encounter cottonwoods, conifers, and the North Platte River. Restaurant, bar. Pool (mineral). Outdoor hot tubs, spa. 9-hole golf course. Horseback riding. Fishing. Cross-country skiing, snowmobiling. | E. Pic Pike Rd. | 307/326–5261 | fax 307/326–5109 | 50 rooms | $99–$299 | AE, DC, MC, V.

SHERIDAN

MAP 9, F1

(Nearby town also listed: Buffalo)

In 1882 John Loucks took a sheet of wrapping paper and on it drew a layout of the town of Sheridan, naming it after Gen. Philip Sheridan, one of the officers under whom Loucks had served in the Civil War. The first round of buildings—wood, with false fronts—gave way to brick and stone structures, many of which remain along Main Street. Those buildings now house businesses and are a part of a district recognized by the National Register of Historic Places in 1982.

Though the region was the territory of the Lakota and Cheyenne Indians until the mid-1800s, cattle ranchers have reigned since. Some of the first large herds of cattle in Wyoming were turned loose in the Sheridan area in the 1870s, and the area became a power center as members of the British nobility established ranches here. People who have ties to British royalty still live and ranch in the area, which is one reason Queen Elizabeth has visited the area and shopped in downtown Sheridan.

Cattleman John B. Kendrick, who later became Wyoming's governor, settled in this area, building a mansion and backing construction of numerous downtown buildings as well. The mansion is now a Wyoming state historic site known as Trail End—the name Kendrick gave it when he brought the first cattle to the area.

With a population of 25,000, Sheridan is known for its ranching heritage, its ropes, and its saddles. Cowboys from all across the country come here to order a custom-made saddle or select the rope with the best feel. Though there are several well-known saddlemakers in Sheridan, the ropes all come from King Ropes, a family-owned business in the heart of the Main Street business district.

Information: **Sheridan Chamber of Commerce** | Box 707, 82801 | 307/672–2485 or 800/453–3650 | fax 307/672–7321 | cvb@visitsheridan.com | www.sheridan.wyo.com.

Attractions

Big Horn Equestrian Center. In the 1880s, aristocratic cattle barons built Wyoming's first polo field. Many of them were "remittance men," possibly second sons or "blackhearts" who were paid to stay away from their homes. You can watch polo games on Sunday afternoon from May through September, and other occasional equestrian events include dressage competitions, steeplechase races, and steer roping. | 800/453–3650.

Bighorn National Forest. No region in Wyoming has a more diverse landscape—lush grasslands, alpine meadows, rugged mountaintops, canyons, and deserts. | 307/672–0751 | www.fs.fed.us/r2/bighorn/ | Camping fees in some locations $8–$14 | Daily.

Bradford Brinton Memorial. Once the Quarter Circle A Ranch, owned by Bradford Brinton, this is now a memorial to a family known for fine art collections and an elegant home. The displays include art by Charles M. Russell, Frederic Remington, and John James Audubon, among others. You'll also see antique furnishings, quilts, rare books, and other memorabilia. | 239 Brinton Rd., Big Horn | 307/672–3173 | $3 | May 15–Labor Day, 9:30–5.

King's Saddlery and Museum. Don King started making saddles decades ago, and he's been collecting saddles for just as long. His craft is on full display in this small downtown museum, along with other cowboy gear. The Saddlery itself is still in business, run by King's sons, and it has a tradition for making some of the finest saddles in the world, even crafting them for royalty. The Kings also make King Ropes, used by professional rodeo cowboys and ranchers. Hundreds of ropes (some of them in neon colors) fill racks at the back of the store, and you'll likely find one or more cowboys there trying them out. | 184 N. Main St. | 307/672–2702 or 800/443–8919 | Free | Mon.–Sat. 8–5.

Main Street Historic District. Historic buildings, most still used by businesses, line Main Street. You can get a pamphlet that maps a tour of structures from local businesses and the Chamber of Commerce. | 307/672–8881.

Trail End Historic Center. When John B. Kendrick brought the first cattle into this area, he established himself as one of the "elite" citizens. Kendrick became Wyoming's governor and a senator, and he lived in this elegant Flemish Revival home completed in 1913. The furnishings at the state historic site are authentic Kendrick items. | 400 Clarendon Ave. | 307/674–4589 | sphs@missc.state.wy.us | commerce.state.wy.us | Free | June–Aug., daily 9–6; Sept.–May, call for hours.

ON THE CALENDAR

JUNE–SEPT.: *Equestrian Events.* Polo games are held every Sunday afternoon, and other equestrian events, including dressage competitions, take place throughout the summer. | Sheridan Equestrian Center | 307/672–2485 or 800/453–3650.

JULY: *Sheridan-Wyo. PRCA Rodeo.* Rodeo events at the Sheridan County Fairgrounds range from steer wrestling to barrel racing, calf roping, and bull riding. | 307/672–2485 or 800/453–3650.

JULY–AUG.: *Concerts.* Free concerts are held every Tuesday evening in Kendrick Park. | 307/672–2485 or 800/453–3650.

AUG.: *Sheridan County Rodeo and Fair.* Youth projects including livestock and crafts are displayed at the fair, which also has entertainment. | 307/672–2485 or 800/453–3650.

SEPT.: *Don King Days.* Featuring Old West activities and rodeo events, this Labor Day celebration at the county fairgrounds honors the best-known saddlemaker in Sheridan. | 307/672–2485 or 800/453–3650.

Dining

Ciao Bistro. Continental. Nine tables are squeezed into this European-style café's cramped downtown quarters. The menu is full of such tempting choices as lamb shank, Chilean sea bass, and horseradish-crusted halibut fillet. | 120 N. Main St. | 307/672–2838 | $10–$30 | MC, V.

Gourmet Galley. American. Despite the name, this restaurant housed in a large log building is best known for basics: steak, chicken, and seafood. You can eat on the large deck that looks out over nearby mountains. Entertainment. Kids' menu. | 850 Sibley Cir | 307/674–5049 | Reservations accepted | $7–$15 | AE, D, DC, MC, V | Closed Sun.

Sanford's Grub, Pub, Brewery. American. The name pretty much says it all. This is a noisy place that caters to the college crowd, but the sandwiches are good and the brews equally so. Particularly popular is the Big Horn Wheat brew. Burgers, steaks, and pasta are also on the menu. | 1 E. Alger Ave. | 307/674–1722 | $6–$18.

Silver Spur. American. You might have to look twice. First to find this downtown breakfast-and-lunch place, and then to decide to go in. It's small and undistinguished, but the helpings are cowboy-size, and the omelettes are well prepared. | 832 N. Main St. | 307/672–2749 | $6–$15 | No credit cards.

Sugarland Restaurant at the Holiday Inn. American. Quiet atmosphere and a diverse menu make this a good choice for dining out. Menu favorites are the beef, seafood, and pasta dishes. Salad bar. Kids' menu | 1809 Sugarland Dr. | 307/672–8931 | $16–$30 | AE, D, DC, MC, V.

Lodging

Best Western Sheridan Center Motor Inn. Just two blocks from the main downtown area—and with a covered walkway over the main street—this is a convenient place to stay. The indoor pool is welcome in winter. Restaurant, bar. Cable TV. 2 pools (1 indoor). Hot tub. Game room. Airport shuttle. | 612 N. Main St. | 307/674–7421 | fax 307/672–3018 | 138 rooms | $80–$82 | AE, D, DC, MC, V.

Big Horn Mountain KOA Campground. This pleasant, shady, and relatively peaceful campground 3½ mi from Sheridan makes roughing it easy with numerous amenities and extras like mini-golf, basketball courts, fishing, and an on-site snack bar. A convenient stopover point for those going on to Yellowstone, it also has five cabins that sleep four or five people and a bunkhouse that sleeps up to eight. Pool. Hot tub, sauna. Playground. Laundry facilities. | 63 Decker Rd. | 307/674–8766 or 800/562–7621 | www.koa.com | 40 tent sites, 100 trailer slots, 5 cabins, 1 bunkhouse | $15 tent site, $19–$22 RV site, $28–$32 cabin | D, MC, V | Closed early Oct.–Mar.

Days Inn. This 1994 hotel is just one block west of I–90 and close to shopping and restaurants. The family rooms have three queen-size beds, and you can also request a room with a Jacuzzi. Complimentary Continental breakfast. Cable TV. Indoor pool. Hot tub. Laundry facilities. | 1104 Brundage La. | 307/672–2888 | fax 307/672–2888. | 46 rooms | $88–$110 | AE, D, DC, MC, V.

Holiday Inn. Five minutes from downtown Sheridan, this hotel is decorated in Western style throughout. The lobby has a four-story atrium with a waterfall and lots of plants. Raquet ball courts are a nice extra. Restaurant, bar, picnic area, room service. In-room data ports, some refrigerators. Cable TV. Indoor pool. Beauty salon, hot tub. Putting green. Exercise equipment. Laundry facilities. Business services. Airport shuttles. Pets allowed. | 1809 Sugarland Dr. | 307/672–8931 | fax 307/672–6388 | 212 rooms | $79–$119 | AE, D, DC, MC, V.

Mill Inn Motel. An old mill by a bridge is incorporated into this motel, which has large guest rooms with pastel spreads, drapes, and rugs. The offices of *American Cowboy* magazine are upstairs, and the walls in the lobby and breakfast room are decorated with Western art prints, boots, saddles, and the like. Complimentary Continental breakfast. Gym. Pets allowed. | 2161 Coffeen Ave. | 307/672–6401 | 45 rooms | $72–$102 | AE, D, MC, V.

Ranch Willow Bed & Breakfast. Built in 1901, this lovely all-stone guest ranch sits on 550 acres of rolling farm land, and is surrounded by huge cottonwood and apple trees. Your hosts include an internationally known furniture-maker who appoints the elegant but homey Western-style rooms and common areas with her unique pieces, and a third-generation Basque sheep farmer, who knows the area inside and out. Great if you want restful and quiet surroundings. The entire guest house is available for larger groups. Continental breakfast, dining room. Some shared bathrooms, no phones or TVs in rooms. Hot tub. | 501 U.S. 14E | 307/674–1510 or 800/354–2830 | fax 307/674–1502 | 4 rooms | $85–$90 room, $270 entire house; 3–night minimum | MC, V.

Spahn's Bighorn Mountain. Bobbie and Ron Spahn have rooms and cabins at their log home 15 mi west of Sheridan. The rooms have tongue-and-groove woodwork and peeled-log beams. You get more than at a traditional B&B: horseback riding, cookouts, and guided tours, including a "moose safari." Full breakfasts are provided; other meals by arrangement. Complimentary breakfast. No air-conditioning, no room phones. Horseback riding. No smoking. | Box 579, Big Horn | 307/674–8150 | fax 307/674–8150 | spahnbb@wave.sheridan.wy.us | wave.sheridan.wy.us/~spahnbb | 2 rooms, 2 cabins | $110–$140 | No credit cards.

SUNDANCE

(Nearby town also listed: Gillette)

Native Americans gathered annually in June for their Sun Dance, a ceremonial gathering akin to a religious rite. The event gave its name to the small town situated just to the northeast of Sundance Mountain and south of the Bear Lodge Mountains. Both sites are sacred to Native Americans, including members of the Crow and Lakota tribes. It's true that outlaw Harry Longabaugh, better known as the Sundance Kid, spent time in the Sundance jail. This town of 1,100, which had an Air Force installation during the 1950s, is surrounded by ranch country and the western portion of the Black Hills.

Information: Sundance Chamber of Commerce | Box 1004, 82729 | 307/283–1000 | fax 307/283–2440.

SUNDANCE

INTRO
ATTRACTIONS
DINING
LODGING

Attractions
Devils Tower National Monument. *See* Gillette, *above..*

Vore Buffalo Jump. Thousands of buffalo bones are piled atop each other at the Vore Buffalo Jump on Frontage Rd., where Native Americans forced buffalo to fall to their deaths in the era when hunting was done with spears rather than fast horses and guns. | 307/283–1000.

ON THE CALENDAR
AUG.: *Crook County Fair and Rodeo.* Projects by local young people are displayed at the Crook County Fairgrounds, from cooking and clothing to livestock projects, with entertainment. | 307/383–1000.

Dining
Aro Restaurant and Lounge. American. This large family diner in downtown Sundance has a cowboys-and-Indians theme and an extensive, well-priced menu. Standards include burgers, prime rib, southwestern smothered burritos, Reuben sandwiches, and a huge Devils Tower brownie sundae dessert. | 205 Cleveland St. | 307/283–2000 | $6–$15 | D, MC, V.

Country Cottage. American. This one-stop shop in the center of town sells flowers, gifts, and simple meals, including submarine sandwiches. | 423 Cleveland St. | 307/283–2450 | $6–$13 | MC, V.

Log Cabin Cafe. American. Locals crowd this small log-cabin restaurant 3 mi from town and full of country crafts for burgers, steaks, and seafood. | U.S. 14 | 307/283–3393 | $3.25–$12 | MC, V.

Lodging

Bear Lodge Motel. This downtown motel has a cozy lobby with a stone fireplace and wildlife mounts on the walls. Hot tub. | 218 Cleveland St. | 307/283–1611 | fax 307/283–2537 | 33 rooms | $64 | AE, D, DC, MC, V.

Best Western Inn at Sundance. Built in 1997, this place has spacious rooms with dark-green carpet and plum-color drapes. Indoor pool. Hot tub. Laundry facilities. | 2719 E. Cleveland St. | 307/283–2800 or 800/238–0965 | fax 307/283–2727 | bestwestern@vcn.com | 44 rooms | $44–$109 | AE, D, DC, MC, V.

Sundance Mountain Inn. This one-story ranch-style motor inn is convenient to I–90 and across the street from area restaurants. Clean, basic rooms, friendly service, and a comfortable poolside area make this a nice place to stay. Continental breakfast. Cable TV. Indoor pool. Hot tub. Laundry facilities. Pets allowed. | 26 Rte. 585 | 307/283–3737 or 888/347–2794 | fax 307/283–3738 | www.sundancewyoming.com/sundancemountaininn.htm | 42 rooms | $79–$89 | AE, D, MC, V.

TETON VILLAGE

MAP 9, B3

(Nearby town also listed: Jackson)

Not any type of incorporated city or town, Teton Village is nevertheless a community that resounds with the sound of clomping ski boots in the winter and the violins, horns, and other instruments of the Grand Teton Music Festival in the summer. The town is made up mostly of the facilities needed to operate the Jackson Hole Ski Resort—a tramway, gondola, and various other lifts, but also has lodging facilities, restaurants, and shops selling everything from snowboards and skis to backpacks and clothing.

Information: **Jackson Chamber of Commerce** | Box E, Jackson 83001 | 307/733–3316 | fax 307/733–5585.

Attractions

Aerial Tramway. Panoramas of Jackson Hole are possible from the aerial tramway that serves skiers in winter at Jackson Hole Mountain Ski Resort. | 307/733–2292 | $15 | Memorial Day–mid-Sept. | www.jacksonhole.com/.

★ **Jackson Hole Mountain Ski Resort.** Jackson's biggest ski resort is known for its 402 inches of powder annually. Snowboarders and skiers both like the scary steeps and vast terrain; at more than 4,000 ft, this is the longest vertical rise in the United States. You can attend camps taught by such pros as Olympic champion Tommy Moe, plus ski and snowboard schools. Of the 22 mi of machine-groomed terrain, 10 percent is beginner, 40 percent intermediate, and 50 percent advanced/expert. A day-care facility opened in 1999. | 307/733–2292, snow reports at 307/733–2291 or 888/333–7766 | info@jacksonhole.com | www.jacksonhole.com/ski | $51 | Dec.–early Apr., daily 9–4.

Two-Can Fly Paragliding. Launch off the 10,450 ft top of Rendezvous Mountain and prepare yourself for a gentle, ½-hr ride along the longest continuous vertical face in the U.S., which offers incredible views of the Teton Mountains and across the Jackson Hole Valley. The fee includes fare up the resort's aerial tramway and a flight instructor, who sits behind you for the flight. | 307/739–2626 | $195 per flight | Late May–late Sept.; flights daily at 8:30 and 10 AM.

ON THE CALENDAR

FEB.: *Cowboy Ski Challenge.* Western music, novelty ski races, a rodeo, a dutch-oven cook-off, cowboy poetry, and a barn dance are part of the activities at this annual winter event. | 307/739–2770.

DEC.–JAN.: *Torchlight Parade.* Ring in Christmas and the New Year at the torchlight parade and fireworks displays. | 307/739–2770.

Dining

Alpenhof. Continental. Etched glass, wood beams, and lots of greenery complete an elegant Bavarian motif at this après-ski place at the base of the Jackson Hole ski area. This is a quiet, elegant place to have a meal after enjoying the slopes. The menu favorites are wild game and local fish. The upstairs Bistro is more relaxed, less expensive, and noisier. Open-air dining. Kids' menu. No smoking. | 3255 W. McCollister Dr. | 307/733–3462 | Reservations accepted | $8–$35 | AE, D, DC, MC, V | Closed early Apr.–mid-May and mid-Oct.–early Dec.

Mangy Moose. American. Folks pour in off the ski slopes for a lot of food and talk at this two-level restaurant plus bar with an outdoor deck. Antiques and oddities abound, including a full-size stuffed caribou suspended from the ceiling complete with a sleigh. The noise level is high, but you get decent fare at fair prices and a chance to try the house Moose Brew beer. Beef dominates the menu, though you can also get buffalo meat loaf. Kids' menu. | 307/733–4913 | $11–$30 | AE, MC, V.

Nick Wilson's Cowboy Cafe. American. At the base of Jackson Hole Mountain, people come to this rustic lodge-style café more for the mountain views, congeniality, and convenience than for the basic burgers and sandwiches. You can also practice on a climbing wall, fish in a pond, or sign up for various resort activities. In the summer, tables are moved to the huge outdoor deck, where standards like cheeseburgers, turkey melts, and Philly cheese steak sandwiches are grilled. | 307/739–2626 | $5–$10 | AE, D, DC, MC, V | Closed April–May, late-Sept.–late-Nov.

Lodging

Alpenhof. This small Austrian-style hotel is in the heart of the Jackson Hole Ski Resort next to the tram. The deluxe rooms have hand-carved alpine furniture and cream-colored walls. Standard rooms are smaller. Restaurant, bar, room service. No air-conditioning. Cable TV. Pool. Hot tub. Cross-country and downhill skiing. Laundry facilities. | 3325 McCollister Dr. | 307/733–3242 or 800/732–3244 (outside WY) | fax 307/739–1516 | alpenhof@sisna.com | www.jacksonhole.com/alpenhof | 43 rooms | $128–$338 | AE, D, DC, MC, V | Closed mid-Oct.–Nov. and Apr.–mid-May.

Best Western Inn at Jackson Hole. You're literally at the base of the ski hill when you stay here. The rooms and family suites all have rustic furnishings and fireplaces, and some have kitchenettes. Restaurant, bar, room service. Cable TV. Pool. 3 hot tubs. Cross-country and downhill skiing. Laundry facilities. | 3345 W. McCollister Dr. | 307/733–2311 | fax 307/733–0844 | 1030346@compuserve.com | 83 rooms, 4 with air-conditioning, 30 with kitchenettes, 11 suites | $89–$199 | AE, D, DC, MC, V.

The Hostel. Although the classic hostel-style accommodations at this lodge-style inn are basic, you can't get closer to the Jackson Hole Ski Resort for a better price. Rooms that sleep four have two twin beds and a bunk bed, and some two-person rooms with king-size beds are available. Popular with young, budget-conscious people, downstairs common areas include a lounge with fireplace, movie room, Internet room, and a ski waxing room. Picnic area. No in-room phones. TV and VCR in common area. Recreation room, library. Laundry facilities. | Box 546, Teton Village | 307/733–3415 | fax 307/739–1142 | www.hostelx.com | 55 rooms | $45–$48 | MC, V.

R Lazy S Ranch. One of the largest, most tried-and-true dude ranches in the Jackson area, this spread, on 325 acres, is bordered by Grand Teton National Park and the Snake River, 1 mi north of Teton Village. All meals are served in the comfortable main lodge and are prepared by a gourmet cook. You stay in individually decorated log cabins, which come in varying sizes. You get riding instruction and half- or full-day riding trips to lakes and mountains, plus overnight pack trips. Full breakfast, dining room, picnic area. No in-room phones, no TVs. | 7800 N. Moose–Wilson Rd. | 307/733–2655; winter, 435/628–6546 for reservations |

TETON VILLAGE

INTRO
ATTRACTIONS
DINING
LODGING

fax 307/734–1120 | www.rlazys.com | 14 cabins | $1,057–$1,435 wk per person (1 wk minimum stay, Sun.–Sun.) | No credit cards.

Resort Hotel at Jackson Hole. Located at the base of Jackson Hole ski area, this hotel is richly decorated in Western style and has a massive stone fireplace in the lobby with large leather chairs. You can ski right from the ski lifts to the private heated walkway. Restaurant, bar. In-room data ports. Pool. Hot tubs, spa. Hiking. Ice-skating. Downhill skiing, ski shop. Convention center. Airport shuttle. | 307/733–3657 | fax 307/733–9543 | jacksonhole@compuserve.com | www.resorthotelatjh.com | 101 rooms | $129–$249 | AE, D, DC, MC, V.

Teton Pines. Teton Village is 7 mi from this convenient and quiet resort, with its own Arnold Palmer–designed 18-hole golf course. The remodeled master bedrooms are spacious and comfortable, and you can also get living room suites. Restaurant, complimentary Continental breakfast, room service. In-room data ports, microwaves, refrigerators. Cable TV. Pool. Hot tub. Driving range, 18-hole golf course, putting green, tennis. Cross-country and downhill skiing. Business services. | Off Teton Village Rd. | 307/733–1005 or 800/238–2223 | fax 307/733–2860 | info@tetonpines.com | www.tetonpines.com | 16 rooms, some with living rooms, 2 3-bedroom townhouses | $325–$450 | AE, DC, MC, V.

THERMOPOLIS

MAP 9, E3

(Nearby town also listed: Riverton)

The city's claim to fame is its mineral hot springs. The area was considered neutral territory by the Native Americans—particularly the Shoshones, who ceded the ground to the government in 1904 in a "gift of the waters." Thermopolis originally started as a replacement to Andersonville when that community dwindled. First called Old Town Thermopolis, it came to be known by the shorter name as people began to promote the beneficial properties of the mineral waters. Hot Springs State Park is now within the town of 3,200, and the Wyoming State Bathhouse is free for those wishing to enjoy the water. When the Shoshones presented the land they did so with the stipulation that the springs should remain available for the free use of all people. You can also use the commercial swimming pools with water slides and soaking pools in the park.

Information: **Thermopolis Chamber of Commerce** | Box 768, 82443 | 307/864–3192 or 800/577–3555 | fax 307/864–3192 | www.thermopolis.com.

Attractions

Boysen State Park. *See* Riverton, *above.* | U.S. 20 | www.state.wy.us/.

Hot Springs County Museum and Cultural Center. Local historical items are on display here. | 700 Broadway | 307/864–5183 | Free | Tues.–Sun.

Hot Springs State Park. You can hike and bike on the trails, watch a buffalo herd, and try the hot mineral springs, either the free ones at the Wyoming State Bathhouse or commercial facilities. Next to the Bighorn River, the park is a quiet place for a picnic. | U.S. 20 | 307/864–2176 or 307/864–3765 (State Bath House) | fax 307/864–3419 | www.state.wy.us | sphs@missc.state.wy.us | Park and bathhouse free; admission charged at commercial pools | Daily.

Old West Wax Museum. Lifelike wax figures of famous and infamous local legends are on display at this eclectic small-town museum. There's one of Cattle Kate, a local cattle rustler, next to a noose, and one of a Native American Indian bison hunt. Downstairs, the Dancing Bear Folk Center (included in the admission price) houses a textile studio, where working looms and quilting blocks are set up; a hands-on exhibit allows you to participate in the making of a mass quilt. Rotating local arts exhibits are also on display, and there is a room dedicated to antique teddy bears. | 119 S. 6th St. | 307/864–9396 | $4.50 | Mid-May–mid-Sept., daily 9–7; Oct.–Apr., weekends 10–5; call for weekday hours.

Wind River Canyon. The granite walls soar nearly straight up in places as the Bighorn River cuts through the canyon. The railroad runs on one side of the river and the highway on the other. | U.S. 20.

Wyoming Dinosaur Center. View dinosaur remains—including "Stan," the second-largest and most complete Tyrannosaurus rex in the world—and artifacts, or dig for yourself at the dinosaur quarry. Learn where to look for dinosaur tracks (there is a track site in the Bighorn Basin 4 mi west of Shell or 8 mi east of Greybull on the Red Gulch Byway). Regular digs scheduled for kids ages 8–13 and ages 13–17. | 110 Carter Ranch Rd. | 307/864–2997 | fax 307/864–5762 | www.thermopwy.net/bhbf/ | $6; dig tours $18 | May 15–Sept. 14, daily 8–8; Sept. 15–May 14, daily 10–4; dig tours 10–4, weather permitting.

ON THE CALENDAR
AUG.: *Gift of the Waters Pageant.* The program, held in Hot Springs State Park, is a re-creation of Shoshone Chief Washakie's ceding the land around the mineral springs to the federal government. | 307/864–3192.
AUG.: *Lions Club Ranch Rodeo.* Ranch hands compete at the fairgrounds in a variety of events from "doctoring" animals to roping, cutting, and penning as they demonstrate skills used daily on ranches. | 307/864–3192.
AUG.: *Outlaw Trail Ride.* Cowboys and cowgirls saddle up for a multiday ride into "outlaw country"— Hole-in-the-Wall. | 307/864–3192.

Dining
Legion Supper Club. American. With a lush view of the adjacent Legion Golf Course, you can often spot wildlife at this elegant restaurant. The specials include seafood-stuffed mushrooms, chicken Tetrazzini, shrimp scampi, filet mignon, and porterhouse steaks. Portions are good, and the popular Holy Hunk of carrot cake feeds two or more. | Airport Hill Rd. | 307/864–3918 | $20–$35 | AE, D, DC, MC, V | Closed Mon.

Safari Dining Room. American. Like a safari hunting lodge, this restaurant in the Holiday Inn of the Waters displays wildlife mounts from around the world. The menu includes great prime rib, steaks, and buffalo. Salad bar. Breakfast buffet. Kids' menu. Sun. brunch. | Hot Springs State Park | 307/864–3131 | $15–$28 | AE, D, DC, MC, V.

Lodging
Holiday Inn of the Waters. The rooms are standard here, but the extra amenities and proximity to the mineral springs set it apart. You can soak year-round in the outdoor mineral hot tub and swim in the pool in summer. A complete health club is nearby, as well as a hiking and jogging trail and a water slide. Special winter lodging-meal-activity packages. Restaurant, bar, room service. In-room data ports, no-smoking rooms. Pool (summer). Outdoor hot tub, massage, sauna, spa, steam room. Health club. Hiking. Laundry service. Pets allowed. | Hot Springs State Park | 307/864–3131 | 80 rooms | $99 | AE, D, DC, MC, V.

Quality Inns & Suites–Plaza Hotel. Renovated and re-opened in 1999, the historic all-brick Plaza Hotel in Hot Springs State Park is now operated by the familiar chain. Comfortable and airy rooms have handcrafted lodgepole furniture and southwestern-style bedspreads, and the two-room suites come with microwaves and refrigerators. You're surrounded by the park and have direct access to the mineral waters. Continental breakfast. In-room data ports. Outdoor pool, hot tub. Conference room. No pets allowed. | 116 E. Park St. | 307/864–2939 or 888/919–9009 | fax 307/864–2927 | hotsprings@wyoming.com | www.qualityinn.com | $110 | AE, D, DC, MC, V.

Super 8. You can park your RV in the large parking area at this new motel at the south edge of town. The single and double rooms and the suite have standard contemporary furnishings. The lobby area is pleasant, with marble floor and a fireplace. No-smoking rooms. Cable TV. Indoor pool. Hot tub. Laundry facilities. | 175 Lane 5, Rte. 20 S | 307/864–5515 | fax 307/864–5447 | www.thermop-super8.com | 52 rooms, 1 suite | $74–$88 | AE, D, DC, MC, V.

TORRINGTON

(Nearby town also listed: Fort Laramie)

Sugar beets and other crops, as well as an active livestock auction, account for Torring-ton's reputation as an agricultural and ranching center, though the community of 5,000 is also home to Eastern Wyoming College.

Torrington is the nearest large town to Fort Laramie National Historic Site, the oldest permanent white community in Wyoming. A compound, known as Fort William, was first established at Laramie as a fur-trading post in 1834 by Robert Campbell and William Sublette. It later evolved into Fort John and eventually became Fort Laramie. Until 1849 the site was privately owned, but then the U.S. Army acquired it as a post for troops assigned to protect travelers on the Oregon-California-Mormon Trail.

Fort Laramie was the most important post in the entire region that now includes Wyoming, portions of Colorado, Nebraska, South Dakota, and Montana. Not only was it a supply point for travelers headed into those parts, it also became important for military operations. Troops headed into the Powder River Basin during the First Sioux War or Red Cloud's War of 1866–68 were generally routed through Fort Laramie. An 1851 treaty with the various Indian tribes that gave white travelers the right to cross Indian lands as they headed toward California and Oregon, and another in 1868, in which the Sioux and other tribes ceded portions of their tribal lands, were both nego-tiated at Fort Laramie.

In 1875, when troops under Lt. Col. George Armstrong Custer located gold in the Black Hills, one soldier rode to Fort Laramie with the news. This set off a chain of events that led to the Second Sioux War or Crazy's Horse's War. That confrontation culminated in the death of Custer and his entire command at the Battle of the Little Bighorn in 1876, and the eventual resettlement of Plains Indians onto reservations.

The history of Fort Laramie is one of fur traders and trappers, overland emigrants, the military, and Native Americans. At the fort, which is now a national historic site, stands the oldest extant building in Wyoming, Old Bedlam.

The military abandoned Fort Laramie in 1890, and the buildings were sold to area farmers and homesteaders. In 1937 the State of Wyoming obtained the property and its remaining structures. A year later the state transferred the site to the National Park Service, which designated it as Fort Laramie National Historic Site.

Information: **Torrington Chamber of Commerce** | 350 W. 21st Ave., 82240 | 307/532–3879 or 800/577–3555 | fax 307/534–2360. **Fort Laramie National Historic Site** | 307/837–2221 | fax 307/837–2120 | www.nps.gov/fola/.

Attractions

Fort Laramie National Historic Site. Near the confluence of the Laramie and North Platte rivers, the fort includes some of the oldest buildings in Wyoming. Costumed interpreters help depict life at a frontier military post, and archaeological excavations are usually underway. The fort interprets four basic Western history themes: frontier military, over-land migration, Native American relations, and the fur trade. | 307/837–2221 | fax 307/837–2120 | www.nps.gov/fola/ | $2 | Daily 8–dusk; visitors center 8–5; Golden Eagle, Golden Age, Golden Access passports accepted.

Homesteader's Museum. Local history displays are the highlight here. | 495 Main St. | 307/532–5612.

Western History Center. Archaeological exhibits are displayed. | 265 Main St. | 307/837–3052 | Tues.–Sun. and by appointment.

JAN.: *Shrine Cutter Races.* Chariot races involves horses pulling small chariots (2-wheeled contraptions) or cutters (small sleighs) down a ¼-mi track on Airport Hill. | 307/532–3879.

AUG.: *Goshen County Fair and Rodeo.* A competition among young people who exhibit their livestock and other projects at the Goshen County Fairgrounds. | 307/532–3879.

SEPT.: *Septemberfest.* This German festival has polka dancing and German-style food. | 307/532–3879.

Dining

Jose Posanos. Eclectic. Locals say this family restaurant has very good Mexican food as well as pizza, pasta, and burgers. Kids' menu. | 1918 Main St. | 308/532–4822 | $8–$18 | MC, V.

Liras. Mexican. Some of the best Mexican food in this part of Wyoming is served in this small restaurant. | Connelly and U.S. 26 N | 307/837–2826 | $12–$17 | V | Closed Mon. No dinner Sun.

Little Moon Lake Supper Club. American. This peaceful fine dining establishment 8 mi east of Torrington, on the Wyoming-Nebraska state line, overlooks a small lake. The interior displays Sioux Indian blankets, hides, and artifacts. The specialties include homemade onion rings, prime rib, rib-eye steak, king crab, and fresh breaded jumbo shrimp. A screened patio filled with large plants offers a lovely setting in the summer. | 316 E. U.S. 26 | 307/532–5750 | $10–$20 | MC, V | Closed Sun.

Lodging

Kings Inn. Convenient to downtown, this is a good stopping point for exploring area attractions. Restaurant, bar. Indoor pool. Spa. Cable TV. | 1555 S. Main St. | 307/532–4011 | 54 rooms | $50–$100 | D, MC, V.

The Maverick. The first motel on the western edge of town, this 1950s-style single-level motor inn has some rooms with kitchenettes and reasonable rates. Cable TV. | U.S. 26 W | 307/532–4064 | fax 307/532–2577 | 10 rooms, 3 kitchenettes | $36, $50 kitchenettes | AE, D, MC, V.

Super 8. Near downtown, this is a modest, modern hotel with some nice extras, such as in-room modem lines and RV parking. Cable TV. | 1548 S. Main St. (U.S. 85) | 307/532–7118 | fax 307/532–7118 | 56 rooms | $45 | AE, D, DC, MC, V.

WHEATLAND

MAP 9, H5

(Nearby towns also listed: Cheyenne, Torrington)

Farming, cattle ranching, and a major power plant dominate the Wheatland area, which in the 1870s was the center of one of the largest cattle empires in the West—the Swan Land and Cattle Company. That operation, owned by Alexander Swan, extended from near Ogallala, Nebraska, to near Baggs, Wyoming—a distance of more than 250 mi. On the Swan, cowboys herded thousands of head of cattle brought north on cattle trails from Texas.

The Swan was one of the first ranches in the state to begin importing blooded breeding stock—primarily Herefords—and it was the original home of the famous black bucking horse, Steamboat. Named one of the five best bucking horses of all time by the National Cowboy Hall of Fame, Steamboat was immortalized on the University of Wyoming football helmet and is widely believed to be the horse used as a model for the Wyoming bucking horse on the license plate. The town now has a population of 8,000.

Information: Platte County Chamber of Commerce | Box 427, 82201 | 307/322–2322 | www.plattechamber.com.

Attractions

Glendo State Park. You can boat and waterski here, and try other water sports as well. The park has a marina, day-use areas, and campsites. | 397 Glendo Park Rd. | 307/735–4433 or 307/735–4216 (marina information) | fax 307/735–4662 | sphs@missc.state.wy.us | www.state.wy.us | $2 resident vehicle, $5 nonresident vehicle | Daily.

Guernsey State Park. The Depression-era Civilian Conservation Corps built the museum here. In the park, you can swim and boat, but fishing is prohibited. | Rte. 317 | 307/836–2334 or 307/836–2900 (museum) | fax 307/836–3088 | sphs@missc.state.wy.us | www.state.wy.us | $2 resident vehicle, $3 nonresident vehicle | Daily.

Laramie Peak Museum. This small-town museum exhibits historic photographs of Wheatland and surrounding areas, and offers you a glimpse of pioneer and early 20th century frontier life in its displays of furniture, tools, and other local artifacts. | 1601 16th St. | 307/322–2322 | Free | May and Sept., weekdays 10–5; Jun.–Aug., Mon., Tues., Thurs., and Fri., 10–8, Wed. 10–5, Sat. 10–3.

ON THE CALENDAR

JUNE: *Chugwater Chili Cook-off.* Chili cooks prepare their own special blends as musicians and cowboy poets provide entertainment. | 307/322–2322.

JUNE: *Glendo Days.* Search for trinkets at the mass flea market, watch the sky fill with colorful hot air balloons, or participate in a fishing tournament at this local summertime festival held 30 mi north of Torrington on I–25. | 307/322–2322.

JULY: *Guernsey Old-Timer's Association Rodeo.* These cowboys aren't kids; they've been roping and riding for years. Here they take part in traditional events at the Guernsey Fairgrounds. | 307/322–2322.

AUG.: *Summer Fun Fest and Antique Tractor Pull.* Farmers and old tractor enthusiasts compete to see which of their tractors can pull the most weight. | 307/322–2322.

AUG.: *Platte County Fair and Rodeo.* 4-H and FFA members exhibit livestock and craft projects at the Platte County Fairgrounds. | 307/322–9504.

Dining

Casey's Timber Haus. American. You can have breakfast or lunch anytime, great hamburgers and daily specials, steaks, seafood, or prime rib in this log cabin–style building with an open cathedral ceiling. | 1803 N. 16th St. | 307/322–1652 | $11–$21 | AE, D, DC, MC, V.

El Rancho Steakhouse. American. This is a Western steak house, no doubt about it. The menu includes steak, shrimp, frogs' legs, and walleye. | 67 El Rancho Rd. | 307/322–5599 | $10.95–$34 | No credit cards | Closed Sun.–Mon. No lunch.

Vimbos. American. Long known as a good place to get a meal in Wheatland, this is a family restaurant that occasionally has Mexican buffets but always serves basic American food. Buffet. Kids' menu. | 203 16th St. | 307/322–3725 | $10–$19 | AE, D, MC, V.

Lodging

Best Western Torchlite Motor Inn. You're right next to I–25 at this inn with a homey lobby and refrigerators in the rooms. Restaurant. Refrigerators. Cable TV. Fitness center. Business services. Airport shuttle. Pets allowed. | 1809 N. 16th | 307/322–4070 | fax 307/322–4072 | 50 rooms | $56 | AE, D, DC, MC, V.

Wyoming Motel. If you're tired of chains, try this locally owned motor inn at the center of town that's well maintained, family-friendly, and affordable. Rooms have wood panelling and are furnished in lilac and fuchsia tones. Refrigerators. Cable TV. | 1101 9th St. | 307/322–5383 or 800/839–5383 | fax 307/322–5385 | cstenson@communicomm.com | www.wyomingmotel.com | 26 rooms | $35 | AE, D, MC, V.

WORLAND

(Nearby town also listed: Thermopolis)

Dad Worland was selling tree seedlings in this area of Wyoming for the Start Nursery Company of Missouri when he decided to become a homesteader and businessman. He claimed land and obtained a supply of whiskey, then opened the Hole-in-the-Wall stage stop. Business was good but Worland recognized the potential of the land if only it had water, so he helped develop a system of irrigation canals, then suggested a town site not far from his own homestead. When it was developed, the town, which now has 5,800 residents, naturally took the name Worland.

From those earliest days of irrigation and agricultural development, the land has been turned into an oasis of wheat and sugar-beet production, making it one of the richest agricultural districts in the state. The sugar beets grown near Worland are processed at the Holly Sugar Company plant—which began operation in the 1920s.

Worland started with a only a few homesteaders, but soon expanded to include immigrants from Japan, Mexico, Russia, and Germany, so that the area became a true melting pot of cultures.

Information: Worland Chamber of Commerce | 120 N. 10th, 82401 | 307/347–3226 | fax 307/347–3025 | wacc@trib.com | worland.com/wacc.

Attractions
Washakie Museum. From dinosaurs and pioneers to geology and Native American history, the displays here have a little of everything. You can see exhibits of artifacts from the Horner Archaeological Site, where bison killing and butchering took place some 11,000 years ago, and a re-created prehistoric cave with Native American pictographs and petroglyphs. | 1115 Obie Sue Ave. | 307/347–4102 | fax 307/347–4865 | wmuseum@trib.com | w3.trib.com/~museum | Free; donations accepted | Oct.–May, Tues.–Sat. 10 to 5; June–Sept., Tues.–Fri. 9–7, Sat., Sun., Mon 9–5.

ON THE CALENDAR
JULY: *Fourth of July Rodeo.* Tensleep holds its annual Fourth of July rodeo and parade at the rodeo arena. | 307/347–3226.
AUG.: *Washakie County Fair.* Youth livestock and craft projects are displayed at the Washakie County Fairgrounds, and there is a parade. | 307/347–3226.

Dining
Crossbow Restaurant. American. A family diner, this place serves simple, basic food. Kids' menu. | 1110 Big Horn Ave. | 307/347–8296 | $7–$15 | MC, V.

Ram's Horn Cafe. American. The café on the town's main street has three rooms including a banquet area, and serves everything from hamburgers to steak. Kids' menu. | 629 Big Horn Ave. | 307/347–6351 | $8–$20 | AE, MC, V.

Tom and Jerry's Steakhouse. American. You can dine in the family steak house, or enjoy your meal in the lounge with a fireplace. The design is contemporary and the specialties are prime rib, steak, and seafood, including shrimp and lobster. Salad bar. Kids' menu. | 1620 Big Horn Ave. | 307/347–9261 | $13–$24 | AE, D, MC, V | Closed Sun. No lunch.

Lodging
Settlers Inn. The rooms have been remodeled with contemporary furnishings, and you're convenient to downtown. Continental breakfast. Business services. Pets allowed. | 2200 Big Horn Ave. | 307/347–8201 | fax 307/347–9323 | 44 rooms | $54 | AE, D, DC, MC, V.

Town House Motor Inn. Family rooms with three queen-size beds distinguish this generally modest and modern inn. Pool. | 119 N. 10th | 307/347–2426 | 23 rooms | $40 | AE, D, MC, V.

Worland Days Inn. All the larger-than-average, clean, earth-toned rooms are on the ground level at this reliable motor inn, which is within walking distance of a handful of restaurants. Continental breakfast. Cable TV. Laundry facilities. Airport shuttle. Small pets allowed. | 500 N. 10th St. | 307/347–4251 or 800/544–8313 | fax 307/347–6500 | 42 rooms | $56 | AE, D, DC, MC, V.

YELLOWSTONE NATIONAL PARK

MAP 9, C1

(Nearby town also listed: Cody)

★ Yellowstone National Park preserves and provides access to natural treasures such as Yellowstone Lake, with its 110-mi shoreline and lake cruises, wildlife, waterfowl, and trout fishing; Grand Canyon of the Yellowstone, 24 mi long, 1,200 ft. deep, in shades of red and ocher surrounded by emerald-green forest; spectacular Mammoth Hot Springs; and 900 mi of horse trails, 1,000 mi of hiking trails, and 370 mi of public roads. Visitors centers throughout the park are the departure points for guided hikes and the sites of evening talks and campfire programs (check the park newsletter *Discover Yellowstone* for details). Park Service literature and warnings about interaction with the wildlife—particularly grizzly bears and bison—should be taken seriously.

Information: Yellowstone National Park | Box 168, Mammoth, WY 82190 | 307/344–7381 or TDD 307/344–2386 | fax 307/344–2014 | www.nps.gov/yell/ | 7-day pass good for both Yellowstone and Grand Teton national parks, $20 per motor vehicle, $10 non-motorized entry permit, $15 motorcycle or snowmobile; $40 annual permit; Golden Age and Golden Eagle permits accepted | Year-round to Mammoth; early May–Sept. other areas; some roads may open later or close earlier due to snowfall; winter season open mid-Dec.–early Mar.

Attractions

Yellowstone Highlights. You can't run out of "firsts," "mosts," or "lasts" when it comes to describing Yellowstone National Park—it was the world's first national park; it is the largest national park in the lower 48; it is, with surrounding wildlands, the center of the last truly intact temperate ecosystem. These are but a few of its features.

A cascading waterfall and rushing river carved the **Grand Canyon of the Yellowstone,** which is 24 mi long and 1,200 ft deep. The red and ochre canyon walls are topped with emerald-green forest.

At **Mammoth Hot Springs,** multicolored travertine terraces formed by slowly flowing hot mineral water, elk are frequent visitors, as they graze nearby.

★ **Norris Geyser Basin,** the hottest and oldest such basin in Yellowstone, is constantly changing. Some geysers or hot springs might suddenly stop flowing, but others blow and hiss into life. Among the features at Norris are Whirligig Geyser, Whale's Mouth, Emerald Spring, and Arch Steam Vent.

You can learn the history of Yellowstone's watchdogs, from turn-of-the-century army troops to today's rangers, at the **Norris Museum,** a small log-cabin museum. Take special note of the architecture of this building.

The huge, though unpredictable, Steamboat Geyser is one of the attractions at **Back Basin,** a big geyser area. Though Steamboat only performs about once a year, when it does, it shoots 300 ft into the air.

The **Porcelain Basin** is a small geyser area that has a 1 mi boardwalk and often a lot of people, but it's a good place to watch the ground bulge and push from underground pressure. The long-standing centerpiece of Yellowstone is **Old Faithful/Upper Geyser Basin.** The mysterious plumbing of Yellowstone has lengthened Old Faithful's eruption cycle somewhat in recent years, but the geyser still spouts the same amount of water–sometimes reaching to 140 ft—and pleases spectators every 80 minutes or so. Sometimes it doesn't shoot so high, but in those cases the eruption lasts longer. To find out when Old Faithful is next expected to erupt, check at the visitors center. Marked trails and bridges lead to Geyser Hill, and you can visit Castle Geyser and Morning Glory Pool as well as the Giantess Geyser and Giant Geyser. Elk and buffalo commonly share the area. In winter, cross-country ski trails converge at Old Faithful.

The Grand Prismatic Spring and Excelsior Geyser Crater are two of the features at **Midway Geyser Basin,** which has some beautiful, richly colored, bottomless pools.

The Great Fountain Geyser is the most spectacular of the features at **Lower Geyser Basin.** But you'll find bubbling mudpots, blue pools, fumaroles, pink mud pots, and the mini-geysers at Fountain Paint Pots here as well.

A small geyser basin and views of Lake Yellowstone are worth stopping for at **West Thumb,** which also has a visitors center and a warming hut if you're here in winter.

You can use the riding trails and have cookouts in the **Tower-Roosevelt** area, check out the Petrified Tree, and hike on trails through the Lamar Valley or to Specimen Ridge with its unusual fossils.

Yellowstone Lake, North America's largest mountain lake, was formed by glaciers. You can boat and fish or simply sit along the shore and watch the waves. In the winter you will sometimes see otters and coyotes in a sort of dance on the ice at the lake's edge.

Yellowstone Institute. This non-profit organization, housed in log cabins in the pastoral Lamar Valley, offers a wide range of summer and winter courses about the ecology, history, and wildlife of Yellowstone. Search with a historian for the trail the Nez Percé took in their flight a century ago, or get tips from professional photographers on how to capture a trumpeter swan on film. Facilities are fairly primitive—guests do their own cooking and camp during some of the courses—but prices are reasonable. Besides, you'll find no better way to get out from behind the windshield and learn what makes the park tick. Some programs are specifically designed for young people and families. | Box 117, Yellowstone National Park | 307/344–2294 | fax 307/344–2485 | www.nps.gov/yell/ya/yellinst.htm.

Yellowstone Outdoor Adventures. With enormous tracts of wilderness, abundant wildlife, innumerable geothermal features and waterfalls, and diverse Rocky Mountain scenery, Yellowstone is still the premier wilderness destination in the lower 48. Visitors throng here in all seasons to experience the Yellowstone backcountry in myriad ways. Contact the park for detailed information about the activities listed below, along with lists of outfitters running trips through the wilderness areas of the park.

Though many people do enjoy **cycling** in Yellowstone, most of the roads are narrow, with little or no shoulder and heavy traffic, making bike riding somewhat hazardous. The road from Grant Village over Craig Pass to Old Faithful is roomier and in better shape than most park roads, though there is no designated bike path.

In winter you use **snowmobiles** to see Yellowstone, when the summer roads become groomed snowmobile trails. You can rent from private companies near the park's main gates, or from Amfac, the park concessionaire, at both Mammoth and Old Faithful. Some people are opposed to snowmobiles because they are noisy and polluting, but as yet no restrictions are in place.

Yellowstone is perhaps the top **cross-country skiing** destination in North America. The ski trails aren't groomed, but there are snowcoach stops in the Old Faithful, Mammoth, and Canyon areas. You can rent equipment at Mammoth and Old Faithful.

You may be one of the many people who think that the way to see Yellowstone in winter is on a **snowcoach tour.** Private companies headquartered at Flagg Ranch (south entrance) or at West Yellowstone provide trips that last from a few hours to an entire day, as does Amfac.

YELLOWSTONE
NATIONAL PARK

INTRO
ATTRACTIONS
DINING
LODGING

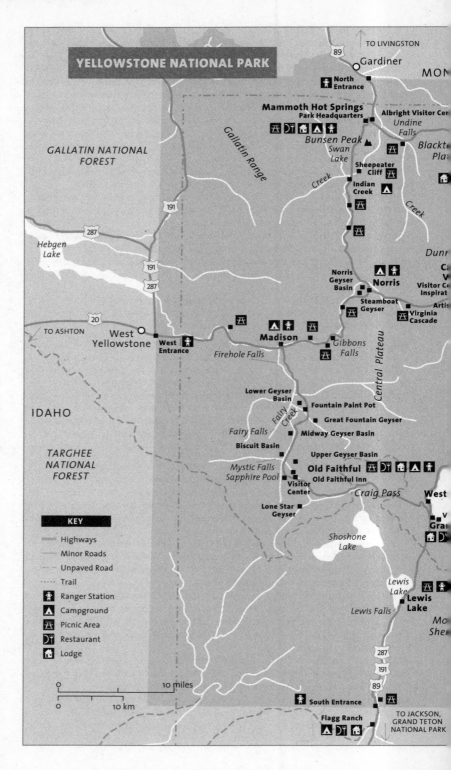

YELLOWSTONE NATIONAL PARK

TO LIVINGSTON

89

Gardiner

MON

North
Entrance

Mammoth Hot Springs
Park Headquarters

Albright Visitor Cen

Undine
Falls

GALLATIN NATIONAL
FOREST

Gallatin Range

Bunsen Peak

Swan
Lake

Blackt
Pla

Sheepeater
Cliff

Indian
Creek

Creek

Creek

191

287

Hebgen
Lake

Dunr

191

Norris
Geyser
Basin

Norris

Ca
V

Visitor Ce
Inspirat

287

TO ASHTON

20

West
Yellowstone

West
Entrance

Madison

Steamboat
Geyser

Virginia
Cascade

Arti

Gibbons
Falls

Central Plateau

Firehole Falls

IDAHO

Lower Geyser
Basin

TARGHEE
NATIONAL
FOREST

Fairy Creek

Fountain Paint Pot

Great Fountain Geyser

Fairy Falls

Midway Geyser Basin

Biscuit Basin

Upper Geyser Basin

Mystic Falls
Sapphire Pool

Old Faithful

Old Faithful Inn

Craig Pass

West

KEY

Visitor
Center

Gra

Highways

Lone Star
Geyser

Minor Roads

Shoshone
Lake

Unpaved Road

Trail

Lewis
Lake

Ranger Station

Lewis
Lake

Campground

Lewis Falls

Mo
She

Picnic Area

Restaurant

Lodge

287

191

10 miles

89

0

10 km

South Entrance

Flagg Ranch

TO JACKSON,
GRAND TETON
NATIONAL PARK

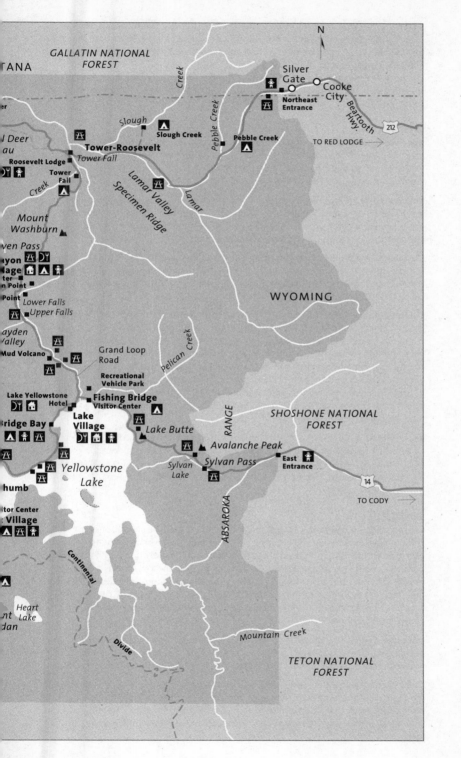

GALLATIN NATIONAL FOREST

TANA

GallatinCreek

Silver Gate

Cooke City

Northeast Entrance

Beartooth Hwy.

212

TO RED LODGE

Slough Creek

Slough Creek

Pebble Creek

Pebble Creek

l Deer
au

Roosevelt Lodge

Tower-Roosevelt

Tower Fall

Tower Fall

Creek

Tower Creek

Lamar Valley
Specimen Ridge

Lamar

Mount Washburn

WYOMING

ven Pass

yon
lage
ter
n Point

Point

Lower Falls
Upper Falls

ayden
Valley

Mud Volcano

Pelican Creek

Grand Loop Road

Recreational Vehicle Park

Lake Yellowstone Hotel

Fishing Bridge
Visitor Center

Lake Village

RANGE

SHOSHONE NATIONAL FOREST

ridge Bay

Lake Butte

Avalanche Peak

Sylvan Pass

East Entrance

Yellowstone Lake

Sylvan Lake

14

TO CODY

humb

ABSAROKA

tor Center
Village

Heart Lake

nt
dan

Continental

Divide

Mountain Creek

TETON NATIONAL FOREST

YELLOWSTONE
NATIONAL PARK

INTRO
ATTRACTIONS
DINING
LODGING

The many rivers and lakes in the park allow for a multitude of **water sports.** You can fish on many of Yellowstone's waters, but you need a license. Boaters embark from Bridge Bay for explorations on Yellowstone Lake. You can swim at certain points on the Firehole River and take guided boat tours through Amfac.

The park has 11 **campgrounds** (under $12) and one RV park, Fishing Bridge ($23), open May–October. You can also camp in the backcountry; check with a ranger to get a back-country permit.

Dining

Lake Yellowstone Dining Room. American. Huge windows give you a view of Lake Yellowstone, and there is generally a musical interlude during the dinner hour. The menu is strong on steaks, prime rib, and trout. Kids' menu. No smoking. | Lake Village | 307/344–7901 | Dinner reservations essential | $12–$18 | AE, D, DC, MC, V | Closed Oct.–May.

Mammoth Hot Springs Hotel. American. After the hustle of exploring Yellowstone during the day, you'll welcome the quiet of the Mammoth Hot Springs Hotel dining room. The service is low-key, and the menu varied, with beef, chicken, and pasta dishes. | Mammoth Hot Springs | 307/344–7901 | Dinner reservations essential | $10–$25 | AE, D, DC, MC, V.

Old Faithful Inn Dining Room. American. The rustic feeling of the Old Faithful Inn carries into the dining room, particularly in the old house section where you can hear the piano. Favorites are local fish and steaks. | 307/344–7901 | Dinner reservations essential | $12–$30 | AE, D, DC, MC, V | Closed mid-Sept.–mid-May.

Old Faithful Snow Lodge. American. From the wood and leather chairs, complete with etched figures of park animals, to the intricate lighting that resembles snow-capped trees and whimsical figures, you'll appreciate the atmosphere of the Old Faithful Snow Lodge, which opened in 1998. This is the only place in the park, aside from Mammoth, where you can enjoy a relaxing, sit-down lunch or dinner during the winter season. The huge windows give you a view of the Old Faithful area, and you can sometimes see the famous geyser as it erupts. Try the French onion soup. The menu also includes beef, chicken, and pasta dishes. | 307/344–7901 | $12–$24 | AE, D, DC, MC, V | Open Dec.–Mar. and May–Oct., 7:30–10:30, 11:30 –2:30, 5:30–10.

Roosevelt Lodge. American. At this rustic log cabin in a pine forest, the menu ranges from barbecued ribs and Roosevelt beans to hamburgers and steak. Chuckwagon cookouts involve one- or two-hour trail rides or stagecoach rides. Kids' menu. | Tower at Roosevelt | 307/344–7901 | Reservations essential for chuckwagon cookouts | $12–$46 | AE, D, DC, MC, V | Closed Sept.–early June.

Lodging

Canyon Lodge. Yellowstone's largest lodging facility, this one is central, busy, and basic, and probably the one you will occupy if you don't make reservations. Pine-frame cabins have modest furnishings, and surround the somewhat ungainly 1970s-style main lodge, which has a gift shop and snack bar. Close to the Yellowstone River, this is a good spot if you opt for convenience over luxury. You can go horseback riding. 3 restaurants, bar, cafeteria. Laundry facilities. | North Rim Dr. | 307/344–7311 | fax 307/344–7456 | www.travelyellowstone.com | 572 cabins, 37 annex rooms | $58–$114 cabins, $129 rooms | AE, D, MC, V | Closed early Sept.–early June.

Dunraven Lodge. This motel-style lodging facility at Canyon Village opened in 1999. Restaurant. | Canyon Village | 307/344–7311 | fax 307/344–7456 | www.amfac.com or www.travelyellowstone.com | 44 rooms | $128 | AE, D, DC, MC, V | Closed mid-Sept.–May.

Grant Village. You get the southernmost accommodations in the park at this complex on the shore of Yellowstone Lake. The rooms are spread through six buildings. You can take sight-seeing tours that start here. Restaurant, bar. No air-conditioning. Laundry facilities. | 307/344–7311 | fax 307/344–7456 | www.amfac.com or www.travelyellowstone.com | 300 rooms | $79–$122 | AE, D, DC, MC, V | Closed Oct.–late May.

Lake Lodge. The main lodge here, a part of which dates to the 1920s, has views of Yellowstone Lake and is nestled among pine groves. Although the basic cabin-style accommodations are similar to other facilities in the park, the cozy lodge and semi-secluded site at the far end of Lake Village Road make this a better choice if you want something more homey. Bar, cafeteria. | 307/344–7311 | fax 307/344–7456 | www.travelyellowstone.com | 186 cabins | $52–$112 | AE, D, MC, V | Closed mid-Sept.–mid-Jun.

★ **Lake Yellowstone Hotel.** Near the shore of Yellowstone Lake, you can relax on the lawn or view the lake from the restaurant. Some rooms have lake views. Cabins are not as close to the shore and do not have lake views. Restaurant, bar. No air-conditioning. | Lake Village | 307/344–7311 | fax 307/344–7456 | www.amfac.com or www.travelyellowstone.com | 194 rooms | $96–$149 | AE, D, DC, MC, V | Closed Oct.–mid-May.

Mammoth Hot Springs Hotel Cabins. One of two park lodgings open in winter, this hotel has some rooms with views of the terraces at Mammoth Hot Springs. Cabins are behind the hotel. Some have hot tubs, but not all rooms or cabins have bathrooms. Bar. No air-conditioning. Ice-skating. Cross-country skiing, snowmobiling. | 307/344–7311 | fax 307/344–7456 | www.amfac.com or www.travelyellowstone.com | 98 rooms, 69 with bath; 128 cabins, 75 with baths | $49–$108 | AE, D, DC, MC, V | Closed mid-Sept.–mid-Dec. and Mar.–May.

Old Faithful Inn. An architectural wonder built in 1903 and later expanded, the log building has a six-story lobby with huge rock fireplaces. Some rooms have views of Old Faithful. Stop by even if you're not staying here. Restaurant, bar. No air-conditioning, some refrigerators, many room phones. | Old Faithful | 307/344–7311 | fax 307/344–7456 | www.amfac.com or www.travelyellowstone.com | 325 rooms, 246 with bath | $75–$159 | AE, D, DC, MC, V | Closed mid-Oct.–Apr.

Old Faithful Snow Lodge. Built in 1998, this lodge sets a new standard for park lodging with its open design, Western furnishings, and unique lighting. Near Old Faithful Geyser, this is one of two lodging facilities in the Old Faithful area that are open in winter. Restaurant, bar. No air-conditioning. Cross-country skiing, snowmobiling. Meeting room. | 307/344–7311 | fax 307/344–7456 | AE, D, DC, MC, V | www.amfac.com or www.travelyellowstone.com | 100 rooms | $121–$148 | Closed mid-Oct.–mid-Dec. and mid-Mar.–May.

Roosevelt Lodge Cabins. The most Western of all Yellowstone lodging, these small cabins have no frills, but they are set in the forest in an area of the park that sees fewer visitors. The lodge also hosts stagecoach rides and cookouts. Restaurant. Horseback riding. | Tower Junction | 307/344–7311 | fax 307/344–7456 | www.amfac.com or www.travelyellowstone.com | 86 cabins, 8 with bath | $37–$73 | AE, D, DC, MC, V | Closed Sept.–early June.

Yellowstone Park Campgrounds. You can choose from multiple camping options throughout Yellowstone, including Fishing Bridge RV Park and developed campgrounds at Bridge Bay, Canyon, Grant Village, and Madison. There are numerous backcountry campsites and some suitable for people with disabilities. Campgrounds generally open in May or June and close in September or October. Due to the presence of bears, food-storage regulations are strictly enforced; at Fishing Bridge RV Park only hard-sided vehicles are allowed. Some campgrounds have coin-operated showers and laundry facilities. Flush toilets. Some pets allowed. | 307/344–7311 | fax 307/344–7456 | www.amfac.com or www.travelyellowstone.com | $15–$27 | AE, D, DC, MC, V | Closed Nov.–early May.

YELLOWSTONE
NATIONAL PARK

INTRO
ATTRACTIONS
DINING
LODGING

Index

A Carousel for Missoula (Missoula, MT), 191

A. Drummond's Ranch (Cheyenne, WY), 435

A'roma (Twin Falls, ID), 99

A-Able Fishing Charters (Kalispell, MT), 179

Abbey Inn (Cedar City, UT), 324

Abravanel Hall (Salt Lake City, UT), 375

Absaroka (Gardiner, MT), 154

Absaroka Mountain Lodge (Cody, WY), 440

Absaroka Ranch (Dubois, WY), 446

Absolute! Restaurant and Brasserie (Salt Lake City, UT), 382

Ackley Lake State Park (Lewistown, MT), 181

Adele's (Carson City, NV), 230

Adriana's (Cedar City, UT), 323

Adrift Adventures Dinosaur (Green River, UT), 331

Adventure Bound River Expeditions (Moab, UT), 343

Adventure Inn (Reno, NV), 282

Aerial Tramway (Teton Village, WY), 498

The Aerie (Salt Lake City, UT), 383

Airport Inn (Hailey, ID), 60

The Albany (Cheyenne, WY), 434

Albeni Falls Dam and Reservoir (Priest Lake Area, ID), 85

Alberta Bair Theater (Billings, MT), 129

Alberto's Restaurant (Bonners Ferry, ID), 38

Albertson College of Idaho (Caldwell, ID), 42

Albi's Steak House (Wallace, ID), 101

Alexis Park Resort (Las Vegas, NV), 269

All Seasons (Park City, UT), 356

Allen Brothers Wilderness Ranch and Outfitting (Lander, WY), 472

Alpenhof (Teton Village, WY), 499

Alpine House (Jackson, WY), 465

Alpine Inn (Alpine, WY), 422

Alpine Slide, Gorgoza Skate Park, and Little Miners' Park (Park City, UT), 353

Alpine Villa Motel (Nampa, ID), 80

Alta Lodge (Salt Lake City, UT), 384

Alta Ski Area (Salt Lake City, UT), 377

Amangani (Jackson, WY), 466

American Computer Museum (Bozeman, MT), 135

American Falls Dam (American Falls, ID), 21

American Heritage Center and Art Museum (Laramie, WY), 475

American West Heritage Center (Logan, UT), 336

Amerisuites Hotel (Boise, ID), 34

Ameritel Inn (Boise, ID), 36

Ameritel Inn (Coeur d'Alene, ID), 49

Ameritel Inn (Idaho Falls, ID), 63

Ameritel Inn (Pocatello, ID), 84

Ameritel Inn (Twin Falls, ID), 99

Amsterdam Inn Bed & Breakfast (Buhl, ID), 40

Anaconda Smoke Stack State Park (Anaconda, MT), 121

Anaconda Visitor Center (Anaconda, MT), 121

Anaconda-Pintler Wilderness (Anaconda, MT), 121

Anasazi State Park Museum (Boulder, UT), 313

Andre's (Las Vegas, NV), 257

Angel Point (Kalispell, MT), 180

Angell's Bar and Grill (Boise, ID), 32

Angie's Silver Dollar Bar (Cody, WY), 437

Anna Miller Museum (Newcastle, WY), 482

Anniversary Inn (Logan, UT), 338

The Anniversary Inn at Kahn Mansion (Salt Lake City, UT), 387

Antelope Butte Ski Area (Greybull, WY), 460

Antelope Island State Park on the Great Salt Lake (Ogden, UT), 348

Anthony's (Jackson, WY), 464

Anton Boxrud Bed & Breakfast (Salt Lake City, UT), 384

Antonio's (Las Vegas, NV), 257

Anvil Motel (Jackson, WY), 466

Apgar Village Lodge (Glacier National Park, MT), 159

Appaloosa Museum and Heritage Center (Moscow, ID), 76

Aqua (Las Vegas, NV), 254

Arapaho Cultural Center Museum and Heritage Center (Lander, WY), 470

Arches National Park (Green River, UT), 330

Arches National Park (Moab, UT), 342

Arches Vineyard (Moab, UT), 342

Archie Bray Foundation (Helena, MT), 173

Archway Inn (Moab, UT), 344

Arco Inn (Arco, ID), 23

Argentine Grill (Salt Lake City, UT), 382

Aristocrat (Las Vegas, NV), 257

Arizona Charlie's (Las Vegas, NV), 260

Armor's (Casper, WY), 429

Armstrong Mansion (Salt Lake City, UT), 387

Aro Restaurant and Lounge (Sundance, WY), 497

Arshel's (Beaver, UT), 307

Art Museum of Missoula (Missoula, MT), 190

Art Works Too & Cowgirl Coffee Cafe (Buffalo, WY), 424

Arts Chateau Museum (Butte, MT), 140

Ashley National Forest (Vernal, UT), 393
Aspen Acres (Ashton, ID), 24
Aspen Lodge Motel (Beaver, UT), 307
Assembly Hall (Salt Lake City, UT), 376
Atlantic City Mercantile
  (Lander, WY), 472
Atlantis (Reno, NV), 280, 281
Aureole (Las Vegas, NV), 254
Averill's Flathead Lake Lodge
  (Bigfork, MT), 127
Ayres Natural Bridge
  (Douglas, WY), 443

B.B. Strands (Boise, ID), 32
Baba Afghan (Salt Lake City, UT), 380
Bacchus Pub (Bozeman, MT), 137
Baci Trattoria (Salt Lake City, UT), 382
Bacilio's (Moscow, ID), 77
Back Basin (Yellowstone National
  Park, WY), 506
Backcountry Bicycle Tours
  (Bozeman, MT), 136
Bad Rock Country Bed & Breakfast
  (Columbia Falls, MT), 145
Bailey's Bar and Grill (Gillette, WY), 452
Baja Cantina (Park City, UT), 355
Baker House Bed and Breakfast (Cedar
  City, UT), 324
Balanced Rock (Buhl, ID), 40
Bald Mountain Lodge (Ketchum, ID), 68
Bald Mountain Ski Resort
  (Orofino, ID), 80
Ballet West (Salt Lake City, UT), 375
Bally's (Las Vegas, NV), 263
Bamboleo (Las Vegas, NV), 254
Bangkok Thai (Salt Lake City, UT), 382
Bannack State Park (Dillon, MT), 148
Banque Club and Exchange
  (Hamilton, MT), 167
Bar Gernika Basque Pub and Eatery
  (Boise, ID), 31
Bar J (Jackson, WY), 464
Baragar House (Coeur d'Alene, ID), 49
Barbary Coast (Las Vegas, NV), 263
Barclay II (Anaconda, MT), 122
Barker-Ewing Float Trips
  (Jackson, WY), 463
Barrister (Helena, MT), 176
Barton's Club 93 (Jackpot, NV), 243
Basque Museum (Boise, ID), 28
Battista's Hole In The Wall (Las
  Vegas, NV), 254
Bavarian Chalet (Ogden, UT), 350
Beamers Hells Canyon Tours and
  Excursions (Lewiston, ID), 71
Bear Creek Lodge (Bonners Ferry, ID), 38
Bear Creek Lodge (McCall, ID), 74
Bear Lake (Montpelier, ID), 74
Bear Lake Loop Bicycle Trail (Garden
  City, UT), 328
Bear Lake National Wildlife Refuge
  (Montpelier, ID), 74
Bear Lake State Park (Garden
  City, UT), 328

Bear Lake State Park
  (Montpelier, ID), 75
Bear Lodge Motel (Sundance, WY), 498
Bear Paw Battleground
  (Chinook, MT), 143
Bear Paw Court (Chinook, MT), 143
Bear River Migratory Bird Refuge
  (Brigham City, UT), 314
Bear River State Park
  (Evanston, WY), 449
Bear Trap (Encampment, WY), 448
Beartooth National Forest Scenic
  Byway (Red Lodge, MT), 196
Beartooth Nature Center (Red
  Lodge, MT), 196
Beartrap Canyon (Ennis, MT), 150
Beaver Creek Park (Havre, MT), 170
Beaver Dam State Park
  (Caliente, NV), 227
Beaver Mountain Ski Area (Garden
  City, UT), 329
Beaverhead County Museum
  (Dillon, MT), 149
Beaverhead Rock State Park
  (Dillon, MT), 149
Beaverhead-Deerlodge National Forest
  (Butte, MT), 141
Beaverhead-Deerlodge National Forest
  (Deer Lodge, MT), 147
Beaverhead-Deerlodge National Forest
  (Dillon, MT), 149
Beaverhead-Deerlodge National Forest
  (Ennis, MT), 150
Beaverhead-Deerlodge National Forest
  (Virginia City, MT), 202
Beaverhead-Deerlodge National
  Forest, Philipsburg District
  (Anaconda, MT), 121
Beavertail State Park
  (Missoula, MT), 189
Beehive House and Lion House (Salt
  Lake City, UT), 374
Bellagio (Las Vegas, NV), 268
Ben's Cafe (Green River, UT), 331
Berlin-Ichthyosaur State Park
  (Austin, NV), 224
Berry Patch Inn (Coeur d'Alene, ID), 49
Bertolini's (Las Vegas, NV), 254
Best Friends Animal Sanctuary
  (Kanab, UT), 334
Best Inn & Suites (Provo, UT), 364
Best Inn and Suites (Caldwell, ID), 42
Best Inn and Suites (Fallon, NV), 237
Best Inn Fillmore (Fillmore, UT), 328
Best Western (Billings, MT), 132
Best Western (McCall, ID), 74
Best Western Airport Motor Inn
  (Boise, ID), 33
Best Western Airport Plaza
  (Reno, NV), 282
Best Western Ameritel Inn Elko
  (Elko, NV), 234
Best Western Antlers Motel
  (Vernal, UT), 395
Best Western Apollo Motor Inn (Twin
  Falls, ID), 99

Best Western Apple Tree Inn
  (Richfield, UT), 366
Best Western Baugh Motel
  (Logan, UT), 338
Best Western Blackfoot Inn
  (Blackfoot, ID), 26
Best Western Burley Inn (Burley, ID), 41
Best Western Butch Cassidy Inn
  (Beaver, UT), 307
Best Western by Mammoth Hot
  Springs (Gardiner, MT), 154
Best Western Caldwell Inn and Suites
  (Caldwell, ID), 43
Best Western Canyonlands Inn
  (Moab, UT), 344
Best Western Capitol Reef Resort
  (Torrey, UT), 393
Best Western Carriage House Inn
  (Price, UT), 361
Best Western Casper (Casper, WY), 429
Best Western Cavanaughs Canyon
  Springs (Twin Falls, ID), 100
Best Western Cavanaughs Colonial
  Hotel (Helena, MT), 176
Best Western Christiania Lodge
  (Ketchum, ID), 68
Best Western Clover Creek Inn
  (Montpelier, ID), 76
Best Western Coral Hills (St.
  George, UT), 369
Best Western Cottontree
  (Rexburg, ID), 87
Best Western Cottontree Inn (Idaho
  Falls, ID), 63
Best Western Cottontree Inn
  (Provo, UT), 364
Best Western Cottontree Inn
  (Vernal, UT), 395
Best Western Dinosaur Inn
  (Vernal, UT), 395
Best Western Douglas Inn
  (Douglas, WY), 444
Best Western Driftwood Inn (Idaho
  Falls, ID), 63
Best Western Dunmar Inn
  (Evanston, WY), 450
Best Western Edgewater resort
  (Sandpoint, ID), 93
Best Western El Ray Inn (Cedar
  City, UT), 324
Best Western Flying Saddle Lodge
  (Alpine, WY), 422
Best Western Foster's Country Inn
  (Laramie, WY), 476
Best Western Gateway Inn
  (Blanding, UT), 310
Best Western Gold Country Inn
  (Winnemucca, NV), 288
Best Western Great Northern Inn
  (Havre, MT), 171
Best Western Green Well
  (Moab, UT), 344
Best Western Hamilton Inn
  (Hamilton, MT), 167
Best Western Heritage Inn (Great
  Falls, MT), 164
Best Western Hi Country Inn
  (Afton, WY), 421
Best Western Hi Desert Inn
  (Tonopah, NV), 286

Best Western High Country Inn (Ogden, UT), 351

Best Western Hitching Post Inn (Cheyenne, WY), 434

Best Western Inn (Roosevelt, UT), 367

Best Western Inn at Jackson Hole (Teton Village, WY), 499

Best Western Inn at Lander (Lander, WY), 473

Best Western Inn at Sundance (Sundance, WY), 498

Best Western Jordan Inn (Glendive, MT), 161

Best Western Kentwood Lodge (Ketchum, ID), 68

Best Western Kings Inn (Powell, WY), 486

Best Western Kootenai River Inn (Bonners Ferry, ID), 38

Best Western Kwataqnuk Resort at Flathead Bay (Polson, MT), 195

Best Western Landmark Inn (Park City, UT), 356

Best Western Lodge at Jackson Hole (Jackson, WY), 466

Best Western Lupine Inn (Red Lodge, MT), 197

Best Western McCarran Inn (Las Vegas, NV), 260

Best Western New Western Motel (Panguitch, UT), 352

Best Western Outlaw Inn (Kalispell, MT), 180

Best Western Paradise Inn (Beaver, UT), 308

Best Western Paradise Inn (Dillon, MT), 149

Best Western Paradise Inn (Fillmore, UT), 328

Best Western Pine Motel (West Yellowstone, MT), 205

Best Western Pinedale Inn (Pinedale, WY), 484

Best Western Pioneer Court (Lusk, WY), 480

Best Western Ponderosa Inn (Billings, MT), 132

Best Western Red Hills (Kanab, UT), 335

Best Western River Terrace (Green River, UT), 331

Best Western Rocky Mountain Lodge (Whitefish, MT), 207

Best Western Ruby's Inn (Bryce Canyon National Park, UT), 317

Best Western Safari (Boise, ID), 33

Best Western Salt Flat Inn (Wendover, UT), 396

Best Western Sawtooth Inn and Suites (Jerome, ID), 65

Best Western Sheridan Center Motor Inn (Sheridan, WY), 496

Best Western Stage Stop Inn (Choteau, MT), 144

Best Western Sunset Motor Inn (Cody, WY), 440

Best Western Templin's Resort (Coeur d'Alene, ID), 49

Best Western Teton West (Driggs, ID), 52

Best Western Thunderbird Resort (Zion National Park, UT), 399

Best Western Torchlite Motor Inn (Wheatland, WY), 504

Best Western Tower West Lodge (Gillette, WY), 452

Best Western Town & Country Inn (Cedar City, UT), 324

Best Western Tyrolean Lodge (Ketchum, ID), 68

Best Western Vista (Boise, ID), 34

Best Western War Bonnet Inn (Miles City, MT), 188

Best Western Wayside Inn (Monticello, UT), 347

Best Western–Salt Lake Plaza (Salt Lake City, UT), 384

Best Western–Big Chief Motel (Battle Mountain, NV), 225

Best Western–Buck's T-4 Lodge (Big Sky, MT), 124

Best Western–Foothills Motor Inn (Mountain Home, ID), 78

Best Western–Lake Mead (Henderson, NV), 241

Best Western–University Inn (Moscow, ID), 77

Best Western–Wallace Inn (Wallace, ID), 101

Beverly's (Coeur d'Alene, ID), 48

Bicycling (Zion National Park, UT), 397

Big Creek Pines Bed & Breakfast (Stevensville, MT), 200

Big Hole Battlefield National Monument (Butte, MT), 141

Big Horn Equestrian Center (Sheridan, WY), 495

Big Horn Mountain KOA Campground (Sheridan, WY), 496

Big Mountain Ski and Summer Resort (Whitefish, MT), 206

Big Rock Candy Mountain (Richfield, UT), 365

Big Sky Motel (Choteau, MT), 144

Big Sky Resort (Big Sky, MT), 124

Big Sky Ski and Summer Resort (Big Sky, MT), 124

Big Sky Water Slide (Columbia Falls, MT), 144

Big Spring Creek Trout Hatchery (Lewistown, MT), 181

Big Springs and Big Springs National Recreation Water Trail (Ashton, ID), 24

Big-Game Hunting (Afton, WY), 421

Big-Game Hunting (Dubois, WY), 445

Bigfork Art and Cultural Center (Bigfork, MT), 125

Bigfork Inn (Bigfork, MT), 126

Bigfork Summer Playhouse (Bigfork, MT), 126

Bighorn (Lovell, WY), 478

Bighorn Canyon National Recreation Area (Hardin, MT), 168

Bighorn Canyon National Recreation Area (Lovell, WY), 477

Bighorn Canyon Visitors Center (Lovell, WY), 478

Bighorn County Historical Museum and Visitor Information Center (Hardin, MT), 168

Bighorn Lodge (Encampment, WY), 448

Bighorn National Forest (Buffalo, WY), 423

Bighorn National Forest (Sheridan, WY), 495

Bill Cody's Ranch Resort (Cody, WY), 440

Billings Area Visitor Center and Cattle Drive Monument (Billings, MT), 129

Billings Inn (Billings, MT), 132

Billings Trolley (Billings, MT), 130

Billy's Giant Hamburgers (Jackson, WY), 464

Bingham County Historical Museum (Blackfoot, ID), 25

Binion's Horseshoe (Las Vegas, NV), 260

bird-watching (Casper, WY), 427

Birds of Prey Float (Boise, ID), 30

Bison Creek Ranch (East Glacier Area, MT), 150

Bistro (Bozeman, MT), 137

The Bit and Spur (Springdale, UT), 390

Bit o'Country Bed & Breakfast (Rawlins, WY), 488

Bitterroot National Forest (Hamilton, MT), 166

Bitterroot National Forest, Darby, Sula, and West Fork Districts (Darby, MT), 146

Bitterroot National Forest, Stevensville District (Lolo, MT), 186

Black Bear Country Inn (Dubois, WY), 446

Black Sandy State Park (Helena, MT), 172

Black Sheep (Cody, WY), 438

Blackwater Creek Ranch (Cody, WY), 440

Blackwell House (Coeur d'Alene, ID), 49

Blaine County Museum (Chinook, MT), 143

Blaine County Museum (Hailey, ID), 60

Blanding Super 8 Motel (Blanding, UT), 310

Bloomington (St. George, UT), 368

Blue and White Motel (Kalispell, MT), 180

Blue Boar Inn (Heber City, UT), 333

Blue Gables Motel (Buffalo, WY), 425

Blue Lion (Jackson, WY), 464

Blue Moon Bar and Grill (Lava Hot Springs, ID), 70

Blue Spruce Inn (Lander, WY), 473

The Bluebird Cafe (Logan, UT), 338

Bluff Walking Tour (Bluff, UT), 311

boat trip (Blanding, UT), 309

Bob Marshall Wilderness Area (Kalispell, MT), 178

Bogus Basin Ski Resort (Boise, ID), 28

Boise Art Museum (Boise, ID), 29

Boise Basin Museum (Idaho City, ID), 61

Boise National Forest (Boise, ID), 29

Boise Park Suite Hotel (Boise, ID), 34
Boise River Inn (Boise, ID), 34
Boise River Tours (Boise, ID), 31
Boise Tour Train (Boise, ID), 30
Bojack's Broiler Pit (Lewiston, ID), 71
Bon Rico (Kemmerer, WY), 470
Bonanza Inn & Casino (Fallon, NV), 237
Bonner County Historical Society Museum (Sandpoint, ID), 92
Bonners Ferry Log Inn (Bonners Ferry, ID), 38
Bonneville Museum (Idaho Falls, ID), 62
Bonneville Speedway Museum (Wendover, UT), 396
Bonnie Springs Old Nevada (Las Vegas, NV), 249
Book Cliff Lodge (Green River, UT), 331
Boomtown (Reno, NV), 281
Boot Hill (Virginia City, MT), 202
Boothill Swords Park Cemetery (Billings, MT), 129
Borrie's (Great Falls, MT), 163
Bottle Creek Ski Trails (Encampment, WY), 447
Boulder City/Hoover Dam Museum (Boulder City, NV), 226
Boulder Hot Springs Hotel (Boulder, MT), 134
Boulder Mountain Lodge (Boulder, UT), 313
Boulder Station (Las Vegas, NV), 264
Boulder View Inn (Torrey, UT), 393
Bowdoin National Wildlife Refuge (Malta, MT), 186
Bowers Mansion (Carson City, NV), 229
Box Canyon Trailhead (Big Timber, MT), 128
Boysen State Park (Riverton, WY), 488
Boysen State Park (Thermopolis, WY), 500
Bozeman's Days Inn and Conference Center (Bozeman, MT), 138
Bradford Brinton Memorial (Sheridan, WY), 495
Breakfast Shoppe (Driggs, ID), 52
Breteche Creek (Cody, WY), 440
Brian Head Ski Resort (Cedar City, UT), 322
Brian Head-Panguitch Lake Scenic Byway (Cedar City, UT), 322
Brick Oven Beanery (Boise, ID), 31
Bricks Restaurant and Wine Bar (Reno, NV), 280
Bridger Bowl Ski Area (Bozeman, MT), 135
Bridger Inn B&B (Bozeman, MT), 138
Bridger Wilderness (Pinedale, WY), 484
Bridger-Teton National Forest (Afton, WY), 421
Bridger-Teton National Forest (Jackson, WY), 461
Bridger-Teton National Forest, Pinedale District (Pinedale, WY), 483
Brigham City Museum-Gallery (Brigham City, UT), 314

Brigham Street Inn (Salt Lake City, UT), 387
Brigham Young Monument (Salt Lake City, UT), 375
Brigham Young University (Provo, UT), 361
Brigham Young Winter Home (St. George, UT), 368
Brighton Ski Resort (Salt Lake City, UT), 377, 384
Brights Cafe (Douglas, WY), 444
Bristlecone Loop (Bryce Canyon National Park, UT), 315
Broker Restaurant (Riverton, WY), 489
Brooks Lake Lodge (Dubois, WY), 446
Brundage Mountain Ski Resort (McCall, ID), 72
Bruneau and Jarbridge Rivers, Bruneau Canyon (Mountain Home, ID), 78
Bruneau Overlook (Bruneau, ID), 39
Bruneau Sand Dunes Park (Bruneau, ID), 39
Bruno's (Billings, MT), 131
Brush Creek Ranch (Saratoga, WY), 493
Bryce Canyon Lodge (Bryce Canyon National Park, UT), 317
Bryce Canyon National Park (Panguitch, UT), 352
Bryce Canyon Pines (Bryce Canyon National Park, UT), 317
Bryce Canyon Pines Restaurant (Bryce Canyon National Park, UT), 317
Bryce Canyon Resort (Bryce Canyon National Park, UT), 318
Bryce View Lodge (Bryce Canyon National Park, UT), 318
Bubba's Bar-B-Que (Jackson, WY), 464
Buccaneer Bay Club (Las Vegas, NV), 257
Buckrail Lodge (Jackson, WY), 466
Budget Host Night's Inn (Richfield, UT), 366
Budget Host Pronghorn (Lander, WY), 473
Budget Inn (Great Falls, MT), 164
Buffalo Bill Dam and Visitor Center (Cody, WY), 437
Buffalo Bill Historical Center (Cody, WY), 436
Buffalo Bill Museum (Cody, WY), 436
Buffalo Bill State Park (Cody, WY), 437
Buffalo Bill Village (Cody, WY), 440
Buffalo Bus Lines (West Yellowstone, MT), 204
Buffalo Café (Twin Falls, ID), 99
Buffalo Joe's Smokehouse (Salt Lake City, UT), 380
Bumbleberry Inn (Springdale, UT), 390
The Bunnery (Jackson, WY), 464
Burggraf's Countrylane B & B (Bigfork, MT), 127
Burgies (Park City, UT), 355
Burn's Saddlery (Salina, UT), 371
Burr Trail Cafe (Boulder, UT), 313
Busy Bee (Kemmerer, WY), 470

Butch Cassidy's Restaurant and Saloon (Montpelier, ID), 75

C. J. Strike Dam (Bruneau, ID), 39
C. M. Russell Museum Complex and Original Log Cabin Studio (Great Falls, MT), 162
C'Mon Inn (Billings, MT), 133
Caboose Motel (Libby, MT), 184
Cache Creek Ranch (Grangeville, ID), 57
Cactus Pete's Hotel-Casino (Jackpot, NV), 243
Cadillac Grille (Jackson, WY), 464
Caesars Palace (Las Vegas, NV), 268
Caesars Tahoe (Stateline, NV), 285
Cafe Basilas (St. George, UT), 369
Cafe Diablo (Torrey, UT), 392
Café Habanero (Logan, UT), 338
Cafe Jacques (Laramie, WY), 476
Cafe Jones (Billings, MT), 131
Cafe Nicolle (Las Vegas, NV), 254
Café Terigo (Park City, UT), 355
Cajun Skillet (Ogden, UT), 350
Cal-Neva Resort (Crystal Bay, NV), 232
Caldos y Mariscos el 7 Mares (Caldwell, ID), 42
Caldron Linn (Burley, ID), 40
Caleb's Country Grill (Fillmore, UT), 328
Calico (Jackson, WY), 464
Caliente Hot Springs Motel (Caliente, NV), 227
Caliente Railroad Depot & Boxcar Museum (Caliente, NV), 227
California (Las Vegas, NV), 264
Cam-Plex (Gillette, WY), 451
Camelot (Laramie, WY), 476
Camp Floyd, Stagecoach Inn State Park and Museum (Provo, UT), 362
Campbell County Recreation Center and Pool (Gillette, WY), 451
Campbell Lodge (Glasgow, MT), 160
campgrounds (Yellowstone National Park, WY), 510
Canefield Mountain Trail System (Coeur d'Alene, ID), 47
Canyon County Historical Society Museum (Nampa, ID), 79
Canyon Ferry Recreation Area (Helena, MT), 172
Canyon Lodge (Yellowstone National Park, WY), 510
Canyon Motel (Buffalo, WY), 425
Canyon Ranch Motel (Springdale, UT), 390
Canyon Rims Recreation Area (Monticello, UT), 346
Canyon Trailrides (Bryce Canyon National Park, UT), 317
Canyonlands By Night (Moab, UT), 343
Canyonlands Field Institute (Moab, UT), 342
Canyonlands Motor Inn (Monticello, UT), 347
Canyonlands National Park (Moab, UT), 342

Canyonlands National Park (Monticello, UT), 346

The Canyons (Park City, UT), 353

Capitol Gorge (Capitol Reef National Park, UT), 321

Capitol Reef Cafe (Torrey, UT), 392

Capitol Reef National Park (Loa, UT), 336

Capitol Reef National Park (Richfield, UT), 365

Capitol Reef National Park (Torrey, UT), 392

Capone's (Coeur d'Alene, ID), 48

Caramel Cookie Waffle (Billings, MT), 131

Carbon County Museum (Rawlins, WY), 486

Caribou National Forest (Montpelier, ID), 75

Carmela Vineyard (Glenn's Ferry, ID), 55

Carmela Vineyards Restaurant (Glenn's Ferry, ID), 55

Carriage House (Las Vegas, NV), 264

Carson Nugget (Carson City, NV), 231

Carson Nugget Steak House (Carson City, NV), 230

Carson Station Hotel Casino (Carson City, NV), 231

Carson Valley Inn (Minden-Gardnerville, NV), 273

Carson Valley Motor Lodge (Minden-Gardnerville, NV), 273

Carver's (Henderson, NV), 241

Casa de Oro (Moscow, ID), 77

Casa Rios (Vernal, UT), 395

Cascade Reservoir (McCall, ID), 73

Casey's Timber Haus (Wheatland, WY), 504

Casino West (Yerington, NV), 289

Casper Mountain and Beartrap Meadow Parks (Casper, WY), 426

Casper Planetarium (Casper, WY), 427

Cassia County Historical Museum (Burley, ID), 40

Cassie's Supper Club (Cody, WY), 438

Cassie's Supper Club and Dance Hall (Cody, WY), 437

The Castle (Virginia City, NV), 287

Castle (White Suphur Springs, MT), 208

The Castle Museum (White Suphur Springs, MT), 208

Castle Valley Inn Bed & Breakfast (Moab, UT), 344

Casual Cove Bed and Breakfast (Cody, WY), 440

Cathay House (Las Vegas, NV), 254

Cathedral Gorge State Park (Caliente, NV), 227

Cathedral of St. Helena (Helena, MT), 173

Cathedral of the Madeleine (Salt Lake City, UT), 376

Cattleman Motel (Lovell, WY), 479

Cavalryman Supper Club (Laramie, WY), 476

Cavanaugh's at Kalispell Center (Kalispell, MT), 180

Cavanaugh's Olympus Hotel (Salt Lake City, UT), 384

Cave Lake State Recreation Area (Ely, NV), 235

Cave Rock (Stateline, NV), 284

Cedar Breaks Lodge (Cedar City, UT), 324

Cedar Breaks National Monument (Cedar City, UT), 322

Cedar Breaks National Monument (Panguitch, UT), 352

The Cedars (Coeur d'Alene, ID), 48

Celtic House and Harp & Thistle (Anaconda, MT), 122

Center Cafe (Moab, UT), 344

Central Montana Museum (Lewistown, MT), 181

Central Nevada Museum (Tonopah, NV), 286

Centre Motel (Elko, NV), 234

Ceyser Park (Billings, MT), 130

Challis National Forest (Challis, ID), 45

Chapala (Boise, ID), 31

Chapala (Las Vegas, NV), 251

Chapel of the Transfiguration (Grand Teton National Park, WY), 453

Chappell Cheese Company (Loa, UT), 336

Charles M. Russell Wildlife Refuge (Glasgow, MT), 160

Charley Montana Bed & Breakfast (Glendive, MT), 161

Charlie Russell Chew-Choo (Lewistown, MT), 182

Charlie's Cafe (Burley, ID), 41

Chart House (Boise, ID), 32

Chart House (Stateline, NV), 284

Chase Suite Hotel (Salt Lake City, UT), 388

Chateau Rouge (Red Lodge, MT), 197

Cheesecake Factory (Las Vegas, NV), 251

Chef in the Forest (Coeur d'Alene, ID), 48

Chef's Coop (Casper, WY), 429

Chef's Palace (Kanab, UT), 335

Cheyenne Botanic Gardens (Cheyenne, WY), 432

Cheyenne Cattle Company (Cheyenne, WY), 434

Cheyenne Frontier Days Old West Museum (Cheyenne, WY), 432

Cheyenne Greenway (Cheyenne, WY), 433

Cheyenne Street Railway (Cheyenne, WY), 433

Chico Hot Springs (Livingston, MT), 185

Chief Black Otter Trail (Billings, MT), 129

Chief Plenty Coups State Park (Billings, MT), 129

Chimayo (Park City, UT), 355

Chinois (Las Vegas, NV), 254

Chinook Motor Inn (Chinook, MT), 143

Chuckwagon Restaurant at Colter Bay (Grand Teton National Park, WY), 455

Churchill County Museum and Archives (Fallon, NV), 237

Ciao Bistro (Sheridan, WY), 495

Circle D Restaurant (Escalante, UT), 327

Circle N (Choteau, MT), 144

Circo (Las Vegas, NV), 254

Circus Circus (Las Vegas, NV), 260

Circus Circus (Reno, NV), 281

City Creek (Pocatello, ID), 83

City of Rocks National Reserve (Burley, ID), 40

CJ's Restaurant (Billings, MT), 131

Claimjumper (Park City, UT), 355

Clark County Heritage Museum (Henderson, NV), 240

Clark House on Hayden Lake (Coeur d'Alene, ID), 49

Clear Creek Bed & Breakfast (Buffalo, WY), 425

Clear Creek Trail (Buffalo, WY), 423

Clear Springs Food (Buhl, ID), 40

Clearlake Waterfowl Refuge (Fillmore, UT), 327

Clearwater Canoe Trail (Seeley Lake, MT), 198

Clearwater Historical Museum (Orofino, ID), 81

Clearwater National Forest (Orofino, ID), 81

Cleveland-Lloyd Dinosaur Quarry (Price, UT), 359

Cliff Lodge (Salt Lake City, UT), 388

Cliffrose Lodge & Gardens (Springdale, UT), 390

Clothes Horse (Fort Hall Indian Reservation, ID), 54

Cloud Peak Inn (Buffalo, WY), 425

Club Edge and Restaurant (Cedar City, UT), 323

Club El Toro (Lander, WY), 473

Cody Coffee Company and Eatery (Cody, WY), 439

Cody Firearms Museum (Cody, WY), 436

Cody Guest Houses (Cody, WY), 441

Cody Nite Rodeo (Cody, WY), 437

Coeur d'Alene Budget Saver Motel (Coeur d'Alene, ID), 50

Coeur D'Alene Inn and Conference Center (Coeur d'Alene, ID), 50

Coeur D'Alene, a Resort on the Lake (Coeur d'Alene, ID), 50

Cohab Canyon (Capitol Reef National Park, UT), 321

Coldwater Creek on the Cedar St. Bridge (Sandpoint, ID), 92

College of Eastern Utah Prehistoric Museum (Price, UT), 360

Collins Mansion Bed & Breakfast (Great Falls, MT), 164

Colonel Bozeman's (Buffalo, WY), 424

Colorado Belle (Laughlin, NV), 270

Colorado River & Trail Expeditions, Inc. (Moab, UT), 343

Colt Service Center (Battle Mountain, NV), 225

Colter Bay Village (Grand Teton National Park, WY), 455
Colters Lodge (Afton, WY), 421
Come on Inn (Bellevue, ID), 25
Comfort Inn (Battle Mountain, NV), 225
Comfort Inn (Billings, MT), 133
Comfort Inn (Boise, ID), 34
Comfort Inn (Bozeman, MT), 138
Comfort Inn (Buffalo, WY), 425
Comfort Inn (Butte, MT), 142
Comfort Inn (Cheyenne, WY), 434
Comfort Inn (Cody, WY), 441
Comfort Inn (Gardiner, MT), 154
Comfort Inn (Great Falls, MT), 164
Comfort Inn (Hamilton, MT), 167
Comfort Inn (Helena, MT), 176
Comfort Inn (Las Vegas, NV), 261
Comfort Inn (Livingston, MT), 185
Comfort Inn (Logan, UT), 338
Comfort Inn (Miles City, MT), 189
Comfort Inn (Payson, UT), 359
Comfort Inn (Pocatello, ID), 84
Comfort Inn (Red Lodge, MT), 197
Comfort Inn (Rexburg, ID), 87
Comfort Inn (Rock Springs, WY), 491
Comfort Inn (Salt Lake City, UT), 384
Comfort Inn (Twin Falls, ID), 100
Comfort Inn (West Yellowstone, MT), 205
Comfort Inn Airport (Salt Lake City, UT), 384
Comfort Inn at Big Sky (Big Sky, MT), 124
Comfort Inn of Blanding (Blanding, UT), 310
Comfort Inn-Airport (Las Vegas, NV), 261
Comfort Inn-Dillon (Dillon, MT), 149
Comfort Suites (Moab, UT), 345
Comfort Suites (St. George, UT), 370
Comstock (Reno, NV), 281
Conrad Mansion (Kalispell, MT), 178
Continental Bistro (Pocatello, ID), 84
Continental Divide (Ennis, MT), 151
Cooney Reservoir State Park (Red Lodge, MT), 196
Copper King Mansion (Butte, MT), 141
Copper Village Museum and Arts Center (Anaconda, MT), 121
Coral Pink Sand Dunes State Park (Kanab, UT), 334
Corral (Afton, WY), 421
Corral Bar, Café & Motel (Big Sky, MT), 125
Corral Motel (Harlowton, MT), 170
Corral Steakhouse Cafe (Big Sky, MT), 124
Cottontree Inn (Rawlins, WY), 488
Cottonwood Butte Ski Resort (Grangeville, ID), 56
Cottonwood Cove Resort and Marina (Laughlin, NV), 270
Cottonwood Inn (Glasgow, MT), 160

Cougar Ranch Bed & Breakfast (Missoula, MT), 192
Council Grove State Park (Missoula, MT), 189
Council Hall (Salt Lake City, UT), 378
Country Cottage (Sundance, WY), 497
Country Inn (Las Vegas, NV), 251
Courtyard by Marriott (Boise, ID), 34
Courtyard by Marriott (Las Vegas, NV), 265
Courtyard by Marriott (Salt Lake City, UT), 384
Covered Wagon (Lusk, WY), 480
Cow Canyon Trading Post (Bluff, UT), 312
Cowboy Grub (Salt Lake City, UT), 380
Cowboy Village Resort at Togwotee (Grand Teton National Park, WY), 456
Cowboy's Smokehouse (Panguitch, UT), 352
CowboyTown Motel (Buffalo, WY), 425
Coyote Café (Las Vegas, NV), 254
The Coyote Inn at Green Valley Spa & Tennis Resort (St. George, UT), 370
Coyote Roadhouse (Bigfork, MT), 126
Craters of the Moon National Monument (Arco, ID), 22
Crazy Mountain Museum (Big Timber, MT), 128
Creekside (Salt Lake City, UT), 382
cross-country skiing (Yellowstone National Park, WY), 507
Crossbow Restaurant (Worland, WY), 505
Crossroads HoJo Inn (Buffalo, WY), 425
Crystal Inn (Brigham City, UT), 315
Crystal Inn (Salt Lake City, UT), 385
Crystal Lake (Lewistown, MT), 181
Cuchina (Salt Lake City, UT), 380
Cunningham's Bed & Breakfast (Glenn's Ferry, ID), 56
Curry Manor (Vernal, UT), 395
Curt Gowdy State Park (Cheyenne, WY), 432
Custer County Art Center (Miles City, MT), 187
Custer National Forest (Hardin, MT), 168
Custer National Forest (Red Lodge, MT), 196
Custer National Forest, Ashland and Sioux Districts (Billings, MT), 129
Cycling (Yellowstone National Park, WY), 507

Dalton's Fine Dining (Payson, UT), 359
Daly Mansion (Hamilton, MT), 166
Dan O'Laurie Museum (Moab, UT), 342
Danish Viking Lodge (Heber City, UT), 333
Darby Pioneer Museum (Darby, MT), 146
Daughters of the Utah Pioneers Museum (Logan, UT), 337
Daughters of Utah Pioneers Museum (Ogden, UT), 348

Davis Dam (Laughlin, NV), 270
Davy Jackson Inn (Jackson, WY), 466
Days Inn (Beaver, UT), 308
Days Inn (Billings, MT), 133
Days Inn (Cheyenne, WY), 434
Days Inn (Cody, WY), 441
Days Inn (Coeur d'Alene, ID), 50
Days Inn (Gillette, WY), 452
Days Inn (Glendive, MT), 162
Days Inn (Great Falls, MT), 164
Days Inn (Jackson, WY), 466
Days Inn (Jerome, ID), 65
Days Inn (Kalispell, MT), 181
Days Inn (Las Vegas, NV), 261
Days Inn (Logan, UT), 338
Days Inn (Missoula, MT), 192
Days Inn (Ogden, UT), 351
Days Inn (Pocatello, ID), 84
Days Inn (Provo, UT), 364
Days Inn (Rawlins, WY), 488
Days Inn (Richfield, UT), 366
Days Inn (Rock Springs, WY), 491
Days Inn (Sheridan, WY), 496
Days Inn (West Yellowstone, MT), 205
Days Inn (Winnemucca, NV), 288
Days Inn Airport (Salt Lake City, UT), 385
Dead Horse Point State Park (Moab, UT), 342
Deano's Pizza (Fillmore, UT), 328
Deer Creek State Park (Heber City, UT), 332
Deer Crossing (Hamilton, MT), 167
Deer Flat National Wildlife Refuge (Nampa, ID), 79
Deer Run Bed & Breakfast (Carson City, NV), 231
Deer Valley Resort (Park City, UT), 353
Deerfield Boutique and Espresso Bar (Buffalo, WY), 424
Defiance House (Blanding, UT), 310
Delicate Arch and Wolfe Ranch (Arches National Park, UT), 305
Delmonico's (Las Vegas, NV), 255
Delta Center (Salt Lake City, UT), 377
Denali Grill and Bakery (Green River, WY), 459
Dent Bridge (Orofino, ID), 81
Depot (Missoula, MT), 192
The Depot (Riverton, WY), 489
Depot Center (Livingston, MT), 185
Desert Edge Brewery (Salt Lake City, UT), 381
Desert Inn (Las Vegas, NV), 268
Desert Princess (Boulder City, NV), 226
Desert Rose Lodge (Bluff, UT), 312
Desert Sage (Boise, ID), 33
Devil's Garden (Arches National Park, UT), 305
Devil's Garden Campground (Arches National Park, UT), 306
Devils Tower National Monument (Gillette, WY), 451

Devils Tower National Monument (Sundance, WY), 497

Diamond D Ranch (Stanley, ID), 95

Diamond Lil's (Salt Lake City, UT), 383

Diamond Peak Ski Resort (Incline Village, NV), 241

Dillon Visitor Center (Dillon, MT), 149

Dinosaur Museum (Blanding, UT), 308

Dinosaur National Monument and Quarry Visitor Center (Vernal, UT), 393

Dinosaur River Expeditions (Green River, UT), 331

Dinosaur River Expeditions (Vernal, UT), 394

Dip Diner (Medicine Bow, WY), 481

Discovery Center of Idaho (Boise, ID), 29

Dive! (Las Vegas, NV), 251

Dixie National Forest (Cedar City, UT), 322

Dixie Red Hills (St. George, UT), 368

DK Motel (Arco, ID), 23

Don Laughlin's Riverside Resort (Laughlin, NV), 270

Don Pedro's Last Outpost (Evanston, WY), 450

Don's Gallery Cafe (Manti, UT), 339

Donna Beam Fine Art Gallery (Las Vegas, NV), 247

Dornan's (Grand Teton National Park, WY), 455

Dornan's Spur Ranch Cabins (Grand Teton National Park, WY), 456

Double Arrow Resort (Seeley Lake, MT), 198

Double Diamond X (Cody, WY), 441

Doubletree (Boise, ID), 34

Doubletree Club Hotel (Boise, ID), 35

Doubletree Edgewater (Missoula, MT), 192

Doubletree-Riverside (Boise, ID), 36

Drai's (Las Vegas, NV), 258

Duck Inn Lodge (Whitefish, MT), 207

Dude Rancher Lodge (Billings, MT), 133

Dunraven Lodge (Yellowstone National Park, WY), 510

Dworshak Dam and Reservoir (Orofino, ID), 81

"E" Center (Salt Lake City, UT), 377

Eagle Canyon Airlines (Las Vegas, NV), 249

Eagle Island State Park (Boise, ID), 29

Earth Science Museum (Provo, UT), 361

Eating Establishment (Park City, UT), 355

Eccles Dinosaur Park (Ogden, UT), 348

Echo Bay Resort and Marina (Overton, NV), 274

Echo Canyon State Park (Caliente, NV), 227

Econo Lodge (Laramie, WY), 476

Econolodge (Casper, WY), 429

Eddie McStiff's Brew Pub (Moab, UT), 344

Eddie's Supper Club (Great Falls, MT), 163

Edelweiss (Kellogg, ID), 66

Edelweiss Haus (Park City, UT), 356

Edge of the Cedars State Park (Blanding, UT), 308

Edgewater Hotel/Casino (Laughlin, NV), 271

Edness K. Wilkins State Park (Casper, WY), 427

Egyptian Theatre (Park City, UT), 353

El Burrito Cafeteria (Billings, MT), 131

El Capitan (Hawthorne, NV), 240

El Capitan Resort & Casino (Hawthorne, NV), 240

El Cortez (Las Vegas, NV), 261

El Jarro (Casper, WY), 429

El Jarros (Lusk, WY), 480

El Mexican (Richfield, UT), 365

El Rancho Boulder (Boulder City, NV), 226

El Rancho Motel (Jackson, WY), 466

El Rancho Steakhouse (Wheatland, WY), 504

El Toro Inn (Havre, MT), 171

El Western (Ennis, MT), 151

Eldorado (Reno, NV), 282

Elephant Head (Cody, WY), 441

Elk Meadows Ski and Summer Resort (Beaver, UT), 306

Elk Street Motel (Rock Springs, WY), 491

Elkhorn State Park (Three Forks, MT), 201

Elkin's (Priest Lake Area, ID), 86

Elmore County Historical Foundation Museum (Mountain Home, ID), 78

Embassy Suites (Salt Lake City, UT), 388

Emerald Pools Trail (Zion National Park, UT), 397

Emeril's New Orleans (Las Vegas, NV), 255

Emerson Cultural Center (Bozeman, MT), 136

Emily A (Seeley Lake, MT), 199

Empress Court (Las Vegas, NV), 259

Enaville Resort (Kellogg, ID), 66

Energy Inn (Kemmerer, WY), 470

Ennis National Fish Hatchery (Ennis, MT), 150

Entrada at Snow Canyon (St. George, UT), 368

Ephraim Co-Op Building (Ephraim, UT), 325

Ephraim Homestead Bed & Breakfast (Ephraim, UT), 325

Ernest Hemingway Memorial (Ketchum, ID), 67

Escalante Outfitters (Escalante, UT), 327

Escalante State Park (Escalante, UT), 326

Escalante's Grand Staircase Bed & Breakfast Inn (Escalante, UT), 327

Eureka Opera House (Eureka, NV), 236

Evel Knievel Jump Site (Twin Falls, ID), 98

Evergreen Restaurant (Ketchum, ID), 67

Excalibur (Las Vegas, NV), 261

Experimental Breeder Reactor Number 1 (EBR-1) (Arco, ID), 23

Factory Stores at Park City (Park City, UT), 353

Fairfield Inn By Marriott (Billings, MT), 133

Fairfield Inn by Marriott (Boise, ID), 35

Fairfield Inn by Marriott (Bozeman, MT), 138

Fairfield Inn by Marriott (Cheyenne, WY), 435

Fairfield Inn by Marriott (Coeur d'Alene, ID), 50

Fairfield Inn by Marriott (Great Falls, MT), 164

Fairfield Inn by Marriott (Las Vegas, NV), 261

Fairmont Hot Springs Resort (Anaconda, MT), 122

Fairview Motel (Kemmerer, WY), 470

Family History Library (Salt Lake City, UT), 375

Family History Library (Salt Lake City, UT), 376

Famous Murphys (Reno, NV), 280

Fan Mountain Inn (Ennis, MT), 151

Far Out West Bed & Breakfast (Saratoga, WY), 493

Farragut State Park (Coeur d'Alene, ID), 47

Fasolini's Pizza Cafe (Las Vegas, NV), 251

Feist Creek Falls Resort (Bonners Ferry, ID), 38

Ferraro's (Las Vegas, NV), 255

Fieldhouse (Bozeman, MT), 136

The Fiery Furnace (Arches National Park, UT), 305

Fiesta (Las Vegas, NV), 261

Finley Point Unit (Polson, MT), 194

Firehole Ranch (West Yellowstone, MT), 205

Firehouse 5 Playhouse (Livingston, MT), 185

1st Avenue West (Kalispell, MT), 179

First Inn Gold (Laramie, WY), 476

First Place (Big Sky, MT), 124

Fishing (Alpine, WY), 422

Fishing (Dubois, WY), 445

Fishlake National Forest (Beaver, UT), 306

Fishlake National Forest (Fillmore, UT), 327

Fishlake National Forest (Richfield, UT), 365

Fitzgeralds (Las Vegas, NV), 261

Fitzgeralds (Reno, NV), 281

Flagg Ranch (Grand Teton National Park, WY), 456

Flaming Gorge Dam and National Recreation Area (Vernal, UT), 394

Flaming Gorge National Recreation Area (Green River, WY), 458

Flaming Gorge National Recreation Area (Rock Springs, WY), 490

Flamingo Hilton (Las Vegas, NV), 265

Flamingo Hilton (Reno, NV), 282

Flamingo Hilton–Laughlin (Laughlin, NV), 271

Flamingo Motel (Coeur d'Alene, ID), 50

Flanigan's Inn (Springdale, UT), 390

Flat Creek (Jackson, WY), 466

Flathead Boat Rentals (Polson, MT), 193

Flathead Lake Biological Station, University of Montana (Bigfork, MT), 126

Flathead Lake State Park (Polson, MT), 193

Flathead Lake State Park, West Shore Unit (Kalispell, MT), 178

Flathead National Forest (Kalispell, MT), 178

Flathead National Forest, Hungry Horse Ranger District, and Spotted Bear Ranger Districts (Columbia Falls, MT), 144

Flathead National Forest, Swan Lake Ranger District (Bigfork, MT), 126

Flathead National Forest, Tally Lake Ranger District (Whitefish, MT), 206

Flathead National Wild and Scenic River (Kalispell, MT), 179

Flathead Raft Co. (Polson, MT), 195

Flathead State Park, Wayfarers Unit (Bigfork, MT), 126

Fleischmann Planetarium (Reno, NV), 278

Floyd Lamb State Park (Las Vegas, NV), 247

Flying V Cambria Inn (Newcastle, WY), 482

Fort Assinniboine (Havre, MT), 170

Fort Bridger State Historic Site (Evanston, WY), 449

Fort Buenaventura State Park (Ogden, UT), 349

Fort Caspar Museum (Casper, WY), 427

Fort Churchill State Historic Park (Yerington, NV), 289

Fort Fetterman State Historic Site (Douglas, WY), 443

Fort Keogh (Miles City, MT), 187

Fort Laramie National Historic Site (Torrington, WY), 502

Fort Owen State Park (Hamilton, MT), 166

Fort Phil Kearny Site (Buffalo, WY), 424

Fort Sherman Museum (Coeur d'Alene, ID), 47

Fort Three Forks (Three Forks, MT), 202

Fort Union Trading Post National Historic Site (Sidney, MT), 199

Forum Shops at Caesars Palace (Las Vegas, NV), 248

Fossil Butte National Monument (Kemmerer, WY), 469

Fossil Country Frontier Museum (Kemmerer, WY), 469

Foundry Grill (Provo, UT), 363

Fountain Motor Inn (Newcastle, WY), 482

4 B's Inn-North (Missoula, MT), 192

4 B's Inn-South (Missoula, MT), 192

Four Corners Inn (Blanding, UT), 310

Four Corners Store, Diner & Country Inn (Newcastle, WY), 482

Four Queens (Las Vegas, NV), 265

Four Seasons (Las Vegas, NV), 269

Four Seasons Inn (Kanab, UT), 335

Four Wind (Gardiner, MT), 154

4 Winds (Jackson, WY), 467

Fourth Street Bistro (Reno, NV), 281

Fourth Ward School (Virginia City, NV), 287

Fox Hollow Bed & Breakfast (Bozeman, MT), 138

Franca's (Cody, WY), 439

Francesco's (Las Vegas, NV), 255

Frank Church–River of No Return Wilderness (Salmon, ID), 90

Franklin Covey Field (Salt Lake City, UT), 377

Fremont (Las Vegas, NV), 261

Fremont County Pioneer Museum (Lander, WY), 471

Fremont Indian State Park and Museum (Richfield, UT), 365

Fremont Street Experience (Las Vegas, NV), 249

Frenchtown Pond State Park (Missoula, MT), 189

Frenchy's Outpost (Alpine, WY), 422

Friday's Station (Stateline, NV), 284

Friendship Inn–Antler Inn (Jackson, WY), 467

Frizzy O'Leary (Priest Lake Area, ID), 86

Frontier Cafe (Stevensville, MT), 200

Frontier Gateway Museum (Glendive, MT), 161

Frontier Grill (Roosevelt, UT), 367

Frontier Montana (Deer Lodge, MT), 147

Frontier Motel (Roosevelt, UT), 367

Frontier Pies (Rexburg, ID), 87

Fruita (Capitol Reef National Park, UT), 321

Fruita Campground (Capitol Reef National Park, UT), 322

Fry Canyon Lodge (Blanding, UT), 310

Fry Canyon Lodge Cafe (Blanding, UT), 309

Galaxie Motel (Brigham City, UT), 315

Galena Lodge (Stanley, ID), 95

Gallatin County Pioneer Museum (Bozeman, MT), 136

Gallatin Gateway (Bozeman, MT), 138

Gallatin Gateway Inn (Bozeman, MT), 137

Gallatin National Forest (Big Timber, MT), 128

Gallatin National Forest (Bozeman, MT), 136

Gallatin National Forest (Gardiner, MT), 154

Gallatin National Forest (Livingston, MT), 185

Gallatin National Forest (West Yellowstone, MT), 203

Gambino's (Moscow, ID), 77

The Gamekeeper (Boise, ID), 33

Gamekeeper's Grille (Park City, UT), 355

Gandolfo's Delicatessen (Provo, UT), 363

Garden City Boardwalk (Garden City, UT), 329

Garden City Park (Garden City, UT), 329

Garduno's (Las Vegas, NV), 252

Gates of the Mountains Wilderness (Helena, MT), 172

Gateway Motel and Campground (Cody, WY), 441

Gateway Resort and Marina (Harrison, ID), 60

Gatsby's (Las Vegas, NV), 259

Genoa House Inn Bed and Breakfast (Genoa, NV), 238

Geological Museum (Laramie, WY), 475

George Henry's (Billings, MT), 131

Georgetown Lake Lodge (Anaconda, MT), 122

Geyser Whitewater Expeditions (West Yellowstone, MT), 204

Gia's (Logan, UT), 338

Giant Springs State Park and State Trout Hatchery (Great Falls, MT), 162

Ginza (Salt Lake City, UT), 381

Givens Hot Springs (Nampa, ID), 79

Glacier Gateway Outfitters (Glacier National Park, MT), 158

Glacier Highland Restaurant (Columbia Falls, MT), 145

The Glacier Institute (Glacier National Park, MT), 158

Glacier Park Inn Bed & Breakfast (Hungry Horse, MT), 177

Glacier Park Lodge (East Glacier Area, MT), 150

Glacier Wilderness Guides/Montana Raft Co. (Glacier National Park, MT), 158

Glendo State Park (Wheatland, WY), 504

Glenn's Ferry Historical Museum (Glenn's Ferry, ID), 55

Glitretind (Park City, UT), 355

Globus (Ketchum, ID), 68

Glory Hole (Reno, NV), 280

Goblin Valley State Park (Green River, UT), 330

Goff Creek Lodge (Cody, WY), 441

Gold Coast (Las Vegas, NV), 261

Gold Hill (Idaho City, ID), 61

Gold Hill Hotel (Virginia City, NV), 287

Gold Spike (Las Vegas, NV), 261

Golden Belle (Billings, MT), 131

Golden Gate (Las Vegas, NV), 262

The Golden Hills Restaurant (Zion National Park, UT), 399

Golden Nugget (Las Vegas, NV), 265

Golden Nugget (Laughlin, NV), 271

Golden Spike National Historic Site (Brigham City, UT), 314

Golden Steer Steak House (Las Vegas, NV), 255

Goldsmith's Bed & Breakfast (Missoula, MT), 193

Golf Courses (St. George, UT), 368

Gonzo Inn (Moab, UT), 345

Good Medicine Lodge (Whitefish, MT), 207

Gordon Biersch (Las Vegas, NV), 252

Gospel Hump Wilderness Area (Grangeville, ID), 58

Goulding's Lodge (Bluff, UT), 312

Goulding's Trading Post and Lodge (Bluff, UT), 311

Gourmet Galley (Sheridan, WY), 496

Governor's Mansion (Salt Lake City, UT), 375

The Granary (Billings, MT), 132

The Granary (Grand Teton National Park, WY), 455

The Grand (Big Timber, MT), 128

Grand and Sierra Bed & Breakfast Lodge (Encampment, WY), 448

Grand Canyon National Park–North Rim (Kanab, UT), 334

Grand Canyon of the Yellowstone (Yellowstone National Park, WY), 506

Grand Encampment Museum (Encampment, WY), 447

Grand Hotel (Big Timber, MT), 129

Grand Staircase–Escalante National Monument (Escalante, UT), 326

Grand Targhee Resort Ski and Summer Resort (Driggs, ID), 53

Grand Targhee Ski and Summer Resort (Driggs, ID), 52

Grand Targhee Ski and Summer Resort (Jackson, WY), 462

Grand Teton National Park (Jackson, WY), 462

Grand Union Hotel (Fort Benton, MT), 152

Grand View Point Overlook Trail (Canyonlands National Park, UT), 320

Grand Wash (Capitol Reef National Park, UT), 321

Grandma Tina's Spaghetti House (Panguitch, UT), 352

Grandview (Priest Lake Area, ID), 86

Granite Hot Springs (Jackson, WY), 462

Granite Park Chalet (Glacier National Park, MT), 159

Granite State Park (Anaconda, MT), 121

Grant Village (Yellowstone National Park, WY), 510

Grant-Kohrs Ranch National Historic Site (Deer Lodge, MT), 147

The Grapevine (Logan, UT), 338

Grappa (Park City, UT), 355

Gray Cliff Lodge (Ogden, UT), 350

Gray Line bus tours (Jackson, WY), 462

Gray Line bus tours (Las Vegas, NV), 249

Gray Line bus tours (Reno, NV), 279

Gray Line bus tours (West Yellowstone, MT), 204

Gray Wolf Inn and Suites (West Yellowstone, MT), 205

Grayson Country Inn (Blanding, UT), 310

Great Basin Bed & Breakfast (Glenn's Ferry, ID), 56

Great Divide Guiding and Outfitters (Glacier National Park, MT), 158

Great Falls Historic Trolley (Great Falls, MT), 163

Great Northern Chalets (Columbia Falls, MT), 145

Great Northern Hotel (Malta, MT), 187

Great Northern Whitewater (Glacier National Park, MT), 158

Great Rift Natural Landmark (American Falls, ID), 21

Great Rocky Mountain Outfitters (Saratoga, WY), 492

Greek Streak (Price, UT), 360

Green Mountain Ski Cabin (Encampment, WY), 447

Green River Comfort Inn (Green River, UT), 331

Green Spring (St. George, UT), 368

Greenbelt (Wheels R Fun) (Boise, ID), 29

Greene Gate Village (St. George, UT), 370

Greenlee's at the Pollard (Red Lodge, MT), 197

Gretchen's (Sun Valley Area, ID), 97

Greybull Motel (Greybull, WY), 461

Greybull Museum (Greybull, WY), 460

Greycliff Prairie Dog Town State Park (Big Timber, MT), 128

Grist Mill Inn Bed & Breakfast (Monticello, UT), 347

Grizzly Discovery Center (West Yellowstone, MT), 203

Gros Ventre River Ranch (Grand Teton National Park, WY), 456

Grouse Mountain Lodge (Whitefish, MT), 207

Grub Steak Expeditions and Tours (Cody, WY), 438

Guernsey State Park (Wheatland, WY), 504

Guinness World of Records Museum (Las Vegas, NV), 248

Gunlock State Park (St. George, UT), 368

Gunnar's Pizza (Afton, WY), 421

Gunnar's Pizza (Alpine, WY), 422

H. Earl Clack Memorial Museum (Havre, MT), 170

H. S. Gilbert Brewery (Virginia City, MT), 202

Habib's (Las Vegas, NV), 252

Hacienda Motel (Saratoga, WY), 494

Hagerman Fossil Beds National Monument (Hagerman, ID), 59

Hagerman Valley Inn (Hagerman, ID), 59

Hales' Half Acre Inn (Pocatello, ID), 84

Hamada of Japan (Las Vegas, NV), 255

Hampton Inn (Casper, WY), 429

Hampton Inn (Idaho Falls, ID), 64

Hampton Inn (Kalispell, MT), 181

Hampton Inn (Missoula, MT), 193

Hampton Inn (Reno, NV), 281

Hampton Inn Salt Lake City–North (Salt Lake City, UT), 385

Hampton Inn Sandy (Salt Lake City, UT), 385

Hangtime Climbing Gym (Park City, UT), 353

Hansel & Gretel's Restaurant (Powell, WY), 485

Hansen Planetarium (Salt Lake City, UT), 378

Hanson's Cafe (Glenn's Ferry, ID), 55

Hanson's Motel (Glenn's Ferry, ID), 56

Harbor Village Resort (Garden City, UT), 330

Harbor Village Restaurant (Garden City, UT), 330

Hard Rock (Las Vegas, NV), 265

Hard Rock Cafe (Las Vegas, NV), 252

Hardman House Motor Inn (Carson City, NV), 231

Harrah's (Las Vegas, NV), 265

Harrah's (Laughlin, NV), 271

Harrah's (Reno, NV), 283

Harrah's (Stateline, NV), 285

Harriman State Park (Ashton, ID), 23

Harris Fine Arts Center (Provo, UT), 361

Harvest Cafe (Buhl, ID), 40

The Harvest House (Springdale, UT), 391

Harvey House Bed and Breakfast (Caldwell, ID), 43

Harvey's (Stateline, NV), 285

Hatch River Expeditions (Green River, UT), 331

Hatch River Expeditions (Vernal, UT), 394

Hatchet Resort (Grand Teton National Park, WY), 456

The Haufbrau (Anaconda, MT), 122

Haus Rustica (Stevensville, MT), 200

Havre Beneath the Streets (Havre, MT), 170

Hawg Smoke Cafe (Idaho Falls, ID), 63

Hawthorne Inn and Suites (Coeur d'Alene, ID), 50

Hawthorne Inn and Suites (Sandpoint, ID), 93

Headwaters Heritage Museum (Three Forks, MT), 201

Heart Mountain Relocation Center (Powell, WY), 485

Heidelberg Inn (Ketchum, ID), 69

Heise Hot Springs and Expeditions (Idaho Falls, ID), 62

Helena National Forest (Helena, MT), 172

Helena's Country Inn & Suites (Helena, MT), 176

Helgeson Place Hotel Suites (Orofino, ID), 82

Hell Creek State Park (Glasgow, MT), 160
Hell's Backbone Grill (Boulder, UT), 313
Hell's Half Acre Lava Flows (Idaho Falls, ID), 62
Hells Canyon Creek (Grangeville, ID), 57
Hells Canyon National Recreation Area (Grangeville, ID), 56
Hells Gate State Park (Lewiston, ID), 71
Henry's Lake State Park (Ashton, ID), 23
Heritage Museum (Libby, MT), 183
Herrett Center for Arts and Science (Twin Falls, ID), 98
Heyburn State Park (St. Maries, ID), 89
Hi-16 Cafe (Newcastle, WY), 482
Hickison Petroglyph Recreation Site (Austin, NV), 224
Hickman Bridge Trail (Capitol Reef National Park, UT), 321
Hidden Creek Ranch (Harrison, ID), 60
Hidden Falls Resort–Holiday Inn Express (Torrey, UT), 393
Hidden Moose Lodge (Whitefish, MT), 207
High Country (Cooke City, MT), 146
Hiking (Zion National Park, UT), 397
Hiking Trails (Grand Teton National Park, WY), 453
Hilander Motel and Steak House (Mountain Home, ID), 79
Hill Aero Space Museum (Ogden, UT), 349
Hill's Resort (Priest Lake Area, ID), 86
Hillcrest (Moscow, ID), 77
Hilltop Inn (Billings, MT), 133
Hilton Salt Lake Center (Salt Lake City, UT), 385
Hines Mansion Bed & Breakfast (Provo, UT), 364
Historic Downtown Laramie Walking Tour (Laramie, WY), 474
Historic Governor's Mansion (Cheyenne, WY), 432
Historic Hat Creek Stage Station (Lusk, WY), 479
Historic Homes (Beaver, UT), 306
Historic Jameson (Wallace, ID), 101
Historic Plains Hotel (Cheyenne, WY), 435
Historic Tours (Casper, WY), 428
Historic Wallace Walking Tour (Wallace, ID), 100
Historical Museum at Fort Missoula (Missoula, MT), 190
Hitching Post Lodge (Jackson, WY), 467
Hitching Rack (Lander, WY), 473
Hockaday Center for the Arts (Kalispell, MT), 179
Hogadon Ski Area (Casper, WY), 427
Hogle Zoo (Salt Lake City, UT), 378
Holding's Little America (Cheyenne, WY), 435
Hole 'n the Rock (Moab, UT), 342
Holiday Inn & Prospector Casino of Ely (Ely, NV), 235

Holiday Inn (Boise, ID), 36
Holiday Inn (Bozeman, MT), 138
Holiday Inn (Casper, WY), 429
Holiday Inn (Cedar City, UT), 324
Holiday Inn (Cody, WY), 441
Holiday Inn (Elko, NV), 234
Holiday Inn (Great Falls, MT), 164
Holiday Inn (Laramie, WY), 477
Holiday Inn (Pocatello, ID), 84
Holiday Inn (Provo, UT), 364
Holiday Inn (Riverton, WY), 490
Holiday Inn (Rock Springs, WY), 491
Holiday Inn (Sheridan, WY), 496
Holiday Inn (West Yellowstone, MT), 205
Holiday Inn Billings Plaza (Billings, MT), 133
Holiday Inn Boardwalk (Las Vegas, NV), 262
Holiday Inn Crowne Plaza Suites (Las Vegas, NV), 265
Holiday Inn Express (Bozeman, MT), 138
Holiday Inn Express (Helena, MT), 176
Holiday Inn Express (Kanab, UT), 335
Holiday Inn Express Airport (Salt Lake City, UT), 385
Holiday Inn Express, Post Falls (Coeur d'Alene, ID), 50
Holiday Inn Hotel and Suites (Price, UT), 361
Holiday Inn of the Waters (Thermopolis, WY), 501
Holiday Inn Resort (St. George, UT), 370
Holiday Inn-Downtown (Salt Lake City, UT), 385
Holiday Inn–Parkside (Missoula, MT), 193
Holiday Motel (Caldwell, ID), 43
Holiday Motel (Jerome, ID), 65
Holiday River and Bike Expeditions (Vernal, UT), 394
Holliday Park (Cheyenne, WY), 432
Holter Museum of Art (Helena, MT), 173
Homestead Family Restaurant (Blackfoot, ID), 26
Homestead Resort (Heber City, UT), 333
Homestead Restaurant (Afton, WY), 421
Homesteader Museum (Powell, WY), 485
Homesteader's Museum (Torrington, WY), 502
Hondoo Rivers and Trails (Torrey, UT), 392
Hong Kong (Gillette, WY), 452
Hong Kong Restaurant (Cody, WY), 439
Hoover Dam (Boulder City, NV), 226
Horse Head Peak (Monticello, UT), 346
Horseshoe Bend Marina (Lovell, WY), 478
Horseshoe Bend Motel (Lovell, WY), 479
The Hostel (Teton Village, WY), 499
Hot Springs County Museum and Cultural Center (Thermopolis, WY), 500

Hot Springs State Park (Thermopolis, WY), 500
Hotel Becker Bed & Breakfast (Hardin, MT), 169
Hotel Higgins (Casper, WY), 429
Hotel McCall (McCall, ID), 74
Hotel Monaco Salt Lake City (Salt Lake City, UT), 388
Hotel Nevada (Ely, NV), 235
Hotel Roberts (Provo, UT), 364
Hotel Wolf (Saratoga, WY), 493, 494
Houston's (Monticello, UT), 346
Houston's Trail's End (Kanab, UT), 335
Hovenweep National Monument (Blanding, UT), 308
Howard Johnson (Lava Hot Springs, ID), 70
Howard Johnson (Lewiston, ID), 72
Howard Johnson (Provo, UT), 364
Howard Johnson Express (Billings, MT), 133
Howard Johnson Inn (Brigham City, UT), 315
Huckleberry Patch (Hungry Horse, MT), 177
Hudson's Hamburgers (Coeur d'Alene, ID), 48
Huff House Inn (Jackson, WY), 467
Hughes River Expeditions (Bruneau, ID), 39
Hugo's Cellar (Las Vegas, NV), 258
Humboldt Museum (Winnemucca, NV), 288
Humboldt-Toiyabe National Forest (Carson City, NV), 229
Humboldt-Toiyabe National Forest (Elko, NV), 233
Humbug Spires Primitive Area (Butte, MT), 141
Hungry Horse Dam (Hungry Horse, MT), 177
Hungry Miner (Rawlins, WY), 487
Hunting for Sapphires (Helena, MT), 173
Hunting moss agates (Glendive, MT), 161
Hyalite Canyon (Bozeman, MT), 136
Hyatt Regency Lake Tahoe (Incline Village, NV), 242
Hydra (Sandpoint, ID), 93
Hyrum State Park (Logan, UT), 337

I. A. O'Shaughnessy Cultural Arts Center (Whitefish, MT), 206
Ichiban (Reno, NV), 280
Idaho Botanical Garden (Boise, ID), 29
Idaho Country Inn (Sun Valley Area, ID), 97
Idaho Falls (Idaho Falls, ID), 62
Idaho Heritage Inn (Boise, ID), 35
Idaho Heritage Museum (Twin Falls, ID), 98
Idaho Museum of Military History (Boise, ID), 29
Idaho Museum of Natural History (Pocatello, ID), 83

Idaho Panhandle National Forests (Coeur d'Alene, ID), 47
Idaho Potato Expo (Blackfoot, ID), 25
Idaho Rocky Mountain Ranch (Stanley, ID), 95
Idaho State Arboretum (Pocatello, ID), 83
Idaho State Historical Museum (Boise, ID), 29
Idaho State University (Pocatello, ID), 83
Ideal Beach Resort (Garden City, UT), 330
Idle Isle (Brigham City, UT), 314
Il Fornaio (Las Vegas, NV), 252
Imperial Palace (Las Vegas, NV), 265
Imperial Palace Auto Collection (Las Vegas, NV), 248
Independence Rock (Casper, WY), 427
Independence Rock (Rawlins, WY), 486
Inn America (Boise, ID), 34
Inn at Incline (Incline Village, NV), 242
Inn at Priest Lake (Priest Lake Area, ID), 86
Inn at Prospector Square (Park City, UT), 356
Inn at Rock Springs (Rock Springs, WY), 491
Inn at Temple Square (Salt Lake City, UT), 385
Inn on the Creek (Heber City, UT), 333
Interconnect Adventure Tour (Park City, UT), 354
Intermountain Lodge (Driggs, ID), 53
Irma Hotel (Cody, WY), 439, 442
Iron Blossam Lodge (Salt Lake City, UT), 388
Iron Horse Bar and Grill (Coeur d'Alene, ID), 48
Iron Mission State Park Museum (Cedar City, UT), 322
Island in the Sky District (Canyonlands National Park, UT), 320
Island Park caldera (Ashton, ID), 24
Ivano's (Sandpoint, ID), 93
Ivo's K-Motel (Heber City, UT), 333
Izaak Walton (Columbia Falls, MT), 145

J. J. Hunan Chinese Restaurant (St. George, UT), 369
J. J. Shaw House Bed and Breakfast Inn (Boise, ID), 36
Jackson Historical Society and Museum (Jackson, WY), 462
Jackson Hole Mountain Ski Resort (Jackson, WY), 462
Jackson Hole Mountain Ski Resort (Teton Village, WY), 498
Jackson Hole Museum (Jackson, WY), 462
Jackson Hole Racquet Club (Jackson, WY), 467
Jackson House Bed and Breakfast (Eureka, NV), 236
Jackson Lake (Grand Teton National Park, WY), 453

Jackson Lake Lodge (Grand Teton National Park, WY), 456
Jackson Lake Lodge Dining Room (Grand Teton National Park, WY), 455
Jackson Lake Lodge Pioneer Grill (Grand Teton National Park, WY), 455
Jacob Hamblin Home (St. George, UT), 368
Jacobson's Cottages (East Glacier Area, MT), 150
Jail House Café (Moab, UT), 344
Jailhouse Motel & Casino (Ely, NV), 235
Jake's (Billings, MT), 132
Jaker's (Idaho Falls, ID), 63
Jaker's (Twin Falls, ID), 99
Jaker's Steak, Rib & Fish House (Great Falls, MT), 164
James Dickinson Library (Las Vegas, NV), 247
Jameson Restaurant and Saloon (Wallace, ID), 101
Jedediah's (Jackson, WY), 465
Jenny Lake (Grand Teton National Park, WY), 453
Jenny Lake Campground (Grand Teton National Park, WY), 456
Jenny Lake Lodge (Grand Teton National Park, WY), 457
Jenny Lake Lodge Dining Room (Grand Teton National Park, WY), 455
Jerome County Historical Museum (Jerome, ID), 64
Jewel Basin Hiking Area (Bigfork, MT), 126
Jewel Basin Hiking Area (Kalispell, MT), 179
Jim & Clara's Dinner Club (Anaconda, MT), 122
Jim Butler (Tonopah, NV), 286
Jim Gatchell Museum of the West (Buffalo, WY), 424
Jimmy D's (Coeur d'Alene, ID), 48
John Ascuaga's Nugget (Sparks, NV), 283
John Atlantic Burr Ferry (Blanding, UT), 309
John Bozeman Bistro (Bozeman, MT), 137
John Deere Tractor Collection (Wolf Point, MT), 209
John Hutchings Museum (Provo, UT), 362
John Wesley Powell River History Museum (Green River, UT), 330
John's Mad House Cafe (Salina, UT), 371
Johnson Mill Bed & Breakfast (Heber City, UT), 333
Jonathan's (Lewiston, ID), 71
Jordanelle State Park (Heber City, UT), 332
Jorgenson's Inn and Suites (Helena, MT), 176
Jose Posanos (Torrington, WY), 503
Joseph Smith Memorial Building (Salt Lake City, UT), 376
Josephine B & B (Billings, MT), 133
Julia Davis Park (Boise, ID), 29

Juliano's (Billings, MT), 132
Jumping Rainbow Ranch (Livingston, MT), 185

Kalispell Grand (Kalispell, MT), 181
Kan Kun (Beaver, UT), 307
Kandahar (Whitefish, MT), 207
Kellogg Mining District Ghost Towns (Kellogg, ID), 66
Kelly Canyon Ski Resort (Idaho Falls, ID), 62
Kelly Inn (Cody, WY), 442
Kelly Inn (West Yellowstone, MT), 205
Kelly's Garden of Eat'n (Beaver, UT), 307
Kennecott Bingham Canyon Mine (Salt Lake City, UT), 378
Kenny's Restaurant (Blanding, UT), 310
Ketchum Grill (Ketchum, ID), 68
Ketchum Korral Motor Lodge (Ketchum, ID), 69
Keyhole State Park (Gillette, WY), 451
Kimball Art Center (Park City, UT), 354
Kimberly Ghost Town (Richfield, UT), 365
King's Saddlery and Museum (Sheridan, WY), 495
Kings Hills National Scenic Byway (White Suphur Springs, MT), 208
Kings Inn (Torrington, WY), 503
Kirkwood Historic Ranch (Grangeville, ID), 57
Knight's British Rail (Driggs, ID), 52
Knob Hill Inn (Ketchum, ID), 69
Kodachrome Basin State Park (Escalante, UT), 326
Kokopelli Inn (Bluff, UT), 312
Kolob Canyons (Zion National Park, UT), 397
Kolob Canyons of Zion National Park (Cedar City, UT), 322
Kootenai National Forest (Libby, MT), 183
Kootenai National Wildlife Refuge (Bonners Ferry, ID), 37
Kootenai Valley Motel (Bonners Ferry, ID), 38
Krug Mansion (Glendive, MT), 161

La Caille (Salt Lake City, UT), 383
La Casita Restaurant (Twin Falls, ID), 99
La Comida (Cody, WY), 439
La Europa Royale (Salt Lake City, UT), 388
La Hacienda (Moab, UT), 344
La Quinta (Cheyenne, WY), 435
La Quinta (Las Vegas, NV), 262
La Quinta (Salt Lake City, UT), 385
La Quinta Inn-Airport (Reno, NV), 281
La Quinta Motor Inn (Las Vegas, NV), 262
Lady Luck Casino (Las Vegas, NV), 265
Lagoon Amusement Park, Pioneer Village, and Water Park (Salt Lake City, UT), 377

Lahontan State Recreation Area (Fallon, NV), 237
Lake Coeur d'Alene (Coeur d'Alene, ID), 47
Lake Elmo State Park (Billings, MT), 130
Lake Lodge (Yellowstone National Park, WY), 511
Lake Mary Ronan State Park (Polson, MT), 194
Lake McDonald Lodge (Glacier National Park, MT), 159
Lake Mead National Recreation Area (Boulder City, NV), 226
Lake Mead National Recreation Area (Laughlin, NV), 270
Lake Mead National Recreation Area (Overton, NV), 273
Lake Pend Oreille (Sandpoint, ID), 92
Lake Powell (Blanding, UT), 309
Lake Powell Air (Moab, UT), 343
Lake Tahoe Horizon (Stateline, NV), 285
Lake Tahoe–Nevada State Park (Incline Village, NV), 242
Lake Yellowstone Dining Room (Yellowstone National Park, WY), 510
Lake Yellowstone Hotel (Yellowstone National Park, WY), 511
Lakeside Inn (Sandpoint, ID), 93
Lakeside Inn (Stateline, NV), 285
Lamb's Restaurant (Salt Lake City, UT), 381
Lame Duck (Jackson, WY), 465
Lamoille Canyon (Elko, NV), 233
Lamplight Restaurant (Monticello, UT), 346
Lamplighter Inn (Powell, WY), 485, 486
Land of Magic (Three Forks, MT), 201
Land of the Yankee Fork State Park (Challis, ID), 45
Lander County Courthouse (Austin, NV), 224
Lander Llama Company (Lander, WY), 472
Landmark Motel (Moab, UT), 345
Landry's (Las Vegas, NV), 252
Lange's Kitchen (Lovell, WY), 478
Laramie Comfort Inn (Laramie, WY), 477
Laramie Peak Museum (Wheatland, WY), 504
Laramie Plains Museum (Laramie, WY), 475
Laredo Del Mar (Las Vegas, NV), 252
Las Vegas Art Museum (Las Vegas, NV), 248
Las Vegas Club (Las Vegas, NV), 266
Las Vegas Hilton (Las Vegas, NV), 268
Las Vegas Motor Speedway (Las Vegas, NV), 249
Las Vegas Natural History Museum (Las Vegas, NV), 248
Last Chance Tour Train (Helena, MT), 173
Latah County Historical Society McConnell Mansion (Moscow, ID), 76
Lava Hot Springs (Lava Hot Springs, ID), 69

Lawrence Park (Kalispell, MT), 179
Lawry's The Prime Rib (Las Vegas, NV), 258
Lazy Acres Campground and Motel (Encampment, WY), 448
Lazy B Motel (Afton, WY), 422
Lazy J (Big Timber, MT), 129
Lazy L and B Ranch (Dubois, WY), 446
Lazy River Cantina (Saratoga, WY), 493
Le Cirque (Las Vegas, NV), 258
Leaf and Bean Coffee House (Bozeman, MT), 137
LeBeau's Drive-in (Garden City, UT), 330
Lee McCune Braille Trail (Casper, WY), 427
Lee Metcalf National Wildlife Refuge (Hamilton, MT), 166
Lee Metcalf Wilderness Area (Stevensville, MT), 200
Lee's Mongolian Barbeque (Ogden, UT), 350
Legacy Inn (Manti, UT), 340
Legal Tender (Evanston, WY), 450
Legion Supper Club (Thermopolis, WY), 501
Lehman Caves (Great Basin National Park, NV), 239
Lehrkind Mansion B&B (Bozeman, MT), 138
Lemhi County Historical Museum (Salmon, ID), 90
Lewis and Clark Caverns State Park (Three Forks, MT), 201
Lewis and Clark Expeditions (Jackson, WY), 463
Lewis and Clark National Forest (Great Falls, MT), 162
Lewis and Clark National Forest, Kings Hill Ranger District (White Suphur Springs, MT), 208
Lewis and Clark National Forest, Musselshell District (Harlowton, MT), 169
Lewis and Clark National Historic Trail Interpretive Center (Great Falls, MT), 162
Lewistown Art Center (Lewistown, MT), 182
Lexie's Cafe (Cheyenne, WY), 434
Libby Dam/Lake Koocanusa (Libby, MT), 184
Liberace Museum (Las Vegas, NV), 248
Liberty Park (Salt Lake City, UT), 374
Lied Children's Discovery Museum (Las Vegas, NV), 248
Lift Tower Lodge (Ketchum, ID), 69
Lillie Langtry's (Las Vegas, NV), 255
Lin Ottinger's Scenic Tours (Moab, UT), 343
Lincoln Monument (Laramie, WY), 475
Lincoln Motel (Austin, NV), 224
Lindey's Prime Steak House (Seeley Lake, MT), 198
Lindley House Bed & Breakfast (Bozeman, MT), 138
Lindo Michoacan (Las Vegas, NV), 252
Lions Park (Cheyenne, WY), 432

Liras (Torrington, WY), 503
Lisa's Fine Foods (Greybull, WY), 460
Little America (Cheyenne, WY), 434
Little America (Green River, WY), 459
Little America Hotel and Towers (Salt Lake City, UT), 386
Little Bear Inn (Cheyenne, WY), 434
Little Bighorn Battlefield National Monument and Custer National Cemetery (Hardin, MT), 168
Little Moon Lake Supper Club (Torrington, WY), 503
The Little Wonder Cafe (Richfield, UT), 366
Littletree Inn (Idaho Falls, ID), 64
Litza's For Pizza (Salt Lake City, UT), 381
Livingston Bar and Grille (Livingston, MT), 185
Lizard Creek Campground (Grand Teton National Park, WY), 457
Llewellyn's (Stateline, NV), 284
Lock, Stock and Barrel (Boise, ID), 33
Lockhart Inn (Cody, WY), 442
Lodge at Mountain Village (Park City, UT), 357
Lodge at Riggins Hot Springs (Riggins, ID), 88
Lodge at Skyhaven (Anaconda, MT), 122
Log Cabin Cafe (Sundance, WY), 497
Log Haven (Salt Lake City, UT), 383
Log House Restaurant (Springdale, UT), 390
Logan House Inn (Logan, UT), 338
Logan State Park (Kalispell, MT), 179
Loghorn Lodge (Medicine Bow, WY), 481
Lollipops (Saratoga, WY), 493
Lolo National Forest (Missoula, MT), 189
Lolo Pass Visitor Center (Orofino, ID), 81
Lone Eagle Grille (Incline Village, NV), 242
Lone Mountain Ranch (Big Sky, MT), 125
Lone Mountain Ranch Dining Room (Big Sky, MT), 124
Lone Pine State Park (Kalispell, MT), 179
Long's Landing Bed & Breakfast (Fort Benton, MT), 152
Longhorn Restaurant (Laramie, WY), 476
Lookout Pass Ski and Recreation Area (Wallace, ID), 100
Los Amigos (Cheyenne, WY), 434
Los Tachos (Monticello, UT), 346
Lost City Museum of Archaeology (Overton, NV), 273
Lost Creek Raceway (Anaconda, MT), 121
Lost Creek Ranch (Grand Teton National Park, WY), 457
Lost Creek State Park (Anaconda, MT), 121
Lost Horse Creek Lodge (Hamilton, MT), 167
Lost Trail Powder Mountain (Darby, MT), 146

Lovelock Inn (Lovelock, NV), 272
Lower Escalante River
  (Escalante, UT), 326
Lower Geyser Basin (Yellowstone
  National Park, WY), 507
Lucky Peak State Park (Boise, ID), 30
Lunch Box (Havre, MT), 171
Luton's Teton Cabins (Grand Teton
  National Park, WY), 457
Luxor (Las Vegas, NV), 266
Lydia's (Butte, MT), 142
Lyon County Museum
  (Yerington, NV), 289

M-K Nature Center (Boise, ID), 30
Macaroni Grill (Las Vegas, NV), 252
Mackenzie River Pizza
  (Bozeman, MT), 137
Mad Mary's (Coeur d'Alene, ID), 49
Mad River Boat Trips, Inc.
  (Jackson, WY), 463
Maddox Ranch House (Brigham
  City, UT), 315
Madison Buffalo Jump State
  Monument (Three Forks, MT), 201
Madison Canyon Earthquake Lake
  Visitors Center (West
  Yellowstone, MT), 203
Madison River Canyon Earthquake
  Area (Ennis, MT), 151
Madison River Outfitters (West
  Yellowstone, MT), 204
Magelby's (Provo, UT), 363
Maggie's Bakery (Hawthorne, NV), 240
Main Salmon Wild and Scenic River
  (Challis, ID), 45
Main Street Artisans Cafe & Gallery
  (Evanston, WY), 450
Main Street Deli (Park City, UT), 355
Main Street Diner (Newcastle, WY), 482
Main Street Historic District
  (Sheridan, WY), 495
Main Street Pizza & Noodle (Park
  City, UT), 355
Main Street Station (Las
  Vegas, NV), 262
Makoshika State Park
  (Glendive, MT), 161
Malad Gorge State Park
  (Jerome, ID), 65
Mallard-Larkins Pioneer Area
  (Orofino, ID), 81
Maltana (Malta, MT), 187
Mama Inez (Idaho Falls, ID), 63
Mammoth Hot Springs (Yellowstone
  National Park, WY), 506
Mammoth Hot Springs Hotel
  (Yellowstone National Park, WY), 510
Mammoth Hot Springs Hotel Cabins
  (Yellowstone National Park, WY), 511
Mangy Moose (Teton Village, WY), 499
Manhattan of Las Vegas (Las
  Vegas, NV), 255
Manti Country Village Inn
  (Manti, UT), 340
The Manti Country Village Restaurant
  (Manti, UT), 339

Manti House Inn (Manti, UT), 340
Manti-La Sal National Forest, La Sal
  Division (Moab, UT), 342
Manti-La Sal National Forest, La Sal
  Division (Monticello, UT), 346
Manti-La Sal National Forest, Manti
  Division (Price, UT), 360
Many Glacier Hotel (Glacier National
  Park, MT), 159
Marcus Daly (Anaconda, MT), 122
Marina Cay Resort (Bigfork, MT), 127
Marjorie Barrick Museum of Natural
  History (Las Vegas, NV), 247
Mark IV Motor Inn (Moscow, ID), 77
Market Grill (Cedar City, UT), 323
Market Street Broiler (Salt Lake
  City, UT), 381
Market Street Grill (Salt Lake
  City, UT), 383
Marrakech (Las Vegas, NV), 255
Marriott Hotel (Salt Lake City, UT), 388
Marshall Mountain Ski Area
  (Missoula, MT), 191
Mary L. Gooding Memorial Park
  (Shoshone, ID), 94
Massacre Rocks State Park (American
  Falls, ID), 21
Matheson Wetlands (Moab, UT), 342
Matthew's Taste of Italy
  (Billings, MT), 132
The Maverick (Torrington, WY), 503
Maverick Mountain Ski Area
  (Dillon, MT), 149
Maxim (Las Vegas, NV), 262
Maxwell's (Cody, WY), 439
Mayflower Cuisinier (Las
  Vegas, NV), 256
Mayor's Inn (Cody, WY), 442
Maze District (Canyonlands National
  Park, UT), 320
McCall Brewing Company
  (McCall, ID), 73
McCormick and Schmick's (Las
  Vegas, NV), 256
McCurdy Historical Doll Museum
  (Provo, UT), 362
McGregors Pub (Pinedale, WY), 484
McReynolds Blacktail Cabins (Grand
  Teton National Park, WY), 457
Meadow House (Grangeville, ID), 58
Meadow Lake Resort (Columbia
  Falls, MT), 145
Medicine Bow Drifters
  (Saratoga, WY), 492
Medicine Bow Museum (Medicine
  Bow, WY), 481
Medicine Bow National Forest, Doug-
  las District (Douglas, WY), 443
Medicine Bow National
  Forest, Laramie District
  (Laramie, WY), 475
Medicine Bow–Routt National
  Forest, Hayden District
  (Encampment, WY), 447
Medicine Lodge State Archaeological
  Site (Greybull, WY), 460

Medicine Rocks State Park (Miles
  City, MT), 187
Medicine Wheel National Historic
  Landmark (Greybull, WY), 460
Medicine Wheel National Historic
  Landmark (Lovell, WY), 478
Menor's Ferry (Grand Teton National
  Park, WY), 453
MGM Grand (Las Vegas, NV), 266
Michael's (Las Vegas, NV), 258
Michel's Christiana (Ketchum, ID), 68
Mickelson's (Nephi, UT), 347
Middle Fork of the Salmon Wild and
  Scenic River (Challis, ID), 45
Midway Geyser Basin (Yellowstone
  National Park, WY), 507
Mikado (Salt Lake City, UT), 381
Milford's Fish House (Boise, ID), 33
Mill House Inn (Carson City, NV), 231
Mill Inn Motel (Sheridan, WY), 496
Mill Steak and Spirits (McCall, ID), 73
Miller's Bakery (Manti, UT), 340
Million Dollar Cowboy Steak House
  (Jackson, WY), 465
Milt's Stage Stop (Cedar City, UT), 323
Mineral County Historical Museum
  (Hawthorne, NV), 239
Mineral Museum (Butte, MT), 141
Mini Golden Inns Motel (Hungry
  Horse, MT), 177
Minnetonka Cave (Montpelier, ID), 75
Miracle of America Museum and
  Historic Village (Polson, MT), 194
Mirage (Las Vegas, NV), 269
Missouri River Headwaters State Park
  (Three Forks, MT), 201
Moki Mac River Expeditions (Green
  River, UT), 331
Mom's Cafe (Salina, UT), 371
Monarch Fisheries (Coeur
  d'Alene, ID), 49
MonDak Heritage Center
  (Sidney, MT), 199
Montana Auto Museum (Deer
  Lodge, MT), 148
Montana Brewing Company
  (Billings, MT), 132
Montana Historical Society Museum
  (Helena, MT), 173
Montana House (Missoula, MT), 191
Montana River Guides (Lolo, MT), 186
Montana Snowbowl
  (Missoula, MT), 191
Montana State University
  (Bozeman, MT), 136
Montana Tech of the University of
  Montana (Butte, MT), 141
Montana Whitewater
  (Bozeman, MT), 136
Monte Carlo (Las Vegas, NV), 259, 267
Monte L. Bean Life Science Museum
  (Provo, UT), 361
Monticello Days Inn
  (Monticello, UT), 347
Monument Valley Navajo Tribal Park
  (Bluff, UT), 311

Monument Valley Visitor Center (Bluff, UT), 311

Moon Time (Coeur d'Alene, ID), 49

Moon's Kitchen Cafe (Boise, ID), 31

Moose Creek Trading Company (Pinedale, WY), 484

Moose Head Ranch (Grand Teton National Park, WY), 457

Moose Visitors Center (Grand Teton National Park, WY), 453

Mormon Station State Historic Park (Genoa, NV), 238

Mormon Tabernacle (Logan, UT), 337

Mormon Temple (Logan, UT), 337

Mormon Temple and Grounds (Manti, UT), 339

Mormon Trail Handcart Visitor Center (Casper, WY), 427

Mormon Trail Handcart Visitor Center (Rawlins, WY), 486

Morning Ray Café & Bakery (Park City, UT), 356

Morrell Mountain Lookout (Seeley Lake, MT), 198

Morton Mansion Bed & Breakfast (Douglas, WY), 444

Mortoni's (Las Vegas, NV), 256

Motel 6 (Ely, NV), 236

Motown Cafe (Las Vegas, NV), 252

Mount Charleston Recreation Area (Las Vegas, NV), 249

Mount Rose Ski Area (Incline Village, NV), 242

Mountain Pine Motel (East Glacier Area, MT), 150

Mountain Sky Guest Ranch (Bozeman, MT), 139

Mountain Village Lodge (Stanley, ID), 95

Moyie Falls (Bonners Ferry, ID), 37

Mt. Air Café (Park City, UT), 356

Mt. Nebo Loop National Scenic Byway (Payson, UT), 358

Murphy's Oyster Bar and Grill (Boise, ID), 31

Museum of Art (Provo, UT), 361

Museum of Church History and Art (Salt Lake City, UT), 376

Museum of Fine Arts and Henry Mellet Gallery (Missoula, MT), 190

Museum of Flight and Aerial Fire Fighting (Greybull, WY), 460

Museum of Mining and Geology (Boise, ID), 29

Museum of Montana Wildlife and Hall of Bronze (Browning, MT), 140

Museum of North Idaho (Coeur d'Alene, ID), 47

Museum of Peoples and Cultures (Provo, UT), 361

Museum of the Mountain Man (Pinedale, WY), 484

Museum of the Northern Great Plains (Fort Benton, MT), 152

Museum of the Plains Indian (Browning, MT), 140

Museum of the Rockies (Bozeman, MT), 136

Museum of the Upper Missouri (Fort Benton, MT), 152

Museum of the Yellowstone (West Yellowstone, MT), 204

My Rancherito (Nephi, UT), 347

Nagle Warren Mansion (Cheyenne, WY), 435

Nani's Genuine Pasta House (Jackson, WY), 465

Naomi Peak Trail (Garden City, UT), 329

Napa (Las Vegas, NV), 259

National 9 High Country Inn (Heber City, UT), 334

National Automobile Museum (Reno, NV), 278

National Bighorn Sheep Interpretive Center (Dubois, WY), 445

National Bison Range (Polson, MT), 194

National Elk Refuge (Jackson, WY), 462

National Outdoor Leadership School (Lander, WY), 471

National Wildlife Art Museum (Jackson, WY), 462

The Nations of the Four Corners Cultural Center (Blanding, UT), 309

Natural Bridge State Park (Big Timber, MT), 128

Natural Bridges National Monument (Blanding, UT), 309

Navajo Loop Trail (Bryce Canyon National Park, UT), 315

Nedra's, Too (Kanab, UT), 335

Needles District (Canyonlands National Park, UT), 320

Nenzel Mansion (Minden-Gardnerville, NV), 273

Nephi Super 8 (Nephi, UT), 348

Nevada Beach (Lake Tahoe, NV), 244

Nevada Beach (Stateline, NV), 284

Nevada City (Virginia City, MT), 202

Nevada City Depot (Virginia City, MT), 203

Nevada Historical Society Museum (Reno, NV), 278

Nevada Museum of Art (Reno, NV), 278

Nevada Northern Railway Museum (Ely, NV), 235

Nevada State Museum (Carson City, NV), 229

Nevada State Museum and Historical Society (Las Vegas, NV), 248

Nevada State Railroad Museum (Carson City, NV), 229

New Frontier (Las Vegas, NV), 262

The New Yorker and the Café at the New Yorker (Salt Lake City, UT), 383

New York-New York (Las Vegas, NV), 267

Newspaper Rock (Monticello, UT), 346

Nez Perce County Museum (Lewiston, ID), 71

Nez Perce National Forest (Grangeville, ID), 57

Nez Perce National Historical Park (Grangeville, ID), 58

Nick Wilson's Cowboy Cafe (Teton Village, WY), 499

Nicolaysen Art Museum and Discovery Center (Casper, WY), 427

Nine Mile Canyon (Price, UT), 360

Nine Quarter Circle Ranch (Big Sky, MT), 125

Ninemile Remount Depot (Missoula, MT), 190

Ninepipe and Pablo National Wildlife Refuges (Polson, MT), 194

1904 Imperial Hotel (Park City, UT), 357

Nora Eccles Harrison Art Museum (Logan, UT), 337

Nordic Valley (Ogden, UT), 349

Norris Geyser Basin (Yellowstone National Park, WY), 506

Norris Museum (Yellowstone National Park, WY), 506

North Beach Cafe (Las Vegas, NV), 252

North Fork Nordic Trails (Cody, WY), 437

North Platte River Trips (Saratoga, WY), 492

Northeastern Nevada Museum (Elko, NV), 233

Northern Forest Fire Laboratory (Missoula, MT), 190

Northern Pacific Depot Railroad Museum (Wallace, ID), 100

Northgate Inn (Challis, ID), 46

Nowlin Creek Inn (Jackson, WY), 467

O. C. Tanner Amphitheater (Springdale, UT), 389

O'Duach'ain Country Inn (Bigfork, MT), 127

O'Fallon Historical Museum (Baker, MT), 123

O'Rourke's Sports Bar and Grill (Driggs, ID), 52

O'Toole's Under the Eaves Guest House (Springdale, UT), 391

Oak Tree Inn (Green River, WY), 459

Oasis Bordello Museum (Wallace, ID), 101

Oasis Cafe (Salt Lake City, UT), 383

Off Broadway (Jackson, WY), 465

Ogden Marriott (Ogden, UT), 351

Ogden Nature Center (Ogden, UT), 349

Old Depot Bed & Breakfast (Encampment, WY), 448

Old Ephraim's Grave (Garden City, UT), 329

Old Faithful Inn (Yellowstone National Park, WY), 511

Old Faithful Inn Dining Room (Yellowstone National Park, WY), 510

Old Faithful Snow Lodge (Yellowstone National Park, WY), 510, 511

Old Fort Hall Replica (Pocatello, ID), 84

Old Idaho Territorial Penitentiary (Boise, ID), 30

Old Mill Inn (Newcastle, WY), 482

Old Miners' Lodge (Park City, UT), 357

Old Mission State Park (Kellogg, ID), 66

Old Montana Prison Museum (Deer Lodge, MT), 148

Old Mormon Fort (Las Vegas, NV), 247

Old Piney Dell (Red Lodge, MT), 197

The Old Spaghetti Factory (Salt Lake City, UT), 381

Old Town Cafe (Missoula, MT), 191

Old Town Grill (Wolf Point, MT), 209

Old Trail Museum (Choteau, MT), 143

Old Tymer (Blanding, UT), 310

Old West Wax Museum (Thermopolis, WY), 500

Old Works Golf Course (Anaconda, MT), 121

Olive Glenn Golf and Country Club (Cody, WY), 437

On Broadway (Helena, MT), 175

Oñati-The Basque Restaurant (Boise, ID), 33

Oop's City Market (Jerome, ID), 65

Opera Theater (Glenn's Ferry, ID), 55

Orange Street Budget Motor Inn (Missoula, MT), 192

Ore House (Ketchum, ID), 68

Oregon Trail DeRail (Glenn's Ferry, ID), 55

Oregon Trail Restaurant (Fort Hall Indian Reservation, ID), 54

Oregon-Mormon-California Trails and The Pony Express (Lander, WY), 471

Original Governor's Mansion (Helena, MT), 172

Orleans (Las Vegas, NV), 262

Ormachea's (Winnemucca, NV), 288

Orofino Scenic Golf and Country Club (Orofino, ID), 81

Osaka (Provo, UT), 363

Oscar's Restaurant (Grangeville, ID), 58

Osprey Inn (Harrison, ID), 61

Our Lady of the Rockies (Butte, MT), 141

Ouray National Wildlife Refuge (Vernal, UT), 394

Outfitting and Big Game Hunting (Lander, WY), 472

Outpost Deli (Choteau, MT), 144

Overland Restaurant (Laramie, WY), 476

Overton Beach (Overton, NV), 273

Owl Hotel (Battle Mountain, NV), 225

Owyhee Plaza Hotel (Boise, ID), 35

Owyhee River (Boise, ID), 30

Oxbow Nature Study Area (Reno, NV), 278

Pack Creek Ranch (Moab, UT), 343, 345

Packard's Grill (Gillette, WY), 452

Paddlefish Fishing (Glendive, MT), 161

Pahaska Teepee Resort (Cody, WY), 442

Painted Porch Bed and Breakfast (Jackson, WY), 467

Painted Rocks State Park (Darby, MT), 146

Paisley Shawl (Casper, WY), 429

Palace Court (Las Vegas, NV), 260

Palace Station Hotel and Casino (Las Vegas, NV), 262

Palais De Jade (Reno, NV), 280

Palisade State Park (Salina, UT), 371

Palm Restaurant (Las Vegas, NV), 256

Pamplemousse (Las Vegas, NV), 256

Pancho & Lefty's (St. George, UT), 369

Panguitch Inn (Panguitch, UT), 352

Panguitch Lake (Panguitch, UT), 352

Panhandle (Bonners Ferry, ID), 38

The Pantry (Rawlins, WY), 487

Papyrus (Las Vegas, NV), 256

Parade Rest Guest Ranch (West Yellowstone, MT), 205

Paradise Guest Ranch (Buffalo, WY), 425

Paradise Inn (Livingston, MT), 186

Paradise Valley Inn Bed and Breakfast (Bonners Ferry, ID), 38

Paris Gibson Square Museum of Art (Great Falls, MT), 163

Paris Tabernacle Historical Site (Montpelier, ID), 75

Park City Marriott (Park City, UT), 357

Park City Mountain Resort (Park City, UT), 354

Park County Museum (Livingston, MT), 185

Park Motel (Montpelier, ID), 76

Park Plaza (Helena, MT), 176

Parker's Model T (Winnemucca, NV), 288

Parkway Inn (Jackson, WY), 467

Parkway Plaza (Casper, WY), 430

Parowan Gap Petroglyphs (Cedar City, UT), 323

Parry Lodge (Kanab, UT), 335

Parson's Pillow Bed & Breakfast (Cody, WY), 442

Pathfinder-Alcova Recreation Area (Casper, WY), 427

Patio Drive-In (Blanding, UT), 310

Paunsagaunt Wildlife Museum (Panguitch, UT), 352

Payette National Forest (McCall, ID), 73

Payette River (McCall, ID), 73

Payson Lake Recreation Area (Payson, UT), 358

Peacock Hill (Moscow, ID), 77

The Peaks (Grand Teton National Park, WY), 455

Peaks to Plains Museum (Red Lodge, MT), 196

Pebble Creek Ski Resort (Pocatello, ID), 83

Peery Hotel (Salt Lake City, UT), 386

Penny's Diner (Green River, WY), 459

The People's Cultural Center (Polson, MT), 195

Peppermill Hotel Casino (Reno, NV), 282

Periodic Spring (Afton, WY), 421

Perrine Memorial Bridge (Twin Falls, ID), 99

Perry's (Ketchum, ID), 68

Pershing County Museum (Lovelock, NV), 272

Peteetneet Academy and Museum (Payson, UT), 359

Peter Schott's (Boise, ID), 33

Peter Yegen, Jr–Yellowstone County Museum (Billings, MT), 130

Philips Supper House (Las Vegas, NV), 256

Phillips County Historical Museum (Malta, MT), 186

Pickle Barrel (Bozeman, MT), 137

Pickleville Playhouse (Garden City, UT), 329

Pictograph Cave State Park (Billings, MT), 130

Pierpont Cantina (Salt Lake City, UT), 381

Pine Butte Swamp Nature Conservancy Preserve (Choteau, MT), 144

Pine Gables Inn B&B (Evanston, WY), 450

Pine Lodge Bar (Encampment, WY), 448

Pine Valley Chapel (St. George, UT), 368

Pines Motel Guest Haus (Driggs, ID), 53

Pineview Reservoir (Ogden, UT), 349

Pioneer Cabin (Helena, MT), 172

Pioneer Cemetery (Idaho City, ID), 61

Pioneer Hotel & Casino (Laughlin, NV), 271

Pioneer House Inn (Bluff, UT), 313

Pioneer Lodge (Springdale, UT), 391

Pioneer Lodge and Restaurant (Springdale, UT), 390

Pioneer Memorial Museum (Salt Lake City, UT), 376

Pioneer Mountains Scenic Byway (Butte, MT), 141

Pioneer Museum (Glasgow, MT), 160

Pioneer Theatre Company (Salt Lake City, UT), 375

Pipe Spring National Monument (Kanab, UT), 334

Pittsburg Landing (Grangeville, ID), 57

Pizza Place (Lusk, WY), 480

Pizza Royal (Lava Hot Springs, ID), 70

Placid Lake State Park (Missoula, MT), 190

Plains Indian Museum (Cody, WY), 437

Plains Trading Post (Douglas, WY), 444

Planet Hollywood (Las Vegas, NV), 253

Platte River Parkway (Casper, WY), 428

Platte Valley Outfitters (Saratoga, WY), 492

The Playmill Theater (West Yellowstone, MT), 204

Plaza (Las Vegas, NV), 263

Plum Creek House (Columbia Falls, MT), 145

Pollard (Red Lodge, MT), 197

Polson-Flathead Historical Museum (Polson, MT), 195

Pomerelle Ski Area (Burley, ID), 41

Pompeys Pillar National Historic Landmark (Hardin, MT), 168

Ponderosa Ranch and Western Theme Park (Incline Village, NV), 242
Ponderosa Restaurant (Escalante, UT), 327
Ponderosa Restaurant and Lounge (Orofino, ID), 82
Ponderosa State Park (McCall, ID), 73
Pony Express (Jackson, WY), 467
Pony Express House (Austin, NV), 224
Poor Boy's Steakhouse (Casper, WY), 429
Poor Richard's (Cheyenne, WY), 434
Poplar Place (Moab, UT), 344
Porcelain Basin (Yellowstone National Park, WY), 507
Porch Swing Bed and Breakfast (Cheyenne, WY), 435
Porcupine Pub and Grille (Salt Lake City, UT), 381
Port Polson Inn (Polson, MT), 195
Porter Park Carousel (Rexburg, ID), 86
Portneuf River (Lava Hot Springs, ID), 70
Powder Mountain (Ogden, UT), 349
Prairie Inn (Evanston, WY), 450
Prairie Schooner (Ogden, UT), 350
Price Canyon Recreation Area (Price, UT), 360
Prichard Art Gallery (Moscow, ID), 76
Priest Lake (Priest Lake Area, ID), 85
Priest Lake State Park (Priest Lake Area, ID), 85
Prime (Las Vegas, NV), 260
Prince of Wales Hotel (Glacier National Park, MT), 159
Prospector Inn (Escalante, UT), 327
Prospector Pizza (Big Timber, MT), 128
Proud Cut (Cody, WY), 439
Providence Inn (Logan, UT), 339
Provo Courtyard by Marriott (Provo, UT), 364
Provo Marriott (Provo, UT), 364
Pryo Mountain National Wild Horse Range (Lovell, WY), 478
Public Beach (Laughlin, NV), 270
Pug Mahon's (Billings, MT), 132
Purple Cow (Hardin, MT), 169

Quality 49er (Jackson, WY), 468
Quality Inn (Beaver, UT), 308
Quality Inn (Gillette, WY), 452
Quality Inn (Idaho Falls, ID), 64
Quality Inn (Richfield, UT), 366
Quality Inn (Sandpoint, ID), 93
Quality Inn Airport Suites (Boise, ID), 35
Quality Inn Downtown (Cedar City, UT), 324
Quality Inn Homestead (Billings, MT), 133
Quality Inn Pine Lodge (Whitefish, MT), 207
Quality Inn–Midvalley (Salt Lake City, UT), 386
Quality Inns & Suites–Plaza Hotel (Thermopolis, WY), 501

Queen's Garden Trail (Bryce Canyon National Park, UT), 315
Questa (Bigfork, MT), 126

R Lazy S Ranch (Teton Village, WY), 499
Rabbit Valley Bakery and Cafe (Torrey, UT), 392
Radisson (Casper, WY), 430
Radisson Airport (Salt Lake City, UT), 386
Radisson Northern (Billings, MT), 133
Radisson Suite Hotel (Ogden, UT), 351
Rafael's (Salt Lake City, UT), 381
Rainbow Bridge National Monument (Blanding, UT), 309
Rainbow Club (Henderson, NV), 241
Rainbow Ranch Lodge (Big Sky, MT), 125
Rainbow Valley (Ennis, MT), 151
Rainsford Inn (Cheyenne, WY), 435
Ram's Horn Cafe (Worland, WY), 505
Ramada Express (Laughlin, NV), 271
Ramada Inn (Boise, ID), 35
Ramada Inn (St. George, UT), 370
Ramada Inn Copper King Park Hotel (Butte, MT), 142
Ramada Inn Copper Queen & Casino (Ely, NV), 236
Ramada Inn–Downtown (Salt Lake City, UT), 386
Ramada Limited (Billings, MT), 134
Ramada Limited (Bozeman, MT), 139
Ramada Limited (Gillette, WY), 452
Ramada Limited (Rock Springs, WY), 491
Ramshorn Bagel and Deli (Dubois, WY), 446
Ranch at Ucross (Buffalo, WY), 425
Ranch Barbecue (Lander, WY), 473
Ranch Willow Bed & Breakfast (Sheridan, WY), 496
The Rancher (Laramie, WY), 476
The Range (Jackson, WY), 465
Range Rider of the Yellowstone Museum (Billings, MT), 130
Range Riders Museum and Pioneer Memorial Hall (Miles City, MT), 187
Rapscallion (Reno, NV), 280
Ravalli County Museum (Hamilton, MT), 166
Rawhide Motel (Lusk, WY), 480
Red Butte Cafe (Salt Lake City, UT), 381
Red Butte Garden and Arboretum (Salt Lake City, UT), 375
Red Canyon River Trips (Cody, WY), 438
Red Lion (Missoula, MT), 193
Red Lion Hotel (Lewiston, ID), 72
Red Lion Inn & Casino (Elko, NV), 234
Red Lion Inn (Winnemucca, NV), 288
Red Lodge Historic District (Red Lodge, MT), 196
Red Lodge Mountain Ski Area (Red Lodge, MT), 196

Red Rock Canyon National Conservation Area (Las Vegas, NV), 247
Redfish Lake Visitor Center (Stanley, ID), 95
Redford Motel (Glenn's Ferry, ID), 56
Reeder's Alley (Helena, MT), 173
Remo's (Pocatello, ID), 84
Rendezvous Beach (Garden City, UT), 329
Rendezvous Trail/Castle Gardens Self-Guided Driving Tour (Riverton, WY), 489
Renegade Rides (Encampment, WY), 447
Reno Hilton (Reno, NV), 282
Residence Inn by Marriott (Boise, ID), 36
Residence Inn by Marriott (Las Vegas, NV), 267
Resort Hotel at Jackson Hole (Teton Village, WY), 500
Restaurant at Salmon River Inn (Riggins, ID), 88
The Restaurant Roy (Provo, UT), 363
Reston Hotel (Salt Lake City, UT), 386
Rex (Billings, MT), 132
Ricardo's (Las Vegas, NV), 253
Ricardo's (Price, UT), 360
Richfield Travel Lodge (Richfield, UT), 366
Rick's Cafe Americain at the Flicks (Boise, ID), 31
Ricks College (Rexburg, ID), 87
Riggins Motel (Riggins, ID), 88
Rim Tours (Moab, UT), 343
Rim Trail (Bryce Canyon National Park, UT), 317
Rimrock Dude Ranch (Cody, WY), 442
Rimview Inn (Billings, MT), 134
Rio Grande Cafe (Salt Lake City, UT), 382
Rio Suite Hotel & Casino (Las Vegas, NV), 269
River Palms Resort & Casino (Laughlin, NV), 271
River Rock Lodge (Big Sky, MT), 125
River Street Inn Bed and Breakfast (Sun Valley Area, ID), 97
River Trips–Idaho Outfitters and Guides Association (Boise, ID), 31
River Trips–Idaho Outfitters and Guides Association (Grangeville, ID), 58
Riverbend Inn, Post Falls (Coeur d'Alene, ID), 51
Riverhorse Cafe (Park City, UT), 356
Riverside Garage and Cabins (Encampment, WY), 448
Riverside Inn (Lava Hot Springs, ID), 70
Riverside Inn (McCall, ID), 74
Riverton Museum (Riverton, WY), 489
Riverview Hotel (Lewiston, ID), 72
Riviera (Las Vegas, NV), 267
Riviera Lodge (Saratoga, WY), 494
Road Creek Inn (Loa, UT), 336
Roal Ridge Restaurant (Alpine, WY), 422

The Robbers' Roost (Torrey, UT), 392
Rock Creek (Red Lodge, MT), 197
Rock Creek (Twin Falls, ID), 99
The Rock Down Under (Hailey, ID), 60
Rock Lodge Resort (Hagerman, ID), 59
Rockford Bay Marina (Coeur d'Alene, ID), 51
Rockpile Museum (Gillette, WY), 452
Rockport State Park (Park City, UT), 354
Rocky Mountain Elk Foundation Wildlife Visitor Center (Missoula, MT), 190
Rocky Mountain Horseback Adventures (Lander, WY), 472
Rodeway Inn (Cedar City, UT), 324
Rodeway Inn (Reno, NV), 281
Rodeway Inn and Historic Olive Hotel (Miles City, MT), 189
Rodeway Inn Pines Resort (Coeur d'Alene, ID), 51
Rodizio Grill (Salt Lake City, UT), 382
Rogers House Bed & Breakfast (Blanding, UT), 310
Romanico Inn (Richfield, UT), 366
Roomers (Riverton, WY), 490
Roosevelt Lodge (Yellowstone National Park, WY), 510
Roosevelt Lodge Cabins (Yellowstone National Park, WY), 511
Rooster's 25th Street Brewing Company (Ogden, UT), 351
Rose's Lariat (Rawlins, WY), 487
Rosebud Battlefield State Park (Hardin, MT), 168
Rosewood Grille (Las Vegas, NV), 258
Ross Park (Pocatello, ID), 83
Round Lake State Park (Sandpoint, ID), 92
Round Valley Ghost Town (Garden City, UT), 329
Roy's Motel (Baker, MT), 123
Royal 7 Budget Inn (Bozeman, MT), 139
Royal Hotel B&B (Lava Hot Springs, ID), 70
Royal Inn (Casper, WY), 430
Royal Motor Inn of Moscow (Moscow, ID), 77
Royal Palace (Cody, WY), 439
Royal Resort (Alpine, WY), 423
Rustic Mountain Lodge (Encampment, WY), 448
Rustic Pine Steakhouse (Dubois, WY), 446
Rustler Lodge (Salt Lake City, UT), 386
Rusty Parrot (Jackson, WY), 468
Rusty's Ranch House (Cedar City, UT), 324
Ruth's Chris Steak House (Las Vegas, NV), 258
Rye Creek Lodge (Darby, MT), 147
Rye Patch State Recreation Area (Lovelock, NV), 272

Sacajawea (Three Forks, MT), 202
Sacajawea Inn (Three Forks, MT), 201

Sacajawea Select Inn (Lewiston, ID), 72
Sacred Sea (Las Vegas, NV), 256
Safari Dining Room (Thermopolis, WY), 501
Sage Room (Stateline, NV), 284
Sagebrush BBQ (McCall, ID), 74
Sagebrush Inn (Baker, MT), 123
Sahara (Las Vegas, NV), 267
Saigon (Las Vegas, NV), 253
Sakelaris Kitchen (Baker, MT), 123
Salmon Lake State Park (Missoula, MT), 190
Salmon National Forest (Salmon, ID), 90
Salmon River (Salmon, ID), 91
Salmon River Coffee Shop (Salmon, ID), 91
Salmon River Lodge (Salmon, ID), 91
Salt Lake Art Center (Salt Lake City, UT), 376
Saltair Bed & Breakfast (Salt Lake City, UT), 386
Sam Woo BBQ (Las Vegas, NV), 253
Sam's Town (Las Vegas, NV), 267
Samba Grill (Las Vegas, NV), 256
San Juan River (Bluff, UT), 312
San Remo (Las Vegas, NV), 267
Sand & Sage Motel (Casper, WY), 430
Sand n Sage Lodge (Hawthorne, NV), 240
Sand's Cafe (Rock Springs, WY), 491
Sanders Bed & Breakfast (Helena, MT), 176
Sandpiper (Boise, ID), 33
Sandpiper (Idaho Falls, ID), 63
Sandpoint Public Beach (Sandpoint, ID), 92
Sanford's Grub, Pub, Brewery (Sheridan, WY), 496
Santa Fe Restaurant (Salt Lake City, UT), 383
Santa Fe Station Hotel & Casino (Las Vegas, NV), 263
Saratoga Historical and Cultural Association Museum (Saratoga, WY), 492
Saratoga Hobo Pool (Saratoga, WY), 492
Saratoga Inn (Saratoga, WY), 493, 494
Saratoga Lake (Saratoga, WY), 492
The Satisfied Ewe (Ephraim, UT), 325
Sawtooth National Forest–Burley Ranger District (Burley, ID), 41
Sawtooth National Recreation Area (SNRA) (Stanley, ID), 94
Sawtooth Valley and Stanley Basin (Stanley, ID), 95
Sawtooth Wilderness (Stanley, ID), 95
Scenic Drive (Arches National Park, UT), 306
Scenic Hills Motel (Salina, UT), 371
Scharf Motor Inn (Deer Lodge, MT), 148
Schwartz's Bed and Breakfast (Bigfork, MT), 127

Schweitzer Mountain Resort (Sandpoint, ID), 92
Scofield State Park (Price, UT), 360
Scott B & B (Billings, MT), 134
Seagull Monument (Salt Lake City, UT), 376
Seasons (Las Vegas, NV), 258
Seasons Restaurant (Seeley Lake, MT), 198
Seedskadee National Wildlife Refuge (Green River, WY), 458
Selkirk Lodge (Sandpoint, ID), 94
Selway River (Orofino, ID), 82
Selway-Bitterroot Wilderness (Orofino, ID), 81
Seminoe State Park (Rawlins, WY), 487
Settlers Inn (Worland, WY), 505
7-11 Ranch (Vernal, UT), 395
Seven K (Boise, ID), 34
Seven Wives Inn (St. George, UT), 370
Sfuzzi (Las Vegas, NV), 253
The Shack (Missoula, MT), 191
Shadow Ridge (Park City, UT), 357
Shalimar (Las Vegas, NV), 253
The Shallow Shaft (Salt Lake City, UT), 383
Shell Falls (Greybull, WY), 460
Shepp Ranch (Riggins, ID), 88
Sheraton (Billings, MT), 134
Sheraton Salt Lake City (Salt Lake City, UT), 388
Sheri Griffith River Expeditions (Moab, UT), 343
Shilo Inn (Coeur d'Alene, ID), 51
Shilo Inn (Elko, NV), 234
Shilo Inn (Helena, MT), 177
Shilo Inn (Idaho Falls, ID), 64
Shilo Inn (Kanab, UT), 335
Shilo Inn (Nampa, ID), 80
Shilo Inn (Salt Lake City, UT), 386
Shilo Inn (Twin Falls, ID), 100
Shilo Inn Airport (Boise, ID), 35
Shilo Inn Nampa Suites (Nampa, ID), 80
Shilo Inn Riverside (Boise, ID), 36
Shooting Star Saloon (Ogden, UT), 351
Shorty's Diner (Hailey, ID), 60
Shoshone Falls Park (Twin Falls, ID), 99
Shoshone Indian Ice Caves (Bellevue, ID), 25
Shoshone Lodge (Cody, WY), 442
Shoshone National Forest (Cody, WY), 437
Shoshone National Forest, Washakie District (Wind River Mountains) (Lander, WY), 471
Shoshone Tribal Cultural Center (Lander, WY), 471
Shoshone-Bannock Tribal Museum (Fort Hall Indian Reservation, ID), 54
Showboat (Las Vegas, NV), 263
Showdown Ski Area (White Suphur Springs, MT), 208
Showthyme (Bigfork, MT), 126

Sierra Silver Mine Tour (Wallace, ID), 101

Signal Mountain (Grand Teton National Park, WY), 453

Signal Mountain Lodge (Grand Teton National Park, WY), 457

Silvana's (Carson City, NV), 230

Silver King Hotel (Park City, UT), 357

Silver Legacy (Reno, NV), 282

Silver Queen (Park City, UT), 357

Silver Queen (Tonopah, NV), 286

Silver Spur (Sheridan, WY), 496

Silverhorn (Kellogg, ID), 66

Silverton (Las Vegas, NV), 263

Silverwood Theme Park (Coeur d'Alene, ID), 47

Simon's Fine Dining (Heber City, UT), 333

Simon's Trolley Square (Salt Lake City, UT), 377

Sinks Canyon State Park (Lander, WY), 471

Sir Galahad's (Las Vegas, NV), 256

Sky Mountain Golf Course (St. George, UT), 368

Sky Ridge Bed & Breakfast (Torrey, UT), 393

Sleep Inn (Billings, MT), 134

Sleep Inn (Boise, ID), 35

Sleep Inn (Bozeman, MT), 139

Sleep Inn (Mountain Home, ID), 79

Sleep Inn (Rawlins, WY), 488

Sleep Inn (Salt Lake City, UT), 387

Sleep Inn of Post Falls (Coeur d'Alene, ID), 51

Sleeping Giant Ski Area (Cody, WY), 437

Slickrock Cafe (Moab, UT), 344

Slickrock Trail (Moab, UT), 342

Smitty's Pancake and Steak House (Idaho Falls, ID), 63

Snake Creek Grill (Heber City, UT), 333

Snake River Bottoms Area (Fort Hall Indian Reservation, ID), 54

Snake River Grill (Hagerman, ID), 59

Snake River Grill (Jackson, WY), 465

Snake River Rafting (Jackson, WY), 463

Snake River Stage Line (Glenn's Ferry, ID), 55

Snake River Wild and Scenic River (Grangeville, ID), 58

Snow Canyon State Park (St. George, UT), 368

Snow College (Ephraim, UT), 325

Snow Family Guest Ranch (Springdale, UT), 391

Snow Flower (Park City, UT), 357

Snow King Resort (Jackson, WY), 468

Snow King Ski Resort (Jackson, WY), 462

Snowbasin (Ogden, UT), 349

Snowberry Inn (Ogden, UT), 351

Snowbird Ski and Summer Resort (Salt Lake City, UT), 377

Snowcoach tour (Yellowstone National Park, WY), 507

Snowed Inn (Park City, UT), 357

snowmobiles (Yellowstone National Park, WY), 507

Snowmobiling (Newcastle, WY), 482

Snowy Range Ski Area (Laramie, WY), 475

Soda Butte Lodge (Cooke City, MT), 146

Soda Springs Geyser (Montpelier, ID), 75

Soldier Mt. Ski Area (Mountain Home, ID), 78

Solitude Float Trips (Jackson, WY), 463

Solitude Mountain Resort (Salt Lake City, UT), 378

Solitude Nordic Center (Salt Lake City, UT), 378

Someday House (Coeur d'Alene, ID), 51

Sorrel River Ranch (Moab, UT), 345

South 40 (Sidney, MT), 199

South Bannock County Society and Museum (Lava Hot Springs, ID), 70

South Pass City State Historic Site (Lander, WY), 471

Southern Nevada Zoological Park (Las Vegas, NV), 249

Southern Utah University (Cedar City, UT), 323

Southgate Golf Club (St. George, UT), 368

Spa Hot Springs (White Suphur Springs, MT), 208

Spaghettini's (Butte, MT), 142

Spago (Las Vegas, NV), 256

Spahn's Bighorn Mountain (Sheridan, WY), 497

Spanish Peaks Brewery and Italian Cafe (Bozeman, MT), 137

Sparks Museum (Sparks, NV), 283

Sperry Chalet (Glacier National Park, MT), 159

Spice of Life (Hamilton, MT), 167

Split Creek Ranch (Grand Teton National Park, WY), 457

Spring City Historic Building Tour (Ephraim, UT), 325

Spring Creek Resort Hotel and Conference Center (Jackson, WY), 468

Spring Meadow Lake State Park (Helena, MT), 173

Spring Mountain Ranch State Park (Las Vegas, NV), 247

Spring Valley State Park (Caliente, NV), 227

Springdale Fruit Company (Springdale, UT), 389

Springville Museum of Art (Provo, UT), 362

Squatter's Pub Brewery (Salt Lake City, UT), 382

St. Anthony Sand Dunes (St. Anthony, ID), 88

St. Francis Xavier Church (Missoula, MT), 190

St. George Golf Club (St. George, UT), 368

St. George Temple and Visitor Center (St. George, UT), 369

St. Joe, Moyie, and Clearwater Rivers (St. Maries, ID), 89

St. Mary Lodge and Resort (East Glacier Area, MT), 150

St. Mary's Mission (Stevensville, MT), 200

St. Paul's Episcopal Church (Virginia City, MT), 202

St. Tropez (Las Vegas, NV), 269

Staff House Mining and Smelting Museum (Kellogg, ID), 66

Stage Coach Inn (West Yellowstone, MT), 206

Stage Deli (Las Vegas, NV), 253

Stagecoach Inn (Buffalo, WY), 425

Stagecoach Inn (Salmon, ID), 91

Stagecoach Motor Inn (Dubois, WY), 446

Stagecoach Museum (Lusk, WY), 479

Stagecoach Restaurant (Bluff, UT), 312

Star Canyon (Las Vegas, NV), 257

Stardust (Wallace, ID), 102

Stardust Resort & Casino (Las Vegas, NV), 267

Starlite Motel (Nephi, UT), 348

State Capitol (Boise, ID), 30

State Capitol (Carson City, NV), 229

State Capitol (Cheyenne, WY), 431

State Capitol (Helena, MT), 172

State Capitol (Salt Lake City, UT), 375

State Line Inn/Silver Smith Hotel-Casino (Wendover, UT), 396

Statehouse Inn (Boise, ID), 36

Station House (Tonopah, NV), 286

Ste. Chapelle Winery and Vineyards (Caldwell, ID), 42

Steak House (Reno, NV), 281

Steak Pit (Salt Lake City, UT), 383

Stefano's (Las Vegas, NV), 257

Stein Eriksen Lodge (Park City, UT), 358

Stephan's (Cody, WY), 439

Sterling Brunch (Las Vegas, NV), 260

Steve's Steakhouse (Richfield, UT), 366

Stevi Cafe (Stevensville, MT), 200

Stillwater Inn Bed & Breakfast (Kalispell, MT), 181

Stonehouse Restaurant (Helena, MT), 176

Stoneridge Resort (Coeur d'Alene, ID), 51

Stoney Desert Inn (Mountain Home, ID), 78

Stratosphere Tower (Las Vegas, NV), 268

Streamside Inn (Cody, WY), 442

The Strip (Las Vegas, NV), 249

Strutting Grouse (Jackson, WY), 465

Sturgeon's Ramada Inn (Lovelock, NV), 272

Su Casa (Rawlins, WY), 487

Sugar Bowl (Encampment, WY), 448

The Sugar House Barbeque Company (Salt Lake City, UT), 382

Sugarland Restaurant at the Holiday Inn (Sheridan, WY), 496

Sullivan's Rococo (St. George, UT), 369
Summit (Stateline, NV), 284
Sun Time Inn (St. George, UT), 370
Sun Valley Lodge and Inn (Sun Valley Area, ID), 97
Sun Valley Lodge Dining Room (Sun Valley Area, ID), 97
Sun Valley Paragliding (Ketchum, ID), 67
Sun Valley Resort (Sun Valley Area, ID), 96
Sun Valley's Elkhorn Resort and Golf Club (Sun Valley Area, ID), 97
Sunbrook (St. George, UT), 368
Sundance (Provo, UT), 362
Sundance Cottages (Provo, UT), 364
Sundance Mountain Inn (Sundance, WY), 498
Sundance Ski Area (Provo, UT), 362
Sundance Summer Theater (Provo, UT), 362
Sundown Lodge (Eureka, NV), 236
Sundowner Motel (Caldwell, ID), 43
Sundowner Station (Riverton, WY), 490
Sunflower Hill Bed & Breakfast (Moab, UT), 345
Sunrise and Sunset Points (Bryce Canyon National Park, UT), 317
Sunrise Inn B&B (Boise, ID), 34
Sunset Station (Henderson, NV), 241
Sunshine Mine Disaster Memorial (Kellogg, ID), 66
Super 8 (Big Timber, MT), 129
Super 8 (Boulder City, NV), 226
Super 8 (Butte, MT), 142
Super 8 (Cheyenne, WY), 435
Super 8 (Coeur d'Alene, ID), 51
Super 8 (Deer Lodge, MT), 148
Super 8 (Dillon, MT), 149
Super 8 (Dubois, WY), 446
Super 8 (Gardiner, MT), 154
Super 8 (Hardin, MT), 169
Super 8 (Helena, MT), 177
Super 8 (Idaho Falls, ID), 64
Super 8 (Lewiston, ID), 72
Super 8 (Lewistown, MT), 183
Super 8 (Libby, MT), 184
Super 8 (Livingston, MT), 186
Super 8 (Lovell, WY), 479
Super 8 (Missoula, MT), 192
Super 8 (Missoula, MT), 192
Super 8 (Moscow, ID), 77
Super 8 (Pocatello, ID), 84
Super 8 (Powell, WY), 486
Super 8 (Rawlins, WY), 488
Super 8 (Red Lodge, MT), 198
Super 8 (Rexburg, ID), 87
Super 8 (Thermopolis, WY), 501
Super 8 (Torrington, WY), 503
Super 8 (Whitefish, MT), 207
Super 8 Lionshead Resort (West Yellowstone, MT), 206
Super 8 Lodge (Billings, MT), 134

Super 8 Lodge–Boise Airport (Boise, ID), 35
Super 8 Teton West (Driggs, ID), 53
Super Budget Inn (Evanston, WY), 450
Svilars (Lander, WY), 473
Swan River Cafe and Dinner House (Bigfork, MT), 127
Swan's Landing (Sandpoint, ID), 93
Sweet Dream Inn (Green River, WY), 459
Sweetwater (Jackson, WY), 465
Sweetwater County Historical Museum (Green River, WY), 458
The Switchback Grille and Trading Company (Springdale, UT), 390

Tabernacle (Salt Lake City, UT), 376
Tabernacle (St. George, UT), 369
Tablerock Brewpub and Grill (Boise, ID), 33
Tacos El Tio Pancho (Mountain Home, ID), 78
Tacos Jalisco (Nampa, ID), 80
Tacos Michoacan (Caldwell, ID), 42
Tag-A-Long Expeditions (Moab, UT), 343
Tahoe Biltmore (Crystal Bay, NV), 232
Tamarack Lodge (Sun Valley Area, ID), 98
Tamarack Lodge and Motel (Hungry Horse, MT), 178
Tamarisk (Green River, UT), 331
Targhee National Forest (Ashton, ID), 24
Tate Geological Museum (Casper, WY), 428
Tautphaus Park Zoo (Idaho Falls, ID), 62
Taylor Outfitting (Lander, WY), 472
Tecumseh's Wyoming Territory Old West Miniature Village and Museum (Cody, WY), 437
Temple (Salt Lake City, UT), 376
Temple Square (Salt Lake City, UT), 376
Temple View Lodge (Manti, UT), 340
Terrace Brook Lodge (Springdale, UT), 391
Territorial Statehouse State Park Museum (Fillmore, UT), 328
Terry Bison Ranch (Cheyenne, WY), 433
Teton Flood Museum and the Old LDS Tabernacle (Rexburg, ID), 87
Teton Mountain Bike Tours (Jackson, WY), 463
Teton Pines (Teton Village, WY), 500
Teton Ridge Ranch (Driggs, ID), 53
Teton Tree House (Jackson, WY), 468
Teton Valley Aviation (Driggs, ID), 52
Teton Wagon Train & Horse Adventure (Jackson, WY), 463
Texas Red's Pit Barbecue and Chili Parlor (Park City, UT), 356
Texas Station (Las Vegas, NV), 263
Thai BBQ (Las Vegas, NV), 253
This Is the Place Heritage Park (Salt Lake City, UT), 375

Thomas and Mack Center (Las Vegas, NV), 248
Thompson Falls State Park (Libby, MT), 184
Thompson-Hickman Memorial Museum (Virginia City, MT), 202
Three Bears (West Yellowstone, MT), 205
Three Island Crossing Oregon Trail History and Education Center (Glenn's Ferry, ID), 55
Three Island Crossing State Park (Glenn's Ferry, ID), 55
Three Rivers Motel (Afton, WY), 422
Three Rivers Ranch (Ashton, ID), 24
Thunder Basin Hotel (Gillette, WY), 452
Thunder Basin National Grassland (Douglas, WY), 443
Thunder Basin National Grassland (Newcastle, WY), 482
Ticaboo Resort (Blanding, UT), 311
Tillerman (Las Vegas, NV), 259
Timberline Steakhouse (Afton, WY), 421
Timbers (Bigfork, MT), 127
Time Out (Powell, WY), 485
Timpanogos Cave National Monument (Provo, UT), 362
TLC Inn (Bozeman, MT), 139
Tom and Jerry's Steakhouse (Worland, WY), 505
Tom's Deli (St. George, UT), 369
Tongue River Reservoir State Park (Hardin, MT), 168
Tonopah Mining Park (Tonopah, NV), 286
Top of the World (Las Vegas, NV), 259
Torch & Toes Bed & Breakfast (Bozeman, MT), 139
Torres Café (Billings, MT), 132
The Torrey Gallery (Torrey, UT), 392
320 Guest Ranch (Big Sky, MT), 125
350 Main (Park City, UT), 356
Tour de Great Falls (Great Falls, MT), 163
Tower-Roosevelt (Yellowstone National Park, WY), 507
Town House Motor Inn (Worland, WY), 506
Towne Center Motel (Mountain Home, ID), 79
Towne Lodge (Idaho Falls, ID), 64
Townhouse Inn (Great Falls, MT), 164
Townhouse Inn (Havre, MT), 171
Trail End Historic Center (Sheridan, WY), 495
Trail of the '49ers Interpretive Center (Battle Mountain, NV), 225
Trail Town and the Museum of the Old West (Cody, WY), 437
Trampas Lodge (Medicine Bow, WY), 481
Trapper Inn (Jackson, WY), 468
Travelodge (Missoula, WY), 192
Travelodge City Center (Salt Lake City, UT), 387
Travelodge Motel (St. George, UT), 370

Travelodge–Downtown (Las Vegas, NV), 263

Travelodge–Las Vegas Strip (Las Vegas, NV), 263

Treasure Island (Las Vegas, NV), 268

The Tree Room (Provo, UT), 363

Treehouse Children's Museum (Ogden, UT), 349

Trenner Memorial Park (American Falls, ID), 22

Triangle Hotel (Monticello, UT), 347

Triple Creek Ranch (Darby, MT), 147

Trolley Tour on Old No. 1 (Butte, MT), 141

Tropicana (Las Vegas, NV), 268

Trout Springs Bed & Breakfast (Hamilton, MT), 167

Tubbs Hill (Coeur d'Alene, ID), 48

Turner Mountain Ski Area (Libby, MT), 184

Tuscany (Cody, WY), 440

Tuscany (Salt Lake City, UT), 384

Tuscany's (Bigfork, MT), 127

Twenty-Fifth Street (Ogden, UT), 349

Twin Falls Park (Twin Falls, ID), 99

Twin Lakes (St. George, UT), 368

Twin Rocks Cafe (Bluff, UT), 312

Two-Can Fly Paragliding (Teton Village, WY), 498

Uinta and Ouray Indian Reservation (Roosevelt, UT), 367

Uinta Basin (Vernal, UT), 394

Uinta County Historical Museum (Evanston, WY), 449

Uinta National Forest (Provo, UT), 362

Ulm Pishkun State Park (Great Falls, MT), 163

Ulrich's Fossil Gallery (Kemmerer, WY), 469

Uncle Looie's (Livingston, MT), 185

Union Station (Ogden, UT), 350

University Inn (Boise, ID), 36

University Inn (Logan, UT), 339

University of Idaho (Moscow, ID), 76

University of Montana (Missoula, MT), 190

University of Nevada–Las Vegas (Las Vegas, NV), 247

University of Nevada–Reno (Reno, NV), 278

University of Utah (Salt Lake City, UT), 375

University of Wyoming (Laramie, WY), 475

University Park Marriott (Salt Lake City, UT), 387

Upper Mesa Falls (Ashton, ID), 24

Upper Missouri National Wild and Scenic River (Fort Benton, MT), 152

Upper Musselshell Museum (Harlowton, MT), 169

Uptown Cafe (Butte, MT), 142

Uptown Cafe (Greybull, WY), 460

USDA Forest Service Aerial Fire Depot (Missoula, MT), 190

USDA Forest Service Smokejumper Visitors Center (Missoula, MT), 190

Utah Field House of Natural History State Park Museum and Dinosaur Gardens (Vernal, UT), 394

Utah Fun Dome (Salt Lake City, UT), 378

Utah Lake State Park (Provo, UT), 363

Utah Museum of Fine Arts (Salt Lake City, UT), 375

Utah Museum of Natural History's (Salt Lake City, UT), 375

Utah Opera Company (Salt Lake City, UT), 376

Utah State University (Logan, UT), 337

Utah Winter Sports Park (Park City, UT), 354

Uxu Ranch (Cody, WY), 443

Vagabond Inn (Reno, NV), 282

Vagabond Lodge Motel (Anaconda, MT), 123

Val-U Inn (Missoula, MT), 192

Val-U Inn (Winnemucca, NV), 288

Valley of Fire State Park (Overton, NV), 273

Vee-Bar Guest Ranch (Laramie, WY), 477

Veedauwoo (Cheyenne, WY), 432

Venture Motor Inn (Libby, MT), 184

Veterans Memorial State Park (Boise, ID), 30

The Victorian Inn (Salina, UT), 371

Village Inn (Challis, ID), 46

Vimbos (Wheatland, WY), 504

Virginia and Truckee Railroad (Virginia City, NV), 287

Virginia City Players (Virginia City, MT), 203

Virginia City-Madison County Historical Museum (Virginia City, MT), 203

Virginian Hotel (Medicine Bow, WY), 481

'Vista Grande (Jackson, WY), 465

Viva Mercado's (Las Vegas, NV), 253

Voodoo Cafe and Lounge (Las Vegas, NV), 259

Vore Buffalo Jump (Sundance, WY), 497

Voss Inn (Bozeman, MT), 139

W. M. Keck Minerals Museum (Reno, NV), 278

W. Pherson House Bed & Breakfast (Ephraim, UT), 325

Wagon Box Restaurant (Buffalo, WY), 425

Wagon Wheel (Pinedale, WY), 484

Wahkpa Chu'gn Archaeology Site (Havre, MT), 170

Walker Lake (Hawthorne, NV), 240

Walkers Grill (Billings, MT), 132

Wallace District Mining Museum (Wallace, ID), 101

Wanda's (Loa, UT), 336

Wapiti Meadow Ranch (Boise, ID), 37

War Bonnet Inn (Butte, MT), 142

War Bonnet Lodge (Browning, MT), 140

War Horse National Wildlife Refuge (Lewistown, MT), 182

Ward Charcoal Ovens Historic State Monument (Ely, NV), 235

Warhawk Air Museum (Caldwell, ID), 42

Warm Springs Ranch Restaurant (Ketchum, ID), 68

Warren Air Force Base (Cheyenne, WY), 432

Warren Engine Company No. 1 Fire Museum (Carson City, NV), 229

Wasatch Mountain State Park (Heber City, UT), 332

Wasatch-Cache National Forest, Logan Canyon (Garden City, UT), 329

Wasatch-Cache National Forest, Logan Canyon (Logan, UT), 337

Washakie Museum (Worland, WY), 505

Washington School Inn (Park City, UT), 358

Washoe Park (Anaconda, MT), 122

Washoe Theatre (Anaconda, MT), 122

water sports (Yellowstone National Park, WY), 510

The Way It Was Museum (Virginia City, NV), 287

Weber State University (Ogden, UT), 350

Weitas Butte, Austin Ridge, and Castle Butte Lookouts (Orofino, ID), 81

Werner Wildlife Museum (Casper, WY), 428

West Coast Idaho Falls Hotel (Idaho Falls, ID), 64

West Coast Park Center Suites (Boise, ID), 37

West Coast Pocatello Hotel (Pocatello, ID), 85

West Glacier Motel (Columbia Falls, MT), 145

West Thumb (Yellowstone National Park, WY), 507

Western Heritage (Bozeman, MT), 139

Western Heritage Center (Billings, MT), 130

Western Heritage Museum (Vernal, UT), 394

Western Hills Motel (Roosevelt, UT), 367

Western History Center (Torrington, WY), 502

Western Inn Spanish Fork (Payson, UT), 359

Western Ins Glacier Mountain Shadows Resort (Columbia Falls, MT), 145

Western Pleasure Guest Ranch (Sandpoint, ID), 94

Western River Expeditions (Green River, UT), 331

Western Timberline Outfitters (Missoula, MT), 191

Western Wyoming Community College Natural History Museum (Rock Springs, WY), 490

Westernaire (Gardiner, MT), 154

Weston Inn (Rawlins, WY), 488

Weston Lamplighter Inn (Vernal, UT), 395

Weston Plaza Hotel (Evanston, WY), 450

Westward Ho Hotel & Casino (Las Vegas, NV), 263

Westwinds Rodeway Inn (Green River, UT), 331

Wet 'n Wild (Las Vegas, NV), 249

Wheeler Historic Farm (Salt Lake City, UT), 378

Wheels Motel (Greybull, WY), 461

Whispering Waters B&B (Priest Lake Area, ID), 86

White Bird Hill Battlefield Auto Tour (Grangeville, ID), 58

White Bird Summit and Road (Grangeville, ID), 58

White Pine County Museum (Ely, NV), 235

White Pine Touring (Park City, UT), 354

White Pine Touring Center (Park City, UT), 354

White Tail Ranch Outfitters, Inc. (Missoula, MT), 191

Whitefish Lake State Park (Whitefish, MT), 206

Whitmore Mansion Bed & Breakfast (Nephi, UT), 348

Whole Famdamily (Lewistown, MT), 183

Wilbur May Museum (Reno, NV), 278

Wild Bunch Cafe (Dubois, WY), 446

Wild Horse Island Unit (Polson, MT), 194

Wild Rivers Expeditions (Bluff, UT), 312

Wilderness Gateway Inn (Seeley Lake, MT), 199

Wilderness River Outfitters (Kalispell, MT), 179

Wildflower (Jackson, WY), 468

Wildflowers Bed & Breakfast (Salt Lake City, UT), 387

Willard Bay State Park (Ogden, UT), 350

Willie Handcart Monument (Lander, WY), 471

Willow Creek Inn (Ephraim, UT), 326

Willow Glen Inn (Cedar City, UT), 324

Winchester State Park (Lewiston, ID), 71

Wind River Canyon (Thermopolis, WY), 501

Wind River Historical Center (Dubois, WY), 445

Wind River Pack Goats (Lander, WY), 472

Windbag Grill (Helena, MT), 176

The Windmill (Billings, MT), 132

Window on the Winds B&B (Pinedale, WY), 484

Wolf Lodge Inn (Coeur d'Alene, ID), 49

Wolf Point Area Historical Society and Museum (Wolf Point, MT), 209

Wolfe Krest Bed & Breakfast (Salt Lake City, UT), 389

Wolfgang Puck's Cafe (Las Vegas, NV), 257

Wonderland Inn (Torrey, UT), 393

Wood River Valley Ski Touring Park (Cody, WY), 437

Woodland Park (Kalispell, MT), 179

Wool House Gallery (Miles City, MT), 187

Worland Days Inn (Worland, WY), 506

World Center for Birds of Prey (Boise, ID), 30

World Museum of Mining and 1899 Mining Camp (Butte, MT), 141

Wort Hotel (Jackson, WY), 468

Wyndham Hotel (Salt Lake City, UT), 387

Wyoming Arts Council Gallery (Cheyenne, WY), 432

Wyoming Children's Museum and Nature Center (Laramie, WY), 475

Wyoming Dinosaur Center (Thermopolis, WY), 501

Wyoming Frontier Prison (Rawlins, WY), 487

Wyoming Game and Fish Visitors Center (Cheyenne, WY), 433

Wyoming Inn (Jackson, WY), 469

Wyoming Motel (Buffalo, WY), 426

Wyoming Motel (Wheatland, WY), 504

Wyoming Pioneer Memorial Museum (Douglas, WY), 444

Wyoming River Trips (Cody, WY), 438

Wyoming State Museum (Cheyenne, WY), 432

Wyoming Territorial Prison and Old West Park (Laramie, WY), 475

Wyoming Transportation Museum (Cheyenne, WY), 432

Wyoming Vietnam Veteran's Memorial (Cody, WY), 437

Xiao Li (Salt Lake City, UT), 382

Xinh-Xinh (Las Vegas, NV), 253

Yardley Inn (Manti, UT), 340

Yarrow Resort Hotel & Conference Center (Park City, UT), 358

Yellow Bay (Polson, MT), 194

Yellowstone Art Center (Billings, MT), 130

Yellowstone Drug Store (Riverton, WY), 489

Yellowstone Highlights (Yellowstone National Park, WY), 506

Yellowstone IMAX Theatre (West Yellowstone, MT), 204

Yellowstone Institute (Yellowstone National Park, WY), 507

Yellowstone Lake (Yellowstone National Park, WY), 507

Yellowstone Mine (Gardiner, MT), 154

Yellowstone Motel (Greybull, WY), 461

Yellowstone National Park Visitors Center (West Yellowstone, MT), 204

Yellowstone Outdoor Adventures (Yellowstone National Park, WY), 507

Yellowstone Park Campgrounds (Yellowstone National Park, WY), 511

Yellowstone Raft Co. (Big Sky, MT), 124

Yellowstone Raft Co. (Gardiner, MT), 154

Yellowstone River Fish Hatchery (Big Timber, MT), 128

Yellowstone Valley Inn (Cody, WY), 443

Yellowstone Village Inn (Gardiner, MT), 154

Yellowtail Wildlife Habitat Management Area (Lovell, WY), 478

Yesterday's Playthings (Deer Lodge, MT), 148

Yogo Inn of Lewistown (Lewistown, MT), 183

Yolie's Churrascaria (Las Vegas, NV), 257

Yuba State Park (Nephi, UT), 347

Z'Tejas Grill (Las Vegas, NV), 257

Z-Bar Motel (Buffalo, WY), 426

Zany's (Lewiston, ID), 72

Zapatas (Cody, WY), 440

ZCMI Mall (Salt Lake City, UT), 377

Zephyr Cove Resort (Lake Tahoe, NV), 244

Zion Canyon Campground Cabins and Motel (Springdale, UT), 391

Zion Canyon Theatre (Springdale, UT), 389

Zion Lodge (Zion National Park, UT), 399

Zion Lodge Restaurant (Zion National Park, UT), 399

Zion National Park (Kanab, UT), 334

Zion National Park (Springdale, UT), 389

Zion National Park (St. George, UT), 369

Zion Nature Center (Zion National Park, UT), 397

Zion Park Inn (Springdale, UT), 391

Zion Park Motel (Springdale, UT), 391

Zion Pizza and Noodle Company (Springdale, UT), 390

Zoo Boise (Boise, ID), 29

Zoom Roadhouse Grill (Park City, UT), 356

ZooMontana (Billings, MT), 130

TALK TO US

Fill out this quick survey and receive a free *Fodor's How to Pack* (while supplies last)

1 Which Road Guide did you purchase?
   (Check all that apply.)
   ❏ AL/AR/LA/MS/TN   ❏ IL/IA/MO/WI
   ❏ AZ/CO/NM   ❏ IN/KY/MI/OH/WV
   ❏ CA   ❏ KS/OK/TX
   ❏ CT/MA/RI   ❏ ME/NH/VT
   ❏ DE/DC/MD/PA/VA   ❏ MN/NE/ND/SD
   ❏ FL   ❏ NJ/NY
   ❏ GA/NC/SC   ❏ OR/WA
   ❏ ID/MT/NV/UT/WY

2 How did you learn about the Road Guides?
   ❏ TV ad
   ❏ Radio ad
   ❏ Newspaper or magazine ad
   ❏ Newspaper or magazine article
   ❏ TV or radio feature
   ❏ Bookstore display/clerk recommendation
   ❏ Recommended by family/friend
   ❏ Other:_____

3 Did you use other guides for your trip?
   ❏ AAA   ❏ Insiders' Guide
   ❏ Compass American Guide ❏ Mobil
   ❏ Fodor's   ❏ Moon Handbook
   ❏ Frommer's   ❏ Other:_____

4 Did you use any of the following for planning?
   ❏ Tourism offices ❏ Internet ❏ Travel agent

5 Did you buy a Road Guide for (check one):
   ❏ Leisure trip
   ❏ Business trip
   ❏ Mix of business and leisure

6 Where did you buy your Road Guide?
   ❏ Bookstore
   ❏ Other store
   ❏ On-line
   ❏ Borrowed from a friend
   ❏ Borrowed from a library
   ❏ Other:_____

7 Why did you buy a Road Guide? (Check all that apply.)
   ❏ Number of cities/towns listed
   ❏ Comprehensive coverage
   ❏ Number of lodgings   ❏ Driving tours
   ❏ Number of restaurants ❏ Maps
   ❏ Number of attractions ❏ Fodor's brand name
   ❏ Other:_____

8 Did you use this guide primarily:
   ❏ For pretrip planning   ❏ While traveling
   ❏ For planning and while traveling

9 What was the duration of your trip?
   ❏ 2-3 days   ❏ 11 or more days
   ❏ 4-6 days   ❏ Taking more than 1 trip
   ❏ 7-10 days

10 Did you use the guide to select
    ❏ Hotels   ❏ Restaurants

11 Did you stay primarily in a
    ❏ Hotel   ❏ Hostel
    ❏ Motel   ❏ Campground
    ❏ Resort   ❏ Dude ranch
    ❏ Bed-and-breakfast   ❏ With family or friends
    ❏ RV/camper   ❏ Other:_____

12 What sights and activities did you most enjoy?
    ❏ Historical sights   ❏ Shopping
    ❏ Sports   ❏ Theaters
    ❏ National parks   ❏ Museums
    ❏ State parks   ❏ Major cities
    ❏ Attractions off the beaten path

13 How much did you spend per adult for this trip?
    ❏ Less than $500   ❏ $751-$1,000
    ❏ $501-$750   ❏ More than $1,000

14 How many traveled in your party?
    ___ Adults   ___ Children   ___ Pets

15 Did you
    ❏ Fly to destination   ❏ Rent a van or RV
    ❏ Drive your own vehicle ❏ Take a train
    ❏ Rent a car   ❏ Take a bus

16 How many miles did you travel round-trip?
    ❏ Less than 100   ❏ 501-750
    ❏ 101-300   ❏ 751-1,000
    ❏ 301-500   ❏ More than 1,000

17 What items did you take on your vacation?
    ❏ Traveler's checks   ❏ Digital camera
    ❏ Credit card   ❏ Cell phone
    ❏ Gasoline card   ❏ Computer
    ❏ Phone card   ❏ PDA
    ❏ Camera   ❏ Other

18 Would you use Fodor's Road Guides again?
    ❏ Yes   ❏ No

19 How would you like to see Road Guides changed?

- ❏ More ❏ Less Dining
- ❏ More ❏ Less Lodging
- ❏ More ❏ Less Sports
- ❏ More ❏ Less Activities
- ❏ More ❏ Less Attractions
- ❏ More ❏ Less Shopping
- ❏ More ❏ Less Driving tours
- ❏ More ❏ Less Maps
- ❏ More ❏ Less Historical information
- ❏ Other:_____

20 Tell us about yourself.

❏ Male   ❏ Female

Age:
- ❏ 18-24   ❏ 35-44   ❏ 55-64
- ❏ 25-34   ❏ 45-54   ❏ Over 65

Income:
- ❏ Less than $25,000   ❏ $50,001-$75,000
- ❏ $25,001-$50,000   ❏ More than $75,000

Name:_____   E-mail: _____

Address:_____   City: _____ State: _____ Zip: _____

Fodor's Travel Publications
Attn: Road Guide Survey
280 Park Avenue
New York, NY 10017

The information herein will be treated in confidence. Names and addresses will not be released to mailing-list houses or other organizations.

Atlas

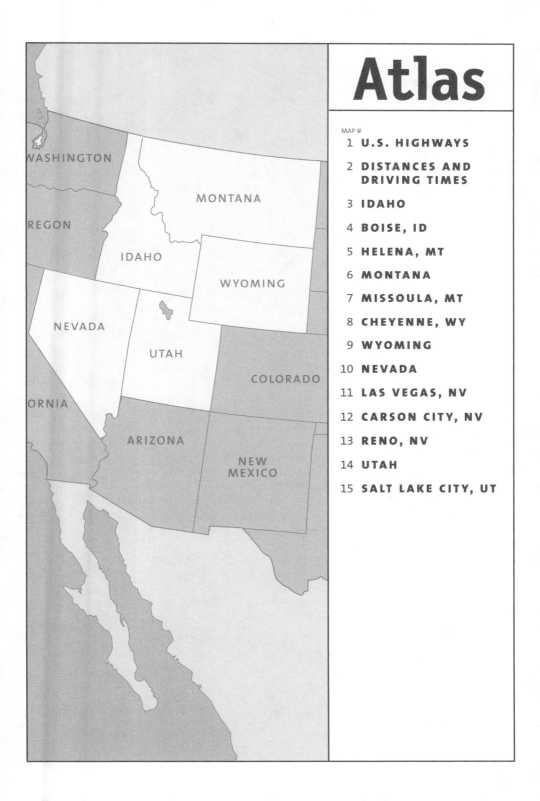

MAP #

1 **U.S. HIGHWAYS**

2 **DISTANCES AND DRIVING TIMES**

3 **IDAHO**

4 **BOISE, ID**

5 **HELENA, MT**

6 **MONTANA**

7 **MISSOULA, MT**

8 **CHEYENNE, WY**

9 **WYOMING**

10 **NEVADA**

11 **LAS VEGAS, NV**

12 **CARSON CITY, NV**

13 **RENO, NV**

14 **UTAH**

15 **SALT LAKE CITY, UT**

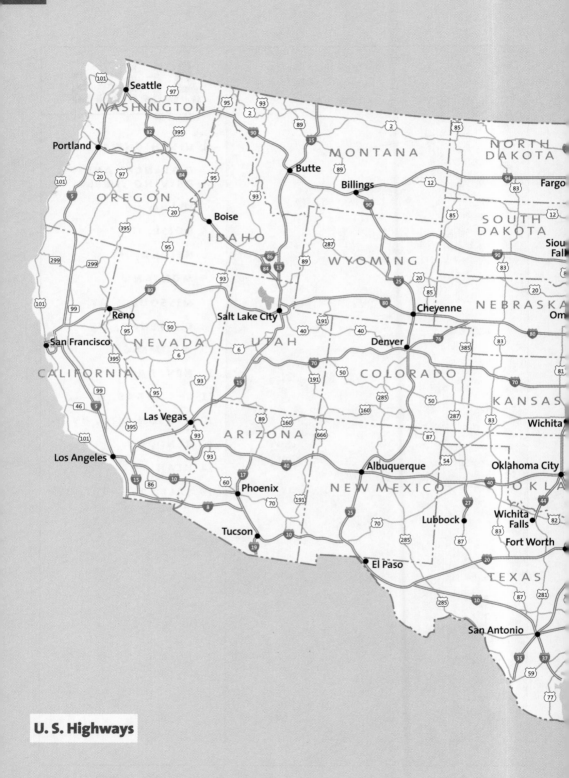

U. S. Highways

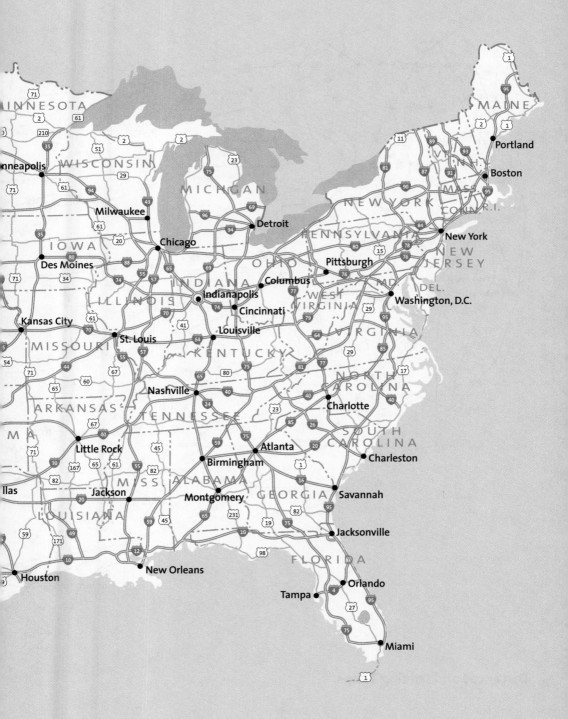

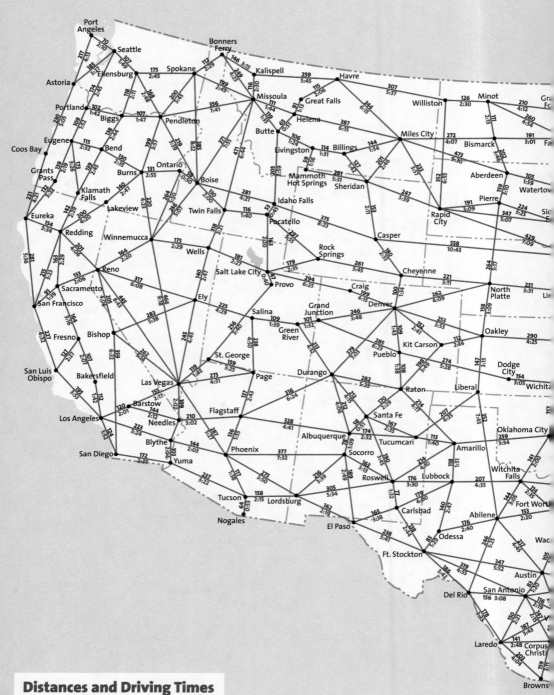

Distances and Driving Times

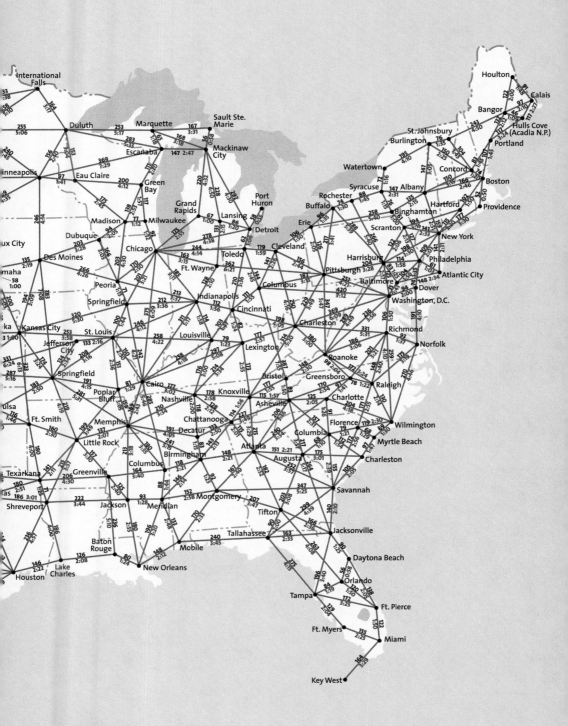

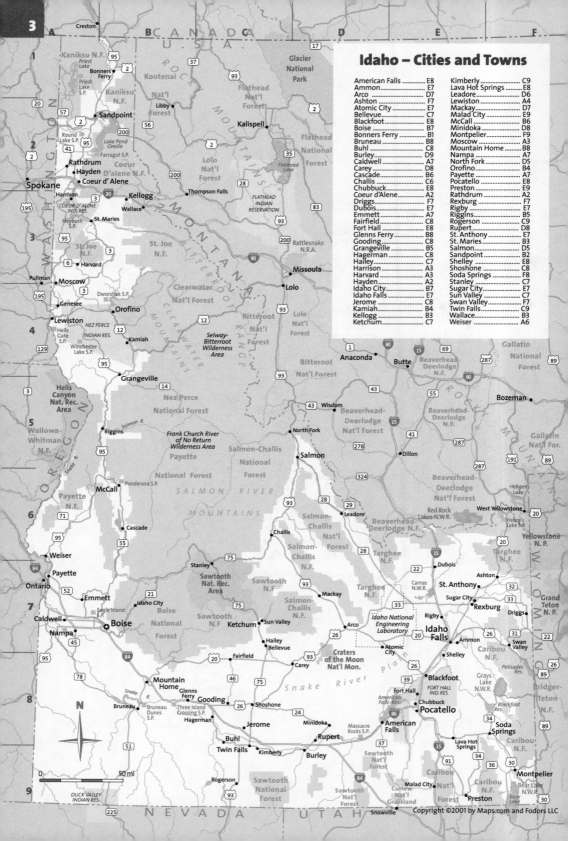

Idaho – Cities and Towns

American Falls	E8
Ammon	E7
Arco	D7
Ashton	F7
Atomic City	E7
Bellevue	C7
Blackfoot	E8
Boise	B7
Bonners Ferry	B1
Bruneau	B8
Buhl	C8
Burley	D9
Caldwell	A7
Carey	C8
Cascade	B6
Challis	C6
Chubbuck	E8
Coeur d'Alene	A2
Driggs	F7
Dubois	E7
Emmett	A7
Fairfield	C8
Fort Hall	E8
Glenns Ferry	B8
Gooding	C8
Grangeville	B5
Hagerman	C8
Hailey	C7
Harrison	A3
Harvard	A3
Hayden	A2
Idaho City	B7
Idaho Falls	E7
Jerome	C8
Kamiah	B4
Kellogg	B3
Ketchum	C7
Kimberly	C9
Lava Hot Springs	E8
Leadore	D6
Lewiston	A4
Mackay	D7
Malad City	E9
McCall	B6
Minidoka	D8
Montpelier	F9
Moscow	A3
Mountain Home	B8
Nampa	A7
North Fork	D5
Orofino	B4
Payette	A7
Pocatello	E8
Preston	E9
Rathdrum	A2
Rexburg	F7
Rigby	E7
Riggins	B5
Rogerson	C9
Rupert	D8
St. Anthony	E7
St. Maries	B3
Salmon	D5
Sandpoint	B2
Shelley	E8
Shoshone	C8
Soda Springs	F8
Stanley	C7
Sugar City	E7
Sun Valley	C7
Swan Valley	F7
Twin Falls	C9
Wallace	B3
Weiser	A6

Copyright ©2001 by Maps.com and Fodors LLC

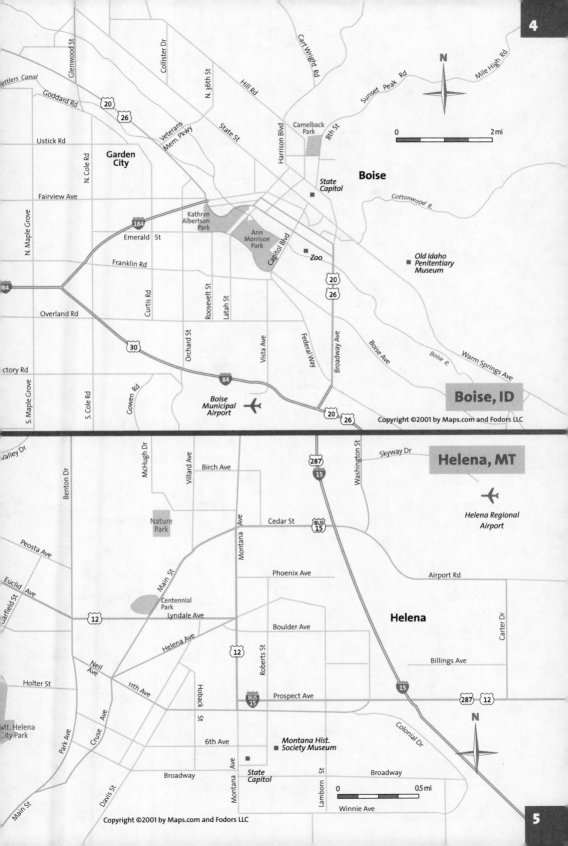

N

0   2 mi

Glenwood St
Collister Dr
Cart Wright Rd
Mile High Rd
Settlers Canal
Goddard Rd
20
26
Veterans Mem. Pkwy
N. 36th St
Hill Rd
State St
Sunset Peak Rd
Ustick Rd
Garden City
N. Cole Rd
Harrison Blvd
Camelback Park
8th St
Boise
Fairview Ave
N. Maple Grove
State Capitol
Cottonwood R.
184
Kathryn Albertson Park
Emerald St
Ann Morrison Park
Old Idaho Penitentiary Museum
Franklin Rd
Curtis Rd
Capitol Blvd
Zoo
84
Overland Rd
Roosevelt St
Latah St
20
26
30
Victory Rd
Orchard St
Vista Ave
Federal Way
Broadway Ave
Boise Ave
Boise R.
Warm Springs Ave
S. Maple Grove
S. Cole Rd
Gowen Rd
84
Boise Municipal Airport
20
26

Boise, ID

Valley Dr
Benton Dr
McHugh Dr
Villard Ave
Birch Ave
287
15
Washington St
Skyway Dr

Helena, MT

Nature Park
Montana Ave
Cedar St
BUS 15
Helena Regional Airport
Peosta Ave
Main St
Phoenix Ave
Airport Rd
Euclid Ave
Garfield St
Centennial Park
Lyndale Ave
12
Boulder Ave
Helena
Carter Dr
Helena Ave
12
Roberts St
Billings Ave
Neil Ave
11th Ave
Holter St
Hoback St
BUS 15
Prospect Ave
287
12
Mt. Helena City Park
Park Ave
Cruse Ave
Colonial Dr
15
N
6th Ave
Montana Ave
Montana Hist. Society Museum
Holter St
Main St
Davis St
Broadway
State Capitol
Lamborn St
Broadway
0   0.5 mi
Winnie Ave

Montana – Cities and Towns

Anaconda......................D6	Choteau......................D4	Fort Benton..............F3	Kalispell....................B3	Seeley Lake..............C4
Baker..........................L5	Columbia Falls........C3	Fort Peck..................J3	Laurel.......................G6	Shelby.......................E2
Belgrade.....................E6	Columbus..................G6	Gardiner....................F7	Lewistown.................G4	Sidney.......................L3
Bigfork.......................C3	Conrad.......................E3	Glasgow.....................I3	Libby.........................A3	Stevensville..............C5
Big Sky.......................E7	Cooke City................F7	Glendive.....................K5	Livingston.................F6	Three Forks..............E6
Big Timber.................G6	Crow Agency.............I6	Grassrange................H5	Lolo..........................C5	Thompson Falls........A4
Billings.......................H6	Cut Bank...................D2	Great Falls.................E4	Malta........................H3	Townsend..................E5
Boulder.......................D6	Darby.........................B6	Hamilton...................B5	Miles City..................J5	Virginia City.............E7
Bozeman.....................E6	Deer Lodge................D5	Hardin.......................I6	Missoula....................C5	W. Glacier..................C3
Broadus......................K7	Dillon........................D7	Harlowton.................G5	Plentywood...............K2	West Yellowstone.....E8
Browning....................D2	Ennis..........................E7	Havre.........................E2	Polson.......................C4	Whitefish...................B3
Butte..........................D6	E. Glacier Park..........C3	Helena.......................C2	Poplar.......................K3	White Sulphur
Chinook......................G2	Forsyth.......................I6	Hungry Horse............C3	Red Lodge..................G7	Springs...................F5
Circle.........................J4	Fort Belknap Agency...H3	Jordan.......................I4	Roundup....................H5	Wolf Point.................J3
				Zortman....................H3

✈ Missoula
Int'l Airport

93

90

200

BUS 90

Flynn Ln

Cemetery Rd

W. Broadway

Scott St

Duncan Dr

Rattlesnake Dr

BUS 90

Mullan Rd

Clark Fork R.

93

Spruce St

Van Buren Ave

200

Missoula

90   12

S. 3rd St

Russell St

Stephens Ave

12

University of
Montana-
Missoula

Lolo

Spurgin Rd

Tower St

Reserve St

14th St

Arthur Ave

Nat'l

Vietnam
Veterans
Memorial

South Ave

Bancroft St

Higgins Ave

Forest

Historical Mus. at
Fort Missoula

Playfair
Park

Spartan
Park

N

Lolo
N.F.

Bitterroot R.

39th St

23rd Ave

Whitaker Dr

Pattee Canyon Rd

0 ————— 2 mi

Copyright ©2001 by Maps.com and Fodors LLC

Riding Club Rd

86
87

219

N

25

Yellowstone Rd

Four Mile Rd

Powderhouse Rd

212

Roundtop Rd

Francis E.
Warren
A.F.B.

0 ————— 2 mi

Cheyenne

Lake
Pearson

L. Terry

Frontier Days
Old West
Museum

Dell Range Blvd

A.F.B.
Museum

Randall Ave

Frontier
Park

✈ Cheyenne
Airport

Converse Ave

Ridge Rd

College Dr

BUS 80   30

Crow Cr.

BUS 87

Pershing Blvd

222

State
Capitol

19th St

Logan Ave

E. Lincolnway

212

210

Happy Jack Rd

Missile Dr

Nationway

Campstool Rd

80

E. Lincolnway

180   5th St

Crow Cr.

80   30

Otto Rd

225

Southwest Dr

Parsley Blvd

College Dr

221

Fox Farm Rd

85

W.H.R.
Reservoir
#1

Swan
Res.

Clear Cr.

212   College Dr

BUS 25

Ave C

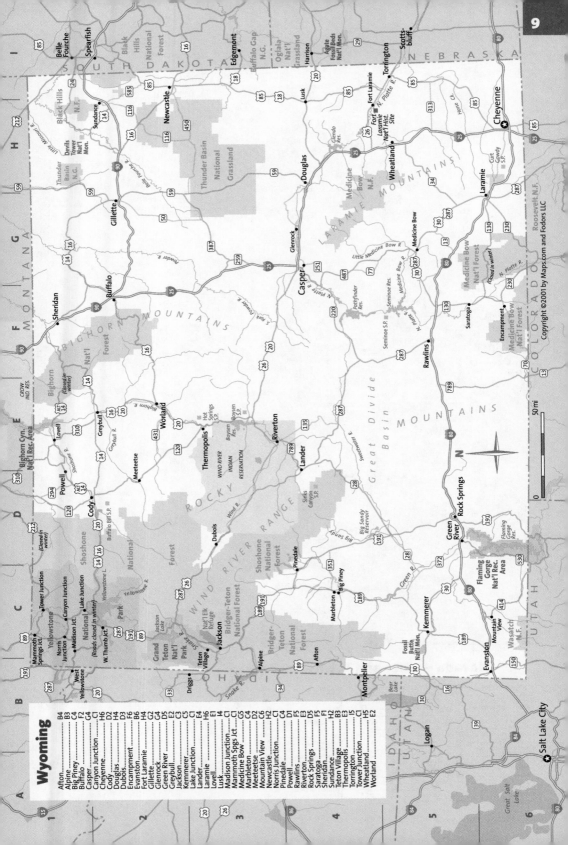

Wyoming

Afton	B4
Alpine	B3
Big Piney	C4
Buffalo	F2
Casper	G4
Canyon Junction	H6
Cheyenne	D2
Cody	H4
Douglas	D3
Dubois	F6
Encampment	B6
Evanston	G2
Fort Laramie	H4
Gillette	G2
Glenrock	D5
Green River	E2
Greybull	C5
Jackson	E4
Kemmerer	E1
Lake Junction	I4
Lander	C1
Laramie	G5
Lovell	H2
Lusk	C1
Madison Junction	G5
Mammoth Spgs Jct	C6
Medicine Bow	C4
Marbleton	H2
Meeteetse	C4
Mountain View	H5
Newcastle	C1
Norris Junction	D1
Pinedale	F5
Powell	B3
Rawlins	D5
Riverton	F1
Rock Springs	F5
Saratoga	H2
Sheridan	B3
Sundance	I5
Teton Village	C1
Thermopolis	H5
Torrington	C1
Tower Junction	H5
Wheatland	E2
Worland	

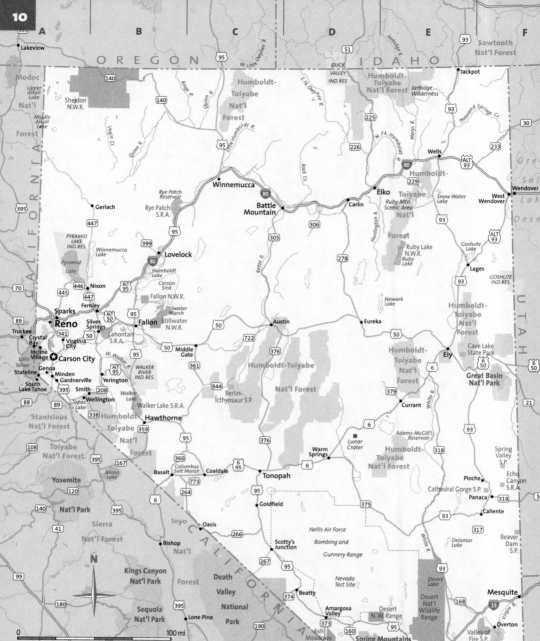

Nevada – Cities and Towns

Amargosa Valley	D7	Gardnerville	A5	Panaca	F6
Austin	C4	Gerlach	A3	Pahrump	D8
Basalt	B6	Goldfield	C6	Pioche	F6
Battle Mountain	C3	Goodsprings	E8	Reno	A4
Beatty	D7	Hawthorne	B5	Scotty's Junction	C6
Boulder City	E8	Henderson	E8	Silver Springs	B4
Caliente	F6	Incline Village	A4	Smith	A5
Carlin	D3	Jackpot	E1	Sparks	A4
Carson City	A4	Lages	E3	Stateline	A5
Coaldale	B6	Las Vegas	E8	Tonopah	C6
Crystal Bay	A4	Laughlin	F9	Virginia City	A4
Currant	E5	Lovelock	B3	Warm Springs	D5
Denio Junction	B1	Mesquite	F7	Wells	E2
Elko	D2	Middle Gate	C4	Wellington	A5
Ely	E4	Minden	A5	West Wendover	F3
Eureka	D4	Nixon	A4	Winnemucca	C2
Fallon	B4	Oasis	C6	Yerington	B5
Genoa	A4	Overton	F7		

Las Vegas, NV

95

Rancho Dr

North Las Vegas

Ann Rd

Ann Rd

93 15

Craig Rd

Nellis Air Force Base

604

Buffalo Dr

Decatur Blvd

Cheyenne Ave

Blvd

Pecos Rd

Las Vegas Blvd

Lamb Blvd

Nellis Blvd

95

Jones Blvd

M. L. King Jr.

Las Vegas

Rancho Dr

Lake Mead Blvd

515

SUMMELIN PKWY

■ *Las Vegas Natural Hist. Museum*

Charleston Blvd

159

■ *Las Vegas Art Mus.*

Sahara Ave

Ft. Apache Rd

Durango Dr

Buffalo Dr

Rainbow Blvd

Spring Mtn. Rd

■ *Wet 'n Wild Water Park*

Maryland Pkwy

Eastern Ave

Desert Inn Rd

582

Desert Wetlands Park

BOULDER HWY

Flamingo Rd

The Strip

■ *Univ. of Nevada Las Vegas*

Tropicana Ave

Decatur Blvd

Paradise Rd

■ *Liberace Museum*

✈ *McCarran Int'l Airport*

Sunset Rd

515 95 93

Sunset

Rd

(under construction)

Sunset Park

Enterprise

Warm Springs Rd

215

Eastern Ave

Pecos Rd

Green Valley Pkwy

Henderson

(under construction)

146

Blue Diamond Rd

160

604

N

15

Lake Mead Dr

Horizon Ridge Pkwy

✈ *Henderson Executive Airport*

146

0   4 mi

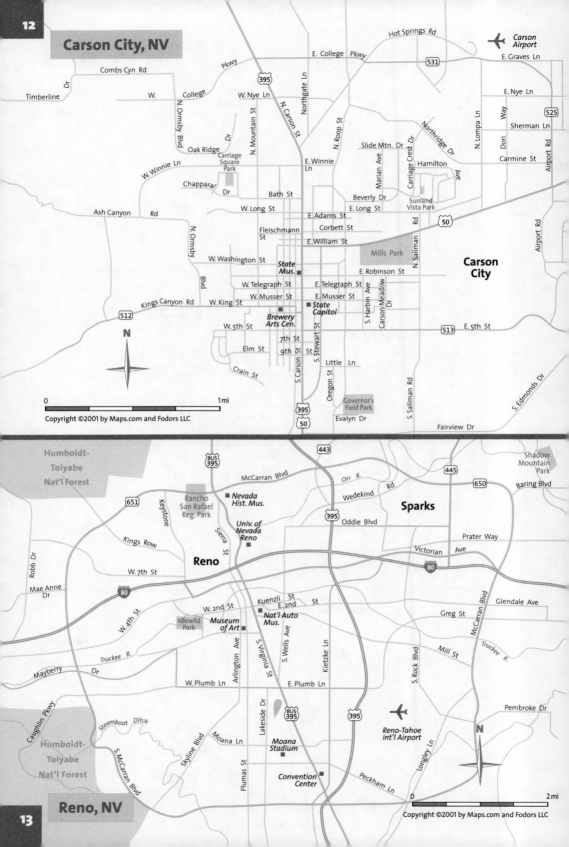

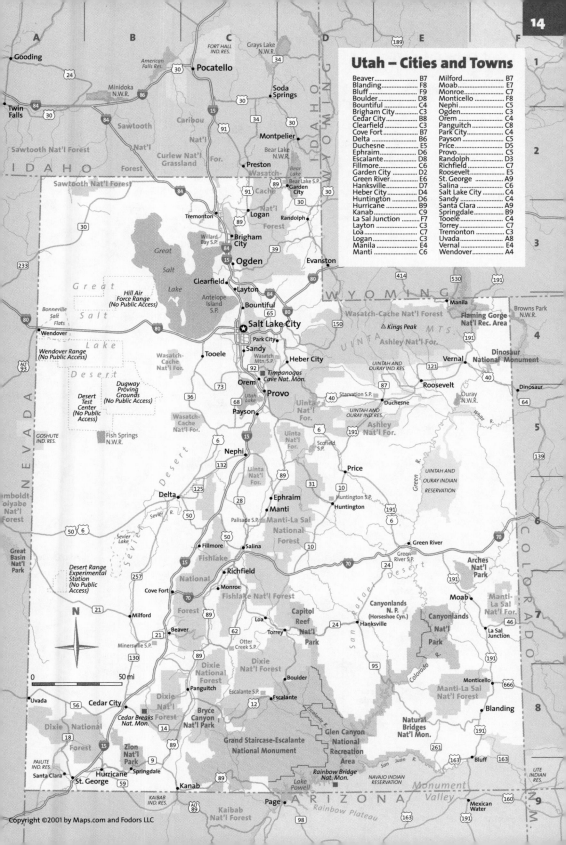

Utah – Cities and Towns

Beaver	B7	Milford	B7
Blanding	F8	Moab	E7
Bluff	F9	Monroe	C7
Boulder	D8	Monticello	F8
Bountiful	C4	Nephi	C5
Brigham City	C3	Ogden	C3
Cedar City	B8	Orem	C4
Clearfield	C3	Panguitch	C8
Cove Fort	B7	Park City	C4
Delta	B6	Payson	C5
Duchesne	E5	Price	D5
Ephraim	D6	Provo	C5
Escalante	D8	Randolph	D3
Fillmore	C6	Richfield	C7
Garden City	D2	Roosevelt	E5
Green River	E6	St. George	A9
Hanksville	D7	Salina	C6
Heber City	D4	Salt Lake City	C4
Huntington	D6	Sandy	C4
Hurricane	B9	Santa Clara	A9
Kanab	C9	Springdale	B9
La Sal Junction	F7	Tooele	C4
Layton	C3	Torrey	C7
Loa	C7	Tremonton	C3
Logan	C3	Uvada	A8
Manila	E4	Vernal	E4
Manti	C6	Wendover	A4

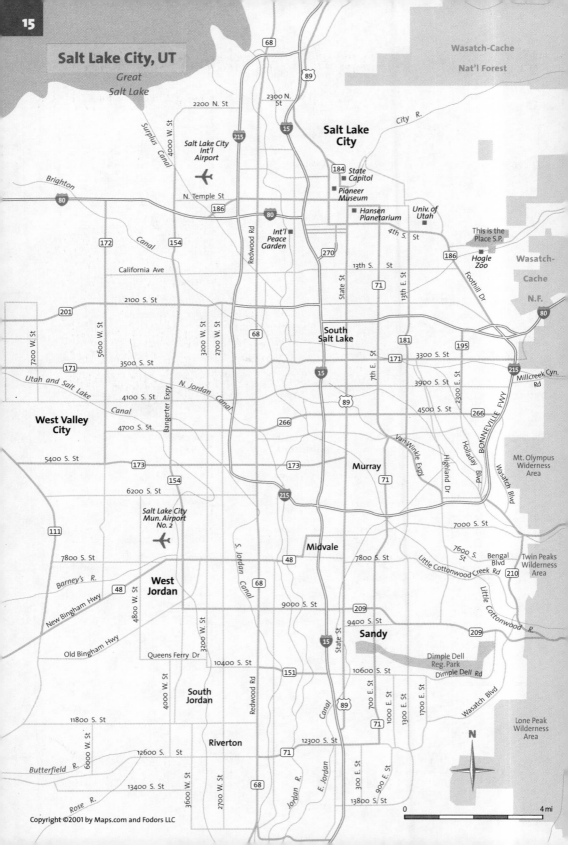